COMPREHENSIVE SCHOOL HEALTH EDUCATION

TOTALLY AWESOME STRATEGIES FOR TEACHING HEALTH™

Sixth Edition

Linda Meeks

Emeritus Professor, The Ohio State University

Philip Heit

Emeritus Professor, The Ohio State University

Randy Page

Professor, Brigham Young University

Boston   Burr Ridge, IL   Dubuque, IA   Madison, WI   New York
San Francisco   St. Louis   Bangkok   Bogotá   Caracas   Kuala Lumpur
Lisbon   London   Madrid   Mexico City   Milan   Montreal   New Delhi
Santiago   Seoul   Singapore   Sydney   Taipei   Toronto

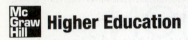

Higher Education

Published by McGraw-Hill, an imprint of The McGraw-Hill Companies, Inc., 1221 Avenue of the Americas, New York, NY 10020. Copyright © 2009, 2007, 2005, 2003. All rights reserved. No part of this publication may be reproduced or distributed in any form or by any means, or stored in a database or retrieval system, without the prior written consent of The McGraw-Hill Companies, Inc., including, but not limited to, in any network or other electronic storage or transmission, or broadcast for distance learning.

This book is printed on recycled, acid-free paper containing a minimum of 50% total recycled fiber with 10% postconsumer de-inked fiber.

1 2 3 4 5 6 7 8 9 0 QPD/QPD 0 9 8

ISBN: 978-0-07-340462-2
MHID: 0-07-340462-4

Editor in Chief: *Michael Ryan*
Publisher: *William Glass*
Sponsoring Editor: *Joseph Diggins*
Marketing Manager: *Nick Agnew*
Director of Development: *Kathleen Engelberg*
Developmental Editor: *Sarah Hill*
Project Manager: *Paul Wells*
Production Service: *Newgen–Austin*
Manuscript Editor: *Mary Ann Short*
Design Manager: *Margarite Reynolds*
Cover Designer: *Margarite Reynolds*
Illustrator: *Deborah Rubenstein*
Production Supervisor: *Richard DeVitto*
Composition: *10/12 New Century Schoolbook by Newgen*
Printing: *45# New Era Matte Plus, Quebecor World, Inc.*

Cover: © Tom Young/Corbis Stock Market

Library of Congress Cataloging-in-Publication Data

Meeks, Linda Brower.
  Comprehensive school health education / Linda Meeks, Philip Heit, Randy Page.—6th ed.
     p. cm.
  Includes index.
  ISBN-13: 978-0-07-340462-2 (alk. paper)
  ISBN-10: 0-07-340462-4 (alk. paper)
  1. Health education (Secondary) 2. Health education (Elementary) I. Heit, Philip.
     II. Page, Randy M.   III. Title.
  RA440.M447 2009
  613.071′2—dc22

                                                                2007026322

The Internet addresses listed in the text were accurate at the time of publication. The inclusion of a Web site does not indicate an endorsement by the authors or McGraw-Hill, and McGraw-Hill does not guarantee the accuracy of the information presented at these sites.

www.mhhe.com

BRIEF CONTENTS

CONTENTS

CHAPTER **3**

The Comprehensive School Health Education Curriculum:
A Blueprint for Implementing
the National Health Education

CHAPTER **9**

Personal Health and Physical Activity **254**

CHAPTER **10**

Alcohol, Tobacco, and Other Drugs **290**

CHAPTER **13**

Environmental Health . . . **385**

CHAPTER **14**

Injury Prevention
and Safety **406**

PREFACE

Tell me, I forget.
Show me, I remember.
Involve me, I understand.

Comprehensive School Health Education: Totally Awesome Strategies for Teaching Health™ has been the leading teacher resource book used to prepare future and current elementary school, middle school, and secondary school teachers to teach health since the publication of the first edition in 1991. It also has been the most widely used teacher resource book selected by state departments of education, school districts, and departments of health for inservice and train-the-trainers programs. As you read about its contents, you will learn why teachers who purchase it find it the most teacher-friendly resource book available for health education.

Section 1. Comprehensive School Health Education includes five chapters and is designed to provide you with a framework for comprehensive school health education. In Chapter 1, you will learn about the six categories of risk behaviors that affect today's students, *Healthy People 2010* and other guidelines for promoting school health, and the eight components in the coordinated school health program. Chapter 2 prepares you for your role in school health services and explains how to provide a healthful and safe school environment. Chapter 3 teaches you how to design comprehensive school health curricula, implement the National Health Education Standards, and effectively assess students, teachers, and school health programs. Chapter 4 describes instructional strategies and technologies you might use in the classroom.

Section 2. Health Content contains more than 200 pages of health content so that you are well informed with up-to-date health knowledge in the ten areas of health: Chapter 5: Mental and Emotional Health; Chapter 6: Family and Social Health; Chapter 7: Growth and Development; Chapter 8: Nutrition; Chapter 9: Personal Health and Physical Activity; Chapter 10: Alcohol, Tobacco, and Other Drugs; Chapter 11: Com-

municable and Chronic Diseases; Chapter 12: Consumer and Community Health; Chapter 13: Environmental Health; and Chapter 14: Injury Prevention and Safety.

Section 3. Totally Awesome Teaching Strategies™ explains the format and how to use Totally Awesome Teaching Strategies™ to help students develop and practice life skills and achieve health goals. Chapter 15 includes Totally Awesome Teaching Strategies™ for each grade level from K to 12 for each of the ten content areas.

Section 4. *The Meeks Heit K–12 Health Education Curriculum Guide* is a state-of-the-art curriculum guide focusing on the National Health Education Standards using the ten content areas. The Curriculum Guide in Chapter 16 can be used as is or can be adapted for a specific school district.

Appendix A. National Health Education Standards: Teaching Masters provides reproducible masters with steps for teaching each of the National Health Education Standards at age-appropriate grade levels: K–2, 3–5, 6–8, and 9–12. **Appendix B** includes a chart of the objectives from ***Healthy People 2010*** relevant for schools. **Appendix C** includes *The Teacher's Encyclopedic Guide for Health Concerns of School-Age Youth . . . from A–Z.* **Appendix D** includes **Health Resources,** a listing of the names and contact information for agencies and organizations in the ten health content areas.

We are committed to helping teachers with the awesome task of providing quality health education.

Linda Meeks
Philip Heit
Randy Page

ACKNOWLEDGMENTS

The authors wish to thank the advisory board, consultants, and publisher's reviewer panel. Their comments and suggestions helped us significantly improve the text. We gratefully acknowledge their expertise and assistance.

We would also like to extend a special thanks to Deborah Rubenstein who provided all of the art for the sixth edition. Her skillfully rendered illustrations are a wonderful addition to the book, and we are grateful to have had the chance to work with her.

Advisory Board

Jane Beougher, Ph.D.
Professor Emeritus
Capital University
Columbus, Ohio

Moon S. Chen, Ph.D., M.P.H.
Associate Director for Cancer Prevention
Professor of Epidemiology and Preventive
    Medicine
School of Medicine
University of California–Davis
Sacramento, California

Karen M. Deasy, M.P.H.
Associate Director, Office of Smoking and Health
Centers for Disease Control and Prevention
Department of Health and Human Services
Atlanta, Georgia

Gary English, Ph.D., CHES
Director, New York Statewide Center for Healthy
    Schools
Little Falls, New York

Deborah Fortune, Ph.D., CHES
Director of HIV/AIDS Project
Association for the Advancement of Health
    Education
Reston, Virginia

Elizabeth Gallun, M.A.
Specialist in CSHE
Maryland Department of Education
Baltimore, Maryland

David Lohrmann, Ph.D., CHES
Associate Professor of Applied Health Science
Indiana University
Bloomington, Indiana

Deborah Miller, Ph.D., CHES
Professor and Health Coordinator
College of Charleston
Charleston, South Carolina

Joanne Owens-Nauslar, Ed.D.
Director of Corporate and Community Relations
Walk4Life, Inc.
Plainfield, Illinois

John Ray, M.S.
Education Specialist
Delaware Department of Education
Dover, Delaware

Spencer Sartorius, M.S.
Assistant Superintendent
Office of Public Instruction
Helena, Montana

Sherman Sowby, Ph.D., CHES
Professor, Health Science
California State University at Fresno
Fresno, California

Deitra Wengert, Ph.D., CHES
Professor, Department of Health Science
Towson State University
Towson, Maryland

Susan Wooley, Ph.D., CHES
Executive Director
American School Health Association
Kent, Ohio

Consultants

Kymm Ballard, M.A.
Physical Education, Athletics, and Sports
    Medicine Consultant
North Carolina Department of Public Instruction
Raleigh, North Carolina

Donna Breitenstein, Ed.D.
Coordinator and Professor of Health Education
College of Education
Appalachian State University
Boone, North Carolina

Brian Colwell, Ph.D.
Professor
Texas A&M University
Department of HLKN
College Station, Texas

Joanne Frasier, Ed.D.
Office of Curriculum Standards
South Carolina Department of Education
Columbia, South Carolina

Dawn Graff-Haight, Ph.D., CHES
Professor and Chairperson
Health and Physical Education
Linfield College
McMinnville, Oregon

Fred Hebert, M.S.
Senior Lecturer
University of Wisconsin–Stevens Point
Stevens Point, Wisconsin

Janet Henke
Middle School Team Leader
Baltimore County Public Schools
Baltimore, Maryland

Russell Henke
Coordinator of Health
Montgomery County Public Schools
Rockville, Maryland

Joe Leake, CHES
Curriculum Specialist
Baltimore County Public Schools
Baltimore, Maryland

Mary C. Marks, Ph.D.
School Health Consultant
California Department of Education
Sacramento, California

J. Leslie Oganowski, Ph.D.
Associate Professor of Health Education
University of Wisconsin–LaCrosse
LaCrosse, Wisconsin

Debra Ogden, M.A.
Coordinator of Health, Physical Education,
    Driver Education and Safe and Drug-Free
    Program
Collier County Public Schools
Naples, Florida

Fred Peterson, Ph.D.
Associate Professor of Child, Adolescent and
    School Health
Department of Kinesiology and Health
    Education
University of Texas
Austin, Texas

Linda Wright, M.A.
Project Director
HIV/AIDS Education Program
District of Columbia Public Schools
Washington, DC

The authors want to acknowledge the colleagues who served on the National Health Education Standards Revision Initiative Advisory Panel. The professional organizations represented included the American Association for Health Education (AAHE), the American Cancer Society (ACS), the American Public Health Association (APHA), the American School Health Association (ASHA), and the Society of State Directors of Health, Physical Education and Recreation (SSDHPER).

NHES Revision Initiative Advisory Panel

Steve Dorman, Advisory Panel Chair
Texas A&M University

Jess Bogli
Oregon Department of Education

Kim Robert Clark
California State University–San Bernardino

Mary Connolly
Cambridge College

Marilyn Jensen
South Dakota Department of Education

Ellen Larson
Northern Arizona University

Mary Marks
California Department of Education

Antoinette Meeks
Florida Department of Education

Linda Morse
New Jersey Department of Education

Fred Peterson
The University of Texas–Austin

Eric Pliner
New York City Department of Education

Becky Smith
American Association for Health Education

Barbara Sullivan
Baltimore County Public Schools

Marilyn Tappe
Minnesota State University

Susan K. Telljohann
University of Toledo

Valerie Ubbes
Miami University

Mary Waters
American Cancer Society

Katherine Wilbur
Maine Department of Education

Publisher's Reviewer Panel

Judith M. Ary
North Dakota State University

Linda Balog
State University of New York at Brockport

Debra Bakker
Calvin College

Susan F. Bowman
Indiana Wesleyan University

Michael R. Davey
Western Illinois University

Michelle Grenier
University of New Hampshire

Shelley Hammill
Winthrop University

Kristin Moline
Lourdes College

Leslie Oganowski
University of Wisconsin–La Crosse

Bruce Ragon
Albany State University

Tara L. Redmond
Columbus State University

Susan E. Tapper
San Francisco State University

HIGHLIGHTS OF THIS EDITION

Highlights of This Edition

- The art for this edition has been completely redrawn to reflect the ethnic diversity of today's youth and the latest developments in technology and lifestyles. Over 230 new illustrations fill the book.
- Content in the areas of school health services and school environment have been streamlined for easier comprehension (Chapter 2).
- The health content chapters (5–14) have been updated to include the latest research and developments in each content area, including new lifestyle health risks for teens; new medical, drug, and vaccination developments; and updated statistics throughout.
- The revised NHES are integrated into the Totally Awesome Teaching Strategies™, and each strategy references blackline Teaching Masters that assist in evaluating students according to NHES.

Chapter and Appendix Highlights

Chapter 1: A Nation at Risk
- Statistics fully updated
- New Section on the Office of Safe and Drug-Free Schools
- New information on the School Health Index

Chapter 2: School Health Services and Healthful School Environment
- New information on the Child Nutrition and WIC Reauthorization Act

Chapter 5: Mental and Emotional Health
- Updated statistics on depression

Chapter 7: Growth and Development
- New section on endometriosis
- New tables on signs and timing of puberty in females and males
- Information on Plan B (emergency contraception) added to Facts about Birth Control Methods section

Chapter 8: Nutrition
- Updated information on food label health claims
- Most recent Nutrition and Physical Activity Guidelines from the American Cancer Society (2006)
- Most recent dietary guidelines to reduce the risk of developing premature cardiovascular disease from the American Heart Association

- New and updated information on common foodborne illnesses
- New section on weight loss surgery

Chapter 9: Personal Health and Physical Activity
- New section on portable music players and their risk for hearing loss
- New information on the proper fit of shoes
- New section on teens and sleep
- New section on Osgood-Schlatter disease

Chapter 10: Alcohol, Tobacco, and Other Drugs
- Additional information on blood alcohol concentration (BAC) and driving under the influence of alcohol
- New data on tobacco advertising and children
- Updated information on the hallucinogenic psilocybin

Chapter 11: Communicable and Chronic Diseases
- Differentiation between the uses of "Sexually Transmitted Disease" and "Sexually Transmitted Infection"
- Information on the HPV vaccination Gardasil
- Updated statistics throughout

Chapter 12: Consumer and Community Health
- New table on health fraud red flags
- Entertainment ratings added for video and computer games
- New information and statistics on Americans without health insurance

Chapter 13: Environmental Health
- Updated information on global warming
- New information on indoor molds
- New section on ad clutter

Chapter 14: Injury Prevention and Safety
- Updated information on child booster seats for motor vehicles
- Expanded coverage of predatory (date rape) drugs

Chapter 15: Using the Totally Awesome Teaching Strategies™
- Revised National Education Standards and Performance Indicators included in Teaching Strategies

- Materials section for each Teaching Strategy identifies one or more blackline Teaching Masters of the revised National Health Education Strategies from Appendix A that can be used with the Evaluation
- Evaluation sections for each Teaching Strategy assess students' mastery of the revised National Health Education Standards

Chapter 16: Using the Meeks Heit K–12 Health Education Curriculum Guide
- Revised National Health Education Standards included in section The Component in a Health Education K–12 Curriculum Guide
- Revised National Health Education Standards and new numbering system contained in the Meeks Heit Umbrella of Comprehensive School Health Education (Figure 16-1)
- Revised Performance Indicators included in Scope and Sequence Chart
- Health Goals and Grade Level Objectives updated to correlate to the revised National Health Education Standards

Appendix A: National Health Education Standards: Teaching Masters
- Grade-level appropriate blackline masters can be made into Teaching Masters for each of the revised National Health Education Standards

Appendix B: Selected Healthy People 2010 Objectives That Relate to Schools and School-Age Youth
- Table containing the Objectives located in the Appendix for easy reference and use

Appendix D: Health Resources
- Resources fully updated and additional resources added

Supplements

Online Learning Center
www.mhhe.com/meeks6e

The Online Learning Center features resources for both the instructor and student.

For the instructor:

- *PowerPoint slides.* A complete set of PowerPoint slides is downloadable. Keyed to the major points in each chapter, the slides can be modified or expanded to adjust to the instructor's teaching style and needs.

- *Instructor's Manual.* The manual includes three sample syllabi, course objectives, and instructor strategies for presenting each chapter.
- *Computerized test bank.* The test bank is available with EZ Test computerized testing software. EZ Test provides a powerful, easy-to-use test maker to create printed quizzes and exams. For secure online testing, exams created in EZ Test can be exported to WebCT, Blackboard, PageOut, and EZ Test Online. EZ Test comes with a Quick Start Guide; once the program is installed, users have access to a User's Manual and Flash tutorials. Additional help is available at www.mhhe.com/eztest.
- *CPS polling questions.* For use with the Classroom Performance System (see below), these questions allow instructors to get real-time results on a variety of polling questions associated with health content chapters. These questions are designed to help you gauge your students' opinions and backgrounds concerning the topics in the health content chapters.

For the student:

- *PowerPoint slides*
- *Chapter health goals and overviews*
- *Chapter self-scoring quizzes*
- *Vocabulary flashcards and crossword puzzles*
- *Appendix D: Health Resources*
- *Web links*

Classroom Performance system

The Classroom Performance System (CPS) brings interactivity into the classroom or lecture hall. CPS is a wireless response system that gives instructors and students immediate feedback from the entire class. Each student uses a wireless response pad similar to a television remote to instantly respond to polling or quiz questions. CPS is the perfect tool for engaging students while gathering assessment data. For more information about using CPS with *Comprehensive School Health Education,* contact your McGraw-Hill sales representative.

PageOut
www.pageout.net

PageOut is a free, easy-to-use program that enables instructors to quickly develop Web sites for their courses. Teachers can use PageOut to create a course home page, an instructor home page, an interactive syllabus, Web links, online discussion areas, an online gradebook, and much more. Contact your McGraw-Hill sales representative to obtain a password for PageOut and for information on their course management systems.

SECTION ONE

1

Comprehensive School Health Education

CHAPTER ONE

A Nation at Risk:

The Need for Comprehensive School Health Education

Perhaps no profession is more vital to the future of this nation than teaching. Every teacher has the potential to affect the lives of many students. Many students are at risk in ways that influence their ability to learn. Some students lack adequate nourishment, sleep, immunizations, and proper clothing. Others are being reared in families in which there is domestic violence, chemical dependency, or some other dysfunction. Still others are managing health conditions, such as asthma, anorexia nervosa, or depression.

Effective teachers are aware of the health status of their students and are committed to work with their students to maintain and improve their health status. Teachers must be positive role models for healthful living. And, of course, teachers must be motivated to create a dynamic and challenging classroom where students can learn and practice life skills and the National Health Education Standards. In other words, today's teachers must be *totally awesome*™. A **totally awesome teacher**™ is committed to promoting health literacy, improving health, preventing disease, reducing health-related risk behaviors in students, and creating a dynamic and challenging classroom where students learn and practice life skills and the National Health Education Standards. Although this task demands training and effort, it has many rewards—the future of this nation depends on students being able to practice life skills for health and achieve health goals.

This *totally awesome*™ teacher resource book, *Comprehensive School Health Education,* was written by teachers who want to make a difference for teachers who want to make a difference. The style of this resource book is teacher-friendly and interactive. This is not a resource book to gather dust on your bookshelf; it is a resource book you can use. Let's discuss how you will be able to use the information in this first chapter. The chapter begins with a review of the six categories of risk behaviors identified by the Centers for Disease Control and Prevention (CDC). You will learn more about the risk behaviors that compromise the health status of today's students. The next section, "Healthy People 2010," discusses objectives targeted for schools and school-age youth to be accomplished by this date. "Healthy People 2010" is followed by the section "CDC School Health Guidelines and Strategies to Promote Healthy Behavior among Children and Adolescents." Being familiar with the CDC guidelines and strategies helps you understand the expectations for school and community-based programs. This is followed by the section on the Office of Safe and Drug-Free Schools.

An entire section of the chapter focuses on the coordinated school health program and its eight components: comprehensive school health education; school health services; healthful and safe school environment; physical education; nutrition services; counseling, psychological, and social services; health promotion for staff; and family and community involvement. It is of utmost importance for you to understand each of the eight components and how they must coordinate to produce an effective school health program. Then the chapter includes a section on a key component of the coordinated school health program—"Comprehensive School Health Education"—where you will examine the Meeks Heit Umbrella of Comprehensive School Health Education. Finally, in the section "Using This *Totally Awesome*™ Teacher Resource Book," you will learn how to implement comprehensive school health education in your school district, school, and classroom.

Six Categories of Risk Behaviors in Today's Students

Four causes are responsible for most deaths of young people: motor vehicle crashes, other unintentional injuries (such as falls, fires, and drownings), homicide, and suicide. Most of these deaths are preventable and are associated with adolescent behaviors such as drinking alcohol, not wearing safety belts, carrying weapons, and engaging in physical fights. Adolescent behaviors result in many health and social problems that cause young people to suffer. For example, approximately 1 million teens become pregnant each year, and approximately 3 million teens suffer new cases of sexually transmitted diseases (STDs) each year. Avoiding sexual activity can prevent these high rates of teen pregnancy and sexually transmitted diseases.

Heart disease, cancer, and stroke are prominent causes of death in adults. Habits established in childhood and adolescence often contribute to these diseases, which do not show up until adulthood. Major causes of these diseases are poor dietary habits, cigarette smoking, alcohol use, and physical inactivity. Childhood and adolescence are times to develop lifestyle habits that foster good health and help prevent disease.

Many of the deaths and illnesses that occur in youths and in adults can be prevented by making healthful behavior choices and avoiding risk

behaviors. A **risk behavior** is an action a person chooses that threatens health. Risk behaviors can cause injury, illness, and premature death. They also can destroy the environment. Examples of risk behaviors are rollerblading without safety equipment, failure to use a safety belt, smoking cigarettes, using alcohol or other drugs, and joining a gang. Most risk behaviors

- are established during youth
- persist into adulthood
- are interrelated
- contribute simultaneously to poor health, education, and social outcomes
- are preventable

The Centers for Disease Control and Prevention (CDC) has identified six categories of risk behaviors in today's students:

1. Behaviors that contribute to unintentional and intentional injuries
2. Tobacco use
3. Alcohol and other drug use
4. Sexual behaviors that contribute to unintended pregnancy, HIV (human immunodeficiency virus) infection, and other sexually transmitted diseases
5. Dietary patterns that contribute to disease
6. Insufficient physical activity

The following sections describe how the six categories of risk behaviors affect today's students. You will learn what many students are doing in their lives and why these risk behaviors place our nation's students at risk. Later, this information will help you understand the importance of the comprehensive school health education program.

Unintentional and Intentional Injuries

The first category of risk behaviors is behaviors that contribute to unintentional and intentional injuries. An **unintentional injury** is an injury caused by an accident. An **intentional injury** is an injury resulting from interpersonal violence or self-directed violence. Intentional injury includes deaths from homicide and suicide. Injuries kill more young people than all diseases combined. Injuries also contribute to substantial suffering and health care costs. For every young person who dies from an injury, many more are hospitalized and treated in emergency rooms. Many young people are disabled by intentional and unintentional injuries. In teenagers, unintentional injuries cause about twice as many deaths as intentional injuries.

UNINTENTIONAL INJURIES

Unintentional injuries are the leading cause of death for children and teens. Some causes of unintentional injuries are motor vehicle accidents, fires, burns, falls, drownings, and poisoning. In recent years, there has been a decline in teen deaths due to accidents (primarily motor vehicle accidents).

Motor Vehicle Related Injuries

There are two primary ways young people sustain motor vehicle related injuries: being struck by a motor vehicle as a pedestrian or being in a motor vehicle crash. Children ages five to nine are the most likely of all age groups to be struck by a motor vehicle and be killed or injured. Unfortunately, children under the age of nine are unable to accurately perceive the distance of oncoming motor vehicles or the speed at

which they are traveling. Teaching them how to cross the street safely is imperative if this risk is to be reduced.

Injuries from being in a motor vehicle crash are the leading cause of death among people one to twenty-four years old. Teenagers and young adults are at particularly high risk for being in motor vehicle crashes. Teens make up only 7 percent of the driving population but 15 percent of all motor vehicle deaths. On the basis of number of miles driven, teens experience three times the number of fatal crashes as all drivers. Teens also are involved in more than 2 million nonfatal crashes each year (National Highway Traffic Safety Administration, 2003).

Inexperience, risk-taking behavior, immaturity, and greater risk exposure place teens at high risk for being involved in a motor vehicle crash. Driving a motor vehicle requires complex skills that take time to develop. Safe driving requires

experience, technical ability, good judgment, and the avoidance of high-risk behaviors. High-risk behaviors such as speeding, inattention, talking on a cell phone or text messaging, and driving under the influence of alcohol or other drugs increase the likelihood of a crash. Peer pressure often encourages risk taking. Driving at night and driving with other teens in the car increase the risk of a crash. Adolescents are much less likely to wear a safety belt, compared to other age groups. Alcohol consumption is often a factor in motor vehicle crashes. Twenty-nine percent of drivers ages fifteen to twenty who died in motor vehicle crashes had been drinking alcohol (National Center for Injury Prevention and Control, 2006). Many teens expose themselves to the effects of drinking and driving. Twenty-nine percent of all high school students report that in the past month they rode with a driver who had been drinking alcohol, and 10 percent report driving after drinking alcohol (Eaton et al., 2006). Adolescents are far less likely to use safety belts than any other group. Twelve percent of high school students report that they rarely or never wear safety belts while riding in a car (Eaton et al., 2006). It is obvious that injury prevention programs must focus on teaching about the dangers of driving while talking on a cell phone or text messaging, driving after drinking alcohol or using other drugs, riding in a car with someone who has been drinking or using other drugs, and the dangers of failing to use safety belts.

Fires

Another leading cause of unintentional injuries in today's students is fire. Most fire-related deaths and injuries occur in the home. More than 3,000 people die each year in home fires (National Fire Protection Association, 2006). In addition, more than 13,000 people are injured in home fires. Of the many who are hospitalized for severe burns, some are disfigured for life. Fires in the home are the leading cause of death for children under the age of fifteen.

Children who live in homes without smoke and heat detectors and those who live in below-standard housing are especially vulnerable to fire-related injuries. Smoke detectors cut in half the chance of dying in a home fire. The National Fire Protection Association (2004) estimates that 93 percent of homes have at least one smoke detector installed. However, one in four homes have smoke detectors that do not function properly, often because batteries are missing or not working. Injury prevention programs should work with children and parents so that they understand the importance of having smoke and heat detectors installed in the home and checking the batteries regularly. Smoke alarms should be installed on every level of the home, including the basement, garage, and attic. They also should be installed outside each sleeping area. New homes are required to have a smoke alarm in each sleeping area as well. Contrary to popular belief, the smell of smoke may not awaken a person who is sleeping. Instead, the poisonous gases and smoke produced by a fire can numb the senses and put a person into a deeper sleep.

Many fatal home fires are caused by improper use and disposal of cigarettes. Children whose parents smoke cigarettes are at high risk of fatal fire injuries. An all-too-common scenario is an adult who smokes falling asleep with a lit cigarette. The risk of falling asleep is enhanced when the person who smokes has been drinking alcohol. Children playing with cigarette lighters and matches are also a significant cause of fires that result in fatalities, injuries, and property damage. Two of every five fires that kill young children are started by children playing with lighters or matches. Injury prevention programs should teach children how dangerous it is to play with matches and lighters. Another important means of protection against fire injury is having a fire escape plan. A fire escape plan should be set up in advance, include at least two different ways to escape from each room, and designate a place outside the home to meet.

Drowning

Drowning is a leading cause of death from unintentional injury in today's students. Drowning as a cause of death is highest among children five and under and among males ages fifteen to twenty-four. Many children who survive near drownings suffer severe and permanent disability.

Many children and adolescents who drown are strong swimmers who became tired or pulled under by the current. Drowning also can result from boating accidents. Many incidents of drowning occur in swimming pools and hot tubs. Many young children are injured or drown in bathtubs, toilets, and sinks.

Young children need to be observed closely when they are near swimming pools and other bodies of water. Many children who drown in swimming pools were out of sight from adults for only five minutes or less. Adults can improve safety and reduce the risk of childhood drownings by installing childproof enclosures to prevent children from entering home swimming pools and whirlpools. Turn-off valves for swimming pools and hot tub

suction drains should be readily accessible in case a child is held under by a suction drain.

As children reach adolescence, they need to be educated about the dangers of participating in boating and other water activities under the influence of alcohol or other drugs. Many adolescent drownings occur in remote, unsupervised areas of lakes, rivers, canals, and the ocean. The risks of swimming in these remote areas (e.g., rough waters, submerged rocks, strong undertow) increase when adolescents use alcohol or other drugs. Alcohol use is involved in 25 to 50 percent of all adolescent drownings (National Center for Injury Prevention and Control, 2006). Drinking alcohol impairs swimming ability and judgment and the ability to recover after being submerged. Alcohol also can delay laryngospasm, a protective reflex that closes the opening to the lungs to prevent water from entering.

Other Unintentional Injuries

Other leading unintentional injuries that cause death and injury include falls, suffocation, poisoning, and bicycling accidents. Falls are the leading cause of injury and death in the home. Most spinal cord injuries are the result of falls. Young children are at particular risk of spinal cord injuries from falls because their sense of balance is not fully developed. Teens injured by falls often have taken unnecessary risks and may have ignored safety precautions or have been showing off. Suffocation due to choking is the leading cause of death among infants. Young children can choke on small objects they put in their mouths, such as small toys, coins, or food. Suffocation also may be due to strangulation. Some children and teens accidentally strangle themselves on material tied around their necks, such as a scarf, that has caught on another object, such as a car door. Children also have been strangled on cords from window coverings, strings on toys, ropes tied into lassoes, and pieces of clothing. Most cases of poisoning in a home result from young children swallowing household products and over-the-counter drugs. Poisoning deaths and injuries also occur as a result of inhaling poisonous substances such as auto exhaust, airplane glue, gasoline, and carbon monoxide. Carbon monoxide is emitted from motor vehicles, stoves, heaters, lawn mowers, and chimneys. Most deaths and serious injuries due to bicycling involve head injuries. Therefore, it is imperative that children and teens be instructed to wear bicycle safety helmets. The most serious injuries occur when bikes collide with motor vehicles.

INTENTIONAL INJURIES

Intentional injuries involving interpersonal violence and self-directed violence take a high toll among today's students. **Violence** is the use of physical force to injure, damage, or destroy oneself, others, or property. Today's students not only are becoming victims of violence but also are routinely witnessing violence in their communities and schools. They are affected by violence in many ways.

Interpersonal Violence

Unfortunately, many students are at risk for violence in their own homes. **Domestic violence** is violence that occurs within a family. Students might witness spousal abuse, abuse in which one parent harms the other. Their brothers or sisters might be violent. They might be victims of child abuse. **Child abuse** is harmful treatment of a minor. Child abuse can include physical abuse, emotional abuse, sexual abuse, and neglect. An estimated 3 million children per year are reported as victims of child abuse and neglect to Child Protection Services (CPS) agencies. More than 1,400 children die from abuse each year (Child Welfare Information Gateway, 2006). A family member is the abusive person in a large proportion of child-abuse cases. Many young people who are abused later become abusive when they are older and become parents if they have not received counseling. A high proportion of violent offenders in prison report that they were abused during childhood.

Other forms of interpersonal violence occur between students. Today's students are more likely to bully one another and to get into fights. **Bullying** is an attempt to hurt or frighten people whom the bully perceives as smaller or weaker.

Most teens have been bullied at one time or another. Bullying often leads to fighting. **Fighting** is taking part in a physical struggle. The first experience children have with fighting is often a fistfight. Forty-three percent of male high school students and 28 percent of female high school students say that they have been in a fight within the past year; 4 percent of students say that they have received medical treatment for injuries from a fight in the past year (Eaton et al., 2006).

Carrying a weapon increases the risk of violence for teens. Guns, knives, razor blades, pipe bombs, brass knuckles, clubs, and stun guns are examples of weapons. Today, many students carry weapons, including guns, or have access to them. Many firearms and handguns are in circulation in this country. Guns and handguns are present in many homes. It is possible for students to obtain a gun from their home without their parents or guardians knowing. Unfortunately, students can buy guns on the street from drug dealers and from pawnshops. Nearly one-fifth of high school students say they carried a weapon (e.g., gun, knife, or club) in the past month. The percentage of high school students who said they carried a firearm on one or more days in the past month is 5.4 percent (9.9 percent of boys and 0.9 percent of girls) (Eaton et al., 2006).

Guns are the weapons most likely to be used to harm teens. Having access to guns and carrying firearms are risk factors for homicide, suicide, and accidental injury. Carrying a gun increases the risk of injury due to accidents, the risk that a gun will be used to settle a fight, the risk that it will be used in a crime, and the risk of it being used for suicide. Among adolescents fifteen to nineteen years old, one in every four deaths is caused by a firearm. Fortunately, the rate of physical fighting and weapon carrying among adolescents declined during the 1990s.

Homicide is the accidental or purposeful killing of another person. The United States has an average of seventeen youth homicides per day. The percentage of homicide victims fifteen to nineteen years of age that are killed with a firearm is 82 percent. Homicide is the leading cause of death for African American youths and the second leading cause for Hispanic youths who are fifteen to twenty-four years of age (National Center for Injury Prevention and Control, 2006). After increasing during the 1980s and early 1990s, homicide rates have declined in recent years. Declines have occurred among urban and rural youths, as well as both African American and Caucasian youths.

Suicide

Suicide is the third leading cause of death among teens and also occurs among younger children. **Suicide** is the intentional taking of one's life. It is a deadly, final solution to temporary problems. Young people who commit suicide usually have experienced depression, anger, hopelessness, alcohol and other harmful drug use, family problems, and relationship problems for which they might have received help. Teen males are much more likely to commit suicide than teen females. However, teen females attempt suicide at a much higher rate than teen males. Youth suicide rates have increased dramatically since 1960. Rates are highest among males and in particular white males. Suicide rates among young African American males have risen dramatically in recent years. Nationwide, 8.4 percent of high school students (10.8 percent of females and 6.0 percent of males) report attempting suicide during the past twelve months in the Youth Risk Behavior Survey (Eaton et al., 2006). The majority of youths who attempt suicide do not receive medical or mental health care. This places them at risk for making another suicide attempt.

Tobacco Use

The second category of risk behaviors in today's students is tobacco use. **Tobacco use** involves the use of cigarettes, pipes, cigars, or smokeless tobacco. Tobacco use is the single most preventable cause of death in the United States. Cigarette smoking annually causes more than 440,000 premature deaths, far more than from alcohol abuse and illegal drugs (National Center for Chronic Disease Prevention and Health Promotion, 2006). Cigarette smoking kills more Americans each year than the combined total deaths caused by suicide, murder, al-

cohol abuse, AIDS (acquired immunodeficiency syndrome) car accidents, illegal drugs, and fires. Cigarette smoking causes nicotine dependence, several kinds of cancer (including lung cancer), chronic obstructive pulmonary disease, emphysema, and numerous other serious health effects. Using smokeless tobacco, including chewing tobacco and snuff, also can harm health. Smokeless tobacco contains many harmful chemicals that can cause nicotine dependence, increases the risk of developing cancer, causes problems with the gums and teeth, and dulls the senses of smell and taste. In addition, breathing environmental tobacco smoke—including sidestream and exhaled smoke from cigarettes, cigars, and pipes—causes serious health problems.

The prevalence of current cigarette smoking (smoking within the past thirty days) among students in grades 8, 10, and 12 increased from 1991 to 1996. Since 1996, there has been a small decline in smoking prevalence in youth in these three grades (Johnston, et al., 2005). Results from the 2005 Youth Risk Behavior Survey show that 22.9 percent of male and 23.0 percent of female high school students are current smokers (have smoked at least one cigarette in the past thirty days). Overall, male students (13.6 percent) were more likely than female students (2.2 percent) to report use of smokeless tobacco in the past month. Nationwide, 14.0 percent of students smoked cigars or cigarillos (little cigars) in the past month (19.0 percent of males and 8.7 percent of females). Seventy percent of students have smoked cigarettes (Eaton et al., 2006).

Tobacco use usually begins in adolescence. Each day in the United States, approximately 4,400 youths ages twelve to seventeen smoke their first cigarette. An estimated one-third of adolescents who smoke are expected to die from a smoking-related disease (Substance Abuse and Mental Health Services Administration, 2003). By experimenting with tobacco, adolescents place themselves at risk for nicotine dependence. Adolescents who began smoking early have more difficulty quitting, are more likely to become heavy smokers, and are more likely to develop smoking-related diseases. Most adolescents who smoke regularly already are addicted to nicotine. Success rates have been low in the cessation programs designed for adolescents. Adolescents are difficult to recruit for formal cessation programs.

Teens who smoke have an increased risk of depression (Killen et al., 2004). Among teens, smoking has been found to be strongly associated

with adverse childhood experiences. Researchers have found an increased risk of cigarette smoking in adolescents who have experienced one or more of the following: emotional, physical, or sexual abuse; a mother who has been battered; parental separation or divorce; and being reared in a household with persons who have abused drugs, suffered from mental illness, or have been incarcerated (Anda et al., 1999). These childhood experiences have a detrimental effect on a child's emotional and social development and behavior and might be responsible for depressed moods. Some adolescents use nicotine to cope with depressed feelings that result from having had adverse childhood experiences. When they feel depressed, they depend on nicotine to elevate or improve their mood. For these adolescents, treatment for nicotine dependence will not be successful unless it also includes treatment for the effects of having had adverse childhood experiences. Some of these adolescents will need treatment from a physician for biochemical depression.

Alcohol and Other Drug Use

The third category of risk behaviors in today's students is alcohol and other drug use. Alcohol and other drug use is dangerous to health and causes numerous family and social problems. Every year, the use of alcohol and other drugs is a factor in numerous traffic fatalities, drownings, fire fatalities, murders, rapes, assaults, child abuse cases, suicides, and deaths from chronic diseases, such as cancer and cirrhosis.

ALCOHOL

Alcohol is a psychoactive drug that depresses the central nervous system, dulls the mind, im-

pairs thinking and judgment, lessens coordination, and interferes with the ability to respond quickly to dangerous situations. The effects of alcohol increase as blood alcohol level increases. This has especially dangerous implications for young people—a smaller body means a higher blood alcohol level and faster impairment of judgment and motor coordination. This is alarming, given that the average age at which students take their first drink of alcohol is between twelve and thirteen. Three-fourths (74.3 percent) of high school students have had at least one drink of alcohol during their lifetime, and 44.3 percent have had a drink of alcohol in the past month. Nationwide, 25.3 percent of students report episodic heavy drinking in the past month. **Episodic heavy drinking** is having five or more drinks on a single occasion (Eaton et al., 2006). Episodic heavy drinking, or binge drinking, is associated with injuries, fights and arguments, rapes and other forms of sexual assault, reckless driving, infection with sexually transmitted diseases (STDs, including HIV), unplanned pregnancy, and other problems among youth.

OTHER DRUGS

The health costs and social costs of illegal drug use are staggering. The economic cost of substance abuse in the United States is estimated at more than $414 billion each year (Physician Leadership on National Drug Policy, 2002). Drug-induced deaths number approximately 14,000 a year. More than 2,400 Americans suffered drug- or gang-related murders in a recent year. The nation's 3.6 million people who are chronic drug users disproportionately spread diseases like hepatitis, tuberculosis, and HIV—more than 33 percent of new AIDS cases can be traced to injecting drug users and their sexual partners. AIDS is the fastest growing cause of death related to the use of illegal drugs. Three-quarters of AIDS cases in females are directly or indirectly linked to injecting drug use (the female either is an injecting drug user or has had sexual contact with someone who is an injecting drug user).

The percentage of children in grades 8, 10, and 12 who used an illicit drug in the past year increased dramatically from 1992 to 1996. However, surveys show that there may have been a slight decline since 1996 (Johnston et al., 2005). Four in ten high school students (38.4 percent) report having tried marijuana, and about one-fifth (20.2 percent) report having used marijuana in the past thirty days (Eaton et al., 2006). The increase in marijuana use seen in the early 1990s was associated with a decreasing belief that marijuana use increased health risks. Increasing use also is associated with increased perception of the availability of marijuana (Johnston et al., 2005).

Adolscents who drink alcohol or smoke cigarettes are at increased likelihood of smoking marijuana and using other illicit drugs. Popular illicit drugs used by some adolescents include marijuana, methamphetamine, ice, cocaine, crack, heroin, LSD, PCP, MDMA (Ecstasy), ketamine (Special K), and methcathinone ("cat"). Some adolescents also abuse anabolic steroids, methylphenidate (Ritalin), rohypnol (roofies), GHB, and inhalants.

Teachers, principals, administrators, and parents must work together to prevent the use of illegal drugs by students. Illegal drug use is having a devastating effect on our students and on society.

Sexual Behaviors That Contribute to Unintended Pregnancy, HIV Infection, and Other STDs

The fourth category of risk behaviors in today's students is sexual behaviors that contribute to unintended pregnancy, HIV infection, and other sexually transmitted diseases (STDs). Less than half (46.8 percent) of all high school students report having had sexual intercourse, and one-third (33.9 percent) report having had intercourse in the past three months. Fourteen percent of students (16.5 percent of males and 12.0 percent of females) have had sexual intercourse with four or more sex partners (Eaton et al., 2006). National surveys show that the proportion of adolescents engaging in sexual activity decreased during the 1990s (Santelli et al., 2000).

Having early sexual experience, and being at a particularly young age at first intercourse, greatly increases a young person's risk of unintended pregnancy and infection with STDs. Youth who begin having sex at younger ages are exposed to these risks over a longer period of time. Sexual intercourse during the teen years, especially first intercourse, usually is unplanned. As a result, teens do not take measures to prevent pregnancy or infection with STDs, including HIV. Youth who have early sexual experience are more likely at later ages to have more sexual partners and more frequent intercourse. The greater the number of sexual partners a person has, the greater the risk of contracting sexually transmitted diseases, including HIV.

HIV INFECTION

Human immunodeficiency virus (HIV) is the pathogen that destroys the body's immune system, allowing the development of AIDS. Currently, there is no cure for AIDS, and AIDS is fatal. During sexual contact, HIV from an infected partner may enter the body of an uninfected partner through exposed blood vessels in small cuts or tiny cracks in mucous membranes. HIV can spread from male to male, male to female, female to male, or female to female. Unprotected sexual intercourse (sexual intercourse without a latex condom) is a risk behavior for HIV infection, yet many students engage in unprotected sexual intercourse. The number of twelve- to twenty-one-year-olds who are infected with HIV is increasing. A significant proportion of young adults who currently have AIDS were infected with HIV during their adolescent years as a result of risk behaviors they practiced.

INFECTION WITH OTHER SEXUALLY TRANSMITTED DISEASES

A **sexually transmitted disease** is a disease caused by pathogens that are transmitted from an infected person to an uninfected person during intimate sexual contact. Common STDs reported in students include chlamydia, gonorrhea, syphilis, chancroid, genital herpes, and genital warts. Chlamydia is the most common STD in the United States. STDs can result in serious consequences, including sterility, increased risk of cancer, blindness and other difficulties in newborns, and severe discomfort. Some sexually transmitted diseases, such as genital herpes, are recurring. For example, a person who is infected with genital herpes always will be infected.

The United States has the highest rates of STDs in the industrialized world, with rates that are fifty to a hundred times higher than other industrialized nations. There are an estimated 15 million new cases of STDs in the United States each year. A quarter of these cases occur in teens (American Social Health Association, 2006). Teenagers are at high risk for becoming infected with an STD because they are more likely to have multiple sex partners, they are more likely to have unprotected intercourse, and their sex partners are likely to be other teens (there is a higher prevalence of STDs among teens than among adults). Compared to older adult females, teen females are more susceptible to cervical infections, such as gonorrhea and chlamydia, due to having an immature cervix. Chlamydia is more common among teenagers than among adults (American Social Health Association, 2006). As many as one in ten adolescent females tested for chlamydia is infected (CDC, 2001).

UNINTENDED PREGNANCIES

Students who choose to be sexually active are at increased risk for having unintended pregnancies. The United States has one of the highest adolescent birthrates among developed nations. Approximately 750,000 American female teens become pregnant each year. Eight in ten pregnancies among teens each year are unintended, and more than one-quarter end in abortion. Fortunately, the rate of teen pregnancy declined during the 1990s (National Campaign to Prevent Teen Pregnancy, 2006).

Most pregnant teens are unmarried, and most are not ready for the emotional, psychological, and financial responsibilities and challenges of parenthood. Teen mothers are likely to have a second birth relatively soon—a high proportion of teen mothers have a second child within twenty-four months of the first birth.

Most teens giving birth prior to 1980 were married, whereas most teens giving birth in recent years are unmarried. Also, pregnant teens are much less likely than older pregnant females to receive timely prenatal care and are more likely to receive no care at all. Pregnant teens also are more likely to smoke and less likely to gain adequate weight during pregnancy. Babies born to these teens are at greatly elevated risk of low birthweight (less than 2,500 grams, or 5 pounds 8 ounces), of serious and long-term disability, and of dying during the first year of life.

Clearly, student sexual behavior is risky and can have serious consequences. Much effort must be directed at encouraging students to choose abstinence from sex and delay the onset of sexual intercourse.

Dietary Patterns That Contribute to Disease

The fifth category of risk behaviors in today's students is dietary patterns that contribute to disease. Seven of the ten leading causes of death are related to nutritional and dietary choices. Poor eating patterns increase the risk of diet-related chronic diseases. Poor eating habits are established early in life, and young people tend to maintain these eating habits as they age. An unhealthful diet is a known risk factor for the three leading causes of death in the United States: coronary heart disease, cancer, and stroke. Other health problems associated with an unhealthful diet are diabetes, high blood pressure, overweight, and osteoporosis. An unhealthful diet accounts for many deaths and substantial chronic illness in the United States each year.

Most young people do not meet recommendations for healthy eating. Unhealthful eating habits can have immediate and lasting effects on their health status. On average, young people consume too much fat, saturated fat, cholesterol, and sodium and not enough fruits, vegetables, and calcium. The diets of most young people lack

servings from each of the healthful food groups, particularly fruits and vegetables. About one-fifth of high school students consume the recommended five or more daily servings of fruits and vegetables, and only 11.6 percent of female and 20.8 percent of male high school students drank three or more glasses of milk per day in the past week (Eaton et al., 2006). Failure to obtain adequate nutrients can result in deficiency diseases such as iron deficiency anemia, which is the most common cause of anemia in the United States. Preventing iron deficiency anemia requires adequate intake of foods high in iron. Vitamin C intake also is important, in part because it helps the body efficiently absorb iron.

Excess consumption of calories and fats can lead to overweight and obesity. Overweight and obesity are increasing among children, adolescents, and adults in the United States (Baschetti, 2005; Anderson & Butcher, 2006; Daniels, 2006). The prevalence of overweight among youths ages six to seventeen has more than doubled since the 1970s. Being overweight in childhood and adolescence is associated with many negative health and social consequences. Overweight children are at increased risk of high blood pressure and elevated blood cholesterol levels. They also might suffer from respiratory disorders and bone and joint problems. Being overweight subjects young people to psychological stress and often exclusion and discrimination from peers and others. Being overweight during childhood and adolescence also is associated with a higher death rate during adulthood. More than one-third of adults in the United States are now obese, compared to one-fourth in 1980.

At the other extreme, today's enormous pressure on young people to attain a slender body build increases the risk that females as young as nine will choose harmful weight-loss practices. Unsafe weight-loss methods can lead to poor growth and delayed sexual development. Dieting is frequently reported by females as young as ten to fourteen years of age (McVey et al., 2004). Female high school students are more likely (54.8 percent) than male students (26.8 percent) to report eating less food, fewer calories, or foods low in fat to lose weight or to avoid gaining weight. Female students also are more likely (17.0 percent) than male students (8.1 percent) to go without eating for more than twenty-four hours to lose or to avoid gaining weight. Taking laxatives or vomiting to lose weight in the past month was reported by 6.2 percent of female students. Further, 8.1 percent of high school females report taking diet pills, powders, or liquids without a doctor's advice to lose weight or to avoid gaining weight (Eaton et al., 2006). Also, the rate of cigarette smoking is higher for adolescent females who diet or who are concerned about their weight than for adolescent females who do not diet or have weight concerns. Some females smoke to control their appetite in order to keep from gaining weight.

Some adolescent and young adult females have eating disorders. An **eating disorder** is a mental disorder in which a person has a compelling need to starve, to binge, or to binge and purge. Anorexia nervosa and bulimia nervosa are types of eating disorders. It is common for eating disorders to begin during adolescence or even earlier in childhood. Many adolescents who have eating disorders have low self-esteem, a negative body image, and feelings of inadequacy. They also might feel anxious and depressed. Eating disorders can cause many severe complications, and the death rates for eating disorders are among the highest for any mental health disorder.

Health problems can result for children who are malnourished. These children develop more infections and subsequently experience more illnesses, miss more school, and are more likely to fall behind in class. Other problems associated with being malnourished include having difficulty concentrating in class, having low energy, and lacking the energy to participate in physical activity. Having a healthful breakfast is an important way for children to start the day off right, nutritionally. Many children and adolescents frequently skip or do not eat breakfast, which impairs their school performance, especially in problem-solving tasks.

Insufficient Physical Activity

The sixth category of risk behaviors in today's students is insufficient physical activity. **Physical activity** is any bodily movement produced by skeletal muscles that results in energy expenditure. Physically active children are energetic. They are more likely to avoid obesity and maintain a healthful body weight. They cope better with stress. Also, physically active children will suffer less chronic disease (e.g., heart disease, high blood pressure, osteoporosis) as adults.

Despite the health benefits of physical activity, many children and adolescents do not get enough physical activity. They are sedentary or less physically active than is recommended. More than half of adults do not get the recommended amount of physical activity, and one-quarter are not physically ac-

tive at all. More than a third of high school students do not engage in vigorous physical activity (Eaton et al., 2006). A disturbing trend is that children and adolescents tend to become increasingly less physically active as they age. Also, fewer children and adolescents are enrolled in daily physical education classes. In 2005, only 33 percent of high school students participated in daily physical education classes, compared with 42 percent of students in 1991 (Eaton et al., 2006). As a result, there has been a significant decline in the percentage of children and adolescents who can perform satisfactorily on a series of physical fitness tests, compared to children and adolescents of previous generations. It appears that sedentary activities such as viewing television, playing video games, and using a computer contribute to a general pattern of physical inactivity among children and adolescents.

Healthy People 2010

The *Healthy People 2010* goals and objectives (www.healthypeople.gov) represent the ideas and expertise of a diverse range of individuals and organizations concerned about the nation's health. *Healthy People 2010* sets two major goals: (1) to increase the quality and years of healthy life and (2) to eliminate health disparities. These goals build on the national initiatives of the past two decades. The 467 objectives are organized into twenty-eight focus areas that include specific diseases, health conditions, or challenges. Many *Healthy People 2010* objectives target actions to reduce or eliminate illness, disability, and premature death among individuals and communities. Others target such challenges as improving access to quality health care, strengthening public health services, and improving the availability and dissemination of health-related information. Each of the 467 objectives has a target for specific improvements to be achieved by 2010. Each reflects the findings of current health-related research and scientific evidence. The objectives that target schools and school-age youth are presented in Appendix B.

CDC School Health Guidelines and Strategies to Promote Healthy Behavior among Children and Adolescents

The Centers for Disease Control and Prevention (CDC) has released a series of documents that provide guidelines and strategies for school health programs to promote healthy behavior among children and adolescents. The CDC developed these guidelines and strategies by reviewing published research, considering the recommendations in national policy documents, convening experts, and consulting with national, federal, and voluntary agencies and organizations. The guidelines and strategies in these documents are intended to help personnel working in schools and community-based programs meet national health objectives by implementing health promotion programs and policies.

The CDC's school health guidelines and strategies contain recommendations that address policy development, curriculum development and selection, instructional strategies, environmental changes, direct interventions, professional development, family and community involvement, program evaluation, and links among components of a coordinated school health program (Fischer et al., 2003). The following guidelines and strategies have been developed by the Centers for Disease Control and Prevention (available at www.cdc.gov/healthyyouth/publications/guidelines.htm):

- *Guidelines for Effective School Health Education to Prevent the Spread of AIDS*
- *Guidelines for School Health Programs to Prevent Tobacco Use and Addiction*
- *Guidelines for School Health Programs to Promote Lifelong Healthy Eating*
- *Guidelines for School and Community Programs to Promote Lifelong Physical Activity among Young People*
- *School Programs to Prevent Skin Cancer*
- *School Health Guidelines to Prevent Unintentional Injuries and Violence*
- *Health, Mental Health, and Safety Guidelines for Schools*
- *Helping the Student with Disabilities Succeed: A Guide for School Personnel*
- *Strategies for Addressing Asthma within a Coordinated School Health Program*
- *Strategies for Establishing a State School Food Safety Program*
- *Six Strategies for Improving School Health Programs by Strengthening Professional Development*

Office of Safe and Drug-Free Schools

The Office of Safe and Drug-Free Schools is the federal agency that provides assistance for drug and violence prevention activities and other activities that promote the health and well-being of students in elementary and secondary schools and institutions of higher education. The office is within the U.S. Department of Education. The Safe and Drug-Free Schools and Communities Act is legislation that provides financial assistance for state and local drug and violence prevention activities in schools. State and local educational agencies as well as other public and private nonprofit organizations are eligible for this funding. The office also provides financial and technical assistance for character and citizenship education activities in elementary and secondary schools. As a result of this assistance many schools and school systems have received funding for implementing drug and prevention programs as well as character education activities. It is important for health education teachers to be aware of this federal assistance.

The Coordinated School Health Program

School health is more than what is taught in the classroom. It also concerns creating programs and policies that promote healthful living. It takes a concerted and coordinated effort to offer the range of health-related activities that improve, protect, and promote the well-being of students, families, and personnel in a school or school district. Currently, emphasis is on encouraging a coordinated school health program to be adopted in every school district. A **coordinated school health program** is a systematic approach schools use to meet the needs of the whole child and maximize the positive effect on students, schools, and communities (Lewallen, 2004). A coordinated school health program requires many components and an organized set of policies, procedures, and activities designed to protect and promote the health, safety, and well-being of students and staff. The goal of a coordinated school health program is to facilitate student achievement and success. A coordinated school health program utilizes personnel, agencies, and programs, both in and out of the school building, and involves several school personnel to address and meet health and social problems. In addition, families, health care personnel, community-based agencies, and others can be active partners in planning and implementing coordinated school health programs (Fischer et al., 2003).

Coordination is a key to a successful school health program. A coordinated school health program is more than a collection of several components and personnel (Lewallen, 2004; Shirer, 2003). Partners have to carefully coordinate services and activities to achieve a program that effectively addresses the complete well-being of students and staff. There needs to be shared commitment and an integration of components. Because many school systems have limited resources, a coordinated approach to school health is practical. Outside agencies can fill gaps that school systems are unable to provide on their own.

A school health coordinating council or school health team coordinates and provides leadership for the school health program (Shirer, 2003). Members typically include parents, students, teachers, school nurses, school administrators, physicians, health educators, a child nutrition director, other school health and mental health professionals, and community members, including representatives from the health department, social services, juvenile justice, voluntary health agencies, mental health agencies, institutions of higher education, and businesses. School health coordinating councils may be at either the school district level or the individual school level. These councils have the primary responsibility for implementing the various components of a coordinated school health program. They coordinate and plan such activities as program planning, fiscal planning, advocacy, liaison with district and state agencies, direct health services, evaluation, accountability, and quality control.

A school health coordinator is central to a well-coordinated school health program (CDC, 2003). A **school health coordinator** is the individual responsible for program administration, implementation, and evaluation of the coordinated school health program. Having an effective school health coordinator can make the difference between having a fragmented program or having a planned, coordinated, and effective school health program (American Cancer Society, 2005). Many coordinators are health educators or school nurses. A coordinator should be familiar with existing community resources; have professional preparation in health education or health services; be able to identify gaps and needs in the school health program; be able to plan, implement, and evaluate a coordinated school health program; and be able to identify and secure some level of outside funding for school health programs (Weiler & Pigg, 2004; Winnail et al., 2004).

Each coordinated school health program is unique and differs from the programs offered in other school systems (Fetro, 1998). Health needs and concerns differ from school to school and community to community. A school in an urban area may have concerns (e.g., gang involvement, traffic problems) that are not faced by a school in a rural area. Schools serving elementary students will address different health concerns than those addressed by secondary schools. Schools differ in what services and instruction are mandated by state or local law or regulation. School systems also differ in availability of and access to health services and health resources. Some schools are unable to provide needed health services; others provide such services. As a result, individual schools need to focus their school health program on the specific needs of their students, families, and staff (Fetro, 1998).

The coordination of these available health resources within a school and the surrounding community benefits students, families, and school personnel. For maximum success, these resources have to be mobilized in ways that make health a priority and a long-term commitment within a school system (McKenzie & Richmond, 1998).

A coordinated school health program that addresses the total well-being of children, families, and school personnel requires many components. The Centers for Disease Control and Prevention (2005) lists the following as components of the coordinated school health program (see Figure 1-1):

1. Comprehensive school health education
2. School health services
3. Healthful and safe school environment
4. Physical education
5. Nutrition services
6. Counseling, psychological, and social services
7. Health promotion for staff
8. Family and community involvement

Incorporating all eight components into a coordinated approach can positively affect the academic success of students as well as provide students with the skills and knowledge to remain healthy. These components also provide a safe and supportive environment that fosters healthful development (Council of Chief State School Officers, 2004).

The School Health Index (SHI) is a self-assessment and planning tool that helps individual schools identify the strengths and weaknesses of their health policies and programs (Brener et al., 2006). This tool is based on the CDC's

FIGURE 1-1

The Coordinated School Health Program

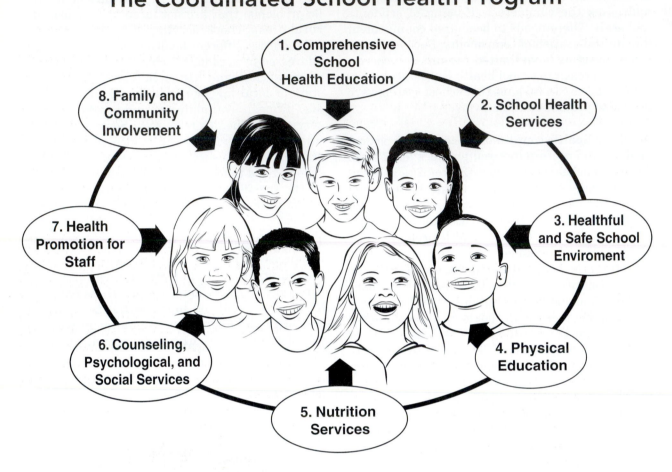

guidelines for coordinated school health programs (www.cdc.gov/healthyyouth).

Comprehensive School Health Education

School health education helps students develop the knowledge and skills they need to avoid or modify behaviors implicated as leading causes of death, illness, and injury during both youth and adulthood. Studies have demonstrated that health education in schools can reduce the prevalence of health-related risk behaviors among young people (Fischer et al., 2003). The **comprehensive school health education curriculum** is an organized, sequential K–12 plan for teaching students information and helping them develop life skills that promote health literacy and maintain

and improve health, prevent disease, and reduce health-related risk behaviors. The comprehensive school health education curriculum addresses the physical, mental, emotional, and social dimensions of health and is tailored to each age level. The curriculum is designed to motivate students and help them maintain and improve their health, prevent disease, and reduce their health-related risk behaviors. It helps students develop and demonstrate increasingly sophisticated health-related knowledge, skills, and practices. Health problems and issues are addressed at developmentally appropriate grade levels. The curriculum is comprehensive and includes a variety of topics:

1. Mental and Emotional Health
2. Family and Social Health
3. Growth and Development
4. Nutrition
5. Personal Health and Physical Activity
6. Alcohol, Tobacco, and Other Drugs
7. Communicable and Chronic Diseases
8. Consumer and Community Health

9. Environmental Health
10. Injury Prevention and Safety

School Health Services

School health services are services designed to appraise, protect, and promote the health of students. Health services differ widely among individual school systems, depending on the resources in the school and community as well as students' health needs. Duncan and Igoe (1998) identified several health services that are offered in various settings:

- Urgent and emergency care
- Timely identification of and appropriate intervention for health problems (e.g., infections, injuries, asthma, emotional difficulties)
- Mandated and necessary screenings for all students (e.g., vision, hearing)
- Assistance with medication during the school day
- Health services for children with special health needs
- Health counseling
- Health promotion for students and staff
- Preventive health services (e.g., immunizations, dental sealants)
- Referrals and links with other community providers

Schools are an ideal place for providing school health services. Most children over age five attend school. Schools provide a favorable setting for preventive health services (e.g., health screening for vision and hearing) and health services that are limited or unavailable to many students. Services and settings vary widely, ranging from traditional core services, such as vision and hearing screenings, to comprehensive primary care in school-based health centers or in off-campus health centers (Story et al., 2006).

School health services are provided mainly by qualified professionals such as physicians, nurses, dentists, social workers, speech pathologists, and other allied health personnel. Teachers also play an important role in school health services. For example, teachers might be called on to participate in various health screenings (e.g., visual testing, scoliosis screening) and to provide emergency care for students involved in sudden illness or accident. Chapter 2 in this book discusses school health services.

A Healthful and Safe School Environment

A **healthful and safe school environment** is a school environment that attends to the physical and aesthetic surroundings and the psychosocial climate and culture that maximize the health and safety of students and staff. Factors involved in the physical environment include the school building and the area surrounding it; any biological agents that might be detrimental to health; and physical conditions such as temperature, noise, and lighting. The psychological environment includes the interrelated physical, emotional, and social conditions that affect the well-being and productivity of students and staff. This includes physical and psychological safety, positive interpersonal relationships, recognition of needs and successes of the individual, and support for building self-esteem in students and staff. In addition to enhancing student health, a healthful and supportive environment fosters learning and academic growth (Anderson & Rowe, 1998). Chapter 2 covers the school health environment.

Physical Education

Physical education is an important part of a coordinated school health program and can improve the health of students, staff, and community members (CDC, 2005). **Physical education** is a planned, sequential K–12 curriculum that provides cognitive content and learning experiences in a variety of activity areas including basic movement skills; physical fitness; rhythms and dance; games; team, dual, and individual sports; tumbling and gymnastics; and aquatics. One of the main goals of the physical education curriculum should be to help students develop a physically active lifestyle that will persist into and throughout adulthood. Therefore, quality physical education should help students develop the attitudes, motor skills, behavioral skills, and confidence they need to engage in lifelong physical activity (Story et al., 2006). Physical education should emphasize skills needed for lifetime physical activities rather than those for competitive sports. Physical education classes should be designed to provide physical activity for students for a large percentage of each class period, and they should be taught by qualified teachers who have been trained to teach the subject (Graham et al., 2004). The CDC (2003) recommends providing an adequate amount of time for physical education classes (at least 150 minutes per week for elementary school students and at least 225 minutes per week for middle and high school students).

Quality physical education in schools can positively impact the health of children and the adults they will become (Johnson & Deshpande, 2000). Physical education can also improve children's academic achievement (Sallis et al., 1999). Yet according to the Centers for Disease Control and Prevention, the number of adolescents who participate in daily physical education has declined in recent years. Nearly half of those ages twelve to twenty-one are not vigorously active on a regular basis (CDC, 2003). Physical education programs can increase students' knowledge about ways to be physically active. Physical education also can be instrumental in increasing the amount of time that school-age youth are physically active in physical education classes (Seefeldt, 1998). Physical education interventions are important strategies for obesity prevention in school children (Budd & Volpe, 2006).

Seefeldt (1998) suggested ways that physical educators in schools can coordinate with the other components of a coordinated school health program. Physical educators can help school nutrition services staff to plan weight-loss and weight-management programs for students and staff who need and would like to participate. Physical educators can contribute to a healthful school environment by ensuring that facilities at the school are safe and free of hazards, and they can increase family and community involvement by offering

activities for families that include physical activity and by encouraging community organizations to use school facilities for physical activity during nonschool hours. There are numerous other ways that physical education can be coordinated in a school health program.

Classroom health education also can complement physical education. Health education can help students acquire the knowledge and self-management skills they need to maintain a physically active lifestyle and to reduce the time they spend in sedentary activities such as watching television. Health and physical educators can collaborate to reinforce the link between sound dietary practices and regular physical activity for weight management. Collaboration also helps these educators to focus on other behaviors that can limit student participation in physical activity, such as using tobacco or other drugs (U.S. Department of Health and Human Services and U.S. Department of Education, 2000).

Nutrition Services

Nutrition services are services that should provide students with nutritionally balanced, appealing, and varied meals and snacks in settings that promote social interaction and relaxation. Those who plan meals and snacks should take into consideration the health and nutrition needs of all students. School nutrition programs should reflect the U.S. Dietary Guidelines for Americans and other quality criteria to achieve nutrition integrity. School nutrition programs should offer an opportunity for students to experience a learning laboratory for applying classroom nutrition and health education and serve as a resource for links with nutrition-related community services. Food service staff have the primary responsibility for providing adequate and appropriate foods (Fitzgerald, 2000). However, the effective operation of school nutrition services requires coordination and cooperation from school administrators, school health coordinators, teachers, families, school nurses, counselors, and other school staff. Food service personnel should play an active role on school health committees (Caldwell, Nestle, & Rogers, 1998; Shirer, 2003).

School nutrition services are aided when supported by community resources and professionals. In addition to the nutrition services provided on-site by school personnel, schools should establish links with qualified public health and nutrition professionals in the community. These professionals can inform families and school staff about nutritional services available in the community, such as the Special Supplemental Program for Women, Infants, and Children (WIC), the Food Stamp Program, the Summer Food Program, and local food and nutrition programs. Qualified public health and nutrition professionals in the community can also serve as resources for nutrition education and health promotion activities for school staff. Voluntary health agencies such as the American Diabetes Association and American Heart Association can provide educational resources and materials to schools for nutrition education.

Counseling, Psychological, and Social Services

Counseling, psychological, and social services are services that provide broad-based individual and group assessments, interventions, and referrals that attend to the mental, emotional, and social health of students. Organizational assessment and consultation skills of counselors, psychologists, and social workers contribute to the overall health of students and to the maintenance of a safe and healthful school environment. Services are provided by professionals such as trained/certified school counselors, psychologists, and social workers. The need for these professionals is particularly highlighted by tragedies, as when schools need to provide services to students when a student or teacher has died. Professionals can provide invaluable services in helping students, staff, and families deal with the shock and grieving process. Personnel such as physicians, nurses, speech and language therapists, special education school staff, and classroom teachers also provide services that contribute to the mental, emotional, and social health of students.

Counseling, psychological, and social services can prevent and address problems, enhance student learning, encourage healthy behavior, and promote a positive school climate. These services are especially needed because of the emotional challenges many students face owing to parental divorce or death, family or peer conflicts, alcoholism, and drug abuse. School counseling and psychological services are capable of intervening in areas of assertiveness training, life skills training, peer interaction, self-esteem, problem solving, and conflict resolution.

It is impossible for schools to offer or fund direct services to meet all of the mental, emotional, and social needs of children. Schools have to develop linkages with community resources so that services can be extended to a greater number of children in need of services. Collaborations between school and community resources help improve school-age youth's access to services. The school health council plays a vital role in this collaboration and in advocating for increased resources for counseling, psychological, and social services (Adelman, 1998).

Health Promotion for Staff

Schools are one of the nation's largest employers, with approximately 4 percent of the total U.S. workforce, comprising nearly 6 million teachers and staff who work in the public school system (Story et al., 2006). The Centers for Disease Control and Prevention (2005) recommends that schools implement quality health promotion programs for staff. Health promotion for staff is health promotion programming—such as health assessments, health education, and health-related physical fitness activities—that protects and promotes the health of school staff. These programs encourage and motivate school staff to pursue a healthful lifestyle, thus promoting better health and improved morale. This commitment can transfer into greater commitment to the health of students and help staff become positive role models for students. Health promotion programs for staff also can improve productivity, decrease absenteeism, and reduce health insurance costs (Council of Chief State School Officers, 2004). For these reasons, health promotion programs for staff make good sense.

It is critical that school staff be offered regular opportunities to cultivate their own physical, mental, and emotional well-being Health promotion can include health education, employee assistance programs, health care, and other activities. Activities that might be offered to school staff include fitness classes, fitness testing and assessment, health screening for early signs of disease (e.g., blood pressure measurements, blood cholesterol testing), smoking cessation classes, nutrition or healthy cooking classes, walking or exercise groups, yoga or meditation classes, conflict resolution training, financial planning sessions, and support groups for various stressful life situations.

Various personnel throughout the school and community can lend their skills and resources to providing health promotion activities for staff. For example, physical education teachers can help plan and provide fitness activities. School food service personnel can teach healthy cooking classes. School psychologists and counselors can stress management and conflict resolution to school staff. School health services personnel, such as nurses, can conduct medical screenings and give immunizations for influenza and other infectious illnesses. Public health and health care professionals in the community are often willing to provide services that would promote the health and well-being of school staff (Allegrante, 1998).

Family and Community Involvement

Family and community involvement is a dynamic partnership in which the school, parents, agencies, community groups, and businesses work collaboratively to address the health needs of children and their families. School health advisory board councils, coalitions, and broad-based constituencies for school health can provide a means to effectively build support for school health program efforts. Schools should be encouraged to actively solicit parent involvement and engage community resources and services to respond more effectively to the health-related needs of students.

There are many ways schools can invite more family and community participation in coordinated school health program activities. Carlyon, Carlyon, and McCarty (1998) have suggested several of the following activities as ways to increase involvement. Health education teachers can send health information for families home with students that reinforces health education lessons. Families and community members can be invited to health fairs held at schools. Schools can encourage family and community involvement in projects that improve the community environment (e.g., recycling programs, providing safe bicycle paths). School staff can invite interested parents or perhaps even community members to participate in health promotion activities such as exercise or smoking cessation classes. School food service personnel can provide information to families about school nutrition programs and recipes for nutritious meals. Facilities available for physical fitness activities can be made available to families and community members. School

counselors can refer families to community services that meet emotional or social needs.

Comprehensive School Health Education

This teacher resource book has been designed to focus on one component of the coordinated school health program: comprehensive school health education. The **comprehensive school health education curriculum** is an organized, sequential K–12 plan for teaching students information and helping them develop life skills that promote health literacy and maintain and improve health, prevent disease, and reduce health-related risk behaviors. The comprehensive school health education curriculum addresses the physical, mental, emotional, family, and social dimensions of health and is tailored to each age level. The following discussion will help you examine the Meeks Heit Umbrella of Comprehensive School Health Education.

The Meeks Heit Umbrella of Comprehensive School Health Education

The **Meeks Heit Umbrella of Comprehensive School Health Education** illustrates how a curriculum can be designed to protect young people from the six categories of risk behaviors identified by the Centers for Disease Control and Prevention by teaching them to comprehend health concepts; analyze influences on health; access valid health information and products and services; use communication skills; use resistance skills; use conflict resolution skills; make responsible decisions; set health goals; practice healthful behaviors; manage stress; be health advocates; and demonstrate good character.

Figure 1-2 shows the Meeks Heit Umbrella of Comprehensive School Health Education protecting young people from raindrops—the six categories of risk behaviors identified by the Centers for Disease Control and Prevention. If young people do not have protection, they will indeed be drenched in troubles! The six categories of risk behaviors from which young people need protection are these:

1. Behaviors that contribute to unintentional and intentional injuries
2. Tobacco use
3. Alcohol and other drug use
4. Sexual behaviors that contribute to unintended pregnancy, HIV (human immunodeficiency virus) infection, and other sexually transmitted diseases
5. Dietary patterns that contribute to disease
6. Insufficient physical inactivity

The design of the Meeks Heit Umbrella of Comprehensive School Health Education illustrates how an effective curriculum is designed. At the top of the umbrella are three stripes, each of which illustrates an important component of a comprehensive school health education curriculum: health literacy, the National Health Education Standards, and performance indicators. These might be defined as follows:

- **Health literacy** is competence in critical thinking and problem solving, responsible and productive citizenship, self-directed learning, and effective communication. When young people are health literate, they possess skills that protect them from the six categories of risk behaviors.
- The **National Health Education Standards** specify what students should know and be able to do regarding health (Joint Committee on National Health Education Standards, 2006). The National Health Education Standards (American Cancer Society, 2007; *Health Education Standards: Achieving Excellence,* Atlanta, Georgia) state that students should be able to do the following:

1. Comprehend concepts related to health promotion and disease prevention to enhance health.
2. Analyze the influence of family, peers, culture, media, technology, and other factors on health behaviors.
3. Demonstrate the ability to access valid information and products and services to enhance health.
4. Demonstrate the ability to use interpersonal communication skills to enhance health and avoid or reduce health risks.
5. Demonstrate the ability to use decision-making skills to enhance health.
6. Demonstrate the ability to use goal-setting skills to enhance health.
7. Demonstrate the ability to practice health-enhancing behaviors and avoid or reduce risks.
8. Demonstrate the ability to advocate for personal, family, and community health.

- The **performance indicators** are a series of specific concepts and skills students should know and be able to do in order to achieve each of the broader National Health Education Standards. For each standard, there are several performance indicators that designate what students should know and be able to do by grades 4, 8, and 11. Young people need to be exposed to a curriculum that helps them master these performance indicators at age-appropriate intervals.

The Meeks Heit Umbrella of Comprehensive School Health Education is divided into ten sections. These ten sections represent content areas for which young people need to gain health knowledge, learn and use life skills, work to achieve and maintain health goals, and master objectives. **Health knowledge** consists of information that is needed to become health literate, maintain and improve health, prevent disease, and reduce health-related risk behaviors. Health knowledge in these content areas contributes to the achievement of the performance indicators identified for each of the National Health Education Standards. Each of the six categories of risk behaviors is included within one or more of these ten content areas; therefore, health knowledge will be obtained for each of the six categories of risk behaviors. Students are not adequately protected with health knowledge alone, however. They need to learn and use life skills. A **life skill** is an ability that maintains and improves a person's health and promotes the health of others. When students have health knowledge and

FIGURE 1-2

The Meeks Heit Umbrella of Comprehensive School Health Education

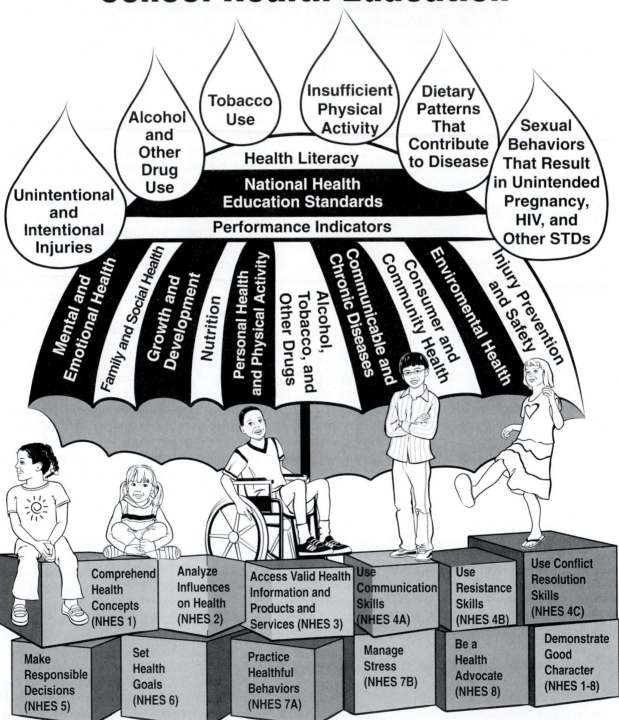

Tobacco Use

Alcohol and Other Drug Use

Insufficient Physical Activity

Dietary Patterns That Contribute to Disease

Health Literacy

National Health Education Standards

Performance Indicators

Unintentional and Intentional Injuries

Sexual Behaviors That Result in Unintended Pregnancy, HIV, and Other STDs

Mental and Emotional Health

Family and Social Health

Growth and Development

Nutrition

Personal Health and Physical Activity

Alcohol, Tobacco, and Other Drugs

Communicable and Chronic Diseases

Consumer and Community Health

Environmental Health

Injury Prevention and Safety

Comprehend Health Concepts (NHES 1)

Analyze Influences on Health (NHES 2)

Access Valid Health Information and Products and Services (NHES 3)

Use Communication Skills (NHES 4A)

Use Resistance Skills (NHES 4B)

Use Conflict Resolution Skills (NHES 4C)

Make Responsible Decisions (NHES 5)

Set Health Goals (NHES 6)

Practice Healthful Behaviors (NHES 7A)

Manage Stress (NHES 7B)

Be a Health Advocate (NHES 8)

Demonstrate Good Character (NHES 1-8)

are able to use life skills, they are better able to achieve health goals. A **health goal** is a healthful behavior a person works to achieve and maintain. **Objectives** are statements that describe what students need to know and do in order to use life skills and achieve health goals. The ten content areas for which students gain health knowledge, learn and use life skills, and work to achieve and maintain health goals are as follows:

1. **Mental and Emotional Health** is the area of health that focuses on developing good character, interacting in ways that help create a positive social-emotional environment, developing healthful personality characteristics, choosing behaviors to promote a healthy mind, expressing emotions in healthful ways, using stress management skills, seeking help if feeling depressed, using suicide prevention strategies when appropriate, coping with loss and grief in healthful ways, and being resilient during difficult times.

2. **Family and Social Health** is the area of health that focuses on developing healthful relationships, working to improve difficult family relationships, making healthful adjustments to family changes, developing healthful friendships, developing dating skills, practicing abstinence from sex, recognizing the negative effects harmful relationships might have on health, developing skills to prepare for marriage, developing skills to prepare for parenthood, and practicing abstinence from sex to avoid the risks of teen marriage and parenthood.

3. **Growth and Development** is the area of health that focuses on keeping body systems healthy, recognizing habits that protect female reproductive health, recognizing habits that protect male reproductive health, learning about pregnancy and childbirth, learning about the growth and development of infants and children, providing responsible care for infants and children, developing a learning style, achieving the developmental tasks of adolescence, developing habits that promote healthful aging, and sharing with one's family feelings about dying and death.

4. **Nutrition** is the area of health that focuses on selecting foods that contain nutrients, evaluating food labels, eating the recommended servings from the MyPyramid, following the Dietary Guidelines, following a healthful diet that reduces the risk of disease, developing healthful eating habits, following the Dietary Guidelines when going out to eat, protecting from foodborne illnesses, maintaining a desirable weight and body composition, and developing skills to prevent eating disorders.

5. **Personal Health and Physical Activity** is the area of health that focuses on having regular examinations, following a dental health plan, being well groomed, getting adequate rest and sleep, participating in regular physical activity, following a physical fitness plan, developing and maintaining health-related fitness, developing and maintaining skill-related fitness, being a responsible spectator and participant in sports, and preventing physical activity-related injuries and illnesses.

6. **Alcohol, Tobacco, and Other Drugs** is the area of health that focuses on following guidelines for the safe use of prescription and over-the-counter drugs, not drinking alcohol, avoiding tobacco use and secondhand smoke, avoiding risk factors and practicing protective factors for drug misuse and abuse, not misusing or abusing drugs, using resistance skills if pressured to misuse or abuse drugs, choosing a drug-free lifestyle to reduce the risk of violence and accidents, choosing a drug-free lifestyle to reduce the risk of HIV infection and unwanted pregnancy, and being aware of resources for the treatment of drug misuse and abuse.

7. **Communicable and Chronic Diseases** is the area of health that focuses on choosing behaviors to reduce the risk of infection with communicable diseases, being aware of immunizations that protect health, choosing behaviors to reduce the risk of infection with respiratory diseases, recognizing ways to manage asthma and allergies, choosing behaviors to reduce the risk of infection with sexually transmitted diseases, choosing behaviors to reduce the risk of HIV infection, choosing behaviors to reduce the risk of cardiovascular diseases, choosing behaviors to reduce the risk of diabetes, recognizing ways to manage chronic health conditions, and choosing behaviors to reduce the risk of cancer.

8. **Consumer and Community Health** is the area of health that focuses on acquiring knowledge of laws to protect health, recognizing rights as a consumer, taking action if consumer rights are violated, making a plan to manage time and money, choosing healthful entertainment, analyzing ways messages delivered through

technology might affect health status, making responsible choices about health care providers and facilities, evaluating ways to pay for health care, investigating health careers, and investigating public and international health needs.

9. **Environmental Health** is the area of health that focuses on staying informed about environmental issues; being aware of organizations and global initiatives to protect the environment; helping to keep the air clean, the water safe, and noise at a safe level; helping improve the visual environment; conserving energy and natural resources; precycling, recycling, and disposing of waste properly; protecting the natural environment; and being a health advocate for the environment.

10. **Injury Prevention and Safety** is the area of health that focuses on following safety guidelines to reduce the risk of unintentional injuries by following safety guidelines for motor vehicle safety; following safety guidelines for severe weather, natural disasters, and national alerts; practicing protective factors to reduce the risk of violence; respecting authority and obeying laws; protecting from physical violence and abuse; protecting from sexual violence and abuse; staying away from gangs; not carrying a weapon; and being skilled in first aid procedures.

Students who participate in comprehensive school health education are enthusiastic, radiant, energetic, confident, and empowered. They are protected from risk behaviors (raindrops, severe thunderstorms, lightning) because the Meeks Heit Umbrella of Comprehensive School Health Education protects them. They have a firm foundation as evidenced by the blocks on which they stand. Each block represents an important life skill they have learned and can use to maintain and improve their health and the health of others. Each block also states the National Health Education Standard that reflects that specific life skill. These life skills enable students to do the following:

- Comprehend Health Concepts (NHES 1)
- Analyze Influences on Health (NHES 2)
- Access Valid Health Information and Products and Services (NHES 3)
- Use Communication Skills (NHES 4A)

- Use Resistance Skills (NHES 4B)
- Use Conflict Resolution Skills (NHES 4C)
- Make Responsible Decisions (NHES 5)
- Set Health Goals (NHES 6)
- Practice Healthful Behaviors (NHES 7A)
- Manage Stress (NHES 7B)
- Be a Health Advocate (NHES 8)
- Demonstrate Good Character (NHES 1–8)

Implementing the Comprehensive School Health Education Curriculum

Approximately 92 percent of schools require health education for students in grades 6 through 12, usually as a separate health course (Grunbaum et al., 2000). The School Health Policies and Programs Study (SHPPS), a national study of secondary schools in the United States, found that the topics most likely to be covered in health classes are alcohol and drug use prevention, HIV prevention, tobacco use prevention, disease prevention and control, nutrition and healthy eating, STD prevention, human growth and development, human sexuality, personal health, and physical activity and fitness (Kann et al., 1995; Lohrmann & Wooley, 1998). The SHPPS also found that required health courses usually last one semester. Only 20 percent of secondary health courses last for an entire school year.

The implementation of comprehensive school health education is facilitated when there is support for qualified and trained teachers, standards-based curricula and assessment, addressing the needs of diverse students, integrating health content into other subject areas, and using principles of effective health education curricula.

QUALIFIED AND TRAINED TEACHERS

Health education is best taught by qualified teachers who have been well trained in content and in the process of teaching life skills. Standards for the preservice preparation of health education teachers have been developed by the Association for the Advancement of Health Education (AAHE) in collaboration with the National Council for Accreditation of Teacher Education (NCATE). Still, many health education teachers, in particular elementary teachers, have not had any preservice preparation in health education teaching methodology. As a result, those teaching health should be given opportunities to participate in health education inservice training programs. Preservice and inservice training programs can help prospective and active teachers implement up-to-date and effective health education methodologies and improve their teaching skills (Allensworth et al., 1997).

STANDARDS-BASED CURRICULA AND ASSESSMENT

The health education curriculum should be periodically evaluated and updated to maximize effectiveness. Curricula should be consistent with the National Health Education Standards as well as state and local standards that support health education. These standards provide a framework for selecting lessons, strategies, activities, and types of assessment to include in the comprehensive school health education curriculum. Learning activities and assessments are tailored to each grade level. The emphasis of comprehensive school health education is on the development of skills that promote health literacy. By promoting health knowledge, health literacy, and the National Health Education Standards, health education also improves the academic achievement and health status of school-age youth (Lohrmann & Wooley, 1998).

A vital part of comprehensive school health education is determining the level of a student's achievement. A curriculum that is based on the National Health Education Standards includes student assessments to determine if these standards are being met. Accompanying each of the National Health Education Standards are performance indicators specifying what students should be able to know and do at grades 4, 8, and 11. These standards and performance indicators include the ten health content areas as well as the six categories of risk behaviors that the Centers for Disease Control and Prevention has identified as the major causes of illness and death. The assessment of student health knowledge and skills has become an expectation in state testing programs, just as assessment in other academic

subjects (e.g., math, reading) is expected (Allensworth et al., 1997).

ADDRESSING THE NEEDS OF DIVERSE LEARNERS

Health education fosters a school culture that supports and challenges all students to do their best. Health education curricula and teachers must consider the needs of diverse learners. This includes bilingual students, students with disabilities, and gifted students. To meet the needs of diverse learners, modifications may be required in instructional materials, instructional time, and types of assessments (Lohrmann & Wooley, 1998).

INTEGRATING HEALTH CONTENT INTO OTHER SUBJECT AREAS

Health education can effectively be integrated into other school subjects. Integration into other courses can complement, but should not replace, planned and sequential health education within a comprehensive school health education curriculum. Classroom time can be maximized by having health education units in other classes (e.g., math, science, language arts, physical education).

USING PRINCIPLES OF EFFECTIVE HEALTH EDUCATION CURRICULA

Research studies have found that effective health education curricula share the following characteristics (Lohrmann & Wooley, 1998):

- Information is accurate, basic, and developmentally appropriate.
- Learning activities engage students in interactive and experiential ways.
- Students are given opportunities to model and practice skills.
- Social and media influences on behavior are addressed.
- Individual values and group norms that support health-enhancing behaviors are strengthened and supported.
- Sufficient time is given to allow students to gain the needed knowledge and skills.
- There is sufficient and effective teacher training.
- Methods and approaches are based on science (research) and theory.

Using This *Totally Awesome*™ Teacher Resource Book

You can make a difference in the lives of students. You can be a *totally awesome teacher*™ who is committed to teaching comprehensive school health education so that your students have an umbrella of protection against the health-related risk behaviors that place our nation's young people at risk. Consider the commitment of the old man in the following adapted story found in *The Star Thrower* by Loren C. Eiseley (1978):

> There was a young man walking down a deserted beach just before dawn. In the distance he saw a frail old man. As he approached the old man, he saw him picking up stranded starfish and throwing them back into the sea. The young man gazed in wonder as the old man again and again threw the small starfish from the sand into the water. He asked, "Old man, why do you spend so much energy doing what seems to be a waste of time?"

> The old man explained that the stranded starfish would die if left in the morning sun. "But, there must be thousands of beaches and millions of starfish!" exclaimed the young man. "How can you make any difference?" The old man looked at the small starfish in his hand and as he threw it to the safety of the sea, he said, "I make a difference to this one."

The old man knew that he made a difference, even if he never had contact with the millions of other starfish on the thousands of other beaches in the world. He knew he could give life back to the starfish whose lives he did touch.

As a *totally awesome teacher*™, you must be as caring and committed to your students as the old man was to the starfish he found on the beach. You will be like the old man as you will not have contact with all youth, but you can make a difference in the lives of the students in your classroom. You can help your students master the National Health Education Standards, learn life skills, and achieve health goals. This will help your students to be like the starfish—alive and healthy.

This *totally awesome teacher*™ resource book is designed to help you with this important task. It provides you with valuable information and teacher-friendly materials that can be used in your classroom or future classroom. This teacher resource book is divided into the following sections:

- Section 1: Comprehensive School Health Education
- Section 2: Health Content
- Section 3: *Totally Awesome Teaching Strategies*™
- Section 4: The Meeks Heit K–12 Health Education Curriculum Guide: A Model for Implementing the National Health Education Standards

Bibliography

Adelman, H. (1998). Counseling, psychological, and social services. In E. Marx & S. F. Wooley with D. Northrop, *Health is academic: A guide to coordinated school health programs* (pp. 142–168). New York: Teachers College Press.

Allegrante, J. P. (1998). School-site health promotion for staff. In E. Marx & S. F. Wooley with D. Northrop, *Health is academic: A guide to coordinated school* health programs (pp. 224–243). New York: Teachers College Press.

Allen, J. A., Haviland, M. L., Healton, C., Davis, K. S., Farrelly, M. C., Husten, C. G., & Pechacek, T. (2003). Tobacco use among middle and high school students—United States, 2002. *Morbidity and Mortality Weekly Report, 52*(45), 1096–1098.

Allensworth, D., Lawson, E., Nicholson, L., & Wyche, J. (1997). *Schools and health: Our nation's investment.* Washington, DC: Institute of Medicine, National Academy Press.

American Cancer Society. (2005). *School health.* Atlanta: Author. Available at www.cancer.org.

American Cancer Society. (2007). *National Health Education Standards: Achieving Excellence.* Atlanta: Author.

American Social Health Association. (2006). *STD/STI-FastFacts.* Research Triangle Park, NC: ASHA. Available at www.ashastd.org/learn/learn_statistic.cfm

Anda, R. F., Croft, J. B., Felitti, V. J., Nordenberg, D., Giles, W. H., Williamson, D. F., & Giovino, G. A. (1999). Adverse childhood experiences and smoking during adolescence and adulthood. *Journal of the American Medical Association, 282,* 1652–1658.

Anderson, A., & Rowe, D. E. (1998). A healthy school environment. In E. Marx & S. F. Wooley with D. Northrop, *Health is academic: A guide to coordinated school health programs* (pp. 96–115). New York: Teachers College Press.

Anderson, P. M., & Butcher, K. F. (2006). Childhood obesity: Trends and potential causes. *The Future of Children, 16*(1), 19–45.

Baschetti, R. (2005). The obesity epidemic. *QJM: An International Journal of Medicine, 98*(4), 319–320.

Brener, N. D., Pejavara, A., Barrios, L. C., Crossett, L., Lee, S. M., McKenna, M., Michael, S., & Wechsler, H. (2006). Applying the School Health Index to a nationally representative sample of schools. *Journal of School Health, 76*(2), 57–66.

Budd, G. M., & Volpe, S. L. (2006). School-based obesity prevention: Research, challenges, and recommendations. *Journal of School Health, 76*(10), 485–495.

Caldwell, D., Nestle, M., & Rogers, W. (1998). School nutrition services. In E. Marx & S. F. Wooley with D. Northrop, *Health is academic: A guide to coordinated school health programs* (pp. 195–223). New York: Teachers College Press.

Carlyon, P., Carlyon, W., & McCarthy, A. R. (1998). Family and community involvement in school health. In E. Marx & S. F. Wooley with D. Northrop, *Health is academic: A guide to coordinated school health programs* (pp. 67–95). New York: Teachers College Press.

Centers for Disease Control and Prevention, Division of Sexually Transmitted Diseases. (2001). *Chlamydia: Disease information.* Atlanta: Author. Available at www.cdc.gov/nchstp/dstd/Fact_Sheets/factschlamydia_info.htm.

Centers for Disease Control and Prevention. (2003). *Ten strategies to promoting physical activity, healthy eating, and a tobacco-free lifestyle through school health programs.* Atlanta: Division of Adolescent and School Health. Available at www.cdc.gov/healthyyouth/physicalactivity/promoting_health/index.htm#strategies.

Centers for Disease Control and Prevention. (2005). *Coordinated School Health Programs.* Atlanta: Division of Adolescent and School Health. Available at www.cdc.gov/healthyyouth/CSHP.

Child Welfare Information Gateway. (2006). *Child Maltreatment 2004: Summary of Key Findings.* Washington, DC: NCCANI.

Council of Chief State School Officers. (2004). *Policy Statement on School Health.* Washington, DC: Author.

Daniels, S. R. (2006). The consequences of childhood overweight and obesity. *The Future of Children, 16*(1), 47–67.

Duncan, P., & Igoe, J. B. (1998). School health services. In E. Marx & S. F. Wooley with D. Northrop, *Health is academic: A guide to coordinated school health programs* (pp. 169–194). New York: Teachers College Press.

Eaton, D. K., Kann, L., Kinchen, S., Ross, J., Hawkins, J., Harris, W. A., Lowry, R., McManus, T., Chyen, D., Shanklin, S., Lim, C., Grunbaum, J. A., & Wechsler, H. (2006). Youth risk behavior surveillance: United States, 2005. In *CDC Surveillance Summaries,* June 9. *Morbidity and Mortality Weekly Report, 55* (SS-5).

Eiseley, L. C. (1978). *The star thrower.* New York: Times Books.

Fetro, J. (1998). Implementing coordinated school health programs in local schools. In E. Marx & S. F. Wooley with D. Northrop, *Health is academic: A guide to coordinated school health programs* (pp. 15–42). New York: Teachers College Press.

Fischer, C., Hunt, P., Kann, L., Kolbe, L., Patterson, B., & Wechsler, H. (2003). Building a healthier future through school health programs. In Centers for Disease Control and Prevention, *Promising practices in chronic disease prevention and control: A public health framework for action.* Atlanta: U.S. Department of Health and Human Services.

Fitzgerald, P. L. (2000). When I grow up. *School Foodservice and Nutrition, 54*(9), 32–40.

Graham, G., Holt-Hale, S. A., & Parker, M. (2004). *Children moving: A reflective approach to teaching physical education* (6th ed.). New York: McGraw-Hill.

Grunbaum, J. A., Kann, L., Williams, B. I., Kinchen, S. A., Collins, J. L., Baumler,

E. R., & Kolbe, L. J. (2000). Surveillance for characteristics of health education among secondary schools—School Health Education Profiles, 1998. In *CDC Surveillance Summaries,* May 18. *Morbidity and Mortality Weekly Report, 49* (SS-8).

Johnson, J., & Deshpande, C. (2000). Health education and physical education: Disciplines preparing students as productive, healthy citizens for the challenges of the 21st century. *Journal of School Health, 70*(2), 66–68.

Johnston, L. D., O'Malley, P. M., Bachman, J. G., & Schulenberg, J. E. (2005). *Monitoring the future national survey results on adolescent drug use: Overview of key findings, 2004* (NIH Pub. No. 05-5726). Betheseda, MD: National Institute on Drug Abuse.

Joint Committee on National Health Education Standards. (2006). *Achieving health literacy: An investment in the future.* Atlanta: American Cancer Society.

Kann, L., Collins, J. L., Pateman, B. C., Small, M. L., Russ, J. G., & Kolbe, L. J. (1995). The School Health Policies and Programs Study (SHPPS): Rationale for a nationwide status report on school health programs. *Journal of School Health, 65*(8), 291–293.

Killen, J. D., Robinson, T. N., Ammerman, S., Hayward, C., & Rogers, J. (2004). Major depression among adolescent smokers undergoing treatment for nicotine dependence. *Addictive Behaviors, 29*(8), 1517–1526.

Lewallen, T. C. (2004). Healthy learning environments. *Education for Life,* August (38). Available at www.ascd.org.

Lohrmann, D. K., & Wooley, S. F. (1998). Comprehensive school health education. In E. Marx & S. F. Wooley with D. Northrop, *Health is academic: A guide to coordinated school health problems* (pp. 43–66). New York: Teachers College Press.

McKenzie, F. D., & Richmond, J. B. (1998). Linking health and learning: An overview of coordinated school health programs. In E. Marx & S. F. Wooley with D. Northrop, *Health is academic: A guide to coordinated school health programs* (pp. 1–11). New York: Teachers College Press.

McVey, G., Tweed, S., & Blackmore, E. (2004). Dieting among preadolescent and young adolescent females. *Canadian Medical Journal, 170* (10), 1559–1561.

National Center for Chronic Disease Prevention and Health Promotion. (2006). *Target-ing tobacco use: The nation's leading cause of death.* Centers for Disease Control and Prevention. Atlanta: Available at www.cdc.gov/nccdphp/publications/aag/aag_osh.htm.

National Center for Injury Prevention and Control. (2006). *Injuries among children and adolescents.* Atlanta: Centers for Disease Control and Prevention. Available at www.cdc.gov/ncipc/factsheets/children.htm.

National Fire Protection Association. (2004). *NFPA fact sheets.* Available at www.nfpa.org.

National Fire Protection Association. (2006). Trends—Home fires. Available at www.nfpa .org.

National Highway Traffic Safety Administration. (2003). *Youth fatal crash and alcohol facts* (Item #2P1093). Washington, DC: Author.

Ogden, C. L., Flegal, K. M., Carroll, M. D., & Johnson, C. L. (2002). Prevalence and trends in overweight among U.S. children and adolescents, 1999–2000. *Journal of the American Medical Association, 288*(14), 1728–1732.

Physician Leadership on National Drug Policy. (2002). *Adolescent substance abuse: A public health priority.* Providence, RI: Center for Alcohol and Addiction Studies.

Sallis, J. F., McKenzie, T. L., Kolody, B., Lewis, M., Marshall, S., & Rosengard, P. (1999). Effects of health-related physical education on academic achievement: Project SPARK. *Research Quarterly for Exercise and Sport, 70*(2), 127–134.

Santelli, J. S., Lindberg, L. D., Abma, J., McNeely, C. S., & Resnick, M. (2000). Adolescent sexual behavior: Estimates and trends from four nationally representative surveys. *Family Planning Perspectives, 32,* 156–165, 194.

Schur, E. A., Sanders, M., & Steiner, H. (2000). Body dissatisfaction and dieting in young children. *International Journal of Eating Disorders, 27,* 74–82.

Seefeldt, V. D. (1998). Physical education. In E. Marx & S. F. Wooley with D. Northrop, *Health is academic: A guide to coordinated school health programs* (pp. 116–135). New York: Teachers College Press.

Shirer, K. (2003). *Promoting healthy youth, schools, and communities: A guide to community-school health councils.* Published in collaboration with the Iowa Department of Public Health, American Cancer Society, American School Health Association, and National Center for Health Education. Available at www .schoolhealth.info.

School Health Services and Healthful School Environment:

Promoting and Protecting Health and Safety

Teachers and other school personnel have great potential to make a positive impact on students in the school environment. Of primary importance is the integral role the teacher plays in promoting and protecting student health. This is made possible by the teacher's access to certain health services and health professionals available through the school system. These health resources can prevent and control communicable disease, provide emergency care for injury or illness, and provide learning opportunities conducive to the maintenance and promotion of individual and community health. One resource you will find helpful is Appendix C, "The Teacher's Encyclopedic Guide for Health Concerns of School-Age Youth," which presents specific information for dealing with special health concerns of children and adolescents.

School Health Services

To promote and protect the health of our school-children, schools must provide a wide range of health services (Committee on School Health, 2001b). **School health services** are services designed to appraise, protect, and promote the health of students and school personnel. These services are delivered through the cooperative

efforts and activities of teachers, nurses, physicians, athletic trainers, allied health personnel (e.g., occupational and physical therapists, speech-language-hearing therapists, audiologists), social workers, and others. Students often are first introduced to school health services through routine health checks and health appraisals, such as hearing tests, vision testing, and scoliosis screening. When physical or emotional problems are suspected or detected through observation or health appraisal, students and their families can be directed to appropriate health resources for further evaluation and help by appropriate school personnel (teachers, school nurses, school physicians, counselors, etc.) or by other appropriate health professionals through referrals.

A system for referring students and families to agencies and health professionals with careful follow-up is a key component of school health services. It is essential that teachers, school health personnel, parents, and administrators consult and coordinate regarding the specific health needs of students. Follow-up services are necessary to make sure that intended health service activities are carried out and properly recorded on each student's health record.

Most schools do not have the money or personnel to offer all of the services that could be included in a comprehensive school health services program. Recognizing this fact, schools are increasingly

Story, M., Kaphingst, K. M., & French, S. (2006). The role of schools in obesity prevention. *The Future of Children, 16*(1), 109–142.

U.S. Department of Health and Human Services and U.S. Department of Education. (2000). *Promoting better health for young people through physical activity and sports: A report to the president.* Atlanta: Centers for Disease Control and Prevention.

Weiler, R. M., & Pigg, M. (2004). The school health portfolio system: A new tool for planning and evaluating coordinated school health programs. *Journal of School Health, 74*(9), 359–364.

Winnail, S., Dorman, S., & Stevenson, B. (2004). Training leaders for school health programs. *Journal of School Health, 74*(3), 79–84.

relying on community support and linkages. This interaction enhances schools' ability to offer the range of services that should be provided to meet the escalating health needs of today's youth (Committee on School Health, 2001b).

Providers of School Health Services

As noted in the previous section, school health services may be provided by an array of personnel, depending on the range of health services offered in a particular school, community resources for health care, available funding, student needs, and local priorities and values. This section examines the vital role of teachers, school nurses, and school health aides in providing school health services.

Teachers

Teachers play a central role in educating students and their families about school health services and helping them gain access to these services. Because teachers have ongoing contact with students in the school environment, they are in a position to observe students in daily situations and see whether students are functioning in healthful or unhealthful ways. The teacher will thus be able to suspect and detect needs and be in a position to refer students to the appropriate person or agency when necessary. The teacher's role does not involve diagnosing diseases, illnesses, or injuries. It involves being supportive in appropriate ways and getting prompt help in emergency situations.

Teachers are often in a position to observe when a student's appearance, behavior, or emotional expression seem unusual. Teachers are responsible for intervening on behalf of the student and should notify the principal, guidance counselor, or school nurse if they notice anything unusual about a student. But referring a student for evaluation or for help does not mean that a teacher's responsibility has been fulfilled, nor does it mean that the student has a major problem. Once a student has been referred, it is important to follow through to be sure that any interventions that

have been recommended are being implemented. For most student health problems that arise in school, the school personnel who play the greatest role are the teacher and school nurse.

School Nurses

The cornerstone of school health services is the school nurse. This professional is invaluable to any coordinated school health program. The school nurse is a health advocate for all children and school staff, working to protect and promote optimal health. The school nurse has many roles. In the course of an average day, a school nurse assumes the roles of care provider, advocate, change agent, educator, therapist, and manager.

School nurses have ample opportunity to directly and indirectly provide health education. For example, school nurses might teach health education classes, offer inservice programs for faculty and staff, implement staff health promotion programs, serve on health education curriculum committees, help in the selection of health education textbooks and other materials, offer parenting skills classes, and counsel students about various health issues. Many nursing preparation programs now offer some training in health education skills.

The U.S. Department of Health and Human Services and professional nursing organizations, such as the National Association of School Nurses (NASN), recommend 1 school nurse for every 750 students (NASN, 2006). Ideally, there should be a school nurse in every school. However, in many school districts there are too few school nurses. Unfortunately, the standards for school nurses in the United States are not uniform, and in many school systems the school nurses are the first staff members to be terminated when there are budget cuts. A small school district might have only 1 nurse for the entire school district. The national average is about 1,200 schoolchildren per school nurse; some school districts have 1 nurse for as many as 10,000 children (Karp, 2000).

Unfortunately, school secretaries or other school staff with no specialized health training are often forced to perform school nurse functions when there is no available school nurse. They are often the only staff available to dispense medication and treat minor injuries (NASN, 2006). These personnel often lack the necessary training for such responsibilities. It is vital that unlicensed assistive personnel (UAP) receive proper training from school nurses when these responsibilities are delegated.

NASN, an organization that supports school nurses, promotes quality standards and practice guidelines for school nursing practice. NASN provides leadership and continuing education opportunities to school nurses. NASN's Web site is www.nasn.org.

School Health Aides

Some school districts employ health aides to assist the school nurse. Health aides may perform tasks such as handling clerical responsibilities, answering telephones, and arranging screening examinations. They might also participate in vision and hearing screenings, take height and weight measurements, arrange for volunteer help, and provide basic first aid as needed in the absence of the school nurse. A health aide working in a school-based health center might also have these duties: making the initial assessment of sick and injured children who come to the clinic; managing of clinic supplies; referring and following up as directed by the school health nurse; setting up and maintaining confidential medical records; and acting as liaison between parents, the school health nurse, and school staff on health-related matters. Health aides can be extremely helpful to the school nurse and the coordinated school health program.

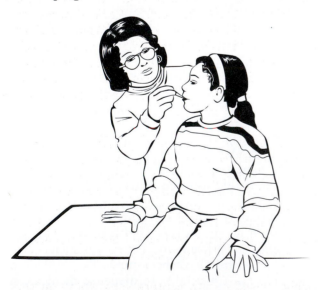

Some states and school districts require that health aides receive first aid training and specific

medication training for school employees. Health aides should be knowledgeable about immunization requirements, common health conditions, communicable diseases, and children's growth and development. Health aides need to understand their limits. They are limited to providing only the health care that has been delegated to them by a supervising school health nurse or other designated school health professional. The administration of oral medicines and cleaning of intermittent catheterizations are two health care tasks that are often delegated to school health aides. State law and school district policy often dictate specific tasks that can be delegated to school health aides. In every instance of delegation, the school nurse retains the responsibility to the student for the quality of the health care that is provided by the school health aide (NASN, 2006). School health aides must be trained, willing, and competent to accept delegated health care/nursing tasks.

Confidentiality of Student Health Information

All school staff must respect the confidentiality of student health information. The federal Family Education Rights and Privacy Act establishes the confidentiality of all student information and records, and parent rights to access these records. In most school districts, health care information about a student cannot be disclosed without signed consent of a parent, a guardian, or the student. Also, families do not have to disclose certain health conditions to school staff. For example, schools do not have the right to know a child's HIV-infection status; families do not have to disclose a child's HIV infection. If this information is disclosed to school staff, the confidentiality of this information must be protected. Another important law that protects privacy of student health records is the Health Insurance Portability and Accountability Act (HIPAA). HIPAA sets standards for the privacy of identifiable health information (NASN, 2004a).

School staff need to be trained in requirements of state law and school policies regarding the confidentiality of student health information. In locations where laws and policies regarding confidentiality are not clear, it is particularly important that school districts develop and implement clear policies about the confidentiality and disclosure of student health information. All school staff must act responsibly to protect the confidentiality of students and families. Health records should be stored with limited access. The security of health records maintained in computers must also be protected.

Community Partnerships for School Health Services

By working in partnership with families, community organizations, businesses, and health care professionals, schools can increase their capacity to offer a comprehensive array of services to meet health needs (NASN, 2005). The degree to which schools should provide health services depends on the needs of the students, the extent to which health service needs are met elsewhere in the community, and the resources of the school district. At a minimum, all schools should provide routine first aid and emergency care, care for students with chronic and episodic illnesses that interfere with learning, operate vision and hearing screenings, maintain immunization and current health assessment records, and make appropriate referrals for further care and attention.

The ideal is a full-service school. **Full-service schools** are schools that attempt to link the delivery of a full scope of educational, social, and health services through cooperative partnerships between schools and community agencies. The goal of full-service schools is to improve the quality of life for individuals and families in the community through the coordinated delivery of health, education, prevention, and social services. Programs developed to integrate services vary from community to community and according to local need. The specific services that are linked through full-service schools might include counseling, mental health services, substance-abuse programs, teen pregnancy programs, dropout prevention, health care, dental care, child-abuse programs, gang-diversion programs, conflict resolution programs, literacy training, job training, tutoring and remedial education, mentoring, after- and before-school care, parenting education, and programs for homeless youth. Other names

for similar programs linking these services include *integrated services programs, school-linked services, community service centers, community centers, community learning centers, family resource centers, and school-based youth services.*

School-Based Health Centers

Young people face financial, legal, family, and cultural barriers to getting adequate health care. To eliminate these barriers, some schools provide school-based health centers that offer a wide range of health services (Center for Health and Health Care in Schools, 2005). A **school-based health center** is an easily accessible location on a school campus where students can go for comprehensive preventive and primary health care services. Many of the children and adolescents who receive services in school-based health centers have no insurance and otherwise lack primary care health services. For many young people, a school health center or a school health clinic is their sole source of physical and emotional care.

Most school-based health centers are located in high schools, but the number in middle and elementary schools is also growing. Still, these health centers exist in only about 2 percent of all U.S. schools (Lawton, 2000). There are an estimated 1,500 school-based centers today (Story, Kaphingst, & French, 2006). Lack of access to health care for children and adolescents is cited as the major reason for the proliferation of school-based health centers in recent years. Other factors, such as the emergence of HIV/AIDS and the decline in the number of traditional school nurses in schools, have also spurred growth.

There has been significant opposition to school-based health centers in some schools and communities, usually around the issues of providing reproductive health care (e.g., provision of birth control services) and parents' rights (Friedrich, 1999). Another reason for opposition is the difficulty of financing school-based health centers in already financially burdened school districts.

School-based health centers vary widely in the type and scope of services they provide. Some school districts require a full-service center to offer a comprehensive array of services. Others might require considerably fewer services. It is not economically feasible to have full-service school-based health centers in every school or school district. The services that might be offered include these:

- Physical examinations—routine exams and required exams for sport participation
- Diagnosis and treatment of minor illnesses and injuries
- Tests for anemia, diabetes, and infections
- Vision, dental, and blood pressure screening
- Treatment of menstrual problems
- Pregnancy prevention
- Diagnosis and treatment of sexually transmitted diseases
- Health care for pregnant teens
- Immunizations
- Counseling for difficulties at home and at school
- Mental health services
- Substance-abuse treatment
- Nutrition education/counseling and weight management
- Smoking prevention and cessation
- AIDS prevention education
- HIV counseling and testing
- Classroom presentations
- Prescriptions
- Referrals to physicians and community agencies for specialized health services

School-based health centers are often staffed by a multidisciplinary team of professionals, which might include physicians, physicians assistants, nurse practitioners, school health nurses, community health nurses, mental health consultants, licensed practical nurses, health assistants, health educators, and outreach workers. Some schools hire part-time physicians to provide primary care services, but this is rare. More often physicians are employed as medical directors or consultants. Some schools hire medical residents in school-based health centers, and this serves as part of their medical training.

Some studies have shown that school-based clinics have reduced visits to emergency rooms, cut health care costs for poor children, and lowered the number of sexually transmitted diseases (Geierstanger et al., 2004; Center for Health and Health Care in Schools, 2005). School-based health centers are prevention oriented. Money can be saved by averting the treatment of simple illnesses or injuries in a school-based health center versus an emergency room. Many hospitalizations can be prevented by interventions at school

for minor illness and injury, chronic illness, and special health care needs. School absenteeism can also be reduced through interventions available through school-based health centers.

Accommodations for Special School Health Services

Schools are required to provide reasonable accommodations for students who have a physical or mental impairment so that those students can receive a free and appropriate education. The rights of students with disabilities are protected and guaranteed by state and federal laws. Section 504 of the Rehabilitation Act of 1973 and the Individuals with Disabilities Education Act (IDEA) are two federal laws that all teachers and prospective teachers should be familiar with. These laws protect students against discrimination and protect their educational rights. Schools and day care centers covered by these laws must accommodate the special needs of qualifying children. The parents of a child with a physical or mental impairment that substantially limits the child's learning or other major life activities may have the right to develop a Section 504 plan or an individual education plan (IEP) with their child's school. These written plans specifically state a child's disability or impairment, the child's needs, and how these accommodations will be delivered. Developing an IEP can be an opportunity for parents and educators to work together as equal participants to identify the student's needs, what specific services should be provided to meet those needs, and what the anticipated outcomes might be. In essence, an IEP is a commitment in writing of the resources the school agrees to provide. Accommodations for special school health services might include allowing a diabetic child to self-administer blood glucose tests in the classroom, having a school nurse administer medication to a child, or providing assistance in feeding a child through a feeding tube. Section 504 plans and IEPs are developed on a case-by-case basis, and a committee is formed for each plan. The committee usually consists of a school administrator or designee, the student's teacher, a parent or legal guardian, and sometimes the student. Parents have the right to bring an advocate, an attorney, and experts to these meetings.

An increasing number of parents are seeking accommodations for their children under these laws. This has resulted in feelings of anxiety among many teachers and other school personnel. Teachers often find themselves responsible for providing services that they do not feel trained or comfortable providing. Under legal provisions, teachers may be required to perform such tasks as suctioning tracheotomy tubes, performing urinary catheterizations, and helping to administer insulin injections. Teachers might fear that they will hurt a child by doing something incorrectly and that they will be held personally liable for such an injury. As a result, teacher responsibility for providing special school health services is currently a controversial educational issue (Temple, 2000).

School-Based Mental Health Services

The American Academy of Pediatrics advocates that school personnel work with pediatric health care professionals and mental health specialists to develop and implement effective school-based mental health services. This is critical because the proportion of children and adolescents who need care and assistance for psychosocial problems has increased substantially in recent years. According to the U.S. surgeon general's report on mental health, 20 percent of children have mental health problems requiring active mental health interventions. School-based programs offer the promise of improving access to diagnosis of and treatment for the mental health problems of children and adolescents. The American Academy of Pediatrics released a policy statement that addresses the need, advantages, delivery models, and challenges of school-based mental health programs (Committee on School Health, 2004). The statement gives recommendations for schools and health care professionals.

Administration of Medications at School

Nonmedical and non-nursing school staff who are designated to administer medications must be adequately trained and supervised. These staff members (or UAP) should be trained in school board policies and procedures governing the administration of oral medications, procedures to follow in administering medication, procedures to follow when there has been an error in dosing or missed doses, required record keeping, emergency and supervising contacts, and confidentiality requirements regarding the administration of medications and student health information. Non-nursing school staff must be trained and supervised by a nurse or medical doctor.

An emergency care plan should be developed for students who might require the administration of emergency medications by injection. Often state or district policies recommend a care plan that includes specific orders from a physician to administer epinephrine or other drugs and any first aid measures that might be necessary. Then if a student with a history of severe reaction to insect stings, food, latex, or other allergens is exposed to the known allergen and develops anaphylaxis, the emergency plan can be implemented. An emergency plan usually requires written permission from a parent or guardian, written orders from a physician, identification of who may administer the medication and requirements for doing so, procedures for notifying parents of emergency treatment, designation of who has responsibility for carrying the emergency medications when students leave school premises but are under the supervision of school staff (e.g., field trips, athletic events), instructions for proper storage of the medication, and a procedure for monitoring the expiration date on the medication. Parents are responsible for keeping school staff informed of changes in physician's orders or a child's condition. Parents are also responsible for supplying and delivering medications to the school. Epinephrine, used to treat severe allergic reactions, is usually administered by automatic-administration devices. These devices are easy to operate and can therefore be used by nonmedical school staff. Older students are often able to self-administer epinephrine through these devices, but many students are too young to do this. An emergency health care plan should also outline when to allow students to self-administer asthma inhalers and when school staff should assist students with asthma inhalers.

Some of the medications administered in schools are controlled substances (e.g., cough syrup with codeine, Ritalin). For these, security measures (such as storing in locked cabinets or locked drawers) are required to prevent theft. Access should be given only to those who need to administer or receive these medications for school use. These medications also need to be secured over school holidays and weekends. Theft of any drugs should be reported to the building principal, the school nurse, and the parents or guardian.

The most common medications dispensed are medications for attention deficit hyperactivity disorder (ADHD). Following ADHD medications, nonprescription medications, asthma medications, analgesics, and antiseizure medications are the most commonly administered drugs in schools. School secretaries are most often designated to dispense the medications, followed by health aides, teachers, parents, and students. The most common medications that students are allowed to self-administer are inhalers for asthma, other asthma medications, insulin, analgesics, gastrointestinal medications, cold remedies, antibiotics, antiseizure medications, and vitamins.

Emergency Care in Schools

Schools must be prepared for students and staff becoming injured or ill during the school day. Every school and district needs to have specific plans for dealing with these situations (NASN, 2004b).

Procedures must be in place for summoning help in emergency situations from local emergency medical services. Individuals in each school need to be identified who are authorized and professionally prepared to make decisions when health emergencies arise. Each school employee needs to know who these individuals are and how to contact them during an emergency. The school health nurse is the ideal person to serve in this role. The school nurse is the person most familiar with students' health conditions and community health care resources. School health nurses should be trained in basic life support, first aid, and the emergency treatment of health conditions such as diabetes, asthma, anaphylactic allergic reactions, and hemophilia. However, because school nurses often cannot be available, other members of the school staff should also be identified and trained to handle emergencies. Training for such non-nursing and nonmedical staff should include first aid, basic life support, and the recognition and treatment of anaphylaxis. This training should be supervised by a school health nurse or school physician. This training should be given to individuals who volunteer to provide service to the school and should include certificates to indicate successful completion of training requirements. Retraining is necessary to keep certification and skills current. In addition, all staff members, including coaches, should be trained in the school district's emergency response plan. Staff should be encouraged to obtain additional emergency response education. In particular, all school staff should be trained in universal precautions to protect against the transmission of bloodborne pathogens. Students should also receive training in emergency lifesaving courses (Committee on School Health, 2001a).

Students with health conditions that may cause them to experience an emergency (e.g., diabetes, food or insect allergies with known anaphylaxis, hemophilia, asthma) should have an individual emergency care plan in place at the school. In the case of an emergency, this plan specifies what emergency treatment is to be given at the school, who is to give the treatment, and how the student is to be transported to a hospital if necessary.

An emergency medical kit should be kept at each school and be available to school staff trained to give emergency care. The kit should be restocked after use. Students and staff members with a history of anaphylaxis need to provide autoinject epinephrine to the school so that it is on hand in the case of an emergency. Because epinephrine becomes inactive over time, expiration dates need to be checked and the drug replaced when expired. In addition, guidelines for emergency care should be available to staff trained to give emergency care.

Schools must inform parents, guardians, or designated emergency contact persons as quickly as possible when a child has been injured at school. Accident reports and other forms as required by a school district must be completed to protect against liability and for insurance purposes (Committee on School Health, 2001a).

In 2003, the American Heart Association introduced the Medical Emergency Response Plan for Schools (MERPS). This public health initiative helps schools respond to life-threatening emergencies in the first minutes before the arrival of emergency medical services (EMS) personnel. MERPS helps school personnel realize that life-threatening emergencies can happen in any school at any time. These emergencies can result from preexisting health problems, violence, unintentional injuries, natural disasters, and toxins. In the same way that schools plan for tornados or fires, school leaders should have an emergency response plan to deal with life-threatening medical emergencies. MERPS encourages every school to develop a program that reduces the incidence of life-threatening emergencies, and maximizes the chances of intact survival from an emergency. Such a program will have the potential to save the greatest number of lives, with the most efficient use of school equipment and personnel.

The American Heart Association plan includes five key elements that are recommended for school medical emergency response plans:

1. *Effective and efficient communication throughout the school campus.*
2. *Coordinated and practiced response plan.*
3. *Risk reduction and injury prevention.*
4. *Training and equipment for first aid and cardiopulmonary resuscitation (CPR).*
5. *Implementation of a lay-rescuer automated external defibrillator (AED) program in schools with an established need.* AEDs can deliver shocks to eliminate abnormal heart rhythms that cause cardiac arrest. AED programs have been shown to improve survival in adults who have cardiac arrest outside of a hospital. See Figure 2-1.

FIGURE 2-1

Using an Automated External Defibrillator (AED)

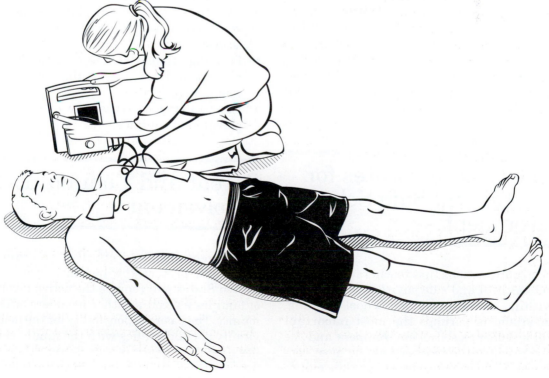

Healthful and Safe School Environment

Schools are responsible for providing a healthful and safe school environment that optimizes opportunities for learning and growth. A healthful and safe school environment is an environment that attends to the physical and aesthetic surroundings and promotes a psychosocial climate and culture that maximizes the health and safety of students and staff. In a healthful and safe school environment, potential hazards have been identified and actions have been taken to reduce the potential for illness or injury. Effective action to create and maintain a healthful and safe school environment requires cooperation from all members of the school staff—teachers, administrators, food service personnel, custodians, teacher aides, clerical workers, school nurses—as well as students and parents. A healthful and safe school environment also includes efforts to enhance the emotional well-being of staff and students and to eliminate hazards in the physical environment.

About one-fifth of the U.S. population, more than 53 million children and about 6 million adults, spend a significant portion of their days in approximately 120,000 public and private school buildings (Environmental Protection Agency, 2005). The school environment consists of the multitude of dynamic conditions that are external to the students, staff, and visitors of particular schools. These conditions not only are physical but also consist of emotional, social, political, and other conditions and circumstances that make up the school environment.

Teachers as Advocates for Healthful and Safe School Environment

There are many actions that teachers can take to develop healthful and safe environmental conditions within the classroom and school building. The classroom is perhaps the most important aspect of a student's school environment and the aspect over which the teacher has the most control. Teachers should do everything they can to provide a safe, comfortable, and nonthreatening environment in the classroom. However, the classroom is but one part of the total school environment. Teachers also should be advocates for a healthful school environment in their entire school building and in their community. This, of course, is a cooperative undertaking involving many people. As health advocates, teachers will work with other school professionals, students, parents, and community organizations to bring about improvements in the total healthful school environment.

Student Involvement

Teachers need to encourage students to take responsibility and become involved in actions that create a healthful school and community environment. Before students can feel responsible, they must develop an attitude of ownership and pride in their school. Such feelings are more likely to develop when students are actively involved in promoting a healthful school environment as well as a healthful community environment. There are many opportunities for student involvement. Here are a few suggestions:

- Working on litter cleanup and recycling projects at school and in the community
- Serving on safety patrols
- Writing letters to community leaders about environmental health or safety concerns
- Attending city or county planning meetings to voice concerns about pressing environmental issues
- Forming student committees to address environmental concerns at the school or in the community
- Fund-raising activities for purchasing safe playground equipment

Parent and Community Involvement

A comprehensive and effective program to improve and protect the health of youth in the United States will require the active involvement of families as well as other members of the community. The basic responsibility for the health and vitality of children lies with the family, but families need the support of schools and other community agencies. Schools are an important part of the community that must rely on and work cooperatively with other community agencies to meet the needs of students. Another important reason for emphasizing parental and community involvement in the school health programs is because it is highly effective. Many of the health problems that youth face are complex and multifaceted, (e.g., sexual abuse, substance abuse, depression), and they require comprehensive approaches. Countering these health problems requires providing young people with services that are often outside the ability of the school system to provide, such as health care, mental health, and social welfare.

This teacher resource text focuses on comprehensive school health education and stresses that the responsibility for health is shared with families and communities (Figure 2-2). For the comprehensive school health education program (see Chapter 1) to work effectively, it must be integrated with other school and community health promotion efforts. Successful integration requires careful planning, interaction, cooperation, and programming. The input of various community agencies, members, and leaders is fundamental to this process. This is often facilitated through the formation of school health advisory committees and community health councils.

FIGURE 2-2

The Responsibility for Health Is Shared

School personnel, students, parents, families, community members, local government, and local health agencies must work together to protect the health of students.

These coalitions can help build support for the school health program and pave pathways for successful school-community health-promotion ventures. School-community health coalitions should strive to bring together organizations and agencies from several community sectors, including education, government, voluntary health agencies, health care providers, charitable organizations, businesses, and parents.

Enhancing Physical Conditions That Facilitate Optimal Learning and Development

The physical conditions of the school environment include such factors as school size, noise, temperature, lighting, and cleanliness. The physical conditions of the school environment play an important role in promoting optimal student well-being. For example, the physical environment increases or decreases the possibility of injuries, the spread of infectious disease, feelings of anxiety and stress, and the potential for learning and development. School professionals should give serious attention to the following factors in order to maximize the potential of students to learn, motivate them to enjoy the process of learning, and create conditions that encourage optimal development (Figure 2-3).

School Size

School and classroom size are important environmental conditions. However, these are conditions over which teachers and other school professionals usually have little control. Student distraction is more likely to occur in large classes compared to small classes. It is more difficult for teachers to give individualized attention to students when a class is large. Small schools are able to offer students greater opportunities to participate in extracurricular activities and exercise leadership roles. Small class size allows teachers to have more interactions with each student. Teacher interaction enhances student learning and satisfaction with school.

Lighting

One of the most critical physical characteristics of the classroom is lighting (McCreery & Hill, 2005). Good lighting is a key to the general well-being of students and teachers who are confined to the classroom environment for several hours per day. Students can experience fatigue, eyestrain, blurry vision, and headaches due to poor indoor lighting. Adequate lighting promotes effective academic work, discourages unsanitary conditions, and encourages high morale. Poor lighting also affects students' ability to perceive visual stimuli and affects their attitude and mood. Some experts have suggested that optimal lighting helps keep students calm and enhances their interest in schoolwork. Proper lighting is necessary for reading and other academic work. Electrical lighting is necessary in most classrooms, especially during cloudy days. School professionals should consult with their local health department or power company to determine if the school's lighting is adequate. Illumination is measured in foot-candles.

Glare is also important, because it detracts from learning and can cause eyestrain that leads to fatigue and tension. Common sources of glare in the classroom are reflections off chalkboards and other surfaces, inadequately shaded windows, and the light from computer screens. Many glare problems can be remedied by simply rearranging desks or computer stations, not standing in front of open windows when instructing students, avoiding the use of teaching materials with glossy finishes, closing window shades when it is bright outside, and not placing posters and charts between windows. Glare and student eyestrain can also be minimized by alternating periods of close eye work with learning activities that rely less on visually demanding tasks, avoiding the use of textbooks and other reading materials with small type, avoiding use of duplicated materials with poor reading quality, writing large on chalkboards and using high-quality chalk, maintaining clean chalkboards, and replacing burned-out lightbulbs or light filaments.

Color Choices

The proper use of color can transform a school's atmosphere from being depressing and monotonous to being inviting, pleasing, and stimulating. Select

FIGURE 2-3

The Physical Conditions Necessary for Optimal Learning

The following factors maximize the potential for students to learn:

1. School size
2. Lighting
3. Color choices
4. Temperature and ventilation

5. Noise control
6. Sanitation and cleanliness
7. Accessibility

wall paint that creates a cheerful, pleasant class-room mood. Certain colors and textures of paint can brighten up a room and, at the same time, maintain a peaceful atmosphere. Light colors enhance the illumination of the lighting system.

Temperature and Ventilation

It is difficult for students to learn in a classroom that is too warm, too stuffy, or too cool. Temperatures that are too high deplete energy from students, making students listless and sluggish. Temperatures that are too low can make students restless and inattentive. Teachers should monitor the temperature of the classroom and frequently ask students if they are comfortable. It is preferable for each classroom to have a thermometer and a thermostat with which a teacher can control the room temperature. Teachers should report temperature and ventilation problems that they cannot control to building principals or custodians.

Optimal classroom temperature varies from region to region and from season to season. In schools that must be heated during the winter, a temperature range of approximately 65 to 70 degrees Fahrenheit is desirable. Because vigorous physical activity causes students to generate more heat, adjustments in room temperature are necessary when students are active. In gymnasiums, a temperature of 65 degrees Fahrenheit or a few degrees cooler may be optimal. Elementary school students have higher metabolic rates and are more active than older students and adults. As a result, they may be more comfortable at a lower temperature than adults. To compensate for this difference, it is often necessary for adults to wear heavier clothing or a sweater in the classroom.

High temperatures and high humidity can make classrooms uncomfortable at the start and end of the traditional school year, particularly in southern states. Air temperature, ventilation, humidity, and air freshness are best controlled through central air conditioning systems, which can be prohibitively expensive for many schools. Window-unit air conditioners are an option, although these can be noisy and make it difficult to carry out classroom activities. In buildings not equipped with air conditioning, teachers should use electrical fans and open windows and doors for air movement. Teachers should make sure that students drink plenty of water to avoid dehydration and be alert for any signs of heat exhaustion in students.

In addition to temperature control, classrooms and other areas in the school need adequate ventilation, or air circulation, to provide comfort, remove body odors, and remove indoor air pollutants. Air movement should be only barely felt; stronger air movement can chill or distract students. Arts and crafts areas might require extra attention to ventilation; exhaust hood systems or other devices may be needed in areas where there are toxic fumes.

Noise Control

Noise control is important in a healthful school environment. Noise can be annoying and distracting, making it difficult for students to learn. Noise can decrease teaching time by forcing teachers to continually pause or by making it difficult for the student and teacher to hear each other. Prolonged noise is stressful for both educators and students and often leads to feelings of anxiety, irritation, frustration, or fatigue. In addition, prolonged exposure to noise is associated with increases in blood pressure, which over time can impair health.

Classroom noise can be controlled by using noise-absorbing materials such as carpeting, ceiling insulation, and acoustical panels, as well as by keeping students' noise to a minimum (Rittner-Heir, 2004). Other school noise control measures include building new schools in quiet neighborhoods away from traffic noise, insulating schools to keep out outside noise, locating noisy activity areas (e.g., gymnasiums, shop classes, the lunchroom) away from other classroom areas, teaching students to avoid shouting in halls and in school buses, and planting shrubs between the school buildings and traffic areas.

Students need to be taught that exposure to loud noise can lead to hearing loss. They should be required to wear earplugs when using noisy equipment. School professionals also need to alert students to the dangers of listening to very loud music through headphones or in cars—such loud noise can be unsafe and lead to eventual deafness.

Sanitation and Cleanliness

A healthful school is sanitary and clean. Sanitation and cleanliness require not only well-trained maintenance staff but also the cooperation of teachers, administrators, and students. **Sanitation** is the protection of health and prevention of disease by removing filth and infectious material from the environment. Sanitation requires cleaning and washing, disinfecting, sewage disposal, waste removal, safe water supply, handwashing, proper food handling and food preservation, and pest control. Personal sanitation procedures such as handwashing should also be stressed for all students and personnel in the school environment. Schools are required by law to maintain a sanitary environment and, in most states, are regularly inspected by public health sanitarians.

Other Physical Environment Concerns

You can probably think of other physical conditions in schools that can negatively or positively impact children's health and development. For example, having adequate space and facilities for physical activity and physical education is important because it encourages and supports physical activity. On the other hand, the physical structure of some school buildings allows for "hidden spaces," away from adult eyes, where students can be in danger of acts of intimidation or violence.

Another major concern about the physical environment is the potential for toxic environmental exposure in the school setting. The list of possible environmental toxins is long but includes such toxins as asbestos, radon, ultraviolet light, lead, mercury, environmental tobacco smoke, carbon monoxide, solvents, pesticides, noise, molds, animal dander, and cockroach parts. Children's metabolism, developing body systems, and exposure to environmental toxins can interact in ways similar to and different than adults. Also, some exposures, while not apparently harmful for adults in similar doses, can result in adverse health effects for children. Childhood exposures may result in health problems years later (NASN, 2004c).

Accessibility

Healthful schools are accepting of students with a wide range of physical abilities and make appropriate accommodations in the physical environment whenever possible. Students with physical disabilities often require modifications in the school environment in order to gain access to the classroom, lunchroom, restroom, playground, and other facilities. This access often requires the installation of special equipment or modification of existing physical facilities to provide ramps, wider doorways, and elevators. Adjustments in time schedules may also be necessary.

Establishing a Positive Emotional Environment

The emotional environment of the school setting deserves special attention. The **emotional environment** is the feelings and sensibilities expressed in the expectations, interpersonal relationships, and experiences that affect the student's development (Figure 2-4). The emotional environment is as fundamental to healthful development as the physical environment is.

Emotionally warm and nonthreatening learning environments promote health and learning. Threatening school environmental conditions take a toll on students as well as school professionals. School professionals who become stressed or burned out find it difficult to be effective teachers and to be supportive of their students.

The teacher's personality and behavior are important determinants of emotional climate. Teachers should consider the following suggestions as ways to enhance the emotional environment of the classroom:

- Have high expectations for student achievement and behavior, and expect all students to succeed.
- Be an effective listener and observer of students.
- Show respect for each student.
- Deal with each student as a unique and valuable person.
- Model respect, concern, and caring for people of all backgrounds.
- Become familiar with students' talents and interests.
- Use firmness, fairness, and friendliness as guiding principles in disciplining students.
- Enforce classroom rules.
- Give immediate attention to behavioral and disciplinary problems, and do not allow pressures to mount.
- Give genuine praise and recognition for student achievement.
- Provide for more successes than failures in student work.
- Have a good sense of humor.
- Be optimistic and enthusiastic.
- Do not allow students to put one another down.
- Get students involved in planning their individual learning goals.
- Make learning fun, relevant, and challenging.
- Avoid speaking to students in a harsh or scolding tone.
- Give appropriate praise, and avoid giving empty praise.
- Get students involved in instructional planning and classroom management.
- Maintain a clean, neat, and orderly classroom.
- Allow students to express feelings and attitudes.
- Accept your limitations and students' limitations.
- Don't overemphasize competitiveness in learning activities and evaluation practices.
- Be sure that the demands you place on students are realistic, meaningful, and appropriate.

FIGURE 2-4

The Emotional Environment Contributes to School Health

The **emotional environment** is the feelings and sensibilities expressed in the expectations, interpersonal relationships, and experiences that affect the student's development.

- Be alert to any behaviors that may indicate emotional problems.

Emotional Security

Students' potential for learning is optimized when students feel secure—not just physically, but also emotionally. **Emotional security** is a feeling of freedom from anxiety in which individuals feel that they can present and express themselves without fear of ridicule, threat, or belittlement. Belittling put-downs are all too common in verbal exchanges between students ("Get a life!" "Hey, stupid!"). In childhood, put-downs are overt and direct. As students grow older, put-downs usually take a more subtle form but can just as surely injure one's emotional security.

Put-downs of any form should not be tolerated in the school setting. Without dismissing or ignoring negative behavior, school professionals should systematically look for and praise the good that they see in students and colleagues. This simple concept is often difficult to implement. Many people are more likely to tear others down than build others up. The power of being a positive builder of other people is immense. Supportive and affirmative behaviors can be taught and then passed on to others by example. When students and staff members feel that another person has treated them with care, compassion, and consideration, they often begin to respond to others within their environment in the same positive manner. Sadly, some students have never had anyone who really cared for them. Feeling cared for is a necessary prerequisite to emotional security. This is an important key to developing supportive, affirming relationships in the classroom and the broader school environment.

An important way to build healthful school environments is for school professionals to model empathetic behavior. Schools need to show high expectations regarding supportive and affirmative behaviors and low tolerance for put-downs. Teaching and modeling these behaviors increases emotional security by building the positive, affirming relationships that are the backbone of a healthful school climate.

Sensitivity to Differences

Today's schools are becoming increasingly diverse—composed of students and staff of various skin colors, religious and ethnic backgrounds, and physical, mental, and emotional capabilities. Every student is unique, different from everyone else in some way. Healthful schools promote attitudes of respect, understanding, and sensitivity to these differences. These attitudes are supported when school professionals model respect, concern, and caring for people of all backgrounds. Schools can also foster sensitivity to differences by incorporating into the curriculum opportunities for

multicultural understanding. School environments characterized by an openness to differences support students and staff in working through any fears that they may have developed about people who are different from themselves.

Providing a Safe School Environment

The potential for injuries occurring in the school environment is a concern. Schools serve a large number of students for many hours a day. School personnel are responsible for the safety of students at school and during school activities, and they share in the responsibility of keeping students safe as they travel to and from school. In addition, the safety of all people who work and visit the school must be protected.

Some school districts are able to employ a safety director or supervisor who can oversee the total school safety program. Other districts or individual schools form safety councils to supervise these activities. Safety councils are formed with representation from teachers, administrators, school support staff, parents, and students. Safety councils establish sound safety policies, procedures, and programs. However, rather than having a separate safety director, these safety functions could be part of the responsibilities of the school health coordinator (see Chapter 1). The school health coordinating council may fulfill the roles and responsibilities of a school safety council. When there is both a safety council and a school health coordinating council in a school system, they should work together.

This section discusses teacher responsibilities, safe school transportation, safe playgrounds, and disaster and emergency preparedness.

Teacher Responsibilities

Classroom teachers have the primary responsibility for instructing students about safety, but they also have other major responsibilities in the school safety program, such as these:

- Properly reporting any accident or injury in or around the school

- Assessing and correcting potential safety hazards in the classroom and total school environment
- Providing proper first aid care to injured students or school employees
- Establishing safety procedures in the classroom
- Providing appropriate supervision of students at all times

LIABILITY PROTECTION AND SAFETY GUIDELINES

Elementary and secondary teachers are becoming increasingly aware that the law defines, limits, and prescribes many aspects of a teacher's daily life. This is an age of litigation, grievances are often brought forth against schools and teachers in the courts, and new legislation seems to be regulating more of school life. In addition to the growing number of local, state, and federal laws, an array of complex case law principles add to the confusion.

The major aspect of safety liability cases stems from charges of negligence relating to a teacher's failure to supervise properly in accordance with his or her *in loco parentis* obligation (to act "in the place of a parent"), contractual obligation, and professional responsibility. **Negligence** is the failure to conduct oneself in conformity with standards established by law for the protection of others against unreasonable risk of injury. Although courts of law do not expect teachers to protect students from unforeseeable accidents or acts of nature, they do require teachers to act as a reasonably prudent teacher should in protecting students from possible harm or injury.

Teachers are responsible for exercising good judgment in adequately supervising the students in their charge. Teachers might be found by a court not to have acted in a reasonably prudent manner when they exercised their duties with carelessness, lack of discretion, or lack of diligence. When an injury results, the teacher may be held liable for negligence as the cause of the injury to the student.

There are several guidelines that teachers should follow to avoid injuries and civil liability:

- Establish and enforce safety rules for all school activities.
- Be familiar with and informed about school, district, and state rules and regulations that pertain to student safety.

- Enforce rules whenever violations occur.
- Be familiar with the liability laws of the state in which the school is located.
- Be aware of the type of insurance policy provided by the district employing the teacher.
- If the school district has no policy, invest in a personal policy for personal protection (the National Education Association, the American Federation of Teachers, and many insurance companies offer policies).
- Become certified in first aid and maintain that certification.
- Always provide adequate supervision of students for all school-related activities.
- Provide higher standards of supervision when students are younger, handicapped, or engaged in potentially dangerous activities.
- Ensure that all equipment used in school activities is in correct working order and checked for safe operation.
- Be at the assigned place at all times.
- Make appropriate arrangements for supervision when it is necessary to leave the classroom or the assigned place of responsibility.
- Inform substitute teachers about any unusual medical, psychological, or handicapping conditions of students placed under their supervision.
- Plan field trips with great care and be sure to provide adequate supervision.
- Do not send students on errands off the school grounds.
- Be sure to file an accident report whenever a student under your supervision has been in an accident.

REPORTING ACCIDENTS

It is important for teachers and other school professionals to complete and file accident reports following any injury. Accident reports not only protect the school and school employees in liability suits, but they also can be helpful in identifying and correcting hazardous conditions at the school site. Accident reports can also provide useful information for evaluating the school safety program. Accident reports should provide the following information:

- Name, age, grade level, and gender of injured student or employee
- Home address of the injured person
- Specific date and time that the accident occurred
- Specific location where the accident occurred

- Detailed description of the nature and degree of the injury and how the injury occurred
- Description of what the injured person was doing, unsafe acts or unsafe conditions, equipment involved, and so on
- Who was present when the injury occurred
- Teacher or school professional in charge when injury occurred
- Whether parent or other individual was notified
- Immediate action taken
- Date of student's or employee's return to activity

Witnesses to the accident should be noted and asked to sign the accident report. The signatures of the school professionals completing the report and the principal also should be included on the report.

Safe Transportation

Students travel to and from school by walking, riding bicycles, riding in automobiles and school buses, or taking public transportation. School professionals must work in conjunction with students, parents, and the broader community to ensure safe school transportation.

A high proportion of school-related pedestrian fatalities occur as students either approach or leave a pickup or dropoff point. All schools should have safe pickup and dropoff points and pedestrian crosswalks in the school vicinity. Pick up and drop off of students should occur only at the curb or at an off-street location protected from traffic. Adequate adult supervision should be provided to assist students when boarding and exiting vehicles; this adult should ensure that students are buckled into a safety restraint while riding and are clear of the path of the vehicle after exiting.

Many secondary students drive themselves to and from school, and many catch rides with other students. Schools must insist that vehicles will be driven in a responsible manner on campus. Unsafe driving practices must not be tolerated. Many school officials impose fines or restrictions on students who display inattentive or irresponsible driving—such as speeding, rapid acceleration, racing, burning tires, or making illegal turns. Such practices place others at risk of injury. The school should enact and enforce policies that protect the safety of students, school staff, and community members.

Many students in urban areas must rely on public transportation to travel back and forth to school. These students should be urged to follow specific guidelines to ensure safety. Students should not travel or wait alone for public transportation, and if the only alternative is to travel or wait alone, waiting should be in well-lighted areas. On public buses, students should sit up front, near the driver. The bus driver is a helper to whom students can go if students are being bothered. If riding on a train, riding in the same car as the conductor is a good idea. Students should always be cautious about talking to strangers and should never go anywhere with strangers. While on public transportation, students should never flash money, transportation passes, or expensive possessions. If mugged, students should give up possessions. Students should always take the safest route, not the shortest route. Students should also be instructed to never play on subway platforms. There is the risk of falling off the subway platform onto the tracks.

Safe Playgrounds

More injuries occur to elementary students on the playground than in any other area of the school (Figure 2-5). Therefore, providing a safe elementary school environment requires close attention to playgrounds and playground equipment. Schools are responsible for providing safe playground equipment, adequately supervising students on the playground, instructing students about safety on the playground, and providing prompt emergency care when students are injured.

Playground equipment injuries most commonly involve students falling or jumping from swings or slides to the surface below. Important factors in the likelihood and severity of injury are the type of surface the student falls on and the height of the apparatus. Falls on pavement are much more likely to result in injury than falls on grass, dirt, or specially designed protective surfaces. Other serious playground equipment injuries involve strangulation by hanging in ropes or chains, falling onto a sharp protrusion, entrapment of a finger or head in a small space or angle, or impact with moving or collapsing equipment.

Safety on Playgrounds

More injuries occur to elementary school students on the playground than in any other area of the school.

Disaster and Emergency Preparedness

Schools must be prepared to deal with a variety of emergencies of natural or human origin: severe weather, fire or explosion, earthquake, a hostage crisis, a bomb threat, and other unforeseen emergency situations. Every school must be ready to take action in the event of such an emergency. Planning in advance of an emergency situation is of paramount importance. This requires formal planning and testing of procedures to maximize the safety of students and staff. School districts are urged to develop emergency plans through the use of emergency planning committees. **Emergency planning committees** are established for the purpose of developing and implementing school emergency plans. Emergency planning committees function best when all of the following are involved in coordination and participation:

- Superintendent's office
- Board of Education

- Principals from each of the levels of schools within the district
- Teachers
- Transportation personnel
- Buildings and grounds personnel
- Health services
- Food services
- Students
- Parents
- Community chief executive officer
- Fire department
- Emergency medical service
- Police agency

School emergency plans should be developed at three levels: district, building, and classroom. A districtwide plan includes general procedures for district personnel to follow when an emergency affects any of the schools within the district's boundaries. The building-level plan should be consistent and compatible with the districtwide plan and specify school procedures to be utilized by an individual building's response to an emergency. At the classroom level, specific step-by-step procedures for teachers and staff during various kinds of emergencies should be detailed.

Emergency preparedness plans should be periodically reviewed, tested, and updated.

After a plan is developed, students and staff should be trained in response techniques that are consistent with the emergency plan. Training should be provided for school staff who have been assigned specific roles and areas of responsibility in the emergency plan. This training should be conducted annually to ensure that school staff and students understand the emergency procedures and to include any changes to school plans. Training also should be coordinated with local emergency management and emergency services personnel in the community. Many school districts use emergency simulations to train students and staff.

Building Violence-Free and Secure School Environments

Characteristics of a Secure Physical Environment

Efforts must be taken to make sure the school campus is a safe and caring place. Effective and safe schools communicate a strong sense of security. School officials can enhance physical safety by taking these steps:

- Supervise access to the building and grounds.
- Reduce class size and school size.
- Adjust scheduling to minimize time in the hallways or in potentially dangerous locations. Traffic flow patterns can be modified to limit potential for conflicts or altercations.
- Conduct a building safety audit in consultation with school security personnel and law enforcement experts. Effective schools adhere to federal, state, and local nondiscrimination and public safety laws, and they use guidelines set by the state department of education.
- Close school campuses during lunch periods.
- Adopt a school policy on uniforms.
- Arrange supervision at critical times (for example, in hallways between classes) and have a plan to deploy supervisory staff to areas where incidents are likely to occur.

- Prohibit students from congregating in areas where they are likely to engage in rule breaking or intimidating and aggressive behaviors.
- Have adults visibly present throughout the school building. This includes encouraging parents to visit the school.
- Stagger dismissal times and lunch periods.
- Monitor the surrounding school grounds—including landscaping, parking lots, and bus stops.
- Coordinate with local police to ensure that there are safe routes to and from school.

In addition to targeting areas for increased safety measures, schools also should identify safe areas where staff and children should go in the event of a crisis.

The physical condition of the school building also has an impact on student attitude, behavior, and motivation to achieve. Typically, there tend to be more incidents of fighting and violence in school buildings that are dirty, too cold or too hot, filled with graffiti, in need of repair, or unsanitary.

The U.S. Department of Education's *Safeguarding Our Children: An Action Guide* (2000) recommends that schools analyze the school environment to identify any hot spots for violent activity. For example, a back hallway leading from the locker commons to the band room may be an area where fights or disruptions occur owing to minimal supervision and poor lighting. Perhaps an analysis also will show that these problems are most likely to occur in the mornings when student traffic increases through the back hallway. Once schools are equipped with such information, they will be in a position to change the environment to minimize opportunities for inappropriate student behavior.

School Violence

Violence is now one of the foremost school concerns. Highly publicized incidences of school shootings have particularly heightened concern about the potential for violence in schools. As a result, teachers, school administrators, parents, and students are grappling with the problem of protecting students and school staff from the violence surrounding them. Educators are faced with such issues as assaults, rapes, suicide, gang membership, and weapon carrying in their schools.

Violence occurs not only in secondary schools but also elementary schools; violence is a concern not only in large urban areas but also smaller cities and rural areas. Beyond the obvious threat that violence poses to students' personal safety, violence also adversely interferes with students' learning and development. When students constantly face a threat of violence at home, at school, or in the community, they put a lot of emotional energy into setting up defenses against their fears; this leaves them with less energy for other developmental tasks, including learning in school. Many young people who live in violent homes feel guilty or responsible for the violence and consequently feel bad or worthless. These feelings not only can distract a student from the tasks of learning but commonly lead young people to feel that they are incapable of learning—which obviously will diminish their motivation to strive for achievement in school.

Students who face the threat of violence or who have suffered trauma from violence have difficulty seeing themselves in meaningful future roles. Students who cannot perceive a positive and secure future for themselves are unable to give serious attention and energy to the tasks of learning and socialization. The unpredictability of violence contributes to a sense of having little or no control over one's life. Students with such a sense of helplessness will have trouble developing the autonomy that is essential for healthful growth and maturation.

Teachers increasingly report feeling threatened by the possibility of violence at school. Many teachers report having been threatened by students. Teachers who are afraid in the school and classroom are less able to teach effectively.

Today's schools must implement policies that build a violence-free and safe school environment for students, staff, and others who come on school premises. To foster learning and healthful development, schools must be free from violence and crime, drugs and drug dealing, and students who carry weapons. For some school systems, this may mean providing such controls as locker searches, hiring police to patrol school premises, and having metal detectors that students must pass before entry. Some school systems have even created separate alternative schools for young people with a history of violent and abusive behavior. Though this option is attracting attention as a means to deal with violence, it is also controversial.

National health objectives target a reduction in the incidence of weapon carrying by youth. When weapons, especially firearms, are carried into schools, the potential for violence escalates. In recent years there have been far too many violent episodes involving weapons on school campuses that have led to tragedy. School personnel are all too familiar with several tragic school shootings.

School Security Measures

In recent years many schools have tightened security and increased the number of school security measures on campus. For example, a middle school in the state of Washington where a teacher and two students were fatally shot made the following changes:

- Hallways have been widened to eliminate areas where students can hide or loiter.
- Restrooms have been redesigned without doors so that parts of the bathroom remain visible to school staff from the outside.
- Video surveillance cameras have been placed in all hallways.
- School staff are required to wear ID badges so that persons not wearing them will be easier to identify as strangers.
- Visitors are required to wear a visible visitor's pass.
- Only one entrance, right by the main office, is open during the day.
- Two security guards walk the hallways, monitor traffic flow, and prevent students from loitering.
- Twice a year the school has a lockdown drill, in which students and teachers practice locking doors and windows, retreat to a designated room, and stay there until they receive notice that all is safe.

A Caring School Community in Which All Members Feel Connected, Safe, and Supported

The U.S. Department of Education's *Safeguarding Our Children* (2000) presents schools and communities with practical steps for developing safe schools. This resource stresses that safe schools support caring relationships between students and staff. Establishing these relationships reduces the causes of interpersonal conflicts (e.g., prejudice) and allows students to gain a sense of belonging, pride, and attachment to the school. These feelings are an important part of keeping students engaged in the educational process and sensitive to the needs of others with whom they interact in school. Establishing these relationships between students and staff makes it more likely that students can share their safety concerns with staff and enhances the opportunities for adults to coach, mentor, and even discipline students if necessary.

Creating caring relationships is not easy, particularly in large and diverse schools. Schools can create and nurture caring environments by organizing the environment to support positive relationships (e.g., by creating small learning communities within schools). In addition, schools can develop effective programs to prevent harassment, bullying, and conflict between groups. These programs will be most effective when they align with social skills instruction, the schoolwide discipline system, and the school's curriculum (U.S. Department of Education, 2000).

Activities to build a school community are varied, but in general, successful community building ensures that students associate positive experiences with their interpersonal interactions in the school environment. In other words, students who are accepted, are respected, and experience interpersonal and academic success will feel good about their school experience. Numerous schoolwide activities can be developed to build a strong sense of community within the school. These activities range from the schoolwide use of an antibias curriculum that teaches children tolerance and to deal with prejudice, to the fair and equal treatment of all students within the school building (U.S. Department of Education, 2000).

Sexual Harassment

Sexual harassment is unwanted and unwelcome sexual behavior. Sexual harassment is not just a problem for adults at the worksite; children and adolescents also are sexually harassed in schools. Recent media accounts have focused on not only adolescents but also students in elementary grades being subjected to severe acts of harassment. Students who are thought to be gay, lesbian, bisexual, or transgendered are at high risk of harassment. Sexual harassment interferes with a student's right to get an education or to participate in school activities. Sexual behavior that constitutes harassment consists of conduct and words that sexually offend, stigmatize, or demean a student. The following are some examples of sexual harassment:

- Touching, pinching, and grabbing body parts
- Sharing sexual notes or pictures
- Writing sexual graffiti
- Cornering another person to force kisses on that person or coerce that person to do something else sexual
- Making suggestive or sexual gestures, verbal comments, or jokes or leering
- Spreading sexual rumors or making sexual propositions
- Pulling another person's clothes off
- Pulling your own clothes off
- Attempted rape and rape

Students deserve a school climate that does not tolerate sexual harassment. Students should be reassured that their school officials have taken steps to stop sexual harassment from happening in the first place and that, if it does happen, immediate actions will be taken to intervene. When school officials fail to respond appropriately, students may come to believe that the school officials will not stand up to injustice. The silence of adults in schools about sexual harassment constitutes negligence and violation of Title IX, a federal law prohibiting harassment and sexual discrimination in schools. Title IX applies to all public and private educational institutions receiving federal aid, including elementary, secondary, and postsecondary schools. This means that all public schools and many private schools are covered. Title IX applies to all school-sponsored activities, including athletics, field trips, extracurricular programs, and bus transportation. Schools must have a clear policy against sexual harassment and establish a clear process for handling sexual harassment complaints.

Schools should develop and enact policies that clearly define what constitutes sexual harassment. Students, staff, and parents should know exactly what constitutes sexual harassment and the consequences offenders will face. Students and parents should be informed of what actions to take if a student feels that she or he is a target of harassment. Recommended actions for students to take include telling someone who will believe them, finding people who will support them (particularly parents), avoiding self-blame, maintaining a written record detailing incidents, saving any notes received from a harasser, reporting incidents to the person at their school responsible for dealing with sexual harassment, clearly informing the harasser that they do not like the behavior, and knowing their rights to file a complaint or lawsuit. Periodic and age-appropriate sexual harassment awareness training should be provided for students, school employees, and parents. Schools should also incorporate age-appropriate sexual harassment awareness into the school curriculum.

Supporting a Drug-Free School Environment

Schools can create an environment that acts as a powerful protective influence in students' lives. Research shows that protective schools may be as effective in decreasing drug use as well-designed prevention curricula. A **protective school** is a school that has a physical and psychological atmosphere that promotes healthy youth development (Bosworth, 2000).

The protective school concept helps educators to recognize that perhaps the best way that a school can prevent students from using drugs is simply to be a good school. This means having a challenging curriculum; high expectations for all students; dedicated, knowledgeable teachers; energetic administrators; a high degree of parent involvement; and an orderly, disciplined learning environment. These factors help students bond to their school.

School Policies

Clear policies regarding use and possession of alcohol and other drugs, both on and off school property, are critical to all members of the school community. Parents, school officials, students, law enforcement officials, and drug and alcohol professionals should all be involved in the development of the policies to make them most effective. School policies should clearly establish that drug use, possession, and sale on school grounds and at school functions will not be tolerated. Policies need to clearly define the off-campus situations of intoxication or impairment that violate school policy. Policies should address both students and school personnel and may include prevention, intervention, treatment, and disciplinary measures.

It is important for established policies to be enforced fairly and consistently. Furthermore, adequate security measures are needed to eliminate alcohol and other drugs from school premises and school functions. It is important that everyone understand the policy and the procedures that will be followed in case of infractions. Copies of the school policy should be made available to all parents, teachers, and students, and the policy should be advertised throughout the school and community. In addition, the school should impose strict security measures to bar access to intruders and to prohibit student drug trafficking. Enforcement policies should correspond to the severity of the school's drug problem.

Drug-Free School Zones

Many communities have established drug-free zones around schools and other areas where young people congregate. A **drug-free school zone** is a defined geographic area around a school designated drug-free for the purpose of sheltering youth from the sale and use of controlled substances. Drug-free school zones show a united front of schools, students, parents, and communities in working together to establish drug-free schools and communities by decreasing drug trafficking around schools. Increased penalties for selling and using drugs have been established for drug-free school zones. The actual area of the zone and the penalties vary from state to state.

Establishing drug-free school zones is an important way to show drug dealers that drugs are not tolerated in a school or community. In many areas, drug-free school zones extend to a 1,000-foot perimeter of school property, school buses, and school bus stops and routes. Drug-free school zones are often designated by signs.

Tobacco-Free School Environment

Environmental tobacco smoke is the combination of sidestream smoke and the mainstream smoke exhaled by a smoker. There is consensus among medical scientists and public health professionals that environmental tobacco smoke (ETS) is a significant cause of health problems in nonsmokers. ETS is a cause of lung cancer and chronic obstructive pulmonary disease in healthful nonsmokers. More nonsmokers die as a result of exposure to ETS than from exposure to any other pollutant. Approximately 50,000 deaths are attributed annually to ETS. About 3,000 of these deaths are due to lung cancer.

The group most affected by ETS is children. Children exposed to ETS are at increased risk of respiratory and middle ear infections, reduced air flow, and asthma. The increased vulnerability of children to ETS makes them a high priority for efforts to protect nonsmokers.

Schools need to do all they can to maintain a tobacco-free environment. A tobacco-free school environment is important for at least two reasons. First, a tobacco-free school environment protects students during the time they spend at school. Second, a tobacco-free school environment reinforces antitobacco messages taught in the health classroom. Federal legislation prohibits smoking in areas that receive federal funds and that serve students. School district policies should be written and enforced so that students and school staff are not exposed to ETS at school or during school activities.

Supporting Healthy Eating and Nutrition

In a healthful school nutrition environment, the messages that are given in the classroom regarding healthy eating are consistent and reinforced with healthful food served in the school dining room and at other school activities. There are many opportunities to practice healthy eating habits throughout the school day and at all school activities when there is a healthful school nutrition environment. Contrast this type of environment to a school that teaches good nutrition in the classroom but sells soda and candy bars to raise money for the school—or a school that offers only school breakfast, and no other meals, during exam week. These schools' messages about healthy eating are not consistent with the schools' policies and practices.

Establishing a healthful school nutrition environment is a shared responsibility requiring teamwork among teachers, parents, school administrators, school food service employees, and others. To help schools meet this challenge, the Centers for Disease Control and Prevention (2000) has developed the *School Health Index: A Self-Assessment and Planning Guide*. This self-assessment and planning tool helps a school identify the strengths and weaknesses of its health and nutrition policies. It also guides schools through the development of an action plan for improvement. This free guide comes in two versions, one for elementary schools and one for middle schools/high schools, and is available through the CDC's Division of Adolescent and School Health (http://apps.nccd.gov/shi or 800-232-463).

School Food Services

School food services should reinforce healthful eating behaviors by serving meals and snacks that reflect the Dietary Guidelines for Americans (see Chapter 8), the Food Guide Pyramid (see Chapter 8), and provide a variety of healthful food choices (Figure 2-6). To achieve this goal, school districts need to offer routine nutrition education for food service personnel. In turn, school food service personnel can also work with classroom teachers in providing nutrition education to students. Students should have the opportunity to choose healthful meals and snacks at school—such as salads, fresh fruit, and low-fat offerings. School health service personnel need to work closely with food service personnel to meet the nutritional needs of students with special nutritional requirements. Many schools now offer healthful foods in vending machines, as alternatives to junk food, and point-of-choice nutritional information in the school food program.

SCHOOL LUNCH

The **National School Lunch Program (NSLP)** is a federally assisted program that provides nutritionally balanced, low-cost or free lunches to

FIGURE 2-6

School Food Services Reinforce Healthful Eating Behaviors

children each school day. It is administered at the federal level by the U.S. Department of Agriculture (USDA) and usually at the state level by state education agencies, which operate the program through agreements with local school districts. The school lunch program was established in 1946 and serves 26 million children each day (USDA, 2004b).

School districts and independent schools that take part in the school lunch program get cash subsidies and donated commodities from the USDA for each meal served. In return, they must serve lunches that meet federal requirements and they must offer free or reduced-price lunches to eligible children.

School meals must meet the Dietary Guidelines for Americans, which recommend that no more than 30 percent of an individual's calories come from fat and less than 10 percent from saturated fat. Regulations also establish a standard for school lunches to provide one-third of the recommended dietary allowances (RDAs) of protein, vitamin A, vitamin C, iron, calcium, and calories.

SCHOOL BREAKFAST

In addition to lunch, many schools now offer breakfast at school. The federal **School Breakfast Program** provides funds to states that provide breakfast programs in schools. Like the NSLP, the School Breakfast Program also is administered by the USDA. Approximately 8.1 million children in more than 78,000 schools and institutions eat breakfast each day under this program (USDA, 2004a). Research is accumulating that shows a link between participation in the School Breakfast Program and improved nutrition and cognitive development in children. Regulations require that all schools participating in the program meet recommendations for the Dietary Guidelines for Americans and provide one-fourth of the daily recommended levels for protein, calcium, iron, vitamin A, vitamin C, and calories.

SPECIAL MILK PROGRAM

The federal **Special Milk Program** provides milk to children in schools and child care institutions that do not participate in other federal child nutrition meal service programs. Schools in the NSLP or School Breakfast Program may also participate in the Special Milk Program to provide milk to children in half-day prekindergarten and kindergarten programs where the children do not have access to the school meal programs. Similar to the meal programs, any child from a family meeting income guidelines is eligible for free milk. Participating schools and institutions receive reimbursement from the USDA for each half pint of milk served (USDA, 2004c).

REAUTHORIZED CHILD NUTRITION LAW

The federal Child Nutrition and WIC (Women, Infants, and Children) Reauthorization Act was signed into law in June 2004. It improves the effectiveness of the NSLP and School Breakfast Program and other child nutrition programs. One of the major aspects of this legislation is that it requires all school districts that provide the school lunch program to develop a wellness policy that addresses nutrition curriculum, physical education, and nutrition services. The policy is to be developed by a school health council composed of individuals from the school and community working together to make the school a healthier place, including parents and students (Zimmerman, 2006). The wellness policy needs to include goals for nutrition education and physical activity and implementation of guidelines and activities for promoting student health and reducing childhood obesity. The Food and Nutrition Service of the USDA provides policy requirements, recommendations, and samples (www.fns.usda.gov).

Providing School-Site Health Promotion for Staff

Most of the focus in this teacher resource has been on the health and vitality of students. Another important aspect of the coordinated school health program, however, is the health and well-being of school employees. Like students, school employees are better able to participate in the learning process when they are healthy. Healthy employees serve as positive role models for students by reinforcing the health principles that students learn in health education. **Health promotion** is the science and art of helping people

move toward an optimal state of health. **Optimal health** is balanced physical, emotional, social, spiritual, and intellectual well-being. **School-site health promotion for staff** is health promotion programming such as health assessments, health education, and health-related physical fitness activities that protect and promote the health of those on the school staff. School-site health promotions for staff is one of the eight compounds of a coordinated school health program (see Chapter 1).

Rationale for Health Promotion for Staff

Schools are one of the largest employers in our nation, employing about 4 percent of the total U.S. workforce (Story, Kaphingst, & French, 2006). Like business and industry, schools are interested in controlling health care costs and in saving taxpayer dollars spent on education. The prospect of saving health care dollars has motivated some school systems to implement health promotion programs for employees. Health promotion programs are invaluable because they help participants improve their overall health, stop smoking, increase physical activity, control weight and blood pressure, and adopt healthful eating behaviors. Health promotion programs also improve employee morale and reduce burnout and stress in educators. Participants in health promotion programs may be admitted to the hospital less often, have shorter lengths of hospitalization, make fewer medical claims costs, and experience lower incidence of lifestyle-related diseases and conditions, such as coronary heart disease, stroke, diabetes, obesity, and certain types of cancer.

There are many reasons for offering health promotion programs for school staff. When employees are healthy, they are able to get more work done and miss work less often. When there is reduced teacher absenteeism, there is less need for substitutes in the classroom; having the regular teacher in class more consistently allows for more time on task for the students and thus more learning. Health promotion activities can also lower job burnout and turnover, allowing for more school resources to be focused on school programs focused on student learning and achievement. Health promotion programs for school staff also increase interest and advocacy for health among school staff members. Teachers participating in health promotion programs are likely to be more interested in teaching students about health in the classroom. Furthermore, school staff are role models for students. Staff who model healthful behavior are a major influence on young people during the times in their lives when their personal habits are being established. Staff involvement in health promotion programs may have a greater impact on promoting student health habits than what teachers say about health in the classroom.

Planning and Implementing Health Promotion Programs

School-site health promotion includes activities designed to promote optimal health. The school is an ideal place for implementing teacher/staff health promotion programs because necessary facilities and personnel are usually in place. It is natural for health education teachers to participate in the planning and operation of school-based health promotion programs along with administrators, nurses, guidance counselors, food service personnel, family life (home economics) teachers, physical educators, and other staff member groups. School buildings have adequate space for instruction, screening, and physical fitness programs. As with any aspect of the school program, administrator support is fundamental to success.

The particular health promotion needs within a particular school or school district can be identified by conducting employee surveys, conducting health risk appraisals, and reviewing health care utilization and cost data. Identifying relevant needs allows program planners to offer program components that will best serve school employees.

Health promotion programs for school staff should consist of the following four components: (1) health screening and assessment, (2) education and activities, (3) organizational policies and environmental change, and (4) an employee assistance program. Health screening and assessment identifies school staff employees who are at risk for major diseases. In addition, health screening and assessment serves as a tool for increasing awareness and action for health promotion and disease prevention. Health screenings that are feasible for school employees include screenings for blood pressure, blood cholesterol, cancer (skin, breast,

colorectal), and tuberculosis and general physical examinations. Several types of health risk appraisal questionnaires are also available to help school staff identify specific health behaviors that will improve health status if modified.

Health promotion programs can offer a variety of educational opportunities and activities designed to promote healthy lifestyle and wise health consumerism among school staff. Offerings take on many forms, such as educational seminars and classes, health education materials (e.g., newsletters, videos, pamphlets, posters, inserts with paychecks), fitness activities and classes, contests and games, health fairs, and the delivery of preventive health services (e.g., immunizations, family planning, pregnancy, and infant care). Health promotion education and activities focus on a wide range of health concerns and may include any of the following:

- Smoking cessation
- Fitness and exercise
- Nutrition and weight control
- Stress management
- Injury prevention
- CPR and first aid training
- Wise use of medical benefits
- Health insurance and managed care plans
- Cancer risk reduction
- Medical self-care
- Blood pressure monitoring
- Mental health
- HIV/AIDS
- Sexually transmitted diseases
- Pregnancy and infant care
- Alcohol and drug use prevention
- Women's health issues and concerns

Organizational policies and environmental changes should support the healthy lifestyle choices of school staff and students. For example, policies restricting or prohibiting smoking in school facilities and on school grounds support the efforts of staff and students to prevent and quit smoking.

The final component is employee assistance programs (EAPs) for school staff. **Employee assistance programs** are work-site-based programs designed to help identify and facilitate the resolution of behavioral, health, and productivity problems that may adversely affect employees' well-being or job performance. The focus of EAPs is wide-ranging, covering alcohol and other drug abuse, physical and emotional health, and marital, family, financial, legal, and other personal concerns that may affect employees. An increasing number of school districts now offer EAPs for teachers and other school personnel.

Schools also are an ideal site for community health promotion centers. Many schools extend the use of their facilities and health promotion program personnel to families of students and other community members. This is a wise use of school facilities that may otherwise stand idle as many as two days and several evenings a week and for three months during the summer. Community- and school-based health promotion programs are one way to make complete use of publicly supported facilities, and they reinforce the role of schools as centers of community life.

Bibliography

Bosworth, K. (2000). *Protective schools: Linking drug abuse prevention with student success.* Tucson: University of Arizona, College of Education. Available at www.drugstats.org.

Center for Health and Health Care in Schools. (2005). *A question and answer session on health care in schools.* Washington, DC: Author. Available at www.healthinschools.org.

Centers for Disease Control and Prevention. (2000). *School health index for physical activity and healthy eating: A self-assessment and planning guide* (elementary school version). Atlanta: Author. Also available at www.cdc.gov/nccdphp/dash.

Committee on School Health, American Academy of Pediatrics. (2001a). Guidelines for emergency medical care in school. *Pediatrics, 107,* 435–436.

Committee on School Health, American Academy of Pediatrics. (2001b). School health centers and other integrated school services. *Pediatrics, 107,* 198–201.

Committee on School Health. (2004). Policy statement: School-based mental health services. *Pediatrics, 113* (6), 1839–1845.

Environmental Protection Agency. (2005). *About healthy school environments.* Available at cfpub2.epa.gov/schools/about.cfm.

Geierstanger, S. P., Amaral, G., Mansour, M., & Walters, S. R. (2004). School-based health centers and academic performance: Research, challenges, and recommendations. *Journal of School Health, 74*(9), 347–352.

Karp, H. (2000). A day in the life of a school nurse. *Parents,* January, pp. 100–106.

Lawton, W. Y. (2000). School clinics take root in state. *Oregonian,* October 10. Retrieved December 1, 2000, from www.oregonlive.com/news/oregonian/index.ssf?/news/oregonian/00/10/lc_31clini10.frame.

McCreery, J., & Hill, T. (2005). Illuminating the classroom environment. *School Planning & Management,* February. Available at www.petrilicom/archive/spm/850.shtm.

NASN. (2004a). *Issue brief: Privacy standards for student health records.* Castle Rock, CO: Author.

NASN. (2004b). *Position statement: Emergency care plans for students with special health care needs.* Castle Rock, CO: Author.

NASN. (2004c). *Issue brief: Environmental concerns in the school setting.* Castle Rock, CO: Author.

NASN. (2005). Roles of the School nurse. *NASN Newsletter,* November, 9–15.

NASN. (2006). *Issue brief: School nursing management of students with chronic health conditions.* Castle Rock, CO: Author.

Rittner-Heir, R. (2004). Healthful school environments. *School Planning & Management,* October. Available at www.peterli.com/archive/spm/760.shtm.

Story, M., Kaphingst, K. M., & French, S. (2006). The role of schools in obesity prevention. *The Future of Children,* 16(1), 109–142.

Temple, L. (2000). Disputed duties: Teaching the disabled. *USA Today,* February 15. Retrieved December 1, 2000, from www.usatoday.com/life/health/child/lhchi129.htm.

USDA. (2004a). *The school breakfast program—Fact sheet.* Available at www.fns.usda.gov/cnd/breakfast/AboutBFast/SBPFactSheet.pdf.

USDA. (2004b). *National school lunch program—Fact sheet.* Available at www.fns.usda.gov/cnd/Lunch/AboutLunch/ NSLPFactSheet.htm.

USDA. (2004c). *Special milk program—Fact sheet.* Available at www.fns.usda.gov/cnd/milk.

U.S. Department of Education. (2000). *Safeguarding our children: An action guide.* Available at www.ed.gov/offices/OSERS/OSEP/ActionGuide.

U.S. Department of Health and Human Services. (1999). *Mental health: A report of the surgeon general.* Rockville, MD: USDHHS, National Institute of Mental Health.

Zimmerman, B. (2005). What do all of these have in common? Linking the Coordinated School Health Program, School Health Council and Child Nutrition and WIC Reauthorization Act of 2004—PL 108-265. *NASN Newsletter,* November.

The Comprehensive School Health Education Curriculum:

A Blueprint for Implementing the National Health Education Standards

The **comprehensive school health education curriculum** is an organized sequential K–12 plan for teaching students the information and skills they need to become health literate and maintain and improve their health, prevent disease, and reduce their health-related risk behaviors. Your role in implementing the comprehensive school health education curriculum is challenging. Because health is essential to the quality of life, you have the opportunity to teach your students skills that will enhance the quality of their lives for years to come.

This chapter will acquaint you with the comprehensive school health education curriculum. After describing the framework for the curriculum—which focuses on health literacy, the National Health Education Standards, and performance indicators—it covers the philosophy for the curriculum, how to design the Scope and Sequence Chart for the curriculum, how to introduce and teach the National Health Education Standards in grade-level appropriate ways, how to create lesson plans using *Totally Awesome™ Teaching Strategies* to motivate students to take responsibility for health, and strategies for assessment.

The Framework for the Curriculum

Accountability, accountability, accountability—this is the emphasis in curriculum development. To ensure accountability, the Joint Committee on Health Education Standards was formed to develop National Health Education Standards designed to help young people become health literate. Having National Health Education standards will help to (1) ensure commonality of purpose and consistency of concepts in health instruction, (2) improve student learning across the nation, (3) provide a foundation for assessment of student performance, (4) provide a foundation for curriculum development and instruction, and (5) provide a guide for enhancing teacher preparation and continuing education (Joint Committee on Health Education Standards, 2006). Performance indicators were developed to assess student mastery of the National Health Education Standards. The National Health Education Standards and the performance indicators were revised by the NHES Review and Revision Panel (American Cancer Society, 2007). The following discussion

examines health literacy, the National Health Education Standards, and the performance indicators.

Health Literacy

Health literacy is competence in critical thinking and problem solving, responsible and productive citizenship, self-directed learning, and effective communication. A **health-literate individual** is a critical thinker and problem solver, a responsible and productive citizen, a self-directed learner, and an effective communicator (Joint Committee on Health Education Standards, 2006).

Imagine a health literacy continuum. At one end of the continuum would be the health-literate individual. By examining a description of the skills that this person has, it will become obvious what skills are lacking in the individual at the opposite end of the continuum.

CRITICAL THINKING AND PROBLEM-SOLVING SKILLS

Young people who are critical thinkers and problem solvers are able to examine personal, national, and international health problems and formulate ways to solve these problems. They gather current, credible, and applicable information from a variety of sources and assess this information before making health-related decisions. They approach health promotion with creative thinking and use responsible decision making and goal setting as tools.

RESPONSIBLE AND PRODUCTIVE CITIZENSHIP

Young people who are responsible and productive citizens feel obligated to keep their community healthful, safe, and secure. They are committed to the expectation that all citizens deserve a high quality of life. They recognize that their behavior affects the quality of life for others, and they avoid behaviors that threaten their personal health, safety, and security and that of others. They work collaboratively with others to maintain and improve health for all citizens.

SELF-DIRECTED LEARNING

Young people who are self-directed learners recognize that they need to gather and use health information throughout life, as the disease prevention knowledge base will change. They gain skills in literacy, numeracy, and critical thinking and expect to gather, analyze, and apply new health information throughout their lives. They embrace learning from others and have the interpersonal and social skills to do so. They internalize self-directed learning and use this process to grow and mature toward a high level of wellness.

EFFECTIVE COMMUNICATION

Young people who are effective communicators express and convey their knowledge, beliefs, and ideas through oral, written, artistic, graphical, and technological media. They demonstrate empathy and respect for others and encourage others to express their knowledge, beliefs, and ideas. They listen carefully and respond when others speak. They are advocates for positions, policies,

and programs that promote personal, family, and community health.

The National Health Education Standards

The **Joint Committee on Health Education Standards** is a committee whose purpose was to identify National Health Education Standards that incorporate the knowledge and skills essential to the development of health literacy. The National Health Education Standards Review and Revision Panel was charged with maintaining the integrity of the NHES by conducting a thorough review and revision (American Cancer Society, 2007). The committee and the review and revision panel both consisted of professionals representing (1) the American School Health Association, (2) the Association for the Advancement of Health Education, (3) the School Health Education and Services Section, the American Public Health Association, and (4) the Society of State Directors of Health, Physical Education, Recreation and Dance. Also included were representatives from institutions of higher education, state education associations, and local education associations, as well as classroom teachers.

The Joint Committee on Health Education Standards (2006) established the following definition and description for health education standards: **Health education standards** "specify what students should know and be able to do. They involve the knowledge and skills essential to the development of health literacy. Those 'skills' include the ways of communicating, reasoning, and investigating which characterize health education."

The National Health Education Standards were revised by the NHES Review and Revision Panel in 2005–2006. The following discussion focuses on the revised National Health Education Standards that appear in *National Health Education Standards: Achieving Excellence* (American Cancer Society, 2007).

HEALTH EDUCATION STANDARD 1

Students will comprehend concepts related to health promotion and disease prevention to enhance health. To be health-literate individuals who are self-directed learners, young people must be able to comprehend concepts of health promotion and disease prevention, including how their bodies function, ways to prevent diseases and other health problems, how their behavior influences their health status, and ways to promote health. As they grow and develop, they must be able to comprehend ways in which physical, mental, emotional, and social changes influence their health status.

HEALTH EDUCATION STANDARD 2

Students will analyze the influence of family, peers, culture, media, technology and other factors on health behaviors. To be health-literate individuals who demonstrate critical thinking, problem solving, and responsible and productive citizenship, young people must be able to recognize, analyze, evaluate, and interpret the influence that a variety of factors have on health and on society. These factors include but are not limited to culture, media, and technology.

HEALTH EDUCATION STANDARD 3

Students will demonstrate the ability to access valid information and products and services to enhance health. To be health-literate individuals who are responsible and productive citizens, young people must be able to recognize and use reliable and credible sources for health information. They must be able to assess health products and services. To do so, they need to develop skills in critical thinking, organization, comparison, synthesis, and evaluation.

HEALTH EDUCATION STANDARD 4

Students will demonstrate the ability to use interpersonal communication skills to enhance health and avoid or reduce health risks. To be health-literate individuals who demonstrate effective communication, young people must be able to interact in positive ways with family members and people in the workplace, school, and community. They must be able to resolve conflict in healthful ways.

HEALTH EDUCATION STANDARD 5

Students will demonstrate the ability to use decision-making skills to enhance health. To be health literate, young people must be able to make responsible decisions. These skills make it possible for young people to apply health knowledge and develop a healthful lifestyle. They are valuable tools that can be used when working with other citizens to improve the quality of life in families, schools, and communities.

HEALTH EDUCATION STANDARD 6

Students will demonstrate the ability to use goal-setting skills to enhance health. To be health literate, young people must be able to set health goals to maintain or improve health.

HEALTH EDUCATION STANDARD 7

Students will demonstrate the ability to practice health-enhancing behaviors and avoid or reduce risks. To be health-literate individuals who are critical thinkers and problem solvers, young people must be able to recognize and practice health-enhancing behaviors that contribute to a positive quality of life. They must recognize and avoid risk-taking behaviors. They must assume responsibility for their personal health.

HEALTH EDUCATION STANDARD 8

Students will demonstrate the ability to advocate for personal, family and community health. To be health-literate individuals who are effective communicators and responsible citizens, young people must have health advocacy skills. They must be able to recognize when and how they might serve as advocates for positive health in their communities.

The Performance Indicators

The Joint Committee on Health Education Standards used performance indicators to assess the National Health Education Standards. **Performance indicators** "are a series of specific concepts and skills students should know and be able to do in order to achieve each of the broader National Health Education Standards" (Joint Committee on Health Education Standards, 2006). The NHES Review and Revision Panel updated the performance indicators (American Cancer Society, 2007). For each of the eight health education standards, there are several performance indicators. The NHES Review and Revision Panel further delineated which performance indicators would be used to assess mastery of the health education standards at the completion of grades 4, 8, and 11.

The Philosophy of the Curriculum

A philosophy is an overall vision of the purpose of the curriculum; it explains the meaning of health and its value. A philosophy should reflect the attitudes and values of society about the purpose of education and the contribution of comprehensive school health education. The following discussion examines the domains of health, the Wellness Scale, and the Model of Health and Well-Being.

The Domains of Health

Health is the quality of life that includes physical, mental-emotional, and family-social health. The term **domains of health** refers to the three kinds of health: physical, mental-emotional, and family-social. **Physical health** is the condition of a person's body. Eating healthful meals and getting exercise and sleep are examples of ways to keep the body in good condition. **Mental-emotional health** is the condition of a person's mind and the ways that a person expresses feelings. The mind requires as much conditioning as the body, if not more. Assessing new information, having challenging conversations, and deciding how to synthesize concepts from different areas are examples of ways to keep the mind in top condition. Taking the time to understand one's own feelings, express them in healthful ways, and meet one's own needs without interfering with the rights of others are ways to stay emotionally healthy. **Family-social health** is the condition of a person's relationships with family members and with others. Focusing on expressing oneself clearly and listening intently when others are speaking are examples of ways to maintain good family-social health. Learning to give affection in appropriate ways and to receive the affection of others also is an aspect of family-social health.

The Wellness Scale

Wellness is another way to describe the quality of life. **Wellness** is the quality of life that includes physical, mental-emotional, and family-social health. The **Wellness Scale** (Figure 3-1) depicts

the range of quality of life, from optimal well-being to high-level wellness, average wellness, minor illness or injury, major illness or injury, and premature death. A person has no control over some factors that influence health and well-being, such as heredity and random acts of violence. However, there are factors over which a person has some degree of control. These factors include the degree to which a person does the following:

1. Comprehends health concepts
2. Analyzes influences on health
3. Accesses valid health information and products and services
4. Uses communication skills
5. Uses resistance skills when appropriate
6. Resolves conflict in healthful and responsible ways
7. Makes responsible decisions
8. Sets health goals
9. Practices healthful behaviors
10. Manages stress
11. Advocates for health
12. Demonstrates good character

Each of the twelve factors directly relates to one or more of the eight National Health Education Standards. A person who has the commitment and skill to perform the identified factors (the National Health Education Standards) has a greater likelihood of having optimal well-being. Each influence can be positive or negative. A positive influence is viewed as a plus (+) and as moving a person in the direction of optimal well-being. A negative influence is viewed as a minus (−) and as moving a person toward illness, injury, or premature death. **Health status** is the sum of the positive and negative influences on a person's health and well-being.

The Model of Health and Well-Being

The **Model of Health and Well-Being** (Figure 3-2) shows the relationship among the three domains of health, the health content areas, and the twelve factors that influence health status. The three domains of health—physical health, mental-emotional health, and family-social health—provide the structure for the outside of the model. In the center of the model is the Well-Being Wheel—which is composed of the ten content

FIGURE 3-1

The Wellness Scale

Factors That Influence Health and Well-Being

Does not comprehend health concepts	Comprehends health concepts
Does not analyze influences on health	Analyzes influences on health
Does not access valid health information and products and services	Accesses valid health information and products and services
Uses ineffective communication skills	Uses effective communication skills
Does not use resistance skills when appropriate	Uses resistance skills when appropriate
Resolves conflict in harmful ways	Resolves conflict in healthful and responsible ways
Makes irresponsible decisions	Makes responsible decisions
Does not set and achieve health goals	Sets health goals
Practices risk behaviors	Practices healthful behaviors
Does not manage stress in healthful ways	Manages stress
Is not concerned about the health of others	Advocates for health
Lacks good character	Demonstrates good character

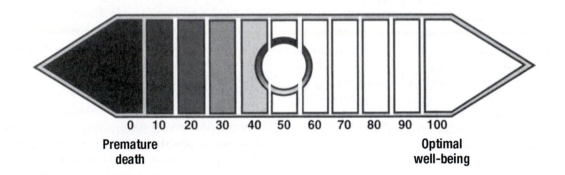

| 0 | 10 | 20 | 30 | 40 | 50 | 60 | 70 | 80 | 90 | 100 |

Premature death   Optimal well-being

Health status is the sum total of the positive and negative influences of the factors that influence health and well-being.

areas of health that make up the comprehensive school health education curriculum:

1. Mental and Emotional Health
2. Family and Social Health
3. Growth and Development
4. Nutrition
5. Personal Health and Physical Activity
6. Alcohol, Tobacco, and Other Drugs
7. Communicable and Chronic Diseases
8. Consumer and Community Health
9. Environmental Health
10. Injury Prevention and Safety

The ten content areas in the Well-Being Wheel are influenced by the degree to which a person com-prehends health concepts; analyzes influences on health; accesses valid health information and products and services; uses effective communication skills; uses resistance skills when appropriate; uses conflict resolution skills; makes responsible decisions; sets health goals; practices healthful behaviors; manages stress; advocates for health; and demonstrates good character. The ten content areas of health influence one another. In turn, each content area influences the three domains of health. The connectedness of the twelve factors that influence health status, the ten content areas of health, and the three domains of health is referred to as **holistic health.** The **holistic effect** is the effect of the twelve factors that influence health and well-being on the whole person.

FIGURE 3-2

The Model of Health and Well-Being

To maintain and improve health, prevent disease, and reduce health-related risk behaviors, students must assume personal responsibility and

1. Comprehend health concepts

2. Analyze influences on health

3. Access valid health information and products and services

4. Use effective communication skills

5. Use resistance skills when appropriate

6. Resolve conflict in healthful and responsible ways

7. Make responsible decisions

8. Set health goals

9. Practice healthful behaviors

10. Manage stress

11. Advocate for health

12. Demonstrate good character

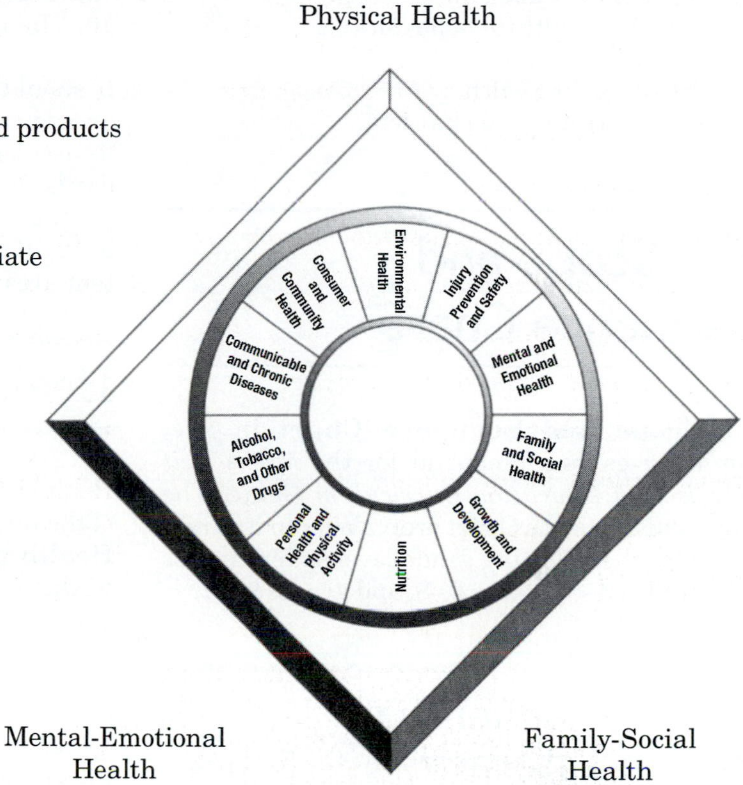

Physical Health

Mental-Emotional Health

Family-Social Health

To visualize holistic health and the holistic effect, visualize the Well-Being Wheel as a large jar of water. All of the ten health content areas and the three domains of health are contained within the jar. Now put a drop of red food coloring into the jar. The red food coloring represents one or more of the following positive influences on health status: comprehension of health concepts; positive health influences; valid health information and products and services; effective communication skills, resistance skills, and conflict resolution skills; responsible decisions; health goals; healthful behaviors; effective stress management; health advocacy; and good character. Red is used because it is the color of blood and represents life-giving behavior. Soon, the entire jar of water becomes red even though only one drop of red food coloring was placed inside. There has been a holistic effect. The whole person has been affected.

Now take another jar of water. This time put a drop of blue food coloring in the jar. The blue food coloring represents one or more of the following negative influences on health status: inability to comprehend health concepts; harmful health influences; inability to access valid health information and products and services; poor communication skills; lack of resistance skills; harmful resolution of conflict; irresponsible decision making; lack of health goals; participation in risk behaviors; inability to manage stress; lack of health advocacy; and poor character. Blue is used to denote illness, injury, and premature death. Soon, the entire jar of water becomes blue even though only one drop of blue food coloring was placed inside. There has been a holistic effect.

The philosophy of the comprehensive school health education curriculum is illustrated by the Model of Health and Well-Being. To maintain and improve health, prevent disease, and reduce health-related risk behaviors, students must assume personal responsibility and do the following:

1. Comprehend health concepts.
2. Analyze influences on health.
3. Access valid health information and products and services.

4. Use effective communication skills.
5. Use resistance skills.
6. Resolve conflict in healthful and responsible ways.
7. Make responsible decisions.
8. Set health goals.
9. Practice healthful behaviors.
10. Manage stress.
11. Advocate for health.
12. Demonstrate good character.

The Scope and Sequence Chart

The **Scope and Sequence Chart** in Section 4 serves as a blueprint for the *Meeks Heit K–12 Health Education Curriculum Guide.* The Scope and Sequence Chart is divided into separate charts for the following grade-level spans: grades K–2, grades 3–5, grades 6–8, and grades 9–12.

The Components of Health Literacy

The components of health literacy (critical thinking and problem solving, responsible and productive citizenship, self-directed learning, and effective communication) are discussed in the introduction to the Scope and Sequence Chart in Section 4. This makes it clear that health literacy drives the content areas, health goals, National Health Education Standards, and objectives that were used in the development of the Scope and Sequence Chart.

The Content Areas

Ten content areas appear as headings within each of the charts for the various grade-level spans. Each of the six categories of risk behaviors is included in one or more of these ten content areas. The ten content areas are as follows:

1. Mental and Emotional Health
2. Family and Social Health
3. Growth and Development
4. Nutrition
5. Personal Health and Physical Activity
6. Alcohol, Tobacco, and Other Drugs
7. Communicable and Chronic Diseases
8. Consumer and Community Health
9. Environmental Health
10. Injury Prevention and Safety

It should be noted that in grades 9–12 there is an additional content area called Life Skills that focuses on the National Health Education Standards. At the other grade-level spans, life skills are taught within the ten content areas. In grades 9–12, life skills are taught both as a separate content area and within the ten content areas.

Health Goals

Health goals appear in the first column under each of the ten content areas within a grade-level span. **Health goals** are healthful behaviors a person works to achieve and maintain. Health goals are stated as "I will . . ." because they indicate that the student is willingly and willfully choosing to be committed to work toward, achieve, and maintain them. One of the purposes of comprehensive school health education is to help students work toward, achieve, and maintain health goals.

The National Health Education Standards

The National Health Education Standards appear in the second column under each of the ten content areas within a grade-level span. The abbreviation *NHES* and a number is used.

NHES 1: Students will comprehend concepts related to health promotion and disease prevention to enhance health.
NHES 2: Students will analyze the influence of family, peers, culture, media, technology, and other factors on health behaviors.
NHES 3: Students will demonstrate the ability to access valid information and products and services to enhance health.
NHES 4: Students will demonstrate the ability to use interpersonal communication skills to enhance health and avoid or reduce health risks.
NHES 5: Students will demonstrate the ability to use decision-making skills to enhance health.

NHES 6: Students will demonstrate the ability to use goal-setting skills to enhance health.

NHES 7: Students will demonstrate the ability to practice health-enhancing behaviors and avoid or reduce risks.

NHES 8: Students will demonstrate the ability to advocate for personal, family, and community health.

In this curriculum, the term *life skill* is used for each of the skills needed to master the National Health Education Standards. **Life skills** are abilities that maintain and improve a person's health and promote the health of others. Each life skill is assigned a number that matches a National Health Education Standard. The following lists the life skills followed by the number of the NHES in parentheses:

- Comprehend Health Concepts (NHES 1)
- Analyze Influences on Health (NHES 2)
- Access Valid Health Information and Products and Services (NHES 3)
- Use Communication Skills (NHES 4A)
- Use Resistance Skills (NHES 4B)
- Use Conflict Resolution Skills (NHES 4C)
- Make Responsible Decisions (NHES 5)
- Set Health Goals (NHES 6)
- Practice Healthful Behaviors (NHES 7A)
- Manage Stress (NHES 7B)
- Be a Health Advocate (NHES 8)
- Demonstrate Good Character (NHES 1–8)

The Objectives (Performance Indicators)

The remaining columns that appear under each of the ten content areas within a grade-level span include behavioral objectives. A **behavioral objective** is a statement of what a student should be able to do after completing a learning experience. When developing the performance indicators, the Joint Committee on Health Education Standards subscribed to the principle that true learning occurs when students function at all levels of cognition identified in Bloom's (1956) *Taxonomy of Educational Objectives*: knowledge, comprehension, application, analysis, synthesis and evaluation (Joint Committee on Health Education Standards, 2006). The NHES Review and Revision Panel adhered to this principle when it updated the performance indicators (American Cancer Society, 2007). Thus the Scope and Sequence Chart in Section 4 restates the performance indicators as behavioral objectives based on Bloom's *Taxonomy*.

WRITING BEHAVIORAL OBJECTIVES

There are five rules for writing behavioral objectives:

- *Rule 1:* A behavioral objective needs to be stated in a way that makes it clear that the expectation is for the student. It would be correct to say, "The *student* will . . ." It would be incorrect to say, "The *lesson* describes . . ." or "The *teacher* will . . ." The first part of a behavioral objective is referred to as the *who*.
- *Rule 2:* A behavioral objective must specify the kind of behavior that will be accepted as evidence. Some words that specify evidence of student behavior are *to list, to compare, to identify, to differentiate, to solve, to write,* and *to recite.* Words that are incorrect because there is no evidence of behavior include *to know, to understand, to have faith in, to believe, to really understand,* and *to appreciate.* Part 2 of a behavioral objective is referred to as the *behavior.*
- *Rule 3:* A behavioral objective must include content about the specific learning experience. For example: The student will identify *the effects of alcohol on the body.* Part 3 of the behavioral objective is referred to as the *content.*
- *Rule 4:* A behavioral objective describes the important conditions under which the

behavior will be expected to occur. These are some examples of conditions: *with textbook open, after seeing a film, using a model of a heart,* and *given a 50-minute time period.* Part 4 of the behavioral objective is referred to as the *condition.*

- *Rule 5:* A behavioral objective must specify the criteria for acceptable performance by describing how well the learner must perform to be acceptable. Thus, the objective "The student will write an essay on the danger signals of heart disease" does not contain acceptable performance criteria. Correctly stated, the objective with criteria would read, "The student will write an essay about heart disease *that includes at least two danger signals.*" Part 5 of the behavioral objective is referred to as the *criteria.*

Figure 3-3, "Constructing a Behavioral Objective," provides examples of two behavioral objectives. Each is broken down into (1) who, (2) behavior, (3) content, (4) condition, and (5) criteria.

CLASSIFYING BEHAVIORAL OBJECTIVES

In addition to constructing behavioral objectives correctly, you will want to be able to distinguish different kinds of desirable student behaviors. Student behaviors can be described as thinking behaviors, feeling or attitudinal behaviors, or action behaviors. These three categories of behavior make it necessary to classify objectives into three domains: the cognitive domain, the affective domain, and the psychomotor or action domain.

The **cognitive domain** is a category of objectives that deals with thinking behavior. Objectives in the cognitive domain emphasize learning and problem-solving tasks and are divided into six classifications (Kibler, Barker, & Miles, 1970):

Low Level
1. **Knowledge objectives** are objectives that require students to reproduce or recall something that they have experienced previously in the same or similar form. Words used in writing knowledge objectives might include *define, recall, describe, identify, list, match, name,* and *recite.*
2. **Comprehensive objectives** are objectives that require students to reproduce or recall something previously experienced in a new form. Words used in writing comprehensive objectives might include *explain, summarize, interpret, rewrite, estimate, confer, infer, translate, rearrange,* and *paraphrase.*

Higher Level
3. **Application objectives** are objectives that require students to use previously experienced procedures or knowledge in new situations. Words used in writing application objectives might include *change, compute, demonstrate, operate, show, use,* and *solve.*
4. **Analysis objectives** are objectives that require students to break down into its component elements something that they have not broken down previously. Words used in writing analysis objectives might include *outline, break down, subdivide, deduce, discriminate, diagram, order, categorize,* and *distinguish.*
5. **Synthesis objectives** are objectives that require students to put something together that they have not put together previously. Words used in writing synthesis objectives might include *combine, compile, compose, create, design, rearrange, plan,* and *produce.*
6. **Evaluation objectives** are objectives that require students to render judgments regarding something for which they have not rendered judgment previously. Words used in writing evaluation objectives might include *justify, appraise, criticize, compare, support, conclude,* and *contrast.*

The **affective domain** is a category of objectives dealing with feelings and attitudes. Objectives in the affective domain contain the behaviors that have emotional overtones and encompass likes and dislikes, attitudes, values, and beliefs and are divided into five classifications (Bloom 1956):

Low Level
1. **Receiving objectives** are objectives that require students to recognize and receive certain phenomena and stimuli.
2. **Responding objectives** are objectives that require students to demonstrate a variety of reactions to stimuli.

Higher Level
3. **Valuing objectives** are objectives that require students to display a behavior with sufficient consistency.
4. **Organizing objectives** are objectives that require students to organize values into a system, determine the interrelationships among them, and establish dominant and pervasive ones.
5. **Characterizing objectives** are objectives that require students to act consistently in

FIGURE 3-3

Constructing a Behavioral Objective

Following are two examples of correctly formulated behavioral objectives:

◊◊◊

With an open textbook, the student will write a balanced menu for one day that includes the correct number of servings from MyPyramid.

Who:	the student
Behavior:	will write
Content:	a balanced menu for one day
Condition:	with an open textbook
Criteria:	that includes the correct number of servings from MyPyramid

◊◊◊

After viewing the film on self-protection, the student will write a pamphlet on child abuse that identifies at least five signs and symptoms of physical abuse.

Who:	the student
Behavior:	will write
Content:	a pamphlet on child abuse
Condition:	after viewing the film
Criteria:	that identifies at least five signs and symptoms of physical abuse

accordance with the values they have internalized at this level.

The **psychomotor domain** is the category of objectives dealing with action behavior. Objectives in the psychomotor domain emphasize some muscular or motor skill, some manipulation of materials or objects, or some act that requires neuromuscular coordination and are divided into four classifications (Kibler, Barker, & Miles, 1970):

Low Level
1. **Gross bodily movement objectives** are objectives that require students to move entire limbs.
2. **Finely coordinated movement objectives** are objectives that require students to coordinate movements of the extremities, usually with the eye and ear.

Higher Level
3. **Nonverbal communication objectives** are objectives that require students to convey a message to a receiver without the use of words.
4. **Speech objectives** are objectives that require students to communicate through speech, such as public speaking.

Introducing and Teaching the National Health Education Standards

Self-responsibility for health is the priority a person assigns to being health literate, maintaining and improving health, preventing disease, and reducing health-related risk behaviors. One goal of comprehensive school health education is to motivate students to assume responsibility for health. **Health promotion** involves informing and motivating students to become health literate, maintain and improve their health, prevent disease, and reduce health-related risk behaviors. Health promotion also involves the environmental constructs and supports that enable students to act on their knowledge and skills.

Health promotion includes effective classroom instruction. Teachers promote health when they make the classroom a laboratory where students learn and use life skills and work to achieve health goals that enable them to master the National Health Education Standards. The following discussion focuses on the eight National Health Education Standards—how to introduce them and how to teach them.

How to Introduce the National Health Education Standards

There is a saying in education: "If you don't know where you are going, you will never get there." What does this mean? It means that before you begin an educational effort, you must identify what you want the outcome to be. The desired outcome for comprehensive school health education is for students to master the National Health Education Standards. Knowing that this is the desired outcome, the first step in teaching ought to be introducing the National Health Education Standards to students. Box 3-1 provides a narrative teachers might use to introduce the National Health Education Standards to middle school students.

How to Teach Health Education Standard 1

Students will comprehend concepts related to health promotion and disease prevention to enhance health.

Comprehend Health Concepts

National Health Education Standard 1 focuses on what students need to know and understand to be healthy. Appendix A, "National Health Education Standards: Teaching Masters," includes teaching masters that identify steps students can follow to

BOX 3-1

How to Introduce the National Health Education Standards

Directions: Teachers might use the following analogy to introduce middle school students to the National Health Education Standards.

Have you ever watched a track meet? One of the events is the hurdles. There are several hurdles between the starting line and the finish line. Runners must practice getting over each hurdle. Each hurdle in the race is as important as the next one. The goal is to get over each hurdle and reach the finish line.

Imagine that you are in a similar event. Your goal is to achieve totally *awesome*™ health. **Totally awesome**™ **health** is the highest level of health possible. It includes keeping your body and mind in excellent condition, expressing your feelings in healthful ways, and having high-quality relationships.

As you begin your health course, you are at the "starting line." Your textbook and your teacher will help you reach your goal. You will learn about eight "hurdles"—the health education standards. A **health education standard** is something you must know and be able to do to be healthy. Each health education standard is important. Therefore, you will need to practice each of the health education standards. This class will be a laboratory where you will participate in activities that help you practice health education standards. With practice, you can master all eight health education standards. When you master all eight health education standards, you will reach your goal—totally *awesome*™ health.

master Health Education Standard 1, Comprehend Health Concepts. The teaching masters are grade-level specific and labeled for use in grades K–2, grades 3–5, grades 6–8, and grades 9–12. The following discussion focuses on the steps students in grades 9–12 can follow to master Health Education Standard 1.

Begin by defining what a health fact is. A **health fact** is a true statement about health. Explain to students that they need to comprehend health facts so that they know why they should be healthy and what to do to be healthy. These are steps students can take to master Health Education Standard 1.

1. *Study health knowledge.* Explain to students that health usually is organized into units. One unit is called Nutrition. Diet and heart disease is one of the many topics covered in the Nutrition unit. The following health fact might be learned when studying diet and heart disease: *Eating broiled chicken is more healthful for the heart than eating fried chicken.*

2. *Ask questions about health knowledge that you don't understand, and make certain you get an answer that you can understand.* Explain to students that asking questions about health facts increases the likelihood of comprehending, or thoroughly understanding, health facts. For example, this question might be helpful: *Why is eating broiled chicken more healthful than fried chicken?* The answer is that saturated fats from frying chicken might cause plaque to form on the artery walls. The plaque might harden, causing atherosclerosis to develop. This reduces blood flow, elevating blood pressure and making it more likely that a thrombus (clot) will lodge in an artery. Asking this question and getting the correct answer increases comprehension of the health fact identified.

3. *Use health knowledge to form health concepts.* Students might answer questions in a textbook or answer questions from their teacher to gain additional comprehension. For example, students might be asked: *Is it more healthful to eat broiled fish or fried fish?* By answering this question, students show that they have used health knowledge to form health concepts. This is another way to increase comprehension.

4. *Use health concepts to promote health and prevent disease.* In this example, students have learned health concepts pertaining to diet and disease. Specifically, they have learned that fried foods contain more saturated fats than do broiled foods. Ask students to suppose they are at a restaurant and have the choice of a broiled chicken sandwich or a fried chicken sandwich. Their comprehension of health concepts helps them choose the broiled chicken sandwich. This, in turn, promotes their health and helps prevent disease.

How to Teach Health Education Standard 2

Students will analyze the influence of family, peers, culture, media, technology, and other factors on health behaviors.

Analyze Influences on Health

National Health Education Standard 2 focuses on people and things that might influence a person's health. Appendix A, "National Health Education Standards: Teaching Masters," includes teaching masters that identify steps students can follow to master Health Education Standard 2, Analyze Influences on Health. The teaching masters are grade-level specific and labeled for use in grades K–2, grades 3–5, grades 6–8, and grades 9–12. The following discussion focuses on the steps students in grades 9–12 can follow to master Health Education Standard 2.

Explain to students that many people and things might influence health. Some influences are positive, whereas others are negative. Knowing the effects an influence might have will help them respond appropriately. Students can take the following steps to analyze influences and master Health Education Standard 2.

1. *Identify people and things that might influence you.* Ask students what people influence them. Their parents or guardian? Their family members? Friends? Heroes from television or sports? Then ask students what things influence them. Do the media have an influence? **Media** are the various forms of mass communication. Are the students influenced by commercials on television? Advertisements on the radio? Ads in magazines or newspapers? Does technology influence them? **Technology** is the use of high-tech equipment to communicate information. Are the students influenced by video games? Advertisements or articles on the World Wide Web? CD-ROMs? DVDs? Does culture influence them? **Culture** is the arts, beliefs, and customs that make

BOX 3-2

Guidelines for Analyzing Influences on Health

1. Does this influence promote healthful behavior?

2. Does this influence promote safe behavior?

3. Does this influence promote legal behavior?

4. Does this influence promote behavior that shows respect for myself and others?

5. Does this influence promote behavior that follows the guidelines of responsible adults, such as my parents or guardian?

6. Does this influence promote behavior that demonstrates good character?

Source: Meeks & Heit, 2003.

up a way of life for a group of people at a certain time. Do family customs influence the students?

2. *Evaluate how the influence might affect your health behavior and decisions.* Explain to students that they can use Box 3-2, *Guidelines for Analyzing Influences on Health.* They can answer *yes* or *no* to each question. Note: All six questions might not apply.

3. *Choose positive influences on health.* Explain that it is important to review answers to the six questions. Was the answer *yes* to the questions that applied? If so, the influence will have a positive effect on health. For example, a television commercial might encourage teens to be drug-free. If the six questions are used to evaluate this commercial, the answer will be *yes* to each question. It is a wise use of time to view this commercial.

4. *Protect yourself from negative influences on health.* Sometimes the answers to one or more of the six questions is *no.* For example, suppose the lyrics of a song on the radio encourage violence and include bad words. *No* answers to the questions indicate that the influence is negative. Explain that one

of the purposes of analyzing influences is to identify possible negative influences and not allow them to affect behavior and attitudes. Whenever possible, it is best to avoid negative influences. For example, a person could turn to a different radio station or turn the radio off to keep from hearing the lyrics. A person should not buy a CD with this song on it.

How to Teach Health Education Standard 3

Students will demonstrate the ability to access valid information and products and services to enhance health.

Access Valid Health Information and Products and Services

National Health Education Standard 3 emphasizes the importance of being able to get what is needed for optimal health. Appendix A, "National Health Education Standards: Teaching Masters," includes teaching masters that identify steps students can follow to master Health Education Standard 3, Access Valid Health Information and Products and Services. The teaching masters are grade-level specific and labeled for use in grades K–2, grades 3–5, grades 6–8, and grades 9–12. The following discussion focuses on the steps students in grades 9–12 can follow to master Health Education Standard 3.

1. *Identify the health information and products and services you need.* Explain to students that there will be times when they need to locate sources of valid health information. Review the sources of health-related information listed in Box 3-3. For example, students might plan to be in the sun and know they must protect against ultraviolet radiation to help protect against skin cancer. They need to locate valid information about the sun protection factor (SPF) for sunscreens. Further explain that they would need to identify a

health product—a sunscreen with a specific SPF. A **health product** is something that is produced and used for health. Identify other health products—dental floss, a stationary bicycle, and first aid ointment. Further explain that sometimes health services must be identified. A **health service** is the help provided by a health care provider or health care facility. A **health care provider** is a trained professional who provides people with health care. Some health care providers are one's dentist, doctor, pharmacist, or a police officer. A **health care facility** is a place where people receive health care. Hospitals and mental health clinics are health care facilities. People who have been sunburned might identify a dermatologist as a health care provider they need to see, and a clinic as a possible health care facility.

2. *Find valid health information and products and services.* Tell students that there are various sources of health-related information (Box 3-3). Ask them to identify where they might get health products. They might get them from a health care provider, from a store, or from their parents or guardian. Ask students where they might locate health services. They might locate them in the telephone directory. They might call a hospital or the American Medical Association for a recommendation. Responsible adults might give a recommendation. They might read an advertisement. Most likely, their parents or guardian will help them obtain health services. Sometimes one will need emergency help. An **emergency** is a serious situation that occurs without warning and calls for quick action. To respond quickly, students must learn the emergency telephone numbers for their area. A 9-1-1 emergency number may summon help from the fire department, police, and emergency medical services. If not, the caller may need to dial the operator (the number 0). See Box 3-4.

3. *Evaluate valid health information and products and services.* Explain to students that health information must be reliable. Use Box 3-5 to identify questions students might ask to decide if health-related information is reliable. Further explain that health products and services also must be evaluated. Use Box 3-6 to identify questions students might ask to decide if health products and services are reliable.

4. *Take action when health information is misleading or health products and services are* *not satisfactory.* Explain to students that they might hear, read, or see inaccurate health information that is not valid. For example, they might find an error in a textbook or hear false information in an advertisement. They

---

BOX 3-3

Some Sources of Health-Related Information

- Health care professionals, such as a physician or dentist
- The Centers for Disease Control and Prevention (CDC)
- The National Health Information Center
- Professional organizations, such as the American Red Cross, American Heart Association, American Cancer Society, American Medical Association, and Association for the Advancement of Health Education
- Textbooks
- Medical journals
- Computer media and networks, such as CD-ROMs and the World Wide Web
- Health teacher
- Videos and television programs

BOX 3-4

How to Make an Emergency Telephone Call

- Remain calm and give your name.
- Tell the exact place of the emergency.
- Tell what happened, the number of people involved, and what has already been done.
- Give the number of the telephone you are using.
- Listen to what the emergency operator tells you to do. Write down directions if necessary.
- Do not hang up until you the operator tells you to do so.
- Stay with the person or persons needing help until emergency care arrives.

BOX 3-5
A Guide to Evaluating Health-Related Information

- What is the source of the information?
- What are the qualifications of the researcher, author, speaker, organization, or group providing the information?
- Is the information based on current research and scientific knowledge, or is it the opinion of certain individuals or groups?
- Have reputable health care professionals evaluated the information and accepted it?
- Is the purpose of sharing the information to inform you or to convince you that you need to buy a specific product or service?
- Is the information provided in a way that educates you without trying to appeal to your emotions?
- Are you able to get additional information if you request it?
- Does the information make realistic claims?

BOX 3-6
Questions to Help Evaluate Health Products and Services

- Do I really need the product or service?
- Do I understand what the product or service does and how to use it?
- Is the product or service safe?
- Is the product or service worth the price?
- Is the product or service of high quality?
- What can I do about the product or service if I am not satisfied?
- What do consumer agencies have to say about the product or service?

BOX 3-7
Federal Agencies That Can Help You with a Complaint

- The **Food and Drug Administration (FDA)** checks and enforces the safety of food, drugs, medical devices, and cosmetics. The FDA has the authority to recall products. A **product recall** is an order to take a product off the market because of safety concerns. The FDA Consumer Affairs Information Line is 1-800-532-4440.
- The **Federal Trade Commission (FTC)** checks advertising practices. The FTC can stop certain advertisements or force an advertiser to change the wording in advertisements.
- The **Consumer Product Safety Commission (CPSC)** establishes and enforces product safety standards. The CPSC has the authority to recall products.
- The **United States Postal Service (USPS)** protects the public when products and services are sold through the mail. Contact your local post office or call the Postal Crime Hotline at 1-800-654-8896.

How to Teach Health Education Standard 4

Students will demonstrate the ability to use interpersonal communication skills to enhance health and avoid or reduce health risks.

Use Communication Skills

National Health Education Standard 4A focuses on communication skills. Appendix A, "National Health Education Standards: Teaching Masters," includes teaching masters that identify steps students can follow to master Health Education Standard 4A, Use Communication Skills. The teaching masters are grade-level specific and

also might not be satisfied with health products and services. If so, it is important that they take action. They might write a letter of complaint or contact one of the federal agencies identified in Box 3-7.

labeled for use in grades K–2, grades 3–5, grades 6–8, and grades 9–12. The following discussion focuses on the steps students in grades 9–12 can follow to master Health Education Standard 4A.

Discuss communication skills. **Communication skills** are the skills that help a person share feelings, thoughts, and information with others. Explain that some people communicate clearly, while others struggle to make themselves understood. Discuss ways to communicate clearly.

When I did not get a return telephone call, I thought you were avoiding me and I was hurt.

1. *Choose the best way to communicate.* There are many choices. When you need to communicate, you might choose to speak to someone in person, speak to someone on the telephone, write a letter, draw a picture, use body language, use facial expressions, use sign language, leave a message on voice mail or an answering machine, or send an e-mail. The choice you make usually depends on what you want to say. For example, if you want to share personal feelings, you might want to choose a private place to talk. If you want to give directions, you might write them on paper or in an e-mail.

2. *Express your thoughts and feelings clearly.* Do not expect others to figure out what you mean. Take responsibility for your thoughts and feelings. Use I-messages instead of you-messages. An **I-message** is a message that shares your feelings and thoughts. It contains a specific behavior or event, the effect of the behavior or event on the person speaking, and the emotions that result. This is an example: "When I did not get a return telephone call, I thought you were avoiding me and I was hurt." This I-message did not attack the other person and allows the person to respond without being defensive. By contrast, a **you-message** is a statement that blames or shames another person. A you-message puts down another person for what he or she has said or done rather than helping you find out more. This is an example: "You were thoughtless and selfish when you did not return my telephone call." Avoid sending a mixed mes-

sage. A **mixed message** is a message that gives two different meanings. To avoid sending a mixed message, the words people use and the tone of their voice when they speak must send the same meaning.

3. *Listen to the other person.* When someone is speaking, pay attention to what the person is saying. Maintain eye contact with the person to show you are listening. Use gestures, such as nodding your head. Do your best to remember what the other person is saying.

4. *Make sure you understand each other.* **Active listening** is a way to respond in a conversation to show that you hear and understand what the speaker is saying. By clarifying, restating, summarizing, or affirming what was said, you show that you are interested in what someone is saying. Using active listening helps you understand exactly what the speaker intended to communicate.

Use Resistance Skills

National Health Education Standard 4B focuses on resistance skills. **Resistance skills,** or **refusal skills,** are skills that are used to say "no" to an action or to leave a situation. Appendix A, "National Health Education Standards: Teaching Masters," includes teaching masters that identify steps students can follow to master Health Education Standard 4B, Use Resistance Skills. The teaching masters are grade-level specific and labeled for use in grades K–2, grades 3–5, grades

6–8, and grades 9–12. The following discussion focuses on the steps students in grades 9–12 can follow to master Health Education Standard 4B.

1. *Say "no" with self-confidence.* Look directly at the person or people to whom you are speaking. Say "no" clearly.
2. *Give reasons for saying "no."* Refer to the six Guidelines for Making Responsible Decisions (Health Education Standard 5).
   - "No, I want to promote my health."
   - "No, I want to protect my safety."
   - "No, I want to follow laws."
   - "No, I want to show respect for myself and others."
   - "No, I want to follow the guidelines of my parents and other responsible adults."
   - "No, I want to demonstrate good character."
3. *Repeat your "no" response several times.* You strengthen your *no* response every time you repeat it. This makes your response more convincing, especially to yourself.
4. *Use nonverbal behavior to match verbal behavior.* Nonverbal behavior is the use of actions to express emotions and thoughts. Shaking your head *no* is an example of nonverbal behavior.
5. *Avoid situations in which there will be pressure to make wrong decisions.* Think ahead. Avoid situations that might be tempting.
6. *Avoid people who make wrong decisions.* Choose to be with people who have a reputation for making responsible decisions. You will be positively influenced by them. You also will protect your good reputation.
7. *Resist pressure to engage in illegal activity.* You have a responsibility to protect yourself and others and to obey the laws of your community.
8. *Influence others to make responsible decisions.* Physically remove yourself when a situation poses immediate risk or danger. If there is not immediate risk or danger, try to turn a negative situation into a positive situation by being a role model for responsible behavior.

Use Conflict Resolution Skills

National Health Education Standard 4C focuses on conflict resolution skills. **Conflict resolution skills** are steps that can be taken to settle a disagreement in a responsible way. Appendix A, "National Health Education Standards: Teaching Masters," includes teaching masters that identify steps students can follow to master Health Education Standard 4C, Use Conflict Resolution Skills. The teaching masters are grade-level specific and labeled for use in grades K–2, grades 3–5, grades 6–8, and grades 9–12. The following discussion focuses on the steps students in grades 9–12 can follow to master Health Education Standard 4C.

1. *Remain calm.* Be patient to stay in control of your emotions. If you are calm, you are less likely to harm yourself or others.
2. *Set a positive tone.* Avoid blaming and shaming, using put-downs, or threats. Instead show that you want to be fair as you work together to resolve the conflict.
3. *Define the conflict.* Have each person describe the conflict, in conversation or writing. Be short and to the point.
4. *Take responsibility for personal actions.* Do not cover up any of your behavior. Apologize if any of your actions were wrong or might have contributed to the conflict.
5. *Listen to the needs and feelings of others.* Do not interrupt when another person is speaking. Use I-messages when it is your turn to respond. Show respect.
6. *List and evaluate possible solutions.* Identify as many solutions as possible. Then examine each solution determining if it is healthful, safe, legal, in accordance with family guidelines and good character, and nonviolent.
7. *Agree on a solution.* Select a responsible solution. State what each party will do. Make a written agreement, if necessary. Restating and summarizing the agreement will help each person honor the agreement.

How to Teach Health Education Standard 5

Students will demonstrate the ability to use decision-making skills to enhance health.

Make Responsible Decisions

National Health Education Standard 5 focuses on how to make responsible decisions. The **Responsible Decision-Making Model** is a series of steps to follow to ensure that decisions lead to actions that do the following:

- Promote health
- Protect safety
- Follow laws
- Show respect for self and others
- Follow guidelines set by responsible adults, such as a person's parents or guardians
- Demonstrate good character

Appendix A, "National Health Education Standards: Teaching Masters," includes teaching masters that identify steps students can follow to master Health Education Standard 5, Make Responsible Decisions. The teaching masters are grade-level specific and labeled for use in grades K–2, grades 3–5, grades 6–8, and grades 9–12. The following discussion focuses on the steps students in grades 9–12 can follow to master Health Education Standard 5.

1. *Describe the situation.* Describe the situation in writing if no immediate decision is necessary. Describe the situation out loud or to yourself in a few sentences if an immediate decision is necessary.
2. *List possible decisions you might make.* List all the possible decisions in writing if no immediate decision is necessary. If you must decide right away, review the possible decisions out loud or to yourself.
3. *Share the list of possible decisions with a parent, guardian, or other responsible adult.* If no immediate decision is necessary, it is wise to delay your decision and get feedback from an adult.
4. *Use six questions to evaluate the possible consequences of each decision.*
   - Will this decision result in actions that promote health?
   - Will this decision result in actions that protect safety?
   - Will this decision result in actions that follow laws?
   - Will this decision result in actions that show respect for myself and others?
   - Will this decision result in actions that follow the guidelines of my parents and other responsible adults?
   - Will this decision result in actions that demonstrate good character?
5. *Decide which decision is most responsible and appropriate.* Rely on the six questions in step 4 as you compare decisions.
6. *Act on your decision and evaluate the results.* Follow through with your decision with confidence.

How to Teach Health Education Standard 6

Students will demonstrate the ability to use goal-setting skills to enhance health.

Set Health Goals

National Health Education Standard 6 focuses on setting health goals. A **health goal** is a healthful behavior a person works to achieve and maintain. Appendix A, "National Health Education Standards: Teaching Masters," includes teaching masters that identify steps students can follow to master Health Education Standard 6. The teaching masters are grade-level specific and labeled for use in grades K–2, grades 3–5, grades 6–8, and grades 9–12. The following discussion focuses on the steps students in grades 9–12 can follow to master Health Education Standard 6.

1. *Write your health goal.* Have each student write his or her health goal in a short sentence beginning with "I will." Explain to students that they can use a health behavior inventory to help them identify a list of possible health goals. A **health behavior inventory** is a personal assessment tool that contains a list of health goals to which a person responds positively (+), "I have achieved this health goal," or to which a person responds negatively (−), "I have not achieved this health goal." Have students take the health behavior inventory in Box 3-8 if they are middle school or high school students. Explain that some health behavior inventories include a variety of health topics, as this one does. Other health behavior inventories might focus on one topic, such as nutrition. Explain that the health goals in this health behavior inventory are not of equal value. For example, "I do not use tobacco products" has more of an effect on the student's own optimal health and well-being than does "I volunteer in school clubs and community organizations and agencies that promote health."
2. *Make an action plan to meet your health goal.* An action plan is a detailed description to meet your health goal. Use the following example. Ask students to imagine that their health goal is "I will get plenty of exercise." They already

have learned how to make a health behavior contract. They might use a health behavior contract as they make their action plan.

3. *Identify obstacles to your plan.* Have students brainstorm obstacles that might interfere with carrying out their plan to get plenty of exercise. Prioritize the obstacles from most to least important and think of ways to deal with the most important ones.

4. *Set up a time line to accomplish your health goal.* Have students identify a possible time line by which they will have established the habit of getting plenty of exercise. What is the date they want to check on their health goal?

5. *Keep a chart or diary in which you record progress toward your health goal.* Explain to students that they might write the kind of exercise and the amount of time they spend doing it on a calendar.

6. *Build a support system.* Have students think of three people who would help them achieve the health goal of getting plenty of exercise. In what ways would these people support them? Suggest that students also might join an exercise group.

7. *Revise your action plan or time line, if necessary.* Explain that it is important not to give up on a health goal. In this situation if the exercise they have planned does not fit into their schedule they might choose kinds of exercise that will.

8. *Reward yourself when you reach your health goal.* Encourage students to choose a reward that fits with their new healthful lifestyle. For example, they might get a T-shirt to wear when getting plenty of exercise.

How to Teach Health Education Standard 7

Students will demonstrate the ability to practice health-enhancing behaviors and avoid or reduce risks.

Practice Healthful Behaviors

National Health Education Standard 7A focuses on practicing healthful behaviors. A **healthful behavior** is an action that

- Promotes health
- Prevents illness, injury, and premature death
- Improves the quality of the environment

Appendix A, "National Health Education Standards: Teaching Masters," includes teaching masters that identify steps students can follow to master Health Education Standard 7A, Practice Healthful Behaviors. The teaching masters are grade-level specific and labeled for use in grades K–2, grades 3–5, grades 6–8, and grades 9–12. The following discussion focuses on the steps students in grades 9–12 can follow to master Health Education Standard 7A.

For grades 9–12, a health behavior contract might be useful. Begin by explaining that a health behavior contract can be used to practice healthful behaviors and reduce health risks. Explain that a **health behavior contract** is a written plan to develop the habit of practicing a health goal. These are steps students can take to make health behavior contracts and master Health Education Standard 7A:

1. *Write your name and date.*
2. *Write the healthful behavior you want to practice as a health goal.* Explain that first a person must decide on a health goal. For example, a person might have stress. **Stress** is the body's reaction to the demands of daily living. A **stressor** is a source or cause of stress. Too much stress is a health risk. Therefore, a person practices healthful behavior and reduces health risks by making a health behavior contract for this life skill: *I will follow a plan to manage stress.*
3. *Write specific statements that describe how this healthful behavior reduces health risks.* For example, these are health facts about stress: *Too much stress can cause you to have a headache and stomachache. Your body gets tired. You are more likely to get colds and flu. You are more likely to have accidents.* Write a few statements about these health risks.
4. *Make a specific plan for recording your progress.* Have students tell what they might do to practice this health goal. For example, these are things they might do to deal with stressors: *Talk to a responsible adult. Get away from the stressor.* These are ways to protect health when a person is stressed: *Get vigorous exercise. Get plenty of sleep and rest. Ask a family member to comfort you.* Choose actions and write them on the plan. Then make a calendar or other way to record what you do. Set a time frame.

BOX 3-8
Health Behavior Inventory

Directions: Read each statement carefully. Each statement describes a behavior you might do. If the statement describes one of your behaviors, place a (+) in front of it. Continue the behavior. If the statement describes a behavior you do not do, place a (−) in front of it. Set a health goal to practice this behavior. Make a health behavior contract for the health goal (see Health Education Standard 7).

MENTAL AND EMOTIONAL HEALTH
( )   1. I cope with stress in healthful ways.
( )   2. I express feelings in healthful ways.

FAMILY AND SOCIAL HEALTH
( )   3. I avoid discriminatory behaviors and prejudice.
( )   4. I handle disagreements without fighting.

GROWTH AND DEVELOPMENT
( )   5. I practice behaviors that contribute to healthful aging.
( )   6. I share my feelings about dying and death.

NUTRITION
( )   7. I read food labels.
( )   8. I will maintain a desirable weight.

PERSONAL HEALTH AND PHYSICAL ACTIVITY
( )   9. I care for my skin, hair, and nails daily.
( ) 10. I will get plenty of exercise.

ALCOHOL, TOBACCO, AND OTHER DRUGS
( ) 11. I do not use tobacco products.
( ) 12. I do not drink alcohol.

COMMUNICABLE AND CHRONIC DISEASES
( ) 13. I use sunscreen to protect myself from the sun.
( ) 14. I have information about my family's history of disease.

CONSUMER AND COMMUNITY HEALTH
( ) 15. I have a budget that I follow.
( ) 16. I participate in school clubs and community activities that promote health and safety.

ENVIRONMENTAL HEALTH
( ) 17. I recycle.
( ) 18. I listen to music at safe levels.

INJURY PREVENTION AND SAFETY
( ) 19. I have a list of emergency telephone numbers.
( ) 20. I wear a safety restraint when riding in a car.

---

5. *Complete the evaluation of how the plan helped you accomplish the health goal.* At the end of the time frame, review how well you did. Did you follow your plan? Did anything get in the way? What did you enjoy about the plan? How might you improve the plan?

Manage Stress

National Health Education Standard 7B also focuses on stress management. Appendix A, "National Health Education Standards: Teaching Masters," includes teaching masters that identify steps students can follow to master Health Education Standard 7B, Manage Stress. The teaching masters are grade-level specific and labeled for use in grades K–2, grades 3–5, grades 6–8, and grades 9–12. The following discussion focuses on the steps students in grades 9–12 can follow to master Health Education Standard 7B.

Explain to students that stress is the body's response to the demands of daily living. A stressor is a source or cause of stress. The **general adaptation syndrome (GAS)** is a series of body changes that result from stress. Students can take the following steps to manage stress:

1. *Identify the signs of stress.* Explain that during the first stage of the GAS, the alarm stage, adrenaline is secreted into the bloodstream. **Adrenaline** is a hormone that prepares the body to react during times of stress or in an emergency. It causes the following body changes: pupils dilate to improve vision, hearing sharpens, saliva decreases, heart rate and blood pressure increase to stimulate blood flow to muscles, bronchioles dilate to increase oxygen supply to muscles, digestion slows to increase blood flow to muscles, and muscles tighten.

2. *Identify the cause of stress.* Ask students to name stressors. Some stressors might be taking a test; giving a speech in front of the class; having a family change such as divorce, remarriage, or the death of a family member; having a fight with a friend; transferring to a new school.

3. *Do something about the cause of stress.* Explain that it is important to do something about the cause of stress. For example, if test taking is a stressor, then the student might need help to gain better study skills. Also, doing relaxation exercises before a test might be helpful.

4. *Take action to lessen the harmful effects of stress.* In addition to doing something about the cause of stress, it is important to lessen the harmful effects of stress. Stress management skills might include writing in a journal, talking to parents, asking friends for support and encouragement, listening to relaxing music, getting physical exercise, reducing the amount of caffeine that is consumed, and playing with a pet.

How to Teach Health Education Standard 8

Students will demonstrate the ability to advocate for personal, family, and community health.

Be a Health Advocate

National Health Education Standard 8 focuses on how students can promote health for themselves and others by being health advocates. A **health advocate** is a person who promotes health for self and others. Appendix A, "National Health Education Standards: Teaching Masters," includes teaching masters that identify steps students can follow to master Health Education Standard 8, Be a Health Advocate. The teaching masters are grade-level specific and labeled for use in grades K–2, grades 3–5, grades 6–8, and grades 9–12. The following discussion focuses on the steps students in grades 9–12 can follow to master Health Education Standard 8.

1. *Select a health-related concern.* Ask students to think of a health-related concern for which they have a strong personal connection.

For example, perhaps a student has known someone who was injured in an automobile accident. This person might not have been wearing a safety belt. As a result, the student is concerned that people remember to wear their safety belts.

2. *Gather reliable information.* Using this example, explain that a health advocate would gather reliable information pertaining to safety belt use. Knowledge of laws pertaining to safety belt use would be helpful. It also would be helpful to know statistics that support safety belt use.

3. *Identify your purpose and target audience.* The purpose of advocating for a health concern might be to educate people about a specific health issue, to get laws passed, or to motivate others to choose healthful and responsible behavior. In this situation, the purpose is to motivate others to wear a safety belt when riding in an automobile. The target audience is the group of people you want to get this message.

4. *Develop a convincing and appropriate message.* Explain to students that they will want to consider how to have the most influence on others. They might make public service announcements. They might design a poster or a pamphlet. They might write an article for the school newspaper. Each of these actions is a way to advocate for health.

How to Create Lesson Plans Using Totally Awesome Teaching Strategies™

Teachers create lesson plans to indicate how they will cover instruction required by state guidelines. Lesson plans identify time allotments for covering specific guidelines required by their school district or state, include creative teaching strategies to motivate and educate students to master health knowledge and skills, and include an effective means of evaluation. This teacher resource book includes *Totally Awesome Teaching Strategies™* that can be used as lesson plans. When a teacher is a substitute teacher or has a substitute teacher, he or she has ready-made and effective lesson plans to use.

A **Totally Awesome Teaching Strategy**™ (Figure 3-4) is a creative and motivating teaching strategy that includes the following:

- *Clever title.* A clever title is set in boldfaced type at the beginning of each strategy.
- *Designated content area.* The content area for which the teaching strategy is designed appears in the upper left-hand corner: Mental and Emotional Health; Family and Social Health; Growth and Development; Nutrition; Personal Health and Physical Activity; Alcohol, Tobacco, and Other Drugs; Communicable and Chronic Diseases; Consumer and Community Health; Environmental Health; and Injury Prevention and Safety. The six categories of risk behaviors identified by the Centers for Disease Control and Prevention are included within one or more of the content areas: behaviors that result in unintentional and intentional injuries; tobacco use; alcohol and other drug use; sexual behaviors that contribute to unintended pregnancy, HIV infection, and other STDs; dietary patterns that contribute to disease; and insufficient physical activity.

- *Designated grade level.* The grade level for which the teaching strategy is appropriate appears directly beneath the designated content area in the upper left-hand corner.
- *Infusion into curriculum areas other than health.* **Infusion** is the integration of a subject area into another area or areas of the curriculum. Teaching strategies are designed to be infused into several curriculum areas other than health education: art studies, foreign language, home economics, language

FIGURE 3-4

A Totally Awesome Teaching Strategy™

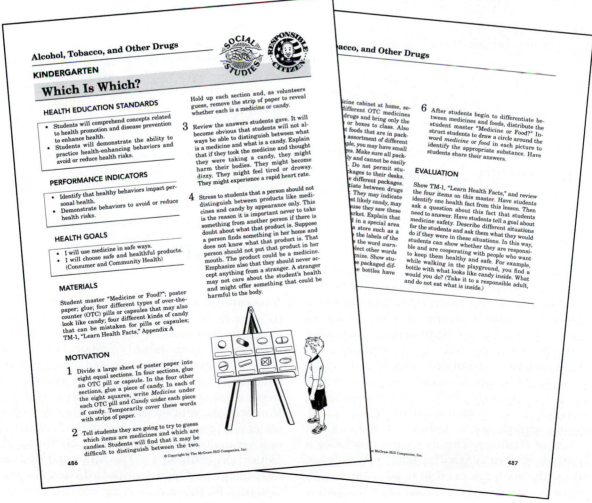

arts, physical education, math studies, music studies, science studies, social studies, and visual and performing arts. The curriculum area into which the teaching strategy is designed to be infused is designated by a symbol that appears to the right of the boldfaced clever title.

- *Health literacy.* **Health literacy** is competence in critical thinking and problem solving, responsible and productive citizenship, self-directed learning, and effective communication (Joint Committee on Health Education Standards, 1995). The teaching strategies are designed to promote competency in health literacy. Four symbols are used to describe the health-literate individual: critical thinker, responsible citizen, self-directed learner, and effective communicator. The symbol designating one of the four components of health literacy appears to the right of the symbol designating curriculum infusion.

- *Health education standard(s).* **Health education standards** are standards that specify what students should know and be able to do. They involve the knowledge and skills essential to the development of health literacy (Joint Committee on Health Education Standards, 2006). The health education standard(s) are listed under the boldfaced subheading.

- *Performance indicator(s).* Performance indicators are the specific concepts and skills students should know and be able to do in order to achieve each of the broader health education standards (Joint Committee on Health Education Standards, 2006). The performance indicator(s) for the teaching strategy are listed under the boldfaced subheading.

- *Health goals.* **Health goals** are healthful behaviors a person works to achieve and maintain. The health goals that are reinforced by using this teaching strategy are listed under this boldfaced subheading.

- *Materials.* The **materials** are items that are needed to do the teaching strategy. The materials used in the teaching strategies are readily available and inexpensive. They are listed under this boldfaced subheading. Teaching masters that identify steps students can follow to master the National Health Education Standards that are used in the evaluation also are listed under this boldfaced subheading.

- *Motivation.* The **motivation** is the step-by-step directions to follow when doing the teaching strategy. The motivation includes a creative way to teach the health knowledge and skills students need to master the health education standards, performance objectives, and health goals. The motivation is listed under this boldfaced subheading.

- *Evaluation.* The **evaluation** is the means of measuring the students' mastery of the health education standards, the performance indicators, the health goals, and the life skills. A suggested way to evaluate students' mastery of at least one of the National Health Education Standards is described under this boldfaced subheading.

- *Multicultural infusion.* **Multicultural infusion** is the adaptation of the teaching strategy to include ideas that promote an awareness and appreciation of the culture and background of different people. Suggestions for adapting the teaching strategy to incorporate learning about people of varied cultures and backgrounds are included under this boldfaced subheading.

- *Inclusion.* **Inclusion** is the adaptation of the teaching strategy to assist and include students with special learning challenges and may include enrichment suggestions for the gifted and reteaching ideas for students who have learning disabilities. Suggestions for adapting the teaching strategy to assist students with special learning challenges are included under this boldfaced subheading.

The effectiveness of comprehensive school health education is very much dependent on the quality and creativity of the teaching strategies that are utilized in the classroom. You will want your lessons to be motivating and challenging. Section 3, *Totally Awesome Teaching Strategies*™, describes *totally awesome teaching strategies*™ that can be used in the classroom.

Assessment Techniques

Assessment is applying a procedure to measure the results of efforts toward a desired goal. The emphasis on accountability in education has made assessment increasingly important in recent years. With regard to comprehensive school health education, there are at least four foci for assessment. First, assessment must measure the efforts that schools, communities, institutions of higher education, and state and national education agencies are making to implement the National Health Education Standards. The following discussion describes the Opportunity-to-Learn Standards designed for this purpose. Second, the curriculum must be assessed. A checklist is provided to use in curriculum assessment. Third, there must be assessment of students' mastery of the National Health Education Standards. Several techniques that can be used to measure progress and mastery are described. Fourth, teacher effectiveness must be assessed. Several techniques for measuring teacher effectiveness are described in the following section of this chapter.

Assessment of the Opportunity-to-Learn Standards

The **Opportunity-to-Learn Standards** "specify directions for the policies, resources, and activities to be conducted in schools, communities, institutions of higher education, and state and national education agencies in order to implement the National Health Education Standards" (Joint Committee on Health Education Standards, 2006). Opportunity-to-Learn Standards are identified for the following:

1. Local education agencies
2. Community education agencies
3. State education agencies
4. Teacher preparation institutions
5. National health agencies

Assessment of the Curriculum

The comprehensive school health education curriculum is an organized, sequential K–12 plan for teaching students the information and skills they need to become health literate, maintain and improve their health, prevent disease, and reduce their health-related risk behaviors. The curriculum should be assessed regularly. The *Comprehensive School Health Education Checklist* (Box 3-9) might be used as an assessment tool.

Assessment of Students

The current emphasis on accountability mandates that assessment be geared toward measuring progress and mastery of the National Health Education Standards and performance indicators. Various techniques might be used.

OBSERVATION

Perhaps the most obvious method involves direct observation of students. The National Health Education Standards and the performance indicators describe what students should be able to do. Teachers can observe students to see what they are doing. For example, are students able to access valid health information using the Internet? Do they make health behavior contracts when they want to achieve a health goal? Are they able to manage stress? Do they analyze ads geared for their age group based on the content of the ad rather than on its emotional appeal? Are they able to communicate effectively? Do students resolve conflicts without fighting? Do they use resistance skills when they are pressured to engage in harmful, unsafe, illegal, or disrespectful actions? Do they demonstrate good character? Are they able to set health goals? Do students use the *Guidelines for Making Responsible Decisions*™ when they have choices to make? Do students advocate for health? This assessment technique is not as subjective as some believe. This chapter provided steps for students to follow to show mastery of the National Health Education Standards. Teachers can use these steps to make their observations. Teachers might share their observations, in confidence, with students and their parents. Teachers might mention situations observed in which students practiced the steps and other situations in which they did not practice the steps. This feedback helps both students and their parents examine behavior.

Cooperative learning is an instructional strategy whereby students work together to understand a particular concept or to achieve a health goal. Cooperative learning provides the opportunity for students to practice interpersonal skills and learn about other students. It also provides the opportunity for students with different skills to share these skills as they work on a project. For example, a student who has difficulty reading but who excels in art might be involved in a cooperative learning project with a student who excels at reading. Together, they might work on a class presentation on risk factors for heart disease. The student who excels in art might help the other student design posters to share with the class. The student who excels in reading might help the other student when they go to the library to find research articles from which they will gather

BOX 3-9

The Comprehensive School Health Education Checklist

_____ 1. *Adheres to a plan in which an adequate amount of time is spent on health education.* The Society of State Directors of Health, Physical Education, and Recreation recommends at least two hours per week of health instruction for the elementary grades. The Society recommends a daily period of health instruction for at least two semesters in the middle and junior high school. For high school, the Society recommends a daily period of health instruction for at least two semesters. These are the minimal recommendations of the Society.

_____ 2. *Focuses on the health education standards and mastery of performance indicators by grades 4, 8, and 11.* Those responsible for designing and implementing the curriculum keep the primary focus on mastery of performance indicators designed to meet the health education standards.

_____ 3. *Provides a foundation of health knowledge.* The content areas, health goals, and health topics that are included in the curriculum are selected to promote mastery of the performance indicators and health education standards.

_____ 4. *Focuses on health literacy.* Health literacy is infused into the lessons so that students become critical thinkers and problem solvers, responsible and productive citizens, self-directed learners, and effective communicators.

_____ 5. *Uses teaching strategies that are motivating and highly interactive.* The classroom is set up as a laboratory in which students learn concepts and develop and practice life skills. "Seeing is believing" and "experiencing is believing" are more than clichés when referring to curriculum implementation. A hands-on, interactive, skill-based approach to learning is used.

_____ 6. *Provides for right- and left-brain learning.* Research indicates that learning may be influenced by the right brain as well as the left brain. Students who learn best from right-brain activities learn more easily with visual lessons including art and music projects. Students who learn best from left-brain activities are more suited to traditional styles of teaching. However, all students respond to variety and involvement and need the challenge of both right- and left-brain learning. By varying teaching style, the classroom remains stimulating.

_____ 7. *Provides opportunities for inclusion of students with special needs.* As teaching strategies are designed to promote mastery of health education standards and performance indicators, provisions are made for students with special needs. For example, a student who has diabetes might complete a health behavior contract in which a daily menu is planned differently than a student who does not have special diet considerations. A student who has a physical disability might be given assistance in learning ways to achieve the benefits from aerobic exercise from sports and games in which she can participate given her limitations. In addition, provisions are made for students with different learning challenges. Students who are able to achieve easily may be given challenging tasks labeled as "challenge" or "enrichment" in the curriculum. When there are students who have difficulty learning, the teacher can focus on reteaching. **Reteaching** is the teaching that occurs when a teacher uses an alternate strategy for instruction after students were not able to garner the concept or life skill from the first instructional strategy.

_____ 8. *Uses a multicultural approach.* The curriculum is multiculturally sensitive. Family health practices vary depending on cultural backgrounds. For example, students may belong to families with different ethnic backgrounds and may have learned to eat specific foods. When teaching about nutrition, examples of diets and food choices typical of the students' families are included. A multicultural approach to curriculum makes

BOX 3-9 (continued)

health education more relevant and it expands the awareness students have of those people around them.

_____ 9. *Provides opportunities for infusion into subject areas other than health.* The teaching strategies are designed to be infused into several curriculum areas other than health education: art studies, foreign language, home economics, language arts, physical education, math studies, music studies, science studies, social studies, and visual and performing arts. Curriculum infusion reinforces learning and helps students understand ways in which educational goals overlap.

_____ 10. *Includes the family.* The family is actively involved. Parents and guardians are kept current on the health issues studied in the classroom. A family newsletter keeps parents and guardians informed as to what students are learning and provides up-to-date health knowledge. Parents and guardians are invited to participate in health behavior contracts. They support the efforts of their children and may, in turn, complete health behavior contracts themselves.

_____ 11. *Uses community resources.* Professionals in the community serve as resources by donating time, supplies, and materials; speaking; and serving on committees. Teachers call national and local health agencies and ask for samples of materials.

_____ 12. *Uses a positive approach.* The attitude of those responsible for health education permeates what happens in the curriculum and then in the classroom. Approaching health and well-being with the attitude that it is rewarding, exciting, and fun to be healthful is more desirable than emphasizing illness and injury. Research indicates that students are more

likely to be motivated by a positive approach than by a scare tactic approach. Positive wording is important. For example, it is better to say, "Most young people do not smoke," than it is to say, "Many young people smoke," It is better to use audiovisuals depicting young people engaging in wellness behaviors than audiovisuals depicting young people engaging in risk behaviors. A picture is worth a thousand words and students should identify with wellness behaviors and healthful situations, not risk behaviors and risk situations.

_____ 13. *Includes technology.* **Technology** is the use of computers, CD-ROM, interactive video, Medline (Medical Literature Analysis and Retrieval System Online), and other forms of high-tech equipment used to communicate and to assimilate, synthesize, analyze, and evaluate information. Those responsible for the curriculum make suggestions for the use of technology within the classroom. The technology should facilitate mastery of the health education standards and performance indicators.

facts. The students help one another master the National Health Education Standards.

Teachers can observe how students communicate during cooperative learning and provide students with important feedback. Teachers also can encourage students to give each other feedback in a constructive manner. In this way, the teacher assesses National Health Education Standard 4, which focuses on interpersonal communications

skills and the component of health literacy labeled "effective communication."

TESTS TO MEASURE HEALTH KNOWLEDGE

The current emphasis in comprehensive school health education is on mastery of the National Health Education Standards and performance indicators. Health knowledge is essential to this task. Teachers can design a variety of tests for this purpose. Box 3-10, *Constructing Tests to Measure Health Knowledge,* provides helpful hints for designing tests.

Selected-response tests, or **multiple-choice tests,** are tests made up of items that have a direct question or an incomplete question stem followed by four or five answer options, from which students must select the correct answer. Selected-response tests, or multiple-choice tests, assess a limited range of health knowledge.

Constructed-response tests are tests made up of items to which students respond by constructing a few words, one or two sentences, or one or two paragraphs. Constructed-response tests might include *completion, short-answer,* and *essay* items. Constructed-response tests assess a limited range of health knowledge.

BOX 3-10

Constructing Tests to Measure Health Knowledge

SELECTED-RESPONSE TESTS, OR MULTIPLE-CHOICE TESTS

Advantages of selected-response tests, or multiple-choice tests:

1. There is a lower chance of guessing correctly than on true/false examinations.

2. It is easy to grade multiple-choice examinations.

3. Students must critically examine several alternatives.

Disadvantages of selected-response tests, or multiple-choice tests:

1. It is time-consuming to prepare them.

2. There must be several responses that are feasible for them to be valid.

3. Students may still guess at answers.

Hints in the construction of selected-response tests, or multiple-choice tests:

1. When writing the directions, use "Select the best answer" to protect against students' finding reasons for more than one choice being correct.

2. Make each possible answer a worthy choice. When one or more of the choices can be ruled out right away, students are guided toward the correct choice without demonstrating mastery of knowledge.

3. Use four or five choices. More than five becomes too cumbersome and confusing, and less than four increases the chance of a correct guess.

Hints for grading selected-response tests, or multiple-choice tests:

1. Have students write answers in capital letters. This minimizes errors in interpreting script.

2. Distribute an answer sheet on which the student can circle the correct choice.

COMPLETION TESTS

A completion test requires students to add missing information to a sentence fragment.

Advantages of completion tests:

1. This type of test requires students to know all aspects of a subject.

2. It is difficult to guess on this type of test.

3. This type of test allows students to organize information.

4. It is easy to write this type of test.

Disadvantages of completion tests:

1. Several answers may correctly complete each item.

2. It takes more time to grade because of the number of possible correct answers.

3. Students will select answers they believe the teacher wants rather than ones they might select.

BOX 3-10 (continued)

Hints for constructing completion tests:

1. Word completion items so that only one response will be correct. For example, "_____ is more potent than marijuana" can be completed with answers other than *Hashish*. However, "_____, which is made from the resin of the hemp plant, is more potent than marijuana" is completed only with *Hashish*.

Hints for grading completion tests:

1. When grading completion answers, place a line through the incorrect answer and not through the question number. This prevents the student from changing the original answer and saying the item was graded incorrectly.

2. If an answer is left blank by a student, place a line through it also. This prevents the student from filling in the blank when the examination is returned and saying the item was misgraded.

ESSAY TESTS

Advantages of essay tests:

1. They are easy to construct, because few questions need be asked.

2. They allow students the opportunity to be creative and show organizational skills.

3. They can be used for any topic in the health education curriculum.

4. They allow students to apply knowledge.

Disadvantages of essay tests:

1. They are difficult to grade.

2. It is sometimes difficult to word them.

3. There is low reliability in scoring them.

4. Students with better writing ability and less knowledge may score well.

5. It is time-consuming to grade them.

Hints in the construction of essay tests:

1. In writing an essay test, be specific. For example, a nonspecific item would be: *Do you feel that smoking in public places should be banned?* A student might write a simple yes or no and provide an accurate response. A better item would be: *Select a position, pro or con, on whether smoking should be banned in public places and provide at least five reasons for your position.*

2. Always make the criteria for acceptable performance clear. In the previous essay item, students were asked to provide "at least five reasons for your position." If this criterion were not identified, those students who provided one reason and those who provided five would have fulfilled what the teacher had asked. It would be unfair to grade them differently.

3. If you plan to count spelling, grammar, creativity, convincing evidence, and so on, be certain to state this on the exam. State how many points each aspect is worth.

4. Assign a point value to each essay item. This will enable students to set priorities in allocating their time when writing answers to more than one question.

5. Take the exam or have a student take the exam before it is given to the class to determine a reasonable amount of time in which it should be completed.

Hints for grading essay tests:

1. Prior to grading essay tests, make a checklist of the items you plan to evaluate and the number of points each is worth. In the previous example, your checklist might include the following: (1) provides at least five reasons (5 points), (2) provides convincing evidence (4 points), (3) is grammatically correct (2 points), and so on. As you read the essay answers, use your checklist for grading. If possible, duplicate this checklist and give it to students before they write their essays.

2. Read only several papers during a time period. During the reading of essay tests, especially those requiring many pages of writing, you might begin by grading objectively and then tire of reading the same kinds of answers. After a while all grades might become similar. Short breaks between sets of papers, such as every five papers, will minimize this effect.

PERFORMANCE ACTIVITIES

Performance activities are activities designed for a single class period in which students participate and make a verbal or written response to indicate health knowledge, attitudes, or skills gained. The *Totally Awesome Teaching Strategies*™ in Chapter 15 of this textbook contain such activities. The activities are intended to motivate students, to provide authentic or lifelike experiences, and to require a response. For example, during a lesson on the effects of smoking, the teacher might ask students to take an eyedropper and use it to drip molasses on an outline of a lung made with posterboard. This demonstration is intended to show students how tar might accumulate in the lungs of a smoker. Some students might put more drops of molasses on the outline than others, indicating that the more a person smokes, the more damage to the lungs. Then the students might be asked to write a warning to be placed on a cigarette package, based on what they observed. Students might write the following warning: *Warning: Cigarette smoking might result in tar accumulating in the lungs, making it difficult to breathe.*

PERFORMANCE PROJECTS

Performance projects are projects designed to be completed outside of class over an extended period of time and require students to complete a product that reveals what they can and will do. A health behavior contract is one example of a performance project. For instance, a student might write a health behavior contract for the health goal: *I will choose behaviors to reduce my risk of cancer.* The student might make a plan for this health goal. The plan might require that the student keep track of something she did each day for one month. The student might record some of the following behaviors: *wore sunscreen with SPF greater than 15, ate five fruits and vegetables, sat in the nonsmoking section of a restaurant.* These behaviors indicate that the student has health knowledge as well as health skills. It also indicates the student's attitude and commitment. Further, it assesses Health Education Standard 7. Another example of a performance project might focus on Health Education Standard 2. A student might keep a journal in which he analyzes ads and commercials for breakfast foods for one week. The student might watch commercials and find ads in magazines and analyze them using the four steps identified in the section "How to Teach the National Health Education Standards."

PORTFOLIO ASSESSMENT

A **portfolio** is a representative collection of a student's work and is used to assess the student's progress or achievement of health knowledge, attitudes, and skills over time or in progress. Portfolios have become increasingly popular as assessment devices. In a classroom portfolio designed for student assessment, a student's works are selected (primarily by the student) and reflected upon to show the student's progress and help the student, teacher, and parents or guardians make evaluations.

When designing a portfolio assessment program, the teacher must first determine the purpose of the portfolio. If the purpose of the portfolio is to track student progress, the teacher must determine which learner goals will be assessed, what samples can demonstrate achievement of these goals, and what criteria will be used to evaluate the contents of the portfolio.

A teacher might decide that students must document the content knowledge of each of the content areas, record a demonstration of a life skill, and collect evidence of critical thinking (Cleary, 1993). Four classes of portfolio documentation have been identified: artifacts, reproductions, attestations, and productions (Collins, 1991). **Artifacts** are actual samples of student works. A health education artifact could be a research paper on a health-related topic, a copy of a test given by the teacher, or a brochure designed to educate about a health-related agency. **Reproductions** are tangible evidence of student participation. Examples of health education reproductions include photographs of a student's involvement in a community cleanup campaign and photographs of a student working at a booth at a school health fair.

Attestations are documents written about the work of the student by someone other than the student. Attestations might include a letter from the organizer of a health fair to thank the student for participating, or a letter describing a student's involvement in a volunteer program at a hospital. **Productions** are works prepared by the student to document knowledge and skills. Productions may include a student's written reflection of the portfolio's contents and captions attached to each document describing the piece and what knowledge or skills the student gained while completing the piece (Cleary, 1993).

One disadvantage of portfolio assessment is the potential difficulty in evaluation. For example,

FIGURE 3-5

Teacher as a Role Model

I'd rather see a sermon
than hear one any day;
I'd rather one should walk
with me than merely
show the way.
The eye's a better pupil,
and more willing than the ear;
Fine counsel is confusing,
but examples always clear.
I soon can learn to do it,
if you'll let me see it done;
I can see your hands in
action, but your tongue
too fast may run.
And the lectures you deliver
may be very fine and true.
But I'd rather get my lesson
by observing what you do.
For I may misunderstand you
and the high advice you give,
But there's no
misunderstanding how
you act and how you live.

RUBRICS AND SCORING

A **rubric** is a written scoring system for student works that measures both health knowledge and health skills, using a point system. Typically, a 4-point system is used. One to 4 points are awarded for mastery of health knowledge, and 1 to 4 points are awarded for mastery of health skills. Students are given the rubric system for scoring when they are given a test or assignment. The rubric might be posted in the classroom. Rubrics are now widely used in health education.

Assessment of Teachers

Socrates said that the unexamined life is not worth living. Perhaps teacher assessment begins with the teacher assessing himself or herself to ascertain whether he or she is committed to being a role model for students. Students are very interested in having teachers who are committed and who "practice what they preach." "Teacher as a Role Model" (Figure 3-5) is a poem that speaks to the importance of the teacher making a commitment to practicing the eight National Health Education Standards and the health goals identified in the Scope and Sequence Chart (in Section 4, *The Meeks Heit K–12 Health Education Curriculum Guide*).

how can a teacher weight and evaluate different documents in each student's portfolio? Should the portfolio be evaluated as a whole, or should each component in the portfolio be evaluated separately? Portfolios are not meant to stand alone as evaluation tools, and standardized tests and other traditional measures are still necessary to accurately gauge student progress (Cleary, 1993). However, the portfolio can provide an in-depth, personalized picture of student progress and an assessment tool that provides hands-on involvement of students, teachers, and parents or guardians. Self-reflection or self-evaluation, an important component of the portfolio, requires that students select their best work, determine strengths and weaknesses of their own samples, and suggest ways they could improve.

BOX 3-11

Likert Scale to Measure Teacher Effectiveness

1. The teacher was interested in teaching health.

2. The teacher motivated me to learn health facts.

3. The teacher motivated me to access valid health information, products, and services.

4. The teacher motivated me to practice health goals.

5. The teacher motivated me to analyze influences on my health.

6. The teacher taught me how to use resistance skills.

7. The teacher demonstrated ways to resolve conflict.

8. The teacher motivated me to use the *Guidelines for Making Responsible Decisions*™.

9. The teacher motivated me to be a health advocate.

10. The teaching strategies used helped me learn how to practice health goals.

11. The teaching strategies used helped me master the eight National Health Education Standards.

12. The class projects and portfolios helped me learn how to practice health goals.

13. The class projects and portfolios helped me master the eight National Health Education Standards.

14. The tests that were given covered content and skills required to master the eight National Health Education Standards.

15. The teacher is a role model—she or he practices what she or he preaches.

Students want to respect their teachers. They want to know that their teachers believe and are committed to what they are teaching. Therefore, an important aspect of teacher assessment is the teacher's self-assessment. A teacher who takes responsibility for his or her health and practices health goals has a positive influence on students. This is why teachers need to regularly review the list of health goals and ask themselves if they practice them. If they do not, effective teachers use the same process they are teaching students—they make health behavior contracts for the health goals they are not currently practicing. This way they demonstrate the lifelong commitment needed to be healthy. Teachers might share their plans and progress with students.

Teachers also might let students know how they practice the life skills for each of the National Health Education Standards. For example, they might share steps they took to resolve a conflict. They might share with students an advertisement they saw in a magazine and the steps they took to analyze this influence on health. They might share ways they advocate for health in the com-

munity or sources they use to access valid health information.

A teacher also might model a commitment to lifelong learning. A teacher who regularly reads up-to-date health information, or takes courses for professional recertification, sends a message to students that lifelong learning is important. This message is especially important because health knowledge changes. Students need to know how important it will be for them to continue to access valid health information after they finish school. They need to have role models for self-directed learning, an important component of health literacy.

LIKERT SCALES

Besides being a role model for students, teachers will want to demonstrate teaching effectiveness. A **Likert scale** is a technique used to measure beliefs and attitudes in which students react to statements with responses of strongly agree, agree, neutral, disagree, or strongly disagree. Teachers might use the *Likert Scale to Measure*

BOX 3-12
Semantic Differential to Measure Teacher Effectiveness

Directions: I would like to learn how you describe our health education class. Below are two headings. Each is followed by pairs of words. Each pair of words is separated by the letters A B C D E, which represent a continuum whose end points are the two words. Circle the letter that best represents your position on the continuum.

YOUR TEACHER

Caring	A B C D E	Uncaring
Well prepared	A B C D E	Not prepared
Healthy	A B C D E	Not healthy
Well informed	A B C D E	Not informed
Open minded	A B C D E	Opinionated

THE UNIT ON NUTRITION

Learned a lot	A B C D E	Did not learn much
Learned life skills	A B C D E	Did not learn life skills
Fair test	A B C D E	Unfair test
Good activities	A B C D E	Boring activities
Included family	A B C D E	Did not include family
Made me think	A B C D E	Did not make me think

Comments: _____

Teacher Effectiveness (Box 3-11) to gain valuable feedback.

SEMANTIC DIFFERENTIALS

A **semantic differential** is a technique used to measure beliefs and attitudes in which students are asked to circle a letter (A-B-C-D-E) to indi-cate their preference on a continuum. The *Semantic Differential to Measure Teacher Effectiveness* (Box 3-12) might be used.

Bibliography

American Cancer Society. (2007). *National Health Education Standards: Achieving excellence.* Atlanta: Author.

Bloom, B. S. (1956). *Taxonomy of educational objectives—The classification of educational goals: Handbook I. Affective domain.* New York: David McKay.

Cleary, M. (1993). Using portfolios to assess student performance in school health education. *Journal of School Health Education, 63,* 377–380.

Collins, A. (1991). Portfolios for biology teacher assessment. *Journal of School Personnel Evaluation Education, 5,* 147–167. Quoted in Cleary (1993).

Joint Committee on Health Education Standards. (2006). *The National Health Education Standards: Achieving Excellence.* Atlanta: Author.

Kibler, R. J., Barker, L., & Miles, D. (1970). *Behavioral objectives and instruction.* Boston: Allyn & Bacon.

Meeks, L., & Heit, P. (2003). *Totally Awesome™ Health.* New York: Macmillan McGraw-Hill.

CHAPTER FOUR

Instructional Strategies and Technologies:

Motivating Students to Learn

I t has often been said that teaching is an art. Most likely, this is because effective teachers select creative ways for their students to learn. They recognize the importance of preparing lessons with the same passion and energy that ballerinas, pianists, and actors have as they prepare for a first-class performance. Effective teachers are indeed artists who recognize the variety of ways in which students learn. They design learning experiences that are challenging, motivating, creative, and captivating. They design learning experiences that help students become health literate and master the performance indicators identified for the National Health Education Standards. This chapter discusses instructional strategies and technologies that can be used in the classroom.

Instructional Strategies

Instructional strategies are teaching methods that help students (1) understand a particular concept or (2) develop and practice a specific life skill or health goal. Chapter 3 discussed Totally Awesome Teaching Strategies™, which are one type of instructional strategy. They serve as creative, challenging, and motivating mini-lessons. A Totally Awesome Teaching Strategy™

contains a clever title, a designated content area, a designated grade level, suggestions for infusion into curriculum areas other than health, health literacy, health education standards, performance indicators, life skills, materials, motivation, evaluation, suggestions for multicultural infusion, and suggestions for inclusion. This section focuses on other types of instructional strategies: lecture, lecture and discussion, role play, brainstorming, buzz groups, panel discussions, debate, cooperative learning, decision making, self-appraisals and health behavior inventories, student presentations, field trips, demonstrations, and guest speakers.

Lecture

Lecture is an instructional strategy involving a verbal presentation. Lecture is often used when many facts need to be covered in a short period of time. The lecture method of teaching can accommodate a large group of students. The following suggestions can increase the effectiveness of lecture:

1. Plan the lecture so that there is a motivating beginning, a presentation of the factual content, and a summary. The beginning and the summary should help students recognize how

the material helps them become health literate and master the performance indicators.

2. Use audiovisuals, such as overhead transparencies or slides, to provide visual support for the verbal presentation and to clarify concepts and facts. Before using audiovisuals, be certain students sitting at the back of the classroom can see and read them.

3. Make the lecture more interesting and personal by adding anecdotes, humor, and fascinating stories.

4. When using notes for lecture, write them on one side of separate sheets or cards so that you can slide from one to the next with ease. Turning pages can be distracting.

5. Give students an outline on which they can take notes on the lecture material. Collect the students' notes periodically and review them to make suggestions. Students who take detailed and organized notes usually retain more information and perform better on tests.

6. Select specific students to gauge the pace of your lecture. Observe these students to determine if they have enough time to grasp the information and take notes. Adjust your pace if necessary.

7. Vary your posture and voice to avoid monotony. Be certain that you can be heard at the back of the classroom. If students cannot hear you, use a microphone.

Lecture and Discussion

Lecture and discussion is an instructional strategy combining a verbal presentation with student dialogue. Student interaction is included when discussion is added to the lecture method. Students have the opportunity to interact with other students as well as with the teacher. Students also have the opportunity to listen to other students. Adding discussion to the lecture method increases the likelihood that students will gain skills needed to become health literate. The following suggestions can increase the effectiveness of lecture and discussion:

1. Plan the lecture so that there is a motivating beginning, a presentation of the factual content, and a summary. The beginning and the summary should help students recognize how the material helps them become health literate and master the performance indicators. As you plan the

lecture, appropriate enough time for student discussion.

2. Use audiovisuals such as overhead transparencies or slides to provide visual support for the verbal presentation and to clarify concepts and facts. Before using audiovisuals, be certain that students sitting at the back of the classroom can see and read them. Ideas generated during student discussion can be written on a blank overhead transparency using a water-base marker. Be certain to write large enough for students sitting in the back of the classroom to read what you have written.

3. Make the lecture more interesting and personal by adding anecdotes, humor, and fascinating stories. Ask students to share experiences they have had that pertain to the material that is being covered.

4. When using notes for lecture, write them on one side of separate sheets or cards so that you can slide from one to the next with ease. Turning pages can be distracting.

5. Insert questions for students in your notes to generate a discussion of points you believe to be important. You can motivate students to use the critical thinking skills needed to become health literate.

6. Give students an outline on which they can take notes of the material to be presented. Include space where students can record what other students have said. Collect the students' notes periodically and review them to make suggestions. Students who take detailed and organized notes usually retain more information and perform better on tests.

7. Encourage students to participate in discussion. Recognize and affirm students for their participation. When a student asks a question that is not relevant at the time, give a short answer and assure the student that you will answer the question in greater detail at the appropriate time. When a student asks a question that you are not able to answer, say that you do not know the answer to the question and offer to find the answer.

8. Have guidelines for participation in order to maintain classroom control. Explain that students must raise their hands and be acknowledged before speaking. Only one student is to speak at a time, while other students listen. Students are to be courteous when they disagree with what is being said.

9. Have a plan of action to use when one or a few students dominate student discussion. For example, you might ask students who have participated to wait until others have had a chance to participate before they speakagain.

10. During student discussion, keep students focused on the topic being addressed. Keep to the allotted time frame so that the lecture material is covered.

Role Play

Role play is an instructional strategy in which students play assigned roles to show how they might act in specific situations.

There are two different kinds of role play. In one kind of role play, students are assigned roles and given specific scripts. During role play, they act according to the specific scripts they have been given. In another kind of role play, students are assigned roles and a situation. During role play, they act according to the role they have been assigned, but the script is spontaneous and depends on what they choose to say. The following suggestions can increase the effectiveness of role play:

1. Use role play to master specific health goals and performance indicators and be certain the script and summary discussion stay focused. For example, suppose role play is used to reinforce the health goal "I will not drink alcohol." When the script for the role play is designed, it might call for one student to be

assigned the role of trying to persuade another student to drink alcohol. Another student might be assigned the role of being the person who is pressured to drink alcohol. The script for the role play might give instructions for the student to resist the pressure. This role play would clearly keep the focus on the health goal "I will not drink alcohol." Now suppose the role play was designed differently. Suppose the student assigned the role of being the student who was pressured was not given instructions to resist the pressure but asked to respond spontaneously to the first student. Suppose that this student did not resist the pressure but agreed to drink the alcohol. At the end of the role play, the discussion must immediately focus on why this action was not responsible behavior. Role play must always culminate in a responsible message that reinforces health goals. Students should never be given a mixed message.

2. Each role play should be limited to three minutes. When role play lasts longer, students often become disinterested and forget the

situation and the responses that need to be processed.

3. Sometimes students are given scripts that contain false information, or they make false or misleading statements when they act in their assigned roles. Correct all misinformation immediately. For example, given the previous situation to use in role play, the student assigned the role of pressuring another student to drink might say, "Drinking one beer will not harm your health." At the culmination of this role play, the teacher must refocus on this false statement and give correct information. The teacher might ask, "How might drinking one beer affect health?" The response might be, "Drinking even one beer slows reaction time. People are more likely to have an accident when their reaction time is slowed."

4. Allow students to volunteer for role play. When selecting students for role play, give them the opportunity to switch roles or to decline. It is difficult to know what life experiences all students have had. Some role plays may include scripts that are too similar to a student's life experience, and this student may feel embarrassed or uncomfortable being assigned a role and having to act this role in front of classmates.

5. Create role plays that help students develop health literacy. A role play might be designed so that students assigned certain roles must think critically and respond quickly to a lifelike situation. This gives students the opportunity to test their skills without experiencing the consequences. A role play might be designed so that students assigned certain roles might practice using words and nonverbal communication to respond to lifelike situations. For example, role play is effective in helping students practice their use of resistance skills. When students practice their use of resistance skills during role play, they are practicing skills needed for effective communication, another component of health literacy. A role play might be designed so that students are assigned roles in which each responds differently to the same situation. The follow-up discussion can focus on which response demonstrated responsible citizenship, still another component of health literacy.

6. Use role reversal within a role play to help students appreciate how one's role can influence one's perceptions and feelings. **Role reversal** is a technique used during role play in which the students switch roles in the middle of the role play. For example, in the situation given previously, the student who is assigned the role of pressuring the other student to drink beer switches to the role of being pressured, in the middle of the role play. The other student switches to the role of pressuring. At the culmination of the role play, the students who were assigned the role reversals can share how they felt as they played each role. A variation might be to assign a student the role of using resistance skills when pressured to drink beer. During the beginning of the role play, the student is not given a script and must rely on her own ideas for resisting the pressure. After several moments, the student might be given a list of reasons to give when resisting the pressure to drink beer. After the role play, this student might be asked which assigned role was most effective. Most likely, the student would recognize that it was easier to use resistance skills when she had the list. This role play might be used to reinforce the need to prepare ahead to say "no" to pressure to act in harmful, unsafe, and illegal ways.

Brainstorming

Brainstorming is an instructional strategy in which the teacher requests a variety of responses to the same question, problem, or trigger statement. There are two ways to use brainstorming: the teacher can state the question, problem, or trigger statement and then facilitate the brainstorming session to generate responses; or the teacher can state the question, problem, or trigger statement and then ask students to break into small groups and generate the list of responses. When brainstorming is done in small groups, the students in each of the groups should select a leader to record their responses. Brainstorming is an appropriate instructional strategy for helping students learn how to make responsible decisions. Brainstorming can be used to help students think creatively and explore several options. The following suggestions can increase the effectiveness of brainstorming. These suggestions might be adapted when the class is divided into small groups for the brainstorming session.

1. During a brainstorming session, record the responses so that students can see them and refer back to them during a discussion. Write the responses on the chalkboard. Write large enough that students in the back of the classroom can read them.

2. Record the responses in the order in which students give them. Do not judge or evaluate the responses by ranking them in any way. This can be done at the culmination of the brainstorming session and will allow for careful and consistent evaluation.

3. Encourage all students to participate when generating the list of responses. If some students do not respond, ask them if a response was given that they might have given. If some students dominate the brainstorming session, ask them to wait to respond further until others have given responses.

4. Have guidelines for the brainstorming session in order to maintain classroom control. Explain that students must raise their hands and be acknowledged before speaking. Only one student is to speak at a time.

5. When using brainstorming to reinforce responsible decision-making skills, give students a situation and ask them to identify as many options as possible. Ask them to avoid judging or evaluating the options, but merely to brainstorm a list. After brainstorming the options, be clear as to the criteria that will be used to evaluate each option. Use the *Responsible Decision-Making Model* (Chapter 16, p. 787). Have students evaluate each option by asking whether the option is healthful, safe, legal, respectful of oneself and others, follows the guidelines of responsible adults such as parents or guardians, and demonstrates character.

Buzz Groups

A **buzz group** is an instructional strategy in which students discuss a topic or issue in small groups. Buzz groups are also referred to as small-group discussions. Buzz groups provide one of the best opportunities for students to practice skills in effective communication, a component of health literacy. The following suggestions can increase the effectiveness of buzz groups:

1. Have a carefully planned strategy for deciding how to place students in buzz groups.

Capitalize on this opportunity for students to practice communication skills. Rather than assigning students to buzz groups with their friends, place them in groups with students they do not know as well. Consider the present communication skills of students. Balance the groups, allowing each group to have at least one student who has good communication skills and at least one student who has fewer skills. By balancing groups in this way, students might learn from one another.

2. Give students a written copy of the topic or issue to be addressed. Give them specific instructions as to how they should proceed. For example, you might ask each group to select a group leader or facilitator. Tell students how long they will have for discussion and what they should accomplish during the allotted time. For example, you might say they are to discuss what they would do if someone tried to pick a fight with them. At the end of a five-minute time period, they are to summarize the suggestions of the group.

3. Never give directions that require members of the buzz group to come to a consensus on a controversial issue. Parents and guardians have the responsibility for teaching children their value system. It is not appropriate to have students take a position on an issue that is contrary to the position of their parents or guardian.

4. When giving instructions for the buzz groups, discuss ways students might communicate effectively in their groups. Discuss the need to stay on task. Emphasize the importance of

encouraging all group members to actively participate and listen.

5. While students are participating in buzz groups, demonstrate your interest and involvement by interacting with each group. Provide suggestions to groups having difficulty staying on task or getting started with their discussion.

6. After the allotted time, ask the leader or facilitator from each group to share the responses of the group with the entire class. Refocus on the health goal that prompted your use of the buzz group. For example, in the situation given, the health goal might have been, "I will use conflict resolution skills." After the students have summarized what group members would do if someone tried to pick a fight with them, the discussion would focus on conflict resolution skills.

7. Allow time for students to evaluate their use of communication skills in the buzz groups. This can be done within the buzz groups or with the class as a whole.

Panel Discussions

A **panel discussion** is an instructional strategy in which two or more students research and report on a topic or issue. Panel members may speak for a set amount of time or they may interact with each other and the audience. The following suggestions can increase the effectiveness of panel discussions:

1. Before assigning panel discussions, discuss how to gather and evaluate health information. Introduce students to reliable sources of health information. Review ways to use the library to obtain information.

2. Give students written instructions for the panel discussions. Clearly state the topic or issue to be addressed. Identify the number of sources that

must be used when gathering information. Explain the role of different panel members. Identify time lines for completion of tasks prior to having the panel discussion in the classroom.

3. Provide class time for at least the first planning session. Ask members of the panel to develop a plan, outline the panel discussion, and assign responsibilities to panel members. Review the plan and make suggestions.

4. After the members of the panel discussion have had time to complete their plans and practice their presentations, meet with them to be certain they are ready for the class presentation. This avoids wasting valuable class time.

5. After the panel presentation, review and clarify information presented. Refocus on the health goal and the performance indicators to be mastered.

Debate

A **debate** is an instructional strategy in which an issue is presented and students identify and defend an approach, solution, or choice. Debate provides the opportunity for students to recognize the importance of being well informed. The

following suggestions can increase the effectiveness of debate:

1. Select appropriate issues for debate. For example, students might debate the following: "For a first offense, any student who starts a fight on school premises should be required to attend a class in conflict resolution training for three successive Saturdays." One student might support or defend this as a helpful solution to reducing the incidence of fighting at school. Another student might challenge this and support a mandatory three-day suspension for the first offense for fighting on school premises.

2. Recognize that some topics are not appropriate for debate in the school setting. For example, students should not be asked to debate whether or not abortion should be legal. Parents and guardians are responsible for influencing the value systems of their children. The topic of abortion and the many issues surrounding this topic should be addressed at home. A further example might be helpful. Students should not be asked to debate whether marijuana use should be made legal. Marijuana use is against the law. Most parents and guardians do not want their children spending time in school developing strategies to defend illegal behaviors.

3. Give students written instructions for the debate. Clearly state the issue to be debated. If students are to select an issue to be debated, screen the issues they select carefully. Adhere to the guidelines in suggestion 2. Identify the number of sources that must be used when gathering information for the debate. Identify time lines for completion of tasks prior to having the debate in the classroom.

4. Provide class time for at least the first planning session for students who will debate the same issue. Ask students to develop a plan, outline possible topics to cover during the debate, and assign responsibilities to those students who will debate the issues. Review the plan and make suggestions.

5. After students have had time to research the issue to be debated and have practiced their presentations, meet with them to be certain they are ready to debate the issue in the classroom. This avoids wasting valuable class time.

6. Before the debate, give specific directions to other students. Ask students to write the issue to be debated at the top of a sheet of paper. Have them fold the paper into two columns and label the columns *For* and *Against*.

Ask students to identify reasons that are *For* and reasons that are *Against* the issue being debated. Under each reason, they are to make a notation whether or not the reason was supported with sufficient evidence. After the debate, have students share what they have written. Discuss the importance of documenting sources of health information and of being well informed on health issues. The processing discussion after the debate should help students learn to evaluate the reliability of information presented by people addressing health issues, a skill needed to meet one of the health education standards.

Cooperative Learning

Cooperative learning is an instructional strategy in which students work together to understand a particular concept or develop a life skill. Cooperative learning provides the opportunity for students to practice communication skills that promote health literacy. Cooperative learning affords the opportunity for students with diverse backgrounds to dialogue and gain further understanding of one another. It also provides the opportunity for students with different skills to share these skills as they work together. The following suggestions can increase the effectiveness of cooperative learning:

1. Select cooperative learning experiences carefully. They should provide an opportunity for students of varied abilities to work together and to succeed. Carefully select students who will be paired together. Assess their varied skills when making selections. Place students who have difficulty learning with students who will be encouraging and supportive.

2. Give specific instructions for the task to be completed. Ask students to develop a plan to complete the task that involves each student. Emphasize the need to combine their strengths and to practice communication skills.

3. When the task is complete, ask students to share what they have learned. Ask students to discuss what they have gained from working together as a team. Ask students to identify the many ways they must work as a team in situations outside the school setting.

4. Avoid using cooperative learning as a basis for grading. When students are aware that a task will be graded, they often focus on the

grade rather than on combining their talents. One or two students might do most of the project because of their concern about the grade.

Decision Making

Decision making is an instructional strategy in which students are given a situation for which a choice must be made and asked to apply a series of steps to determine which choice leads to responsible actions. The authors of this book have developed the *Responsible Decision-Making Model* (Chapter 16, p. 787) for use with this instructional strategy. This model is a series of steps to follow to ensure that decisions lead to actions that (1) promote health, (2) protect safety, (3) obey laws, (4) show respect for oneself and others, (5) follow guidelines set by responsible adults such as parents and guardians, and (6) demonstrate character. Being able to make responsible decisions is a skill needed to become health literate. The following suggestions can increase the effectiveness of responsible decision making:

1. Help students distinguish between problem solving and responsible decision making. The difference focuses on the first step. In problem solving, the first step is to "identify the problem." In responsible decision making, the first step is to "identify the situation." For example, the student may be asked to examine this scenario, "You are at a party and someone offers you an alcoholic beverage." Using the problem-solving approach, this scenario would be stated as being the "problem." Students would be asked to "identify the problem." Given the responsible decision-making approach, students would be asked to "clearly describe the situation they face." The responsible decision-making approach helps students to be more empowered for the following reason. In the problem-solving approach, they are told they have a problem that must be solved. In the responsible decision-making approach, they are told they are facing a situation. If they make a decision that results in a responsible action, they avoid having a problem.
2. Emphasize the importance of using the six criteria that are stated in step 4 of the *Responsible Decision-Making Model*. Explain that these criteria help them to be objective and to avoid being convinced that a decision or action is responsible when it is not. For example, given the previous example, suppose several of their friends decided to drink an alcoholic beverage. The actions of their friends would not be an acceptable reason for choosing to drink an alcoholic beverage. It is not one of the criteria to be used to decide if an action or decision is responsible.
3. Emphasize the importance of gathering and evaluating information in making responsible decisions (a health education standard). When using the *Responsible Decision-Making Model*, a student may need to gather and evaluate information to learn if a particular decision will result in an action that meets the six criteria. Given the previous example, the following information is helpful: Drinking alcohol irritates the stomach lining (interferes with health). Drinking alcohol slows reaction time (interferes with safety). Drinking alcohol is against the law for minors (against the law). Drinking alcohol depresses the central nervous system and interferes with judgment (may result in actions that do not show respect for oneself or others). Most parents and guardians do not want their minor children drinking alcohol (against family guidelines). Drinking alcohol is against school rules (shows a lack of character).

Self-Appraisals and Health Behavior Inventories

A **self-appraisal** or **health behavior inventory** is a personal assessment tool that contains a list of actions to which a student responds positively (+), "I practice this action," or to which the student responds negatively (−), "I do not practice this action." A positive response indicates that a student has made a choice to practice a life skill that results in an action that promotes health literacy, maintains and improves health, prevents disease, and reduces health-related risk behaviors. A negative answer indicates that the student chooses actions that may interfere with health literacy, harm health, and increase the risk of disease or injury and premature death. The following suggestions can increase the effectiveness of a health behavior inventory:

1. When you ask students to complete a health behavior inventory, explain that the actions being assessed are not of equal value. For example, the following two statements might appear on the same health behavior

inventory: *I do not use tobacco products,* and *I volunteer in school clubs and community organizations and agencies that promote health.* Although both of these actions are desirable, choosing not to use tobacco products is of greater value in becoming health literate, maintaining and improving health, preventing disease, and reducing health-related risk behaviors than is choosing to volunteer in school clubs and community organizations.

2. If you choose to design a health behavior inventory to be given to students after you have covered a content area to assess what the students intend to do, add the word *will* to each statement. For example, a statement might be *I will not use tobacco products.* Students then respond *yes* or *no* to indicate what they intend to do as a result of what they have just learned. In this case, you are assessing intended actions, not current actions.

3. After students complete a health behavior inventory, have them summarize what they have learned about their behavior.

4. Some health behavior inventories contain statements that may be an invasion of family and student privacy. Be certain to follow school policy when selecting health behavior inventories for use in the classroom.

Student Presentations

A **student presentation** is an instructional strategy in which a student makes an oral presentation or demonstration on a health topic that he has researched in depth. This instructional strategy helps students develop effective communication skills and gather and evaluate health information. The following suggestions can increase the effectiveness of student presentations:

1. Work with students to select topics that directly support mastery of the health education standards. For example, Health Education Standard 2 is *Students will analyze the impact of family, peers, culture, media, technology, and other factors on health behaviors* (Joint Committee on Health Education Standards, 2006). A student might make an oral presentation on the impact the media has on the incidence of violence. When students are selecting topics, be certain that they know why they are appropriate.

2. Give students the criteria for acceptable performance (grading) before they give student presentations. A written list of criteria is helpful and usually improves the performance of students. For example, the student presentation might be worth 25 points. You might award 5 points for a creative presentation style, 10 points for having used accurate sources of information, and 10 points for having made at least three relevant points about the impact of the media on the incidence of violence. By establishing the criteria prior to the student presentations, you will not be swayed by the halo effect and reward students who are entertaining but who have not adequately evaluated health information and made relevant points. You will not unjustly penalize students who were not entertaining but who did adequately evaluate health information and make relevant points.

3. Encourage students to practice their presentations and to develop an effective communication style. Offer to help them prior to their presentation. Suggest practicing the student presentation at home with their families or in front of a mirror. Encourage students to use audiovisuals, such as posters, photographs, slides, or overhead transparencies.

Field Trips

A **field trip** is an instructional strategy in which students visit a site outside the school to gather information or develop a health goal. A field trip might involve a visit to a health museum, a health agency, a waste treatment plant, or a fire department.

1. Be aware of school district policy regarding field trips. For example, a school district may require that parents or guardians sign a consent form that has been approved by the school board. There may be a requirement as to how many adults must be available to supervise students during a field trip. Check the school district policy covering liability. Check your personal liability or professional liability coverage. Remember, the consent of parents or guardians does not waive the teacher from being responsible for protecting the health and safety of students.

2. After discussing the proposed field trip with the individuals at the site, follow with a letter. State the purpose of the field trip and the number of students who will attend,

and describe your expectations. In most cases, individuals are better prepared to meet the needs of your students when they have this information clearly stated in writing.

3. Prepare students for the field trip. Give them relevant information. Clarify your reasons for taking the field trip and your expectations. If students are to write reaction papers or complete other learning experiences after the trip, tell them before the trip. Set guidelines for student behavior for the field trip and identify consequences for breaking guidelines.

4. After the trip, process the learning experience. Have students write thank you notes to the individuals who participated at the field trip site and to parents, guardians, or other adults who assisted with the trip. Write a letter to the individuals with whom you planned the trip and provide appropriate feedback.

Demonstrations

A **demonstration** is an instructional strategy in which the teacher or other appropriate person demonstrates a concept or life skill. A teacher may want to depict a form of physical abuse. The teacher might take two eggs. The teacher breaks the first egg into a bowl. The egg yolk will be visible. The teacher might say this is the brain of a child. Then the teacher might shake the second egg vigorously and explain that shaking a child is a form of physical abuse. The teacher then breaks the egg into a bowl. The yolk will be scrambled and can be used to show what might happen to the brain as a result of the vigorous shaking. Students can observe the brain damage that often results from this kind of child abuse. Teachers also can demonstrate life skills such as brushing and

flossing teeth. The following suggestions can increase the effectiveness of demonstrations:

1. Be certain to have all the materials needed for the demonstration. Try the demonstration before using it with students. Have the materials organized and ready to avoid wasting class time.

2. Adequately prepare students for the demonstration. For example, in the demonstration using the two eggs, the teacher might ask students to note the difference between the two egg yolks.

3. After the demonstration, process the information or the life skill that was presented. When appropriate, such as when a life skill has been demonstrated, have students repeat the demonstration.

Guest Speakers

A **guest speaker** is a person who will speak to students about his or her expertise or experience regarding a health topic or life skill. A guest speaker might also demonstrate a concept or life skill. There usually are many qualified guest speakers in a community.

Health care professionals and health educators at health agencies often are available as guest speakers. Guest speakers may have audiovisuals or other resources that the teacher does not have access to. Using a guest speaker can provide a change of pace for the students and pique their interest. The following suggestions can increase the effectiveness of using a guest speaker in the classroom:

1. Have a specific purpose in mind when using a guest speaker as an instructional strategy. Carefully select the guest speaker. Whenever possible, select guest speakers who are highly recommended by other competent teachers and who have previously spoken to students of this specific age level.

2. When contacting a guest speaker, be specific as to why you are inviting the person to your classroom, the expected outcomes, the date and time period, the location, and the age and number of students. Share any concerns or school district policies related to the topic or life skill to be addressed. For example, if a guest speaker is contacted to address the topic of suicide prevention, it may be helpful for the guest speaker to be aware of the curriculum guidelines for this topic at the grade level of the students to whom she is speaking. In addition, if there has been a recent suicide or suicide attempt in the school, the guest speaker should be informed so she will be prepared should students begin to share feelings. Ask the guest speaker if she has any specific requests for audiovisual equipment or room setup.

3. Prepare students for the guest speaker. Collect questions for the speaker ahead of time and send them to the speaker. Have students prepare questions for the class period. Explain your expectations for the class time to be spent with the guest speaker.

4. After the guest speaker's visit, process the learning experience. Obtain feedback from students. Ask students to write thank you notes to the guest speaker. Their thank you notes should provide specific feedback to the guest speaker. For example, a student might share something that he learned or a reason he is now motivated to practice a specific health goal.

5. Keep a file on guest speakers. After having a guest speaker, summarize feedback from the students and record it. Make notations as to whether or not the guest speaker's visit to the classroom met expectations. Refer back to your file before inviting a guest speaker for another visit to the classroom.

Educational Technologies

Educational technologies are teaching methods that involve the use of high-tech equipment, including computers, CD-ROMs, and online communication. Technology can enhance a curriculum by making learning relevant and interactive (Farrington & Eleey, 1994). Students can use technology to learn to write, research, and evaluate sources of information (Herndon, 1994). Technology can be used to support students' learning and as a management and communication tool for teachers. This section of the chapter discusses the hardware and software available, including the parts of the computer and software programs such as word processing and spreadsheets. It discusses telecommunications, including the Internet and the World Wide Web and their uses in the classroom, and multimedia and virtual reality. The section ends with the "Directory of Selected Health-Related World Wide Web Sites."

Hardware

A **computer** is a machine that accepts, processes and outputs data. A computer needs hardware and software. **Hardware** is the electronic components that form a computer. Hardware includes the hard drive, keyboard, monitor, modem,

printer, and any other equipment. **Software** is a computer program.

There are two main kinds of personal computer operating systems. These are Windows and Macintosh. Both Windows and Macintosh allow users to manage files and run software programs on personal computers. The Windows operating system was developed by Bill Gates and is the most widely used operating system on the market. Through a graphical user interface, Windows users can navigate through icons on their computers. Macintosh has the ability to allow users to use equivalents of Windows such as Microsoft Office. Macintosh is considered to have graphics capabilities that are easier to use than Windows.

Two of the most important features of a computer are the processor speed and the RAM (random access memory). The processor speed is how fast the computer can process information. Generally the faster the processor speed, the more expensive the computer. Processor speed is measured in gigahertz (GHz). RAM is "temporary" memory—a software program is copied to RAM when it is in use and removed from RAM when it is closed. The more memory (RAM) a computer has, the more

programs it can run at one time. Most software programs specify a minimum RAM requirement to run the program effectively. RAM is measured in megabytes (MB).

Many computers include the following components:

- A *hard drive* is a device that reads and enters data onto a hard disk (a more "permanent" memory).
- A *keyboard* is a device that allows you to enter letters, digits, and other symbols into a computer.
- A *monitor* displays computer output.
- A *mouse* is a device that controls the movement of the cursor on the screen. The cursor signifies where the computer will enter data or perform other operations, like open a folder.
- A *computer speaker* is a device that is connected to a computer and plays audio.
- A *printer* is a device that makes a "hard" (paper) copy of the text or illustrations created on a computer.
- A *floppy disk drive* is a device that can read and write to floppy disks, which, despite their name, are rigid. As CD-ROMs and DVDs (digital video disks) continue to surpass floppy

disks in storage capacity, the use of floppy disks is declining.

- A *CD-ROM drive* is a device used to play CD-ROM disks. *ROM* stands for "read-only memory." CD-ROM disks contain data that can be read by a computer. CD-ROMs hold more data than floppy disks, but new data cannot be recorded on a CD-ROM. Data can be saved on other kinds of CDs: CD-R (CD-recordable) and CD-RW (CD-rewritable). Most computers now feature drives that can read both CD-ROMs and DVDs.

- A *Zip drive* is a special floppy disk drive that holds high-capacity zip disks. Zip disks can hold much larger amounts of data than CD-ROMs or floppy disks.

- A *modem* is an electronic device that enables a computer to transmit and receive data over telephone or cable lines. A modem allows a computer to communicate with other computers. This is also called "going online." Internal modems are installed inside the computer. External modems plug into the outside of a computer.

Other kinds of hardware that can be valuable for classroom use include DVDs, laser disc players, scanners, digital cameras, and LCD projectors.

DIGITAL VIDEO DISK

A **DVD** is a special type of CD that can hold extensive amounts of computer data, audio, and video. The DVD is a relatively new technology that has the potential of replacing the traditional VCR and the laser disc player. Many DVDs now allow you to both play back information and record it. DVDs are known for their exceptional picture and sound quality, and the large amount of information they can store. One advantage for classroom use over film projectors and videotapes is that DVDs provide immediate access to information because they do not have to be fast-forwarded or rewound, like a tape does. An increasing number of programs and movies are now available on DVD.

DVDs can also be used for high-capacity computer data storage. They can hold far more data, and data of a greater variety, than CDs or Zip disks, which makes DVDs especially useful for storing video and audio files created on a computer.

LASER DISC PLAYER

A *laser disc* is a large metal disk that permanently stores large amounts of information. A laser disc player is analogous to a VCR. Like VCRs, laser disc players are hooked up to televisions or computer monitors. The players read information stored on laser discs but are currently unable to record on a laser disc. Laser discs have better clarity than videos, and when they are paused the picture is clear, not fuzzy. Like the DVD player, laser disc players can access information immediately, because there is no tape to fast-forward or rewind.

SCANNER

A **scanner** is equipment used to copy material from a "hard-copy" source (paper, plastic, etc.) to a computer. Scanners can be used to copy photographs, pages from books, or other hard copy. Some are handheld, others lie flat like copy machines. An example of an educational use for a scanner would be a student who scans photos from books to include in a book report. A teacher might use a scanner to copy illustrations for a bulletin board display.

DIGITAL CAMERA

A **digital camera** stores pictures in digital form on a small disk instead of on film. The digital pictures can be viewed immediately in the camera's viewing screen and loaded into the computer, where they can be digitally altered and printed out. A student might use a digital camera for a project on the human body by taking a photo of himself with a digital camera, loading it into the computer, and labeling the parts of his body using a photo-editing software program. Instead of the traditional portfolio, a student might make an electronic portfolio by taking pictures of her larger projects, such as dioramas or artwork, with a digital camera. A teacher might use a digital camera to take photos of new students to print for their personnel records.

LCD

An **LCD** is a device that displays computer output on a screen larger than a monitor. An LCD projecter allows a large group of people, such as a classroom of students, to see the information and is similar in concept to an overhead projector. A student might use an LCD projector to show the class illustrations of first aid procedures found on the Internet. A teacher might use an LCD to show students' electronic portfolios at parent night. A popular software program used with the projectors is PowerPoint.

Software

Software is a computer program. System software includes the operating system and other programs that control computer functions. Application software includes word processors, databases, and games. Software is usually stored on the hard disk or on a CD-ROM that is loaded into the computer for use. Much software is available geared toward the educational market.

Word processing is using a computer to produce documents. Word-processor software allows you to create a document, store it electronically, make changes to it, and print it. For example, a student might use word-processing software to write a report on trends in teen smoking, and use the editing features to later update the report with more recent statistics. A teacher might use word-processing software to send health newsletters home to parents.

A **spreadsheet** is a table of numerical data arranged in columns and rows. When you change an entry, called a cell, the program will automatically make any necessary adjustments based on the formula that the user has specified. Spreadsheet programs often include graphics features that produce charts and graphs from the data. For example, a student might enter data about costs of health insurance from different companies into a spreadsheet and print it out in a bar graph to compare the data. A teacher might use a spreadsheet to calculate budget costs for school supplies for the year.

A **database** is a collection of related information organized for quick access to specific items of information. Some databases, such as an address book, support only text. Other databases, such as hypertext, allow text, graphics, video, and audio to be linked together. Databases can be searched to find information quickly. For example, a student might use a database to create a phone directory of local health organizations. A teacher might use a database as a grade book, to record and average students' grades. Databases that can be accessed on the Internet include ERIC (Education Resources Information Center) and CANCERLIT.

DESKTOP PUBLISHING

Desktop publishing is similar to word processing but uses page layout programs to produce professional-looking materials, such as newsletters and books. Desktop publishing programs offer WYSIWYG (what you see is what you get) capabilities to see on screen what a document will look like when it is printed. Nowadays word-processing software incorporates basic desktop publishing features. A student might use desktop publishing to create a banner about MyPyramid to decorate the classroom. A teacher might use desktop publishing to create a class newsletter to distribute to students and their parents (Thomas, 1987/1988).

Telecommunications

One of the most popular uses for a computer has become communicating with others. Going on line can open up the world to a classroom. Students and teachers can access information resources from multiple sources while they are sitting in their own classrooms. Online communication allows access to a vast array of resources and allows people who are great distances apart to communicate and collaborate with each other (Grauman, 1994). It enables students and teachers to gain access to hundreds of libraries without ever leaving the place where the computer is located. They can disseminate information to others. Links with cable television and satellite systems allow interactive, two-way communication between students and teachers, regardless of location. In some schools, students are taught by instructors long distance in a face-to-face, interactive manner (Gilder, 1994).

The **Internet** is an online telecommunications system that links most online networks worldwide. The Internet originated with the United States Department of Defense and the National Science Foundation. Millions of people worldwide use the Internet. Users should always practice safety guidelines on the Internet (see Box 4-1). Users can access information that has been posted by other people, post their own messages, and communicate with others in real time. The Internet can be accessed through special accounts. The most common kind of account is with a telecommunication company, such as Comcast, or a commercial online service, such as America Online, or local Internet service providers (ISPs). These services are subscriber based and often charge a monthly fee.

The Internet can be compared to the world's largest library. Virtually any type of information can

BOX 4-1

Internet Safety Guidelines

The U.S. Department of Education offers safety guidelines for children who use the Internet. Consider making the following information available to parents:

- Make sure your children understand what you consider appropriate for them. What kinds of sites are they welcome to visit? What areas are off limits? How much time can they spend and when? How much money, if any, can they spend? Set out clear, reasonable rules and consequences for breaking them.
- Make online exploration a family activity. Put the computer in the living room or family room. This arrangement involves everyone and helps you monitor what your children are doing.
- Pay attention to games your older child might download or play online. Some are violent or contain sexual content.
- Look into software or online services that filter out offensive materials and sites. Options include standalone software that can be installed on your computer and devices that label or filter content directly on the Web. In addition, many Internet service providers and commercial online services offer site blocking, restrictions on incoming e-mail, and children's accounts that access specific services. Often, these controls are available at no additional

cost. Be aware, however, that children are often smart enough to get around these restrictions. Nothing can replace your supervision and involvement.

Discuss the following safety guidelines with your students:

- Never give out personal information (including your name, home address, phone number, age, race, family income, school name or location, or friends' names) or use a credit card online without a parent's or guardian's permission.
- Never tell your password to anyone, not even your friends.
- Never arrange a face-to-face meeting with someone you meet online unless your parent or guardian approves of the meeting and goes with you to a public place for the meeting.
- Never respond to messages that make you feel confused or uncomfortable. Ignore the sender, end the communication, and tell a parent, guardian, or another trusted adult right away.
- Never use bad language or send mean messages online.
- Recognize that people you meet online are not always who they say they are and that online information is not necessarily private.

Source: U.S. Department of Education (1997).

---

be found on the Internet. For example, students who are studying consumer health might look up the risks of health-related products from journals, government documents, and consumer Web sites. A teacher also can review countless journals, magazines, and consumer information to stay up to date with health-related information. It is important to remember that not all information on the Internet is accurate or reliable. Students need to be media literate (see Box 4-2).

E-MAIL

The most commonly used Internet service is e-mail. **E-mail** is the system of instantaneously transmitted electronic messages. Through e-mail, users can send messages to people they know or people they don't know. E-mail can contain hyperlinks, and long documents and multimedia files can be transmitted as attachments to e-mail. A

user can obtain an e-mail address and software needed to access the Internet through an ISP.

Classroom uses for e-mail include these:

- Students can e-mail penpals ("E-pals" or "Key-Pals") in other cities, states, or countries. For example, if a class is studying nutrition around the world, the teacher can help the student find e-mail penpals to interview about cultural differences in nutrition and diet.
- Students can contact, interview, and establish e-mail relationships with experts in a field they are studying or in which they have an interest. Experts might even become their mentors. For example, a student who is interested in working in the field of biomedical research might e-mail someone at the National Institutes of Health and request an interview to learn more about a career in the field of medicine. The

BOX 4-2

Media Literacy and the Internet

Students should be taught to recognize that sources on the Internet are not all reliable and might contain inaccurate, even dangerous, information. Students should always identify and evaluate sources of health information online. They should be taught to use the principles of media literacy as guidelines when online.

Media literacy is the ability to recognize and evaluate messages sent through various forms of mass communication.

A media-literate person

- Can distinguish reality from what is being presented
- Recognizes that the creators of the message have a motive
- Understands that the motive behind media is usually profit
- Knows that media are meant to influence your thinking
- Enjoys media in a deliberately conscious way
- Has a sense of his or her own values regardless of what the media say

professional might respond and keep in touch with the student after the project ends.

- Teachers can use e-mail to keep parents updated on their child's progress and class events and to otherwise communicate with them.

WORLD WIDE WEB

The **World Wide Web** ("the Web") is a vast collection of linked Internet documents that use hypertext. Hypertext is a way to connect related pieces of information in computer databases or documents nonsequentially. Hypertext includes hyperlinks, or "links," which are highlighted text or graphics. Clicking on a hyperlink takes you to another document or Web page.

The advantage of hypertext is that, if you want more information about a particular subject mentioned in a hypertext document, you can usually just click on it to read further detail. In fact, documents can be, and often are, linked to other documents by completely different authors—much like footnoting, but you can get the referenced document instantly. Hyperlinks might contain text, graphics, video, and audio.

A **Web site** is a collection of documents listed under one uniform resource locator (URL). The URL is an address for the Web site. For example, the URL for the American Heart Association is www.americanheart.org. The last three letters in an URL help identify who hosts the Web site. The following are common suffixes and organizational affiliations:

- com—commercial
- org—not-for-profit organization
- edu—educational
- gov—government
- net—networking

The first page of a Web site is called the home page. Web sites can consist of a single home page or an unlimited number of pages. Browsing the Web also is called "surfing" the Web.

Much of the information online is available to the public. This results in more Web sites than one person could ever look at. There are Web sites available that serve as indexes to the information on the web. A **search engine** is a program that looks for Web sites that include key words and provides a list of relevant Web sites. A user can type in a word or phrase, and the search engine will return a list of Web sites that match the description. For example, a teacher who wants to find the latest information about HIV/AIDS could search using the key words *HIV* and *AIDS*. A menu of topics and subtopics would appear, along with the addresses of Web sites, sometimes annotated. Many search engines offer special searches that are geared toward children and are limited to material appropriate for children.

Major search engines and Web indexes include these:

- AltaVista (www.altavista.com)
- WebCrawler (www.webcrawler.com)
- Excite (www.excite.com)
- Yahoo (www.yahoo.com)
- Google (www.google.com)
- Ask.com (www.ask.com)
- Wikipedia (www.wikipedia.org)

The Web can be a valuable classroom tool:

- Students can search the Web for information about virtually any topic they are studying or in which they have an interest. For example, a student who is studying physical activity can read about sports, exercise, and the Presidential Fitness Program.
- Teachers can search Web sites to be up to date on the latest health-related information. For example, a teacher might search Web sites produced by newspapers and magazines for a key word or key phrase on a subject, such as *drug abuse in teens,* to use in their lessons.
- Teachers and students can create Web sites on a subject area or contribute to a school Web site. Web sites might include school and classroom newspapers and school calendars.
- Teachers can use the Web to continue their professional development. Many colleges and universities offer classes online for college credit. Nonaccredited classes and online education geared toward almost any subject can also be found online (Joint Committee on Health Education Standards, 2006).

CHAT

Chat is real-time text conversation between people "in" a special online area, called a "chat room." All conversation is accessible to all users who are in the chat room while the conversation is taking place. Users also can instantaneously communicate privately one on one with other users via instant messaging programs. For example, a teacher might enter a chat room for teachers who are discussing school violence. A moderator might monitor the chat, and an expert might be part of the discussion.

BULLETIN BOARDS

A computer **bulletin board** is a service that allows users to post and obtain messages. A bulletin board allows people to offer input where others can read and respond to it. Because many bulletin boards are not monitored, student use should be regulated. Teachers might use a bulletin board geared for teachers to find new health lesson ideas and post their own.

VIDEOCONFERENCING

Videoconferencing is a conference between people in different locations who can see and hear each other using electronic communications.

Videoconferencing is similar to talking on the telephone, except that video of the people on the phone can be seen. An example of videoconferencing use in the classroom is a professor at a college teaching a class in another state.

Evaluating Web Sites

Not all Web sites are credible. Here are some criteria to determine if a Web site is valid.

- *The source.* Determine if the author is credible. Is this someone you have heard about or is he or she known in the field? The sponsor of the site is also important. For example, sites that have .gov for government resources or .edu for educational or research material usually provide valid content.
- *The content.* Not all material on a Web site is valid. Look for bias or opinions that may be overemphasized. Many people set up their own Web sites, and these Web sites may contain inaccurate content. Be wary of Web sites that contain spelling errors and use poor grammar. Content should also be comprehensive, have depth of information, and a time span covered. The Web site should also have been updated, and the content should be current. There should also be links to credible resources.
- *Style.* Check out the layout of the Web site. Is it easy to navigate? For example, does the Web site offer users the ability to go back, home, go to top, and so on.

Multimedia

Multimedia is any form of video or audio used with technology. Multimedia includes the use of text, graphics, video, and sound in an interactive format. For example, a student using a multimedia approach to a report on first aid might include a video clip of a person demonstrating a first aid procedure, a scanned photograph of medical equipment, and an audio clip narrating the report (Wilst, 1987). Hypermedia is a type of multimedia program that allows a user to view data as if it were a book, without having to follow a sequential order. Hypermedia programs refer to each "page" as a card in a stack, as in a stack of index cards. Each card can include a different use of text, graphics, video, and audio. For example,

Directory of Selected Health-Related World Wide Web Sites

Thousands of health-related Web sites are available to the public, and more are being added every day. There are Web sites devoted to individual health topics, such as nutrition and disease. Examples of Web sites that are particularly useful to health educators are included in this directory.

GENERAL HEALTH INFORMATION RESOURCES

The following portals offer health-related information and links to other related Web sites. Many search engines offer health categories in which health information and health links to other sites can be found.

DrKoop.com is the Web site by a company led by Dr. C. Everett Koop, former United States surgeon general.
www.drkoop.com

HealthAtoZ is a health and medical resource developed by health care professionals.
www.healthatoz.com

Healthfinder is the guide to reliable health information offered by the U.S. Department of Health and Human Services.
www.healthfinder.org

*Healthlink*USA includes a health topic index and allows a search for information from more than a thousand selected Web sites.
healthlinkusa.com

HealthWeb is a collaborative project of several health sciences libraries.
www.healthweb.org

Intellihealth is a comprehensive health resource company that is a subsidiary of Aetna U.S. Healthcare.
www.intellihealth.com

Kidshealth.org is a site for child-related health information sponsored by the Nemours Association.
www.kidshealth.org

Mayo Oasis is the website of the Mayo Clinic.
www.mayoclinic.com

Mdchoice.com offers free access to online, physician-reviewed information.
www.mdchoice.com

Medscape is a Web site for health professionals.
www.medscape.com

PubMed is the U.S. National Library of Medicine's search service, which provides access to more than 11 million databases in Medline and other related databases and includes links to online journals.
www.pubmed.gov

Reutershealth.com is the Reuters health news service.
www.reutershealth.com

HEALTH AND MEDICAL JOURNALS

American Journal of Psychiatry
ajp.psychiatryonline.org

American Journal of Preventive Medicine
www.elsevier.com/wps/find/journaldescription.cws_home/600644/description#description

American Journal of Medicine
www.elsevier.com/wps/find/journaldescription.cws_home/525049/description#description

British Medical Journal
www.bmj.com

JAMA (Journal of the American Medical Association)
www.jama.ama-assn.org

The Lancet
thelancet.com

New England Journal of Medicine
content.nejm.org

HEALTH-RELATED ORGANIZATIONS

Alliance for Health, Physical Education, Recreation and Dance
www.aahperd.org

Alcoholics Anonymous
www.alcoholics-anonymous.org

American Cancer Society
www.cancer.org

American Dental Association
www.ada.org

American Heart Association
www.americanheart.org

American Lung Association
www.lungusa.org

American Medical Association (AMA)
www.ama-assn.org

American Public Health Association
www.apha.org

American School Health Association
www.ashaweb.org

American Social Health Association
www.ashastd.org

Centers for Disease Control
and Prevention
www.cdc.gov

Department of Health and
Human Services
www.hhs.gov

Food and Drug Administration
www.fda.gov

National Association for Sport
and Physical Education
www.aahperd.org

National Cancer Institute
www.cancer.gov

National Dairy Council
www.nationaldairycouncil.org

National Health Information
Center (NHIC)
www.health.gov/nhic

National Institute on Drug
Abuse (NIDA)
www.nida.nih.gov

National Institutes of Health (NIH)
www.nih.gov/

National Library of Medicine
www.nlm.nih.gov

National Mental Health Association
www.nmha.org

National Safety Council
www.nsc.org

President's Council on Physical
Fitness and Sports
www.surgeongeneral.gov

Women's Sports Foundation
www.womenssportsfoundation.org

a student might use hypermedia to design a report with graphics and sound about the risks of smoking.

Whiteboards

Electronic and interactive whiteboards are communication vehicles the teacher can use in the classroom to present information in health education. The whiteboard works with dry erase markers and is connected to a computer so that notes written on the whiteboard can be downloaded into the computer and printed or shared by e-mail. The whiteboard also serves as a projection screen for the computer. Using a PowerPoint presentation, a teacher can write notes on top of an image being projected. A special pen works either as a highlighter or as a mouse that is activated by touching the pen to the screen.

Bibliography

Farrington, G. C., & Eleey, M. (1994). Penn's plans for integrating emerging technologies. *Technological Horizons in Education, 22,* 104–106.

Gilder, G. (1994). The convergence of the twain: Computers and fiber optics are coming together in cheap and powerful ways. *Electronic Learning, 13*(8), 30–31.

Graumann, P. J. (1994). The road to the information superhighway: Are we almost there yet? *Technology and Learning, 14*(2), 28–34.

Herndon, J. P. (1994). School as waystation on the information highway. *Technological Horizons in Education, 22,* 78–82.

Joint Committee on Health Education Standards. (2006). *The National Health Education Standards: Achieving health literacy.* Questions about the National Health Education Standards might be directed to the American Cancer Society; the American School Health Association; the Association for the Advancement of Health Education; the School Health Education and Services Section, American Public Health Association; and the Society of State Directors of Health, Physical Education, Recreation and Dance. For copies of *The National Health Education Standards,* call or write the American Cancer Society, 1599 Clifton Road NE, Atlanta, GA 30329 (1-800-ACS-2345).

Thomas, S. B. (1987/1988). Microcomputer telecommunications: Basic principles for health education research. *Health Education, December/January* 16–19.

U.S. Department of Education. (1997). *U.S. Department of Education Parents Guide to the Internet—November 1997.* Available at www.ed.gov/PDFDocs/97–6609.pdf. Accessed October 25, 2006.

Wilst, W. H. (1987/1988). Update on computer-assisted video instruction in the health sciences. *Health Education,* December/January 8–12.

SECTION 2 TWO

Health Content

CHAPTER FIVE

Mental and Emotional Health

HEALTH GOALS FOR MENTAL AND EMOTIONAL HEALTH

1. I will develop good character.
2. I will interact in ways that help create a positive social-emotional environment.
3. I will develop healthful personality characteristics.
4. I will choose behaviors to promote a healthy mind.
5. I will express emotions in healthful ways.
6. I will use stress-management skills.
7. I will seek help if I feel depressed.
8. I will use suicide-prevention strategies when appropriate.
9. I will cope with loss and grief in healthful ways.
10. I will be resilient in difficult times.

Mental and emotional health is the area of health that focuses on developing good character, interacting in ways that help create a positive social-emotional environment, developing healthful personality characteristics, choosing behaviors to promote a healthy mind, expressing emotions in healthful ways, using stress-management skills, seeking help if feeling depressed, using suicide-prevention strategies when appropriate, coping with loss and grief in healthful ways, and being resilient during difficult times. This chapter teaches young people important life skills for mental and emotional health. See the Scope and sequence chart in the Meeks Heit K–12 Health Education Curriculum Guide (Chapter 16) to identify mental and emotional health content that is appropriate for specific grade levels.

Health Goal #1

I Will Develop Good Character

Values and Character

People hold certain values. A value is a standard or belief. An example of a value is that it is important to always tell the truth. A **family value** is a standard that is held by members of a family. Individuals learn family values and other values from their parents or guardian. For example, a

family may give high value to education. The family encourages all the children to learn new ideas and new skills to do well in school.

Character is a person's use of self-control to act on responsible values. **Self-control** is the degree to which a person regulates her own behavior. For example, suppose a person who values honesty is accidentally given too much change by a grocery store clerk. Because this person values honesty and has good character, she uses self-control and avoids the temptation to keep the extra change.

Suppose a person who values his health is moving down the buffet line at a restaurant, making food selections. Self-control helps keep him from taking too much food. Self-control helps him practice moderation. **Moderation** is placing limits to avoid excess. Although the food looks delicious, the person practices moderation and does not overeat.

A person who has good character has the self-control to delay gratification when appropriate. **Delayed gratification** is the voluntary postponement of an immediate reward in order to complete a task before enjoying a reward. For example, suppose a student who values education has a test tomorrow morning and needs to study for the exam tonight. Tonight is also the decisive NBA

championship game, and this student would like very much to watch the game on television instead of study for the test. Instead, she uses self-control. She chooses to study tonight and decides to videotape the game and watch it tomorrow evening.

People who have good character set limits for themselves. Their behavior reflects responsible values. They practice delayed gratification when it is appropriate.

Self-Esteem

Self-esteem is an important indicator of a person's mental health. **Self-esteem** is one's belief about one's own worth. **Positive self-esteem** is a person's belief that he is worthy and deserves respect. **Negative self-esteem** is a person's belief that he is not worthy and does not deserve respect.

It is important to encourage young people to develop positive self-esteem based on responsible actions, for several reasons. People with positive self-esteem are more likely to practice life skills. They take responsibility for their health by keeping their body, mind, and relationships in top condition. People with positive self-esteem are more likely to be proactive in making important decisions. People who realize that they are special do not have to go along with the crowd to feel accepted. They rely on their own judgment and make responsible decisions. People with positive self-esteem appreciate their own uniqueness. They are confident and do not give in to pressure to be like everyone else. People with positive self-esteem have a firm foundation for difficult times. They understand that everyone experiences difficult times. They know difficult times will pass, and they do not give up because they believe in themselves. People with positive self-esteem are more likely to take calculated risks to mature. People who believe in themselves do not worry about failing. They are not overwhelmed if they have unsatisfactory results when they try something new, because they believe in their abilities. They are willing to take another calculated risk.

A related concept to self-esteem is self-efficacy. **Self-efficacy** is a person's belief in his or her capacity or ability to perform a behavior or skill in a desired way. People with high self-efficacy are confident that they can achieve personal goals (Beckman, Hawley, & Bishop, 2006).

People with positive self-esteem also expect others to treat them with respect. Because their own actions are worthy, they have self-respect. **Self-respect** is a high regard for oneself because one behaves in responsible ways. Other people will tend to be respectful toward a person who behaves responsibly and has self-respect.

Self-respect should not be confused with conceit. **Conceit** is excessive appreciation of one's own worth.

Developing Good Character and Improving Self-Esteem

To possess good character, one's actions must reflect responsible values. People should periodically conduct a character check on themselves. They do this by listing responsible values and then conducting a self-evaluation to determine whether one's own actions reflect these values. Another good character check is to ask for feedback from responsible adults who have good character. If a person's actions do not reflect the list of responsible values, she should change her behavior to reflect these values. Behaving in ways that contradict responsible values does not build character.

To improve self-esteem, one's belief statements must be responsible. Individuals have the power to control the belief statements that play in their minds. Negative belief statements, such as "I am worthless" or "I will fail no matter how hard I try," can be changed. A person must have a set of belief statements that motivate him to behave in responsible ways. This helps him feel good about himself. This is a key to healthful, positive self-esteem.

A person who has self-respect will treat herself in special ways. Other people will notice the behavior and will show her respect. Here are some guidelines for individuals to follow to show self-respect:

1. *Pay attention to your appearance.* Being well groomed is one of the first indicators of self-respect. When you carefully choose what to wear and have a neat appearance, you put your best foot forward. You feel more self-confident when you look your best.

2. *Make a list of responsible actions and review the list often.* Knowing that your actions are responsible will help keep you from getting down on yourself. It is important to give yourself credit for behaving in responsible ways. You should change any of your behaviors that is not responsible.

3. *Be a friend to yourself by enjoying activities, such as hobbies, by yourself.* Being by yourself gives you quiet time to get in touch with your thoughts and feelings. Developing a talent or hobby helps you feel unique.

4. *Write your feelings in a journal.* Writing about your feelings is a good way to examine what is happening in your life. Writing about feelings also is a way to vent feelings such as anger, resentment, and disappointment. Reviewing what you have written can help you gain self-knowledge.

5. *Make spending time with family members a priority.* If you have a loving, supportive family, members of the family believe each individual in the family is special. They build each other up and encourage one another. When a person is down, family members help the person change his or her attitude.

6. *Care for other people in the way you would like to be cared for.* Helping others gives you a sense of your own value.

7. *Let other people know what helps you feel special.* Never take it for granted that others know how to make you feel special. It is important to be honest in expressing your feelings and desires to others.

8. *Support the interests of family members and friends, and ask them to support your*

interests. For example, suppose your sister plays on the volleyball team. Attending her volleyball games supports this sister. Other family members can ask this sister to attend the activities in which they participate.

9. *Ask family members and friends to tell you examples of your actions that have shown character.* This feedback can help guide you in developing self-control to act responsibly.

10. *Get plenty of exercise to generate feelings of well-being.* After vigorous exercise, beta-endorphins are released into the bloodstream. **Beta-endorphins** are substances produced in the brain that create a feeling of well-being.

An important movement in education is character education. Character education involves efforts to positively influence the character of students (Elkind & Sweet, 2004). Character education helps students learn. Qualities such as caring, responsibility, respect for oneself and others, fairness, trustworthiness, citizenship, and self-restraint promote a healthy, safe, and supportive learning environment (Michigan State Board of Education, 2004).

Health Goal #2

I Will Interact in Ways That Help Create a Positive Social-Emotional Environment

---

Social-Emotional Environment

The **social-emotional environment** is the quality of the contacts a person has with the people with whom he or she interacts. An individual's interactions with members of his or her family influence that person's social-emotional environment. A young person's interactions with peers and adults in the community also have an influence. A positive social-emotional environment improves health status by allowing a person and others to comfortably communicate needs, wants, and emotions.

Social-Emotional Environment and Health Status

A positive social-emotional environment exists when a person receives plenty of social-emotional boosters. A **social-emotional booster** is an interpersonal contact that helps a person feel encouragement and support, choose responsible behavior, and recognize options. In a positive social-emotional environment, people around an individual encourage him or her to take calculated risks and give praise when the person does things well. They recognize and appreciate that the person is special and unique and provide compliments when that person uses self-discipline and chooses responsible behavior. The person then feels the support needed to take calculated risks. When the person is tempted to do something wrong, he or she is more likely to decide against it. The person is less likely to feel depressed or down over circumstances in his or her own life. He or she is better able to recognize that there are options, even for the most difficult circumstances.

A negative social-emotional environment exists when a person experiences too many social-emotional pollutants. A **social-emotional pollutant** is an interpersonal contact that closes options or may cause a person to feel discouraged and alone or to choose wrong behavior. In this type of environment, people around an individual are disrespectful, put the person down, or gossip about the person. They try to manipulate, control, or abuse the person in some way. They behave in ways that are wrong, and they want the person to do the same. These people do not want the individual to improve his or her circumstances, and tell the individual that he or she cannot change the way things are. Actions such as these create a negative social-emotional environment.

Here are ten ways that a positive social-emotional environment improves health status:

- Improves self-respect
- Provides support for responsible behavior
- Provides the support and encouragement you need to take calculated risks
- Allows you to correct mistakes, forgive yourself, and move on
- Helps you to be resilient
- Helps you to be optimistic
- Reduces stress

- Helps to prevent and relieve depression
- Helps to prevent feelings of loneliness and alienation
- Reduces the risk of psychosomatic disease

Strategies to Improve the Social-Emotional Environment

There are strategies that young people can use to improve the social-emotional environment. These strategies focus on improving one's interactions with others.

1. *Minimize or avoid contact with people who put you down.* Evaluate the positive and negative effects of various relationships such as peers, family, and friends. Consider how these relationships affect your physical and emotional health. Minimize or avoid contact with persons who treat you with disrespect.

2. *Use positive self-statements if you are with a person or group of persons who are negative.* Evaluate the dynamics of your relationships with peers and family. Evaluate the dynamics of the social groups to which you belong. You may not be able to avoid certain people or groups of people. Suppose you are with a person or group of persons who are negative or who put you down. Pretend you have a shield of armor surrounding and protecting you from their words. Continue to say positive statements to yourself to avoid listening to their negative words and putdowns.

3. *Spend time with a mentor.* The significant people in your life may not give you social-emotional boosters. They may ignore your needs, wants, and emotions. Find a mentor with whom you can spend time and get the social-emotional boosters you need. Communicate your needs, wants, and emotions to your mentor.

4. *Join a support group.* The people in the support group can provide you with social-emotional boosters. Within the group, you can experience a positive social-emotional environment. You can practice expressing your needs, wants, and emotions in a safe setting.

5. *Expand the network of people with whom you communicate needs, wants, and emotions.* Remember, you need social-emotional boosters to maintain physical and emotional health. If you are not getting them, consider finding new friendships that provide them. Participate in new activities at school and in your community.

6. *Give others social-emotional boosters.* Contribute to the quality of the social-emotional environment by supporting and encouraging peers, friends, and family members. Encourage them to communicate their needs, wants, and emotions. When you do, you help others maintain their physical and emotional health.

Health Goal #3

I Will Develop Healthful Personality Characteristics

Personality

Personality is an individual's unique pattern of characteristics. An individual's personality is what makes that person different from others. There are many influences on personality, including heredity, environment, attitudes, and behaviors. Heredity helps determine one's intellectual abilities, temperament, and talents. It might influence athletic and artistic capabilities. It might influence how resilient a person is. Environment includes everything around a person and influences the opportunities that the person has. Where a person lives and the people with whom one has contact influences personality. A person's attitudes show through in the person's personality. Behavior, or what a person does, also affects personality.

Personality Characteristics That Promote Good Health

Personality characteristics are often used to describe a person. The following personality characteristics promote good health:

- Ambition
- Compassion
- Confidence
- Cooperativeness
- Courage
- Dedication
- Enthusiasm
- Faithfulness
- Generosity
- Honesty
- Hopefulness
- Loyalty
- Optimism
- Patience
- Perceptiveness
- Persistence
- Reliability
- Resilience
- Resoluteness
- Respectfulness
- Responsibility
- Security
- Self-determination
- Self-discipline
- Sincerity

Health Goal #4

I Will Choose Behaviors to Promote a Healthy Mind

Mental Alertness and Mental Health

To be alert is to be quick to perceive and act, to be watchful and intelligent. People who are alert are interested in what is going on in their lives. They understand that they will have problems and disappointments, but they do not allow those problems and disappointments to overwhelm them. People who are mentally alert understand that their minds need exercise just as their bodies do. They read for fun and for information. They challenge themselves with word puzzles or jigsaw puzzles. They read newspapers to be aware of what is going on in their neighborhood and in the world. They never stop learning about new ideas and new ways of doing things. They choose to promote their mental health.

Mentally healthy people generally feel good about themselves, have satisfying relationships, and set realistic goals for themselves. Their life experiences are not always positive, but they learn to cope. On the other hand, people who are not able to cope might suffer from some form of mental disorder. The difference between mental health and having a mental disorder is often very slight. The symptoms of many mental disorders can be controlled with medicines, so that people with these disorders can continue to have a normal life in society. Other mental disorders are more serious and more complicated to treat and recover from.

Addictions

An important part of well-being is coping with difficult situations and problems. Some people do not acknowledge problems or deal with problems in appropriate ways. They might instead use drugs or rely on harmful behaviors as a way of coping. They develop addictions. An **addiction** is a compulsion to repeatedly take a drug or engage in a specific behavior.

One of the most familiar of addictions is drug addiction. Some people drink alcohol to avoid dealing with problems. They feel a compelling need or urge to drink alcohol whenever they feel bored, lonely, or frustrated. They depend on alcohol to avoid their problems and change their mood. Some depend on other drugs, such as cocaine, methamphetamine, or heroin. Drug addiction is also referred to as chemical dependence and drug dependence. You will learn more about addiction/dependence in Chapter 10.

Even a behavior that is neutral or healthy can become an addictive behavior when carried to extreme. For example, a person who feels compelled to shop when unhappy might cross the line from shopping to shopping addiction, and people who

exercise to extremes to avoid facing problems have an addiction.

Addictions can harm physical health, jeopardize safety, harm relationships, cause legal problems, and cause financial problems. Using drugs—such as nicotine, alcohol, cocaine, marijuana, or heroin—harms body organs. Exercising to extremes can cause injuries. Because alcohol and other drugs change the way a person thinks, a person who is using these might choose unsafe actions and have accidents. Drug use can lead to fights that result in injuries and is a major cause of motor vehicle accidents that result in injury or death. People with thrill-seeking addiction take unnecessary risks that can result in injury or death.

People with addictions focus most of their attention on a drug or a behavior. They neglect their relationships. They deny their addictions and begin to lie or be secretive. They are unable to share feelings in healthful ways. As a result, their relationships with family and friends suffer. A person using drugs can get arrested and jailed for using and possessing drugs. Young people can be suspended from school. People with shopping addiction often overspend. They might borrow credit cards or steal to pay for purchases. They get into financial difficulty and might even break the law to continue their addiction. People with drug addiction might spend large amounts of money on drugs. People with gambling addiction might continue betting when they do not have money.

Signs that might indicate that a person has an addiction include these:

- Having a compulsion to repeatedly take a drug or engage in a behavior
- Taking a drug or engaging in a behavior instead of dealing with feelings of anxiety, depression, boredom, or loneliness
- Feeling bad about oneself after taking a drug or engaging in a behavior
- Taking a drug or engaging in a behavior even when there are negative consequences
- Attempting to stop taking a drug or engaging in an addictive behavior, but failing at these attempts.

Table 5-1 lists several types of addictions and the characteristics of people with these addictions.

GETTING HELP FOR ADDICTIONS

People often deny that they have addictions and refuse to get help. They may need to be confronted by family members or other caring people. A **formal intervention** is an action by people, such as family members, who want a person to get treatment. The people involved in a formal intervention prepare ahead of time, reviewing what the person has said and done, and how the person's addiction affects them. A trained counselor can help them prepare. During a formal intervention, these people confront the person with the addiction, perhaps with the counselor present. They are specific as they tell the person what they have observed and why that person needs treatment.

There are different approaches to treatment for addictions. Individual therapy is treatment that involves a trained professional and the person with an addiction. Group therapy involves a trained professional who works with more than one person at a time. Family therapy involves a trained professional who works with the person and family members. Some people who have addictions must be hospitalized, and some must be treated for physical health problems.

People who have been treated for an addiction may have a relapse. A **relapse** is a return to a previous behavior or condition. These people return to their addiction when they feel depressed, anxious, or lonely. To avoid relapse, people must stick to their plan for recovery. Part of any recovery plan for people with addictions is to have a support network. The purpose of the support network is to allow an individual to feel secure enough to share

TABLE 5-1

TYPES OF ADDICTIONS

TYPE	DESCRIPTION	CHARACTERISTICS (People with This Addiction):
Drug Addiction	The compelling need for a drug even though it harms the body, mind, or relationships	• Feel the need for drugs when anxious, bored, or depressed • Depend on drugs to change their moods • Use drugs to avoid facing problems • Usually deny that they use drugs to change moods and avoid facing problems
Exercise Addiction	The compelling need to exercise	• Make exercise the focus of their lives • Exercise to relieve tension and to feel in control of their lives • Put their exercise routine ahead of family, friends, job, studying, and other responsibilities • May push themselves to the limit and injure themselves • Feel depressed, anxious, unhappy, or have difficulty sleeping if they do not exercise
Eating Disorders	A mental disorder in which a person has a compelling need to starve, binge, or binge and purge	• Usually have negative self-esteem and often do not feel good about their appearance • Want more control over their lives and substitute harmful eating habits for the control they think they are lacking
Gambling Addiction	The compelling need to bet money or other valuables	• Often are bored and restless • Get a high when they place bets • Have a history of betting during childhood that progresses into adulthood • Often have other addictions as well
Nicotine Addiction	The compelling need for nicotine; also known as nicotine dependence	• Develop their schedule around smoking or chewing tobacco • Rely on nicotine to relieve tension or boredom
Perfectionism	The compelling need to do everything perfectly	• Often repeat the same task because they are never satisfied with their performance • Are overly critical of themselves and others • Feel that nothing is ever good enough for them • Adults in their lives often had unrealistic expectations of them during their childhood

Type	Description	Characteristics
Relationship Addiction	The compelling need to be connected to another person	• Use relationships like they would use drugs • Feel a constant need to be with a certain person • Are often described as being needy • Cause the person with whom they have a relationship to feel suffocated and drained of energy • Have a need to be with another person to "fill up" their feelings of emptiness or to relieve them of feelings of depression and insecurity
Sexual Addiction	The compelling need for sexual activity without any commitment to a sexual partner	• Might participate in several forms of sexual behavior, such as prostitution, masturbation, exhibitionism, rape, or incest • Develop life problems as a result of their sexual activity
Shopping Addiction	The compelling need to purchase things	• Like other forms of addiction, harbor deep feelings of insecurity • Feel a high from shopping and use shopping to relieve negative feelings such as depression, anxiety, or insecurity • Feel in control and powerful when they make purchases • Often face severe financial problems as well as emotional and relationship problems
Television Addiction	The compelling need to watch TV and other forms of entertainment media (e.g., DVDs, movies); a similar form of addiction is found among people who excessively use computers	• Plan their schedules around the television programs they watch • Might watch television and similar forms of entertainment media for seven hours or more a day • When they become anxious or bored, they turn on the TV to get a quick fix • Unable to manage their time and get other things done • Often do not become involved in other pursuits and activities • May suffer from poor grades or poor physical fitness
Thrill-Seeking Addiction	The compelling need to take unnecessary risks	• Enjoy high-risk situations and are willing to take dangerous dares • During risky experiences, there are biochemical changes in the brain • Get hooked on and frequently seek the feelings from biochemical changes that result from high-risk activities • May take unnecessary risks and may injure themselves or others
Workaholism	The compelling need to work to fill an emptiness	• Feel the need to work whenever they can • Do not enjoy themselves when they are not working or studying • Keep from dealing with other aspects of their lives (e.g., emotions, relationships) because of the long working hours • Need the constant praise they may get from work • Get a high from work that helps them to overcome feelings of depression; anxious, tense, or upset when they are not working

feelings and needs. People in the support network also provide encouragement.

Codependence

People involved with other people who have an addiction often want to rescue the person with an addiction and fix the individual's problems. **Codependence** is a compulsion to control, take care of, and rescue people by fixing their problems and minimizing their pain. A **codependent** is a person who wants to rescue and control another person. People with codependence usually do the following:

- Deny their feelings
- Focus on fixing other people's problems
- Try to control other people
- Feel responsible for what other people say or do
- Seek approval from others
- Have difficulty having fun
- Have difficulty allowing others to care for them
- Try to protect others from the harmful consequences of their behavior
- Do not meet their own needs
- Avoid living their own lives by concentrating on other people

People with codependence are enablers. An **enabler** is a person who supports the harmful behavior of others. For example, an enabler might lend money to someone with gambling addiction or make excuses for a friend who uses drugs. An enabler might praise someone who exercises to extremes for being in condition. These responses encourage people with addictions to continue their addiction.

People with codependence might benefit from individual, group, or family therapy. They also may benefit from being in a support group. A **support group** is a group of people who help one another deal with an addiction, a particular disease, or difficult situation.

Mental Disorders

A **mental disorder** is an illness of the mind that can affect the thoughts, feelings, and behaviors of a person, preventing him or her from leading a happy, healthful, and productive life. The cause of a mental disorder can be organic or functional. Organic mental disorders are caused by physical injuries and illnesses that affect the brain. Some causes include strokes, brain tumors, automobile accidents, alcoholism, sexually transmitted diseases, and meningitis. Functional mental disorders have causes that are not physical. Some causes include environmental conditions, stress, traumatic experiences, and poor coping skills. When compared to other diseases (such as cancer and heart disease), major mental illness, including clinical depression, bipolar disorder, schizophrenia, and obsessive-compulsive disorder, is the most common cause of disability in the United States.

The American Psychiatric Association (2000) classifies mental disorders according to their common patterns of behaviors. Six categories of mental disorders are affective disorders, anxiety disorders, dissociative disorders, personality disorders, somatoform disorders, and schizophrenia.

AFFECTIVE DISORDERS

An **affective disorder** is a disorder involving extreme moods. The exact causes of affective disorders are not known, but they are more common in some families. Three types of affective disorders are clinical depression, bipolar disorder (manic-depressive disorder), and seasonal affective disorder. **Clinical depression** involves long-lasting feelings of hopelessness, sadness, or helplessness. In **bipolar disorder,** or **manic-depressive disorder,** a person's moods vary from extreme happiness to depression. **Seasonal affective disorder** is a type of depression caused by reduced exposure to sunlight.

ANXIETY DISORDERS

An **anxiety disorder** is a disorder in which real or imagined fears prevent a person from enjoying life. People who have an anxiety disorder may have panic attacks. A panic attack is a period of intense fear and anxiety that is accompanied by body changes. Body changes may include increased heart rate, sweating, shaking, shortness of breath, discomfort, nausea, loss of control, chills, hot flashes, and fear of dying. Types of anxiety disorders include general anxiety disorder, phobia, obsessive-compulsive disorder, and post-traumatic stress disorder. **General anxiety disorder** is a recurring state of anxiety, fear, restlessness, and tenseness. A **phobia** is an excessive fear of certain objects, situations, or people. **Obsessive-compulsive disorder** is the urgent need to repeat a thought or an action. **Post-traumatic stress disorder (PTSD)** is a condition in which the aftereffects of a past event keep a person from living in a normal way.

DISSOCIATIVE DISORDERS

A **dissociative disorder** is a disorder in which a person has memory loss, confused identity, or more than one identity. Two types of dissociative disorders are amnesia and dissociative identity disorder. **Amnesia** is the inability to recall past experiences. **Dissociative identity disorder** is a rare mental disorder in which two or more personalities coexist within the same person.

PERSONALITY DISORDERS

A **personality disorder** is a disorder in which a person's patterns of thinking, feeling, and acting interfere with daily living. There are many types of personality disorders. A person with **antisocial personality disorder** has patterns of behavior that conflict with society. A person with **avoidant personality disorder** avoids all social contact. A person with **dependent personality disorder** cannot function without the advice and help of others. A person with **histrionic personality disorder** has emotional outbursts and constantly draws attention to himself or herself. A person with **narcissistic personality disorder** is boastful, conceited, and inconsiderate of others. A person with **passive-aggressive personality disorder** uses overly compliant behavior to mask anger or resentment.

SOMATOFORM DISORDERS

A person with **somatoform disorder** has symptoms of disease for which no physical cause can be found. Two types of somatoform disorders are hypochondria and conversion disorder. A person with **hypochondria** is constantly worried about illness. A hypochondriac constantly feels aches and pains and worries about developing some illness or disease. A person with **conversion disorder** experiences sudden health changes as a result of an emotional state. Health changes that might occur include sudden loss of vision or hearing, loss of sensation in the skin, or paralysis of a body part.

SCHIZOPHRENIA

Schizophrenia is a disorder in which there is a split or breakdown in logical thought processes. The split results in unusual behaviors. Actions, words, and emotions are confused and usually are inappropriate. A person with this disorder may appear desperate and withdraw into an inner world of fantasy. **Paranoid schizophrenia** is a type of schizophrenia in which a person has delusions of either persecution or grandeur. People with delusions of persecution believe they are being persecuted by others. People with delusions of grandeur see themselves as unusually great.

HELP FOR PEOPLE WITH MENTAL DISORDERS

People with medical disorders can be helped through formal interventions, evaluations, medications, therapy, support groups, and recovery plans. A formal intervention may be needed to help people who deny their condition and refuse to get help. People with mental disorders may need both a medical evaluation and a psychological evaluation. Some people with mental disorders need medication that must be prescribed by a physician. People with mental disorders might benefit from sharing their feelings and needs. Family members also may benefit from being in support groups. People with mental disorders must have a long-range recovery plan. They must continue their therapy and medication when recommended to prevent a relapse.

Health Goal #5

I Will Express Emotions in Healthful Ways

Emotions and the Mind-Body Connection

People experience many emotions. An emotion is a specific feeling. Feeling depressed, optimistic, disgusted, rejected, or envious are examples of emotions. Other examples are feeling afraid, lonely, angry, loving, anxious, nervous, resentful, excited, sad, frustrated, shy, guilty, stressed, happy, surprised, jealous, or thrilled.

Emotions affect both the mind and the body. The response to an emotion is mental as well as physical. The **mind-body connection** is the close relationship between mental and physical responses. Your body responds to the way you think, feel, and act. When you are stressed, anxious, or upset, your body can tell that something isn't right. For example, high blood pressure or a stomach ulcer might develop after a particularly stressful or upsetting life event (American Academy of Family Physicians, 2005).

Being unable to express emotions in healthful ways can harm the body. A **psychosomatic disease** is a physical disorder caused or aggravated by emotional responses. Health professionals are increasingly using the term *psychophysiologic illness* for these conditions. A person who does not know how to handle an argument with friends might get a stomachache or a headache. A person who has asthma—a chronic condition in which breathing becomes difficult—might worry about not having enough money to pay a bill and in response have difficulty breathing. This emotional response (worry) aggravated a physical disorder (asthma).

Remember that good health status includes the condition of the body, mind, emotions, and relationships. To promote good health status, one must pay attention to the mind-body connection. Expressing emotions in healthful ways is essential for healthful relationships.

to deny their feelings. **Denial** is a condition in which a person refuses to recognize what she is feeling because it is extremely painful. Denial can take many forms, such as minimizing problems, blaming problems on others, making excuses for problems, pretending that a problem does not exist, changing the subject to avoid threatening topics, and avoiding issues. Recognizing and expressing feelings can help an individual understand and cope with negative feelings such as anger, anxiety, and jealousy.

Expressing Emotions in Healthful Ways

Communication is the exchange of feelings, thoughts, or information with one or more persons. The way a person expresses and shares feelings, thoughts, and information influences how well this person relates with others. A person who expresses feelings in healthful ways is more likely to have a healthy mind and body. A person who expresses feelings in harmful ways or keeps feelings bottled up inside might not relate well with others. Being unable to express feelings can have a negative effect on a person's health.

DIFFICULTY IN COMMUNICATING

Many young people do not learn to recognize and express their feelings as they mature. For example, children who grow up in dysfunctional families often find it difficult to express their feelings. They might not even understand what they are feeling, much less why. Instead, they learn

GUIDELINES FOR EXPRESSING EMOTIONS IN HEALTHFUL WAYS

A person can learn to express emotions in healthful ways by following five guidelines:

1. *Identify the emotion.* What emotions am I experiencing?
2. *Identify the source of the emotion.* Why do I feel this way?
3. *Decide whether or not there is the need to respond right away.* Should I talk to a parent, guardian, or other responsible adult about the emotions? Should I try to sort out my emotions by myself? Do I need more information before I respond? Do I need to rehearse what I will say before I respond?
4. *Choose a responsible and healthful response.* What I-message might I use? (I-messages are explained in the next section of this chapter.) Would it be helpful to express my emotions by writing in a journal? Could I write a poem, sculpt clay, or draw a picture to express my emotions?

5. *Protect your health.* Do I need extra sleep? Do I need to work off my strong emotions with vigorous exercise? Am I aware of any physical disorders that might be connected to the emotional response I am experiencing? (If so, I might need to see a physician.) Am I able to function in daily activities? (If not, I might need to consider counseling.)

I-Messages and You-Messages

Using I-messages is a healthful way to express feelings. An **I-message** is a statement that focuses on a specific behavior or event, how that behavior or event affects the speaker, and the emotions the speaker feels as a result. When a person uses I-messages, she assumes responsibility for sharing feelings, because I-messages refer to the person speaking, her feelings, and her needs. An example of an I-message is "When you picked me up late for the game, we were late, and I was angry with you." An I-message gives the other person an opportunity to respond without being on the defensive. For example, in response to the I-message, the other person might say, "I understand why you are angry with me. I would feel the same way." A **you-message** is a statement that blames or shames another person. A you-message puts down the other person and puts him on the defensive. This kind of message would provoke a much different response from another person. An example of a you-message is "You are rude and selfish to pick up the phone when I am trying to have a conversation with you."

Active Listening

An important part of learning to communicate effectively is to learn to listen carefully. Listening carefully shows interest in the other person. **Active listening** is a way of responding that shows that the listener hears and understands. An active listener might respond in four different ways to let the other person know that she is really hearing and understanding. The listener might ask for more information (clarifying response): "Will you give me another chance to pick you up for an event so that I can show you that I will be on time?" The listener might repeat in her own words what the speaker said (restating response): "So what you are telling me is that you are angry with me because I picked you up late." The listener might summarize the main idea (summarizing response): "I can see that the problem is that you missed part of the game because I picked

you up late." The listener might acknowledge and show appreciation for the speaker's feelings (confirming response): "I don't blame you for feeling angry, and I appreciate that you told me how you feel."

Nonverbal Communication and Mixed Messages

In addition to words, actions also express emotions. **Nonverbal communication** is the use of actions to express emotions and thoughts. For example, twisting one's hair often expresses anxiety. Tapping one's foot might express impatience. Smiling usually indicates pleasure, and frowning usually indicates displeasure or sadness. These are examples of actions that send a message to anyone who is observing.

Individuals should avoid sending mixed messages when expressing feelings. A **mixed message** is a message in which behaviors (verbal or nonverbal) do not match in meaning. Suppose a student would like to get to know a classmate better. He smiles, but when there is an opportunity to speak to the other person, he walks away without speaking. The other person might be confused as to which message (the smile or the walking away) is the real message. Words and facial expression can also send different meanings: A person who apologizes with a smirk on her face gives a mixed message. Mixed messages are difficult to understand.

Anger-Management Skills

Anger is an emotion varying in intensity from mild irritation to intense rage that is often accompanied by physiological changes that prepare the body for fighting. Anger is usually a response to being hurt, frustrated, insulted, or rejected. An **anger trigger** is a thought or event that causes a person to be angry. Perhaps someone is hit and feels physical pain. Or a person may be frustrated over a situation or is rejected by peers and becomes angry. An **anger cue** is a body change that occurs when a person is angry. The response to anger is often called the fight-or-flight response because the body changes prepare a person for an emergency. These body changes include rapid breathing, increase in heart rate, rise in blood pressure, increased sweating, and dryness of the mouth.

Hidden anger is anger that is not recognized or is expressed in an inappropriate way. The following types of behavior may be signs of hidden anger: being negative, making cruel remarks to others, being sarcastic, procrastinating, blowing up easily, having little interest in anything, being bored, sighing frequently, and being depressed. Hidden anger adversely affects health. When these feelings are not recognized and expressed, they usually increase. Hidden anger builds and eventually cannot be kept hidden; then it is expressed in outbursts, temper tantrums, or fights. A person with hidden anger may experience tense facial muscles, stiff or sore neck and shoulder muscles, ulcers, headaches, high blood pressure, some types of cancer, and weight loss or gain.

Some people are always angry. They have a chip on their shoulder and seem ready to blow up. They exhibit **hostility syndrome**—a physical state in which the body is in the fight-or-flight state at all times. In other words, the person's body always feels that an emergency is about to happen. Because the person's body is on overdrive and gets little rest, the immune system, the body system that fights disease, does not work well.

People with hostility syndrome have lowered brain serotonin levels. **Serotonin** is a chemical in the body that helps regulate primitive drives and emotions. People with lowered brain serotonin levels can become very aggressive. Low levels are also associated with depression and anxiety disorders.

People with hidden anger may express their anger in harmful ways. They may express their anger with projection. Projection is attributing to others the emotions or responsibilities that one does not want to recognize in one's self. For example, a person who scores poorly on a test may say the test was unfair and blame a teacher for his or her failure. People with hidden anger may express anger with displacement. **Displacement** is the releasing of anger on someone or something other than the cause of the anger. For example, a person angry about a family situation might destroy public property.

It is not harmful to feel angry. Feeling angry is a normal and healthful response to many situations. However, it is essential to learn to control one's anger and to express anger in appropriate ways. **Anger-management skills** are healthful ways to control and express anger. The following ten skills help a person manage anger:

1. *Keep an anger self-inventory.* An anger self-inventory helps you examine your anger. The questions in the inventory can help you recognize anger cues. You can then decide whether you are overreacting to a situation or person and whether the situation or person is worth your attention. If your anger is justified, you can examine ways to respond. The following is a sample of questions for an anger self-inventory:
   • What am I feeling?
   • What is causing me to feel this way?
   • Is my anger justified?
   • Am I still angry? (If yes, continue.)
   • What are healthful ways to express my anger?

2. *Use self-statements to control anger.* **Self-statements** are words you can say to yourself when you experience anger triggers and cues. Here are some examples:
   • *I can manage this situation.*
   • *I will take a few deep breaths before I say anything.*
   • *I'll just count to ten. One, two, three, . . .*
   • *I am in control as long as I keep cool.*
   • *I am not going to explode over this.*

3. *Use I-messages instead of you-messages.* An I-message can be used to express your anger about another person's behavior. Using I-messages keeps communication lines open. The other person can respond without feeling threatened.

4. *Write a letter.* Writing a letter is a safe way to express your anger. You can state your reasons for being angry without being interrupted, and you can read the letter and make changes before sending it. Or you can hold on to the letter until you've cooled down. You might even decide not to send the letter.

5. *Write in a journal.* Writing in a journal can help you vent your anger. The journal can consist of writing the answers to the questions in an anger self-inventory. Reviewing your answers to these questions can help you learn more about your anger.

6. *Reduce the effects of anger cues with physical activity.* Vigorous physical activity can relieve anger cues. Try dancing, jogging, swimming, martial arts, weightlifting, or rollerblading, for instance.

7. *Use safe physical actions to blow off steam.* Express your anger in a physical way that

will not have harmful consequences to yourself or to others:

- Stomp on the floor.
- Scream into a pillow.
- Hit a pillow.
- Squeeze a tennis ball.
- Throw a fluff ball.

8. *Keep a sense of humor.* Telling a joke or poking fun at a situation or yourself (in a good-spirited way that does not attack others) can lighten up a situation. Laughing reduces the effects of anger cues.

9. *Rehearse what to do in situations that you know are your anger triggers.* Think of situations that get you angry. Imagine what you would say and do in these situations to control anger. Then rehearse in front of a mirror or with a friend, parent, or counselor.

10. *Talk with a parent or mentor.* Responsible adults can help you recognize your anger triggers and cues. These people can help you choose and support healthful actions.

Health Goal #6

I Will Use Stress-Management Skills

Understanding Stress

Stress is the body's response to the demands of daily living. Stress is what you feel when you react to pressure, either from the outside world (school, family, friends) or from inside yourself (wanting to fit in, wanting to do well in school) (American Academy of Family Physicians, 2006). A **stressor** is a source or cause of stress. Stressors can be physical, mental, social, or environmental. Exercising until exhausted is a physical stressor. Working to get a challenging assignment done is a mental stressor. Having an argument with a friend is a social stressor. Being in a room filled with cigarette smoke is an environmental stressor.

Eustress is a healthful response to a stressor that produces positive results. For example, a person might diligently train for a race, and win the race. This person would feel terrific and gain confidence from the fact that she accomplished a goal. **Distress** is a harmful response to a stressor that produces negative results. A person might postpone efforts to meet a deadline and end up not completing the assignment. He might then be so angry at himself for getting a poor grade that he compounds his disappointment by not doing other assignments.

The General Adaptation Syndrome

Everyone experiences stress. It cannot be avoided. The body responds to stress with a series of changes. **General adaptation syndrome (GAS)** is a series of body changes that result from stress. GAS occurs in three stages: the alarm stage, the resistance stage, and the exhaustion stage.

In the **alarm stage,** the first stage of GAS, the body gets ready for quick action. During this stage, adrenaline is released into the bloodstream. **Adrenaline** is a hormone that helps the body react during times of stress or in an emergency. Heart rate and blood pressure increase, digestion slows, muscles contract, respiration and sweating increase, and mental activity increases. The pupils dilate so the person can see sharply, and hearing sharpens as well. There is a burst of quick energy. Sometimes the alarm stage is called the fight-or-flight response because it gets a person ready to take action or to run away for protection.

In the **resistance stage,** the second stage of GAS, the body attempts to regain internal balance. The body is no longer in the emergency state. Adrenaline is no longer secreted. Heart rate and blood pressure decrease, and digestion begins again. Muscles relax, respiration returns to normal, and sweating stops.

The first two stages of GAS are normal and healthful. When experiencing a stressor, the alarm stage helps a person to respond. Then in the resistance stage, the body regains internal balance.

However, some people are not able to manage stress well, and their bodies remain in the alarm stage for long periods of time. People who do not know positive actions to take in response to stress force their bodies to stay ready for an emergency, and eventually they become exhausted. In the **exhaustion stage,** the third stage of GAS, wear and tear on the body increases the risk of injury, illness, and premature death.

How Stress Affects Health Status

Stress has a holistic effect. This means that a stressor in any of the ten areas of health can affect one or more of the other areas. Suppose a teenager's parents get divorced. The teenager may find it difficult to study (mental and emotional health), to eat (nutrition), and to sleep (personal health and physical activity). The original stressor, the divorce, creates other stressors that affect the teen's health status. Stress can affect all ten areas of health.

MENTAL AND EMOTIONAL HEALTH

Prolonged stress makes it difficult to think clearly and concentrate. Grades and work performance may be affected. A person may feel edgy, express emotions inappropriately, and develop psychosomatic diseases. Physical disorders such as headaches, stomachaches, and ulcers are common examples of psychosomatic diseases. Other physical disorders, such as asthma and chronic fatigue syndrome, also can be aggravated by stress.

FAMILY AND SOCIAL HEALTH

Prolonged stress in a relationship can cause changes inside the body. The number of white blood cells that fight disease may decrease. This increases the likelihood that a person will become ill.

GROWTH AND DEVELOPMENT

Stress during puberty might cause growth impairment. Also, teens who are uncomfortable with their body changes might be more likely to develop an eating disorder.

NUTRITION

When a person is stressed, the body secretes adrenaline. This causes the body to use up its supply of vitamins B and C. Additional vitamins B and C are needed. Consuming caffeine can trigger the alarm stage of GAS to begin. Some people respond to stress by eating sweets.

PERSONAL HEALTH AND PHYSICAL ACTIVITY

Some people respond to stress by exercising to the point of exhaustion. Too much exercise can diminish the effectiveness of the immune system. The person may become ill, fatigued, and run down. Also, when continuing stress burns up the available vitamin C in the body, the person's gums may bleed.

ALCOHOL, TOBACCO, AND OTHER DRUGS

The use of drugs, like tobacco, marijuana, cocaine, alcohol, or tranquilizers, can decrease a person's ability to cope with stress. Stimulant drugs, like cocaine and nicotine, trigger the alarm stage of the GAS. Alcohol and tranquilizers depress the part of the brain responsible for reasoning and judgment, diminishing the person's decision-making skills.

COMMUNICABLE AND CHRONIC DISEASE

Periods of being overwhelmed and frustrated may suppress the body's immune system, making the person more susceptible to communicable diseases, such as flu and the common cold. Prolonged stress might increase a person's risk of cancer. Cancer cells are more likely to develop, multiply, and spread. Being stressed keeps the body in the alarm stage of GAS. Heart rate and blood pressure remain high. This can damage the heart and blood vessels, increasing the risk of cardiovascular disease.

CONSUMER AND COMMUNITY HEALTH

Boredom is a stressor. Boredom results from a lack of challenge. People who are bored with their lives may turn to harmful behavior. Shopping addiction, television addiction, video game addiction, and gambling addiction are more common in people who are stressed from boredom.

ENVIRONMENTAL HEALTH

Loud noise, such as rock music and concerts, heavy traffic, and airports, initiates the alarm stage of GAS. A person exposed to loud noises is more likely to make mistakes and have accidents.

INJURY PREVENTION AND SAFETY

Stress is a major contributing factor in almost all kinds of accidents. People who are frustrated, aggressive, and angry because of stress in their lives may not be able to concentrate on safe driving. These people have higher accident rates.

SOURCES OF STRESS

Stress can result from the accumulation of daily hassles as well as from life crises. **Daily hassles** are the day-to-day stressors of normal living. Hassles may include concerns about physical appearance, relationships with peers, worries about school assignments or grades, being criticized, or losing belongings.

Stress-Management Skills

A person who does not learn to manage stress can develop poor health. Long periods of stress cause the body to work too hard by keeping blood pressure and heart rate higher than normal. The muscles tire from being tensed for long periods of time. In addition, the immune system does not function as efficiently as it should. The **immune system** is the body system that fights disease.

Stress-management skills are techniques that can be used to cope with the harmful effects produced by stress. One type of skill focuses on doing something about the cause of stress. Learning and using responsible decision-making skills can help solve the stressor that is causing stress. A second type of skill focuses on keeping the body healthy and relieving anxiety; exercising and eating a healthful diet are effective skills of this kind. Consider the following stress-management skills:

1. *Use responsible decision-making skills.* When you apply the steps in the model to a difficult situation, you will feel less anxious and more in control. You will develop confidence to cope both with everyday hassles and with life crises.
2. *Get plenty of rest and sleep.* Without rest and sleep, you will find it difficult to reduce stress levels. When you are resting, your blood pressure lowers, heart rate slows, and muscles relax. After sleep, you will feel invigorated and ready to face the day's challenges.
3. *Participate in physical activities.* Physical activity relieves tension by providing a physical outlet for the energy that builds up with stress.
4. *Use a time management plan.* If you are overwhelmed by the number of tasks to complete in a day, try keeping a daily calendar. Write down what you need to do and the order to follow to complete the list. It is sometimes best to tackle the more difficult tasks first.
5. *Write in a journal.* Writing is a healthful way to express feelings, and it can help you work through stress. You might choose to share a journal with a parent, mentor, or trusted friend, or you might not.
6. *Develop friendships.* When you are with friends, you can share feelings and experiences without being judged. Friends can listen and offer suggestions that might help ease your stress.
7. *Talk with parents and other trusted adults.* Parents or other trusted adults can listen and offer encouragement and suggestions from their own life experiences.
8. *Help others.* Helping others can give you a different outlook on a situation. Helping people less fortunate than yourself can make your own stressful situations seem less important.
9. *Express affection in appropriate ways.* Expressing affection in appropriate ways can give you a feeling of closeness, which in turn will relieve your stressful feelings.
10. *Care for pets.* Taking care of and holding a pet is comforting and relaxing. The physical contact involved in the care helps reduce feelings of stress.
11. *Reframe your outlook.* You might reframe your outlook and view life's obstacles as challenges. **Reframing** is changing your outlook in order to see a situation in a more positive way.
12. *Keep a sense of humor.* A good laugh is a positive way to manage stress. A hearty laugh will relax you and lower your heart rate, blood pressure, and muscular tension.
13. *Use breathing techniques.* Deep and relaxed breathing can produce calmness and stop the alarm stage.

Health Goal #7

I Will Seek Help if I Feel Depressed

Recognizing Depression

Depression affects people of all ages and ethnic backgrounds. About 5 percent of children and adolescents suffer from depression (American

Academy of Child and Adolscent Psychiatry, 2005). Some of the characteristics of depression include the following (National Mental Health Association, 2005):

- Persistent sadness
- Loss of pleasure and interest in activities once enjoyed
- Fatigue or loss of energy
- Restlessness, irritability
- Sleep disturbances
- Weight or appetite changes
- Lack of concentration or difficulty making decisions
- Feelings of worthlessness, hopelessness, low self-esteem, anger, or guilt
- Thoughts or expressions of suicide or death

Minor depression is a mood disorder accompanied by feelings of hopelessness, sadness, or helplessness. It is diagnosed when two to four of the symptoms listed are present and last for at least two weeks. *Minor depression* might go away, or it might become chronic. This means a teen continues to have mild depression. *Dysthymic disorder* is a long-lasting form of depression. With this disorder, a person displays two or more of these symptoms. *Major depression* is a mood disorder accompanied by long-lasting feelings of hopelessness, sadness, or helplessness. Major depression is a serious medical illness that should be distinguished from normal temporary feelings of sadness after a loss, such as the death of a relative or friend. According to the American Medical Association (2003), major depression affects 14 million people in the United States each year.

Childhood and Adolescent Depression

It was once thought that children were not capable of being depressed before the age of puberty. This notion has now been overturned by studies showing that children experience feelings that are described as major depression, and even preschoolers can experience symptoms such as sadness and lack of energy that are characteristic of depression in teenagers and adults (Voelker, 2003). The following symptoms of depression are common in children and adolescents:

- Increased irritability, anger, or hostility
- Being bored
- Reckless behavior

- Outbursts of shouting, complaining, unexplained irritability, or crying
- Poor school performance and frequent absences
- Fear of death
- Alcohol or substance abuse
- Frequent nonspecific physical complaints such as headaches, muscle aches, stomachaches, and fatigue

Causes

In childhood, boys and girls seem to be at equal risk for depressive disorders, though during adolescence girls are twice as likely as boys to develop depression. Children who develop major depression are more likely to have a family history of the disorder, often a parent who experienced depression at an early age (Voelker, 2003). Other suspected causes include the following:

- *Inability to cope with a life crisis.* Some teens are unable to get through life crises that most teens can cope with, such as the loss of a boyfriend or girlfriend, moving to a new neighborhood, or failing to make an athletic team. Some teens experience severe life crises, such as being a victim of crime, witnessing a tragic event, or being in a natural disaster such as an earthquake, flood, or tornado. Some teens develop PTSD after experiencing a life crisis. Teens who have PTSD often are depressed.
- *Changes in brain structure.* During the teen years, the brain is still developing. Between the ages of fourteen and seventeen, there is a "pruning," or clearing, of the gray matter. The gray matter consists of closely packed and interconnected nerve cells. It is found in the outer layers of the cerebrum. The cerebrum is the largest part of the brain and controls the ability to memorize, think, and learn. Gray matter also is found in some regions deeper within the brain. The pruning process involves clearing out unused brain-cell connections. When this process is complete, teens can focus more intently and learn things more deeply. Scientists have learned that there is a significant increase in mental disorders when this clearing-out process takes place. Research is being conducted to find out why.

- *Genetic predisposition.* The inheritance of genes that increase the likelihood of developing a condition is called genetic predisposition. Some teens may be genetically predisposed to having depression. The closer a teen is connected to a biological family member who is depressed, the greater the likelihood that the teen may become depressed. For example, a teen whose mother suffers from depression is more at risk than if the teen's aunt suffers from depression.
- *Low serotonin levels.* A chemical that is involved in controlling states of consciousness and mood is serotonin. Serotonin levels fluctuate and are not the same in all people. Teens who have lowered serotonin levels are more at risk for depression (Brock et al., 2005).
- *Traumatic family events.* Teens who have experienced traumatic family events are at increased risk for depression. Examples of traumatic family events include parents' divorce; the serious illness of a family member; the death of a family member; a parent losing a job; a family member going to jail; the murder, abduction, or sudden absence of a family member; a family member engaged in a war; or abuse by a family member (physical, emotional, or sexual).
- *Physical illness and disorders.* Teens who have certain physical disorders and are ill may experience depression. For example, heart disease, cancer, diabetes, and stroke may cause depression. Some nutritional deficiencies, such as a lack of vitamin B, also may cause depression.
- *Alcohol or other drug use.* Teens who drink alcohol and abuse other drugs have much higher rates of depression. Their brains are not fully developed, and depressant drugs have an even greater effect on their mood. Teens who suffer from depression and use alcohol and other depressant drugs become even more depressed.

RISKS

Most teenagers feel down in the dumps once in a while. In many cases, they bounce back after speaking with a parent, guardian, mentor, or other trusted adult and using coping strategies for depression. But some teens do not bounce back from depressed feelings. It is not healthy to suffer from major depression or lasting mild depression.

- *School performance.* Teens who are depressed are tired and have difficulty concentrating. This affects their ability to memorize, think, and learn. They are apathetic and have difficulty getting motivated to do schoolwork. School absence and poor grades are warning signs of teen depression. Teens who do poorly in school limit the options they will have in the future.
- *Social isolation.* Young people who are depressed often withdraw from friends. They stop participating in enjoyable activities, such as athletic events, clubs, and get-togethers. This can make their depression worse. Those who are socially isolated miss the opportunity to gain social skills, which makes it difficult for them to develop and maintain healthful relationships.
- *Drug addiction.* Drug addiction is the compelling need to take a drug, even though it harms the body, mind, and relationships. Young people who are depressed might depend on alcohol and use other drugs to escape from problems or change their mood.
- *Other addictions.* Teens might depend on certain behaviors to change their mood. Some of these behaviors, such as exercising, are healthful and may help with depression. However, when a specific behavior is taken to extremes, it can become an addiction.
- *Physical illnesses.* When people are depressed, their body's immune system is suppressed. The immune system is less able to fight off pathogens. People who are depressed are more susceptible to colds and flus. There is some evidence that long-lasting periods of depression increase the risk of some cancers.
- *Mental disorders.* Depressed teens are at increased risk for having major depression in adulthood. They are also at increased risk for developing bipolar disorder and personality disorders in adulthood.
- *Suicide attempts.* Depressed teens have a sense of hopelessness and helplessness. When these feelings are coupled with other risk factors, such as drug use, eating disorders, or social isolation, the risk of making a suicide attempt increases.

Treatment for Depression

Depression is a treatable disease and more than 80 percent of individuals who receive treatment experience significant improvement (Brock et al., 2005). Unfortunately, fewer than half of people with depression seek help. Children and adolescents who are depressed often suffer for years before they are diagnosed. The following are types of treatment for depression.

PHYSICAL EXAMINATION

A physical examination is needed to evaluate health status. Poor health status, such as illness, might be a cause of depression. Depression also might be a cause of poor health status because it is associated with symptoms such as sleeplessness and loss of appetite. Depression also suppresses the immune system, which increases the risk of illness.

THERAPY

Young people who are depressed may benefit from therapy. **Cognitive behavior therapy** is a form of psychotherapy that involves behavior therapy and cognitive therapy. Behavior and cognitive therapies help a person modify behavior and the person's way of thinking. Other forms of therapy, such as individual counseling or a combination of therapy and medication, also can be beneficial. Therapy can change a young person's hopeless and negative thinking. It can help a young person gradually resume former responsibilities and patterns of daily living.

MEDICATION

A physician will determine if a young person will benefit from taking prescription drugs for depression. An **antidepressant** is a drug used to relieve depression. There are different kinds of antidepressant drugs. Some antidepressants regulate serotonin levels, which play a role in regulating a person's mood. Antidepressant drugs can take several weeks to become effective and require medical supervision to check for side effects Several antidepressant drugs have not been approved by the Food and Drug Administration for persons under age eighteen. However, physicians sometimes prescribe them in what is referred to as "off-label" use. This is a common procedure for several prescription drugs that are being studied. The National Institutes of Health is studying the long-term effects of different antidepressants used by teens.

One of these concerns is increased risk of suicide in children and teens taking antidepressants. The Food and Drug Administration (FDA) acknowledges that antidepressants may increase the risk of suicidal thoughts in some young people (Rados, 2005). As a result, the manufacturers of these drugs are now required to add a "black box" warning to the labels of all antidepressant medications.

This warning describes this risk and emphasizes the need to closely monitor patients taking these drugs (Pharmaceutical News, 2005; Center for Drug Evaluation and Research, 2004). Some common antidepressants are Prozac (fluoxetine hydrochloride), Paxil (paroxetine hydrochloride), Zoloft (sertaline hydrochloride), and Celexa (citalopram hydrobromide) (Food and Drug Administration, 2005). Fluoxetine is the only one approved for the treatment of depression in children.

Another medication that may be associated with depression and possibly suicide is Accutane (isotretinion), a drug used to treat severe acne. Some people using Accutane report feeling depressed or having suicidal thoughts. No one knows for sure if Accutane caused these feelings and thoughts.

Coping with Depression

These are strategies that teachers and other adults can encourage young people to use for coping with depression.

- Talk with a parent, guardian, mentor, or other trusted adult.
- Stay connected with friends.
- Practice healthful behaviors, such as eating nutritious meals and getting exercise.
- Use anger-management skills.
- Practice stress-management skills.
- Avoid the use of alcohol and other drugs.
- Take steps to develop resiliency.
- Seek treatment if these strategies do not relieve depression.

Health Goal #8

I Will Use Suicide-Prevention Strategies When Appropriate

Suicide Prevention

Suicide is the number three cause of death among people ages fifteen to twenty-four. Some view suicide as a way to escape problems, gain attention, or get even with those who have rejected them. There is always a better choice than suicide.

SUICIDE ATTEMPTS

Suicide attempts are usually a cry for help. Young people who make a suicide attempt are often depressed, discouraged, and lack hope (Page et al., 2006). They want others to know that they are in a lot of pain. Many people think about suicide at least once in their lives. For most of these people the thought is fleeting, but many others dwell on it. Each year, almost a half million young people attempt suicide for such reasons as being alienated from family and friends, having difficulty coping with body changes and sexuality, or the death of a parent. Most of these people do not receive help and continue down a path of depression, hopelessness, and withdrawal from others.

SUICIDAL TENDENCIES

People who are at risk for attempting suicide tend to have one or more of the following characteristics:

- Aggressive behavior
- Perfectionistic behavior
- Feelings of hopelessness
- Low self-esteem
- Inadequate social skills
- Mental disorders
- Depression
- Hidden anger

People who attempt suicide may have had a difficult life experience, such as a breakup of a relationship, an unwanted pregnancy, or failure at school. People are more likely to attempt suicide if they

- abuse alcohol or other drugs;
- have experienced the death of a parent, parental separation, or parental divorce;
- feel alienated from family and friends;
- are teased or rejected by peers; or
- have difficulty coping with body changes and sexuality.

Youth with feelings of alienation, cultural and societal conflict, academic anxiety, and feelings of victimization are at high risk of suicide. Native American youth, sexual minority youth (lesbian, gay, bisexual, and transgender), and youth in the juvenile justice system are at high risk of suicide (Technical Assistance Partnership for Child and Family Mental Health, 2005).

RECOGNIZING WARNING SIGNS OF SUICIDE

Young people who are thinking about attempting suicide often provide warning signs. By trying to warn others, they are crying out for help and hoping someone will step in and help them. The following are some of the warning signs that might be given by a young person who is considering suicide:

- Making a direct statement about killing herself, such as "I wish I was never born."
- Making an indirect statement about killing himself, such as "I wonder where I can get a gun."
- Having a change in personality.
- Withdrawing from family and friends.
- Losing interest in her personal appearance.
- Having a preoccupation with death and dying.
- Making frequent complaints about physical symptoms that can be related to emotions, such as stomachaches.
- Using alcohol and other drugs.
- Losing interest in schoolwork.
- Giving away his possessions.
- Talking about getting even with others.
- Failing to recover from a disappointment or a loss.
- Running away from home.
- Talking about a close friend or relative who has committed suicide.

SUICIDE-PREVENTION STRATEGIES

Suicide-prevention strategies are techniques that can be used to help prevent a person from thinking about, attempting, or completing suicide. The following are important suicide prevention strategies:

1. *Keep suicide hotline numbers available.* One national suicide hotline service is the National Youth Suicide Hotline. The toll-free phone number is 800-621-4000. This twenty-four hour hotline is staffed by trained volunteers who listen to problems and offer support and help. They provide information on resources, youth programs, and support groups available in the young person's community.

2. *Take action when a person feels depressed.* Try to determine what the source of the depression is. Help the person make a list of her strengths and the positive aspects of her life. This person should decide on a plan of action that will relieve her depressed feelings.

3. *Help the person build a network of support.* A support network is a network of people who care and might include family members, friends, school counselors, clergy, and teachers. They will listen, offer advice, and help during difficult times.

4. *Help the person become involved in rewarding activities.* Rewarding activities provide an opportunity to be productive. This helps raise a person's self-esteem.

5. *Take action if someone shows warning signs.* It is important to get help for anyone who is depressed or demonstrates suicidal tendencies. Here are guidelines:
   - Do not ignore any warning signs or treat them lightly.
   - Ask a responsible adult for help.
   - Let the person know you care. Be concerned and show respect.
   - Listen and try not to be shocked by what the person says.
   - Ask the person directly if she or he is considering suicide. The person will either be relieved to talk about it or will deny having such thoughts.
   - Help the person think of better ways to solve problems.
   - Identify other supportive people with whom the person can talk.
   - Get professional help. Call a suicide hotline or school officials, the person's parents and physician, clergy, or the police.
   - Do not leave the person alone. Stay with the person, at least until professionals take over.

- Use a contract for life. A **contract for life** is a written agreement in which a suicidal person promises not to hurt himself or herself for a certain period of time or until after he or she has received professional help.

Health Goal #9

I Will Cope with Loss and Grief in Healthful Ways

Loss and Grief

The feeling that occurs when someone dies or a life situation changes or ends is **loss. Grief** is intense emotional suffering caused by a loss, disaster, or misfortune. **Anticipatory grief** is grief experienced prior to a loss. It is the feelings a person has when he or she knows someone or something that is cherished or valued is about to die or change. No one goes through life without experiencing loss and grief.

Causes of Loss and Grief

The causes of loss and grief include a change in the family, changes in living conditions, the death of a friend, suicide, the death of a well-known person, tragedies in the news, and the loss of special belongings.

- *Change in the family.* Family changes that cause feelings of loss and grief might include death of a family member, divorce of parents, serious or terminal illness, or death of a family pet. Almost 1 million children in the United States are living in a single-parent household because of the death of the other parent (Lohan, 2006).
- *Changes in living conditions.* A change in living conditions can trigger feelings of loss and grief. A family member might lose a job or be temporarily laid off. A change in a family's economic situation may result in not being able to afford house payments and having to move into a smaller house or apartment. In severe situations, a family might be evicted from a home, apartment, or trailer, and may become homeless or live in a shelter. Young

people experience loss when these events take place. Homelessness and poverty are major risk factors for teen depression.

- *Death of a friend.* The death of a friend is very traumatic. **Out-of-order death** is the death of a person that occurs at an unexpected time in his or her life cycle.
- *Suicide.* When a suicide or several suicides (known as cluster suicides) occur, it is especially difficult for young people. The young people might wonder if they could have done anything to prevent the suicide(s). They might feel guilty because they are still alive. Most communities and schools offer counseling when teen suicide occurs. Young people need to talk through their feelings of grief.
- *Death of a well-known person.* This might be a political leader, actor, sports figure, or other person that the public has grown to know and love. Even though the person was not known personally, some might experience loss or grief when a person dies. You imagine what it might be like to be a member of the person's family. You feel their sense of grief and loss.
- *Tragedies in the news.* Most likely, you watched news coverage of the tragedies that occurred on September 11, 2001. You might have watched news coverage of wars, murders, terrorist bombings, tornadoes, floods, hurricanes, or earthquakes. These events can trigger feelings of loss and grief. You value human life and are saddened when life and property are lost. You have empathy for people who are affected by loss or death.
- *The end of something special.* It is common and normal to experience feelings of loss and grief when something ends. For example, people often experience these feelings at the end of a period of their lives that has been special (e.g., graduation from high school or college). Although you are looking forward to the future, you may be sad about leaving school and friends. Parents and guardians usually experience this feeling of loss when a grown child moves away from home. Feelings of loss and grief also arise when a special relationship breaks up.
- *Holidays.* Feelings of loss and grief can intensify during holidays and certain days that mark anniversaries, birthdays, and other important dates that relate to a loved one who has died.

Some symptoms of loss and grief are the following:

- Numbness
- Shock
- Loss of appetite
- Intestinal upsets
- Sleep disturbances
- Loss of energy
- Shortness of breath
- Confusion
- Crying spells
- Moodiness
- Outbursts of anger
- Depression

Drug and Alcohol Use and Loss and Grief

Feelings associated with grief and loss may range from numbness and isolation to anger and resentment or sadness and depression. Some people may turn to a form of self-medication in an attempt to feel better or to escape the feelings of grief. Using alcohol or other drugs as a coping mechanism for feelings of grief is not a solution. Although these substances may produce a temporary feeling of relief for some people, in the long run, these substances will not help a person get through the grieving process. The feelings of grief remain after the effects of the drugs have worn off. In many cases, these substances may actually make a person feel worse, emotionally and physically, after their use.

Positive ways to cope with grief include talking about feelings with close friends, family members, or a trusted teacher or religious leader. Expressing feelings in writing, such as keeping a journal, can help as well. It is also important to stay healthy by taking care of one's body through exercising, eating a balanced diet, and getting enough sleep. Grief counseling with a professional counselor or therapist can also be extremely helpful for someone who is struggling with the grieving process.

Five Stages of Loss and Grief

People experience a variety of emotions that must be worked through before they can accept what has happened to them. The five stages of loss and grief are psychological stages: denial, anger, bargaining, depression, and acceptance. These stages are described in Health Goal #10 (I will be resilient in difficult times). A person might spend different amounts of time in each stage of loss and grief. One might backslide. For example, a person might work through his feelings and gain acceptance, only to backslide to feeling depressed. Or a person might skip one stage and move to the next stage. Some get stuck in one of the five stages. People who become stuck in one of these stages of loss and grief usually need help.

Dealing with a Terminal Illness

The five-step grieving process can be illustrated by the example of people with terminal illnesses. Someone who learns from a doctor that she has a terminal illness may first refuse to believe that she is dying. She may pretend the information the doctor told her is wrong. The second stage is anger. Someone with terminal illness in this stage may direct his anger at his family, friends, physicians, or other medical professionals. Anger can turn into bargaining. People who are dying try to avoid death by making deals and promises. When they realize bargaining will not change the outcome, they become depressed. Once a terminally ill person accepts that she is dying, she begins to say good-bye, shares special feelings and thoughts, and tries to enjoy the remainder of her life.

Different people may spend different amounts of time in each of the stages. Some people progress through the stages, whereas others get stuck or go backward. Family members and friends of terminally ill people may go through similar stages.

Healthful Ways to Respond to a Loss

There are no rules about grieving and no right way to grieve. Each person experiences grief in his or her own way. Trying to behave according to others' expectations during this difficult time only adds stress to the situation. Some people suffer greatly, but they might express their feelings through art, writing, exercise, or another outlet. Others, especially teenagers, might enter a state of denial and feel numb for weeks or months after a death or another loss. As the numbness fades,

they may need support as they deal with their feelings.

Crying is a healthful expression of emotions and helps to release bottled-up tension. Trying too hard to control painful emotions can block healing and make the process take longer. At the same time, there is no correct schedule for grieving. People let go of a loved one or recover from another loss in different ways and are ready to let go at different times.

The response to loss and grief differs based on (1) who we are, (2) whom or what we have lost, and (3) how much our day-to-day life is changed. The following information provides guidelines for responding when someone close to you is dying, when someone you know is grieving a loss, and when you are grieving a loss. Remember, everyone responds to loss and grief in his or her own way. Young people should be encouraged to talk to parents, guardians, mentors, or other trusted adults if they have any questions.

GRIEVING A LOSS

Here are some guidelines for handling grief in a healthful way:

1. Talk with a parent, guardian, mentor, or other trusted adult.
2. Ask your friends to comfort and support you.
3. Have someone stay by your side for a period of time if you prefer to not be alone.
4. Give yourself time to grieve, including some alone time.
5. Express feelings in healthful ways:
    *   Give yourself permission to cry.
    *   Use I-messages to express feelings.
    *   Use anger-management skills if you are angry.
    *   Use strategies for coping with depression to help with your sadness.
    *   Write your feelings in a journal. Writing about feelings helps relieve sadness and depression.
6. Maintain a normal schedule and routine as much as possible.
    *   Begin slowly to avoid becoming too tired.
7. Protect your health.
    *   Physical activity will relieve tension and will release beta-endorphins, substances that give you a feeling of well-being.
    *   Moderate your intake of sugar and caffeine. This reduces stress.
    *   Maintain your sleep and rest schedule. Go to bed when you normally sleep. Wake up

when you normally would wake up. Avoid napping when you normally would be awake.
- Use breathing techniques. Inhale with slow, deep breaths through your nose. Slowly exhale through the mouth. Repeat four or five times.
- Avoid harmful behaviors as ways of coping. For example, do not smoke, drink alcohol, or use other harmful drugs.

8. Seek help if you are unable to make adjustments or have lingering anger and depression.

WHEN SOMEONE CLOSE TO YOU IS DYING

When someone close to you is dying, both you and the person who is dying experience anticipatory grief. The person who is dying grieves the loss of his or her life. You grieve the loss of the person you care about or love. The time you have left to be together and share becomes very special. You can make wise use of the precious moments you have.

WHAT TO DO IF SOMEONE YOU KNOW IS DYING

- Spend time with the friend or family.
- Share loving feelings and memories.
- Share your feelings of loss and pain.
- Encourage the person to talk about his or her death.
- Listen carefully to the person's feelings and thoughts about the past, present, and future.
- Reassure the person with affection, hold hands, or hug.
- Share your grief with family members and friends.
- Continue your daily routine if possible.
- Consider what you will do to keep alive the memory of the person.
- Allow yourself time to grieve.

WHEN SOMEONE YOU KNOW IS GRIEVING A LOSS

You may know someone who is grieving the loss of a close friend or loved one. You also can comfort this person. Make yourself available. Remember, friends support one another during difficult times. Another way to comfort the person is to do something thoughtful for the person. You might

send a card or call the person. You might offer to help the person with meals or errands. You can show your support for someone who is grieving by attending memorial services.

Have empathy for the person's loss. Do not lessen the loss by making statements such as "She would have wanted it this way." Instead say, "I am sorry you feel sad. I am here to support you." Encourage the person to talk about his or her grief, and be able to recognize signs of grief that are not healthful. A person who remains severely depressed or who relies on alcohol or other drugs may need help.

Health Goal #10

I Will Be Resilient in Difficult Times

Some people are more resilient than others. They are prepared for life crises and respond to them in healthful ways. The following steps will help people be prepared to deal with difficult situations:

1. Work on your relationships with members of your family.
2. Develop a close relationship with a mentor.
3. Choose friends who are supportive and who have responsible behavior.
4. Do not put off dealing with difficult situations.
5. Avoid choosing harmful behaviors as a way of coping with tough times.
6. Ask for support when you need it.
7. Discuss available support groups with a parent, guardian, or other responsible adult.
8. Be involved in school and community activities.

Coping with Life Crises

Sometimes life is quite difficult. Events happen over which a person has no control—a loved one dies; a parent loses a job; an earthquake, fire, flood, or tornado ruins property; there is a car accident. There are also less serious disappointments in life, such as not making an athletic team, arguments, or breaking up with a boyfriend or girlfriend, which can also make life difficult at times. A **life crisis** is an experience that causes a high level of stress.

Everyone has ups and downs, but some people seem to have more difficult times than other people. Difficult times don't have to last, though. People who hang in, or persevere, are resilient. To be **resilient** is to be able to adjust, recover, bounce back, and learn from difficult experiences.

Most people respond to life crises by working through a series of five emotional responses identified by Elisabeth Kübler-Ross (1997):

1. *Denying,* or refusing to believe that the crisis is happening.

2. *Being angry* about what is happening.
3. *Bargaining,* or making promises, hoping it will change what is happening.
4. *Being depressed* when recognizing the outcome is unlikely to change.
5. *Accepting* what is happening, adjusting, and bouncing back.

Interventions in communities and schools that help youth develop resiliency have promise for enhancing positive youth development (Ungar, 2005). These programs focus on prevention strategies that help reduce risk factors and strengthen protective factors.

CHAPTER SIX

Family and Social Health

HEALTH GOALS FOR FAMILY AND SOCIAL HEALTH

11. I will develop healthful family relationships.
12. I will work to improve difficult family relationships.
13. I will make healthful adjustments to family changes.
14. I will develop healthful friendships.
15. I will develop dating skills.
16. I will practice abstinence from sex.
17. I will recognize harmful relationships.
18. I will develop skills to prepare for marriage.
19. I will develop skills to prepare for parenthood.
20. I will practice abstinence from sex to avoid the risks of teen marriage and parenthood.

Optional Health Goal: I will learn facts about birth control methods.

Family and social health is the area of health that focuses on developing healthful family relationships, recognizing ways to improve family relationships, adjusting to family changes, developing healthful friendships, developing dating skills, practicing abstinence, recognizing harmful relationships, developing skills to prepare for marriage, developing skills to prepare for parenthood, and avoiding the risks of teen marriage and parenthood. This chapter provides the health information that is needed to teach young people important life skills for family and social health.

Health Goal #11

I Will Develop Healthful Family Relationships

The Healthful Family

The basic unit of society is a family. A **family** is a group of people to which we belong. Families may consist of a group of people who are related by blood, adoption, marriage, or a desire for mutual support. Entrance into a family also occurs by invitation and agreement. Family structures vary from traditional married families to single-parent families to families built around partnerships with or without marriage. Each family is different, but all families share certain characteristics with other families.

A **healthful family** is a family that practices skills that promote loving, responsible relationships. Healthful family relationships are those that have a positive effect on physical and emotional health. A **dysfunctional family** is a family that does not promote loving, responsible relationships.

The **family continuum** indicates the degree to which a family promotes skills needed for loving, responsible relationships (see Figure 6-1). This continuum shows the two extremes of family life: the healthful family and the dysfunctional family. Studying and discussing the continuum is an important way to learn about relationships.

FIGURE 6-1

The Family Continuum

The *Family Continuum* indicates the degree to which a family promotes skills needed for loving and responsible relationships. The majority of families rank somewhere in between the ends of the continuum because family members practice some but not all of the behaviors and skills of a healthful family.

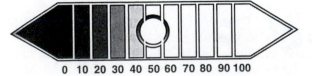

0 10 20 30 40 50 60 70 80 90 100

Skills Learned in a Healthful Family

In reality, most families are not perfect. After all, families are made up of family members who are human, and to be human is to have strengths as well as weaknesses. Many families possess some of the characteristics of a healthful family, but no family is perfect all of the time. This section of the chapter reviews twelve skills that are taught in healthful families.

Characteristics of dysfunctional families are these:

- Chemical dependence
- Other addictions
- Perfectionism
- Violence
- Physical abuse
- Emotional abuse
- Neglect
- Sexual abuse
- Abandonment
- Mental disorders

In a healthful family, parents teach their children the following:

- Self-respecting behavior
- Healthful attitudes toward sexuality
- Effective communication
- A clear sense of values
- Responsible decision making
- Ways to resolve conflict
- Effective coping skills
- Ways to delay gratification
- Ways to express affection and integrate love and sexuality
- How to give and receive acts of kindness
- A work ethic
- Respect for rules and laws

LEARNING SELF-RESPECTING BEHAVIOR

Self-respecting behavior is treating oneself in healthful and responsible ways. It is an outgrowth of the ways children were treated by the adults who raised them from birth. Children receiving love feel accepted and feel good about themselves. Children who are well cared for learn to take care of themselves. They learn not to choose behaviors that harm them. Children raised in a healthful family also know the difference between self-respecting and self-centered behavior.

Self-centered behavior is behavior that fulfills personal needs with little regard for the needs of others. Self-centered behavior does not contribute to healthful family relationships.

LEARNING HEALTHFUL ATTITUDES TOWARD SEXUALITY

Sexuality includes the feelings and attitudes a person has about his or her body, sexual identity, and sexual orientation. Sexuality also includes a person's feelings and attitudes regarding his or her body and the sexual orientation of others. It is an integral part of a person's self-esteem and body image. A person's sexual behavior is also a part of sexuality. Sexuality is influenced from birth and much is learned from parents. Parents can help their children develop healthful attitudes about sexuality by having open discussions about sex and sexuality at an early age in their children's lives. It is important for parents to model healthful attitudes about sexuality. In a healthful family, parents or guardians discuss puberty with children. They explain the changes in feelings and emotions that accompany puberty. Their openness and sensitivity help children learn how to understand their sexuality.

LEARNING EFFECTIVE COMMUNICATION

Children first learn how to communicate in their family. In a healthful family, children feel secure practicing communication skills. Then they feel secure in using communication skills in other relationships.

LEARNING A CLEAR SENSE OF VALUES

In a healthful family, parents or guardians teach their children values. They behave in ways that are consistent with the values they teach. They discuss their values with their children. Children observe the everyday behavior of their parents and guardians and this behavior confirms what these adults say. Children tend to internalize their parents' values and behaviors and behave in similar ways. Parents' values become the standard of what their children think and believe. When parents are clear and consistent about their values, they provide a clear sense of values for their children.

LEARNING TO MAKE RESPONSIBLE DECISIONS

In a healthful family, parents and guardians serve as role models for decision making. Children observe their parents and guardians using the decision-making process: carefully evaluating options before deciding what to do, weighing the consequences of possible actions, and making responsible decisions. The children learn from this to do the same. In a healthful family, parents or guardians expect responsible behavior from their children. They set guidelines and make their expectations clear. They specify clear consequences for breaking family guidelines. Children learn that there always are consequences for wrong behavior. This helps children when they are pressured by peers. They think about consequences and say "no" to wrong behaviors. When children have difficulty saying "no," they can turn to their parents or guardians for support. If children make mistakes, their parents or guardians help them learn from it.

LEARNING TO RESOLVE CONFLICTS

In a healthful family, parents or guardians teach their children to resolve conflicts in healthful ways. They listen to both sides of a disagreement and work to find an acceptable solution. Conflicts are resolved without violence. Children learn healthful ways to resolve family conflicts, and this gives them the skills to resolve conflicts in other relationships.

LEARNING EFFECTIVE COPING SKILLS

In a healthful family, parents or guardians want their children to develop emotional strength. They encourage their children to share their feelings during a life crisis. From this example, children learn skills that help them cope during difficult times later in their lives.

LEARNING TO DELAY GRATIFICATION

In a healthful family, parents or guardians teach their children the importance of delayed gratification. Being able to delay gratification is especially important in relationships. Children learn that it is not appropriate to be sexually active in their teenage years. They learn that waiting until marriage to express intimate sexual feelings protects their health and follows their family guidelines.

LEARNING TO EXPRESS AFFECTION AND INTEGRATE LOVE AND SEXUALITY

In a healthful family, parents or guardians teach their children how to express affection. The parents' expressions of warm feelings help their children feel loved. They also teach their children appropriate ways to express affection. The children learn who has the right to touch them, and when, and how. In a healthful family, parents or guardians teach their children that sex and love belong together in a committed marriage. The children learn that sex belongs in marriage and to practice delayed gratification.

LEARNING TO GIVE AND RECEIVE ACTS OF KINDNESS

In a healthful family, parents or guardians demonstrate acts of kindness and express thankfulness. They do kind things for family members and for other people in the community. They accept and are grateful for acts of kindness from others. As children observe their parents or guardians giving and receiving, they learn to act in similar ways. They are willing to give to others and express thankfulness. They are able to receive kind acts from others. Giving and receiving are both needed to sustain healthful relationships.

LEARNING A WORK ETHIC

In a healthful family, parents or guardians teach their children a work ethic. Parents and guardians work hard and serve as role models for their children. As children observe their parents or guardians, they learn to do their best and not give up when work is challenging. They learn the rewards that result from hard work. They learn to demonstrate a work ethic by completing schoolwork, doing household chores, participating in athletics, holding a part-time job, or doing volunteer work.

LEARNING RESPECT FOR RULES AND LAWS

In a healthful family, children respect family rules and the law of the land. Parents or guardians set and enforce guidelines for behavior. The children respect their parents or guardians and do not break their guidelines. They recognize that if a guideline is broken, there will be consequences. Parents and guardians use appropriate discipline, such as taking away certain privileges. In a healthful family, parents or guardians also serve as role models for their children. They, too, respect authority by obeying laws and rules. As children observe their parents' behavior, they learn to obey laws and rules set by authority figures such as teachers, principals, and police officers.

LEARNING TO VALUE THE NEEDS OF OTHERS

Children raised in a healthful family learn the difference between self-respecting behavior and self-centered behavior. Self-centered behavior consists of actions that fulfill personal needs with little regard for the needs of others.

Being a Loving Family Member

Always remember that parents or guardians are human. They may try hard but fall short. This is the reason that family relationships will not be perfect and family life will not always be healthful. Yet the struggle to have the best family life possible is worth the effort. Each individual has the task to be the very best family member he or she can be. This is best accomplished by choosing actions that promote healthful family relationships, making a promise to be a loving family member, and spending time with one's family.

Health Goal #12

I Will Work to Improve Difficult Family Relationships

Family Relationships

Family relationships are the connections a person has with family members. Members of the extended family are family members in addition to parents, brothers, and sisters. The **extended family** might include stepparents, stepbrothers, stepsisters, grandparents, aunts, uncles, and foster brothers and sisters. Other significant adults or children may be included also.

Dysfunctional Family Relationships

The term dysfunctional family was first used to describe families in which there was alcoholism. The family member with alcoholism did not function in healthful ways. The family members who lived with that alcoholism also began to function in ways that were harmful. The term *dysfunctional family* is now applied to all families in which members relate to one another in destructive and irresponsible ways. This section of the chapter examines the causes of dysfunctional families.

CHEMICAL DEPENDENCE IN THE FAMILY

The lives of family members who are drug dependent become dominated by the need to obtain and use drugs. The drugs, in turn, cause changes in thinking and behaving. There is more violence in families in which there is drug dependence. There is also more sexual abuse. Children who are raised in a family in which there is chemical dependence are at risk for being harmed by violence. They might use drugs to cope with difficult times. There is evidence that chemical dependence may be inherited. Children and teens with a family history of chemical dependence who experiment with alcohol and other drugs have an increased risk of developing chemical dependence. Family members may develop codependence.

OTHER ADDICTIONS IN THE FAMILY

Besides chemical dependence, the following addictions contribute to dysfunctional family life: eating disorders, exercise addiction, perfectionism, gambling addiction, shopping addiction, television addiction, thrill-seeking addiction, and workaholism. A family member with an addiction becomes obsessed with the addiction, which becomes a top priority. Family life is neglected. Children who live with a family member who has an addiction may develop codependence. They may develop the same or other addictions as ways of coping.

PERFECTIONISM IN THE FAMILY

Perfectionism is an addiction that can affect other family members. Parents or guardians who are perfectionists are overly critical of themselves and their children. Children who live with a perfectionistic parent or guardian may feel inadequate and insecure. These children also may become perfectionists. They may criticize others and never be satisfied with anything. They may be overly critical with themselves. Their behavior is self-destructive and harms their relationships with others.

VIOLENCE IN THE FAMILY

The family member who is violent usually is very controlling. Often, the violent family member abuses drugs. Other family members try to keep peace by avoiding disagreements. They may blame themselves when the family member has violent outbursts. Between acts of violence, the family member who is violent may be kind, gentle, and apologetic. But the cycle of drug use and violent outbursts continues.

Children who live in homes with domestic violence are at risk. They might be injured by the family member who is violent. They might copy the behavior of the family member who is violent and become controlling and violent. These children are at risk for becoming juvenile offenders. Children and teens who are sexually abused are also at risk for becoming pregnant or infected with HIV and other sexually transmitted diseases (STDs).

ABUSE IN THE FAMILY

A family member who is abusive is controlling and moody. Sometimes, family members who are abusive are drug dependent. Their need for control and their moodiness increase when they are under the influence of drugs. Children who live with a family member who is abusive may be afraid and confused. They cannot understand why a family member who is abusive can be loving at one moment and abusive the next. They want to believe they are loved. For this reason, they deny their feelings about the abuse and cover up the abuse. They might blame themselves for the abuse and believe they deserve to be abused.

ABANDONMENT IN THE FAMILY

Parents who abandon their children are not available for them. Their absence from their children's lives can cause their children pain, suffering, and confusion. Children who have been abandoned have difficulty getting close to others. They may feel that if they get close to someone, that person too might abandon them. Children who have been abandoned might push away others. Or they might be very needy. They might demand the attention of others to fulfill childhood needs that were not met.

MENTAL DISORDERS IN THE FAMILY

Families in which one or more family members have a mental disorder have special stressors. Suppose a family member suffers from clinical depression. Other family members might respond in a healthful way. They might recognize that this family member has a mental disorder that requires treatment. They are sensitive to this but do not let this person's depression dominate their lives. In a dysfunctional family, family members do not respond in a healthful way. They may feel responsible for the family member's depression and feel guilty. They may try to "fix" the family member's depression and attempt to cheer up the depressed family member. When the family member remains depressed, they feel personally responsible. They may allow the family member's depression to dominate family life.

Recognizing Codependence

Family members living in a dysfunctional family may develop codependence. **Codependence** is a problem in which people neglect themselves to care for, control, or try to "fix" someone else. People who have codependence are called codependent. (See Chapter 5 for more information on codependence.)

The Tree of Codependence (Figure 6-2) illustrates how dysfunctional family life can lead to codependence. The roots are labeled with behaviors that occur in dysfunctional families. The branches are labeled with feelings and behaviors that describe people who are codependent.

People who are codependent struggle in their relationships. They have difficulty developing intimacy. **Intimacy** is deep and meaningful sharing between two people. People with codependence avoid intimacy by choosing one extreme or another:

1. They focus on trying to please other people and deny their own needs or
2. They avoid being close to other people to keep from being hurt.

The following questions are helpful in recognizing codependent feelings and behavior in a family member:

1. *Does the person try to hide his or her anger?* Hidden anger is anger that is not recognized and is expressed in an inappropriate way.
2. *Is the person a people pleaser?* People pleasing is needing the approval of others to feel good about oneself.
3. *Is the person a caretaker?* A caretaker assumes responsibility for the problems of others so (s)he will be needed.
4. *Is the person a controlling person?* A person who is controlling wants others to do as (s)he says so (s)he can feel secure.
5. *Does the person fear abandonment?* A person who fears abandonment is worried that something will be taken away from him or her.
6. *Does the person fear authority figures?* A person who is constantly criticized by authority figures may fear authority figures.
7. *Does the person have frozen feelings?* A person whose feelings have been met with disapproval, anger, or rejection may stop recognizing his or her feelings.
8. *Does the person lack self-confidence?* A person who lacks self-confidence always worries that (s)he will make a mistake or fail.
9. *Is the person overly responsible?* A person who is overly responsible takes on too much and does tasks that others should do themselves.
10. *Does the person isolate himself or herself?* A person who isolates himself/herself withdraws when he/she is uncomfortable.

FIGURE 6-2

The Tree of Codependence

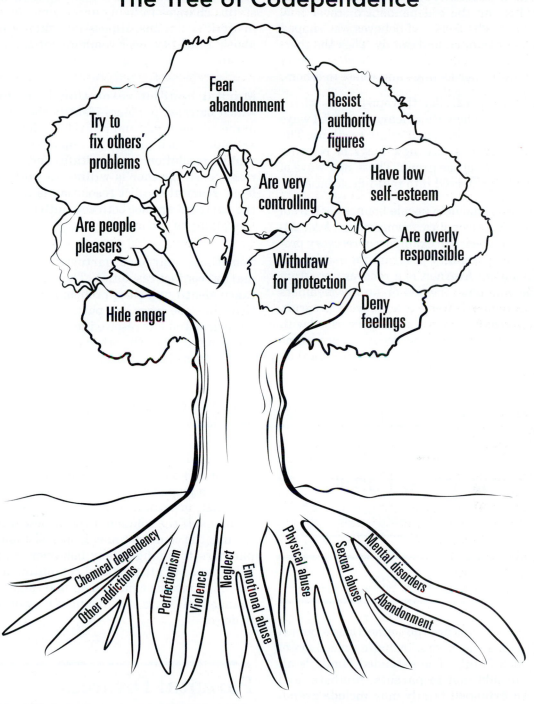

Improving Dysfunctional Family Relationships

There is hope for recovery from codependence. Family members can learn how to relate in responsible and healthful ways. It is important to recognize that parents, guardians, and family members may choose behaviors that are harmful and are not responsible. Their actions and behaviors may be wrong, but it is still important to give them love and respect as much as possible. Young people can recognize that they may be copying a parent's or guardian's harmful behavior and change their own behavior. Family members always are responsible for their own actions.

Individual and group therapy can help ensure recovery from codependence. In individual therapy, a skilled therapist works one on one with the codependent, helping the codependent discover how much of what (s)he feels and believes was shaped by his or her dysfunctional family. Then the therapist helps the codependent learn healthier ways to express his or her feelings and relate to others.

In group therapy, a skilled therapist works with a group of people to help them learn healthful ways to express their feelings and relate to others. The group members practice new ways of relating within the safety of the group. These new ways of relating are transferred into real-life situations.

Recovery programs help people bounce back from codependence. Alcoholics Anonymous (AA), Al-Anon, and Al-Ateen are examples of recovery programs. AA is a recovery program for people who have alcoholism. Al-Anon is a recovery program for people who have friends or family members with alcoholism. Al-Ateen is a recovery program for teens who have a family member or friend with alcoholism. There are also recovery programs that address codependence, gambling, workaholism, and many other addictions.

Health Goal #13

I Will Make Healthful Adjustments to Family Changes

Extended Families

Family relationships are the connections a person has with family members, including members of the extended family. The extended family is all relatives in addition to parents, brothers, and sisters. An extended family may include grandparents, aunts, uncles, cousins, stepparents, stepbrothers, and stepsisters.

Marital Stress and Conflict

For marriages to succeed and be satisfying, married partners need to pay attention to their relationship. When a marriage is taken for granted, the quality of the marriage declines and the partners lose intimacy. The most common stressors in marriage are changes in financial status, changes in living arrangements, changes in work situations, illness of a family member, abuse, infidelity, poor communication, and alcohol and other drug dependency.

Marital conflict resolution is a process in which married partners identify their problems, agree on solutions, and reestablish intimacy. The attitude of each partner is important in marital conflict resolution. In a healthful and caring marriage, each partner is willing to work on problems. Marital conflict resolution is impossible if the partners are not both committed to restoring the quality of the marriage.

Sometimes marriage partners need help with marital conflict resolution. They may need assistance identifying their problems or finding solutions. In some cases, one partner is aware there is a problem and has resolved to do something about the situation, but the other partner does not recognize there is a problem. This is often the case in a marriage in which one partner abuses drugs. The partner who abuses drugs denies that a problem exists. Outside intervention may be needed to help resolve the problem.

A married couple might recognize a problem but not be able to solve it. A marriage counselor, such as a member of the clergy, psychologist, psychiatrist, or social worker, can present possible solutions. If the solution involves new ways of behaving, the counselor may help assist one or both partners to change their behavior. Again, the importance of attitude and commitment is obvious. A counselor cannot help marriage partners change their ways of behaving if they do not want to do so.

Parental Divorce

Married couples are not always able to solve their problems and reestablish intimacy. About two-thirds of all first marriages end in marital separation or divorce. **Marital separation** is a cessation of cohabitation between a married couple by mutual agreement or judicial decree. **Divorce** is a legal way to end a marriage in which a judge or court decides the terms with respect to property, custody, and spousal support.

STAGES IN THE DIVORCE PROCESS

Most married couples who divorce experience a six-stage process. Marital separation may occur at any time during the six stages, but it often occurs in an earlier stage. In the first stage of divorce, the marriage deteriorates and partners show less affection and begin to detach from one another. One or both partners do not meet the needs of the other. The first stage may last several years.

In the second stage of divorce, one or both partners seek legal counsel. This begins the process of discussing the grounds for the divorce and issues regarding property, custody of children, and financial support. During this stage of divorce, the different options for ending the marriage are examined. An **annulment** is a legal way to end a marriage in which it is decided that the marriage was not legally binding. A **dissolution** is a legal way to end a marriage in which the marriage partners decide the terms with respect to property, custody, and support.

In the third stage of divorce, issues regarding property and support payments are finalized. The property in a marriage usually refers to the home and household furnishings the couple owns, jewelry, cars, life insurance, money in savings accounts, stocks, and other investments. One partner may agree to pay spousal support to the other. Usually, the partner paying spousal support is the partner who has the greater ability to earn money. Spousal support often is based on the potential earning power of one partner versus the other, the length of the marriage, and the other assets in the marriage.

In the fourth stage of divorce, issues of custody, visitation rights, and child support are negotiated. **Single custody** is an arrangement in which one parent keeps legal custody of a child or children. The **custodial parent** is the parent with whom a child or children live and the parent who has the legal right to make decisions about the health and well-being of a child or children. Sometimes the parents or the court decides upon joint custody of a child or children. **Joint custody** is an arrangement in which both partners keep legal custody of a child or children. A child or children may live with one parent or may alternate living arrangements, spending time with one parent and then the other. In joint custody, both parents maintain the legal right to make decisions about the health and well-being of their child or children. This arrangement requires that meaningful communication between the parents be maintained after the marriage has ended.

Visitation rights are guidelines set for the visitation of children by the parent who does not have custody. In some cases, visitation rights are very specific and include the exact number of days and a specific amount of time the visiting parent can spend with a child or children. Some guidelines may be set with regard to a parent moving to a new location and the effects of the move on visitation. Recently, the court has begun to look at other aspects of visitation, such as grandparents' rights. **Grandparents' rights** are the visitation rights with grandchildren courts have awarded to grandparents when their son's or daughter's marriage ends.

In the fifth stage of divorce, each of the partners establishes a new identity with family, friends, and coworkers. This stage often is difficult. In fact, some people going through divorce delay telling others about the divorce because they fear it will affect their relationships with them. These former relationships may have been based on the individual being part of a couple. Some family members and friends might take sides and feel angry or disappointed with one or both partners.

In the sixth stage of divorce, each of the partners makes emotional adjustments to the new lifestyle that results from being divorced. This stage of divorce affects both marriage partners and their children.

SUGGESTIONS FOR CHILDREN AND ADOLESCENTS WHOSE PARENTS DIVORCE

Divorce is tough for children and adolescents. The following guidelines can help children and teens cope with the divorce of their parents:

1. *Practice stress-management skills.* Remember, you have experienced a major life stressor.
2. *Avoid using alcohol and other drugs to numb painful feelings.* Work through your anger, disappointment, and sadness without using drugs.
3. *Recognize that becoming sexually active will not fill the emptiness you feel as a result of your family's breakup.* In most cases, this behavior will make you feel even more empty and alone.

4. *Choose healthful ways to express your anger over your family's breakup.* Delinquent behavior will make your life even more difficult.

5. *Be aware of your feelings of rejection and betrayal and ask for help.* Do not allow these feelings to keep you from forming healthful friendships and dating relationships. Responsible adults can help you learn to connect with others.

Adjustments to Divorce

Divorce requires adjustments. Separation and divorce require building a new life. Major adjustments must be made by the formerly married partners and their child or children.

ADJUSTMENTS MADE BY FORMERLY MARRIED PARTNERS

Often, one marriage partner has a more difficult time adjusting to the divorce than the other. Usually, one partner feels much better off for getting divorced, while the other partner does not feel better off. Usually, the partner who initiated the divorce feels better off.

Partners differ in their immediate responses to divorce. Some people become very involved in work; others begin to date excessively, seeking reassurance that they are still attractive; others withdraw; and still others are too depressed to function. Women usually must make more economic adjustments after a divorce than men. Many women experience a drop in their standard of living and must adjust to living on much less money. Both women and men who divorce are more at risk for health problems because of added stress.

ADJUSTMENTS MADE BY CHILDREN AFTER PARENTS SEPARATE OR DIVORCE

Separation and divorce are very different experiences for children and adults. At least one of the married partners wanted the divorce and felt it was for the best. Children do not have this kind of control over their situation. They usually feel that they have had no control over this decision that influences something fundamental to their development—an intact family structure.

Most children have the same initial reaction to separation and divorce—they feel vulnerable and

fearful. Young children exhibit these fears by having difficulty sleeping or having nightmares. Teens exhibit these fears through a loss of concentration and a need to either cling to others or withdraw from others.

Divorced parents may spend less time with their children. Most divorced fathers do not have custody of their children and have infrequent or no contact with their children. Any lack of parenting takes its toll on the children. Many children start to get poorer grades. Many are at risk for becoming depressed, becoming sexually active, abusing alcohol and other drugs, or engaging in delinquent behavior.

Some children might have to adjust to parental dating. This can cause stress. If parental dating begins before or soon after the divorce, children might feel angry and might believe that the new person caused the breakup. Children often fantasize about their parents getting back together. They may continue to hope for a reconciliation for many years.

When parents date, children can resent the time and attention the parent is giving to that new person. They may be jealous of anyone the parent dates, and they may try to disrupt the relationship in order to regain the parent's attention.

Children of divorce tend to have two traits in common: fear of rejection and fear of betrayal. These traits may affect all their relationships. For example, teen females whose parents divorce often fear abandonment. As a result, they may try to have many boyfriends at the same time so there always will be a backup. They may seek an older boyfriend to be the father figure they do not have. They are more likely to get into harmful relationships and not end them. Teen males whose parents divorce often feel awkward with females. These teens often hold back their feelings in dating and have difficulty trusting others. Some throw themselves into sports or work rather than into developing and maintaining relationships.

Single-Custody Families

A **single-custody family** is a family in which a child or children live with one parent who has custody. This term is used instead of *single-parent family* because a child or children may have two living parents. However, only one of the parents has custody or responsibility for them. When both parents have custody and responsibility, a child or children live in a joint-custody family. The non-custodial parent may or may not be considered as part of a child living in a joint-custody situation.

There often are differences between living in a single-custody family and living in a joint-custody family. Most children raised in a single-custody family live with their mothers. They are more likely to be economically disadvantaged. This means they will lack many of the resources that other families have available, from good medical care to clothing, food, and shelter. This makes living in a single-custody family more stressful than living in a two-parent family. In a two-parent, or joint-custody family, both parents share custody of children.

After divorce, many teens live with their mothers and have little or no contact with their fathers. Unless there is another male figure, such as a grandfather, in their lives, these teens do not experience the benefits of having a male role model. The single-custody parent has the sole responsibility for supervising the children. If the parent works outside the home, there is less time for supervising children and for being involved in their academic performance. This could account for less time for parents to spend with their children and could account for poor academic performance.

Following are several suggestions for children and teens who live in single-custody families:

1. *Recognize the financial pressures on your parent.* Discuss ways to help control expenses.
2. *Schedule time to be with your parent.* Parents have many demands on their time. If you arrange a set time to be together, you and your parent will have time together to look forward to.
3. *Look for a mentor who can be a role model for you.* Try to find a mentor who is the same sex as the parent who does not live with you. A mentor is an adult who will care about you and spend time with you. Organizations like Big Brothers and Big Sisters can pair you with an adult mentor who can give you support and advice. Children should be sure that any mentor is screened and approved.
4. *Pay attention to your academic performance.* You do not have to have two parents to be interested in your schoolwork. Take more responsibility for yourself. Think about getting a tutor or additional after-school help if you need it.

5. *Discuss with your parent your fears and concerns about your parent's dating.* Your parent can reassure you of your importance and remind you that dates do not replace you. Your parent also can discuss with you any other concerns you have.

Remarriage of a Parent

A **blended family,** or **stepfamily,** is a family consisting of the marriage partners, children that one or both of them had previously, and the children they have by their marriage to one another. Many blended families include a stepfather whose new wife has custody of her children. The stepfather also might have visitation rights with children of his former marriage. In some blended families, the father has custody of his children, but this is not a common arrangement. Some blended families include joint-custody arrangements.

The two greatest sources of conflict in a blended family are determining which set of rules the children will follow and adjusting to a new budget. Often children in a blended family are expected to follow rules that are different from the rules they were raised with. Suppose that one set of children in a blended family was raised with clear guidelines in which consequences were identified for inappropriate behavior; and suppose that the other children in the family had little discipline and were allowed to behave as they pleased. Blending these two sets of children into one framework for discipline will likely cause conflict. Another issue is the rules for children who live with the other parent and come to visit the blended family. All parents and stepparents involved need to communicate about how to blend these children into the family during visitation, rules the children must follow, and how to discipline the children.

Decisions about the budget in a blended family can be challenging. Parents and stepparents have many decisions to make about how to spend money. When money is spent on one child for a birthday or other special circumstances, it may not be available for the needs of other children. The two sets of children may have been raised with different guidelines for spending money.

Other issues that are important in blended families arise from the new relationships that are formed. The success of the blended family often depends on how stepsiblings interact. Clear guidelines for interaction must be set by parents. For example, teens from different families who are living together may find each other attractive. Parents must establish that acting on the attraction is not acceptable. Guidelines for resolving conflict also must be set for the family.

Many teens who live in blended families resent their stepparent. They may think that their stepparent does not like them or that their stepparent does not treat them well. However, with effective communication and mutual respect they can establish a healthful relationship with their stepparent.

Following are several suggestions for children and teens whose parents remarry:

1. *Respect the new guidelines for behavior.* Although you might not like the new rules, the rules should be obeyed.
2. *Help your family follow a budget.* Recognize that your parents have the challenging task of providing for a larger family.
3. *Interact in healthful ways with your stepbrothers and stepsisters.* Discuss guidelines for behavior when interacting with new siblings.
4. *Interact in healthful ways with your stepparent.* Use effective communication skills and mutual respect to establish a healthful relationship with your stepparent.

Other Situations Requiring Adjustment

IF A PARENT LOSES A JOB

The loss of a job can be devastating to a parent and stressful for the family. The parent who loses the job might become depressed and disappointed, lose self-confidence and feel embarrassed, worry about losing the respect of family members and friends, and be anxious and worried about how the family will survive. There may be an adjustment period before the parent feels energized and ready to find another job. The parent may need training or other help before getting another job. Children and teens who have a parent who has lost a job also may be anxious and worried. They may wonder, "What should I say to my parent?" "What should I say to other people?" "What changes will this bring about in where

and how we live?" "How will the loss of income affect me?"

Following are suggestions for children and teens who have a parent who has lost a job:

1. *Give your parent emotional support and encouragement.*
2. *Discuss with your parents what to say to people outside the family.* Discuss which family discussions are private and what information can be shared with others.
3. *Discuss what changes will occur in the family budget.* Recognize that money might be tight. Do not spend money on things that are not needed. Perhaps you can contribute money from a part-time job.

IF A PARENT GOES TO JAIL

When a parent is sentenced to jail, the family experiences a great deal of stress. One of the most immediate stressors may be a shortage of money, if the parent was the main source of income for the family. Legal fees can be expensive, and arrangements must be made to pay these fees. The family may be eligible for money from the government for rent and food stamps. However, some families are left with no source of support.

The loss of income can result in other changes. The family may have to move to another place or move in with relatives. Suppose the parent who goes to jail is a single parent. Children who live with this parent may end up living with other relatives or be placed in foster care. **Foster care** is an arrangement in which an unrelated adult assumes temporary responsibility for a child.

Children who have a parent who is sentenced to jail may have to deal with the response from society. If the crime was widely publicized, people may make cruel remarks. They may be angry about the parent's crime. This may require a child or teen to be resilient. It can be embarrassing to listen to comments about a parent's wrong behavior. Other people might assume that the child or teen is like the parent who committed the crime and that the child or teen also will commit crimes.

Children who have a parent who is sentenced to jail must recognize that they are not responsible for what has happened. Their guilty parents chose wrong actions, for which there are consequences. The children did not choose this behavior. They do not have to behave in similar ways. They can choose to follow the law.

Following are suggestions for children and teens who have a parent in jail:

1. *Discuss your feelings with a trusted adult.* You might feel ashamed, angry, confused, betrayed, and anxious because your parent is in jail. Share your feelings with another adult you trust, such as your other parent, a teacher, or a counselor.

2. *Ask about changes that might result.* These questions can be directed to your other parent, a teacher, a counselor, a social worker, or legal advisor. Your questions might include these:
   - Will there be any changes in our living arrangements?
   - Will my family's financial situation change?
   - Will my family responsibilities change (e.g., will I have to look after younger siblings)?
   - What kind of contact will I be allowed to have with my jailed parent?
   - When will my jailed parent be eligible for parole or release from jail?

3. *Do not accept blame for your parent's illegal actions.* Some young people blame themselves for their parent's imprisonment. They might wonder if they could have prevented the parent's criminal behavior if they had noticed wrong behavior sooner or done something differently. This is faulty thinking. Sometimes a parent is imprisoned based on an action a child took, such as calling the police. If this is the case for you, remember that your action may have protected innocent people. You did not commit a crime. Your parent committed a crime and must pay the consequences.

4. *Pledge to not engage in illegal behavior.* Children who have a parent in jail are more at risk for committing a crime themselves. You do not have to behave in similar ways. You can make responsible decisions that follow the law.

Health Goal #14

I Will Develop Healthful Friendships

A **healthful friendship** is a balanced relationship that promotes mutual respect and healthful behavior. Having healthful friendships improves the quality of life. Friends take a personal interest in each other. They support each other in their successes and encourage each other during difficult times. Friends often participate in social activities together.

There is an old saying: "A friend is a gift you give yourself." Good friends share interests, help each other solve problems, teach each other new things, and help each other feel good about themselves. There is another old saying: "To have a friend, you must be a friend." Making new friends takes time and effort, but it is worth it.

Initiating Friendships

Before initiating a friendship, it is smart to make a background check on the person. There are questions young people should ask themselves about a prospective friend:

- What do I know about this person?
- Does this person have good character?
- Do my parents or guardian know this person?
- Will my parents or guardian approve of my spending time with this person?

A friendship should be pursued only if the person has good character and the person's parents or guardians approve. There always is an element

of risk involved in initiating a friendship. The person who is invited to start a friendship might not want a friendship. Young people should be instructed to consider the possible opening moves that might be taken in initiating a friendship. Is waiting in the hall after class to begin a conversation or calling a person on the telephone the best strategy? Of course, most opening moves involve risk (such as rejection) as well as the possibility of reward—the reward of having an opportunity to develop a new friendship.

CARRYING ON A CONVERSATION

Many young people worry about how to talk with another person. Success in developing new friendships often depends on having the ability to carry on a conversation. Conversation skills increase when Conversation Keepers are used. The Conversation Keepers and Conversation Killers (Table 6-1) are dos and don'ts for having conversations.

HANDLING REJECTION

Everyone experiences rejection at times. How should a person respond to rejection? Should a person become angry and try to get even when rejected? Should a person who is experiencing rejection bury feelings and pretend not to care? These responses destroy relationships. Instead, hurt,

anger, or disappointment should be expressed in a healthful way. Here are guidelines:

- Use I-messages to share your feelings with the person who rejected your gestures of friendship.
- Share your feelings with a trusted adult if you are unable to share them with the person who rejected your friendship gestures.
- Reaffirm your high self-worth even when a person rejects your friendship.

Two characteristics, shyness and loneliness, make it difficult for people to make new friends. **Shyness** is a condition characterized by discomfort, inhibition, and awkwardness in social situations. Young people who are shy withdraw from interacting and expressing themselves with others. As young people who are shy are encouraged to interact with others, small successes will increase their self-confidence.

Loneliness is a condition that is characterized by unpleasant, painful, or anxious feelings as a result of having fewer or less satisfying relationships than desired. Feelings of loneliness often are temporary. However, many young people feel alienated and lonely because of changes in their personal lives, such as the separation or divorce of their parents or moving away from their friends.

TABLE 6-1	
CONVERSATION KEEPERS	CONVERSATION KILLERS
Asking questions	Talking about yourself
Showing interest in what someone else is saying	Appearing disinterested in what someone else is saying
Listening carefully	Interrupting someone
Responding to others	Changing the topic
Considering other ideas	Being a know-it-all
Using correct grammar	Using slang words
Encouraging another person	Bragging
Being positive	Complaining
Sharing your ideas and feelings	Talking about others
Encouraging someone to talk	Dominating the conversation
Making eye contact	Avoiding eye contact

Balanced Friendships

A friendship requires the commitment of two people. A **balanced friendship** is a friendship in which two people give to and receive from each other acts of kindness. Giving and receiving are valuable to a friendship. There are many ways to give to a friendship, such as listening when a friend is discouraged, helping a friend celebrate a success, or buying a friend a special gift on a special occasion. There are ways to receive in a friendship, too, such as listening to a friend's compliments or accepting a friend's gifts or help. When a friend goes the extra mile, a person should express gratitude.

In balanced friendships, there generally is an equal exchange of giving and receiving, though the giving and receiving might not be balanced at all times. For example, if a friend is sick or is going through difficult times, there may be the need to do more giving than usual. The friend may need more giving at these times. But, after a period of time, the friend is able to reciprocate. This shift back and forth is healthful.

Some people form one-sided friendships. A **one-sided friendship** is a friendship in which one person does most of the giving and the other person does most of the receiving. There are at least two reasons why a person might choose to do most of the giving in a friendship. First, people who do most of the giving in a friendship may be people pleasers. A **people pleaser** is a person who constantly seeks the approval of others. People pleasers are insecure. They choose to do most of the giving so that they will be liked and noticed by others. However, their giving does not result in what they really want—healthful and balanced friendships. Another reason why people might do most or all of the giving in their friendships is that they do not know how to receive acts of kindness from others. They are uncomfortable accepting gifts of time or support from others. They have never learned to rely on others to meet any of their needs. So they play the role of the giver in most of their relationships.

People who do most or all the receiving in their friendships often are described as "takers" or "users." They take from others or use others to get their needs met. They have little interest in meeting the needs of their friends. They believe they always should come first, they want to be in control

of most decisions, and they are self-centered and selfish. People who are takers or users do not have healthful and balanced friendships. They do not know how to become close to others.

Ending Friendships

Changing friendships is a part of growing up. Friendships change for many reasons. A friend may move away and not keep in touch. A friend may break a confidence and the relationship is never the same again. Sometimes interests change, and new friends replace old ones. However, there are times when a person needs to be objective about a friend and decide if that person truly is a friend. For example, if a friend regularly encourages wrong actions or actions contrary to one's own values, it might be time to end the friendship.

Health Goal #15
I Will Develop Dating Skills

Dating

The social life of preadolescents usually involves same-sex group activities, mostly with close friends. Young teens are still interested in group activities, but their groups tend to include both sexes. Gradually, members of the group begin to date each other. Dating is an extension of friendship. Adolescents need to learn to develop and sustain successful and satisfying dating relationships in order to prepare for more important decisions regarding commitment and marriage. Dating provides the opportunity for young people to learn more about themselves and others. Dating affords adolescents the opportunity to do the following:

- *Strengthen self-esteem.* Being liked and accepted by friends is especially important during adolescence. Asking someone to share an activity and having this person accept affirms a young person's belief about his or her attractiveness and desirability. Feeling good about a dating experience allows an adolescent to gain confidence in the way (s)he is managing his or her social life.

- *Improve social skills.* Dating provides an opportunity to practice social skills, such as meeting another person's parents or guardian for the first time, making a mutual decision about what to do on a date, using good manners, and taking part in conversations.
- *Develop skills in intimacy.* Skills for intimate relationships can be learned and practiced. A sense of trust and a sense of caring are important in the development of intimacy.
- *Understand personal needs.* In a healthful relationship, people develop an understanding of one another's needs, and they desire to meet these needs in healthful ways.

Establishing Dating Standards

A common concern of parents, guardians, and teens is the appropriate time for young people to begin dating. Parents and guardians do not want dating to interfere with their children's emotional, social, and psychological development. Evidence shows that dating at a young age can have negative consequences.

Teens who begin dating before age fifteen may seem to be confident and self-assured, but they tend to be more superficial than their peers. Early dating can interfere with the development of an independent sense of identity. Teens who begin dating early may base their identity on their dating experiences rather than on developing their uniqueness. Parents or guardians are concerned that their children will not remain abstinent if they begin dating too early. Their concerns are supported by research findings (Brooks-Gunn & Furstenberg, 1989; Small & Bogenschneider, 1994). Teens who begin dating at a young age and form steady relationships are more at risk for becoming sexually active.

Young people should be encouraged to be involved in "intelligent dating" rather than "brainless dating" (Covey, 2006). "Intelligent dating" is establishing and following the standards for dating discussed in this section.

Before accepting a date, young people need to establish standards for dating. Standards can be shared with parents or guardians and with persons chosen to date. The following is a list of six dating standards for young people that encourage "intelligent dating":

1. *Give your parents or guardian background information on the person you will be dating.* What is his or her name? How old is she or he? Where does (s)he attend school? How can his or her parents or guardian be reached? Your parents or guardian need this information to discuss whether it is appropriate for you to date this person.

2. *Tell your parents or guardian your exact plans.* When will the date occur? What activity has been planned? Details need to be shared. The timing of the date should not interfere with family activities or with school or work responsibilities. The activity should be appropriate.

3. *Arrange for safe transportation.* If you or your date have a driver's license, your parents or guardian will emphasize that you obey traffic laws and speed limits and do not drink alcohol or use other drugs. If you will be relying on your parents or guardian for transportation to and from activities, your dating arrangements must fit into your parents' or guardian's schedule. Another option is to rely on older teens for transportation. Your parents or guardian will want to check out the person who will be driving. Your parents or guardian should be assured that drinking alcohol or using other drugs will not be tolerated. You also need a plan about what to do if the person who is driving violates traffic laws or exceeds the speed limit. Never get into a car if the driver has been drinking alcohol or using other drugs. Instead, call home for help whenever such a problem arises.

4. *Establish a reasonable curfew.* A **curfew** is a fixed time when a person is to be at home. Your parents or guardian will establish how late you can stay out. Having a curfew helps guarantee your safety and relieves your parents or guardian of needless worry.

5. *Establish a personal code of conduct.* The privilege to date is accompanied by the responsibility to use wise judgment. Issues regarding wise judgment need to be clear. For example, your parents or guardian will have certain expectations regarding adult supervision of your activities. Will you be at your date's home when no adults are present? Money is another issue that needs discussion. How much can be spent? Who should pay for what? Young people also should be aware of their parents' or guardian's guidelines for sexual behavior. Remember, your parents or guardian establish guidelines to protect you.

6. *Establish the expected code of conduct for the person you will date.* Your parents or guardian may discuss the importance of your

being respected by anyone you date. No one you date should ever act in a way that shows disrespect for you or your parents or guardian. Your date should never encourage you to disobey your parents' or guardian's guidelines, say cruel words to you, hit or shove you, force you to show affection or to be sexually active, drink alcohol, or use other harmful drugs. If your date acts in these ways, discuss what you should do about it with your parents or guardian.

Dating Skills

The following dating skills are competencies that help a person on a date:

1. *Do not base your self-worth on your ability to get a date.* If someone turns down a date with you, it does not mean that you are a loser. It is never appropriate to consider oneself a success or failure based on another person's acceptance or rejection of your invitation.
2. *Asks questions and get the facts before accepting a date.* It is important to know what activities will be included in a date.
3. *Decline a date when there will be pressure to drink or be sexually active.*
4. *Honor your dating commitments and don't change your plans if someone better comes along.* Character is essential in dating. It is important to always treat people with respect. Try to understand how you would feel if someone canceled plans with you for someone else. You should always keep commitments you make with others. One strategy is to set a date with the second person for a different time.
5. *Recognize the advantages of dating a variety of people rather than going steady.* The teen years provide an opportunity to practice dating skills. Going steady allows you to practice these skills only up to a point. Asking out different people and accepting other invitations provides additional opportunities. You will learn to handle rejection when you are turned down by someone who does not want to go out with you. Having a variety of dating experiences will help you meet new people and gain self-confidence.
6. *Make a fast exit from a date when you find yourself in a situation that violates your parents' or guardian's guidelines.* The faster you leave a bad situation, the better. There can be serious consequences if you decide to stay. Remember that your parents gave you the privilege to date. This privilege is based on their belief in your trustworthiness and responsibility. If your date will not leave, you should still make a fast exit. Call your parents, your guardian, or another responsible adult to pick you up.
7. *Don't hesitate to call your parents or guardian if you're on a date and need help.*
8. *Feel comfortable about staying home when you don't want to date.* Going out, or dating, should be a choice. You might not be ready for dating or might not be interested in it right now. Never date because you feel pressured to do so.
9. *Be clear about your expectations when you give or receive a gift in a dating situation.* Whenever a gift is given in a dating situation, expectations must be clear between the giver of the gift and the receiver. In most cases, a gift is something that is voluntarily given with no strings attached. Then it becomes the property of the person to whom it was given. Sometimes young people exchange rings or other gifts to indicate that they are going steady. It should be made clear if the gift given is the receiver's property only as long as the two are a couple.
10. *Be honest and kind when you turn someone down for a date.* This situation should be handled with class and is an opportunity for you to practice social graces. Thank the person for the invitation. It is okay to directly and gently decline the invitation for the date. The best policy is to avoid dishonesty. It is okay to say that you are not interested in going out. Never say that you are busy when you are not.

Health Goal #16

I Will Practice Abstinence from Sex

Benefits of Abstinence from Sex

Abstinence from sex is voluntarily choosing not to be sexually active. Most parents want schools to teach the many benefits of abstinence from sex. According to a study conducted by the Kaiser Family Foundation (2003), only 23 percent of teens ages fifteen to seventeen agree that sexual activity is appropriate for teens their age. Very few (2 percent) consider sex under the age of fifteen appropriate.

Among the two-thirds of teens in the Kaiser Family Foundation study who reported that they had not had sexual intercourse, a high percentage reported that the following influenced their decision not to have sex:

- Concern about pregnancy (94 percent)
- Concern about HIV/AIDS (92 percent)
- Concern about sexually transmitted diseases (92 percent)
- Feeling they are too young (91 percent)
- Because of what their parents taught them about sex (91 percent)
- Because of what they learned in sex education (89 percent)
- Because of religious or moral values (84 percent)
- Concern for personal reputation (83 percent)

Young people benefit in many ways from practicing abstinence from sex. Practicing abstinence from sex is a responsible decision for several reasons:

1. *Practicing abstinence promotes health.* Practicing abstinence until marriage reduces the risk of becoming infected with HIV and developing AIDS, becoming infected with other sexually transmitted diseases (STDs), or becoming a teenage parent.
2. *Practicing abstinence protects safety.* Practicing abstinence reduces the risk of violence from suicide and child abuse that is associated with teen parenthood.
3. *Practicing abstinence follows laws.* Practicing abstinence helps young people avoid being prosecuted for having sex with a minor. In most states, having sex with a person who has not reached the legal age of consent is considered corruption of a minor. The **legal age of consent** is that age when a person is legally able to give permission. A person who has a mental disability might not understand what it means to give permission, even if this person is not a minor. A person can be prosecuted for having sex with a minor or with someone who has a mental disability. Practicing abstinence also helps young people avoid behavior for which they can be prosecuted for date rape.
4. *Practicing abstinence shows respect for self and others.* Practicing abstinence helps a

person maintain a good reputation because that person acts responsibly. Supporting another's decision to be abstinent shows respect for that person. Other young people respect those who behave in responsible ways.

5. *Practicing abstinence follows the guidelines of responsible parents and other responsible adults.* Young people avoid having conflicts with their parents when they follow family guidelines. Parents want their children to live quality lives. They set high standards for their children's behavior. They know that there are serious consequences that occur from being sexually active. They want to protect their children from serious consequences.
6. *Practicing abstinence demonstrates good character.* Practicing abstinence shows that a young person is self-disciplined and can delay gratification. This demonstrates good character and the upholding of the young person's family's values.
7. *Practicing abstinence promotes dignity, respect, responsibility, strength, health, and sexual fidelity in marriage.* Sexual fidelity in marriage is sexual faithfulness and involves a promise to have sex only with one's marriage partner. Sexual fidelity, or faithfulness, promotes dignity, respect, and responsibility within marriage. It helps promote trust, a foundation for any strong marriage. Sexual fidelity helps protect the health of marriage partners. When marriage partners are faithful to one another, they do not need to worry about the sexual transmission of diseases. Sexual fidelity helps marriage partners uphold their vows and helps them keep their commitment. When teens practice abstinence from sex in their dating relationships, they reserve sex for the marriage relationship. This helps keep sex within marriage very special.

Setting Limits for Expressing Physical Affection

Young people need to develop a sense of personal responsibility to protect against risky sexual behavior. One of the benefits of abstinence from sex for teens is self-respect and feeling important enough to protect themselves from risky sexual behavior (Page & Page, 2007). Knowing how to set limits for expressing affection helps people maintain their self-respect and the respect of their dating partners. Setting limits helps people keep their sexual feelings under control. Sexual feelings are feelings that result from a strong physical and emotional attraction to another person. Sexual feelings may occur when you see a certain person, kiss or touch that person, look at a picture, or read certain material. Sexual feelings might occur in response to having certain thoughts.

It is important to understand how physical expressions of affection can intensify sexual feelings. When two people are attracted to each other, they might physically express their affections by kissing or hugging. These ways of physically expressing affection are enjoyable—and can result in sexual feelings.

The couple's expressions of affection might not stop with a hug or a casual kiss. The couple might continue to prolonged kissing. Prolonged kissing further intensifies sexual feelings. Caressing or touching also strengthens sexual feelings. Intimate physical expressions of affection cause physical changes to occur in the body. There is increased blood flow to the reproductive organs. In the male, the penis fills with blood and becomes erect. This intensifies sexual feelings in the male. In the female, there is increased blood flow to the vagina and clitoris, creating arousal and a warm feeling.

These physical changes prepare the body for sex even if the couple previously had decided to abstain from sex. Their bodies now say, "Yes, I am ready for sex!" even though their brains say, "No, I do not want to be sexually active!" In essence, the body attempts to override the brain's message to say "no" to being sexually active. Young people need to keep the brain's message in charge in order to practice abstinence. The following are some ways to set limits for physical expressions of affection:

1. Limit physical expressions of affection to hand holding, hugging, and casual kissing, to keep your brain in control of your decisions and actions.
2. Tell the other person your limits before expressing affection.
3. Do not date anyone who does not respect your limits.
4. Avoid drinking alcohol and using other drugs that dull your brain and interfere with your wise judgment.

5. Do not date others who drink alcohol or use other drugs that dull their brain and interfere with their wise judgment.

Resisting Negative Peer Pressure to Be Sexually Active

Resistance skills are skills that help a person say "no" to an action or leave a situation. The following are guidelines for young people for resisting negative peer pressure to be sexually active.

1. *Be confident and say, "No, I do not want to be sexually active."* You can best do this by looking directly at the other person while you speak. Clearly state your limits for physical expressions of affection.
2. *Give reasons for choosing to practice abstinence.* You can use the six guidelines from the *Responsible Decision-Making Model* to develop your reasons for saying, "No, I do not want to be sexually active."
   I practice abstinence to promote my health.
   * I do not want to become infected with HIV and develop AIDS.
   * I do not want to become infected with other STDs, such as genital herpes and genital warts.
   * I do not want to become a teenage parent.
   I practice abstinence to protect the safety of others.
   * I do not want to risk being a stressed teen parent who neglects or abuses a child.
   * I do not want my partner or myself to be prosecuted for having sex with a minor.
   * I do not want to be accused of date rape.
   I practice abstinence to show respect for myself and others.
   * I want to protect my good reputation and the reputation of others.
   * I want to uphold my personal values.
   * I want to protect my health and the health of others.
   I practice abstinence to follow the guidelines of my parents and other responsible adults.
   * I want to practice family values.
   * I do not want to disappoint or disobey my parents or guardian.
   I practice abstinence because I want to demonstrate good character.
   * I want to have a good reputation.
   * I do not want to feel guilty or anxious.

- I want to postpone sexual intercourse until marriage.

3. *Use the broken-record technique and repeat several times your same reason for practicing abstinence.* When getting continued pressure, repeat your reasons for practicing abstinence. You will sound like a broken record. Each time you give the same response, you are more convincing to those who didn't want to believe your message.

4. *Use nonverbal behavior to support your message that you do not want to be sexually active.* Don't lead another person on or "go too far" when you express affection. Your behaviors should match the limits you have set for your behavior.

5. *Avoid situations in which you might be pressured to be sexually active.* Avoid situations in which you are vulnerable, such as being in someone else's bedroom. Other situations to avoid include parties at which alcohol or drugs are being used; watching movies, videos, and television shows that imply that being sexually active is okay; or reading books and magazines that are filled with pictures and stories that encourage sexual promiscuity.

6. *Avoid being with anyone who pressures others to be sexually active.* Expect the people you date to respect your limits. Do not date anyone who pressures you to have sex. It is wise to avoid individuals who brag about "scoring" or having "sexual conquests." Date people your own age. Older people might exert additional pressure on you to have sex. Pay attention to the advice of your parents or guardian when they tell you to avoid certain people.

7. *Know and obey the laws regarding sex that protect you.* Tell a parent or guardian if an adult makes sexual advances toward you. Also, tell them if a person rapes or tries to rape you.

8. *Influence your friends to practice abstinence.* Be confident and share with your friends your decision to practice abstinence. Encourage your friends who are sexually active to begin practicing abstinence.

Changing Behavior

Some young people who have been sexually active in the past learn from their experience. They gain knowledge as they experience the negative consequences of their activity. They begin to recognize that being sexually active was not the best choice. They understand the benefits of practicing absti-

nence from sex. They might feel guilty or anxious about having been sexually active. They might take another look at the facts—the risk of HIV infection, other STDs, and unwanted pregnancy. These young people may regret that they have not followed their family guidelines. They may have given in to pressure to have sex and now regret having done so. Young people who practice abstinence can be proud of their behavior. Steps young people who have been sexually active can take to change their behavior include these:

1. Write a list of reasons for choosing abstinence.
2. Talk to a trusted adult about your past behavior and your decision to start practicing abstinence.
3. Consider the negative health consequences that might have occurred from being sexually active.
4. Set new limits for expressions of affection.
5. Have a frank discussion with a partner with whom you were previously sexually active.
6. Get reassurance from your current dating partner that she or he will practice abstinence.
7. Break off your relationship with your dating partner if she or he will not agree to practice sexual abstinence.
8. Reevaluate the influence of your friends.
9. Be honest and direct about your commitment to practice abstinence in new relationships.
10. Avoid behaviors that impair wise judgment, such as using alcohol or other drugs and being in tempting situations.

Health Goal #17

I Will Recognize Harmful Relationships

A **relationship** is a connection a person has with another person. A person's health status is affected by the quality of the relationships she has with others. A person may have different kinds of relationships. In general, relationships are usually healthful or harmful. A **healthful relationship** is a relationship that promotes self-respect, encourages productivity and health, and is free of violence and drug misuse and abuse. A **harmful relationship** is a relationship that harms self-respect, interferes with productivity and health, and includes violence or drug misuse and abuse.

Harmful Ways of Relating

Some people lack self-respect and don't respect others. They are not interested in the health of others and do not encourage others to be productive and do their best. They relate to others in harmful ways. This section of the chapter includes ten profiles of people who relate in harmful ways.

THE PEOPLE PLEASER

The *people pleaser* constantly seeks the approval of others. A people pleaser will do almost anything to be liked, including harmful behavior such as using alcohol or other drugs. Other people describe people pleasers as "doormats" because others can walk all over them with no consequences. People pleasers sabotage their chances to have healthful relationships because others do not respect them.

THE ENABLER

The *enabler* supports the harmful behavior of others. The enabler might deny or overlook another person's harmful behavior, such as drinking, gambling, or cheating, and make excuses or cover up for that person. The enabler also might contribute to another person's harmful behavior—for instance, placing bets for a friend who has a gambling problem or drinking with a person who has a drinking problem. Enablers sabotage their chances to have healthful relationships when they do not require others to behave responsibly. As a result, enablers cannot get their own needs for attention, affection, and support met.

THE CLINGER

The *clinger* is needy and dependent. The clinger feels empty inside and constantly turns to another person to feel better. When the clinger has this person's attention or affection, the clinger feels better. But no amount of attention or affection keeps the clinger feeling fulfilled. The clinger keeps demanding more and eventually "suffocates" the other person because the clinger wants all of the other person's time or attention. Clingers sabotage their chances to have healthful relationships by not giving other people space. When people pull away, the clinger is threatened and clings even more.

THE FIXER

The *fixer* tries to fix other people's problems. Fixers take on problems that are not their responsibility but are the responsibility of another person. Fixers are quick to give advice. They will identify different possible solutions to the other person's problems and try them for the person. In the process of getting involved with another person's problems, fixers avoid their own feelings and problems. Fixers sabotage their chances to have healthful relationships because healthy people do not want others to solve their problems. Healthy people solve their own problems with the support of others but do not want others to take over.

THE DISTANCER

The *distancer* is emotionally unavailable to others. The distancer keeps other people from getting too close in a number of ways, such as being too busy to spend time with other people and avoiding sharing feelings. Distancers keep others at a distance to avoid getting hurt. Distancers sabotage their chances to have healthful relationships by not risking emotional involvement.

THE CONTROLLER

The *controller* is possessive, jealous, and domineering. The controller seeks power. Controllers might tell another person what to do, what to wear, and what to believe, and they do not like to share the object of their attention with anyone else. The controller might monopolize a girlfriend's or boyfriend's time. Controllers sabotage their chances to have healthful relationships by not respecting the interests or opinions of others and trying to dominate others. Healthy people want to participate in the decisions made in a relationship, and they do not want another person trying to control them.

THE CENTER

The *center* is self-centered. It is almost as if the center is wearing a badge that says "ME, ME, ME." If you talk to the center on the telephone, the center will do most of the talking and will show little interest in what you have to say. Centers want to do what they want to do when they want to do it and are not too concerned about what other people want to do or how other people feel. Centers sabotage their chances to have healthful relationships by focusing on being the center of attention and ignoring others' needs.

THE ABUSER

The *abuser* is a person who is abusive. The abuser might constantly put others down or harm others. The abuser might threaten, begin fights, and act in other violent ways, such as forcing another person to have sex. Other people find the abuser's behavior confusing because abusers tend to alternate periods of abusiveness with periods of gentleness. However, after calmer periods the abusive behavior returns. Abusers sabotage their chances to have healthful relationships by threatening and harming others. Stay away from a person you suspect may be an abuser. This person can harm you physically or emotionally.

THE LIAR

The *liar* does not tell the truth. Honesty is a foundation in any healthful relationship—people base many of their responses to others on what others tell them in conversations and actions. When a liar does not tell the truth, other people respond based on false information, doing and saying things they might not have done or said had they known the truth. This is exactly what the liar wants. Liars will lie about themselves to try to look good, pretending to be something they are not in order to impress others. Their relationships are based on lies. The liar avoids the truth to manipulate others into the responses the liar wants. Liars sabotage their chances to have healthful relationships by lying to others to get the response they want.

THE PROMISE BREAKER

The *promise breaker* is not reliable. The promise breaker will make plans with another person and then be a no-show, opting instead to do something better that has come along. Promise breakers might promise to change their ways, but that's merely another broken promise. Promise breakers sabotage their chances to have healthful relationships by not keeping their word. Other people doubt the promise breaker's sincerity and commitment.

Interactions in Harmful Relationships

The interactions, or dynamics, in harmful relationships often explain why people end up in such relationships. People who relate in harmful ways often are drawn to each other, as if they have a magnetic attraction toward being in a relationship together. Being together helps them play out their profiles as a people pleaser, enabler, clinger, fixer, distancer, controller, center, abuser, liar, or promise breaker. Following are some examples of interactions that can help explain why some people end up in harmful relationships.

MATCH-UP: A PROMISE BREAKER AND A PEOPLE PLEASER

The promise breaker makes plans to go to a movie with a people pleaser. When the promise breaker gets another, more interesting invitation, she cancels the plans. The people pleaser is angry but keeps his anger inside, accommodating the promise breaker by agreeing to go to the movie at a later date. The people pleaser makes the promise breaker's life easy by not objecting to being treated badly. The promise breaker helps perpetuate the people pleaser's unassertiveness by treating him badly. The promise breaker needs to learn to keep commitments. The people pleaser must set limits and tell others how he feels about their behavior.

MATCH-UP: A CONTROLLER AND AN ENABLER

The controller is typically a very jealous teen male who demands all of his girlfriend's attention. He objects when she spends time with her girlfriends and has angry outbursts if a male classmate speaks to her. He is suspicious and accuses his girlfriend of seeing other guys. She, in turn, is an enabler and makes excuses for him. She tells herself, "He loves me so much that he wants me with him all the time." When she gives up her other friends to spend all her time with him, she supports his wrong behavior. If she tells a friend about her boyfriend's "love" for her, the friend might think she is in a loving relationship—not recognizing that it is a harmful relationship and that both of them relate in harmful ways. The boyfriend must respect his girlfriend's right to have friends and encourage her to run her own life. The girlfriend must take responsibility for her life, not allow her boyfriend to control her, and not deny her own feelings and needs.

MATCH-UP: A CLINGER AND A DISTANCER

An example of a clinger might be a female who was raised in a divorced family. Her father abandoned the family when she was ten years old, and she rarely speaks with him. She was very hurt and feels the loss of her father's presence in the home. Deep down inside, she fears that she will be abandoned again. As a result, she is afraid to be vulnerable and close. She becomes attracted to a distancer. The distancer is the perfect match because he is emotionally unavailable. Both the clinger and the distancer are afraid to be close. They protect themselves in different ways. The clinger chases someone who cannot be close. The distancer runs away from relationships and does not get emotionally involved with the clinger. He spends some time with her and then backs off. She then chases harder. They continue to play into each other's game. Both the clinger and the distancer must change to have healthful relationships. The clinger must address the emptiness she feels and develop greater self-confidence. The distancer must address his fears of sharing feelings and becoming close to others.

CHANGING PROFILES IN DIFFERENT RELATIONSHIPS

There are many match-ups of people who relate in harmful ways, such as a center and a fixer, and a people pleaser and an abuser. It is important to know that a person can be described one way in one relationship and a different way in another relationship. For example, suppose a female has several healthful relationships with close friends and is an enabler only when she is with her boyfriend. She needs to examine what it is about this relationship that causes her to relate in harmful ways.

What to Do about Harmful Relationships

The following are suggestions of how young people can address harmful relationships:

1. *Evaluate each of your relationships on a regular basis.* List ways you relate to others that concern you. List ways other people relate to you that concern you. Ask a parent, guardian, or other trusted adult to review the lists with you. This adult might recognize behaviors in one of your relationships that you do not recognize.
2. *Recognize when you must end a harmful relationship rather than work to change it.* End a relationship with anyone who chooses illegal

behavior. End a relationship with anyone who threatens your health or safety. End a relationship when your parents or guardian ask you to do so. Get help from a trusted adult if the harmful relationship is with a family member.
3. *For any existing harmful relationship, identify changes in behavior that must occur for you to stay in that relationship.* List changes you expect in yourself. For example, you might write, "I will not make plans and cancel them because I have something better to do." List changes you expect the other person to make. For example, you might write, "I expect [person's name] to tell the truth at all times."
4. *Talk to a parent, guardian, or other trusted adult about the changes you expect in the relationship.* Share your concerns about the relationship. Describe your own behaviors you expect to change. Describe the behaviors you expect the other person to change. Discuss whether your expectations are realistic. Discuss whether or not it is wise to continue the relationship. Discuss your other relationships. Do you notice any similarities? Discuss ways to improve your relationship skills.
5. *Have a frank discussion with the other person in the relationship, sharing your concerns and expectations.* State your concerns and your expectations. Ask the other person to state his or her concerns and expectations. Discuss whether or not the relationship should be continued. Make a plan to work on the relationship if you want to continue together.
6. *Set a future date in which you will evaluate the relationship again.* Identify a realistic time frame for making the necessary changes. When the set date arrives, evaluate whether or not your expectations have been fulfilled.

Health Goal #18
I Will Develop Skills to Prepare for Marriage

Preparing for Marriage

A **traditional marriage** is an emotional, spiritual, and legal commitment a man and a woman make to one another. Most people marry at least once and have expectations in their marriage. Marriage provides intimacy and companionship as well as feelings of well-being. Marriage provides a framework for sustaining the family unit and having and raising children. Children and adolescents can learn information about marriage that will help them make decisions in the future.

When two people choose to marry, they are choosing to share their lives with one another. Intimacy plays a vital role in a marriage relationship. **Intimacy** is deep and meaningful sharing between two people. There are many kinds of intimacy, but for a marriage to be sustained over the years, four kinds of intimacy are particularly important: philosophical, psychological, creative, and physical.

Philosophical intimacy is the sharing of beliefs and values. Marriage partners share how their beliefs influence their decisions. Marriage partners share the values that determine their day-to-day priorities. For example, one partner might value his or her relationship with parents. As a result, spending holidays with these parents is a priority to this partner. The other partner recognizes and respects this priority, even though this particular value may not be as important to him or her.

Psychological intimacy is the sharing of needs, emotions, weaknesses, and strengths. Marriage partners share their needs, such as the need for a hug or the need to have someone who will listen. Marriage partners share and rejoice in their individual successes and ask one another for support when they have a disappointment. When they share weaknesses, they feel accepted rather than rejected. Psychological intimacy deepens through the years.

Creative intimacy is the sharing of efforts to accomplish tasks and projects. This kind of sharing goes beyond discussion and emotional responses. Marriage partners engage in many cooperative efforts. For example, they may work together to make their apartment or house a home. They may choose furniture together, plant a garden, and select wallpaper. Marriage partners may plan a vacation together. They may take lessons to learn a sport they can enjoy together. Raising children also involves creative intimacy. Marriage partners plan activities they can participate in with his or her children. They share child-raising responsibilities, such as discipline. For marriage partners to have creative intimacy, each partner must do his or her share of the work with a willing attitude. Marriage partners must agree on expectations and on who does what.

Physical intimacy is the sharing of physical affection and includes a wide range of behaviors that express warmth and closeness. Marriage partners show physical affection when they touch, caress, hold hands, kiss, or have sexual intercourse. To be physically intimate, marriage partners should be sexually attracted to one another. Each marriage partner should have a healthful attitude about sex. The commitment marriage partners make to each other gives them a sense of security that enhances physical intimacy.

Potential marriage partners can assess the warmth and closeness they feel for each other without having sexual intercourse. Sex before marriage *does not* predict sexual satisfaction during marriage. Remember, it is a responsible decision to wait until marriage to have sex. Because sex before marriage does not involve a commitment, there is no feeling of security. Real intimacy is not involved.

Predicting Success in Marriage

The following factors are important in helping to predict whether a marriage will be a success:

1. *Age.* Couples who marry during their teen years have a high divorce rate. Couples who marry when they are in their twenties or

older usually enjoy more success. Marriage partners who are similar in age have greater success in marriage than marriage partners with large age differences, because they are at similar stages of development.

2. *Reasons for marriage.* Couples who marry to love and nurture one another and to share intimacy are more likely to succeed at marriage than those who marry to escape a difficult and unhappy family situation, to get even with parents, or to escape loneliness.

3. *Length of the relationship and engagement.* Longer relationships and engagements provide the opportunity for couples to examine their relationship and to develop intimacy. Longer relationships are usually associated with success in marriage.

4. *Similar attitudes about children and child raising.* Discussing attitudes toward having and raising children contributes to a successful marriage. Couples might discuss these issues before they are married: if and when they want children, how many children they want, how they intend to raise their children. Couples should work through any disagreement on these issues before they are married.

5. *Similar interests.* Although marriages can sustain differences in interests, the old saying "Opposites attract" might not apply when predicting success at marriage. Differences present stressors that must be worked out. Couples who are similar with regard to race, ethnic background, religious beliefs, socioeconomic status, interests, lifestyles, education, and intelligence are more likely to stay married.

6. *Commitment to sexual fidelity.* Physical intimacy in marriage provides a closeness and a feeling of security. Sexual fidelity is important in establishing trust. Couples who honor a commitment to sexual fidelity and who trust each other are more likely to succeed at marriage.

7. *Good character.* People who have good character make responsible decisions. They are self-disciplined. They are aware that their actions will affect the quality of their marriage.

8. *Parents' success at marriage.* People whose parents are divorced are more likely to get divorced themselves. This might be because their parents were not good role models for resolving conflicts and maintaining a marriage.

9. *Parental attitudes toward the potential marriage partner.* A marriage is more likely to succeed when a person's parents approve of the future husband or wife.

10. *Careful selection of marriage partner.* A marriage is more likely to succeed when people are cautious when selecting a mate. This includes considering the factors that contribute to successful marriage when selecting a partner.

Marriage Commitment

Divorce rates are rising. To help ensure that their marriage will last, marriage partners must be committed to actions that honor their wedding vows. When two people marry, they take vows, or make promises. This is what commitment is. A commitment involves responsible actions. People cannot promise how they will feel for a lifetime; however, they can promise how they will act. Marriage partners can behave in the ways they have promised to behave.

Teen Marriage Is Risky

One way to reduce the number of separations and divorces is to reduce the number of teen marriages. More than 75 percent of teen marriages end in divorce. There are many reasons why teen marriages do not succeed. Teens need to master the developmental tasks of adolescence before tackling the tasks that are appropriate for the stages of marriage. Robert Havighurst (1948), a sociologist, identified developmental tasks of adolescence. A *developmental task* is an achievement that needs to be mastered to reach the next level of maturity. The following discussion explains why teen marriage interferes with reaching the next level of maturity necessary for a successful marriage.

TASK 1—DEVELOP HEALTHFUL FRIENDSHIPS WITH MEMBERS OF BOTH SEXES

Teen marriage does not give teens enough time to develop healthful friendships with members of both sexes. During adolescence, teens need to have friendships with members of both sexes. They need to learn how to communicate and how to develop friendships. They need to be selective and learn to evaluate friendships. To do this, they must identify characteristics of people they admire. Examining issues such as trust, honesty, and loyalty is important. Having friendships with members of both sexes helps teens learn more about themselves, which is an important aspect of forming personal identity. They need to gain a sense of who they are. Teen marriage cuts short the time spent developing friendships with members of both sexes. Teens who marry are less likely to have a support network of mature friends who will be helpful during the stressful first years of marriage.

Task 2—Become Comfortable with Your Maleness or Femaleness

Teen marriage does not give enough time for the teens to become comfortable with their maleness or femaleness. Dating helps young people to respond to people of the opposite sex. Having the opportunity to date different people is very beneficial. Teens who marry pass up much of the fun that their peers have participating in social activities.

Task 3—Become Comfortable with Your Body

Teen marriage does not give the teen enough time to become comfortable with his or her body. Teenagers' bodies are still growing and developing. Hormonal changes that accompany puberty cause new feelings as well as body changes. **Puberty** is the stage of growth and development when the body becomes capable of producing offspring. Teens may notice that their moods change. They need time to adjust to these changes in their emotions, just as they need time to be comfortable with changes in their bodies. Teens might marry solely because they feel strong sexual attraction. They might lack the skills needed to tell the difference between love and sexual attraction. As a result, they can make mistakes in selecting a marriage partner.

Task 4—Become Emotionally Independent from Adults

Teen marriage does not give teens enough time to become emotionally independent from adults. One of the reasons teens are described as rebellious is that they challenge their parents or guardian. They might do this as a way to show independence. At times, teens still may want to be dependent on their parents or guardian; at other times, they want to break away from their influ-

ence. This is normal. After all, teens are learning to be adults and preparing to run their own lives. Teens need the safety and security that parents or guardians provide, and they need their help as they test ways of becoming independent. Teens who marry are faced with adulthood without the safety and security of being parented themselves when they really need it. If they marry and live with parents or guardians who continue in the parent role, the teens are unable to master one of the primary tasks of the first stage of marriage—to create a family with their partner.

Task 5—Learn Skills Needed Later for a Successful Marriage and Parenthood

Teen marriage does not give teens enough time to learn skills needed later for a successful marriage and parenthood. As teens mature and complete developmental tasks, they acquire skills they can use later when they marry and become parents. Teens need to develop effective communication skills to help them achieve intimacy in adulthood. Intimacy is deep and meaningful sharing between two people. Teens also need to develop conflict resolution skills to learn how to settle disagreements when they are married and become parents. Teens who marry have not had time to fully develop these and other skills necessary for marriage and parenthood.

Task 6—Prepare for a Career

Teen marriage does not give teens enough time to prepare for a career. During adolescence, young people are gaining skills and self-knowledge to help them prepare for a career. Education should be a top priority. The goal is to have the skills needed to get a job, support oneself, and be financially independent. Teens who marry usually have difficulty completing their education. When they try to get a job, they have difficulty competing with their skilled peers who stayed in school. As a result, they earn less money. If they rely on parents or a guardian for financial support, they are not able to achieve their own financial independence. Living with limited income places stress on a marriage.

Task 7—Have a Clear Set of Values to Guide Behavior

Teen marriage does not give teens enough time to develop a clear set of values to guide behavior. A value is a standard or belief. Parents or guardians teach teens many values that help guide choices and behavior. Adolescents are beginning to achieve emotional independence from their parents or guardian, and they take a second look at the values they have learned from their parents or guardian. Teens gain confidence when they move from the attitude "These are my parents' or guardian's values" to "These are my values." Teens who marry might do so before they are certain of their own values, and they might marry someone who has different values.

TASK 8—UNDERSTAND AND ACHIEVE SOCIALLY RESPONSIBLE BEHAVIOR

Teen marriage does not give teens enough time to understand and achieve socially responsible behavior. Adolescence has been described as the "me" stage. During early and middle adolescence, teens tend to focus on their personal needs, and they might spend much time thinking about their appearance, social life, and friends. In the next few years, this focus will change. Older teens will look at the world around them and identify ways to be helpful. Teens who marry do not have the time to get involved in their community and help others. The demands of a teen marriage take up all of their time.

Health Goal #19

I Will Develop Skills to Prepare for Parenthood

Things to Consider before Becoming a Parent

Being a parent is one of the most important tasks in society. Children benefit from living with a loving father and mother who are married and respect one another. Many children do not live with both their parents. Perhaps a parent died. Perhaps their parents are divorced. The parent with whom they live might be loving and have good parenting skills. Some children who live with both parents have a loving parent and an abusive parent. These kinds of situations change the structure of the family. The ideal situation is for children to live with two loving, married parents.

There are three *R*s that young people might consider before becoming a parent:

R: The *reasons* for wanting to have a child.
R: The *resources* needed to raise a child.
R: The *responsibilities* one will have as a parent.

REASONS FOR BECOMING A PARENT

Being ready for parenthood means being ready to focus on someone else's needs in addition to one's own. The best reason to have a child is the desire to love and guide a child. Children need help in growing and developing. They need to be taught how to be responsible.

Other reasons for wanting to become parents focus more on the parent's needs than on the child's need. Some people want to build up their ego by having a child who looks like them, will carry on the family name, or will inherit the family business, money, or property. Others want to compensate for something that is missing in their life and may have a child to save their marriage, make up for an unhappy childhood, or help them feel more secure as a woman or a man. Still others feel a need to conform to what their peers are doing or what others expect and may therefore have a child to please their parents or guardian, to do what their friends are doing, or to keep from being criticized for being childless.

RESOURCES NEEDED FOR PARENTHOOD

Financial resources are needed for parenthood. A couple who are considering having a child must evaluate their financial resources. These are some of the costs of parenthood a couple might expect:

- Health and hospitalization insurance
- Prenatal care
- Maternity clothes
- Delivery and postpartum care for the mother and baby in a hospital or a birth center or at home
- Hospitalization for the baby
- Pediatrician's hospital visits, regular well-baby checkups, required immunizations, sick visits, medications
- Nursery furnishings: bassinet, crib, bedding, linens, bathtub, stroller, highchair, chest, car seat, infant carrier, toys
- Clothing for the baby
- Diapers or diaper service
- Formula, food, and vitamins for the baby

- Baby supplies: bottles, swabs, baby wipes, diaper rash ointment, tissues, powder, baby soap and shampoo, oil
- Child care or day care

For many families, there is the additional cost of lost income during the mother's maternity leave. One of the parents may cut back to part-time work or stop working altogether after the birth of a baby. The first year of child rearing is expensive. These financial considerations must be considered when deciding if and when to become parents.

RESPONSIBILITIES OF PARENTHOOD

When people become parents, they take responsibility for raising a child. Whether the child is newborn or adopted, there are certain promises parents should make. The ten promises listed here can be called the Parent Pledge to a Child:

1. I will set aside a quantity of time as well as quality time to spend with you.
2. I will learn about your age-appropriate development so that I can have realistic expectations for you.
3. I will teach you rules to ensure your health and safety.
4. I will give you love and affection.
5. I will teach you with a positive attitude, avoiding criticism.
6. I will teach you my moral and ethical values.
7. I will teach you self-discipline and self-control with effective discipline, not child abuse.
8. I will provide economic security for you.
9. I will recognize that you have rights, and I will respect those rights.

10. I will raise you in a stable, secure family that is free from substance abuse (free from the abuse of alcohol, tobacco, marijuana, and other drugs).

Responsible Parenting

Parenting involves having more than loving feelings for a child. Being a responsible and caring parent is not an easy task. It involves developing intimacy with a child, caring for a child as he or she grows and develops, and helping a child develop self-discipline and self-control.

DEVELOPING INTIMACY WITH A CHILD

Developing intimacy with a child is one of the responsibilities of parenting. The early lessons children learn from their parents with regard to intimacy influence their ability to become intimate with others.

Children can learn **philosophical intimacy** from parents. Responsible parents teach their children beliefs and values. They discipline their children when their children act in wrong ways. This helps their children know how to behave. It helps them develop good character.

Children can learn **psychological intimacy** from parents. Responsible parents are trustworthy and accepting. Their children can talk to them about sensitive topics. Responsible parents encourage and support their children when their children have disappointments.

Children can learn **creative intimacy** from parents. Responsible parents give their children their first feelings of teamwork. They ask their children to help with tasks in the home. They share fun projects.

Children can learn about **physical intimacy.** Responsible parents express physical affection for children in appropriate ways. Babies who receive soft touches and are spoken to, held, and looked at frequently by the mother and father in the first few days of life cry less and smile and laugh more than babies who are not treated in these ways. Children who are loved learn to feel secure in ways of expressing affection. They are able to receive affection from others.

CARING FOR CHILDREN AS THEY GROW AND DEVELOP

Responsible parents help their children develop emotional, social, verbal, intellectual, and motor skills. They understand that age-appropriate skills help keep their children safe from harm. They understand emotional development and reassure their children if they are fearful or anxious. They obtain medical help for their children when needed.

HELPING CHILDREN DEVELOP SELF-DISCIPLINE AND SELF-CONTROL

Responsible parents discipline their children. **Discipline** is training that develops self-discipline and self-control. **Preventive discipline** is training in which a parent explains correct behavior and the consequences of wrong behavior. Suppose a child gets a new bicycle for his birthday. His mother explains her expectations. For example, she says she expects the child to put away the bicycle after riding it. She further explains that if the child does not put the bicycle away, (s)he will not be permitted to ride the bicycle for three days.

Behavior modification is a disciplinary technique in which positive rewards are used to encourage desirable behavior and negative consequences are used to stop undesirable behavior. For example, a father might praise his daughter for remembering to put away her bicycle, or he might plan a special reward. On the other hand, the parent wants to change undesirable behavior. The child who leaves the bicycle in an unsafe place may not be permitted to ride the bicycle for three days.

Logical consequences discipline is a disciplinary technique in which the child is allowed the opportunity to experience the results of undesirable behavior so that he will want to change the undesirable behavior. An example might be a child who frequently forgets to take his or her packed lunch to school. The child calls the parent and asks the parent to bring the forgotten lunch to school. The parent disciplines the child by refusing to take the forgotten lunch to school. The child experiences the consequences—no lunch. As a result, the child is not as forgetful in the future.

Physical punishment is a disciplinary technique in which an act is used to teach a child not to repeat undesirable behavior. Slapping and spanking are examples of physical punishment.

Slapping and spanking appear to be helpful in only two instances. First, when a child is young, a parent might slap the child's hand to prevent a behavior that might harm the child. For example, the parent might slap the hand of a child who is trying to put a fork in an electrical outlet. Second, a parent might use a very light slap on the young child's buttocks or hand to get the child's attention. The slap should not be severe enough to hurt or injure the child.

Spanking is usually ineffective in teaching long-range discipline and self-control. For example, consider two examples: a child who does not put away his or her bicycle and a child who forgets to take his or her packed lunch to school. If a child is spanked for either of these behaviors, the discipline creates fear rather than changing undesirable behavior. The other approaches to discipline that were discussed are more effective than physical punishment in teaching the desired behavior. Spanking usually creates hostility and anxiety in children. In many cases, physical punishment is physical abuse.

The parents who are most effective in helping their children learn self-discipline and self-control are those who do the following:

1. Set limits for their children
2. Are consistent in their actions
3. Are neither too strict nor too permissive
4. Discuss acceptable behavior with their children
5. Listen to their children and pay attention to their feelings

Child Abuse

Abuse is one characteristic of dysfunctional families. **Abuse** is harmful treatment. There are four kinds of abuse: physical, emotional, neglect, and sexual. **Physical abuse** is harmful treatment that physically injures a person. **Emotional abuse** is putting down another person and making the person feel worthless. **Neglect** is failure to provide proper care and guidance. **Sexual abuse** is sexual contact that is forced on a person.

Physical abuse is not the same as discipline. Physical abuse is harmful. Discipline is training. Suppose a parent, stepparent, or guardian slaps or kicks a child and says, "I'll teach you to follow my rules." Actions such as these are not appropriate forms of discipline. They are acts of violence. Physical abuse includes striking a child with a belt buckle, rope, or other object to inflict harm. Burning, bruising, cutting, or breaking bones on purpose also are forms of physical abuse. These actions are not methods of discipline. They do not develop self-control and self-discipline.

Emotional abuse may be difficult to recognize. Suppose a parent, stepparent, or guardian puts down a child. Perhaps the parent, stepparent, or guardian makes comments such as "You are worthless" or "You will never amount to anything." Comments like these make a child feel inadequate. They harm the child's self-respect and are considered abusive. Emotional abuse should not be confused with constructive criticism. Responsible adults also look at their other behaviors to determine if they are forms of emotional abuse. For example, suppose a parent, stepparent, or guardian pushes a child to excel in beauty pageants, athletics, or other activities without allowing the child to have a healthful, normal childhood. These actions are examples of harmful emotional abuse.

Sexual abuse is a topic that is very difficult for most people. The thought of a parent, stepparent, or guardian having sexual contact with a child is upsetting. However, both males and females can be abused by adult family members.

Sexual abuse often is a family secret. Family members might not talk about the abuse and might hide the abuse from people outside the family. There are different forms of sexual abuse. Incest is having sex with a family member. Many people believe incest and sexual abuse are synonymous, but acts other than incest can be considered sexual abuse. Showing young people pornographic pictures or taking pornographic pictures of them is sexual abuse. Inappropriate touching of body parts is sexual abuse. These actions are inappropriate behaviors.

Neglect covers a wide range of actions. There are laws that further define neglect. For example, children under a certain age must have adult supervision. If parents, stepparents, or guardians work, children must be in the care of a responsible adult—children cannot be left at home alone. If children are not supervised, parents, stepparents, or guardians are guilty of neglect. There are many other forms of neglect, such as not giving children adequate food or clothing or not obtaining for children the medical care they require.

Individuals can choose to be responsible parents. Every child deserves parents, stepparents, or guardians who love them and act lovingly toward them.

CYCLE OF ABUSE

Young people who have been abused are at risk for abusing others. The **cycle of abuse** is the repeating of abuse from one generation to the next. Young people who have been abused learned to interact with others in much the same way as their family members interact. They want to control others and they use wrong actions to do so. They practice the wrong actions they have learned. This is one reason why people who have been abused often need help before they are ready to have children. They need to sort through the confusion, secrecy, and wrong actions that occurred while they were growing up. Then the cycle of abuse can be stopped.

Health Goal #20

I Will Practice Abstinence from Sex to Avoid the Risks of Teen Marriage and Parenthood

Teen Pregnancy Is a Major Problem

According to the National Campaign to Prevent Teen Pregnancy (2002), the United States has one of the highest rates of teen pregnancy among industrialized nations. Four in ten girls become pregnant at least once before age twenty, accounting for more than 900,000 teen pregnancies annually. About 40 percent of pregnant teens are seventeen years of age or younger, and 79 percent of births to teen mothers are out of wedlock. There are nearly half a million teen births each year. Almost one-half of all teen mothers and more than three-quarters of unmarried teen mothers begin receiving welfare within five years of the birth of their first child. Teen mothers are likely to have a second birth relatively soon—about one-fourth of teen mothers have a second child within twenty-four months of the first birth—which can further impede their ability to finish school or keep a job and to escape poverty.

Risks Associated with Being a Baby Born to Teen Parents

A discussion of teen pregnancy and parenthood often begins with the risks to the teen mother and father. Instead, let's begin with the correct focus. A loving, caring, and responsible person considers the effects of his or her behavior on others. Teens are at risk for producing unhealthy babies.

- *Low birth weight*. A teen female's body is still developing and maturing. For proper growth, her body needs adequate rest and balanced nutrition. Many teen females do not have healthful habits. Because a developing baby relies on the mother-to-be for its nutrition, whatever the mother-to-be eats, smokes, or drinks gets into the baby's bloodstream. Even if a teen female changes her habits as soon as she knows she is pregnant, the developing baby already has relied on her until her pregnancy becomes known. This means the baby may have been inadequately nourished for six to eight weeks or more. Most pregnant teens delay getting prenatal care and many do not receive any prenatal care. As a result, teen mothers are at risk for having a baby with a low birth weight. A low birth weight is a weight at birth that is less than 5.5 pounds (2.5 kilograms). Low-birth-weight babies are more likely to have physical and mental problems than are babies of normal birth weight.
- *Damaged heredity material*. The health habits of a teen father-to-be also affect a developing baby. The habits of the father-to-be affect the quality of the hereditary material contained in his sperm. Some substances that can damage a male's sperm are related to poor lifestyle choices such as smoking, drinking alcohol, and taking other drugs. Lead, pesticides, benzene, and anesthetic gases also can damage sperm. Males who plan to be fathers should avoid these substances for at least three months prior to conception. Because most teen pregnancies are not planned, a teen female should understand that the habits of a father-to-be may seriously affect the quality of his sperm.
- *Inadequate parenting skills*. Parenting takes knowledge and skill. Babies born to teen parents are at risk of having parents with inadequate parenting skills. Every parent has a twenty-four-hour job caring for his or her child. However, a teen has responsibilities that include school, his or her social development, and other learning experiences. Having a baby in addition to those responsibilities can be overwhelming to a teen, and the baby can suffer as a result.

Risks Associated with Teen Parenthood

- *For females*. Pregnancy places many demands on a female's body. The demands on a female who is a teen are even greater because her body is still growing. A pregnant teen is at risk of developing anemia and toxemia of pregnancy. **Anemia** is a condition in which the oxygen-carrying material in the blood is below normal. If the pregnant teen is anemic, the developing baby will be seriously affected because the baby depends on the mother's blood for oxygen and nutrients. **Toxemia of pregnancy** is a disorder of pregnancy characterized by high blood pressure, tissue swelling, and protein in the urine. If severe, toxemia of pregnancy can progress to seizures and coma. Pregnant teens and teen mothers are at risk in other ways. Pregnancy and parenthood disrupt education and career plans. Dating opportunities are limited for an unmarried teen raising a child. She does not have as much time or money as her peers. Males, other than the baby's father, may not want to get involved with someone who has a baby.
- *For males*. Teen fathers have the responsibility of providing for the care of their babies. Some states have passed laws that require teen fathers to pay child support until their child is eighteen Many teen fathers drop out of school to earn money to provide child support. They are less likely to graduate from high school or college than their peers who did not become fathers when they were teens. Teen fathers usually do not marry the mother of their children. If they do marry the mother of their child, they often divorce within five years. As a result, teens who become fathers often spend only a small amount of time with their children about once a week. Children do not thrive as well when there is a lack of contact with their father. Fathers also can feel the emptiness of not being close to their children.

Faulty Thinking and Teen Pregnancy

Faulty thinking is a thought process in which a person ignores or denies information. Faulty thinking is dangerous. It can lead to actions that cause harm. It is a factor in teen pregnancy and parenthood. The following are examples of faulty thinking that can lead to teen pregnancy.

- *Faulty thinking: I can have a baby now; my mother had a baby when she was a teen and she managed okay.* The **generational cycle of teen pregnancy** occurs when a teen whose mother was a teen parent becomes pregnant. Only 70 percent of teen females who have babies finish high school, and the likelihood that any of these teen females will get a higher education is slim. As a result, the downward cycle of low income and poverty begins for a teen mother and her baby. She is less likely to marry or stay married to the baby's father than is a woman who has her first baby in her twenties. By the time her baby is five years old, a teen mother is less likely to own a home or have savings in the bank than a female who waits to have a baby. The cycle of low income and poverty is too often perpetuated as a teen mother raises a child in poverty who becomes a teen mother.

- *Faulty thinking: I'll be the center of attention if I have a baby.* Unmarried actresses who have babies often receive a lot of publicity. From this exposure, teens can get the idea that being a parent is fun and easy without stopping to think that these actresses may have full-time nannies, cooks, and housekeepers that care for their needs and the needs of their babies. Teens also can have this faulty thinking when they observe people making a fuss over another teenager's baby. They don't stop to consider what the teen mother's life is like most of the time.
- *Faulty thinking: I (she) won't get pregnant if it's our first time.* One out of ten females becomes pregnant before the age of twenty. Few of these females planned on getting pregnant. A female can become pregnant the first time she has sex. She can become pregnant even if she is being careful. She can become pregnant even if her partner says he is being careful.
- *Faulty thinking: I can drink alcohol and still stay in control of my decisions about sex.* Alcohol is a depressant drug that numbs the part of the brain that controls reasoning and judgment. Many teens who are sexually active were drinking alcohol the first time they had sex. They didn't plan to have sex.
- *Faulty thinking: It's up to her to set the limits; after all, "boys will be boys."* Although the female carries the unborn child, the male also is responsible for the pregnancy. The male and female are legally and morally responsible for the baby when it is born. A teen male must recognize the significance of fatherhood, set limits, and take responsibility. A teen male is not ready to provide the emotional and financial support that a mother and baby need.

Optional Health Goal

I Will Learn Facts about Birth Control Methods

A Word from the Authors

Teachers should learn the guidelines for teaching facts about birth control methods from their state departments of education and from their local school districts. Some state departments of education and some school districts require that facts about birth control methods be taught in middle school and high school. It is our recommendation that teachers who teach facts about birth control methods convey the following message to their students: Knowing facts about birth control methods helps teens prepare for adulthood when they might choose to marry and plan a family. Practicing abstinence is the expected standard for teens. Practicing abstinence reduces the risk of infection with HIV and other STDs and prevents pregnancy. The following content on this optional health goal is intended for teachers to educate them on facts about birth control methods. It is the teachers' responsibility to stay informed about the latest medical research on birth control methods if state and local guidelines call for teaching this information.

Facts about Birth Control Methods

Birth control methods are ways to alter the conditions necessary for conception or pregnancy to occur. Birth control methods might involve chemical, physical, or surgical methods of preventing fertilization or implantation of an ovum. Table 6-2, Facts to Know about a Birth Control Method, lists and describes what facts might be included in a discussion of birth control methods. Table 6-3, Facts about Birth Control Methods, identifies different birth control methods and provides facts about each. It does not include instructions for correct use. This information might be obtained from a current publication produced by the federal government. State and local guidelines determine the extent to which instructions for correct use of various birth control methods are discussed in health education classes. Note that the theoretical and actual user effectiveness percentages included in Table 6-3 are

for adult users. Facts pertaining to actual user effectiveness for teens are not available. Table 6-3 does not include information on who should not use these methods and the cost for each. Again, state and local guidelines determine the extent to which these facts are discussed in health education classes.

TABLE 6-2

FACTS TO KNOW ABOUT A BIRTH CONTROL METHOD

How it works: The way the birth control method works to prevent pregnancy.

Effectiveness: How well the birth control method works for adult users stated as a percentage.

- **Theoretical effectiveness:** The percentage that tells how well the birth control method works for adult users if it is used every time, always used in the correct way, and used by adults who have no preexisting conditions that reduce how well it works.

- **Actual user effectiveness:** The percentage that tells how well the birth control method works for most adult users; this percentage takes into consideration adults who do not use it every time, adults who do not use it in the correct way, and adults who have conditions that reduce how well it works.

Other benefits from consistent use: Benefits the users get from the birth control method that are in addition to it being used to prevent pregnancy.

Side effects: Unwanted changes, including health risks, that might occur when the birth control method is used.

FACTS ABOUT BIRTH CONTROL METHODS

TABLE 6-3

BIRTH CONTROL METHOD	HOW IT WORKS	EFFECTIVENESS	OTHER BENEFITS FROM CONSISTENT USE	SIDE EFFECTS
Abstinence from sex is voluntarily choosing not to be sexually active.	Choosing abstinence from sex until marriage is the expected standard for adolescents. Choosing abstinence from sex follows the *Responsible Decision-Making Model.* The **Responsible Decision-Making Model** is a series of steps a person can follow to assure that her or his decisions lead to actions that promote health, protect safety, follow laws, show respect for self and others, follow guidelines set by responsible adults, and demonstrate good character.	Abstinence from sex is the only birth control method that is 100% effective.	Health Goal #16 in this chapter lists several benefits that come from practicing abstinence.	There are no side effects.
The **combination pill** is a pill that combines estrogen and progestin to change the natural menstrual cycle and to prevent ovulation. The combination pill differs from the progestin-only pill, or mini-pill, in that it contains estrogen. A female will resume her natural menstrual cycle	The combination pill changes the natural menstrual cycle in several ways. It decreases the amount of follicle stimulating hormone (FSH) that is secreted. FSH is needed for ovulation to occur. Thus, the combination pill helps prevent ovulation. The combination pill also	The theoretical effectiveness for adult users of the combination pill is 99%–100%. The actual user effectiveness for adults is 97%–98%. The actual user effectiveness for adults is lower because some females forget to take their pills or do not take them according to the directions.	Females who take combination pills might experience a regular twenty-eight-day menstrual cycle, reduced menstrual flow, less chance of having anemia, fewer menstrual cramps and less pain, reduced incidence of ovarian cysts, reduced chance of endometriosis, reduced	Females might experience the following side effects: nausea and vomiting; headaches; weight gain and fluid retention; spotting or bleeding between menstrual periods; vaginitis; recurring yeast infections; vaginal discharge; nervousness; depression; mood changes; fatigue;

if she stops taking the combination pill. **Progestin** is the synthetic form of the hormone progesterone.	changes the uterine lining, making it difficult for a fertilized ovum to implant in the uterine lining. It thickens cervical mucus, which makes it difficult for sperm to move through the cervix into the uterus.		risk of uterine and ovarian cancer, and reduced risk of pelvic inflammatory disease (PID).	dizziness; decreased sex drive; darkening of the skin on the upper lip, under the eyes, on the chin, or on the forehead; and changes in vision. Females who smoke are at increased risk for having circulatory diseases and strokes. Females who have gallbladder problems might have additional side effects. To date, there is no evidence that combination pills cause cancer. A female should contact her physician if she has side effects.
The **progestin-only pill**, or **mini-pill**, is a pill that contains progestin, which changes the natural menstrual cycle and prevents ovulation. The progestin-only pill differs from the combination pill in that it contains only a small dose of progestin and no estrogen. A female will resume her normal menstrual cycle if she stops taking the progestin-only pill.	The progestin-only pill changes the natural menstrual cycle in several ways. It decreases the amount of FSH that is secreted. FSH is needed for ovulation to occur. Thus, the progestin-only pill helps prevent ovulation. It changes the uterine lining, making it difficult for a fertilized ovum to implant in the uterine lining. The progestin-only pill also thickens cervical mucus, which makes it difficult for sperm to move through the cervix in the uterus.	The theoretical effectiveness for adult users of the progestin-only pill is greater than 99%. The actual user effectiveness for adults is lower because some females forget to take one or more pills or might not take pills according to the directions. Vomiting, diarrhea, and antibiotic use also lower actual user effectiveness for adults. The actual user effectiveness for adults is slightly lower during the use of the first three to six pill packs.	Females who take progestin-only pills might experience a reduced menstrual flow, fewer menstrual cramps and less pain, reduced risk of uterine and ovarian cancers, and reduced risk of PID.	The changes in the natural menstrual cycle might result in very irregular menstrual periods. Some females will have no menstrual periods at all. More females stop taking the progestin-only pill than stop taking the combination pill because their menstrual periods are very irregular. A female should contact her physician if she has side effects.

continued

BIRTH CONTROL METHOD	HOW IT WORKS	EFFECTIVENESS	OTHER BENEFITS FROM CONSISTENT USE	SIDE EFFECTS
Injectable progestin is a shot of synthetic progesterone that is given every three months to change the natural menstrual cycle and to prevent ovulation.	Injectable progestin changes the natural menstrual cycle in several ways. It decreases the amount of FSH that is secreted. FSH is needed for ovulation to occur. Thus, injectable progestin helps prevent ovulation. Injectable progestin also changes the uterine lining, making it difficult for a fertilized ovum to implant in the uterine lining. Injectable progestin also thickens the cervical mucus, which makes it difficult for sperm to move through the cervix into the uterus.	The theoretical effectiveness for adult users of injectable progestin is greater than 99%. The actual user effectiveness for adults is 99%.	Females who are on injectable progestin might experience a reduced menstrual flow, fewer menstrual cramps and less pain, reduced risk of uterine and ovarian cancers, and reduced risk of PID.	The changes in the natural menstrual cycle might result in very irregular menstrual periods. Some females will have no menstrual periods at all.
Plan B is an emergency contraceptive measure that can be taken up to three days (seventy-two hours) after unprotected sex. **Emergency contraception** is a method of preventing pregnancy after a contraceptive fails or after unprotected sex. It is not for routine use; it is a backup method to birth control. It is available without a prescription for females eighteen and older or with a prescription for	Two pills are taken: the first as soon as possible (within seventy-two hours of unprotected sex), and the second twelve hours after the first. The pills contain a large dose of the hormone levonorgestrel, which prevents the release of an egg from the ovary. It also may prevent fertilization of an egg and its implantation in the uterus, which usually occurs seven days or more after release of an egg	The risk of pregnancy can be reduced by up to 89%. Plan B is not meant to be used consistently as a birth control method.	Plan B should not be used consistently; it should be used only for infrequent, emergency protection.	There are no major side effects associated with Plan B. Some females may experience their next period earlier or later than usual or may experience other minor side effects commonly associated with birth control pills (nausea, dizziness, breast tenderness, stomach pain, or headache). Plan B pills contain higher levels of the hormone levonorgestrel than do

Method	How It Works	Effectiveness	Benefits	Side Effects
females seventeen and younger.	from the ovary. Plan B will not do anything to a fertilized egg already attached to the uterus. The pregnancy will continue.			daily oral hormonal contraceptives.
The transdermal contraceptive patch, or **Ortho Evra,** is a skin patch applied to the lower abdomen, buttocks, or upper body that slowly releases progestin and estrogen into the bloodstream to prevent pregnancy. A new patch is put on once a week for three weeks; then the patch is not worn during the fourth week in order for a female to have a menstrual period.	The transdermal contraceptive patch changes the natural menstrual cycle in several ways. It decreases the amount of FSH that is secreted. FSH is needed for ovulation to occur. Thus, the transdermal patch helps prevent ovulation. The transdermal patch also changes the uterine lining, making it difficult for a fertilized ovum to implant in the uterine lining. The transdermal patch also thickens cervical mucus, which makes it difficult for sperm to move through the cervix into the uterus.	The effectiveness of the transdermal contraceptive patch is similar to that for the combination pill. The theoretical effectiveness for adult users of transdermal contraceptive patch is 99%. The actual user effectiveness is lower because some females forget to apply the patch or fail to apply it as directed. The patch is less effective in females who weigh more than 198 pounds.	The benefits of the transdermal patch are similar to those for the combination pill because of the estrogen and progestin that is released. Less frequent dosing is required in comparison to taking the combination pill. Females who use the transdermal patch might experience a regular twenty-eight-day menstrual flow, less chance of having anemia, fewer menstrual cramps and less pain, reduced incidence of ovarian cysts, reduced chance of endometriosis, reduced risk of uterine and ovarian cancer, and reduced risk of PID.	The side effects of the transdermal patch are similar to those for the combined birth control pill. Users may experience skin reactions where the patch is applied.
The vaginal contraceptive ring, or **NuvaRing,** is a flexible ring about two inches in diameter that is inserted into the vagina where it remains for three weeks releasing progestin and estrogen to prevent pregnancy. A new ring	The vaginal contraceptive ring changes the natural menstrual cycle in several ways. It decreases the amount of FSH that is secreted. FSH is needed for ovulation to occur. Thus, the vaginal contraceptive ring helps prevent ovulation. The	The effectiveness of the vaginal contraceptive ring is similar to that for the combination pill. The theoretical effectiveness for adult users of the vaginal contraceptive ring is 99%. The actual user effectiveness is lower because some females	The vaginal contraceptive ring is easy to insert and needs to be inserted only once a month. The benefits of the vaginal contraceptive ring are similar to those for the combination pill because of the estrogen and progestin that is released.	The side effects of the vaginal contraceptive ring are similar to those for the combined birth control pill. It may also cause vaginal irritation, vaginal discharge, or headache.

continued

BIRTH CONTROL METHOD	HOW IT WORKS	EFFECTIVENESS	OTHER BENEFITS FROM CONSISTENT USE	SIDE EFFECTS
must be inserted each month. The ring is self-inserted, so a female does not need to rely on a health care professional to insert it. The ring is removed for menstruation and is replaced when menstruation is completed.	vaginal contraceptive ring also changes the uterine lining, making it difficult for a fertilized ovum to implant in the uterine lining. The vaginal contraceptive ring also thickens cervical mucus, which makes it difficult for sperm to move through the cervix into the uterus.	may fail to reinsert a new ring each month or fail to apply it as directed. A female should use a backup method of contraception for the first week of use, because the ring is not effective until after seven days of continuous use (unless already using oral contraceptives or another hormonal method). The effectiveness of a vaginal ring may be lowered when taken with certain medications, including antibiotics and anti-seizure, tuberculosis, and migraine medications.	Less frequent dosing is required in comparison to taking the combination pill. Females who use the vaginal contraceptive ring might experience a regular twenty-eight-day menstrual cycle, reduced menstrual flow, less chance of having anemia, fewer menstrual cramps and less pain, reduced incidence of ovarian cysts, reduced chance of endometriosis, reduced risk of uterine and ovarian cancer, and reduced risk of PID.	
The **diaphragm** is a dome-shaped cup that fits over the cervix to help prevent sperm from entering a uterus. It is made of soft rubber or latex and has a flexible, semirigid rim. A spermicide always should be used with the diaphragm.	The diaphragm provides a barrier that reduces the risk that sperm will enter the uterus and move into the fallopian tubes. If the barrier is effective, sperm cannot reach the ovum and fertilize it. The spermicide that is used with the diaphragm also forms a barrier. It contains a chemical that might kill some sperm. The spermicide provides additional protection if the diaphragm is inserted incorrectly or becomes	The theoretical effectiveness for adult users of the diaphragm with spermicide is 94%. The actual user effectiveness for adults is approximately 80%. The actual user effectiveness for adults is lower because some females who use a diaphragm do not use it every time, do not insert it properly, do not use additional spermicide when necessary, or remove the diaphragm too soon. The diaphragm also might	There are no other benefits from correct use.	A female whose diaphragm is too large might experience cramping and pain. A female whose diaphragm is too small might have difficulty removing it. Some females have higher incidences of urinary tract infections from using the diaphragm. A female should contact her physician if she has these side effects. Some males and females are allergic to the materials from which the diaphragm is made.

Method	How It Works	Effectiveness	Other Benefits	Side Effects
	dislodged during sexual intercourse. This is why the diaphragm always should be used with a spermicide.			Some males and females are allergic to the substances in spermicide. They might experience irritation. Some females might experience burning.
The **cervical cap** is a rubber or plastic dome that fits snugly over the cervix to provide a barrier to help prevent sperm from entering the uterus. A spermicide should be used with the cervical cap.	The cervical cap relies on suction to fit snugly over the cervix. It provides a barrier that reduces the risk that sperm will enter the uterus and move into the fallopian tubes. If the barrier is effective, sperm cannot reach the ovum and fertilize it. The spermicide that is used with the cervical cap also forms a barrier. It contains a chemical that might kill some sperm. The spermicide provides additional protection if the cervical cap is inserted incorrectly or becomes dislodged during sexual intercourse. This is why the cervical cap always should be used with a spermicide.	The theoretical effectiveness for adult users of the cervical cap with spermicide is 74–91%. The actual user effectiveness for adults is approximately 60–80%. This is because the cervical cap might become dislodged during sexual intercourse.	There are no other benefits from correct use.	Although rare, the cervical cap may irritate or cause ulcers to form on the cervix. A female should contact her physician if she has these side effects. Some males and females are allergic to the material from which the cervical cap is made. Some males and females are allergic to the substances in spermicide. They might experience irritation. Some females might experience burning.
A **spermicide** is a foam, cream, jelly, film, or suppository that forms a barrier and contains a chemical that might kill some sperm.	Spermicides form a barrier to reduce the risk that sperm will enter the uterus and move into the fallopian tubes. If the barrier is effective, sperm cannot reach the ovum and fertilize it. Foams, creams, and jellies work in the same way. An	The theoretical effectiveness for adults users of spermicide is 94%. The actual user effectiveness for adults is 74%. Spermicide used by itself is not an effective birth control method.	According to the CDC Division of STD Prevention, to date there is no evidence that spermicides provide protection against infection with STDs, including HIV.	Some males and females are allergic to the substances in spermicide. They might experience irritation. Some females experience burning, especially with the use of suppositories.

continued

BIRTH CONTROL METHOD	HOW IT WORKS	EFFECTIVENESS	OTHER BENEFITS FROM CONSISTENT USE	SIDE EFFECTS
	applicator inserts these spermicides deep into the vagina near the cervix. Some suppositories froth and form a thick barrier to sperm. Other suppositories and film simply melt and form a barrier.			
The **male condom** is a thin sheath of latex, natural skin, or polyurethane that is placed over the erect penis to collect semen during ejaculation. The male condom is also called a rubber or prophylactic. A spermicide always should be used with the male condom. Other than abstinence from sex, the use of a male latex condom with a spermicide is the most effective way to reduce the risk of sexual transmission of pathogens that cause some STDs, including HIV.	When used properly, the male condom collects semen from ejaculate. It provides a barrier that reduces the risk that sperm will be ejaculated into the vagina. If no sperm enter the vagina, sperm cannot enter the uterus and move to the fallopian tubes. Sperm cannot reach an ovum and fertilize it. The spermicide that is used with the male condom also forms a barrier. It contains a chemical that might kill some sperm. The spermicide provides additional protection if the male condom slips off, breaks, or is removed incorrectly and sperm gets into the vagina. This is why the male condom always should be used with spermicide.	The theoretical effectiveness for adult users of the male condom with a spermicide is 97%. Actual user effectiveness for adults is 86%. These effectiveness ratings are for reducing the risk of conception *not reducing the risk of transmission of pathogens that cause some STDs, including HIV.*	The correct use of the male condom with a spermicide reduces the risk of sexual transmission of pathogens that cause some STDs, including HIV. However, *the male condom with spermicide is not 100% effective in reducing the risk of transmission of pathogens that cause some STDs, including HIV.*	Some males and females are allergic to the materials from which the male condom is made. These materials might cause irritation or allergic reaction. Some males think the use of a condom reduces sensitivity. There is no scientific data to prove this belief. Some males and females are allergic to the substances in spermicides. They might experience burning.

The **female condom** is a soft, polyurethane pouch that is inserted deep into the vagina to collect semen during ejaculation. It is about seven inches long and has flexible rings at both ends. The female condom should always be used with a spermicide. The use of a female condom with a spermicide reduces the risk of sexual transmission of pathogens that cause some STDs, including HIV. However, the female condom with a spermicide is not as effective as the male condom with a spermicide in reducing the risk of sexual transmission of pathogens that cause some STDs, including HIV.	When used properly, the female condom fits loosely inside the vagina and collects semen from the ejaculate. It provides a barrier that reduces the risk that sperm will be ejaculated into the vagina. If no sperm enter the vagina, sperm cannot enter the uterus and fertilize the ovum. The spermicide that is used with the female condom also forms a barrier. It contains a chemical that might kill some sperm. The spermicide provides additional protection if the female condom slips out of place, breaks, or is removed incorrectly and sperm get into the vagina. This is why the female condom should always be used with a spermicide.	The theoretical effectiveness for adult users of the female condom is 95%. These effectiveness ratings are for reducing the risk of conception *not reducing the risk of transmission of pathogens that cause some STDs, including HIV.* The female condom is more difficult to use than the male condom. This is why there is a greater chance of incorrect use.	The correct use of the female condom with a spermicide reduces the risk of sexual transmission of pathogens that cause some STDs, including HIV. However, *the female condom with spermicide is not 100% effective in reducing the risk of transmission of pathogens that cause some STDs, including HIV.*	Some males and females are allergic to polyurethane. This material might cause irritation or allergic reaction. Some males and females are allergic to the substances in spermicides. Some females might experience burning.
The **intrauterine device (IUD)** is a small device that fits inside the uterus and helps prevent pregnancy. Currently, there are two IUDs approved for use by the Food and Drug Administration (FDA): the progestin-releasing IUDs and the Copper T IUD. IUDs are placed inside the uterus by a health care professional.	The IUD is believed to work in a variety of ways. The IUD might help prevent the movement of sperm. The sperm are not able to move through the cervix, into the uterus and fallopian tubes. The IUD might increase the speed at which an ovum moves down a fallopian tube. This shortens the amount of time that the ovum is in the fallopian	The theoretical effectiveness for adult users of the IUD is 98%–99%. The actual user effectiveness for adults might be influenced by the type of IUD, the presence of copper or progestin, the ages and number of children of the female, and the correct position of the IUD.	The progestin-releasing IUD decreases menstrual flow and reduces menstrual cramps.	Pelvic infections sometimes occur during the first three weeks following insertion. These infections need immediate treatment. Symptoms of pelvic infection include a high temperature, tenderness in the pubic area, and a discharge from the cervix. Females who use the Copper T IUD might have increased menstrual flow, spotting,

continued

BIRTH CONTROL METHOD	HOW IT WORKS	EFFECTIVENESS	OTHER BENEFITS FROM CONSISTENT USE	SIDE EFFECTS
	tube. In turn, this shortens the time in which fertilization can take place. These are ways the IUD helps prevent conception. The IUD also might help prevent implantation. The IUD might cause changes in the lining of the uterus, making it difficult for a fertilized ovum to implant itself in the uterine lining. One of the IUDs approved for use releases progestin. Progestin alters the normal menstrual cycle, further adding to the effectiveness of the IUD. The other IUD approved for use, the Copper T, contains copper. The copper is toxic to sperm and might kill some sperm.			and menstrual cramps. These side effects are most noticeable during the first three months after insertion. Severe pain and bleeding might be signs that the IUD has been expelled. A female should contact her physician if she has these side effects.
The **basal body temperature method** is a birth control method in which a female uses her basal body temperature (BBT) to predict ovulation. The BBT is the temperature of a healthy person upon waking after at least three hours of sleep. A BBT thermometer can be	The BBT method is based on a slight rise in temperature (0.4°F–0.8°F) shortly before, during, and right after ovulation. The slight rise in the BBT is caused by the secretion of the hormone progesterone. The BBT remains slightly higher until a female begins	The theoretical effectiveness for adult users of the BBT method is 98%. The actual user effectiveness for adults is lower because of stress, illness, drug use, or other factors that might affect the BBT.	A female who keeps a record of her BBT has important information about her menstrual cycle. She will know approximately when she ovulates. She will know how to recognize her fertile period when she and her husband want to conceive. A fertile period	There are no side effects.

purchased at a pharmacy without a prescription.	her menstrual period. A female practices abstinence from sex from the first day of menstrual bleeding until her BBT has been elevated for three consecutive mornings.		is the days in a female's menstrual cycle during which sexual intercourse can lead to conception.	There are no side effects.
The **calendar method** is a birth control method in which a female records the length of her menstrual cycle on a calendar to predict her fertile period. A **fertile period** is the days in a female's menstrual cycle during which sexual intercourse can lead to conception.	The calendar method helps a female predict the days in her menstrual cycle when she might conceive if she has sexual intercourse. A female follows specific instructions to calculate her fertile period so she will know which days are unsafe for her to have sexual intercourse. Abstinence from sex must be practiced or backup birth control methods must be used during the predicted fertile period.	The theoretical effectiveness for adult users of the calendar method is 85% if a female has regular menstrual periods and abstains from sexual intercourse on all days of her predicted fertile period. The actual user effectiveness for adults is closer to 65%. This lower effectiveness rate is due to females having irregular menstrual cycles. Also, many females take risks and actually do not abstain from sexual intercourse on all the days of their predicted fertile period.	A female who uses the calendar method has important information for her physician. She will have a calendar that shows when she began and ended her last eight menstrual periods. She will know the length of her menstrual periods for at least eight months. She will know how to predict her fertile period when she and her husband want to conceive.	
Sterilization is any procedure by which an individual is made permanently incapable of reproduction. **Tubal ligation** is a method of female surgical sterilization that includes the use of clips, rings, and cauterization to	Tubal ligation ("tying the tubes") blocks the fallopian tubes so there is no way for a mature ovum to move through the tube to the uterus. This reduces the risk of a sperm and an ovum uniting. Vasectomy blocks the passage of	The theoretical effectiveness for adults who have had a sterilization procedure is 99%–99.5%. The actual effectiveness is about 99%. Tubal ligation is immediately effective, although for absolute effectiveness, a backup	Sterilization is a highly effective, permanent, and one-time expense. These procedures appear to be safe; however, more research is ne eded on the safety of Essure. Sterilization does not affect hormones or the menstrual cycle.	Females having tubal ligation may experience some pain for a short time after the surgery at the site of the incision. About 2% of females may experience minor complications, including bleeding, fever, abdominal pain, or infection. A male

continued

BIRTH CONTROL METHOD	HOW IT WORKS	EFFECTIVENESS	OTHER BENEFITS FROM CONSISTENT USE	SIDE EFFECTS
block the fallopian tubes. **Vasectomy** is a method of male sterilization in which the vas deferens is resected (cut off) and tied. A newer method of sterilization is the Essure Permanent Birth Control System, which is the first nonsurgical alternative and was approved by the Food and Drug Administration in November 2002.	sperm through the vas deferens, so that sperm is prevented from entering a male's ejaculate. In the Essure Permanent Birth Control Method, a thin tube is used to thread a tiny springlike device through the vagina and uterus into each fallopian tube. The device, which remains in the tube, irritates the tube's lining, causing scar tissue to form and eventually plugging the tube. It takes about three months for the scar tissue to grow.	method should be used until the first menstrual cycle. Failure may occur if the tubes rejoin or if there is surgical error. Vasectomy failure can also occur if there is surgical error. Early studies of the Essure Permanent Birth Control System show that it is extremely effective in preventing pregnancy in females whose Essure devices were implanted successfully.		may experience some swelling and pain in the area of the scrotum for a few days following a vasectomy. These methods are irreversible and are inappropriate for individuals who may wish to have more children.

Sources: Nemours Foundation; Food and Drug Administration; Consumer Reports.

CHAPTER SEVEN

Growth and Development

HEALTH GOALS FOR GROWTH AND DEVELOPMENT

21. I will keep my body systems healthy.
22. I will recognize habits that protect female reproductive health.
23. I will recognize habits that protect male reproductive health.
24. I will learn about pregnancy and childbirth.
25. I will learn about the growth and development of infants and children.
26. I will provide responsible care for infants and children.
27. I will develop my learning style.
28. I will achieve the developmental tasks of adolescence.
29. I will develop habits that promote healthful aging.
30. I will share with my family my feelings about dying and death.

Growth and development is the area of health that focuses on keeping body systems healthy, recognizing habits that protect female reproductive health, recognizing habits that protect male reproductive health, learning about pregnancy and childbirth, learning about the growth and development of infants and children, providing responsible care for infants and children, developing a learning style, achieving the developmental tasks of adolescence, developing habits that promote healthful aging, and sharing with one's family one's feelings about dying and death. This chapter provides the health information that is needed to teach young people important life skills for growth and development.

Health Goal #21
I Will Keep My Body Systems Healthy

The human body is a marvelous machine, and much can be done to keep it functioning in healthful ways. The body is made of cells, tissues, and organs that form body systems. A **cell** is the smallest living part of the body. A **tissue** is a group of similar cells that work together. An **organ** is a body part consisting of several kinds of tissue that do a particular job. A **body system** is a group of organs that work together to perform a main body function.

People can help their bodies perform at their best by learning about the human body and by knowing how to take care of it. For a person's body to achieve the best possible performance, the body systems must work at their highest levels. It is important to understand that the body functions as a result of all body systems working together.

Nervous System

The **nervous system** carries messages to and from the brain and spinal cord and all other parts of the body. The nervous system is composed of two divisions: the central nervous system and the peripheral nervous system.

The **central nervous system** consists of the brain and spinal cord. The **peripheral nervous system** consists of the nerves that branch out from the central nervous system to the muscles, skin, internal organs, and glands. The sense organs continually send messages—such as odors, sights, or tastes—to the brain through the peripheral nervous system. These messages go to the central nervous system. The central nervous system in turn relays responses to these messages

to the muscles and glands as the body responds to changes in the environment.

BRAIN

The Society for Neuroscience (2006) describes the human brain as the most complex living structure known in the universe.

The **brain** is a mass of nerve tissue that acts as the control center of the body. The human brain weighs about three pounds (1.35 kilograms) and can store more information than all the libraries in the world put together. The brain creates ideas and controls thinking, reasoning, movement, and emotions. The brain has three major parts: the cerebrum, the cerebellum, and the brain stem.

The **cerebrum** is the largest part of the brain and controls the ability to memorize, think, and learn. The cerebrum also determines a person's intelligence and personality. It consists of two halves, called hemispheres, divided by a deep groove. The right hemisphere controls the left side of the body and the left hemisphere controls the right side of the body. The **cerebellum** is the part of the brain that controls and coordinates muscle activity. It also helps maintain balance. The ability to catch a ball is a function of the cerebellum. The **brain stem** is the part of the brain that controls the functions of the internal organs.

SPINAL CORD

The **spinal cord** is a thick column of nerve cells that extends from the brain down through the spinal column. The spinal cord carries messages between the brain and the body. It keeps the brain informed of changes in the body and in the environment, often creating changes in movement and organ function. The spinal cord is protected by the backbone.

NERVE CELLS

The nervous system is composed of cells called neurons. A **neuron** is a nerve cell that is the structural and functional unit of the nervous system. Some neurons in the spinal cord may be several feet long. A neuron consists of a cell body, an axon, and dendrites. A cell body is the main body of the neuron. An **axon** is an elongated fiber that carries impulses away from the cell body to the dendrites of another neuron. Dendrites are branching fibers that receive impulses and carry them to the cell body.

Sensory and motor neurons work together to help an individual respond to the environment. Sensory neurons carry impulses from the sense organs to the spinal cord and brain. Motor neurons carry responding impulses to muscles and glands from the brain and spinal cord. Motor neurons tell muscles and glands what to do.

REFLEX ACTION

When a person touches something hot and instantly pulls away from it, the person is experiencing a reflex action. A **reflex action** is an involuntary action in which a message is sent to the brain via the spinal cord, is interpreted, and is responded to immediately. Sensory neurons carry a message to the spinal cord and brain. The brain interprets the message. Motor neurons carry the message back to the muscles, which move the hand quickly away from the hot surface. Reflex actions do not involve conscious thought and take only a fraction of a second. Reflex actions help keep people safe.

Cardiovascular System

The **cardiovascular system** transports nutrients, gases, hormones, and cellular waste products throughout the body. The cardiovascular system consists of the blood, blood vessels, and heart.

BLOOD

The blood carries nutrients, oxygen, carbon dioxide, and cellular waste products to and from cells. The average-size adult has about ten pints (4.7 liters) of blood. Blood is composed of plasma and blood cells. **Plasma** is the liquid component of blood that carries blood cells and dissolved materials. It is about 95 percent water. Plasma contains two major types of blood cells: red blood cells and white blood cells. **Red blood cells** transport oxygen to body cells and remove carbon dioxide from body cells. Red blood cells contain large quantities of hemoglobin. **Hemoglobin** is an iron-rich protein that helps transport oxygen and carbon dioxide in the blood. New red blood cells are constantly produced in bone marrow, which is the spongy interior of some bones. **White blood cells** attack, surround, and destroy **pathogens** that enter the body and prevent them from causing infection. A pathogen is a germ that causes disease. The number of white blood cells in the blood increases when a person has an infection.

White blood cells are discussed in more detail in the section on the immune system. Plasma also consists of particles called platelets. A **platelet** is a particle that helps the blood clot. Blood clots stop the bleeding when blood vessels are injured.

BLOOD VESSELS

There are three major types of blood vessels: arteries, veins, and capillaries. An **artery** is a blood vessel that carries blood away from the heart. Arteries have thick muscular walls that move the blood between heartbeats. A **vein** is a blood vessel that returns blood to the heart. Veins have thinner walls than arteries. A **capillary** is a tiny blood vessel that connects arteries and veins. Capillaries have thin walls that allow the transfer of nutrients, oxygen, carbon dioxide, and cellular waste between the blood and the body cells.

A **coronary artery** is a blood vessel that carries blood to the heart muscles. Coronary arteries supply the heart with food and oxygen. A **pulmonary artery** is a blood vessel that carries blood from the heart to the lungs to pick up oxygen and release carbon dioxide.

HEART

The **heart** is a four-chambered muscle that pumps blood throughout the body. The chambers are called atria and ventricles. An **atrium** is one of the upper two chambers of the heart. A **ventricle** is one of the lower two chambers of the heart. The heart is divided into the right atrium, right ventricle, left atrium, and left ventricle. Blood returning from the body flows constantly into the right atrium and into the right ventricle.

A **vena cava** is one of two large veins that returns blood rich in carbon dioxide to the right atrium. Carbon dioxide is a waste product of body cells. This blood flows from the right atrium into the right ventricle. From the right ventricle, the blood is pumped through the pulmonary arteries to the lungs, where carbon dioxide is released and oxygen is absorbed as the blood circulates in capillaries around the air sacs in the lungs. This oxygen-rich blood returns in pulmonary veins to the left atrium and flows into the left ventricle. Contractions of the heart muscle pump the blood through the aorta to the body. The **aorta** is the main artery in the body. The aorta branches into smaller arteries through which blood flows to all parts of the body.

Heart rate is the number of times the heart contracts each minute. **Pulse** is the surge of blood that results from the contractions of the heart. **Blood pressure** is the force of blood against the artery walls.

Immune System

The **immune system** removes harmful organisms from the blood and combats pathogens. The immune system is composed of lymph, lymph nodes, lymph vessels, tonsils, thymus, and spleen. The immune system protects the body from pathogens, germs that cause disease. When white blood cells attack pathogens, the pathogens are filtered into the lymph. **Lymph** is a clear liquid that surrounds body cells and circulates in lymph vessels. Lymph carries harmful pathogens and other small particles to lymph nodes. A **lymph node** is a structure that filters and destroys pathogens. Pathogens also are removed by the spleen. The **spleen** is an organ on the left side of the abdomen that filters foreign matter from the blood and lymph.

The immune system plays an important role in immunity. **Immunity** is the body's resistance to disease-causing agents. An **antibody** is a special protein that helps fight infection. The **thymus gland** is a gland that causes white blood cells to become T cells. A **T cell** is a white blood cell that destroys pathogens. A **B cell** is a white blood cell that produces antibodies. Antibodies cover the surface of pathogens and make it difficult for them to attack the body.

Respiratory System

The **respiratory system** provides body cells with oxygen and removes carbon dioxide that cells produce as waste. Air enters the respiratory system through the nose or mouth during inhalation. Mucus in the nasal passages and sinuses warms and moistens the air and traps dust particles and pathogens. **Mucus** is a thick secretion that moistens, lubricates, and protects mucous membranes. A **mucous membrane** is a type of tissue that lines body cavities and secretes mucus.

Air moves from the nose or mouth through the pharynx to the trachea. The **pharynx** is the throat. The **epiglottis** is a flap that covers the entrance to the trachea when a person swallows foods or beverages. During inhalation, the epiglottis opens and air flows into the trachea. The **trachea** is a tube through which air moves to the lungs. The trachea is sometimes called the windpipe. The trachea is lined with cilia. **Cilia** are hairlike structures that remove dust and other particles from the air.

Next the air enters the bronchi. The **bronchi** are two tubes through which air moves to the lungs. The **lungs** are the main organs of the respiratory system. Where the bronchi enter the lungs, they branch into smaller tubes called bronchioles. The **bronchioles** are small tubes divided into alveoli. The **alveoli** are microscopic air sacs. The walls of the alveoli are so thin that gases can easily pass through them. Two exchanges take place in the alveoli: oxygen passes through the walls of the alveoli into the capillaries, and carbon dioxide passes from the capillaries through the walls of the alveoli into the alveoli. During exhalation, carbon dioxide passes out of the body. Blood rich in oxygen flows from the lungs to the heart, where it is pumped to the body cells.

Skeletal System

The **skeletal system** serves as a support framework, protects vital organs, works with muscles to produce movement, and produces blood cells. There are 206 bones in the skeletal system of an adult. **Bone** is the structural material of the skeletal system. **Periosteum** is a thin sheet of outer tissue that covers bone. It contains nerves and blood vessels. The nerves cause us to feel pain when we suffer a blow to the bone. **Bone marrow** is the soft tissue in the hollow center area of most bones where red blood cells are produced.

Cartilage is a soft, connective tissue on the ends of some bones. It acts as a cushion where bones meet. For example, the disks between vertebrae are cartilage and serve as shock absorbers, and cartilage forms a cushion in the knee and hip joints. A **ligament** is a tough fiber that connects bones. Sprained ankles and knees involve stretched or torn ligaments. A **joint** is the point where two bones meet. There are several types of joints in the body.

Muscular System

The **muscular system** consists of muscles that provide motion and maintain posture. There are more than 600 muscles in the body. Muscles are divided into two major groups. A **voluntary muscle** is a muscle a person can control. Muscles in the arms and legs that a person uses to move are voluntary muscles. An **involuntary muscle** is a muscle that functions without a person's control. Muscles in the stomach and other internal organs are involuntary muscles.

There are three types of muscle tissue in the body. **Smooth muscle** is involuntary muscle tissue found in many internal organs. **Skeletal muscle** is muscle tissue that is attached to bone. Skeletal muscles help move your body. **Cardiac muscle** is a unique kind of muscle tissue found only in the heart. It differs from other muscle tissue in its structure. The contractions in cardiac muscles are generated by nerve stimulation.

A **tendon** is tough tissue fiber that attaches muscles to bones. Muscles work in pairs to move the body. While one muscle in the pair contracts and shortens, the other relaxes and lengthens.

Endocrine System

The **endocrine system** consists of glands that control many of the body's activities by producing hormones. A **gland** is a group of cells, or an organ, that secretes hormones. A **hormone** is a chemical messenger that is released directly into the bloodstream. Hormones control many of the body's activities.

PITUITARY GLAND

The **pituitary gland** is an endocrine gland that produces hormones that control growth and other glands. It is located just below the hypothalamus in the brain and is about the size of a pea. Hormones from the pituitary gland influence growth, metabolism, development of the reproductive organs, uterine contractions during childbirth, and many other body functions. The pituitary gland often is called the master gland because it releases hormones that affect the working of the other glands. The pituitary hormones do the following:

- Regulate the development of bones and muscles
- Affect the reproductive organs
- Affect the functioning of the kidney, the adrenal gland, and the thyroid glands
- Stimulate the uterus to contract during childbirth

THYROID GLAND

The **thyroid gland** is an endocrine gland that produces thyroxine. **Thyroxine** is a hormone that controls metabolism and calcium balance in the body. **Metabolism** is the rate at which food is converted into energy in body cells. The thyroid gland is located near the upper portion of the trachea.

PARATHYROID GLAND

The **parathyroid glands** are endocrine glands that secrete hormones that control the amount of calcium and phosphorus in the body. All four parathyroid glands are located on the thyroid gland.

PANCREAS GLAND

The **pancreas** is a gland that produces digestive enzymes and insulin. **Insulin** is a hormone that regulates the blood sugar level. If the pancreas fails to produce enough insulin, a person develops diabetes mellitus. **Diabetes,** or **diabetes mellitus,** is a disease in which the body produces little or no insulin.

ADRENAL GLANDS

The **adrenal glands** are endocrine glands that secrete several hormones, including adrenaline. **Adrenaline** is a hormone that prepares the body to react during times of stress or in an emergency. The adrenal glands also secrete hormones that affect the body's metabolism. The two adrenal glands are located on the kidneys.

OVARIES

The **ovaries** are female reproductive glands that produce ova and estrogen. **Ova** are egg cells, or female reproductive cells. There are two ovaries in the female body. **Estrogen** is a hormone produced by the ovaries that stimulates the development of female secondary sex characteristics and affects the menstrual cycle.

TESTES

The **testes** are male reproductive glands that produce sperm cells and testosterone. There are two testes in the male body. **Testosterone** is a hormone that produces the male secondary sex characteristics.

Digestive System

The **digestive system** breaks down food into nutrients that can be used by the body. The digestive system also allows nutrients to be absorbed by body cells and eliminates waste from the body. **Digestion** is the process by which food is changed so that it can be absorbed by the body's cells.

MOUTH

When food is chewed in the mouth, the teeth break it into smaller pieces. The mouth contains **salivary glands** that release saliva, which contains a chemical that begins the digestion of carbohydrates. **Saliva** is a fluid that helps soften food so that it can be swallowed more easily.

ESOPHAGUS

When food is swallowed, it moves into the **esophagus,** a tube connecting the mouth to the stomach. Food passes to the stomach by the process of **peristalsis,** a series of involuntary muscle contractions. Peristalsis can move food to the stomach even in a person who is doing a headstand.

STOMACH

The **stomach** is an organ that releases acids and juices that mix with the food and produce a thick paste called chyme. The stomach also produces a layer of mucus to protect its lining from the strong acids that it releases. After about four hours of churning the food, muscles in the stomach force the food into the small intestine.

SMALL INTESTINE

The **small intestine** is a coiled tube in which the greatest amount of digestion and absorption takes place. The small intestine is about twenty-one feet (6.3 meters) long and is lined with villi. **Villi** are small folds in the lining of the small intestine. The villi increase the surface area and allow more food to be absorbed. Several enzymes are produced in the lining of the small intestine. An **enzyme** is a protein that regulates chemical reactions.

LIVER

The **liver** is a gland that releases bile to help break down fats, maintain blood sugar level, and filter poisonous wastes. Bile flows to the small intestine to help in the digestion of fats. The **gallbladder** is an organ that stores bile. The liver produces bile, which is transported to the small intestine to aid in digestion. Several other enzymes that aid digestion in the small intestine come from the pancreas.

PANCREAS

The **pancreas** is a gland that produces digestive enzymes and insulin. A portion of the pancreas produces enzymes for the digestive system; another portion produces hormones for the endocrine system. Enzymes from the pancreas break down proteins, starches, and fats in the small intestine.

LARGE INTESTINE

After food passes through the small intestine, it enters the large intestine, also called the colon. The **large intestine** is a tube extending from the small intestine in which undigested food is prepared for elimination from the body. When the large intestine is full, it contracts, and solid wastes leave the body through the rectum and anus. The **rectum** is a short tube at the end of the large intestine that stores wastes temporarily. The **anus** is the opening to the outside of the body at the end of the rectum.

Urinary System

The **urinary system** removes liquid wastes from the body and maintains the body's water balance. The organs of the urinary system are the kidneys, ureters, bladder, and urethra.

KIDNEYS

A **kidney** is an organ that filters the blood and excretes waste products and excess water in the form of urine. **Urine** is a pale yellow liquid composed of water, salts, and other waste products. The body has two kidneys. They lie on either side of the spinal column just above the waist.

URETERS

A **ureter** is a narrow tube that connects the kidneys to the urinary bladder. The ureters carry urine from the kidneys to the urinary bladder.

URINARY BLADDER

The **urinary bladder** is a muscular sac that stores urine. As the urinary bladder fills with urine, it expands. When it reaches its capacity, the urinary bladder releases urine into the urethra.

URETHRA

The **urethra** is a narrow tube extending from the urinary bladder to the outside of the body through which urine passes out of the body.

Integumentary System

The **integumentary system** covers and protects the body and consists of skin, glands associated with the skin, hair, and nails. The skin is the largest organ in the body. It has nerve cells that help the person detect pain, pressure, touch, heat, and cold. The skin protects some body parts against injury, prevents microorganisms from entering the body, and helps maintain a healthful body temperature.

The skin helps with the removal of wastes from the body and helps the person sense the environment. It also helps protect from ultraviolet radiation through the presence of melanin. **Melanin** is a pigment that gives the skin its color and protects the body from the ultraviolet rays of the sun.

The skin is made up of two layers. The **epidermis** is the outer layer of skin cells. These cells are constantly shed and replaced. The epidermis does not contain blood vessels or nerve endings. New skin cells are produced in the deepest layer of the epidermis. The **dermis** is a thick layer of cells

below the epidermis that contains sweat glands, hair follicles, sebaceous (oil) glands, blood vessels, and nerves. A **sweat gland** is a gland that helps cool the body by releasing sweat through the pores to evaporate on the surface of the skin. A **sebaceous gland** is a small oil-producing gland that helps protect the skin. **Sebum** is the oil produced by sebaceous glands. Skin has several types of nerve cells that help detect pain, pressure, touch, heat, and cold. Below the dermis is a layer of fatty tissue called the subcutaneous layer. A large portion of the body's fat is stored in this layer.

Because skin is the largest organ in the human body, it also is the most vulnerable organ. Several types of conditions affect the skin. Common skin conditions include birthmarks and scars. A birthmark is an area of discolored skin that is present at birth. Birthmarks include various types of freckles and moles and can be removed by a physician. A scar is a mark left on damaged tissue after the tissue has healed. A person who is badly cut or severely burned will develop a scar. Some people are more likely than others to develop scars. These people might get large, thick scars from small cuts or burns.

Warts and ringworm are other common skin conditions. A **wart** is a contagious growth that forms on the top layer of the skin. Warts are caused by a viral infection. They usually grow in groups and can be spread by contact. Warts can be treated with over-the-counter drugs. However, if warts spread, they should be treated by a physician. **Ringworm** is a skin condition that causes small, red, ring-shaped marks on the skin. Ringworm is caused by a fungal infection and can be spread by physical contact. Physicians usually treat ringworm with ointments or creams. However, severe cases of ringworm may require treatment with antifungal tablets.

Nails and hair also are part of the integumentary system. Nails are made up of dead cells and keratin. **Keratin** is a tough protein that makes up nails and hair. **Hair** is a threadlike structure consisting of dead cells filled with keratin. Hair protects the skin from harmful sun rays and helps maintain body temperature. Hair varies in color, texture, and amount for each person. A full head of hair can contain 100,000 to 200,000 hairs. Each hair grows from a follicle. A **hair follicle** is a pit on the surface of the skin that contains nutrients a hair needs to grow. The roots of hair are made up of living cells. As new hair cells are produced, old hair cells are pushed up through the scalp.

Health Goal #22

I Will Recognize Habits That Protect Female Reproductive Health

During adolescence, a female's body matures. The girl develops secondary sex characteristics and has her first menstrual period. Her body becomes capable of reproduction, even though the adolescent is not prepared to be a parent.

Puberty in Females

Puberty is the stage of growth and development when the body becomes capable of producing offspring. When a female is around eight years old, her pituitary gland increases its production of a hormone called follicle stimulating hormone (FSH), which travels through the bloodstream to the ovaries and causes them to secrete estrogen. **Estrogen** is a hormone produced by the ovaries that stimulates the development of female secondary sex characteristics and affects the menstrual cycle. **Secondary sex characteristics** are physical and emotional changes that occur during puberty. During puberty, a girl must learn to accept these physical changes and manage her emotions in responsible ways. See Table 7-1 for more information on the signs of puberty in females and when they occur.

MANAGING EMOTIONS DURING PUBERTY

During puberty, a girl may notice that she has sudden emotional changes and sexual feelings. Estrogen and other hormones cause these changes. Hormone levels fluctuate, and as a result the girl might experience sudden changes in her emotions. Everyday occurrences, such as school assignments or family responsibilities, may produce intense feelings. She might be puzzled or confused by some of her reactions. But she should know that most changes in mood are normal. Of course, she must take responsibility for behaving in responsible ways even though her emotional feelings may change rapidly. The increase in estrogen also produces sexual feelings. Sexual feelings result from a strong physical and emotional attraction to an-

TABLE 7-1

SIGNS AND TIMING OF PUBERTY IN FEMALES

Breast Development
- First visible sign of sexual maturation (in four out of five girls) is appearance of breast buds, which generally takes place around age 10 or 11 years
- Full breast development takes three to four years and is generally complete by age 14

Hair Development and Growth
- Appearance of pubic hair, which becomes darker, curlier, and coarser
- Auxiliary hair that develops under the arms, on the arms and the legs, and to a slight degree on the face

Menstruation
- Most dramatic sign of sexual maturity
- Occurs at an average age of 12.8 years, ranging from 11 to 13 years
- Early menstrual cycles are often irregular and painful, often without ovulation
- After one or two years the cycles tend to become more regular and with ovulation

Source: Pinyerd & Zipf, 2005.

other person. Adolescent females must set limits, stick to these limits, and practice abstinence.

ACCEPTING PHYSICAL CHANGES

The physical changes that occur during puberty become noticeable between the ages of eight and fifteen. The maturing process that happens in puberty is affected by a female's heredity, diet, health habits, and health status. For example, a female with an inadequate diet might mature more slowly, and a female who overtrains for a sport might have a delayed menstrual cycle. During puberty, a female must become comfortable with her maturing body. A female is more likely to have a positive body image when she is well educated about her anatomy and physiology. Knowing that females mature at different rates can be comforting. A female should avoid comparing her body to those of other females of the same age. She should ask her parents, guardian, or physician when she has questions about her growth and development.

EARLY SEXUAL DEVELOPMENT IN FEMALES

Signs of sexual development in females appear at younger ages today than in the past. One in seven Caucasian females starts to develop breasts or pubic hair by age eight. Nearly one out of every two African American females shows these signs by the age of eight (Lemonick, 2000). Early sexual maturation causes pressures that young females are not prepared to handle. They feel pressure to act like teens or even adults. In a sense, they are pushed prematurely out of childhood. Early maturing females also often have to cope with pressures from males who are interested in them sexually. This is difficult for young females to deal with.

Researchers have not been able to identify with certainty the reasons for the increase in early sexual maturity in females. Some scientists believe that it may be due in part to the increase in obesity. Overweight females tend to mature earlier, and very thin females, such as those with anorexia nervosa, tend to mature later than normal. Some other scientists think that a chemical contained in food might be the reason, and still others believe that seeing sexualized messages might trigger brain chemicals that jump-start sexual development (Lemonick, 2000).

The Female Reproductive System

The **female reproductive system** consists of organs in the female body that are involved in producing offspring. The external female reproductive organs are called the vulva. The vulva consists of the mons veneris, the labia majora, the labia minora, the clitoris, and the hymen. The **mons veneris** is the fatty tissue that covers the front of the pubic bone and serves as a protective cushion for the internal reproductive organs. During puberty, hair begins to cover the mons veneris and the labia majora. The **labia majora** are the heavy folds of skin that surround the opening of the vagina.

The **labia minora** are two smaller folds of skin located within the labia majora. The clitoris and the openings of the urethra and the vagina are located within the labia minora. The **clitoris** is a small, highly sensitive structure located above the opening of the urethra. The clitoris is richly supplied with blood vessels and nerve endings.

The **hymen** is a thin membrane that stretches across the opening of the vagina. The hymen has small openings in it. Some females do not have a hymen. Other females often break or tear the hymen when they ride bicycles or horses, exercise strenuously, or insert their first tampon.

The internal female reproductive organs are the ovaries, fallopian tubes, uterus, and vagina. The **ovaries** are female reproductive glands that produce ova and estrogen. A female is born with between 200,000 and 400,000 immature ova in her ovaries. About 375 of these ova will mature and be released in a female's lifetime. During puberty, the ova begin to develop. Each developing ovum is enclosed in a small, hollow ball called a follicle. Each month during the menstrual cycle, an ovum matures and is released from its follicle. **Ovulation** is the release of a mature ovum from one of the two ovaries.

When an ovum is released from an ovary, it enters one of the fallopian tubes. A **fallopian tube** is a tube four inches (ten centimeters) long that connects an ovary to the uterus. A female has two fallopian tubes, one connected to each ovary. During the menstrual cycle, a mature ovum moves through a fallopian tube to the uterus. If fertilization occurs, it usually occurs in the fallopian tube. An ovum that is not fertilized either disintegrates in the uterus or leaves the body in the menstrual flow. The uterus is a muscular organ that receives and supports the fertilized egg during pregnancy and contracts during childbirth to help with delivery. The **cervix** is the lowest part of the uterus and connects the uterus to the vagina. The **vagina** is a muscular tube that connects the uterus to the outside of the body. The vagina serves as the female organ for sexual intercourse, the birth canal, and the passageway for the menstrual flow.

The Menstrual Cycle

The **menstrual cycle** is a monthly series of changes that involve ovulation, changes in the uterine lining, and menstruation. **Menstruation** is the period in the menstrual cycle in which the unfertilized egg and the lining of the uterus leave the body in a menstrual flow. Females often describe menstruation as their "period." On average, the menstrual cycle occurs over twenty-eight to thirty-two days. This means a female will have her period every twenty-eight days. However, many females have slightly longer or slightly shorter cycles, and many teens have irregular cycles—the length of their menstrual cycle varies from month to month. Menstrual flow usually lasts about five days, but this also can vary. The menstrual cycle usually follows this pattern:

Days 1–5. Menstrual flow leaves the body. The menstrual flow consists of about two ounces (56 grams) of blood. Some females may notice small viscous lumps in their flow. These are small pieces of uterine lining. At this time, a new ovum is maturing in an ovary.

Days 6–12. The uterine lining begins to thicken. The uterus prepares for ovulation and the possibility that an ovum will be fertilized.

Days 13–14. Ovulation occurs: A follicle in an ovary bursts, and an ovum is released into one of the fallopian tubes.

Days 15–20. The corpus luteum secretes hormones to support a pregnancy. The corpus luteum is formed when the remains of the burst follicle close. The **corpus luteum** is a temporary gland that secretes progesterone. **Progesterone** is a hormone that changes the lining of the uterus. As the uterine lining changes, it prepares to support a fertilized ovum. If an ovum is fertilized, the corpus luteum continues to secrete progesterone throughout pregnancy.

Days 21–28. The corpus luteum disintegrates if an ovum is not fertilized. No more progesterone is secreted. The cells in the lining of the uterus die without progesterone. The unfertilized ovum disintegrates. The menstrual cycle begins again.

Female Reproductive Health

It is important for each female to assume responsibility for her health. Females should be informed about products for absorbing menstrual flow, reducing menstrual cramps, toxic shock syndrome, premenstrual syndrome, missed menstrual cycles, pelvic examinations, breast self-examinations, mammography, and protecting reproductive health.

PRODUCTS FOR ABSORBING MENSTRUAL FLOW

Pads, panty shields or liners, and tampons are products that can be used to absorb the menstrual flow. A pad is a thick piece of cotton that absorbs the menstrual flow as it leaves the vagina. A pad should be changed every four to six hours. A panty shield or liner is a thin strip of cotton that is worn inside underpants to collect the menstrual flow. It is usually worn on days when flow is light and may be worn with a tampon for extra protection. A tampon is a small tube of cotton placed inside the vagina to absorb the menstrual flow. The tampon collects the menstrual flow before any of the flow leaves the vagina. A female who wears a tampon can swim during her period without fear that the menstrual flow will get on her bathing suit or into the water. Tampons should be changed at least every four to six hours.

REDUCING MENSTRUAL CRAMPS

Some females have painful menstrual cramps in the lower abdomen caused by contractions of the uterus. A warm bath and moderate exercise may relieve the cramps. Reducing the amount of caffeine and sodium in the diet also may reduce menstrual cramps. A young female can speak with her parents, guardian, or physician about using medications, such as ibuprofen, that reduce menstrual cramps.

TOXIC SHOCK SYNDROME

Toxic shock syndrome (TSS) is a severe illness resulting from infection with toxin-producing strains of staphylococcus. Early flu-like symptoms of TSS include a high fever of more than 102 degrees Fahrenheit (39 degrees Celsius), vomiting, diarrhea, dizziness, fainting, and a rash like a sunburn. These symptoms may progress to a sudden drop in blood pressure. Complications of TSS include kidney and heart failure and difficulty in breathing. About 95 percent of TSS cases occur in females who are menstruating. Bacteria in the vagina secrete a toxin that gets into the bloodstream. Females should be careful when using tampons and change them at least four or five times a day. Regular tampons changed often are better than super-absorbent tampons worn for longer periods of time. A pad should be worn at night. Tampon use should be discontinued if fever or other signs appear. Prompt medical care is needed if symptoms occur.

PREMENSTRUAL SYNDROME

Premenstrual syndrome (PMS) is a combination of physical and emotional symptoms that affect a female a week to ten days prior to menstruation. These symptoms may include weight gain, bloating, swollen breasts, headaches, backache, constipation, mood swings, cravings, anxiety, and depression. A female can help reduce weight gain, bloating, and swelling by avoiding caffeine and salt. This reduces the chances that she will retain fluids. She also can exercise regularly to produce beta-endorphins that improve mood and reduce anxiety and depression. A physician can prescribe medications to reduce the symptoms of PMS.

MISSED MENSTRUAL CYCLES

Amenorrhea is the absence of menstruation. Some females do not start a menstrual cycle at puberty. This type of amenorrhea may be caused by underdeveloped female reproductive organs, poor general health, or emotional stress. Some females miss menstrual cycles after they have begun menstruating. This type of amenorrhea is often caused by pregnancy or by a reduction in red blood cell levels resulting from stress, overtraining, eating disorders, drastic weight loss, or anemia.

PELVIC EXAMINATIONS

A **pelvic examination** is an examination of the internal female reproductive organs. A Pap smear usually is done when this examination is performed. A **Pap smear** is a screening test in which cells scraped from the cervix are examined to detect cervical cancer.

BREAST SELF-EXAMINATION

A **breast self-examination (BSE)** is a screening procedure for breast cancer in which a female checks her breasts for lumps and other changes. A physician or a nurse performs the breast exam when a female has checkups. A female should check her technique with a physician or nurse to be certain she is performing BSE properly. Females should begin BSEs when they reach age twenty.

MAMMOGRAPHY

Mammography is a highly sensitive X-ray screening test used to detect breast lumps and is a highly effective tool in the early detection of cancer. A **mammogram** is the image of the breast tissue created by mammography and is read by a qualified physician. The American Cancer Society recommends that a female should have a baseline mammogram between the ages of thirty-five and forty; a female should have a routine mammogram every one to two years during her forties; a female should have a yearly mammogram after the age of fifty.

Each month, there is a buildup of fluid and fibrous tissue in a female's breasts in preparation for pregnancy. When a pregnancy does not occur, the body must reabsorb these unneeded substances by draining and emptying them into lymph nodes. Occasionally, the drainage causes congestion, and cysts and fibroadenomas are formed. A cyst is a sac that is formed when fluid becomes trapped in a lymph duct. A **fibroadenoma** is a lump that is formed when fluid becomes trapped in a lymph duct. The result is fibrocystic breast condition, a condition in which cysts and fibroadenomas cause lumpiness, breast tenderness, and discomfort. The exact causes of this condition are unknown, but the condition is believed to be related to hormones.

ENDOMETRIOSIS

Endometriosis can affect females of all ages. To understand endometriosis it is important to know first what the endometrium is. The **endometrium** is the tissue that lines the uterus. **Endometriosis** is a condition that occurs when tissue similar to the endometrium is found outside its normal location. These growths outside the surface of the uterus are called **endometrial implants** and they can occur on the ovaries, the fallopian tubes, the ligaments that support the uterus, the internal area between the vagina and rectum, and the lining of the pelvic cavity (American Academy of Family Physicians, 2007).

Pelvic pain and mild cramps during menstruation are the two most common symptoms of endometriosis in young females. However, other symptoms such as painful or frequent urination or pain associated with exercise or after a pelvic exam might also be caused by endometriosis.

The cause of endometriosis is not known. There is no cure for endometriosis, but females can be treated for symptoms. It is important for any female who suspects endometriosis to see a health care professional for proper diagnosis and proper care. Proper treatment can make a difference in improving the quality of a female's life and is particularly important in terms of preserving fertility for future childbearing. It is important for all females to understand that endometriosis is not a sexually transmitted disease (STD).

PROTECTING REPRODUCTIVE HEALTH

Following are seven suggestions for females to help them protect their reproductive health:

1. *Keep a calendar in which you record information about your menstrual cycle.* Keep track of the number of days in each cycle. Keep track of the number of days of menstrual flow. Know the date of your last menstrual period. Make a note of any cramps, mood swings, or heavy menstrual flow. Share this information with your parents or guardian and your physician.

2. *Practice good menstrual hygiene habits.* Change your pads, panty shields, or tampons every four to six hours. Wear a pad or panty shield at night to reduce the risk of TSS. Change your underwear often and wash your genitals daily to avoid vaginal odor.

3. *Choose habits that prevent or reduce menstrual cramps.* Exercise regularly and reduce the amount of caffeine and salt in your diet.

4. *Perform monthly breast self-examinations.* Begin the habit of monthly BSE. Perform BSE each month after your menstrual flow stops.

5. *Have regular medical checkups.* Take along your calendar with the information you have recorded about your menstrual cycles when you go in for physician checkups. Go over your recorded information with your physician. Your parents or guardians and your physician will determine the appropriate age for you to begin to have a pelvic examination and Pap smear.

6. *Seek medical attention when you are showing signs of infection.* Vaginal discharge, lumps, and rashes are symptoms of infection. This may indicate infection with a sexually transmitted disease.

7. *Practice abstinence from sex.* Abstinence from sex is choosing not to be sexually active. Practicing abstinence prevents teen pregnancy and infection with sexually transmitted diseases.

Health Goal #23

I Will Recognize Habits That Protect Male Reproductive Health

During adolescence, a male's body matures. He develops secondary sex characteristics. His body becomes capable of reproduction, even though he is not prepared to be a parent.

Puberty in Males

Puberty is the stage of growth and development when the body becomes capable of producing offspring. During puberty the male's pituitary gland increases its production of luteinizing hormone, which travels through the bloodstream to the testes and causes them to secrete testosterone. **Testosterone** is a hormone that produces male secondary sex characteristics. The secondary sex characteristics are physical and emotional changes that occur during puberty. During puberty, males must learn to accept these changes. See Table 7-2 for more information on the signs of puberty in males and when they occur.

MANAGING EMOTIONS

During puberty, a male might notice that he has sudden emotional changes and sexual feelings. Testosterone causes these changes. Testosterone levels fluctuate, and a male experiences sudden

TABLE 7-2

SIGNS AND TIMING OF PUBERTY IN MALES

Genital Development
- Increase in testicular size occurs at about age 12 years, ranging from 9.5 to 13.5 years
- Testes and scrotum enlarge
- Penis lengthens and widens, taking several years to reach full adult size

Sperm Production
- Sperm production coincides with growth of testes and penis at about age 13.5 to 14 years

Hair Development and Growth
- Pubic hair grows after the increase in testicular size
- Facial hair appears about three years after the onset of pubic hair growth, first on the upper lip and followed by growth on the sides of the face and on the chin (there is considerable variation in hair growth due to genetic factors)

Source: Pinyerd & Zipf, 2005.

changes in his emotions. He might become angry or say things he does not mean to say. He may feel insecure or edgy for no reason. A male might be puzzled or confused by having such intense feelings. But he should know that changes in emotions are normal during puberty. Teen males are accountable for the way they respond to their emotional changes.

The increase in testosterone also produces sexual feelings. Sexual feelings result from a strong physical and emotional attraction to another person. Males must set limits, stick to these limits, and practice abstinence.

ACCEPTING PHYSICAL CHANGES

In males, the physical changes that occur during puberty become noticeable between the ages of twelve and fifteen. The maturing process that happens in puberty is affected by heredity, diet, health habits, and health status. For example, a male who lifts weights may develop a more muscular body than a male who does not. A male who is short for his age may have biological relatives who are short.

During puberty, a male must become comfortable with his maturing body. A male's body image is his perception of his body's appearance. A male is more likely to have a positive body image when he is knowledgeable about male anatomy and physiology. For example, the growth spurt occurs later in males than it does in females. Also, males mature at very different rates. A male who is short in stature suddenly may have a growth spurt of several inches. A male should ask his parents, guardian, or physician the questions he has about growth and development. He should avoid comparing his body to those of other males. For example, a teenage male should not compare his body to a professional athlete's body. Professional athletes are older and have completed training programs that have affected their bodies.

The Male Reproductive System

The **male reproductive system** consists of organs in the male body that are involved in producing offspring. The external organs of the male reproductive system are the penis and the scrotum. The **penis** is the male sex organ used for reproduction and urination. The **scrotum** is a sac-like pouch that holds the testes and helps regulate their temperature. The **testes** are male reproductive glands that produce sperm cells and testosterone. The scrotum hangs from the body so that the testes have a lower temperature than the rest of the body. This allows the testes to produce sperm. **Sperm** are male reproductive cells.

The internal male reproductive organs include the testes, seminiferous tubules, epididymis, vas deferens, seminal vesicles, ejaculatory duct, prostate gland, Cowper's glands, and urethra. The testes are divided into several sections that are filled with seminiferous tubules. The **seminiferous tubules** are a network of coiled tubules in which sperm are produced. **Spermatogenesis** is the process by which sperm are produced.

After sperm are produced in the seminiferous tubules, they move to the epididymis. The **epididymis** is a comma-shaped structure along the upper rear surface of the testes where sperm mature. Some sperm are stored in the epididymis, but most move to the vas deferens after they mature.

The **vas deferens** are two long, thin tubes that act as a passageway for sperm and a place for sperm storage. They extend from the epididymis in the scrotum up into the abdomen. The walls of the vas deferens are lined with cilia. The contractions of the vas deferens, along with the actions of the cilia, help transport sperm. In the abdomen, the vas deferens circle the bladder and connect with the ducts of the seminal vesicles to form the ejaculatory duct. The **seminal vesicles** are two small glands that secrete a fluid rich in sugar that nourishes sperm and helps them move. The **ejaculatory duct** is a short, straight tube that passes into the prostate gland and opens into the urethra. The urethra serves as a passageway for sperm and urine to leave the body.

The **prostate gland** is a gland that produces a fluid that helps keep sperm alive. The prostate gland is located beneath the bladder and surrounds the urethra. Without the fluid from the prostate gland, fertilization would be almost impossible because many sperm would die. **Cowper's glands** are two small glands that are located beneath the prostate gland. They secrete a clear, lubricating fluid into the urethra.

An **erection** is a process that occurs when the penis swells with blood and elongates. An erection may be accompanied by ejaculation. **Ejaculation** is the passage of semen from the penis and is a result of a series of muscular contractions. **Semen** is the fluid that contains sperm and fluids from the seminal vesicles, prostate gland, and Cowper's glands. After ejaculation, the penis returns to a nonerect state.

Male Reproductive Health

It is important for each male to assume responsibility for his health. Males should be informed about circumcision, inguinal hernia, mumps causing sterility, digital rectal examination, testicular self-examination, and protecting reproductive health.

Nocturnal Emissions

Once a male begins producing sperm, the testes constantly manufacture sperm. Some of the sperm is stored in the epididymis and the stored sperm are occasionally released as part of the normal process to make room for new sperm. This can occur automatically during sleep, and when it does it is known as a "nocturnal emission" or "wet dream." Males entering puberty should be assured that nocturnal emissions are a normal part of maturation.

Circumcision

The end of the penis is covered by a piece of skin called the foreskin. **Circumcision** is the surgical removal of the foreskin from the penis. This procedure usually is performed on the second day after birth. Circumcision may reduce the risk of urinary infections and cancer of the penis. Males who are not circumcised should pull the foreskin back and cleanse the penis regularly to prevent smegma from collecting. **Smegma** is a substance that forms under the foreskin consisting of dead skin and other secretions.

Inguinal Hernia

In a developing male fetus, the testes pass from the abdomen into the scrotum through the inguinal canal during the seventh month of pregnancy. Then the inguinal canal closes to keep the intestines from also passing into the scrotum. In some males, the inguinal canal does not completely close off. The intestines pass into the inguinal canal and the male develops an inguinal hernia. An **inguinal hernia** is a hernia in which some of the intestine pushes through the inguinal canal into the scrotum. Lifting heavy objects sometimes stresses this area and is the cause of the hernia. An inguinal hernia can be painful and can be repaired surgically.

Mumps and Sterility

Mumps is a viral infection that affects the salivary glands. Mumps usually occurs in childhood. There is a vaccine to prevent mumps. But some people do not get mumps in childhood, and they do not get the mumps vaccine. If a male has mumps after puberty, the virus can affect his testes. The virus causes swelling in the testes. The seminiferous tubules can be crushed and become incapable of producing sperm. This causes sterility. Sterility is the inability to produce offspring.

Digital Rectal Examination

Prostate cancer is the second most common cancer in males. A major symptom of prostate cancer is an enlarged prostate. Physicians use digital rectal examinations to examine males for symptoms of prostate cancer. A **digital rectal examination** is an examination in which the physician inserts a finger into the rectum and examines the internal reproductive organs and the rectum for irregularities. The American Cancer Society recommends that males over the age of forty have a digital rectal examination annually.

Testicular Self-Examination

Testicular cancer is one of the most common cancers in males between the ages of fifteen and thirty-four. The best way to detect testicular cancer is by doing regular testicular self-examinations. A **testicular self-examination** is a screening procedure for testicular cancer in which a male checks his testes for lumps or tenderness. If detected early, testicular cancer has a high rate of cure. Teen males should begin the habit of performing testicular self-examinations.

Protecting Male Reproductive Health

Following are seven suggestions for males to help them protect their reproductive health:

1. *Bathe or shower daily.* Keep your external reproductive organs clean to prevent infection and odor.
2. *Bend at your knees and keep your back straight when you lift heavy objects.* Using the correct

technique when lifting heavy objects can help prevent the risk of an inguinal hernia.

3. *Wear protective clothing and equipment when you participate in sports and physical activities.* Some sports have athletic supporters that provide extra support for the penis and testes. Wear protective equipment, such as a cup, to prevent injury to these organs.

4. *Perform testicular self-examinations.* Testicular cancer is one of the most common cancers in younger males. Teen and adult males should examine their testes for lumps and tenderness.

5. *Have regular medical checkups.* During a medical checkup, a physician examines and discusses the ways your body is changing. A physician also will answer any questions you have about your reproductive system.

6. *Seek medical attention when you show signs of infection.* A discharge from the penis, tenderness in the scrotum, lumps, and rashes are symptoms of infection with sexually transmitted diseases (STDs).

7. *Practice abstinence from sex.* Abstinence from sex is choosing not to be sexually active. Practicing abstinence prevents teen pregnancy and infection with sexually transmitted diseases, including HIV.

Health Goal #24

I Will Learn about Pregnancy and Childbirth

Conception

Conception or **fertilization** is the union of an ovum and a sperm. One ovum matures and is released from an ovary each month. Ovulation usually occurs on about the fourteenth day before the expected beginning of the next menstrual period. Once an ovum is released, it enters a fallopian tube. As the ovum moves through the fallopian tube, it can be fertilized if sperm are present. Conception usually occurs in the upper third of a fallopian tube.

At conception, heredity is determined. **Heredity** is the passing of characteristics from biological parents to their children. All body cells, except sperm and ova, contain twenty-three pairs of chromosomes. A **chromosome** is a threadlike structure that carries genes. A **gene** is a unit of hereditary material. One pair is called the sex chromosomes. Females have two X chromosomes; males have an X chromosome and a Y chromosome. Ova and sperm contain only one set (not pairs) of twenty-three chromosomes. Every ovum contains an X chromosome. Every sperm contains either an X chromosome or a Y chromosome. The Y chromosome determines maleness: when a Y sperm fertilizes an ovum, the fertilized egg has the chromosomal characteristics (XY) to develop into a male; when an X sperm fertilizes an ovum, the fertilized egg has the chromosomal characteristics (XX) to develop into a female.

All chromosomes carry genes that contain hereditary material. **Sex-linked characteristics** are hereditary characteristics transmitted on the sex chromosomes. The X chromosome carries genes for traits such as color vision and blood clotting. The Y chromosome does not carry matching genes for those or other traits. Therefore, when the X and Y chromosomes are present together, the genes on the X chromosome control these traits.

Some couples receive genetic counseling to prepare for parenthood. In some cases, the physician may recommend that a pregnant female have a test for possible genetic defects in the fetus or embryo. **Genetic counseling** is a process in which a trained professional interprets medical information concerning genetics to prospective parents. **Amniocentesis** is a diagnostic procedure in which a needle is inserted through the uterus to extract fluid from the amniotic sac. The **amniotic sac** is a pouch of fluid that surrounds a fetus. Cells extracted from the amniotic fluid are analyzed to determine if any genetic defects are present in the fetus or embryo. Ultrasound is another diagnostic procedure used to monitor the fetus. Ultrasound uses high-frequency sound waves to provide an image of the developing baby. The image is evaluated by the physician. Parents who know that their baby will be born with a birth defect can make advance preparations for caring for the baby after birth.

Pregnancy

After conception, the fertilized egg begins cell division and moves through the fallopian tube. The egg is a cluster of cells by the time it reaches the uterus. This cluster of cells attaches to the endometrium, the lining of the uterus. **Embryo** is the name given to a developing baby through the second month of growth after conception. **Fetus** is the name given to a developing baby from the ninth week until birth. The outer cells of the embryo and the cells of the endometrium form the placenta. The **placenta** is an organ that anchors the embryo to the uterus. Other cells form the umbilical cord. The **umbilical cord** is a rope-like structure that connects the embryo to the placenta. Blood from the mother carries nutrients and oxygen to the embryo through the cord. Waste products from the embryo move to the mother's bloodstream through the cord to be excreted.

PREGNANCY DETERMINATION

The first sign of pregnancy is the absence of a menstrual period. However, a missed period does not always indicate pregnancy. A female may skip her menstrual period because of stress, diet, physical activity, or illness. If conception has occurred, she usually has other symptoms of pregnancy, such as tenderness in her breasts, fatigue, a change in appetite, and morning sickness. Morning sickness is nausea and vomiting during pregnancy. Some pregnant females have spotting or light irregular menstrual flow.

A female who misses a period and also has other symptoms of pregnancy should have a pregnancy test. A physician or nurse practitioner can administer this test and send it to a lab for confirmation. Some pregnancy tests also are sold in drugstores. However, a pregnancy should be confirmed by a physician or nurse.

PRENATAL CARE

Prenatal care is care given to the mother-to-be and baby before birth. Prenatal care includes routine medical examinations, proper nutrition, reasonable exercise, extra rest and relaxation, childbirth and child care education, avoidance of drugs and other risk behaviors, and the practice of common sense.

A pregnant female needs a well-balanced diet. Premature birth or low birthweight can result when a developing baby does not receive adequate nutrients. **Premature birth** is the birth of a baby before it is fully developed, or less than thirty-eight weeks from time of conception. A **low birthweight** is a weight at birth that is less than 5.5 pounds (2.5 kilograms). Premature birth and low birthweight are associated with mental retardation and infant death.

A pregnant female needs to check with her physician before taking any prescription or over-the-counter drugs. Drugs present in her bloodstream can pass into the developing baby's bloodstream and can harm the developing baby. For example, tranquilizers taken early in pregnancy can cause birth defects. Some drugs prescribed for acne also can cause birth defects. Hormones, such as those in birth control pills, can cause birth defects. Aspirin may interfere with blood clotting in both the pregnant female and her developing baby.

A female should not drink alcohol during pregnancy. **Fetal alcohol syndrome (FAS)** is the presence of severe birth defects in babies born to mothers who drank alcohol during pregnancy. FAS includes damage to the brain and to the nervous system, facial abnormalities, small head size, below normal IQ, poor coordination, heart defects, and behavior problems.

A pregnant female should not smoke or inhale sidestream smoke from tobacco products. Females who smoke have smaller babies in poorer general health than babies of nonsmoking females. Smoking and breathing smoke increase the risk of complications, miscarriage, and stillbirth during pregnancy. A **miscarriage** is the natural ending of a pregnancy before a baby is developed enough to survive on its own. Babies born to mothers who smoke also may be at risk for heart disease in adulthood.

A pregnant female should not use other harmful drugs, such as marijuana, crack, cocaine, or heroin. Babies born to mothers who use these drugs can be born prematurely and have low birthweight, and they might be born addicted to drugs. Some research indicates that caffeine may be linked to birth defects. Caffeine is found in coffee, chocolate, cola drinks, tea, and some prescription and over-the-counter drugs. A mother-to-be should follow her physician's advice about caffeine.

Childbirth

Labor is the process of childbirth. There are signs that indicate the beginning of labor. Muscular contractions of the uterus start, become more intense, last longer, and become more frequent. The amniotic sac may rupture before or shortly after labor begins. A discharge or gushing of water from the vagina indicates the sac has broken. There may be bloody show. Bloody show is the discharge of the mucous plug that sealed the cervix during pregnancy. There are three distinct stages of labor.

STAGE 1: DILATION OF THE CERVIX

The first stage of labor is the longest stage. It can last from two hours to an entire day. Dilation or widening of the cervix occurs. The cervical opening enlarges eight to ten centimeters, wide enough for the baby to move through.

STAGE 2: DELIVERY OF THE BABY

The second stage begins when the cervix is completely dilated and ends with the delivery of the baby. The baby moves farther down into the birth canal, usually head first. The mother-to-be pushes, and the muscles in her uterus contract to push the baby out. **Crowning** is the appearance of the baby's head during delivery. Once the baby has been eased out of the birth canal and begins breathing on its own, the umbilical cord is cut.

STAGE 3: DELIVERY OF THE PLACENTA

The third stage of labor is the expulsion of the afterbirth. The **afterbirth** is the placenta, which is expelled shortly after delivery. If this does not occur naturally, the physician removes the placenta.

When the baby is breathing on its own, the umbilical cord is clamped and cut off. A stump remains on the navel. It dries up and falls off in a few days. The physician gives the baby an Apgar score. The **Apgar score** is a rating of physical characteristics of an infant one to five minutes after birth. Characteristics such as heart rate, color, respiratory effort, and reaction to sucking are scored and used to predict the health of the baby.

The **postpartum period** is the span of time that begins after the baby is born. Hormones produce changes in the mother's body. The breasts secrete a watery substance believed to provide the baby with immunity to certain diseases. The breasts also secrete a hormone that stimulates the breasts to secrete milk. Some studies show that breast-fed babies have fewer cases of respiratory illnesses, skin disorders, constipation, and diarrhea.

MULTIPLE BIRTHS

Some pregnancies result in the birth of two or more babies at the same time. Two babies born at the same time are called twins. Identical twins are two babies that develop from the same egg and sperm. Identical twins develop when one fertilized ovum divides at a very early stage of development and the two resultant cell clusters continue their development separately. This results in twins of the same sex who are genetically identical and are very similar in appearance. Fraternal twins are two babies that develop when two ova are released from an ovary and are fertilized at the same time by different sperm. Fraternal twins are no more alike genetically than non-twin siblings. Three babies born at the same time are called triplets; four are quadruplets; five are quintuplets; and six are sextuplets. Multiple births of more than three babies are rare.

CHILDBIRTH CLASSES

Childbirth classes prepare prospective parents for childbirth. Hospitals, health centers, and other organizations offer these classes. The classes include detailed information about the process of childbirth. A nurse or other health care practitioner answers questions and helps with concerns. Special exercise classes also are offered for pregnant females to help them stay fit during pregnancy and prepare for childbirth. A pregnant female should obtain permission from her physician before participating in exercise classes.

Complications during Pregnancy and Childbirth

ECTOPIC PREGNANCY

An **ectopic pregnancy** is a pregnancy that occurs outside the uterus. The embryo becomes implanted in the fallopian tube or another location in the abdomen. Symptoms include cramping, severe abdominal pain, and spotting. Surgery often is needed to remove the embryo.

RH INCOMPATIBILITY

Rh incompatibility is a mismatch between the blood of a pregnant female and the blood of the developing baby. The female's blood produces an antibody that attacks a substance in the developing baby's blood. Rh incompatibility may occur when the female's blood is Rh negative and the developing baby's is Rh positive. An injection of an antibody to the Rh factor is given to the female to prevent risk during future pregnancies.

TOXEMIA OF PREGNANCY

Toxemia of pregnancy is a condition characterized by a rise in the pregnant female's blood pressure, swelling, and leakage of protein into the urine. Untreated toxemia can result in the death of the female or the developing baby.

MISCARRIAGE

Miscarriage is the natural ending of a pregnancy before a baby is developed enough to survive on its own. Miscarriages occur most often during the first trimester. They may be caused by a defect in the fetus or a medical condition of the fetus or the pregnant female. Signs of miscarriage include cramping, severe pain, spotting, and bleeding.

CESAREAN SECTION

Cesarean section is a procedure in which a baby is removed surgically from the mother. A physician makes a surgical incision through the mother's abdomen and uterus and removes the baby. A Cesarean section may be performed if an unborn baby is too large to pass through the mother's pelvis or is not positioned correctly, or if the physician determines that a vaginal delivery may be dangerous to the health of the mother or baby. Recovery time from a delivery by Cesarean section often is longer than recovery from a vaginal delivery.

STILLBIRTH

Stillbirth is a fully developed baby born dead. Stillbirth may be caused by a defect in the baby or a medical condition of the baby or pregnant female.

Health Goal #25

I Will Learn about the Growth and Development of Infants and Children

Infancy consists of the period from birth to about two years of age. The first years of life are a time of incredible growth and development. Although there is uniformity in the growth and development of most children, no two children develop exactly alike. Children differ in physical, cognitive, social, and emotional growth patterns. They also differ in the ways they interact with and respond to their environment as well as play, affection, and other factors. An understanding of infant growth and development patterns and concepts is necessary for parents and caregivers to create a nurturing and caring environment that will stimulate optimal growth in young children.

Types of Development

Physical development refers to physical changes in the body and involves changes in weight, height, motor skills, vision, hearing, and development of the senses and perceptions. Physical growth is rapid during the first two years of life. With each physical change, a child acquires new abilities. By repeating motor actions, an infant builds physical strength and muscular coordination.

Cognitive development refers to the development of skills such as reasoning, language acquisition, problem solving, and knowledge acquisition. Children learn through their senses (e.g., sight, touch, hearing, taste) and through multiple interactions with people and things in the environment. As children grow and interact with their environment, they go through various stages of cognitive development.

Emotional development is the expression of feelings about one self, others, and things. **Social development** is relating to others. These two types of development are often grouped together because they are closely interrelated growth patterns and are referred to as social-emotional development. Social-emotional development includes developing feelings of self-esteem, trust, and friendship. It also includes developing skills to socialize and interact effectively with others.

Developmental Milestones

Developmental milestones are the physical or behavioral signs of development or maturation in infants and children. Observing developmental milestones helps to determine the growth and development progress of an infant over time. A comprehensive list of developmental milestones is available from the American Academy of Pediatrics (see www.aap.org).

Health Goal #26

I Will Provide Responsible Care for Infants and Children

Preteens and teens often have opportunities to be child-sitters. A child-sitter is a person who provides care for infants and children with the permission of a parent or guardian. Young people may look after a younger brother or sister or be asked by neighbors or other adults to look after their children. Teachers and other adults have a role in preparing young people to be child-sitters. Preteens and teens need to learn how to care for young children three to eight years old.

Preparation for Child-Sitting

A responsible child-sitter is prepared. A responsible child-sitter is

- Observant and alert
- Calm during emergencies
- Able to follow instructions
- Trained in first aid and familiar with universal precautions
- Able to recognize safety hazards
- Able to communicate with adults
- Able to communicate with young children
- Able to supervise young children
- Patient
- Friendly

Young people can evaluate their preparedness for child-sitting by determining whether the following statements are true for them:

1. I have taken a first aid course, and I am familiar with universal precautions.
2. I have taken a child-sitting course offered by the American Red Cross or by another organization.
3. I have a parent's or guardian's approval to child-sit.
4. I have checked to make sure I am available to child-sit.
5. I have discussed with the parents or guardian the hours I will child-sit and the payment.
6. I have arranged for transportation to and from the job.
7. I have met the child or children and learned their names and ages.
8. I have familiarized myself with the house and where everything is.
9. I have discussed pets and rules for them.
10. I have discussed what privileges I will have in regard to such things as the telephone, food, and visitors.
11. I know the address and telephone number of the home where I will be child-sitting.
12. I know what time to arrive.

13. I know what time the parents or guardian will be home.
14. I know the address and telephone number of the parents or guardian.
15. I know who to contact if the parents or guardian cannot be reached.
16. I know emergency telephone numbers, including police, fire, and poison control.
17. I know whether 911 service is available.
18. I know the name and telephone number of the child's physician.
19. I know the child's mealtimes.
20. I know the child's nap times and bedtime.
21. I know what health problems the child has.
22. I know what medications the child needs.
23. I know what allergies the child has.
24. I know what the child is and is not allowed to do.
25. I know what the child's favorite activities and toys are.

Caring for Infants and Toddlers

Learning the characteristics of infants and toddlers allows a young person to know what to expect when child-sitting. Children newborn to one year old need to feel secure, like to be with people, cry when hungry or uncomfortable, like to touch and hold things, like to look at hands and faces, and like to put things in their mouths. Children one year old to three years old need to feel secure; want to be independent; want to eat, drink, and get dressed without help; like to play, build things, and watch what others are doing; like to do the same thing over and over again; and may have temper tantrums if they don't get what they want.

A responsible child-sitter never leaves an infant or toddler alone. A responsible child-sitter never shakes or hits an infant or toddler. Young people need to consult a parent or guardian if an infant or child persists in a behavior they find difficult or inappropriate. They need certain skills to provide responsible care for an infant or toddler. These skills include the following:

• Knowing what to do when a baby cries
• Knowing what to do if they suspect that an infant or toddler is sick
• Knowing how to diaper a baby
• Knowing how to bathe a baby
• Knowing how to give a baby a bottle
• Knowing how to burp a baby
• Knowing how to pick up and hold a baby

Caring for Young Children

Children three to five years old share common characteristics, as do those five to eight years old. Children three to five years old enjoy playing with friends and communicating with others, like to learn numbers and play simple games, like to be independent and do things for themselves, like to learn new words and names for things, can be very active, and can be very aggressive. Children five to eight years old need to socialize with others besides family members, want to be a part of conversations with family members, usually have more self-confidence than those three to five years old, like to ask questions about almost everything, and are influenced by what adults say and do.

A responsible child-sitter never leaves a young child alone. A responsible child-sitter never shakes or hits a child. Young people need to consult a parent or guardian if a young child persists in a behavior they find difficult or inappropriate. They need certain skills to provide responsible care for young children who are three to eight years old. These skills include the following:

• Knowing what to do when a child is afraid
• Knowing what to do if a child has a tantrum
• Knowing how to help a young child
• Knowing what to do when a child refuses to go to bed
• Knowing what to do if a young child appears to be sick

Health Goal #27

I Will Develop My Learning Style

Learning Styles

Individuals gain and process information in different ways. A **learning style** is the way a person

SATURATED FAT

- Remember what they hear
- Repeat word for word what someone else has said
- Remember every word of a song
- Prefer to listen rather than take notes
- Perform better on oral tests than on written tests

Here are some tips for auditory learners:

1. Tape-record information you need to recall.
2. Play the tape several times when studying.
3. Read or say information aloud to yourself.
4. Study by having someone give you an oral test.
5. Make a song of words or facts you need to remember.

KINESTHETIC LEARNERS

A **kinesthetic learner** is a person who learns best by acting out something, touching an object, or repeating a motion. People who are blind often become kinesthetic learners. For example, they may recall a location by using their cane to feel a sidewalk or curb. Kinesthetic learners do the following:

- Remember objects they have touched
- Remember facts from being in a role play
- Perform better on tests requiring demonstration than on oral or written tests
- Can act out a story or concept

Here are some tips for kinesthetic learners:

1. Associate information with a feeling or smell.
2. Role-play situations in which you recall facts.
3. Demonstrate concepts you have learned.
4. Make a story to help yourself remember facts.

GLOBAL LEARNERS

A **global learner** is a person who learns best by combining visual, auditory, and kinesthetic ways of learning. Here are some tips for global learners:

1. Assess which learning style works best for you in specific situations.
2. Experiment with the tips given for the other kinds of learners.

gains and processes information. Educators have identified four kinds of learners.

VISUAL LEARNERS

A **visual learner** is a person who learns best by seeing or creating images and pictures. Visual learners do the following:

- Picture the words they read or hear
- Store what they see, read, or hear in images or pictures rather than in words (for example, visual learners are more likely to remember the face, rather than name, of a person they have met for the first time)
- Perform better on written tests than on oral tests

Here are some tips for visual learners:

1. Take notes and review them often.
2. Color-code or highlight notes to be reviewed.
3. Make a mental picture of key words.
4. Remember lists by using a mnemonic (memory-assisting) device or code.

AUDITORY LEARNERS

An **auditory learner** is a person who learns best by listening or by discussing a topic. Auditory learners do the following:

Learning Disabilities

A **learning disability** is a disorder in which a person has difficulty acquiring and processing information. There are different types of learning disabilities:

- *Dyslexia.* **Dyslexia** is a learning disability in which a person has difficulty spelling, reading, and writing. People who have dyslexia may reverse letters and numbers. They may read from right to left.
- *Attention deficit disorder.* **Attention deficit disorder (ADD)** is a learning disability in which a person is restless and easily distracted. People who have ADD cannot keep their attention focused on what they are doing. They have difficulty completing tasks. They may daydream.
- *Attention deficit hyperactivity disorder.* **Attention deficit hyperactivity disorder (ADHD)** is a learning disability in which a person is easily distracted and also is hyperactive. To be hyperactive is to not be able to sit still or stand still. People who have ADHD cannot keep their attention focused on what they are doing. They are restless and fidgety. They may be impulsive.
- *Tracking disorder.* **Tracking disorder** is a learning disability in which a person has difficulty following a series of words or images. People who have tracking disorder have difficulty staying on the same line as they read. Or they may have difficulty catching a baseball thrown from the outfield to home plate.

LEARNING ABOUT SUPPORT FOR PEOPLE WITH LEARNING DISABILITIES

People who have difficulty acquiring and processing information can take diagnostic tests to find out if they have a learning disability. If they have a learning disability, a plan to increase their learning can be drawn up. A variety of professionals will work with these individuals and their parents or guardians. These professionals may include a counselor, school psychologist, teacher, and tutor.

Schools may offer special education classes for students with learning disabilities. The curriculum and teaching techniques are adapted to the needs of students who require help in order to learn to their full capacity. There may be fewer students in the class to allow the teacher more time with each student. Many students with learning disabilities remain in the same classroom with other students. Their teachers provide special help when needed. For example, a student who has dyslexia might take an oral test rather than a written one. Some students with learning disabilities may get extra help outside the classroom. For example, a student might work with a speech pathologist or a reading specialist after school. Many students have a tutor. A tutor is a person who works with individual students to help them with schoolwork. You will be more sensitive to people with learning disabilities if you understand the following five facts; if you have a learning disability, these facts may help you understand yourself more fully. People with learning disabilities:

1. Are capable of learning
2. Can learn strategies that help them acquire and process information
3. May need special education classes or a tutor
4. Need support and encouragement from classmates and family members
5. Can be very successful

Health Goal #28

I Will Achieve the Developmental Tasks of Adolescence

Developmental Tasks of Adolescence

The **developmental tasks of adolescence** are achievements that need to be mastered to become a responsible, independent adult. Robert Havighurst (1948), a sociologist, identified eight developmental tasks that needed to be mastered.

TASK 1: DEVELOP HEALTHFUL FRIENDSHIPS WITH PEOPLE OF BOTH SEXES

Healthful friendships involve mutual respect, flexibility, trust, honesty, and the opportunity to share feelings. Through healthful friendships, individuals learn how to communicate effectively,

cooperate, and resolve conflict. These skills will help in the workplace and in marriage. Friends provide support and companionship throughout life.

Young people achieve task 1 by

1. Initiating a new friendship with a responsible person
2. Evaluating current friendships to make sure they are healthful
3. Making efforts to be a good friend to others

TASK 2: BECOME COMFORTABLE WITH YOUR MALENESS OR FEMALENESS

A **sex role** is the way a person acts and the feelings and attitudes a person has about being a male or female as well as the expectations he or she has for other males and females. Early sex roles are influenced by families. Regardless of whether a person is a male or female, a person should feel free to express a variety of emotions and participate in a variety of activities. Being able to express several aspects of one's personality and being able to have a wide variety of interests and to gain acceptance reinforce one's comfort level with regard

to masculinity and femininity. A person who likes and accepts his or her sex role is more likely to accept the masculinity and femininity of others.

Sexual orientation is a person's sexual attraction to people of the opposite sex, same sex, or both sexes. A heterosexual is a person who has a sexual preference for someone of the opposite sex. A homosexual is a person who has a sexual preference for someone of the same sex. A bisexual is a person who has a sexual interest in people of both sexes.

Young people achieve task 2 by

1. Participating in a variety of social activities
2. Considering what society expects males to be like
3. Considering what society expects females to be like
4. Discussing unrealistic, uncertain, or uncomfortable expectations about sex roles with a responsible adult, such as a parent or guardian

TASK 3: BECOME COMFORTABLE WITH YOUR BODY

Adolescence is a period of transition that involves physical, social, emotional, and intellectual changes. When adolescents' bodies develop secondary sex characteristics, they become adultlike. Physically, adolescents are now capable of producing offspring, although adolescents are not ready to marry and parent children. Adolescents must become comfortable with the ways their bodies are changing. They must develop a positive body image. **Body image** is a person's perception of her or his body's appearance. Being proud that one's body is female or male is an important part of developing healthy sexuality.

Young people achieve task 3 by

1. Discussing any concerns about their body with a responsible adult
2. Maintaining a healthful appearance
3. Practicing habits that will keep their body in top condition
4. Performing regular breast self-examinations or testicular self-examinations

TASK 4: BECOME EMOTIONALLY INDEPENDENT FROM ADULTS

Parents or guardians provide emotional security throughout one's childhood. They shield and help young people sort out things. As adults, individuals can still stay close to their parents. However, the balance of responsibility now starts to shift to the young person. Young people may still ask parents for feedback but must become responsible for themselves and independent from their parents or guardians.

Young people achieve task 4 by

1. Using the *Responsible Decision-Making Model* (see page 787) when making a decision
2. Keeping a journal; decisions that did not turn out as expected should be noted; a young person can analyze what might have been done differently
3. Staying close to parents or guardians by sharing decisions and emotions with them

TASK 5: LEARN SKILLS NECESSARY FOR MARRIAGE AND PARENTING

Adolescence is a time for learning about intimacy. **Intimacy** is deep and meaningful sharing between two people. **Self-disclosure** is the act of making one's thoughts and feelings known to another person. During adolescence, individuals practice self-disclosure. Self-disclosure may bring a person closer to someone. Young people are sometimes disappointed by those to whom they have disclosed their thoughts and feelings. Such disappointments help young people learn to trust their instincts about other people. They learn whom they can safely share their feelings with. Later on, this will help them select a marriage partner with whom they can be intimate. During adolescence, young people also can practice relating to infants and young children. They can learn skills that will help them if they become a parent.

Young people achieve task 5 by

1. Analyzing whether they make wise choices about who to share their thoughts and feelings with
2. Reviewing relationships that have not been healthful and supportive
3. Discontinuing all relationships that have been destructive
4. Practicing relating to infants and children

TASK 6: PREPARE FOR A CAREER

Adolescence is a time to begin preparing for a career. During adolescence, young people gain skills and knowledge about themselves that help them prepare for a career. Adolescents need to make decisions that will affect their careers. Does the adolescent need to continue her or his education to be able to get the kind of job and income she or he wants? Will the young person attend college or a vocational school? Is there some other training in which the young person is interested? Adolescents should select their high school courses carefully. They will benefit from talking to adults who are engaged in the type of career that interests them. They may want to be a volunteer or get a part-time job to gain experience.

Young people achieve task 6 by

1. Working with a high school guidance counselor to select the right courses to prepare for the career they are interested in
2. Studying hard
3. Getting a high school diploma
4. Speaking with adults who have careers of interest
5. Participating in volunteer opportunities
6. Getting a part-time job

TASK 7: HAVE A CLEAR SET OF VALUES TO GUIDE BEHAVIOR

Parents or guardians teach a set of values to guide their children's behavior. But as children mature, their values must be in their hearts as well as their heads. A young person must believe in these values and want them to guide his or her behavior. Wanting to practice values because one believes in them is to have values in one's heart.

Young people achieve task 7 by

1. Examining how the values they have learned from parents or guardians have guided their behavior
2. Identifying what they want to stand for
3. Examining whether their behavior is consistent with the values they say are important to them

TASK 8: UNDERSTAND AND ACHIEVE SOCIALLY RESPONSIBLE BEHAVIOR

To be a responsible adult, a person must have a social conscience. A **social conscience** is a desire to contribute to society and to live a socially responsible life. To do this, young people must move beyond thinking about themselves to thinking about the lives of others. What can one do to enrich the quality of life within one's home, school, family, community, nation, and world?

Young people achieve task 8 by

1. Participating in volunteer activities that benefit others, such as collecting food for the needy
2. Joining clubs at school that volunteer in the community
3. Looking for ways to help out at home

Planning for the Future

A **goal** is a desired achievement toward which a person works. A **short-term goal** is something a person plans to achieve in the near future. A **long-term goal** is something a person plans to achieve after a period of time. Setting and achieving personal goals does not need to be an overwhelming task. Following are seven steps a person can take to successfully reach a goal:

1. *State the goal.* Write the goal in a short sentence. Be as specific as possible. Share the goal with your parents or guardian. Is the goal clear? Is it realistic? Is it achievable?
2. *Make an action plan.* An **action plan** is a detailed description of the steps you will take to reach a goal. You might need to identify short-term goals to help you make progress toward a long-term goal.
3. *Identify obstacles to your plan.* Brainstorm about obstacles that might interfere with your plan. Ask what might keep you from being able to accomplish your goal.
4. *Set up a time line.* When will your action plan begin? When do you expect to achieve your goal? Have you considered your other obligations and responsibilities? Is this a realistic time line?
5. *Keep a chart or diary in which you record progress toward your goal.* Seeing your progress will encourage you to stick to your goal and your action plan.
6. *Build a support system.* Consider people who will help you reach your goal. Ask them for ideas and help.
7. *Revise your goal, plan, or time line if necessary.* Sometimes people realize that their plans are not working out as they expected and that they must make changes. If you find that you must make changes in your plan, make them. Do not give up on your goal. When you change your action plan, do not lower your standards.

KEYS TO A SUCCESSFUL FUTURE

There are eight keys that will help unlock the door to a successful future.

Key 1: *Assess your strengths.* Try to find where your strengths lie. Take tests prepared by professionals to assess your strengths. Talk to your parents or guardians, a school counselor, and other responsible adults.

Key 2: *Assess your interests.* There are interest inventories to help individuals determine what they like to do. A school counselor will answer any questions you have about these.

Key 3: *Identify and use your resources.* You must make things happen for yourself. Go out and find people who can advise you about your goals and help you reach them. Use resources in your community, such as the library or youth center, to help you reach your goals.

Key 4: *Set goals and make plans to reach them.* Always consider avenues of self-improvement. Set new short-term and long-term goals when appropriate.

Key 5: *Develop a work ethic.* A **work ethic** is an attitude of discipline, motivation, and commitment toward tasks. People increase their self-respect when they have a work ethic. Others know they can count on a person with a work ethic. A person with a work ethic is committed and motivated.

Key 6: *Keep your priorities in order.* The ability to prioritize will help you be successful. You may need to give up some things in order to reach your goal. Carefully pick and choose what your priorities are. Which things must you do and which can you give up?

Key 7: *Manage your time wisely.* Time management is critical in school, on the job, and in personal life. Create a realistic schedule that you can follow. Determine how much time you need to spend on school and work to be successful. Consider how much time you need for family responsibilities. This helps you know how much time you have for your social life.

Key 8: *Develop a positive attitude.* What you believe in, you can achieve.

Health Goal #29

I Will Develop Habits That Promote Healthful Aging

Aging

There are several ways to measure a person's age. **Chronological age** is the number of years a person has lived. **Biological age** is a measure of how well a person's body systems are functioning. **Social age** is a measure of a person's involvement in leisure activities. Nothing can be done to change a person's chronological age, but health habits can affect biological and social age.

Gerontology is the study of aging. A **gerontologist** is a person who specializes in the study of aging. Some gerontologists believe that aging begins the day a person is born. Others believe that aging begins when a person stops growing.

Gerontologists have developed the following theories about the causes of aging:

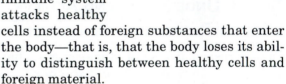

- The *wear-and-tear theory* maintains that, like any machine, the human body simply wears out.
- The *waste-product theory* hypothesizes that waste products accumulate in body cells, damaging the cells and causing them to lose their normal ability to function.
- The *anti-immune theory* proposes that the body's immune system attacks healthy cells instead of foreign substances that enter the body—that is, that the body loses its ability to distinguish between healthy cells and foreign material.
- The *cell-error theory* maintains that as body cells divide, errors are introduced into the genetic material; as the errors are reproduced during subsequent cell division, more and more cells accumulate errors, resulting in aging.
- The *brain theory* suggests that the brain initiates and controls the aging process by a mechanism that is not completely understood.

Physical, mental, and social changes occur during middle and late adulthood.

Physical Changes in Middle and Late Adulthood

As we age, our body systems also age. Some changes are due to a person's heredity. Other changes may be due to one of the other factors that influence health status. Changes occur in each body system.

THE NERVOUS SYSTEM

As people age, their reaction time slows. Eyesight diminishes as ocular muscles weaken. Body senses diminish due to a loss of nerve cells. Touch, taste, smell, and hearing may be affected. Some short-term memory may be lost, but intelligence is not affected. The loss and degeneration of nerve cells also can cause Parkinson's disease. **Parkinson's disease** is a brain disorder that causes muscle tremors, stiffness, and weakness. To minimize such changes in their nervous system, older people should exercise their minds and bodies regularly.

THE CARDIOVASCULAR SYSTEM

As people age, their heart may become less efficient. Blood might not circulate as well. Blood vessels might lose their elasticity and become clogged, causing increased blood pressure. Resting heart rate may increase and oxygen consumption decrease. To minimize such changes in their cardiovascular system, older people should maintain a desirable weight, exercise regularly, and eat a low-fat diet.

THE IMMUNE SYSTEM

As people age, their immune system becomes less efficient in protecting the body. Older people have less resistance to communicable diseases and are more likely to develop chronic diseases. A chronic disease is an illness that develops and lasts over a long period of time. To minimize such changes in their immune system, older people should have regular physical examinations, eat a healthful diet, and get regular flu shots if so advised by a physician.

THE RESPIRATORY SYSTEM

As people age, their lungs become less elastic. They may not be able to hold the same volume of air as in earlier years and may get short of breath. They have an increased risk of chronic bronchitis, emphysema, and flu. **Chronic bronchitis** is a recurring inflammation of the bronchial tubes. Emphysema is a condition in which the alveoli lose most of their ability to function. To minimize such changes in their respiratory system, older people should avoid secondhand smoke, avoid getting cold and wet in severe weather, exercise regularly, and not smoke.

THE SKELETAL SYSTEM

As people age, their bones become less dense and, when broken, take longer to heal. There may be less fluid between the bones in the spinal column, so an older person may become shorter with age. Many people develop arthritis as they age. **Arthritis** is a painful inflammation of the joints. Some older people, especially females, develop osteoporosis. **Osteoporosis** is a condition in which the bones become thin and brittle. To minimize such changes in their skeletal system, older people should maintain a desirable weight, exercise regularly, and eat foods containing calcium.

THE MUSCULAR SYSTEM

As people age, their body composition changes. Their muscle mass and strength decrease, and their percentage of body fat increases. To minimize such changes in their muscular system, older people should exercise regularly, being careful to lift objects correctly.

THE ENDOCRINE SYSTEM

As people age, there are changes in their hormone levels. Some people who are overweight or who have a hereditary tendency may develop diabetes mellitus. **Diabetes,** or **diabetes mellitus,** is a disease in which the body produces little or no insulin. To minimize such changes in their endocrine system, older people should maintain a desirable weight and have regular blood tests.

THE DIGESTIVE SYSTEM

As people age, their metabolism slows and their weight may increase. They absorb fewer nutrients from foods. Their liver may be less effective at breaking down toxic substances. Some older people have difficulty digesting fatty foods. Gum disease and the loss of teeth can make it difficult to eat. Some older people may lose their appetites, eat less, and become malnourished. To minimize such changes in their digestive system, older people should maintain a desirable weight, eat a balanced diet, limit alcohol consumption, and eat smaller meals more often.

THE URINARY SYSTEM

As people age, their bladder may decrease in size so that they have to urinate more frequently. Their kidneys also may produce less urine. To minimize such changes in their urinary system, older people should drink at least eight glasses of water each day.

THE INTEGUMENTARY SYSTEM

As people age, their skin becomes drier and may wrinkle. Age spots may appear on the skin. (Extended exposure to sunlight earlier in life can affect how skin ages.) Hair thins and grays. Some males become bald, and some females develop bald spots. To minimize such changes in their integumentary system, older people should regularly check their skin and hair for signs of aging, wear sunblock and a hat to reduce their exposure to ultraviolet radiation, and use lotions to keep their skin moist.

THE REPRODUCTIVE SYSTEM

As people age, their bodies produce fewer sex hormones. **Male climacteric** is a decrease in testosterone in males, accompanied by symptoms such as hot flashes, depression, insomnia, and fatigue. When women go through menopause, their estrogen level falls and menstruation ceases. Approaching and after menopause, some females experience hot flashes, depression, insomnia, headaches, fatigue, and short-term memory loss. A female's risk of developing heart disease increases as her estrogen level falls. Some females choose estrogen replacement therapy. **Hormone replacement therapy (HRT)** is a combination of estrogen and progesterone that is taken to reduce the symptoms of menopause and to help prevent osteoporosis.

Mental Changes in Middle and Late Adulthood

As people age, they can lose some short-term memory. Some older people develop dementia. **Dementia** is a general decline in all areas of mental functioning. Dementia is usually due to brain disease or mental impairment. Alzheimer's disease is a type of dementia. **Alzheimer's disease** is a progressive disease in which the nerve cells in the brain degenerate and the brain shrinks in size. Symptoms vary, but there are usually three stages. In the first stage, the person is forgetful, loses interest, and feels anxious and depressed. In the second stage, the person is disconnected and restless and has increased memory loss, especially for recent events. In the third stage, the person becomes very disoriented, confused, and completely dependent on others. Older people should work to

stay mentally sharp by using their mental skills, drink at least eight glasses of water each day, limit their intake of alcohol, and not abuse drugs. They should be cautious and try to avoid accidents that may affect their mental function.

Social Changes in Middle and Late Adulthood

People who are aging have the same social needs as younger adults. They need friends with whom they can talk and engage in social activities. Most older people who stay active socially have better mental and physical health. Some older people suffer from depression. **Clinical depression** is long-lasting feelings of hopelessness, sadness, or helplessness. Exercise, therapy, and prescription medications are used to treat clinical depression.

Being a Caregiver

As people age, they may develop chronic diseases or other health conditions and require special care. Most older people turn to family members and friends for assistance and support. These family members and friends are caregivers. A **caregiver** is a person who provides care for a person who needs assistance. Most people are caregivers for an elderly family member at some time in their lives.

There are important factors to consider when an individual is a caregiver for a family member:

- The type of care the family member needs
- The type of care the family member will accept
- The cost of the type of care needed
- The insurance coverage and financial resources of the family member
- The type of care the caregiver is able or willing to provide
- The types of care provided by resources in the community

RESOURCES FOR CAREGIVERS

1. *Senior centers.* Senior centers are facilities where older people can be involved in classes and social activities. Most senior centers provide meals.
2. *Transportation assistance.* Some community agencies and senior centers provide buses or

vans to transport older people to a physician, grocery store, or senior center.

3. *Friendly visitors or companions.* Friendly visitors or companions are volunteers who regularly visit older people who are alone. They check on their needs and provide companionship.

4. *Telephone reassurance programs.* Telephone reassurance programs are staffed by volunteers who regularly call older people who are alone. They check on the older person's needs and provide companionship by telephone.

5. *Home-delivered meal programs.* Organizations such as Meals-on-Wheels deliver food to older people who are shut-ins.

6. *Gatekeeper and home observation programs.* Service people who work for the post office or a public utilities company may be trained to notice changes that might affect the needs of the elderly and to report these changes for investigation and action.

7. *Home health care organizations.* Home health care organizations offer a variety of services including nursing care, medical treatment, and therapy in the home.

8. *Personal emergency response devices.* Personal emergency response devices are mechanical devices that help older people call for help even if they are not able to reach or use the telephone.

9. *Adult day care programs.* Adult day care programs provide health care, social activities, meals, therapy, and transportation.

10. *Respite care.* **Respite care** is care provided by someone who is temporarily relieving a family member of caregiving responsibilities. Adult day care programs are examples of respite care.

11. *Nursing homes or convalescent centers.* Nursing homes or convalescent centers are facilities that provide twenty-four-hour care. Medical care is provided at nursing homes.

12. *Hospice care.* A **hospice** is a facility or home services for people who are dying and their families.

Habits That Promote Healthful Aging

To stay healthy, people of all ages need something worthwhile and satisfying to do. In adolescence, individuals may be engaged in school activities,

sports, and hobbies. In early and middle adulthood, a person may be engaged as a parent, as a volunteer, or in a career outside the home. During late adulthood, a person may enjoy satisfying hobbies and volunteer work. People in late adulthood need someone to love to stay healthy. Throughout life, individuals will have better health if they stay involved with family and friends. These people help a person feel loved and supported. They encourage a person. Research shows that having a pet to love and care for also improves health.

People also need something to hope for in order to stay healthy. Having something to look forward to gives people a reason to take care of themselves. Having events to look forward to gives a person a reason to keep going. As a person ages, having a reason to keep going is very important. Elderly people benefit from such things as looking forward to the birth of a grandchild or great-grandchild, or the graduation of a grandchild.

Following are ten habits that promote healthful aging:

1. Eat a healthful, balanced breakfast each day.
2. Follow the Dietary Guidelines.
3. Exercise regularly.
4. Do not smoke or use other tobacco products.
5. Get plenty of rest and sleep.
6. Have regular physical examinations.
7. Balance work with play.
8. Choose activities that keep the mind alert.
9. Develop healthful relationships with family members and friends.
10. Practice stress-management skills.

Health Goal #30

I Will Share with My Family My Feelings about Dying and Death

Dying and Death

The reality is that everyone will die some day. Death is a normal part of the life cycle. Acknowledging and accepting this reality can give a person's life meaning and purpose. Fear of death ural. However, people are more accepting of death if they take the time to sort out the meaning and purpose of life and learn the facts about death.

Death is the permanent cessation of function of all vital organs. At one time, people were pronounced dead when their heart and lungs stopped functioning. But today, life-support systems can prolong life by performing the functions of the heart and lungs. A **life-support system** is mechanical or other means to support life. An example is the use of a respirator to force air into the lungs. The advent of life-support systems made it necessary to define death in legal terms. **Legal death** is brain death or the irreversible cessation of circulatory and respiratory functions. **Brain death** is the irreversible cessation of all functions of the entire brain, including the brain stem.

DECISIONS ABOUT ONE'S OWN DEATH

Many people discuss the way they want to die. Some people want to be near family members and close friends at the time of their death. According to an article in *Time* magazine (Cloud, 2000), seven out of ten Americans want to die at home, but three-fourths instead die in medical institutions; more than a third of people who are dying spend at least ten days in intensive-care institutions, where many endure torturous attempts at a cure; and many families and physicians ignore the wishes of dying people.

People are living longer than they did in the past. This has made people think more about issues related to life-support systems and legal death. People now have the right to make living wills. A **living will** is a document that tells what treatment a person wants in the event that she or he no longer can make medical decisions. A living will differs from a regular will. A regular will states how possessions shall be distributed after death. For example, a regular will might state exactly how much money to spend on care for children or other relatives.

A living will focuses on issues of medical treatment. A living will might name someone to make decisions about the person's medical treatment if the person is no longer able to do this. For example, a person who has gone into a coma (a state of unconsciousness) cannot make decisions. In a living will, a person might state that (s)he refuses medical intervention. A refusal of medical intervention is a person's refusal of specific life-support systems when there is no reasonable expectation of recovering or regaining a meaningful life. People

can state which life-support systems they refuse. These might include antibiotics, machine or forced feedings or fluids, cardiac resuscitation, respiratory support, or surgery. The request also may state that treatment be limited to providing comfort, such as the administration of painkillers.

People wanting to be near family members and close friends at the time of their death can consider hospice care. **Hospice** is a facility or home services for people who are dying and their families. Two criteria must be met before a person is eligible for hospice care. The person must have a terminal illness (an illness that will result in death), and the person must be expected to die in less than six months. Hospice care can be provided at a hospital, in another facility, or in someone's home. When hospice care is provided at a facility, the atmosphere is homelike. Whenever possible, hospice care is provided in the person's home. Usually medications are given to keep the person as comfortable as possible. Family members and friends stay with the person who is dying. Hospice volunteers assist the family in caring for the person.

Grief

Grief is intense emotional suffering caused by a loss, disaster, or misfortune. When someone dies, people who have been close to this person grieve. People who are dying grieve the loss of their own life. **Anticipatory grief** is grief experienced prior to a loss. The person who is dying grieves the loss of his or her life. People who care about the dying person grieve their anticipated loss of that person.

THE FIVE STAGES OF GRIEF

There are five stages of grief (Kübler-Ross, 1997). The **five stages of grief** are five psychological stages of grieving: denial, anger, bargaining, depression, and acceptance. These five stages describe the common grieving process in people who are dying:

Stage 1: *Denial*. People who are dying refuse to believe that they are dying.

Stage 2: *Anger*. People who are dying are angry. They might direct their anger at family members, friends, their physician, or other medical professionals.

Stage 3: *Bargaining*. People who are dying try to bargain with God for more years of life.

Stage 4: *Depression*. People who are dying become very sad when bargaining does not work. They know they will die and will not be around for future events.

Stage 5: *Acceptance*. People who are dying begin to say good-bye and to share special feelings and thoughts with family and friends.

The five stages also describe the common grieving process in people who know a family member or friend is dying.

Stage 1: *Denial*. Family members and friends of someone who is dying refuse to believe that a person they care about or love is dying.

Stage 2: *Anger*. Family members and friends of someone who is dying are angry and direct their anger at the person who is dying, at other people who are close to them, or at medical professionals.

Stage 3: *Bargaining*. Family members and friends of someone who is dying make deals and promises, hoping this will allow the person they care about to survive.

Stage 4: *Depression*. Family members and friends of someone who is dying become very sad when bargaining does not work. They imagine what life will be like without that person.

Stage 5: *Acceptance*. Family members and friends of someone who is dying begin to say good-bye and to share special feelings and thoughts with that person.

WHEN SOMEONE CLOSE IS DYING

There are several things that can be done to help someone who is dying. Here are some things to consider:

1. Spend time with the friend or family member who is dying.
2. Share loving feelings and memories.

3. Share feelings of loss and pain.
4. Encourage the person to talk about her or his death.
5. Listen carefully to the person's feelings and thoughts about the past, present, and future.
6. Reassure the person with affection; hold hands or hug.
7. Share feelings of grief with family members and friends.
8. Continue a daily routine if possible.
9. Consider what can be done to keep alive the memory of the person.
10. Allow time for personal grieving.

The time left to be together with the dying person becomes very special. These precious moments can be used wisely—even if the person is in a coma. Frequent visits may be helpful to the person doing the visiting as well as the person in the coma. Many people who come out of a coma remember words that were spoken to them when they were unconscious. They also remember being comforted. Comfort can be rendered by holding the person's hand and speaking to the person. Expressing feelings also helps both individuals.

WHEN SOMEONE IS GRIEVING A LOSS

Following are some suggestions that can help a person give support to someone grieving a loss:

1. *Be available*. Friends support one another during difficult times.
2. *Do something thoughtful for the person*. Consider sending a card or calling the person. An offer to help with meals or errands can benefit the person.
3. *Attend memorial services*.
4. *Have empathy for the person's loss*. Do not lessen the loss by making statements such as "She would have wanted it this way." Instead say, "I am sorry you feel sad. I am here to support you."
5. *Encourage the person to talk about his or her grief*.
6. *Recognize signs of grief that are not healthy*. A person who remains severely depressed, or who relies on alcohol or other drugs, may need help.

8

CHAPTER EIGHT

Nutrition

HEALTH GOALS FOR NUTRITION

31. I will select foods that contain nutrients.

32. I will evaluate food labels.

33. I will eat the recommended daily amounts of food from MyPyramid.

34. I will follow the Dietary Guidelines.

35. I will follow a healthful diet that reduces the risk of disease.

36. I will develop healthful eating habits.

37. I will follow the Dietary Guidelines when I go out to eat.

38. I will protect myself from foodborne illnesses.

39. I will maintain a desirable weight and body composition.

40. I will develop skills to prevent eating disorders.

Nutrition is the area of health that focuses on selecting foods that contain nutrients, evaluating food labels, eating the recommended daily amounts of food from MyPyramid, following the Dietary Guidelines, planning a healthful diet that reduces the risk of disease, developing healthful eating habits, following the Dietary Guidelines when going out to eat, protecting oneself against foodborne illnesses, maintaining a desirable weight and body composition, and developing skills to prevent eating disorders. This chapter provides the health information needed to teach young people important life skills for nutrition.

Health Goal #31

I Will Select Foods That Contain Nutrients

All foods are made up of nutrients. A **nutrient** is a substance in food that helps with body processes, helps with the growth and repair of cells, and provides energy. There are six basic classes of nutrients needed for health: proteins, carbohydrates, fats, vitamins, minerals, and water.

No one food contains all the nutrients needed for health.

Energy is measured in calories. A **calorie** is a unit of energy produced by food and used by the body. Calories are supplied by proteins, carbohydrates, and fats. Because these nutrients supply energy (calories), they are often called macronutrients. Vitamins, minerals, and water are necessary for healthy body function but do not supply calories to one's diet. For good health, most people should increase complex carbohydrates consumption and reduce protein, simple sugar, and fat consumption. Most diet-related diseases result from excess calories and an increased consumption of fat. Low intake of vitamins, minerals, and water also can affect health adversely.

Proteins

A **protein** is a nutrient needed for growth; for building, repairing, and maintaining body tissues; and for supplying energy. Proteins form part of every cell in the body. Proteins make up more than 50 percent of total body weight. The skin, nails, and hair are mostly proteins. Proteins help the body maintain strength and resist infection. Each gram of protein provides four calories of energy. A daily diet deficient in proteins can stunt a person's growth, impair the development of certain tissues, and impair mental development. Excess protein is burned as energy or stored as fat.

There are two kinds of proteins: complete proteins and incomplete proteins. A **complete protein** is a protein that contains all of the essential amino acids. Amino acids are the building blocks that make up proteins. Sources of complete proteins include meat, fish, poultry, milk, yogurt, eggs, and soybeans. Soybeans are the only plant food that provides all nine of the essential amino acids. The body needs twenty amino acids to function properly. The body can produce only eleven of these amino acids. **Essential amino acids** are the nine amino acids the body cannot produce. These nine essential amino acids must come from the foods we eat.

An **incomplete protein** is a protein that does not contain all of the essential amino acids. Incomplete proteins come from plant sources and fall into three general categories: grains (whole grains, pastas, and corn), legumes (dried beans, peas, and lentils), and nuts and seeds. Different plant sources of incomplete proteins can be combined to obtain all of the essential amino acids.

Carbohydrates

Carbohydrates are the main source of energy for the body. Carbohydrates include sugars, starches, and fiber. Carbohydrates supply four calories of energy per gram of food. Your body can store only limited amounts of carbohydrates. Excess carbohydrates are converted and stored as fat. Sources of carbohydrates include vegetables, beans, potatoes, pasta, breads, rice, bran, popcorn, and fruit.

There are two types of carbohydrates: simple carbohydrates and complex carbohydrates. **Simple carbohydrates** are sugars that enter the bloodstream rapidly and provide quick energy. Sugars are found naturally in fruits, honey, and milk. Processed sugar, or table sugar, is added to many foods during processing. Processed sugar is found in cakes, candy, and other sweet desserts as well as in ketchup, spaghetti sauce, and soda pop. Simple carbohydrates provide calories but few vitamins and minerals.

Complex carbohydrates are starches and fiber. Most of the calories in most people's diets come from complex carbohydrates. Sources of complex carbohydrates include grains, such as bread and pasta, and vegetables, such as potatoes and beans. **Starch** is a food substance that is made and stored in most plants. Starches provide long-lasting energy. **Fiber** is the part of grains and plant foods that cannot be digested. Fiber also is known as roughage. Fiber helps move food through the digestive system, preventing constipation and other intestinal problems. When eating foods that contain fiber, a person feels full. Eating foods with fiber reduces blood cholesterol level and the risk of developing heart disease. Good sources of fiber include wheat, bran, cereals, fruit, and vegetables. When eaten, complex carbohydrates are changed by saliva and other digestive juices to a simple sugar called glucose. Cells use some glucose to provide energy and heat. The remaining glucose is changed to glycogen. Glycogen is stored in the muscles. When there is a need for energy, glycogen is converted to glucose.

Fats

A **fat** is a nutrient that provides energy and helps the body store and use vitamins. One gram of fat supplies nine calories of energy. Fats supply more than twice the number of calories supplied by proteins and carbohydrates. Fats store and transport fat-soluble vitamins. A fat-soluble vitamin is a vitamin that dissolves in fat and can be stored in the body. Fat-soluble vitamins include vitamins A, D, E, and K. Fats are stored as fat tissue that surrounds and cushions internal organs. Fats contribute to the taste and texture of many foods. The body needs fats to maintain body heat, store and use vitamins, maintain an energy reserve, and build brain cells and nerve tissues.

There are two main types of fats: saturated fats and unsaturated fats. **Saturated fat** is a type of fat from dairy products, solid vegetable fat, and meat and poultry. Saturated fats usually are in solid form when at room temperature. Saturated fats contribute to the level of cholesterol in a person's blood. **Cholesterol** is a fatlike substance made by the body and found in certain foods. Cholesterol in food is called dietary cholesterol. Dietary cholesterol is found in foods of animal origin, such as meats and dairy products. A person's blood cholesterol level is a combination of dietary cholesterol and cholesterol produced by the body. A person's blood cholesterol level can be lowered by eating fewer saturated fats. Maintaining a healthful cholesterol level lowers the risk of heart disease and some cancers.

Unsaturated fat is obtained from plant products and fish and is usually liquid at room temperature. There are two types of unsaturated fats: polyunsaturated fats and monounsaturated fats. Polyunsaturated fats include sunflower, corn, and soybean oils. Monounsaturated fats include olive and canola oils.

Visible fat is fat that can be seen when looking at food. For example, fatty areas can be seen on some meats and on greasy potato chips. **Invisible fat** is fat that cannot be seen when looking at food, such as the eggs and shortening in a piece of cake. ***Trans*-fatty acids** are fatty acids that are produced when polyunsaturated oils are hydrogenated (have hydrogen added). Scientific evidence shows that consumption of saturated fat, *trans* fat, and dietary cholesterol raises low-density lipoprotein (LDL, or "bad") cholesterol level, which increases the risk of coronary heart disease (CHD).

Vitamins

A **vitamin** is a nutrient that helps the body use carbohydrates, proteins, and fats. Vitamins do not supply energy. There are two types of vitamins: fat soluble and water soluble. A **fat-soluble vitamin** is a vitamin that dissolves in fat and can be stored in the body. There are four fat-soluble vitamins: vitamins A, D, E, and K. Fat-soluble vitamins are stored primarily in the liver. A **water-soluble vitamin** is vitamin that dissolves in water and cannot be stored in the body. Examples of water-soluble vitamins are B complex and vitamin C.

People who do not eat a balanced diet may have vitamin deficiencies. Symptoms of vitamin C deficiency include loosened teeth and gum disease. Symptoms of vitamin D deficiency include rickets, poor teeth, and soft bones in adulthood. Diseases associated with vitamin deficiency are rare in the United States and are most common in underdeveloped countries. Many people take vitamin supplements. Vitamin supplements usually contain synthetic forms of particular vitamins. However, a person who eats a balanced diet that contains all the food groups will get adequate amounts of vitamins from foods. There have been many claims that vitamin supplements will improve health. Certain groups of people, such as the elderly, athletes, or people who have illnesses that impair normal digestion, might benefit from supplements. However, foods are the best source of nutrients. One danger of taking supplements is that people tend to think that if everyone needs a small amount of vitamins, taking a larger amount of vitamin supplements will multiply the benefits. Instead, high doses of many vitamins can be toxic.

Minerals

A **mineral** is a nutrient that regulates many chemical reactions in the body. There are two types of minerals: macro minerals and trace minerals. Macro minerals are required in amounts greater than 100 milligrams. Examples of macro minerals are calcium and sodium. Trace minerals are needed in very small amounts. Examples of trace minerals are iron and zinc. Trace minerals are as important to the body as macro minerals.

Three important minerals are iron, calcium, and sodium. **Iron** is an important component of hemoglobin and functions as a carrier of oxygen in the body. Iron deficiency can lead to anemia, a condition in which the body is unable to produce sufficient red blood cells. A person who does not get enough iron is susceptible to illnesses and infection, and may have a poor appetite, feel weak, and be continually tired. Iron deficiency results in a decrease in the body's ability to transport oxygen. The best way to get an adequate amount of iron is to eat a variety of foods, such as seafood, green leafy vegetables, lean red meats, and whole-grain breads.

Calcium builds bones and teeth and maintains bone strength. Calcium also functions in the contraction of muscles and in blood clotting. All cells in the body need calcium. Good sources of calcium are milk and milk products, dark green leafy vegetables, calcium-fortified foods (orange juice, cereal, bread, soy products, tofu products), dried beans, and nuts.

Sodium regulates and maintains the balance of fluids in the body. Table salt is a major source of sodium. Sodium also occurs naturally in many foods and is added to many processed foods, such as salted snacks and canned foods. Most people can get adequate sodium in their diet without adding extra salt to their food.

Water

Water is a nutrient that is involved with all body processes, makes up the basic part of the blood, helps to remove waste, regulates body temperature, and cushions the spinal cord and joints. Water makes up more than 60 percent of body mass. Water carries nutrients to all body cells and waste products from the cells to the kidneys. Water leaves the body in the form of perspiration and urine. A person can live without other nutrients for months but can survive without water only for about three days. Even slight dehydration can make a person feel tired.

Dehydration is a condition in which the water content of the body has fallen to a low level. Dehydration is caused by a lack of water intake, a dry environment, fever, vomiting, or diarrhea. The sense of thirst tells a person when his or her body needs water, yet a person can be dehydrated before feeling thirsty. For example, hot weather and exercise can cause dehydration before the person gets a feeling of thirst. Signs of dehydration can include dizziness, fatigue, weakness, dry mouth, flushed skin, headache, blurred vision, difficulty swallowing, dry skin, hot skin, rapid pulse, and frequent need to urinate.

It is important to drink at least six to eight glasses of water a day. Other good sources of water, besides water itself, include juice, milk, and soup. Water is also found in many foods, such as fruits and vegetables. Soda pop should not be substituted for water. Soda pop and drinks containing caffeine act as diuretics. **Diuretics** flush water from the body, increasing the amount of urine excreted.

Nutrient Density

Nutrient density refers to the amount of nutrients in a food as compared to the calories. Foods low in calories and high in nutrients are nutrient rich (dense). Foods high in calories and low in nutrients are nutrient poor. Nutrient-rich foods should be consumed frequently, whereas nutrient-poor

219

...uld be limited. A challenge is to help
...and adolescents select snacks that are
...rient dense.

Fresh fruits and vegetables, low-fat milk, and
low-fat cottage cheese are examples of foods high
in nutrient density. Examples of food with low
nutrient density include french fries, onion rings,
soda pop, candy bars, ice cream, cookies, and
cake. The amount of nutrients relative to calories
in these foods is low.

Health Goal #32

I Will Evaluate Food Labels

Food Labels

Food labels help people make healthful food
choices. A food label is a panel of nutrition information that is required on all processed foods
regulated by the U.S. Food and Drug Administration (FDA). A **food label** is required by law to
include the following elements:

- Name of the food
- Net amount in weight or volume
- Name and address of manufacturer, distribu-
  tor, or packager
- Ingredients
- Nutrient content

The Nutrition Facts Label

Nutrition Facts is the title of the information
panel that is required on most foods (Figure 8-1).

Serving size is the listing of the amount of food
that is considered a serving. Serving size should
be read carefully. Where one might expect three
cookies to be one serving, the label might say that
one cookie is one serving. Serving size listings on
food labels are now uniform for similar products.
The servings are determined by the FDA, not by
the manufacturer of the product.

Servings per container is the listing of the
number of servings in the container or package.
This must also be read carefully. The label on a

FIGURE 8-1

Nutrition Facts Label

Nutrition Facts
Serving Size 1 cup (265g)
Servings per Container 2

Amount per Serving	
Calories 235 Calories from Fat 30	
	% Daily Value*
Total Fat 3g	5%
Saturated Fat 1g	5%
Trans Fat 0.5g	
Cholesterol 30mg	10%
Sodium 775mg	32%
Total Carbohydrate 34g	11%
Dietary Fiber 9g	36%
Sugars 5g	
Protein 18g	

Vitamin A 25%	•	Vitamin C 0%
Calcium 12%	•	Iron 20%

*Percent Daily Values are based on a 2,000
calorie diet. Your daily values may be higher
or lower depending on your calorie needs:

		Calories	2,000	2,500
Total Fat	Less than		65g	80
Sat Fat	Less than		20g	25g
Cholesterol	Less than		300mg	300mg
Sodium	Less than		2,400mg	2,400mg
Total Carbohydrate			300g	375g
Dietary Fiber			25g	30g

Calories per gram:
Fat 9 • Carbohydrate 4 • Protein 4

bottle of juice might say 90 for the number of calories but might also say that the bottle contains
two servings; a person who drinks the whole
bottle will be consuming 180 calories. The listed
calories and nutrients must be multiplied by the
number listed for servings per container to determine the total number of calories and nutrients
in a container or package.

Calories listing states the number of calories in
one serving of the food.

Calories from fat states the number of calories
from fat in one serving of the food. The FDA now
requires food manufacturers to list *trans* fat (i.e.,
trans-fatty acids) on Nutrition Facts and some
Supplement Facts panels. Since 1993, the FDA
has required that saturated fat and dietary cholesterol be listed on food labels. By adding *trans*
fat on the Nutrition Facts panel (required by January 1, 2006), consumers now know for the first
time how much of all three—saturated fat, *trans*
fat, and cholesterol—are in the foods they choose.
This revised label, which includes information on
trans fat as well as saturated fat and cholesterol,
will be of particular interest to people concerned
about high blood cholesterol and heart disease.

However, all Americans should be aware of the risk posed by consuming too much saturated fat, *trans* fat, and cholesterol.

Percent daily value is the portion of the recommended daily amount of a nutrient provided by one serving of the food. For total carbohydrate, dietary fiber, vitamins, and minerals, the goal is to consume 100 percent of the recommended daily amount each day.

The percent daily value figure is based on dietary goals recommended for most adults and children over age four. Notice that the footnote states that the percent daily values are based on a diet of 2,000 calories. A person's recommended diet may consist of more or less than 2,000 calories. Extremely active people may need an intake of 2,500 calories. Maximum recommended limits for total fat, saturated fat, cholesterol, and sodium are listed for both a 2,000-calorie and 2,500-calorie diet. Values for vitamins A and C and the minerals calcium and iron are required on all food labels. Values for other vitamins and minerals may be added but are not required by law.

Along with Nutrition Facts, other information can be found on a food label. This information may be included on the Nutrition Facts panel, or it might be found elsewhere on the packaging. Included in this information is a listing of ingredients, food additives, and other important facts.

The food label is *not* required on fresh fruits and vegetables; food served in restaurants; food sold by vendors; bakery, deli, and candy products; spices; coffee and tea; fresh meats; and foods in very small packages.

Ingredients Listing

Almost all foods must have an ingredients listing. Ingredients are the substances that make up the particular food. The **ingredients listing** is the list of ingredients in a food. This listing is not a part of the Nutrition Facts label but is found somewhere else on the label. Ingredients are listed by weight, beginning with the ingredient that is present in the greatest weight. For example, if a soup label lists tomatoes first, that means that by weight the soup contains more tomatoes than any other ingredient. The ingredients list should be read carefully to determine the true amount of an ingredient. For example, total sugar content might be extremely high but might be listed in smaller amounts, broken down into sucrose, fructose, and glucose.

Dates

People should be aware of the dates that are included on a food label or elsewhere on the packaging. Dates are listed in three ways:

- *Sell By:* The last date on which the product should be sold (although it can be stored past this date)
- *Best If Used By:* The date by which the product should be used, to ensure quality
- *Expiration Date:* The date after which the product should not be used

Food Additives

Food labels must list additives. **Food additives** are substances intentionally added to food. Food additives may add nutrients, flavor, color, or texture. They may prevent spoilage or help foods age quickly. They also improve taste and appearance.

Foods may be enriched or fortified to increase their nutrient value. In an **enriched food,** nutrients lost during processing have been added back into the food. In a **fortified food,** nutrients not usually found in the food have been added. For example, some orange juice products are fortified with calcium. Folic acid is now added to all enriched grain products and iron has been added to enriched grains for many years.

Health Claims

Food labels also include claims from manufacturers about the various health qualities of the food product. Before current regulations were in place, the wording of these claims was not regulated. This allowed food manufacturers to make whatever claims they desired to sell a food. The FDA instituted regulations to help protect consumers. Table 8.1 lists the common claims and the conditions the FDA requires manufacturers and producers to comply with for each claim.

Health Goal #33

I Will Eat the Recommended Daily Amounts of Food from MyPyramid

MyPyramid

MyPyramid is an educational tool designed to help individuals make healthful food and physical activity choices based on the *2005 Dietary Guidelines for Americans* (Figure 8-2). It also is called

TABLE 8-1

FDA REQUIREMENTS FOR FOOD CLAIMS

Claims for Calories	**Per Serving**
Calorie-free	Less than five calories
Low calorie	Forty calories or less
Claims for Fat	
Fat-free	Less than a half gram fat or saturated fat
Saturated-fat-free	Less than a half gram saturated fat and less than a half gram *trans*-fatty acids
Low fat	Three grams or less total fat
Low saturated fat	One gram or less saturated fat
Reduced fat or less fat	At least 25 percent less fat than the regular version
Claims for Sodium	
Sodium-free or salt-free	Less than five milligrams of sodium
Very low sodium	Thirty-five miligrams or less sodium
Low sodium	One-hundred-forty milligrams or less sodium
Reduced sodium or less sodium	At least 25 percent less sodium than the regular version
Claims for Cholesterol	
Cholesterol-free	Less than two milligrams
Low cholesterol	Twenty milligrams or less
Reduced cholesterol or less cholesterol	At least 25 percent less cholesterol than the regular version
Claims for Sugar	
Sugar-free	Less than a half gram sugar
Reduced sugar	At least 25 percent less sugar than the regular version
Claims for Fiber	
High fiber	Five grams or more fiber
Good source of fiber	2.5 to 4.9 grams fiber

FIGURE 8-2

Anatomy of MyPyramid

Anatomy of MyPyramid

One size doesn't fit all

USDA's MyPyramid symbolizes a personalized approach to healthy eating and physical activity. The symbol has been designed to be simple. It has been developed to remind consumers to make healthy food choices and to be active every day. The different parts of the symbol are described below.

Proportionality

Proportionality is shown by the different widths of the food group bands. The widths suggest how much food a person should choose from each group. The widths are just a general guide, not exact proportions. Check the Web site for how much is right for you.

Variety

Variety is symbolized by the 6 color bands representing the 5 food groups of the Pyramid and oils. This illustrates that foods from all groups are needed each day for good health.

Gradual Improvement

Gradual improvement is encouraged by the slogan. It suggests that individuals can benefit from taking small steps to improve their diet and lifestyle each day.

Activity

Activity is represented by the steps and the person climbing them, as a reminder of the importance of daily physical activity.

Moderation

Moderation is represented by the narrowing of each food group from bottom to top. The wider base stands for foods with little or no solid fats or added sugars. These should be selected more often. The narrower top area stands for foods containing more added sugars and solid fats. The more active you are, the more of these foods can fit into your diet.

Personalization

Personalization is shown by the person on the steps, the slogan, and the URL. Find the kinds and amounts of food to eat each day at MyPyramid.gov.

MyPyramid.gov
STEPS TO A HEALTHIER YOU

GRAINS VEGETABLES FRUITS OILS MILK MEAT & BEANS

USDA U.S. Department of Agriculture
Center for Nutrition Policy and Promotion
April 2005 CNPP-16

USDA is an equal opportunity provider and employer.

the MyPyramid food guidance system. You will learn more about the Dietary Guidelines in the next section of this chapter (see Health Goal #34).

MyPyramid provides individuals with daily food intake patterns. **Daily food intake patterns** are recommendations on what and how much to eat for good health. The United States Department of Agriculture has set up a Web site (MyPyramid.gov) that includes tables of suggested amounts of food to consume (daily food intake patterns) from the basic food groups, subgroups, and oils to meet recommended nutrient intakes at twelve different calorie levels. The calorie levels include a wide range (1,000 to 3,200) to accommodate the needs of different individuals of various activity levels (see Figure 8-3). The tables help individuals select the daily amount of food from each food group at a particular calorie level. Figure 8-3 includes the daily amounts for the following food groups: fruits, vegetables, grains, meats and beans, milk, and oils. Each food group also is described. Specific amounts of foods to be eaten are given in measurable amounts (e.g., cups, ounces, tablespoons). This differs from the original Food Guide Pyramid, which recommended the number of servings to be eaten rather than specified amounts. MyPyramid helps estimate daily calorie needs by providing a chart for males and females based on age and physical activity level (see Figure 8-3). Also included in the tables is discretionary calorie allowance. **Discretionary calorie allowance** is the remaining amount of calories in a food intake pattern after accounting for the calories needed for all of the food groups. The discretionary calorie allowance can be used to increase the amount of nutrient-dense foods or to select foods that are not in their most nutrient-dense form, sweetened beverages, additional foods, or additions to foods (e.g., salad dressing, sugar, butter). For many people, the discretionary calorie allowance is totally used by the foods they choose in each food group.

The MyPyramid symbol (Figure 8-2) is simple in design. It symbolizes a personalized approach to healthy eating and physical activity. Figure 8-2 describes how the MyPyramid symbol and slogan encourages activity, moderation, personalization, proportionality, variety, and gradual improvement.

Individuals are encouraged to follow the daily food intake recommendations found on the My Pyramid.gov Web site (also shown in Figure 8-3). Individuals can also find out what and how much they need to eat each day by going to the Web site

and plugging in their height, weight, and age to get more personal recommendations. Those wanting to evaluate their current diet and physical activity pattern can go to the Web site and click on the MyPyramid Tracker. This Web-based interactive tool helps consumers compare their diet and physical activity to current health recommendations. Individuals can enter the foods they eat and their physical activities for a day and obtain the energy balance between them. MyPyramid Tracker provides each user with detailed, personalized results.

Vegetarian Diets

In a **vegetarian diet,** vegetables are the foundation and meat, fish, and poultry are limited or eliminated. There are four kinds of vegetarian diets. A **vegan diet** excludes foods of animal origin. A **lacto-vegetarian diet** excludes eggs, fish, poultry, and meat. A **lacto-ovo-vegetarian diet** excludes fish, poultry, and red meat. A **semivegetarian diet** excludes red meat.

People follow a vegetarian diet for different reasons. Consider the health benefits. Animal products are sources of fats, saturated fats, and cholesterol. A diet low in fats, saturated fats, and cholesterol helps reduce blood cholesterol and reduces the risks of developing high blood pressure, heart disease, diabetes, and breast and colon cancer. Such a diet also makes it easier to maintain a healthful weight. Of course, a person can eat red meat occasionally and still obtain these health benefits.

Young people choosing a vegetarian diet should discuss their choice with their parents or guardian and a physician or dietitian. Teens need to get enough protein, B vitamins, and calcium for growth and development. Foods of animal origin are a source of complete protein. Foods of plant origin are sources of incomplete protein. Teens who do not eat foods of animal origin must combine different sources of incomplete protein to get all the essential amino acids. For example, a teen might eat a vegetable burger and a serving of beans at the same meal or vegetarian chili topped with cheese. Because foods of animal origin are the only natural source of vitamin B_{12}, a physician or dietitian may recommend vitamin supplements. Dairy foods are the best source of calcium. Teens who eliminate or restrict dairy products must discuss with a physician or dietitian how to get enough calcium.

FIGURE 8-3

MyPyramid: Food Intake Patterns

The suggested amounts of food to consume from the basic food groups, subgroups, and oils to meet recommended nutrient intakes at 12 different calorie levels. Nutrient and energy contributions from each group are calculated according to the nutrient-dense forms of foods in each group (e.g., lean meats and fat-free milk). The table also shows the discretionary calorie allowance that can be accommodated within each calorie level, in addition to the suggested amounts of nutrient-dense forms of foods in each group.

DAILY AMOUNT OF FOOD FROM EACH GROUP

CALORIE LEVEL[1]	1,000	1,200	1,400	1,600	1,800	2,000	2,200	2,400	2,600	2,800	3,000	3,200
Fruits[2]	1 cup	1 cup	1.5 cups	1.5 cups	1.5 cups	2 cups	2 cups	2 cups	2 cups	2.5 cups	2.5 cups	2.5 cups
Vegetables[3]	1 cup	1.5 cups	1.5 cups	2 cups	2.5 cups	2.5cups	3 cups	3 cups	3.5 cups	4 cups	4 cups	4 cups
Grains[4]	3 oz-eq	4 oz-eq	5 oz-eq	5 oz-eq	6 oz-eq	6 oz-eq	7 oz-eq	8 oz-eq	9 oz-eq	10 oz-eq	10 oz-eq	10 oz-eq
Meat and Beans[5]	2 oz-eq	3 oz-eq	4 oz-eq	5 oz-eq	5 oz-eq	5.5 oz-eq	6 oz-eq	6.5 oz-eq	6.5 oz-eq	7 oz-eq	7 oz-eq	7 oz-eq
Milk[6]	2 cups	2 cups	2 cups	3 cups	3 cups	3 cups	3 cups	3 cups	3 cups	3 cups	3 cups	3 cups
Oils[7]	3 tsp	4 tsp	4 tsp	5 tsp	5 tsp	6 tsp	6 tsp	7 tsp	8 tsp	8 tsp	10 tsp	11 tsp
Discretionary calorie allowance[8]	165	171	171	132	195	267	290	362	410	426	512	648

1 **Calorie Levels** are set across a wide range to accommodate the needs of different individuals. The following table "Estimated Daily Calorie Needs" can be used to help assign individuals to the food intake pattern at a particular calorie level.

2 **Fruit Group** includes all fresh, frozen, canned, and dried fruits and fruit juices. In general, 1 cup of fruit or 100% fruit juice, or 1/2 cup of dried fruit can be considered as 1 cup from the fruit group.

3 **Vegetable Group** includes all fresh, frozen, canned, and dried vegetables and vegetable juices. In general, 1 cup of raw or cooked vegetables or vegetable juice, or 2 cups of raw leafy greens can be considered as 1 cup from the vegetable group.

VEGETABLE SUBGROUP AMOUNTS ARE PER WEEK

CALORIE LEVEL	1,000	1,200	1,400	1,600	1,800	2,000	2,200	2,400	2,600	2,800	3,000	3,200
Dark green veg.	1 c/wk	1.5 c/wk	1.5 c/wk	2 c/wk	3 c/wk	3 c/wk	3 c/wk	3 c/wk	3 c/wk	3 c/wk	3 c/wk	3 c/wk
Orange veg.	.5 c/wk	1 c/wk	1 c/wk	1.5 c/wk	2 c/wk	2 c/wk	2 c/wk	2 c/wk	2.5 c/wk	2.5 c/wk	2.5 c/wk	2.5 c/wk
Legumes	.5 c/wk	1 c/wk	1 c/wk	2.5 c/wk	3 c/wk	3 c/wk	3 c/wk	3 c/wk	3.5 c/wk	3.5 c/wk	3.5 c/wk	3.5 c/wk
Starch veg.	1.5 c/wk	2.5 c/wk	2.5 c/wk	2.5 c/wk	3 c/wk	3 c/wk	6 c/wk	6 c/wk	7 c/wk	7 c/wk	9 c/wk	9 c/wk
Other veg.	3.5 c/wk	4.5 c/wk	4.5 c/wk	5.5 c/wk	6.5 c/wk	6.5 c/wk	7 c/wk	7 c/wk	8.5 c/wk	8.5 c/wk	10 c/wk	10 c/wk

4 **Grains Group** includes all foods made from wheat, rice, oats, cornmeal, and barley, such as bread, pasta, oatmeal, breakfast cereals, tortillas, and grits. In general, 1 slice of bread, 1 cup of ready-to-eat cereal, or 1/2 cup of cooked rice, pasta, or cooked cereal can be considered as 1 ounce equivalent from the grains group. **At least half of all grains consumed should be whole grains.**

5 **Meat & Beans Group** In general, 1 ounce of lean meat, poultry, or fish, 1 egg, 1 tbsp. peanut butter, 1/4 cup cooked dry beans, or 1/2 ounce of nuts or seeds can be considered as 1 ounce equivalent from the meat and beans group.

FIGURE 8-3 (*CONTINUED*)

MyPyramid: Food Intake Patterns

6 **Milk Group** includes all fluid milk products and foods made from milk that retain their calcium content, such as yogurt and cheese. Foods made from milk that have little to no calcium, such as cream cheese, cream, and butter, are not part of the group. Most milk group choices should be fat-free or low-fat. In general, 1 cup of milk or yogurt, 1 1/2 ounces of natural cheese, or 2 ounces of processed cheese can be considered as 1 cup from the milk group.

7 **Oils** include fats from many different plants and from fish that are liquid at room temperature, such as canola, corn, olive, soybean, and sunflower oil. Some foods are naturally high in oils, like nuts, olives, some fish, and avocados. Foods that are mainly oil include mayonnaise, certain salad dressings, and soft margarine.

8 **Discretionary Calorie Allowance** is the remaining amount of calories in a food intake pattern after accounting for the calories needed for all food groups—using forms of foods that are fat-free or low-fat and with no added sugars.

ESTIMATED DAILY CALORIE NEEDS

To determine which food intake pattern to use for an individual, the following chart gives an estimate of individual calorie needs. The calorie range for each age/sex group is based on physical activity level, from sedentary to active.

	Calorie Range		
Children	**Sedentary**	$\rightarrow$	**Active**
2–3 years	1,000	$\rightarrow$	1,400
Females			
4–8 years	1,200	$\rightarrow$	1,800
9–13	1,600	$\rightarrow$	2,200
14–18	1,800	$\rightarrow$	2,400
19–30	2,000	$\rightarrow$	2,400
31–50	1,800	$\rightarrow$	2,200
51+	1,600	$\rightarrow$	2,200
Males			
4–8	1,400	$\rightarrow$	2,000
9–13	1,800	$\rightarrow$	2,600
14–18	2,200	$\rightarrow$	3,200
19–30	2,400	$\rightarrow$	3,000
31–50	2,200	$\rightarrow$	3,000
51+	2,000	$\rightarrow$	2,800

Sedentary means a lifestyle that includes only the light physical activity associated with typical day-to-day life.

Active means a lifestyle that includes physical activity equivalent to walking more than 3 miles per day at 3 to 4 miles per hour, in addition to the light physical activity associated with typical day-to-day life.

U.S. Department of Agriculture, Center for Nutrition Policy and Promotion, April 2005

Strict vegans can meet protein requirements by eating complementary combinations of plant foods. Complementary combinations of plant foods can provide adequate amounts of essential amino acids. Examples of complementary combinations are peanut butter and whole-grain bread, and corn and beans. Eating several grains, fruits, vegetables, legumes, nuts, and seeds each day helps ensure that all essential amino acids are included in the diet.

Health Goal #34

I Will Follow the Dietary Guidelines

The Dietary Guidelines

The Dietary Guidelines for Americans are recommendations for diet choices for healthy Americans who are two years of age or older. The Dietary Guidelines for Americans are a result of research done by the U.S. Department of Agriculture and the U.S. Department of Health and Human Services. The Dietary Guidelines were first published in 1980. They are updated every five years to reflect new scientific information about diet (Ballard-Barbash, 2001). For example, the 2000 guidelines for the first time emphasized being physically active each day (Troiano, Macera, & Ballard-Barbash, 2001) and keeping food safe (Woteki, Facinoli, & Schor, 2001).

Unlike previous versions of the Dietary Guidelines, which were written for the general public, the 2005 guidelines are oriented toward policymakers, health and nutrition educators, nutritionists, and health care providers and contain more technical information. The purpose of the 2005 guidelines is to summarize and synthesize knowledge regarding individual nutrients and food components into recommendations for a pattern of eating that can be adopted by the public. The Dietary Guidelines' report identifies forty-one key recommendations (twenty-three for the general public and eighteen for special populations) that are grouped into nine focus areas: adequate nutrients within calorie needs, weight management, physical activity, food groups to encourage, fats, carbohydrates, sodium and potassium, alcoholic beverages, and food safety. The key recommendations for the general population are shown

in Figure 8-4. In general, the recommendations are based on accumulated scientific evidence for lowering the risk of chronic disease (cardiovascular disease, Type 2 diabetes, hypertension, osteoporosis, and certain cancers) and promoting health. The recommendations encourage most Americans to eat fewer calories, be more physically active, and make wiser food choices. The information in the Dietary Guidelines will help health and nutrition education experts develop educational materials and nutrition education programs (U.S. Department of Health and Human Services and U.S. Department of Agriculture, 2005a).

A booklet has been developed for the general public that is based on the 2005 Dietary Guidelines that is titled *Finding Your Way to a Healthier You* (U.S. Department of Health and Human Services and U.S. Department of Agriculture, 2005b). It encourages and provides guidance to individuals to make smart choices from every food group, find a balance between food and physical activity, and get the most out of the calories they eat. It encourages a healthy eating plan that emphasizes fruits, vegetables, whole grains, and fat-free or low-fat milk and milk products; includes lean meats, poultry, fish bean, eggs, and nuts; and is low in saturated fats, *trans* fats, cholesterol, salt (sodium), and added sugars. Individuals are encouraged to look at food labels and compare them with what nutrients they are also getting to decide whether the food is worth eating. This booklet and the Dietary Guidelines for Americans are available online at www.healthierus.gov/dietaryguidelines.

Health Goal #35

I Will Follow a Healthful Diet That Reduces the Risk of Disease

Diet affects a person's health status in the present as well as in the future. A healthful diet is needed for growth and development. It provides energy for daily activities, including exercise. Children and teens who eat a healthful diet reduce their risk of developing certain diseases as adults. For instance, a healthful diet reduces the risk of cancer, cardiovascular diseases, diabetes, hypoglycemia, and osteoporosis.

FIGURE 8-4

2005 Dietary Guidelines for Americans

Key Recommendations for the General Population

ADEQUATE NUTRIENTS WITHIN CALORIE NEEDS
- Consume a variety of nutrient-dense foods and beverages within and among the basic food groups while choosing foods that limit the intake of saturated and trans-fats, cholesterol, added sugars, salt, and alcohol.
- Meet recommended intakes within energy needs by adopting a balanced eating pattern, such as the U.S. Department of Agriculture (USDA) Food Guide or the Dietary Approaches to Stop Hypertension (DASH) Eating Plan.

WEIGHT MANAGEMENT
- To maintain body weight in a healthy range, balance calories from foods and beverages with calories expended.
- To prevent gradual weight gain over time, make small decreases in food and beverage calories and increase physical activity.

PHYSICAL ACTIVITY
- Engage in regular physical activity and reduce sedentary activities to promote health, psychological well-being, and a healthy body weight.
  - To reduce the risk of chronic disease in adulthood, engage in at least 30 minutes of moderate-intensity physical activity, above usual activity, at work or home on most days of the week.
  - For most people, greater health benefits can be obtained by engaging in physical activity of more vigorous intensity or longer duration.
  - To help manage body weight and prevent gradual, unhealthy body weight gain in adulthood, engage in approximately 60 minutes of moderate- to vigorous-intensity activity on most days of the week while not exceeding caloric intake requirements.
  - To sustain weight loss in adulthood, participate in at least 60 to 90 minutes of daily moderate-intensity physical activity while not exceeding caloric intake requirements. Some people may need to consult with a health care provider before participating in this level of activity.
- Achieve physical fitness by including cardiovascular conditioning, stretching exercises for flexibility, and resistance exercises or calisthenics for muscle strength and endurance.

FOOD GROUPS TO ENCOURAGE
- Consume a sufficient amount of fruits and vegetables while staying within energy needs. Two cups of fruit and 2 1/2 cups of vegetables per day are recommended for a reference 2,000-calorie intake, with higher or lower amounts depending on the calorie level.
- Choose a variety of fruits and vegetables each day. In particular, select from all five vegetable subgroups (dark green, orange, legumes, starchy vegetables, and other vegetables) several times a week.
- Consume 3 or more ounce-equivalents of whole-grain products per day, with the rest of the recommended grains coming from enriched or whole-grain products. In general, at least half the grains should come from whole grains.
- Consume 3 cups per day of fat-free or low-fat milk or equivalent milk products.

FATS
- Consume less than 10 percent of calories from saturated fatty acids and less than 300 mg/day of cholesterol, and keep trans-fatty acid consumption as low as possible.
- Keep total fat intake between 20 to 35 percent of calories, with most fats coming from sources of polyunsaturated and monounsaturated fatty acids, such as fish, nuts, and vegetable oils.
- When selecting and preparing meat, poultry, dry beans, and milk or milk products, make choices that are lean, low fat, or fat-free.
- Limit intake of fats and oils high in saturated or trans-fatty acids, and choose products low in such fats and oils.

CARBOHYDRATES
- Choose fiber-rich fruits, vegetables, and whole grains often.
- Choose and prepare foods and beverages with little added sugars or caloric sweeteners, such as amounts suggested by the USDA Food Guide and the DASH Eating Plan.
- Reduce the incidence of dental caries by practicing good oral hygiene and consuming sugar- and starch-containing foods and beverages less frequently.

SODIUM AND POTASSIUM
- Consume less than 2,300 mg (approximately 1 teaspoon of salt) of sodium per day.

FIGURE 8-4 *(CONTINUED)*

2005 Dietary Guidelines for Americans

- Choose and prepare foods with little salt. At the same time, consume potassium-rich foods, such as fruits and vegetables.

ALCOHOLIC BEVERAGES

- Those who choose to drink alcoholic beverages should do so sensibly and in moderation, defined as the consumption of up to one drink per day for women and up to two drinks per day for men.
- Alcoholic beverages should not be consumed by some individuals, including those who cannot restrict their alcohol intake, women of childbearing age who may become pregnant, pregnant and lactating women, children and adolescents, individuals taking medications that can interact with alcohol, and those with specific medical conditions.
- Alcoholic beverages should be avoided by individuals engaging in activities that require attention, skill, or coordination, such as driving or operating machinery.

FOOD SAFETY

- To avoid microbial foodborne illness:
  - Clean hands, food contact surfaces, and fruits and vegetables. Meat and poultry should not be washed or rinsed.
  - Separate raw, cooked, and ready-to-eat foods while shopping, preparing, or storing foods.
  - Cook foods to a safe temperature to kill microorganisms.
  - Chill (refrigerate) perishable food promptly and defrost foods properly.
  - Avoid raw (unpasteurized) milk or any products made from unpasteurized milk, raw or partially cooked eggs or foods containing raw eggs, raw or undercooked meat and poultry, unpasteurized juices, and raw sprouts.

Note: The Dietary Guidelines for Americans 2005 contains additional recommendations for specific populations. The full document is available at www.healthierus.gov/dietaryguidelines.

Diet and Cancer

The American Cancer Society (2006) publishes Nutrition and Physical Activity Guidelines to advise health care professionals and the general public about dietary and other lifestyle practices that reduce cancer risk. The guidelines, updated in 2006, are based on the current scientific evidence on diet and physical activity in relation to cancer risk:

Maintain a healthy weight throughout life.

- Balance caloric intake with physical activity.
- Avoid excessive weight gain throughout life.
- Achieve and maintain a healthy weight if currently overweight or obese.

Adopt a physically active lifestyle.

- Adults: Engage in at least 30 minutes of moderate to vigorous physical activity, above usual activities, on 5 or more days of the week; 45 to 60 minutes of intentional physical activity are preferable.
- Children and adolescents: Engage in at least 60 minutes per day of moderate to vigorous physical activity at least 5 days per week.

Eat a healthy diet, with an emphasis on plant sources.

- Choose foods and beverages in amounts that help achieve and maintain a healthy weight.
- Eat 5 or more servings of a variety of vegetables and fruits each day.
- Choose whole grains in preference to processed (refined) grains.
- Limit consumption of processed and red meats.

If you drink alcoholic beverages, limit consumption.

- Drink no more than 1 drink per day for women or 2 per day for men.

The American Cancer Society emphasizes the importance of eating a variety of fruits and vegetables each day. Eating vegetables and fruits is associated with a lower risk of lung, oral, esophageal, stomach, and colon cancer. Many compounds in fruits and vegetables may be protective against cancer (Kushi et al., 2006).

- **Phytochemicals** are a wide variety of compounds produced by plants to protect against insects or perform other important biological functions for plants. Phytochemicals may play a role in reducing cancer risk.

- **Antioxidants** are substances that protect and repair cells damaged as result of normal metabolism (oxidation). Antioxidants include vitamin C, vitamin E, carotenoids (e.g., beta-carotene), and many other phytochemicals.
- **Lycopene** is the red-orange carotene pigment found primarily in tomatoes and tomato-based foods. Lycopene also is found to a lesser extent in pink grapefruit and watermelon. Because consumption of tomato products reduces the risk of some cancers, it is suspected that lycopene is the nutrient responsible for the lowered risk.
- **Vitamin C** is a water-soluble vitamin found in many vegetables and fruits, particularly oranges, grapefruit, and peppers. Eating foods rich in vitamin C is associated with a reduced risk for cancer.
- **Folate** is a B vitamin found in many vegetables, beans, fruits, whole grains, and fortified breakfast cereals. Grain products produced in the United States are fortified with folate. A deficiency of folate in the diet may increase the risk of cancers of the colon, rectum, and breast. Folate consumption through vegetables, fruits, and enriched grain products may reduce cancer risk.
- **Fiber** is the part of grains and plant foods that cannot be digested. Good sources of fiber are beans, vegetables, whole grains, and fruits. Fiber consumption and reduced cancer risk are weakly associated. However, eating foods high in fiber is recommended because these foods have other significant health benefits.

Diet and Cardiovascular Diseases

A **cardiovascular disease** is a disease of the heart and blood vessels. Another term for cardiovascular disease is heart disease. Cardiovascular diseases are a leading cause of premature death and disability. The risk of developing premature cardiovascular diseases can be reduced by practicing the following dietary recommendations from the American Heart Association (Lichtenstein et al. 2006):

- Balance calorie intake and physical activity to achieve or maintain a healthy body weight.
- Consume a diet rich in vegetables and fruits.
- Choose whole-grain, high-fiber foods.
- Consume fish, especially oily fish, at least twice a week.

- Limit your intake of saturated fat to less than 7 percent of energy, *trans* fat to less than 1 percent of energy, and cholesterol to less than 300 milligrams per day by
  — choosing lean meats and vegetable alternatives
  — selecting fat-free (skim), 1 percent-fat, and low-fat dairy products
  — minimizing intake of partially hydrogenated fats
- Minimize your intake of beverages and foods with added sugars.
- Choose and prepare foods with little or no salt.
- If you consume alcohol, do so in moderation.
- When you eat food that is prepared outside of the home, follow these recommendations.

Diet, Diabetes, and Hypoglycemia

Diabetes, or **diabetes mellitus,** is a disease in which the body produces little or no insulin. **Insulin** is a hormone that regulates the blood sugar level. Without treatment, a person with diabetes will have a high blood sugar level. Diabetes is treated first by diet and exercise. If needed, medications or insulin may be used. A physician and dietitian can work with someone with diabetes to make a plan. The person may be advised to do the following:

- Eat complex carbohydrates and protein to provide long-lasting energy.
- Limit total carbohydrate intake, especially sweets.
- Eat six small meals a day to maintain a constant blood sugar level.
- Have regular examinations to test blood sugar levels and reevaluate diet.
- Maintain desirable weight.

Hypoglycemia is a condition in which the pancreas produces too much insulin, causing the blood sugar level to be low. Normally, when a person eats, the blood sugar level increases. As blood sugar level increases, the pancreas secretes insulin into the bloodstream. When proteins and complex carbohydrates are eaten, insulin is secreted at a slower rate. People with hypoglycemia experience a rapid increase in blood sugar followed by a sudden drop. When their blood sugar level drops, they feel dizzy, weak, irritable, and confused. They may have headaches and feel hungry.

To relieve these symptoms, they need to eat again to restore their blood sugar level.

People with hypoglycemia follow a diet similar to people who have diabetes and may follow the same guidelines:

- Eat complex carbohydrates and protein to provide long-lasting energy.
- Limit the amounts of sweets. (Simple sugars increase blood sugar and the need for insulin.)
- Eat six small meals a day to maintain a constant blood sugar level.
- Have regular examinations to test blood sugar levels and reevaluate diet.
- Maintain desirable weight.

Osteoporosis

Osteoporosis is a decrease in bone density. Osteoporosis causes bones to fracture easily. The disease develops unnoticed over many years, with no symptoms or discomfort, until a fracture occurs. It often causes a loss of height and dowager's hump in the elderly. A **dowager's hump** is a severely rounded back due to reduced bone mass in the spine. Osteoporosis is a major cause of death in elderly females. Females are ten times more likely than males to have severe osteoporosis.

Calcium and phosphorus form the hard substance in bone. Calcium is a mineral that is essential to bone growth. During the growing years, a child's body needs calcium to build strong bones and to create a supply of calcium reserves. Building bone mass in childhood and adolescence is a good investment for future health. A deficiency of calcium during growth, especially in females, increases the risk for osteoporosis.

Eating a balanced diet is critical to obtaining enough calcium. Dairy products, including milk, yogurt, and cheese, are excellent sources of calcium. A serving of milk, which is eight ounces, provides 300 milligrams of calcium. Green leafy vegetables, such as broccoli and collard greens, are good sources of calcium. For a person whose diet is calcium deficient, calcium supplements may be advised. A person should talk to a physician before taking a calcium supplement.

Inadequate calcium intake in adolescence can contribute to osteoporosis later in life. Bone growth occurs more rapidly in adolescence than in any other time in life. Bones approach maximum density during childhood, adolescence, and young adulthood, so obtaining enough calcium, and hence bone density, during childhood and adolescence is critical to reduce the risk of osteoporosis later in life. A daily intake of 800 milligrams of calcium a day is recommended for children ages four through eight. For older children nine through eighteen, 1,300 milligrams a day is recommended. To meet this recommendation, adolescents need to consume four to five servings of dairy foods or other calcium-rich foods daily.

It is typical for teen and preteen girls to consume only one or two servings of dairy foods a day. One reason for this may be their belief that milk and other dairy products will make them fat. They are often unaware that skim or low-fat dairy foods will not increase caloric intake or weight. Skim and low-fat dairy foods contain as much calcium as whole milk. For example, an eight-ounce serving of skim milk has 80 calories and 300 milligrams of calcium. Eight ounces of 2 percent milk contains 120 calories, and the same amount of whole milk contains 150 calories. Two percent and whole milk also provide approximately 300 milligrams of calcium. Another reason young people do not get enough calcium is soda pop consumption. Soda pop is often a replacement for milk. Consumption of milk by children and adolescents has decreased since the late 1970s, while intake of soda pop has increased (Amschler, 1999).

Another reason that some people fail to meet calcium needs is lactose intolerance. This is discussed in the following section.

Food Allergies and Intolerances

A **food allergy** is an abnormal response of the immune system to food. The body mistakes a protein in food (allergen) as a threat and produces an antibody to it. Food allergies can cause severe illness, and some may be deadly. A person who suspects a food allergy should see a physician. The physician first may consider other possibilities that lead to the symptoms. If a food allergy is diagnosed, the physician might recommend that the person completely avoid the food causing the allergy or might recommend some other treatment, such as medication. The foods that most commonly cause allergic reactions in adults are shellfish, peanuts, fish, and eggs. In children, foods such as eggs, milk, and peanuts commonly cause allergic reactions. Symptoms of food allergies include

- Vomiting
- Diarrhea
- Abdominal cramps
- Hives
- Swelling
- Sneezing
- Asthma
- Difficulty breathing
- Itching
- Nausea

Food allergies are actually quite rare. According to the International Food Information Council (2003), only about 2 percent of adults have food allergies. Infants are more likely than adults to have a food allergy. Between 4 and 8 percent of infants and young children have food allergies. Many infants outgrow their food allergies.

The most severe food allergy reaction is called anaphylaxis. **Anaphylaxis** is a severe reaction to an allergen that results in serious symptoms, such as itchy tongue or mouth, throat tightening, wheezing, shock, or cardiac arrest. Immediate medical help is needed to treat anaphylaxis. The treatment usually includes an injection of epinephrine. Fortunately, anaphylactic reactions are rare. They occur most often when a person is eating away from home.

What many people think are food allergies are actually food intolerances. A **food intolerance** is an abnormal response to food that is not caused by the immune system. It merely means that a food is not tolerated well.

LACTASE DEFICIENCY

Lactase deficiency is a condition in which lactase, an enzyme that breaks down the milk sugar present in the cells of the small intestine, is missing. This condition results in **lactose intolerance**—the inability to digest lactose, which is found in most dairy products. As the undigested lactose moves through the lower gastrointestinal tract, it releases gases that cause discomfort. The symptoms of lactase deficiency include abdominal pain, bloating, and diarrhea.

Lactase deficiency is the most common form of food intolerance. Many people become lactose intolerant as adolescents or adults. They feel ill or uncomfortable after eating or drinking dairy products. Some people feel a little uncomfortable after eating a lot of dairy foods. Others have severe problems after eating even a small amount of foods containing lactose. Drinking skim or low-fat milk will not help. It is not fat, but lactose, that causes the symptoms. Some people with lactose intolerance find relief of symptoms through over-the-counter lactose remedies. Others choose to drink and eat lactose-free products, such as lactose-free milk, soybean milk, or milk substitute. Lactose also is found in some foods that are not considered dairy foods, such as some cold cuts and baked products.

CELIAC DISEASE

Celiac disease, also known as celiac sprue, is intolerance to gluten due to an unknown genetic defect. Gluten is a part of wheat, rye, and certain other grains. The symptoms of celiac sprue include tiredness, breathlessness, weight loss, diarrhea, vomiting, and abdominal pain. People with celiac sprue must stick to a restricted diet and avoid eating any form of gluten.

ABNORMAL REACTIONS TO FOOD ADDITIVES

Food additives can cause allergic reactions. Monosodium glutamate (MSG) is a common cause of food intolerance. A flavor enhancer added to many foods, it can cause headaches, feelings of warmth, and chest pain in some people. MSG is often added to Chinese and other Asian foods. Coloring agents, such as yellow dye number 5, also have been associated with food intolerance. Coloring agents may cause a rash or digestive problems. Sulfites added to foods also can cause food intolerance. Sulfites can be found in wines, potatoes, and packaged foods. Sulfites are especially harmful to people with asthma, who might react by going into shock.

Health Goal #36

I Will Develop Healthful Eating Habits

Motives for Eating

Often people eat simply because they are hungry. **Hunger** is the physiological need for food. Following are examples of eating motivated by hunger:

- Eating breakfast because they have not eaten since the night before
- Eating a sports nutrition bar after burning many calories playing in a strenuous soccer game
- Eating an extra helping of vegetables at dinner because they are having a teenage growth spurt and sense a need to eat more
- Eating after a medical test before which they had to fast for twelve hours

A desire to eat also comes from factors other than hunger. The following are examples of eating for reasons other than hunger:

- Gorging on chips because they feel stressed out about a test
- Treating themselves to a pizza because they feel rejected because they were not invited to a party
- Cooking themselves some Tuscan pasta because they've spent the past three hours reading cookbooks

People need to eat when they are hungry. They need to eat to obtain the nutrients that are necessary for good health.

- People do not need to eat to manage stress.
- People do not need to eat when tempted by the sight or smell of food.
- People do not need to eat when feeling rejected, depressed, anxious, bored, or lonely.

- People do not need to eat to have something to do at a party where they feel uncomfortable.
- People do not need to eat because other people are eating.

To develop healthful eating habits, people must understand why they eat. They should plan breakfast, lunch, dinner, and snacks to satisfy their hunger. They must recognize when they are eating for reasons other than hunger. Then they must evaluate whether eating for this reason promotes their health or harms their health. Suppose a person eats a few slices of pizza with friends half an hour after eating dinner, solely for the purpose of being just like those friends; this is not a healthful reason to eat pizza.

Eating is not the best way to handle feeling rejected, depressed, anxious, bored, or lonely. Relying on eating as a coping mechanism can lead to harmful eating habits, such as eating disorders.

Planning a Healthful Breakfast and Lunch

The word *breakfast* means "break the fast." After a night's sleep, the body has been fasting (going without food for several hours) and is running out of energy. Eating a healthful breakfast provides the energy a person needs to begin the day. Eating a healthful breakfast also jump-starts metabolism. **Metabolism** is the rate at which food is converted into energy in body cells. Metabolism slows down during sleep. After eating, the body begins to use the nutrients in the foods and metabolism speeds up again. Eating a healthful breakfast also helps one to feel alert and provides the recommended nutrient intakes needed from MyPyramid. The Dietary Guidelines should be followed when choosing foods and beverages for breakfast.

Eating a healthful breakfast begins the day in a healthful way. Lunch is also a must. A well-balanced lunch provides energy for afternoon activities, making it possible to remain alert and able to do work. Eating lunch readies a person to participate in activities after lunch. A person who skips lunch may experience a midafternoon feeling of tiredness. MyPyramid helps in choosing foods and beverages for lunch.

When making breakfast and lunch choices, a person should do the following:

- Eat foods high in proteins.
- Eat fruits or drink fruit juice.
- Eat vegetables or drink vegetable juice.
- Eat foods, such as cereal or bread, that are sources of grain and fiber.

The following are poor choices for breakfast and lunch:

- Skipping foods that are a source of protein
- Surviving on a doughnut, sweet roll, or candy bar
- Eating fatty foods, greasy foods, or fried foods
- Pigging out on salt-cured foods, such as ham or bacon

COMMON EXCUSES
FOR SKIPPING BREAKFAST

"I have no time for breakfast" is a common excuse. People who are pressed for time can prepare breakfast the night before or choose foods that are easy to prepare in a hurry—such as skim milk, juice, bagels, cold cereal, and reduced-fat peanut butter on whole-grain bread. Some people contend that skipping breakfast will help them to lose weight. However, eating breakfast jump-starts metabolism, causing more calories to be burned, and skipping breakfast usually causes a person to eat more calories during the rest of the day. A breakfast containing protein, such as an omelet made from egg substitute, helps maintain energy level throughout the morning and is low in calories. Some people say that they don't eat breakfast because they don't like breakfast foods. But just about any food can be eaten for breakfast—veggie pizza, tuna fish, beans and rice, tamales.

Planning Dinner and Snacks

Breakfast helps start the day, and a healthful dinner helps complete daily nutrition requirements. Eating a nutritious dinner requires careful planning at first. After evaluating the foods that have been eaten so far that day, a person can select, for dinner, foods that provide nutrients that properly supplement the nutrients obtained at breakfast, lunch, and between meals. For people who are less physically active in the evening (and this is

most of us), dinner should supply no more than one-third of daily caloric intake. Following are some helpful hints for dinner choices:

- Eat a variety of foods.
- Round out daily nutrition requirements.
- Eat early in the evening rather than close to bedtime.
- Avoid caffeine to prevent difficulty falling asleep.
- Avoid spicy foods if they interfere with getting a good night's sleep

Snacks also require planning to be healthful. People should eat snacks to quell hunger and to get needed nutrients (see MyPyramid). People should not snack out of boredom, loneliness, anxiety, or depressed feelings, or just to take a break from hard work such as homework. Snacking for these reasons leads to harmful eating habits. A person should follow the Dietary Guidelines when choosing snacks. The following are guidelines for snacking:

1. Select snacks that provide nutrient contributions specified in MyPyramid. For example, a person who has not yet eaten enough vegetables during the day might choose to snack on raw carrots.
2. Limit snacks that are high in sugar.
3. Limit snacks that are high in fats and saturated fats.
4. Limit snacks that are high in salt.
5. Carry healthful snacks, to avoid the temptation to buy snacks from vending machines. (The same foods also cost more from a vending machine than from a grocery store.)
6. Consider the following healthful snack choices: fat-free yogurt, fruit, plain popcorn, low-salt pretzels, veggies, low-fat granola, low-sugar cereals, crackers, rice cakes, reduced-fat peanut butter, cottage cheese, bagels, bean dip, shrimp, juice, and low-fat cheese.

Students Are Flunking Healthy Eating

A report by six leading medical associations (American Academy of Family Physicians, American Academy of Pediatrics, American Dietetic Association, National Hispanic Medical Association, the National Medical Association, and the U.S. Department of Agriculture [2000]) cited a number of statistics showing that today's children and youth tend to have unhealthy eating patterns that can have negative consequences for their health. Following are some of those statistics:

- Only 2 percent of youth meet all recommendations of the Food Guide Pyramid; 16 percent do not meet any of the recommendations.
- Less than 15 percent of schoolchildren eat the recommended number of fruit servings, less than 20 percent eat the recommended number of vegetable servings, less than 25 percent eat the recommended number of grain servings, and only 30 percent consume the recommended number of milk group servings on any given day.
- Only 16 percent of schoolchildren meet the guidelines for saturated fat on any given day.
- Teenagers drink twice as much carbonated soda as milk, and only 19 percent of girls aged nine to nineteen meet the recommended intakes for calcium.
- About 12 percent of students report skipping breakfast. Only 11 percent report eating a breakfast that contains foods from three food groups and food energy intakes greater than 25 percent of the recommended dietary allowance (RDA). The likelihood of eating breakfast declines with the age of the student.

Nutrition and Sports

Many young people are physically active, enjoy sports, or are members of athletic teams. Young people are often puzzled about what is the best diet when participating in sports and whether certain foods or eating habits improve athletic performance. Young people who participate in sports should be counseled to get answers to their questions from well-qualified professionals. A physician or dietitian can provide answers.

Young people need to carefully evaluate advertising claims that specific foods and beverages enhance performance. These advertisements are designed to sell the products, not to enhance people's health. Food labels should also be examined to learn nutrition information.

This section of the chapter examines how the following products and practices affect performance in sports and health status: vitamin supplements, salt tablets, sport drinks, energy bars, carbohydrate loading, protein supplements, creatine, "making weight," and precompetition meals.

VITAMIN SUPPLEMENTS

A supplement is something that is added to the diet to enhance performance. For example, a person might take extra vitamins to improve performance. **Megadosing** is taking vitamins in excessive amounts. To date, there is no evidence that megadosing will improve sport performance. Some vitamins in excess can be toxic.

SALT TABLETS

Some people also might try to enhance performance by taking salt tablets. Because their skin is salty during physical activity, some people believe the salt must be replaced. Other people think that they need salt to keep the body from losing too much water. However, most people get ten times the salt they need. What many people do not, and should, replace is the water they lose through physical activity. The best advice is to forget the salt tablets and drink plenty of water.

SPORT DRINKS

On TV, there are many ads for sport drinks that help replace electrolytes lost during physical activity. An **electrolyte** is a nutrient that becomes electrically charged when in a solution such as a body fluid. Sodium and potassium are electrolytes. Electrolytes are important because they need to be in just the right balance for a person to have a normal heartbeat. Sport drinks should be used to replace *fluid*. They should not be used to maintain electrolyte balance. A physician or dietitian can advise a person on how to maintain a healthful electrolyte balance. Many sport drinks are high in sugar and calories. The best (and least expensive) way to maintain a healthful electrolyte balance is to eat foods with potassium, follow the Dietary Guidelines for salt intake, and drink plenty of water.

ENERGY BARS

Many energy bars look like candy bars. They are supposed to contain ingredients that enhance performance. People should read the food label before purchasing an energy bar. Many energy bars contain the main ingredient in candy bars—sugars. They are high in calories. Some energy bars are made from fruits, nuts, and grain. These energy bars are mostly carbohydrate and provide quick energy. The nuts are a source of protein, but usually the amount is too small to provide long-lasting energy. Some energy bars contain more grams of protein. These energy bars provide longer-lasting energy than the energy bars made of sugar.

CARBOHYDRATE LOADING

Carbohydrate loading is an eating strategy in which a few days of a very low carbohydrate intake is followed by a few days of a very high carbohydrate intake. This strategy, referred to as "carbo loading," is supposed to load the muscle with glycogen prior to strenuous physical activity. Experts have mixed opinions about the advantages of carbohydrate loading.

PROTEIN SUPPLEMENTS

Soy and whey in premade energy drinks or powders are the forms in which protein supplements are usually found. When taken in liquid form, they are sometimes called "protein shakes." Many who consume these products believe that the protein helps them build muscle. Health and fitness experts say that the amount of protein needed each day is about one gram of protein per pound of body weight. Most people easily meet or exceed this requirement. Any excess protein is converted to fat and not to muscle.

CREATINE

Creatine is an amino acid that is made naturally in the liver, kidneys, and pancreas. It is also found naturally in meat and fish. It is a popular dietary supplement. Many teenagers and young adults use creatine as a way to increase their performance in sports or as a way to more become more muscular. It is recommended that creatine be taken only under medical supervision. There is suspicion that creatine use could be linked to such adverse effects as cramping, diarrhea, nausea, dizziness, dehydration, incontinence, muscle strain, high blood pressure, and abnormal liver and kidney function.

"MAKING WEIGHT"

There is pressure for participants in some sports, such as wrestling or boxing, to maintain a certain weight, or "make weight." Other sports in which participants might be overly concerned about their weight include gymnastics, swimming, dancing, cheerleading, and running. Excessive concern about weight can lead to eating disorders.

PRECOMPETITION MEALS

It is generally recommended that athletes consume a pregame meal two to three hours before competition. Eating immediately before a competi-

tion can decrease an athlete's performance. Foods to avoid in a precompetition meal include these:

- Spicy foods, which might cause gastrointestinal problems
- Fried foods, which might cause gastrointestinal problems
- Sugary foods, which might cause gastrointestinal problems
- Caffeine, which can increase nervousness and stimulate the flow of urine

Health Goal #37

I Will Follow the Dietary Guidelines When I Go Out to Eat

Ordering from a Restaurant Menu

People can eat a healthful diet whether eating at home or in a restaurant. In a restaurant, as well as in the home, the Dietary Guidelines and MyPyramid can be followed in choosing foods that are low in fat, saturated fat, cholesterol, sugar, and salt. Food choices at restaurants should include fruits, vegetables, and grains. Some menus designate some foods as "heart healthy" or "light." Diners can ask about the ingredients in foods and should, especially if they have a food allergy or food intolerance. Diners at a restaurant can request that their food be prepared in a healthful way—such as without butter or salt, or broiled instead of fried—or that meat be cooked well done to ensure that pathogens are destroyed by thorough cooking. Diners should never be shy about asking for substitutions or about ingredients and preparation.

Ordering Fast Foods

Fast foods are foods that can be served quickly. Fast foods include TV dinners and foods served at fast-food restaurants. Fast foods are convenient and quick, but they can be expensive, and they can be high in calories, fat, and sodium. Fast

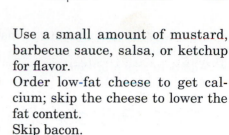

Burger and Fries

Here is your order: 65 gms of fat and 700 mg of sodium.

- Use a small amount of mustard, barbecue sauce, salsa, or ketchup for flavor.
- Order low-fat cheese to get calcium; skip the cheese to lower the fat content.
- Skip bacon.

When Ordering Chicken

Extra crispy usually means extra fattening. To make a healthful choice, consider the following when ordering chicken:

- Order grilled chicken.
- Avoid fried and breaded chicken.
- Choose white meat over dark meat.
- Remove the skin or order it skin-free.
- Order chicken sandwiches without mayonnaise and special sauces.
- Choose a whole-wheat or oat bran bun for additional fiber.
- Skip the fried and fattening chicken wings.

When Ordering Pizza

Two slices of a stuffed-crust pizza may contain more than twice the calories of a thin-crust pizza. To make healthful choices, consider the following when ordering pizza:

- Try pizza without cheese.
- Avoid pepperoni, sausage, and bacon.
- Order vegetables, such as broccoli, peppers, mushrooms, or spinach.
- Add pineapple for an extra serving of fruit.
- Skip extra cheese; it adds extra fat.

foods are frequently advertised on television and in other forms of mass media. Follow these three guidelines when ordering fast foods:

1. Ask the fast-food restaurant for nutrition information about the foods and beverages it serves. Read the information before ordering.
2. Choose foods and beverages that supply nutrient and energy needs as specified in My-Pyramid.
3. Follow the Dietary Guidelines and order foods that are low in fats, saturated fats, cholesterol, sugars, and salt. Include vegetables, fruits, and grains.

When Ordering a Burger

The average single burger at a fast-food restaurant contains anywhere from ten to twenty-six grams of fat. A double bacon cheeseburger can contain as much as seventy grams of fat. To make a healthful choice, consider the following when ordering a burger:

- Order the small or junior-size burger—the smaller the burger, the lower the fat, calories, and sodium content.
- Order the burger lean and emphasize that it should be cooked thoroughly.
- Choose a whole-wheat or oat bran bun for additional fiber.
- Order burgers without mayonnaise and special sauces.

When Getting a Salad

Just because a product is called salad doesn't mean it is low in fat. Tuna, chicken, potato, and pasta salads may contain lots of mayonnaise. A Caesar salad contains eggs, oils, and cheese. A chef's salad may contain cheese and ham. To make healthful choices, consider the following when getting a salad:

- Load up on fresh vegetables.
- Choose fat-free or low-fat salad dressings.
- Add fresh fruit.
- Order low-fat or fat-free cheese.

- Choose dark green lettuce instead of ice-berg lettuce.
- Add beans as a protein source.
- Add grilled chicken as a protein source.

WHEN SELECTING SIDE DISHES

Choose several side dishes, such as a side salad and baked potato, for a filling but low-calorie meal. To make a healthful choice, consider the following when selecting side dishes:

- Eat a salad with low-fat or fat-free dressing.
- Choose a plain baked potato instead of french fries.
- Skip the sour cream, bleu cheese, and bacon bits on baked potatoes.
- Have a side of steamed vegetables, such as corn, without butter.
- Choose vegetable soup on the side.
- Limit fried sides, such as onion rings.
- Don't add extra salt.

WHEN ORDERING BREAKFAST

A muffin may have as many calories and grams of fat as a piece of cake. Order low-fat or fat-free muffins. To make a healthful choice, consider the following when ordering breakfast:

- Order a fiber-rich, low-sugar cereal with skim or low-fat milk.
- Choose a low-fat bran muffin instead of a doughnut.
- Have a bagel or English muffin instead of a croissant or biscuit.
- Choose Canadian bacon rather than bacon or sausage.
- Drink fruit juice or eat fresh fruit.
- Order an omelet made of egg whites or egg substitute.

WHEN SELECTING DESSERTS AND DRINKS

If a food or beverage is sweet, it probably contains sugar. Watch out for the sugar content in fast-food desserts and beverages. To make healthful choices, consider the following when selecting desserts and drinks:

- Limit soda pops.
- Choose fat-free or low-fat yogurt shakes and sundaes.
- Drink fruit juices.
- Top yogurt sundaes with fresh fruits.
- Limit pies, cakes, and other fatty desserts.

New Food Options for Healthful Eating When Eating Out

Many fast-food restaurants cater to nutrition-conscious consumers by offering more menu choices for healthful eating. Compared to a few years ago, there is a varied assortment of salads, with low-fat dressings available, and other low-fat menu items. For example, a leading fast-food restaurant now offers a Penne Pasta Salad with Italian-style chicken. This item has 266 calories and its calories are less than 5 percent fat even with the dressing. This same restaurant currently also offers a fruit bag that consumers can substitute for french fries in children's meals. Young people and adults can opt to select a salad or baked potato instead of french fries when ordering a combo meal. Some fast-food restaurants offer a greater assortment of grilled chicken menu items and veggie burgers as healthful alternatives to fried chicken and hamburgers. Other healthful alternative trends include sandwiches with vegetables (e.g., pita bread sandwiches), lettuce wraps for sandwiches instead of buns, and low-fat yogurt with fruit. It is likely that a greater assortment of healthful food choices will become available at fast-food restaurants in response to consumer demand for these products.

Ethnic Restaurants

An **ethnic restaurant** is a restaurant that serves food that is customary for people of a specific culture. When eating at an ethnic restaurant, use MyPyramid and the Dietary Guidelines to choose foods that are low in fat, saturated fat, cholesterol, sugars, and salt.

Although eating habits in America are blended from many different traditions, ethnic diets and foods are considered to be those that have maintained their distinctiveness in America. Ethnic diets consist of foods and eating customs from other cultures. Ethnic diets reflect not only particular foods but also ways of combining them and cooking them. Many Americans eat a variety of ethnic foods—Italian, Chinese, and Mexican are among the most popular. Food traditions have been introduced to our society by people who have emigrated from other countries and have specific eating habits.

Every type of ethnic cooking has its own nutritional benefits and potential disadvantages. For example, benefits of the traditional Chinese diet include low fat intake, a high proportion of plant products, and low proportion of animal proteins. However, many foods in Chinese restaurants in America are high in sodium, and when cooked in oil or fried they may be high in fat. Food served in Mexico features rice and beans, which are low in fat and high in protein. However, many meals at Mexican restaurants in the United States feature meat, cheese, and sour cream, which are very high in fat.

Health Goal #38

I Will Protect Myself from Foodborne Illnesses

Foodborne Illnesses

A **foodborne illness** is an illness caused by consuming foods or beverages that have been contaminated with pathogens. There are many different disease-causing pathogens (e.g., bacteria, viruses, parasites) that can contaminate foods and beverages. In addition, poisonous chemicals or toxins can cause foodborne illnesses if they are present in food. As a result, there are many different foodborne illnesses. More than 250 different foodborne illnesses have been described by health officials.

According to the Centers for Disease Control and Prevention (CDC) (2005c), an estimated 76 million cases of foodborne illness occur each year in the United States. The majority of these cases are mild and cause symptoms for only a day or two. Some cases are more serious. The CDC estimates that there are 325,000 hospitalizations and 5,200 deaths related to foodborne illness each year. The most severe cases tend to occur in the very old, the very young, those who have an illness already that reduces their immune system function, and healthy people exposed to a high dose of a pathogen.

After someone swallows pathogens, there is a delay, called the incubation period, before the symptoms of illness begin. This delay ranges from hours to days, depending on the kind of pathogen and the dose. During the incubation period, the pathogens pass through the stomach into the intestine, attach to the cells lining the intestinal walls, and begin to multiply there. Some pathogens stay in the intestine, some produce a toxin that is absorbed into the bloodstream, and some can directly invade the deeper body tissues.

Symptoms of a foodborne illness could begin one-half hour to several hours after eating the contaminated food. Common symptoms of foodborne illness are cramps, nausea, diarrhea, vomiting, and fever. If symptoms are severe, or if the person is young, elderly, or pregnant, prompt medical care is needed. A laboratory test will identify the specific pathogen causing an illness. Treatment includes drinking fluids and bed rest.

There are many kinds of foodborne illness. Treatment depends on the symptoms. Illnesses that cause diarrhea or vomiting can lead to dehydration if a person loses a lot of fluid and electrolytes. **Electrolytes** are salts needed by the body for good health. Replacing the lost fluid and electrolytes and keeping up fluid intake is important to treating illness associated with diarrhea and vomiting. If diarrhea is severe, a person should drink an oral rehydration solution such as Pedialyte, CeraLyte, or Oralyte to replace the lost fluid and prevent dehydration. Sport drinks such as Gatorade might not replace the losses correctly and should not be used to treat diarrheal illness. Products containing bismuth subsalicylate (e.g., Pepto-Bismol) can reduce the duration and severity of simple diarrhea. If diarrhea and cramps occur, without bloody stools or fever, taking an antidiarrheal medication may relieve symptoms. However, if there is high fever or blood in the stools, these medications should be avoided because they can make the illness worse.

COMMON SERIOUS FOODBORNE ILLNESSES

The most commonly recognized foodborne illnesses are those caused by the bacteria *Salmonella, Campylobacter,* and *E. coli* O157:H7, and by noroviruses.

1. *Campylobacter* is a bacterial pathogen that causes fever, diarrhea (often bloody), and abdominal cramps. *Campylobacter* bacteria are the second-most frequently reported cause of foodborne illness (Food Safety and Inspection Service, 2006). Infection usually is caused by consuming unpasteurized milk, raw or undercooked meat or poultry, or other contaminated food or water.

2. **Salmonella** is a bacterial pathogen that is widespread in the intestines of birds, reptiles, and mammals. It can spread to humans through a variety of foods of animal origin. The illness it causes, salmonellosis, typically includes fever, diarrhea, and abdominal cramps. In persons who have a weakened immune system, it can invade the bloodstream and cause life-threatening infections. The CDC's Food Diseases Active Surveillance Network (Food Net) identifies salmonellosis as the most common bacterial foodborne infection reported.

3. **E. coli 0157:H7** is a bacterial pathogen that causes infection that often leads to bloody diarrhea and occasionally to kidney failure. In 3 to 5 percent of cases, a complication called hemolytic uremic syndrome (HUS) occurs several weeks after the initial symptoms. This severe complication includes temporary anemia, profuse bleeding, and kidney failure. Though most illness from *E. coli* has been associated with eating undercooked, contaminated ground beef, people have become ill from eating contaminated bean sprouts or fresh leafy vegetables such as lettuce and spinach. Transmission of *E. coli* also occurs from person-to-person contact in day care centers and in families. Transmission occurs from swimming in or drinking sewage-contaminated water. In the fall of 2006, about 200 people became infected after eating contaminated spinach in twenty-six states (Centers for Disease Control and Prevention, 2005c).

4. **Noroviruses** are a group of viruses that cause the "stomach flu" (gastroenteritis) in people. Other names for this group of viruses include Norwalk-like viruses, caliciviruses, and small round-structured viruses. The illness caused by noroviruses is not related to influenza ("the flu"), which is a respiratory illness caused by influenza virus. The symptoms of norovirus illness usually include nausea, vomiting, diarrhea, and some stomach cramping. An important cause of infection is eating food or drinking beverages that are contaminated with noroviruses. Also, because these viruses are found in the feces or vomit of people who are infected, having contact with a person who is infected can result in infection as can touching surfaces or objects contaminated with noroviruses.

Some common diseases are occasionally spread through food, even though they are usually spread in other ways. These include infections caused by *Shigella,* hepatitis A, and the parasites *Giardia lamblia* and *Cryptosporidia.* Even strep throat is spread occasionally through food.

Some foodborne illnesses are caused by the presence of a toxin that was produced by a pathogen in the food. For example, the bacterium *Staphylococcus aureus* can grow in some foods and produce a toxin that causes intense vomiting. The rare but deadly disease known as botulism occurs when the bacterium *Clostridium botulinum* grows and produces a powerful paralytic toxin in foods. The toxin produces illness even if the microbes that produced them are no longer there.

Other toxins and poisonous chemicals can cause foodborne illnesses. People can become ill if a pesticide is inadvertently added to a food, or if naturally poisonous substances are used to prepare food. Every year, people become ill after eating poisonous mushrooms that were mistaken for safe species. Several people also become ill every year from eating poisonous reef fishes.

Food Safety

Many years ago typhoid fever, tuberculosis, and cholera were common foodborne illnesses in the United States. Improvements in food safety, such as the pasteurization of milk, safe canning, and disinfection of water supplies, have helped to reduce the prevalence of foodborne illnesses. People who farm, produce food, and work to prepare food in other ways play a role in food safety. People need to keep and prepare foods safely in their homes, and to be alert when they eat out and purchase foods. This section of the chapter presents guidelines for keeping food safe and avoiding tainted food.

AT THE STORE
- Check expiration dates, and do not buy or eat outdated foods.
- Choose foods in cans and packages that are free of dents, cracks, rust, holes, bulges, and tears.
- Check that products marked "keep refrigerated" are stored in a refrigerated case and that frozen foods are frozen solid.
- Open egg cartons to check to see if the eggs are whole, clean, and chilled.
- Take foods and beverages that are refrigerated or frozen directly home for proper storage.

IN THE REFRIGERATOR

- Set the refrigerator temperature below 40 degrees Fahrenheit.
- Set the freezer thermometer at or below 0 degrees Fahrenheit.
- Pay attention to the "Use by" date and the "Keep refrigerated" instructions on any food.
- Do not store foods or beverages in metal cans.
- Do not store foods or beverages that have not been prepared or served safely—throw it out.
  When in doubt,
  Throw it out.

IN THE KITCHEN

- Wash hands with hot, soapy water for at least twenty seconds before and after preparing food.
- Keep juices from raw meat, chicken, and fish from contacting other foods and from having contact with utensils and surfaces that might contact other foods. This prevents cross-contamination of pathogens from one food to another.
- Use a separate sponge or towel to clean surfaces on which there was raw food; do not let these cleaning items have contact with other surfaces or items, such as cooking utensils.
- Cover cuts or sores with bandages or plastic gloves before preparing food.
- Thaw frozen foods in the microwave or in the refrigerator—never at room temperature.
- Wash fruits and vegetables with running water.
- Cook eggs until they are firm, not runny.
- Use a meat thermometer to make sure meat is thoroughly cooked.
- Do not taste foods that are not cooked thoroughly.
- Read the label and follow safety instructions on the package—such as *"Keep Refrigerated"* and the *"Safe Handling Instructions."*

ON THE TABLE

- Place cooked food in a clean dish for serving.
- Do not use the same plate for both preparing and serving foods, unless it has been washed in between.
- Wash utensils before using them.
- Do not let cooked food sit at room temperature for more than two hours.
- Keep hot foods hot and cold foods cold.

- Do not eat or drink unpasteurized juices, raw sprouts, raw (unpasteurized) milk, or products made from unpasteurized milk.
- Do not eat raw or undercooked meat, poultry, eggs, fish, or shellfish (clams, oysters, scallops, mussels).

LEFTOVERS

Foods or beverages that look or smell unusual should be thrown out. Discard any perishable food left out at room temperature for more than two hours. Refrigerated foods and beverages should be checked for maximum storage times; foods and beverages that have been in the refrigerator for longer than their maximum storage time should be thrown out:

- *Milk:* Four to five days after the sell-by date
- *Orange juice:* Up to a week after opening
- *Refrigerated raw chicken:* Three days
- *Hard cheese:* One to two months after opening
- *Cold cuts and hot dogs:* Three to five days
- *Eggs:* Three to five weeks
- *Foods taken home in restaurant doggie bags:* Three days

AT A RESTAURANT

- Carefully select which restaurants to patronize. Find out how restaurants did on their most recent inspections, and use that score to help guide your choice. In some areas, the latest inspection score is posted in the restaurant.

- When ordering a hamburger, ask for it to be cooked to a temperature of 160 degrees Fahrenheit. Send it back if it is still pink in the middle.
- Before ordering food that is made with many eggs pooled together, such as scrambled eggs, omelets, or French toast, ask the waiter whether it was made with pasteurized eggs—and choose something else if it was not.

REPORT FOODBORNE ILLNESSES

Suspected foodborne illnesses should be reported to the local health department. The local public health department is an important part of the food safety system. Reports of suspected foodborne illnesses from concerned citizens are how outbreaks are first detected. This helps protect others from possible infection. It is important for individuals to cooperate if they are contacted by a public health official about an illness, even if they are not ill.

Food Safety Offenders

There many situations in which people share food. This means there are many opportunities to contaminate foods and beverages with germs. Beware of the following food safety offenders.

1. The "double-dipper" puts a piece of food into a dip and takes a bite, then puts the same piece of food back in the dip and finishes it. Double-dipping contaminates food with germs. Other people who eat the same dip ingest these germs. People should not double-dip; they should put a scoop of dip on their own plate to use for dipping.
2. The "pop-swapper" drinks from another person's can, glass, or bottle, getting germs on it. Another person then drinks from the same can, glass, or bottle, ingesting those germs. People shouldn't pop-swap; they should pour a beverage into separate glasses when sharing a beverage.
3. The "careless cook" tastes foods while preparing them, getting germs into the foods. People should not be careless cooks; they should use a clean utensil each time they taste foods while preparing them.
4. The "container contaminator" takes a sip or bite from a container of beverage or food, contaminating it with germs, then puts it back

for others to drink or eat (and ingest germs). People should not be container contaminators; they should use a glass or clean utensil to take a sip of a beverage or bite of food.

5. The "bite burglar" takes a bite of another person's food and gives it back, or takes bits of food off another person's plate, contaminating the other person's food. People should not be bite burglars; they should cut off a piece of food or use a clean utensil and put a portion on their own plate before eating.

Health Goal #39

I Will Maintain a Desirable Weight and Body Composition

Desirable Weight and Body Composition

Desirable weight is the weight that is healthful for a person. A physician or a dietitian can help a person determine desirable weight. Factors that determine a person's desirable weight include age, height, gender, body frame, basal metabolic rate, percentage of muscle tissue, and activity level. The physician or dietitian will ask the person's age, measure height and current weight, and evaluate the other factors.

Body frame is the approximate weight and density of the bone structure. The type of body frame a person has (small, medium, or large) can be determined by measuring the wrist. A wrist measurement of less than 5 1/2 inches (12.25 centimeters) is a small frame. A wrist measurement between 5 1/2 inches (12.25 centimeters) and 6 1/4 inches (15.7 centimeters) indicates a medium frame. A wrist measurement over 6 3/8 inches (15.9 centimeters) indicates a large frame.

The **basal metabolic rate (BMR)** is the number of calories the body uses at rest. A **calorie** is a unit of energy produced by food and used by the body. There are tests to determine thyroid gland function and BMR. A physician will determine if these tests are necessary. The physician or dietitian will ask about activity level. Physical activity increases BMR. Because the thyroid gland

plays an important role in regulating the body's metabolic rate, it is often important to determine proper functioning of this gland.

A physician or dietitian will emphasize the importance of having a **healthful body composition.** The percentage of body fat can vary. There are two kinds of body fat. **Essential body fat** is the amount of body fat needed for optimal health. The body needs to have some fat for many reasons, such as dissolving fat-soluble vitamins before they can be used by the body. Adipose tissue is fat that accumulates around internal organs, within muscle, and under the skin. A person who has a high percentage of adipose tissue has a higher risk of developing cardiovascular diseases, cancer, diabetes, and arthritis.

A healthful percentage of body fat for teen males is about 11 to 17 percent. A healthful percentage of body fat for teen females is about 16 to 24 percent. There are different tests to measure the percentage of body fat. One test uses calipers to measure the thickness of skinfolds. A more accurate test involves underwater weighing. A quick test to determine whether one has too much body fat is to pinch a fold of skin on the upper arm, then estimate its thickness. A person has an excess of body fat if the pinched fold is more than one inch (2.5 centimeters) thick.

Another way to assess body weight is to by a comparison of weight in relation to height, or body

mass index (BMI). Body mass index can be determined by BMI charts (see www.health.gov/dietaryguidelines/dga2000/document/aim.htm#weight_top), body mass index calculators (see www.cdc.gov/nccdphp/dnpa/bmi/index.htm), or by using mathematical formulas (weight in kilograms divided by height in meters squared). A person who has a BMI of 18.5 to 24.9 is considered healthy, whereas a person who has a BMI of 25 to 29.9 is considered overweight, and a person who has a BMI of 30 or higher is considered obese. The further a person's BMI is above the healthy range, the higher the weight-related risk. BMI should not be used to evaluate the weight of those who are frail and elderly, body builders, or women who are pregnant or breastfeeding. People who have extra weight from muscle, not fat, might have a high BMI and still be healthy.

BMI is used differently to assess overweight and obesity in children and teens. In children, the percentage of body fat changes as they grow, and girls and boys differ in their percentage of body fat as they mature. BMI-for-age is plotted on gender-specific growth charts developed by the Centers for Disease Control and Prevention. These charts are used for children and teens two to twenty years of age. Children and adolescents are considered overweight if they are at or above the 95th percentile of their sex-specific BMI-for-age growth chart.

Weight Management

Weight management is a diet and exercise plan to maintain or attain a desirable weight and body composition. A **weight management plan** is based on caloric intake and caloric expenditure. **Caloric intake** is the number of calories a person takes in from foods and beverages. Caloric expenditure is the number of calories a person uses for basal metabolism, digestion, and physical activity. To maintain weight, a person's caloric intake must be the same as caloric expenditure. To gain weight, caloric intake must be greater than caloric expenditure. To lose weight, caloric intake must be less than caloric expenditure.

To make a weight management plan, a person must know about calories and body fat. One pound of body fat is equal to 3,500 calories. To gain one pound, a person must, over a period of time (such as a week), take in 3,500 more calories than are expended. To lose one pound, caloric intake, over a period of time, must be 3,500 calories less than caloric expenditure. There are various ways to achieve this. The person could simply eat less (lower caloric intake) and not increase physical activity (unchanged caloric expenditure), but the recommended method is to both keep caloric intake at a healthful level and increase physical activity to burn more calories.

Gaining Weight

Underweight is a body weight that is 10 percent or more below desirable body weight. People who are underweight may be malnourished. **Malnutrition** is a condition in which the body does not get the nutrients required for optimal health. Most malnourished people have inadequate vitamin and mineral intake. Children and teens who are malnourished may not have the nutrients they need for proper growth, and they may lack energy. There are other reasons why a young person might be underweight, such as having a disease or an eating disorder. Young people who are underweight should have a physical examination to determine the cause. They should work with a physician or dietitian to develop a healthful plan for weight gain.

Following are steps to help a person achieve healthful weight gain:

1. *Have a physical examination.*
2. *Have a physician or dietitian determine the number of pounds you need to gain.*
3. *Have a physician or dietitian help you design a plan for weight gain.* Remember, one pound of body fat is equal to 3,500 calories. Suppose you want to gain five pounds. You might want to gain one pound a week for five weeks. You will then need to increase your caloric intake by 3,500 calories a week to gain a pound each week. This means you need to take in 500 more calories each day (3,500 calories divided by seven days 5 500 calories). This calculation assumes, of course, that you do not also increase your level of physical activity (caloric expenditure).
4. *Increase the daily amounts from each food group in MyPyramid, except for the fats, oils, and sweets group.* Eat extra amounts from each of these groups:
   • Grains
   • Vegetables
   • Fruits
   • Milk
   • Meat and beans
5. *Follow the Dietary Guidelines and do not develop harmful eating habits.* Good eating

habits are essential in attempts to gain weight. The Dietary Guidelines should be followed to form good eating habits. Choose low-fat and lean foods from the meat, poultry, fish, dry beans, eggs, and nuts group. Select broiled, baked, steamed, or poached foods rather than fried foods. Use egg substitutes. Choose low-fat or fat-free foods from the milk, yogurt, and cheese group. Do not develop harmful eating habits that are difficult to break. For example, don't pig out on greasy, salty french fries.

6. *Eat healthful snacks between meals.*
7. *Exercise to increase your muscle mass.* It might be healthful for much of your weight gain to be muscle rather than fat (your physician or dietician can tell you what body composition you need to develop). Remember that to gain weight, you must increase your caloric intake when you increase your caloric expenditure in exercise.
8. *Drink plenty of fluids.*
9. *Ask your family and friends to support your efforts to gain weight.*
10. *Keep a journal of your food and beverage intake and your weight gain.* Review the information in your journal with your physician or dietitian.

Losing Weight

Overweight is a body weight that is 10 percent or more over desirable body weight. **Obesity** is a body weight that is 20 percent or more over desirable body weight. People who are overweight or obese need to have a physical examination. Usually their condition is caused by overeating and lack of physical activity. However, there may be other causes. A physician can check for other causes, such as an underactive thyroid gland.

People who are overweight or obese are at risk for developing cardiovascular diseases, diabetes, and certain cancers. They also have more accidents and more injuries, and they are less likely to be satisfied with their relationships.

Following are steps to help a person achieve healthful weight loss:

1. *Have a physical examination.*
2. *Have a physician or dietitian determine the number of pounds you need to lose.*
3. *Have a physician or dietitian help you design a plan for your weight loss.* Remember, one pound of body fat is equal to 3,500 calories. Suppose you want to lose ten pounds. You

might want to lose two pounds a week for five weeks. This means you need to burn 1,000 more calories per day than you take in. (Two pounds = 3,500 × 2 = 7,000 calories, or 1,000 calories a day for seven days.) A physician or dietitian can advise you on how best to make this change. Most likely, the health care professional will recommend that you decrease your caloric intake and increase your physical activity. For example, you might reduce your daily caloric intake by 500 calories and engage in physical activity to burn an extra 500 calories per day.

4. *Select the appropriate daily amounts from MyPyramid.* Do not leave out any food group. Each food group contains nutrients that are needed for optimal health. Instead, select low-calorie foods and beverages from each food group. Read food labels to determine serving sizes and calories.

5. *Follow the Dietary Guidelines.* Be especially careful to choose low-fat and fat-free foods that also are low in calories. Trim fat from foods. Select broiled, baked, poached, and steamed foods rather than fried foods. Limit sugars and salt. Select sensible portion sizes.

6. *Keep on hand ready-to-eat, low-calorie snacks.* Keep snacks like celery sticks and carrots in the refrigerator. Carry an apple, celery sticks, or other fruits or vegetables to eat between classes and appointments. Satisfy your appetite and quell your hunger with these snacks, so you won't be tempted to eat high-calorie foods.

7. *Participate in regular physical activity.* Physical activity increases BMR. Try to engage in physical activity early in the morning and again later in the day. Physical activity tones muscle. Vigorous physical activity causes the body to secrete beta-endorphins, hormones that improve mood. These can help you keep your spirits up when you are working on losing weight.

8. *Drink plenty of fluids.* Your body needs plenty of water to burn fat, and there is a chance of developing gallstones if you do not drink enough water.

9. *Ask your family and friends to support your efforts to lose weight.* Discuss the changes in lifestyle that your weight loss efforts will require. For example, your friends might eat pizza on Fridays. You might ask them to eat something lower in calories on Fridays while you're losing weight. Ask friends and family members to provide support by volunteering to make some changes that will make it easier for you to stick to your weight loss efforts. Ask for encouragement.

10. *Keep a journal of your food and beverage intake, your exercise (caloric expenditure), and your weight loss.* Your physician or dietitian will recommend a way to record your food and beverage intake, exercise, and weight loss. Review the information recorded in your journal with your physician or dietitian.

The Dietary Guidelines advise that people who are overweight lose weight gradually. Losing 10 percent of body weight over six months, with a loss of one-half pound to two pounds per week is usually safe (Flegal, Troiano, & Ballard-Barbash, 2001).

Weight-Loss Strategies

The suggestions for gradual weight loss presented in this chapter should be followed after checking with a physician or dietitian. These suggestions help a person to develop healthful eating habits. After reaching desirable weight, a person gradually adds more calories to the diet to maintain weight. Some people try other weight-loss strategies. These strategies are described in this section.

FAD DIETS

A **fad diet** is a quick weight-loss strategy that is popular for a short time. The Grapefruit Diet and the Cabbage Soup Diet are examples of fad diets. Some people try one fad diet after another. They try such a variety of diets that they never develop healthful eating habits. They lose weight and gain it back when they resume their former eating habits. Some fad diets are dangerous. A person needs a balanced diet for optimal health, and the only way to obtain a balanced diet is to get the correct number of servings from each food group in MyPyramid. Examples of popular fad diets are the Atkins Diet, the South Beach Diet, Sugar Busters, the Carbohydrates Addicts Diet, Pritikin, Eat Right for Your Blood Type, the Beverly Hills Diet, and the 5-Day Miracle Diet. Discuss these diets with a physician before using them to lose weight. Figure 8-5 is a nutrition fact sheet prepared by the American Dietetic Association that reviews facts about these diets.

LIQUID DIETS

A **liquid diet** is a diet in which beverages are substituted for some or all meals. Some liquid diets

FIGURE 8-5

A Review by the ADA of Popular Diets That Might Appeal to Young People

DIET	DESCRIPTION
"New" Atkins Diet	One of the most popular and well-known fad diets. This diet restricts carbohydrates. It focuses on eating mostly protein and recommends adding vitamin and mineral supplements. Dieters are promised that the diet will increase the body's metabolism so that it will burn fat and build muscle mass. Low-carb bars and food products from Atkins Nutritionals, Inc., are promoted in the diet. The diet demonizes carbohydrates and restricts fruits and vegetables, whole grains, legumes, and low-fat dairy foods. These recommendations contradict the Dietary Guidelines and much of what health professionals recommend for good health.
Zone Diet	Dieters are presented with a complex eating plan that divides meals into proportions of 40 percent carbohydrates, 30 percent proteins, and 30 percent fats. Eating in this manner supposedly places the body into the "Zone," which is a state of peak physical performance. The diet is complicated and requires constantly measuring portions and counting calories. Health experts recommend that following the Dietary Guidelines is superior to this diet.
South Beach Diet	The South Beach diet consists of three phases. The "detoxification" phase is the first two weeks of the diet and is characterized by banning carbohydrates including fruit, bread, rice, pasta, and baked goods. Dieters can eat portions of meat, poultry, shellfish, vegetables, eggs, and nuts during the first phase, but only in moderate portions. In the next phase, dieters can eat certain carbohydrates that the diet defines as "good carbs." The third phase allows dieters to eat just about anything, but in moderation. This diet is a low-calorie diet with an average intake of about 1,500 calories a day. The diet promotes the idea that the faster one digests sugars and starches, the more weight one will gain. Health experts are concerned that the first phase of the diet promotes weight loss too fast and could be potentially dangerous for some people.
Sugar Busters	This diet promotes that all sugars are "toxic." Sugars, including those from complex carbohydrates and starches, are demonized because they produce excess insulin causing the body to store sugar and fat and make cholesterol. The diet provides a list of acceptable foods and foods to avoid. Health experts stress that there is no evidence that excess insulin release causes obesity in healthy people.
Beverly Hills Diet	The premise of this diet is that enzymes found in food "activate" the human body. Each of the three food groups—proteins, carbohydrates and fats—contain their own set of enzymes to break down food so that the body can properly digest it. The diet advocates that it is when you eat and what foods you eat together that matters. Health experts stress that this is incorrect because the enzymes necessary for digestion are found *within* the body, not in the foods we eat. The diet also promotes that becoming fat is a result of indigestion, that when food is not properly digested, it "causes fatness." Health experts stress that the opposite of this is true; if foods are not properly digested, they cannot be absorbed by the body. The diet also recommends consuming a single food for an entire day. This is clearly not in alignment with recommendations from credible nutrition and health experts and organizations. Another concern is that the diet does not mention physical activity as a strategy for losing and maintaining weight.

Source: American Dietetic Association (2004). *Nutrition fact sheet: Popular diets reviewed.* Chicago, IL: ADA and The DietChannel.com (www.dietchannel.com).

are obtained only at a diet center, hospital, or physician's office and must be followed under medical supervision. Before beginning a medically supervised liquid diet, a person has a physical examination and extensive blood tests. An electrocardiogram is required to check the condition of the heart. While on the liquid diet, a person has medical supervision with blood tests at set intervals. The person must drink plenty of fluids, will urinate frequently, and might take an over-the-counter product to help with bowel movements. The person may attend classes to learn more about eating habits. When the weight-loss goal is reached, a maintenance plan must be followed. The maintenance plan is designed to help the person practice healthful eating habits.

Some liquid diets are sold in supermarkets and drugstores and are used without medical supervision. These liquid diets can be dangerous. They provide few calories and can have side effects. People who rely on them do not learn healthful eating habits and often gain back any weight they have lost.

PRESCRIPTION MEDICATIONS

An **anorectic drug** is a drug that decreases appetite. Medical supervision is required when a person takes anorectic drugs for obesity. The person must have a physical examination, electrocardiogram, and regular blood tests and usually will follow a special diet and meet regularly with a dietitian. Some anorectic drugs—such as phentermine, fenfluramine, and dexfenfluramine—have been determined to be unsafe. People must be careful in using these drugs. People should ask their physicians if long-term studies have been conducted on the safety and effectiveness of prescribed anorectic drugs.

OVER-THE-COUNTER DIET PILLS

Over-the-counter diet pills are pills that can be purchased in drugstores, grocery stores, or health food stores, or by mail order without a prescription. Some of these diet pills claim to suppress appetite. Others claim to fill the stomach and curb hunger. These diet pills can be dangerous, addictive, and ineffective. Side effects may include headaches, heart palpitations, dizziness, nervousness, drowsiness, rapid pulse rate, and sleeplessness. The warning labels on these diet pills advise against use by anyone with high blood pressure, diabetes, depression, or cardiovascular, kidney, or thyroid disease. People who use these diet pills

often do not get a balanced diet and might have malnutrition.

LAXATIVES AND DIURETICS

A **laxative** is a drug that helps a person have a bowel movement. A **diuretic** is a product that increases the amount of urine excreted. Some people mistakenly take these for weight loss. However, the weight loss from their use is temporary, as it is only fluid loss. The calories a person has consumed are still used by the body and stored as fat. And ridding the body of fluids can be dangerous. It can decrease the amount of potassium in the blood, which can interfere with normal heart function. Other side effects include abdominal pain, nausea, diarrhea, bloating, loss of bowel function, and dehydration.

WEIGHT-LOSS SURGERY

The decision to undergo surgery to reduce weight is a serious one. Severe possible health risks and long-term consequences are associated with weight-loss surgery. Therefore, weight-loss surgery is performed only for adolescents who are severely obese and who have not had long-term success with all other means of weight-loss and who have compromised health because of their obesity. Those who undergo weight-loss surgery must commit to lifelong lifestyle changes to avoid weight regain and improve chances of avoiding obesity-related diseases. Weight-loss surgery does not guarantee that a person will lose all excess weight or that the weight will be kept off. Surgery does not replace the long-term need for a healthful diet and regular physical activity (Lucile Packard Children's Hospital, 2006).

Gastric bypass surgery is a surgical technique that reduces the patient's stomach size and narrows the connection between the stomach and small intestine, leading to a decrease in the amount of food a person can eat. A surgeon staples the stomach across the top to create a small pouch and adds a bypass from the pouch to the middle of the small intestine. The resulting small pouch can hold only about an ounce of food. Some of the risks associated with gastric-bypass surgery are blood clots in the legs, leaking from the staples in the stomach, pneumonia, gallstones, bleeding stomach ulcer, and intolerance to certain foods.

Another surgical technique is *laparoscopic adjustable gastric banding,* in which an adjustable band is placed around the upper part of the stomach to reduce its capacity. This creates a new small stomach pouch that can hold only a small amount of food. As the person loses weight, the surgeon can adjust the band.

Healthful Weight in Children

Children need food for proper growth, but food with too many calories combined with too little physical activity can lead to overweight. The percentage of children who are overweight has increased dramatically in recent years (CDC, 2005). Adults can encourage healthful weight by offering children grain products, vegetables and fruits, low-fat dairy products, beans, lean meat, poultry, fish, or nuts. Adults set an example when children see them eating healthful foods. Children should be offered only small amounts of food high in fat or added sugars. Adults should encourage children to participate in physical activities and should regularly join children in physical activity. Children should have limits set on how much time they can spend in sedentary activities such as watching television or playing computer or video games (American Academy of Pediatrics, 2001; Dietz, 2005).

The Obesity Epidemic

Obesity threatens to become the leading health problem in the 21st century unless actions are taken to curb it. Obesity is described as epidemic in the United States (Dietz, 2005), and the World Health Organization (2002) describes obesity as an "escalating global epidemic" in many parts of the world that is spreading into the developing countries. About 31 percent of American adults are obese, and about 40 percent will be obese by 2010 if the current trend continues (Hellmich, 2003). From 1986 to 2000, the proportion of Americans who were severely obese (body mass index of 40 or higher) quadrupled, increasing at a rate twice as fast as that of milder obesity (Sturm, 2005). The proportion of Americans with severe obesity jumped from 1 in 200 adults in 1986 to 1 in 50 in 2000. The overweight and obesity epidemic is not restricted to adults. The prevalence of overweight and obesity among children and adolescents also has been increasing worldwide (Schmidt, 2003) and in the United States (CDC, 2005). According

to the Centers for Disease Control and Prevention (2004), each year an estimated 400,000 Americans die of causes related to obesity and physical inactivity. The CDC (2004) reports that obesity is on the increase among children and adults and in both males and females. This is an unfortunate trend because obesity decreases the quality of life and increases the risk of heart disease and certain types of cancer. It is also a major cause of diabetes, which increased in prevalence in both adults and children in the last decade (Dietz, 2005).

There are many reasons for an increase in obesity. For many, food is plentiful in the United States. People take less time for meal preparation and often eat junk food and snacks. They drink soda pop instead of healthful beverages. Research has found that soda pop consumption is one factor that accounts for an increase in obesity among children (Ludwig, Peterson, & Gortmaker, 2001). And soda pop consumption is increasing among children (Bellisle & Rolland-Cachera, 2001). In general, people of all ages are not as physically active as they should be to prevent obesity (Dietz, 2005).

Health Goal #40

I Will Develop Skills to Prevent Eating Disorders

The Addictive Nature of Eating Disorders

An **eating disorder** is a mental disorder in which a person has a compelling need to starve, to binge, or to binge and purge. To binge is to eat large amounts of food over a short period of time. To purge is to rid the body of food by vomiting or by using laxatives and diuretics. Eating disorders are addictions. An **addiction** is a compelling need to take a drug or engage in a specific behavior. Young people with eating disorders feel compelled to starve, eat to excess, vomit, use laxatives and diuretics, or exercise to extremes to control their weight. As with other addictions, attitudes and coping styles exacerbate eating disorders.

It is important to note that people can have an eating disorder, regardless of their gender. Some people mistakenly believe that only females can have eating disorders, yet males also can have eating disorders. Perhaps 5 to 10 percent of people who have eating disorders are male. However, it might be higher because many males do not seek treatment for an eating disorder because of the social stigma of having a problem that is often perceived as being a "female problem." Also, health care professionals may fail to recognize eating disorders in males. Like females, males need professional treatment for successful recovery. Males develop eating disorders for the same reasons women do. The signs, symptoms, and treatment needs for eating disorders in males are similar to those of females. Males, however, tend to develop eating disorders at older ages than females.

Risks for Developing Eating Disorders

There are several reasons why some youth are at risk for developing eating disorders. Seven of these reasons are discussed next.

REASON 1: TOO MUCH EMPHASIS ON APPEARANCE

Body image is a person's perception of his or her body's appearance. Teens who have a positive body image like what they see when they look in the mirror. They are not uncomfortable if they are shorter, taller, or less muscular than other teens. Teens who have a negative body image are dissatisfied when they look in the mirror. They want to have a different appearance. They may develop body image distortion. **Body image distortion** is having an inaccurate visual perception of one's body; for example, some slender persons see themselves as fat and feel fat. Too much exposure to the mass media can cause some teens to develop a negative body image. Television shows and magazine ads predominantly portray teens who are thin or muscular and attractive. Teens who lack self-confidence may begin to compare themselves to actors, models, and professional athletes.

REASON 2: DISCOMFORT WITH SEXUAL MATURITY

Puberty brings the development of secondary sex characteristics. Some teens have difficulty with these changes. For example, some females are uncomfortable when their breasts begin to develop; they slouch and wear baggy clothes to hide their breasts and feel anxious and embarrassed about their body changes. Some females are uncomfortable when menstruation begins; rather than accept their maturing body, they may find menstruation disgusting. Males may feel uncomfortable about growing a beard or having wet dreams. These teens might choose harmful ways to cope with their feelings. They may starve or binge and purge rather than talking about their feelings. Teens going through puberty should be reassured that these changes are completely normal and are signs of growing up.

REASON 3: PERFECTIONISM

Perfectionism is a compelling need to do everything perfectly. Teens who are perfectionists are overly critical of themselves. Perfectionism results from feeling inadequate and insecure. Some teens become perfectionists because adults had unrealistic expectations of them during their childhood. Perfectionistic teens tend to go overboard when they go on a diet and end up with an eating disorder.

REASON 4: NEED FOR CONTROL

Some teens feel compelled to control every situation. These teens may have had traumatic childhoods. Perhaps they were raised in families with alcoholism or abuse and did not have responsible adults they could rely on to protect them. They might constantly have been in danger of a parent, guardian, or other adult family member becoming drunk or physically or sexually abusive. As a result, these teens have difficulty trusting the unknown and feel more secure when they control situations. They diet or exercise to extremes as a way to show control.

REASON 5: INABILITY TO EXPRESS EMOTIONS

Some teens are not able to express their emotions. They have difficulty when they feel frustrated, lonely, depressed, or anxious. They substitute other behaviors for the healthful expression of these emotions. For example, some teens eat high-fat foods like ice cream when they feel lonely or rejected. Some teens pig out on chips and other junk food when they are frustrated by homework assignments. Such teens turn to food for comfort. They rely on excessive eating as a way to satisfy their emotional needs. Some other teens starve themselves when they have emotional needs.

REASON 6: SOCIAL PRESSURE FROM MEDIA AND PEERS

Social pressures from the media and peers appear to be a major cause in the increase in eating disorders. The images of very thin and attractive people that young females see in the visual media shape their self-perception, even though such thinness can be unhealthy, and for many females it is unrealistic to aspire to be as physically attractive as TV actors and models. And the women featured in the media keep getting thinner. The result is that females of a healthful weight often think of themselves as being fat and may take drastic measures to lose weight. More than half of all teenage females (62.3 percent) report that they are trying to lose weight (Grunbaum et al., 2004). One-third of third-grade females report wanting to lose weight, and one-fourth report dieting to lose weight (Robinson et al., 2001).

REASON 7: PRESSURE FELT BY ATHLETES

Both males and females in certain sports may feel pressure to lose weight or body fat. This is particularly true in sports and activities such as wrestling, gymnastics, cheerleading, figure skating, swimming, ballet, and track. Pressure to lose weight can lead to unhealthy weight-control practices and eating disorders. Rapid weight-loss attempts may lead student athletes to use diet pills or laxatives, cut back on water intake, or exercise too intensely. At a time when they need extra nutrients from food to maintain their stamina, teens may instead be putting considerable stress on their bodies and compromising their athletic performance. Teens need to be aware that if a coach encourages weight loss—or weight gain—they should seek advice from their parents or guardian and a physician. Adults should be prepared to intervene when they believe that a coach is demanding rapid weight loss. The American Academy of Pediatrics recommends undertaking weight reduction during the off-season so there's less risk of overstressing the body.

Adults should observe young people for warning signs that may indicate eating disorders. The more warning signs that are observed, the greater the likelihood that a young person may be experiencing an eating disorder. The following are warning signs that young people may have an eating disorder:

1. Constantly comparing themselves to others
2. Being unhappy with their physical appearance
3. Wearing baggy clothes to hide body changes, such as breasts (females)
4. Thinking it is disgusting to have menstrual periods (females)
5. Never being satisfied with anything they do
6. Perceiving parents or guardians as never being satisfied with anything they do
7. Having felt unsafe during childhood (from alcoholism, physical abuse, or sexual abuse in the family)
8. Feeling secure only when in control of a situation
9. Not knowing what to do when feeling lonely, frustrated, rejected, or depressed
10. Eating, starving, excessively exercising, or purging when feeling uncomfortable

Anorexia Nervosa

Anorexia nervosa is an eating disorder involving self-starvation and being 15 percent or more below desirable weight. The person also may exercise to extremes, vomit, and use laxatives and diuretics. Anorexia nervosa usually is referred to as anorexia. People with anorexia nervosa are obsessed with being thin and do not recognize when they have become dangerously thin. When they look at their bodies in the mirror, they see themselves as fat even when they are very thin. Many people with anorexia nervosa are obsessed with exercise. Most are perfectionists. Most are good students and are obedient and respectful. Most have a parent or guardian who has set very high expectations for them. As a result, they feel inadequate and controlled. The one thing they can control is whether or not they eat, so to gain back control they starve themselves. When their parents or guardians pressure them, they become even more committed to starving. People with anorexia nervosa usually deny that they are starving themselves.

The incidence of anorexia nervosa in American females has been rising steadily since the 1930s (Schur, Sanders, & Steiner, 2000). The greatest increases in anorexia are among young women fifteen to twenty-four years of age. Anorexia also is increasing among younger females, ages ten to fourteen.

HEALTH CONSEQUENCES

Many physical problems are associated with anorexia nervosa. People with anorexia may have the following:

- A weight loss to 15 percent or more below desirable weight
- Dehydration, constipation, abdominal pain, and nausea
- Hair loss
- Hormonal changes
- Damage to heart, kidneys, and other body organs
- Decrease in heart rate and blood pressure
- Impaired immune system function
- Absence of menstruation, in females
- Malnutrition

Without treatment, 10 percent of people with anorexia nervosa will die. Other people with anorexia nervosa will have permanent damage to body organs. People with anorexia nervosa may

- Have negative self-confidence
- Lack self-respect
- Have frequent bouts with depression
- Withdraw from others
- Be at risk for attempting suicide

TREATMENT

Treatment for anorexia nervosa involves a team of professionals—physicians, nurses, dietitians, and mental health professionals. A treatment plan is developed that deals with the person's physical and emotional health problems. A hospital stay may be necessary to treat for dehydration and malnutrition. Intravenous feedings may be required to supply nutrients. Tests are required to assess and treat damage to body organs. Mental health professionals work with the person who is anorexic and with the family. The person must recognize and deal with the emotional problems that caused the eating disorder. Often, the family is involved in therapy. The person may need to achieve independence from a controlling parent or guardian.

Bulimia

Bulimia is an eating disorder in which a person binges and purges. The binging involves eating large amounts of food in a short period of time. This is followed by purging, or ridding the body of foods that were eaten. People with bulimia may vomit or use laxatives or diuretics to purge. Bulimia is far more common than anorexia nervosa. Most cases of bulimia occur in people who want to lose weight. They are obsessed with their body shape and size. They try to follow a diet but are unsuccessful. So they turn to starvation to lose weight. Then they feel compelled to eat and go on a binge. After the binge, they feel guilty and worry about weight gain. Then they feel compelled to purge. The binge-purge cycle dominates their lives. People who have a negative body image are at risk for bulimia. Other people at risk include those who were raised in families in which there was alcoholism or abuse. These young people are insecure and depressed, and they hide their insecurity and depression from others. Denying their feelings increases the likelihood that they will binge and purge.

BULIMIC BEHAVIOR

Unlike people with anorexia nervosa, those with bulimia usually know they have a problem. They feel guilty and ashamed but are unable to change their behavior. At first, they find purging disgusting. Then they get used to it. Usually they do not want anyone to know they binge and purge. They hide their behavior. They might not eat at their friends' homes. If they eat out, they choose restaurants where they can vomit without anyone knowing. Some people, though, do not hide their bulimic behavior—they become friends with others who have bulimia, and they binge and purge together and share laxatives and diuretics.

People with bulimia may do the following:

- Binge in private, eating regular amounts when with others
- Have one secret place in which to binge, such as a closet
- Steal food or hide it in a secret place
- Think about food constantly and plan each binge carefully
- Buy or steal special treats or elaborate dishes for a binge
- Gulp or stuff in food quickly while bingeing so as not to be discovered
- Steal money to purchase food or steal food from the stores
- Exercise and diet excessively between binges

HEALTH CONSEQUENCES

Many physical problems are associated with bulimia. People with bulimia may have

- Dissolved tooth enamel
- Tooth decay
- Sore gums
- Enlarged salivary glands
- Swollen cheeks
- Water loss
- Depletion of potassium
- Increase in blood pressure
- Damage to the colon, heart, and kidneys
- Impaired bowel function

People with bulimia may

- Have a negative body image
- Lack self-respect
- Be insecure and depressed
- Deny their feelings

TREATMENT

It is difficult to diagnose bulimia. Many people with bulimia have desirable weight and are successful at hiding their behavior. Treatment for bulimia involves a team of professionals—physicians, nurses, dentists, dietitians, and mental health professionals. A treatment plan is developed that deals with physical and emotional health problems. Tests are required to assess and treat damage to body organs. A dentist may repair teeth and treat gums. Tests for BMR may be used. Some people with bulimia have a metabolic condition. They do not feel full after eating. This condition is corrected. Those people with bulimia need help with their emotional health. They need to recognize the reasons why they developed bulimia. People who have been raised in families with alcoholism, physical abuse, or sexual abuse must sort out their feelings and develop new ways of coping. Young people with a negative body image and who lack self-respect must gain self-confidence.

Binge-Eating Disorder and Obesity

Binge-eating disorder is an eating disorder in which a person cannot control eating and eats excessive amounts. The diagnosis is made when a person binges two or more times per week for six months. Teens with binge-eating disorder cannot resist the urge to eat when they see food. They eat too much, too often. They are obsessed with eating.

Binge-eating disorder is more common in females but also occurs in males. People with binge-eating disorder have difficulty expressing emotions and coping. They turn to food as a substitute for coping. After a time, they are addicted to food. They might stuff themselves in private while pretending to diet when they are with others, but they are not successful at hiding their disorder. Most people with binge-eating disorder are overweight. Family and friends know they have a weight problem but may not realize that the cause is an eating disorder. Individuals with binge-eating disorder may not understand that they need medical and psychological help. They may think they will lose weight if they can find the right diet. But their attempts at weight loss are never successful. Until they are treated for binge-eating disorder, they continue to be overweight. Binge-eating disorder is a common cause of obesity. **Obesity** is being 20 percent or more above desirable body weight.

HEALTH CONSEQUENCES

Many physical problems are associated with binge-eating disorder and obesity. People who are overweight or obese may have

- Skeletal difficulties because their bones must support excessive weight
- Increase in heart rate and blood pressure
- Increased risk of developing cardiovascular diseases, high blood pressure, diabetes, and certain types of cancer

More than 80 percent of teens who are obese are still obese as adults. Teens with binge-eating disorder may

- Lack self-respect
- Have negative self-esteem
- Have a negative body image
- Have frequent bouts of depression
- Do not feel accepted by peers
- Withdraw from social activities
- Substitute eating for relationships

TREATMENT

Treatment for binge-eating disorder and obesity involves a team of health care professionals. A treatment plan is developed that deals with physical and emotional problems. A complete physical examination is required. Blood tests and an electrocardiogram are needed. Existing health conditions are treated. A weight-loss plan is designed. The person on the weight-loss plan has medical supervision with blood tests at set intervals. People who are obese are placed on liquid diets. They see a physician each week, have regular blood tests, and may have an electrocardiogram at set intervals. The Food and Drug Administration has approved anorectic drugs for people who are obese. An **anorectic drug** is a prescription drug that decreases appetite. People receiving these drugs must meet certain restrictions and be supervised by a physician. After weight loss, people must learn new eating habits. They are put on a supervised weight-maintenance plan to prevent relapse. To change their eating habits, they need to examine the reasons why they developed binge-eating disorder. If not, they will relapse and begin to overeat again. Therapy, nutrition classes, and support groups help prevent relapse.

9

CHAPTER NINE

Personal Health and Physical Activity

HEALTH GOALS FOR PERSONAL HEALTH AND PHYSICAL ACTIVITY

41. I will have regular examinations.
42. I will follow a dental health plan.
43. I will be well groomed.
44. I will get adequate rest and sleep.
45. I will participate in regular physical activity.
46. I will follow a physical fitness plan.
47. I will develop and maintain health-related fitness.
48. I will develop and maintain skill-related fitness.
49. I will be a responsible spectator and participant in sports.
50. I will prevent physical activity-related injuries and illnesses.

Personal health and physical activity is the area of health that focuses on having regular examinations, following a dental health plan, being well-groomed, getting adequate rest and sleep, participating in regular physical activity, following a physical fitness plan, developing and maintaining health-related fitness, developing and maintaining skill-related fitness, being a responsible spectator and participant in sports, and preventing injuries and illnesses related to physical activity. This chapter provides the health knowledge needed to teach young people important life skills for personal health and physical activity.

Health Goal #41

I Will Have Regular Examinations

Physical Examinations

A physical examination is a series of tests that measure health status. Physical examinations may be performed by a physician with assistance from other health care professionals.

For good health, a person should have a physical examination at least every two years. Individuals who have special health conditions, such as a chronic disease (e.g., asthma, diabetes) or a pregnancy, may require physical examinations or regular checkups with their physician on a more frequent basis. Ideally, a school-age child should have a physical exam each year (Advocate Health Care, 2005). Some schools require physical examinations before enrollment. Several school systems require physical examinations prior to participation in school sports activities.

Physical exams are important because they give parents an opportunity to determine their child's growth and development. A physical exam makes it possible for a physician to recognize any health problems at their earliest stages, when problems can be most effectively treated. Annual checkups also provide an opportunity to talk about health issues of special concern regarding school-age children, such as nutrition, exercise, and injury. Physical exams also provide a good time for a health care provider to discuss with adolescents sensitive issues like sexuality, alcohol and drug use, smoking, self-esteem, and eating disorders. These discussions can be between the doctor and a teen alone, or they can include the parents, depending on how the parent and child feel. These discussions can help a child adopt healthy habits that can prevent disease in the teenage years and later in life (Advocate Health Care, 2005).

WHAT TO EXPECT IN A PHYSICAL EXAMINATION

During a physical examination, a health history is taken. A **health history** is a record of a person's health habits, past health conditions and medical care, allergies and drug sensitivities, and health facts about family members. Health care professionals ask several questions to obtain a health history. It is helpful to bring health-related information to the examination in order to provide accurate answers to the questions. This information becomes a part of a person's permanent health record. A **health record** is a file that includes a health history and the results of the physical examination. The health record is updated each time a person visits his or her physician. The health record is an important tool the physician uses to provide the best possible health care. With every appointment, patients may be asked to update their health history. Knowing their own health history and their family health history can give people important insight into the type of care that they should be receiving.

Physical examinations can vary in what they cover. In a typical physical examination, the physician checks height, weight, body temperature, pulse rate, respiratory rate, blood pressure, general appearance, skin, eyes, ears, nose, mouth, neck, lungs, heart, breasts, lymph nodes, back, reproductive organs, rectum, legs, feet, bones, joints, and reflexes. A physical examination may also include an electrocardiogram and a number of laboratory tests, such as urinalysis and blood tests. An **electrocardiogram (ECG)** is a record of the electrical impulses of the heart that is used to diagnose disorders of the heart. A **urinalysis** is a set of urine tests that check for normal kidney function and urinary tract infections. A **blood test** is an analysis of blood for blood components, chemicals, pathogens, and antibodies.

A physician usually discusses the results of a physical examination with the person receiving the exam or the parents or guardian of children and teens. If the physician diagnoses any health problems or conditions, a treatment plan will be discussed. Individuals should be certain to ask questions about anything they do not understand. A physician also may advise a patient to change some health habits. People are wise to never put off adopting lifestyle changes that can improve their health status.

Some symptoms that are observed in a physical examination may require prompt or further medical attention. A **symptom** is a change in a body function from the normal pattern. A diagnosis is made after reviewing symptoms. A **diagnosis** is the determination of a person's problem after taking a health history, studying symptoms, or getting test results. A physician may recommend a treatment plan or make a referral to a specialist for further diagnosis or treatment.

A physician should be contacted when a person has any of the following symptoms:

- Shortness of breath
- Loss of appetite for no obvious reason
- Blood in the urine or in a bowel movement
- Blood in the mucus or saliva
- A constant cough
- Fever of 100 degrees Fahrenheit (37.7 degrees Celsius) or higher for more than one day
- Swelling, stiffness, or aching in the joints
- Severe pain in any body part
- Frequent or painful urination
- Sudden weight gain or loss
- Dizziness
- Any warning sign of cancer
- Any warning sign of heart attack or stroke

Eye Care

The sense of sight adds quality to life. People who have the sense of sight use it to acquire more than 80 percent of their knowledge. Eye examinations, correcting refractive errors, understanding eye conditions, and protecting eyes are important ways to preserve the sense of sight.

EYE EXAMINATIONS

Eye examinations are performed by ophthalmologists and optometrists. An **ophthalmologist** is a physician who specializes in medical and surgical care and treatment of the eyes. Ophthalmologists can diagnose and treat all types of eye conditions, test vision, perform surgery, and prescribe corrective lenses. An **optometrist** is an eye care professional who is specially trained in a school of optometry. Optometrists can test vision and prescribe corrective lenses.

During an eye examination, an eye care professional reviews a person's health history and examines the eyes for vision problems, checking for refractive errors, color blindness, lazy eye, cross-eye, eye coordination, depth perception, eye disease, and general eye health. This helps determine if correction is necessary.

VISUAL ACUITY AND REFRACTIVE ERRORS

Visual acuity is sharpness of vision. Refractive errors can interfere with visual acuity. A **refractive error** is a variation in the shape of the eyeball that affects the way images are focused on the retina and blurs vision. The retina is the inner lining of the eyeball.

Refractive errors include myopia, hyperopia, astigmatism, and presbyopia. **Myopia,** or nearsightedness, is a refractive error in which distant objects appear blurred and close objects are seen clearly. Eyes of nearsighted people are longer than average. The images they see are focused in front of the retina. As the body grows during adolescence, nearsightedness often worsens. **Hyperopia,** farsightedness, is a refractive error in which close objects appear blurred and distant objects are seen clearly. Eyes of farsighted people are shorter than average. The images they see are focused behind the retina. **Astigmatism** is a refractive error in which irregular shape of the cornea causes blurred vision. The cornea is the transparent front part of the outer shell of the eyeball. Astigmatism affects both distant and close vision. A person can have astigmatism and either myopia or hyperopia. **Presbyopia** is a refractive error caused by weakening of eye muscles and hardening of the cornea.

CORRECTING REFRACTIVE ERRORS

Refractive errors can be corrected with eyeglasses or contact lenses. They help the eye focus images on the retina so that visual acuity is restored. People with presbyopia may wear bifocals. **Bifocals** are lenses that correct for both close and distant vision.

Most eyeglass lenses are made of plastic or nonbreakable glass. A protective coating may be added to prevent glare and protect the eyes against ultraviolet radiation. Contact lenses can be hard or soft and are worn directly on the cornea. It is important to clean and store the lenses correctly to help prevent eye infection.

Myopia also can be corrected with surgery. **Radial keratotomy** is a type of surgery that improves myopia by changing the curve of the cornea. The surgeon makes several incisions in the cornea that flatten it out and allow images to focus directly on the retina. **Photorefractive keratectomy** is laser surgery that reshapes the cornea to improve myopia. Some risks may be involved in both types of surgery.

Eye Conditions and Diseases

Eyes can be affected by conditions and diseases. **Conjunctivitis** is an inflammation of the eye membranes that causes redness, discomfort, and discharge. Another name for conjunctivitis is pinkeye. The eyelids of a person who has conjunctivitis may stick together. Causes include bacterial infection, allergies, contact lenses, certain drugs, and secondhand smoke. Pinkeye caused by bacteria is highly contagious. Pinkeye usually is not serious unless the infection spreads to the deeper tissues in the eye, which can result in a permanent loss of vision.

Two eye conditions may affect visual acuity in middle and late adulthood. **Glaucoma** is a condition in which the pressure of the fluid in the eye is high and may damage the optic nerve. The optic nerve is the bundle of nerve fibers that transmit messages from the retina to the brain. Regular eye examinations are important for early detection of glaucoma. The increased pressure of glaucoma can be prevented with early treatment. A **cataract** is a clouding of the lens of the eye that obstructs vision. Seeing through an eye with a cataract in it is like trying to see through a steamy window. Images are hazy and out of focus. Cataract surgery involves removing the cloudy lens and implanting an artificial lens. Risks may be involved in this type of surgery.

Eye Protection

Most eye injuries involve people under the age of 25. Ninety percent of eye injuries could be prevented if people protected their eyes properly.

Each year, more than 40,000 sport-related eye injuries are treated in hospital emergency rooms in the United States (Rodriguez & Lavina, 2003). One-third of victims are children. The most common injuries associated with sports are abrasions and contusions, detached retinas, corneal lacerations, hemorrhages, and loss of an eye. High-risk sports for eye injuries include basketball, baseball, hockey, football, lacrosse, racquetball, and soccer. Sports such as racquetball and hockey often cause eye injuries due to the high speed of the objects used in the sport. For example, a hockey puck travels at 90 to 100 miles (153 to 170 kilometers) per hour. Another recreational activity that poses high risk of eye injuries is paintball sports

(Parker & Simon, 2004). Eye injuries in sports can be prevented by wearing polycarbonate eye protectors. Normal prescription eyeglasses, made of hardened glass or plastic, are not designed to withstand the force of a collision with the objects used in sports. Contact lenses can make sport-related eye injuries worse by scraping and cutting the surface of the eye.

Many eye injuries that can lead to permanent eye damage and loss of vision are caused by BB guns, slingshots, and fireworks. The BB pellet can cause severe damage to the interior of the eye, whether or not the eye is penetrated. Penetration of the eye by the BB pellet can lead to total loss of the eye, requiring the surgical removal of the eye. Chemicals, such as chlorine, also can damage the eyes. Chlorine and other substances in water irritate the eyes. Wearing goggles can protect the eyes from these substances when swimming. Safety goggles should be worn if working around dangerous chemicals such as bleach, insecticides, or cleaning products that can splash into the eyes and cause injury.

Long exposure to ultraviolet (UV) radiation in sunlight also causes severe eye damage. Wearing a wide-brimmed hat and sunglasses with 99 to 100 percent UV protection reduces risk of eye damage from UV radiation. It is important to check the label information when purchasing sunglasses. Following are terms found on sunglasses labels and some relevant information about them:

- *Blocks at least 99 percent of all UV light.* Long exposure to UV light can cause eye damage.
- *Blocks 90 percent of infrared light.* Sunlight has low levels of infrared light. Infrared rays are not believed to be harmful to the eyes.
- *Blue-blocking.* It is not known whether blue light is harmful to the eyes. Filtering out blue light leaves a yellow or orange tint on what's seen. These lenses help vision in snow and haze.
- *Polarized.* Polarization cuts reflected glare. These lenses are good for water sports and driving. They might not have adequate UV protection.
- *Mirror-coated.* These lenses have a metallic finish. They protect from glare but usually offer little UV protection.
- *Photochromatic.* These lenses darken in bright light. They become clear in weaker light. They do not always offer UV protection.
- *Single-gradient lenses.* These lenses are shaded at the top and the bottom but not in

the middle. They are useful for skiing, tennis, and sailing, but they do not always block UV light.

Ear Care

The sense of hearing adds to the quality of life, so care of the ears is important. The outer ear should be cleansed frequently with a soft, clean washcloth. Objects of any size, including cotton-tipped swabs, should never be inserted into the ear because these objects might puncture the eardrum. A puncture would allow dirt or microorganisms to get into the ear and cause infection and could lead to hearing loss. Proper cleansing of the outer ear also helps avert wax buildup in the ear canal. After bathing or swimming, the ears should be thoroughly and gently dried with the corner of a clean towel. Earplugs help prevent ear infections such as swimmer's ear, a painful and itchy bacterial infection of the external ear canal that develops after long periods of swimming or bathing. If an infection develops in the ear, scratching or inserting cotton swabs into the ear will only aggravate the condition. A physician should be consulted whenever an ear becomes infected, because infection of the middle ear can affect hearing.

Proper ear care also includes having regular ear examinations and tests for hearing loss. People should also take care to protect against hearing loss; for instance, they should avoid exposure to loud music in vehicles and through headphones.

Ear Examinations

Ear examinations are performed by audiologists or by otolaryngologists. An **audiologist** is a specialist who diagnoses and treats hearing and speech-related problems. An **otolaryngologist (ENT)** is a physician who diagnoses and treats disorders of the ears, nose, and throat. An ENT can diagnose ear conditions, test hearing, recommend hearing devices, and perform surgery.

A common way to test for hearing loss is to use an **audiometer,** a machine that measures the range of sounds a person hears. The results provide data on the type and extent of hearing loss and show whether the loss is due to problems in the middle or inner ear or to nerve damage. A tympanogram is a measure of the vibrations of the eardrum and

air pressure in the eustachian tube. The **eustachian tube** is the tube that connects the middle ear and the back of the nose. It allows fluid to drain from the middle ear and regulates air pressure on both sides of the eardrum. If the middle ear fills with fluid, the eardrum will not vibrate as it should. Air pressure increases in the eustachian tube and may affect hearing.

A physician should be contacted if any of the following symptoms are observed:

- Pain in the ears
- Drainage from the ears
- Difficulty hearing people talking
- Difficulty hearing on the telephone
- A need to turn up the volume on the TV to a point that others complain it is too loud
- Difficulty determining what direction sounds are coming from
- Difficulty understanding what is being said in a noisy room
- Difficulty hearing in social situations

Hearing Loss

One in every ten people has hearing loss. More than half of all eighteen-year-olds have some hearing loss. Hearing loss ranges from mild to profound deafness. Causes of hearing loss include premature birth, respiratory distress at birth, birth defects, exposure to drugs or infection before birth, viral infections, middle ear infections, high fevers, and injuries.

Exposure to noise also can lead to hearing loss. In fact, noise-induced hearing loss is the second most common kind of hearing loss, after age-related hearing loss (Rabinowitz, 2000). **Noise-induced hearing loss** is the slow loss of hearing caused by too much noise. Hearing loss happens when too much noise hurts the hair cells in the inner ear. Noise-induced hearing loss usually happens slowly. There is no pain. Right after hearing loud noise, a person may notice a "ringing" sound in their ears. They might have trouble hearing people talk. After several hours or even a few days, these symptoms usually go away but the hearing loss remains. Early signs of noise-induced hearing loss include the following (Rabinowitz, 2000):

- Having trouble understanding what people say, especially in crowded rooms
- Needing to turn the TV sound higher
- Having to ask people to repeat what they just said to you

- Not being able to hear high-pitched sounds, like a baby crying or a telephone ringing in another room

The only way to find out if a person has a hearing loss is to have his or her hearing tested by a trained professional. In addition to causing hearing loss, exposure to loud or constant noise causes stress, fatigue, irritability, and tension. Exposure to noise places even children and young adults at risk of hearing loss.

Hearing loss is either conductive or sensorineural. In **conductive hearing loss,** sound is not transported efficiently from the outer to the inner ear. Conductive hearing loss is caused by excessive wax buildup, ear injury, birth defects, or middle ear infection. In **sensorineural hearing loss,** there is damage to the inner ear or acoustic nerve. The acoustic nerve connects the inner ear to the brain. Generally, sensorineural hearing loss is permanent. Some people with sensorineural hearing loss receive cochlear implants. A **cochlear implant** is an electronic device that is implanted in the ear to restore partial hearing to the totally deaf.

Noise-induced hearing loss is one of the most common causes of nerve deafness (sensorineural hearing loss) (Rabinowitz, 2000). Approximately 10 million Americans have this kind of hearing problem. Noise-induced hearing loss lasts forever. Hearing aids can help, but they can't fully correct it. This kind of hearing loss can be prevented by staying away from loud noises.

PORTABLE MUSIC PLAYERS AND RISK TO HEARING

Audiologists warn that listening to loud music on portable music players, such as MP3 players and iPods, poses serious risk of hearing loss. These devices can pump music through headphones directly into the ear canal at dangerously high decibel levels. Because they hold thousands of songs and can play for hours without recharging, users tend to listen continuously for hours at a time. Hearing experts warn that continuous listening to an MP3 player, even at levels that do not seem loud to a listener, can damage the hair cells in the inner ear that transmit sound impulses to the brain. Individuals listening at eighty-five decibels for eight hours can develop hearing loss. MP3 players and other personal stereo devices produce sound levels well in excess of this level. The volume is likely at an unsafe level if other

people can hear the music from earbuds or headphones or if a person can't hear other loud sounds around them.

Hearing loss experts caution that increasing a sound level by three decibels and listening for half as long will produce the same amount of hearing loss. Many MP3 player users listen for several hours a day! Further, many young users do not seem concerned about putting their hearing at risk by using these devices.

Young people need to be informed about safe listening guidelines. A rule of thumb is to listen at about half the maximum level. So on a scale of 1 to 10, a person should be listening to a volume level of about 5 or less. The higher the volume, the less time should be spent listening. Some audiologists suggest a 60 percent/60-minute rule, in which a device is used for no more than about an hour a day and at levels below 60 percent of maximum volume. If listeners lower the volume further and use headphones designed to block other noise, they can safely listen for longer periods of time. To minimize hearing loss, audiologists also recommend that listeners switch from earbud-style headphones to over-the-ear headphones.

ASSISTIVE HEARING DEVICES

Many people with hearing loss use assistive hearing devices. An **assistive hearing device** is a device that helps a person with hearing loss communicate and hear. The most common assistive hearing device is the hearing aid.

Even with a hearing aid, certain situations may pose problems for people with hearing loss. For example, using the telephone may be difficult. A person with hearing loss may need a telephone amplifier that increases the volume on the telephone.

Background noise also can cause problems for people with hearing loss—especially when listening to the TV, radio, or stereo. Increasing the volume to overcome the background noise may make the sound too loud for others. Headphones and other headsets can be connected directly to a TV, radio, or stereo—but these can make the problem worse by bringing very loud noise directly to the ear canal. Television caption devices allow a person to read the audio portion of a TV program. Many people with hearing loss use signaling devices to deal with special circumstances, such as flashing lights that alert them that the phone is ringing, someone is at the door, or the smoke detector has been activated.

PROTECTING AGAINST HEARING LOSS

The following are ways to protect against hearing loss:

1. Do not insert any objects, including cotton-tipped swabs, into the ears. These objects may puncture the eardrum.
2. Clean the outer ear with a soft, clean washcloth to avoid wax buildup.
3. Use the corner of a dry, clean towel to gently dry the ears after bathing or swimming.
4. Contact a physician if the ears become infected or there are signs of hearing loss.
5. Keep the volume of radios, compact disc players, personal stereos (iPods and other MP3 players), and TVs at safe levels.
6. Avoid listening to music through headphones at unsafe levels.
7. Wear protective earplugs when operating loud machinery, using power tools, or attending rock concerts. Hearing protection devices, like earplugs, earmuffs, and canal caps, are sold in drugstores and hardware stores. Different brands offer different amounts of protection. If you are not sure which kind is best for you, or how to use it correctly, ask your doctor. Often the best kind is the one that you feel comfortable in so you can wear it when you need it.

Health Goal #42

I Will Follow a Dental Health Plan

Dental decay is one of the most common health conditions affecting school-age children. Dental decay is a preventable health problem that begins early in life. According to the Surgeon General's report Oral Health in America (U.S. Department of Health and Human Services, 2000a), 17 percent of children two to four years old have already had decay. By the age of eight, approximately 52 percent of children have experienced decay, and by the age of seventeen, dental decay affects 78 percent of children. Poor children suffer twice as many dental caries as their more affluent peers, and their disease is more likely to go untreated. Among low-income children, almost 50 percent of tooth decay remains untreated and

can result in pain, dysfunction, underweight, and poor appearance—problems that can greatly reduce a child's capacity to succeed in the educational environment. Professional care is necessary for maintaining oral health, yet 25 percent of poor children have not seen a dentist before entering kindergarten. The social impact of oral diseases in children is substantial. More than 51 million school hours are lost each year to dental-related illness. Poor children suffer nearly twelve times more restricted-activity days than children from higher-income families. Pain and suffering due to untreated dental diseases can lead to problems in eating, speaking, and attending to learning.

Dental health problems can usually be avoided by following a dental health plan. A **dental health plan** is a plan for taking care of the teeth and gums that includes frequent brushing and flossing, reduction of cavity-promoting foods, avoidance of tobacco, protecting the teeth from injury, regular dental examinations, and cleaning of the teeth by a dental hygienist.

Types of Teeth

Babies begin to get teeth at about six months of age; by age two, a complete set of teeth (known as "baby teeth") is present. These teeth will be replaced by thirty-two permanent teeth. There are four different types of permanent teeth. **Incisors** are the eight teeth in the front and center of the mouth that have a flat, sharp edge that cuts up food. **Cuspids** are the four teeth in the corners of the mouth that have a long, heavy root and a pointed cusp that tears food. **Bicuspids** are the eight teeth in back of the cuspids; they have one or two roots and two cusps that tear and crush food. **Molars** are the twelve teeth in the back of the mouth; they have two or three roots and several cusps that grind food.

Dental Checkups

The American Academy of Pediatric Dentistry recommends a dental checkup at least twice a year for most children. Children with an increased risk of tooth decay, unusual growth patterns, or poor oral hygiene need more frequent dental visits. People who are not aware of any dental problems should still have a checkup. A dentist can find and correct problems before they become painful or obvious. When a dental problem has had time to develop, the treatment often is painful and costly.

Teeth Cleaning

A thorough cleaning by a dental hygienist is recommended two times a year. A **dental hygienist** is a trained dental health professional who works under the direction of a dentist to provide dental care by removing dental plaque and calculus that have built up on teeth. **Dental plaque** is an invisible, sticky film of bacteria on teeth, especially near the gum line. **Calculus** is hardened plaque. Plaque builds and continues to harden. Calculus is difficult to remove through brushing and must be done by a trained dental health professional. A fluoride treatment may be given to strengthen teeth and help prevent cavities. The dental hygienist also will give instructions for brushing and flossing teeth.

X-rays

X-rays of the teeth may be taken to detect tooth decay or other dental problems. X-rays show the insides of the teeth, gums, and supporting bones and can show problems that a dentist cannot see by examination alone. Dentists are careful to minimize the patient's exposure to radiation when taking X-rays, and they use lead aprons and shields to protect the patient.

Whitening

Human teeth naturally are somewhat yellow. As a person ages, the teeth become more yellow. Using tobacco and drinking coffee are two habits that affect the color of teeth. Natural yellowing does not place a person at higher risk of dental problems. There are treatments to whiten teeth. The only reason to get such treatment is cosmetic. Whitening kits are available over the counter, but there are possible side effects.

Dental Sealants

A **dental sealant** is a thin, plastic coating painted on the chewing surfaces of the back teeth to prevent tooth decay. The chewing surfaces of the back teeth are most susceptible to tooth decay. They are rough and uneven because they have small pits and grooves. Food and germs can

get stuck in the pits and stay there a long time. Toothbrush bristles have a difficult time brushing away the food and germs.

Sealants are painted on as a liquid and quickly harden to form a shield over a tooth that protects the teeth from the food, bacteria, and acid that lead to tooth decay. Many dentists recommend that children get sealants on their permanent molars before any decay occurs. The first molars come in between the ages of five and seven. The permanent molars come in between the ages of eleven and fourteen. Teenagers without decay or fillings also may get sealants.

Dental Veneers

A **dental veneer** is a thin shell of ceramic material used to cover teeth. Dental veneers are used to improve the appearance of the front teeth. They also are used to treat broken or chipped teeth, large gaps between teeth, permanently stained or discolored teeth, and crooked teeth.

Dental veneers are attached directly to the existing teeth. The dentist takes an impression of a person's tooth to make an exact copy. Bonding material is used to adhere the veneer to the tooth. Veneers can last for up to ten years, depending on how well a person takes care of them. They are resistant to stains and chipping. However, nail biting and chewing on hard objects such as ice and hard candies can damage them.

Tooth Decay

During a regular examination, a dentist will check for cavities and problems of the teeth and gums. A **cavity** is an area of tooth decay. The chief cause of dental decay is plaque, the invisible, sticky film of bacteria on teeth, especially near the gum line. The bacteria found in plaque ingest sugars and starches and excrete an acid waste product that is corrosive to teeth. This acid causes tooth decay by dissolving the hard enamel and dentin of the teeth. **Dentin** is the hard tissue that forms the body of the tooth. A dentist may put a filling into a cavity. A filling is the material that a dentist uses to repair a cavity in a tooth. Sometimes tooth decay progresses into the pulp of the tooth. The **pulp** is the living tissue within a tooth. If the pulp becomes irreversibly damaged or dies, a root canal must be performed. A **root canal** is a dental procedure performed to save a tooth in which the pulp has died or is severely diseased.

PERIODONTAL DISEASE

When brushing and flossing are ignored, plaque and calculus build up on the teeth. **Periodontal disease** is a disease of the gums and other tissues supporting the teeth. Plaque formation and acid production by bacteria in the plaque can cause periodontal disease. This disease is the main cause of tooth loss in adults. The early stage of periodontal disease is called gingivitis. **Gingivitis** is a condition in which the gums are red, swollen, and tender and bleed easily. The condition worsens if it is not treated. The gums pull away from the teeth. Pockets form between the teeth and gums. The pockets fill with more bacteria, pus, plaque, and calculus, which causes bad breath and infection. Particles of food also become trapped in the pockets and begin to decay. The supporting bones and ligaments that connect the root to the tooth can be destroyed. The teeth may loosen and fall out.

MALOCCLUSION

During a dental examination a person is checked for malocclusion. **Malocclusion** is the abnormal fitting together of teeth when the jaws are closed. An **orthodontist** is a dental health professional who specializes in correcting malocclusion. Malocclusion can make it difficult for a person to bite and speak properly. It also affects a person's appearance. Malocclusion can make it difficult to clean teeth thoroughly, which can lead to gum disease, tooth loss, and abnormal wearing of teeth.

Malocclusion usually is corrected by removing some teeth or by applying braces. **Braces** are devices that are placed on the teeth and wired together to help straighten teeth. About 4.5 million people in the United States are wearing braces or other appliances to straighten teeth (Bren, 2005). Teeth with braces need to be cleaned very well in order to prevent cavities, because food tends to collect under the braces. Braces usually are worn for eighteen to twenty-four months. A dentist or orthodontist will provide an estimate of the time before beginning treatment. After braces are removed, a retainer is usually worn. A **retainer** is a device worn to keep the teeth from moving back to their original locations. When a person has a retainer, it is critical not to forget to wear it and to keep it clean. A new alternative to braces is Invisalign, which uses a series of clear removable aligners instead of wires and brackets. They are custom-made from impressions made of the teeth. Unlike braces, the aligners are removable for eating, brushing, and flossing (Bren, 2005).

Keeping the Teeth and Gums Healthy

Good dental health requires taking care of the teeth and gums. Otherwise dental problems such as tooth decay and periodontal disease may develop. Improper care of the teeth can also put a person at risk for dental injuries. To keep teeth and gums healthy, a person needs to brush and floss teeth daily, obtain a source of fluoride, eat a healthful diet, and wear a mouthguard when participating in sports.

TOOTHBRUSHING

Daily toothbrushing helps remove plaque from the exposed surfaces of the teeth. It also freshens breath. Teeth should be brushed at least twice a day. If possible, brush after every meal. The toothbrush should be soft bristled to prevent injury to the gums. The toothbrush also needs to be long enough to easily reach all of the teeth. A toothpaste that contains fluoride should be used. Fluoride strengthens the teeth and helps prevent tooth decay. It is important to take time to brush teeth carefully. This means brushing the outer, inner, and chewing surfaces of the teeth and tongue with gentle and short strokes. Old toothbrushes should be discarded and new toothbrushes should be used every three to four months.

FLOSSING

Flossing helps remove dental plaque and bits of food between teeth. Flossing can reach areas that brushing cannot. Flossing plays an important part in preventing gum disease. **Dental floss** should be wrapped around one finger on each hand and then moved gently between the teeth to the gum line. Bend the floss around the edges of each tooth, one edge at a time, and slide the floss up and down. The floss should continually be rotated between the fingers so that clean floss is used. This reduces the introduction of bacteria from other teeth.

FLUORIDE

Fluoride can help prevent tooth decay. **Fluoride** is a mineral that strengthens the enamel of teeth. Teeth with strong enamel are resistant to tooth decay because they are able to withstand attacks from acid in the mouth. Fluoride also helps repair areas of teeth that have begun to be dissolved by acid. There are two primary ways to get fluoride: by ingesting fluoride and through water and other products that contain fluoride. **Systemic fluoride** is fluoride that is ingested into the body. A **dietary fluoride supplement** is a product that is prescribed by a dentist or physician for prevention of tooth decay. Supplements come as lozenges, drops, and tablets. They should be used only by children living in areas without water fluoridation. For best results, dietary fluoride supplements should begin when a child is six months old. In areas without water fluoridation, supplements should be taken until age sixteen. A **topical fluoride** is a fluoride product that is applied directly to the teeth. Fluoride toothpastes and mouth rinses are available for purchase without a prescription.

Community water fluoridation is the process of placing fluoride in community water supplies to a level that is optimal for dental health. The water supply of some communities does not need fluoridation because fluoride already appears naturally at an optimal level for dental health. The optimal level is 0.7 to 1.2 parts fluoride per million parts water. More than one-third of the U.S. population (100 million people) has no access to community water fluoridation (U.S. Department of Health and Human Services, 2000a). People without a fluoridated water supply can use dietary fluoride supplements.

DIET

Teeth-damaging acids form in the mouth every time one eats a sugary or starchy food. The acids continue to affect the teeth for at least twenty minutes before they are neutralized and can't do any more damage. The more times sugary snacks are eaten during the day, the more often bacteria is fed the fuel it needs to cause tooth decay. Certain kinds of sweets can do more damage than others. Compared to foods that are chewed quickly and swallowed, gooey or chewy sweets spend more time sticking to the surface of teeth, giving the teeth a longer sugar bath. Sugary foods such as candies, cakes, cookies, and soda pop are not the only culprits. Starchy snacks, especially potato snacks like chips, can also break down into sugars once they are in the mouth. People should think about when, and how often, they eat sugary and starchy snacks. Do they nibble sugary snacks many times throughout the day? Or do they eat them only right after a meal? Another factor is how long the sugary or starchy food stays in the mouth and whether it is sticky. Many snacks are less harmful to teeth than chewy, sticky, sugary foods. Low-fat choices like raw vegetables, fresh fruits, and whole-grain crackers or bread are smart choices. Eating foods that contain vitamin C keeps gums healthy. Eating healthful foods can help protect from tooth decay and gum disease, as can brushing teeth after snacks and meals.

MOUTHGUARDS

Dentists advise using mouthguards when playing sports, to protect the teeth and face. Dentists see many oral and facial injuries that might have been prevented by the use of a mouthguard. Mouthguards come in several varieties. **Custom-made mouthguards** are mouthguards made from a cast model of the teeth. They are more expensive than other types of mouthguards, but they provide the best fit and protection. Custom-made mouthguards also prevent concussions caused by blows to the chin because they cushion the jaw. These mouthguards do not interfere with speech or breathing.

Ready-made commercial mouthguards are sold in sporting goods stores. Made of rubber or polyvinyl, they are the least expensive mouthguards. However, they also are the least effective in protecting the teeth and face. If a person becomes unconscious, mouthguards that are not custom-fit can lodge in the throat and possibly cause an airway obstruction. Another option is a mouthguard that is shaped to fit the individual's teeth. The mouthguard is placed in hot water to soften, then placed in the mouth and bitten into with one's natural bite. The mouthguard hardens to this shape, protecting the teeth in their natural closed bite. This kind of mouthguard tends to become either brittle or bitten through after being used for a while. People with braces find it difficult to wear mouthguards because noncustom mouthguards do not provide much protection to the tops of their teeth. Mouthguards should be worn at all times during athletic competition—in practices as well as in games. Mouthguards need to be kept clean by rinsing them with water or mouthwash after each use. No one should be allowed to use another person's mouthguard.

Health Goal #43
I Will Be Well Groomed

Grooming is keeping the body clean and having a neat appearance. Good grooming practices require the regular cleansing of the hair, skin, nails, and feet, as well as wearing clean clothes. Good grooming practices help protect health by reducing the spread of germs from one part of the body to another part and from one person to another. Good grooming also improves a person's emotional and social health. People with clean bodies and a neat appearance are more attractive to other people. Young people who are not well groomed could be rejected or ostracized by their peers, which will only reduce their feelings of self-worth. On the other hand, being well groomed and having a neat appearance enhances self-confidence and fosters acceptance by peers and adults.

Caring for Hair

The hair on the scalp grows an average of 0.5 inch (1.25 centimeters) per month. The rate of growth varies according to the hair length, the season, and the person's gender.

- Short hair grows faster than long hair.
- Hair cut infrequently grows more slowly.
- Hair grows faster during the day than at night.
- Hair grows faster in warm weather.
- Participating in physical activity may speed hair growth.

One's hair makes a statement about one's personal style. Taking good care of one's hair is an important part of grooming. Healthy hair is shiny and flexible. Unhealthy hair is dull, limp, or oily.

WASHING AND STYLING HAIR

Many products can be used to wash hair. A product that meets the needs of the hair's style and condition should be selected. The more acid a shampoo has, the more it smoothes down the hair. Shampoos designed for oily hair have more detergent than shampoos for dry or normal hair. Some people follow their shampoo with a conditioner. Some people use a shampoo to control dandruff. **Dandruff** is a condition in which dead skin sheds from the scalp, producing white flakes.

Hair is properly washed by wetting it thoroughly with warm water and working shampoo into the hair with the fingertips until there is a good lather. A person with oily hair should not rub the scalp vigorously; rubbing can stimulate the oil glands in the scalp. Thorough rinsing removes suds and loosens scalp flakes. If a conditioner is used after the shampoo, it needs to be rinsed out well. A towel is then used to squeeze extra water from the hair and pat it dry. Wet hair should be combed gently. Brushing wet hair may cause it to break. The hair should then be allowed to dry naturally, or dried with a hair dryer on a warm or cool setting. Hair dryers set on hot can cause hair to become dry and brittle and have split ends. Curling irons and hot rollers also can damage the hair.

Ingredients in hair products may cause skin reactions and harm eyes. Incorrect use or overuse of hair products can damage hair. Some consumers using hair dyes have reported hair loss, burning, redness, and irritation from hair dyes. Allergic reactions to dyes include itching, swelling of the face, and even difficulty breathing (Meadows, 2001). When applying hair chemicals at home or in a hair salon, consumers and beauticians should be careful to keep them away from the eyes. The U.S. Food and Drug Administration has received reports of injuries from hair relaxers and hair dye accidentally getting into eyes. When using or storing any hair chemical, it is critical to keep it away from children to prevent ingestion and other accidents, and to follow product directions carefully.

CARING FOR DIFFERENT TYPES OF HAIR

The type of hair that a person has depends on the type of hair that one inherits from his or her parents and therefore from the part of the world where one's ancestors originated. Hair type depends on the race or mixture of races from which a person has descended. Scientists have identified three types of hair based on race: Asian, African, and Caucasoid. These three types of hair look different, and each type responds differently to hair treatments and elements such as heat and humidity (Gray, 2003).

Asian Hair

People with Asian ancestry have black hair that is very straight. The hair shaft is usually thick and round. The angle of the follicles causes hair to grow straight and perpendicular to the scalp. The density of Asian hair on the scalp (follicles per unit area of skin) is less than that typically observed in Caucasians. Asian hair grows about 1.3 centimeters a month. Asian hair is on average the thickest and most coarse hair compared to Caucasian and African American hair. Asian hair tends to be highly porous, absorbing and retaining moisture more quickly. Highly porous hair tends to color and perm faster. It is important to use gentle solutions and customize the amount of recommended time for color and perm applications.

African Hair

People with African ancestry have hair that is black and tightly curled. The hair shafts are oval in shape. African hair is slightly more dense than Asian hair and grows almost parallel to the scalp, twisting around itself as it grows. The density is about the same as in Caucasians. African hair is the slowest growing of all, at less than 0.9 centimeter a month. African hair follicles produce more oils and sebum than follicles in other races, but due to the coil in the hair fiber, the oils are not evenly distributed along the length. The hair fiber is typically very dry; therefore, African hair needs more hair oils to supplement its natural oil production and help keep the hair fiber flexible. Also, tightly coiled hair is difficult to brush and comb, so using oils helps reduce the friction and static from combing and make the hair more manageable. African hair is easily damaged by heat and chemicals. It is vulnerable to the drying effects of products such as relaxers, perms, and permanent hair colorings. African hair requires more intensive conditioning and moisturizing.

Caucasian Hair

The hair of the Caucasoid group is the most mixed and varied of the three racial groups. Caucasian hair fibers grow at an oblique angle to the scalp, and it may be curly, wavy, or straight. The fiber can be circular or oval in cross section and is on average thinner than Asian hair. The color ranges

from pale blond to black and every possible shade in between. The diameter of the hair also varies widely. As far as rate of growth is concerned, Caucasian hair comes between the other two at 1.2 centimeters a month, but it has the highest density of all. Density can range from 100,000 to 150,000 hair follicles. Hair follicle density varies, and density can be approximately related to hair color. Red-haired people have the least dense scalp hair growth of Caucasians, blonds the most dense, and brown-haired people somewhere in the middle. Hair care for people in this group varies depending on the hair's characteristics.

HAIR REMOVAL

In addition to removing unwanted hair with tweezers and shaving hair with razors and shaving cream or shaving gels, other products are available. **Depilatories** are chemicals that dissolve hair at the skin's surface. **Waxing** is applying hot wax to the skin. A strip of cloth or paper is pressed onto the hot wax. The strip is then quickly pulled away, taking hairs with it. **Laser hair removal** is the use of a laser to cause damage to hair follicles while sparing damage to surrounding tissues. **Electrolysis** is the use of a hair-thin metal probe that delivers electricity to cause damage to hair follicles. Some hair removal products and procedures can cause severe skin reactions in certain people. If these products are not used correctly, the skin or hair follicles may be damaged.

HEAD LICE

Lice are insects that pierce the skin and secrete a substance that causes itching and swelling. Head lice attach to hair on the head and other body parts. To prevent infection with head lice, individuals should avoid sharing brushes, combs, or hats with other people. More information about head lice is given in Appendix C.

Caring for Skin and Nails

Skin is considered to be the largest organ in the body. The average-sized adult has seventeen square feet of skin. Skin protects the body from invasion of microbial agents and ultraviolet rays from the sun. It serves a sensory function by relaying messages from the outside world to the brain. Skin also helps eliminate toxins and wastes from the body through perspiration. Within the skin are millions of cells that make up nerve endings, blood vessels, and sweat glands. Skin is a complex organ that requires good care. The remainder of this section provides information on skin reactions, acne, sunbathing and tanning booths, fingernail care, body odor, foot odor, and foot problems.

Skin Reactions

Some people have sensitive skin that reacts to grooming products. Many products with strong scents irritate skin and can cause allergic reactions. A person who has a reaction, such as a rash, to a grooming product should stop using the product. If the rash does not clear up, a dermatologist or other physician should be contacted. A **dermatologist** is a physician who specializes in care of the skin.

Acne

Many teens develop acne. **Acne** is a skin disorder characterized by inflammation of skin glands and hair follicles and the eruption of pimples. Teens with acne get three main types of skin afflictions: pimples, whiteheads, and blackheads. Pimples occur when a clogged pore becomes infected with bacteria. Whiteheads occur when a clogged pore is not exposed to air. Blackheads occur when a pore becomes clogged with excess oil and dead skin cells.

Acne most commonly appears on the face, neck, shoulders, upper arms, or chest. It usually appears first during puberty, when hormones stimulate oil glands to produce and secrete more oil. Factors that make acne worse include stress, certain medications, menstrual cycle, exposure to sun, oily or heavy cosmetics, popping or picking acne, perspiring, and putting pressure on the face for an extended period of time. Heredity plays a role in acne. The risk of developing acne is greater if your parents, brother, or sister had acne. Acne is not caused by foods or beverages such as chocolate, soda pop, or greasy foods. Acne is not caused by having a dirty face or body. Acne cannot be spread from one teen to another. A recent study showed that a high proportion of young people with acne have misconceptions about the causes and effective treatment of acne (Tan, Vasey, & Fung, 2001).

There is no cure for acne. However, there are many ways to treat acne. The skin should be kept clean and washed gently with a clean washcloth and rinsed well. A physician can recommend a special soap or over-the-counter topical medication. Acne sores should not be squeezed, picked

at, scrubbed, or popped. These actions can cause infection and scars. Hair should be kept away from the face, because hair touching skin causes excess oil. A person with acne should limit time in the sun to reduce perspiration and select cosmetics that are water based.

A dermatologist should be consulted for severe acne, acne that does not clear up, or acne accompanied by signs of infection. Severe, untreated acne can result in permanent scarring.

Sunbathing and Tanning Booths

Some exposure to sunlight is necessary for the body to produce vitamin D, but overexposure can have harmful effects on the skin—such as sunburn. Sunburn is a burn caused by overexposure to sunlight. Ultraviolet rays from the sun destroy cells in the outer layer of the skin and damage blood vessels. The affected skin becomes red and tender and may blister. Exposure to the sun should be limited to prevent sunburn, even if conditions are hazy. A tan is not safe or healthy. It is the skin's attempt to protect itself from damage.

Exposure to the sun's ultraviolet (UV) rays appears to be the most important environmental factor in developing skin cancer (Rados, 2005). Long-term exposure to the sun's harmful rays increases the risk of developing skin cancer and premature wrinkles. Exposure can be reduced with protective clothing and sunscreen with a sun protection factor (SPF) of at least 15. Sunscreens work by absorbing or reflecting UV rays. Research shows that only a small proportion (approximately 20 percent) of school-age youths report always taking sun protection measures, including the frequent use of sunscreens (Coogan, et al., 2001). Further, even though most parents have been alerted about the need to protect their children from sunburns, many do not take effective sun protection behaviors for their children (for instance, many parents of light-skinned children view a tan as healthy), which results in sunburns (Robinson, Rigel, & Amonette, 2000). Children's sunburn could be reduced by more children seeking shade, wearing protective clothing, limiting sun exposure during peak hours, and effectively using sunscreens. It is estimated that 50 to 80 percent of the skin's lifetime sun damage occurs in childhood and adolescence; sunburns during these critical periods increases the risk of developing melanoma later in life. Be careful with baseball caps because they do not protect the ears from sun exposure.

Proper application of sunscreen is important. Use adequate amounts (at least one ounce) when at the pool or beach or during other sun exposure. Apply sunscreen at least thirty minutes prior to sun exposure. Limit exposure to the sun between 10 A.M. and 3 P.M., when UV radiation is most intense. Do not use sunscreen that is leftover from last year. Use sunscreen that has been recently purchased—check the date on the label. Children under six months of age should not have sunscreen applied on their skin. Keep their skin protected from the sun. When outdoor activity is a must, the American Cancer Society recommends that individuals *slip* on a shirt, *slop* on some sunscreen with an SPF of 15 or higher, *slap* on a hat, and *wrap* sunglasses on your face to protect from the sun's strong rays.

Some people believe that tanning booths prevent future sunburn and are a safe alternative to sunbathing because they emit only a certain type of UV radiation. They are mistaken. Tanning booths are dangerous and a risk factor for developing premature wrinkles and skin cancer (Rados, 2005).

Lotions and sprays that contain dihydroxyacetone (DHA) are effective in making the skin appear tanned. DHA is a colorless sugar that interacts with dead cells located in the upper layer of the epidermis, making the skin appear tanned. The tanned color usually lasts about five to seven days after the application. Products are available in shades of light, medium, or dark. They can produce an attractive tan without the risks of sun or tanning bed exposure.

TATTOOS AND BODY PIERCINGS

Unsterile tattooing equipment and needles can transmit communicable disease such as hepatitis C. Therefore, it is extremely important that all tattooing equipment be clean and sterilized before use.

Removing tattoos and permanent makeup can be difficult. Because the skill levels of tattoo artists vary, the pigment can be placed in the skin improperly. Before getting a tattoo, it is critical to ask for references. Although a tattoo may look fine when it is applied, it can fade and the pigments can migrate, causing a blurred appearance. Also, styles change, so what seemed stylish can later become outdated or even cause embarrassment. Changing tattoos or permanent makeup is not as easy as changing your mind. Even with advances in laser technology, tattoo removal can be painful, expensive, and require several treatments. In some cases, complete removal without scarring is not possible.

Allergic reactions to tattoo pigments are rare, but when they occur, they can be troublesome. Some people who have developed allergic reactions have had to suffer with them for many years.

The American Red Cross prohibits donors from donating blood for one year after getting tattooed. Tattooing exposes blood and body fluids; therefore, a person who gets tattooed risks getting a disease or infection that is carried through the blood, such as hepatitis B and C, tetanus, and HIV.

Body piercings have become very popular. The most popular body part pierced in both males and females is the earlobe. Other common piercing sites include the navel, upper part of the ear, nose, tongue, eyebrows, lips, and nipples. Before piercing one's body, the person should be aware of the risks.

There is a risk of acquiring an infection anytime that the skin barrier is pierced. For this reason, it is critical that equipment used to perform body piercing is sterile. The site of a body piercing needs to be kept clean with soap and water. Any redness or swelling that appears at the piercing site should be reported to a doctor. The same is true if any pus develops at the site. One suggestion for keeping the wound moist and to assist in healing is to apply petroleum jelly. Sometimes allergic reactions to the jewelry or over-the-counter antibiotic ointments develop. Other risks associated with body piercings include bleeding, scarring, and permanent holes or marks in the body. Oral piercings have special risks. They can lead to chipped or broken teeth, choking from mouth jewelry that becomes loose, difficulty speaking, and a high risk of infection.

FINGERNAIL CARE

The fingernails can collect dirt and bacteria. They should be trimmed regularly to keep them clean. Nails should be trimmed straight across and not too close to the skin. It is important to not bite or pick at fingernails or cuticles. A **cuticle** is the nonliving skin that surrounds the nails. If hands are dry, moisturizing cream will help prevent hangnails. A **hangnail** is a strip of skin torn from the side or base of a fingernail. Hangnails can be trimmed with nail scissors and covered until healed. Picking at a hangnail can tear the skin and cause infection.

BODY ODOR

Body odor, or what children call "BO," occurs when perspiration combines with dirt, oils, bacteria, and dead skin cells on the body. Sweat glands beneath the dermis allow perspiration to escape through the pores. Regular bathing and use of an antiperspirant or deodorant help prevent body odor. An **antiperspirant** is a product used to reduce the amount of perspiration. Most antiperspirants coat the skin and reduce the flow of sweat leaving the body. A **deodorant** is a product that reduces the amount of body odor, may reduce the amount of perspiration, and contains fragrance to cover up odor. Washing clothes regularly also reduces (residual) body odor.

FOOT ODOR

Foot odor is caused by bacteria that collect on the bottom of feet and between the toes. To prevent foot odor, the feet should be regularly washed with soap. Toenails should be scrubbed with a nail brush. Other measures to avoid foot odor include drying the feet well, wearing clean socks every day, and letting shoes air out after wear.

FOOT PROBLEMS

Several problems can affect the feet. **Athlete's foot** is a fungus that grows on feet. Athlete's foot is treated with special foot powders or creams. An **ingrown toenail** is a toenail that grows into the skin. An ingrown toenail can cause swelling and infection. Toenails should be clipped straight across to reduce the risk of ingrown toenails. A **blister,** a raised area containing liquid, is caused by a burn or by an object rubbing against the skin. If a blister breaks and oozes fluid, clean the area, treat it with an antiseptic, and cover it with a sterile bandage. A **callus** is a thickened layer of skin caused by excess rubbing. Determine what causes the rubbing and make changes to stop it. A **corn** is a growth that results from excess rubbing of a shoe against the foot or from toes being squeezed together. Special pads can be used to reduce pain caused by corns. A **bunion** is a deformity in the joint of the big toe that causes swelling and pain. Wearing low-heeled shoes with a square toe or open toes helps prevent bunions. Medical help should be obtained if a foot problem interferes with walking or lasts for a period of time.

Many foot problems can be averted by properly fitting shoes. Shoes need to be properly fitted and selected for various activities. Buy athletic and work shoes that meet the stability, support, protection, and cushioning requirements for what you do. Beware of high-heeled shoes. Females are at risk for developing a variety of foot and posture problems as a result of wearing high heels. Platform shoes have been known to cause sprained ankles and other injuries associated with falls. Low-heeled shoes with plenty of room in the toe are safer and healthier.

Health Goal #44

I Will Get Adequate Rest and Sleep

Adequate rest and sleep are essential to keep mentally alert, maintain a good disposition, stay physically well, and maintain proper growth. During rest and sleep the body rebuilds and re-energizes itself. **Rest** is a period of relaxation. A person can be awake or asleep and be resting. **Sleep** is a state of deep relaxation in which there is little movement or consciousness.

Types of Sleep

During sleep, the brain continues to process information and the body continues to undergo changes. A person moves through stages of sleep during each night of sleep. The first stage is a transition between being awake and asleep. Each subsequent stage progresses to deeper sleep and unresponsiveness. Heart rate slows by about ten to fifteen beats per minute. Blood pressure decreases. Fewer breaths are taken per minute. Muscles lose tension. Brain waves become much slower. It takes about one hour to get to the stage of deepest sleep.

There are two kinds of sleep. When a person is in the deepest stage of sleep, he or she begins rapid eye movement (REM) sleep. **Rapid eye movement (REM) sleep** is the period of sleep during which virtually all dreaming occurs. This stage is characterized by rapid eye movements behind closed eyelids. Brainwave activity increases to the awake level even though the person is sound asleep. Muscles of the face, arms, legs, and trunk remain relaxed. The eyes dart back and forth in rapid motion. People who are awakened during REM sleep recall vivid dreams. Adults spend about one-fourth of a night's sleep in REM sleep. Infants spend half of their sleep in REM sleep. **Nonrapid eye movement (NREM) sleep** is the period of sleep in which the eyes are relaxed. NREM sleep can range from very light to very deep sleep. It takes about ninety minutes to go through the stages of sleep. After REM sleep, the sequence starts again. Throughout the night, the stages of sleep repeat.

The Need for Sleep

Young people who are not getting enough sleep lack the vitality and concentration needed to perform well in school, in sports, and in other activities. Lack of sleep also increases risk for certain illnesses. People who do not get enough sleep have a weakened immune system and are more accident prone. Sleep is needed to restore physical, emotional, and mental energy. Sleep is even critical to growth. Growth occurs during rest and sleep, when growth hormone is released.

Inadequate sleep and sleep loss can have serious effects on adolescents. Sleep researchers believe that insufficient sleep in teens and young adults can contribute to difficulties (National Sleep Foundation, 2000):

1. *Increased risk of unintentional injuries and death.* Sleep loss is a major cause of traffic crashes. One-sixth of all traffic crashes in the United States are due to sleep loss and fatigue. Drivers age twenty-five and younger cause more crashes due to inadequate sleep than any other age group. Alcohol, even in small amounts, increases a sleep-deprived driver's inability to control a motor vehicle. This accounts for greater risk of traffic crash and injury. Sleepiness also contributes to nontraffic injuries in the workplace and in the home.

2. *Low grades and poor school performance.* Getting less sleep, having later bedtimes, and having irregular sleep schedules are associated with low grades and poor school performance. Students who get enough sleep are more alert in school and struggle with sleepiness in classes less often. They are able to complete their homework because they are more alert.

3. *Negative moods (e.g., anger, sadness, and fear), difficulty controlling emotions, and behavior problems.* Sleepy adolescents are more likely to have negative moods and behavior problems. It is harder to control emotions when one is tired. High school girls with later weeknight bedtimes and who stay up late on weekends report more feelings of depression than do girls with earlier bedtimes. Inadequate sleep may also play a role in disorders such as attention deficit hyperactivity disorder (ADHD) and conduct disorders.

4. *Increased use of stimulants.* Young people are likely to use stimulants such as caffeine and nicotine to counteract the effects of inadequate sleep.

The amount of rest and sleep needed varies from person to person according to a person's level of physical activity and usually decreases with age. Infants spend most of their time sleeping. First- and second-graders usually sleep for eleven to twelve hours; sixth-graders may average nine or ten hours. Adolescents require 8½ to 9¼ hours of sleep each night (Johnson, 2004). Adolescents often require extra sleep and rest because of rapid physical growth and to deal with the demands of a busy lifestyle. It is typical for adolescents to feel sleepy during the daytime, even when they are getting an optimal amount of sleep. The natural time for adolescents to fall asleep changes to a later time in the evening—at around 11 P.M. or later.

Many adolescents do not get enough sleep. This is especially true during the school week. Only about one in seven adolescents gets 8½ hours or more on school nights. Weekend sleep schedules are much different than weekday sleep schedules.

Adolescents sleep on average about two hours more on weekend nights than on weekday nights. One of the most important needs of adolescents is to establish and maintain a consistent sleep-wake schedule.

Research shows that children with a television set in their rooms go to bed significantly later on weekdays and weekends. Even if the TV set is not in their bedroom, children and teens who watch more TV go to bed later than other youths who watch less TV. Youth who are highly involved with playing computer games and using the Internet report less sleeping time and more daytime tiredness. Thus, media choices strongly influence young people's sleeping habits (Van den Bulck, 2004).

Most adults need about eight hours of sleep, but the range of normal sleep for adults ranges from five to ten hours. Feeling rested and energetic during the day is a good sign that a person has had enough sleep. However, too much sleep can make a person feel sluggish, so more is not always better.

A person for whom any of the following are true may need to get more rest and sleep:

- Feels irritable during most of the time being awake
- Always has to have an alarm clock to wake up
- Thinks about and craves more sleep during the day
- Has to rely on caffeine to keep awake during the day
- Dozes off during class or work
- Dozes off while watching television
- Feels tired most of the day
- Feels tired most of the time when playing sports or participating in enjoyable activities

SLEEPY TEENS

The National Sleep Foundation (NSF) 2006 *Sleep in America* poll reveals some very interesting facts about adolescent sleep, or in many cases lack of it. According to the poll, only 20 percent of adolescents report that they get an optimal nine hours of sleep on school nights and nearly half say they actually sleep less than eight hours on school nights. The poll found that many teens try to make up for lost sleep by napping and sleeping late on weekends. Thirty-eight percent took at least two naps per week in the two weeks preceding the survey, and most adolescents reported sleeping between 1.2 and 1.9 hours longer on nonschool nights. A common means of coping with sleep loss by teens is frequently consuming caffeinated beverages. Almost one-third (31 percent) say that they drink two or more caffeinated beverages a day. Not getting enough sleep can lead to dangerous and unhealthy behaviors, such as giving up on exercise or driving while drowsy. More than a quarter (28 percent) of adolescents say they felt too tired or sleepy to exercise, and about half (51 percent) who drive say they've driven while drowsy during the past year.

An interesting finding of the *Sleep in America* poll is an association between the amount of sleep and mood. Teens were asked questions to gauge their mental health, mood, behavior, and attitude. More than half (55 percent) of adolescents who scored in the best-mood category said, "I had a good night's sleep" every night or almost every night versus only 20 percent of those in the worst-mood category. This finding is not really surprising because sleep experts caution that lack of sleep can cause teens to act out and succumb to feelings of anxiety, depression, and hopelessness. Further, insufficient sleep can lead to difficulty with focus, attention, and concentration. Teens with these feelings and symptoms find it difficult to excel in school and are likely to suffer from irritability and mood disorder. The poll also showed that a high proportion of teens frequently fall asleep in school, arrive late, or miss school because of oversleeping. An interesting finding of the poll regarding success in school is that A and B students report going to bed earlier and getting more sleep than students with poorer grades.

The busy routines of teens and the early starting time of the school day contribute to sleep deprivation. The average school day for teens begins around 6:30 A.M. More than half of high school students start school before 8 A.M. and must leave their homes for school on average by 7:10 A.M. Busy school days and afternoon and early evening activities mean that more than half (55 percent) of high school students don't go to bed until after 11 P.M. on school nights.

The poll found that a high proportion of teens have "sleep stealers," such as televisions, computers, cell phones, and MP3 players, in their bedrooms. These electronic devices frequently take away sleep time when they are used near bedtime or in the bedroom. The poll showed the following percentages of adolescents have these devices in their bedrooms:

- 90 percent—MP3 players or radios
- 57 percent—televisions

- 21 percent—Internet access in the bedroom
- 43 percent—video games
- 42 percent—cell phones in the bedroom

Getting Adequate Sleep and Rest

To get a good night's sleep, it helps to establish a regular time to go to bed at night and to get up in the morning. Quiet activities such as reading, taking a warm bath, and listening to relaxing music encourage sleep. These activities help the transition between wakefulness and sleep. Nightly rituals such as brushing teeth, setting the alarm clock, and organizing materials for the next day also encourage sleepiness. Napping during the day is a good way to catch up on sleep, but sometimes this practice makes it hard to fall asleep at night. A person who has a lot of difficulty falling asleep at night might have to avoid napping completely.

Having a quiet and comfortable place to sleep is necessary for a good night's sleep. A medium-hard mattress supports a person's back and makes it easier to fall asleep and sleep restfully. A dark room, carpets and rugs that muffle sounds, and earplugs also can help.

Certain substances, when taken into the body, make falling asleep difficult. Caffeinated beverages should be avoided during the evening because they induce wakefulness. The nicotine in cigarettes is also a stimulant that can make falling asleep difficult. Alcoholic beverages and some sleeping medications suppress REM sleep and cause restlessness and waking. Eating large amounts of food just before going to bed can interfere with sleep, but hunger pangs can also keep a person awake. People should not drink fluids in the hours before bedtime to avoid having to get up and empty the bladder.

The body is programmed to feel sleepy during the nighttime hours and to be active during the daylight hours. People who work at night and try to sleep during the day must constantly fight their biological sleep clock. The same is true for people who fly to other time zones. They get jet lag because they cannot maintain a regular sleep-wake schedule. They feel tired and sluggish and may have difficulty falling asleep.

Not being able to fall asleep now and then is normal. Continual failure to be able to fall asleep may be insomnia. **Insomnia** is the prolonged inability to fall asleep, stay asleep, or get back to sleep once a person is awakened during the night. Insomnia becomes a pattern and can cause problems during the day, such as tiredness, a lack of energy, difficulty in concentrating, and irritability. Insomnia affects people of all ages.

Relaxing and Resting

Being able to relax and rest is important in counteracting physical and mental fatigue and in coping with stress. People should take time for the things they enjoy doing. Participating in enjoyable activities such as hobbies, interests, and entertainment can be energizing. These activities take one's mind off problems and worries. Participating in sports promotes relaxation by providing a physical outlet for stress and tension. People who feel uptight can relax with some moderate physical activity, such as going for a walk, shooting some hoops, or kicking around a soccer ball.

Health Goal #45

I Will Participate in Regular Physical Activity

Physical activity is any bodily movement produced by skeletal muscles that results in energy expenditure. **Regular physical activity** is physical activity that is performed on most days of the week.

The lack of regular physical activity is a serious problem in the United States. A majority of adults in the United States are not physically active at levels that promote and maintain health (Macera et al., 2005). Physical inactivity is more prevalent among those with lower income and education. One-third (31 percent) of high school students do not participate regularly in vigorous or moderate physical activity (Eaton et al., 2006). Physical activity levels begin to decline as children approach their teenage years and continue to decline throughout adolescence (Sturm, 2005).

Low levels of physical activity among young people may be one factor responsible for the steep

increases in childhood obesity seen in recent years. The percentage of young people who are overweight has tripled since 1980 (Story, Kaphingst, & French, 2006). Because a pattern of inactivity begins early in childhood, it is imperative to promote physical activity among children.

When physical inactivity is combined with poor diet, the impact on health is devastating, accounting for an estimated 350,000 deaths per year (Mokdad et al., 2005). Tobacco use is the only behavior that kills more people.

The Health Benefits of Regular Physical Activity

The landmark *Physical Activity and Health: A Report of the Surgeon General* (U.S. Department of Health and Human Services, 1996) identified substantial health benefits of regular participation in physical activity:

- People who are usually inactive can improve their health and well-being by becoming even moderately active on a regular basis.
- Physical activity need not be strenuous to achieve health benefits.
- Greater health benefits can be achieved by increasing the amount (duration, frequency, or intensity) of physical activity.

A lifestyle of regular physical activity during childhood and adolescence, which continues into and throughout adulthood, is important for health and well-being (Nieman, 2003). Research indicates that physical activity in childhood and adolescence may positively influence health status during childhood and adolescence, as well as throughout adulthood (Blair, Cheng, & Holder, 2001; Malina, 2001). *Physical Activity and Health: A Report of the Surgeon General* (U.S. Department of Health and Human Services, 1996) outlined the following eleven benefits of regular physical activity.

REDUCES THE RISK OF PREMATURE DEATH

Life expectancy is the number of years a person can expect to live. **Premature death** is death before a person reaches her or his predicted life expectancy. Children and teens don't usually think ahead to middle and late adulthood. However, they should know that participating in regular physical activity right now will affect the quality of their life in middle and late adulthood. By being physically active, young people are preparing early to live a long and healthful life.

REDUCES THE RISK OF CARDIOVASCULAR DISEASE

Cardiovascular disease is a disease of the heart and blood vessels. During physical activity, cardiac output increases to provide muscle cells with oxygen. **Cardiac output** is the amount of blood pumped by the heart each minute. Cardiac output is equal to heart rate multiplied by stroke volume. **Stroke volume** is the amount of blood the heart pumps with each beat. Regular physical activity makes the threadlike muscle fibers of the heart thicker and stronger. As a result, stroke volume increases. The heart does not have to beat as often to maintain the same cardiac output. Resting heart rate is lowered.

Regular physical activity influences blood lipid levels. **High-density lipoproteins (HDLs)** are substances in the blood that carry cholesterol to the liver for breakdown and excretion. **Low-density lipoproteins (LDLs)** are substances in the blood that carry cholesterol to body cells. Vigorous physical activity increases the number of HDLs, which reduces the risk of developing atherosclerosis. **Atherosclerosis** is a disease in which fat, or plaque, accumulates on artery walls, narrowing the arterial passageways and reducing blood flow.

Regular physical activity reduces the likelihood of developing coronary thrombosis. **Coronary thrombosis** is the narrowing of one of the coronary arteries by a blood clot. This causes a section of the heart muscle to die from lack of oxygen. Regular physical activity helps prevent platelets from clumping together to form a blood clot. It also enhances the breakdown of blood clots.

Regular physical activity also improves coronary collateral circulation. **Coronary collateral circulation** is the development of additional arteries that can deliver oxygenated blood to the heart muscle. When you work out, your heart muscle needs oxygen. Small arteries branch off existing arteries to provide the additional blood flow. These additional routes for blood flow are helpful should a person develop blockage in a coronary artery. This makes a person less likely to die from a heart attack.

REDUCES THE RISK OF DEVELOPING TYPE 2 DIABETES

Type 2 diabetes is a type of diabetes in which the body produces insulin but it cannot be used by cells. More than 90 percent of people who have diabetes have Type 2 diabetes. People who are overweight are at risk for developing Type 2 diabetes. The risk is greatest in people with excess fat around the waist, abdomen, and upper body and within the abdominal cavity. People who are physically inactive have the greatest risk of developing Type 2 diabetes. They have higher blood glucose levels and insulin values than do people who are physically active. One negative consequence that is linked to the child obesity epidemic is the appearance of Type 2 diabetes in recent years among adolescents. Type 2 diabetes was previously so rarely seen in children that it came to be called "adult-onset diabetes." Now, an increasing number of teenagers and preteens must be treated for Type 2 diabetes (CDC, 2005).

REDUCES THE RISK OF DEVELOPING HIGH BLOOD PRESSURE

Regular physical activity reduces the risk of developing atherosclerosis. When the arteries remain elastic, they can dilate when the body needs more oxygenated blood. Resting blood pressure stays in normal range. **Blood pressure** is the force of blood against the artery walls. When the arteries are elastic, dynamic blood pressure remains low. **Dynamic blood pressure** is the measure of the changes in blood pressure during the day. Sudden changes in blood pressure can cause stroke. A **stroke** is a condition caused by a blocked or broken blood vessel in the brain.

REDUCES HIGH BLOOD PRESSURE

People who already have high blood pressure must pay attention to the risk factors over which they have control. They have control over their weight. Regular physical activity helps them to maintain desirable weight or to lose weight if needed. Regular physical activity helps prevent plaque from collecting on artery walls. Clear arteries remain elastic and are able to dilate when more oxygenated blood is needed. This helps prevent increases in blood pressure.

REDUCES THE RISK OF DEVELOPING COLON CANCER

Regular physical activity helps speed the movement of waste through the colon, resulting in more regular daily bowel movements. Having daily bowel movements decreases the risk of colon cancer.

REDUCES FEELINGS OF DEPRESSION AND ANXIETY

Regular physical activity improves circulation to the brain. As a result, a person feels more alert. Regular physical activity also causes the body to produce higher levels of norepinephrine and beta-endorphins. **Norepinephrine** is a substance that helps transmit brain messages along certain nerves. **Beta-endorphins** are substances produced in the brain that create a feeling of well-being. These two substances help reduce the risk of depression and provide some relief of symptoms in people who are suffering from depression. Regular physical activity counterbalances the bodily changes that occur in the first stage of stress by using up the adrenaline that is secreted during the stress response. This helps the body return to its normal state and reduces the risk of stress-related diseases. Regular physical activity relieves anxiety by providing a physical outlet when a person is stressed.

Helps Control Weight

Regular physical activity increases metabolic rate, burns calories, and shrinks fat cells. Regular physical activity also helps regulate the hypothalamus in the brain. As a result, appetite decreases. Each of these factors helps to maintain desirable weight. In fact, inactivity is a major factor contributing to overweight and obesity.

Regular physical activity also affects body composition. **Body composition** is the percentage of fat tissue and lean tissue in the body. Having too much fat tissue is a risk factor for cardiovascular disease, diabetes, cancer, and arthritis. Regular physical activity also favorably affects fat distribution, reducing the accumulation of fat in the abdominal area, which reduces the risk of developing cardiovascular diseases.

Helps Build and Maintain Healthy Bones, Muscles, and Joints

Weight-bearing physical activity is essential for normal skeletal development in children and teens. It continues to be essential for maintaining peak bone mass as young people age. A lifetime habit of weight-bearing activities, such as running, walking, and roller-blading, prevents bones from becoming brittle. **Osteoporosis** is a condition in which the bones lose calcium and become thin and brittle. This condition can be prevented and managed with regular physical activity and diet. Females also might take estrogen replacement therapy after menopause. Research has also shown that physical activity has a protective effect against hip fracture among elderly people (Norton et al., 2001).

Regular physical activity helps joints as well as bones. Stretching helps muscles lengthen, which allows the joints to move freely and easily through the full range of motion. Regular physical activity provides positive benefits for people who have arthritis. **Arthritis** is a painful inflammation of the joints. Moderate physical activity reduces the swelling around the joints. It increases the pain threshold and energy levels of people who have arthritis. As a result, people with arthritis are better able to cope with their condition.

Helps Older Adults Become Stronger and Better Able to Move About without Falling

Regular physical activity may help prevent accidents by improving muscular strength, balance, and reaction time. Accidents, especially falls, are a primary cause of fractures and other injuries in older adults.

Promotes Psychological Well-Being

People who participate in regular physical activity have higher levels of norepinephrine and beta-endorphins. These substances promote feelings of well-being. Regular physical activity promotes psychological well-being in other ways as well. Improved appearance from muscle tone and reduced body fat may boost self-confidence. The routine of regular physical activity increases self-discipline and promotes self-respect. Completing a workout gives a person a feeling of accomplishment. Through its effects on psychological well-being, physical activity may help increase students' capacity for learning.

Physical Activity Guidelines for Youth

The first physical activity guidelines for children ages five to twelve were released in 1998 (Corbin & Pangrazi, 1998). In 2004, the physical activity guidelines for children were revised, and the recommended amount of activity was increased (National Association for Sport and Physical Education, 2004). The first of four new guidelines recommends *at least sixty minutes, and up to several hours, of physical activity per day.* This is not surprising given the fact that inactivity has contributed to the recent obesity epidemic and sedentary living is a known threat to health. The purpose of the guidelines is to provide parents, physicians, teachers, youth physical activity leaders, school administrators, and others dedicated to promoting physically active lifestyles for children with suggestions about appropriate physical activity for preadolescent children. The following are the recommendations for children ages five to twelve:

- Children should accumulate *at least sixty minutes, and up to several hours,* of age-appropriate physical activity on all, or most, days of the week. This daily accumulation should include moderate and vigorous physical activity with the majority of the time being spent in activity that is intermittent in nature.

- Children should participate in *several bouts of physical activity lasting fifteen minutes* or more each day.
- Children should participate each day in *a variety of age-appropriate physical activities* designed to achieve optimal health, wellness, fitness, and performance benefits.
- *Extended periods (periods of two hours or more) of inactivity are discouraged* for children, especially during the daytime hours.

In the guidelines, physical activity is broadly defined and includes exercise, sport, dance, and other movement forms. Most children will have a difficult time meeting these guidelines unless they have sufficient opportunity for physical education and recess at school and for participation in sports after school hours. These guidelines support the Healthy People 2010 goal of achieving more physical education in schools since long school days without activity lead to long periods of inactivity.

An international consensus conference developed physical activity guidelines for adolescents (Corbin, Pangrazi, & Masurier, 2004; Sallis & Patrick, 1994). These guidelines call for all adolescents to be physically active daily, or nearly every day, for at least thirty minutes as part of play, games, sports, work, transportation, recreation, physical education, or planned exercise in the context of family, school, and community activities. Further, the guidelines recommend that adolescents engage in three or more sessions per week of activities that last twenty minutes or more and that require *moderate to vigorous* levels of exertion. These guidelines are consistent with American College of Sports Medicine guidelines for adults (ACSM, 2000).

Award programs from the President's Council on Physical Fitness and Sports can help youth meet physical activity guidelines. The activity requirements for the President's Challenge Award constitute a set of standards for youth and adults to achieve. To receive the President's Active Lifestyle Award (PALA), youth ages six to seventeen must participate in sixty minutes of physical activity a day for at least five days per week, for a total of six weeks. This is consistent with the sixty-minute standard for children. The program also allows youth to achieve the award by accumulating at least 13,000 steps for males or 11,000 steps for females recorded on a pedometer (President's

Council on Physical Fitness and Sports, 2003). However, it should be noted that fitness experts are concerned that a higher step count than currently recommended for the PALA standards may be required to achieve good health (Corbin, Pangrazi, & Masurier, 2004).

Health Goal #46

I Will Follow a Physical Fitness Plan

Following a Physical Fitness Plan

To become physically fit, a person must participate in physical activities that develop each of the components of health-related and skill-related fitness. A **physical fitness plan** is a written plan of physical activities to develop each of the components of fitness and a schedule for doing them. There are six steps to follow when designing an individualized plan for health-related fitness:

1. *Design a physical fitness plan in the form of a health behavior contract.* A health behavior contract is a written plan to develop the habit of practicing a life skill.
2. *Use the FITT formula.* The **FITT formula** is a formula in which each letter represents a factor for determining how to obtain fitness benefits from physical activity: F = frequency, I = intensity, T = time, and T = type.
3. *Include a warmup and a cooldown.* A warmup consists of three to five minutes of easy physical activity to prepare the muscles and joints to do more work. A cooldown consists of five to ten minutes of reduced physical activity to help the body return to the nonexercising state. A warmup and cooldown reduce the risk of injuries related to physical activity.
4. *Include aerobic exercises to develop cardiorespiratory endurance and a healthful body composition.* Aerobic exercises should be performed three to five days a week at the target heart rate and should burn 1.8 calories for each pound of body weight. The time spent in the workout depends on how many calories the activity burns.
5. *Include resistance exercises to develop muscular strength and muscular endurance.*

Resistance exercise can be performed by lifting one's own weight, lifting free weights, or working with weight machines. Resistance exercises should be performed two to four days a week with a day of rest in between each workout. The amount of resistance and the repetitions performed should be recorded. Increase resistance gradually. Perform three sets of eight to twelve repetitions of each exercise with free weights or weight machines. Perform additional repetitions when the resistance weight is body weight, as when doing pushups or situps.

6. *Include static stretching exercises to develop flexibility.* Perform static stretching exercises two to three days a week. Hold each stretch for thirty seconds. Rest for thirty to sixty seconds between stretches. Repeat each stretch three to five times. A flexibility workout should last for fifteen to thirty minutes. Also include static stretching exercises as part of a warmup and cooldown to reduce the risk of injuries.

The following are some ways to stay motivated to follow a physical fitness plan:

1. Select a variety of physical activities.
2. Work out with a friend.
3. Work out with family members.
4. Reward oneself when reaching goals.
5. Record progress, to feel a sense of accomplishment.
6. Listen to energetic music while working out.
7. Have a backup plan for bad weather.
8. Organize the day so it is easy to work out.
9. Join a sports club or team.
10. Take lessons to improve a fitness skill.

Health Goal #47

I Will Develop and Maintain Health-Related Fitness

Health-Related Fitness

Physical fitness is the ability to perform physical activity and to meet the demands of daily living while being energetic and alert. There are several components of physical fitness. These components are grouped into health-related

fitness and skill-related fitness. **Health-related fitness** is the ability of the heart, lungs, muscles, and joints to function at optimal capacity. The next section of this chapter will describe skill-related fitness. There are five components of health-related fitness:

1. **Cardiorespiratory endurance** is the ability of the circulatory and respiratory systems to supply oxygen during sustained physical activity.
2. **Muscular strength** is the maximum amount of force a muscle can produce in a single effort.
3. **Muscular endurance** is the ability of the muscle to continue to perform without fatigue.
4. **Flexibility** is the ability to bend and move the joints through the full range of motion.
5. **Healthful body composition** is a high ratio of lean tissue to fat tissue in the body.

Exercise

Exercise is planned, structured, and repetitive bodily movement done to improve or maintain one or more components of physical fitness. There are five kinds of exercises: aerobic, anaerobic, isometric, isotonic, and isokinetic.

Aerobic exercise uses large amounts of oxygen continually for an extended period of time. Aerobic exercises are vigorous, continuous, and rhythmic. They improve cardiorespiratory endurance, muscular strength, and body composition.

Anaerobic exercise is activity that is performed at high intensity that exceeds the body's capacity to use oxygen during the exertion. Anaerobic exercises cause lactic acid to gather in the muscles. Lactic acid is a waste product that is produced when muscles work without the presence of oxygen. Running sprints and playing basketball are two examples of anaerobic exercises.

Isometric exercises involve tightening for about five to eight seconds with no body movement. Pressing the palms of the hands together at chest level for at least five seconds is an isometric exercise. Isometric exercises can be done almost anywhere and require little or no equipment. Holding your breath when you perform isometric exercises can cause your blood pressure to rise. Isometric exercises should not be performed by people with heart conditions.

An **isotonic exercise** is one in which a muscle or muscles move a moderate amount of weight eight to fifteen times. Weight lifting, pushups, curlups, and jumping jacks are isotonic exercises. When performing isotonic exercises, increase resistance gradually. Isotonic exercises improve muscular strength and endurance and increase flexibility. Performing isotonic exercises at high intensity for a specified amount of time can improve cardiorespiratory endurance.

An **isokinetic exercise** is an exercise that involves using special machines that provide weight resistance through the full range of motion. Isokinetic exercises promote muscular strength, muscular endurance, and flexibility.

THE FITT FORMULA

In the **FITT formula,** each letter represents a factor for determining how to obtain fitness benefits from physical activity:

F *Frequency* is how often a person will perform physical activities.

I *Intensity* is how hard a person will perform physical activities.

T *Time* is how long a person will perform physical activities.

T *Type* is the kind of physical activities that a person will perform to develop a fitness component or obtain a specific benefit.

Cardiorespiratory Endurance

Cardiorespiratory endurance is the ability of the circulatory and respiratory systems to supply oxygen during sustained physical activity. This section discusses the benefits of cardiorespiratory endurance, developing a cardiorespiratory endurance program, warming up and cooling down, maintaining cardiovascular endurance, and measuring cardiorespiratory endurance.

BENEFITS OF CARDIORESPIRATORY ENDURANCE

There are several benefits of cardiorespiratory endurance (Sharkey, 2002). Cardiorespiratory endurance:

1. Helps the heart and lungs function more efficiently.

2. *Improves metabolic rate.* Physical activities that promote cardiorespiratory endurance burn calories. They raise the resting metabolic rate for up to twelve hours.

3. *Promotes healthful aging.* Physical activities that promote cardiorespiratory endurance activate antioxidants. Antioxidants slow or prevent reactions that produce free radicals, which can damage body cells. Free radicals are believed to be one cause of aging.

4. *Improves insulin sensitivity.* Physical activities that promote cardiorespiratory endurance improve insulin sensitivity. This helps with the metabolism of carbohydrates, fats, and proteins and lowers the risk of developing diabetes.

5. *Reduces the harmful effects of the alarm stage of general adaptation syndrome.* During the first stage of stress—the alarm stage—hormones are secreted. Epinephrine and cortisol, two of these hormones, put the body in a state of emergency. Too much of these two hormones increases the risk of developing cardiovascular diseases and can suppress the immune system. This increases the risk of developing certain kinds of cancers. Physical activities help prevent having too much of these two hormones in the bloodstream.

6. *Improves the muscles' ability to use lactic acid.* Muscles produce **lactic acid** during vigorous exercise, and it is one of the factors that cause cramps. Physical activities that promote cardiorespiratory endurance

provide a training effect. They lengthen the time people can exercise without feeling fatigue or cramping.

7. *Increases the level of high-density lipoproteins and decreases the level of low-density lipoproteins.* High-density lipoproteins (HDLs) carry cholesterol to the liver for breakdown and excretion. Low-density lipoproteins (LDLs) carry cholesterol to body cells. Physical activities that promote cardiorespiratory endurance increase HDLs and decrease LDLs. This reduces the risk of developing cardiovascular diseases.

8. *Improves the function of the immune system.* A person with good cardiorespiratory endurance may have fewer colds and upper respiratory infections. (Caution: Too much strenuous physical activity can depress the function of the immune system.)

9. *Protects against some types of cancer.* Physical activities that promote cardiorespiratory endurance speed the movement of food through the gastrointestinal tract. A person is more likely to have daily bowel movements. This decreases the risk of developing colon cancer.

10. *Improves psychological well-being.* Physical activities that promote cardiorespiratory endurance cause beta-endorphins to be secreted into the bloodstream. Beta-endorphins are substances produced in the brain that create a feeling of well-being.

Developing a Cardiorespiratory Endurance Program

Cardiorespiratory endurance is developed by following the FITT formula:

Frequency: Participate in physical activity three to five days a week. Start with three days and work up to five days. Training less than three days a week does not produce fitness benefits. Training more than five days a week can lead to injury and can stress the immune system.

Intensity: Perform physical activity within the target heart rate. **Target heart rate** is a heart rate of 75 percent of the individual's maximum heart rate. **Maximum heart** rate is 220 beats per minute minus the person's age.

Time: The length of time physical activity is performed will depend on the intensity. As a general rule, continue to perform physical activity until 1.8 calories have been burned for each pound of body weight. For example, people might walk for forty-five to sixty minutes at four miles (6.4 kilometers) per hour, but the workout would be shorter if they picked up the pace and ran. For example, they might run briskly for twenty to twenty-five minutes.

Type: Choose aerobic activities, such as aerobic dancing, backpacking, badminton, basketball, bench-stepping, bicycling, cross-country skiing, field hockey, handball, hiking, hockey, in-line skating, jogging, karate, lacrosse, racquetball, jumping rope, rowing, rugby, running, soccer, stairwalking, swimming, and walking.

Warming Up and Cooling Down

A critical aspect of participating in physical activities to improve cardiorespiratory endurance is warming up and cooling down. A **warmup** is a period of three to five minutes of easy physical activity to prepare the muscles to do more work. This preliminary warmup activity gets blood flowing to active muscles. The muscles work better when their temperature is slightly above resting level. The warmup also gets synovial fluid spreading throughout the joints. **Synovial fluid** is fluid that lubricates and provides nutrition to the cells on the surface of joints. These body changes enhance performance and decrease the chances of injury. A **cooldown** is a period of five to ten minutes of reduced physical activity after the workout to help the body return to a nonexercising state. As a person cools down, heart rate, breathing, and circulation return to normal. The cooldown is a good time to do stretching exercises because the muscles are warm and won't be injured by stretching.

Maintaining Cardiorespiratory Endurance

A person will notice steady improvement for about four to six weeks when beginning a training program. A person has to gradually increase intensity and time during training sessions to become more fit. The more fit one becomes, the more difficult it will be to make gains. When a person reaches an acceptable level of cardiorespiratory fitness, it is time to begin a maintenance program. Training should continue at the same intensity on at least three nonconsecutive days of the week.

MEASURING CARDIORESPIRATORY ENDURANCE

The one-mile run/walk test is a test to measure cardiorespiratory fitness, based on how long it takes a person to complete one mile (1.6 kilometers) of brisk walking and the person's heart rate at the end of the walk. Age, gender, and body weight also are considered. A fast time and a low heart rate are desirable.

This test should be performed on a track. On most tracks four laps is a mile. A person who cannot run the entire mile should walk part way. The person should be instructed to stop if she or he feels dizzy or sick. Individuals can time themselves or be timed by partners. Before the test, a person should warm up. At the end of the test, a person should cool down. The score on the test is the time it takes to run or walk the mile. A person can take a baseline one-mile run/walk test to assess current cardiorespiratory endurance. Later tests can determine progress in cardiorespiratory endurance.

Muscular Strength and Endurance

Muscular strength is the maximum amount of force a muscle can produce in a single effort. Muscular endurance is the ability of the muscle to continue to perform without fatigue. This section discusses the benefits of muscular strength and endurance, developing a conditioning program for muscular strength and endurance, warming up and cooling down, maintaining muscular strength and endurance, and measuring muscular strength and endurance.

BENEFITS OF MUSCULAR STRENGTH AND ENDURANCE

Muscular strength and endurance do the following:

1. Help a person perform everyday tasks, such as carrying schoolbooks, climbing stairs, and lifting objects
2. Help maintain correct posture
3. Reduce the risk of low back pain
4. Reduce the risks of being injured

5. Help a person enjoy physical activities without tiring
6. Improve body composition by increasing muscle mass and decreasing fat tissue
7. Improve self-image because muscles are firm and the body is toned
8. Keep bones dense and strong
9. Make the surfaces of joints less susceptible to injury

DEVELOPING A CONDITIONING PROGRAM FOR MUSCULAR STRENGTH AND ENDURANCE

A conditioning program should include resistance exercises. A **resistance exercise** is an exercise in which a force acts against muscles. To obtain resistance, a person can lift his or her own weight, lift free weights, or work with weights on a weight machine. A **repetitions maximum** is the maximum amount of resistance that can be moved a specified number of times. **Repetitions** are the number of times an exercise is performed in one set. A **set** is a group of repetitions followed by a rest period. A person builds muscular strength by doing maximum resistance exercises only a few times. A person builds muscular endurance with less resistance and more repetitions.

Weight training is a conditioning program in which free weights or weight machines provide resistance for muscles. Isometric, isotonic, and isokinetic exercises are used for weight training. Isometric exercises, such as tightening abdominal muscles, can be performed using an immovable object, such as a wall, to provide resistance. Isotonic or isokinetic exercises, such as pushups or situps, can be done using body weight as resistance. Free weight can be also used to do isotonic and isokinetic exercises. A **free weight** is a barbell or dumbbell. A collar is a device that secures weights to a barbell or dumbbell. Weight machines also can be used for isotonic and isokinetic exercises. A **weight machine** is an apparatus that provides resistance to a muscle or group of muscles. A person should obtain the advice of a coach or trainer when beginning to use free weights or a weight machine.

A person should follow the FITT formula:

Frequency: Train with weights two to four days a week, with a day of rest between workouts.

Intensity: Keep a record of the amount of resistance and number of repetitions. Begin with a weight that can be moved easily for eight to twelve repetitions. Add more weight until three sets of ten to twelve repetitions can be done. A heavy weight and a low number of repetitions (one to five) build muscular strength. A lighter weight and a high number of repetitions (twenty to twenty-five) build muscular endurance.

Time: Perform eight to twelve repetitions of each exercise to build muscular strength and endurance. Perform at least one set of each exercise. Perform three sets for maximum fitness benefits.

Type: Exercises that use body weight for resistance include abdominal crunch, bent arm hang, curlup twist, dips, pullups, pushups, side leg raises, sitting tuck, situps, squats, and stride jump. Exercises that use free weights or weight machines include bench press, bicep curl, decline press, flies, half squats, kickbacks, lateral pull-downs, lateral raises, leg curls, leg extensions, leg presses, seated overhead presses, seated rows, shrugs, squats, tricep extensions, and tricep pull-downs.

WARMING UP AND COOLING DOWN

Before a weight-training session, a person should warm up by walking or easy jogging for three to five minutes. This warms the muscles and lubricates the joints for harder work. A person can warm up specific muscle groups before using free weights or weight machines by doing a set of eight to ten repetitions at low weight resistance. For example, a helpful warmup is performed at one-half the weight resistance used for the workout exercise. A person can cool down by walking or easy jogging for five to ten minutes. This should be followed by stretching exercises to prevent muscle soreness. (Also, stretching should be considered after completing the sets of repetitions planned for each muscle group.)

MAINTAINING MUSCULAR STRENGTH AND ENDURANCE

A person will improve rapidly during the first four to six weeks of training. After six weeks, goals need to be evaluated. It is helpful to work with a trainer or coach to determine what to accomplish. Muscular strength and endurance are maintained by continuing to train two or three days a week, with rest days between workouts.

MEASURING MUSCULAR STRENGTH AND ENDURANCE

Muscular strength is tested by measuring the maximum amount of weight a person can lift at one time. Muscular endurance is tested by counting the maximum amount of time a person can hold a muscular contraction or the maximum number of repetitions of a muscular contraction a person can do. Pullups also are used to measure muscular strength and endurance.

Flexibility

Flexibility is the ability to bend and move the joints through the full range of motion. This section discusses the benefits of flexibility, developing flexibility, warming up and cooling down, and measuring flexibility.

BENEFITS OF FLEXIBILITY

Flexibility

1. Improves quality of life; a person can bend and move easily and without pain
2. Helps prevent and relieve symptoms associated with arthritis
3. Helps prevent low-back pain
4. Helps prevent injuries to muscles and joints
5. Decreases the likelihood of having accidents, such as falls
6. Improves performance in sports, such as golf and tennis, that require a range of motion

DEVELOPING FLEXIBILITY

To develop flexibility, the FITT formula needs to be followed:

Frequency: Stretching exercises need to be performed two to three times a week and as part of a cooldown for weight training.

Intensity: Stretches should be held for fifteen to thirty seconds. Between each stretch there should be rest for thirty to sixty seconds. Stretching exercise should be repeated three to five times.

Time: Include exercises to stretch the muscles that work each of the major joints in the body. This will probably take fifteen to thirty minutes.

Type: Two techniques for stretching muscles that move joints are static stretching and ballistic stretching. **Static stretching** is stretching the muscle to a point where a pull is felt and holding the stretch for fifteen to thirty seconds. Static stretching is safe and effective. **Ballistic stretching** is rapidly stretching the muscle with a bouncing movement. Fitness experts warn against ballistic stretching because it can cause injuries. Stretching exercises for flexibility can be done using free weights and weight machines; stretches that do not require equipment include across-the-body, ankle flex, calf stretcher, lateral stretch, side launch, sit and reach, spine twist, step stretch, towel stretch, and upper back stretch.

WARMING UP AND COOLING DOWN

The warmup and cooldown are critical when doing stretching exercises. Warming up can be done by walking or easy jogging for three to five minutes. This increases blood flow to muscles to get them ready for more work. A person should begin gradually with slow stretches. A workout needs to finish with a cooldown period. Walking and easy jogging after stretching improve circulation. Easy stretches keep muscles from being sore.

MEASURING FLEXIBILITY

The V-sit reach test assesses flexibility by measuring how far a person can lean forward. A line is marked on the floor as the baseline. A measuring line is drawn perpendicular to the midpoint of the baseline. The point where the baseline and the measuring line intersect is "zero" point. The person sits on the floor with the measuring line between the legs and soles of the feet placed immediately behind the baseline. The heels should be eight to twelve inches apart. The person clasps thumbs so that hands are together, palms down, and places them on the measuring line. The person slowly reaches as far forward as possible, keeping fingers on the baseline and feet flexed. The score is the number of inches the person reaches on the

measuring line (President's Council on Physical Fitness and Sports, 2003).

Healthful Body Composition

Healthful body composition is a high ratio of lean tissue to fat tissue in the body. **Overfat** is having too high a percentage of body fat. This section discusses the benefits of healthful body composition, warming up and cooling down, measuring one's percentage of body fat, and establishing a program to develop and maintain healthful body composition.

BENEFITS OF HEALTHFUL BODY COMPOSITION

Healthful body composition

1. Reduces the risk of obesity
2. Reduces the risk of coronary heart disease
3. Reduces the risk of developing diabetes
4. Reduces the risk of developing high blood pressure
5. Reduces the risk of having a stroke
6. Improves appearance and self-image

WARMING UP AND COOLING DOWN

When participating in physical activities to develop and maintain healthful body composition, there needs to be adequate warmup and cooldown. When developing and maintaining healthful body composition, a person should be performing the same physical activities used to develop cardiorespiratory endurance. The same guidelines for warming up and cooling down need to be followed. The warmup should include three to five minutes of easy physical activity. The cooldown should include five to ten minutes of reduced physical activity. Stretching exercises during cooldown are advised.

MEASURING PERCENTAGE OF BODY FAT

One test to measure the percentage of body fat uses calipers to measure the thickness of skinfolds. A more accurate test involves underwater weighing. A quick test to determine overfatness is to pinch a fold of skin on the upper arm—if the skinfold thickness exceeds one inch (2.5 centimeters), the person might have too much body fat.

DEVELOPING A PROGRAM TO DEVELOP AND MAINTAIN HEALTHFUL BODY COMPOSITION

To develop and maintain healthful body composition, a person should eat a healthful diet and participate in physical activities to promote cardiorespiratory endurance. Again, the FITT formula needs to be followed:

Frequency: Participate in physical activity three to five days a week.

Intensity: Perform physical activity at the target heart rate.

Time: The length of time that physical activity is performed depends on the intensity. As a general rule, physical activity should be performed until 1.8 calories have been burned for each pound of body weight.

Type: Select aerobic activities, such as aerobic dancing, backpacking, badminton, basketball, bench-stepping, bicycling, cross-country skiing, field hockey, handball, hiking, hockey, in-line skating, jogging, karate, lacrosse, racquetball, jumping rope, rowing, rugby, running, soccer, stairwalking, swimming, or walking.

Health Goal #48

I Will Develop and Maintain Skill-Related Fitness

Skill-Related Fitness

In addition to the health-related components of fitness, there are skill-related components. **Skill-related fitness** is the capacity to perform well in sports and physical activities. Fitness skills are skills that can be used in sports and physical activities. There are six fitness skills: agility, balance, coordination, reaction time, speed, and power. Heredity is an important influence on these fitness skills. However, most fitness skills can be developed and improved.

AGILITY

Agility is the ability to rapidly change the position of the body. Physical activities in which people change directions quickly require agility. For example, agility is needed to change directions to hit a tennis ball or to make a jump shot in basketball.

BALANCE

Balance is the ability to keep from falling when in a still position or moving. Balance is needed when skiing down a mountain slope, riding a bicycle, performing on the balance beam, or using in-line skates.

COORDINATION

Coordination is the ability to use the senses together with body parts during movement. One type of coordination is hand-eye coordination. **Hand-eye coordination** is the use of the hands together with the eyes during movement. Hitting a tennis ball requires keeping the eyes on the ball while swinging the racket with the hands. Batting in baseball requires keeping the eyes on the ball while swinging the bat at the ball with the hands. Without hand-eye coordination, a person would have difficulty playing sports such as tennis and baseball. There are many other examples of coordination. For instance, kicking a soccer ball or a football requires foot-eye coordination: the eyes must focus on the ball as the foot moves toward it to kick it.

REACTION TIME

Reaction time is the time it takes a person to move after hearing, seeing, feeling, or touching a stimulus. The less time that elapses, the quicker the reaction time. The time it takes a person to get into position to catch a thrown ball is reaction time. The time it takes a runner to begin to push off out of the starting block after the start signal is reaction time.

SPEED

Speed is the ability to move quickly. After grabbing a rebound under the opponent's basket, speed is needed to dribble the length of the basketball court to make a basket. When one's tennis opponent hits a drop shot close to the net, speed is needed to get to the ball before it bounces twice. Many sports and physical activities require speed.

A person must run fast when playing soccer, football, lacrosse, and baseball.

POWER

Power is the ability to combine strength and speed. To throw a discus far requires power. In baseball, throwing a fastball requires power. In the high jump, power is needed to impel the body high into the air.

Lifetime Sports and Physical Activities

Lifetime sports and physical activities are sports and physical activities that can be engaged in throughout a person's life. There are many advantages to participating in lifetime sports and physical activities. Lifetime sports and physical activities often become long-lasting habits that ensure that a person will be physically active throughout life. Participating in different lifetime sports and physical activities can improve different areas of physical fitness and different fitness skills. Social interaction with friends and family members is another important benefit of lifetime sports and physical activities. This section discusses examples of lifetime sports and physical activities, including their benefits and safety considerations.

BASKETBALL

Playing basketball improves cardiorespiratory endurance and muscular endurance. Learning how to dribble, shoot, and pass the ball improves agility, balance, and coordination. When playing basketball, a person burns 500 to 600 calories per hour. Common basketball injuries include sprained ankles, sprained knees, and eye injuries. Basketball injuries can be avoided by wearing protective equipment such as a mouthguard, eye protection, and elbow and knee pads. Stretching and warming up before playing is another way to prevent injuries.

CROSS-COUNTRY SKIING

Cross-country skiing helps maintain and improve fitness. The leg and arm movements involved in cross-country skiing improve muscular endurance and cardiorespiratory endurance. Depending on the difficulty of the terrain, cross-country skiing also improves balance, coordination, power, and reaction time. Cross-country skiing burns 700 to 800 calories per hour. This activity effectively reduces the percentage of body fat.

Safety is important when cross-country skiing. A person cross-country skiing must be aware of natural dangers such as avalanches, freezing temperatures, and UV radiation from the sun. Skiers must know their physical abilities, skill level, and limitations. A person should also know how to prevent and treat illnesses and injuries, such as hypothermia, frostbite, pulled muscles, and broken bones.

GOLF

Walking the length of a golf course improves cardiorespiratory endurance. A person burns close to 1,060 calories when walking an eighteen-hole round of golf. Riding in a cart is less strenuous and burns far fewer calories. Swinging a club to hit the ball also has fitness benefits. Learning how to hit the ball can improve balance, coordination, and power. The repeated swinging motion used in a round of golf also improves muscular endurance. To avoid injuries, golfers should always stretch before playing.

IN-LINE SKATING

In-line skating provides a vigorous cardiorespiratory workout that burns 350 to 550 calories per hour. The wide range of movements improve muscular strength and muscular endurance and promote agility, balance, coordination, and power. Safety is an important factor of in-line skating. In-line skaters need to use the proper equipment, follow safety rules, and carry a water bottle to avoid dehydration and heat exhaustion.

MARTIAL ARTS

Different martial arts promote different levels of physical fitness and fitness skills. Karate training combines vigorous cardiorespiratory workouts with skill training. The different movements involved in karate training improve agility, coordination, and reaction time. Most martial arts involve substantial physical contact that can result in shoulder, elbow, and wrist injuries. Broken toes and fingers also are common. To avoid serious injuries, protective equipment needs to be worn and safety guidelines followed.

BICYCLING

The peddling motion of cycling promotes muscular endurance, muscular strength, and cardiorespiratory endurance. Balance, coordination, and reaction time are important when facing steep trails and obstacles. To avoid injuries and accidents, bikers must maintain control of the bike, use proper equipment, and keep a watchful eye on other bikers.

ROCK CLIMBING AND WALL CLIMBING

Rock and wall climbers use their arms to pull them up the climbing surface and to maintain position. This improves muscular strength and muscular endurance. Agility, coordination, and reaction time are important in rock and wall climbing because each move requires analyzing both the terrain and one's abilities to climb it. Rock and wall climbing burn almost 600 calories per hour. Safety is always a concern when rock and wall climbing. To avoid injuries and accidents, a person should receive proper instruction and know the safety rules.

RUNNING AND JOGGING

Running and jogging improve health-related fitness. They improve cardiorespiratory endurance and also help reduce body fat and cholesterol levels. Running at twelve miles (19.2 kilometers) per hour burns almost 1,500 calories per hour. Jogging at a moderate pace burns 500 to 750 calories per hour. Running on hills or other inclines can triple the calories burned, depending on the incline. Injuries to watch out for include pulled muscles, tendinitis, and shin splints, which result from overuse of muscles. To avoid these and other types of injuries, a person should always follow training principles. Runners and joggers should carry a water bottle to avoid dehydration and heat exhaustion.

SWIMMING

Swimming provides many fitness benefits. For example, the crawl stroke involves making a windmill action with the arms while quickly kicking the feet. The crawl helps improve coordination, power, and speed. The crawl also promotes cardiorespiratory endurance, muscular endurance, and muscular strength. Swimming the crawl stroke at one mile per hour burns almost 420 calories per hour. Other strokes involve other fitness skills and different levels of health-related fitness. The most common swimming injuries are tendinitis and pulled muscles that result from overuse of muscles. Injuries are avoided by warming up and stretching before swimming. A person should learn cardiopulmonary resuscitation (CPR) and basic first aid and follow water safety guidelines if choosing swimming as a lifetime sport.

TENNIS

Tennis is enjoyed by many people and this activity can positively impact health, particularly when it is played at an intensity that demands high physical activity. Tennis can build leg and arm strength, eye-hand coordination, flexibility, and agility. Many players say that tennis is a great stress reliever and that there are important social benefits when playing with others.

WALKING

Walking provides a moderate cardiorespiratory workout. Walking burns 150 to 550 calories per hour, depending on the intensity of the walk. Many physicians and health professionals recommend walking as an easy way to maintain physical fitness. Safety is an important aspect of walking, especially when walking on the street. Most injuries to walkers are caused by traffic accidents. For this reason, it is important to be familiar with traffic laws and traffic patterns. The safest direction to walk is facing the traffic. Stretching before walking helps walkers to avoid minor injuries. Walkers should carry a water bottle to avoid dehydration and heat exhaustion.

Health Goal #49

I Will Be a Responsible Spectator and Participant in Sports

Responsible Sport Spectatorship

Young people often attend sport events at school. They also may attend other sporting events in the community. They may be fans of college or professional teams. Young people can learn to be responsible sport spectators. Students who are

responsible sport spectators can make the following claims:

1. I recognize that I represent my school when I attend sport events.
2. I will learn the rules for the sport events I follow.
3. I will not boo or hiss officials, referees, players, coaches, or other fans.
4. I will show respect for officials and referees and their decisions.
5. I will respect the decisions of the coaches.
6. I will applaud the good play and sportsmanship of players for both teams.
7. I will respond with enthusiasm when cheerleaders ask me to participate.
8. I will express disapproval for rough play and poor sportsmanship.
9. I will not say or yell critical comments.
10. I will stay in control of my emotions.
11. I will not instigate or participate in any confrontations or fights.
12. I will not damage property at the opposing team's school.
13. I will not attend sport events under the influence of alcohol or other drugs.
14. I will not bet or gamble on sport events.
15. I will consider ways to support sport teams, such as being a cheerleader or a member of the band.
16. I will make encouraging remarks to participants when they lose or do not play well.
17. I will be a loyal and supportive fan during a losing as well as a winning season.
18. I will not throw paper, soda pop, or anything else at the officials when I do not agree with a call.
19. I will not make unkind remarks about any member of the opposing team.
20. I will not run onto the court or field before or immediately after play is completed.

The following experience illustrates the importance of responsible sports spectatorship. At a basketball game in Detroit between the Detroit Pistons and the Indiana Pacers in November 2004, a brawl ensued after a fan threw a cup of liquid at a player for the Indiana Pacers. The player proceeded into the stands to confront the fan. This ignited a melee between a number of players and several fans. Nine spectators were injured as a result, and several players were suspended from playing future games. Five players from the Indiana Pacers and five spectators were charged with misdemeanor assault and battery, including the spectator who threw the liquid-filled cup.

Responsible Sport Participation

A responsible sport participant does the following:

1. *Puts forth maximum effort.*
2. *Has realistic expectations.* The odds of making it to the pros for a high school male athlete are 1 in 6,000. The odds of making it to the NBA for a high school male are an even longer shot—1 in 10,000.
3. *Keeps grades a priority.*
4. *Manages time effectively.*
5. *Avoids the use of alcohol and other drugs.*
6. *Does not bet on sport events.*
7. *Has a healthful attitude toward winning and losing.*
8. *Does not instigate or participate in fights.*

9. *Shows respect for officials, referees, coaches, and other players.*
10. *Cooperates with teammates.*

Drug Tests

Presently, few high schools require sport participants to take drug tests. However, drug testing is common at the college, professional, and Olympic levels. Sport participants who undergo drug testing are asked for a urine sample, which is sent to a lab for analysis to detect drug metabolites. **Drug metabolites** are chemicals that, when present in urine, indicate that the person has used a banned substance. Banned substances that are tested for include steroids, cocaine, and marijuana. A sport participant guilty of using one or more banned substances may be dropped from an athletic team and suspended from school.

Health Goal #50

I Will Prevent Physical-Activity-Related Injuries and Illnesses

The most common risk associated with physical activity is injury to the musculoskeletal system—the bones, joints, tendons, and muscle (Division of Nutrition and Physical Activity, 2006). These injuries are usually not serious, often require no treatment other than a few days of rest, and can be minimized by taking sensible precautions. Most of these types of injuries may be prevented by gradually working up to the desired level of activity and by avoiding excessive amounts of activity at one time.

The CDC's Division of Nutrition and Physical Activity counsels that, to avoid soreness and injury, people who have not been regularly active and are thinking about increasing their level of physical activity should start out slowly, incorporating a few minutes of increased activity into their day, gradually building up to the desired amount of activity, and giving their bodies time to adjust.

The following tips should be kept in mind to help prevent common injuries associated with participating in physical activity (Division of Nutrition and Physical Activity, 2006):

- Listen to your body—monitor your level of fatigue, heart rate, and physical discomfort.
- Be aware of the signs of overexertion. Breathlessness and muscle soreness could be danger signs.
- Be aware of the warning signs and signals of a heart attack, such as sweating, chest and arm pain, dizziness, and lightheadedness.
- Use appropriate equipment and clothing for the activity.
- Take three to five minutes at the beginning of any physical activity to properly warm up your muscles through increasingly more intense activity. As you near the end of the activity, cool down by decreasing the level of intensity. (For example, before jogging, walk for three to five minutes, increasing your pace to a brisk walk. After jogging, walk briskly, decreasing your pace to a slow walk over three to five minutes. Finish by stretching the muscles you used—in this case primarily the muscles of the legs.)
- Start at an easy pace—increase time or distance gradually.
- Drink plenty of water throughout the day to replace lost fluids (at least eight to ten 8-ounce. cups per day). Drink a glass of water before you get moving, and drink another half cup every fifteen minutes that you remain active.

Training Principles

Training principles are guidelines to follow to obtain maximum fitness benefits and reduce the risk of injuries and illnesses. There are six training principles:

1. The **principle of warmup** states that a workout should begin with three to five minutes of easy exercise to increase blood flow, raise the temperature in muscles, stretch muscles, and increase joint lubrication. To follow this principle, a person should begin the warmup by walking or by jogging slowly. As the person warms up, blood flow increases to the muscles being used. This raises the person's temperature and gets the person ready to do more work. Heart rate increases gradually as one warms up. Synovial fluid lubricates the surfaces of the joints. Once muscles are warmed, a person should do some static stretching.

2. The **principle of cooldown** states that a workout should end with five to ten minutes of reduced exercise to help the heart rate,

breathing rate, body temperature, and circulation return to the nonexercising state. The cooldown should include walking or slow jogging and static stretching. During cooldown, heart rate should gradually slow to less than one hundred beats per minute. Body temperature should cool and return to normal. Blood that pooled in the legs should begin to flow back to the heart.

3. The **principle of specificity** states that a workout should include a specific type of exercise to obtain the desired fitness benefits. A person who wants to improve cardiorespiratory endurance might choose aerobic exercises such as running, swimming, and in-line skating for their workout. Aerobic exercises provide the specific fitness benefit desired. To be good at a particular sport, a person can improve skills specific to that sport. For example, a gymnast who performs on a balance beam should work on balance and coordination.

4. The **principle of overload** states that a workout must include exercise beyond what a person usually does to gain additional fitness benefits. People who want to develop strength in the arm muscles must work the arm muscles more than usual. They might lift free weights and add additional weight to gain overload and work the arm muscles more.

5. The **principle of progression** states that the amount and intensity of exercise during workouts must be increased gradually.

6. The **principle of fitness reversibility** states that fitness benefits are lost when training stops. Within two months of stopping regular workouts, a person can lose up to 50 percent of the fitness benefits previously gained.

Injuries Related to Physical Activity

Participation in physical activity includes the risk of injury. There is greater risk of injury when training is extreme or too hard. The following are injuries related to physical activity.

OVERUSE INJURY

An **overuse injury** is an injury that occurs from repeated use or excessive overload. A person who does too much too fast can develop an overuse injury.

MICROTRAUMA

A **microtrauma** is an injury that is not recognized or becomes worse as a person continues to work out. Microtraumas are so small that they do not show up on X-rays or during superficial examinations.

BRUISE

A **bruise** is a discoloration of the skin caused by bleeding under the skin. Ice should be applied to reduce bleeding and swelling.

MUSCLE CRAMP

A **muscle cramp** is the sudden tightening of a muscle. Sharp pains may signal muscle cramps. Muscle cramps can occur in any muscle. They often are caused by fatigue and dehydration. Precautions for exercising in hot weather and static stretching help prevent muscle cramps. When muscles cramp, the person should drink plenty of fluids and gently massage the muscles that have cramped.

MUSCLE STRAIN

A **muscle strain** is overstretching of a muscle that may result in tearing a muscle or tendon. A warmup of walking, easy jogging, and static stretching helps prevent muscle strain. Use the RICE treatment if muscle strain occurs. The RICE treatment (rest, ice, compression, and elevation) is a technique for treating musculoskeletal injuries.

SHIN SPLINT

A **shin splint** is an overuse injury that results in pain in the front and sides of the lower leg. There may be tenderness over the shin and some swelling. Shin splints might be prevented by wearing proper footwear and running on even surfaces. A workout should begin with static stretching of the muscles of the front of the lower leg to avoid shin splints. In most cases, shin splints clear up after a week or two of rest. On the first day, ice can be applied four times a day for twenty minutes. Check with a physician before taking aspirin or other drugs to reduce pain and inflammation.

SIDE STITCH

A **side stitch** is a dull, sharp pain in the side of the lower abdomen. Side stitch can be prevented by warming up and following the FITT formula. A workout needs to be planned with appropriate frequency, intensity, and time. To relieve side stitch, a person should bend forward while pressing a hand firmly at the point of the pain.

SPRAIN

A **sprain** is partial or complete tearing of a ligament. A **ligament** is a tough fiber that connects bones. Sprains occur from injuries that twist the tissue around a joint. Careful shoe selection helps prevent strains. High-top athletic shoes help support ankles, and wider-soled shoes such as cross-trainers can prevent ankle twisting. Weak ankles can be taped by a trainer, or an ankle or knee brace can be worn for extra support. Sprains should be given RICE treatment.

STRESS FRACTURE

A **stress fracture** is a hairline break that results from repetitive jarring of a bone. Most stress fractures are overuse injuries. Stress fractures can be serious. A stress fracture can be a microtrauma, undetected on an X-ray or during superficial examination. Stress fractures can be prevented by following the FITT formula and not overdoing exercise. The treatment for stress fractures depends on the severity and the area that is affected. Rest is important.

TENDINITIS

Tendinitis is inflammation of a tendon. A **tendon** is tough tissue fiber that attaches muscles to bones. Pain and swelling occur in joints. Tendinitis in the elbow is called tennis elbow. Other joints commonly afflicted by tendinitis are the knees, shoulders, and backs of ankles. A warmup with static stretching helps prevent tendinitis. Choose exercises to develop muscle strength. The RICE treatment should be used for tendinitis. Tendinitis can take as long as a month to heal. A physician should be consulted before taking aspirin or other drugs to relieve pain and inflammation.

OSGOOD-SCHLATTER DISEASE

Osgood-Schlatter disease is a painful swelling just below the knee that is seen most often in active, athletic adolescents, usually between ages ten and fifteen. The disease is believed to be caused by repeated overuse before growth of the lower leg bone is complete. It is common in adolescents who play soccer, basketball, and volleyball and who participate in gymnastics. Osgood-Schlatter disease affects more boys than girls (Cassas, 2006; Patel, 2006). This condition can be diagnosed by physical examination. Rest is needed, and the application of ice and nonsteroidal anti-inflammatory drugs such as ibuprofen are helpful treatment measures.

Participating in Physical Activity during Extreme Weather Conditions

This section discusses participating in physical activity in cold weather, hot weather, polluted air, and high altitude.

COLD WEATHER

Cold-temperature-related illnesses are conditions that result from exposure to low temperatures. When working out in very cold weather, a person must protect against frostbite and hypothermia. **Frostbite** is the freezing of body parts, often the tissues of the extremities (fingers and toes). Signs of frostbite include numbness in the affected area, waxy appearance of skin, and skin that is cold to the touch and discolored. **Hypothermia** is a reduction in body temperature to lower than normal. Hypothermia results from overexposure to cool temperatures, cold water, moisture, and wind. People with hypothermia will shiver and feel cold. Pulse rate slows down and becomes irregular as body temperature drops. Without treatment, a hypothermic individual can become unconscious and die. To prevent cold-temperature-related illnesses, a person should follow these guidelines:

1. *Check the windchill before exercising in cold weather.*
2. *Postpone exercise if the windchill is dangerous.*
3. *Postpone exercise if conditions are icy and wet.*
4. *Wear several layers of lightweight clothing.* Dressing too warmly causes sweating, which can cause chilling. The innermost layer of clothing should be made of polypropylene or thermax, fabrics that transport moisture away from the skin. Over this layer should be a garment of dacron or fleeced polyester, which serves as a good insulator. The top layer should be a windbreaker of waterproof material that keeps out moisture but allows perspiration to filter out.
5. *Wear gloves, a hat, and ski mask to protect the fingers, ears, and nose.*
6. *Wear two pairs of socks or thermal socks to protect the toes.*

Hot Weather

Heat-related illnesses result from exposure to temperatures that are higher than normal. When working out during hot weather, a person must protect against heat cramps, heat exhaustion, and heat stroke. **Heat cramps** are painful muscle spasms in the legs and arms due to excessive fluid loss through sweating. **Heat exhaustion** is extreme tiredness due to the body's inability to regulate its temperature. Signs of heat exhaustion include a very low body temperature; cool, moist, pale, and red skin; nausea and headache; dizziness and weakness; and fast pulse. **Heat stroke** is a life-threatening overheating of the body. Sweating ceases, so the body cannot regulate its temperature. Signs of heat stroke include high body temperature; rapid pulse; rapid respiration; hot, wet, and dry skin; weakness; dizziness; and headache. To prevent heat-related illnesses a person should follow these guidelines:

1. Check the heat index before exercising in hot weather.
2. Postpone exercise if the heat index is dangerously high.
3. Plan to work out at the time of day when the temperature is lowest.
4. Drink plenty of fluids before and during the workout.
5. Avoid vigorous workouts on extremely hot and humid days.
6. Wear porous clothing that allows air to pass through it and sweat to evaporate.
7. Wear light-colored clothing that reflects the sun.
8. Avoid wearing rubberized and plastic clothing. This kind of clothing traps heat and perspiration and causes fluid loss and increased body temperature.
9. Wear a hat, sunglasses, and sunscreen.

Air Pollution

Air pollution influences the safety and effectiveness of workouts. When air is polluted, a person has to breath more often to deliver oxygen to body cells. Air pollution can cause shortness of breath. The media issues warnings when the pollution standard index (PSI) is high. The **pollution standard index (PSI)** is a measure of air quality based on the sum of the levels of five different pollutants. It is best not to work out outdoors when the PSI is high.

High Altitude

Being in a high altitude places extra demands on the body. Think of the extra demands of the high altitude as being a form of overload. The body must adjust to these extra demands. Unacclimated individuals should shorten their workouts at first. For example, a person who takes a trip to the mountains to snow ski should avoid hard skiing for the first two days. Unacclimated people who exercise too much can develop altitude sickness. Signs of altitude sickness include shortness of breath, chest pain, and nausea.

Alcohol, Tobacco, and Other Drugs

HEALTH GOALS FOR ALCOHOL, TOBACCO, AND OTHER DRUG USE

51. I will follow guidelines for the safe use of prescription and OTC drugs.

52. I will not drink alcohol.

53. I will avoid tobacco use and secondhand smoke.

54. I will not be involved in illegal drug use.

55. I will avoid risk factors and practice protective factors for drug misuse and abuse.

56. I will not misuse or abuse drugs.

57. I will use resistance skills if pressured to misuse or abuse drugs.

58. I will choose a drug-free lifestyle to reduce the risk of HIV infection and unwanted pregnancy.

59. I will choose a drug-free lifestyle to reduce the risk of violence and accidents.

60. I will be aware of resources for the treatment of drug misuse and abuse.

Alcohol, tobacco, and other drugs constitute an area of health that focuses on following guidelines for the safe use of prescription and over-the-counter (OTC) drugs, not drinking alcohol, avoiding tobacco use and secondhand smoke, not being involved in illegal drug use, avoiding risk factors and practicing protective factors for drug misuse and abuse, not misusing or abusing drugs, using resistance skills if pressured to misuse or abuse drugs, choosing a drug-free lifestyle to reduce the risk of HIV infection and unwanted pregnancy, choosing a drug-free lifestyle to reduce the risk of violence and accidents, and being aware of resources for the treatment of drug misuse and abuse. This chapter provides the health knowledge needed to teach young people important life skills relating to alcohol, tobacco, and other drugs.

Health Goal #51

I Will Follow Guidelines for the Safe Use of Prescription and OTC Drugs

Drugs and Drug Use

A **drug** is a chemical substance that affects the way the body or mind functions. Some drugs harm health. These drugs include alcohol, tobacco, cocaine, methamphetamine, Ecstasy, and marijuana. Other drugs promote health. These drugs include OTC drugs and prescription drugs, such as insulin for diabetes. Drugs intended to promote health can harm health if the user does not follow guidelines for their safe use.

People use drugs in responsible and irresponsible ways. **Responsible drug use** is the correct use of legal drugs to promote health and well-being. An example of responsible drug use is taking a prescription drug for its intended purpose according to a physician's instructions.

Drugs can be misused and abused. **Drug misuse** is the incorrect use of a prescription or an OTC drug. Examples of drug misuse include taking medicine leftover from a previous illness and using another person's prescription drug. Other examples include mixing medications without consulting a physician and driving or drinking alcohol after taking certain medications. **Drug abuse** is the intentional use of a drug without medical or health reasons. Taking an illegal drug is drug abuse. Using a substance for purposes other than those intended by the manufacturer (e.g., inhaling gasoline or solvents) is drug abuse. Both legal and illegal drugs are abused. Drug misuse and abuse can destroy health and relationships.

Ways Drugs Enter the Body

To produce an effect, a drug has to enter the body. Drugs can be taken by mouth, injection, inhalation, absorption, or implantation.

BY MOUTH

The most common way of taking a drug is by swallowing it. A drug in the form of a pill, capsule, or liquid may be swallowed. After being swallowed, a drug travels to the stomach and small intestine. Then it is absorbed into the bloodstream. Not all drugs can be taken by mouth, because digestive juices in the stomach destroy certain drugs or make them ineffective.

BY INJECTION

Some drugs are injected using a syringe and needle. A drug that is injected goes directly under the skin into a muscle or blood vessel. Drugs must be in liquid form to be injected into the body. A drug that is injected into a blood vessel produces effects very quickly. Injecting drugs without medical supervision is a risk factor for infection with HIV and hepatitis B.

BY INHALATION

Some drugs are inhaled through the nose or mouth and enter the bloodstream in the lungs. Drugs that are inhaled produce effects very quickly. People with asthma may inhale drugs that open their air passages. Some drugs that are inhaled, such as the nicotine from cigarette smoke, harm health. They irritate the tissues that line the lungs and throat. Long-term inhalation of harmful drugs can cause respiratory diseases.

BY ABSORPTION

A drug that is absorbed enters the bloodstream through the skin or mucous membranes. Ointments, creams, lotions, sprays, and patches contain drugs that are absorbed. They may be applied to the skin or mucous membranes of the eyes, nose, mouth, vagina, or anus. A **skin patch** is a patch worn on the body that contains a drug that is absorbed through the skin. A **suppository** is a wax-coated form of a drug that is inserted into the anus or vagina. When the wax melts, the drug is absorbed into the bloodstream. **Buccal absorption** is the absorption of a drug between the cheek and gum. Nicotine is absorbed into the bloodstream when chewing tobacco is placed in the mouth. **Sublingual absorption** is the absorption of a drug when it is placed under the tongue.

Some people believe that snorting is a type of inhalation, but actually a drug taken through snorting is absorbed. **Snorting** is sniffing drugs through the nose so that they can be absorbed through the mucous membranes of the nasal passages. Snorting drugs can damage the nose and nasal passages. When cocaine is snorted in its powdered form, its effects are not felt as rapidly as when it is smoked (inhaled).

BY IMPLANTATION

Some drugs are implanted, or placed, under the skin where they can be released into the bloodstream. For example, some forms of cancer therapy involve implanting drugs under the skin.

Other Factors That Determine Drug Effects

Other factors besides the ways a drug enters the body also determine the effects of a drug. The dose is the amount of a drug that is taken at one time. The larger the dose, the greater the effect of the drug. How a person feels is another factor. If a person is depressed, taking a drug that slows body functions can make the person more depressed. Weight, age, and health also influence the effects a drug will have. Drugs have an increased effect on a person who is young or who has a low body weight or poor health status. When two or more drugs are taken together, their interaction can alter the effects of the drugs, counteract the effects of one or more of the drugs, or increase the effects.

Prescription Drugs

A **medicine** is a drug that is used to treat, prevent, or diagnose illness. A **prescription drug** is a medicine that can be obtained only with a written order from a licensed health professional. A **prescription** is a written order from a physician or other licensed health professional. A prescription lists the patient's name; name of the drug; form of the drug, such as pills or liquid; dosage level; directions for use; physician's name, address, phone number, and signature; U.S. Drug Enforcement Agency registration number; and refill instructions. Prescription drugs are intended to be used only according to the directions on the prescription.

Obtaining or using prescription drugs without a prescription is illegal. By law, prescription drugs must be prepared and sold by licensed pharmacists. A **pharmacist** is an allied health professional who dispenses medications that are prescribed by certain licensed health professionals. Prescription drugs are obtained from a pharmacy. A **pharmacy** is a place where prescription drugs are legally dispensed. A pharmacist fills a prescription with either a brand-name or a generic drug. The prescription states whether the pharmacist can substitute a generic drug for a brand-name drug. A **brand-name drug** is a drug with a registered name or trademark given to a drug by a pharmaceutical company. A **generic drug** is a drug that contains the same active ingredients as a brand-name drug. Generic drugs usually are less expensive. The generic and brand-name versions of a particular drug usually have therapeutical equivalence. **Therapeutical equivalence** is when two drugs are chemically the same and produce the same medical effects.

GUIDELINES FOR THE SAFE USE OF PRESCRIPTION DRUGS

Following are guidelines for the safe use of prescription drugs:

1. Contact a physician if the drug does not seem to be producing the desired effects.
2. Report new or unexpected symptoms to a physician.
3. Do not stop taking the drug if you are starting to feel better.
4. Carefully follow the instructions on the label.
5. Follow instructions for storing the prescription drug.
6. Keep all prescription drugs out of the reach of children.
7. Never take prescription drugs that have been prescribed for another person.
8. Keep prescription drugs in their original containers.
9. Dispose of prescription drugs that are no longer needed.
10. Never take prescription drugs that appear to have been tampered with, are discolored, or have a suspicious odor.
11. Check the expiration date on the medication. Do not use if it is past that date.

COMMON TYPES OF PRESCRIPTION DRUGS

More than 10,000 different prescription drugs are available in the United States. Prescription drugs are used to treat and prevent a variety of health conditions. The following are some common types of prescription drugs:

1. A **prescription analgesic** is used to relieve pain.
2. An **antibiotic** is used to treat bacterial infections.
3. An **antidepressant** is used to treat depressive disorders.
4. An **antiepileptic** is used to prevent and control epileptic seizures.

5. An **antihypertensive drug** is used to lower elevated blood pressure.
6. An **antiulcer drug** is used to treat the discomfort of ulcers.
7. A **bronchodilator** widens air passages to facilitate breathing in people with asthma.
8. A **hypnotic** produces drowsiness and sleep.
9. A **lipid-lowering drug** lowers blood cholesterol levels.
10. A **sedative** has a calming effect on a person's behavior.

OFF-LABEL DRUG USE

Once the Food and Drug Administration (FDA) has approved a drug for marketing, it does not regulate how and for what uses physicians prescribe a drug. A physician may prescribe a drug for uses, treatments, or patient populations that are not on the FDA-approved labeling for a particular drug. **Off-label drug use** is the use of a drug that a physician has prescribed for treatments other than those specified on the label. Off-label use is believed to be widespread for drugs prescribed to children. This is because very few studies evaluate the efficacy and risk of medications in children.

Off-label use is legal. The FDA acknowledges that unapproved uses may be appropriate in certain situations. Often physicians and health care professionals are aware of advances in medical knowledge concerning the treatment of a disease, and they have this knowledge before the FDA can revise drug labels. According to the American Medical Association, when a physician prescribes a drug for a use not on the approved label, he or she has the responsibility to be well informed about the drug and to base such use on a firm scientific rationale or on sound medical evidence. There are many issues concerning off-label drug use that medical groups and the FDA are trying to resolve.

Over-the-Counter Drugs

An **over-the-counter (OTC) drug** is a drug that can be purchased without a prescription. OTC drugs can be purchased in stores such as a grocery store or drugstore. OTC drugs usually are taken to relieve signs and symptoms of an illness, not to cure an illness. The U.S. Food and Drug Administration (FDA) requires that OTC drugs

have labels with detailed information about the drug and its use.

An **indication for use** is a symptom or condition for which the OTC drug should be used. A **contraindication for use** is a symptom or condition for which the OTC drug should not be used.

GUIDELINES FOR THE SAFE USE OF OTC DRUGS

Following are guidelines for the safe use of OTC drugs:

1. Children and adolescents should obtain permission from their parents or guardian to take an OTC drug.
2. Do not purchase an OTC drug if the tamper-resistant packaging is broken. A **tamper-resistant package** is a package that is sealed to assure the buyer that the package was not opened previously. The FDA requires that all OTC drugs be placed in tamper-resistant packages.
3. Carefully follow the directions for use.
4. Ask a pharmacist or physician questions about the use of an OTC drug.
5. Do not take more than the recommended dose.
6. Do not take an OTC drug if a condition listed under contraindications is present.
7. Stop using the OTC drug and notify a physician if experiencing unwanted side effects. A **side effect** is an unwanted body change that is not related to the main purpose of a drug.
8. Do not take more than one OTC drug at a time without telling a pharmacist or physician.
9. Do not take an OTC drug after the expiration date. The effectiveness of a drug may change with time.
10. Do not participate in risky activities while taking an OTC drug that can cause drowsiness. For example, do not drive a motor vehicle, ride a bicycle, play a contact sport, or operate machinery while taking an OTC drug that can cause drowsiness.

COMMON TYPES OF OTC DRUGS

More than 300,000 different OTC products are available in the United States. OTC drugs are used to treat and prevent a variety of health conditions. Following are the major drug classes

16. Ophthalmics to promote eye hygiene and treat eye infections.
17. Vitamins and minerals to provide diet supplementation.
18. Antiperspirants and deodorants to suppress body odor.

Monitoring the Safety and Effectiveness of Drugs

Ingredients in legal drugs must be listed as safe and effective by the U.S. Food and Drug Administration (FDA). The FDA is a federal agency that monitors the safety of cosmetics and food and the safety and effectiveness of new drugs, medical devices, and prescription and OTC drugs. The FDA must approve any new drug before it is distributed legally. The drug must be tested to learn about drug effects and side effects before it can be used by people.

approved by the FDA for OTC status and the main uses of these products:

1. Analgesics and anti-inflammatories to relieve pain, fever, and inflammation.
2. Cold remedies to relieve cold symptoms.
3. Antihistamines and allergy products to relieve allergy symptoms.
4. Antitussives to relieve and suppress coughing.
5. Stimulants to diminish fatigue and drowsiness.
6. Sedatives and sleep aids to promote sleep.
7. Antacids to relieve indigestion from rebound activity.
8. Laxatives to relieve constipation.
9. Antidiarrheals to relieve minor diarrhea.
10. Bronchodilators and antiasthmatics to assist breathing.
11. Dentrifices and dental products to promote oral hygiene.
12. Acne medications to treat and prevent acne.
13. Sunburn treatments and sunscreens to treat and prevent skin damage from ultraviolet rays.
14. Dandruff and athlete's foot medications to treat and prevent specific skin conditions.
15. Contraceptives and vaginal products to prevent pregnancy and treat vaginal infections.

Why Some Drugs Are Removed from the Market

An important mission of the Food and Drug Administration (FDA) is to make sure that drugs are safe and effective. According to the FDA, a safe drug is a drug in which the drug's benefits outweigh its risks for the intended population and use. It is important to realize that safe does not mean harmless, because every drug comes with risks. Also, the risks of drugs that treat serious and life-threatening illnesses, such as cancer, are higher. But on the other hand, they save lives.

If the FDA deems that a drug's benefits outweigh its risks, the drug is approved for marketing. The FDA's Center for Drug Evaluation and Research (CDER) continues to evaluate approved drugs through a surveillance system that monitors a drug's safety on an ongoing basis. Sometimes problems with the drug that were not recognized before approval are identified through surveillance. This makes it possible for the FDA to act quickly to communicate new information about risks to consumers and health care professionals.

The FDA takes seriously any reports of adverse effects from drugs. When important new risks about a drug are discovered, the risks are added to the drug's labeling and doctors are informed of the new information through letters and other means of education. On rare occasions, it is necessary for the FDA to reconsider the approval decision of a drug. If the adverse effects are serious or frequent, the FDA may decide that the drug should no longer be marketed and pull it from the market. The FDA asks companies to voluntarily withdraw such drugs. If a company refuses, the FDA can force removal of a drug from the market.

Examples of drugs that have recently been removed from the market are Fen-Phen, Vioxx, Bextra, Baycol, and Seldane. Millions of people used Fen-Phen as a weight-loss drug. In 1997, it was withdrawn from the market following evidence that it might cause heart valve defects and primary pulmonary hypertension. Vioxx is a drug that relieved the pain and inflammation resulting from arthritis and menstrual cramps, but it was associated with an increased risk of heart attack and stroke. The drug's manufacturer voluntarily withdrew Vioxx from the market in 2004. A drug similar in actions and adverse effects to Vioxx is the drug Bextra, also used to treat arthritis and menstrual cramps. The FDA asked the manufacturer of Bextra to withdraw the drug on the basis that its use also increased risk of heart attack and stroke. Baycol is an anticholesterol drug that was removed from the market in 2001. Seldane is an antihistamine that was used for the treatment of allergies until the product was linked to serious heart problems when used in conjunction with certain drugs. As a result, the manufacturer of Seldane and the generic form of the drug (terfenadine) quit marketing and distributing these drug products.

A single report of a drug reaction in a 39-year-old woman ultimately contributed to the removal of Seldane from the market. Ten days after being prescribed Seldane, this woman was admitted to the hospital due to fainting episodes. She experienced serious changes in her heart rhythm that caused her death. Her case was reported in *JAMA, Journal of the American Medical Association,* and this prompted further investigations of abnormal heart rhythms related to Seldane. The case also brought attention to the fact that when Seldane was taken in conjunction with the antibiotic drug erythromycin, the risk was heightened (Meadows, 2004).

Health Goal #52
I Will Not Drink Alcohol

Alcohol and Alcoholic Beverages

Alcohol is a drug found in certain beverages that depresses the brain and nervous system. Alcohol is made by fermentation. **Fermentation** is a process in which yeast, sugar, and water are combined to produce alcohol and carbon dioxide. Alcohol is consumed in alcoholic beverages.

The most common alcoholic beverages are beer, wine, and liquor.

- **Beer** is an alcoholic beverage that is made by fermenting barley, corn, or rye. Most beers are about 4 percent alcohol. **Malt liquor** is beer that has a higher alcohol content than regular beer. **Light beer** is beer that has fewer calories than regular beer but about the same alcohol content.
- **Wine** is an alcoholic beverage made by fermenting grapes or other fruits. Most wines are about 12 to 14 percent alcohol. A **wine cooler** is a carbonated, fruit-flavored alcoholic beverage that is 1.5 to 6 percent alcohol.
- **Liquor** is an alcoholic beverage that is made by distillation. **Distillation** is a process that uses a fermented mixture to obtain an alcoholic beverage with a high alcohol content. Whiskey, bourbon, rye, rum, gin, vodka, tequila, and brandy are types of liquor. Liquor may also be called distilled spirits. Most liquors are about 40 percent alcohol.

Proof is a measure of the amount of alcohol in a beverage. The proof of a beverage is double the percentage of alcohol in the beverage. For example, a beverage with 20 percent alcohol is 40 proof.

Blood Alcohol Concentration

Alcohol enters the bloodstream within minutes after drinking it. About 20 percent of the alcohol that a person drinks is absorbed into the bloodstream through the walls of the stomach. The rest of the alcohol is absorbed through the walls of the intestine. Alcohol affects the body immediately after it is swallowed. The alcohol is absorbed by the stomach and intestines. Then it moves quickly into the bloodstream and affects every cell in the body. A small amount of the alcohol is excreted through urine, perspiration, or breath. Most of the alcohol is changed to harmless waste by the liver. The liver can change only about one drink per hour. If people have more than one drink, the excess alcohol builds up in the body. Eventually, all of the alcohol is excreted. The effects of alcohol intensify as the concentration of alcohol in the blood increases. **Blood alcohol concentration (BAC)** is the amount of alcohol in a person's blood. BAC is given as a percentage. The higher the BAC, the greater the effects of alcohol on the body. The alcohol in a drink goes to all the body tissues before being excreted.

An alcoholic beverage that contains about one-half ounce (14 grams) of alcohol is considered one drink of alcohol. One-half ounce (14 grams) of alcohol is about the amount of alcohol in one can of beer, four to five ounces (112 to 140 grams) of wine, or one (1.5 ounces of 80-proof liquor) mixed drink. Drinking more than this causes BAC to rise. Alcohol is a toxin. A **toxin** is a substance that is poisonous. If too large an amount is swallowed, the stomach will reject it. This causes a person to vomit. The body attempts to break down alcohol as quickly as possible to remove it from the body. However, a large amount of alcohol in the body takes a long time to be excreted. This is why people who drink alcohol at night may still feel its effects the next morning. These people may still be drunk the next day. There is no way to speed alcohol through the body. Coffee, showers, and fresh air do not break down alcohol.

FACTORS THAT AFFECT BAC

The following factors influence blood alcohol concentration:

1. *Amount of alcohol consumed.* The number of drinks people have affects their BAC. The alcohol content of each drink determines the effects of the alcohol.
2. *Speed at which alcohol is consumed.* Drinking at a faster rate increases BAC. Drinking alcohol quickly is dangerous and can be fatal. When people chug, slam, or down several alcoholic beverages in a short period of time, the liver does not have time to break down the alcohol. The alcohol does not leave the body. BAC can reach life-threatening levels.
3. *Body size.* About two-thirds of the body is made up of fluid (water). When alcohol is consumed, it is absorbed and mixes evenly with this fluid. A larger person has more fluid in the body. As a result, the alcohol will be more dilute in a larger person than in a smaller person.
4. *Percentage body fat.* Body fat does not absorb as much alcohol as lean body tissue. For example, suppose two people of the same weight but different body composition have a drink. The person with the higher percentage of body fat will have a higher BAC after one drink than the person with a lower percentage of body fat (because this person has more lean body tissue).
5. *Gender.* BAC rises faster in females than in males. Most females have a higher percentage of body fat than most males. Females are also typically smaller than makes. Certain hormones also make females more sensitive than males to the effects of alcohol. Females are more susceptible to the effects of alcohol immediately before and after the onset of menstruation. Females also have less than males of a certain stomach enzyme that breaks down alcohol before it enters the bloodstream.
6. *Feelings.* Feelings such as stress, anger, and fear can affect BAC by speeding up the rate of alcohol absorption into the bloodstream.
7. *Amount of food eaten.* Alcohol passes more quickly into the bloodstream when the stomach is empty than when it is full.
8. *Presence of other drugs in the bloodstream.* The presence of certain drugs in the bloodstream increases the effects of alcohol. For example, tranquilizers and painkillers increase the depressant effects of alcohol.
9. *Age.* Elderly people are more sensitive to the effects of alcohol than younger people are. The bodies of elderly people contain a lower volume of blood than the bodies of younger people.
10. *Drinking carbonated beverages.* The alcohol in carbonated beverages passes into the bloodstream more quickly than the alcohol in noncarbonated drinks. Carbonated alcoholic beverages include beer, sparkling wine, champagne, and liquor mixed with carbonated beverages.

EFFECTS OF ALCOHOL AT INCREASING BAC LEVELS

The effects of alcohol on people intensify as BAC increases. Remember that the factors listed earlier can influence BAC.

BAC of 0.02 (about one drink in an hour)—People feel relaxed. They may have increased social confidence and become talkative. Thinking and decision-making abilities may be impaired.

BAC of 0.05 (about two drinks in an hour)—Areas of the brain that control reasoning and judgment are impaired. Others may be able to tell that people have been drinking. People feel warm, relaxed, and confident. Speech may be slurred. People may say or do things they usually would not say or do. They may not realize that what they are saying or doing is not appropriate. There is a decrease in muscular coordination, and reaction time is slowed.

BAC of 0.08 (about three to four drinks in an hour)—Balance, speech, vision, and hearing are slightly impaired. People whose BAC has reached this level are considered legally intoxicated in most states.

BAC of 0.10 (about five drinks in an hour)—Reasoning, judgment, self-control, muscular coordination, and reaction time are seriously impaired. People no longer can make responsible decisions. However, they may claim not to be affected by the alcohol. They have slurred speech and walk with a stagger. They may have unpredictable emotions. In many states, they are considered legally drunk. However, a bill passed by the U.S. Congress in October 2000 lowered the legal blood alcohol limit to 0.08 in most states. States that do not lower the legal level of blood alcohol to 0.08 will lose federal highway funds.

BAC of 0.12—People usually become confused and disoriented. Their vision may be blurred. They may lose control of coordination and balance, become nauseous, and vomit.

BAC of 0.20—Emotions are unpredictable and may change rapidly. For example, people may quickly switch from crying to laughing. They may pass out.

BAC of 0.30—People whose BAC has reached this level have little or no control over their mind and body. Most people cannot stay awake to reach this BAC.

BAC of 0.40—People whose BAC has reached this level are likely to be unconscious. Their breathing and heartbeat slow down. They may die.

BAC of 0.50—People whose BAC has reached this level may enter a deep coma and die.

DANGERS OF BINGE-DRINKING AND HAZING

Drinking alcohol quickly—chugging, downing, doing shots, funneling, or gulping—is especially dangerous. Binge-drinking also is extremely dangerous. **Binge-drinking** is often defined as drinking five drinks in a row by males and four in a row by females on a single occasion. Binge-drinking and drinking quickly can cause BAC to rise to dangerous levels very rapidly. People may become unconscious or dangerously drunk.

Some young people drink quickly playing drinking games. Some drinking games are races to finish large quantities of alcohol. Others involve drinking as a punishment for losing the game. Young people have died from playing drinking games. Drinking often is used as a hazing activity. In a **hazing activity,** a person is forced to participate in a dangerous or demeaning act to become a member of a club or group. Some young people have been forced to drink large quantities of alcohol during hazing activities. Some have died from these hazing activities. Young people should not participate in hazing activities. Hazing activities are against the law in most states and violate the rules of most schools. Incidences of hazing should be reported to a parent, guardian, or other responsible adult.

Effects of Alcohol on the Body

Alcohol is a leading cause of death. Almost every part of the body is harmed when people drink large quantities of alcohol. People who drink regularly usually require more health care than other people. Heavy drinking harms most of the body systems.

NERVOUS SYSTEM

Drinking alcohol harms the brain and other parts of the nervous system. It can destroy nerve cells and cause blackouts and seizures. People who drink heavily may develop dementia. Dementia is a general decline in all areas of mental functioning. People with dementia caused by alcohol can recover if they stop drinking.

DIGESTIVE SYSTEM

Drinking alcohol increases the risk of developing cancers of the mouth, esophagus, and stomach. When people drink alcohol, their mouth, esophagus, and stomach are directly exposed to alcohol. The cells in the linings of these organs change and may become cancerous. Drinking alcohol also stimulates the secretion of stomach acids that can injure the inner lining of the stomach and cause ulcers. An **ulcer** is an open sore on the skin or on a mucous membrane. Ulcers usually are inflamed and painful.

Drinking alcohol also increases the risk of developing liver disease. As alcohol is oxidized in the liver, it poisons the liver. When the liver is poisoned by alcohol, it goes through three stages of disease. In the first stage, the liver becomes enlarged with fatty tissue. People with a fatty liver usually do not feel sick. In the second stage, alcoholic hepatitis develops. **Alcoholic hepatitis** is a condition due to alcohol in which the liver swells. People with this condition may have yellowing of the skin and eyes, abdominal pain, and fever. Alcoholic hepatitis can cause serious illness or death. The third stage is cirrhosis. **Cirrhosis** is a disease of the liver caused by chronic damage to liver cells. Cirrhosis can cause liver failure and death. A liver transplant is the only effective treatment for people with advanced cirrhosis.

Heavy drinking increases the risk of developing pancreatitis. **Pancreatitis** is inflammation of the pancreas. People with pancreatitis are at risk for developing diabetes mellitus, or diabetes, a disease in which the body produces little or no insulin. Heavy drinking also can lead to pancreatic cancer.

Heavy drinking also can cause malnutrition. Malnutrition is a condition in which the body does not get the nutrients required for optimal health. People who drink usually eat less food and eat a poorly balanced diet. Drinking also interferes with the digestion and absorption of nutrients. Thiamine, folate, vitamin A, and zinc are commonly deficient in people who drink alcohol. Alcohol-related nutritional deficiencies can cause anemia.

IMMUNE SYSTEM

Drinking alcohol depresses the function of the immune system. This increases the risk of developing certain illnesses, such as respiratory infections, tuberculosis, and certain cancers. Long-term drinking lowers the number of infection-fighting cells in the body and decreases the ability of these cells to fight pathogens.

CARDIOVASCULAR SYSTEM

Drinking alcohol can damage the organs of the cardiovascular system. People who drink are at increased risk for developing cardiovascular diseases, high blood pressure, and stroke. Heavy drinking increases the risk of cardiomyopathy. **Cardiomyopathy** is a disease in which the heart muscles weaken and enlarge and blood cannot be pumped effectively. Drinking alcohol also causes blood vessels to widen, giving a false feeling of warmth. People who have been drinking alcohol can lose body heat and get frostbite or hypothermia in cold weather.

SKELETAL SYSTEM

Drinking alcohol causes the body to lose calcium. Calcium is necessary for proper development and maintenance of the skeletal system and bones. Frequent, long-term use of alcohol is a risk factor for developing osteoporosis. **Osteoporosis** is a condition in which the bones become thin and brittle. People who have osteoporosis are at high risk for breaking bones.

URINARY SYSTEM

Alcohol increases urine flow. Long-term, heavy drinking can cause kidney failure.

REPRODUCTIVE SYSTEM

Drinking alcohol can have significant effects on the reproductive system during puberty. In females, it can delay the first menstrual cycle, cause irregular periods, and impair breast development. Females who drink as teens may have an increased risk of developing breast cancer later in life. In males, drinking can decrease the size of the testes and the development of muscle mass. It can delay the age at which the voice deepens and reduce the amount of body and facial hair.

Effects of Drinking during Pregnancy

Drinking alcohol at any time during pregnancy is harmful to a developing baby. When a pregnant female drinks, the alcohol quickly reaches the developing baby through the bloodstream. Drinking is especially harmful during the early months of pregnancy when the fetal body systems are being formed.

Drinking alcohol during pregnancy can cause miscarriage and stillbirth. A **miscarriage** is the natural ending of a pregnancy before a baby is developed enough to survive on its own. A **stillbirth** is a baby that is born dead. Drinking during pregnancy also increases the risk of bleeding, premature separation of the placenta, and several other complications.

Babies exposed to alcohol during pregnancy may be shorter and smaller than other babies. Pregnant females who have been drinking heavily during the last three months of pregnancy are more likely to have a low-birthweight infant. A **low-birthweight infant** is an infant that weighs less than five pounds (2.2 kilograms) at the time of birth. Low-birthweight infants are at risk for respiratory problems, feeding problems, infections, and long-term developmental problems.

Newborn babies with mothers who are alcohol dependent or drink alcohol during the last months of pregnancy may have symptoms of alcohol withdrawal shortly after they are born. These babies may have sleeping problems, abnormal muscle tension, shakes, and abnormal reflexes. They cry more frequently than other babies.

Babies of mothers who drink alcohol during pregnancy may also be born with fetal alcohol syndrome. **Fetal alcohol syndrome (FAS)** is the presence of severe birth defects in babies born to mothers who drank alcohol during pregnancy. Babies with FAS may have small eye openings, a small head, and retarded physical and mental growth. FAS is a leading cause of mental retardation and birth defects.

Prenatal alcohol exposure does not always result in FAS, although there is no known safe level of alcohol consumption during pregnancy. Most individuals affected by alcohol exposure before birth do not have the characteristic facial abnormalities and growth retardation identified with FAS, yet they have brain and other impairments that are just as significant. Alcohol-related neurodevelopmental disorder (ARND) describes the functional or mental impairments linked to prenatal alcohol exposure, and alcohol-related birth defects (ARBD) describes malformations in the skeletal and major organ systems (National Foundation for Fetal Alcohol Syndrome, 2003).

Effects of Alcohol on Thinking and Decision Making

Drinking alcohol adversely affects thinking and decision making in many ways. Drinking alcohol can cause a person to make wrong decisions, give a false sense of security, interfere with judgment, make a person feel invincible, increase the likelihood of giving in to negative peer pressure, intensify sexual feelings, dull reasoning, slow reaction time, impair coordination, intensify emotions, and cause hangovers and blackouts.

WRONG DECISIONS

Young people who are drinking alcohol might not follow the guidelines for making responsible decisions. They might make choices that they would not make if they were not under the influence of alcohol, and these choices might endanger their health and safety. While they're drinking they might break the law and family guidelines, lose self-respect and the respect of others, and ruin their reputations.

FALSE SENSE OF SELF-CONFIDENCE

Drinking alcohol can give a false sense of self-confidence in social situations. A person who is shy and insecure should never drink to be more social. People should never use alcohol as a crutch. Because alcohol affects communication and reasoning, they may find out later that they did or said things that were not appropriate or were out of character. For example, a person may drink and suddenly have the courage to talk to someone she really likes. She talks to this person and believes they had a good conversation, but later finds out that she slurred her words.

IMPAIRED JUDGMENT

Drinking alcohol can interfere with judgment. People who are drinking might say or do things they usually would not say or do, such as insult another person or share a secret they were supposed to keep. The next day they might find out that they have lost a friend.

FEELINGS OF INVINCIBILITY

Drinking alcohol can make people feel invincible and lead them to do things that are daring or dangerous, sometimes injuring themselves or others. For example, some young people who were drinking alcohol jumped from rooftop to rooftop, misjudged the distance, and were seriously injured in falls.

GIVING IN TO NEGATIVE PEER PRESSURE

Drinking alcohol can increase the likelihood that a person will give in to negative peer pressure. A person who has been drinking is more likely to be persuaded by peers to do things they would not normally do. Suppose a person drinks too much alcohol and is talked into experimenting with marijuana. The person has engaged in two risk behaviors that are harmful and illegal.

INTENSIFIED SEXUAL FEELINGS AND IMPAIRED REASONING

Drinking alcohol can intensify a person's sexual feelings and dull reasoning. Alcohol can make sexual feelings difficult to control. Because reasoning is also dulled, a person might participate in unplanned sexual activity. Most teens who have been sexually active were drinking before they had sex. More than one-half of teen females who become pregnant report that they were under the influence of alcohol when they had sex. Many teens become infected with sexually transmitted diseases (STDs) and HIV when their drinking leads to sex.

IMPAIRED REACTION TIME AND COORDINATION

Drinking alcohol slows reaction time and impairs coordination. A person who is drinking cannot respond as quickly as usual. For example, a person who is usually a responsible pedestrian might cross the street as the light turns yellow, rather than waiting, after having a few alcoholic drinks. The person might be struck by a car.

AGGRESSIVE BEHAVIOR

Drinking alcohol can cause a person to become aggressive. Many people are more likely to argue and get into fights when they are drinking. Many

acts of violence, such as physical abuse and murder, occur after someone has been drinking. For example, at a party, one teen male who has been drinking alcohol might accidentally spill a drink on another male who has been drinking. Although both boys might usually resolve conflict without violence, the fact that both have been drinking could turn the spilled drink into an angry, violent fight.

INTENSIFIED EMOTIONS

Drinking alcohol intensifies emotions. A person who is a bit sad might, after a few drinks, end up feeling extremely sad, depressed, desperate, jealous, or angry. Drinking to numb depressed feelings is very dangerous. Most teens who attempt suicide have been drinking alcohol or taking other drugs.

HANGOVERS

A **hangover** is an aftereffect of using alcohol and other drugs. A hangover may involve a headache, increased sensitivity to sounds, nausea, vomiting, tiredness, and irritability. Hangovers can interfere with fulfilling one's responsibilities, such as school, job, physical activity, and family activities. Some young people think that it is not dangerous for people in high school and college to drink and get drunk now and then. They believe faulty statements, such as "Everybody parties when they are in school" or "Drinking is okay to celebrate prom night." They say they will stop this behavior when they are older. However, drinking alcohol one time can have serious consequences. Drinking now and then can lead to drug dependence. Some experts claim that people who start drinking as teens are more at risk for developing alcoholism than people who start drinking as adults.

BLACKOUTS

People who drink alcohol may have blackouts. A **blackout** is a loss of memory for what happened during a period of time. People who have been drinking may do something risky, embarrassing, or violent and not remember this behavior later. People who have blackouts may find themselves in a place and not remember how they got there. These people may have participated in sexual behavior and not remember it. Other people might not be able to tell that a person is having a blackout. They might later tell the person what he did while drinking, and he might find it difficult to believe.

Drinking Alcohol and the Risk of Violence and Illegal Behavior

Studies show that alcohol is the drug most likely to be involved in violence (National Institute on Alcohol Abuse and Alcoholism, 2000). When people drink alcohol, their judgment is not clear. They make unwise decisions, their behavior changes, and they are less predictable. They may become depressed and consider harming themselves. Their feelings may get stronger. They may become very angry and harm others. Drinking alcohol increases the risk of violence and illegal behavior.

VIOLENCE

Alcohol, more than any other drug, has been linked with violence. People who drink alcohol often have a false sense of confidence and little regard for the feelings and safety of others. They may act on angry or aggressive feelings and harm others. Young people who drink or spend time with people who drink are at risk for fighting, abuse, and murder. They also are more likely to engage in illegal behaviors, such as shoplifting, vandalism, and selling drugs.

DOMESTIC VIOLENCE

A leading cause of divorce and broken families is domestic violence. **Domestic violence** is violence that occurs within a family. Most acts of domestic violence occur after a family member has been drinking alcohol. Each year, many children are seriously abused by a parent or guardian who uses alcohol.

RAPE

Drinking alcohol is a risk factor for rape. **Rape** is the use of physical force (threatened or actual) to force sex on a person without the person's consent. **Acquaintance rape** is rape committed by a person who is known to the victim. People who have been drinking may become victims of acquaintance rape, and people who have been drinking are more likely to commit rape. Inhibitions are reduced, thinking is impaired, and sexual feelings are increased. A person may not acknowledge that the other person is saying "no." People who commit rape after drinking are accountable in a court of law. People who get someone drunk in order to have sex also can be charged with rape.

SUICIDE

Drinking can intensify feelings of sadness and depression. Alcohol is a factor in many suicide attempts. These people were not thinking clearly and could not see another way of coping with their problems.

LAWBREAKING

Drinking and buying alcohol is against the law for teens. In most states, a person must be twenty-one years old to purchase alcohol. A minor is a person who is under the legal age. Minors who drink or purchase alcohol risk being arrested, fined, and jailed. It is illegal for someone who is over the legal age to buy alcohol for a minor. Using fake identification to buy alcohol is also illegal.

VIOLATING SCHOOL POLICIES

Children and teens who drink alcohol during school hours or bring alcohol to school are violating school policies. Most schools suspend or expel students who break school alcohol policies. Teens who drink are more likely than other teens to drop out of school and to have lower grades. Teens who drink might skip school to drink or to recover from hangovers.

DRINKING WHILE DRIVING

People who drink alcohol and drive might be injured or killed, and they also might injure or kill passengers, other motorists, and pedestrians. Alcohol-related motor vehicle accidents are a leading cause of death and spinal injury in young people. Many teens who have been involved in alcohol-related accidents later report they did not realize at the time that the alcohol had impaired their ability to drive.

Drinking and driving by teens is a health issue that health educators should emphasize in health education classes and other prevention activities. Motor vehicle crashes are the number one killer of teens, and alcohol use is frequently involved in these crashes. In the past two decades, increased education and new laws have helped to reduce the number of alcohol-related deaths among teens. This is good news, but there are still too many deaths and injuries from alcohol-related crashes.

Drinking is dangerous when driving because alcohol slows reaction time and impairs judgment and coordination—vital skills needed to drive a car safely. The more alcohol consumed, the greater the impairment. All states in the United States have adopted a 0.08 BAC as the legal limit for operating a motor vehicle for drivers age 21 or older. However, drivers under age 21 are not allowed to operate a motor vehicle with any level of alcohol in their system. When a driver is suspected of driving under the influence, blood alcohol concentration is measured by either a blood alcohol test or a breathalyzer. Individuals need to understand that impairment due to alcohol use begins to occur at levels well below the legal limit.

Alcoholism

Alcoholism is a disease in which there is physical and psychological dependence on alcohol. *Alcohol dependence* is another term for alcoholism. Alcohol dependence can destroy the lives of those who drink and the lives of those around them. Alcoholism is a factor in automobile accidents, injuries, suicide, violence, job loss, divorce, serious illness, and death. Alcoholism often causes family dysfunction and relationship difficulties.

People with alcoholism have difficulty controlling their drinking. They often feel overwhelmed by the desire for another drink. Some people with alcoholism do not drink often, but they are out of control when they do.

Alcoholism causes people's personalities to change. Moods and emotions change rapidly, and behavior becomes unpredictable and irresponsible. Feelings of anger, paranoia, and depression can increase.

People with alcoholism continue to drink alcohol even though it causes many problems. They are in denial. **Denial** is refusing to admit a problem. Many alcoholics deny that there is a connection between their problems and their drinking.

People with alcoholism may go through several stages. They may try to stop drinking. This often occurs after they do something they regret, such as abuse a family member. They promise to quit drinking, but they usually do not. When they stop drinking, they may suffer from alcohol withdrawal syndrome. **Alcohol withdrawal syndrome** is the reaction of the body to the

sudden stopping of drinking. People with alcohol withdrawal syndrome feel nauseous, anxious, and agitated. They may vomit, have tremors ("the shakes"), trouble sleeping, and delirium tremens. **Delirium tremens** is a severe form of alcohol withdrawal syndrome in which there are hallucinations and muscle convulsions.

Effects of Alcoholism on the Family

Alcoholism affects entire families. People with alcoholism often have difficulties with relationships, money, and jobs. They might have accidents or become ill as a result of drinking. They might neglect or injure family members. Family members might not bring friends home because they fear that the person with alcoholism will embarrass them or become violent. Many family members of people with alcoholism are codependent, blaming themselves for the drinking problem.

Children whose parents abuse alcohol are more likely to have problems with alcohol. Alcohol abuse is lower in families in which parents or guardians clearly disapprove of drinking.

TREATMENT FOR ALCOHOLISM

People with alcoholism need treatment. This involves treatment for people with the disease as well as counseling for family members and friends. Treatment usually involves short-term or long-term stays at a recovery facility and may involve recovery programs. **Alcoholics Anonymous (AA)** is a recovery program for people who have alcoholism. **Al-Anon** is a recovery program for people who have friends or family members with alcoholism. **Al-Ateen** is a recovery program for teens who have a family member or friend with alcoholism. **Adult Children of Alcoholics (ACOA)** is a recovery program for children who have one or more parents, a guardian, or a caregiver with alcoholism. After completing a recovery program, people with alcoholism need support.

Alcohol Advertising

The alcohol beverage industry is one of the leading industries in terms of spending money to advertise its products. People of all ages see alcohol advertisements. The purpose of alcohol advertising, of course, is to convince people to buy a specific alcohol product.

Alcohol advertisers spend large amounts of money advertising their products on TV and in magazines. Alcohol companies also spend a great deal of money on billboard advertising in neighborhoods. Billboards and other public alcohol signage put people in these neighborhoods at increased risk of developing irresponsible drinking habits. The Internet is another area where alcohol ads appear in large numbers. There are numerous Web sites that people of all ages can access that promote alcohol use. Some of these Web sites use specific ways to attract young people to the company's products.

One way that young people are influenced by TV ads is the time that these ads are shown. For example, many young people watch football, basketball, hockey, and baseball games that may be on during the daytime or nighttime on weekends. In addition, many companies place advertisements in popular magazines that young people read. This is another way to get the attention of young people. A study by the Center on Alcohol Marketing and Youth (2005) found that more than half of the money that alcohol companies spend for magazine advertising goes to magazines that have high readership of underage youths, ages twelve to twenty.

A great deal of alcohol advertising focuses on associating drinking with "coolness" and "having a good time." Alcohol advertisements tend to show attractive people drinking and having fun. Young people may think that drinking is cool and that they need to drink to have fun like the people in the ads.

Health Goal #53

I Will Avoid Tobacco Use and Secondhand Smoke

Nicotine

Nicotine is a stimulant drug found in tobacco products, including cigarettes and chewing tobacco. Nicotine stimulates the nervous system and is highly addictive. It dulls the taste buds,

constricts the blood vessels, and increases heart rate and blood pressure. When tobacco smoke is inhaled into the lungs, nicotine is absorbed into the bloodstream and quickly reaches the brain. Nicotine also can be absorbed into the bloodstream from smokeless tobacco that is placed in the mouth. When the "pick-me-up" effect of nicotine wears off, a user is motivated to use more tobacco.

TOBACCO PRODUCTS THAT CONTAIN NICOTINE

Tobacco is a plant that contains nicotine. Tobacco can be smoked in cigarettes, cigars, and pipes. A **cigarette** is dried and shredded tobacco wrapped in paper. A **bidi** is a small, hand-rolled, filterless cigarette made in India that contains more tar and nicotine than regular cigarettes. They resemble marijuana joints in appearance and are quite popular with young people. They also come in such flavors as mango, orange, chocolate, watermelon, raspberry, vanilla, and menthol. A **clove cigarette** is a cigarette that has a mixture of ground cloves and tobacco. Clove cigarettes contain higher amounts of tar, nicotine, and carbon monoxide than regular cigarettes. They also contain **eugenol,** a chemical that numbs the back of the throat and reduces the ability to cough. A **cigar** is dried and rolled tobacco leaves. **Pipe tobacco** is shredded tobacco that is smoked in a pipe. **Smokeless tobacco** is tobacco that is chewed or snorted but not smoked. Chewing tobacco and snuff are forms of smokeless tobacco. **Chewing tobacco** is a tobacco product made from chopped tobacco leaves that is placed between the gums and cheek. **Snuff** is a tobacco product made from powdered tobacco leaves and stems that is snorted or placed between the gums and cheek.

NICOTINE DEPENDENCE

Nicotine is a powerfully addictive drug. Nicotine goes straight to the brain and acts on areas of the brain that control feelings of pleasure. Nicotine causes an increase in dopamine, which creates intense feelings of pleasure and satisfaction. Many health experts and health organizations have declared that nicotine is as addictive as heroin, cocaine, and alcohol. Nicotine dependence causes more premature death and disease than all other forms of drug dependence combined. People who regularly use tobacco develop a tolerance to nicotine. They need more and more to produce the desired effect. At first, the desired effect is to feel the stimulation that nicotine causes. Later, it is to lessen the craving for nicotine. People develop a physical dependence on nicotine when the body becomes accustomed to its effects. Psychological dependence develops when people feel the need to smoke or chew tobacco at certain times or for specific reasons.

People who try to quit using tobacco often have nicotine withdrawal syndrome. **Nicotine withdrawal syndrome** is the body's reaction to quitting tobacco products. People with nicotine withdrawal syndrome feel a craving for tobacco; may be anxious, irritable, and restless; may have headaches and difficulty concentrating; can become frustrated and angry; and have heart palpitations and increased appetite.

Experimenting with tobacco puts young people at risk for nicotine dependence. According to the U.S. surgeon general (U.S. Department of Health and Human Services, 2000b), the probability of becoming addicted after one exposure is higher for nicotine than for other addictive substances such as heroin, cocaine, and alcohol. Young people have a harder time quitting smoking than people who start smoking when they are older. They also are more likely to become heavy smokers and to die of a disease caused by smoking.

Health Consequences of Tobacco Smoking

Tobacco smoke contains many harmful chemicals in addition to nicotine. Scientists estimate there are more than 4,000 different chemicals in tobacco smoke. Several carcinogens have been found in tobacco smoke. A **carcinogen** is a chemical that is known to cause cancer. Most of the carcinogens in tobacco smoke are found in tar. **Tar** is a sticky, thick substance formed when tobacco is burned. Tar coats and irritates respiratory tissues and is a major cause of lung cancer. Another dangerous substance that forms when tobacco is burned is carbon monoxide. **Carbon monoxide** is an odorless, tasteless gas that interferes with the ability of blood to carry oxygen.

CANCER

Smoking causes lung cancer and increases the risk of many other types of cancer. Lung cancer kills more people that any other cancer. According to the American Cancer Society (2006), more

females used to die of breast cancer than any other cancer, but today more females die of lung cancer than of breast cancer. This is due to higher rates of smoking among females. It is rare for someone who has never smoked to develop lung cancer. Lung cancer almost always causes death. Most people with lung cancer die within five years of learning that they have cancer.

Smoking also is a major risk factor for cancer of the throat, mouth, esophagus, pancreas, and bladder. The American Cancer Society (2006) reports that one-third of all cancer deaths are due to tobacco use and that nine out of every ten cases of lung cancer are caused by smoking cigarettes.

RESPIRATORY DISEASES

Smoking prevents the lungs from working effectively. When a person smokes, tar lines the lungs and air passages. Tobacco also harms the cilia in the nose, throat, and bronchial tubes. **Cilia** are hairlike structures that remove dust and other particles from inhaled air and prevent harmful substances from reaching the lungs. Cilia are destroyed after a person has smoked for several years. This increases the risk of respiratory infection. Smoking aggravates asthma. **Asthma** is a condition in which the bronchial tubes become inflamed and constrict, making breathing difficult.

Smoking is a risk factor for **chronic obstructive pulmonary disease (COPD),** a disease that interferes with breathing. Examples of COPDs are chronic bronchitis and emphysema. **Chronic bronchitis** is a recurring inflammation of the bronchial tubes that causes mucus to line the bronchial tubes. People must cough often to remove the mucus. Coughing cannot remove all the harmful matter from the air passages. This increases the risk of lung infection and interferes with the ability to breathe.

Emphysema is a condition in which the alveoli in the lungs lose most of their ability to absorb oxygen from inhaled air and pass it into the bloodstream or remove carbon dioxide from the bloodstream. As a result, it is difficult to get oxygen into the bloodstream and carbon dioxide builds up in the body because it cannot be removed from the bloodstream. It becomes increasingly difficult for people with emphysema to be active. Some people with emphysema must remain in bed and use special equipment to get an adequate amount of oxygen. Emphysema cannot be cured.

CARDIOVASCULAR DISEASES

The ingredients in tobacco smoke also harm the cardiovascular system. Smoking is a major cause of death from heart and blood vessel diseases, blood clots, and stroke. Smoking speeds up the development of fat deposits on the arteries and damages the inner lining of arteries. Fat deposits reduce the space in the artery through which blood can flow. The risk of developing blood clots increases.

A clot in an artery in the heart can cause a heart attack. A **heart attack** is the death of cardiac muscle caused by a lack of blood flow to the heart. A clot in the brain can result in a stroke. A **stroke** is a condition caused by a blocked or broken blood vessel in the brain. Strokes can cause paralysis or be fatal. Smoking also is a risk factor for aortic aneurysm. An **aortic aneurysm** is a bulging, weakened area in the aorta. The aorta is the main artery in the body. An **aneurysm** is the result of a weakening in an artery wall.

The nicotine in tobacco smoke raises a person's resting heart rate by close to twenty beats per minute. This and inhaled carbon monoxide place extra strain on the heart. Carbon monoxide replaces oxygen in some red blood cells, so the heart must pump faster to deliver enough oxygen to the cells for them to survive. The combination of nicotine and carbon monoxide in tobacco smoke may be responsible for the large numbers of smokers who develop heart disease.

ACCIDENTS

Cigarette smoking is a leading cause of fires. Many fires start when a smoldering cigarette ignites bedding, mattresses, and other household furniture. Many people each year, of all ages, are seriously injured or die when a lit cigarette causes a fire. Explosions often are ignited by a lit cigarette as well. Cigarette smoking also is a factor in many motor vehicle accidents—drivers who smoke are frequently distracted by trying to light a cigarette or by dropping a lit cigarette. Eye irritation caused by tobacco smoke also can distract a driver, reduce vision, and contribute to fatigue.

OTHER HEALTH PROBLEMS

Smoking can harm other areas of the body in addition to the ones discussed earlier. Smokers are more likely to develop gum disease and to lose teeth and supporting gum tissues. Smoking may cause or worsen ulcers in the stomach and small intestine. Smoking causes ulcers to become inflamed and painful. Smoking during pregnancy harms the developing baby. Studies show that quitting smoking during pregnancy could prevent 5 percent of infant deaths, 20 percent of low birthweight in babies, and 8 percent of premature deliveries.

Health Consequences of Breathing Secondhand Smoke

A lit cigarette burns for about twelve minutes. During those twelve minutes, people who are near the smoker will breathe in secondhand smoke. **Secondhand smoke,** or **environmental tobacco smoke,** is exhaled smoke and sidestream smoke. **Sidestream smoke** is smoke that enters the air from a burning cigarette, cigar, or pipe. *Passive smoking* and *involuntary smoking* are other terms used to describe breathing in secondhand smoke. Sidestream smoke has even more tar, nicotine, carbon monoxide, ammonia, and benzene than mainstream smoke. **Mainstream smoke** is smoke that is inhaled into the smoker's mouth and lungs.

Secondhand smoke is more than just an annoyance. It harms the health of anyone who inhales it. Secondhand smoke is the most hazardous form of indoor air pollution. It can cause lung cancer in nonsmokers and increase their risk of developing heart disease and respiratory problems. People who already have heart disease or respiratory problems are especially affected. Secondhand smoke is a major health risk for children with parents who smoke. These children are at increased risk for ear infections, bronchitis, and pneumonia. The lungs of children exposed to secondhand smoke may not develop properly. Secondhand smoke is an irritant that causes the eyes to burn and can irritate the nose, throat, and airways. Many people report having headaches after breathing secondhand smoke.

The Environmental Protection Agency (EPA) has classified secondhand smoke as a Group A carcinogen. A **Group A carcinogen** is a substance that causes cancer in humans.

People are exposed to secondhand smoke in many places. Children are most likely to be exposed at home. Adults who do not smoke are most likely to be exposed at work. People also are exposed to secondhand smoke in social situations such as parties and in public places such as restaurants.

Many steps are being taken to protect nonsmokers from secondhand smoke. Laws are being passed to prevent smoking inside public buildings, schools, and workplaces. Airlines have restricted smoking during flights. Many businesses no longer allow smoking in their office buildings or factories. People are showing greater concern for their health and the health of others.

It is not always easy to avoid secondhand smoke. Following are examples of ways to avoid secondhand smoke:

1. Speak up to the person who is smoking, while still being polite. Inform people about health concerns related to smoking.
2. Ask smokers not to smoke in indoor areas that are shared.
3. Encourage a nonsmoking policy for the home.
4. Encourage family members who smoke to quit smoking and to go outside if they must smoke.
5. Request seating in nonsmoking sections of restaurants or in public areas.

Health Consequences of Smokeless Tobacco

Smokeless tobacco is manufactured and sold in two forms. Chewing tobacco is a tobacco product made from chopped tobacco leaves that is placed between the gums and cheek. Snuff is a tobacco product made from powdered tobacco leaves and stems that is snorted or placed between the gums and cheek. Nicotine is released from smokeless tobacco, absorbed through the linings of the mouth or nose, and carried to the brain in the bloodstream. The effects of the nicotine can last for several hours if the tobacco is kept in the mouth. Smokeless tobacco has most of the same harmful ingredients as other tobacco products.

NICOTINE DEPENDENCE

Smokeless tobacco causes nicotine dependence. Every time people use smokeless tobacco, they feel the "pick-me-up" effects of nicotine. The body becomes accustomed to these effects, leading to craving and a repeated use of tobacco. The body

develops a tolerance to the effects. Craving and tolerance both are signs of nicotine dependence.

HARMFUL CHEMICALS

Smokeless tobacco contains many chemicals that harm health, including formaldehyde, lead, nitrosamines, cadmium, and polonium. All forms of smokeless tobacco contain carcinogens.

CANCER

Smokeless tobacco increases the risk of developing cancer. Smokeless tobacco and its irritating juices are in contact with the gums, cheeks, and lips for long periods of time. This causes changes in the cells of the mouth called leukoplakia. **Leukoplakia** are abnormal cells in the mouth that appear as white patches of tissue. These abnormal cells can develop into cancer. Using smokeless tobacco also increases the risk of cancer of the larynx, pharynx, and esophagus.

GUM AND TEETH PROBLEMS

Smokeless tobacco causes problems with the gums and teeth. It permanently stains teeth, causes bad breath, and can leave tiny particles of tobacco on the teeth. Chewing tobacco includes particles that scratch and wear away teeth. The sugar in smokeless tobacco mixes with dental plaque to form acids that cause tooth decay. Smokeless tobacco also can cause the gums to pull away from the teeth, exposing the roots. The teeth become more sensitive and are more likely to fall out.

DULLED SENSES

Smokeless tobacco dulls the senses of smell and taste. As a result, people who use smokeless tobacco often eat more salty and sweet foods. These foods are harmful if eaten in large amounts.

Tobacco Advertising and Promotion

Tobacco manufacturers are not allowed by law to put tobacco ads on TV or radio. Tobacco manufacturers still manage to promote their products in many ways, such as by distributing clothing and other items that display their logos and symbols—people who wear or use these items are walking ads for the tobacco company. Tobacco companies also promote their products by offering merchandise in exchange for coupons found on cigarette packs or smokeless tobacco containers and by sponsoring sporting events and rock concerts. They want people to associate their product and their logo with excitement and glamour. Such advertising does an end run around the laws that prohibit advertising tobacco products on television.

The American Academy of Pediatrics (2006) report *Children, Adolescents, and Advertising* notes that tobacco companies spend $30 million per day, or $11.2 billion per year, on advertising and promotion. Tobacco advertising exerts a powerful effect. The report presents research findings showing that exposure to tobacco advertising may be a stronger risk factor for smoking than having family members and peers who smoke. In fact, one-third of all adolescent smoking may be due to tobacco advertising and other promotions.

APPEALS TO USE TOBACCO

Tobacco companies spend billions of dollars each year to convince people to use tobacco. They want people to think tobacco use is "in" and to take attention away from the warnings. Many tobacco ads are designed to appeal to children and teens. People in the ads are models who are attractive, healthy looking, and well dressed. They are having fun and are very appealing to the ads' target audiences. Unfortunately, many young people are persuaded by these ads. What these ads fail to say is that smoking cigarettes does not make a person look attractive, healthy, or well dressed and that others are likely to be turned off by the smoking behavior, the stinky breath, and the stained teeth. Tobacco ads also do not say that more than 400,000 people die each year from smoking. They do not show people dying of lung disease or restricted to bed because of emphysema. They do not show family members grieving the death of loved ones who used tobacco. They do not show how difficult it is to quit using cigarettes or other forms of tobacco.

Tobacco companies claim they do not design ads that target children. But on the Internet, tobacco companies appeal to children by using interactive games, giveaways, and chats to promote their products. They promote the idea that using tobacco products makes a person seem more grownup and cool.

A very troubling tactic employed by tobacco companies to sell more cigarettes to young people is the introduction of candy-flavored cigarettes and smokeless tobacco. RJ Reynolds introduced a series of candy-flavored cigarettes, which include flavors such as pineapple and coconut, citrus, toffee, and mocha mint. Brown & Williamson markets spit tobacco with berry, apple, wintergreen, vanilla, and cherry flavors. Candy-flavored cigarettes have exotic names such as Twista Chill Lime, Kauai Kolada, Winter Warm Toffee, and Midnight Berry that sound like beverages or ice cream flavors. Some of the flavored cigarettes are priced to make them more affordable to children. Brown & Williamson also promotes Kool cigarettes with hip-hop music themes and images that have particular appeal to African American youths.

Quitting Tobacco Use

There are many reasons to quit using tobacco. People who quit using tobacco live longer than those who continue to use tobacco. They reduce their risk of heart disease, stroke, emphysema, chronic bronchitis, and some forms of cancer.

There are even more immediate rewards to quitting smoking. Within a day after a person stops smoking, the body begins to heal itself from the

damages caused by tobacco. Breathing is easier, and smoker's cough is less frequent. The sense of taste and smell improve.

Quitting tobacco use takes planning and effort. Following are guidelines to help a person quit using tobacco:

1. *List your reastons for wanting to quit.* Focus on all the things you do not like about using tobacco. For example, think about the mess, the inconvenience, the waste of money, the way it makes you smell, the cravings, and the dangers. Ask family members and friends to add to your list of reasons.

2. *Decide upon a date to quit.* Set a target date to quit and know what to expect. Understand that nicotine withdrawal symptoms are temporary. Understand that quitting is not easy, but it is possible. Expect to experience pressures to use tobacco when you are feeling stressed.

3. *Make a health behavior contract.* Make a health behavior contract with the life skill "I will stop using smokeless tobacco" or "I will stop smoking." Describe the effect that the life skill will have on your well-being. Design a plan to quit using tobacco. Determine how you will evaluate your progress.

4. *Think about the situations in which you smoke or use smokeless tobacco.* Change your daily routines to avoid situations when you use tobacco. For example, go for a walk instead. Stay busy and active.

5. *Get help from a health care professional.* Make an appointment with a school nurse or a physician to help with your plan. A physician might prescribe a low-dose nicotine patch, nicotine chewing gum, a nicotine inhaler, or nicotine nasal spray. A **nicotine patch** is a patch worn on the skin of the upper body or arms that releases nicotine into the bloodstream at a slow rate. **Nicotine chewing gum** is chewing gum that releases nicotine when chewed lightly and then held between the teeth and cheek. A **nicotine inhaler** is a device that provides nicotine vapor when air is inhaled through the device. **Nicotine nasal spray** is a spray that administers nicotine to the mucous membranes in the nose. Nicotine patches, chewing gum, inhalers, and nasal sprays release nicotine into the bloodstream without the cancer-causing chemicals found in tobacco. They help people cope with cravings for tobacco and withdrawal from nicotine.

They can gradually eliminate the need for nicotine. However, there can be side effects. Using nicotine gum can result in sore jaws, upset stomach, nausea, heartburn, loosened dental fillings, and problems with dentures. Nicotine patches can cause redness, itching, swelling, nervousness, dry mouth, and inability to sleep. Nicotine inhalers and nicotine nasal sprays can be irritating to the nasal passages. A physician may also prescribe buproprion. **Buproprion** is a prescription antidepressant drug approved by the FDA as a smoking cessation aid that does not contain nicotine. Buproprion can be used alone or together with nicotine patch, chewing gum, inhaler, or nasal spray.

6. *Join a tobacco cessation program.* A **tobacco cessation program** is a program to help a person stop smoking or using smokeless tobacco. Tobacco cessation programs are offered by local chapters of the American Cancer Society, the American Lung Society, and the American Heart Association, health departments, schools, and hospitals.

7. *Get help from others.* Telling family members and friends of your decision to quit enlists their encouragement and support. It may also be helpful to ask a friend or family member who uses tobacco to quit at the same time.

8. *Throw away all tobacco products.* Get rid of items associated with tobacco use, such as ashtrays, lighters, and matches.

9. *Be prepared for temptation.* For the first few weeks or longer after quitting, you might get urges to use tobacco. These cravings will be strongest in situations where you used to use tobacco the most. It is best to stay away from people who use tobacco as much as possible during this time. When you get the urge to use tobacco, substitute another activity.

10. *Participate in activities that keep your mind off using tobacco.* Try vigorous exercise to release beta-endorphins. Beta-endorphins may help relieve tension caused by quitting. Participating in other activities, such as working on a hobby or going to a movie, also may help.

11. *Avoid weight gain.* Eating a healthful diet with the proper amount of protein, carbohydrates, and fat is essential when quitting. A healthful diet should also include plenty of fruits and vegetables, and you can enjoy low-fat and low-calorie snacks. Participating in physical activity regularly will help you avoid weight gain. Avoid the temptation to overeat.

12. *Keep your guard up.* The urge to use tobacco often comes at predictable times. Continue to plan ahead for these situations. Find ways to cope with these urges.

13. *If you slip up and use tobacco, keep trying to quit.* Do not feel discouraged. Slipping up does not have to mean failure. Think of it as a setback. Figure out why you slipped up and how to avoid it the next time.

Health Goal #54

I Will Not Be Involved in Illegal Drug Use

Controlled Substances

The abuse of controlled substances threatens the health of the user and may cause behaviors that threaten the health and safety of others. A **controlled drug** is a drug whose possession, manufacture, distribution, and sale are controlled by law. A prescription is needed to obtain controlled drugs. **Illegal drug use** is the use of a controlled drug without a prescription. It is illegal to buy or sell controlled drugs on the street. Many controlled substances are psychoactive drugs. Psychoactive drugs act on the central nervous system and alter a user's moods, perceptions, feelings, personality, or behavior.

Stimulants

Stimulants are a group of drugs that speed up the activities of the central nervous system. Stimulants are sometimes called "uppers" because they make people feel alert, awake, and active. They increase blood pressure, heart rate, and breathing rate. Young people use legal and illegal stimulants to get a high, to stay awake, and to lose weight.

The use of stimulants is always followed by a "crash." A crash is the intense down period that follows a stimulant high. People who crash feel fatigued, weak, sleepy, very sad, and depressed. People who use stimulants often take larger amounts of stimulants to avoid the crash. They develop physical and psychological dependence.

Types of Stimulants

Cocaine is a highly addictive stimulant that is obtained from the leaves of the coca bush. It can be snorted, injected, or smoked. It takes about three minutes for cocaine to reach the brain when it is snorted, about fifteen seconds when it is injected into a vein, and seven seconds when it is smoked. Cocaine stimulates the stress response and may cause death by heart attack, stroke, or seizure. Trying cocaine even once can be fatal. Cocaine is also known as

- Coke
- Blow
- Gold dust
- White lady
- Snow

Crack is purified cocaine that is smoked to produce a rapid and intense reaction. It is named for the sound it produces when smoked. Crack is even more addictive than regular cocaine. Crack is a type of freebase cocaine. The effects of crack and freebase cocaine are ten times greater than those of snorted cocaine. People who use crack may become rapidly addicted. Trying crack even once can be fatal. Crack is also known as rock.

Amphetamines are chemically manufactured stimulants that are highly addictive. They used to be taken as diet pills. They no longer are sold for this purpose because of possible harmful effects.

A **look-alike drug** is a drug manufactured to resemble another drug and mimic its effects. Many look-alike drugs are made to appear as amphetamines. Look-alike amphetamines contain large amounts of legal, nonprescription stimulants such as caffeine.

Methamphetamine is a highly addictive central nervous system stimulant in the amphetamine family that can be injected, snorted, smoked, or ingested orally. Methamphetamine users feel a short yet intense rush when the drug is initially administered. The effects of methamphetamine include increased activity, decreased appetite, and a sense of well-being that can last from twenty minutes to twelve hours. The drug has limited medical uses for the treatment of narcolepsy, attention deficit disorders, and obesity. Methamphetamine can easily be manufactured in clandestine laboratories using store-bought materials and is the most prevalent synthetic drug manufactured in the United States. The manufacturing of methamphetamine is called "cooking." Cooking a batch of meth can be very dangerous due to the fact that the chemicals used are volatile and the by-products are toxic. Meth labs present a danger to the meth cook, the community surrounding the lab, and the law enforcement personnel who discover the lab. The ease of manufacturing methamphetamine and its highly addictive potential has caused the use of the drug to increase throughout the nation. The methamphetamine problem was originally concentrated in the West but has spread throughout the entire country.

Yaba, the Thai name for a tablet form of methamphetamine mixed with caffeine, has appeared in many areas in the United States. These tablets are popular in Southeast and East Asia where they are produced. The tablets are small enough to fit in the end of a drinking straw and are usually reddish orange or green with various logos. There are indications that methamphetamine tablets are popular within the rave scene because of the tablet's similar appearance to club drugs such as Ecstasy (Office of National Drug Control Policy, 2003). Ice is a form of pure methamphetamine that is smoked. Methamphetamine is also known as

- Meth
- Crank
- Crystal meth
- Crystal tea
- Crystal
- Ice

Ephedrine is a stimulant that is found naturally in the ephedra plant. Ephedrine can also be made synthetically in a laboratory. It used to be a common ingredient in decongestants, bronchodilators, and diet pills. A **decongestant** is a drug used to relieve a stuffed-up nose. A **bronchodilator** is a drug that is taken to make breathing easier. Ephedrine is sometimes prescribed to relieve asthma. The U.S. Food and Drug Administration (FDA) banned the over-the-counter sale of decongestants and bronchodilators that contain ephedrine. Ephedrine and a related drug, pseudoephedrine, are used in the illegal manufacture of methamphetamine.

MDMA is a stimulant that also has mild hallucinogenic properties. MDMA, known as "Ecstasy," reduces inhibitions and anxiety and produces feelings of empathy for others and extreme relaxation. In addition to stimulation, MDMA suppresses the need to eat, drink, or sleep. These effects enable users to endure all-night dance parties known as "raves." MDMA can damage the brain. It can also cause the body to overheat, leading to heatstroke. The risk of heatstroke is heightened when Ecstasy is taken at a rave in hot, crowded conditions (U.S. Drug Enforcement Administration, 2001).

The use of MDMA has moved into settings other than nightclubs and raves, such as private homes, high schools, college dorms, and shopping malls. In addition to the dangers associated with MDMA itself, users are also at risk of being given a substitute drug. For example, PMA (para-methoxyamphetamine) is an illicit, synthetic hallucinogen that has stimulant effects similar to MDMA. However, when users take PMA thinking they are really ingesting MDMA, they often think they have taken weak Ecstasy because PMA's effects take longer to appear. They then ingest more of the substance to attain a better high, which can result in overdose and death. Adulterants may be added to Ecstasy without the user's knowledge. The majority of the MDMA in the United States is produced in western Europe, primarily the Netherlands. Traffickers smuggle MDMA into the United States through express mail services, commercial flights, and airfreight shipments to deliver their merchandise (Office of National Drug Control Policy, 2002). MDMA is also known as

- Ecstasy
- XTC
- E
- X
- Adam

Methylphenidate is a stimulant that is used to treat **attention deficit hyperactivity disorder (ADHD),** a learning disability in which a person is easily distracted and also is hyperactive. Methylphenidate stimulates a portion of the brain that helps a person pay attention and reduces hyperactivity.

Caffeine is a stimulant found in chocolate, coffee, tea, some soda pops, and some prescription and over-the-counter drugs. It is the most widely used stimulant and is not a controlled substance. Caffeine produces a quick pick-me-up effect. It increases the likelihood of having irregular heartbeat, irritates the stomach, and increases urine production. Some people develop caffeinism. **Caffeinism** is poisoning due to heavy caffeine intake.

HEALTH CONSEQUENCES

The illegal use of stimulants can harm health in the following ways:

1. *By causing immediate death.* Within minutes, people who have taken a stimulant may have seizures, stop breathing, and die. People who lack a chemical in the liver needed to break down cocaine can have an immediate fatal reaction. MDMA and other drugs that are sometimes sold as Ecstasy can cause body temperature to rise as high as 107 to 109 degrees Fahrenheit. A number of deaths have resulted from the overheating that can happen when taking these drugs. Mixing other drugs with stimulants increases the risk of overdose and possible death.

2. *By harming the body.* People who use stimulants may experience body tremors, vomiting, a racing heart, increased alertness, and quickened movements. Stimulants raise heart rate and blood pressure, which can lead to the breaking of a blood vessel in the brain. This can cause a stroke. Snorting stimulants causes sores and burns in and around the nose. People who snort large amounts may develop holes between their nostrils and have a runny nose, sore throat, and hoarse voice.

3. *By harming the mind.* People who use stimulants can become confused, anxious, aggressive, and paranoid. Their emotions change. They may hallucinate. A hallucination is an imagined sight, sound, or feeling.

4. *By causing dependence.* The body builds up tolerance to stimulants very quickly. Some people who use stimulants increase their doses rapidly and become physically dependent. This can occur after using stimulants only one time.

5. *By increasing the risk of becoming infected with HIV and hepatitis B.* People infected with HIV or hepatitis B may leave infected blood on a needle after injecting themselves with stimulants. If the needle is used by other people, the infected blood can enter their bodies and infect them.

6. *By increasing the risk of accidents, violence, and crime.* Stimulants impair reasoning and judgment, often resulting in accidents. They increase feelings of anger and aggressiveness and can lead to violence. Selling and buying cocaine and other stimulants often is associated with gangs and violence. Laboratories that produce illegal stimulants may explode and emit toxic gases.

7. *By causing teeth grinding.* MDMA can cause the muscles in the jaws to clench. When this happens, users will grind their teeth. This can cause a wearing down of the enamel of the teeth and other oral problems.

Sedative-Hypnotics

Sedative-hypnotics are drugs that depress the central nervous system. A **sedative** is a drug that has a calming effect on a person's behavior. A **hypnotic** is a drug that produces drowsiness and sleep. Sedative-hypnotics include tranquilizers and sleeping pills. They are highly addictive and are illegal without a prescription.

TYPES OF SEDATIVE-HYPNOTICS

The two major types of sedative-hypnotics are barbiturates and benzodiazepines. A **barbiturate** is a type of sedative-hypnotic that used to be prescribed to help people sleep and to relieve tension, Today, physicians rarely prescribe barbiturates because they are very addictive and dangerous. **Benzodiazepines** are sedative-hypnotics that often are prescribed by physicians to treat anxiety. They are commonly known as tranquilizers. Benzodiazepines also are prescribed to relax muscles and as anticonvulsants. An **anticonvulsant** is a drug that is taken to prevent or relieve epileptic seizures. Benzodiazepines are dangerous unless used under medical supervision. An example is flunitrazepam, the "date rape drug." Sedative-hypnotics are also known as

- Roofies
- Barbs
- Bank bandits
- Ludes
- Reds
- Blockbusters

GHB (gamma hydroxybutyrate) is a central nervous system depressant that was banned by the FDA in 1990. GHB was originally sold in health food stores and marketed to body builders because of its supposed ability to release a growth hormone and stimulate muscle growth. It is easily manufactured, and kits for making it are advertised over the Internet. At low doses, GHB causes drowsiness, dizziness, nausea, and visual disturbances. At higher doses, unconsciousness, seizures, severe respiratory depression, and coma can occur. Several GHB-related deaths have occurred. GHB is primarily available in liquid form and is usually sold by the cupful. It is some-times used as a date-rape drug. A few drops of GHB slipped into a drink can render a victim un-conscious within twenty minutes. Victims have no memory of what happened while they were un-conscious, and the drug is difficult to trace, often leaving the body within twenty-four hours (Nor-denberg, 2000).

HEALTH CONSEQUENCES

The illegal use of sedative-hypnotics can harm health in the following ways:

1. *By causing immediate death.* Combining sedative-hypnotics with alcohol is extremely risky and can be fatal. Alcohol multiplies the depressive effects of sedative-hypnotics on the central nervous system. This combination of drugs slows respiration and can cause coma and death.
2. *By harming the body.* Sedative-hypnotics slow body functions. People who take sedative-hypnotics may have slurred speech, lack of coordination, clammy skin, dilated pupils, and an inability to stay awake.
3. *By harming the mind.* People who take seda-tive-hypnotics cannot use reasoning and judgment to make responsible decisions. They may be lazy and constantly tired. Some people who take sedative-hypnotics develop clinical depression.
4. *By causing dependence.* The use of barbitu-rates and benzodiazepines can lead to physi-cal dependence. People physically dependent on barbiturates or benzodiazepines have with-drawal if they stop taking the drug. With-drawal symptoms include anxiety, sweating, difficulty sleeping, restlessness, agitation, and muscle tremors. People who are physi-cally dependent can have seizures, hallucina-tions, and elevated blood pressure and heart rate. Withdrawal from sedative-hypnotics can be fatal.
5. *By increasing the risk of becoming infected with HIV and hepatitis B.* People who use sedative-hypnotics cannot make responsible decisions. They might have sex with a person infected with HIV or hepatitis B and become infected themselves.
6. *By increasing the risk of accidents, violence, and crime.* Sedative-hypnotics impair reason-ing and judgment, cause confusion, reduce muscular coordination, and slow reaction time. It is risky to use sedative-hypnotics when driving a car, riding a bicycle, or operat-

ing machinery. Sedative-hypnotics also cause feelings of anger and aggressiveness and can lead to violence. Selling and buying sedative-hypnotics is illegal.

Narcotics

Narcotics are drugs that slow down the central nervous system and relieve pain. They slow down body functions, such as breathing and heart rate. Narcotics often are prescribed by physicians as analgesics. An **analgesic** is a drug that relieves pain. Narcotics also are used to suppress coughs and control diarrhea. Narcotics should be used only with the supervision of a physician.

TYPES OF NARCOTICS

Some narcotics are made from opium and mor-phine. Opium is a white, milky fluid from the seedpod of the poppy plant. **Morphine** is a nar-cotic found naturally in opium that is used to con-trol pain. Morphine is one of the strongest pain relievers used in medicine. It can cause addiction and severe withdrawal symptoms. **Codeine** is a painkiller produced from morphine. **Heroin** is an illegal narcotic derived from morphine. It often is injected, snorted, smoked, and taken as a pill. People who inject heroin are at high risk for infec-tion with HIV and hepatitis B. **Black-tar heroin** is heroin produced in Mexico that is dark in color and sticky in texture. Heroin is also known as

- Smack
- Junk
- Horse
- Chiva

Many people have become addicted to narcotic painkillers. One of these is Oxycontin. **Oxycontin** is a narcotic drug that is prescribed for chronic or long-lasting pain. This medication's active ingre-dient is oxycodone, which is also found in drugs like Percodan and Tylox. Physicians often pre-scribe this drug for cancer patients or those with chronic, long-lasting back pain. It is prescribed as a timed-release tablet that provides about twelve hours of relief from chronic pain. Oxycontin abus-ers either crush or dilute the tablet before ingest-ing or injecting the drug. This eliminates the timed-release action of the Oxycontin and causes a quick, powerful high. The high from taking

Oxycontin in these ways is similar to the feeling that results from taking heroin. It also increases the risk of addiction (Center for Substance Abuse Treatment, 2001).

HEALTH CONSEQUENCES

The illegal use of narcotics can harm health in the following ways:

1. *By causing immediate death.* Narcotic drugs suppress the central nervous system. Large doses of narcotic drugs slow down breathing and can cause coma and even death.
2. *By harming the body.* People who use narcotics may experience euphoria, drowsiness, nausea, rapid heartbeat, and clammy skin. Large doses can induce sleep and may cause vomiting. Narcotics can be especially dangerous to people who have respiratory problems. Narcotics interfere with breathing and coughing. People allergic to narcotics may develop a skin rash.
3. *By harming the mind.* People who use narcotics cannot use reasoning and judgment to make responsible decisions. They may become depressed and lazy. Their emotions may change and they may have mood swings.
4. *By causing dependence.* Repeated use of narcotics results in increasing tolerance. This leads to physical dependence. People physically dependent on narcotics have withdrawal if they stop taking the drug. They may become deeply depressed, have mood swings, and be very sensitive to pain. Narcotics also cause psychological dependence. People who use narcotics become preoccupied with taking and obtaining the drug. They often lack energy and motivation and neglect themselves and their responsibilities. They may suffer from malnutrition, infection, illness, or injury. They may rob or steal to get narcotics.
5. *By increasing the risk of becoming infected with HIV and hepatitis B.* People who are infected with HIV or hepatitis B may leave blood on a needle after injecting themselves with narcotics. If the needle is used by other people, the infected blood may enter their bodies and infect them. Heroin and morphine are narcotics that usually are injected.
6. *By increasing the risk of accidents, violence, and crime.* People who use narcotics may fall in and out of sleep. This is called "nodding out." Nodding out can cause an accident if a person is driving a car, riding a bicycle, or operating machinery. When people who smoke nod out, they can suffer burns or start a fire.

Hallucinogens

Hallucinogens are drugs that interfere with the senses and cause hallucinations. A hallucination is an imagined sight, sound, or feeling. Hallucinogens also are called psychedelic drugs. The effects of hallucinogens may last for several hours or days.

TYPES OF HALLUCINOGENS

LSD is an illegal hallucinogen sold in the form of powder, tablets, liquid, or capsules. LSD also is taken in the form of blotter acid. **Blotter acid** is a small paper square that contains LSD. LSD causes the pupils to dilate, skin to become flushed, and heart rate and body temperature to increase. People who take LSD may have terrifying hallucinations known as a "bad trip." They often believe they are invincible. LSD is also known as

- Acid
- Trips
- Lucy
- Diamonds
- Microdots

PCP (angel dust) is a hallucinogen that can act as a stimulant, sedative-hypnotic, or painkiller. It is sold illegally in the form of liquid, powder, or pills and is swallowed, smoked, and sniffed. People who use PCP feel restless, disoriented, anxious, isolated, angry, aggressive, and invincible. Users may experience a feeling of being "out of the body" and detached from their environment. A PCP user may appear to be in a trance. PCP is also known as

- Angel dust
- Zombie
- Rocket fuel
- Hog

Ketamine is a hallucinogen that is used as an anesthetic drug in veterinary medicine. It is sold illegally in the form of liquid, powder, or pills. Most of the ketamine that is used illegally has been stolen from veterinarians' offices. Its effects are similar to those of PCP, but ketamine is less potent than PCP and its effects last for a shorter time. It is sometimes given to unsuspecting victims as a date-rape drug. Ketamine is also known as

- Special K
- Vitamin K
- K
- Cat valium
- Bump

Mescaline is an illegal hallucinogen made from the peyote cactus. **Psilocybin** and **psilocyn** are hallucinogenic substances contained in certain mushrooms. The hallucinogenic mushrooms are generally grown in Mexico and Central America. They are dried and can be eaten or brewed and consumed as tea. The effects of psilocybin and psilocin are similar to LSD and mescaline. Hallucinogenic mushrooms are also known as

- Magic mushrooms
- Shrooms
- Mushrooms

MDMA (discussed in the "Stimulants" section) is a stimulant that also acts a mild hallucinogen.

HEALTH CONSEQUENCES

The illegal use of hallucinogens can harm health in the following ways:

1. *By harming the body.* Hallucinogens cause vomiting, nausea, loss of muscle control, chills, sweating, stomach cramps, and an increase or decrease in heart rate, body temperature, blood sugar level, and blood pressure.
2. *By harming the mind.* Hallucinogens impair short-term memory and affect perception of time. People who take hallucinogens may believe something is real when it is not. They cannot control their emotions, may have mood swings, and may take unnecessary risks that can harm health. They also can have flashbacks. A **flashback** is a sudden hallucination a person has long after having used a drug.
3. *By causing dependence.* People who regularly use hallucinogens may develop tolerance. They then need to take more and more of the drug to get the same effects.
4. *By increasing the risk of accidents, violence, and crime.* Hallucinogens impair reasoning and judgment, slow reaction time, and a person's ability to judge distances. Some hallucinogens increase feelings of anger and aggressiveness and can lead to violence.

Marijuana

Marijuana is the dried leaves and tops of the cannabis plant, which contains THC. **THC** is a drug found in the cannabis plant that produces psychoactive effects. THC is a fat-soluble drug that settles and builds up in the fatty organs of the body, including the brain, heart, and liver. Marijuana usually is smoked or eaten. A marijuana cigarette is called a joint. The effects of smoking or eating marijuana depend on the amount of THC. In the past, marijuana contained 1 to 5 percent THC. Today's marijuana is much more potent. It usually contains 8 to 15 percent THC. Marijuana is also known as

- Chronic
- Reefer
- Ganja
- Mary Jane
- Pot
- Grass
- Weed

Hashish is a drug that is made from marijuana. It is smoked alone, mixed with tobacco, or eaten in cookies or candies. **Hashish oil** is the liquid resin from the cannabis plant. Hashish oil is placed on cigarettes or in hashish pipes and then smoked. Hashish and hashish oil are stronger than marijuana. Marijuana, hashish, and hashish oil are considered gateway drugs. A gateway drug is a drug whose use increases the likelihood that a person will use other harmful drugs.

HEALTH CONSEQUENCES

The illegal use of marijuana can harm health in the following ways:

1. *By harming the body.* People who use marijuana feel relaxed, euphoric, and drowsy, and have an increased appetite. Eating marijuana brownies can cause nausea and vomiting. Smoking marijuana damages the lungs and respiratory system. Marijuana smoke contains many of the same carcinogens as tobacco smoke. Long-term use of marijuana can affect the reproductive system. Marijuana use by a pregnant female may harm the developing baby.
2. *By harming the mind.* Marijuana causes short-term memory loss and impairs concentration. People who smoke marijuana of-

ten lose their train of thought. They may say and do things they later regret. They may take unnecessary risks that harm health. Marijuana causes amotivational syndrome. **Amotivational syndrome** is a persistent loss of ambition and motivation. Marijuana can cause drowsiness and sleep and loss of interest in daily activities, such as school and work. People who use marijuana might not pursue goals or maintain a nice appearance. People who use marijuana can have flashbacks weeks or months after using it, similar to the flashbacks experienced by people who have used hallucinogens.

3. *By causing dependence.* People who use marijuana develop tolerance after high doses and long-term use. They can also develop psychological dependence. They become preoccupied with using and obtaining marijuana. They may feel they have to use marijuana to enjoy other activities. It is not clear whether marijuana causes physical dependence and withdrawal symptoms.

4. *By increasing the risk of becoming infected with HIV and hepatitis B.* People who use marijuana cannot make responsible decisions. A person who has smoked marijuana may have sex with a person who is infected with HIV or hepatitis B and become infected.

5. *By increasing the risk of accidents, violence, and crime.* Marijuana impairs a person's ability to judge distances and slows a person's reaction time. A person under the influence of marijuana is more likely to cause a motor vehicle accident or have an accident operating machinery.

According to the publication *What Americans Need to Know About Marijuana* (Office of National Drug Control Policy, 2003), marijuana is the most widely used illicit drug. Further, this report states that despite the fact that many people might believe that marijuana is helpful as a medicine, current research has not demonstrated this to be the case.

Anabolic-Androgenic Steroids

Steroids are drugs that are related to hormones. One type of steroid is an anabolic-androgenic steroid. An **anabolic-androgenic steroid** is a steroid that is related to male sex hormones.

These steroids promote the growth of skeletal muscles (anabolic effects), the development of male sexual characteristics (androgenic effects), and also cause some other effects. Many people refer to anabolic-androgenic steroids as steroids. Steroids are injected or taken by mouth. Their effects include deepening of the voice, growth of facial and body hair, increase in muscle size, and increase in aggressiveness. Physicians prescribe anabolic-androgenic steroids to treat certain medical conditions. Using anabolic-androgenic steroids without the supervision of a physician is illegal. Steroids are taken to improve athletic performance and strength. The use of steroids is banned in most sports. Many people use steroids to build muscles and improve their appearance.

Corticosteroids are drugs that are similar to cortisol. **Cortisol** is a natural hormone produced by the adrenal glands. Corticosteroids are used to treat allergic conditions, arthritis, multiple sclerosis, and other diseases. They cause many side effects, including weight increase, mood swings, and headaches.

STEROID SUPPLEMENTS

Dehydroepian-drosterone (DHEA) and androstenedione ("andro") can be purchased legally without a prescription through many commercial sources, including health food stores. They are often referred to as dietary supplements, although they are not food products. These substances, known as steroidal supplements, can be converted into testosterone (an important male sex hormone) or a similar compound in the body. Whether such conversion produces sufficient quantities of testosterone to promote muscle growth or whether the supplements themselves promote muscle growth is unknown. Medical experts are concerned about the side effects of steroidal supplements. If large quantities of these compounds substantially increase testosterone levels in the body, they also are likely to produce the same side effects as anabolic steroids. As a result, individuals should understand that there are risks for serious side effects and should not take supplements with "andro."

In 2004, the Food and Drug Administration (FDA) sent letters to several companies asking them to stop distributing products sold as dietary supplements that contain androstenedione warning them that they could face enforcement penalties if they do not take appropriate actions. The FDA has concluded that there is inadequate information to establish that a dietary supplement containing androstenedione can reasonably be expected to be safe. The FDA is also encouraging Congress to consider legislation to classify these products as controlled substances.

HEALTH CONSEQUENCES

The illegal use of steroids can harm health in the following ways:

1. *By harming the body.* Many young people believe that steroids only improve a person's appearance. However, steroids cause acne, oily skin, rashes, purple and red spots, and bad breath. Steroids increase the risk of heart disease and stroke. Steroids cause fluid to build up in the body, which leads to high blood pressure. Steroids also lower the level of high-density lipoproteins (HDLs) in the blood. This increases the risk of heart disease and stroke. Steroids harm the reproductive system. In males, using steroids causes reduced sperm count, sterility, baldness, painful urination, swelling of the prostate gland, and shrinking of the testicles. Males who use steroids may also develop large breasts. In females, using steroids causes missed menstrual periods, shrinking of the uterus, hair growth on the face and body, and a deepened voice. The breasts of females who use steroids may become smaller. Steroid use is particularly risky for teens because they are still growing. Using steroids may cause bone growth to stop. A teen who uses steroids may end up with large muscles but permanently stunted growth. People who use steroids often injure their tendons because their muscles grow but their tendons do not become stronger.

2. *By harming the mind.* Using steroids often causes severe emotional changes. People who use steroids may become angry and aggressive, and have roid rages that result in violence. **Roid rage** is an outburst of anger and hostility caused by using steroids.

3. *By causing dependence.* People who regularly use steroids may develop physical or psychological dependence. When they stop using steroids, they become very depressed, anxious, and restless. They may be tired, have frequent headaches, feel nauseous, and become sick. If they start using steroids again, these symptoms disappear.

4. *By increasing the risk of becoming infected with HIV and hepatitis B.* People who are infected with HIV or hepatitis B may leave blood on a needle after injecting themselves with steroids. If another person uses the needle, the infected blood may enter this person's body and the person becomes infected.

5. *By increasing the risk of accidents, violence, and crime.* People who use steroids may have roid rages that result in violence. Many people illegally buy and sell steroids. They are breaking the law and can spend time in jail.

Inhalants

Inhalants are chemicals that affect mood and behavior when inhaled. Nonmedical inhalants are not controlled drugs. Most inhalants are chemicals that are not produced to be inhaled or used as drugs. Inhalants often are the first drug a young person uses because they are easily accessible. Inhalants produce a very quick high because they are inhaled. However, the high usually lasts only a few minutes. There are several ways to use inhalants. **Huffing,** or **sniffing,** is inhaling fumes to get high. **Bagging** is inhaling fumes from a bag to get high. Inhalants also are

inhaled from balloons, aerosol cans, and other containers.

TYPES OF INHALANTS

Many kinds of substances are used as inhalants. The following are just some of them:

- Amyl nitrite and butyl nitrite
- Fingernail polish remover
- Furniture polish
- Gasoline
- Glue
- Hairspray
- Laughing gas (nitrous oxide)
- Lighter fluid
- Liquid wax
- Marker fluid
- Paint thinner
- Paper correction fluid
- Rubber cement
- Shoe polish
- Spray paint
- Transmission fluid

HEALTH CONSEQUENCES

The use of nonmedical inhalants can harm health in the following ways:

1. *By causing immediate death.* Inhalants can cause heart failure and instant death. They also cause the central nervous system to slow down. This interferes with breathing and may cause suffocation. People who use inhalants may become unconscious and have seizures. They could choke on their own vomit if they get sick.
2. *By harming the body.* People who use inhalants may experience euphoria, nausea, vomiting, headache, dizziness, and uncontrollable laughter. Inhalants reduce the flow of oxygen to the brain and can cause permanent brain damage. People who use inhalants may have an irregular heartbeat, difficulty breathing, and headaches. Inhalants damage the immune system, heart, kidneys, blood, and bone marrow. Some inhalants can cause leukemia and lead poisoning.
3. *By harming the mind.* People who use inhalants cannot make responsible decisions because reasoning and judgment are impaired. They can have hallucinations that may cause them to harm themselves or others.
4. *By causing dependence.* People who use inhalants can develop psychological or physical

dependence. They need to take more and more of the inhalant to get the desired effects.
5. *By increasing the risk of accidents, violence, and crime.* Inhalants impair reasoning and judgment. They also affect vision, coordination, and reaction time. Inhalants can cause disorientation and confusion. People who use inhalants do not have the mental functioning needed to drive and make responsible decisions.

Health Goal #55

I Will Avoid Risk Factors and Practice Protective Factors for Drug Misuse and Abuse

---

Risk Factors

Research has identified risk factors that increase a young person's risk of drug misuse and abuse (Figure 10-1). A **risk factor** is something that increases the likelihood of a negative outcome. Certain risk factors put some teens more at risk than others for harmful drug use. Some of these risk factors involve a young person's behavior or the environment in which the teen lives. Young people with risk factors are at risk for using harmful drugs and need to recognize this risk. Young people have varying degrees of control over their risk factors for drug misuse and abuse. For example, a young person does not have control over living in a neighborhood in which drugs are easy to buy, but she does have control over her choice of friends. Risk factors refer to only the statistical likelihood that a young person might use harmful drugs. Having certain risk factors for drug use does not mean that a young person has an excuse to use harmful drugs. A person always has control. Figure 10-1 presents thirteen risk factors for drug use.

WARNING SIGNS OF DRUG USE

Any of the following warning signs might indicate drug use in young people:

- Slurred speech
- Reddened eyes and use of eyedrops

FIGURE 10-1

Risk Factors That Make Young People Vulnerable to Drug Use

1. *Lacking self-respect.* Young people who lack self-respect believe they are unworthy of love and respect. They are at risk because they believe drugs will numb the negative feelings they have about themselves. They may not have enough confidence to say "no" to negative peer pressure.

2. *Being unable to express emotions in healthful ways.* Young people who have difficulty expressing emotions are more likely than other teens to use harmful drugs. Young people who cannot cope with stress, anger, and depression may think that drugs will help numb these feelings. They may use drugs instead of expressing their feelings honestly.

3. *Having friends who use drugs.* One of the strongest risk factors for drug use is having friends who use drugs. Drug users tend to pressure others to use drugs with them. They want others to support their unsafe and illegal habits. They might continue to pressure a person who has said "no."

4. *Being unable to delay gratification.* **Delayed gratification** is voluntarily postponing an immediate reward in order to complete a task before enjoying a reward. Drug use is a form of instant gratification—choosing an immediate reward regardless of potential harmful effects. Immediate pleasure is more important to people who use drugs than maintaining good health and staying safe.

5. *Having access to drugs.* The temptation to use drugs is greater when drugs are easily available. Having access to drugs includes living in a neighborhood where drugs are sold, going to a school where people sell drugs, and knowing people who sell drugs.

6. *Being rejected by peers.* Young people who feel rejected by peers may use drugs to try to numb feelings of loneliness or to fit in. They often are not interested in another young person's personality. They are friends with anyone who can supply them with drugs or will use drugs with them.

7. *Having a biological family member who is drug dependent.* Certain individuals may inherit a genetic predisposition to drug abuse. A **genetic predisposition** is the inheritance of genes that increase the likelihood of developing a condition. Children born to parents who have alcoholism are more likely to have alcoholism than children born to nonalcoholic parents.

8. *Having difficult family relationships.* Children who live in families that do not manage conflict healthfully often have difficult family relationships. These children have an increased risk of drug use. They might not follow family guidelines. They may not have a responsible adult with whom they can share feelings. Difficult family relationships often create a stressful atmosphere. These children may turn to drugs to cope with stress and numb their feelings.

9. *Having role models who use drugs.* A role model may be someone a teen knows, such as a friend or family member: Or a role model may be a celebrity, such as a sport star or entertainer. Some teens have role models who use drugs and act like it is sexy, macho, or cool. Young people who admire role models who use drugs may use drugs to be like their role models.

10. *Using drugs early in life.* Drug use during early childhood and adolescence is a risk factor for harmful drug use. Young people who begin drug use at an early age are more likely to become drug dependent when they are adults.

11. *Doing poorly in school or having a learning disability.* Young people who get poor grades in school are more at risk for drug use than their peers who have better grades. Children and adolescents who have learning disabilities are at special risk. They may become frustrated and feel inadequate if they compare themselves to peers who do not have learning disabilities. They may use drugs to numb these feelings.

12. *Being uninvolved in school activities and athletics.* Children and teens who do not participate in school activities and athletics are more likely to use harmful drugs. They are more likely to be bored and to have more time to spend using drugs.

13. *Lacking respect for authority and laws.* Teens who lack respect for authority and laws are more at risk for drug use. They disregard the guidelines of parents or guardians and other responsible adults. They disregard community laws and may not care that using drugs is against the law.

- Glassy eyes and a blank stare
- A sloppy appearance
- Use of breath fresheners
- A long-term runny nose and sniffling
- Having friends who use drugs
- Giving up friends who do not use drugs
- Joining a gang
- Skipping school
- Poor school performance
- Missing money or objects of value
- Changing eating habits
- Mood swings and hostility
- A lack of energy and motivation

Protective Factors

A **protective factor** is something that increases the likelihood of a positive outcome. A protective factor is a shield that helps a young person resist the temptation to use drugs and behave in other harmful ways. The more protective factors a young person practices, the lower the risk that the youth will abuse drugs. Figure 10-2 lists thirteen protective factors that reduce the risk of drug use.

Health Goal #56

I Will Not Misuse or Abuse Drugs

Risks of Using Drugs

There are many risks involved in using drugs such as alcohol, marijuana, cocaine, and methamphetamine. Even experimenting with a drug "just once" can have consequences.

1. *Using drugs can lead to overdose.* People who use drugs can overdose on them. To overdose is to take an excessive amount. A drug overdose can cause serious injury or death. Both people who have taken a drug for a long time and those who take a drug for the first time can overdose. An overdose often is the result of taking more than one drug at a time. Drugs have different effects on people; two people might take the same amount of a drug, and one might feel few effects whereas the other might overdose.

2. *Using drugs can cause accidents.* Drugs slow reaction time, impair coordination, and impair judgment. People under the influence of drugs often think they can perform tasks they cannot, such as drive safely. Most deaths caused by motor vehicle accidents involve a person under the influence of alcohol. Many people under the influence of drugs are struck by motor vehicles as well.

3. *Using drugs increases the risk of HIV infection, sexually transmitted diseases (STDs), and unwanted pregnancy.* Drugs affect people's ability to make responsible decisions. Some drugs intensify sexual feelings. Teens who have been sexually active often were under the influence of drugs. This increases the likelihood of unwanted pregnancy and of having sex with a person infected with HIV or another STD. People who share needles to inject drugs are at risk for infection with HIV and hepatitis B.

4. *Using drugs can harm relationships.* People who use drugs often harm relationships with friends and family members. They might say and do things when under the influence of drugs that later they regret. They might think that what they are saying or doing is appropriate even though it is not. This can cause misunderstandings and conflict.

FIGURE 10-2

Protective Factors That Serve as a Coat of Armor and Promote Resiliency

1. *Having self-respect.* Young people who have self-respect feel confident about themselves. They want to take care of their health and to stay safe. They know that using drugs harms health. Young people who have self-respect make responsible decisions. They are less likely to give in to negative peer pressure than other young children and adolescents.

2. *Practicing resistance skills.* Young people who practice resistance skills do not give in to pressure to use drugs. They are able to say "no." They stand up to peers who want them to use drugs. They know that peers who pressure them are not concerned for their health and safety.

3. *Having friends who do not misuse and abuse drugs.* Young people who have friends who are drug-free have less temptation than other teens to experiment with drugs. Drug-free friends do not pressure others to use drugs. They encourage others to participate in drug-free activities.

4. *Being able to delay gratification.* When young people are able to delay gratification, they use self-control. They recognize that using drugs interferes with their long-term goals. They know that using drugs in an attempt to "feel good now" will have negative consequences later.

5. *Being resilient, even when living in an adverse environment.* An **adverse environment** is an environment that interferes with a person's growth, development, and success. Children and adolescents may be exposed to drugs in their neighborhood, school, or home. A young person might have a parent or guardian who is drug dependent. However, a young person who is resilient knows that drugs only lead to more problems. Young people who live in an adverse environment can be resilient if they recognize that they can control their own behavior and decisions.

6. *Having social skills.* Using social skills reduces the risk of harmful drug use. Those who lack social skills often have difficulty relating to others and may feel rejected by peers. Having social skills helps children and teens make and keep friends. They develop close bonds with others and have a sense of belonging.

7. *Having a set of goals and plans to reach them.* Young people who have goals are more likely to evaluate the consequences of their actions. They recognize that drug use will interfere with their goals and that using drugs now may affect their entire future.

8. *Having healthful family relationships.* Young people who are close to family members are less likely than other teens to use harmful drugs. Having a supportive relationship with parents or guardians is especially important. It motivates young people to behave in responsible ways. Following family guidelines and remaining drug-free helps to keep the respect and trust of one's family. A young person who does not have a supportive adult family member can find a mentor. A **mentor** is a responsible person who guides another person. A mentor encourages a young person to stay drug-free.

9. *Having a positive role model.* Children and adolescents often choose to copy the behavior of their role models. Having a role model who does not use drugs shows young people they can be successful and worthy of admiration without using drugs.

10. *Having stress management skills.* Young people who are able to manage stress in healthful ways do not use drugs to cope with stress. They recognize that using drugs can cause more stress.

11. *Having anger management skills.* Young people who are able to manage anger in healthful ways do not use drugs to cope with anger. They recognize that drugs might make them violent and lose control.

12. *Being involved in school activities and athletics.* Young people who are involved in school activities and play on athletic teams are less likely than other teens to use harmful drugs. School activities and athletics take time. Participating in such activities leaves teens with less free time. These teens are less likely to be bored. Schools usually have eligibility requirements for participation in school activities. For example, young people who use drugs often are ineligible to participate in school activities. Teens who enjoy these activities do not want to lose the privilege of participation.

13. *Having respect for authority and laws.* Young people who have respect for authority and laws are less likely to use harmful drugs. They follow guidelines of parents or guardians and other responsible adults. They respect the laws of the community and know that drug use is against the law.

5. *Using drugs can prevent people from developing social skills.* People who are uncomfortable in a social situation might use drugs to relax. They rely on drugs to get through social situations. They will not develop the social skills needed for healthful relationships.

6. *Using drugs can lead to violence and illegal behaviors.* Drugs change the way people think and act. People who use drugs often become angry and aggressive and may harm other people. Most homicides, suicides, and episodes of abuse occur when people are using drugs. People who have been using drugs also are more likely to be involved in illegal behaviors such as damaging property and shoplifting.

7. *Using drugs can lead to drug dependence.* Many drugs stimulate the pleasure center of the brain. The pleasure center of the brain is the part of the brain that contains specialized nerve cells that release dopamine. **Dopamine** is a chemical that triggers feelings of pleasure. Certain drugs activate the release of dopamine. This is the major reason why people repeatedly use drugs and become drug dependent.

Drug Dependence

Drug dependence is the continued use of a drug even though it harms the body, mind, and relationships. *Chemical dependence, chemical addiction,* and *drug addiction* are other terms for drug dependence. Drug dependence impairs judgment and common sense. Drugs become more important to the user than school, work, family, and relationships. People who are drug dependent often try to quit using drugs, but they usually are not successful. People who use drugs may become physically and psychologically dependent on them.

PHYSICAL DEPENDENCE

Physical dependence is a condition in which a person develops tolerance to a drug and taking the drug becomes necessary to prevent withdrawal symptoms. **Tolerance** is a condition in which the body becomes accustomed to a substance. People with a high tolerance to a drug need a greater amount of the drug to produce the same effect as people with a low tolerance would get from a smaller amount of the drug. For example, people may feel certain effects from drinking their first can of beer. After a few weeks of drinking one beer, they may need to drink two cans of beer to achieve the same effect. Later on, they may need three cans of beer.

Withdrawal symptoms are unpleasant reactions that occur when a person who is physically dependent on a drug no longer takes it. Withdrawal symptoms include chills, muscular twitching, fever, nausea, vomiting, and cramps. People who are physically dependent on a drug must continue taking the drug to avoid withdrawal symptoms.

PSYCHOLOGICAL DEPENDENCE

Psychological dependence is a strong desire to continue using a drug for emotional reasons. People with psychological dependence may or may not be physically dependent. Psychological dependence sometimes is described as a strong craving for drugs. For example, the pleasurable feelings that a drug produces may be desired again and again, or people may rely on a particular drug that they believe helps reduce stress or anxiety. If they stop taking the drug for a short time, they crave the drug but do not go through physical withdrawal. Psychological dependence can become so severe that people become obsessed with the drug and may center their life around buying and taking it.

SYMPTOMS OF DRUG DEPENDENCE

According to the *Diagnostic and Statistical Manual of Mental Disorders* (American Psychiatric Association, 2000), people are drug dependent if they have had three or more of the following symptoms in the past year:

1. Developing tolerance to a drug
2. Experiencing withdrawal symptoms when stopping the use of a drug
3. Taking large amounts of a drug or taking a drug for a long period of time
4. Trying to quit taking a drug with no success
5. Spending lots of time obtaining a drug, using a drug, or recovering from the effects of drug use
6. Giving up important activities, such as work or school, because of drug use
7. Continuing to use a drug even though it is causing problems, such as physical illness or injury

PROGRESSION TO DRUG DEPENDENCE

The path to drug dependence begins with experimentation with a drug or drugs. People may be tempted to experiment with drugs because they do not want to feel left out when friends are using a drug, they are curious about a drug's effects, or they enjoyed the feeling they got when they first tried the drug. This is likely to lead to using the drug again and again. Tolerance may develop, so that the drug no longer has the same pleasurable effects. Users may suffer from withdrawal symptoms when they stop using the drug. Such a person is likely in denial, not admitting that drug use is causing any problems. She probably claims that she can stop using the drug at any time. Problems in her life intensify, and she does things that she later regrets. She has become drug dependent. She might decide to quit using the drug, but she cannot stick with the decision.

Unhealthy Responses to a Family Member's Addiction

The behavior of people who are drug dependent profoundly affects family members. A **codependent** is a person who wants to rescue and control another person. Family members who are codependent may respond to a drug-dependent person by playing one of the following roles: chief enabler, family hero, scapegoat, lost child, or mascot. However, it is important to realize that many respond in healthy ways.

CHIEF ENABLER

An **enabler** is a person who supports the harmful behavior of others. People who are drug dependent may have several family members and friends who are enablers. There usually is a chief enabler. The **chief enabler** is the family member who tries to smooth over the problems caused by the drug-dependent person. This person tries to make things appear normal to people outside the family. The chief enabler most often is the spouse of the drug-dependent person.

FAMILY HERO

The **family hero** is a family member who tries to do everything right. Family members know they can count on this person to be successful, reliable, and responsible. When a parent or guardian is drug dependent, the family hero often is the oldest child. The family hero also may be a younger sibling of a drug-dependent child. The family hero often takes care of housekeeping responsibilities and parents younger children. The family hero might believe that if she were a better child, the parent or guardian would stop using drugs.

SCAPEGOAT

The **scapegoat** is a child who is blamed as the cause of problems in the family. For example, a person who has been drinking might say to family members, "I wouldn't have had to drink if he didn't get into trouble at school." The blaming takes attention away from the drug-dependent parent or guardian. Scapegoats are labeled as not being able to do anything right. They often become rebellious and use drugs. They have little self-respect and feel resentment and anger toward other family members.

LOST CHILD

The **lost child** is a child who helps the family maintain balance by not causing problems or getting in the way. This child requires little attention in the family. The lost child avoids conflict, withdraws from others, and is shy or quiet. The lost child is not disruptive and will not demand any attention.

MASCOT

The **mascot** is a family member who relieves tension by acting in a funny or entertaining way. For example, a mascot will tell jokes or attempt to be cute. Family members feel better because this person makes them laugh and feel good. The mascot usually is one of the younger children in the family. A mascot has a hard time growing out of this role as an adult. The mascot feels lonely, insecure, and inadequate.

Health Goal #57

I Will Use Resistance Skills if Pressured to Misuse or Abuse Drugs

Peer Pressure to Use Drugs

Peer pressure is influence that people of similar age or status place on others to behave in a certain way. Peer pressure can be negative or positive. For example, peers might pressure other young people to do well in school. This pressure is positive. **Positive peer pressure** is influence from peers to behave in a responsible way. Positive peer pressure helps a person maintain self-respect and good character. If peers pressure a young person to use drugs, their influence is negative. **Negative peer pressure** is influence from peers to behave in a way that is not responsible.

Young people who use drugs sometimes pressure their peers to use drugs. They do this because they want support for their wrong behavior. They think that if others are using drugs with them, their behavior is not wrong. Also, if they get caught, they won't be the only ones in trouble. Young people who use drugs are uncomfortable when their peers stand up to their pressure. They do not like being reminded that drug use is harmful, unsafe, and illegal.

Some young people who use drugs pressure their peers to use drugs because they want them to embarrass themselves. Some young people who use drugs get their peers to use drugs without knowing it. They might slip a drug into peers' glasses when they are not looking. Young people who use drugs do not care about the consequences or consider the harmful effects the drug may have. They are not concerned that their behavior is disrespectful and illegal.

Some young people who use drugs pressure their peers to use drugs because they know drugs impair judgment. For example, suppose that a teen male wants a teen female to have sex with him and that she says "no" when she is sober. The male knows that she is more likely to agree to have sex with him after drinking alcohol. He might get her to drink so much that she does not know what she is doing. He has sex with her without her consent. He does not realize or care that having sex with someone who does not give consent is rape.

Young drug users might use statements like the following to try to get their peers to use drugs:

- "You're not afraid, are you?"
- "Everybody is doing it."
- "Don't mess up the fun for everyone else."
- "Don't be a nerd."
- "Nobody will know but me and you."
- "It can't hurt just this one time."
- "If you won't do it, don't bother to come."
- "It really is safe."
- "Don't worry, we've been doing this for a long time."
- "It will be fun."
- "You will feel better than you ever have before."

Resisting Pressure to Use Drugs

Following are some of the reasons not to use drugs, which a young person can think or say out loud when pressured to use drugs:

- I don't want to betray the trust of my parents or guardian.
- I don't want to break the law and get arrested.
- I don't want to become violent and harm others.
- I don't want to say something I will regret later.
- I don't want to experience blackouts.
- I don't want to hallucinate.
- I don't want to become depressed and consider suicide.
- I don't want to spend time in jail.
- I don't want to become addicted.
- I don't want to risk overdosing.
- I don't want to increase my risk of developing cirrhosis of the liver, cancer, or cardiorespiratory diseases.
- I don't want to be suspended from school.
- I don't want to get kicked off my athletic team.
- I don't want to waste money.
- I want to think clearly.
- I want to stay in control and stick to my decision to choose abstinence.
- I want others to respect me.
- I want to be a role model for my younger siblings.
- I want to have social skills without relying on drugs.
- I want to be able to react quickly to prevent accidents.

SHOWING CHARACTER

It takes character to resist peer pressure to use drugs. **Character** is a person's use of self-control to act on responsible values. To maintain respect, a person needs to have good character. It is also important to choose friends who have good character. Throughout life, people must sharpen their skills in noticing the difference between people who have good character and those who do not have good character. It is important to always remember that people who do not have good character can bring other people down. They can influence others in ways that cause a person to lose self-respect.

Using Resistance Skills

Some young people have a difficult time resisting peer pressure. They lack self-confidence. They may plan to say "no," but they give in when they are pressured. Negative peer pressure takes many forms. Sometimes it is direct. Young people who use drugs make persuasive statements. Sometimes it is indirect. Young people might not be pressured directly but might still choose to go along with the crowd.

Most young people face peer pressure to smoke cigarettes, chew tobacco, drink alcohol, sniff inhalants, smoke marijuana, use cocaine, or take other drugs. It is important for them to always resist the pressure to use drugs. Resistance skills are skills that help a person say "no" to an action or to leave a situation. The following are guidelines for young people to use resistance skills when pressured to use drugs:

1. *Saying "no" to drug use with self-confidence.*
   - Look directly at the person to whom you are speaking.
   - Say "no" in a firm voice.
   - Be confident because you are being responsible.
   - Be proud because you are obeying laws and respecting family guidelines.
2. *Giving reasons for saying "no" to drug use.*
   - Explain that drug use is harmful, unsafe, and illegal.
3. *Using the broken-record technique.*
   - Repeat the same response several times to convince the person pressuring you that you will not change your mind.
4. *Using nonverbal behavior to match verbal behavior. What a person does and says should be consistent.*
   - Do not pretend to use a drug.
   - Do not pretend to sip a beer.
   - Do not hold or pass a cigarette or marijuana joint.
   - Do not touch a syringe or needle used to inject drugs.
   - Do not agree to buy a drug for someone else.
   - Do not do or say anything that indicates that you approve of harmful drug use.
   - Do not keep drugs for someone else.
5. *Avoiding being in situations in which there will be pressure to use harmful drugs.*
   - Think ahead about what peers will be doing when they invite you to join them.
   - Ask if there will be drug use before you put yourself in a situation.
   - Do not go anywhere you know there will be drug use.
   - Attend only drug-free activities.
6. *Avoiding being with people who use drugs.*
   - Choose friends who do not use drugs.
   - Stay away from people who use or sell drugs.
7. *Resisting pressure to engage in illegal behavior.*
   - Learn the laws that apply to drug use in your community and state.
   - Do not break drug use laws.
   - Stay away from people who break laws pertaining to drug use.
   - Stay away from areas where people use and sell drugs.
8. *Influencing others to choose responsible behavior.*
   - Suggest drug-free activities.
   - Encourage those who pressure you to use drugs to change their behavior.
   - Be aware of places where teens who use drugs can get help.

Drug Use Is Never an Excuse for Wrong Behavior

Some people use alcohol and other drugs as an excuse for something they say or do. A teen who has been drinking and does something embarrassing might think he can laugh it off. He thinks that what he did will not affect his reputation, because he was drinking. Or suppose a teen uses drugs and then has sex. Later, the teen says, "I only had sex with the person because I was on drugs and couldn't help it." Or suppose a teen takes drugs and then does something illegal. Being high is not a defense for breaking the law. This is faulty thinking. People are responsible for what they say and do at all times, even when they are drunk or have been taking other drugs.

Being a Drug-Free Role Model

A **drug-free role model** is a person who chooses a drug-free lifestyle, knows and follows laws and policies regarding drugs, and educates others about the risks of using drugs. Adults should help young people choose a drug-free lifestyle. A **drug-free lifestyle** is a lifestyle in which a person does not misuse or abuse drugs. People who choose a drug-free lifestyle have more control over their lives. They take responsibility for their behavior and decisions. They do not risk their health and safety or the health and safety of others. They follow laws and respect the guidelines of parents or guardians and other responsible adults. They know and follow policies regarding drug use. They know and follow the laws and school policies regarding legal and illegal drugs and drug use. They encourage others to follow these policies and educate others about the risks of drug use. Most schools or communities have a drug prevention program for which young people might volunteer. Some peer programs offer special training to become a peer leader or counselor. A **peer leader** is an older student who teaches younger students about drugs and how to resist pressure to use them.

Health Goal #58

I Will Choose a Drug-Free Lifestyle to Reduce the Risk of HIV Infection and Unwanted Pregnancy

---

A Drug-Free Lifestyle

A drug-free lifestyle is a lifestyle in which a person does not misuse or abuse drugs. People who choose a drug-free lifestyle protect themselves from the harmful effects of drugs. There are other ways a drug-free lifestyle protects health: People with this lifestyle stay in control of their reasoning and judgment and avoid risky behaviors, lowering their risk of HIV infection and unintended pregnancy.

Reducing the Risk of HIV Infection and Unwanted Pregnancy

Human immunodeficiency virus (HIV) is a pathogen that destroys infection-fighting T cells in the body. People who are infected with HIV can develop AIDS. **Acquired immunodeficiency syndrome (AIDS)** is a condition that results in a breakdown of the body's ability to fight infection.

Teenagers who use drugs are four times more likely to have an unwanted pregnancy than teens who do not use drugs. Two people are involved in creating every unwanted teen pregnancy—a male and a female. For this reason, teen males as well as teen females must examine why unwanted pregnancies occur.

There are important reasons why teens who use drugs increase their risk of HIV infection and unwanted pregnancy:

1. *People who use drugs may not stick to their decision to practice abstinence from sex.* People who drink alcohol or use marijuana or other drugs that impair reasoning and judgment do not think clearly. During drug use, they are not clear as to the consequences of their behavior. Many teens who have been sexually active were under the influence of alcohol during their first sexual experience. Remember, one sexual contact can cause HIV infection or unwanted pregnancy and change a person's life.

2. *Teens who use drugs are less likely to be in control of their sexual feelings.* To control sexual feelings, teens must set limits for expressing affection. However, these limits are easy to surpass when teens are under the influence of drugs. Drugs can intensify sexual feelings very quickly.

3. *Teens who use drugs are more likely to excuse their wrong sexual behavior by saying that they were under the influence of drugs at the time.* Some teens plan ahead to use drugs so they will have an excuse for wrong sexual behavior. For example, they may drink too much, have sex, and later say they would not have had sex if they had not been drinking. They do not think about other future consequences for their actions, such as unwanted pregnancy.

4. *People who are drug dependent might have sex as a way of getting drugs.* People who are drug dependent have a compelling need for drugs. If they don't have the money to support their drug habit, they might engage in prostitution to get money to buy drugs. Prostitution is sexual activity for pay. Some people who are drug dependent exchange sex for drugs. Prostitution and the exchange of sex

for drugs is illegal and increases the risk of HIV infection.

5. *People who are involved in injection drug use might share a needle with infected blood on it.* When people inject drugs, the needle or syringe they use will have droplets of their blood on it. If the needle or syringe has been previously used by a person infected with HIV, a person who uses that same needle or syringe to inject drugs will also be injecting droplets of blood infected with HIV. Injection drug use is illegal and increases the risk of HIV infection.

6. *Teens who use drugs are more at risk for committing rape or being raped.* When teens use drugs, they are less likely to think about the consequences of their behaviors. Females under the influence of drugs may take risks they usually would not take. For example, they might spend time with a male of whom their parents or guardian do not approve. They might agree to go to a party where there are no adults. They might leave a party at night and walk home alone. They might drink too much, pass out, and not even know that they were raped when they were unconscious. Males under the influence of drugs can become more aggressive. Their judgment is impaired, and they might not respect their own or a female's sexual limits. Rape can result in HIV infection or unwanted pregnancy. Using drugs is never a defense for rape.

Health Goal #59

I Will Choose a Drug-Free Lifestyle to Reduce the Risk of Violence and Accidents

Risk of Violence

Drugs alter the way people think and feel, which affects the way they behave. Many drugs increase the risk that people will become violent. Drug trafficking also increases the risk of violence. Young people need to learn to protect themselves from the violence associated with drug trafficking.

ALCOHOL

Alcohol depresses the nervous system and changes mood and behavior. People who are angry, aggressive, or depressed experience even more intense feelings when they drink alcohol. They might act on these feelings and harm themselves or others. For example, most fights and assaults are associated with alcohol use. Most young people who attempt suicide have been drinking alcohol. Many young people who have been abused were abused by adults under the influence of alcohol. Most cases of homicide involve drinking.

STIMULANTS

Stimulants can cause people to become impulsive, paranoid, and irrational when they believe other people are going to harm them. As a result, they may begin fights in which they and others are harmed.

MARIJUANA AND HALLUCINOGENS

People who use marijuana or hallucinogens may experience hallucinations. They worry and feel threatened after having hallucinations. They may resort to violent actions.

PCP

People who use PCP can become very angry, aggressive, and irritable. They may have hallucinations and severe depression. They are difficult to control. They may harm people who try to control their actions.

ANABOLIC-ANDROGENIC STEROIDS

People who use anabolic-androgenic steroids have mood swings and outbursts of anger called "roid rages." During roid rages, they may harm others. Use of anabolic-androgenic steroids also is associated with severe depression. People who use these steroids are at risk for making suicide attempts.

SEDATIVE-HYPNOTICS

People who take high doses of sedative-hypnotics can become angry, aggressive, agitated, and violent.

DRUG TRAFFICKING

Drug trafficking is the illegal production, distribution, transportation, selling, or purchasing of drugs. All people who are involved in drug trafficking are criminals. Many people who are involved in drug trafficking belong to gangs. Drug trafficking is dangerous. Most people associated with drug trafficking own and use weapons to protect their territory, or turf, from their competitors. They may injure or murder people who are on their turf. Some of the people who are injured or murdered are their competitors or people who owe them money. Many drive-by shootings are related to drug trafficking. Law enforcement agents may also be injured or murdered as they try to put a stop to drug trafficking. Other people who are injured or murdered may be innocent victims who have been caught in the crossfire of a gang war.

Young people can protect themselves from violence associated with drug trafficking in the following ways:

1. *By not associating with anyone who produces, distributes, transports, sells, or purchases drugs.*
2. *By not associating with gang members or people who belong to a gang.*
3. *By staying away from people who own weapons.*
4. *By staying away from areas in which there is drug trafficking.*
5. *By staying away from gang turf.*
6. *By helping one's school enforce a safe and drug-free school zone.* A **safe and drug-free school zone** is a defined area around a school for the purpose of sheltering young people from the sale of drugs and use of weapons. There are increased penalties for using and selling drugs and having weapons in this zone.

Risk of Accidents

Drug use increases the risk of accidents, for a number of reasons. People who have been using drugs are not able to think clearly and use wise judgment. They may take risks that they normally would not take. They may engage in foolish behavior. For example, they may play driving games such as chicken or accept a dare to walk on a train track with a train coming. People who have been using drugs have a slower reaction time and have less coordination and balance. As a result, they do not respond quickly to prevent accidents. For example, when driving they might be unable to turn the wheel in time to avoid hitting another

motor vehicle. People who use drugs cannot judge the distance of an oncoming car. They might be hit by an oncoming vehicle because they are not able to hear the vehicle when they are walking.

Drug users have dulled senses. Their senses of hearing, smell, touch, and sight are not sharp. They may not respond quickly to sounds that warn them of danger. They may not smell smoke or fire. They may not experience hot, cold, or pain as they should. Their vision is blurry and their depth perception can be affected.

Health Goal #60

I Will Be Aware of Resources for the Treatment of Drug Misuse and Abuse

How Young People Can Help a Person Who Needs Intervention

Many young people know someone who misuses or abuses drugs. The person could be a family member, a close friend, or someone on a school team. Young people need to be trained to not participate in the drug-dependent person's denial. **Denial** is refusing to admit a problem. Most people who are drug dependent are in a state of denial. They do not admit that they are dependent on drugs. They do not recognize how their behavior is affecting other people. Because people who are drug dependent are in a state of denial, they do not seek treatment. Other people must intervene.

Following are four steps for a young person to take when they want to get help for someone who is misusing or abusing drugs:

1. *List the person's specific behaviors and signs of drug abuse.* Write out a detailed list that describes specific situations, dates, and behaviors.
2. *Share the list with a responsible adult.* The adult can review what you have written and decide on appropriate steps to take. If the adult with whom you share the list does not

respond, share the list with another responsible adult.

3. *Know that you have made a responsible decision by sharing the list with an adult.* Recognize that people who look the other way or make excuses for a person who abuses drugs are enablers. Feel proud that you have made a responsible decision.

4. *Follow the advice of the adult who takes action.* The adult may choose to contact a trained counselor or other health care professional. There may be a formal intervention.

Formal Intervention

A **formal intervention** is an action by people, such as family members, who want a person to get treatment. The goal is to help drug-dependent people recognize the effects of their drug misuse or abuse. A trained counselor guides people through the formal intervention process.

A formal intervention should be carefully planned with a trained counselor. The counselor usually holds a planning session before the intervention. The people who will be involved discuss the person's drug use and its consequences. The formal intervention is practiced and rehearsed. The trained counselor will make sure that a treatment program is selected ahead of time and that the appropriate arrangements are made.

During a formal intervention, family members, friends, and other significant people talk to the person who is drug dependent, describing the person's behavior and how it affects them. Specific situations in which the person's behavior caused negative consequences are discussed. The people involved in the intervention explain that they

want the person who is drug dependent to get treatment.

It is best for the drug-dependent person to enter treatment immediately after the formal intervention. A person who is drug dependent is likely to come up with excuses not to enter treatment, given time to think about it. Family members often have packed a suitcase and made plans to take the person to a treatment facility immediately following the formal intervention.

HONEST TALK

Family members, friends, and employers who use honest talk and I-messages often are successful at convincing a person who is drug dependent to agree to treatment. **Honest talk** is the straightforward sharing of feelings. An **I-message** is a statement that describes a specific behavior or event and how that behavior or event affected the speaker. People who are healthy recognize when other people are drug dependent. They use honest talk and I-messages to express their feelings. For example, a person might say the following:

- "I feel that I cannot trust you when you lie about your drug use, and this distresses me."
- "I cannot bring friends over because I don't know if you have been drinking; this makes me sad."
- "I cannot relax when you are out drinking with your friends because I worry that you might have an accident."

Treatment

People who are drug dependent need help to discontinue their drug use. It is important to make sure that people get the treatment approach that will work best for them. Treatment programs do not only focus on getting people off drugs. They also try to teach people to live more effectively than before. This helps prevent relapse. A **relapse** is a return to a previous behavior or condition.

DETOXIFICATION

Detoxification usually is the first stage of treatment programs. **Detoxification** is the process in which an addictive substance is withdrawn from the body. Detoxification often causes people to suffer withdrawal symptoms. **Withdrawal symptoms** are unpleasant reactions that occur when a person who is physically dependent on a drug no longer takes it. Physicians give some people in detoxification medications to ease their withdrawal symptoms.

INPATIENT CARE

Inpatient care is treatment that requires a person to stay overnight at a facility. The facility may be a hospital or drug treatment center. The main advantages of inpatient care are the medical supervision and the drug-free setting. Inpatient care may last from a few weeks to a year, but most inpatient drug treatment programs last for twenty-eight days.

OUTPATIENT CARE

Outpatient care is treatment that does not require a person to stay overnight at a facility. Outpatient care is offered by many hospitals and community treatment centers. People in outpatient drug treatment programs can work or attend school while recovering from drug dependence.

HALFWAY HOUSES

A **halfway house** is a live-in facility that helps a person who has been through drug treatment gradually adjust to living independently in the community. Halfway houses provide food, shelter, and drug treatment. They provide a supportive, drug-free environment for living. Halfway house residents often learn job skills and receive counseling about ways to live responsibly.

RECOVERY PROGRAMS

There are many recovery programs available for people who are drug dependent. In these programs, people recovering from drug dependence give one another feedback and support. Narcotics Anonymous is a recovery program that helps people deal with narcotics dependence. Cocaine Anonymous is a recovery program that helps people deal with cocaine abuse. There also are recovery programs for other drug dependencies.

SCHOOL RESOURCES

Many schools offer resources to help students with drug problems. A school may participate in a student assistance program. A **student assistance program** is a school-based program to help prevent and treat alcoholism and other drug dependencies. Some schools also have recovery groups for students.

PROGRAMS FOR PEOPLE AFFECTED BY OTHER PEOPLE'S DRUG DEPENDENCE

Treatment programs are available for people affected by other people's drug dependence. These programs often focus on helping people who are codependent and enablers. It is difficult for people to stop being codependent and enablers because they do not want to let the person who is drug dependent suffer the consequences of his or her drug use. People who are drug dependent may become angry when their codependents try to end their enabling behavior.

11
CHAPTER ELEVEN

Communicable and Chronic Diseases

HEALTH GOALS FOR COMMUNICABLE AND CHRONIC DISEASES

61. I will choose behaviors to reduce my risk of infection with communicable diseases.

62. I will be aware of immunizations that protect health.

63. I will choose behaviors to reduce my risk of infection with respiratory diseases.

64. I will recognize ways to manage asthma and allergies.

65. I will choose behaviors to reduce my risk of infection with sexually transmitted diseases.

66. I will choose behaviors to reduce my risk of HIV infection.

67. I will choose behaviors to reduce my risk of cardiovascular diseases.

68. I will choose behaviors to reduce my risk of diabetes.

69. I will recognize ways to manage chronic health conditions.

70. I will choose behaviors to reduce my risk of cancer.

Communicable and chronic diseases is the area of health that focuses on choosing behaviors to reduce risk of infection with communicable diseases, being aware of immunizations that protect health, choosing behaviors to reduce risk of infection with respiratory diseases, recognizing ways to manage asthma and allergies, choosing behaviors to reduce risk of infection with sexually transmitted diseases, choosing behaviors to reduce risk of HIV infection, choosing behaviors to reduce risk of cardiovascular diseases, choosing behaviors to reduce risk of diabetes, recognizing ways to manage chronic health conditions, and choosing behaviors to reduce risk of cancer. This chapter provides the health knowledge needed to teach young people important life skills for communicable and chronic diseases.

Health Goal #61

I Will Choose Behaviors to Reduce My Risk of Infection with Communicable Diseases

Communicable Diseases

A **communicable disease,** or **infectious disease,** is an illness caused by pathogens that can be spread from one living thing to another.

Fungi can live on the skin, mucous membranes, and lungs and cause disease in the process. Some diseases caused by fungi are athlete's foot, ringworm, jock itch, nail infections, and thrush.

PROTOZOA

Protozoa are tiny, single-celled organisms that produce toxins that cause disease. Malaria, African sleeping sickness, and dysentery are diseases caused by protozoa.

A **pathogen** is a germ that causes disease. For example, people develop the flu when pathogens that cause influenza enter their body. There are many types of pathogens that cause disease.

BACTERIA

Bacteria are single-celled microorganisms. There are more than a thousand types of bacteria. Most bacteria are beneficial, but close to a hundred types are known to cause disease. Bacteria cause disease by releasing toxins. A toxin is a poisonous substance. Some diseases caused by bacteria are syphilis, gonorrhea, strep throat, tuberculosis, tetanus, diphtheria, and Lyme disease.

RICKETTSIA

Rickettsia are pathogens that grow inside living cells and resemble bacteria. Two diseases caused by rickettsia are typhus and Rocky Mountain spotted fever.

VIRUSES

A **virus** is the smallest known pathogen. When a virus enters a cell, it takes over the cell and causes it to make more viruses. Newly produced viruses then are released and take over other cells. In this way, viruses spread rapidly. Some viral diseases are the common cold, mumps, hepatitis, mononucleosis, chickenpox, HIV, rabies, Ebola, and influenza.

FUNGI

Fungi are single- or multicelled parasitic organisms. Fungi obtain their food from organic materials, such as plant, animal, or human tissue.

HELMINTHS

A **helminth** is a parasitic worm. People can become infected with helminths when they eat undercooked pork or fish or practice poor hygiene. Some helminths, such as tapeworms, pinworms, and hookworms, can infect the human digestive tract. Other helminths can infect muscle tissue and blood.

The Spread of Pathogens

Pathogens are spread in a variety of ways. They may be spread through direct contact with an infected person, as in shaking hands, intimate kissing, sexual intercourse, receiving a transfusion of the person's blood, touching ulcers or open sores, or handling body fluids such as blood or urine. They may be spread through the air by coughing or sneezing. Contact with contaminated objects spreads pathogens. This includes sharing a needle with an infected person to inject drugs or get a tattoo and using objects such as combs, toothbrushes, razors, or eating utensils touched by an infected person. Contact with animals and insects, such as handling or being bitten by an infected animal or insect, also spreads pathogens. So does contact with contaminated food and water, as in drinking infected water or eating infected food, undercooked meats and other foods, or improperly canned or prepared foods. Pathogens are also spread by people who do not wash their hands after using the restroom.

The Immune System

The **immune system** removes harmful organisms from the blood and combats pathogens. The immune system is composed of body organs, tissues, cells, and chemicals. The skin is the first line of defense. Unbroken skin acts as a barrier to prevent pathogens from entering the body. Perspiration and oils on the skin kill pathogens. Tears also contain chemicals that kill pathogens and prevent them from entering the eyes. The mucus and hairs that line the inside of the nose trap and destroy pathogens, and many are killed by saliva in the mouth. Many pathogens that are swallowed are destroyed by stomach acids.

LYMPHOCYTES

Lymphocytes are white blood cells that help the body fight pathogens. When a pathogen enters the body, lymphocytes multiply in lymph tissue to fight infection. Two types of lymphocytes are B cells and helper T cells. A **B cell** is a white blood cell that produces antibodies. An **antibody** is a special protein that helps fight an infection. A **helper T cell** is a white blood cell that signals B cells to produce antibodies.

Soon after a pathogen invades the body, helper T cells send signals to B cells to produce antibodies. B cells enter the lymph nodes and other lymph tissues. From there, these cells enter the blood. Antibodies then travel through the blood to destroy the pathogen. Antibodies can make pathogens ineffective and sensitive to macrophages. **Macrophages** are white blood cells that surround and destroy pathogens. Antibodies attach to pathogens and make them easier for macrophages to destroy. Destroyed pathogens enter lymph, are filtered in the lymph nodes, and are removed by the spleen.

The immune system helps people develop immunity. **Immunity** is the body's resistance to disease-causing agents.

ACTIVE IMMUNITY

Active immunity is resistance to disease due to the presence of antibodies. For example, after a person has contracted the chickenpox virus, antibodies to that virus remain in the body after the person has recovered; the antibodies protect the person from developing chickenpox. Active immunity also can result from being given a vaccine.

PASSIVE IMMUNITY

Another type of immunity is passive immunity. **Passive immunity** is immunity that results from introducing antibodies into a person's bloodstream. The antibodies may be from another person's blood. This type of immunity is short term and is used when the risk of developing a disease is immediate. For example, a person who has not had hepatitis B immunizations and travels to a country where it is widespread may be given an injection with hepatitis B antibodies. Another example of passive immunity is the protection babies have for the first few months of life because of the antibodies they received before birth from their mothers. Also, babies who are breast-fed receive some antibodies from breast milk.

Health Goal #62

I Will Be Aware of Immunizations That Protect Health

An **immunization,** or **vaccine,** is a substance containing dead or weakened pathogens that is introduced into the body to increase immunity. Immunizations commonly are given by injection and orally. Immunizations cause the body to make antibodies for a specific pathogen. If these pathogens enter the body again, the antibodies destroy them.

Immunization Recommendations

Immunization recommendations change rapidly, so keeping up with new recommendations can be challenging. The annual Recommended Childhood Immunization Schedule is an important source of information about immunizations and is available through the Centers for Disease Control's National Immunization Program Web site (www .cdc.gov/nip) and your local health department.

RECOMMENDED IMMUNIZATIONS FOR CHILDREN AND ADOLESCENTS

All children should be immunized against hepatitis B, diphtheria, tetanus, pertussis (whooping cough), *Haemophilus influenzae* Type b, polio, measles, mumps, rubella (German measles), varicella (chickenpox), and pneumococcal pneumonia. Some of these immunizations can be given in the same shot, such as MMR (measles, mumps, and rubella) and DTaP (diphtheria, tetanus, and acellular pertussis). Several immunizations are given in a series of doses. For example, DTaP is recommended to be given at two months of age, four months, six months, and between fifteen to eighteen months. In addition, tetanus and diphtheria are recommended again at age eleven to twelve and every ten years thereafter.

Hepatitis A vaccine is recommended for children and adolescents in selected states and regions and for certain high-risk groups. In 2003, influenza vaccine was recommended annually for children older than six months with certain risk factors such as asthma, sickle cell disease, and diabetes. In addition, annual influenza vaccination was recommended for all healthy children ages six to twenty-three months to avoid influenza-related hospitalization.

Health officials recommend a well-child office visit at eleven to twelve years of age to evaluate the immunization status for varicella, hepatitis B, and the second dose of MMR. Also, a tetanus immunization is recommended if it has not been given in the past five years. Preadolescents and adolescents should be screened for high-risk conditions that indicate the need for influenza, pneumococcal, or hepatitis A vaccines.

Despite the availability of effective immunizations, almost one-quarter of children in the United States lack at least one of the basic childhood immunizations (American Academy of Pediatrics, 2003). Children who are poor or who live in inner-city or rural areas have lower immunization rates than do children in the general population. The Healthy People 2010 target for vaccine coverage among children is 90 percent for all recommended vaccines.

RECOMMENDED IMMUNIZATIONS FOR ADULTS

The Advisory Committee on Immunization Practices (ACIP) recommends that adults receive a tetanus immunization if they have not had a booster within the past ten years. When adults reach age fifty they should be screened for high-risk conditions such as chronic cardiac or pulmonary diseases (except asthma) that indicate the need for pneumococcal vaccine. The pneumococcal vaccine

is given once. In addition, they should start getting an annual influenza vaccination if they have not previously done so. The optimal time for getting an influenza vaccination is from mid-October through November. However, December is not too late for influenza vaccination.

Adults who are high risk for certain diseases might require vaccination. Intravenous drug users, individuals with multiple sexual partners, household contacts of people with chronic hepatitis B infection, and residents of institutions for the developmentally disabled, and nursing home and long-term care facility residents would benefit from hepatitis B vaccine. Health care workers, because they are more likely to come in contact with infected persons, should also be immunized against hepatitis B. College students living in dormitories, particularly freshmen, are also advised to be immunized for meningococcal disease. Veterinarians and animal handlers may be at increased risk of rabies and hepatitis A infection and should consider vaccination from these diseases. Rabies vaccination is also recommended for spelunkers. Travelers to foreign countries may benefit from vaccinations for certain diseases.

Pregnant women should not receive MMR and varicella vaccinations until after delivery because these vaccines could lead to birth defects in a developing fetus or embryo. However, inactivated influenza vaccine is recommended for women who will be in the second or third trimester of pregnancy during influenza season. Vaccination is recommended after the first trimester.

Health Goal #63

I Will Choose Behaviors to Reduce My Risk of Infection with Respiratory Diseases

---

Infectious Respiratory Diseases

Many diseases affect the respiratory system. Some of these are infectious; others are not. An infectious disease is a communicable disease—it can be spread from one person to another. Five infectious respiratory diseases are discussed in this section: the common cold, influenza, pneumonia, strep throat, and tuberculosis. The following will be discussed for each disease: the cause, methods of transmission, symptoms, diagnosis and treatment, and prevention.

The Common Cold

The **common cold** is a respiratory infection caused by more than 200 different viruses. One-third of all colds are caused by rhinoviruses. A **rhinovirus** is a virus that infects the nose. High levels of stress can increase a person's chances of catching a cold. Being exposed to cold weather or getting wet or chilled does not cause a cold.

METHODS OF TRANSMISSION

Cold viruses are released into the air when an infected person coughs or sneezes. The viruses can remain in the air for a while, and people can inhale them and become infected. They also can become infected by shaking hands with an infected person or by touching objects contaminated with the viruses—if they then touch a mucous membrane with the virus-contaminated hand (rub their eye or nose, touch inside their mouth), the viruses can pass into their bloodstream.

SYMPTOMS

Symptoms include runny nose, watery eyes, difficulty in breathing, sneezing, sore throat, cough, and headache and can last from two to fourteen days.

DIAGNOSIS AND TREATMENT

People with colds need to get plenty of rest and drink plenty of fluids. Over-the-counter (OTC) medicines may help relieve some symptoms, but they will not cure or shorten the length of a cold. Gargling with warm salt water can bring relief to a sore throat. Applying petroleum jelly to the nose may help an irritated nose.

PREVENTION

The most effective way to keep from getting a cold is to wash the hands frequently and not touch the nose or eyes. Sneeze or cough into a facial tissue. Whenever possible, avoid close contact with anyone who has a cold. To keep colds from spreading in a family, wash dishes and other objects thoroughly in hot, soapy water or in a dishwasher.

Influenza

Influenza, or the **flu,** is a highly contagious viral infection of the respiratory tract. Most people recover within a week or two, but it can be life-threatening for elderly people, newborn babies, and people with chronic diseases. The flu can lead to pneumonia. Flu viruses are constantly changing, making it difficult for the immune system to form antibodies to new variations of the flu virus. The illness that people often call "stomach flu" is not influenza.

METHODS OF TRANSMISSION

Flu viruses spread primarily from person to person as they enter the air when people cough and sneeze. They can enter the body through the mucous membranes of the eyes, nose, or mouth. Flu can spread rapidly in crowded places. The infected person who spreads it often does not show symptoms yet. An infected person is particularly contagious during the first three days of infection.

SYMPTOMS

Symptoms include headache, chills, sneezing, stuffy nose, sore throat, and dry cough, followed by body aches and fever.

DIAGNOSIS AND TREATMENT

A physician usually determines if people have the flu by their symptoms and by whether the flu is present in the community. Treatment consists of bed rest and drinking lots of fluids. Aspirin or acetaminophen may relieve fever and discomfort. Children and teens should not take aspirin to relieve symptoms as it may increase the chances of developing **Reye's syndrome.** Reye's syndrome is a disease that causes swelling of the brain and deterioration of liver function. Antibiotics are not effective against flu viruses but may help prevent the pneumonia that sometimes follows it.

PREVENTION

Avoid direct contact with an infected person and with objects that might be contaminated by them. Wash the hands often. Flu shots are highly recommended for people over age sixty-five; for people with chronic illnesses such as diabetes, heart disease, lung disease, and asthma; for people with a history of respiratory infections; and for people who care for the sick or elderly.

Pneumonia

Pneumonia is an infection in the lungs caused by bacteria, viruses, or other pathogens.

METHODS OF TRANSMISSION

Pneumonia bacteria and viruses can be spread by direct contact with an infected person or with contaminated objects. Untreated respiratory infections and allergies also can lead to pneumonia.

SYMPTOMS

Symptoms include shortness of breath, difficulty breathing, coughing, chest pain, weakness, fever, and chills.

DIAGNOSIS AND TREATMENT

Laboratory tests, chest X-rays, and physical examination are used. Prompt treatment is critical. Antibiotics are used to treat bacterial pneumonia. Viral pneumonia is much more difficult to treat. Severe cases may require hospital care.

PREVENTION

Avoid direct contact with people infected with pneumonia and with contaminated objects. Wash the hands often. Get prompt treatment for respiratory infections and allergies.

SARS

Severe acute respiratory syndrome (SARS) is a viral respiratory illness caused by a coronavirus, called SARS-associated coronavirus (SARS-CoV). SARS was first reported in Asia in February 2003. Over the next few months, the illness spread to more than two dozen countries in North America, South America, Europe, and Asia. The SARS global outbreak of 2003 was contained; however, it is possible that the disease

could reemerge (Centers for Disease Control and Prevention, 2005).

METHODS OF TRANSMISSION

The main way that SARS seems to spread is by close person-to-person contact. The virus that causes SARS is thought to be transmitted most readily by respiratory droplets (droplet spread) produced when an infected person coughs or sneezes. Droplet spread can happen when droplets from the cough or sneeze of an infected person are propelled a short distance (generally up to three feet) through the air and deposited on the mucous membranes of the mouth, nose, or eyes of persons who are nearby. The virus also can spread when a person touches a surface or object contaminated with infectious droplets and then touches his or her mouth, nose, or eye. In addition, it is possible that the SARS virus might spread more broadly through the air (airborne spread) or by other ways that are not now known (Centers for Disease Control and Prevention, 2005).

SYMPTOMS

In general, SARS begins with a high fever. Other symptoms may include headache, an overall feeling of discomfort, and body aches. Some people also have mild respiratory symptoms at the outset. About 10 to 20 percent of patients have diarrhea. After two to seven days, SARS patients may develop a dry cough. Most patients develop pneumonia. There is not enough information about the new virus to determine the full range of illness that it might cause (Centers for Disease Control and Prevention, 2005).

DIAGNOSIS AND TREATMENT

The CDC recommends that patients with SARS receive the same treatment that would be given for any patient with serious pneumonia. SARS-CoV is being tested against various antiviral drugs to see if an effective treatment can be found. Several laboratory tests can be used to detect SARS-CoV from blood, stool, and nasal secretions. Blood tests also can be performed to detect SARS-CoV antibodies produced after infection.

PREVENTION

To minimize the risk for SARS among U.S. residents, the public health system took careful and thorough precautions to prevent the spread of SARS. People who were suspected of having SARS were isolated from others and received care. People arriving from affected parts of the world (who might have been exposed to SARS) received information about SARS and instructions on what they should do if they became ill. SARS patients and their contacts were monitored to help prevent spread of the disease.

Strep Throat

Strep throat is a bacterial infection of the throat. If it is not treated promptly, rheumatic fever can occur. **Rheumatic fever** is an autoimmune action in the heart that can cause fever, weakness, and damage to the valves in the heart.

METHODS OF TRANSMISSION

Strep throat bacteria are spread by coughing, sneezing, and close contact with an infected person.

SYMPTOMS

Symptoms include fever and severe sore throat. The throat may appear very red, and small patches of pus may be visible.

DIAGNOSIS AND TREATMENT

A throat culture is needed. Antibiotics are prescribed to kill the bacteria and to prevent spread of the infection. Rest and fluids help the body fight the infection.

PREVENTION

Avoid contact with infected persons and disinfect objects they have used. Wash hands often.

Tuberculosis

Tuberculosis is a bacterial infection of the lungs. People with weakened immune systems, such as those with AIDS and the frail elderly, are highly susceptible to tuberculosis. People who are homeless or malnourished or inject drugs are at increased risk for tuberculosis.

METHODS OF TRANSMISSION

Tuberculosis bacteria become airborne through coughing and sneezing by an infected person. Only people with active tuberculosis are con-tagious. Tuberculosis is not likely to be spread through items or objects that have been touched by a person with the disease.

SYMPTOMS

Symptoms include extreme tiredness, coughing, night sweats, loss of appetite, weight loss, low-grade fever, and chills. Advanced symptoms include spitting up bloody sputum, shortness of breath, and chest pain.

DIAGNOSIS AND TREATMENT

A **tuberculin skin test** is the injection of a protein substance under the skin in the forearm. If within two days a red welt forms around where the protein was injected, the person has been exposed to tuberculosis. The tuberculin skin test does not confirm that a person has tuberculosis. Chest X-rays and sputum samples are used to confirm a diagnosis. Although antibiotics are used to treat tuberculosis, some tuberculosis pathogens have become resistant to them. A full course of antibiotic treatment is necessary to successfully treat tuberculosis.

PREVENTION

Avoid direct contact with people infected with tuberculosis. Any person who has had contact with an infected person should have a tuberculin skin test. People who have a positive tuberculin skin test or who frequently are in close contact with someone who has tuberculosis may need antibiotics. **Isoniazid** is a drug that prevents tuberculosis in people in close contact with infected people. Rooms with good ventilation and air flow reduce the risk of the spread of tuberculosis.

Health Goal #64

I Will Recognize Ways to Manage Asthma and Allergies

Asthma

Asthma is a condition in which the bronchial tubes become inflamed and constricted, making breathing difficult. Asthma is a serious condition

that is common in children, teens, and adults. It is the leading cause of school absence and hospitalization for children under the age of fifteen.

SYMPTOMS AND TRIGGERS

Asthma is a chronic disease that cannot be cured. Symptoms of asthma include coughing, wheezing, and shortness of breath. People with asthma have sensitive lungs that react to certain asthma triggers. **Asthma triggers** are substances that cause the airways to tighten, swell, and fill with mucus. The airways become narrow and blocked, and it is difficult to breathe. Asthma triggers include tree pollens; grasses and weeds; dust and mold; dogs, cats, or other animals; cigarette smoke; air pollution; red tide (see Chapter 13 for more information); having a cold or the flu; aspirin or other OTC drugs; perfumes and fragrances; odors from sprays and paints; insecticides; certain foods; and smoke from burning wood, paper, or other items. Asthma also can be triggered by emotional stress, especially during childhood and adolescence. Asthma attacks can be very serious. An **asthma attack** is an episode of coughing, wheezing, and shortness of breath experienced by a person who has asthma. Some people may become extremely sick from asthma attacks and need to be hospitalized. Some people have died from them.

Most children who suffer from asthma continue to have asthma as adults. However, for about one-fourth of children with asthma, the symptoms decrease significantly as they get older. Sometimes asthma does not develop until the person is an adult.

EXERCISE-INDUCED ASTHMA

Exercise-induced asthma (EIA) is a condition in which a person has difficulty breathing during or shortly after strenuous physical activity. The symptoms of EIA can be mild or severe and include coughing, wheezing, shortness of breath, and chest pain. Some people with EIA suffer an asthma attack only with exercise. A high percentage of people with EIA suffer asthma from allergies to airborne substances such as air pollutants, dust, and animal dander. Exposure to cold, dry air during physical activity is a major trigger.

EIA can be prevented by avoiding exercise. However, because regular physical activity improves health status, it is important to learn to manage EIA. Proper medication allows most people who have EIA to participate in regular physical activity. EIA often can be reduced and prevented by improving physical fitness. Breathing warm, moist air usually helps the condition. Swimming and other indoor water sports provide an ideal environment for people who have EIA. People with EIA frequently breathe in puffs of medication from an inhaler before they exercise to prevent the EIA from starting.

Preventing Asthma Attacks

People who have asthma can prevent asthma attacks by avoiding asthma triggers, by recognizing warning signs, and by taking certain medications. If they fail to recognize these signs, their symptoms may get worse. People who have asthma should plan what to do when they notice warning signs and symptoms of asthma. The plan should be made with a physician. Parents, guardians, and school personnel should be involved in drawing up a plan for children and teenagers who have asthma. Six warning signs and symptoms of asthma are

- Coughing
- Wheezing
- Shortness of breath
- Tightness in the chest
- Rapid breathing
- Itchy or sore throat

Managing Asthma

Most people who have asthma can live a normal life that includes participation in physical activity and sports. They can become free of symptoms by learning how to manage their asthma. The following are guidelines for managing asthma:

1. *Get medical treatment and advice from a physician who treats people with asthma.*
2. *Make a daily management plan and an emergency plan with a physician.*
3. *Avoid asthma triggers.*
4. *Use a peak flow meter every day if a physician recommends one.* A **peak flow meter** is a small device that measures how well a person is breathing.
5. *Know the warning signs and symptoms of asthma attacks.*
6. *Take medications as directed by a physician.*
7. *Keep on hand the medications required for emergencies.*
8. *Know when and how to get medical help for severe asthma attacks.*
9. *Avoid taking sleeping pills or sedatives if unable to sleep because of asthma.* They slow down breathing and can make it more difficult to breathe.
10. *Avoid smoking and breathing secondhand smoke.*
11. *Practice stress management skills.*
12. *Participate in regular physical activity if recommended by a physician.*

Allergies

An **allergy** is an overreaction of the body to a substance that, in most people, causes no response. An **allergen** is a substance that produces an allergic response. Most allergens are harmless substances. They come into contact with the skin, respiratory airways, the eye's surface, or stomach.

The most common airborne allergens are animal dander, feathers, pollens, and mites. Animal dander is flakes of dead skin or dander from an animal. People who have allergy symptoms such as dizziness, nausea, skin rash, drops in blood pressure, or difficulty in breathing when they are near cats, dogs, horses, or other animals are allergic to animal dander. Many people believe it is the hair of the animal to which they are allergic, but it actually is the flakes of dead skin.

Pollen is a yellowish powder made by flowers and grass. Pollen from flowers, flowering trees and plants, and grass may become airborne and trigger an allergic response. The most common response is hay fever. **Hay fever** is a common term for seasonal respiratory allergies. Symptoms include coughing, sneezing, and inflammation of the nasal mucous membranes. Hay fever occurs most often in the spring and fall. People who have hay fever may take medicine or have shots to lessen their response to pollen.

Some people are allergic to feathers in bedding and pillows. They can use pillows and quilts with synthetic stuffing. Some people are allergic to house dust because it usually contains small fragments of mites and their feces. **Mites** are tiny, eight-legged animals that resemble spiders. Skin tests can be used to identify allergens that produce allergic reactions. A **skin patch test** involves putting allergens on a patch, taping the patch to the skin, and observing the reaction. A **wheal** is a round skin lump that indicates sensitivity to a particular allergen. Another test involves using a needle to place allergens under the skin and observing the reaction. A wheal again indicates sensitivity to a particular allergen.

People who have allergies might want to consider getting allergy shots (immunotherapy). Allergy shots help the body build a type of immunity to specific allergens that eventually can prevent or "block" the allergen from triggering symptoms when a person is exposed to the substance. Allergy shots work better against some allergens than others. For example, allergy shots seem to be the most effective against venoms and allergens that are inhaled, such as pollens, dust, molds, and animal dander. Allergy shots are usually safe and effective and can be given to children as young as four or five years old. However, reactions and side effects occur in some people.

Health Goal #65

I Will Choose Behaviors to Reduce My Risk of Infection with Sexually Transmitted Diseases

A **sexually transmitted disease (STD)** is a disease caused by pathogens that are transmitted from an infected person to an uninfected person during intimate sexual contact. Some public health professionals and medical experts suggest replacing the term *sexually transmitted disease* with *sexually transmitted infection* (STI). The preference for *STI* stems from the fact that several of the most common STDs have no signs or symptoms for the majority of persons infected or that the signs and symptoms are so mild that they can easily be overlooked. Common infections such as chlamydia, gonorrhea, herpes, and human papillomavirus (HPV) can therefore cause infection but may not result in any medical symptoms for a person—hence no disease. However, the literature in general describes the infections discussed in this section as STDs. The Centers for Disease Control and Prevention refers to these infections as STDs. The American Social Health Association refers to them as STDs/STIs. Our choice in this section is to follow the CDC and refer to the infections as STDs.

At present, there are about twenty microorganisms that are known to be transmissible by intimate sexual contact. These organisms are responsible for spreading about fifty different diseases. More than 19 million new cases of STDs are reported each year in the United States (American Social Health Association, 2006).

Eight sexually transmitted diseases are discussed in this section: chlamydia, genital herpes, genital warts, gonorrhea, pubic lice, syphilis, trichomoniasis, and viral hepatitis. The following will be discussed for each disease: the cause, methods of transmission, symptoms, diagnosis and treatment, and complications.

Chlamydia

CAUSE

Chlamydia is an STD that is caused by the bacterium *Chlamydia trachomatis,* which produces inflammation of the reproductive organs. It is the most common STD in the United States. Each year there are almost 3 million new cases of chlamydia, many of which are in adolescents and young adults (American Social Health Association, 2006).

METHODS OF TRANSMISSION

Chlamydia is spread by intimate sexual contact with an infected partner. An infected female may pass the infection to her newborn baby during delivery. During delivery, the *Chlamydia* bacteria can enter the baby's eyes or lungs. If not treated, the baby can become blind or develop pneumonia.

SYMPTOMS IN MALES

One-fourth of infected males have no symptoms. *Chlamydia* bacteria can continue to multiply in a male who does not know he is infected. Males with symptoms may have painful urination, a discharge from the penis, inflammation of the urethra, and pain or swelling in the scrotum. Symptoms usually appear within one to three weeks after exposure. Some males never have symptoms but still can infect a sexual partner.

SYMPTOMS IN FEMALES

One-half of infected females have no symptoms. A female may not know she has chlamydia until complications develop. Symptoms include inflammation of the vagina and cervix, a burning sensation during urination, and an unusual discharge from the vagina.

DIAGNOSIS AND TREATMENT

A physician uses a cotton swab to collect a sample of the discharge, which is examined in a laboratory for the presence of the *Chlamydia* bacterium. Antibiotics are used to treat chlamydia. Infected persons must take all the prescribed antibiotics, even after the symptoms disappear. A follow-up visit to a physician is necessary to be sure that the infection is cured. All sex partners of persons infected with chlamydia should be checked and treated.

COMPLICATIONS

Pelvic inflammatory disease (PID) is a serious infection of the internal female reproductive organs. Many cases occur in females infected with chlamydia but who had no symptoms. PID can cause a scarring of the fallopian tubes, which can block the tubes and cause sterility. To be sterile means to be unable to produce children. Ectopic pregnancy is also linked to PID. An **ectopic pregnancy,** or **tubal pregnancy,** occurs when a fertilized egg implants in a fallopian tube instead of in the uterus. This condition results in the death of the fetus and can be fatal for the pregnant female. If left untreated, chlamydia can cause sterility in males. A baby born to a mother with chlamydia may develop pneumonia or a serious eye infection that can lead to blindness if not treated promptly. Babies infected with chlamydia usually develop pneumonia within three to six weeks after birth.

Genital Herpes

CAUSE

Genital herpes is an STD caused by the herpes simplex virus (HSV), which produces cold sores or fever blisters in the genital area and mouth. **Herpes simplex virus Type 1 (HSV-1)** is a virus that causes cold sores or fever blisters in the mouth or on the lips. HSV-1 also may cause genital sores. **Herpes simplex virus Type 2 (HSV-2)** is a virus that causes genital sores but also may cause sores in the mouth. The viruses remain in the body for life. It is estimated that as many as one in four people in the United States have genital herpes, yet up to 90 percent are unaware they have it (American Social Health Association, 2006).

METHODS OF TRANSMISSION

Genital herpes is spread by intimate sexual contact with an infected person. Infected people are highly contagious when blisters break and form red, painful open sores. Through touch, they can spread them to other areas of the body. If they have lesions in the mouth and place their fingers there and then touch the genitals or eyes, the virus is spread.

SYMPTOMS

Symptoms of genital herpes occur within a week after contact with an infected partner. Early symptoms can include an itching or burning sensation; pain in the legs, buttocks, or genital area; vaginal discharge; or a feeling of pressure in the abdominal area. Clusters of small, painful blisters that may develop into open sores appear in the genital area. Other symptoms that accompany the outbreak of the blisters can be fever, headache, muscle aches, painful or difficult urination, vaginal discharge, and swollen glands in the groin area. The symptoms may last from two to four weeks and then disappear. In some people, these symptoms may reappear during times of stress or illness.

DIAGNOSIS AND TREATMENT

The sores of genital herpes usually are visible. Diagnosis is made by growing the virus from a swab of the ulcers. Blood tests can be given to detect the presence of antibodies to HSV in the blood. They can distinguish whether people have HSV-1 or HSV-2. There is no known cure for genital herpes. **Acyclovir** is an antiviral drug approved for the treatment of herpes simplex infections. It relieves symptoms and prevents some recurrences of genital herpes. Sores need to be kept clean and dry, and hands need to be washed after contact with the sores.

COMPLICATIONS

Genital herpes sores are painful and disrupt people's lives. People with genital herpes fear recurrences and spreading the infection to others. Genital herpes increases the risk of infection with HIV. HIV can easily enter the body through broken blisters if people infected with herpes have intimate contact with a person who has HIV. Episodes of genital herpes can be long-lasting and severe in people with weak immune systems. An infected female can infect her baby during vaginal delivery.

Genital Warts

CAUSE

Genital warts is an STD caused by certain types of the human papillomavirus (HPV) that produces wartlike growth on the genitals. More than sixty types of HPV have been discovered, several of which can cause genital warts.

METHODS OF TRANSMISSION

Genital warts are very contagious and are spread during intimate sexual contact and by direct contact with infected bed linens, towels, and clothing. They can be spread from a female to her baby during vaginal delivery of the baby.

SYMPTOMS

Most people with HPV do not develop symptoms. For those who do, genital warts appear three to eight months after infection. They usually are soft, are red or pink, and resemble a cauliflower. Sometimes they are hard and yellow gray. In addition to appearing on or near the genitals, they may develop in the mouth. In males, genital warts usually appear on the tip of the penis. They also may be found on the shaft of the penis, on the scrotum, or in the anus. In females, genital warts may appear on the vulva, on the labia, inside the vagina, on the cervix, or around the anus.

DIAGNOSIS AND TREATMENT

A physician inspects the warts to make a diagnosis. Several new laboratory tests can identify specific types of HPV. These tests may be helpful in determining whether or not the infection is likely to progress to cancer and be spread from a pregnant female to a newborn. A Pap smear also may be given to females who are sexually active because of the increased risk of cervical cancer. No treatment is available that will completely get rid of the virus causing genital warts. Once infected, people will always have the virus in their bodies. Medication can be placed on genital warts, and laser surgery can remove them. Genital warts can be frozen and removed by using liquid nitrogen but may reappear after removal.

GARDASIL

Gardasil is a new vaccine recently approved by the Food and Drug Administration (FDA) to prevent cervical cancer in females between the ages of nine and twenty-six. The vaccine works against four types of human papillomavirus (HPV), including the two types that cause most cervical cancers and the two types that cause most genital warts. HPV is the most common sexually transmitted infection in the United States, and it increases the risk of cervical cancer among those who are infected by it. The Centers for Disease Control and Prevention (CDC) estimates that about 6.2 million Americans become infected with genital HPV each year and that over half of all those sexually active become infected at some time in their lives.

Because Gardasil prevents HPV it is important that it be given before females become sexually active. The CDC's Advisory Committee on Immunization Practice (ACIP) recommends that Gardasil be routinely given to girls when they are eleven or twelve years of age. Gardasil can be started as early as age nine, and can also be given to females, ages thirteen to twenty-six.

Giving Gardasil to children raises concerns in many parents who are not in favor of giving a vaccine against an STD to preteens. There are concerns that giving a vaccine against an STD might encourage promiscuity, since it could foster the belief that it protects against STDs. Two reliable sources of up-to-date information about Gardasil are the FDA (www.fda.gov) and CDC (www.cdc.gov) Web sites.

COMPLICATIONS

Besides being an embarrassment, several types of HPV increase the risk of cancers of the cervix, vulva, anus, and penis. Genital warts often enlarge during pregnancy and make urination difficult for a pregnant female. Genital warts on the vaginal wall make delivery of the baby very difficult. Babies born to a mother with genital warts can develop warts in their throats. To prevent blocking of the airway, an infected baby may need laser surgery to remove the warts from the throat.

Gonorrhea

CAUSE

Gonorrhea is a highly contagious STD caused by the gonococcus bacterium *Neisseria gonorrhoeae*. Gonorrhea infects the linings of the genital and urinary tracts of males and females.

METHODS OF TRANSMISSION

Gonorrhea is spread by intimate sexual contact with an infected person. A baby born to an infected female can become infected during childbirth if the bacteria enter the baby's eyes.

SYMPTOMS IN MALES

Males usually have a white, milky discharge from the penis and a burning sensation during urination. They may experience pain and increased urination within two to ten days after infection. They might be contagious even if they do not have symptoms.

SYMPTOMS IN FEMALES

Many infected females have no symptoms. If symptoms appear, they include a burning sensation when urinating and a discharge from the vagina and usually appear within two to ten days after sexual contact with the infected partner. Severe symptoms, such as abdominal pain, bleeding between menstrual periods, vomiting, or fever, can occur if gonorrhea is not treated.

DIAGNOSIS AND TREATMENT

Gonorrhea is diagnosed through a microscopic examination of the discharge. The Gram stain is a test that involves placing a smear of the discharge on a slide stained with a dye. The test is accurate for males but not for females. The preferred method for females is the culture test, which involves placing a sample of the discharge on a culture plate and letting it grow for up to two days. Antibiotics are used to treat gonorrhea. Some strains are resistant to some antibiotics, making treatment difficult. People with gonorrhea should take the full course of prescribed medication. A follow-up visit to a physician is necessary. All sex partners of infected people should be tested even if they have no symptoms. Most states require that the eyes of newborn babies be treated with silver nitrate or other medication immediately after birth to prevent gonococcal infection of the eyes in case the mother was infected.

COMPLICATIONS

The bacteria can spread to the bloodstream and infect the joints, heart valves, and the brain. Gonorrhea in both males and females can cause permanent sterility. It is a major cause of pelvic inflammatory disease (PID). In newborns, gonococcal infection can lead to blindness.

Pubic Lice

CAUSE

Pubic lice is infestation of the pubic hair by pubic, or crab, lice that survive by feeding on human blood. **Lice** are insects that pierce the skin and secrete a substance that causes itching and swelling.

METHODS OF TRANSMISSION

Lice can be spread from one person to another through intimate sexual contact. Because lice can live outside the body for as long as a day, people can become infected by sleeping on infested sheets, wearing infested clothing, sharing infested towels, and sitting on a toilet seat that has been used by a person who has lice.

SYMPTOMS

The main symptom is itching in the pubic area. The lice may be visible as little black spots on body parts that have dense hair growth.

DIAGNOSIS AND TREATMENT

A physician examines the body to find the lice. Pubic lice and their nits are easily diagnosed because they are visible by the naked eye or through a magnifying glass. **Nits** are tiny white lice eggs that attach to body hair. A prescription drug is used as a shampoo to kill the lice. OTC preparations also are used. After the lice are killed, itching may continue because the skin has been irritated and requires time to heal. Certain medications can stop the itching.

COMPLICATIONS

The major health problem is the discomfort from itching and irritation.

Syphilis

CAUSE

Syphilis is an STD caused by the spirochete bacterium *Treponema pallidum*. A **spirochete** is a spiral-shaped bacterium. Syphilis spirochetes enter the body through tiny breaks in the mucous membranes and then burrow their way into the bloodstream.

METHODS OF TRANSMISSION

Syphilis is spread by intimate sexual contact with an infected person. The spirochete also can be transmitted from a pregnant female to her fetus.

SYMPTOMS

Primary syphilis is the first stage of syphilis. The first symptom of syphilis is a chancre. A **chancre** is a painless, open sore that appears at the site where the spirochetes entered the body. This might be on the genitals or in the mouth. Chancres appear within ten days to three months after exposure to syphilis. Because a chancre is painless and sometimes occurs inside the body, it may not be noticed. Chancres contain spirochetes, so syphilis can spread to people who have contact with a chancre. The chancre will disappear within a few weeks whether or not a person is treated. However, the pathogens for syphilis remain in the body and the disease progresses to secondary syphilis.

Secondary syphilis is the stage of syphilis characterized by a skin rash and begins anywhere from three to six weeks after the chancre appears. The skin rash may cover the whole body or appear in only a few areas, such as the hands or soles of the feet. People are very contagious during secondary syphilis. The rash heals within several weeks or months. Other symptoms, such as fever, tiredness, headache, sore throat, swollen lymph glands, and loss of weight and hair, may occur during this stage. The symptoms will disappear without treatment and may come and go during the next one or two years.

DIAGNOSIS AND TREATMENT

People with a suspicious skin rash or sore in the genital area should be checked by a physician. A blood test will detect the presence of the spirochetes that cause syphilis in any stage of the disease. Syphilis is treated with antibiotic drugs. People being treated for syphilis need to have regular blood tests to check that the pathogens are no longer present. Treatment in the later stages cannot reverse the damage done to body organs in the early stages of the disease.

COMPLICATIONS

If secondary syphilis is not treated, it may become latent syphilis. **Latent syphilis** is a stage of syphilis in which there are no symptoms but the spirochetes are still present and may damage tissues and organs. Latent syphilis can last for years and even for decades. Some people with latent syphilis will not suffer any further damage from the disease. However, people who are infected will develop late syphilis. **Late syphilis,** or **tertiary syphilis,** is the final stage of syphilis in which spirochetes damage body organs. The spirochetes damage the heart, eyes, brain, nervous system, bones, joints, or other body parts. Mental illness, blindness, paralysis, heart disease, liver damage, and death may occur. The damage to body organs cannot be reversed. If a pregnant female has syphilis, the fetus is at risk. The pregnancy may result in a miscarriage, stillbirth, or fetal death. More than two out of three babies born to a mother with syphilis are born with syphilis. Babies with syphilis may have skin sores, rashes, fever, hoarse crying, a swollen liver and spleen, yellowish skin, and anemia and are at high risk for being born with mental retardation and other birth defects.

Trichomoniasis

CAUSE

Trichomoniasis is an STD caused by the single-celled protozoan *Trichomonas vaginalis.* The most common site of infection in males is the urethra. In females, the most common site of infection is the vagina.

METHODS OF TRANSMISSION

Trichomoniasis is spread during intimate sexual contact with an infected person. It can be transmitted even when no symptoms are present and without sexual contact. The protozoa can survive for up to twenty-four hours on damp towels. Sharing infected towels is a means of transmission. Females who use vaginal sprays and douches may change the natural condition of their vagina enough to create a favorable environment for the protozoa to multiply.

SYMPTOMS IN MALES

Symptoms include a thin, whitish discharge from the penis and painful or difficult urination. Most males do not experience any signs or symptoms with trichomoniasis.

SYMPTOMS IN FEMALES

While trichomoniasis affects both males and females, symptoms are more common in females. About half of all infected females have no symptoms. There may be a yellow-green or gray vaginal discharge that has an odor, painful urination, irritation and itching in the genital area, and, on rare occasions, pain in the abdomen.

DIAGNOSIS AND TREATMENT

A smear of the discharge is examined under a microscope. The drug metronidazole (Flagyl) is used to treat trichomoniasis. People taking this drug should not drink alcohol—mixing the two drugs can cause severe nausea and vomiting.

COMPLICATIONS

Trichomoniasis may cause pregnant females to deliver low-birthweight or premature babies. Trichomoniasis in pregnant women may also cause premature rupture of the membranes and preterm delivery. The genital inflammation caused by trichomoniasis might also increase a female's risk of acquiring HIV infection if she is exposed to HIV. Trichomoniasis in a female who is also infected with HIV can increase the chances of transmitting HIV infection to a sex partner.

Viral Hepatitis

CAUSE

Viral hepatitis is a viral infection of the liver. Several different viruses cause hepatitis, including hepatitis A (HAV), hepatitis B (HBV), hepatitis C (HCV), delta hepatitis (HDV), and hepatitis E (HEV).

METHODS OF TRANSMISSION

All types of viral hepatitis, except infection by HEV, are known to be spread through intimate sexual contact. HBV, HCV, and HDV also are spread through sharing contaminated drug needles. HAV is most commonly spread by contaminated food and water. HEV is spread mainly through contaminated water in areas with poor sanitation. HBV can be spread from a pregnant female to her baby.

SYMPTOMS

Many infected people have no symptoms. When symptoms are present, they may be mild or severe. The most common early symptoms are mild fever, headache, muscle aches, tiredness, loss of appetite, nausea, vomiting, or diarrhea. Later symptoms may include dark and foamy urine, pale-colored feces, abdominal pain, and jaundice. **Jaundice** is yellowing of the skin and whites of the eyes. Infection with each type of virus can produce different symptoms.

DIAGNOSIS AND TREATMENT

Blood tests confirm viral hepatitis. A physician also can observe symptoms. Treatment consists of bed rest, a healthful diet, and avoidance of alcoholic beverages. Drugs may be prescribed to improve liver function. Vaccines are now available for lifelong immunity to hepatitis A and hepatitis B. Immunoglobulin also is available to provide immediate and short-term protection against hepatitis B.

COMPLICATIONS

Many cases of hepatitis are not a serious threat to health. Others are long-lasting and can lead to liver failure and death. Viral hepatitis increases the risk of developing liver cancer.

Reducing the Risk of STDs

The risk of STDs is reduced by the following responsible actions:

1. *Abstaining from sex until married.* The pathogens that cause STDs are transmitted during intimate sexual contact in which body fluids are exchanged. People who abstain from sex avoid the risk behaviors in which STDs are transmitted and will not become infected with incurable STDs. They also avoid the legal and moral complications that would arise if they were to infect another person.

2. *Changing behavior and being tested for STDs and HIV if one has been sexually active.* People who have been sexually active should immediately begin to practice abstinence. In addition, they should see a physician or visit a clinic to be tested for STDs. A person who is infected requires prompt treatment. Remember, a person can be infected and not have symptoms. A person who is infected with an STD has a legal and moral obligation to disclose this to any potential marriage partner because there is no cure. Teenagers should discuss past sexual behavior with their parents or guardian and ask for their help and support.

3. *Having a monogamous marriage if choosing to marry in the future.* A **monogamous marriage** is a marriage in which partners have sex only with each other. If both partners are disease-free when they enter the marriage, monogamy provides security and protects partners from infection with STDs, including HIV.

4. *Choosing a drug-free lifestyle.* Drugs dull reasoning and judgment. A person using drugs may not think clearly and might not stick to a decision to practice abstinence until marriage. As a result, a person may become infected with STDs.

5. *Avoiding use of injection drugs.* Sharing a needle, syringe, or injection equipment for drug use is a risk behavior for STDs.

6. *Changing behavior if using drugs.* A person who misuses or abuses drugs should see a physician or go to a clinic and get tested for STDs. A person who is infected needs prompt treatment. A person who is drug dependent usually needs treatment for quitting drugs. Young people who are misusing or abusing drugs should ask their parents or guardian for their help and support.

7. *Avoiding sharing a needle to make tattoos or to pierce ears and other body parts.* Sharing a needle to make a tattoo or pierce ears and other body parts is a risk behavior. Tattooing and piercing should be performed only by qualified people who use sterile equipment.

8. *Following universal precautions.* **Universal precautions** are steps taken to prevent the spread of disease by treating all human blood

and certain body fluids as if they contain HIV, HBV, and other pathogens. Universal precautions should always be followed when there is contact with a person's blood and other body fluids. Wearing disposable latex gloves and washing the hands with waterless antiseptic hand cleanser after removing them are behaviors that should always be practiced. The use of a face mask or shield with a one-way valve is essential if performing first aid for breathing emergencies. Touching objects that have had contact with a person's blood should be avoided. When performing first aid, a person should not eat or drink anything or touch the mouth, eyes, or nose.

Health Goal #66

I Will Choose Behaviors to Reduce My Risk of HIV Infection

HIV Infection

The Centers for Disease Control and Prevention (2007) estimates that approximately 40,000 persons in the United States become infected with HIV each year. The **human immunodeficiency virus (HIV)** is a pathogen that destroys infection-fighting T cells in the body. When HIV enters the body, it attaches to a molecule called CD4 on helper T cells. HIV then takes control of the helper T cells and reproduces more HIV. As HIV reproduces and makes more HIV, it attacks the other helper T cells and takes control of them. Some signs of HIV infection may include flulike symptoms, such as fever, sore throat, skin rash, diarrhea, swollen glands, loss of appetite, and night sweats. These signs may come and go as the helper T cell count fluctuates. See Figure 11-1.

OPPORTUNISTIC INFECTIONS

People are susceptible to many opportunistic infections when they are infected with HIV. An **opportunistic infection** is an infection that develops in a person with a weak immune system. The pathogens that cause opportunistic infections already are present in the bodies of most people but usually are harmless unless a person has HIV or some other disease that weakens the immune system.

There are many opportunistic infections. **Thrush** is a fungal infection of the mucous membranes of the tongue and mouth. White spots and ulcers cover the infection. Infections of the skin and mucous membranes also appear. There may be sores around the anus, genital area, and mouth. **Oral hairy leukoplakia** is an infection with fuzzy white patches found on the tongue. *Pneumocystis carinii* **pneumonia (PCP)** is a form of pneumonia that may affect people infected with HIV.

People who are infected with HIV are at risk for developing tuberculosis. They also are at risk for developing cancers. **Kaposi's sarcoma (KS)** is a type of cancer that affects people who are infected with HIV. KS causes purplish lesions and tumors on the skin and in the linings of the internal organs. These lesions spread to most of the linings of the body.

EFFECTS ON THE NERVOUS SYSTEM

HIV destroys brain and nerve cells. **AIDS dementia complex** is a loss of brain function caused by HIV infection. There is gradual loss of a person's ability to think and move, personality change, and loss of coordination. As AIDS dementia complex progresses, confusion increases and memory loss becomes severe.

WASTING SYNDROME

People who have AIDS may develop **HIV wasting syndrome,** a substantial loss in body weight that is accompanied by high fevers, sweating, and diarrhea.

AIDS

To date, half of all people infected with HIV have developed AIDS within ten years. A person infected with HIV who has 200 or fewer helper T cells (also known as CD4 cells) per microliter of blood or has an opportunistic infection has AIDS (acquired immunodeficiency syndrome).

HIV Transmission

People who are infected with HIV have HIV in most of their body fluids. HIV is spread from infected persons to others by contact with certain body fluids. These body fluids are blood, semen, vaginal secretions, and, in a few cases, breast milk. Minute traces of HIV have been found in saliva, sweat, and tears. To date, there have

FIGURE 11-1

How HIV Attacks the Immune System

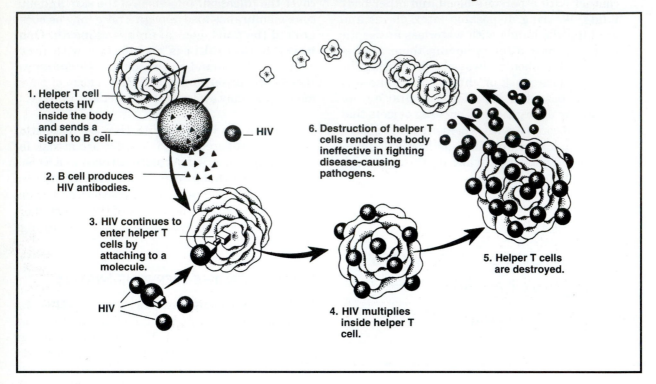

1. Helper T cell detects HIV inside the body and sends a signal to B cell.

— HIV

2. B cell produces HIV antibodies.

3. HIV continues to enter helper T cells by attaching to a molecule.

HIV

6. Destruction of helper T cells renders the body ineffective in fighting disease-causing pathogens.

5. Helper T cells are destroyed.

4. HIV multiplies inside helper T cell.

---

been no documented cases of HIV transmission through saliva, sweat, or tears. HIV is transmitted by contact with infected body fluids.

HAVING SEXUAL CONTACT WITH AN INFECTED PERSON

During sexual contact, HIV from an infected person may enter the body of an uninfected partner through exposed blood vessels in small cuts or tiny cracks in mucous membranes. HIV can spread from male to male, male to female, female to male, or female to female. HIV transmission can occur if the male ejaculates or if he withdraws before ejaculation. This is because HIV is present in the preejaculatory fluid. Increased risks from sexual contact include the following:

1. *Having multiple sex partners.* The greater the number of sex partners people have, the more likely they will have sex with someone who is infected with HIV.
2. *Having sex with a prostitute.* Because male and female prostitutes have a large number of sexual partners, people who have sex with them are at an increased risk for being infected with HIV. Prostitutes also are known to use injecting drugs.

3. *Having other sexually transmitted diseases.* STDs that produce sores or lead to bleeding or discharge provide body openings through which HIV can spread more easily. Genital sores provide an exit point for infected people and an entry point for uninfected people for transmission of HIV in blood, semen, and vaginal secretions.

OPEN-MOUTH KISSING

The Centers for Disease Control and Prevention warns against open-mouth kissing with a person infected with HIV because of the possibility of contact with infected blood if the infected person has open sores in the mouth.

SHARING NEEDLES, SYRINGES, OR OTHER DRUG INJECTION EQUIPMENT

An **injecting drug user** is a person who injects illegal drugs into the body with syringes, needles, and other injection equipment. When an infected person injects drugs, droplets of HIV-infected blood remain on the needle, syringe, or other injection equipment. A second person who uses that needle, syringe, or other injection equipment to inject drugs will also inject HIV-infected blood. Then this person will be infected with HIV.

SHARING NEEDLES TO MAKE TATTOOS OR TO PIERCE BODY PARTS

Droplets of HIV-infected blood remain on the needle when an infected person uses a needle to make a tattoo or to pierce ears or other body parts. A second person who is given a tattoo using that needle will get the HIV-infected blood in his or her body and could become infected.

HAVING CONTACT WITH THE BLOOD OR OTHER BODY FLUIDS, MUCOUS MEMBRANES, OR BROKEN SKIN OF AN INFECTED PERSON

People who handle the body fluids of a person who is infected with HIV risk having HIV enter their bodies through small cuts or tears on their skin or through blood splashing in the eyes. People who use something such as a razor or toothbrush that may have droplets of infected blood on it risk having the infected blood enter their bodies through small cuts or tears in the mucous membranes or skin. Touching the mucous membranes or broken skin of an HIV-infected person may result in contact with exposed blood vessels. HIV-infected blood can enter the body through small cuts or tears on the skin.

RECEIVING A TRANSFUSION OF INFECTED BLOOD OR BLOOD PRODUCTS

In the United States, the FDA controls blood donations, blood donor centers, and blood labs. All donors are screened. After donation, blood is tested for HIV, hepatitis B, and syphilis. People traveling to countries other than the United States should inquire about the safety of the blood supply. A person cannot become infected with HIV by donating blood at a site that uses only sterile needles and follows universal precautions (such as the Red Cross or hospitals).

RECEIVING AN INFECTED TISSUE TRANSPLANT (ORGAN DONATION)

In the United States, screening and testing procedures have reduced the risk of being infected by human tissue transplants. Potential donors for all human tissues must be tested for HIV, hepatitis B, and hepatitis C. They also must be screened for risk behaviors and symptoms of AIDS and hepa-

titis. Imported tissues must be accompanied by records showing that the tissues were screened and tested. If no records are available, tissues are shipped under quarantine to the United States. People having tissue transplants outside the United States should check screening and testing procedures.

BEING BORN TO A MOTHER WITH HIV INFECTION

A pregnant female infected with HIV can transmit HIV through the umbilical cord to her developing embryo or fetus. A baby also can be infected while passing through the mother's vagina at birth. Infected blood in the vagina can enter the baby's blood through a cut on the baby's body. A nursing baby can become infected with HIV through the breast milk of an infected mother. Of pregnant females infected with HIV, 15 to 30 percent infect their babies with HIV through perinatal transmission. **Perinatal transmission** is the transfer of an infection to a baby during pregnancy, during delivery, or after birth through breast milk.

WAYS HIV IS NOT TRANSMITTED

To date, there have been no documented cases of HIV transmission through saliva, sweat, or tears. HIV is not spread through casual contact, such as the following:

- Closed-mouth kissing
- Hugging
- Touching, holding, or shaking hands
- Coughing or sneezing
- Sharing food or eating utensils
- Sharing towels or combs
- Sharing bathroom facilities or water fountains
- Sharing a pen or pencil
- Being bitten by insects
- Donating blood
- Eating food prepared or served by someone else
- Attending school
- Using a telephone or computer used by someone else
- Swimming in a pool
- Using sports and gym equipment

HIV Testing

It is impossible to tell if people are infected with HIV by the way they look. They may look and feel healthy and not have symptoms and still spread the virus to others. Therefore, anyone who has engaged in a risk behavior or been in a risk situation for HIV transmission should be tested for HIV.

An HIV antibody test is the only way to tell whether a person is infected with HIV. When HIV enters the body, the immune system responds by making antibodies. The HIV antibody test detects HIV antibodies in the blood and tells whether people are infected. HIV antibodies usually show up in the blood within three months after infection, but could take up to six months. The test will detect antibodies in most people infected within six months. It does not tell if people have AIDS or when they will get AIDS. HIV antibodies do not protect from disease or prevent someone from infecting others with HIV.

ELISA is a blood test used to check for antibodies for HIV. If an ELISA test is positive, it is repeated to confirm the result. If two or more ELISA tests are positive, a Western blot test is given. **Western blot** is a blood test used to check for antibodies for HIV and to confirm an ELISA test. It is more specific and takes longer to perform. Used together, ELISA and Western blot are correct more than 99.9 percent of the time.

The FDA has approved use of a few home collection kits for HIV antibody testing. A home collection kit for HIV testing allows a person to take a blood sample at home, place drops of blood on a test card, mail the card to a lab, and call a toll-free number to get HIV results. The blood sample contains a personal identification number that the caller gives when using the toll-free number for the test results. The tests usually are available within a week. If the test is positive, a counselor usually comes on the telephone. Many health care professionals are concerned about people being told over the telephone that they are HIV positive. Teens who need to be tested for HIV should talk to their parents or guardian and decide together where to have testing done.

A positive test result means a person is HIV positive. A person who is **HIV positive** has antibodies for HIV present in the blood. A person who is **HIV negative** does not have antibodies for HIV present in the blood. A person who engaged in a risk behavior this past week might test HIV negative today because antibodies for HIV do not show up in the blood right away.

Scientists are working to develop better HIV tests. Recently the Food and Drug Administration (FDA) approved the OraQuick Rapid HIV-1 Antibody Test, which detects antibodies to HIV-1 found in blood specimens obtained by fingerstick or venipuncture. Results of the test can be read in as little as twenty minutes. As is true of all HIV screening tests, a reactive test result needs to be confirmed by an additional, more specific test. The OraSure HIV-1 oral fluid specimen device is the only FDA-approved device for collecting oral fluid for testing. The oral fluid is tested to see if it contains HIV antibodies. It requires no needles, and blood is not involved. The sample is sent to a laboratory for HIV antibody testing. This test is very accurate, and health officials are hopeful that it will attract people who are fearful of taking a blood test.

Treatment for HIV Infection and AIDS

There is no cure for HIV infection or AIDS. Treatment focuses on slowing the progression of the virus by taking drugs and practicing healthful habits. Early treatment is critical in slowing the rate at which HIV multiplies. This, in turn, delays the progression of HIV to AIDS. The FDA has approved several drugs for HIV and HIV-related conditions.

Before a person starts HIV treatment, a physician will take a complete health history, perform a physical examination, and perform several blood tests. These include a viral load test and CD4+ T cell count. A **viral load test** is a test that measures the amount of HIV in a person's blood. This test is important because it shows how far a person's HIV infection has progressed and it provides a basis to determine how well HIV treatment is working. A CD4+ T cell count is a test that determines the number of CD4+ T cells in a sample of blood. This test shows how well a person's immune system is working. It also provides a basis to determine how well HIV treatment is working.

Antiretroviral drugs are drugs used to slow virus replication. **Virus replication** is the virus copying itself or reproducing or multiplying. Antiretroviral drugs slow the progression of HIV disease. The FDA has approved three classes of antiretroviral drugs:

- *Nucleoside reverse transcriptase inhibitors (NRTIs):* zidovudine (AZT), didanosine (ddl), zalcitabine (ddC), stavudine (d4T), lamivudine (3TC), Combivir (AZT and 3TC), and abacavir (Ziagen).
- *Protease inhibitors (PIs):* saquinavir (Invirase and Fortovase), ritonavir (Norvir), indinavir (Crixivan), and nelfinavir (Viracept).
- *Non-nucleoside reverse transcriptase inhibitors (NNRTIs):* nevirapine (Viramune), delavirdine (Rescriptor), and efavirenz (Sustiva).

The preferred treatment for HIV is highly active antiretroviral therapy. **Highly active antiretroviral therapy (HAART)** is a triple drug combination. HAART might include two NRTIs and one PI, or two NRTIs plus efavirenz, or two NRTIs plus ritonavir and saquinavir.

A viral load test can help to determine whether antiretroviral drugs are working. A person should have viral load tested two to four weeks after starting treatment. If the drugs are working, viral load should decrease and continue to decrease as the person continues to take antiretroviral drugs. Throughout HIV treatment, viral load should be tested every three to four months to make sure the drugs are still working.

People who are infected with HIV or who have developed AIDS should practice healthful habits. They should eat healthful foods, get enough rest and sleep, exercise, and avoid alcohol, tobacco, and other drugs. People who have HIV wasting syndrome need to follow food safety practices. Their weakened immune system leaves them vulnerable to illnesses that are spread in contaminated food. They should avoid eating nonpasteurized dairy products, raw eggs, and raw seafood. They should cook food thoroughly before eating it. They should wash their hands and eating utensils with soap and hot water.

Scientists have made progress in the treatment of HIV and AIDS. They continue to test vaccines and research ways to keep people with HIV and AIDS as healthy as possible as long as possible. Some people may import for their personal use unapproved, but promising, drugs for HIV and life-threatening AIDS-related diseases. Because there are many scams, the FDA initiated an AIDS Health Fraud Task Force to explain how to identify phony health products and to distribute general information about HIV infection.

TREATMENT DURING PREGNANCY

A female who is HIV positive and pregnant should talk to a physician as soon as possible about treatment of HIV. There is no way to determine for sure if her baby will be born HIV positive. However, there are steps that can be taken to reduce the risk of transmitting HIV to the baby.

Currently, the only drug proven to reduce the risk of transmitting HIV to the baby is zidovudine (AZT). Treatment should begin after the fourteenth week of pregnancy and continue until delivery. During labor, zidovudine will be given to the mother intravenously. After birth, the baby will receive zidovudine for the first six weeks of life.

Reducing the Risk of HIV Infection

There are several ways to reduce the risk of infection with HIV:

1. *Abstain from sex until married.* HIV is transmitted during intimate sexual contact in which body fluids are exchanged. High-risk behaviors for HIV infection include having multiple sex partners and having sex with a prostitute.
2. *Do not engage in open-mouth kissing with a person who is infected with HIV.* The CDC warns against open-mouth kissing because of the possible contact with infected blood.
3. *Change behavior if sexually active in the past.* People who have been sexually active in the past should be tested for HIV and other STDs. Teenagers who have been sexually active should abstain from sex until marriage. People who have been sexually active should make an appointment with a physician or go to a clinic and be tested for HIV and other STDs. Young people can ask their parents or guardian to help and support them as they change their behavior.
4. *Have a monogamous marriage if choosing to marry.* A **monogamous marriage** is a

marriage in which the partners have sex only with each other.

5. *Do not inject illegal drugs.* Sharing a needle, syringe, or injection equipment for injecting drug use is a risk behavior for HIV infection.

6. *Change behavior if ever have injected illegal drugs.* A person who has injected drugs in the past should be tested for HIV and other STDs and, if needed, get help for drug misuse and abuse.

7. *Do not share a needle to make tattoos or to pierce ears or other body parts.* Sharing a needle to make a tattoo or to pierce ears or other body parts is a risk behavior. Tattooing and piercing should be performed only by qualified people who use sterile equipment.

8. *Follow universal precautions.* **Universal precautions** are steps taken to prevent the spread of disease by treating all human blood and certain body fluids as if they contain HIV, HBV, and other pathogens. It is important to always follow universal precautions when having contact with the blood, other body fluids, mucous membranes, or broken skin of a person. Disposable latex gloves should be worn and the hands washed with a waterless antiseptic hand cleanser after removing them. The use of a face mask or shield with a one-way valve when performing first aid for breathing emergencies also provides protection. One should not touch objects that have had contact with a person's blood.

9. *Ask at the dentist whether dental pieces and accessories are sterilized (autoclaved) between patients.* To **autoclave** is to sterilize with steam under pressure. The FDA, CDC, and American Dental Association recommend autoclaving.

10. *Inquire about the safety of having a transfusion or tissue transplant.* A person should not give blood if he or she engages in risk behavior. The FDA controls blood donations in the United States. All donors are screened and checked against a list. After donation, blood is tested for HIV, hepatitis B, and syphilis. As a result, there is little risk of HIV infection from blood transfusions in the United States. In countries other than the United States, anyone who might need a blood transfusion should inquire about the safety of the blood supply. Since 1993 all potential donors of human tissues in the United States must be tested for HIV, hepatitis B, and hepatitis C. Imported tissues must be accompanied by records showing the tissues were screened and tested.

Health Goal #67

I Will Choose Behaviors to Reduce My Risk of Cardiovascular Diseases

Cardiovascular Diseases

A cardiovascular disease is a disease of the heart and blood vessels. Cardiovascular diseases account for almost half of all deaths in the United States, and they disable millions more people each year. The American Heart Association (2007) cites statistics showing that nearly 900,000 Americans die of cardiovascular diseases each year. Taken as a whole, cardiovascular disease is the cause of more deaths than the next five causes of death combined (American Heart Association, 2007).

ARTERIOSCLEROSIS AND ATHEROSCLEROSIS

Arteriosclerosis is a general term for several conditions that cause hardening and thickening of the arteries. Some arteriosclerosis occurs naturally as people age. One type of arteriosclerosis is **atherosclerosis,** a disease in which fat is deposited on artery walls. The fatty deposits may harden and form plaque. **Plaque** is hardened deposits. Medical scientists believe that high blood cholesterol levels, a high-fat diet, high blood pressure, and smoking can cause injury to the lining of arteries and contribute to plaque buildup. The buildup of plaque in artery walls may begin as early as two years of age. It does not develop suddenly in later life.

CORONARY HEART DISEASE

Coronary heart disease (CHD) is a disease in which the coronary arteries are narrowed or blocked. A **coronary artery** is a blood vessel that carries blood to the heart muscles. The coronary arteries encircle the heart and continuously nourish it with blood. Plaque buildup in the coronary arteries causes coronary heart disease, which can cause a heart attack.

Heart Attack

A **heart attack** is the death of cardiac muscle caused by a lack of blood flow to the heart. **Myocardial infarction (MI)** is the medical term for heart attack. A coronary artery that is narrowed by plaque might become clogged by a blood clot. If this happens, blood flow to the heart muscle is blocked. A heart attack can result in disability or death. The warning signs include uncomfortable pressure or pain in the center of the chest; pain that spreads to the shoulders, neck, jaw, or back; lightheadedness; fainting; sweating; nausea; and shortness of breath. The American Heart Association (AHA) warns that not all of these signs occur in every heart attack. The AHA advises that people get medical help immediately when some of these symptoms occur.

Angina Pectoris

Angina pectoris is chest pain that results from narrowed coronary arteries. The pain occurs because the heart is not getting an adequate amount of oxygen. Sudden physical exertion, vigorous exercise, or excessive stress can cause angina pectoris in people with coronary heart disease. Many people with coronary heart disease take nitroglycerin pills to relieve chest pains. **Nitroglycerin** is a drug that widens the coronary arteries, allowing more oxygen to get to the cardiac muscle. Angina pectoris is a warning sign for a heart attack. A heart attack may occur if the narrowing that causes angina pectoris is very severe.

Heart Rhythm Abnormalities

The heart must beat in rhythm to effectively pump blood throughout the body. **Arrhythmia** is a heart condition in which the heart sometimes beats very slowly or very fast for no obvious reason. The heart may skip beats or beat irregularly. Various drugs are available to treat arrhythmia. People who do not improve after taking drugs may need to have surgery to implant a pacemaker. A **pacemaker** is a device that is implanted in the heart to stimulate normal heart contractions.

Congestive Heart Failure

Congestive heart failure is a condition that occurs when the heart's pumping ability is below normal capacity and fluid accumulates in the lungs and other areas of the body. Causes of congestive heart failure are heart attack, atherosclerosis, birth defects, high blood pressure, and rheumatic fever. Drugs that improve the heart's pumping ability and get rid of excess fluids are used to treat congestive heart failure. Reducing the amount of sodium in the diet is helpful.

Rheumatic Fever

Rheumatic fever is when the immune system attacks the heart and can cause fever, weakness, and damage to the valves in the heart. **Rheumatic heart disease** is permanent heart damage that results from rheumatic fever. The symptoms of rheumatic fever are painful, swollen joints and skin rashes. Rheumatic fever is most common in children and teens. Prevention of rheumatic fever involves getting prompt treatment for strep throat.

Stroke

A **stroke,** or **cerebrovascular accident,** is a condition caused by a blocked or broken blood vessel in the brain. Brain cells in the area of the blocked or broken blood vessel are deprived of the oxygen they need. The brain cells die within minutes, and the affected area of the brain and the parts of the body controlled by those brain cells cannot function. One of the most common causes of a stroke is a blood clot in an artery in the brain. Strokes also can be caused if an aneurysm in the brain bursts. An **aneurysm** is a weakened area of a blood vessel. Strokes also can be caused by a head injury. A stroke may result in paralysis, disability, or death. High blood pressure, cigarette smoking, high blood cholesterol, and having heart disease or diabetes are major risk factors for stroke.

Reducing Risk of Cardiovascular Diseases

Scientific studies have identified several cardiovascular disease risk factors (Kuller et al., 2006). **Cardiovascular disease risk factors** are characteristics of people and ways they might behave that increase the possibility of cardiovascular disease. The greater the number of cardiovascular disease risk factors people have, the greater their risk of cardiovascular disease. The severity of a risk factor also determines its importance. For example, of two people whose only risk factor is a high blood cholesterol level, the one with the higher level is more at risk for cardiovascular disease.

Some cardiovascular disease risk factors cannot be controlled. These include age, gender, race, and having blood relatives with cardiovascular disease. The risk of cardiovascular disease increases with age. Four out of five people who die of heart attack are over the age of sixty-five. Males have a higher incidence of cardiovascular disease than females. However, after menopause the incidence of cardiovascular disease increases in females. People whose family members and other close relatives have suffered a premature heart attack also have an increased risk. A **premature heart attack** is a heart attack that occurs before age fifty-five in males and age sixty-five in females. Some cardiovascular disease risk factors can be controlled. The seven actions that follow can help control cardiovascular disease risk factors.

MAINTAIN A HEALTHY BLOOD CHOLESTEROL LEVEL

The risk of a heart attack rises as blood cholesterol level increases. **Cholesterol** is a fatlike substance made by the body and found in certain foods. It is a normal part of the blood and causes problems when the level is too high. People can check their blood cholesterol level by having a small amount of their blood analyzed and, if cholesterol is high, getting a lipoprotein analysis. A **lipoprotein analysis** is a measure of two main types of lipoproteins in the blood. **Low-density lipoproteins (LDLs)** are substances in the blood that carry cholesterol to body cells. **High-density lipoproteins (HDLs)** are substances in the blood that carry cholesterol to the liver for breakdown and excretion. The higher the HDL level in the blood, the lower the risk of developing heart disease. Saturated fat raises blood cholesterol level. **Saturated fat** is a type of fat from dairy products, solid vegetable fat, and meat and poultry. Reducing the amount of saturated fat in the diet can help lower blood cholesterol level. People who are overweight can lower their total blood cholesterol level by losing excess weight. Physical activity and quitting smoking also helps increase the level of HDLs.

CHOOSE A HEART-HEALTHY DIET

A **heart-healthy diet** is a low-fat diet rich in fruits, vegetables, whole grains, nonfat and low-fat milk products, lean meats, poultry, and fish. Sugars, sweets, fats, oils, and salt are limited. Choosing a heart-healthy diet can help control factors that influence the risk of cardiovascular disease, such as blood cholesterol level, blood pressure, and weight. A heart-healthy diet includes foods that contain antioxidants. An **antioxidant** is a substance that protects cells from being damaged by oxidation. A balanced diet that includes antioxidants may lower the risk of heart disease. Vitamins C and E, beta-carotene, and selenium are antioxidants. Fruits and vegetables are good sources of antioxidants. See Chapter 8 for more information about choosing a heat-healthy diet, including a diserssion of *trans* fat.

AVOID TOBACCO PRODUCTS AND SECONDHAND SMOKE

Tobacco smoke contains carbon monoxide, which affects the heart by reducing the amount of oxygen available in the blood. A smoker's heart, lungs, brain, and other organs do not receive enough oxygen. Nicotine in tobacco causes an increase in heart rate and blood pressure that results in wear and tear on the heart and blood vessels, narrowing of the arteries, and reducing blood flow. People who use tobacco products are more likely to have heart attacks, high blood pressure, blood clots, strokes, aneurysms, and other disorders of the cardiovascular system. Smokers are about three times more likely than nonsmokers to die from coronary heart disease. Exposure to secondhand smoke also increases the risk of cardiovascular disease. People who quit using tobacco products reduce their risk of dying from cardiovascular disease. Fifteen years after quitting, an ex-smoker has the same risk of coronary heart disease as people who have never smoked.

MAINTAIN HEALTHFUL BLOOD PRESSURE

High blood pressure is a blood pressure of 140/90 mm Hg (millimeters of mercury) or greater for an extended time. The heart has to work extra hard to pump enough blood and oxygen to the body. This often contributes to artery walls becoming scarred, hardened, and less elastic. Keeping blood pressure within the normal range reduces the risk of cardiovascular disease. There usually are no symptoms of high blood pressure. The only way people can tell if they have high blood pressure is to have it checked. High blood pressure that is left untreated can contribute to heart attack, stroke, kidney failure, or vision problems. People can keep their blood pressure low, or lower their high blood pressure, by making lifestyle choices. They can lose weight if they are overweight; participate regularly in

risk than those who carry weight on their hips. They are at increased risk for heart disease, stroke, high blood pressure, high blood cholesterol, and diabetes. The key to controlling weight is balancing the calories eaten with the calories burned. Cutting down on calories and engaging in regular physical activity can help people lose and keep off weight.

PARTICIPATE IN REGULAR PHYSICAL ACTIVITY

Participating in physical activity helps control blood cholesterol, blood pressure, body weight, and diabetes. When physical inactivity is combined with poor diet, the impact on health is devastating, accounting for 400,000 deaths per year (Centers for Disease Control and Prevention, 2005). Physical activity does not have to be painful or overly strenuous to be healthful. Thirty minutes of physical activity a day can build a healthy cardiovascular system. Regular physical activity prevents and lowers high blood pressure. It increases HDL levels and helps maintain healthy body weight. The body is better able to use insulin, which helps control diabetes. Diabetes also is a risk factor for cardiovascular disease. Regular physical activity decreases the tendency to form blood clots, helps reduce stress, and contributes to a stronger cardiovascular system.

physical activity; avoid tobacco products and secondhand smoke; get an adequate amount of potassium, calcium, and magnesium in their diet; and choose foods low in fat, cholesterol, and sodium. Many people who have high blood pressure can lower it by reducing the amount of sodium in their diet. When lifestyle choices do not improve blood pressure, a physician might prescribe antihypertensives. **Antihypertensives** are drugs that lower hypertension, or high blood pressure.

MAINTAIN A HEALTHFUL BODY WEIGHT

Excess body weight increases the risk of cardiovascular disease because the heart must work harder to pump blood to the body. Being overweight increases the risk of high blood cholesterol, high blood pressure, and diabetes. When overweight people lose weight, they lower their level of LDLs, increase their level of HDLs, and lower their blood pressure. How weight is distributed in the body also makes a difference. People who carry fat around the waist have a greater

MANAGE STRESS

Being stressed causes the heart to pump more often than it should. Stress increases resting blood pressure. It also increases blood cholesterol levels in some people. It can lead to excess smoking or eating and an inability to sleep well. People can control stress using stress-management skills. **Stress-management skills** are techniques to prevent and deal with stressors and to protect against the unhealthful effects produced by the stress response. They include using responsible decision-making skills, keeping a time management plan, having a support network of friends, participating in physical activity, and getting plenty of rest and sleep.

An Emerging Culprit

New scientific studies suggest that inflammation is important in the development of atherosclerosis (the process in which fatty deposits build up in the lining of arteries). **Inflammation** is the process by which the body responds to injury. Evidence is also accumulating that inflammation is a common trigger of heart attacks, even when the buildup of fatty deposits in the lining of arteries is minimal.

In an article in *U.S. News and World Report,* Katherine Hobson (Oct. 20, 2003, p. 42) describes the suspected process and theory of inflammation's role in heart attack:

> The fatty plaques that gum up arteries were once thought to be the result of too much low density lipoprotein—LDL, the "bad cholesterol"—hanging around and clogging the vessels, much like a hairball in a drain. Now there's a more complex theory, involving inflammation. When those LDL particles sit around for long enough, they oxidize and cause the blood vessel walls to become "sticky." The sticky walls in turn attract specialized white blood cells—monocytes and T cells—and suck them into the inner wall of the artery. A complicated cascade of chemical events follows, but the bottom line is that it's the immune system's inflammatory response—not just the bad cholesterol itself—that gums up the works, causing strokes and heart attacks.

Inflammation can be measured by a test that looks for high levels of a chemical called C-reactive protein, one of many that increase during inflammation. **C-reactive protein (CRP)** is a protein produced by the liver as part of the normal immune system response to injury or infection. It is one of the most studied markers of the possible role of inflammation in heart disease. Some experts predict that it may become a standard part of physical exams and might identify people at high risk for heart disease who in the past might not have been considered at high risk due to normal or low blood cholesterol levels. Studies are underway to determine whether CRP

is a better predictor of heart disease than high blood cholesterol (Hackam & Anand, 2003).

Health Goal #68

I Will Choose Behaviors to Reduce My Risk of Diabetes

Diabetes

Diabetes, or **diabetes mellitus,** is a disease in which the body produces little or no insulin. **Insulin** is a hormone that regulates the blood sugar level. If the pancreas fails to produce enough insulin, a person develops diabetes. Diabetes disrupts metabolism. **Metabolism** is the rate at which food is converted into energy in body cells. **Glucose** is a simple sugar that is the main source of energy for the body. Normally, insulin regulates the amount of glucose in the blood and the delivery of glucose into body cells. If there is not enough insulin, or if the body does not use the insulin, glucose levels build up in the blood. This causes the excess glucose to overflow into urine and pass out of the body. Because glucose is the main source of energy, the body loses its source of fuel even though the blood contains large amounts of glucose.

There are three types of diabetes: Type 1 diabetes, Type 2 diabetes, and gestational diabetes. There are 20.8 million children and adults in the United States, or 7 percent of the population, who have diabetes. One-third of these people are unaware that they have the disease (American Diabetes Association, 2007). Experts estimate that by the year 2025 the incidence of diabetes in the United States will double (Gorman, 2003). African Americans, Native Americans, Hispanics, and Asians have higher rates of diabetes than non-Hispanic white Americans. Diabetes is also a global problem; the prevalence of diabetes is expected to triple in Africa, the eastern Mediterranean, the Middle East, and Southeast Asia and to double in Europe (Gorman, 2003).

TYPE 1 DIABETES

In **Type 1 diabetes,** the body produces little or no insulin. Type 1 diabetes is considered an autoimmune disease. An **autoimmune disease** is a disease that results when the immune system produces antibodies that turn against the body's own cells. In Type 1 diabetes, the immune system attacks and destroys cells that produce insulin. Genetic factors and viruses are thought to trigger the body's immune system to attack these cells. Five to 10 percent of people who have diabetes have Type 1. Type 1 used to be called juvenile-onset diabetes because it appears most often in children and young adults. Type 1 usually appears suddenly and progresses quickly. Symptoms of Type 1 include increased thirst, frequent urination, constant hunger, weight loss, blurred vision, and extreme tiredness. These symptoms are caused by the buildup of sugar in the blood and the loss of sugar in the urine. People who have Type 1 need daily injections of insulin to stay alive. They also need to follow a special diet.

TYPE 2 DIABETES

In **Type 2 diabetes,** the body produces insulin but it cannot be used by cells. Type 2 diabetes is the most common type of diabetes. About 90 to 95 percent of people who have diabetes have Type 2. Type 2 used to be called adult-onset diabetes because it used to appear most often in adults over age forty. However, this term is no longer appropriate because Type 2 is now appearing increasingly in children and adolescents. The onset of Type 2 diabetes is usually gradual, and the symptoms are not as noticeable as those of Type 1 diabetes. As a result, Type 2 diabetes may go undetected for many years. Symptoms include feeling tired, frequent urination, unusual thirst, weight loss, blurred vision, frequent infections, and slow healing of sores. About 80 percent of people who have Type 2 diabetes are overweight. Type 2 diabetes often can be treated through weight loss, diet, physical activity, and oral medications. Blacks, Hispanics, American Indians, Asian Americans, and Pacific Islanders are at particularly high risk for Type 2 diabetes (Bren, 2004).

Although Type 2 diabetes still tends to most frequently strike people in their fifth or sixth decade, more children and adolescents are getting it. Type 2 diabetes has been rising steadily in children and teens, especially black, Hispanic, and Native American youths (Bren, 2004). This is of grave concern because these young people likely face a lifetime of problems, including higher risks of blindness, heart disease, and stroke. The fact that increasing numbers of young people are now developing Type 2 diabetes is a warning sign that many people need to make changes in their

lifestyle or this problem will continue to escalate (Gorman, 2003).

GESTATIONAL DIABETES

Gestational diabetes occurs in some females during pregnancy. Insulin is produced, but the body does not respond to it. The resistance to insulin is caused by hormones the placenta produces during pregnancy. Gestational diabetes usually is treated with diet, not with oral medications because these might harm the baby. Gestational diabetes usually disappears after the birth of the baby. Women who have had gestational diabetes are at higher risk of developing Type 2 diabetes.

Managing Diabetes

People who have diabetes must manage their disease to avoid the devastating complications of diabetes. Managing diabetes involves monitoring blood glucose levels to make sure they do not become too low or too high. Blood-testing kits are available that allow diabetics to test their own blood glucose levels. The test involves pricking a finger to draw a drop of blood and placing the blood on a strip of specially coated material. The strip is placed into a machine that measures blood glucose levels. People who have diabetes might test their glucose level several times a day. In this way, they can see how their body responds to meals, exercise, and insulin shots or oral medication. Research shows that people who have diabetes and keep their blood sugar levels as close to normal as possible have a reduced risk of developing complications (American Diabetes Association, 2007).

People who have Type 1 diabetes need daily injections of insulin to keep their blood glucose levels safe. Insulin injections must be balanced with meals and daily activities. Many people who have Type 2 diabetes are able to control their diabetes with diet and exercise exclusively. Because most people who have Type 2 diabetes are overweight, losing weight is an important part of the treatment. Some people who have Type 2 diabetes also need oral medication or insulin injections to lower blood glucose levels. People who have diabetes need to consult a physician who can monitor the disease and check for complications. Complications can affect almost every area of the body. Diabetes can lead to blindness, heart disease, stroke, kidney failure, loss of circulation to the legs and feet, nerve damage, and premature death. This year more than 200,000 Americans will die from diabetes (Gorman, 2003).

Reducing the Risk of Diabetes

Diabetes is not a contagious disease. A person cannot be infected by someone who has the disease. A person cannot get diabetes from eating too much sugar. However, certain factors increase the risk of developing diabetes. People can remember these risk factors by considering four *F*s:

- *Fat* (being overfat and overweight)
- *Female* (being female)
- *Family* (having a family history)
- *Forty* (being forty years of age or older)

People cannot control three of the four risk factors—being female, having a family history of diabetes, and being over forty years of age. However, they can maintain a healthful weight and percentage body fat. They can exercise regularly and eat the right amount of calories to maintain a healthful body weight. The best way to prevent or delay Type 2 diabetes is to maintain a desirable body weight and to keep physically active. Being overweight reduces the body's ability to produce and use insulin. Physical activity has a positive influence in decreasing blood glucose levels. Physical activity also helps the body respond to insulin. A major study showed that making modest changes in diet and physical activity delayed Type 2 diabetes for at least three years in people who were at high risk (Gorman, 2003). Medical scientists do not know how to prevent Type 1 diabetes.

Health Goal #69

I Will Recognize Ways to Manage Chronic Health Conditions

Chronic Health Conditions

It is estimated that 5 to 15 percent of young people have chronic health conditions. Chronic health conditions are recurring or persistent.

Chronic health conditions can cause great suffering and, in some cases, death. People who have chronic health conditions have to cope with changes in their health status over long periods of time. They need to take care of themselves and might take medications or have special diets to follow. They may need surgery or other medical care. They may require assistance with daily activities. Often, they must work through feelings of anxiety, fear, and isolation. There are many chronic health conditions.

ARTHRITIS

Arthritis is the painful inflammation of joints. Arthritis affects the muscles, tendons, and ligaments that surround joints. There are two major types of arthritis. **Osteoarthritis** is the wearing down of the moving parts of joints. **Rheumatoid arthritis** is a condition in which joints become deformed and may lose function.

CEREBRAL PALSY

Cerebral palsy is a disorder of the nervous system that interferes with muscle coordination. Possible causes include too much pressure on the head during childbirth, head injury, lead poisoning, accidental injury, and certain illnesses. People with cerebral palsy might stand and walk in an awkward manner and have difficulty speaking, hearing, and seeing. They may be mentally retarded, although a portion have normal or high intelligence.

CHRONIC FATIGUE SYNDROME

Chronic fatigue syndrome (CFS) is a condition in which recurring tiredness makes it difficult to function in normal ways. Symptoms include headache, sore throat, low-grade fever, fatigue, and weakness. People with CFS also may have tender lymph glands, muscle and joint aches, and the inability to concentrate. CFS symptoms may recur for more than six months. CFS may begin during periods of high stress. CFS may develop after mononucleosis in the teens. There is no known cure.

CYSTIC FIBROSIS

Cystic fibrosis is a condition in which large amounts of abnormally thick mucus are produced, particularly in the lungs and pancreas. Body organs, such as the lungs and pancreas, may be damaged by accumulations of this mucus. Signs and symptoms of cystic fibrosis include coughing, wheezing, difficulty breathing, vomiting, and constipation. The sweat of people with cystic fibrosis contains an excessive amount of salt. Physicians use a sweat test to diagnose cystic fibrosis. Many people who have cystic fibrosis survive into adulthood. Cystic fibrosis is caused by an abnormal gene.

DOWN SYNDROME

Down syndrome is a genetic disorder in which a child is born with an extra chromosome in each cell. Children born with Down syndrome have mental retardation, short arms and legs, and a flattened face with upward slanting, almond-shaped eyes. The heart and other organs also may be affected.

EPILEPSY

Epilepsy is a disorder in which abnormal electrical activity in the brain causes a temporary loss of control of the mind and body. A **seizure** is a period in which a person loses control over mind and body. **Petit mal** is a small seizure in which a person loses consciousness for a few seconds. **Grand mal** is a major seizure in which a person may have convulsions. During a convulsion, the body stiffens and twitching may occur. People who are having major seizures can be helped by removal of objects that may injure them. Do not place anything in the mouth. Although people of any age can get epilepsy, it primarily affects children, teens, and young adults. Epilepsy can be caused by head injury, brain tumor, stroke, poisoning, or infection. Heredity also plays a role in some cases of epilepsy.

HEMOPHILIA

Hemophilia is an inherited condition in which the blood does not clot normally. A minor injury to a person with hemophilia can lead to uncontrolled bleeding. Spontaneous bleeding also occurs. Hemophilia occurs almost exclusively in males. A defective gene is passed from the father to his offspring. To inherit hemophilia, a female must get the defective gene from both parents.

MIGRAINE

Migraine is severe head pain that is caused by dilation of blood vessels in the brain. The symptoms may include severe throbbing, blurred vision, nausea, and vomiting. In some cases, the pain is so severe that people cannot attend school or work.

MULTIPLE SCLEROSIS

Multiple sclerosis (MS) is a disease in which the protective covering of myelin on nerve fibers in the brain and spinal cord is destroyed. It is believed that the immune system attacks the myelin, resulting in scarring of nerve fibers. People who have MS experience tingling and numbness in the body and may feel tired and dizzy. They may have these symptoms for several weeks to several months. Relapses may follow illness or periods of stress. Some people who have MS are not able to walk or care for themselves. There is no cure for MS. MS is more common in young adults.

MUSCULAR DYSTROPHY

Muscular dystrophy is a genetic disease in which the muscles progressively deteriorate. There is gradual loss of muscle function. Muscular dystrophy is rare. The most common type affects males. There is no cure.

NARCOLEPSY

Narcolepsy is a chronic sleep disorder in which people are excessively sleepy, even after adequate nighttime sleep. People who have narcolepsy often become drowsy and fall asleep in inappropriate situations. They may fall asleep without warning several times each day. This often interrupts their daily lives and interferes with school or work. The cause of narcolepsy is unknown. Symptoms usually appear in the teen years. Although there is no cure, there is treatment.

PARKINSON'S DISEASE

Parkinson's disease usually affects people over the age of fifty. Signs and symptoms include rigid posture, slow movement, fixed facial expression, and a shuffling walk. Symptoms may become worse when a person is tired or emotionally distressed. The intellect is not affected until late in the disease, although speech becomes slow.

PEPTIC ULCER

Peptic ulcer is an open sore on the lining of the esophagus, stomach, or first part of the small intestine. The most common symptom is a burning pain in the abdomen. There may be upset stomach, back pain, and bleeding. Peptic ulcers can be fatal if they are not treated. Peptic ulcer is caused by a bacterial infection, which is treated with antibiotics.

SICKLE-CELL ANEMIA

Sickle-cell anemia is a condition in which the red blood cells are sickle shaped and are fragile and easily destroyed. The sickle-shaped cells do not easily pass through tiny blood vessels. Symptoms appear after six months of age and include fatigue, headache, and shortness of breath. Children who have sickle-cell anemia are at increased risk for developing pneumonia and other infections. There is no cure. In the United States, it occurs primarily in African Americans.

SYSTEMIC LUPUS ERYTHEMATOSUS

Systemic lupus erythematosus (SLE) is an autoimmune condition in which connective tissue becomes inflamed. SLE affects the skin, kidneys, joints, muscles, and central nervous system. There may be bleeding in the central nervous system, kidney failure, or heart failure. Symptoms include fatigue, fever, loss of appetite, nausea, joint pain, and weight loss. A red, blotchy rash may develop on the cheeks and nose. SLE occurs most often during the teen years and is more common in females than males.

Health Goal #70

I Will Choose Behaviors to Reduce My Risk of Cancer

Cancer

All cells in a person's body usually divide in an orderly pattern to produce more cells. This enables the body to grow and repair itself. Normal cell division is under precise control. But sometimes there are problems, and cells do not divide in the usual way. **Cancer** is a group of diseases in which cells divide in an uncontrolled manner. These cells can form a tumor. A **tumor** is an abnormal growth of tissue. Tumors can be benign or malignant. A **benign tumor** is a tumor that is not cancerous and does not spread to other parts of the body. Benign tumors rarely are life-threatening. They usually can be removed and do not grow back. A **malignant tumor** is a tumor

that is cancerous and may spread to other parts of the body. **Metastasis** is the spread of cancer. Cancer cells can break away from a malignant tumor, enter the bloodstream or lymphatic system, and travel to other parts of the body where they form tumors.

Cancer is not contagious. A person cannot get cancer from another person. Cancer also is not caused by an injury, such as a bump or bruise.

People of all ages get cancer. However, nearly all types of cancer are more common in middle-aged and elderly people than they are in young people. The most common type of cancer for both males and females is skin cancer. The next most common type among males is prostate cancer. Among females, it is breast cancer. Lung cancer is the leading cause of cancer deaths in both males and females (American Cancer Society, 2007).

Risk Factors, Signs and Symptoms, and Early Detection

Although the causes of cancer are not completely understood, many risk factors for cancer have been identified. These risk factors increase people's chances of getting cancer. Some people are fearful of cancer. They do not realize that many types of cancer can be prevented or successfully treated when detected early. They can improve the chance that cancer will be detected early if they have regular physical examinations, perform certain self-examinations, and are aware of risk factors for and signs and symptoms of cancer.

Cancer Treatment

Many people who have cancer are treated successfully. In some cases, the cancer is cured. In other cases, the progress of the cancer is slowed, life is prolonged, and quality of life is improved. Common treatment approaches for cancer include surgery, radiation therapy, chemotherapy, and immunotherapy.

Surgery is the most common treatment for cancer. If tumors are confined to a particular site, physicians can remove the cancerous tissue from the body. If tumors are spread out, surgery is more difficult to perform. Surgery often is combined with radiation therapy and chemotherapy.

Radiation therapy is treatment of cancer with high-energy radiation to kill or damage cancer cells. Radiation therapy usually is performed using a machine that generates radiation. It also is performed by placing radioactive materials in or near the cancer. Radiation therapy may produce side effects, such as fatigue, nausea, and vomiting. The skin also may become red and blistered in the areas that are treated. Radiation therapy does not make patients radioactive.

Chemotherapy is treatment with anticancer drugs. These drugs kill cancer inside the body. Chemotherapy works mainly on cancer cells, but healthy cells can be harmed as well. Almost all people taking chemotherapy experience unwanted side effects, such as nausea, vomiting, hair loss, and fatigue. Most of these side effects do not last long and will gradually go away. Nausea and vomiting usually stop a day or two after each treatment. If hair is lost, it usually grows back after the treatment has stopped. Many people wear wigs, caps, or scarves until their hair grows back. Fatigue may last several months.

Immunotherapy is a process in which the immune system is stimulated to fight cancer cells. One type of immunotherapy involves injecting patients with cancer cells that have been made harmless by radiation. The immune system responds by producing antibodies that attack cancer cells in the body. Other types of immunotherapy involve injecting patients with other substances that stimulate the immune system.

Reducing the Risk of Cancer

Some risk factors for cancer cannot be controlled. For example, people cannot control their heredity. However, almost all cancers are associated with choices over which people do have control. There are things people can do to help reduce their risk of developing cancer:

1. *Know the warning signs of cancer.* Detecting cancer in the early stages increases the chances that it can be treated successfully. The American Cancer Society recommends that people learn seven early warning signs of cancer, for which the mnemonic is the acronym *CAUTION:*
   - **C**hange in bowel or bladder habits
   - **A** sore that does not heal
   - **U**nusual bleeding or discharge
   - **T**hickening or lump in a breast or elsewhere
   - **I**ndigestion or difficulty in swallowing
   - **O**bvious change in a wart or mole
   - **N**agging cough or hoarseness
2. *Choose a tobacco-free lifestyle.* Tobacco use is the most preventable cause of cancer death. Tobacco products contain many carcinogens. A **carcinogen** is a chemical that is known to cause cancer. Using tobacco products and being exposed to secondhand smoke are leading causes of cancer death. Cases of lung cancer would be greatly reduced if people would never begin to smoke. People who smoke one pack of cigarettes a day are ten times more likely than nonsmokers to get lung cancer. Exposure to secondhand smoke increases the risk of lung cancer for nonsmokers. Smokeless tobacco increases the risk of cancers of the mouth, gums, and throat. Individuals who use tobacco products should quit immediately to reduce cancer risk.
3. *Protect against the sun and avoid tanning booths and sunlamps.* **Ultraviolet (UV) radiation** is a type of radiation that comes from the sun and also is emitted by sunlamps and tanning booths. Repeated exposure to UV radiation increases the

risk of skin cancer, including malignant melanoma. **Malignant melanoma** is the form of skin cancer that is most often fatal. The sun's harmful UV rays are strongest during the summer between 10 A.M. and 3 P.M. Avoid exposure to the sun during these hours. People who are in the sun should wear protective clothing and use sunscreens that have a sun protection factor (SPF) of at least 15. Tanning booths or sunlamps should never be used. People should check their skin regularly and consult a physician if they notice any abnormal growths.

4. *Follow dietary guidelines.* Eating a variety of foods is important so that a person's body has a combination of nutrients. Several servings of a variety of fruits and vegetables should be eaten each day. Fruits and vegetables contain antioxidants that help prevent cancer. Several servings of fiber-rich foods, such as whole-grain cereals, legumes, vegetables, and fruits, need to be eaten. Fatty foods should be avoided. Foods that are smoked, salted, or nitrite-cured should be limited or omitted.

5. *Maintain desirable weight and a healthful body composition.* People who are overweight and have a high percentage body fat are more at risk for developing cancer. Regular exercise and weight management are essential to reduce cancer risk.

6. *Avoid drinking alcohol.* Drinking alcohol may cause changes in body cells. Alcohol also drains from the body vitamins needed for optimal health. Drinking alcohol increases the risk of cancer of the liver, throat, mouth, breast, and stomach. Chances of developing cancer are multiplied further if a person drinks alcohol and smokes tobacco or marijuana.

7. *Avoid exposure to dangerous chemicals and airborne fibers.* The following are some of the many substances that have been found to increase the risk of cancer: benzene, benzidene, vinyl chloride, uranium, radon, nickel, cadmium, asbestos, and pesticides. Wearing rubber gloves and a mask when exposed to dangerous chemicals reduces exposure. Protective clothing should be worn if exposed to airborne fibers.

8. *Avoid air pollution.* Polluted air contains many carcinogens. People should avoid the exhaust from cars, buses, and trucks. People should have their homes tested for **radon,** an odorless, colorless radioactive gas that is released by rocks and soil. It can collect and be trapped in basements and crawl spaces. Inhaling radon can increase the risk of lung cancer.

9. *Avoid infection with HIV and sexually transmitted diseases (STDs).* Many people who are infected with HIV develop Kaposi's sarcoma and other cancers. Women who have genital warts are at increased risk for cervical cancer. Choosing abstinence is an important way to reduce the risk of cancer. So is choosing not to inject drugs, such as steroids and heroin. Contact with blood and body fluids should be avoided.

10. *Know one's family cancer history.* Some cancers, such as breast, colon, and ovarian cancers, occur more frequently in certain families. This could be due to heredity or to the family's environment and lifestyle habits. Individuals should be aware of family members and other relatives who have had cancer. If a family member or other relative has had cancer, regular cancer checkups and keeping one's physician informed are essential.

Consumer and Community Health

HEALTH GOALS FOR CONSUMER AND COMMUNITY HEALTH

71. I will acquire knowledge of laws to protect health.
72. I will recognize my rights as a consumer.
73. I will take action if my consumer rights are violated.
74. I will make a plan to manage time and money.
75. I will choose healthful entertainment.
76. I will analyze ways messages delivered through technology might affect health status.
77. I will make responsible choices about health care providers and facilities.
78. I will evaluate ways to pay for health care.
79. I will investigate health careers.
80. I will investigate public and international health needs.

Consumer and community health is the area of health that focuses on acquiring knowledge of laws to protect health, recognizing rights as a consumer, taking action if consumer rights are violated, making a plan to manage time and money, choosing healthful entertainment, analyzing the ways that messages delivered through technology might affect health status, making responsible choices about health care providers and facilities, evaluating ways to pay for health care, investigating health careers, and investigating public and international health needs. This chapter provides the health knowledge needed to teach young people important life skills for consumer and community health.

Health Goal #71

I Will Acquire Knowledge of Laws to Protect Health

A **consumer** is a person who chooses sources of health-related information and buys or uses health products and services. **Consumerism** is the practice of obtaining reliable and tested products, services, and information. Suppose someone purchases a product and it is defective or parts are missing. Suppose someone buys a service and the provider does not provide what is expected. Consumers would not be satisfied and would have every right to take action.

Laws That Protect Health

There are many laws that protect health and aim to prevent disease and injury. There are different types of laws that govern people's actions. In the United States, individuals are subject to the laws and regulations made by their city, county, state, and federal governments. It is best to think of laws as a hierarchy with federal laws at the top, local laws at the bottom, and state laws somewhere in between.

Federal laws are laws that are enacted by the United States Congress. No federal or state law may violate a federal law. Federal laws must be followed by every state in the country. If a state law contradicts a federal law, the federal law preempts the state law, and the state will be required to abide by the federal law. An example of a federal law that protects health is the Occupational Safety and Health Act. This law requires that employers provide workplaces that are free from serious recognized hazards and comply with occupational safety and health standards. Another federal law designed to protect health is the Clean Air Act. This law sets standards for air quality. Another is the Public Health Improvement Act. This law provides for grants to state and local health departments to update laboratories, improve electronic information networks and emergency response systems, and train staff. The law is designed to strengthen the ability of public health departments to respond to health threats like drug-resistant diseases and terrorist attacks.

Various federal agencies are responsible for enforcing federal laws. For example, the Food and Drug Administration has the responsibility (or shares the responsibility with other federal agencies) of enforcing several federal laws that protect health, such as the Federal Food, Drug, and Cosmetic Modernization Act; the Food Quality Protection Act; the Federal Meat Inspections Act; and the Controlled Substances Act.

Federal laws do not cover all areas of the law, and in those instances, state or local laws can help to protect the public. **State laws** are laws that are enacted by state legislatures. State laws apply to everyone within the state. These laws cannot violate the state constitution, federal constitution, or federal law. State laws vary widely from state to state because it is up to each state to enact its own state laws. An example of state laws that protect the health of individuals and communities by preventing disease are school-entry immunization laws. All states require vaccination before children enter school. During the late 1970s, these laws were vigorously sought by school nurses, public health providers, family physicians, and parents who wanted to better protect the health of children entering school. The requirements of these laws vary from state to state. All states will exempt children from vaccination for medical reasons, and some will exempt children for religious and philosophical reasons.

County and municipal governments also enact laws. **Ordinances** are laws enacted by county and municipal governments through the authority granted to them by the state. Ordinances apply to everyone within the county or municipality limits. These ordinances may not violate state or federal laws. An example of an ordinance that protects the health of citizens is a local law that requires the use of bicycle helmets. In recent years, a number of counties and municipalities have enacted ordinances that require bicycle helmet use. Many of these ordinances were passed in states that do not have state laws requiring helmet use. There is no federal law requiring bicycle helmet use, and less than half of all states have bicycle helmet use laws. Does the county or city in which you live require the use of a bicycle helmet?

Young people need to realize that ordinances vary widely from locality to locality. Health teachers can help students become familiar with the laws that protect health in the state and city or county of residence. It is fairly easy to obtain a copy of state laws and local ordinances from the World Wide Web. Most state governments have a Web site that contains links to state laws. The same is often true for many city or county governments. Another option is to call the information number for a county or city government.

Health Goal #72

I Will Recognize My Rights as a Consumer

Consumer Rights

Consumer rights are the privileges that a consumer is guaranteed. There are four consumer rights that often are called "The Consumer Bill of

Rights" (see Table 12-1). By exercising consumer rights, individuals become intelligent consumers and thereby avoid being misled by inaccurate information and protect their health and the health of others.

It is important to remember that consumer rights are a privilege. Along with those privileges come responsibilities. It is a consumer's responsibility to use products and services in the manner in which they are intended. It is a consumer's responsibility to choose products and services that are affordable. And it is a person's responsibility to notify government agencies and businesses if these products or services do not meet expectations.

Tips for Being a Successful Consumer

To be a successful consumer, it is wise to shop around and compare quality and prices before purchasing a product or service. Take time to

TABLE 12-1

CONSUMER RIGHTS

CONSUMER RIGHT	PRIVILEGE
The right to choose	The ability to choose from various products and services available at competitive prices with the guarantee of satisfying quality
The right to be heard	The ability to have consumer well-being advocated when making and implementing government policy and when developing products and services
The right to safety	The protection from products, services, and production methods that are unhealthy or unsafe
The right to be informed	The ability to obtain information needed to make educated choices and the protection from false or misleading advertising and labeling
The right to satisfaction of basic needs	The ability to obtain vital products and services
The right to redress or remedy	The ability to reach an acceptable solution for a complaint, including compensation for misrepresentation, poor quality products, and unsatisfactory service
The right to consumer education	The ability to be aware of consumer rights and responsibilities and to act on them
The right to environmental health	The ability to live and work in an environment that is not unhealthy to present and future generations

consider all of the facts before making a decision. Do not be pressured into signing or buying anything. Check a company's reputation before doing business with it. Get a written estimate of repair costs. Never accept verbal guarantees or warranties in place of written ones. Read and understand contracts before signing. Make sure to never sign incomplete contracts. Keep copies of all contracts, warranties, guarantees, and receipts. Use caution when giving out credit card or bank account numbers. Avoid "too good to be true" offers. Never pay money to collect a "prize." Be suspicious if you must decide *immediately* to take advantage of the offer.

Health Fraud

Health fraud is the advertising, promotion, and sale of products and services that have not been scientifically proven safe and effective. A **quack** is a person or company who is involved in health fraud.

The Food and Drug Administration (FDA) identified categories in which health fraud is most frequent:

- Instant weight-loss schemes
- AIDS cures
- Arthritis products
- Cancer treatments
- Baldness treatments
- Nutritional supplements

There are several reasons why people must protect themselves from health fraud:

1. A person does not want to waste money on products or services that do not do what they are claimed to do.
2. A person does not want to use products or services that cause harm or injuries.
3. A person does not want to delay valuable medical treatment.

Health fraud often is targeted at young people and elderly people. Young people, particularly teens, who are overly concerned about their looks are vulnerable. They may buy useless products to clear up acne, build muscles, or lose weight quickly.

Elderly people with chronic health problems and life-threatening diseases are vulnerable. They may buy useless products and medicines, hoping that these will provide quick cures or recapture their youth.

The following questions can be used to recognize and protect against health fraud. Quacks often use these methods to sell products and services. A yes answer to any of these questions might indicate quackery or health fraud:

1. Is there a promise to cure a condition that medical scientists cannot cure?
2. Is there a promise of quick or painless results?
3. Is there a claim that a product or treatment works by a secret formula or in a mysterious way?
4. Is the product or treatment sold over the telephone, door to door, or by mail order?
5. Is the product available only through a PO box address?
6. Is the product or service promoted by a little-known person or group?
7. Is the product or service promoted on the back pages of magazines?
8. Is the product or service promoted through infomercials or in newspaper ads that look like articles?
9. Are there testimonials from people who claim that they were cured by the product or service?
10. Are celebrity endorsements used to promote the product or service?
11. Does the seller claim that the medical profession does not recognize the product or service?
12. Are tactics that play on emotions used to sell the product or service?
13. Are there claims that the product or service is effective for many unrelated disorders?
14. Does the seller say it is not necessary to talk to a physician about using the product or service?
15. Does the product fail to have labels that provide directions for use or cautions about use?
16. Does the seller claim that traditional medical treatment is more harmful than healthful?
17. Does a seller make claims that a product is "all-natural"?
18. Do providers of a treatment lack credentials from accredited schools?

Before buying a product that might be phony, a person should take the following steps:

- Contact the Better Business Bureau or a consumer protection office to check for complaints against the company.
- Ask about the refund or exchange policy.
- Read the warranty to find out what must be done if there is a problem.
- Check to see if a PO box can be found.
- Do not respond to any prize or gift offer that requires paying any money.

TABLE 12-2

HEALTH FRAUD RED FLAGS

Michelle Meadows advises consumers in the November–December 2006 issue of *FDA Consumer* to learn how to evaluate health-related claims in order to avoid becoming a victim of health fraud. Consumers need to avoid Web sites and other sources that offer quick and dramatic cures for serious diseases. The following are red flags that consumers need to watch for:

- Statements that the product is a quick and effective cure-all or a diagnostic tool for a wide variety of ailments. "Beneficial in treating cancer, ulcer, prostate problems, heart trouble, and more . . ."
- Statements that suggest the product can treat or cure diseases. "Shrinks tumors, cures impotency . . ."
- Promotions that use words like "scientific break-through," "miraculous cure," "secret ingredient," and "ancient remedy."
- Text that uses impressive-sounding terms like "hunger stimulation point" and "thermogenesis" for a weight-loss product.
- Undocumented case histories or personal testimonials by consumers or doctors claiming amazing results. "After eating a teaspoon of this product each day, my pain is completely gone . . ."
- Limited availability and advance payment requirements. "Hurry! This offer will not last."
- Promises of no-risk money-back guarantees. "If after 30 days you have not lost at least four pounds each week, your uncashed check will be returned to you."
- Promises of an easy fix.

Health Goal #73

I Will Take Action if My Consumer Rights Are Violated

Consumer Protection

Federal, state, and local government agencies play important roles in consumer protection. Professional associations help consumers by monitoring the credentials of their members and their actions. Private organizations provide additional assistance to consumers.

FEDERAL AGENCIES

Several federal agencies play a role in consumer protection. The **Consumer Information Center** provides free and low-cost publications on numerous consumer topics. The **Consumer Product Safety Commission (CPSC)** establishes and enforces product safety standards, receives consumer complaints about the safety of products, and distributes product safety information. The CPSC has authority to recall products. A **recall** is an order to take a product off the market due to safety concerns. The **Federal Bureau of Investigation (FBI)** is responsible for federal criminal offenses, including investigation of health fraud such as insurance scams. The **Federal Trade Commission (FTC)** enforces consumer protection laws and monitors trade practices and the advertising of foods, drugs, and cosmetics. The **Food and Drug Administration (FDA)** monitors the safety of cosmetics and food and the safety and effectiveness of new drugs, medical devices, and prescription and over-the-counter (OTC) drugs. The **National Health Information Center (NHIC)** is an agency that refers consumers to organizations that can provide health-related information. The **U.S. Department of Agriculture (USDA)** enforces standards to ensure the safe processing of food and oversees the distribution of food information to the public. The USDA also publishes consumer pamphlets on nutrition and food safety topics. The **U.S. Postal Service (USPS)** offers postal services and works to protect the public from crimes and fraud involving mail. Some of these crimes are sending unsolicited sexually oriented advertising, mailing child pornography, mailing bombs or materials designed to harm people (e.g., anthrax), consumer fraud schemes, and mail theft.

STATE AND LOCAL AGENCIES

Two important agencies that play a role in consumer protection are local health departments and state health departments. Responsibilities of local health departments include investigating consumer complaints, collecting health statistics, and offering maternal and child care programs, alcohol and other drug abuse programs, health education, and communicable disease control. Responsibilities of state health departments include investigating consumer complaints, collecting and distributing health information, and preventing and controlling disease. Another valuable resource for consumer protection is your state's office of attorney general. This office usually investigates allegations of fraud or illegal business practices. Consumers can file a consumer complaint with this office. This office also usually provides resources for consumer protection.

PRIVATE ORGANIZATIONS

There are private organizations that play a role in consumer protection. The **Council of Better Business Bureaus** is a nonprofit organization that monitors consumer complaints and advertising and selling practices. It provides listings of businesses that have received consumer complaints and publishes materials to help educate consumers about advertising and selling practices. **Consumer's Union (CU)** is an organization that tests products and publishes a magazine, *Consumer Reports,* that provides comparison ratings for product performance and safety. The CU also publishes books and pamphlets on consumer topics. The **Center for Science in the Public Interest (CSPI)** is a nonprofit organization that conducts activities to improve government and industry policies regarding food, nutrition, and other health concerns. The CSPI publishes educational materials for consumers. The **National Council Against Health Fraud (NCAHF)** is an organization that provides legal counsel and assistance to victims of health fraud. NCAHF provides many educational materials to consumers on the topic of health fraud.

TAKING ACTION IF CONSUMER RIGHTS ARE VIOLATED

Suppose a person purchases a product and it is defective or is missing parts. Or suppose someone buys a service and the provider does not provide what is expected. The consumer would not be satisfied and would have every right to take action, because consumer rights have been violated.

Even informed consumers sometimes buy a product or use a service that does not meet expectations. Consumers can report their complaints to one of the agencies or organizations discussed in this section of the chapter. If they do not know where or how to make a complaint, they can contact the local health department for advice.

There are specific actions that adults can teach young people to take when their consumer rights have been violated:

1. *Talk to parents or guardian and agree on a plan of action.*
2. *Save all paperwork related to the purchase in a file.*
3. *Contact the business that sold the item or performed the service.* Describe the problem and the desired action the business should take to remedy the problem (e.g., wanting money back, exchanging the product).
4. *Keep a record of actions.* Write down the name of the person who was contacted and a summary of the conversation.
5. *Allow time for the person who was contacted to resolve the problem.*
6. *Write a letter to the company headquarters if not satisfied with the actions taken to resolve the problem.* The letter should be addressed to the consumer office or the company president. Include the following information: date and place of purchase, a description of the product or service, what went wrong, and the desired action the business should take to remedy the problem. Include copies of all documents such as receipts or warranties. Do not send the originals. Keep a copy of the letter in files.
7. *Send a copy of the letter to a consumer group, the state's attorney general, or the local Better Business Bureau if the company does not respond in an adequate amount of time.* Contact the local or state consumer protection agency right away if there is suspicion that a law has been broken.
8. *Advise the company that groups responsible for consumer protection have been notified.*
9. *Inform the news media when there is a belief that an ad for a product or service is deceptive or inaccurate.*
10. *Consider the legal actions that one's family might take.*

Health Goal #74

I Will Make a Plan to Manage Time and Money

Time Management

There only are so many hours in the day, so people must consider their priorities. **Time management** is organizing time to accomplish priorities. Time management contributes to optimal health status. Optimal health status is the highest level of health a person can achieve. People who organize their time and include priorities in their lives will be balanced and will be less stressed. People who manage time and accomplish priorities are less likely to develop psychosomatic illnesses. There are twelve priorities for achieving optimal health status:

1. Time for family members
2. Time for friends
3. Time for oneself
4. Time for chores and job responsibilities
5. Time for schoolwork
6. Time for school activities
7. Time for physical activities
8. Time for mental activities such as reading and learning
9. Time for hobbies and entertainment
10. Time for rest and sleep
11. Time for healthful eating
12. Time for helping others

TIPS FOR STAYING ORGANIZED

Young people will find the following tips helpful for staying organized:

1. *Keep a calendar or organizer as a reminder of when important tasks need to be done.* Important events need to be written down. Use the calendar to plan large projects.
2. *Keep a daily to-do list.* Make a list of daily tasks that you must complete. Carry it with you and update it each morning or night. Number the list in the order of importance. Check off each task as you complete it.
3. *Keep your room and locker neat.* This helps you find materials quickly and not get stressed by things getting lost. It helps you avoid being late because you have to hunt for something.

Managing Money

Financial health is a health topic that many have failed to consider, but it is very important for at least two reasons. First, people who manage their money wisely experience less stress. They are not anxious and worried about paying bills or overspending. They are less likely to develop premature heart disease or cancer because of stress. Second, people who manage their money wisely will have the money they need to pay for health care. An important step in knowing how to manage money is being able to make a budget.

People should base their spending decisions on their budgets. They need to check the budget before making a purchase. They should not purchase something if it is more than the budget allows.

People should avoid the temptation to purchase on credit. Many people charge expenses on a credit card. A **credit card** is a card used for payment that the owner of the card agrees to make later. Each month the cardholder receives a statement of the expenses charged on the credit card. The person pays the bill in full or in part. If the person pays only part of the bill, interest is charged on the remaining balance. **Interest** is additional money that is paid for the use of a larger sum of money. Interest can add up. Credit cards are convenient, but they should be used with caution. People should not have more charges on their credit card than they can pay off in one month. They can go into debt if they make a habit of charging more than they can pay off each month. **Debt** is the condition of owing.

People need to avoid borrowing money. Some people often borrow money from friends and family members. This practice can be risky. There may be disagreements if people who borrow money do not repay it.

MAKING A BUDGET

Following are steps to take to make a budget:

1. *List income.* **Income** is money received. A student's income may include an allowance, money from part-time jobs, and gifts of money.

2. *List expenses.* **Expenses** are amounts of money needed to purchase or do something. Student expenses include clothing, snacks, and entertainment, and any money the student contributes to family and to savings. Savings is money set aside for future use. Savings might be used for college or vocational school or for emergencies.

3. *Keep a balanced budget.* A **balanced budget** is a plan in which a person's income is equal to or more than expenses. Compare expenses to income. If the expenses are greater than the income, evaluate the way the money is being managed. People can cut back on expenses or make a plan to earn more money. Children and teens should evaluate the budget with their parents or guardian.

GUIDELINES FOR COMPARISON SHOPPING

Comparison shopping is evaluating products and services using the following five criteria:

- *Price:* the cost
- *Convenience:* something that saves time or effort
- *Features:* the outstanding characteristics
- *Quality:* the degree of excellence of a product or service
- *Warranty:* a written assurance that a product or service will be repaired or replaced if a problem occurs

A person should ask several questions before buying a product: Is this something that I need? Can I afford this? Will I still enjoy this product a month from now? Can I purchase the same item at a different store or location for less money? Does this product appeal to me mainly because of its name brand? Would a different brand be less expensive and just as good? Is the quality of the item a good value for the price?

Health Goal #75

I Will Choose Healthful Entertainment

Entertainment is something that is designed to hold the interests of people. Entertainment can include a variety of activities. For example, a person might play sports, participate in a hobby,

shop, or go to museums or concerts for entertainment. One thing that has had a major impact on our choices for entertainment is technology. Technology has brought different opportunities into our lives, not only for learning, but also for entertainment. Think about the technology that people use on a daily or weekly basis, such as telephones, computers, or videos. The list goes on.

Media Entertainment

Many forms of entertainment are available through media and technology. For example, most people have one or more televisions in their homes. Two other popular forms of media entertainment are going to movies and renting videos or DVDs. The radio is another source of entertainment for many people. People who enjoy music often listen to the radio, CDs, and MP3 players as well as attend live concerts. Many also enjoy video or computer games. An increasing number of people use computers for many reasons, including entertainment.

Young people over the age of eight spend on average six hours and twenty-one minutes a day using various forms of media outside of school (Rideout, Roberts, & Foehr, 2005). Serious concerns have arisen over the many hours that young people spend using media entertainment. One concern is that time spent with media entertainment often takes away from activities that might serve as better uses of a young person's time, such as doing homework, participating in sports and physical activities, working, or reading. Many are also concerned about the growing use of profanity, sexual content, and violence found in so much of today's media entertainment. There is an increasing trend for this type of content in today's media, and most adults do not want young people to be exposed to it. Network prime-time shows often depict sexual situations, and rarely discuss any of the risks and responsibilities associated with sex. Many popular movies also commonly depict sexual situations and include nudity. Foul language also has increased on TV, in movies, and in popular music. People on talk shows often use offensive language and put-downs and get into fights with one another. There is also a serious problem with the easy availability of inappropriate material on the Internet.

Evaluating Entertainment Media

Individuals need to be selective in making decisions about the television programs, movies, music, and other forms of entertainment they choose. There are many quality entertainment choices. However, there is a lot of entertainment that does not contribute to optimal health and well-being. Young people should be guided to choose entertainment that lifts spirits and encourages positive feelings; contributes to good character; meets family guidelines; and does not have inappropriate content such as violence, sex, and profanity. Also, harmful drug use should not be portrayed as acceptable behavior. Use the Questions for Evaluating Entertainment Media to guide your media entertainment selections (see Table 12-3).

The **V-chip** is a small electronic device that allows television programs to be blocked. Parents or guardians can use it to block programs they feel are not appropriate for their children. As of January 2000, all televisions with screens that are thirteen inches or larger are required to contain a V-chip. Computer software programs are also available to block access to certain sites containing inappropriate material on the Web. These are helpful programs for parents because of the abundance of inappropriate material on the Internet.

Health Goal #76

I Will Analyze Ways Messages Delivered through Technology Might Affect Health Status

Entertainment can add to the joy of life, bringing relaxation, recreation, and stimulation. The right type and amount of entertainment can be a healthy outlet for stress and pressure. Good entertainment can uplift spirits and elevate mood. Positive feelings are important to health.

Entertainment choices can also have a negative influence on health status. There are a number of ways that inappropriate entertainment choices can harm a person's health:

1. *A risk of becoming a couch potato.* A cause of physical inactivity is spending lots of time watching television and in other activities that involve lots of sitting. Spending too much time watching television, playing video games, or being on the computer can lead one to become a couch potato. A typical teenager watches television an average of four hours a day. It is typical for young people watching television or playing video games to snack on high-fat, high-calorie foods. This increases their risk of weight gain and other health problems. Young people who are not physically fit have less energy, and this creates a vicious circle because participating in sports and other physical activities is not enjoyable for kids who are out of shape.

2. *A risk of becoming desensitized.* Many television programs and movies include violence. Young people who watch a lot of violent programs are at risk for being desensitized to violence. **Desensitization** is the effect of reacting less and less to exposure to something. Young people who are exposed to lots of media violence begin to see violence as a way of life. Watching violence over and over again can increase the likelihood of acting in violent ways. A typical child views 8,000 murders and 100,000 acts of violence on television from ages three to twelve (Perle, 2007). Some television programs and movies show other forms

TABLE 12-3

QUESTIONS FOR EVALUATING ENTERTAINMENT MEDIA

1. Who paid for the medium? Why?
2. What message does the medium convey to you and to others?
3. What kind of lifestyle is presented? Is it realistic or glamorized? Does it portray risky behaviors, such as smoking or drug use, in an appealing way?
4. What values are expressed?
5. Does it contain inappropriate material?
6. What does the medium attempt to persuade you to do?
7. In what ways is the medium presenting a healthy or unhealthy message?
8. How did listening or viewing the medium make you feel? What impression did it leave on you?
9. Would you recommend that others see or hear the medium? Why or why not?
10. Does the medium live up to your guidelines for personal behavior? Does it follow your family guidelines?
11. Does the medium have a rating that is appropriate for your age and values?

ENTERTAINMENT RATINGS

Television shows are rated according to the following system:

TV-Y	Suitable for children ages two to six. Not expected to frighten younger children.
TV-Y7	Suitable for children ages seven and above who can distinguish between pretend and reality. May include mild fantasy or comedic violence.
TV-Y7-FV	Directed toward older children—same as TV-Y7, but with more intense fantasy violence.
TV-G	General audience. Suitable for all ages; contains little or no violence, suggestive dialogue, sexual situations, or strong language.
TV-PG	Parental guidance suggested. May be unsuitable for younger children; may contain moderate violence, some sexual situations, some coarse language, or some suggestive dialogue.
TV-14	Parents strongly cautioned. May be unsuitable for children under age fourteen; may contain intense violence or sexual situations; very coarse language or very suggestive dialogue.
TV-MA	Mature audiences only. Suitable for adults; may be unsuitable for children under age seventeen; may contain graphic violence, explicit sexual activity, or indecent language.

Movies are rated by the film industry according to the following system:

G	General audience. Suitable for all ages; contains little or no violence, suggestive dialogue, or sexual situations; no strong language; and no drug and alcohol use content.
PG	Parental guidance suggested. May be unsuitable for younger children;may contain moderate violence, some sexual situations, some coarse language, or some suggestive dialogue.
PG-13	Parents strongly cautioned. May be unsuitable for children under age thirteen; may contain intense violence or sexual situtions; very coarse language, or very suggestive dialogue.
R	Restricted. A child under age seventeen must be accompanied by an adult; may contain extreme violence, nudity, sexual situations and language,or drug and alcohol use content.
NC-17	No one under seventeen admitted. Suitable for adults only; may contain extreme gore or violence, extreme sexual situations and language, or frequent drug and alcohol use content.

Video and computer games are rated according to the following system:

EC	Early childhood. May be suitable for ages three and older. Contains no material that parents would find inappropriate.
E	Everyone. May be suitable for ages six and older. May contain minimal cartoon, fantasy, or mild violence and infrequent use of mild language.

TABLE 12-3–(CONTINUED)	
E10+	Everyone ten and older. May be suitable for ages ten and older. May contain more cartoon, fantasy, or mild violence; mild language; and minimal suggestive themes.
T	Teen. May be suitable for ages thirteen and older. May contain violence, suggestive themes, crude humor, minimal blood, simulated gambling, and infrequent use of strong language.
M	Mature. May be suitable for ages seventeen and older. May contain intense violence, blood and gore, sexual content, and strong language.
AO	Adults only. Suitable for ages eighteen and older. May include prolonged scenes of intense violence and graphic sexual content and nudity.

Some CD labels say, "Parental Advisory—Explicit Content," which indicates that the recording may contain strong language or expressions of violence, sex, or substance abuse. Individual record companies provide these labels voluntarily.

of inappropriate material. They may show or talk about people having sex or using drugs. They may use vulgar and offensive language.

3. *A risk of seeing solutions to life's problems modeled in unrealistic ways.* Watching television and movies can influence young people's views on how problems and situations can be effectively solved. A young person might think that things in life happen the way they do on a television program. For example, soap operas and popular teen programs often portray life in an unrealistic way. People on television programs may get into difficult situations, such as unwed parenthood or drug use, and then find simple solutions. In real life, solutions are not as simple as those presented on television programs.

4. *A risk of developing entertainment addiction.* **Entertainment addiction** is the compelling need to watch television or other entertainment media. People with entertainment addiction watch many hours of TV each day or spend hours with other forms of entertainment (e.g., going to movies, listening to music, playing computer games, or surfing the Internet). They center their lives around their favorite TV shows or other forms of entertainment. They spend so much time being entertained that they have little time left to become involved in healthful activities. Relationships with family and friends suffer. They may put off doing homework and chores. They have little time to participate in physical activities and are at increased risk of being overweight. Entertainment addiction might be used as a way to cope with feelings like loneliness, shyness, depression, and anxiety.

5. *A risk of using entertainment as a way to avoid, or as a substitute for, relationships.*

Some people might find it easier to talk to others through a computer than to have relationships with people in person. E-mail and chat-line friends should never be a substitute for healthful relationships with family and friends.

6. *A risk of being persuaded to become sexually promiscuous.* People portrayed in television shows and movies often are sexually promiscuous. Consider the impact on a person who watches many television shows and movies in which the actors are promiscuous. This can cause a person to have unrealistic views about the way to live. Being promiscuous is not a satisfying lifestyle. Behaving in this way can lead to infection with sexually transmitted diseases or HIV infection. An unwanted pregnancy might occur.

7. *A risk of becoming persuaded to use alcohol, tobacco, or other drugs.* Actors in movies and television programs often smoke and drink. They light up or pour a drink often during times of stress or suspense. People who frequently see this behavior may begin to believe that a cigarette or a drink is the answer when life gets difficult. Television programs and movies usually do not show the misery that accompanies years of cigarette smoking or the adverse consequences of alcohol and other drug use.

8. *A risk of becoming persuaded to believe that violence is okay.* Many movies and television programs contain depictions of violence. Rappers and other musical artists may perform songs and raps with violent lyrics. People who are exposed frequently to these media might begin to believe that violence against others is okay. Violence against anyone is not okay.

I Will Make Responsible Choices about Health Care Providers and Facilities

Health Care Providers

A health care provider is a trained professional who provides people with health care. Physicians, health care practitioners, and allied health professionals are health care providers.

PHYSICIANS

A **physician** is an independent health care provider who is licensed to practice medicine. Physicians obtain medical histories, perform physical examinations, give diagnoses to patients, and are licensed to prescribe medications. Some physicians are licensed to perform surgery. There are two main types of physicians. A **medical doctor** is a physician who is trained in a medical school and has a doctor of medicine (MD) degree. An **osteopath** is a physician who is trained in a school of osteopathy and has a doctor of osteopathy (DO) degree. **Osteopathy** is a therapy that uses manipulation to treat a wide range of health problems directly or indirectly relating to the musculoskeletal system (muscles, joints, and ligaments) of the body. Osteopathy is based on the principle that restoring harmony and balance to the musculoskeletal system influences all levels of the body. Osteopaths believe that manipulations of the musculoskeletal system during times of illness allow the body to restore itself to health. Medical doctors and osteopaths can choose to work in primary care or become specialists. **Primary care** is general health care. Physicians who provide primary care often are the first health care providers that a patient consults. They can refer patients to specialists. A **specialist** is a professional who has specialized training in a particular area. Almost two-thirds of physicians are specialists.

The following are types of physician specialists:

Cardiologist—A physician who specializes in the treatment of the heart and blood vessels

Dermatologist—A physician who specializes in the care of the skin

Family practice physician—A physician who provides general care

Gastroenterologist—A physician who specializes in disorders of the digestive tract

Geriatrician—A physician who specializes in the treatment of the elderly

Gynecologist—A physician who specializes in female reproductive health

Internist—A physician who specializes in diagnosis and nonsurgical treatment of the internal organs

Neurologist—A physician who specializes in disorders of the nervous system

Obstetrician—A physician who specializes in the care and treatment of pregnant women and their unborn babies

Oncologist—A physician who specializes in the treatment of tumors and cancer

Ophthalmologist—A physician who specializes in medical and surgical care and treatment of the eyes

Orthopedist—A physician who specializes in the treatment of muscles, bones, and joints

Otolaryngologist (ENT)—A physician who diagnoses and treats disorders of the ears, nose, and throat

Pathologist—A physician who conducts lab studies of tissues, cells, and blood and other body fluids

Pediatrician—A physician who specializes in the care of children and adolescents

Plastic surgeon—A physician who specializes in surgery to correct, repair, or improve body features

Psychiatrist—A physician who specializes in the treatment of mental disorders

Radiologist—A physician who specializes in the use of radiation for the diagnosis and treatment of illness and disease

Urologist—A physician who specializes in the treatment of urinary disorders and the male reproductive system

Health Care Practitioners

A **health care practitioner** is an independent health care provider who is licensed to practice on a specific area of the body. Health care practitioners can provide general or specialized care. In addition to physicians, podiatrists, dentists, and optometrists are health care practitioners. A **podiatrist** is a doctor of podiatric medicine (DPM) who specializes in problems of the feet. A **dentist** is a doctor of dental surgery (DDS) or a doctor of medical dentistry (DMD) who specializes in dental care. An **optometrist** is an eye care professional who is specially trained in a school of optometry.

An **allied health professional** is a trained health care provider, such as a nurse, audiologist, dental hygienist, pharmacist, and physical therapist, who practices under the supervision of a physician or health care practitioner. More information about health care providers is found at the end of this chapter.

CHOOSING HEALTH CARE PROVIDERS

Some people pose as health care providers and make money treating people, but do not have reliable credentials. It is important to carefully choose reliable health care providers to protect health status. Health care providers are listed in the yellow pages of the telephone directory. Local chapters of the American Medical Association (AMA) and the American Dental Association (ADA) also keep lists of their members. Hospitals often have lists of physicians they will recommend, and a trusted physician or other health care provider may offer recommendations.

It is important to choose a primary care physician who will provide basic medical care and help prevent illness. Primary care physicians are most often family practitioners, pediatricians, or internists. The primary care physician should be familiar with the patient's medical history and health care needs and will refer a patient to a specialist if further diagnosis or treatment is needed.

After visiting a health care provider for the first time, a person should ask the questions that follow. The responses to these questions will help determine whether the person is satisfied with the health care provider or needs to find a different one.

- Did I feel comfortable sharing my needs and concerns with the health care provider?
- Did the health care provider answer my questions?
- Did the health care provider make a plan to address my health care needs?
- What are the credentials of the health care provider?
- What hospital affiliations does the health care provider have?
- What arrangements can be made for care on weekends and after hours?
- Who will provide care if the health care provider is out of town or unavailable?
- Does the health care provider emphasize prevention of illness and injury?
- How much are fees?
- How are fees paid?
- Is this health care provider eligible for payment if I have a health care plan?
- How long is the wait to get an appointment with the health care provider?
- How long is the wait in the office for an examination or visit?

Health Care Facilities

A **health care facility** is a place that provides health care. People should be aware of the types and locations of health care facilities in their community. They also should know the hours the facilities are open, the services they provide, and the fees they charge.

A **hospital** is a health care facility where people can receive medical care, diagnosis, and treatment on an inpatient or outpatient basis. **Inpatient care** is treatment that requires a person to stay overnight at a facility. **Outpatient care** is treatment that does not require a person to stay overnight at a facility. There are different types of hospitals:

- A **private hospital** is a hospital that is owned by private individuals and operates as a profit-making business.

- A **voluntary hospital** is a hospital that is owned by a community or organization and does not operate for profit.
- A **government hospital** is a hospital that is run by the federal, state, or local government for the benefit of a specific population. For example, the Veteran's Administration operates hospitals for military veterans.
- A **teaching hospital** is a hospital that is associated with a medical school or school of nursing. Teaching hospitals provide training for health professionals in addition to the regular services of most hospitals.

A **walk-in surgery center** is a facility where surgery is performed on an outpatient basis. The cost of outpatient surgery averages less than one-third to one-half the cost of inpatient fees. Many health insurance companies encourage or require patients who need certain types of surgery to choose outpatient surgery in walk-in surgery centers. However, certain types of surgery require inpatient care.

A **health center** is a facility that provides routine health care to a special population. For example, there are health centers that provide health care to low-income families. A **health department clinic** is a facility in most state and local health departments that keeps records and performs services. A **mental health clinic** is a facility that provides services for people who have mental disorders. Many mental health clinics are open twenty-four hours a day, seven days a week, to help people in crisis situations.

An **extended care facility** is a facility that provides nursing, personal, and residential care. Extended care facilities also provide care for people who need assistance with daily living. Nursing homes and convalescent centers are examples of extended care facilities. Home health care may be more convenient and affordable than staying in an extended care facility. **Home health care** is care provided within a patient's home. Home health care organizations offer a variety of services, including nursing care, medical treatment, and therapy in the home.

Many patients receive hospice care in their home or in the home of a loved one. Others receive hospice care in hospices. **Hospice** is a facility or home care for people who are dying and their families. Hospice services usually provide care twenty-four hours a day. Hospice care extends after the patient dies. Contact and support from hospice staff continues for at least a year after a family member dies.

EMERGENCY ROOMS

An **emergency room** is a facility within a hospital where emergency services are provided without an appointment. Emergency rooms are open at night and on weekends when other care is not available. Fees for emergency room services are higher than for visits to a physician's office.

Some people rely on hospital emergency rooms as their source of primary care and go there for conditions that are not emergencies. As a result, many emergency rooms are very crowded. People without urgent problems may have to wait a long time to get care. Physicians working in emergency rooms may have many people to examine. Emergency rooms should be used only for urgent medical care.

A **freestanding emergency center,** or **urgent care center,** is a facility that is not part of a hospital that provides emergency care. Freestanding emergency centers do not require an appointment. Many freestanding emergency centers are open twenty-four hours a day, seven days a week. Their fees are lower than those of hospital emergency rooms but higher than for visits to a physician's office.

There are certain symptoms for which a person should seek immediate medical attention, including these:

- Difficulty breathing or shortness of breath
- Chest or upper abdominal pain or pressure
- Fainting
- Sudden dizziness, weakness, or change in vision
- Change in mental status, such as unusual behavior, confusion, or difficulty waking up
- Sudden, severe pain anywhere in the body
- Bleeding that cannot be stopped
- Severe or persistent vomiting
- Coughing up or vomiting blood
- Suicidal or homicidal feelings

Patients' Bill of Rights

All patients in a hospital have certain rights. They have the right to

- Receive respectful care
- Be given complete information regarding their diagnosis, treatment, and prognosis

- Receive information necessary for their informed consent prior to any procedure
- Refuse treatment
- Have privacy regarding care and records
- Be granted requests for services within reason
- Be advised of any experimental procedure
- Expect continuity of care; receive explanation of the bill
- Know hospital regulations

Health Goal #78

I Will Evaluate Ways to Pay for Health Care

The price of health care has soared. The United States spends $2.2 trillion a year on health care, or $7,129 per person (Appleby, 2006). High-tech equipment, disease epidemics, malpractice lawsuits, and an increase in the number of tests performed on patients are some of the reasons. America's obesity epidemic is also causing a rise in spending for health care. As health care costs have soared, it has become much more difficult for people to pay for health care. Health care can be unexpected and expensive.

Health Insurance

Many people use health insurance to pay for health care costs. **Health insurance** is financial protection that provides benefits for sickness or injury. When a person purchases insurance, the insurance provider agrees to pay for or reimburse the costs of care. The insurance provider calculates that over a long period of time it will take in more money than it will pay out.

An **insurance policy** is the legal document issued to the policyholder that outlines the terms of the insurance. Insurance policies are issued by insurance companies and the federal government. Insurance policies vary greatly regarding coverage, costs, and limitations. A premium must be paid at certain periods of time. A **premium** is a specific amount of money that will guarantee that an insurance company will pay for health services as specified in the insurance policy. Premiums for health insurance provided by private insurance companies are paid by the individual, by the company where the individual works, or by a combination of both.

Some insurance policies pay the entire cost of medical care. Others pay a portion. A **deductible** is an amount that insurance does not cover that must be paid by the individual. A **co-payment** is the portion of the medical fee the individual must pay.

Managed care is an organized system of health care services designed to control health care costs. Managed care insurance plans control the types of health care that insured people receive. They also limit what is paid out for specific kinds of care. Health maintenance organizations and preferred provider organizations are two kinds of managed care.

A **health maintenance organization (HMO)** is a business that organizes health care services for its members. HMOs try to provide care at a reduced cost. Except for emergency care, policyholders are covered only for services received directly from the HMO or from outside providers with specific approval. HMOs encourage regular checkups for preventive health care.

A **preferred provider organization (PPO)** is a health insurance plan that has a contract with a group of health care providers who agree to provide health care services at a reduced rate. A **preferred provider** is a health care provider who appears on a list that has been approved by the health insurance provider. People covered under these plans must select preferred providers within the plan or pay a higher cost for health services.

Federal and state governments offer health care payment for some people. The major sources of insurance coverage include Medicare, Medicaid, coverage for veterans, and coverage for government employees. **Medicare** is a government health insurance plan for people sixty-five years of age and older and for people who have received Social Security disability benefits for two years. Medicare covers a portion of a person's health care costs. The rest is paid by the person, other programs such as Medicaid, or supplemental insurance programs. **Medicaid** is a health insurance plan for people with low incomes that is managed and paid for by the government. The state government and federal government divide the costs of the health care. Medicaid programs are different from state to state.

Malpractice insurance is insurance that health care providers and health care facilities purchase to provide coverage for malpractice lawsuits. Malpractice lawsuits are claims made by patients that a health care provider did not provide appropriate health care treatment. The great number of malpractice lawsuits is one reason health care costs have risen. Health care providers have to pay a great deal for malpractice insurance.

The rising number of people without health insurance is a critical problem for our nation. Nationally, nearly 16 percent of the population, or 46.6 million people, lack health insurance (Appleby, 2006). People without insurance are more likely to skip routine medical care and seek assistance instead at emergency rooms or urgent care centers, where costs are much higher. They also are less likely to receive recommended screenings to detect cancer when it is most treatable and other preventive screenings. It is also a sad fact that an increasing number of elderly people and children have no health care coverage.

Evaluating Health Insurance

Health insurance should cover standard risks of illness and injury for family members. It also should cover special conditions family members might have that require ongoing medical attention. There are two kinds of expenses. A **covered expense** is a medical expense that is paid for under the terms of a health insurance plan. An exclusion is a service for which a health insurance plan will not pay. People must study health insurance plans carefully in order to know exactly what services are covered and excluded.

Health insurance plans are not all the same. Some cost more than others, and some cover more than others. People must evaluate health insurance plans in terms of their own and their family's needs. They should take the following actions:

1. Obtain and read carefully a copy of the health insurance plan.
2. Ask questions of representatives from the health insurance plan.
3. Shop around for health insurance plans.
4. Choose plans that give the most comprehensive coverage at the most affordable price.

Some insurance providers will not sell insurance to people they consider high risks, such as people with disabilities or preexisting conditions. A **preexisting condition** is a health problem that a person had before being covered by the insurance. According to law, people must disclose all health information to the insurer. If they do not, the insurance provider may cancel the contract.

The following questions are helpful in evaluating health insurance coverage:

1. Is the entire family covered?
2. Are regular checkups covered?
3. Are the needed services covered?
4. Are immunizations covered?
5. Is maternity care covered?
6. Is vision or dental care covered?
7. Are psychological services covered?
8. Is physical therapy covered?
9. Are there time limits for extended treatment?
10. What is not covered?
11. How much are the deductibles?
12. How many days in the hospital are covered?
13. Is there a waiting period before coverage begins?
14. Are there limitations on choices of health care providers or facilities?
15. Is the insurance renewable or can the company cancel it in certain situations?

TYPES OF COVERAGE IN HEALTH INSURANCE PLANS

Health insurance plans offer five basic types of coverage:

1. **Medical insurance** is insurance that pays physician's fees, laboratory fees outside a hospital, and fees for prescription drugs.
2. **Major medical insurance** is insurance that pays for extra expenses not covered by other insurance policies. Major medical insurance might cover treatment for diseases such as cancer or AIDS.
3. **Hospitalization insurance** is insurance that pays the cost of a hospital stay.
4. **Surgical insurance** is insurance that pays for fees related to surgery.
5. **Disability insurance** is insurance that replaces income lost because of accidents or illnesses that require a period of recovery.

I Will Investigate Health Careers

Health Careers

A **health career** is a profession or occupation in the health field for which one trains. A health career may be of interest to many students. A health class is a good opportunity for students to learn about health careers. Jobs in the health field are growing at a higher rate than in many other fields. This section introduces several of the many health careers available.

AUDIOLOGIST

An **audiologist** is a specialist who diagnoses and treats hearing and speech-related problems. An audiologist tests for hearing problems, prescribes hearing aids and devices, plans hearing conservation programs, and teaches speech or lip reading. An audiologist must have a master's degree and a state license.

CERTIFIED ATHLETIC TRAINER

A **certified athletic trainer** is a specialist who works with athletes to maintain fitness and prevent and treat injuries. A certified athletic trainer treats emergency athletic injuries, assists with rehabilitation, educates athletes concerning safety and injury prevention, and can refer athletes for further medical treatment. A certified athletic trainer has a bachelor's degree, and possibly a master's degree, and must be certified by the National Athletic Trainers Association (NATA). Many states require certified athletic trainers to have a state license.

CLINICAL PSYCHOLOGIST

A **clinical psychologist** is a psychologist who has a PhD and has had an internship in a psychiatric setting. A clinical psychologist helps people deal with mental disorders, stressors, and life crises; provides individual, group, and family psychotherapy; and plans behavioral modification programs. A clinical psychologist must have a doctoral degree in clinical psychology and a state license.

COMMUNITY HEALTH EDUCATOR

A **community health educator** is a health educator who focuses on educating people in a specific community. A community health educator identifies community health problems and needs and plans health promotion programs in the community. A community health educator must have a bachelor's degree in health education or a related area and might need to be a certified health education specialist (CHES). Community health educations are frequently also known as public health educators.

DENTAL HYGIENIST

A **dental hygienist** is a trained dental health professional who works under the direction of a dentist to provide dental care. A dental hygienist cleans teeth, provides preventive dental care, teaches people how to practice good oral hygiene, examines patients' teeth and gums, and takes and develops dental X-rays. A dental hygienist must have an associate's or bachelor's degree, certification from an accredited school of dental hygiene, and a state license.

DENTIST

A **dentist** is a doctor of dental surgery (DDS) or a doctor of medical dentistry (DMD) who specializes in dental care. A dentist diagnoses, treats, and prevents problems of the teeth and mouth, examines X-rays, removes decay and fills cavities, repairs fractured teeth, removes teeth, and places protective sealants on teeth. A dentist must have a DDS or DMD degree and a state license.

DIETITIAN

A **dietitian,** or **nutritionist,** is a specialist who counsels people about diet and nutrition. A dietitian plans nutritional programs, supervises the preparation of foods, evaluates diets, develops menus for people with health problems, and consults with other health care providers about nutrition. A dietitian must have a bachelor's degree in dietetics, foods and nutrition, food systems management, or a related field and might need certification as a registered dietitian (RD) and a state license.

EMERGENCY MEDICAL TECHNICIAN

An **emergency medical technician (EMT)** is a health care professional who gives health care to people in emergency situations before they reach the hospital. There are three types of emergency medical technicians. An EMT-basic gives immediate care to people in emergency situations and transports them to medical facilities. An EMT-intermediate has the same responsibilities as an EMT-basic but also can administer intravenous fluids, use defibrillators to give lifesaving shocks to a person with a stopped heart, and perform other intensive care procedures. An EMT-paramedic has the same responsibilities as an EMT-intermediate but also can administer drugs orally and intravenously, read EKGs, perform endotracheal intubations, and use monitors and other complex equipment. An EMT-basic must be at least eighteen years old, have a driver's license, have a high school diploma or equivalent, and have basic EMT training and state certification. An EMT-intermediate must have intermediate EMT training and state certification. An EMT-paramedic must have EMT-paramedic training and state certification.

GUIDANCE COUNSELOR

A **guidance counselor** is a specialist who assists students with personal, family, education, and career decisions and concerns. A guidance counselor helps students develop job-finding skills, provides college counseling, and helps students develop life skills they need to prevent and deal with problems. A guidance counselor must have a master's degree in counseling and state school counseling certification and might need a teaching certificate.

HEALTH EDUCATION TEACHER

A **health education teacher** is a teacher who specializes in health education. A health education teacher promotes the development of health knowledge, life skills, and positive attitudes toward health and well-being in students. A health education teacher works with students and their family members, school principals, teachers, counselors, nurses, and community members. A health education teacher must be certified to teach school and is usually required to have a major or minor in health education.

HEALTH SERVICES MANAGER AND ADMINISTRATOR

A **health services manager and administrator** is a professional who manages a health services organization. A health services manager and administrator plans, organizes, coordinates, and supervises a health services organization. A health services manager and administrator must have a bachelor's or master's degree in health service administration, business administration, public health, public administration, or another related field. Health services managers and administrators usually are not required to have special training or a state license. However, a nursing home administrator must have special training and a state license.

LICENSED PRACTICAL NURSE

A **licensed practical nurse (LPN),** or **licensed vocational nurse (LVN),** is a nurse who, under the direction of registered nurses or physicians, provides nursing care for people who are sick or injured. A licensed practical nurse must have a high school diploma or equivalent and training as a practical nurse and might need a state license.

MEDICAL WRITER

A **medical writer** is a writer who specializes in the areas of medicine and health. A medical writer might write for the media, such as a newspaper column on medicine or an article for a medical journal, or might write brochures, newsletters, and information sheets for hospitals, medical schools, health organizations, and medical companies. Medical writers also write for online medical services.

OCCUPATIONAL THERAPIST

An **occupational therapist** is a health professional who helps people who have disabilities learn to make adjustments. An occupational therapist assists people who have disabilities to develop, recover, or maintain daily living and work skills. An occupational therapist must have a bachelor's degree in occupational therapy and might need a state license.

PHARMACIST

A **pharmacist** is an allied health professional who dispenses medications that are prescribed by certain licensed health professionals. A pharmacist prepares and dispenses drugs, provides information to patients about drugs, and consults with health care professionals about drugs. A pharmacist must have either a bachelor's degree or a graduate degree in pharmacy and a state license and must complete an internship under a licensed pharmacist.

PHARMACOLOGIST

A **pharmacologist** is a specialist in the composition of drugs and their effects. A pharmacologist studies the effects of drugs on the body and mind, researches the safety and effectiveness of drugs, and develops new drugs. A pharmacologist must have a bachelor's degree or master's degree in pharmacy, chemistry, medicine, or another related field.

PHYSICAL THERAPIST

A **physical therapist** is an allied health professional who helps people rehabilitate their physical disabilities and injuries. Physical therapists help improve mobility, relieve pain, and limit permanent physical disability in people who are physically disabled or injured. They teach people exercises to speed recovery and test strength and range of motion to evaluate recovery. A physical therapist must have certification from an accredited program in physical therapy and a state license.

PHYSICIAN

A **physician** is an independent health care provider who is licensed to practice medicine. Physicians obtain medical histories, perform physical examinations, and give diagnoses to patients. Physicians are licensed to prescribe medications to patients. Specially trained physicians are licensed to perform surgery. There are two main types of physicians. A **medical doctor** is a physician who is trained in a medical school and has a doctor of medicine (MD) degree. An **osteopath** is a physician who is trained in a school of osteopathy and has a doctor of osteopathy (DO) degree. Medical doctors and doctors of osteopathy must have a state license.

RADIOLOGIC TECHNOLOGIST

A **radiologic technologist** is an allied health professional who works under the direction of a radiologist. A radiologic technologist prepares patients for X-ray examination, takes and develops X-rays, and assists with the other imaging procedures, such as ultrasound scanning and magnetic resonance imaging (MRI). Radiologic technologists also prepare radiation therapy for patients who have cancer. A radiologic technologist usually has an associate's or bachelor's degree in radiologic technology and a state license.

RECREATIONAL THERAPIST

A **recreational therapist** is a health care professional who plans and directs medically approved recreational activities. Recreational therapists use recreational activities to help patients maintain physical, emotional, and mental well-being. They instruct patients in relaxation techniques to reduce stress and tension. A recreational therapist must have an associate's or bachelor's degree in recreational therapy and might need a state license or other certification.

REGISTERED NURSE

A **registered nurse (RN)** is a nurse who is certified for general practice or for one or more of several nursing specialties. A registered nurse monitors patients and records symptoms, assists physicians during examinations and treatments, administers medications, assists in the recovery and rehabilitation of patients, and provides emotional care for patients and their families. A registered nurse must have a degree from an accredited nursing school and both a national and a state license. Nurses who want to specialize to be clinical nurse specialists, nurse practitioners, or nurse anesthetists must have additional training.

SCHOOL PSYCHOLOGIST

A **school psychologist** is a psychologist who works with students, parents, school personnel, and teachers to solve learning and behavioral problems. School psychologists test students' intellectual, emotional, and behavioral skills. They work with students who have disabilities or are gifted and talented, and they teach students conflict resolution skills. A school psychologist must have a graduate degree in psychology and a state license and complete a one-year internship with a school psychologist.

SOCIAL WORKER

A **social worker** is a person who helps people with a wide range of social problems. A social worker investigates, treats, and gives aid to people who have social problems, such as mental illness, lack of job skills, serious health conditions, financial difficulties, disability, substance abuse problems, child or domestic abuse, and unwanted pregnancy. A social worker must have a master's degree in social work (MSW) and a state license.

SPEECH PATHOLOGIST

A **speech pathologist** is an allied health professional who helps people overcome speech disorders. Speech pathologists work with people who suffer from speech and language disorders and people who have oral motor problems that cause eating and swallowing difficulties. They also counsel parents or guardians and family members of these people. A speech pathologist must have a master's degree in speech pathology and a state license.

Health Goal #80

I Will Investigate Public and International Health Needs

Public health is the use of organized community efforts to prevent disease and injury and promote health. **Public health programs** are planned activities that are carried out to prevent disease and injury and promote health. The public health approach is quite different from the medical or health care approach, which treats people one at a time. Public health emphasizes the prevention of disease and the promotion of healthy behaviors rather than the treatment of people after they are sick. Many public health activities are invisible to the public, but they quickly become apparent when there are wide-scale health threats, such as a communicable disease outbreak; a bioterrorist threat; contamination in the air, food, or water; or escalating chronic disease.

Public health is a wise investment for communities, states, and nations because it helps people live longer and enjoy good health, and it saves money. Public health focuses on prevention and can help our nation save billions of dollars. Speaking about the importance of public health, former U.S. surgeon general C. Everett Koop said, "Health care is vital to all of us some of the time but public health is vital to all of us all of the time."

U.S. Public Health Agencies

Public health in the United States is carried out through a system of federal, state, and local agencies. The system includes local public health departments, state health departments, and federal public health agencies.

LOCAL AND STATE HEALTH DEPARTMENTS

One of the most important public health agencies is your local public health department. A **local public health department** is a local government agency that offers programs and services aimed at protecting and promoting the health of a specific community. Local public health departments often serve a particular city or county (or counties).

Each state is served by a state health department. A **state health department** is a state government agency that offers programs and services aimed at protecting and promoting the health of the state and provides support to local health departments. State health departments often provide funding to local health departments to aid them in carrying out their public health programs. State health departments also provide training and technical expertise to local health departments and enforce state public health laws.

FEDERAL AGENCIES

The **Centers for Disease Control and Prevention (CDC)** is the lead federal public health agency for protecting the health and safety of people in the United States. The CDC works with state and local health departments as well as other agencies in communities, states, and the nation to monitor health, detect and investigate health problems, conduct research to enhance prevention, develop and advocate sound public health policies, implement prevention strategies, promote healthy behaviors, foster safe and healthful environments, and provide leadership and training. The CDC is a large organization with headquarters in Atlanta, Georgia. CDC employees work in several other states, and some employees are assigned to work overseas.

The CDC is an agency of the U.S. Department of Health and Human Services (HHS). The Department of Health and Human Services includes other important federal public health agencies:

- The National Institutes of Health (NIH) supports research projects on diseases such as cancer, Alzheimer's, diabetes, arthritis, heart ailments, and AIDS, and it includes eighteen separate health institutes, the National Center for Complementary and Alternative Medicine, and the National Library of Medicine.
- The Food and Drug Administration (FDA) is responsible for assuring the safety of foods and cosmetics and the safety and efficacy of pharmaceuticals, biological products, and medical devices. The products that the FDA regulates represent twenty-five cents out of every dollar in our nation that people spend.
- The Indian Health Services (IHS) operates hospitals, health centers, and school health centers, and health stations for the American Indians and Alaska Natives.
- The Health Resources and Services Administration (HRSA) provides access to essential health services for low-income and uninsured people, as well as in rural and urban neighborhoods where health care is scarce. The HRSA works with many state and community organizations to support programs that ensure healthy mothers and children, increase the number and diversity of health care professionals in underserved communities, and provide supportive services for people with HIV infection.
- The Substance Abuse and Mental Health Services Administration (SAMHSA) works to improve the quality and availability of substance abuse prevention, addiction treatment, and mental health services, and it provides federal grant money to states to support and maintain substance abuse and mental health services.
- The Centers for Medicare and Medicaid Services (CMS) manages the Medicare and Medicaid programs and manages the State Children's Health Insurance Program.

Public Health Needs

Public health has done an extraordinary job of meeting public health needs in the past one hundred hundred years. There has been remarkable improvement in the health and life expectancy of our nation's population during the past century. Since 1900, the average lifespan of persons in the United States increased by more than thirty years. Advances in public health are responsible for twenty-five years of this gain. Significant improvements in the quality of life during the past century are also the result of public health.

Although public health has made great improvements in the health of our population, many public health problems remain. Public health problems that need more attention include injuries, teen pregnancy, control of high blood pressure, and smoking and substance abuse. Growing threats from the resurgence of infectious diseases, and increases in violence, demands of an aging population, and escalating costs of health care are other examples of immediate and challenging concerns for public health officials. As our population grows in terms of the number of older adults, health problems such as Alzheimer's disease, arthritis, long-term care, and inadequate home health care will also become more intense. There are growing threats to our environment that concern public health officials.

NEWLY RECOGNIZED INFECTIOUS DISEASES

Although public health has had major successes in fighting infectious diseases such as smallpox, measles, and polio, today's public health professionals are having to deal with an ever-expanding group of newly recognized infectious diseases such as E coli, cyclospora, cryptosporidium, hantavirus, West Nile virus, Ebola, and SARS (see Chapter 11 for more information on SARS). While the number of new infectious diseases rises, the illnesses once controlled through the use of antibiotics are reemerging as public health threats by becoming resistant to the antibiotics used to fight them.

BIOTERRORISM

There is also the threat of bioterrorism. **Bioterrorism** is the use or threatened use of bacteria, viruses, or toxins as weapons. Although a number of infectious agents could potentially be used as weapons, those of most concern are smallpox, anthrax, botulism, and plague. Public health officials are working hard to protect our nation from the threat of bioterrorism.

NEW PROBLEMS

New problems will also present themselves. As our world changes in certain ways, we see increasing threats to public health. In today's world, there is an increase in international travel. This heightens the possibility that infectious disease agents can spread rapidly from one area of the world to another. Overcrowding in cities with poor sanitation increases the risk of certain infectious diseases. Increases in food distribution throughout the world raise the likelihood that foodborne illness will be spread. There is an increase in the number of people in developing countries taking up unhealthy habits such as smoking, eating high-fat foods, and avoiding physical activity. These lifestyle factors increasingly place individuals at risk of heart attack.

International Health Needs

In many ways, the world is a healthier and safer place today than it used to be. Progress has been made in reducing the impact of many infectious diseases. Smallpox has been eradicated from the world, and efforts toward eliminating polio are proving successful. Throughout the world, more people than ever before have access to clean water and food, so there are fewer waterborne and food-related illnesses. In more affluent parts of the world, cigarette smoking rates are decreasing and so are death rates from motor vehicle accidents. However, the World Health Organization points out that in other ways the world is becoming more dangerous. Lifestyles of populations are changing around the world to be more in line with wealthy societies. These changes bring new risks to the health of these populations—such as tobacco use, excessive drinking of alcohol, obesity, physical inactivity, high blood pressure, and high blood cholesterol. Poverty also continues to cause an enormous amount of disease and poor health conditions throughout the world.

POVERTY

The major cause of health conditions resulting from underweight and undernutrition, unsafe water, poor sanitation and hygiene, iron deficiency, and indoor smoke from cooking fires is poverty. Many people in the United States are not aware that in poor countries today there are 170 million underweight children, mainly due to lack of food. More than 3 million will die this year as a result. On the other hand, more than 1 billion adults worldwide are overweight, and at least

300 million are obese. Among these, about half a million people in North America and western Europe combined will die this year from obesity-related diseases (World Health Organization, 2002).

POOR NUTRITION

According to the World Health Organization (2002), about one in fourteen deaths in the world is due to childhood and maternal underweight. **Undernutrition** is a deficiency in calories, protein, vitamins, or minerals as a result of inadequate diet and frequent infection. It is a huge problem in developing countries in which most of the population is poor. The most serious and deadly form of undernutrition is protein-energy malnutrition. **Protein-energy malnutrition (PEM)** is undernutrition that results from inadequate calorie intake. The World Health Organization stresses that PEM plays an important role in at least half the child deaths that occur in the world each year. Infants and young children with protein-energy malnutrition are likely to have stunted growth and are vulnerable to infections.

Lack of access to food is not the only cause of undernutrition. Poor feeding practices, such as inadequate breast-feeding, offering the wrong foods to children, and giving too little food to children, also contribute to undernutrition. Health workers in developing countries play an important role in checking the nutritional status and feeding practices of every child under two years of age and those with a low weight for their age. They counsel parents on the correct foods for each age group and help them to overcome various feeding problems. They can teach mothers about the health benefits of breast-feeding. The World Health Organization stresses that a modest increase in breast-feeding rates could prevent up to 10 percent of all deaths of children under age five. When a mother breast-feeds, her children have a lowered risk of diarrhea and respiratory infections.

LACK OF WATER AND SANITATION

Water is important for many aspects of life, and access to clean water is very important to good health. Therefore it is unfortunate that in many places in the world water is wasted, tainted, or taken for granted. According to the World Health Organization (WHO), one-fifth of the world's population lacks access to safe water. WHO predicts that if current trends continue, two out of every three people on Earth will suffer moderate to severe water shortages in little more than two decades from now. When it comes to the need for clean water, the poor and developing countries suffer the most. Millions of people worldwide lack access to safe drinking water and adequate sanitation. More than 2 million children die each year from water-related diseases. The lack of clean water and sanitation is one of the world's most pressing crises.

MALARIA

Malaria is serious, life-threatening disease transmitted by mosquitoes. The cause of malaria is a parasite that is transmitted from person to person through the bite of a female *Anopheles* mosquito. Four out of ten people in the world are at risk of contracting malaria. According to the World Health Organization, it causes about 1 million deaths each year and makes more than 300 million people sick. Although malaria is found in many regions of the world, most cases of malaria occur in Africa. WHO says that malaria kills one African child every thirty seconds. Those who survive an episode of malaria are at risk of brain damage or an impaired ability to learn.

Unfortunately, there is no effective vaccine for malaria. Mosquito nets treated with insecticide can reduce malaria transmission. Prompt access to treatment and medicines can help save lives from malaria.

HIV INFECTION

HIV infection is a global epidemic. This epidemic continues to expand in some of the most populated regions and countries of the world. Countries with many poor people are vulnerable to the HIV epidemic. According to the Joint United Nations Programme on HIV/AIDS (UNAIDS, 2006), 39.5 million people throughout the world are living with the HIV virus. The region of the world that has been hit hardest by the HIV/AIDS epidemic is sub-Saharan Africa, where about 25 million are affected. Of the 2.9 million people throughout the world who died from HIV/AIDS in 2006, 2.1 million were living in sub-Saharan Africa.

HIV/AIDS is expanding rapidly in the Baltic states (e.g., Latvia, Lithuania, Estonia), Ukraine, the Russian Federation, and some central Asian republics (Tajikistan, Uzbekistan, Kazakhstan). Much of this increase is believed to be the result of increased risk from injecting drugs. This region of the world has seen a marked decrease in its standard of living. Unemployment is rampant, and poverty levels are increasing. These factors may be a cause of the increase in injecting drug use. Also, heroin from Afghanistan has flooded into this area in recent years.

The HIV/AIDS epidemic is growing in China and India, the two most populated countries in the world. A million people are now living with HIV in China, and 4 million are living with HIV in India. UNAIDS warns that if present trends continue, there will be 10 million people living with HIV in China a decade from now. UNAIDS predicts that the global HIV/AIDS epidemic will continue to grow unless efforts to protect the world's population against this epidemic increase.

TOBACCO USE

According to the World Health Organization (2002), tobacco kills almost 5 million people each year. It is predicted that this number of deaths could double by the early 2020s. More than two-thirds of these deaths will occur in the developing countries of the world where there have been large increases in smoking prevalence, especially among males. On the other hand, tobacco use has been decreasing in many industrialized countries. Tobacco use contributes to malnutrition when people spend money on tobacco instead of food. For example, the World Health Organization (2002) says that it has been estimated that if poor people in Bangladesh did not smoke, 10.5 million fewer people would be malnourished.

International Disasters

A powerful earthquake struck in the Indian Ocean off the coast of the Indonesian island Sumatra on December 26, 2004. The earthquake created huge waves, called tsunamis, which swept across a broad stretch of coastland in South Asia and affected India, Sri Lanka, Indonesia, Thailand, Myanmar (Burma), Malaysia, Bangladesh, and the Maldives. The waves caused extensive loss of life and damage. More than 150,000 people were reported killed, including 50,000 children. Thousands were left homeless. Clean drinking water became scarce as a result of flooding and contamination. Outbreaks of waterborne diseases were a major concern, and hospitals were damaged. There was an urgent need for medical supplies. Many people throughout the United States

and other nations desired to help the people that were affected by this disaster.

What can people do to help during an international disaster or a disaster within your country? The best way to assist victims of disaster is through financial donations to reputable relief or response organizations. Monetary contributions allow relief organizations to purchase the most urgently needed items as close to the disaster site as possible. When purchases of needed supplies are made near the disaster, they get to victims as quickly as possible. It also eliminates some of the expensive transportation costs needed to ship supplies. Generous contributions to organizations such as the Red Cross, Médecins Sans Frontières (MSF), CARE International, the United Nations Children's Fund (UNICEF), and many others further the relief and response that these agencies are able to provide.

Another way of helping is through in-kind donations. However, the donations of goods such as clothing, canned goods, toys, furniture, and hygiene items require a tremendous amount of time, money, and personnel to sort, clean, and distribute. In-kind donations can come at the expense of emergency activities that relief workers are attempting to perform. Shipping donated goods is also costly in the aftermath of a disaster when transportation to a disaster site is often difficult or nearly impossible. For these reasons, the most immediate, beneficial form of help is a monetary contribution to a relief organization. Organized in-kind donations, however, may be a very important source of help for a disaster region after the emergency response and during the recovery period of a disaster. Young people can give valuable service to this kind of effort.

Another form of helping is volunteering. Volunteers from outside a disaster region are usually not needed until the recovery period. Until this time, there are rarely enough accommodations (beds, food, water) in an affected area for all those who might wish to travel to the area to help. The best volunteers are those who have been trained by a response organization, understand effective procedures and services for helping, and heed physical and emotional dangers. Other sought-out qualifications for volunteers include prior disaster relief experience, fluency in the language spoken in the disaster-stricken area, and expertise in technical fields (e.g., medicine, communications, water/sanitation engineering). Volunteers may be needed for as long as three to four months when there has been extensive damage, such as the tsunami of 2004. Many organizations also seek volunteers to work in nonemergency situations in the developing world.

13

CHAPTER THIRTEEN

Environmental Health

HEALTH GOALS FOR ENVIRONMENTAL HEALTH

81. I will stay informed about environmental issues.
82. I will be aware of organizations and global initiatives to protect the environment.
83. I will help keep the air clean.
84. I will help keep the water safe.
85. I will help keep noise at a safe level.
86. I will help improve the visual environment.
87. I will help conserve energy and natural resources.
88. I will precycle, recycle, and dispose of waste properly.
89. I will protect the natural environment.
90. I will be a health advocate for the environment.

Environmental health is the area of health that focuses on staying informed about environmental issues; being aware of organizations and global initiatives to protect the environment; helping keep the air clean; helping keep the water safe; keeping noise at a safe level; helping improve the visual environment; conserving energy and natural resources; precycling, recycling, and disposing of waste properly; protecting the natural environment; and being a health advocate for the environment. This chapter provides the health knowledge that is needed to teach young people important life skills for environmental health.

Health Goal #81

I Will Stay Informed about Environmental Issues

Environmental Issues

The **environment** is everything around a person. It includes the air people breathe, the water they drink, the food they eat, and the noise they hear. It includes Earth and everything in, on, and around Earth. Environment is an important part

of people's everyday lives. The environment and people depend on one another—the actions that people take affect the quality of the environment, and the environment affects the quality of people's lives. **Global environmental issues** are environmental concerns that can affect the quality of life of people everywhere. Five environmental issues that interest many people around the globe are population growth, poverty and hunger, the greenhouse effect and global warming, destruction of the ozone layer, and destruction of rain forests.

POPULATION GROWTH

Population growth is an important environmental issue. Nearly 6.6 billion people live on Earth, and the population is growing by 200,000 people each day (Department of Economic and Social Affairs, 2005; U.S. Census Bureau, 2007). Worldwide improvements in health have led to population growth—people are living longer, and fewer infants are dying. As population grows, the demand for Earth's resources increases. Some nations with high population growth are not able to produce enough food to feed all of their people; the land suitable for growing crops might be covered with dwellings, the country might have few natural resources, droughts might kill crops. As the number of people increases, so does the demand for health services and other public services. More than two-thirds of the world's population live in developing countries in Africa, Asia, and South America. A **developing country** is a country that is working to achieve an acceptable standard of health conditions. A **developed country** is a country that has achieved an acceptable standard of health conditions. Most developed countries keep on working to further improve conditions. In developing countries, the faster rate of population growth is both

impelled by and impedes solving the poor standards of health conditions.

POVERTY AND HUNGER

Poverty and hunger exist in all parts of the world. **Poverty** is a condition of not having sufficient resources to eat and live healthfully. People who are poor and hungry are more at risk for disease and might have stunted growth. Some suffer from malnutrition. **Malnutrition** is a condition in which the body does not receive either the energy nutrients or the balance of nutrients required for optimal health. Malnourished individuals are more likely to be depressed, hostile, and stressed. Poverty is responsible for many environmental problems faced by developing nations.

GREENHOUSE EFFECT AND GLOBAL WARMING

Some gases, such as carbon dioxide, trap heat near Earth's surface and prevent it from escaping into the atmosphere, similar to how the enclosing glass warms the air in a greenhouse—the glass permits light to enter but prevents heat from escaping. The **greenhouse effect** is a process in which water vapor and gases in the atmosphere absorb and reflect infrared rays and warm Earth's surfaces. Greenhouse gases such as carbon dioxide, ozone, methane, and chlorofluorocarbons (CFCs) have warmed Earth's surface during the past one hundred years. **Global warming** is an increase in Earth's temperature. Global warming has caused glaciers to melt and sea levels to rise. The greenhouse effect and global warming are affected by burning fuels that produce greenhouse gases. These fuels currently are widely used as sources of energy. Scientists predict that global warming causes weather patterns to change and that flooding and droughts could increase.

In February 2007, an international panel of scientists released a report that predicted that global warming due to greenhouse gas emissions will continue for centuries to come. This panel, the Intergovernmental Panel on Climate Change of the United Nations, blamed carbon dioxide and other greenhouse gases produced by human activity as the main cause of the global warming that has taken place since 1950. The scientists said that some health effects from climate change will result, including heat waves, heavy rainfall, and severe droughts. For example, flooding and drought bring many associated health problems, such as contaminated water supplies and the spread of infectious diseases. The Centers for Disease Control and Prevention is creating an action plan in response to the threat of climate change to address the health risks posed by global warming

THINNING OF THE OZONE LAYER

Ozone is a form of oxygen. The ozone layer is a protective layer of the upper atmosphere that traps ultraviolet (UV) radiation from the sun and prevents it from reaching Earth's surface. Too much UV radiation is harmful to living tissue and is associated with skin cancer, cataracts, and other health conditions and can harm farms and forests. The use of certain chemicals increases the amount of UV radiation that reaches Earth, because when they are released into the air these chemicals rise into the upper atmosphere and destroy the ozone layer. **Chlorofluorocarbons (CFCs)**—a group of gases that, because they are easy to compress and expand, are used as propellants in aerosol sprays and as coolants in air conditioners, insulation, and refrigerators—are a leading cause of the thinning of the ozone layer.

REDUCTION OF RAIN FORESTS

Rain forests are located near the equator in countries of Latin America, Africa, and Asia. A **tropical rain forest** is a hot, wet forested area that contains many species of trees, plants, and animals. Rain forests cover about 7 percent of the land on Earth (Fanning, 2007). Rain forest vegetation is very important to the global environment. Rain forests add oxygen to, and remove carbon dioxide from, the atmosphere; are a source of food, rubber, and timber; and are home to half the world's plant and animal species. Many of the active ingredients in prescription drugs are extracted from plants in tropical rain forests, and it is believed that there are many more beneficial substances in rain forest vegetation that have not yet been discovered or understood.

Some rain forests face reduction by deforestation. **Deforestation** is the cutting down of trees for timber or other land uses. Many of the world's rain forests have been destroyed in this century. Many developing countries clear the forests for agriculture and housing areas. Rain forest wood is harvested for fuel and wood products and lumbered to clear land for industries such as gold mining. Change in weather patterns also has contributed to deforestation. Like other green plants, trees produce oxygen and absorb carbon dioxide. Deforestation diminishes the sources of oxygen for Earth's atmosphere and increases the levels of carbon dioxide. It also can permanently kill off many species of plants and animals. This diminishes **biodiversity**, the variety of life forms on Earth. This variety gives humans food, vegetation, and medicine. About 25 percent of modern drugs originate in the rain forests.

Staying Informed about Environmental Issues

There are many ways to stay informed about environmental issues. Popular media are sources of environmental information—radio and TV newscasts and other programs often deal with environmental issues, and many magazines and journals continually report on environmental issues. Environmental agencies and organizations have Web sites.

Health Goal #82

I Will Be Aware of Organizations and Global Initiatives to Protect the Environment

Environmental Agencies and Organizations

Governmental and some nongovernmental agencies and organizations are reliable sources of information about environmental issues. A number of regulatory agencies have been established to protect the environment and the general public. A **regulatory agency** is an agency that enforces laws to protect the general public.

Many state regulatory agencies that protect the environment are known as departments of environmental quality or environmental protection. On the local level, the public health department is the environmental regulatory agency. Local public health departments enforce environmental standards and regulations and provide information on the environment. Many nongovernmental environmental organizations also advocate for the environment, educate the public on environmental issues, and organize projects to improve the environment. There are also international environmental laws.

Some of the primary federal agencies charged with protecting the environment and their functions are explained here:

- The **Environmental Protection Agency (EPA)** is a federal regulatory agency responsible for reducing and controlling environmental pollution. Pollution is any change in air, water, soil, noise level, or temperature that has a negative effect on life and health. The EPA publishes information on environmental issues and regulations. The EPA Web site (www.epa.gov) has resources that health teachers can use in teaching.
- The **Occupational Safety and Health Administration (OSHA)** is a federal regulatory agency responsible for workplace environment. It sets and enforces standards for a safe and healthy workplace.
- The **National Institute for Occupational Safety and Health (NIOSH)** is a federal regulatory agency that conducts research on health hazards in the workplace.

Federal Acts to Regulate the Environment

Congress has enacted many federal laws to regulate the environment. Examples of important federal environment acts are the following:

1. The **Clean Air Act** allows the EPA to set standards for major air pollutants. **Pollutants** are harmful substances in the environment.
2. The **Comprehensive Environmental Response, Compensation, and Liability Act** provides federal funding to clean up uncontrolled or hazardous waste sites and oil and chemical spills.
3. The **Clean Water Act** sets regulations on wastes going into water and on the operation of waste treatment plants and makes it illegal to release pollutants into the water.
4. The **Safe Drinking Water Act** protects the quality of drinking water. It also sets standards for owners and operators of public water systems.
5. The **Endangered Species Act** protects animal and plant species that are threatened with extinction. Extinction is the death of all members of a species of animal or plant. The act makes it illegal to remove an endangered species from its natural habitat. A habitat is a place where an animal or plant lives.
6. The **National Environmental Policy Act** requires all government agencies to consider and assess the impact on the environment before taking any action that might affect the environment.
7. The **Toxic Substances Control Act** authorizes the EPA to set standards for the manufacturing, use, transportation, and disposal of toxic substances.
8. The **Occupational Safety and Health Act** establishes minimum safety and health standards that all employers must meet.

Nongovernmental Advocates

There also are nongovernmental environmental organizations that advocate for the environment, educate the public on environmental issues, and organize projects to improve the environment. Some nongovernmental advocates help specific parts of the environment, like local water sources or local air quality. Other groups work to improve the overall environment. Many companies also work to lessen their impact on their environment. The Sierra Club and Greenpeace are examples of nongovernmental environmental organizations. The Sierra Club is the largest and most influential grassroots environmental organization in the United States.

Health Goal #83

I Will Help Keep the Air Clean

Air Quality

The quality of air that people breathe changes depending on the materials that are in the atmosphere, the layer of gases that surrounds Earth. Many kinds of substances are found in air. Natural substances that result from such events as dust storms, forest fires, or erupting volcanoes contribute materials to the atmosphere. Human activity also releases materials into the atmosphere. Burning fuels to provide heat, electric power, and transportation release gases and solid particles. Materials released into the environment that can damage health are pollutants.

The Environmental Protection Agency (EPA) measures air quality in all major cities in the United States daily. The Air Quality Index (AQI) indicates how clean the air is and if it will affect people's health status. It considers ground-level ozone, particulate matter, carbon monoxide, and nitrogen and sulfur dioxides. Many newspapers and TV stations report on the current air quality. It is important to pay attention to these reports in order to know the quality of the air. There may be times when it is not advisable to exercise outdoors because of poor air quality. This is especially true for people with respiratory problems.

Air Pollution

Air pollution is a contamination of the air that causes negative effects on life and health. Natural events such as dust storms, forest fires, and erupting volcanoes cause some air pollution. However, most air pollution is caused by people. Over the years, as the human population has grown, air pollution has increased.

EFFECTS ON HEALTH STATUS

The quality of the air people breathe is affected when materials are released into Earth's atmosphere, the layer of gases that surrounds Earth. Many kinds of waste substances, when released into the air, contribute to air pollution. These include chemicals, smoke, harmful gases, and solid particles such as soot. Air pollution harms health status in various ways. For example, pollutants in the air can interfere with the action of cilia in the respiratory system. Cilia are hairlike structures that remove dust and other particles from the air. Pollutants can damage or destroy cilia. This increases the likelihood of respiratory diseases and infections such as asthma, emphysema, bronchitis, and lung cancer. Air pollution also contributes to heart disease, eye and throat irritation, and a weakened immune system. Even healthy people

who exercise and stay fit can become ill in areas where air pollution is concentrated.

EFFECTS OF AIR POLLUTION ON CHILDREN

According to the American Academy of Pediatrics (Committee on Environmental Health, 2004), children are more vulnerable to the adverse effects of air pollution than adults are. The developing lungs of children are highly susceptible to damages from exposure to air pollutants. The higher breathing rates of children, the higher level of physical activity, and the greater time spent outdoors mean that children are exposed to more air pollutants than adults. Numerous studies are finding harmful health effects from air pollution at levels once considered safe. Children exposed to air pollution are at increased risk of respiratory tract illness, worsening of asthma, and impaired lung function. Levels of ozone and particulates (see the next section) are unhealthful in many parts of the United States.

Sources of Air Pollution

Sources of air pollution include fossil fuels, particulates, motor vehicle emissions, smog, and indoor air pollution.

FOSSIL FUELS

A **fossil fuel** is a fuel that is formed from plant or animal remains as a result of pressure over many years. Coal, oil, gasoline, and natural gas are fossil fuels. Fossil fuels are the major sources of energy on Earth. They also are a leading source of air pollution because when they are burned they produce carbon monoxide, carbon dioxide, nitrogen oxides, sulfur oxides, and other solid substances. **Carbon monoxide** is an odorless, tasteless gas. It is poisonous and reduces the ability of blood to carry oxygen to body cells. Although it is a normal part of the atmosphere, in large amounts it pollutes the air.

When fossil fuels are burned, sulfur oxides and nitrogen oxides are released into the atmosphere. **Sulfur oxides** are sulfur-containing chemicals that irritate the nose, throat, and eyes and smell like rotten eggs. **Nitrogen oxides** are nitrogen-containing chemicals that appear as a yellow-brown haze in the atmosphere and irritate the respiratory system. The combination of sulfur oxides and nitrogen oxides with water vapor in the air results in **acid rain**—rain or another form of precipitation that has a high acid content. Acid rain destroys plants and crops, changes the composition of water in lakes, causes fish to die, and damages buildings.

PARTICULATES

Particulates are tiny particles in the air. Soot, ash, dirt, dust, and pollen are particulates. Particulates harm the cilia and other surfaces of the respiratory system. Very tiny particulates escape the cilia and travel deep into the lungs, where they damage the lungs and can cause coughing, wheezing, asthma attacks, respiratory infections, bronchitis, and lung cancer.

MOTOR VEHICLE EMISSIONS

Motor vehicle emissions are substances released into the atmosphere by motor vehicles burning fuel, particularly gasoline. Emissions include carbon monoxide, airborne lead, sulfur oxides, and nitrogen oxides. Inhaling motor vehicle emissions increases the risk of respiratory diseases, including lung cancer, asthma, and bronchitis.

SMOG

Smog is the haze that results when water vapor in the air combines in the presence of sunlight with motor vehicle emissions and the smoke and particles from factories. Smog is a threat to the health of the elderly and to people who have respiratory illnesses. The amount of smog often is increased by thermal inversions. In a **thermal inversion,** a layer of warm air forms above a layer of cool air, preventing air circulation and trapping pollutants in the cooler layer.

Smog also contains harmful gases, such as **ozone**—a form of oxygen. Most ozone is found in the upper atmosphere of Earth, where it is produced naturally when sunlight reacts with oxygen. This high-altitude ozone layer helps protect Earth from the sun's harmful rays. However, the ozone formed close to Earth's surface by chemical reactions between sunlight and pollutants is a health hazard. It helps form more smog and can irritate the eyes, lungs, and throat and produce headaches, coughing, and shortness of breath.

INDOOR AIR POLLUTION

There is air pollution indoors as well as outdoors. Pollutants can be even more concentrated indoors because they are trapped. Secondhand smoke is an indoor air pollutant. **Secondhand smoke, or environmental tobacco smoke,** is exhaled smoke and sidestream smoke. Secondhand smoke has been declared a Group A carcinogen by the EPA. A **Group A carcinogen** is a substance that causes cancer in humans. Breathing secondhand smoke is a major cause of lung cancer and increases the risk of respiratory infections and asthma.

Wood-burning stoves, gas appliances, unvented kerosene heaters, and poorly vented furnaces and stoves also are sources of indoor air pollution. Wood-burning stoves emit particulates, carbon monoxide, and sulfur dioxide. Faulty space heaters, furnaces, and water heaters can release carbon monoxide and cause carbon monoxide poisoning, which can be fatal. Signs of carbon monoxide poisoning include headaches, nausea, vomiting, fatigue, dizziness, and unconsciousness.

Building materials can be sources of indoor air pollution. Formaldehyde is a colorless gas with a strong odor. Formaldehyde can be found in plywood, furniture, and other wood products and in insulation, cosmetics, upholstery, carpets, floor coverings, household appliances, and cigarette smoke. Breathing formaldehyde causes shortness of breath, coughing, dizziness, eye irritation, headaches, nausea, asthma attacks, and cancer.

Asbestos is a heat-resistant mineral found in many building materials. Building materials that contain asbestos may be found in many older buildings and homes, heating systems, floor and ceiling tiles, shingles, and insulation around household pipes. Asbestos fibers can get into the air. Breathing asbestos has been linked to lung and gastrointestinal cancer.

Many cleaning agents and some hobby supplies, such as glues, also release toxic fumes into the air. Inhaling toxic fumes from some cleaning agents and some types of glues can cause respiratory damage and may harm the brain.

Radon is an odorless, colorless radioactive gas that is released by rocks and soil. Radon can enter homes through cracks in the floors and basement walls and through drains and sump pumps. Many homes have unsafe radon levels. Inhaling radon increases the risk of lung cancer. You can purchase a radon detector for monitoring the radon levels in a home.

Sick building syndrome (SBS) is an illness that results from indoor air pollution. SBS is very risky for the elderly, infants, and people with asthma. Signs of SBS include headaches, irritated eyes, nausea, dizziness, drowsiness, hoarseness, and respiratory conditions. Symptoms usually disappear when people leave the building and get fresh air.

Indoor molds are molds that grow on indoor surfaces that are wet. Molds have the potential to cause health problems. Molds produce allergens (substances that can cause allergic reactions), irritants, and in some cases, potentially toxic substances. Inhaling or touching mold or mold spores may cause allergic reactions in sensitive individuals. Allergic responses include hay fever–type symptoms, such as sneezing, runny nose, red eyes, and skin rash. Allergic reactions to mold are common. They can be immediate or delayed. Molds can also cause asthma attacks in people with asthma who are allergic to mold. In addition, mold exposure can irritate the eyes, skin, nose, throat, and lungs of both mold-allergic and non-mold-allergic people. Symptoms other than the allergic and irritant types are not commonly reported as a result of inhaling mold. More research is needed to learn more about mold and health effects (Office of Air and Radiation, 2006).

Keeping the Air Clean

Everyone has a responsibility to help keep the air free from pollutants and protect the atmosphere. No one should rely on others to keep the air they breathe clean. The following are twenty actions individuals can take to keep the air clean:

1. Do not smoke. Carbon monoxide and other chemicals from cigarette smoke pollute the air.
2. Support laws that restrict tobacco smoking in indoor areas. Make your home a smoke-free environment. If you have family members or friends who smoke, encourage them to quit.
3. Avoid driving at high speeds. Driving at high speeds burns more fuel and releases more pollutants into the atmosphere.

4. Do not leave a motor vehicle running when it is not being driven.
5. Drive a motor vehicle that gets good gas mileage and uses only unleaded gas or use a vehicle that uses a less polluting source of energy.
6. Service motor vehicles to keep the engine running efficiently. Keep a logbook of the maintenance schedule.
7. Walk or ride a bicycle when going short distances.
8. Use public transportation whenever possible.
9. Carpool with others to school activities and other social gatherings.
10. Have your home checked for asbestos. Have any asbestos removed or sealed in place.
11. Check the radon level in your home. Home testing kits are available at hardware stores. Seal cracks in the floor and basement walls and install fans to lower the radon level by moving air out.
12. Install a carbon monoxide detector.
13. Check often to see that space heaters, furnaces, water heaters, or wood-burning stoves are working properly.
14. Change the filter in the furnace regularly.
15. Make sure that all laminated or chemically treated wood products are sealed to eliminate formaldehyde fumes.
16. Limit your use of household cleaners that give off toxic fumes.
17. Use hobby supplies such as glues only in well-ventilated areas.
18. Use nontoxic glues and paints.
19. Do not burn trash or yard waste.
20. Plant trees whenever possible. Trees produce oxygen and absorb carbon dioxide.

Another action that some are taking to keep the air clean is driving a hybrid car. A **hybrid car** is a car that uses a mixture of technologies such as internal combustion engines, electric motors, batteries, hydrogen, and fuel cells to improve gasoline mileage performance. They are environmentally friendly alternatives to traditional internal combustion engine vehicles. Less air pollution is emitted from a hybrid car as a result of improved gasoline mileage and reduced tailpipe emissions. Decreased gasoline fuel consumption is a key to decreasing pollution emissions. Consumers are also excited that hybrid cars are able to get twenty to thirty more miles per gallon of gasoline than standard automobiles (Layton & Nice, 2007).

I Will Help Keep the Water Safe

Clean and Safe Water Needs

Water covers two-thirds of Earth's surface. About 97 percent of the water supply is saltwater. More than 2 percent is frozen in ice caps and glaciers. Less than 1 percent of the water on Earth is freshwater. **Freshwater** is water that is not contaminated or salty. People need clean freshwater to live. We use water to drink, prepare food, bathe, and for many other personal purposes and for industrial purposes and to generate power and irrigate crops. The freshwater we use comes from lakes, streams, rivers, reservoirs, and wells. We need to conserve this water and keep it clean and safe.

HOME WATER USE

The water used in the home comes from either a groundwater source, such as a well, or from a surface-water source, such as a lake or reservoir. After water is used at home, it usually goes into a septic tank in the backyard or is returned to a sewage treatment plant through a sewer system. The average person uses eighty to one hundred gallons of water per day. Following are average daily water uses for one person:

- Toilets—thirty-five gallons
- Baths and showers—twenty-eight gallons
- Clothes washing—eighteen gallons
- Faucets—thirteen gallons
- Dishwashing—three gallons

Water Pollution

Water is necessary for life. A human being will die within a few days without water to drink. **Water pollution** is contamination of water that causes negative effects on life and health. Water can be contaminated in many ways. Sewage, chemicals, radioactive wastes, and other substances dumped or accidentally spilled in or near sources of freshwater can cause contamination.

When pollutants are dumped near water sources, they enter the water source as water runoff. **Runoff** is water that runs off the land into a body of water. When snow melts, when it rains, or when people water lawns, parks, or crops, some of the water is absorbed by the ground. The rest of the water flows over the surface of the land until it reaches a river, stream, or lake. Some of the water runoff soaks into the ground until it reaches an underground stream known as groundwater. As the water runoff flows, it picks up pollutants dumped in or on the ground and carries them to freshwater supplies. The many kinds of pollutants carried by water runoff include

toxic chemicals, fertilizers, sediments, and radio-active waste.

TOXIC CHEMICALS

Toxic chemicals—such as cleaning agents, paints, pesticides, weedkillers, solvents, and oil—often find their way into streams, rivers, and lakes. Factories and industries might dump or release them directly into bodies of water, or they might be carried by water runoff. These chemicals can kill plants, fish, and other animals. Humans who eat contaminated fish may become ill.

PCBs are chemicals called polychlorinated biphenyls. They were used in appliances such as electrical equipment, pigments, and carbonless copy paper. The manufacture of PCBs stopped in the 1970s when they were found to present substantial health risk. PCB contamination typically results from releases at manufacturing plants or explosions of electrical equipment. In the body, PCBs collect in fatty tissues and in the liver. People who drink PCB-contaminated water are at risk for birth defects, reproductive disorders, liver and kidney damage, and cancer.

Dioxins are a group of chemicals used in insecticides. Small amounts of dioxins are produced naturally by forest fires and volcanic eruptions. Paper mills also produce dioxins as by-products of the chemicals used to bleach pulp and paper. Dioxins often are found in fish that live downstream from paper mills. People who eat these fish can become ill.

Lead, a heavy metal, can enter the water supply from lead pipes and water lines in older houses. Lead affects most body systems. The body system most sensitive to lead poisoning is the central nervous system, particularly in children. Lead can damage nerve cells, kidneys, and the immune system. The effects of lead are the same whether it is inhaled, swallowed, or absorbed through the skin.

FERTILIZERS

When fertilizers enter natural waterways, they cause an overgrowth of algae and other plant life. The balance between plants and animals is disrupted by this eutrophication. **Eutrophication** is the buildup of excess nutrients in water; this causes an overgrowth of plants that deplete oxygen and can kill much of the animal life in the water.

TRIHALOMETHANES

Trihalomethanes are harmful chemicals produced when chlorine attacks pollutants in water. Most water treatment systems use chlorine to purify water. Drinking water that contains trihalomethanes is dangerous. Trihalomethanes increase the risk of certain cancers, birth defects, and disorders of the central nervous system.

SEDIMENTS

Sediments are suspended solids that settle to the bottom of bodies of water. As sediments fill lakes and streams, they destroy the feeding grounds of fish and other animals. The rapid construction of homes, streets, office buildings, and malls has contributed to sedimentation. Areas that are covered with cement and asphalt cannot absorb rainwater, and the resultant heavy runoff causes erosion when it finally flows onto soft ground, washing eroded soil into waterways.

RADIOACTIVE WASTE

Low-level radioactive waste is any radioactive by-product, typically resulting from such activities as nuclear research and the development of nuclear medicines. Low-level radioactive waste can pollute water and affect plants, fish, and other animals.

THERMAL POLLUTION

In many factories, power plants, and nuclear reactors, water is used to cool machinery. In the cooling process, the heat from the machinery is absorbed by the water. When the heated water is returned to the water supply, thermal pollution can result. **Thermal pollution** is a harmful condition caused by the addition of heated water to a water supply. When the temperature of the water supply rises, the water's oxygen level decreases. As a result, many plants and animals die.

MICROORGANISMS

Microorganisms such as parasites and bacteria may enter water supplies from human or animal sewage. The improper operation of a septic tank or the failure of a waste treatment plant to properly treat sewage can be the source of microorganism contamination. Microorganism contamination can cause illness.

One microorganism that occasionally gets into water systems is *Giardia lamblia*, a parasite that lives in the intestines of humans and other mammals and causes giardiasis. **Giardiasis** is a stomach and intestinal infection that causes abdominal cramps, nausea, gas, and diarrhea. **Dysentery** is a severe infection of the intestines, causing diarrhea and abdominal pain.

Millions of people in developing countries become sick each year from microorganisms. In many developed countries, the public is alerted at once if the water supply is found to contain microorganisms. Beaches might be closed, and people might be advised to boil water to eliminate microorganisms. Water contamination often results from natural disasters, such as earthquakes and floods. Contamination also can occur when heavy rains interfere with waste treatment.

RED TIDES

Red tides occur throughout the world. **Red tides** are caused by the rapid growth, or bloom, of certain microscopic algae that usually results in a marked discoloration of the water. Red tide blooms occur naturally in certain coastal areas when certain environmental conditions arise that promote the explosive growth of a species of algae known as dinoflagellates. The environmental conditions that promote red tide include warm surface temperature, high nutrient content in the water, low salinity of the water, and calm seas. Rain followed by sunny weather in the summer months is often associated with red tide blooms. This phenomenon is called "red tide" because the high concentration of algae turns the water a rusty or reddish color. However, red tides are not always red; the water may appear greenish, brownish, purplish, or even remain its normal color during a bloom.

The algae that causes red tides off the coast of southern states, including Florida, is not the same as the algae that can proliferate along the coast of New England. In Florida, the species that causes most red tides is *Karenia brevis*, which produces a poison called a brevetoxin. The red tide off coastal Florida can cause noxious fumes, shut down beaches, and poison sea life. Toxic gases can cause itching and tearing eyes, headaches, coughing, sneezing, runny noses, shortness of breath, and other respiratory problems in humans. People with severe or chronic respiratory conditions (such as emphysema or asthma) are advised to avoid red tide areas because the fumes can slightly lower lung capacity. People with asthma are particularly susceptible to asthma attacks. Red tide is also believed to affect pets, especially dogs, the same way it affects humans. Fish, manatees, dolphins, and other sea life are often killed by red tides and wash up on beaches. Red tides off the New England coast contaminate only shellfish (e.g., oysters and clams), making them unsafe for animals and humans to eat. Swimmers, fish, and popular seafood such as lobster or shrimp are not affected. Scallops also are not affected because people do not eat the part that absorbs the poison. Only shellfish that filter seawater for food can build up dangerous concentrations of toxin in their meat. Red tides have damaged the seafood industry, shoreline quality, and local economies in affected areas.

Keeping Water Safe

Steps have been taken to reduce water pollution. The Environmental Protection Agency (EPA) requires public suppliers to notify people if water does not meet safety standards or if required monitoring has not taken place. The **Clean Water Act (CWA)** sets regulations on wastes going into water and the operation of waste treatment plants. This act makes it illegal to release pollutants into the water. The **Safe Drinking Water Act (SDWA)** protects the quality of drinking water. This law sets standards for owners and operators of public water systems. Laws enacted by local governments also help protect

BEACH CLOSED
RED TIDE

people from water pollution, and new methods being used by manufacturers and companies have helped reduce water pollution.

It is easy to think that personal and individual habits and activities have little impact on the quality of the water. However, each person has a great influence on the quality of the water that is available where she or he lives. The following are some ways individuals can help keep the water safe:

1. Do not pour toxic chemicals down the drain or into the toilet. Dispose of them at hazardous waste collection centers.
2. Do not pour toxic chemicals on the ground. These substances can contaminate groundwater supplies in water runoff.
3. Use phosphate-free detergents and biodegradable soaps and shampoos. A **biodegradable product** is a product that can be broken down by living organisms into harmless and usable materials.
4. Let water run for at least thirty seconds when you first turn it on. Water that has stood in the pipes might have absorbed lead. Or boil water for ten minutes before drinking it if there's a chance that it might contain microorganisms.
5. Pump out your septic tank once a year.
6. Support community efforts to clean up rivers, lakes, and streams and to preserve wetlands.
7. Support local and state legislation to control water pollution.
8. Do not dump garbage or toxic chemicals into lakes, streams, rivers, ponds, storm sewers, or ditches.
9. Do not dispose of plastics, such as plastic cups and bags, in waterways.
10. Select yard plants that require little or no fertilizer.
11. Plant trees and shrubs to discourage water runoff and soil erosion.
12. Convert yard trimmings into compost. As plant materials decay, they can be used as a soil conditioner, gradually releasing nutrients to a lawn or garden. This allows less fertilizer to be used.
13. Contact the public health department or water company if water from a faucet has an unusual appearance, smell, or taste. It could be contaminated. Use bottled water until the water is tested and pronounced safe to drink.
14. Follow the recommendations of the public health department or water company in regard to drinking water.
15. Test drinking water for lead contamination if you suspect that there is lead in it.

Health Goal #85
I Will Help Keep Noise at a Safe Level

Sounds and Noise

Sounds can be a source of relaxation and pleasure. Sounds can also be a source of noise. **Noise** is a sound that produces discomfort or annoyance. Noise can cause health problems and is a leading pollutant of the environment.

The sounds people hear are produced by sound waves. **Sound waves** are vibrations of air. When someone beats a drum, the drum vibrates and moves the air around and creates sound waves that reach people's ears. Different types of sound waves produce sounds at different pitches. **Pitch** is how high or low a sound is. Some sounds have a high pitch, such as a whistle. Other sounds have a low pitch, such as a motor vehicle engine. Sounds have different amplitudes. **Amplitude** is the loudness of a sound. A **decibel (dB)** is a unit used to measure the loudness of sounds. Sounds that measure more than seventy dB harm the environment and animal and human health.

Noise Pollution

Noise pollution is a loud or constant noise that causes hearing loss, stress, fatigue, irritability, and tension. It is a stressor that can harm health. The body responds to noise pollution as a threat and goes through the **general adaptation syndrome (GAS)**—a series of body changes that result from stress. Prolonged exposure to noise pollution can cause ulcers, headaches, and high blood pressure. Noise pollution also can cause accidents by preventing people from hearing warnings and interfering with their ability to concentrate and perform. It also can cause sleeplessness, increase irritability, and provoke violent reactions. Prolonged noise pollution can cause hearing loss.

According to OSHA, daily exposure of eight hours a day or more to noise levels averaging over 85 dB will result in hearing loss. Noise below 85 dB also can damage hearing, but it will take longer. Noises above 120 dB can cause immediate and permanent hearing damage. An **acoustic trauma** is an immediate and permanent loss of hearing caused by a short, intense sound. Exposure to loud noises can cause people's ears to ring or feel full. This ringing sensation or full feeling is a symptom of **temporary threshold shift (TTS),** the temporary loss of the ability to hear certain frequencies and amplifications. A **sound frequency** is the number of sound waves produced per minute.

Noise-induced permanent threshold shift is a permanent loss of the ability to hear certain frequencies and amplifications. Hearing becomes muffled, and the person might develop tinnitus—a ringing, buzzing, or hissing sensation in the ears that can reach levels equivalent to 70 dB. Tinnitus can impair concentration, be a source of great frustration, and interfere with one's ability to sleep, hold a conversation, and learn.

Following are examples of noises that can cause permanent hearing loss after eight hours:

- Vacuum cleaner—80 dB
- Power lawnmower—85 dB
- City traffic—90 dB
- Motorcycle—90 dB
- Garbage truck—100 dB
- Chain saw—100 dB
- Car horn—110 dB
- Boom stereo in car—115 dB

Following are examples of noises that can cause immediate and permanent hearing loss:

- Jackhammer (3 feet away)—120 dB
- Earphones on loud—125 dB
- Rock music—130 dB
- Rivet gun—130 dB
- Jet engine (100 feet away)—135 dB
- Air raid siren—140 dB
- Gunshot—140 dB
- Rocket launch—180 dB

The environment of our homes often results in noise pollution. Several home appliances such as dishwashers (65 dB), vacuum cleaners (80 dB), coffee grinders (80 dB), garbage disposals (80 dB), electric mixers (75 dB), and hair dryers (75 dB) create a lot of noise. Although most of these appliances do not by themselves produce hazardous levels of noise, there can be a cumulative effect when two or more sounds of equal volume are emitted at the same time. This problem can be compounded when the volume on the radio, stereo, or television is cranked up to be audible over noisy appliances. Over time, the accumulation of these noises could cause harm to our ears. Unless we make a conscious decision to reduce decibel levels, a peaceful evening at home can be as damaging to our ears as several hours in a nightclub (National Campaign for Hearing Health, 2004).

Keeping Noise at Safe Levels

Everyone should know which sounds are safe and which are not, so they can keep noise at a safe level. Many young people use earphones to listen to music at a high volume that can exceed safety limits and cause permanent hearing loss. Rock concerts and personal sound systems also can cause hearing loss. For example, "kicker" stereos can reach 145 dB, which is louder than a jet engine.

It is critical for people to be able to recognize when a sound is too loud. A sound near you is unsafe in the following cases:

- You must raise your voice to be heard.
- You cannot hear words said by someone less than two feet (sixty centimeters) away.
- You experience pain or ringing in your ears.
- You feel unsteady, dizzy, or nauseated in the presence of the sound or when the sound stops.

- Other sounds are muffled when the sound stops.
- Other people can hear your music from the headset or earphones you are wearing.

The following are actions that people can take to avoid noise pollution:

1. *Keep the volume of radios, compact disc players, stereos, and TVs at safe levels.* Lower the volume if it is too loud. Set the volume so that a normal conversation can be carried on.
2. *Avoid listening to music through headphones or headsets at unsafe levels.* Headphones and headsets cover your ears. They produce sounds that immediately reach your ears and can cause hearing loss.
3. *Wear protective earplugs when operating loud machinery or using power tools.* Most drugstores sell earplugs made from foam, rubber, silicone, or wax. Earplugs used to protect hearing are not the same as earplugs designed for swimming.
4. *Wear protective earplugs when attending loud concerts.* Many music performers wear earplugs to protect their hearing when they perform.
5. *Use your fingers to protect your ears if you don't have earplugs.* Pressing your fingers over the ear canal opening can temporarily protect you from sounds that are too loud.
6. *Distance yourself from loud sounds if you cannot avoid exposure to the sounds and don't have earplugs.* Sit at a safe distance from performers and speakers when attending a loud concert. Keep objects between you and the sound to help reduce the sound's intensity. Trying to carry on a conversation in such circumstances will only add to noise levels and can cause stress.
7. *Be considerate of others.* Be careful not to expose others, including pets, to noise. Many people will not tolerate noise. This could lead to legal warnings or penalties. For example, other people might call the police if you are having a party and making too much noise.
8. *Avoid drinking alcohol.* Drinking alcohol intensifies the impact of noise.

Health Goal #86

I Will Help Improve My Visual Environment

The Visual Environment

The **visual environment** is everything people see around them. The visual environment includes what we see when we wake up in the morning, when we look out the window, and when we travel to work or school.

A positive visual environment is visually appealing. Think about how differently people feel when they see buildings that are well cared for and a community park with flowers (a positive visual environment) and when they see buildings with broken windows, peeling paint, and graffiti (a negative visual environment). **Graffiti** is defacement of a public surface with markings. A negative visual environment contains visual pollution. **Visual pollution** is sights that are unattractive, such as litter, graffiti, and dilapidated buildings.

Visual pollution also includes materials that are displayed in inappropriate places. For example, billboards advertising alcohol and tobacco products used to be found near schools and playgrounds. Federal law now prohibits advertisements for alcohol or tobacco on billboards within a certain distance from schools. A blinking neon sign hanging in a bedroom window also is visual

pollution. Areas that are visually polluted seem to invite more visual pollution. For example, people are more likely to dump garbage and throw litter in places that already are polluted. They assume that if an area is polluted, one more piece of litter will not make any difference.

The visual environment also includes indoor surroundings. A positive indoor visual environment might be a room that is free of clutter and litter and that is freshly painted. Visual pollution in an indoor environment might include clutter and trash.

AD CLUTTER

Ads seem to be everywhere we look. The amount of advertising that we are exposed to has gone up dramatically in recent years. People are exposed to about 5,000 ads a day now compared to only 500 ads a day in the 1970s (CBS News, 2006). Advertisers and agencies are desperately trying to find new ways to stand out in the advertising glut and grab people's attention. To reach people, they have had to become much more creative and more invasive. Have you noticed that it seems that the goal of marketers and advertisers is to cover every blank space with a brand logo, a promotion, or an advertisement? They plaster logos and ads on buildings, buses, parking stripes, floors, subway tunnels, scoreboards, and even in front of urinals and toilets. They digitally insert virtual products within TV shows and video games, making advertising part of the entertainment instead of a break from the entertainment. The amount of product placements in movies has increased as well.

This ad clutter is really an assault on our senses. It is in-your-face advertising that produces an information overload. It often feels to be "in your face." People have to screen it out because they cannot absorb that much information. Many forms of ad clutter can be construed as visual pollution, especially when our living spaces are plastered with ads and our entertainment choices are infiltrated with ads and other product placements.

Positive Visual Environment and Health Status

Following are some of the ways a positive visual environment improves health status:

1. *Improves mood.* The sight of an attractive painting or a sunrise can be energizing. The sight of a beautiful sunset can inspire a sense of awe.
2. *Improves motivation.* The sight of a clean desk and a neat room can help people feel motivated. People are better able to focus and concentrate when they are not distracted by visual pollution.
3. *Helps relieve stress.* Certain sights can be calming. People who are stressed may find that looking out the window at a pleasant scene relaxes them.
4. *Contributes to quality of life.* Communities in which there is visual pollution, such as graffiti and litter, often are at high risk for crime and violence. The value of property is lower. People may not have pride in the community. Improving the visual environment is linked to a decrease in crime and violence, an increase in property value, and an increase in community pride.
5. *Improves social health.* People share visual environments with one another. In fact, each person is a part of other people's visual environment. The way a person appears and the way he or she cares for the visual environment can affect those around them. Being well groomed and having a clean and healthful appearance can improve everyone's social health. It demonstrates that people care for themselves and have self-respect.

Improving the Visual Environment

When they look around at their visual environment, most people will see things that could be improved. The following are ways to improve the visual environment:

1. *Pick up clutter.* Organize belongings so they are stored neatly. Keep an area free of clutter in which to work on projects.
2. *Clean up litter.* Throw litter in the trash. Keep trash cans available to decrease the likelihood that other people will litter.
3. *Put up pictures.* Cover bare or cracked walls with pictures or other decorations. Decorations can add warmth and increase the visual interest of a room.
4. *Add plants and other living things.* Consider adding a plant, an aquarium, or a terrarium

to a home. A **terrarium** is a transparent container that holds plants and perhaps small animals. Plants add color and can improve the atmosphere. (Bedrooms should not have a lot of plants because plants absorb oxygen at night.)

5. *Improve the view outside windows.* Hang a bird feeder, clean up litter, plant a tree.
6. *Change the colors.* Colors can impact mood. Bright red, yellow, and orange have an energizing effect. Blues and greens have a relaxing effect.
7. *Organize a cleanup campaign.* Many organizations and community groups sponsor cleanup campaigns in the community in which people can participate. Other efforts include cleaning up abandoned buildings, picking up litter in parks, and planting trees and flowers.
8. *Write to community leaders about visual pollution in the community.* Write letters to officials explaining concerns about such visual pollution as abandoned buildings and graffiti.

Health Goal #87

I Will Help Conserve Energy and Natural Resources

Energy and Natural Resources

Energy and natural resources are an important part of the environment. A **natural resource** is anything obtained from the natural environment to meet people's needs. Energy is the ability to do work. The **law of conservation of energy** is a scientific principle that says that energy cannot be created or destroyed but can be changed in form. For example, plants use light energy to combine water and carbon dioxide to form sugar. The sugar in plants provides energy for animals and people. Plants are a natural resource that people use for food. Many resources are sources of energy.

FOSSIL FUELS

Fossil fuel is a fuel that is formed from plant or animal remains as a result of pressure over many years.

- **Coal** is a black or brown solid that contains stored energy from decayed plant material. It is the most abundant fossil fuel in the United States.
- **Petroleum,** or **crude oil,** is a black liquid energy source that is trapped in rock beneath Earth's surface. It is removed by drilling wells and pumping the oil through pipelines to tankers or oil refineries. An **oil refinery** is a processing plant that produces gasoline, heating oil, diesel oil, or asphalt from petroleum. Oil also is used to produce fertilizers, pesticides, plastics, synthetic materials, paint, and medical products. After coal, oil is the cheapest fuel.
- **Natural gas** is an energy source that is found underground, above deposits of oil. Methane, propane, and butane are types of natural gas. Natural gas is the cleanest-burning fossil fuel.

OTHER SOURCES OF ENERGY

There are other sources of energy besides fossil fuels:

- **Nuclear energy** is produced by splitting atoms of uranium into smaller parts. **Uranium** is a radioactive substance that is mined. It is used to power nuclear reactors, which split atoms to produce steam. The steam is used to generate electricity. Nuclear energy is one of the more expensive sources of energy.
- **Hydroelectric power** is electricity generated from flowing or falling water. Dams are built to store water and direct its flow through turbines. A **turbine** is an engine that rotates. Hydroelectric power is an inexpensive source of energy.
- **Solar energy** is the energy of the sun. Solar energy can be converted into electrical energy or heat. Currently solar energy systems are very expensive. However, solar energy could prove to be an almost unlimited source of power.
- **Biomass** is organic plant matter produced by solar energy from the sun's rays. It includes wood, sewage, agricultural wastes, and algae. All of these can be used as sources of energy when they are burned. **Bagasse,** a biomass source of energy, is a fibrous waste produced during the processing of sugarcane. **Gasohol,** another biomass, is a blend of grain alcohol and gasoline that is used as a fuel source.

- **Geothermal energy** is heat transferred from underground sources of steam or hot water. It can be used to heat homes, produce electricity, and power industrial plants.
- **Wind energy** is energy from wind. Wind turbines change wind energy into electricity.
- **Hydrogen power** is energy produced by passing electrical current through water to burn the hydrogen. Hydrogen yields a high amount of energy.

Conservation of Energy and Natural Resources

Most people take energy for granted and do not realize how much energy they use—or how much they waste. We can all conserve energy by developing habits that use less energy and by using energy-saving devices. **Conservation** is the saving of resources. The following are ways to conserve energy supplied by natural resources:

1. Turn off lights when leaving a room.
2. Use fluorescent lights except for reading.
3. Use light bulbs with a low wattage except when reading or when doing activities that require adequate lighting.
4. Turn off electrical appliances such as TVs, stereos, and radios when not in use.
5. Use rechargeable instead of disposable batteries.
6. Use fans instead of air conditioning.
7. Plant fast-growing trees near your home to keep it cooler.
8. Wear an additional layer of warm clothing in cold weather instead of turning up the heat.
9. Install weather stripping around windows and seal air leaks around doors to prevent heat loss.
10. Turn down the thermostat at night and when away from home.
11. Reduce the amount of hot water used for showers or baths.
12. In warm weather, dry clothes on a clothesline.
13. Purchase energy-efficient products for the home.
14. Try to use a motor vehicle that gets thirty miles (forty-eight kilometers) or more per gallon of gas.
15. Carpool or use public transportation whenever possible.
16. Ride a bike to save fuel whenever possible.
17. Walk instead of driving a motor vehicle whenever possible.
18. Service the furnace once a year and replace furnace filters frequently.

Water is necessary for all forms of life to survive. Following are ten ways people can conserve water:

1. Install a low-flow showerhead to reduce the amount of water used in showering.
2. Take shorter showers.
3. Take a shower instead of a bath.
4. Check faucets and pipes for leaks.
5. Run a washing machine only for a full load of clothes.
6. Do not allow water to run constantly while washing and rinsing dishes.
7. Run a dishwasher only for a full load.
8. Water the lawn only at the coolest time of the day, and do not water for long periods of time.
9. Plant trees in the yard, because they store water and release it into the ground.
10. Keep drinking water in the refrigerator instead of allowing tap water to run until it is cool enough to drink.

Health Goal #88

I Will Precycle, Recycle, and Dispose of Waste Properly

Solid Waste

The amount of solid waste thrown away every day in the United States averages four pounds (1.8 kilograms) per person. **Solid waste** is discarded solid materials, such as paper, metals, plastics, glass, leather, wood, rubber, textiles, food, and yard waste. Most solid waste is dumped in landfills. A **landfill** is a place where waste is dumped in layers and buried.

We brought our own bags.

6. Do not use plastic wrap or aluminum foil.
7. Avoid purchasing food items in single-serving containers.
8. Do not purchase non-biodegradable products.
9. Do not buy items that have a lot of packaging.
10. Do not use plastic or paper bags unless required to.

Solid waste is a problem that affects many parts of the environment. It pollutes the air, water, and soil. The landfills where solid wastes are dumped take up space and can contaminate water supplies and pollute the air.

Precycling

Some solid wastes can be precycled. **Precycling** is a process of reducing waste. It includes purchasing products in packages or containers that have been or can be broken down and used again, purchasing products that have little packaging, and repairing existing products rather than throwing them out and buying new ones. Here are some tips for precycling:

1. Do not purchase paper items not made from recycled paper.
2. Do not purchase beverages that are not in returnable or refillable containers or containers made of materials that can be broken down and used more than once.
3. Do not use disposable diapers made of plastic, paper, or some other throw-away material.
4. Do not use just one side of a sheet of paper.
5. Do not use paper napkins or paper towels to dry the hands.

Recycling

Recycling is the process of re-forming or breaking down a waste product so that it can be used again. Recycling can reduce the amount of solid waste in landfills and the pollution caused by wastes that are nonbiodegradable. Nonbiodegradable waste cannot be broken down by natural processes and can last for hundreds of years. Plastics, aluminum cans, and glass are nonbiodegradable wastes. Waste that is biodegradable can be broken down by living organisms; examples are foods and certain paper products. Recycling is not always appropriate. However, when it is, it can help conserve natural resources because it reduces the need for raw materials. Recycling involves collecting reusable material, processing and marketing it, and reusing it for a new product. Many communities have recycling programs or centers. Recycling can help reduce the amount of raw materials, energy, and water used and cut down the amount of air pollution created by normal processing. Six commonly recycled materials are paper, glass, used petroleum products, yard trimmings, plastics, and aluminum.

Waste Disposal

Individuals, families, industries, businesses, and farms all produce huge amounts of waste. This waste can be disposed of in several different ways, including landfills, incineration, composting, and deep-injection wells.

LANDFILLS

There are two types of landfills. A **sanitary landfill** is a waste disposal land site where solid waste is spread in thin layers, compacted, and covered with a fresh layer of dirt daily. The dirt contains bacteria to help break down the organic material in the garbage. A **secure landfill** is a landfill that has protective liners to reduce or prevent leachate from escaping through water runoff. Leachate is the liquid that drains from a landfill. Hazardous wastes and nonbiodegradable materials should not be sent to a landfill.

INCINERATION

An **incinerator** is a furnace in which solid waste is burned and energy is recovered in the process. Incinerators reduce the volume of solid waste but can release pollutants into the atmosphere. Some incinerators use the heat produced by burning to create steam that generates electricity. For safety reasons most biohazardous waste is incinerated. **Biohazardous waste,** or **medical waste,** is infectious waste from medical facilities. It includes syringes, needles, tubes, blood vials, and other items that can contain tissues and body fluids from a person or animal.

COMPOSTING

Compost is a mixture of decayed organic material generally used to fertilize and condition the soil. **Composting** is the use of naturally occurring soil bacteria to break down plant remains into humus. **Humus** is a soil conditioner. In some communities, yard waste is separated from other kinds of waste and transported to compost landfills. Many individuals have their own compost piles. Food wastes such as meat and eggs should not be composted because they will attract flies and rodents. A **mulching lawn mower** cuts grass clippings into small pieces that can be left on the lawn to decompose naturally, thereby reducing yard waste and creating a natural lawn fertilizer.

HAZARDOUS WASTE

Hazardous waste is any solid, liquid, or gas that is harmful to humans or animal or plant life. Hazardous waste includes paints, solvents, cleaners, acids, alkalis, pesticides, petroleum products such as gasoline and motor oil, and other toxic chemicals. Proper disposal of hazardous waste is very important to environmental health. Hazardous waste can leach out of landfills and escape into the environment. Hazardous waste cannot be incinerated because it might cause an explosion. One way that hazardous waste might be disposed of is in deep-injection wells. A **deep-injection well** pumps waste into porous rock far below the level of groundwater. However, there are often problems when disposing of hazardous waste in deep-injection wells, such as cracks and undetected faults, that can allow wastes to migrate.

Health Goal #89

I Will Protect the Natural Environment

The Natural Environment

The **natural environment** is everything around a person that is not made by people—including plants, animals, insects, mountains, oceans, and the sky. The natural environment influences **quality of life**—the degree to which a person lives life to the fullest.

APPRECIATING THE NATURAL ENVIRONMENT

Just thinking about nature and the natural environment can give a sense of awe and appreciation. Areas that have been set aside for enjoying and appreciating nature include community parks, nature preserves, state parks, and national parks. Following are some of the many kinds of places where people can enjoy the natural environment and improve their quality of life:

- A **nature preserve** is an area restricted for the protection of the natural environment.
- A **wildlife sanctuary** is a place reserved for the protection of plants and animals.
- **National parks** and **state parks** are government-maintained areas of land open to the public.
- A **community park** is an area of land kept for natural scenery and recreation.
- A **nature trail** is a path through a natural environment.

- A **recreational trail** is a path designed for recreational activities, such as walking, jogging, in-line skating, biking, and hiking.
- A **beach** is the shore of a body of water covered by sand, gravel, or rock.
- A **zoo** is a park in which animals are cared for and shown to the public.
- A **garden** is an area where trees, flowers, and other plants are grown and landscaping is maintained.
- A **conservatory** is a greenhouse in which plants are grown and displayed to the public.

The Natural Environment and Health Status

The natural environment improves health status. In the natural environment, a person can find the following:

1. A quiet place to spend time alone. This contributes to well-being. It gives a person time to collect thoughts.
2. A place to spend time with family members and friends—such as a zoo, a park, or a beach.
3. A place to participate in outdoor physical activities, such as hiking, in-line skating, swimming, or playing basketball.
4. A place to enjoy leisure time. **Leisure time** is time free from work or duties. During leisure time, some people collect leaves, observe the stars, watch birds, or participate in physical activities.
5. A place to relieve stress. Most people feel more relaxed after walking through a park, spending time at a zoo or at a nature preserve, or visiting a conservatory.

Protecting the Natural Environment

People need to take responsibility for preserving the natural environment. Following are ten actions people can take to help protect the natural environment:

1. *Follow all rules.* Many places created to help people enjoy the natural environment post rules to follow. Rules might involve staying in certain areas, keeping pets on a leash, and following safety guidelines.
2. *Do not leave belongings behind.* Whatever a person takes into a natural area should go with them when they leave the area.
3. *Do not litter or leave other objects.* Bring garbage bags to collect trash and other wastes.
4. *Do not destroy or harm the environment.* Leave as little trace as possible of having been in a natural environment. Do not damage trees or plants. Do not carve initials in trees. Do not write graffiti on rocks, trees, bridges, trail signs, buildings, or anywhere else.
5. *Do not take things out of the natural environment.* Leave everything in its place so that you do not harm the natural habitat. A **habitat** is a place where an animal or plant normally lives. Do not pick flowers. Do not break branches off trees. Do not take animals or other objects from the natural environment.
6. *Do not feed wild animals.* Feeding wild animals makes them dependent on humans for food. They do not learn to feed themselves. Many animals starve to death after people leave the area. Feeding wild animals also makes them more dangerous to humans because they lose their natural fear of humans; this can result in their being killed by animal control officers.
7. *Stay on trails.* Trails are designed to protect people from possible dangers and to protect the natural environment. On narrow trails, walk single file rather than side by side when hiking with two or more people, to make sure everyone stays on the trail.
8. *Keep fires small and make sure they are extinguished before leaving.* Follow park rules for building fires. Make sure that fires are completely out before leaving the area. Do not build fires if they are not allowed.
9. *Be considerate of others when in the natural environment.* Do not make loud noises, such as screaming or playing loud music. Do not monopolize equipment and facilities. Walk or ride on the appropriate side of trails.
10. *Do not drink out of lakes and streams or consume wild plants.* Many lakes and streams are polluted with microorganisms and other pollutants that harm health. Many wild plants are poisonous and can cause illness or death. Consuming wild plants takes from the natural environment.

I Will Be a Health Advocate for the Environment

Health Advocacy for the Environment

Health advocacy is taking responsibility to improve the quality of life. A **health advocate for the environment** is a person who promotes a healthful environment. Health advocates for the environment take actions to improve the quality of the environment. They avoid actions that may threaten the environment. Health advocates for the environment work together with other people to promote environmental health. They encourage others to join them in taking responsibility for the environment. They have successfully influenced the passage of laws that protect the environment.

Anyone can be a health advocate for the environment and a role model to others by taking responsibility for the environment. There are a variety of ways to become an effective health advocate for the environment:

1. *Take responsibility for your personal actions regarding the environment.* Do not allow circumstances or peer pressure to make you forget or avoid your responsibility to promote a healthy environment. Instead, take advantage of the opportunity to be both a health advocate for the environment and a role model for your friends.
2. *Stay informed about environmental issues that affect the community, the nation, and the world.* New discoveries are made every day. New technology brings about change rapidly. Keep current on the changes and how they affect environmental issues. Read about environmental issues in newspapers and magazines, and learn about factors that may harm the environment. Recognize that scientists and environmental groups have differing options about environmental issues. Make sure that information comes from a reliable source.

3. *Take actions to promote the environment.* Review this chapter for actions you can take to promote the environment. Look for ways to protect and improve the environment, such as conserving water and energy, recycling, building a compost pile, planting trees, and not littering.
4. *Encourage others to protect the environment.* Share the information you have learned in this chapter with your family and friends. Invite others to join you in efforts to protect the environment.
5. *Volunteer to work on environmental improvement projects in the community.* Identify environmental organizations or groups involved in improving your community. Young people should first obtain permission from a parent or guardian to volunteer to help these organizations or groups.
6. *Organize environmental improvement projects.* Being a health advocate for the environment involves taking responsibility. If you see a need for improvement in an area of the environment, such as air or water pollution, don't wait for someone else to organize an environmental improvement project. Choose a way to improve the environment and take action.

Opportunities for Health Advocacy for the Environment

People do many things to play a role in helping the environment. When the National Community Service Trust Act was passed in 1933, it started a strong push to help the environment. This national service initiative allows people who want to help the environment to receive financial aid to help them pay for college.

High school students between the ages of sixteen and eighteen can enroll in summer programs in which they can work for a month at a time in outdoor settings on public lands. Experience is not needed. Participants can learn about careers in conservation. It's a productive way to spend the summer and also learn about the environment.

People can participate in various community-service programs. They can work on special projects such as taking steps to beautify the community. One example is people picking up trash along the side of the road or planting flowers in a local park.

The federal government started a program called AmeriCorps. AmeriCorps is similar to the Peace Corps, but instead of working in another country, AmeriCorps participants work in the United States. When people work for AmeriCorps, they perform a number of tasks to help the community. In turn, the participants receive a small stipend or funds to help pay for a college education or to repay a student loan. People in AmeriCorps undertake many environmental activities, such as beautifying communities and creating vegetable gardens in previously unusable land. These actions help the environment and the community.

Injury Prevention and Safety

HEALTH GOALS FOR INJURY PREVENTION AND SAFETY

91. I will follow safety guidelines to reduce the risk of unintentional injuries.

92. I will follow safety guidelines for severe weather, natural disasters, and national alerts.

93. I will follow guidelines for motor vehicle safety.

94. I will practice protective factors to reduce the risk of violence.

95. I will respect authority and obey laws.

96. I will protect myself from physical violence and abuse.

97. I will protect myself from sexual violence and abuse.

98. I will stay away from gangs.

99. I will follow guidelines to help reduce the risk of weapon injuries.

100. I will be skilled in first-aid procedures.

I**njury prevention and safety** is the area of health that focuses on following safety guidelines to reduce the risk of unintentional injuries; following safety guidelines for severe weather, natural disasters, and national alerts; following guidelines for motor vehicle safety; practicing protective factors to reduce the risk of violence; respecting authority and obeying laws; protecting oneself from physical violence and abuse; protecting oneself from sexual violence and abuse; staying away from gangs; following guidelines to help reduce weapon injuries; and being skilled in first-aid procedures. This chapter provides the health knowledge needed to teach young people important life skills for injury prevention and safety.

Health Goal #91

I Will Follow Safety Guidelines to Reduce the Risk of Unintentional Injuries

Unintentional Injuries

An **unintentional injury** is an injury that results from an accident. Unintentional injuries are the leading cause of death for children, teenagers, and young adults. They are also a leading cause of visits to emergency rooms and stays in hospitals. Unintentional injuries occur in the home, in the community, and in the workplace.

Unintentional Injuries in the Home

Many accidents occur in the home, and that is where young children and older people are most likely to experience unintentional injury and death. A few easy and inexpensive steps can be taken to make the home a safe environment.

FALLS

Falls are a leading cause of injury and death in the home. Half of all falls are caused by hazards such as poor lighting, loose carpets, trailing wires, and  unsteady stair rails. Most spinal cord injuries are the result of falls. Young children are at particular risk because their sense of balance is not fully developed. Many teens injured by falls have taken unnecessary risks and have ignored safety precautions or have been showing off. Teens have been injured and killed from falls off rooftops, bridges, mountains, and windows in high buildings. Many elderly people also suffer from falls in the home. Fall injuries break bones and often result in death for elderly people.

Young people need to be taught the following ways to reduce the risk of falls:

- Do not take risks in high places, such as going too close to a dropoff or hanging out a window.
- Use a sturdy ladder when climbing to reach an object. Keep your body in the center of the step to avoid losing balance. Face the ladder when climbing down.
- Place infants or young children in a playpen, crib, or safety seat when they must be out of your sight.

- Use appropriate child safety devices to block stairways and windows.
- Do not run in the home.
- Be cautious if wearing shoes with slippery bottoms or high heels.

FIRES

Most deaths and injuries related to fires occur in the home. Most home fires are caused by improper use and disposal of cigarettes, cigarette lighters, and matches. All homes should be equipped with a fire extinguisher, a heat detector, and at least one smoke detector on each floor. A **smoke detector** is an alarm that sounds when it detects smoke. A **heat detector** is a device that sounds an alarm when the room temperature rises above a certain level. The batteries in these detectors should be checked frequently to ensure that they are working. They should be changed every six months. A fire escape plan should be set up in advance and should include at least two different ways to escape from each room and should designate a meeting place outside the home.

Take the following actions if a fire occurs in the home:

1. Alert everyone in the home or building.
2. Place a cloth, wet if possible, over the face.
3. Crawl out of the building on hands and knees to stay below the smoke line.
4. Feel doors for heat before opening. Do not open doors that are warm or hot. Open cool doors slowly.
5. Stuff rugs, blankets, or clothes around door cracks to stop smoke from entering if you are unable to leave a room. Call out of a window for help.
6. Call 911 or the fire department after you have escaped.
7. Meet family members at the designated meeting place.
8. Do not go back into a burning building.
9. Tell fire officials if people or animals are inside the building.
10. Have ropes or ladders available to help family members escape from two-story houses.

Following are some ways to reduce the risk of fires:

- Have a no-smoking policy in the home.
- Keep all matches, cigarette lighters, and flames out of children's reach.
- Do not overload electrical outlets or run cords under rugs.

- Do not leave small electrical appliances such as irons or electric hair-styling products plugged in for long periods of time.
- Frequently check food that is cooking on a stove.
- Check burning candles frequently.

POISONING

Poisoning is a harmful chemical reaction from a substance that enters the body. It includes reactions to drugs. Other substances that can be poisonous when swallowed include household cleaners, polish, ammonia, nail polish remover, antifreeze, insecticides, rat poison, and certain plants. Taking very high doses of vitamin and mineral supplements also can result in poisoning. Most cases of poisoning in a home are the result of young children swallowing household products and over-the-counter (OTC) drugs. Certain substances, such as auto exhaust, airplane glue, gasoline, and carbon monoxide, cause poisoning when inhaled. Carbon monoxide is an odorless, tasteless gas emitted from motor vehicles, stoves, heaters, lawn mowers, and chimneys.

Following are some ways to reduce the risk of poisoning:

- Use childproof containers on potential poisons and keep them out of the reach of children.
- Place warning stickers on any potential poisons.
- Place childproof latches on the doors of all cabinets in which harmful substances are kept.
- Do not keep a motor vehicle or lawn mower running in a closed garage.
- Do not use outdoor grills indoors.
- Check chimneys for blockage and have them cleaned regularly.

AIRWAY OBSTRUCTION

Suffocation is an obstruction of the airway by an external object that blocks the mouth and nose, such as plastic bags, pillows, or blankets. **Choking** is the result of an obstruction of the airway by an internal object, such as food or small toys. Young children can choke on objects they place in their mouths—such as small toys, coins, or food. Strangulation also causes airway suffocation. Strangulation is the result of external compression of the airway when an object, such as a cord, string, jewelry, or crib slats, compresses the neck. Some young people have strangled themselves on material worn around their neck, such as a scarf, that caught on another object, such as a car door. Children have strangled on cords from window coverings, strings on toys, ropes tied into lassoes, and pieces of clothing.

Following are some ways to reduce the risk of suffocation:

- Keep small objects out of the reach of children.
- Do not allow children to play with plastic bags or toys that are not appropriate for their age.
- Check sleeping infants and children to be sure their breathing is not blocked by a pillow, blanket, or stuffed toy.
- Cut food into small pieces that are easy to swallow.
- Do not tie a rope or cord around the neck, even as a joke.

Unintentional Injuries in the Community

Young people often are injured in the community. They may be injured because they disregard safety guidelines. Peers may influence them to be daring. They may be stressed or overtired and careless or less alert. They risk injury when they ride a bicycle and can be at risk for drowning when near bodies of water.

DROWNINGS

Drowning is the third leading cause of accidental death. Drownings most often occur when people are swimming or playing in water. Many people who drown are strong swimmers who become tired or are pulled under by the current. Drownings also can result from boating accidents. Alcohol is a major factor in drownings and most boating accidents, so people should not drink alcohol and swim or boat. Many drownings occur in swimming pools, and young children also drown in bathtubs, hot tubs, toilets, and sinks.

Following are some ways to reduce the risk of drowning:

- Learn to swim and have training before participating in water sports.
- Never swim or use a hot tub alone and do not leave children alone near water.

- Wear a personal flotation device (life jacket) when boating or participating in water sports.
- Swim only in well-lit designated areas safe for swimming and in sight of a lifeguard.
- Stay out of the water in threatening weather such as thunderstorms and hurricanes.
- Leave the water if you have cramps or are tired.
- Enforce an alcohol-free policy around water.
- Never boat with others who speed or do not follow safety guidelines.
- Have training before boating or participating in water sports.
- Do not overload a boat or personal watercraft such as a jet ski.
- Check the depth of water before entering.
- Install a childproof fence and latches around swimming pools.
- Do not walk on untested ice.

BICYCLING INJURIES

Most deaths and serious injuries due to bicycling involve head injuries. The most serious injuries occur when bikes collide with motor vehicles.

Following are some ways to reduce the risk of bicycling injuries:

- Wear a bicycle helmet.
- Obey the traffic rules followed by motor vehicle drivers, and obey traffic lights.
- Ride on the right, with the flow of traffic.
- Check that the bicycle and all safety equipment, such as brakes, lights, and reflectors, are in good condition.
- Wear clothing that will not get caught in the chain of the bicycle.
- Wear reflective clothing at night, and use bicycle lights.
- Wear shoes at all times.
- Watch for the sudden opening of motor vehicle doors.
- Walk the bicycle across busy streets.
- Do not ride with another person on the bicycle.
- Beware of unsafe road conditions such as ice and potholes.

SCOOTER INJURIES

Scooters have become very popular. Most scooter injuries occur to children under age fifteen. Most injuries result when riders fall from the scooter. Most injuries are fractures or dislocations to the arms and hands.

Following are some ways to reduce the risk of scooter injuries:

- Wear a helmet and pads to protect the knees and elbows.
- Always ride the scooter on the sidewalk or paved off-road paths.
- Stay away from cars or other vehicles.
- Avoid streets or other surfaces with water, sand, gravel, or dirt.
- Do not ride the scooter at night.

Unintentional Injuries in the Workplace

The workplace is second only to the home as the most frequent site of unintentional injuries. Common workplace injuries to young people involve driving a motor vehicle or heavy equipment such as tractors and using power tools. Machine-related accidents, electrocution, and homicide also account for many deaths in the workplace. Most injuries to teenagers in the workplace occur in food preparation and food service jobs. The most common types of injuries in food service are sprains, strains, cuts, bruises, scrapes, heat burns, fractures, and dislocations.

LAWS PROVIDING PROTECTION IN THE WORKPLACE

According to law, an employer must meet safety guidelines for healthful working conditions. The **Occupational Safety and Health Act** is a series of safety and health standards that all employers must meet. Recognized health hazards must be eliminated. Employees regularly review safety regulations. New employees must be trained on equipment and made aware of hazards.

The Fair Labor Standards Act (FLSA) contains child labor laws to protect the health and safety of minors. The act limits the hours minors under age sixteen can work and prohibits employing minors under age eighteen to work dangerous jobs. Examples of jobs that the FLSA bans to minors are logging, mining, roofing, and manufacturing or storing explosives.

REPETITIVE STRAIN INJURY

An increasingly common workplace injury is **repetitive strain injury (RSI)**—injury from repeated physical movements. RSI damages tendons, nerves, muscles, and other soft body tissues. Using computer devices, such as keyboards and mice, often contributes to the injury. Symptoms include tingling, tightness, pain, and stiffness in the hands, wrists, fingers, arms, or elbows; weakness in the hands; and a need to massage the hands, wrists, and elbows. To prevent RSI when typing, sit straight and relax the hands and wrists. Keep the computer screen at eye level and position the keyboard so hands and wrists are straight. Take regular breaks when using a computer.

Health Goal #92

I Will Follow Safety Guidelines for Severe Weather, Natural Disasters, and National Alerts

Guidelines for Severe Weather, Natural Disasters, and National Alerts

Families should prepare themselves for a severe weather emergency, a natural disaster, or national alerts by taking action. Families can contact their local emergency management office or chapter of the American Red Cross for a copy of their emergency plans. Families should learn the warning signals for their community, such as sirens or announcements. Know which emergencies can occur in your area. Know your city's evacuation routes. The most important thing that families and individuals can do is develop an emergency plan. A plan should do the following:

- Specify how the family will get together in case they are in separate locations. Include two meeting places—one near your home in case of fire and one outside your neighborhood in case of evacuation.
- Identify one emergency contact person in the area and one contact person out of town.
- Ensure that all family members know the name and phone number of these two people.

- Teach all family members how and when to turn off gas, electricity, and water.
- Prepare an emergency supply kit.

The following items should be in your emergency kit at all times: a flashlight with extra batteries; a radio with extra batteries; a first-aid kit; important papers, including family records, a list of emergency contact numbers, and a copy of your family's emergency plan; waterproof bags for valuables and mementos; rubber gloves; and rain gear and sturdy shoes.

The following items should be put into your emergency kit when severe weather, natural disasters, or national alerts are predicted: a supply of medication; candles and waterproof matches: a supply of water (one gallon per person per day); nonperishable food and a nonelectric can opener; any special requirements for babies, older adults, or disabled individuals; cash and credit cards; and blankets or sleeping bags.

During all of the following severe weather situations, listen to the radio or watch TV for the latest emergency information, and keep your emergency kit close by. Evacuate immediately if instructed to do so.

LANDSLIDES

A **landslide** is a movement of a mass of earth or rock. If there is a risk of landslides, take the following actions.

- Listen to the radio or watch TV for the latest developments.
- Evacuate immediately if instructed to do so.
- Look for landslide warning signs such as doors or windows cracking; new cracks in walls or foundations; cracks widening on the ground or pavement; water breaking through ground surface in new locations; fences, utility poles, or trees tilting or moving; and a faint rumbling sound increasing in volume.

A person who is inside during a landslide should stay inside and take cover under a desk, table, or other piece of sturdy furniture. A person who is outdoors should try to get out of the path of the landslide; run to the nearest high ground in a direction away from the path; run to the nearest shelter, such as a building or group of trees, if debris is approaching; and curl into a tight ball and protect his or her head if escape is not possible.

FLOODS

A **flood** is a temporary condition of partial or complete deluge of normally dry land by an overflow of inland or tidal water, or the rapid accumulation of surface waters from any source. A **flash flood** is a flood that occurs suddenly. Flash floods are the number one weather-related cause of death in the United States. If there is a risk of floods, people should take the following actions:

- Listen to the radio or watch TV for the latest developments.
- Fill bathtubs, sinks, and jugs with clean water in case the water supply becomes contaminated. Bring outdoor belongings indoors, if time permits.
- Move valuable household possessions to the upper floors or to safe ground.
- Be prepared to evacuate.
- Turn off utilities at the main switch and turn off the main gas valve if instructed to do so.
- Evacuate immediately if instructed to do so.

A person who is inside during a flood should turn on a radio or TV for the latest emergency information and keep an emergency supply kit handy. A person who is outdoors should climb to higher ground and stay there and avoid walking through flood waters of more than several inches. A person in a motor vehicle should not drive through flood waters and should not attempt to move the vehicle if it stalls, but should abandon the vehicle and climb to higher ground.

EARTHQUAKES

An **earthquake** is a violent shaking of Earth's surface caused by the shifting of plates that make up Earth's crust. If there is a risk of earthquakes, people should take the following actions:

- Keep the emergency supply kit close by.
- Identify safe places in the room, such as against an inside wall or under a piece of heavy furniture.
- Evacuate immediately if instructed to do so.

A person who is indoors during an earthquake should do the following:

1. Take cover under a piece of heavy furniture or against an inside wall and hold on tightly.
2. Stay inside.
3. Do not try to leave a building.
4. Be prepared for aftershocks.

A person who is outdoors during an earthquake should do the following:

1. Move into the open, away from buildings, street lights, and utility wires.
2. If on a bridge, get off as soon as possible.
3. Be prepared for aftershocks.

TORNADOES

A **tornado** is a violent, rapidly spinning windstorm with a funnel-shaped cloud. A **tornado watch** is an emergency alert that is issued when weather conditions are such that a tornado is likely to develop. A **tornado warning** is issued when a tornado has been sighted or an alert indicated by radar. If there is a risk of tornadoes, people should take the following actions:

- Gather family members together.
- Be prepared to move to the safest place.
- Listen to the radio or watch TV for the latest developments.
- Keep the emergency supply kit available.
- Evacuate immediately if instructed to do so.

A person who is indoors during a tornado should do the following:

1. Go at once to the basement, storm cellar, or lowest level of the building or an inner hallway or small inner room without windows.
2. Stay away from windows and corners.
3. Get under a piece of sturdy furniture, such as a large, heavy table, and hold on to it.
4. Protect one's head and neck.
5. If in a mobile home, get out and find shelter elsewhere.

A person who is outdoors during a tornado should do the following:

1. Seek shelter indoors.
2. Lie in a ditch or low-lying area or crouch near a building.
3. Use arms to protect head and neck.

A person who is in a motor vehicle during a tornado should do the following:

1. Not try to drive out of or away from a tornado.
2. Get out of the vehicle immediately.
3. Seek shelter indoors.
4. Lie in a ditch or low-lying area or crouch near a building.
5. Use arms to protect head and neck.

HURRICANES

A **hurricane** is a tropical storm with heavy rain and winds in excess of seventy-four miles (118.4 kilometers) per hour. If there is a risk of hurricanes, people should take the following actions:

- Listen to the radio or watch TV for the latest developments.
- Bring outdoor objects indoors.
- Secure buildings by closing and boarding up windows.
- Fill bathtubs, sinks, and jugs with clean water in case the water supply becomes contaminated.
- Store valuables and personal papers in a waterproof container on the highest level of the building. Hurricanes often involve flooding, and this will help to protect these items from water damage.
- Store emergency foods that will last for several days and that do not require refrigeration.
- Have fresh batteries on hand for flashlights and portable radios.

A person who is indoors during a hurricane should do the following:

1. Secure the home by unplugging appliances and turning off the electricity and the main water valve.
2. Evacuate immediately if instructed to do so.
3. Stay inside, away from windows.
4. Keep a supply of flashlights and extra batteries handy.
5. Avoid open flames, such as candles, as a source of light.
6. Turn off major appliances to reduce power.
7. Evacuate mobile homes.

WILDLAND FIRES

A **wildland fire** is a fire that occurs in the wilderness. If there is a risk of wildland fires, people should take the following actions:

- Listen to the radio or watch TV for the latest developments.
- Take down flammable drapes and curtains and close all blinds and window coverings.
- Close gas valves and turn off pilot lights.
- Turn on a light in each room for visibility in heavy smoke.
- Place valuables that would not be damaged by water in a pool or pond.
- Leave sprinklers on roofs and on anything that might burn, if adequate water is available.
- Evacuate immediately, if asked to do so.

During a wildland fire, a person should do the following:

1. Not attempt to outrun the fire if trapped.
2. Crouch in a body of water if possible.
3. Cover the head and upper body with wet clothing.
4. Seek shelter in a cleared area or bed of rocks if water is not available.
5. Breathe the air close to the ground through a wet cloth.

ELECTRICAL STORMS

An **electrical storm** is a storm that has lightning and thunder. A **severe thunderstorm watch** is an emergency alert that is issued when the weather conditions are such that a severe thunderstorm is likely to develop. A **severe thunderstorm warning** is an alert that is issued when a severe thunderstorm has been sighted or indicated by radar. If there is a risk of electrical storms, a person should take the following actions:

- Review the safety guidelines for tornadoes and flash floods, which may accompany thunderstorms.
- Listen to a battery-operated radio for the latest weather developments.
- Unplug the TV.
- Bring outdoor objects indoors.
- Close and board up windows.

To avoid electrocution, a person who is indoors during an electrical storm should do the following:

1. Not handle any electrical equipment or telephones.
2. Avoid bathtubs, water faucets, and sinks.
3. Avoid open doors, windows, and all electrical equipment.
4. Unplug computers, stereos, and other electrical equipment.
5. Avoid using a shower.

To avoid being hit by lightning, a person who is outdoors during an electrical storm should do the following:

1. Go inside a building or motor vehicle, if possible.
2. Go to an open space away from trees and other high objects and squat low to the ground, if it is not possible to go indoors.
3. Stand in the woods in an area protected by a low clump of trees and away from high trees.

4. Avoid tall structures such as towers, fences, and telephone or power lines.
5. Avoid golf clubs, tractors, fishing rods, bicycles, and camping equipment.
6. Stay away from bodies of water.
7. Crouch forward with feet together and hands on knees if you feel your hair stand on end, which indicates that lightning is about to strike.
8. Do not lie flat on the ground, as this exposes your body to conduct electricity if lightning hits the ground near you.

WINTER STORMS

A **winter storm** is a storm in the form of freezing rain, sleet, ice, heavy snow, or blizzards. If there is a risk of winter storms, a person should listen to the radio or watch TV for the latest developments and make preparations to survive being isolated and without electricity. A person who is indoors during a winter storm should remain indoors until the storm has passed and close all windows and doors. A person who is outdoors or in a motor vehicle should do the following:

1. Seek shelter immediately.
2. Travel only if necessary.
3. In case of evacuation, pack a motor vehicle with winter storm supplies, including sand, shovel, rope, scraper, flares, heavy blanket, warm clothing, drinking water, emergency food, candles, and matches.

The Homeland Security Advisory System

The world changed on September 11, 2001, when terrorists attacked the United States. Our nation is at risk for terrorist acts now and most likely in the future. Individuals and organizations must be watchful, prepared, and ready to respond to terrorist acts. The **Homeland Security Advisory System** is a system of the U.S. federal government to inform federal, state, and local authorities and the American people of the risk of terrorist acts. Risk includes both the likelihood of a terrorist attack occurring and the possible severity of the attack. This national alert system has five warnings, known as threat conditions. Each threat condition has a description and a corresponding color.

This system helps people to make rational decisions about how to react to the threat. A specific threat condition means that organizations need to take specific actions to reduce their vulnerability to terrorist attacks. When the threat condition increases to a higher level, organizations need to be ready to respond in the event of a terrorist act. Threat conditions can apply to the entire nation, a geographic region, or an industrial area.

Health Goal #93

I Will Follow Guidelines for Motor Vehicle Safety

Motor Vehicle Safety

Motor vehicle accidents are the leading cause of death for children, teenagers, and adults. According to the National Highway Traffic Safety Administration, teenagers are involved in three times as many fatal crashes as other drivers. Young people need to understand the risks of driving motor vehicles and learn guidelines for motor vehicle safety.

OBTAINING A VALID DRIVER'S LICENSE

Anyone who wants to obtain a driver's license must pass a written test and a driving test. Many young people take a driver education course to gain the knowledge and skills they need to pass these tests. The courses are required in several states and are offered by schools, community organizations, and private companies. Young people need to check on state laws and opportunities to learn driving skills. They may have to get a learner's permit or a graduated license first. A **learner's permit** is an authorization to drive when supervised by a licensed driver of a certain age. A **graduated license** is a conditional license given to new drivers. People with a graduated license have restricted driving privileges, such as being allowed to drive only during the day. The likelihood of accidents in the first year of driving is high.

BEING A DEFENSIVE DRIVER

A defensive driver is a driver who guards against the unsafe actions of other drivers. Defensive

Avoiding Traffic Violations

A **traffic violation** is any violation of the current traffic code. After a certain number of citations for traffic violations, a driver's license can be revoked, or taken away for a period of time. Motor vehicle insurance rates will increase. The person may have to attend additional driver education classes. Serious violations, such as speeding, driving without a license, and driving under the influence of alcohol or other drugs, can result in imprisonment, a criminal record, fines, and the risk of injuring or killing oneself and others.

driving is one way to reduce the risk of accidents. It includes taking the following actions:

- Observe traffic laws and speed limits.
- Make sure the intersection is clear before entering it when the light turns green.
- Never tailgate.
- Stay alert.
- Avoid distractions such as loud music, talking on a cellular phone, or eating while driving.
- Listen to traffic reports and adjust plans accordingly.
- Check that all parts of the motor vehicle are working properly.

Avoiding High-Risk Driving

High-risk driving is dangerous driving that can result in accidents. It includes behaviors such as speeding, trying to beat red lights or a train, racing other drivers, jumping hills, drinking and driving, doing "doughnuts" or "fishtails," and hanging out of motor vehicles. These behaviors are dangerous not only to drivers but to passengers as well. A person should not ride in a motor vehicle with a driver who chooses high-risk driving. Anyone who is in such a vehicle should ask the driver to stop or get out and call another person for a ride.

Avoiding Drinking and Driving

Drinking is a leading cause of motor vehicle accidents. Alcohol impairs judgment, reaction time, and motor skills. It is against the law for people under the age of twenty-one to drink alcohol.

Wearing Safety Belts

A **safety belt** is a seat belt and shoulder strap. Safety belts should be worn by the driver and all passengers at all times. The lap belt should be snug and low across the hips and pelvis, and the shoulder belt should be snug and fit across the chest and collarbone.

Air bags provide additional protection for occupants of motor vehicles. An air bag is a cushion in motor vehicles that inflates upon impact. Air bags cushion people from being thrown into the wheel, dashboard, and windshield. Air bags are not a substitute for safety belts. Air bags often are effective in protecting people involved in frontal crashes but offer little protection in side, rear, and rollover crashes.

The National Highway Traffic Safety Administration recommends that all children under the age of twelve ride in the back seat of a motor vehicle. This protects them from injury from air bags and puts them farthest away from most impacts. All infants and small children must be placed in a child safety restraint placed in the back seat of a motor vehicle. A child safety restraint is a seat designed for a small child that is secured in the back seat of a motor vehicle. Motor vehicle safety seats for small infants face the rear. Seats for older infants face the front. Children should start using a booster seat when they grow out of their child safety seats (usually when they weigh about forty pounds). They should continue to ride in a booster seat until the lap and shoulder belts in the car fit properly, typically when they are four feet nine inches tall (National Highway Traffic Safety Administration, 2006). All fifty states and the District of Columbia have child restraint laws but these laws vary widely from state to state. Many states are expanding their legislation to require booster seats for older children. Only a few states have mandated the back seating position for children.

Motor Vehicle Violence

People need to protect themselves from violence while driving or riding in motor vehicles. Some people pretend to be offering help to people who have motor vehicle trouble and then assault them. Others hitchhike and rob or injure people who stop and give them a ride. Some motorists become violent toward other motorists. **Road rage** is any display of aggression by an angry or impatient driver or passenger of a motor vehicle. Examples include verbal abuse, hand gestures, intimidating stares, driving in an intimidating manner, throwing objects at or bumping other vehicles, and threatening other drivers. People who have road rages injure others by fighting, hitting them with a vehicle, or using weapons such as firearms. The reasons drivers and passengers give for their road rage include another motorist driving slowly, playing loud music, refusing to allow them to pass or cutting them off, taking a parking space, tailgating, or failing to signal. The American Automobile Association (AAA) Foundation for Traffic Safety recommends that, to avoid drivers and passengers who are inclined to develop road rage, a person should avoid eye contact with an aggressive driver, stay calm and not react to a person who is trying to provoke a reaction, keep a safe distance from people who are driving unpredictably, and report incidences of road rage to the police or 911.

Carjacking is motor vehicle theft that occurs by force or threat of force while the driver or passengers are still in the motor vehicle. People can protect themselves by following these strategies:

- Have a cell phone to use in case of emergency.

- Keep the fuel tank full and your vehicle in good condition to prevent breakdowns.
- Carry a flashlight, road flares, and a "send help" sign in case your vehicle breaks down.
- Stay in your vehicle and keep your doors locked and your windows rolled up if someone other than a police officer stops to offer help.
- Never leave children in an unattended vehicle.
- Never leave keys in the ignition or the engine running. Lock your vehicle at all times and keep your keys with you.
- Keep valuables out of sight.
- Check the seats before getting into a vehicle.
- Try to drive and park in safe, well-lit areas.
- If you think you are being followed, go to a public place and call the police.
- Keep your vehicle in gear when at a stoplight.
- Be cautious of anyone approaching your vehicle when it is stopped.
- Drive to a nearby phone and call 911 if someone needs help.
- Never hitchhike or pick up a hitchhiker.
- Do not resist if an armed person demands your vehicle.
- Get a latch for the inside of your trunk so that you can escape if forced inside.

Health Goal #94

I Will Practice Protective Factors to Reduce the Risk of Violence

Violence

Violence is the use of physical force to injure, damage, or destroy oneself, others, or property. **Nonviolence** is the avoidance of the threatened or actual use of physical force to injure, damage, or destroy oneself, others, or property. A **perpetrator of violence** is a person who commits a violent act. A **victim of violence** is a person who has been harmed by violence. There are different kinds of violence.

BULLYING

Bullying is intentional psychological, emotional, or physical harassment of one person or group. A **bully** is a person who hurts or frightens people who are perceived to be smaller or weaker.

Bullying often occurs at school or between home and school. It includes exclusion from a peer group, inducing fear or a sense of inferiority, taking money or property by force, and violence. Most children and teens have been bullied at one time or another. In fact, three-fourths of high school students say they have been bullied. Bullying is violent behavior and wrong.

FIGHTING

Fighting is taking part in a physical struggle. About 40 percent of high school students say they have been involved in at least one fight per year. Eight percent of high school students say that in the last thirty days they have been in a fight that caused someone to need medical treatment for an injury. Males are more likely than females to get into fights. Fighting is risky. Many young people are injured in fights. In most murders of young people, the violence began with a fight.

ASSAULT

Assault is a physical attack or threat of attack. There are more assault injuries to teenagers than any other age group. Some assaults occur because one person wants to harm another person. Other assaults result from other types of crime. For example, a teen might push down another teen to take a possession from him or her. One out of four people who have been assaulted require emergency medical treatment.

HOMICIDE

Homicide is the killing of one person through the act, advantage, or mistake of another. Homicide is murder, manslaughter, an excusable homicide, or a justifiable homicide. Murder is the death of a person as a result of intentional actions. Manslaughter is the death of a person as a result of neglect, abuse, or recklessness. Murder and manslaughter are unlawful homicides. Some unlawful homicides follow fights between people who know each other, whether they be family, friends, or acquaintances.

An excusable homicide is the death of a person as a result of an accident while doing any lawful act, without criminal negligence or any unlawful intent. Justifiable homicide is the death of a person as a result of the intention to kill or to do serious bodily injury under circumstances that the law holds sufficient to pardon the person who commits it. Justifiable homicides include a police officer acting in obedience to a lawful warrant and a person killing in lawful self-defense. The acts of excusable and justifiable homicides are lawful. Homicide is the second leading cause of death in teens.

SEXUAL HARASSMENT

Sexual harassment is unwelcome sexual advances, requests for sexual favors, and other verbal or physical conduct of a sexual nature when submission to or rejection of this conduct creates an intimidating, hostile, or offensive environment. Federal law makes it clear that sexual harassment should never occur in a school. Unfortunately, sexual harassment is a too common occurrence in schools.

RAPE

Rape is sexual penetration without consent obtained by force or threat of harm or when the victim is incapable of giving consent. An important part of this definition is the phrase "without consent." The law interprets "without consent" to mean that if a person does not agree willingly to have sex, there is no consent. People under a certain age and people who do not have certain mental abilities are considered unable to give consent even if they willingly agree to have sex. A person who has sex with someone without consent is guilty of committing rape.

CHILD ABUSE

Child abuse is harmful treatment of a minor that can cause injury or psychological damage. Child abuse may involve physical abuse, emotional abuse, sexual abuse, or neglect. The most common type of child abuse is neglect, followed by physical, sexual, and emotional abuse. A family member is the perpetrator 85 to 90 percent of the time. Children and teens have a right to be protected and safe. No one has the right to abuse them.

DOMESTIC VIOLENCE

Domestic violence is abuse used by one person in a relationship to control the other. Domestic violence, including physical assault, sexual abuse, and stalking, is criminal behavior. Emotional, psychological, and financial abuse are not criminal behaviors, but they are abuse and can lead to criminal behaviors.

Domestic violence can happen frequently or once in a while. Half of all married couples say that violence has occurred at least once during their marriage. About one-third of all female murder victims in the United States are killed by a current or former intimate partner (Bureau of Justice Statistics, 2005).

Domestic violence also includes violence between other family members. It is estimated that one-half of all families have experienced some type of domestic violence. Roommates may also experience domestic violence.

Parent abuse is the abuse of parents by their children and is a type of elder abuse. **Elder abuse** is physical, emotional, or psychological harm done to an older adult. Elder abuse also can be financial exploitation or when a caregiver intentionally or unintentionally neglects an older adult.

Risk Factors for Violence

A **risk factor** is something that increases the likelihood of a negative outcome. Risk factors refer only to the statistical probability that something negative will happen. This does not mean that a person will actually behave in violent ways or be harmed by others. Individuals have varying degrees of control over risk factors. For example, we do not have control over the family in which we are raised or whether we are born rich or poor, but we do have control over whether we carry a weapon to school. Knowing about risk factors is an important step in protecting oneself and others from violence.

The following are risk factors that increase the likelihood that a person will be a perpetrator or victim of violence:

1. Failing to recognize violent behavior
2. Lacking self-respect
3. Being raised in a dysfunctional family
4. Living in an adverse environment
5. Lacking social skills
6. Being unable to manage anger
7. Being unable to manage stress
8. Not participating in physical and recreational activities
9. Having suicidal tendencies
10. Resolving conflict in harmful ways
11. Practicing discriminatory behavior
12. Lacking responsible decision-making skills
13. Being unable to resist negative peer pressure
14. Using alcohol and other harmful drugs

15. Carrying a weapon
16. Belonging to a gang
17. Challenging authority and breaking laws
18. Failing to take precautions to protect oneself
19. Avoiding recovery after being a victim of violence
20. Repeating violence after being a juvenile offender

Protective Factors for Violence

A **protective factor** is something that increases the likelihood of a positive outcome. Protective factors refer only to the statistical probability that one's health, safety, and well-being will be protected. There is a chance that a person's health, safety, or well-being will be affected in negative ways by something beyond the person's control—such as being hit by a stray bullet from a drive-by shooting. However, the more protective factors that apply to a person, the more likely that person is to be protected from violence. Protective factors promote **resiliency**—the ability to adjust, recover, and learn from change, illness, or misfortune without becoming overwhelmed or acting in inappropriate ways. A young person's level of resiliency determines how well he or she can overcome adversity and hold up under pressure. High levels of resiliency help a person come out of situations stronger.

The following are protective factors that reduce the likelihood that a person will be a perpetrator or victim of violence:

1. Recognizing violent behavior
2. Having self-respect
3. Being raised in a healthful family
4. Living in a nurturing environment
5. Having social skills
6. Being able to manage anger
7. Being able to manage stress
8. Participating in physical and recreational activities
9. Practicing suicide-prevention strategies
10. Being able to resolve conflict
11. Avoiding discriminatory behavior
12. Making responsible decisions
13. Being able to resist negative peer pressure
14. Avoiding the use of alcohol and other harmful drugs

15. Staying away from weapons
16. Staying away from gangs
17. Showing respect for authority and obeying laws
18. Practicing self-protection strategies
19. Participating in recovery when having been a victim of violence
20. Changing behavior after having been a juvenile offender in the past

Using Assertive Behavior to Reduce the Risk of Violence

A person's behavior can influence the likelihood that he or she will be a perpetrator or victim of violence. **Passive behavior** is holding back ideas, feelings, and decisions. People who have passive behavior find conflict very unsettling. As a result, they back off when there is a disagreement. They keep their anger to themselves. Bottled-up anger will continue to grow when it is not expressed. People with passive behavior may explode and lash out. They are at risk for being perpetrators of violence. People with passive behavior also are at risk for being victims of violence. This is because they do not stand up for themselves or do not expect others to treat them with respect. If others harm them, they may keep it a secret in order to avoid conflict.

Aggressive behavior is the use of words or actions that are disrespectful toward others. Aggressive people are controlling. They are at risk for being perpetrators of violence. They might use force or intimidation to convince others to do what they want them to do. People who are aggressive also are at risk for being victims of violence, because their actions can provoke others into retaliation or into defending themselves by using violence.

Assertive behavior is the honest expression of ideas, feelings, and decisions while respecting the rights and feelings of others. Assertive people respect others and expect others to respect them. They are not controlling, forceful, or intimidating. They express anger in appropriate ways. They communicate in healthful ways and are able to resolve conflicts without fighting. As a result, the risk for being perpetrators of violence decreases. People with assertive behavior also are less likely to be victims of violence. Because they expect to be treated with respect, they do not allow others to take advantage of them. People with assertive behavior confront disrespectful behavior and do not ignore it.

Health Goal #95

I Will Respect Authority and Obey Laws

Laws and Authority

Laws that are regulated by people in positions of authority govern all societies. A **law** is a rule of conduct or action that is recognized to be binding. Laws are enforced by a controlling authority. **Authority** is the power and right to apply laws and rules. Laws usually represent the beliefs of a majority of people in a community, state, or nation. Every citizen has the responsibility to know and obey existing laws.

Laws are designed to protect the rights of people in a community, state, or nation. Many laws protect the health and safety of people and are intended to prevent violence and injury.

Why Do Some Youths Challenge Authority and Break Laws?

Young people who have a solid moral code respect authority and obey laws. What about youths who challenge authority and break laws? Why might they choose behaviors that put themselves and others at risk for injury? Why might they be involved in actions that promote violence? Consider the three stages of moral development. In the first stage, children base their ideas of right and wrong on how their past behaviors were rewarded or punished. Parents, guardians, and other caregivers made choices about rewards and punishments. If they were very clear as to what behavior they expected, the child had clear guidelines for behavior. If adults always followed through and gave consistent consequences for wrong behavior, the child learned that wrong behavior would have negative outcomes.

Hey, don't pick on him!

Juvenile Offenders

A **juvenile offender** is a minor who commits a criminal act. Juvenile offenders are involved in **delinquent behavior**—illegal actions committed by a juvenile. Delinquent behavior includes serious crimes, such as homicide, rape, drug trafficking, prostitution, robbery, assault, burglary, auto theft, and arson. Delinquent behavior also includes **status offenses**—behaviors for which an adult would not be arrested, such as truancy, alcohol use, running away, defying parents or guardians, and breaking curfew.

Many juvenile offenders who are arrested stop committing crimes and do not become repeat offenders. They fear being arrested, put on probation, or sentenced to serve time in a correctional facility. Other juvenile offenders mature and change their behavior. Another group of juvenile offenders responds favorably to rehabilitation. **Rehabilitation of juvenile offenders** is the process of helping juvenile offenders change wrong behaviors into responsible behavior. Juvenile offenders may experience the following consequences:

Some young people are raised in families in which they are not shown clear expectations for their behavior. Their parents, guardian, or other caregivers might not discipline them for wrong behavior, or they might discipline them in an inappropriate way, such as with physical abuse. As a result, these young people do not develop a conscience and do not feel obligated to do what is right. When they behave in wrong ways, they do not feel guilty. These young people need mentors to help them examine the difference between right behaviors and wrong behaviors. A **mentor** is a responsible person who guides another person. When troubled teens have a mentor, they have someone to whom they are accountable for right actions.

Peer groups have a tremendous influence on youths between the ages of ten and thirteen. Suppose members of a person's peer group respected authority and obeyed laws. Then that person would behave in the same way. However, some teens hang out with the wrong crowd, such as peers who get into trouble or gang members. These teens will behave as their peers do. To change their behavior, troubled teens must break away from peers who behave in wrong ways.

Some teens put their rights ahead of the rights of others. They want what they want right now. They do not care about the rights of others or consider the effects of their actions on others. If they harm someone, they do not care. Young people who have no principles to guide their behavior get themselves in trouble. They are dangerous. They may become juvenile offenders.

1. *Probation.* **Probation** is a sentence in which an offender remains in the community under the supervision of a probation officer for a specific period of time. Probation is the most common sentence judges give to juvenile offenders. More than two-thirds of juvenile offenders are sentenced to probation. Judges set restrictions and conditions on juvenile offenders during probation. For example, juvenile offenders might be ordered to obey laws, obey parents or a guardian, attend school, avoid contact with other juvenile offenders, take drug tests, and make some form of restitution. **Restitution** is making up for what has been taken, damaged, hurt, or done. It might involve making a payment, returning stolen property, or performing community service.

2. *Spending time in a correctional facility.* Juvenile offenders who engage in illegal behavior or violate the terms of their probation may be sent to a correctional facility. These include detention centers, training schools, ranches, forestry camps, farms, halfway houses, and group homes. **Juvenile detention** is the temporary physical restriction of juveniles in special facilities until the outcome of their legal case is decided. Detention centers are secure

custody facilities where juvenile offenders are kept. Detention centers also are known as juvenile halls. Juvenile offenders usually are held in detention centers for a period of several hours to ninety days while they wait for their court hearing. They are held there because they may be a threat to others, their home environment is unacceptable, or they need physical or mental health treatment.

3. *Incarceration in prison.* Some people feel that the best way to deal with juvenile offenders is to treat them as adults and keep them in prison. These people are concerned about juvenile offenders who repeat crimes. Many states have changed their laws so that teens as young as fourteen years old can be tried as adults for any crime. People who are opposed to trying juvenile offenders as adults feel that the results would be negative. They are afraid juvenile offenders will spend time in prison without changing their behavior. They are concerned about the influence adult criminals might have on juvenile offenders. They also are concerned that juvenile offenders will be sexually and physically abused by adult criminals while they are in prison.

4. *Diversion.* **Diversion** is an approach to rehabilitation that involves sending juvenile offenders somewhere to learn how to obey laws. Juvenile offenders may be sent to social agencies, child welfare departments, mental health agencies, substance abuse clinics, shoplifters' programs, crisis intervention programs, or runaway shelters. Youth Service Bureaus offer services such as drop-in centers, school outreach programs, and crisis intervention programs.

5. *Boot camp.* A **boot camp** is a camp that uses rigorous drills, hard physical training, and structure to teach discipline and obedience. At boot camp, juvenile offenders live under very strict rules. They might have to wake up at 5 A.M. and go to bed at 9 P.M. They might not be allowed to watch television, listen to the radio, or swear. Most boot camps include education and therapy efforts. Many juvenile offenders end up in boot camp in exchange for reduced sentences.

6. *Parole and aftercare.* **Parole** is a conditional release from a sentence in a correctional facility. **Aftercare** is support and supervised services that juvenile offenders receive when they are released to live in the community. Once out on parole, juvenile offenders are assigned an aftercare officer who makes certain they follow the conditions of their parole and stay out of trouble. Juvenile offenders who do not follow the conditions of their parole are returned to correctional facilities.

Teens who have been juvenile offenders can change their behavior by doing the following:

- Improving difficult family relationships or finding a supportive substitute family
- Spending time with a mentor
- Asking trusted adults for feedback on their behavior
- Working to improve their self-respect
- Choosing friends who obey laws
- Making restitution for their wrong actions
- Becoming involved in school activities
- Developing job-related skills
- Volunteering in the community
- Attending a support group
- Avoiding alcohol and other drugs

Health Goal #96

I Will Protect Myself from Physical Violence and Abuse

Self-Defense Strategies

A person can avoid unnecessary risks that jeopardize safety by using self-defense strategies. **Self-defense strategies** are strategies that can protect people from violence. The first line of self-defense is for a person to be aware of the people and situations around him or her. Awareness involves the ability to "read" people and situations. People who are aware of their surroundings can avoid many acts of random violence. **Random violence** is violence over which a person has no control.

Awareness is not being afraid or suspicious. A person's degree of awareness should be determined by the situation the person is in. For example, a young person should be more aware when walking alone at night than when shopping in a mall with friends.

The sooner a person becomes aware of a threat, the more options he or she has to respond to it. If a person sees or senses that a situation may be dangerous, the person should change the route of travel and prepare to run or defend himself or herself.

Successful self-defense is not about winning a fight; it is about avoiding one. If it is not possible to avoid a fight, a person should try to defuse it. If it cannot be defused, a person should try to escape from it. If escape is not possible, a person may have to fight his or her way out of the situation.

If you are attacked, there is only one rule: you must survive. A person needs to do everything possible—scream, scratch, hit, kick, or attack with a common object—to end the threat or to have enough time to escape.

A trusted adult needs to know if a young person suspects that a person or situation is dangerous. Adults can talk with young people about self-defense.

There are strategies one can use to reduce the risk of random violence. Trusting one's gut feeling that a person or situation may be dangerous is critical. Avoid the person or situation whenever possible. It's better to be safe and risk embarrassment than to be in a situation that may be unsafe. Give up personal belongings rather than risk being harmed. Yell, "Call 911!" or say to someone nearby, "Walk me to the store on the corner. I'm being followed."

Young people should be encouraged to use the following self-defense strategies:

- Know where you are going.
- Do not walk too close to buildings.
- Carry yourself with confidence.
- Have your keys ready when you approach your car or building.
- Do not label key chains with your name or address.
- Vary your routine.
- Drive or walk different routes every day.
- Do not talk about your plans where strangers can overhear you.
- Always carry a cell phone or enough change for a telephone call.

Hazing

Most young people want to be a part of a group. Being a part of a group helps form a sense of identity and fulfills needs for belonging and friend-

ship. Some groups require an initiation to become a member or to stay a part of the group. When groups use humiliation, ridicule, embarrassment, mental or physical discomfort, or dangerous activities to initiate a person into a group, the behavior is called hazing. **Hazing** is the physical or emotional abuse a person endures while trying to become or stay part of a group, regardless of that person's willingness to participate.

Hazing is more than playing pranks; it is about attempting to establish power and control over others, which sets up the climate for abuse to occur. Hazing is dangerous and can easily get out of hand because some teens may be willing to do just about anything to belong to a group—even engage in dangerous or illegal behavior. Some groups may force teens to steal, take drugs, or break other laws in order to belong to the group. Other groups verbally or emotionally abuse teens during hazing.

Teens and college students have died or been injured during hazing incidents—in motor vehicle accidents or from falling, drowning, or being beaten. Some teens have died of alcohol poisoning after being forced to drink large quantities of alcohol during initiation ceremonies.

In some hazing incidences, young people have been forced to drink large amounts of water. This is risky because water dilutes the sodium in the body and can lead to dangerous changes in heart rhythm. This is what happened to a California college student who was forced to drink five gallons of water during a pledge to join a fraternity. The autopsy ruled that the cause of death was cardiac dysrhythmia, a deadly heart rhythm caused by an electrolyte imbalance (Teague, 2005).

A young person who is being threatened by hazing should tell a parent or guardian, a coach, a counselor, a school administrator, or a law enforcement official. Young people should be taught that they can create ways to form bonds within a group that are not in any way humiliating, demeaning, or hurtful. Groups can institute community-building initiation activities, such as playing recreational games together, participating in a ropes course, taking on a fund-raising activity or a service project, or by group members becoming mentors for younger students.

Many schools have strict antihazing rules and written policies, and these schools take strong disciplinary action against members of a group who have been responsible for hazing. Hazing is against the law in most states. Young people should learn what their state law says about hazing and what the legal penalties are for violating antihazing laws.

Bullying

Most children and teens have experienced what it feels like to be bullied. Three out of every four teens will be bullied during their school years. About one-third of teens say that they have been bullied three or more times in the past year. According to the National Crime Prevention Council, 60 percent of teens witness bullying at least once a day.

Bullying is repeatedly doing or saying things to intimidate or dominate another person. A **bully** is a person who hurts or frightens people who are perceived to be smaller or weaker. Bullying someone is violent behavior and it is wrong. No one has the right to hurt or intimidate others.

Bullying can be physical or verbal. Bullying may include taunting, making fun of or isolating someone; name-calling; pushing, hitting, poking, pinching, hair-pulling, kicking, or other physical abuse; spreading rumors, telling lies, or setting someone up to get in trouble; taking money or possessions from someone; making faces or obscene gestures at someone; excluding someone; pressuring someone to do something he or she doesn't want to do; and sexually harassing someone in any way.

Bullying differs from teasing. Usually the one doing the teasing knows and cares about the person being teased. Teasing can turn into bullying, however, if it becomes cruel, causes someone distress, or becomes one-sided and repeated.

WHY IS BULLYING HARMFUL?

Victims of bullying can receive physical injury from their abuse. They may also grow fearful of being in places where they are subjected to bullying. The stress that results from this fear can lead to school absences, trouble sleeping at night, difficulty concentrating on schoolwork, depression, and other stress-related symptoms. Continually facing intimidation is tough on a person's self-esteem. Because they feel helpless to stop harassment from bullies, victims may also see themselves as helpless in other areas of their lives. Some victims of bullying retaliate for the abuse in violent ways, including suicide and murder.

Young people who bully are at risk of criminal behavior. They often lack the social skills needed to be successful in life. If they do not learn to improve their social skills, they will have problems relating to others throughout their lives. Bullies are more likely to drop out of school and may have difficulty keeping a job.

Peers of victims who are bullied are also affected by bullying. Students may not associate with a victim out of fear of also being bullied. They may not report bullying out of fear that the bullies will retaliate. Some who witness bullying experience feelings of guilt because they did not stand up to the bully or offer to help stop the abuse. Because of group pressure, students who witness bullying are sometimes drawn into the bullying behavior.

WHO IS BULLIED?

Young people who are bullied tend to be quiet and shy, and they do not make asser-

That's not right.

tive responses when someone bullies them. They may lack friends and social support at school. They may not be confident about their physical abilities and strength. They tend to be smaller and physically weaker than peers.

Children and adolescents who are perceived as different are sometimes victims of bullying. Someone who is overweight or who has a speech impediment, a physical disability, or a learning disability is at an increased risk of being bullied. Sometimes being a member of a different religious faith or race incites incidents of bullying.

Those who are bullied are usually younger than the bullies. They feel that nobody will help them or be able to stop the bullying, and they do not tell because they fear the bullying may become worse as a result.

How to Handle Bullying

Sometimes bullying stops when a person takes actions to stop it. Bullies continue as long as it works, because it makes them feel powerful. Many bullies will stop if they know they do not threaten their victim.

Strategies to avoid becoming a victim of bullying include having confidence that the bullying can be dealt with in a peaceful way. Young people should recognize that violence may put them at further risk of injury. Humor can often be used to defuse a tense situation. Young people can be assertive as a way to handle bullying. Standing up for one's feelings and needs is important. Young people can say "no" to a bully's demands and look the bully in the eye. A bully needs to be told to stop the threats. Young people should know that it is okay to walk away and ignore further taunting. A young person who fears physical harm in the school setting should find a teacher or move toward friends who can provide support. It is imperative that persistent bullying is reported to an adult. Telling an adult rarely makes the situation worse and may help both the one being bullied and the bully.

Child Abuse

Child abuse is the harmful treatment of a minor that can cause injury or psychological damage. Child abuse may involve physical abuse, emotional abuse, sexual abuse, or neglect. Most cases of child abuse occur behind closed doors and are not reported. The most common type of child abuse is neglect, which is followed by physical abuse and emotional abuse.

Physical Abuse

Physical abuse is maltreatment that harms the body. A student who is unusually bruised or burned might be suffering from physical abuse. Other signs that a child has been physically abused include bites, internal injuries, fractures, and abrasions on different body parts.

Neglect

Neglect is maltreatment that involves the lack of proper care and guidance. A parent or guardian might not provide adequate supervision, food, shelter, clothing, or medical care.

Emotional Abuse

Emotional abuse is maltreatment that involves nonphysical assault, such as constant criticism, threats, rejection, and withholding love or guidance. Emotional abuse is discussed further later in this section.

Sexual Abuse

Sexual abuse is the maltreatment that occurs when an adult, an adolescent, or an older child uses power to involve a minor in inappropriate sexual activity. There are no age limits for victims of sexual abuse. Even infants can be abused. Sexual abuse includes activities such as fondling, intercourse, exhibitionism, and commercial exploitation through prostitution or the production of pornographic materials.

Child Abuse Laws

Every state (and the District of Columbia) has laws that identify mandatory reporters. A **mandatory reporter** is a person who is required by law to report suspected child abuse. Any person, however, may report incidents of child abuse or neglect. Mandatory reporters usually include professionals who work with children, such as health care workers, mental health professionals, teachers and other school personnel, law enforcement officials, and child care providers. In some states, any person who suspects child abuse is required to report it.

In most cases, the identity of the person reporting the suspected child abuse remains confidential.

Reports of child abuse are often made to child welfare agencies or to the police, and they are usually investigated rapidly. If an investigation shows that a child is in danger, that child will likely be placed in protective custody or in a foster home.

Mental and Emotional Abuse

Mental and emotional abuse is difficult to identify because the effects are not as obvious as those of physical abuse. Mental and emotional abuse is dangerous to victims. A victim might have low self-esteem. Children who are emotionally abused are more likely to attempt suicide.

Mental and emotional abuse is about power and control. It can be found in any type of relationship, including parent-child, dating, marriage, employer-employee, peers, and teacher-student relationships. Mental and emotional abuse includes the following abusive behaviors:

- *Rejection.* Refusing to acknowledge a person's presence, making a person feel inferior, or devaluing a person's thoughts and feelings is rejection.
- *Degradation.* Insulting, ridiculing, imitating, or diminishing the identity, dignity, and self-worth of a person is degradation.
- *Terrorization.* Inducing fear or threatening to or placing a person in a dangerous environment is terrorization.
- *Isolation.* Restricting social contact or contact with family members or limiting freedom within a person's environment is isolation.
- *Corruption and exploitation.* Socializing a person to accept illegal ideas or behaviors, using a person for advantage or profit, or training a person to serve the interests of the abuser is corruption and exploitation.
- *Denying emotional responsiveness.* Failing to provide care in a sensitive and responsive manner, being detached and uninvolved, or ignoring a person's mental health is denying a person emotional responsiveness.

A child who is being mentally or emotionally abused may show the following signs:

- Is depressed or apathetic
- Experiences behavioral difficulties
- Withdraws from peers

- Is developmentally or mentally delayed
- Exhibits behaviors such as facial tics or rocking motions
- Reacts fearfully to authority
- Verbally reports that she or he is being emotionally abused

Domestic Violence

Domestic violence is abuse used by one person in a relationship to control the other. This form of violence takes many forms and can happen frequently or once in a while. It occurs at all levels of society and in all communities. Domestic violence is about power and control, and it includes physical abuse, isolation from family or friends, emotional abuse, economic abuse by withholding money, intimidation, stalking, or sexual assault.

Victims of domestic violence become fearful, angry, and confused about what is happening. Escape may seem impossible. These victims live in difficult circumstances. Because they usually live in the same home as the offender, they often face repeated and prolonged attacks. Relationships that exhibit signs of domestic violence go through the following three phases:

- *Buildup or escalation phase.* Frustration, anger, and tension build up inside the domestic violence offender. The offender becomes increasingly controlling or cruel. He or she sometimes uses alcohol or other drugs to deal with feelings. The victim often becomes submissive in an attempt to keep the offender calm.
- *The acute battering (explosion) phase.* This is the phase when abuse and battering occur. **Battering** is intentional, harmful touching of another person without the person's consent. Battering "unloads" the tension that has built up. If the victim resists or fights back, the offender may become even more violent. Following abuse, victims usually feel fearful, trapped, depressed, and helpless.
- *Honeymoon phase.* In this phase, the offender has unloaded his or her tension and feels physical relief. The offender is usually ashamed of the violence and may express remorse. The offender often apologizes, gives the victim gifts, or pleads for forgiveness. The offender may even threaten to commit suicide if the victim leaves or may promise to enter a treatment program. The victim often succumbs to these

promises, believing that the offender will change. After a while, something triggers the cycle again.

Victims of domestic violence need to know that the abuse is not the victim's fault and the victim does not deserve it. Alcohol or drugs may be involved in the abuse, but these substances do not cause it. Waiting for offenders to change and trying harder to please this person will not work. The abuse will get worse, not better. Victims should talk about the abuse with someone they trust. Victims should be aware of the emergency services available, and they should be prepared to use them when necessary. Children who learn violence at home are at risk of having violent relationships.

DOMESTIC VIOLENCE LAWS

Most domestic violence cases are handled by state and local authorities. State domestic violence laws prohibit physical abuse and threatened or attempted physical abuse. Most state laws also prohibit sexual abuse, emotional abuse, and even financial exploitation.

All states have laws that allow victims of domestic violence to obtain protective orders. A **protective order** is an order of the court issued by a judge to prohibit a domestic violence offender from committing further acts of violence, harassing or threatening the victim, and going near the victim's home or place of work.

Sometimes protective orders also require a domestic violence offender to pay for child support, spousal support, alternative housing for the victim, or to provide compensation for damages caused by the violence. Sometimes the protective order requires the domestic violence offender to attend counseling. Protective orders are enforced by the police, and violation of them is a criminal offense.

More states are strengthening laws that deal with domestic violence. Some states prohibit domestic violence offenders from owning or possessing guns. Some states require domestic violence training for law enforcement personnel, prosecutors, judges, and medical and mental health professionals. Some states order that domestic violence offenders be monitored electronically when they are released from custody. Some states are increasing funding for services and counseling for victims.

Dating Violence

Dating violence is when one person in a dating relationship uses physical, emotional, or sexual abuse to control the other person. Dating violence is more than just arguing and fighting. Dating violence occurs when one or both partners have not learned positive ways of solving problems and dealing with intense emotions.

WARNING SIGNS

Dating violence can happen to males or females. There are signs that might indicate that a person is prone to dating violence. Young people should be aware of partners who are jealous and possessive and who try to control them by giving orders, not taking their opinions seriously, or making all decisions.

Partners who tell another partner where they can or cannot go or with whom they can or cannot talk may be prone to dating violence. A dating partner who tries to keep a person away from his or her friends and family and who makes family and friends concerned about the person's well-being and safety may be prone to dating violence. Partners who use alcohol or other drugs or try to get a person to use alcohol or other drugs are prone to dating violence. Also, those who are cruel to animals are prone to dating violence.

Men or women who abuse dating partners usually were abused as children, quickly lose their temper, find great enjoyment watching violent movies or playing violent video or computer games, and have strict ideas about the roles of men and women in relationships.

Whenever one's dating partner seems to act differently around others, has unpredictable mood swings, and frightens or threatens the person, he or she is showing signs of dating violence. If someone calls his or her partner a name, tries to lower the partner's self-esteem, says that the partner wouldn't be anything without him or her, says that no one else would ever go out with the partner, puts the partner down, makes fun of or embarrasses the partner in front of others, then he or she is committing dating violence. If a partner is physically abusive, pressures or is forceful for sex, thinks that physical abuse is romantic or sexy, has abused former partners, and blames his or her abusive behavior on the partner, then he or she is committing dating violence.

Victims of dating violence need to recognize that the dating violence is not their fault and that no one deserves to be in a violent dating relationship. Young people who are victims of dating violence must not ignore it—hoping that it will go away is not enough to make it go away. These young people need to get out of violent relationships. They must tell someone they trust and who can help. They must also understand that they should not spend time alone with an abuser.

Recovering from Violence

The emotional pain that follows violence often is deeper and lasts longer than the physical injuries. Victims of violence may need help to recover from violence, and perpetrators of violence need to change violent behavior.

Victims of violence may experience different reactions after being harmed. Their responses may be influenced by the way they usually act or by the kind of violence they experienced. They may be highly emotional, depressed, and cry often. They may avoid others. They may neglect everyday tasks and have difficulty concentrating. They may have difficulty sleeping or have nightmares and flashbacks. They usually are very angry and afraid. They may try to numb their feelings with alcohol or drugs.

POST-TRAUMATIC STRESS DISORDER

Some victims are able to recover without help. However, most do not recover quickly or easily. **Post-traumatic stress disorder (PTSD)** is a condition in which a person mentally relives a stressful experience again and again. PTSD is common in people who have experienced violence. The signs of PTSD include sleep problems, irritability, and trouble concentrating. When something reminds them of the experience, people with PTSD respond with much emotion.

SECONDARY VICTIMIZATION

Victims often experience additional pain after the violence. Secondary victimization is the hurtful treatment victims may receive after they experience violence. For example, many victims must attend the perpetrator's trial and may have to answer painful questions. Also, others may try to find fault with the victim's behavior because if they can find fault, they can convince themselves that this type of violence will never happen to them. Secondary victimization usually is not intentional.

VICTIM RECOVERY

Victim recovery is a person's return to physical and emotional health after experiencing violence. Victim recovery may include treatment for physical injuries, treatment for emotional pain, support from family and friends, repayment for money or property losses, or education in self-protection skills. The purpose of recovery programs is to help victims survive the pain, heal, and move forward with self-confidence. Survivors of violence are resilient.

Victims may need a medical examination if they have experienced physical injuries. They may need blood tests to determine if they have become infected with any STDs. Victims also may need help with trust issues. To have close relationships, people must feel safe. Victims also may lack self-respect and allow others to harm them. Without help, they may continue to allow others to treat them with disrespect. Victims also may need to learn better ways to protect themselves. Victims who do not fully recover are at risk for behaving in violent ways. This is especially true if violence occurred in the family. Victims who were abused by parents or a guardian may become abusive parents themselves someday.

PERPETRATOR RECOVERY

People who behave in violent ways usually want to stop. Many believe they cannot help it. They are wrong. A person can stop behaving in violent ways, but changing violent behavior is not easy. Violence is usually learned as a child, and it becomes ingrained when a person repeatedly uses it to deal with problems. But it also can be unlearned. It is important for children who are abused to receive treatment and counseling so that they do not become abusive themselves. Perpetrators of violence must want to change.

Perpetrators must expect that change may occur only after a long period of time. Perpetrators need education and counseling in order to change. Being arrested, being barred by protective orders from seeing victims, spending time in jail or prison, being placed on probation or on a sexual offender list, and receiving clear messages from family, friends, and authorities help deter a person from using violence in the future.

There are signs that a perpetrator's behavior is changing. The person no longer blames others for his or her behaviors. The person does not do or say things that frighten others. The person respects others' feelings. The person's family and friends feel comfortable during time spent together. Others feel safe around the person. The person does not attempt to control others. The person has received treatment for any alcohol or other drug use problems.

Health Goal #97

I Will Protect Myself from Sexual Violence and Abuse

Images of sexual violence are all too common in television shows, movies, and music videos. Some music lyrics make references to sexual violence. These images and references can lead to mistaken ideas about rape, sexual abuse, sexual harassment, and stalking, which can put young people at risk. Sexual violence is always wrong. It is never the victim's fault.

Rape

Sexual assault is any type of unwanted sexual contact. Rape is a form of sexual assault. **Rape** is sexual penetration without consent obtained by force or threat of harm or when the victim is incapable of giving consent. Though many people may believe that sexual assault is the same thing as rape, rape is only one form of sexual assault. Verbal threats, grabbing, or unwanted fondling are some other forms of sexual assault.

Though anyone can be a victim of rape, the majority of victims are female. And, although anyone can be a perpetrator of rape, the majority of perpetrators are male. A perpetrator of rape can be a stranger to a victim, though most perpetrators know the victim in some way. In all forms of sexual assault and rape, anger and a need for power usually are the motivating factors. All forms of sexual assault and rape are forms of violence, and all are unethical and illegal.

ACQUAINTANCE AND DATE RAPE

The majority of rape cases involve a form of rape called acquaintance rape. **Acquaintance rape** is when a person who is raped knows the rapist. **Date rape** is when rape occurs in a dating situation.

High school students and college students are sometimes confused about date rape. They may believe that sex without consent is acceptable in some situations. Sex without consent is never acceptable—it is rape. Rape is never the victim's fault. Circumstances do not change this definition of unlawful behavior.

Suppose a male believes that males should be aggressors and females should be resisters. He might believe that when a female says "no" she really means maybe or yes. As a result, he ignores messages of nonconsent and forces the female to have sex. He is guilty of committing rape. In a situation like this, females must be consistent, say "no" clearly, and not encourage sexual advances. Males must stop when a female says "no." Forcing a person to have sex is rape.

Suppose a male believes that cuddling or kissing indicates a desire to have sex. He might believe a female says "no" because she does not want to appear too "easy," and so he becomes more forceful. As a result, he ignores her resistance and forces sex. He is guilty of committing rape. In a situation like this, females need to keep their limits clear when they express affection. If a male becomes more forceful, the female must resist more forcefully. She must say "no" firmly and yell, scream, or run away if necessary. Males must stop when a female says "no." Again, forcing a person to have sex is rape.

Suppose a female puts herself in a risk situation. Perhaps she goes into a male's bedroom when no adults are home. Do her actions indicate consent to have sex even if she says "no"? No, they do not. If a male forces a female to have sex, even when she is in a risk situation, he has committed rape. Females should avoid putting themselves in risk situations because it can be difficult to defend themselves or to get help if sexual advances occur. Males must always stop when a woman says "no."

Suppose a female wears sexy clothes, such as a very short skirt, a tight sweater, or a low-cut dress. Is she "asking for it" because she dresses in this way? No, she is not. People have the right to dress as they please. If a male assumes she wants to have sex and forces her to do so, he has committed rape. While people have the right to wear what they want without the threat of harm, it is important to realize that others might not respect this right. Males must realize that the clothing a woman wears does not equal consent for sex. Forced sex is always rape. The perpetrator is always the one at fault.

LAWS CONCERNING DATE RAPE

As mentioned earlier, rape is the threatened or actual use of physical force to get someone to have sex without giving consent. An important part of this definition are the words "without consent." There are laws to interpret what "without consent" means.

If a person does not willingly agree to have sex, there is no consent, and sex in this case is considered rape. The law states that people under a certain age and people who do not have certain mental abilities are considered unable to give consent, even if they agree to have sex. A person who has sex with someone described as not able to give consent is guilty of committing rape.

Anyone under the influence of alcohol or other drugs cannot give legal consent to have sex. In other words, having sex with someone who has been drinking or using drugs can be considered date rape in a court of law, even if the person did not say "no." Drunkenness or being high on drugs is not a legal defense against date rape.

ALCOHOL AND OTHER DRUG USE

The use of alcohol and other drugs greatly increases the possibility that date rape might occur because of the following reasons:

- *Increased likelihood of getting into a risk situation.* Suppose a female has been drinking alcohol or smoking marijuana. She might not be thinking clearly and leave a party with a male she does not know. She might go to a male's home when no adults are there and listen to music in his bedroom. She is now in a risk situation. It may be difficult for her to defend herself from sexual advances or rape.
- *Impaired judgment.* Suppose a male makes sexual advances toward a female. The female tries to make her limits for expressing affection clear to him. She says "no." If the male has been drinking or using other drugs, he is unable to think clearly. He does not respect

his female companion's response and rapes her because his judgment is impaired.
- *Intensified feelings and the need for control.* Date rape is an act of violence. A person who is a rapist often has an increased need to control a companion. The rapist may try to get the victim in an isolated location and then use threats or intimidation to control and assault the victim. He or she also is more likely to act on that need after using alcohol or other drugs. Indeed, many rapes have reportedly happened after alcohol or other drug use has occurred.

Predatory Drugs

Predatory drugs is a term used to identify drugs that can be used to facilitate sexual assault. These drugs are sometimes called date-rape drugs. Awareness of these drugs began in the late 1990s, as law enforcement officials noticed a new, disturbing trend of rape cases that involved the drugging of victims with chemicals such as Rohypnol, GHB, and ketamine. Predatory drugs are dangerous because they can be slipped into a person's beverage without his or her knowledge. A person might not be able to see, smell, or taste the drug. People have died after these drugs have been slipped into their drinks. People need to be very careful in any type of social setting and should avoid setting a drink down and leaving it alone if planning to continue drinking it.

According to the Drug Enforcement Administration (2007), the following are dangers of predatory drugs:

- These drugs render the victim incapable of resisting sexual advances.
- Sexual assaults facilitated by these drugs can be difficult to prosecute or even recognize because:
  —Victims may not be aware that they ingested a drug at all. The drugs are invisible and odorless when dissolved in water. They are somewhat salty tasting, but are indiscernible when dissolved in beverages such as sodas, juice, liquor, or beer.
  —Due to memory problems induced by these drugs, the victim may not be aware of the attack until 8–12 hours after it occurred.
  —The drugs are metabolized quickly, so there may be little physical evidence to support the claim that the drugs were used to facilitate an assault.

—Memory impairment caused by the drugs also eliminates evidence about the attack.

ROHYPNOL

Rohypnol is a drug that is sometimes referred to as roofies, rophies, R2, roaches, Mexican valium, or the forget-me pill. It is a prescription sedative/depressant that is used as a treatment for insomnia or as a preanesthetic in other countries. Roofies are not manufactured or sold legally in the United States. When dissolved in liquid, including water, the drug is often undetectable. It is tasteless and odorless.

The effects of roofies include impaired judgment and motor skills, as well as memory loss, including amnesia. Dizziness, drowsiness, confusion, and a state of semiconsciousness also can result. All of these effects increase in intensity and duration if roofies are taken in combination with alcohol or other drugs. Noticeable effects occur within twenty minutes of ingestion. The effects can last up to thirty-six hours if the drug has been combined with alcohol.

GHB

GHB, sometimes called liquid Ecstasy, Clear X, Liquid X, liquid dream, and Chemical X, is a colorless, odorless liquid that is a depressant/anesthetic. Although GHB used to be marketed as a body-building supplement, the manufacture, distribution, and possession of GHB has been illegal in the United States since 2000. The effects of GHB include dizziness, nausea, drowsiness, amnesia, hallucinations, and coma. The effects can be felt within ten to fifteen minutes after ingestion and can last as long as seventy-two hours if the drug is mixed with alcohol or other drugs.

KETAMINE

Ketamine, also called Special K, Super K, KO, and Ket Kat, is a legal drug used as a veterinary sedative or as an anesthetic on humans. Effects include delirium, hallucinations, amnesia, and coma. If ingested, the effects can be felt in about ten to twenty minutes and are short lived compared to those of roofies and GHB, lasting only three hours.

All of these drugs leave the user vulnerable to sexual attack. They remain detectable in the body for only about forty-eight hours after use. If an assault is not reported immediately, there might be no physical evidence that these drugs were used in a sexual attack.

Sexual Abuse

Sexual abuse is maltreatment that typically involves inappropriate sexual behavior between an adult and a child, but it also can occur between a person under the age of eighteen and a younger child. Sexual abuse can take many different forms. It can consist of a single incident of sexual contact, or it can consist of repeated incidents of sexual contact.

Sexual abuse behaviors can include rape, incest, or any type of sexual contact between an adult and child. Exploitation of children under the age of eighteen can consist of promoting minors to engage in sex acts, using minors to produce pornography, or encouraging and promoting prostitution. All forms of sexual abuse are wrong, and the adult perpetrator is always the one at fault. Victims of sexual abuse are never the ones at fault.

INCEST

Incest is sexual abuse in which the abuser is a close relative of the child. Incest is the most common form of sexual abuse. Children often do not recognize incest as abuse. The child might view it as favoritism. Incest is always wrong, and the adult perpetrator is always the one at fault. Although victims might feel that they did something to cause the abuse, they need to understand that they are not to blame. Incest is never the fault of the victim.

A child or teen who is sexually abused might have difficulty sharing information about the abuse. The young person might fear that his or her parent will be penalized by law enforcement authorities or that the family will break up. As a result, he or she is reluctant to report the abuse. The young person needs to realize that these things might occur but that he or she needs to report the abuse to make it stop. The abuser needs to get help to stop the abuse. The young person also needs to get help to recover from the abuse.

A young person also might feel unjustly ashamed and guilty. A young person might disclose sexual abuse immediately after an incident, or it may take several months or even years before he or she discloses the abuse or it is discovered by someone else. Often a young person does not disclose sexual abuse out of fear that a perpetrator will harm him or her further. He or she also is likely to feel shame and embarrassment, which hinder disclosure. The young person should remember that the abuse is not his or her fault and that seeking help can stop it from occurring.

LAWS AND SEXUAL ABUSE

All states have laws that prohibit sexual abuse and require teachers and health professionals to report suspected cases of abuse. The identity of the person who is reporting the suspected abuse remains confidential when an abuse case is filed with child welfare agencies or the police. If an investigation reveals that a child is in danger, that child will be placed in protective custody or in a foster home.

Sexual Harassment and Stalking

Sexual harassment is unwanted sexual behavior that ranges from making sexual comments to forcing another person into unwanted sexual acts. Examples of sexual harassment include telling sexual jokes, making inappropriate gestures, staring at someone in a sexual manner, and touching someone in sexual ways. **Stalking** is repeatedly engaging in harassing or threatening behavior, such as following or making harassing phone calls to a person.

Adults need to tell young people who are victims of sexual harassment the following:

- *Ask the person who is harassing you to stop.* Be direct about what behavior is bothering you. The person might interpret a lack of response as encouragement.
- *Keep a record of what happened.* Write down the date and time, describe the situation and behavior, and explain how you handled the situation. Save any notes, letters, or pictures.
- *Check to see if there are guidelines to follow for the specific situation.* For example, if the harassment occurred at school, check school guidelines; if the harassment occurred at work, check work guidelines.
- *Report the harassment to the appropriate person in charge.* This person may be a boss, teacher, or school counselor.

- *Determine if you want to take legal action.* Sexual harassment is against all companies' policies. It also is a violation of the Civil Rights Act of 1964.

Adults need to tell young people who are victims of stalking the following:

- *Tell a trusted adult.* Tell your parents or guardian and school officials what is happening. As much as possible, avoid being alone.
- *Keep a record of each incident of stalking.* Write down the date, time, what was said, and what happened.
- *Save evidence.* Evidence would include notes and letters that might have been written to you and answering machine tapes with messages left on them.
- *Try to obtain a restraining order.* A **restraining order** is an order by a court that forbids a person from coming within a certain distance of the victim.
- *Contact the police department to report the stalking.* Consider pressing charges against the person who is stalking you.
- *Seek counseling.* Seek appropriate counseling or join a support group for victims of stalking.

SEXUAL HARASSMENT AND STALKING LAWS

Sexual harassment. Sexual harassment is illegal. A federal law, Title VII of the Civil Rights Act of 1964, strictly prohibits sexual harassment in the workplace. Title IX, also a federal law, makes it clear that sexual harassment should never occur in a school. People have a right to be free from sexual harassment, and these laws help to protect their rights. Many states also have laws that protect against sexual harassment. In addition, most schools have developed policies to deal with sexual harassment. Many schools and places of employment train employees on how to prevent and deal with sexual harassment.

Stalking. Some people who stalk others are trying to form a relationship or extend a relationship with the person they are stalking. In some cases, a stalker takes further action, and stalking leads to injury or murder. Before antistalking laws began to be passed in the 1990s, victims of stalking had few opportunities for protection. Many were victimized by prolonged intimidation and physical harm because there were no laws available to protect victims from stalking crimes. In 1992, the U.S. Congress passed an antistalking law to serve as a model for states. This law encouraged states to pass similar laws, making stalking a felony offense with stiff penalties.

In 1994, the Violence Against Women Act (VAWA) made it a federal crime for a person to cross a state line with the intent to injure, harass, or intimidate that person's spouse or intimate partner. Since California became the first state to pass an antistalking law, all states and the District of Columbia have passed antistalking laws. These laws give law enforcement agencies more power to arrest and prosecute stalkers, and they give more protection to stalking victims. Victims of stalking need to become familiar with the current antistalking laws in the state and community in which they live. Support groups also offer information.

Recovery for Survivors of Sexual Violence

Survivors of sexual violence and abuse often experience feelings of anger, fear, shock, confusion, and depression. In many instances, they blame themselves for what happened. The world that they may have felt was safe and predictable is suddenly unsafe and unpredictable. The survivor may ask, "Why me?"

The purpose of recovery programs is to help victims survive the pain, heal, and move forward with self-confidence. This may be difficult for survivors. Recovery does not mean that they forget what happened. Instead, recovery is being able to understand and believe that being a victim was not their fault. A survivor will never forget what has happened, but with time and effort, a survivor can accept the reality and work through his or her feelings. Survivors of rape or sexual abuse can and do recover. Recovery can be a powerful and positive step in the survivor's life. There are several steps survivors can take to fully recover:

- *Talk about what happened.* It is important to share feelings, thoughts, and experiences. Survivors need a support network of family members and trusted friends who can help them through the recovery process. Survivors of sexual violence and abuse need to get a complete examination. They need to have physical injuries treated. They might need blood tests to determine if they have become infected with a sexually transmitted disease and might need to be tested for pregnancy.
- *Seek counseling.* Survivors may need counseling and support services for emotional trauma. School counselors and physicians can tell them about the counseling and support services offered in the community. There are support groups for survivors of sexual violence and abuse. Survivors might ask school counselors or look in the local phone directory or newspaper to find support groups.
- *Practice self-defense strategies.* Survivors can gain confidence so that they can protect themselves from further harm. They can learn about risk situations and how to avoid them. They can learn and practice self-defense strategies. Most of all, they can try to remain hopeful and optimistic about the future. Survivors might not believe it right away, but the world is a wonderful place, and recovery and happiness are possible.

RECOVERY EFFORTS FOR RAPE SURVIVORS

A **rape survivor** is a person who has been raped. Rape survivors often need treatment for both physical injuries and emotional damage. A rape survivor should not take a shower after a rape until a medical exam has been performed. This is so that health status can be determined and evidence collected. Rape survivors may become infected with HIV or other STDs. Female rape survivors may become pregnant.

- *Rape trauma syndrome.* After the rape, survivors might be in shock or feel frightened or guilty. They might feel responsible for the rape. They might wonder why they were chosen to be the rapist's victim. They might not want other people to know what happened to them. Some rape survivors experience rape trauma syndrome. **Rape trauma syndrome** is a condition in which a rape survivor experiences emotional responses and physical symptoms over a period of time. After a rape, survivors might feel ashamed, angry, afraid, guilty, and powerless. Physical symptoms include nausea, headaches, and sleeplessness. Emotional responses may last from several weeks to several years. Rape survivors might experience problems when becoming intimate with a person of the opposite sex. Many survivors fear retaliation from the rapist. They often change their living habits by changing their telephone numbers, moving, or moving in with others. To recover and to avoid the lasting effects of rape trauma syndrome, survivors need treatment for both physical injuries and emotional damage. Sometimes victims are examined by sexual assault nurse examiners (SANEs), who are trained to deal with the emotional damage caused by rape, as well as physical injuries.

- *Resources.* Many resources are available to help rape survivors in their recovery. Rape crisis centers are available in many communities. Hospitals and women's centers also offer counseling and support groups. Rape victims can call the National Sexual Assault Hotline at 1-800-656-HOPE (4673) for information on local support groups and resources.
- *Providing support for a rape victim.* If *you* know someone who has been raped, there are ways that you can provide support. Be sure never to blame the victim for the rape. Give the victim time to feel comfortable with discussing the rape, but encourage the victim to share feelings and thoughts when he or she feels ready. When the victim does share those experiences, thoughts, or feelings with you, believe what the victim says about the experience and the feelings. Try to be supportive but not overly protective. Realize that it might take weeks, months, or years for the victim to begin working through the recovery process. As the person feels more comfortable, encourage the victim to get help from a rape crisis center, a counselor, or mental health professional.
- *Advice for family members and friends.* Friends, family members, spouses, boyfriends, or girlfriends of people who are victims of sexual assault also are victims. This is because the crime has affected their lives too. Husbands, wives, boyfriends, or girlfriends of sexual assault victims might feel angry, inadequate, and guilty. They might worry that their partner is pregnant or infected with a sexually transmitted disease, including HIV. Family members might have similar worries and fears. Family members might want to seek counseling to help them work through this difficult time.

RECOVERY FOR PERPETRATORS

People who have committed sexual violence do not have to continue being violent. These people can get help and change their behavior. Young people who have committed acts of sexual violence may be able to change their behavior so that they do not commit such acts in the future.

Changing this behavior requires entering and completing a treatment program that offers help from mental health professionals. Treatment programs include relapse prevention, which helps individuals develop skills so that they do not return to a previous pattern of inappropriate behavior.

Relapse prevention should teach offenders to understand any thoughts, feelings, or situations that trigger acts of sexual violence. It also helps individuals in treatment to identify thinking patterns that contribute to committing acts of sexual violence.

Health Goal #98

I Will Stay Away from Gangs

A gang is a group of people involved in violent and illegal activities. Some gangs consist of a few neighborhood teens. Others have thousands of members who cooperate in highly organized illegal activities. Gang violence is an increasing problem. Gangs have moved from big cities to smaller cities, suburbs, and rural areas.

Recognizing Gangs

Gang members come from families of all income levels. They may live in big cities, small towns, or rural areas. However, most gang members have some common characteristics:

1. *Gang members band together as a group.* Gang members hang out only with other gang members. They refer to their groups as "crews" or "posses."
2. *Gang members play specific roles.* Gangs have clear structures. A **hard-core gang member** is a senior gang member who has the most influence. Most gangs have several hard-core members who are leaders and tell others what to do. A **regular gang member** is a person who belongs to the gang and obeys the hard-core gang members. A **wanna-be** is a child or teen who is not a gang member but might wear gang clothing and engage in violent or criminal behavior to prove worthy of being a gang member. A **could-be** is a child or teen who is interested in belonging to a gang, perhaps to

emulate a family member or friend who is a member. Many could-bes are younger friends and family members of gang members.

3. *Gang members follow specific rules.* Gangs have strict rules for the behavior of gang members. These rules are set by hard-core gang members. The rules might be written down in a code book. There are harsh consequences for gang members who break the rules. The rules might include hanging out only with other gang members and committing certain crimes.

4. *Gang members operate within a territory.* Gang members refer to their territory as their "turf." They might draw graffiti on buildings to mark their turf. They consider members of other gangs to be trespassers if they enter their turf. Gang members might injure or kill people who trespass onto their turf.

5. *Gang members wear certain colors or types of clothing.* Gang members identify themselves with a certain color or style of dress. They may choose one specific color to wear or one particular item of clothing to wear, such as a scarf or colored shoelaces.

6. *Gang members have their own vocabulary, logos, and signals.* Gang members invent code words to use among themselves. They invent ways to identify themselves as members of the gang, such as hand signals and handshakes. Gangs also identify themselves by writing graffiti, or "tagging." Gang logos are used as graffiti as a public statement of turf and of intimidation.

7. *Gang members identify themselves by nicknames.* A person who joins a gang is given a nickname, or street name. Nicknames are used to disguise gang members when they are involved in illegal activity.

8. *Gang members often have tattoos.* Gang members get tattoos to identify themselves as members of the gang. Tattoos are a sign that a member is pledging to be in the gang for life.

Risks of Belonging to a Gang

Belonging to a gang is risky. It usually means being with young people who have enemies. Rivalry exists among gangs. Gang rivalry results in fighting, homicide, and other acts of violence. Gang members have sought revenge against rival gang members for insults, trespassing on gang turf, and personal disputes. If gang members feel they have been insulted or cheated, they feel their honor is at stake. They must restore their honor by seeking revenge. Revenge might include an assault or a drive-by shooting. Family members of gang members are at risk as well. Gang members often retaliate against the family members of rival gang members. Gang members often carry weapons to protect themselves from rival gangs. They also are involved in illegal weapon sales. Gang members often are involved in illegal drug use and drug trafficking. These activities can lead to violence.

Gang members may commit crimes to gain respect from other gang members. A **prestige crime** is a crime committed to gain status among other gang members. A gang member may assault a member of another gang, participate in a drive-by shooting, or steal in an effort to establish a tough reputation.

Gang members also participate in violence against their own gang members. Gang members who do not follow orders are beaten.

Teens who want to join a gang must participate in violent behaviors before they are admitted. These teens must go through an initiation period to prove they are "worthy" of gang membership. During the initiation period, they are subject to any gang member's demand at any time. They must commit violent crimes to prove themselves. Teens who are going through initiation often commit the most serious crimes so that the gang members do not have to do the dirty work themselves. Initiation demands may include murder, drug trafficking, weapons dealing, getting tattoos, carving or burning gang symbols into the skin, robbery, beating up other people, participating in a drive-by shooting, or beating up or killing members of rival gangs. Initiation could involve **jumping-in**—an initiation rite in which a potential gang member is beaten by other members of the gang. The potential gang member may have to fight all of the other members of the gang, either one by one or all at once. This initiation rite might continue for hours or even days. Teens have been severely injured or killed by jumping-in. Initiation for females may involve being "sexed-in." This means they are forced to have sex with one or more male gang members. This puts them at risk for infection with HIV, other STDs, and unwanted pregnancy.

Sometimes teens are used by gang members. They might believe they are being initiated into a gang when gang members demand they participate in criminal or sexual activities. Afterward these teens are told they are not worthy of being members of the gang.

Reasons for Gang Membership

Young people might seek gang membership to get a sense of belonging. However, in reality, being a gang member does not give a sense of belonging. Teens who are gang members are considered property of the gang. Gang leaders believe they own their members and can use them to do whatever they want. Gang members are accepted and "liked" by other gang members only if they behave the way gang leaders want them to. Gang members who break a rule or have a different opinion than other gang members may be injured or killed. Gang members always have to watch out for breaking a rule or getting on the wrong side of a gang leader.

Young people might seek gang membership as a way to get more money. Some gang members make their money from drug trafficking, stealing, and other illegal activities. When large amounts of money and illegal activities are involved, violence follows. Gang members are more likely to get a criminal record from these activities than make money. A person who has a criminal record often has more difficulty finding a job. Gang members are at high risk of dropping out of school. Not having an education increases the risk of poverty.

Young people might seek gang membership as a way of escaping family problems by being in a gang. Many gang members have been raised in dysfunctional families where there is physical abuse, sexual abuse, drug abuse, or neglect. Teens who think about joining a gang may believe they will be escaping the abuse—that, unlike their family, the gang will care for them and pay attention to them. However, these same abusive behaviors continue among gang members. Gangs are even more dysfunctional. Gang leaders abuse gang members. Fighting, drug abuse, and rape are common among gang members.

Young people might seek gang membership to get protection. Gang members might offer protection, but once a teen is a member of a gang the risks of harm and threats from others are greatly increased. Teens are harmed being initiated into gangs. They are constantly at risk of being harmed by rival gang members. Involvement in drug trafficking and criminal activity also increases their risk of being harmed.

Protection from Gangs

Young people can resist pressure to join gangs by taking specific actions. For example, they can use resistance skills to stay away from gang members, avoid gang turf and places where gang activity takes place, be aware of gang colors in the community and in nearby communities, avoid listening to music that supports gang activities, not stay out late at night, not write graffiti, spend time with family members and mentors, obey laws and respect authority, avoid alcohol and other drug use, and set goals and make plans to reach them.

Some young people who live in communities in which there are gangs have formed antigang gangs. An **antigang gang** is a group of teens who stay together to avoid pressure and protect themselves from gang members. The goal of antigang gangs is for teens to continue with daily activities without being pressured or threatened by gang members. Antigang gangs walk together as a group to and from school and make arrangements to escort one another to school activities. An adult may accompany them for additional protection. These teens recognize that gang members are less likely to pressure them to join a gang when they are in a group. They do not hang out around gang members or participate in gang activities. They do not wear gang clothing or take other actions to identify themselves as a group. Antigang gangs are informal, and any teen who wants to avoid gangs can become involved.

Leaving a Gang

Young people who joined gangs when they were younger often were not aware of what being in a gang involves. Gang members often realize that being in a gang is not what they had hoped for. They recognize that it is risky, stressful, and, at times, boring. However, they may be afraid to try to leave the gang. They know that other gang members may harm them or their family members if they leave. Some gangs allow members to leave, or jump out, if they survive a severe beating. However, many do not survive. Other gangs say they will not allow gang members to leave under any circumstances. However, it is not too late for teens who are in gangs. Help is available. Many teens have successfully left gangs and started lives without gangs, violence, and fear. Law enforcement officers have helped protect many gang members who wanted to leave their gangs. Many communities have gang counselors who help gang members leave gangs. Teens who want to leave a gang may move to another neighborhood, community, or state to be safe. Others return to their neighborhood and avoid gang members. The best way to avoid having to leave a gang is not to join one in the first place.

Health Goal #99

I Will Follow Guidelines to Help Reduce the Risk of Weapon Injuries

According to several surveys, one in five high school students has carried a gun, knife, or club to school or elsewhere. Young people are more likely to use weapons to solve disagreements today than they were in the past. In many cases, fighting with fists has been replaced by fighting with guns and weapons.

Carrying a Weapon Can Increase Risk of Injury

A **weapon** is a device used for fighting. Guns, knives, razor blades, pipe bombs, brass knuckles, clubs, and stun guns are examples of weapons. Guns are the weapons most likely to be used to harm teens. Young people sometimes carry guns or other weapons (with parental permission) to hunt animals or to go target shooting. However, there are many situations in which it is unsafe to carry a weapon. Carrying a weapon can increase the risk of injury:

1. *Carrying a weapon increases the risk of injury due to accidental discharge.* Every day, teens die or are seriously injured in gun accidents.

Most victims were "fooling around with the gun." They might not have known how to handle the gun or might have been showing off the gun to impress others or gain status. They might have thought the gun was not loaded and wondered what it would be like to pull the trigger. They might have been handling a gun that was bought illegally. Or they might have been with a person who was handling a gun for one of the reasons stated earlier.

2. *Carrying a weapon increases the risk that it will be used to settle a disagreement or fight.* Young people who carry a weapon might use the weapon if they get into a fight. If they had not had the weapon, they might have settled their disagreement in a more rational way. But when emotions are strong and someone has a weapon, it is easy to use it. Once the weapon has been used, there is no way to take back any injury that has been inflicted. If a teen has a weapon, there also is the possibility that another person will wrestle it away and use it to get even.

3. *Carrying a weapon increases the risk of it being used in a crime.* Young people who commit crimes may intend to use a weapon only to frighten their victim. But they may actually use the weapon if the victim puts up a fight.

4. *Carrying a weapon, particularly a gun, increases the risk of suicide.* Sometimes young people experience hard times. They may feel depressed and not know how to handle their situation. They may be taking drugs. These situations can lead to thoughts of suicide. In most cases, thoughts of suicide pass. However, if a weapon is available, a teen might use it.

Reducing the Risk of Being Injured by a Weapon

There are actions that young people should be encouraged to take to reduce the risk of being injured by a weapon:

1. *Do not purchase a weapon illegally.* Most states have laws forbidding the sale of guns to people under the age of eighteen. If you want to purchase a gun for hunting, ask your parents or guardians for permission. You need to learn how to use the gun and to keep it in a safe place. It should not be carried at inappropriate times.

2. *Do not carry a concealed weapon.* Carrying a concealed weapon without a permit is against

the law in some states for a person of any age. Follow laws that provide protection.

3. *Do not carry a weapon to school.* Students need to understand that they are forbidden to carry a weapon to school. The violation of this could result in suspension from school or not being able to graduate. Students need to understand that they have a responsibility to keep their school safe.

4. *Encourage others to avoid buying, carrying, or concealing a weapon.* You can be a positive influence. The fewer weapons there are in a community, the safer all will be.

5. *Do not pretend to use a weapon.* Pretending can be misinterpreted. This behavior may threaten others into violence. For example, suppose a person points his finger in his pocket to pretend that he has a gun. Another person may respond with violence for self-protection.

6. *Avoid being around people who buy, carry, conceal, or use weapons.* Your safety depends on staying away from people who have weapons. They might be involved in other crimes, such as drug trafficking.

7. *Do not argue with someone who has a weapon.* In these situations, it is important to keep your distance. Do not attempt to provoke or argue with this person. Weapons often are used to inflict injury when someone becomes emotional. Therefore, it is important to remain calm.

8. *Avoid being in situations in which there will be weapons.* If you know that others will carry a weapon to a specific event, stay away from the event.

9. *Do not touch any weapon you find.* The weapon may have been used in a crime. If so, it may have fingerprints on it that would help solve the crime. The exact location of the weapon may also be important.

10. *Tell a responsible adult if you find a weapon.* Someone needs to know the location of the weapon. A responsible adult, such as a parent, guardian, teacher, or law enforcement officer, can make arrangements, remove the weapon, and put it in a safe place.

Gun Safety

Some people, such as police officers, use guns for their occupation, while others use them for hunting or target shooting. Many of these people use and store their guns safely. However, it is important for everyone to know general gun safety guidelines to help reduce the risk of injury. The following information is what you can tell young people about gun safety:

At home. If you have guns in your home, be sure they are stored unloaded in a secured, locked container, such as a gun safe or strong-box, with the key in a secure place out of the reach of children. Guns that cannot be locked up should be stored unloaded with a durable trigger lock. Ammunition should be stored in a secure container away from the gun. All guns should be out of the sight and reach of children.

Away from home. If you happen to see a gun that is not safely locked up at a neighbor's house, at school, or on the street, there are some guidelines to follow. First, do not touch the gun. The gun may be loaded, and it is a serious risk to you and those around you if not handled properly. A gun you see at school or on the street may have been used in a crime. Second, leave the area at once. If the gun is loaded and someone decides to pick it up or play with it, everyone in the area is in immediate danger. Last, immediately tell a responsible adult, such as a parent, guardian, teacher, or law enforcement officer, where the gun is located.

Additional actions. Along with knowing what to do if you see a gun, it is also important to know additional actions you can take to reduce the risk of being injured by a gun.

Suppose you want to purchase a gun for hunting. Ask your parents or guardian for permission. Learn how to use the gun. Make sure it is stored unloaded in a locked container.

Avoid being in situations that are unsupervised by parents or guardians where there will be access to guns. You cannot be certain what will happen if another person has a gun and does not know how to use it correctly.

Always follow laws because they protect you and others. Do not carry a gun to school or have one in your car. Remember, it is illegal to carry a weapon to school. Do not pretend you are going to use a gun. Pretending can be misinterpreted, and this may lead to violence. If you know that someone at your school is keeping a gun or other weapon there, immediately tell a teacher or your principal. Also inform school authorities if you know that someone is planning to bring a gun or other weapon to school. You will help to keep yourself and others safe by keeping weapons out of your school.

Do not provoke or argue with someone who has a gun. Keep your distance. Remember, guns often are used to inflict injury when someone becomes emotional. Remain calm.

Gun Laws

The Youth Handgun Safety Act, part of the Omnibus Violent Crime Control and Law Enforcement Act of 1994, federally prohibits the possession of a handgun or ammunition by a person under the age of eighteen or the private transfer of a handgun or ammunition to a juvenile. The law includes a number of exceptions, such as possessing a firearm for farming, hunting, and other specific uses. Some states have established different age limits. There is no federal minimum age for possession of a long gun (rifle or shotgun).

Laws on carrying a concealed weapon specify the conditions under which individuals may carry weapons in public. A **concealed weapon** is a weapon partially or fully hidden from view. These laws include weapons such as guns, knives, and clubs, and they vary widely from state to state. Some states prohibit carrying concealed weapons. In most states, a permit is required to carry a concealed weapon.

The Gun-Free Schools Act requires school districts to have policies that require any student who brings a firearm to school to be expelled. This act also requires that these students

be referred to the criminal justice or juvenile delinquency system.

Health Goal #100

I Will Be Skilled in First Aid Procedures

All teachers should become prepared to respond to emergencies and be skilled in first aid. Health teachers should be trained and certified in first aid and CPR. An **emergency** is a serious situation that occurs without warning and calls for quick action. **First aid** is the immediate and temporary care given to a person who has been injured or suddenly becomes ill. The "Guide to First Aid Procedures" that follows explains how to maintain a first-aid kit, make an emergency telephone call, obtain consent to give first aid, follow universal precautions, and administer firstaid procedures. Knowing first aid procedures allows you to respond quickly in an emergency and helps you stay calm if someone is injured or ill. First aid is also an important part of health education for students. Health education teaches students how to give proper first aid.

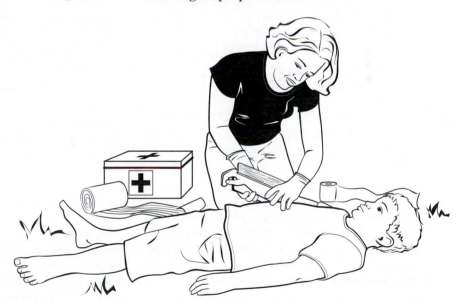

A Guide to First Aid Procedures

This guide explains how to maintain a first-aid kit, make an emergency telephone call, obtain consent to give first aid, follow universal precautions, and administer first-aid procedures. A person who knows first aid procedures can respond quickly to an emergency and will not panic if someone is injured or ill.

FIRST AID KITS

It is important to keep first-aid kits where they might be needed. You will probably want to have a first-aid kit in your classroom. It is also good to keep a first-aid kit at home and in your car. A first aid kit can be purchased from a drugstore or the local chapter of the American Red Cross. Kits can also be assembled using items that you have purchased yourself. Keep in your first-aid kit items needed to follow universal precautions (see the section "Universal Precautions"). Add to your personal first-aid kit special medicines you or family members need. Check first-aid kits often. Some items have expiration dates and will need to be replaced on expiration. Have a flashlight in or next to all first-aid kits and make sure batteries are fresh.

EMERGENCY TELEPHONE CALLS

Always follow school district policy during any emergency in the school setting. In many communities, calling 911 will reach assistance for fire, police, and medical emergencies. The local phone book will say whether your community uses 911 for emergency assistance. Dial the operator (the number 0) if you do not know the correct number to call. When you call 911, an emergency dispatcher will answer the telephone. An **emergency dispatcher** is a person who decides whom to contact when there is a call for help. The call may be directed to the police, fire station, poison control center, rescue squad, or emergency medical team.

You should follow these instructions when making an emergency telephone call:

1. Remain calm and speak clearly.

2. Describe the exact location of the emergency. Give the address and ways for emergency personnel to find the location (e.g., name the closest intersection or a landmark).
3. Give your name, what happened, the number of people involved, the condition of the injured people, and the help that has been given.
4. Give the telephone number of the telephone you are using. This makes it possible for someone to call you back if you get disconnected or if the dispatcher needs more information.
5. Listen carefully if you are told how to care for the victim. Write down directions if necessary. Give these directions to other people who are caring for the victim.
6. Do not hang up the telephone until you are told to do so.
7. Return to the victim. Provide care if appropriate. Stay with the victim until help arrives.

CONSENT TO GIVE FIRST AID

You must have consent to give first aid. There are two types of consent. **Actual consent** is oral or written permission from a mentally competent adult to give first aid. Tell the victim who you are, what you plan to do, and the first-aid training you have had. If the person gives you permission, this is actual consent. Do not give first aid to a conscious adult who does not give you permission. A parent or guardian must give actual consent if the victim is a child or is not mentally competent. A supervising adult with legal permission from parents to care for an infant or child, such as a teacher or school staff member, also can give actual consent. Do not give first aid to a conscious infant or child when a parent or guardian says "no." Do not give first aid to a conscious infant or child when a supervising adult with legal permission to care for an infant or child says "no." Implied consent is permission to give first aid to

• A mentally competent adult victim who is unconscious

of a fracture of the skull include bleeding from the head or ears, drowsiness, and headache.

When you suspect a fracture, call the local emergency number and obtain medical care immediately. Follow these steps to provide first aid for fractures:

1. Treat for bleeding and shock.
2. Keep the injured part from moving. Use a splint when appropriate. If the victim has a head injury, keep the victim still.
3. Apply ice to the break or crack to prevent swelling.
4. Follow universal precautions. Control bleeding.
5. Get prompt medical help.

DISLOCATIONS

A **dislocation** is the movement of a bone away from its joint. Dislocations often are accompanied by stretched ligaments. The signs of a dislocation are pain, swelling upon movement, loss of movement, and deformity. Call the local emergency number and obtain medical care immediately. Follow these steps to provide first aid for a dislocation:

1. Splint above and below the dislocated joint.
2. Apply cold compresses.

SPRAINS

A **sprain** is an injury to the ligaments, tendons, and soft tissue around a joint caused by undue stretching. The signs of a sprain include pain that increases with movement or weight bearing, tenderness, and swelling. Follow these steps to provide first aid for sprains:

1. Apply RICE treatment.
2. Get prompt medical help if you suspect a fracture.

STRAINS

A **strain** is an overstretching of muscles or tendons. One of the most common strains involves the muscles of the back. Signs of strain include pain, swelling, stiffness, and firmness in the area. Follow these steps to provide first aid for strains:

1. Administer RICE treatment.
2. Get prompt medical help for a severe strain.

RICE TREATMENT

RICE treatment consists of rest, ice, compression, and elevation:

Rest: Rest the injured part for twenty-four to seventy-two hours. Longer rest is required for severe injuries. Do not exercise the injured area until there is complete healing.

Ice: Apply cold water, a cold compress, or ice pack for twenty minutes as soon as possible after the injury occurs. Apply several times a day for one to three days. Wrap ice in a cloth before placing on the skin. Applying cold reduces pain, swelling, inflammation, and tissue damage.

Compression: Wrap the injury with an elastic bandage to limit swelling. The compression should not be so tight that it restricts blood flow. Remove the wrap periodically and check for good circulation.

Elevation: Raise the injured body part above the level of the heart to reduce swelling and drain blood and fluid from the area.

SUDDEN ILLNESS

A **sudden illness** is an illness that occurs without warning. Often it is difficult to determine whether the situation is an emergency. Signs of sudden illness may include dizziness and confusion, weakness, changes in skin color, nausea, vomiting, and diarrhea. Seizures, paralysis, slurred speech, difficulty seeing, and severe pain may also indicate sudden illness. Call the local emergency number and obtain medical care immediately for a sudden illness. Follow these steps to provide first aid for sudden illness:

1. Give first aid for life-threatening conditions.
2. Keep the victim calm.
3. Cover the victim with a blanket if he is chilled.

4. Do not give an unconscious victim anything to eat or drink.
5. Get prompt medical attention.

FAINTING

Follow these steps to provide first aid for fainting:

1. Put the victim on her back if she is not vomiting. If she is vomiting, turn her onto her side.
2. Elevate the victim's legs eight to twelve inches above the level of the heart. (Do not elevate the legs if you suspect a head or back injury.)
3. Loosen tight clothing.
4. Do not splash water on the victim, slap the victim's face, or use smelling salts.

SEIZURES

Follow these steps to provide first aid for a seizure:

1. Place something under the victim's head to cushion the head from injury.
2. Remove objects that might injure the victim.
3. Loosen the clothing around the victim's neck.
4. Do not restrain the victim.
5. Do not place anything in the victim's mouth or between the teeth.
6. Look for a medical alert tag.

HEAT-RELATED ILLNESSES

Heat-related illnesses are conditions that result from exposure to temperatures higher than normal. Heat cramps, heat exhaustion, and heat stroke are the most common heat-related illnesses.

HEAT CRAMPS

Heat cramps are painful muscle spasms in the legs and arms due to excessive fluid loss through sweating. Follow these steps to provide first aid for heat cramps:

1. Have the victim rest in a cool, shaded area.
2. Give the victim cool water to drink.
3. Stretch stiff muscles gently.

HEAT EXHAUSTION

Heat exhaustion is extreme tiredness due to the body's inability to regulate its temperature. Heat exhaustion can be life threatening. A victim of heat exhaustion will have a body temperature that is below normal. Other signs of heat exhaustion include cool, moist, pale, or red skin, nausea, headache, dizziness, fast pulse, and weakness. Call the local emergency number and obtain medical care immediately for heat exhaustion. Follow these steps to provide first aid for heat exhaustion:

1. Have the victim rest in a cool place.
2. Have the victim lie down and elevate the feet.
3. Give the victim cool water to drink.
4. Observe the victim for signs of heat stroke.

HEAT STROKE (SUNSTROKE)

Heat stroke is an overheating of the body that is life threatening. Sweating ceases, so that the body cannot regulate its temperature. The victim has a high body temperature and rapid pulse and respiration rate. The skin becomes hot and dry. A victim feels weak and dizzy and has a headache. A victim may be unconscious. Call the local emergency number and obtain medical care immediately for heat stroke. Follow these steps to provide first aid for heat stroke:

1. Have the victim rest in a cool place.
2. Remove heavy clothing.
3. Wrap the victim in cool, wet towels or sheets.
4. Place ice packs near the neck, armpits, and groin.
5. Continue cooling until the victim's body temperature reaches 102 degrees Fahrenheit (38.9 degrees Celsius).
6. Treat any other injuries.

COLD-TEMPERATURE-RELATED ILLNESSES

Cold-temperature-related illnesses are conditions that result from exposure to low temperatures. The most common cold-temperature-related emergencies are frostbite and hypothermia.

FROSTBITE

Frostbite is the freezing of body parts, often the tissues of the extremities. Frostbite may involve the fingers, toes, ears, and nose. People exposed to subfreezing temperatures or snow are at risk for developing frostbite. Signs of frostbite include numbness in the affected area, waxy appearance of skin, and skin discolored and cold to touch. Call the local emergency number and obtain medical care immediately for frostbite. Follow these steps to provide first aid for frostbite:

1. If a medical facility is nearby, do not attempt rewarming—take the victim to the medical facility. Take the following steps only if medical help is not available.
2. Remove any clothing or jewelry that interferes with circulation.
3. Handle the affected area gently.
4. Soak the affected body part in water that has a temperature between 100 degrees Fahrenheit (37.8 degrees Celsius) and 105 degrees Fahrenheit (40.6 degrees Celsius). Test the water by having someone who has not been exposed to the cold place a hand in the water. Water that is too warm for the hand is too warm to use for the victim. Warming usually takes twenty-five to forty minutes, until the tissues are soft.
5. Apply warm, moist cloths to warm the ears, nose, or face.
6. Do not rub the affected body part.
7. Do not allow a victim to walk on frostbitten toes or feet, even after rewarming.
8. Slightly elevate the affected part.
9. Place dry, sterile gauze between the toes and fingers to absorb moisture and prevent them from sticking.

HYPOTHERMIA

Hypothermia is a reduction of the body temperature so that it is lower than normal. Hypothermia results from overexposure to cool temperatures, cold water, moisture, and wind. An air or water temperature as high as 50 degrees Fahrenheit (11.7 degrees Celsius) can cause hypothermia.

Most cases of hypothermia are mild. The victim will shiver and feel cold. But if the exposure continues, the pulse rate slows and becomes irregular, the body temperature drops, and the victim loses consciousness. Hypothermia can cause death if not treated. Call the local emergency number and obtain medical care immediately for hypothermia. Hypothermia victims should be handled gently and moved to a warm environment whenever possible. Follow these steps to provide first aid for hypothermia:

1. Get the victim into a warm environment.
2. Handle the victim gently.
3. Remove any wet clothing, and replace it with dry clothing.
4. Place something warm above and below the victim, such as blankets.
5. Cover the victim's head.

For mild hypothermia (body temperature above 90 degrees Fahrenheit [32.2 degrees Celsius]):

6. Warm the victim. Use an electric blanket or tub of water with a temperature no greater than 105 degrees Fahrenheit (40.6 degrees Celsius). Keep the victim's legs and arms out of the water. Do not cover the victim's arms or legs with the electric blanket.
7. Place hot packs on the victim's head, neck, chest, and groin. Be careful not to burn the victim.

For profound hypothermia (body temperature below 90 degrees Fahrenheit [32.2 degrees Celsius]):

8. Do not rewarm a victim who can be transported to a medical facility within twelve hours.
9. Calm the victim.
10. Move the victim as little as possible.
11. Do not give CPR to the victim unless there is no pulse. If CPR is initiated, continue administering CPR until the victim is transported to a medical facility.

Bibliography for Health Content

Advocate Health Care. (2005). Children's physicals: Tune-ups for growing kids. Available at www.advocatehealth.com.

American Academy of Child and Adolescent Psychiatry. (2005). Facts for families. Available at www.aacap.org/publications/factsfam/index.htm.

American Academy of Family Physicians. (2005). *Mind/body connection: How your emotions affect your health.* Shawnee Mission, KS: Author. Available at familydoctor.org/782.xml.

American Academy of Family Phsicians. (2006). *Teens and stress: Who has time for it?* Available at familydoctor.org/278.xml.

American Academy of Family Physicians, American Academy of Pediatrics, American Dietetic Association, National Hispanic Medical Association, National Medical Association, U.S. Department of Agriculture. (2005). Prescription for change: Ten keys to promote healthy eating in schools. In USDA Food and Nutrition Service, *Changing the scene: Improving the school nutrition environment.* Washington, DC: Author.

American Academy of Family Physicians. (2007). *Information for teens: Endometriosis.* Available at www.kidshealth.org/teen/sexual_health/girls/endometriosis.html.

American Academy of Pediatrics. (2001). Children, adolescents, and television. *Pediatrics, 107,* 423–426.

American Academy of Pediatrics. (2003, October). Increasing immunization coverage. *Policy Statement, 112,* 993–996.

American Academy of Pediatrics. (2006). Policy statement: Children, adolescents, and advertising. *Pediatrics, 118*(6), 2563–2569.

American Cancer Society. (2006). *Cancer facts and figures 2006.* Atlanta: Author.

American Cancer Society. (2006). *The complete guide—nutrition and physical activity.* Available at www.cancer.org/docroot/PED/Content/PED_3_2X_DIET_Activity_Factors_That_Affect_Risks_ASP.

American Cancer Society. 2007. *Cancer facts and figures* 2007. Atlanta: Author.

American College of Sports Medicine. (2000). *ACSM's guidelines for exercise testing and prescription* (6th ed.). Philadelphia: Lippincott, Williams, & Wilkens.

American Diabetes Association. (2007). *All about diabetes.* Available at www.diabetes.org/about-diabetes.jsp.

American Heart Association. (2000a). *CPR for family and friends.* Dallas: Author.

American Heart Association. (2000b). *Heartsaver CPA in schools.* Dallas: Author.

American Heart Association. (2005). *Heart and stroke statistics—2005 update.* Dallas: Author.

American Heart Association. (2007). *Cardiovascular disease statistics.* Available at www.americanheart.org.

American Medical Association. (2003). JAMA Patient Page: Depression. *Journal of the American Medical Association, 289,* 3198.

American Psychiatric Association. (2000). *Diagnostic and statistical manual of mental disorders* (4th ed.) *(DSM-IV-TR).* Washington, DC: Author.

American Social Health Association. (2006). *STD/STI statistics—fast facts.* Available at www.ashastd.org/learn/learn_statistics.cfm.

Amschler, D. H. (1999). Calcium intake in adolescents; An issue revisited. *Journal of School Health, 69*(3), 120–22.

Appleby, J. (2006, October 16). Consumer unease with U.S. health care grows. *USA Today.* Available at www.usatoday.com/money/industries/health/2006-10-15-health-concern-usat_x.htm.

Ballard-Barbash, R. (2001). Designing surveillance systems to address emerging issues in diet and health. *Journal of Nutrition, 131,* 437S–439S.

Beckman, H., Hawley, S., & Bishop, T. (2006). Application of theory-based health behavior change techniques to the prevention of obesity in children. *Journal of Pediatric Nursing, 21*(4), 266–275.

Bellisle, F., & Rolland-Cachera, M. (2001). How sugar-containing drinks might increase adiposity in children. *The Lancet, 357,* 4909.

Blair, S. N., Cheng, Y., & Holder, J. S. (2001). Is physical activity or physical fitness more important in defining health benefits? *Medicine and Science in Sports, 33,* S379–S399.

Bren, L. (2004). Diabetes prevention, treatment. *FDA Consumer, 38*(4), 18–19.

Bren, L. (2005). Straight talk on braces. *FDA Consumer, 39*(1), 20–25.

Brock, K., Nguyen, B., Liu, N., Watkins, M., & Reutzel, T. (2005). The use of antidepressants in school-age children. *Journal of School Nursing, 21*(6), 318–322.

Brooks-Gunn, J., & Furstenberg, F. F. (1989). Adolescent sexual behavior. *American Psychologist, 44*(2), 249–257.

Bureau of Justice Statistics, U.S. Department of Justice. (2005). *Homicide trends in the U.S.: Intimate homicide*. Available at www.ojp .usdoj.gov/bjs/homicide/intimates.htm.

Cassas, K. J. (2006). Childhood and adolescent sports-related overuse injuries. *American Family Physician, 73*(6), 1014–1022.

CBS News. (2006, September 16). *Cutting through advertising clutter*. Available at www.cbsnews .com/stories/2006/09/17/sunday/main2015684 .shtml.

Center for Drug Evaluation and Research. (2004). *FDA Public Health Advisory: Suicidality in Children and Adolescents Being Treated with Antidepressant Medications*. Washington, DC: Food and Drug Administration. Available at www.fda.gov/cder/drug/antidepressants/ default.htm.

Center for Substance Abuse Treatment. (2001, April). Oxycontin®: Prescription drug abuse. *CSAT Advisory: Breaking News for the Treatment Field, 1*(1), 1–4.

Center on Alcohol Marketing and Youth. (2005). *Youth overexposed: Alcohol advertising in magazines, 2001 to 2003*. Available at camy.org/ research/mag0405.

Centers for Disease Control and Prevention. (2004). Physical activity and good nutrition: Essential elements to prevent chronic diseases and obesity. Available at www.cdc.gov/ nccdphp/aag/aag_dnpa.htm.

Centers for Disease Control and Prevention. (2005a). *Fact sheet: Basic information about SARS*. Available at www.cdc.gov/ncidod/sars/ factsheet.htm.

Centers for Disease Control and Prevention. (2005b). The burden of obesity in the United States: A problem of massive proportions. *Chronic Disease: Notes and Reports, 17*(2), 4–9.

Centers for Disease Control and Prevention. (2005c). *Foodborne illnesses*. Available at www.cdc.gov/ncidod/dbmd/diseaseinfo/files/ foodborne_ilness_FAQ.pdf.

Centers for Disease Control and Prevention. (2007). *A glance at the HIV/AIDS epidemic*. Available at www.cdc.gov/hiv/resources/ factsheets/At-A-Glance.htm.

Cloud, J. (2000, September 18). A kinder, gentler death. *Time,* pp. 60–67.

Consumer Reports (2005, February). Your comparative guide to contraceptives. Available at www.consumerreports.org/cro/health-fitness/ health-care/condoms-and-contraception-205/ acomparative-guide/index.htm.

Coogan, P. F., Geller, A., Adams, M., Benjes, L. S., & Koh, H. K. (2001). Sun protection practices in preadolescents and adolescents: A school-based survey of almost 25,000 Connecticut schoolchildren. *Journal of the American Academy of Dermatology, 44,* 512–519.

Committee on Environmental Health, American Academy of Pediatrics. (2004). Ambient air pollution: Health hazards to children (policy statement). *Pediatrics, 114*(6), 1699–1707.

Corbin, C. B., & Pangrazi, R. P. (1998). *Physical activity for children: A statement of guidelines*. Reston, VA: National Association for Sport and Physical Education.

Corbin, C. B., Pangrazi, R. P., & Masurier, G. C. L. (2004). Physical activity for children: Current patterns and guidelines. *President's Council on Physical Fitness and Sports Research Digest, 5*(2), 1–8.

Covey, S. (2006). *The 6 most important decisions you'll ever make*. New York: Fireside.

Department of Economic and Social Affairs of the United Nations Secretariat, Population Division. (2005). *World population prospects: The 2004 revision,* and *World urbanization prospects: The 2003 revision*. Available at esa. un.org/unpp.

Dietz, W. H. (2005). CDC's response to the obesity epidemic. *Chronic Disease: Notes and Reports, 17*(2), 2–3.

Division of Nutrition and Physical Activity. (2006). Tips for avoiding activity-induced injuries. Atlanta: Centers for Disease Control and Prevention. Available at www.cdc.gov/nccdphp/ dnpa/physical/life/avoiding_injury.htm.

Drug Enforcement Administration. (2007). *What are predatory drugs?* Available at www.dea .gov/concern/predatory.html.

Eaton, D. K., Kann, L., Kinchen, S., Ross, J., Hawkins, M. A., Harris, W. A., Lowry, R., McManus, T., Chyen, D., Shanklin, S., Lim, C., Grunbaum, J. A., & Wechsler, H. (2006). Youth risk behavior surveillance: United States, 2005. *Morbidity and Mortality Weekly Report, 55*(SS05), 1–10.

Elkind, D. H., & Sweet, F. (2004). *How to do character education*. San Francisco: Live Wire

Media. Available at www.goodcharacter.com/Article_4.html.

Fanning, K. (2007). All about the rain forest: Saving the world's rain forest. *Scholastic News.* Available at teacher.scholastic.com/scholasticnews/indepth/rainforest/rainforest.asp.

Fleagal, K. M., Troiano, R. P., & Ballard-Barbash, R. (2001). Aim for a healthy weight: What is the target? *Journal of Nutrition, 131,* 440S–450S.

Food and Drug Administration. (2003, December). Birth control guide. FDA Consumer Magazine. Available at www.fda.gov/fdac/features/1997/babytabl.html.

Food and Drug Administration. (2005). *Medication guide: About using antidepressants in children and teenagers.* Washington, DC: Author.

Food Safety and Inspection Service. (2006). *Factsheets on food safety.* Available at www.fsis.usda.gov/fact_sheets.

Gorman, C. (2003, November 30). Why so many of us are getting diabetes. *Time.* Available at www.time.com/time/magazine/article/0,9171,1006377,00.html.

Gray, J. T. (2003). The world of hair. Online reference from Procter and Gamble, Hair Care Research Center. Available at www.pg.com/science/haircare/ hair_twh_toc.html.

Grunbaum, J. A. Kann, L., Kinchen, S. A., Ross, J. G., et al. (2004). Youth risk behavior surveillance—United States, 2003. *Morbidity and Mortality Weekly Report, 53*(SS-2), 1–96.

Hackam, D. G. & Anand, S. S. (2003). Emerging risk factors for atherosclerotic vascular disease: A critical review of the evidence. *Journal of the American Medical Association, 290,* 932–940.

Hadley, A. A., Ogden, C. L., Johnson, C. L., Carroll, M. D., Curtin, L. R., & Flegal, K. M. (2004). Prevalence of overweight and obesity among U.S. children, adolescents, and adults, 1999–2002. *Journal of the American Medical Association, 291*(23), 2847–2850.

Havighurst, R. J. (1948). *Developmental tasks and education.* Chicago: University of Chicago Press.

HealthDay. (2007, February 2). Global warming poses health threats: Floods, drought, infectious diseases expected to become worse, experts say. Available at www.healthfinder.gov/news/newsstory.asp?docID=60162.

Hellmich, N. (2003, October 14). Obesity predicted for 40% of America. *USA Today,* p. 7D.

Hobson, K. (2003, October 20). The body on fire. *U.S. News & World Report,* pp. 42–44.

International Food Information Council. (2003, July/August). Food sensitivities, allergies, and intolerances: Separating fact from fiction. *Food Insight,* 1–4.

Johnson, K. (2004). Adolescent sleep patterns: Biological, social, and psychological influences. *Journal of the American Academy of Child and Adolescent Psychiatry, 43*(3), 374–375.

Kaiser Family Foundation. (2003, October). Virginity and the first time: A series of national surveys of teens about sex. *SexSmarts* (Publication 3368). Survey conducted in collaboration with *Seventeen* magazine. Available at www.kff.org/entpartnerships/3368-index.cfm.

Krauss, R. M., Eckel, R. H., Howard, B., Appel, L. J., Daniels, S. R., Deckelbaum, R. J. Erdman, J. W., Kris-Etherton, P., Goldberg, I. J., Kotchen, T. A., Lichtenstein, A. H., Mitch, W. E., Mullis, R., Robinson, K., Wylie-Rosett, J., St. Jeor, S., Suttie, J., Tribble, D. L., & Bazzarre, T. L. (2001). AHA scientific statement: AHA dietary guidelines revision 2000: A statement for healthcare professionals from the Nutrition Committee of the American Heart Association. *Journal of Nutrition, 131,* 132–146.

Kübler-Ross, E. (1997). *On Death and Dying.* New York: Simon & Schuster.

Kuller, L. H., Arnold, A. M., Psaty, B. M., Robbins, J. A., O'Leary, D. H., Tracy, R. P., Burke, G. L., Manolio, T. A., & Chaves, P. H. (2006). 10-year follow-up of subclinical cardiovascular disease and risk of coronary heart disease in the Cardiovascular Health Study. *Archives of Internal Medicine, 166,* 71–78.

Kushi, L. H., Byers, T., Doyle, C., Bandera, E. V., McCullough, M., Gansler, T., Andrews, K. S., Thun, M. J., & the American Cancer Society 2006 Nutrition and Physical Activity Guidelines Advisory Committee. (2006). American Cancer Society guidelines on nutrition and physical activity for cancer prevention: Reducing the risk of cancer with healthy food choices and physical activity. *CA Cancer Journal for Clinicians, 56,* 254–281.

Layton, J., & Nice, K. (2007). How hybrid cars work. Available at www.howstuffworks.com/hybrid-car.htm.

Lemonick, M. D. (2000, October 30). Teens before their time. *Time,* pp. 66–74.

Li, S., Chen, W., Srinivasan, S. R., Bond, M. G., Tang, R., Urbina, E. M., & Berenson, G. S.

(2003). Childhood cardiovascular risk factors and carotid vascular changes in adulthood: The Bogalusa Heart Study. *Journal of the American Medical Association, 290,* 2271–2276.

Lichtenstein, A. H., Appel, L. J., Brands, M. Carnethon, M., Daniels, S., Franch, H. A., Franklin, B., Kris-Etherton, P. Harris, W. S., Howard, B., Karanja, N., Lefevre, M., Rudel, L., Sacks, F., Van Horn, L., Winston, M., & Wylie-Rosett, J. (2006). Diet and lifestyle recommendations revision 2006: A scientific statement from the American Heart Association Nutrition Committee. *Circulation, 114,* 82–96.

Lohan, J.A. (2006). School nurses' support for bereaved students: A pilot study. *Journal of School Nursing, 22*(6), 48–52.

Ludwig, D. S., Peterson, K. E., & Gortmaker, S. L. (2001). Relation between consumption of sugar-sweetened drinks and childhood obesity: A prospective, observational analysis. *The Lancet, 357,* 505–508.

Lucile Packard Children's Hospital. (2006). Adolescent bariatric surgery. Available at www.lpch.org/clinicalspecialtiesservices/clinicalsepcialities/centerhealthyweight/bariatricsurgery.htm.

Macera, C. A., Ham, S. A., Yore, M. M., Jones, D. A., Ainsworth, B. E., Kimsey, C. D., & Kohl, H. W. (2005). Prevalence of physical activity in the United States: Behavioral Risk Factor Surveillance System, 2001. *Preventing Chronic Disease, 2*(2), A17. Available at www.cdc.gov/ pcd/issues/2005/apr/04_0114.htm.

Malina, R. M. (2001). Physical activity and fitness: Pathways from childhood to adulthood. *American Journal of Human Biology, 13*(2), 162–172.

Meadows, M. (2001). Heading off hair-care disasters: Use caution with relaxers and dye. *FDA Consumer, 35*(1), 21–24.

Meadows, M. (2004). Preventing serious drug interactions. *FDA Consumer, 38*(4), 12–17.

Meadows, M. (2006). Cracking down on health fraud. *FDA Consumer, 40*(6). Available at www.fda.gov/fdac/606_toc.html.

Michigan State Board of Education. (2004). *Policy on quality character education.* Michigan Department of Education. Available at www.michigan.gov/documents/Character_policy_final_94134_7.pdf.

Mokdad, A. H., Marks, J. S., Stroup, D. F., & Gerberding, J. L. (2005). Correction: Actual causes of death in the United States, 2000. *Journal of the American Medical Association, 293,* 293–294.

National Association of Sport and Physical Education. (2004). *Physical activity guidelines for children ages 5–12* (2nd ed.). Reston, VA: Author.

National Campaign for Hearing Health. (2004). *Toxic noise.* Available at www.hearinghealth.net/cms/index.cfm?displayArticle=16.

National Campaign to Pevent Teen Pregnancy. (2002, February). *Not just another single issue: Teen pregnancy prevention's link to other critical social issues.* Washington, DC.

National Campaign to Prevent Teen Pregnancy. (2006). *National teen pregnancy and birth data.* Washington, DC: Author. Available at www.teenpregnancy.org/resources/data/national.asp.

National Foundation for Fetal Alcohol Syndrome. (2003). What is fetal alcohol syndrome? Available at www.nofas.org/faqs.aspx?id=9.

National Highway Traffic Safety Administration. (2006). *Traffic safety facts research note 2005: Misuse of child restraints.* Washington, DC: U.S. Department of Transportation.

National Institute on Alcohol Abuse and Alcoholism. (2000). *10th special report to the U.S. Congress on alcohol and health.* Washington, DC: United States Department of Health and Human Services, National Institutes of Health.

National Mental Health Association. (2005). *Depression: What you need to know.* Alexandria, VA: Author. Available at www.nmha.org/infoctr/factsheets/21.cfm.

National Oceanic and Atmospheric Administration. (2007). Global warming: Frequently asked questions. Available at lwf.ncdc.noaa.gov/oa/climate/globalwarming.html.

National Sleep Foundation. (2000). *Adolescent sleep needs and patterns: Research report and resource guide.* Washington, DC: Author.

National Sleep Foundation. (2006). *2006 Sleep in America Poll.* Washington, DC: Author. Available at www.sleepfoundation.org/site/c.hulxkjmolxf/b.2417353/k.6764/Sleep-in-America_Polls.htm.

Nemours Foundation. (2006). About birth control: What you need to know. Available at kidshealth.org/teen/sexual_health/contraception/contraception.html.

Nice, K. (2005). How hybrid cars work. Available at www.auto.howstuffworks.com/hybrid-car.htm.

Nieman, D. C. (2003). *Exercise testing and prescription: A health-related approach.* New York: McGraw-Hill.

Nordenberg, T. (2000, March/April). Death of the party: All the rave—GHB's hazards go unheeded. *FDA Consumer,* pp. 14–19.

Norton, R., Galgali, G., Campbell, A. J., Reid, I. R., Robinson, E., Butler, M., & Gray, H. (2001). Is physical activity protective against hip fracture in frail older people? *Age and Ageing, 30*(3), 262–264.

Office of Air and Radiation. (2006). *A brief guide to mold, moisture, and your home.* Washington, DC: U.S. Environmental Protection Agency. Available at www.epa.gov/mold/moldguide.html.

Office of National Drug Control Policy. (2002, April). *Drug policy information clearinghouse fact sheet: MDMA (Ecstasy).* Available at www.whitehousedrugpolicy.gov/.

Office of National Drug Control Policy. (2003a). *Drug policy information clearinghouse fact sheet: MDMA (Ecstasy).* Available at www.whitehousedrugpolicy.gov/ drugfact/meth amphetamine/index.html.

Office of National Drug Control Policy. (2003b, October). *What Americans need to know about marijuana: Important facts about our nation's most misunderstood illegal drug.* Available at www.whitehousedrugpolicy.gov/publications/amer_know_marij.

Page, R. M., & Page, T. S. (2007). *Promoting health and emotional well-being in your classroom* (4th ed.). Sudbury, MA: Jones & Bartlett.

Page, R. M., Yanagishita, J., Suwanteerangkul, J., Zarco, E. P., Lee, C. M., & Miao, N. F. (2006). Hopelessness and loneliness among suicide attempters in school-based samples of Taiwanese, Philippine and Thai adolescents. *School Psychology International, 27*(5), 583–598.

Parker, J. F., & Simon, H. K. (2004). Eye injuries due to paintball sports: A case series. *Pediatric Emergency Care, 20*(9), 602–604.

Patel, D. R. (2006). Musculoskeletal injuries in sports. *Primary Care, 33*(2), 545–579.

Perle, L. (2007, March). Talking to kids about TV and movie violence. Commonsense Media. Available at www.commonsensemedia.org.

Pharmaceutical News. (2005, March 3). Antidepressants prescribed to children will have Black Box labels warnings. *Pharmaceutical News.* Available at www.news-medical.net/?id=8163.

Pinyerd, B., & Zipf, W. B. (2005). Puberty—timing is everything! *Journal of Pediatric Nursing, 20*(2), 75–87.

President's Council on Physical Fitness and Sports. (2003). *The president's challenge: Physical activity and fitness awards program.* Bloomington, IN: The President's Challenge.

Rabinowitz, P. M. (2000). Noise-induced hearing loss. *American Family Physician, 61,* 2749–2762.

Rados, C. (2005a). Safeguards for children taking antidepressants strengthened. *FDA Consumer, 39*(1). Available at www.fda.gov/fdac/features/2005/105_kids.html.

Rados, C. (2005b). Teen tanning hazards. *FDA Consumer, 39*(2), 8–9.

Rideout, V., Roberts, D. F., & Foehr, U. G. (2005). *Generation M: Media in the lives of 8–18 year-olds.* Menlo Park, CA: Kaiser Family Foundation.

Robinson, J. K., Rigel, D. S., & Amonette, R. A. (2000). Summertime sun protection used by adults for their children. *Journal of the American Academy of Dermatology, 42*(5), 746–753.

Robinson, T. N., Chang, J. Y., Haydel, K. F., & Killen, J. D. (2001). Overweight concerns and body dissatisfaction among third-grade children: The impacts of ethnicity and socioeconomic status. *Journal of Pediatrics, 138,* 181–187.

Rodriquez, J. O., & Lavina, A. M. (2003). Prevention and treatment of common eye injuries in sports. *American Family Physician, 67,* 1481–1496.

Rushton, J. L., Forcier, M., & Schectman, R. M. (2002). Epidemiology of depressive symptoms in the National Longitudinal Study of Adolescent Health. *Journal of American Child Adolescent Psychiatry, 41*(2), 199–205.

Sallis, J. F., & Patrick, K. (1994). Physical activity guidelines for adolescents: Consensus statement. *Pediatric Exercise Science, 6,* 302–314.

Schmidt, C. W. (2003). A weighty issue for children. *Environmental Health Perspectives, 111*(13), A701–A707.

Schur, E. A. Sanders, M., & Steiner, H. (2000). Body dissatisfaction and dieting in young children. *International Journal of Eating Disorders, 27,* 74–82.

Sharkey, B. J. (2002). *Fitness and Health* (5th ed.). Champaign, IL: Human Kinetics.

Small, S., & Bogenschneider, K. (1994). *Youth at risk for early sexual activity and teenage parenthood.* Wisconsin Youth Futures Technical Report 11. Madison, WI: University of Wisconsin-Madison, Cooperative Extension Service. Available at www.cyfernet.org/research/youthfut11.html.

Society for Neuroscience. (2006). *Brain facts: A primer on the brain and nervous system.* Washington, DC: Author.

Story, M., Kaphingst, K. M., & French, S. (2006). The role of schools in obesity prevention. *The Futures of Children, 16*(1), 109–142.

Sturm, R. (2005). Childhood obesity—what we can learn from existing data on societal trends, part 2. *Preventing Chronic Disease, 2*(2), A20. Available from www.cdc.gov/pcd/issues/2005/apr/04_0039.htm.

Tan, J. K., Vasey, K., & Fung, K. Y. (2001). Beliefs and perceptions of patients with acne. *Journal of the American Academy of Dermatology, 44*(3), 439–444.

Teague, S. (2005, February 9). H20 hazing harmful to health. The Orion Online. Available at www.theorion.com/media/storage/paper889/news/2005/02/09/APledgesDeath/H2O-Hazing.Harmful.To.Health-1507285.shtml.

Technical Assistance Partnership for Child and Family Mental Health. (2005). *Preventing tragedy: Bringing an end to youth suicide.* Washington, DC: T. A. Partnership. Available at www.tapartnership.org/specialtopics/preventing_tragedy.asp.

Troiano, R. P., Macera, C. A., & Ballard-Barbash, R. (2001). Be physically active each day: How can we know? *Journal of Nutrition, 131,* 451S–460S.

UNAIDS. (2006). *UNAIDS/WHO AIDS epidemic update: December 2006.* Available at www.unaids.org/en/HIV_data/epi2006.

Ungar, M. (2005a). *Handbook for working with children and youth: Pathways to resilience across cultures and contexts.* London: Sage.

Ungar, M. (2005b). Resilience among children in child welfare, corrections, mental health and education settings: Recommendations for service. *Child and Youth Care Forum, 34*(6), 445–464.

U.S. Census Bureau. (2007). *World population information–population clocks.* Available at www.census.gov/ipc/www/world.html.

U.S. Department of Agriculture and U.S. Department of Health and Human Services. (2000). *Nutrition and your health: Dietary guidelines for Americans* (5th ed.). Home and Garden Bulletin No. 232, Washington, DC: U.S. Government Printing Office.

U.S. Department of Health and Human Services. (1996). *Physical activity and health: A report of the surgeon general.* Atlanta U.S. Department of Health and Human Services, Centers for Disease Control and Prevention, National Center for Chronic Disease Prevention and Health Promotion.

U.S. Department of Health and Human Services. (2000a). *Oral health in America: A report of the surgeon general—executive summary.* Rockville, MD: U.S. Department of Health and Human Services, National Institute of Dental and Craniofacial Research, National Institutes of Health.

U.S. Department of Health and Human Services. (2000b). *Reducing tobacco use: A report of the surgeon general.* Atlanta: U.S. Department of Health and Human Services, Centers for Disease Control and Prevention, National Center for Chronic Disease Prevention and Health Promotion.

U.S. Department of Health and Human Services and U.S. Department of Agriculture. (2005a). *Dietary guidelines for Americans* (6th ed.). Washington, DC: U.S. Government Printing Office.

U.S. Department of Health and Human Services and U.S. Department of Agriculture. (2005b). *Finding your way to a healthier you: Based on the Dietary Guidelines for Americans.* Washington, DC: U.S. Government Printing Office.

U.S. Drug Enforcement Administration. (2001). *Statement of Asa Hutchinson, administrator, Drug Enforcement Administration, before the Senate Caucus on International Narcotics Control, December 4.* Available at www.usdoj.gov/dea/pubs/cngrtest/ ct120401.html.

Van den Bulck, J. (2004). Television viewing, computer game playing, and Internet use and self-reported time to bed and time out of bed in secondary-school children. *Sleep, 27*(1), 101–104.

Voelker, R. (2003). Researchers probe depression in children. *Journal of the American Medical Association, 289,* 3078–3079.

World Health Organization. (2002). *The world health report 2002: Reducing risks, promoting healthy life.* Available at www.who.int/whr/en.

Woteki, C. E., Facinoli, S. L., & Schor, D. (2001). Keep food safe to eat. Healthful food must be safe as well as nutritious. *Journal of Nutrition, 131,* 502S–509S.

Zimmerman, R. K., Middleton, D. B., & Smith, N. J. (2003). Vaccines for persons at high risk due to medical conditions, occupation, environment, or lifestyle, 2003. *Journal of Family Practice, 52*(1), S22–S35.

SECTION 3 THREE

Totally Awesome Teaching Strategies™

Totally Awesome Teaching Strategies™

Totally Awesome Teaching Strategies™ are designed to help students become health literate and master the performance indicators established for each of the National Health Education Standards.

KINDERGARTEN

Which Is Which?

HEALTH EDUCATION STANDARDS

- Students will comprehend concepts related to health promotion and disease prevention to enhance health.
- Students will demonstrate the ability to practice health-enhancing behaviors and avoid or reduce health risks.

PERFORMANCE INDICATORS

- Identify that healthy behaviors impact personal health.
- Demonstrate behaviors to avoid or reduce health risks.

HEALTH GOALS

- I will use medicine in safe ways.
- I will choose safe and healthful products. (Consumer and Community Health)

MATERIALS

Student master "Medicine or Food?"; poster paper; glue; four different types of over-the-counter (OTC) pills or capsules that may also look like candy; four different kinds of candy that can be mistaken for pills or capsules; TM-1, "Learn Health Facts," Appendix A

MOTIVATION

1 Divide a large sheet of poster paper into eight equal sections. In four sections, glue an OTC pill or capsule. In the four other sections, glue a piece of candy. In each of the eight squares, write *Medicine* under each OTC pill and *Candy* under each piece of candy. Temporarily cover these words with strips of paper.

2 Tell students they are going to try to guess which items are medicines and which are candies. Students will find that it may be difficult to distinguish between the two.

Hold up each section and, as volunteers guess, remove the strip of paper to reveal whether each is a medicine or candy.

3 Review the answers students gave. It will become obvious that students will not always be able to distinguish between what is a medicine and what is a candy. Explain that if they took the medicine and thought they were taking a candy, they might harm their bodies. They might become dizzy. They might feel tired or drowsy. They might experience a rapid heart rate.

4 Stress to students that a person should not distinguish between products like medicines and candy by appearance only. This is the reason it is important never to take something from another person if there is doubt about what that product is. Suppose a person finds something in her home and does not know what that product is. That person should not put that product in her mouth. The product could be a medicine. Emphasize also that they should never accept anything from a stranger. A stranger may not care about the student's health and might offer something that could be harmful to the body.

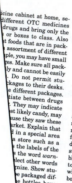

cine cabinet at home, se-
different OTC medicines
drugs and bring only the
or boxes to class. Also
t foods that are in pack-
assortment of different
ple, you may have small
es. Make sure all pack-
ly and cannot be easily
. Do not permit stu-
ckages to their desks.
tiate between drugs
. They may indicate
st likely candy, may
use they saw these
rket. Explain that
d in a special area
a store such as a
s the labels of the
e the word *warn-*
lect other words
nize. Show stu-
e packaged dif-
e bottles have

6 After students begin to differentiate between medicines and foods, distribute the student master "Medicine or Food?" Instruct students to draw a circle around the word *medicine* or *food* in each picture to identify the appropriate substance. Have students share their answers.

EVALUATION

Show TM-1, "Learn Health Facts," and review the four items on this master. Have students identify one health fact from this lesson. Then ask a question about this fact that students need to answer. Have students tell a goal about medicine safety. Describe different situations for the students and ask them what they would do if they were in these situations. In this way, students can show whether they are responsible and are cooperating with people who want to keep them healthy and safe. For example, while walking on the playground, you find a bottle with what looks like candy inside. What would you do? (Take it to a responsible adult, and do not eat what is inside.)

e McGraw-Hill Companies, Inc.

CHAPTER FIFTEEN

Using the Totally Awesome Teaching Strategies™

A teaching strategy is a technique that a facilitator or teacher uses to help a student (1) understand a particular concept, or (2) develop and practice a specific life skill. *Totally Awesome Teaching Strategies*™ are teaching strategies that contain a clever title, designated content area, designated grade level, suggestions for infusion into curriculum areas other than health, health literacy, health education standards, performance indicators, health goals, materials, motivation, evaluation, and suggestions for multicultural infusion and inclusion. Totally Awesome Teaching Strategies™ are designed to help students become health literate and master the performance indicators established for each of the National Health Education Standards. This chapter contains Totally Awesome Teaching Strategies™. The following discussion describes their unique design.

The Design of the Totally Awesome Teaching Strategies™

The **Totally Awesome Teaching Strategies**™ include the following:

- *Clever title*. A clever title is set in boldfaced type on the left side of the page.
- *Designated content area*. The content area for which the teaching strategy is designed appears in the upper left-hand corner: Mental and Emotional Health; Family and Social Health; Growth and Development; Nutrition; Personal Health and Physical Activity; Alcohol, Tobacco, and Other Drugs; Communicable and Chronic Diseases; Consumer and Community Health; Environmental Health; and Injury Prevention and Safety. A teaching strategy may include content from more than one content area. The additional content areas for which the teaching strategy is appropriate are identified in parentheses next to the life skills/health goals. The six categories of risk behaviors identified by the Centers for Disease Control and Prevention are included within one or more of the content areas: behaviors that contribute to unintentional and intentional injuries; tobacco use; alcohol and other drug use; sexual behaviors that contribute to unintended pregnancy, HIV infection, and other sexually transmitted diseases (STDs); dietary patterns that contribute to disease; and insufficient physical activity.
- *Designated grade level*. The grade level for which the teaching strategy is appropriate appears directly beneath the designated content area in the upper left-hand corner.

FIGURE 15-1

Curriculum Infusion

Symbols used to designate the curriculum areas into which the teaching strategies are infused.

- *Infusion into curriculum areas other than health.* **Infusion** is the integration of a subject area into another area or areas of the curriculum. Teaching strategies are designed to be infused into several curriculum areas other than health education: art studies, foreign language, home economics, language arts, physical education, math studies, music studies, science studies, social studies, and visual and performing arts. The curriculum area into which the teaching strategy is designed to be infused is designated by a symbol that appears to the right of the boldfaced clever title (Figure 15-1).
- *Health literacy.* **Health literacy** is competence in critical thinking and problem solving, responsible and productive citizenship, self-directed learning, and effective communication. The teaching strategies are designed to promote competency in health literacy. Four symbols are used to describe the health-literate individual: critical thinker, responsible citizen, self-directed learner, and effective communicator (Figure 15-2). The symbol designating one of the four components of health literacy appears to the right of the symbol designating curriculum infusion.
- *Health education standards.* Health education standards are standards that specify what

students should know and be able to do. They involve the knowledge and skills essential to the development of health literacy (Joint Committee on Health Education Standards, 2006). The health education standard is listed under this boldfaced subheading.
- *Performance indicators.* Performance indicators are the specific concepts students should know and skills they should be able to perform in order to achieve each of the broader health education standards (Joint Committee on Health Education Standards, 2006). The performance indicator for the teaching strategy is listed under this boldfaced subheading.
- *Health goals.* **Health goals** are actions that promote health literacy, maintain and improve health, prevent disease, and reduce health-related risk behaviors. The life skills for the primary content area are listed first under this boldfaced subheading. Life skills for other content areas covered in the teaching strategy appear in italics and are identified in parentheses.
- *Materials.* The **materials** are the items needed to do the teaching strategy. The materials used in the teaching strategies are readily available and inexpensive. They are listed under this boldfaced subheading. Teaching masters that identify steps to follow to master the

FIGURE 15-2

Health Literacy

Symbols used to designate the category of health literacy promoted by the teaching strategies.

National Health Education Standards used in the evaluation also are listed under this bold-faced subheading.

- *Motivation.* The **motivation** portion presents step-by-step directions to follow when doing the teaching strategy. The motivation includes a creative way to teach the health knowledge and skills students need to master the health education standards, performance objectives, and life skills. The motivation is listed under this boldfaced subheading.

- *Evaluation.* The **evaluation** is the means of measuring the students' mastery of the health education standards, the performance indicators, and the life skills. A suggested way to evaluate students' mastery of at least one of the National Health Education Standards is described under this boldfaced subheading.

- *Multicultural infusion.* **Multicultural infusion** is the adaptation of the teaching strategy to include ideas that promote an awareness and appreciation of the culture and background of different people. Suggestions for adapting the teaching strategy to incorporate learning about people of varied cultures and backgrounds are included under this bold-faced subheading.

- *Inclusion.* **Inclusion** is the adaptation of the teaching strategy to assist and include students with special learning challenges and may include enrichment suggestions for the gifted and reteaching ideas for students who are learning disabled. Suggestions for adapting the teaching strategy to assist students with special learning challenges are included under this boldfaced subheading.

The effectiveness of comprehensive school health education is very much dependent on the quality and creativity of the teaching strategies that are utilized in the classroom. You will want your lessons to be motivating and challenging. This section of the book presents *totally awesome teaching strategies*™ that can be used effectively in the classroom.

FAMILY HEALTH Newsletter

Dear Parent,

Your child will be learning life skills for health in school. Health goals are actions that promote health literacy, maintain and improve health, prevent disease, and reduce health-related risk behaviors. Health goals are learned and practiced for a lifetime.

Your child will practice other skills as he or she learns life skills for health. My health lessons are creative and meaningful. They help your child develop skills in art, language arts, visual and performing arts, foreign languages, social studies, math, music, physical education, home economics, and science. They also help your child become a critical thinker and problem solver, a responsible and productive citizen, a self-directed learner, and an effective communicator. I have included lessons to help your child gain an appreciation of people who are different from your child.

I will teach your child how to make wise choices. I will encourage your child to do the following:

- Make choices that are healthful.
- Make choices that are safe.
- Make choices that follow school laws and school rules.
- Make choices that show you care about others.
- Make choices that follow family rules.

I also will teach your child ways to say "no" when she or he is pressured by others to do something harmful, unsafe, illegal, or something that harms others or is against family rules.

From time to time, I will be sending you a Dear Parent Letter. Each Dear Parent Letter will tell you what your child is learning. I also will be sending you a copy of a Health Plan. A Health Plan is a plan that helps your child develop a healthful habit. For example, your child might have a Health Plan that includes brushing and flossing the teeth each day. You can help your child develop this habit. You can go over the Health Plan with your child and encourage your child to complete the Health Plan.

I want to work with you to keep your child healthy and safe. Should you have any questions, please write them on the back of this letter. Have your child return the letter to me. I will be in touch with you.

I hope today finds you and your family in good health.

Warm regards,

FAMILY HEALTH Newsletter

Dear Parent,

Your child will be learning life skills for health in school. Health goals are actions that promote health literacy, maintain and improve health, prevent disease, and reduce health-related risk behaviors. Health goals are learned and practiced for a lifetime. Your child will practice other skills as she or he learns life skills for health. My health lessons are creative and meaningful. They help your child develop skills in art, language arts, visual and performing arts, foreign languages, social studies, math, music, physical education, home economics, and science. They also help your child become a critical thinker and problem solver, a responsible and productive citizen, a self-directed learner, and an effective communicator. I have included lessons to help your child gain an appreciation of people who are different from him or her.

I will use *The Responsible Decision-Making Model* to help your child learn how to make responsible decisions. I will encourage your child to evaluate each possible decision by asking the following questions:

- Will this decision result in an action that promotes my health and the health of others?
- Will this decision result in an action that promotes my safety and the safety of others?
- Will this decision result in an action that is legal?
- Will this decision result in an action that shows respect for myself and others? Will this decision result in an action that follows the guidelines of responsible adults including my parent(s) or guardian?

I also will teach your child resistance skills he or she can use when pressured by peers to engage in actions that are harmful, unsafe, illegal, or which show disrespect for others and for family guidelines.

From time to time, your child will bring home Health Behavior Contracts. A Health Behavior Contract is a written guide that helps your child develop a healthful habit. For example, your child might have a Health Behavior Contract that asks her or him to eat four servings of vegetables each day. You can help your child develop this habit. You can review the Health Behavior Contract with your child. You can discuss ways to get these four servings each day. You can encourage your child to have a healthful diet.

I want to work with you to keep your child healthy and safe. Should you have any questions, please write them on the back of this letter. Have your child return the letter to me. I will be in touch with you.

I hope today finds you and your family in good health.

Warm regards,

FAMILY HEALTH Newsletter

Dear Parent,

More than likely you are aware that many young people participate in risk behaviors with devastating results. Risk behaviors threaten self-esteem, harm health, and increase the likelihood of illness, injury, and premature death. The Centers for Disease Control and Prevention has identified six categories of risk behaviors of special concern:

1. Behaviors that contribute to unintentional and intentional injuries
2. Tobacco use
3. Alcohol and other drug use
4. Sexual behaviors that contribute to unintended pregnancy, HIV infection, and other sexually transmitted diseases
5. Dietary patterns that contribute to disease
6. Insufficient physical activity

These risk behaviors usually are established at a young age and continue into adulthood. Fortunately, they can be prevented. One way to prevent risk behaviors is to educate young people and help them develop life skills for health. This is the purpose of the health education course your child is taking. Your child will gain health knowledge and develop health goals in many areas of health: Mental and Emotional Health; Family and Social Health; Growth and Development; Nutrition; Personal Health and Physical Activity; Alcohol, Tobacco, and Other Drugs; Communicable and Chronic Diseases; Consumer and Community Health; Environmental Health; and Injury Prevention and Safety. It is my hope that your child will make a commitment to being healthy and do the following:

- Use health knowledge
- Choose wellness behaviors instead of risk behaviors
- Choose to be in healthful situations
- Choose to have healthful relationships
- Make responsible decisions that promote health, protect safety, protect laws, show respect for self and others, follow your guidelines, and demonstrate good character
- Use resistance skills and say "no" to peers when pressured to do something harmful, unsafe, illegal, disrespectful, or in conflict with the guidelines you have set
- Possess protective factors including a supportive and nurturing environment
- Be resilient or capable of recovering, bouncing back, and learning from misfortune, change, or pressure
- Be health literate and have competency in critical thinking and problem solving, responsible and productive citizenship, self-directed learning, and effective communication

I want to work closely with you, as I believe the home and school are important in educating students about health. Should you have any questions or suggestions, please contact me.

I hope today finds you and your family in good health.

Warm regards,

KINDERGARTEN

My Choices

HEALTH EDUCATION STANDARDS

- Students will comprehend concepts related to health promotion and disease prevention to enhance health.
- Students will demonstrate the ability to use goal-setting skills to enhance health.
- Students will demonstrate the ability to practice health-enhancing behaviors and avoid or reduce health risks.

PERFORMANCE INDICATORS

- Identify that healthy behaviors impact personal health.
- Identify a short-term personal health goal and take action toward achieving the goal.
- Demonstrate behaviors to avoid or reduce health risks.

HEALTH GOALS

- I will make responsible decisions.
- I will say "no" to wrong decisions.

MATERIALS

Student master "Make Wise Choices to Be at Your Best"; student master "Say No"; red construction paper; green construction paper; TM-18, "Make Wise Decisions," Appendix A

MOTIVATION

1 Give each student a copy of the student master "Make Wise Choices to Be at Your Best." Explain the importance of making wise choices. Wise choices are healthful. Have students point to the girl eating the apple. She makes a healthful choice. Have students tell you another healthful choice.

2 Have students point to the boy who is skating. Explain that he is careful when he skates. He does not skate in the street. He wears a helmet, knee pads, and elbow pads. Wise choices are safe. Have students tell you another safe choice.

3 Have students point to the boy who is holding his baby sister. Explain that he holds his sister because he cares about her. Wise choices show that a person cares about others. Have students tell ways they can show they care about others.

4 Have students point to the boy who is holding the stop sign. He is on the safety patrol at his school. He helps boys and girls follow school rules. He helps them cross the street. Wise choices follow laws and school rules. Have students tell other choices that follow laws and school rules.

5 Have students point to the girl setting the table for dinner. She is following family rules. All families have rules. The rules may tell what time the children must be in bed. Children who follow this rule are ready for bed at this time. The rules may tell children where toys are to be kept. Children who follow this rule put their toys back in this place when they are done playing. Have students share a rule from their families.

6 Have students point to the girl putting her toy away. She works hard to keep her room clean. She does what her parents ask her to do. The girl is showing good character.

7 Explain to students that some choices are not wise. It would not be wise for the boy to skate in the street. It would not be wise for him to skate between parked cars. It would not be wise to talk to a stranger. It would not be wise to smoke a cigarette. If someone tries to get you to do something that is not a wise choice, say "no."

8 Give each student a copy of the student master "Say No." Explain that when someone tries to get them to do something that is not a wise choice, they can say "no." Go over the steps on the student master "Say No."

Mental and Emotional Health

EVALUATION

Explain to students they must know the four steps to make wise decisions. Then review TM-18, "Make Wise Decisions."

Give each student a sheet of red construction paper and a sheet of green construction paper. They can print NO on the red construction paper and YES on the green construction paper. Explain that you are going to ask them to make choices that demonstrate responsible decisions. If the choice is wise, they should hold up the green paper and say YES. If the choice is not wise, they should hold up the red paper and say NO, showing that they are using their resistance skills. Then they should tell you why they said no.

1. Let's eat an apple. (YES)
2. Let's run across the street. (NO. It is not safe.)
3. Let's call your parent to say you came to my house to play. (YES)
4. Let's ride double on my bike. (NO. It is not safe. It is against the law.)
5. Let's wait until the light is green to cross the street. (YES)
6. Let's push to get ahead in line to go down the slide. (NO. It is not safe. It does not show I care about others.)
7. Let's play inside my house. No grown-up is home. (NO. It does not follow my family rules.)
8. Let's smoke a cigarette. (NO. It is not good for my health.)
9. Let's call someone an ugly name. (NO. It does not show I care about others.)
10. Let's play with matches. (NO. It is not safe.)

MULTICULTURAL INFUSION

Have students do the same evaluation. This time, teach them how to say "yes" and "no" in other languages. For example, in French *yes* is *oui* (sounds like "we") and *no* is *non* (sounds like "nawh"). When students hold up the green paper, they will say *oui*. When students hold up the red paper, they will say *non*.

Student Master

Make Wise Choices to Be at Your Best

Make choices that
are healthful.

Make choices that follow
laws and school rules.

Make choices
that are safe.

Make choices that
show good character.

Make choices that show
you care about others.

Make choices that
follow family rules.

Say No

SAY NO

1. Look at the person.

2. Say, "No."

3. Tell them why you are saying no.

4. Do not change your mind.

KINDERGARTEN

My Family

HEALTH EDUCATION STANDARDS

- Students will comprehend concepts related to health promotion and disease prevention to enhance health.
- Students will demonstrate the ability to practice health-enhancing behaviors and avoid or reduce health risks.
- Students will demonstrate the ability to use interpersonal communication skills to enhance health and avoid or reduce health risks.

PERFORMANCE INDICATORS

- Identify that healthy behaviors impact personal health.
- Demonstrate healthy practices and behaviors to maintain or improve personal health.
- Demonstrate healthy ways to express needs, wants, and feelings.

HEALTH GOALS

- I will get along with my family.
- I will follow safety rules for home and school. (Injury Prevention and Safety)

MATERIALS

Student master "My Family"; crayons; small paper bags; old magazines; TM-10, "Communicate," Appendix A

MOTIVATION

1 Introduce the term *family*. A **family** is a group of people who are related or who live together. Bring old magazines to class and cut out pictures that show families engaged in healthful activities. Be sure to show different kinds of families such as single-parent families, families with two parents, families with one or several children, families with grandparents, and families of different cultures.

2 Show the class the pictures of families. For each picture, have students tell what they think the people in the family are doing to enjoy themselves and each other. Have students also tell how the families differ.

3 Explain to students that there are many different kinds of families and that all family members can spend meaningful times with each other. Explain that each member of a family has a responsibility to keep other members safe, regardless of the activity the family is enjoying. For example, you might show a family at a cookout and point out that the young children in the family are kept away from the fire so that they do not become harmed.

4 Emphasize that parents or guardians have a responsibility to protect their children from harm. Children should appreciate the decisions or choices their parents or guardians must make to help keep them safe.

5 Distribute copies of the student master "My Family," and have students draw a picture that shows them doing something with one or more of their family members. Emphasize that their pictures should show they are doing something enjoyable and also safe.

473

6 After students complete their pictures, have them share what they have drawn. Students should explain not only what they are doing but also when it is safe to do this activity. Give each student a small paper bag. Decorate your own bag first and explain to students that they will make a family member puppet. Students can color the different parts of the face and draw facial features such as eyes and ears. The puppet will represent a family member they like. When they finish their puppets, they will introduce the puppet to the class. Students are to pretend that the puppet is the family member. They are to talk as if they are the puppet and tell why they are a good family member. Begin this activity by demonstrating your own puppet. Place the paper bag on your hand in order to show students the hand puppet. Say something like, "Hi, I'm Mother Puppet and I love everyone in my family. I help my children do their homework. I talk to them when they are sad." Select students to take turns with their puppets.

EVALUATION

Explain to students that using good communication skills promotes good health. Then review TM-10, "Communicate."

Have students share information about family activities that give them an opportunity to do things with members of their family and a chance to get to know one another better. Also have them share how their family members influence them to make responsible or wise choices. For example, a parent might insist that their child wear a helmet when riding a bicycle.

MULTICULTURAL INFUSION

Have students share activities they do with family members that are common to their cultural background. For example, students may go to certain places with family members on special occasions. They may celebrate certain holidays or eat certain foods.

Student Master

My Family

Name

Draw your family.
Show your family doing something fun and safe.

SOCIAL STUDIES

CRITICAL THINKER

KINDERGARTEN

Being Sensitive toward Others

HEALTH EDUCATION STANDARDS

- Students will comprehend concepts related to health promotion and disease prevention to enhance health.
- Students will demonstrate the ability to advocate for personal, family, and community health.

PERFORMANCE INDICATORS

- Recognize that there are multiple dimensions of health.
- Make requests to promote personal health.

HEALTH GOAL

- I will try different ways of learning.

MATERIALS

Student master "Being Helpful to Others"; paper; writing instruments; blindfolds; a book that can be read to the class; TM-1, "Learn Health Facts," Appendix A

MOTIVATION

1 Explain to students that as they grow they have different things they need. Students need food, friends, help from family members, and an education. Have students brainstorm to list the kinds of things they need every day.

2 Explain to students that sometimes people are not able to perform activities in the same way as others because their learning styles and needs may be different. Some people learn by reading, and others are more visual learners. Some have learning problems. Some have bodies that do not work in the same ways as others. For example, some people have a visual impairment. They cannot see clearly or see at all. Some people have a hearing impairment. They

may not be able to hear as well as others, or they may not be able to hear at all.

3 This activity will help students develop a sensitivity toward people who have special needs. Ask students to take a sheet of paper and draw a simple picture. Next give students blindfolds or ask them to close their eyes if you do not have blindfolds. Keeping their eyes closed, students are to try to find a sheet of paper and something with which to write. Continuing to keep their eyes closed, students are to draw the same pictures as they did when their eyes were open.

4 Discuss with students how it felt to try to do tasks when their eyes were closed. Students will say they were scared or frustrated. Explain that there are many people who either were born with a visual impairment or lost their sight at some time during their lives. These people learn and continue to make adjustments so they can perform tasks.

5 Take a book and begin to read it to the class. As you read it, gradually lower your voice so that it is barely heard. However, keep your lips moving so that it appears you are still talking. Have students share how they felt when they could not hear what you were saying. Explain that a person who has a hearing impairment may be able to hear only slightly or may not be able to hear at all. Yet these people have many of the same needs as everyone else.

6 Tell students that people who are not able to see or hear still have the same needs as everyone else. In addition, these people may sometimes need help. Ask students to share how they might help others who may have visual or hearing impairments. For example, a student might help a person who has a visual impairment by offering his or her arm to guide the person. A student might speak more slowly and look at a person who has a hearing impairment so that person can read their lips. *Lip reading* is watching another person's lips as they form words.

7 Distribute the student master "Being Helpful to Others." Explain that the person in the wheelchair has a disability. This person cannot walk. A friend helps the person in the wheelchair move to another place. Have students color the picture. Students can share their pictures and tell how they would help a person in a wheelchair.

EVALUATION

Review the health facts in this lesson. Then explain the four items in TM-1, "Learn Health Facts." Walk into class and pretend that you have a visual impairment. Tell students that you need to perform certain tasks and that they are to tell you how they would help you.

For example, you may say that you need to find a pencil or that you need to walk to the back of the room. You might have students practice what they would actually do to help you. You can also pretend that you have a hearing impairment. How might students talk to you? What other ways might students help communicate to you? Ask students how they might help older family members who have visual or hearing impairments. How might they help other students who have physical disabilities? How might they help another student who has a learning style that is different than their own? It is also important for students to understand that people who have disabilities need to have the opportunity to perform tasks without the help of others. All people need a sense of accomplishment.

Being Helpful to Others

Name _____

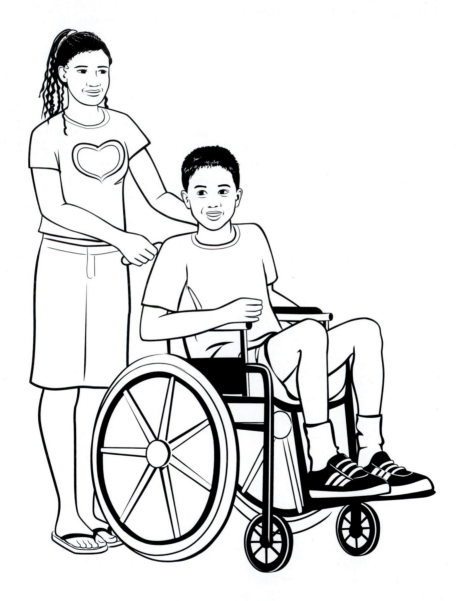

Be Helpful to Others

KINDERGARTEN

Healthful Foods Help Me Grow

HEALTH EDUCATION STANDARDS

- Students will comprehend concepts related to health promotion and disease prevention to enhance health.
- Students will demonstrate the ability to practice health-enhancing behaviors and avoid or reduce health risks.
- Students will demonstrate the ability to use goal-setting skills to enhance health.

PERFORMANCE INDICATORS

- Identify that healthy behaviors impact personal health.
- Demonstrate healthy practices and behaviors to maintain or improve personal health.
- Identify a short-term personal health goal and take action toward achieving the goal.

HEALTH GOALS

- I will eat the recommended daily amounts of food from MyPyramid.
- I will follow the Dietary Guidelines.
- I will eat healthful meals and snacks.
- I will choose habits that prevent heart disease. (Communicable and Chronic Diseases)
- I will choose habits that prevent cancer. (Communicable and Chronic Diseases)

MATERIALS

Student master "Healthful Food Choices"; student master "Healthful Foods I Like"; paper plates for each student; scissors; old magazines; crayons; TM-24, "Practice Healthful Habits," Appendix A

MOTIVATION

1 Cut out pictures from magazines that show healthful foods such as fruits and vegetables as well as foods that are not healthful such as candy and cake. Explain to students that certain kinds of foods are important in helping them grow. These foods are fruits, such as oranges, grapes, and apples, and vegetables, such as carrots, lettuce, and broccoli. Fruits and vegetables come from plants. Other kinds of foods that may be healthful come from another group that is made up of milk, yogurt, and cheese. Some foods come from animals and are kinds of meats including chicken and fish. Yet other kinds of foods come from breads, cereal, rice, and pasta. (It is not necessary for students at this age group to identify the six major nutrients found in these foods: water, proteins, carbohydrates, fats, vitamins, and minerals. However, healthful foods will contain some or all of these nutrients.) The purpose of this strategy is to have students select foods from MyPyramid that are healthful and to try to avoid foods that are made up mostly of fats, oils, and sweets.

2 After reviewing the material about healthful foods, explain to students that certain foods such as candy or cake may not be healthful because they contain sugar and oils. Fried foods may contain large amounts of fat. (You may choose to demonstrate the presence of oil or fat in food by taking a slice of a sponge cake or fried potato and pressing a tissue upon it. Students will see the oil.) Eating fatty foods can lead to cardiovascular disease. Some foods may also contribute to cancer. Explain to students that they can substitute healthful foods for foods high in fats, oils, and sweets.

3 Distribute paper plates and scissors to each student. Distribute a copy of the student master "Healthful Food Choices." Have students color the healthful foods the appropriate colors (1, red tomato, 2, orange carrots, and 3, brown breads). They are to put an X through the food that is not healthful (the slice of cake). In addition, they are to trace the corresponding numbers that reflect the number of items in each box. After completing the colors

and numbers, students are to cut around the box and place their healthful foods on the plate. Students can be selected to identify their healthful foods and the number of healthful foods in the pictures. They can also identify the food they would avoid (the one with the X placed through it).

4 You can expand this activity to identify other healthful foods and other foods that can be avoided. You can also have students look through magazines and identify foods that are healthful and foods that can be avoided because they may not be nutritious.

EVALUATION

When beginning the evaluation, review TM-24, "Practice Healthful Habits." Give examples of different kinds of foods to students. You may cut out pictures of foods from magazines and show them to students, or you may tell the class about these foods. For each food identified, have students give a thumbs-up if the food is health-ful or a thumbs-down if the food is not healthful. Have them identify foods that have been fried and can contribute to clogged arteries and perhaps even cancer. You also can evaluate the student responses on the student master, which indicate if they were able to distinguish between healthful and harmful foods. Distribute the student master "Healthful Foods I Like." Ask students to draw a healthful food in each of the four boxes and to color that food. Have the students share their masters with others.

MULTICULTURAL INFUSION

Explain that certain cultures have a basic food. For example, rice has been a basic food of Asia, and wheat bread has been a basic food of Europe throughout history. In certain cultures, people eat red meats but not fish. Students may bring in foods that are common in a certain culture. Students may share these foods with the class. As each food is identified it can be categorized, such as coming from a plant or an animal, or belonging to a group such as fruits, vegetables, milk, or cereal.

Student Master

Healthful Food Choices

Name_____

Color the food.
Trace the number.
Draw an X through the picture of the food that
is not healthful.

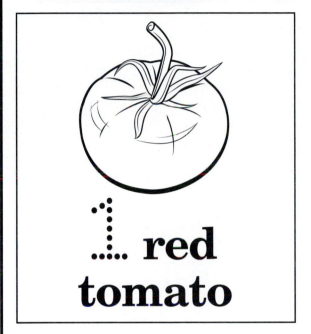

1. **red
tomato**

2. **orange
carrots**

3 **brown
breads**

4 **slice of
cake**

Student Master

Healthful Foods I Like

Name _____

Draw one healthful food in each box.
Color the four foods.

Personal Health and Physical Activity

KINDERGARTEN

A Restful Experience

HEALTH EDUCATION STANDARDS

- Students will comprehend concepts related to health promotion and disease prevention to enhance health.
- Students will demonstrate the ability to practice health-enhancing behaviors and avoid or reduce health risks.
- Students will demonstrate the ability to use goal-setting skills to enhance health.

PERFORMANCE INDICATORS

- Identify that healthy behaviors impact personal health.
- Demonstrate behaviors to avoid or reduce health risks.
- Identify a short-term personal health goal and take action toward achieving the goal.

HEALTH GOALS

- I will get plenty of sleep and rest.
- I will get plenty of exercise.
- I will choose habits that prevent heart disease. (Communicable and Chronic Diseases)

MATERIALS

Student master "Whose Heart Works Hard?"; any battery-operated toy; TM-27, "Manage Stress," Appendix A

MOTIVATION

1 Bring a battery-operated toy to class. Show students the toy and explain that the toy can operate only if the battery inside the toy is charged. Show students the battery. Start up the toy and let students see how the toy operates. Explain that the battery inside the toy serves as energy for that toy. The battery gives the toy its energy to work.

2 Explain to students that they need energy to do everything. Have students share what they do every day. They may say they play with their friends, they read, and they go to school. Explain that they need **energy** to do these activities. Explain that they get their energy from food, whereas the toy gets its energy from the battery.

3 Explain that the human body needs to rest after it has used energy. The more energy the body uses, the more important it is to rest. For example, if someone is involved in an activity for an hour, that person may feel tired. It is important to rest when feeling tired.

4 The following activity will demonstrate why people need rest. Have students make a tight fist. Explain that you are going to ask them to open their fists wide and then shut them tight. You are going to count from one to ten with each opening and closing of the fist. At the count of one, students will open their fists. At the count of two, students will close their fists. At the count of three, they will open their fists again, and so on. As students open and close their fists, they are to count from one through ten with you. Students will do sets of opening and closing their fists four times. Each time, you are to speed up the count.

5 After the fourth time, students will notice that their hands feel tired. At this point, have students rest their fists. Explain that they need to rest because they feel tired. Emphasize that when they feel tired they need to rest, otherwise an injury may occur. Explain that if you had not given them a rest, eventually they would not have been able to open and close their fists continually. At first, students would have noticed that they began to open and close their fists more slowly before stopping completely. Explain that by resting, students are allowing their bodies to return to a more energized state so that they can continue to perform activities again.

6 Explain that there are different ways to rest. Students can sleep. They can sit

483

quietly and color in a coloring book. They can watch an educational show on television.

7 Next, introduce the function of the heart. Explain that the **heart** works somewhat like a fist in that it always moves as it pumps blood throughout the body. The harder a person exercises, the faster the heart beats. When a person is at rest, the heart beats more slowly. Point to your ribs and explain that the heart is located underneath. Emphasize that resting one's body also allows the heart to beat fewer times in a given period of time. Explain that the heart rests between beats, but it can rest in a different way by beating fewer times when you rest. Emphasize that exercise helps the heart become healthier and promotes physical fitness. By exercising and resting, a person can help keep healthy.

8 Distribute the student master "Whose Heart Works Hard?" to students. Instruct students to color the circles red if the person is resting and the heart is not working hard. Tell students to color the circles green if the person is physically active and the person's heart is working hard.

EVALUATION

Explain that rest helps relieve stress by referring to TM-27, "Manage Stress." Students are going to identify ways they can rest. Tell them you are going to begin a sentence. The sentence is "I rest by . . ." Have students complete the sentence by telling ways they rest. Also have students explain how adequate rest and sleep in combination with exercise promote physical fitness and reduce the risk of cardiovascular disease.

Personal Health and Physical Activity

Whose Heart Works Hard?

Name _____

Color the circles green if the heart works hard.
Color the circles red if the heart rests.

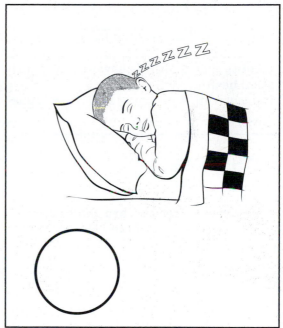

485

KINDERGARTEN

Which Is Which?

HEALTH EDUCATION STANDARDS

- Students will comprehend concepts related to health promotion and disease prevention to enhance health.
- Students will demonstrate the ability to practice health-enhancing behaviors and avoid or reduce health risks.

PERFORMANCE INDICATORS

- Identify that healthy behaviors impact personal health.
- Demonstrate behaviors to avoid or reduce health risks.

HEALTH GOALS

- I will use medicine in safe ways.
- I will choose safe and healthful products. (Consumer and Community Health)

MATERIALS

Student master "Medicine or Food?"; poster paper; glue; four different types of over-the-counter (OTC) pills or capsules that may also look like candy; four different kinds of candy that can be mistaken for pills or capsules; TM-1, "Learn Health Facts," Appendix A

MOTIVATION

1 Divide a large sheet of poster paper into eight equal sections. In four sections, glue an OTC pill or capsule. In the four other sections, glue a piece of candy. In each of the eight squares, write *Medicine* under each OTC pill and *Candy* under each piece of candy. Temporarily cover these words with strips of paper.

2 Tell students they are going to try to guess which items are medicines and which are candies. Students will find that it may be difficult to distinguish between the two.

Hold up each section and, as volunteers guess, remove the strip of paper to reveal whether each is a medicine or candy.

3 Review the answers students gave. It will become obvious that students will not always be able to distinguish between what is a medicine and what is a candy. Explain that if they took the medicine and thought they were taking a candy, they might harm their bodies. They might become dizzy. They might feel tired or drowsy. They might experience a rapid heart rate.

4 Stress to students that a person should not distinguish between products like medicines and candy by appearance only. This is the reason it is important never to take something from another person if there is doubt about what that product is. Suppose a person finds something in her home and does not know what that product is. That person should not put that product in her mouth. The product could be a medicine. Emphasize also that they should never accept anything from a stranger. A stranger may not care about the student's health and might offer something that could be harmful to the body.

Alcohol, Tobacco, and Other Drugs

5 From your medicine cabinet at home, select about five different OTC medicines and prescription drugs and bring only the empty containers or boxes to class. Also select five different foods that are in packages. Try to get an assortment of different packages. For example, you may have small jars or paper packages. Make sure all packages are closed tightly and cannot be easily opened by students. Do not permit students to take the packages to their desks. Have them look at the different packages. Ask them to differentiate between drugs (medicines) and candy. They may indicate that some products, most likely candy, may be easily identified because they saw these products in the supermarket. Explain that the drugs are purchased in a special area of a supermarket or in a store such as a drugstore. Show students the labels of the different products such as the word *warning* or the word *tablets*. Select other words students can see and recognize. Show students that medicines may be packaged differently. For example, some bottles have special caps.

6 After students begin to differentiate between medicines and foods, distribute the student master "Medicine or Food?" Instruct students to draw a circle around the word *medicine* or *food* in each picture to identify the appropriate substance. Have students share their answers.

EVALUATION

Show TM-1, "Learn Health Facts," and review the four items on this master. Have students identify one health fact from this lesson. Then ask a question about this fact that students need to answer. Have students tell a goal about medicine safety. Describe different situations for the students and ask them what they would do if they were in these situations. In this way, students can show whether they are responsible and are cooperating with people who want to keep them healthy and safe. For example, while walking in the playground, you find a bottle with what looks like candy inside. What would you do? (Take it to a responsible adult, and do not eat what is inside.)

Medicine or Food?

Name _____

Look at the picture.
Circle the correct word.

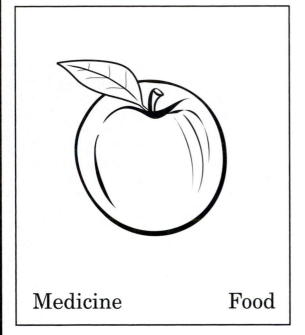

Medicine   Food

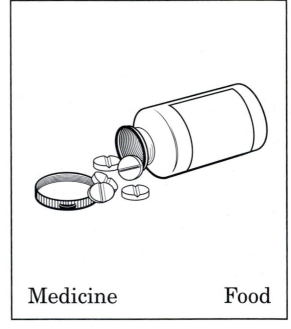

Medicine   Food

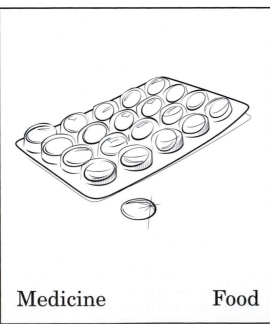

Medicine   Food

Medicine   Food

Communicable and Chronic Diseases

KINDERGARTEN

Your Germs Are Spreading

HEALTH EDUCATION STANDARD

- Students will comprehend concepts related to health promotion and disease prevention to enhance health.

PERFORMANCE INDICATORS

- Identify that healthy behaviors impact personal health.
- Describe ways to prevent communicable diseases.

HEALTH GOAL

- I will protect myself and others from germs.

MATERIALS

Family master, "Cold Tips"; dark-colored felt; chalk dust or powder; two hand puppets; TM-1, "Learn Health Facts," Appendix A

MOTIVATION

1 Explain to students that germs are spread through the air in many different ways. Explain that most people their age get a cold at least two times in a year. In other words, between one birthday and the next, most people their age will have two colds.

2 Review the signs and symptoms of a cold. Explain to students that they might know they have a cold when their nose feels stuffy. They may have a runny nose and their eyes may have a large number of tears. They may have a sore throat or they may have a headache. Not all people who have colds experience the same kinds of symptoms.

3 Explain that a cold is a disease that is spread from one person to another. A disease is being ill or not feeling well. There

are many kinds of diseases, but you are going to talk only about the common cold. Explain that the cold is common because many people get colds. Explain that one way people get colds from other people is through coughing or sneezing. For example, if you have a cold and you cough into the face of another person, that person can breathe in, or inhale, your germs. When these germs get into the other person's body, that person can then become ill.

4 To demonstrate how germs spread through the air when a person coughs, take the dark piece of felt and tape it to the wall or chalkboard. Place a hand puppet on each hand. Place chalk dust or powder in the mouth of one puppet. Hold the puppets in front of the felt. As the puppets are talking to each other, pretend to cough. As you manipulate the puppet, cough sideways across the mouth of the puppet that has the powder in its mouth. When you do this, students will notice that specks of chalk dust or powder splatter on the felt. Explain to the class that the chalk dust or powder represents germs. Have the students notice that the "germs" are now near the puppet that did not cough. Explain that the "germs" may enter the body of the other puppet. Ask the class how this can happen. (When the other puppet breathes in, or inhales, the germs can enter the body. When this happens, the person may also become ill.)

5 Explain to students that the puppet who was not ill could have been better protected. Ask students how this could have happened. (The puppet who was ill could have placed its hand over its mouth when it coughed. This would have slowed the spread of the germs.) Emphasize to students that if they have a cold, they can help protect others by covering their mouth when they cough. They can also cover their nose when they sneeze. These actions will reduce the spread of germs throughout the air. It is always helpful to provide students with healthful hints. For example, when people sneeze, they should not pinch their nostrils shut. The air from a sneeze needs to leave the nose, otherwise a person may create health problems in other parts of the body such as the ears.

6 Distribute the family master "Cold Tips" and have students take it home to share with a parent.

Select students to try your puppets. Under the same circumstances (the cough), have students tell you what they should do to stop the spread of germs from a cough. Students should demonstrate that they know how to help prevent colds from spreading. Point out that crowded conditions increase the risk of spreading a cold to others. Review student answers for accuracy.

EVALUATION

Reread the information in TM-1, "Learn Health Facts," to review how to apply information about preventing the spread of germs.

Family Master

Cold Tips

Dear Parent,

Your child is learning how to protect himself/herself if (s)he has a cold or is around others who have a cold. Speak with your child and review the tips on this sheet.

1. Always carry tissues or a handkerchief if you have a cold and are sneezing or coughing.

2. Cover your mouth and nose when you cough or sneeze.

3. Try to avoid going near others when you have a cold.

4. Wash your hands if you touch the same object that the person who has a cold has touched.

5. Get rest and drink plenty of healthful fluids if you have a cold. Water and fruit juices are good fluids to drink.

6. Do not take aspirin if the cold may actually be the flu. A person who has muscle aches, fever, or a sore throat may have the flu. Taking aspirin if a person really has the flu can cause an illness called Reye's syndrome.

7. See a doctor if the signs of a cold last more than five days and you do not feel better.

8. Do not leave used tissues around because someone else may touch them and catch the germs from the sick person.

9. Do not play sports or engage in heavy physical activity.

10. Avoid close contact with others until signs of the cold disappear.

Consumer and Community Health

KINDERGARTEN

Protectors

HEALTH EDUCATION STANDARDS

- Students will demonstrate the ability to advocate for personal, family, and community health.
- Students will demonstrate the ability to access valid information and products and services to enhance health.

PERFORMANCE INDICATORS

- Make requests to promote personal health.
- Identify trusted adults and professionals who can help promote health.

HEALTH GOAL

- I will cooperate with health helpers.

MATERIALS

Old magazines with pictures; scissors; TM-7, "Find Health Facts and Get Help," Appendix A

MOTIVATION

1 Explain that there are many people in a home, school, and community who can talk with young people about any concerns. These people are interested in protecting young people from harm.

2 You can explain that a *teacher* can help protect boys and girls in school. Adults in a family help keep children in the family safe and secure. A teacher helps children learn how to cross the street safely. A teacher also helps children learn how to solve problems by talking with them. A firefighter helps keep children safe from harm by fire and smoke. A police officer helps children keep safe from others and from danger. A member of the clergy helps children and their families solve problems.

3 Cut pictures from magazines that show people in the family, school, and community who protect health and safety. You may cut out a picture of a parent and a baby. You may cut out a picture of a guard at a school crossing guiding children across the street as they walk to school. Cut out several pictures that show different people helping boys and girls.

4 Show the pictures you have cut out to the class. When you show each picture, have a volunteer imagine and tell a story about the picture. The story should include how the picture illustrates a responsible adult protecting health by following school rules and laws.

EVALUATION

Introduce TM-7, "Find Health Facts and Get Help," to review ways to access health information. Have students name a responsible adult in

Consumer and Community Health

their community and tell how this person helps keep them safe. In doing so, they should demonstrate that they will seek help from people who will protect their physical and emotional health and their safety.

MULTICULTURAL INFUSION

Show people of different cultures doing something to help protect the health and safety of boys and girls. Explain that no matter what country people come from, there are responsible adults who care about the safety of children.

Environmental Health

KINDERGARTEN

My Friend, My Home

HEALTH EDUCATION STANDARD

- Students will comprehend concepts related to health promotion and disease prevention to enhance health.

PERFORMANCE INDICATOR

- Identify that healthy behaviors impact personal health.

HEALTH GOALS

- I will help protect the environment.
- I will help stop pollution.

MATERIALS

The poem "My Friend, My Home"; globe; art paper; crayons or markers; TM-1, "Learn Health Facts," Appendix A

MOTIVATION

1 If possible, take students to sit outside during this lesson. Talk to students about the difference between things made by nature and things made by people. Ask students to name things that they can see that are made by nature (trees, grass, flowers). Tell students that air and water are also part of nature. Explain that all living things—people, plants, and animals—need air and water to live. Ask students to name ways they use air and water every day. (We breathe the air. We drink water and wash in it.)

2 Read the poem "My Friend, My Home" aloud. Have students act out these ideas as you say them: playing in the air and the shining sun, tiny creatures running, putting toes in running water, rain coming down and flowers growing, students being

kind to the earth. Tell students that these activities are what the poem is about. Have students close their eyes and ask them to imagine each activity as you slowly read the poem again.

3 Have students name the parts of nature they heard in the poem (air, sun, breeze, water, flowers). Ask students what the poet was referring to as "my friend, my home" (the Earth). Then ask why they think the poet called the Earth "my friend, my home," and a living place. (Students might say because we live here; because the Earth takes care of us; because people, plants, and animals live here.) Explain that people need to take care of the Earth and all living things. Ask students to tell ways that they might take care of things made by nature (water the grass, stay out of flower gardens, be careful and kind to animals).

4 Tell students that keeping air and water clean is also important. Explain that clean air and water help all living things live and grow. Point out that people everywhere are working very hard to keep the earth safe and clean. Ask students what they might

do to help keep the world clean. (Throw litter away in trash cans; ask people they know to keep the world clean.) Tell them that another way students can help keep the earth safe and clean is to ask an adult before throwing something away or spraying something in the air. Explain that litter, especially sprays and liquids, can be washed into rivers and streams by the rainfall.

EVALUATION

When you return to the classroom, have each child make an "I Love You, Earth" card. It should include these words and include a picture showing activities that promote clean air and clean water. Display the cards on classroom walls with a globe nearby. Show TM-1, "Learn Health Facts," and review health facts they used to draw their cards.

My Friend, My Home

The air,
the shining sun,
a place where tiny creatures run.

The quiet breeze
across my face—
the Earth is such a living place.

Clear water runs
across my toes,
rains down
to make the flowers grow.

My friend, my home
for every day—
I'll keep it safe in every way.

KINDERGARTEN

Avoid That Car

HEALTH EDUCATION STANDARDS

- Students will demonstrate the ability to practice health-enhancing behaviors and avoid or reduce health risks.
- Students will demonstrate the ability to access valid information and products and services to enhance health.

PERFORMANCE INDICATORS

- Demonstrate behaviors to avoid or reduce health risks.
- Identify ways to locate school and community health helpers.

HEALTH GOALS

- I will follow safety rules for home and school.
- I will cooperate with health helpers. (Consumer and Community Health)

MATERIALS

Teaching master "What Do You Remember?"; transparency projector; a cardboard carton from the grocery or appliance store; chair; scissors; pencil; TM-7, "Find Health Facts and Get Help," Appendix A

MOTIVATION

1 Ask students if they have ever been walking down the street when a car with a stranger inside stopped and the stranger wanted to ask a question. Ask students to describe what they did. Some students may say that they approached the car. Others might say that they did not approach the car and ran away. Explain that most people who are traveling in cars and who stop to ask someone a question are nice. But you cannot tell if a person inside a car is nice or not. Tell students that the following activity will describe what they can do if they are approached by a stranger in a car.

2 Cut one of the large sides from a carton. Then draw an outline of a car in the shape of a convertible, and cut around the outline. You will need this shape because you will place a chair behind it so it appears that you are driving. You also will be able to reach out from the side of the car.

3 Select a student to stand ten feet away from the car. Tell this student to pretend he is walking down the street and to do what you say. Pretend you have a photograph of a puppy and say to the student, "Excuse me. I lost my puppy and I have a picture of her. Could you come over here so I can show you her picture? She is lost, and I want to know if you saw her." As the student approaches the car, reach out and grab him by the arm. Then tell the class that if you were a stranger who wanted to harm this person, you easily could have dragged him into the car.

4 With this example in mind, emphasize that you should never approach a car with a stranger inside. Reinforce the concept that most strangers are nice people; however, there are certain rules that need to be followed in situations involving strangers, and keeping away from strangers in automobiles is one of those rules.

5 Explain to students that when approached by a stranger inside a car, they should run in the direction *opposite* to the car's direction. They are to run in the opposite direction because if a person inside the car wanted to attack them, the car would need to travel backward or turn around and that would be difficult to do. If a person were to run away in the same direction as the car was traveling, it would be much easier for the stranger to catch this person. Explain to students that it is also important to remember as much as possible about the car and the stranger. For example, the student

could remember the color of the car, what kind of car it was, and what the stranger was wearing. You can practice this aspect of the activity by drawing and attaching a license plate to the car. Do not tell the class what you have done. Then have another student volunteer to be walking along the street. Pretend that you stopped your car and asked this student to come closer to see the photograph of your lost puppy. Tell the student to act in the correct way. (Run away in the opposite direction the car is traveling.)

EVALUATION

Before beginning this evaluation, review TM-7, "Find Health Facts and Get Help." Have students tell what they would do if they were walking down the street and were approached by a stranger in a car. (They would run away in the direction opposite the direction the car was traveling.) By running away, the student is protecting himself or herself from a person who might harm him or her and is cooperating with people who are concerned with the student's safety. Tell students to close their eyes and to try to remember certain facts such as the numbers on your license plate and three things about you (the stranger). They may think about such items as the color of your dress or shirt, your hair color, or whether you were wearing glasses. Then ask students to tell you what they remember without looking up to see you or the car. Review student answers to your questions for thoroughness and accuracy. Make a transparency of the teaching master "What Do You Remember?" Do not tell students what you have in mind. Show the transparency and after ten seconds, turn off the transparency projector, then ask students to tell you what they remembered about the picture. Assess how many facts students remembered about the person or the car. Students should remember the sex of the driver (male), his characteristics (mustache), his clothing (hat with the letter *S*), and the car (two-door sedan).

Teaching Master

What Do You Remember?

Mental and Emotional Health

GRADE 1

You Are So Very Special

HEALTH EDUCATION STANDARDS

- Students will demonstrate the ability to practice health-enhancing behaviors and avoid or reduce health risks.
- Students will demonstrate the ability to use interpersonal communication skills to enhance health and avoid or reduce health risks.

PERFORMANCE INDICATORS

- Demonstrate healthy practices and behaviors to maintain or improve personal health.
- Demonstrate healthy ways to express needs, wants, and feelings.

HEALTH GOAL

- I will choose actions for a healthy mind.

MATERIALS

Student master "I Am Special"; shoe box; decorative paper such as scrap wallpaper; tape; small pocket mirror; TM-10, "Communicate," Appendix A

MOTIVATION

1 To get ready for this lesson, prepare a special box that you will bring to class. Take a shoe box for which you no longer have use. Decorate the cover and all sides of the shoe box by pasting decorative paper to it. On the inside bottom of the shoe box, place a mirror that is held in place by tape.

2 Stand in front of your class, holding the shoe box so that it is visible to everyone. Do not say a word to the class. Students will begin to wonder what is inside the shoe box. After several seconds, tell the students that each of them will have the opportunity to see what is inside the shoe box. Tell

students there are two rules to follow when you do this activity. First, they cannot tell anyone else what is inside the box. Second, they must identify what is special about what is inside the box. Explain to students that what is inside the box is very special.

3 Approach each student, and tilt the box so that she will see her face as she peeks inside. Reiterate to each student that it is important to remember what is special about what she sees inside the box. (Emphasize that you are asking students "What is special about what you see inside the box?" not "What do you see inside the box?" This way you will avoid responses such as "I saw myself inside the box.")

4 After students have had the opportunity to see their faces reflected in the mirror inside the box, have them share what was so special about what they saw. You can add that what is inside the box is a special gift. Discuss the concept that people like receiving gifts and that gifts help make people feel good. Explain that you can be a gift to others. You can share happy feelings with people and give the gift of helping them to feel good about themselves. You also can talk about what makes you special and important. You can discuss how you look and what you like to do with others. You can discuss qualities students have that others like.

5 Distribute the student master "I Am Special." Explain that there is a mirror inside the bottom of the shoe box. Each student is to pretend that he is looking inside the box and sees a reflection of his face. Students are to draw their faces and show their picture to the class. Then they are to share how they are special.

EVALUATION

Explain to students that a part of feeling good about themselves is related to communicating well with others. Review the information

500

on TM-10, "Communicate." Then review what makes them feel good. On the chalkboard, write the following incomplete statement. "I feel good about myself because. . . ." Go around the room and have students name a characteristic they have that makes them feel good about themselves. An optional activity is to show students a picture of a person who looks happy. Students in the class can brainstorm ideas about why the person in the picture feels happy. They can make up a story about a situation that happened to make that person feel special and important. You can then have students relate these stories to their own experiences. For example, they may indicate that the person in the picture has a birthday and received a new toy. Receiving a new toy can help make a person feel happy and special. Students can then share an experience they have had in which they received a toy and why that helped them feel happy.

MULTICULTURAL INFUSION

You can choose to show pictures from magazines depicting people of different cultures. These pictures will show people who appear happy, and maybe something in the picture will show why this person appears happy. For example, a person may be eating a particular ethnic food, and this person is smiling because she likes this food. This is a good opportunity to infuse different cultural aspects about health and how these aspects impact a person's health.

I Am Special

Name _____

Pretend this is a box with a mirror taped to the bottom. Pretend you look inside. Draw your face. Tell why you are special.

Family and Social Health

GRADE 1

One, Two, a Friend for You

HEALTH EDUCATION STANDARDS

- Students will demonstrate the ability to use interpersonal communication skills to enhance health and avoid or reduce health risks.
- Students will demonstrate the ability to practice health-enhancing behaviors and avoid or reduce health risks.

PERFORMANCE INDICATORS

- Demonstrate listening skills to enhance health.
- Demonstrate healthy practices and behaviors to maintain or improve personal health.

HEALTH GOALS

- I will get along with my family.
- I will help others take care of their health.

MATERIALS

Student master "Friendly Faces"; paper; pencils; TM-24, "Practice Healthful Habits," Appendix A

MOTIVATION

1 Ask students if they have ever heard of the nursery rhyme "One, Two, Buckle My Shoe." You can tell students the first few lines for this nursery rhyme:

One, two,
Buckle my shoe;
Three, four,
Shut the door;
Five, six,
Pick up sticks;
Seven, eight,
Lay them straight.

2 Tell students that they are going to learn a new version of this nursery rhyme. However, this new version will emphasize the importance of being a good friend. Have students sing the song using the new words:

One, two,
I like you;
Three, four,
I'll smile more;
Five, six,
I'll eat a mix;
Seven, eight,
Of foods that are great.

3 Distribute the student master "Friendly Faces." Students are to draw friendly faces next to each number so that the number of friendly faces matches the number to its left. For example, a student will draw one friendly face next to the number 1, two friendly faces next to number 2, and so on. Collect the papers and check that the drawings match the numbers.

4 You can continue this activity with extended math instruction. For example, you can point to the number 8 and ask students, "How many faces would remain if two of the friendly faces went away?" (Six friendly faces.) You can present math problems that correspond to your students' abilities.

EVALUATION

Have each student select a number from 1 through 5. You can have them pick from random numbers in an envelope. For each number, students are to tell ways to be a good friend. For example, a student who selects the number 3 will tell three ways to be a good friend; a student who selects the number 5 will tell five ways to be a good friend, and so on. Knowing how to choose good friends is a healthful behavior that can be repeated. Reinforce this concept by referring to TM-24, "Practice Healthful Habits."

503

Student Master

Friendly Faces

Name _____

Look at each number.
Draw the correct number of faces by each number.

1.

2.

3.

4.

5.

6.

7.

8.

Growth and Development

GRADE 1

Unique Me

HEALTH EDUCATION STANDARD

- Students will demonstrate the ability to practice health-enhancing behaviors and avoid or reduce health risks.
- Students will comprehend concepts related to health promotion and disease prevention to enhance health.

PERFORMANCE INDICATORS

- Demonstrate healthy practices and behaviors to maintain or improve personal health.
- Recognize that there are multiple dimensions of health.

HEALTH GOALS

- I will act in ways that show I am special.
- I will share feelings. (Mental and Emotional Health)

MATERIALS

Student master "This Is Me"; markers or crayons; ink pad; index cards; a card for each student; TM-24, "Practice Healthful Habits," Appendix A

MOTIVATION

1 Distribute an index card to each student. Tell each student to draw a picture of himself or herself that includes as many unique features as possible. This will be a drawing of the student without a head, but have students leave space so that they can add a head later. Have several students share their headless drawings with the class and indicate what is special about their drawings.

2 Have students press their thumbs on the ink pad to make a thumbprint where their heads should be on their pictures. Each student will now have a complete body. Students are to write their names on their cards. Post each card on the bulletin board.

3 Explain to students that the "heads" on the cards may look alike from a distance. However, there is something unique about each of the "heads." Have students observe the details of the "heads." Then ask students what they observed. Students will indicate that each "head" is different because each fingerprint is unique. Explain that no two people have the same fingerprints. Fingerprints are a physical feature that makes one person different from another. Have students share other ways people differ from each other because of their physical features. Emphasize that although people may look similar from a distance, on closer inspection they are different. For example, thumbprints look alike from a distance, but on close inspection they are different. Explain that people are born with other unique features. A person has no control over these features, and it is these unique features that help make each person special.

4 Discuss the different kinds of features people have and how each of these features may differ. For example, people have eyes. But some people have brown eyes, others have green eyes, and yet others have blue eyes. Tell students about hair. Have students identify different color hair. Discuss the kind of hair people have, such as long or short or curly or straight. Introduce other physical features, such as whether someone is tall or short. Distribute the student master "This Is Me." Have students draw a full picture of themselves. Then have them fill in the blanks. You can review the blanks and help them fill in the missing information.

EVALUATION

Randomly distribute the cards that were displayed on the bulletin board. Be sure that each student has another student's card. Each student is to go to the student whose card she or he has and tell that student two features observed on the card that make that student special. Explain that being nice to others is a healthful thing to do. Show TM-24, "Practice Healthful Habits," and ask students to name other healthful things they do.

This Is Me

Name _____

Draw a picture of yourself from head to toe.
Answer the questions.

My hair color is _____ .

My eye color is _____ .

My hair is _____ .

Healthful Food Grab Bag

HEALTH EDUCATION STANDARDS

- Students will demonstrate the ability to practice health-enhancing behaviors and avoid or reduce health risks.
- Students will demonstrate the ability to use decision-making skills to enhance health.

PERFORMANCE INDICATORS

- Demonstrate behaviors to avoid or reduce health risks.
- Differentiate between situations when a health-related decision can be made individually or when assistance is needed.

HEALTH GOALS

- I will eat healthful meals and snacks.
- I will eat the recommended daily amounts of food from MyPyramid.

MATERIALS

Student master "A Smile or a Frown"; student master "My Fruit Diary"; one orange; a slice of bread; a banana; grains of rice; a tomato; corn flakes; a brown paper bag; TM-1, "Learn Health Facts," Appendix A

MOTIVATION

1 In this activity, students will learn how they can identify foods by using only the sense of touch. They will learn that they may identify a food by how soft or hard a food may feel, how a food is shaped, or by the texture of a food. They also will learn that foods that are nutritious will provide the body with energy and contain substances needed to maintain body tissues and to regulate body processes. The body uses six major classes of nutrients. The following descriptions of these nutrients are included for the teacher's reference: Proteins are essential for growth and development and the repair of all body tissues. Some foods that contain protein are meat and cheese. Carbohydrates are the main source of energy for the body. Examples of carbohydrates are starches that are found in pasta. Fats provide additional energy and help the body store certain vitamins. Fats that are healthful for the body can be found in animals that fly or swim, such as poultry and fish. Vitamins help chemical reactions that take place inside the body. Different kinds of foods contain specific kinds of vitamins. Minerals regulate the many chemical reactions in the body. Foods such as leafy green vegetables contain minerals. Water, although not considered a food, is a nutrient that makes up about 60 percent of the body mass.

2 Introduce the term *nutritious* to the class. Explain that foods that are nutritious are healthful. They help the body grow. Explain that some foods are not nutritious. They contain a large amount of sugar or other substances such as saturated fats that are not healthful for the body. Explain that these foods may include different kinds of candy, potato chips, and ice cream. Emphasize to students that they should make healthful selections whenever possible.

3 Explain that students can use their sense of touch to identify many healthful kinds of foods. Explain that you are going to play a game called "Feel the Food." You will place different foods, one at a time, inside a bag. You will select several student volunteers to come to the front of the room. Each student will place one hand inside the bag. Students may not look at what is inside the bag. They will feel what is inside the bag. They are to describe what they feel inside the bag. Then the student should guess what the food is in the bag. If the student is not able to guess, the other students in the class can try to guess the name of the food based on the description of that food given by the student whose hand is in the bag. For example, the student may be feeling the

tomato. That student may say that it feels very smooth, it is soft, and it is round.

4 Explain to students that only nutritious foods will be inside the bag. You want students to begin to develop an awareness of those foods that are nutritious and are as free as possible from substances such as sugar, saturated fats, and salt. This also is an opportunity for students to begin to describe the characteristics of nutritious foods.

EVALUATION

Show TM-1, "Learn Health Facts," to review how students learn facts. Students can pretend they have identified a healthful food that is in a bag. Select one student at a time to close his eyes and pretend that his hand is inside the bag. That student is to think of a food and describe it to the class. The class must identify the food the student is imagining. Be sure that students identify only healthful foods. You can also distribute the student master "A Smile or a Frown." Students are to take this master home and complete it with a parent. Have students return their masters the next day and review their answers. Emphasize the importance of eating healthful foods. Distribute the student master "My Fruit Diary." Explain that a diary is a record a person keeps to tell what she or he is doing. Have students keep a diary that shows how many fruits they eat for one week. The recommended number of servings from the fruit group for students of this age group is three servings each day. Have students write the names of fruits they eat each day. Their parent can help them keep track of the fruits eaten by helping them record the information. Review the student diaries after a week.

A Smile or a Frown

Name _____

Dear Parent,

Your child is learning about healthful foods to eat. For example, your child is learning to avoid foods that are high in sugar, fats, and salt and to eat healthful foods instead. Different kinds of foods are listed on this sheet. Have your child determine whether the food pictured is healthful and nutritious or harmful and not nutritious. Next to each food is a face that has no mouth. Have your child draw a smile (⌣) for the mouth if the food is healthful and a frown (⌢) for the mouth if the food is not nutritious. Have your child provide you with reasons why he or she made the particular choice.

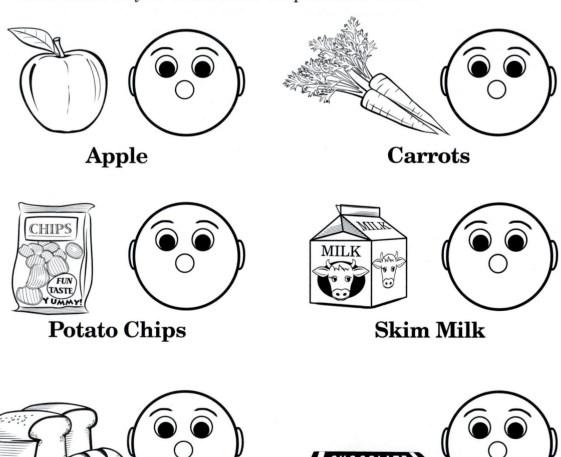

Apple

Carrots

Potato Chips

Skim Milk

Bread

Chocolate

My Fruit Diary

Name _____

Write the names of the fruits you eat each day.
Ask a parent or adult to help you.
Try to eat three fruits each day.

Monday _____

_____

Tuesday _____

_____

Wednesday _____

_____

Thursday _____

_____

Friday _____

_____

Saturday _____

_____

Sunday _____

_____

Personal Health and Physical Activity

Teeth with a Bite

SCIENCE STUDIES · CRITICAL THINKER

HEALTH EDUCATION STANDARDS

- Students will comprehend concepts related to health promotion and disease prevention to enhance health.
- Students will demonstrate the ability to use goal-setting skills to enhance health.

PERFORMANCE INDICATORS

- Identify that healthy behaviors impact personal health.
- Identify a short-term personal health goal and take action toward achieving the goal.

HEALTH GOALS

- I will take care of my teeth.
- I will take care of my body. (Growth and Development)

MATERIALS

Student master "Which Do My Teeth Need?"; student master "How I Care for My Teeth"; transparency projector; carrot; a large photo from a magazine that highlights the face of a person who has a nice smile with teeth very evident (make two transparencies of this picture, and in one of the transparencies, darken several teeth so it appears that this person lost some teeth); TM-18, "Make Wise Decisions," Appendix A

MOTIVATION

1 Tell the class that you are going to review three reasons why having healthy teeth is important. Begin by having a student come to the front of the room. Ask this student to take a bite of the carrot and then chew what is inside her mouth. Then tell this student to pretend she has no teeth and to take another bite of the carrot. To pretend that this student has no teeth, ask her to place her lips over her front teeth. Then ask this student to take another bite of the carrot. The student will not be able to bite the carrot because her teeth are covered by her lips. Explain to the students that they have just observed what it would be like not to be able to bite because they had missing teeth. Ask the students, "What is one purpose of teeth?" (One purpose of teeth is to help people chew food.)

2 Discuss the second purpose of teeth. Show students the transparency of a person who has a wide smile with bright, clean teeth. Ask students, "What do you notice about this person?" (Students will indicate this person has a nice smile or a nice appearance.) Then show the students the next transparency of the same person. Explain that this person decided not to care for his teeth, as shown by the darkened spaces that show missing teeth. Then ask the students, "What do you think about this person's appearance?" (Students will probably laugh at first and then say this person does not have a nice appearance.) Explain that another purpose of teeth is to help people have a nice appearance. It is important to recognize that many students in your class have lost or are losing teeth. Remind students that everyone loses their baby or primary teeth. Emphasize that this is normal and that boys and girls who lose their teeth still look cute. But you want your students to understand that it is important to keep their adult or permanent teeth. The person in the picture lost his or her permanent teeth.

3 Review the third purpose of teeth. Tell students you want them to say the following tongue twister: *She sells seashells by the seashore.* Have the class repeat this sentence with you. Now have students pretend they lost their teeth and place their lips over their front teeth. After students do this, have them repeat the tongue twister again. Then ask students, "Why couldn't I understand what you were saying?" (Students will say that they could not speak clearly when they had teeth missing.) Thus,

you can indicate that another purpose of teeth is to help people speak clearly.

4 You can use this activity to reinforce that there are behaviors students can follow to help ensure that their teeth remain healthy. Emphasize that students should brush their teeth after meals, floss every evening, avoid sticky and sweet foods that stick to the teeth, and eat dairy products such as milk and yogurt that help keep teeth hard.

5 Distribute the student master "How I Care for My Teeth" and encourage students to record their healthful dental practices.

EVALUATION

Use the information in TM-18 to review how to make choices that promote dental health. Provide students with a copy of the student master "Which Do My Teeth Need?" Have students color the products that are healthful for teeth. Have students place an X through those products that are not healthful for teeth. Evaluate the students' papers for accuracy. Also, have students share their masters with a parent.

Student Master

Which Do My Teeth Need?

Name

Dear Parent,
Your child is learning about healthful behaviors that are important for dental health. (S)he has learned that it is important to brush twice each day, floss each day, eat foods high in calcium such as milk products including yogurt and cheese, and avoid foods that contain large amounts of sugar and that stick to teeth. Check your child's work on this page. Your child should color the pictures that show something healthful related to teeth, and your child should place a large X through the pictures that show something that is not healthful for teeth.

Dental Floss

Toothbrush

Candy

Milk

Marshmallows

Cheese

Student Master

How I Care for My Teeth

Name _____

Dear Parent,
Your child is learning the importance of following good dental health practices. Your child should brush his or her teeth at least two times each day and eat foods high in calcium, such as foods that contain milk. Help your child keep this diary by helping him or her enter the requested information. Keep this diary for one week.

Place a check in the appropriate block each time you brush your teeth that day.

Monday	Tuesday	Wednesday	Thursday	Friday	Saturday	Sunday

List the names of foods you eat each day that help your teeth.

Monday _____

Tuesday _____

Wednesday _____

Thursday _____

Friday _____

Saturday _____

Sunday _____

ungs

HEALTH EDUCATION STANDARDS

- Students will demonstrate the ability to practice health-enhancing behaviors and avoid or reduce health risks.
- Students will demonstrate the ability to use decision-making skills to enhance health.

PERFORMANCE INDICATORS

- Demonstrate behaviors to avoid or reduce health risks.
- Identify situations when a health-related decision is needed.

HEALTH GOALS

- I will not use tobacco.
- I will not use drugs that are against the law.

MATERIALS

Teaching master "Smoky Lungs"; transparency projector; cigarettes; two clear plastic sandwich bags; two straws; cotton balls; tape; TM-12, "Say No," Appendix A

MOTIVATION

1 Explain to students that they will observe how ingredients from cigarette smoke can harm the lungs. To review how the lungs function, stuff cotton balls inside a clear plastic bag. Insert a straw through the top of the bag. Wrap the top of the bag around the straw, about one inch from the bottom. Tape the wrapped bag around the straw to form a lung (bag) with the windpipe (straw) going inside. At this point, the connection between the straw and the bag should be airtight.

2 To prepare for this experiment, construct another plastic bag lung at home. Find a person who smokes. When he or she is

ready, ask that person to smoke a cigarette without inhaling the smoke. Do not use a cigarette that has a filter tip. Have the person blow the smoke from the cigarette through the straw into the bag with cotton. Each time the person blows smoke into the bag, squeeze the bag so that the smoke is released. After doing this procedure for two cigarettes, the cotton balls will turn brown from the tar deposited by the cigarette smoke. Bring this bag to class.

3 Show students the clean plastic bag lung containing fresh cotton. Explain to students how a lung works. Explain that the cotton balls represent air sacs inside the lungs and that the air sacs hold fresh air that is carried throughout the body by the blood. The bag is the lung and the straw is the windpipe. Blow a puff of air into the lungs through the windpipe. Have students observe how the lung inflates or becomes bigger. You can also have the class observe how you inhale and notice that your chest cavity expands. Now squeeze the air out of the lung through the windpipe. Students will notice that the lung deflates and becomes smaller. Have students observe how you exhale and how your chest becomes smaller because the air is escaping from your lungs. Explain that the lung you have shown students is clean. The lung has not been exposed to tobacco, specifically, not cigarette smoke.

4 Show the class the bag you prepared with cigarette smoke, and have students observe this lung. Students will notice that the cotton inside is brown. Explain that the cotton, or air sacs, inside that lung changed color because of smoke that entered the lung from a cigarette. Explain that cigarette smoke contains tar, which is a dark, sticky substance. Explain that the smoke from only two cigarettes was blown into the lung. Tell students that when a person smokes, the tar from the cigarette smoke begins to cover the lungs. This can cause a person to have difficulty breathing. It also can cause a person to develop many kinds of illnesses.

5 You can pass the bag representing the smoker's lung around the room and ask students to smell the contents of the lung through the opening of the straw. Students will notice an awful odor. Remind students that the lung you passed around contained the ingredients from only two cigarettes. Tell students that smokers may smoke a pack or more of cigarettes each day for many years. A pack contains twenty cigarettes. Have students imagine how the lungs of someone who smokes a pack of cigarettes each day might look.

6 Review the harmful effects of tobacco on the body. Explain that it harms the lungs. It causes many kinds of illnesses. You can also mention that smoking harms the heart as well as the throat and many other body parts. It makes the teeth yellow, and it causes an unpleasant odor.

7 Show the teaching master "Smoky Lungs." Have students visualize smoke from a cigarette entering the lung by moving from the mouth, down the windpipe, and into the lungs.

EVALUATION

Hold up a large trash bag and tell students to imagine you are holding a large lung. Provide each student with a sheet of white paper. Tell students you would like them to draw a picture of something healthful a person could do instead of smoking. They might also draw a picture showing the use of resistance skills to say "no" to pressure to use tobacco. Students are to write their name on their paper. Then have each student roll the sheet of paper around so that it appears they have made a large cigarette. Tell students you want them to roll their papers so that their pictures are on the inside. Tape the students' papers so that they stay in the shape of a cigarette. Explain to students that they have just created cigarette tips. They are to place their "cigarette tips" inside the large trash bag. Have each student pick out a cigarette from the bag (lung). They are to read the name of the person whose picture they have chosen and then describe what "healthful tip" is inside the picture. Use this opportunity to have students share positive activities people can do instead of smoking. Then show TM-12, "Say No," and review what to do when someone is offered a cigarette.

Teaching Master
Smoky Lungs

Communicable and Chronic Diseases

GRADE 1

Friend or Foe?

HEALTH EDUCATION STANDARDS

- Students will comprehend concepts related to health promotion and disease prevention to enhance health.
- Students will demonstrate the ability to practice health-enhancing behaviors and avoid or reduce health risks.

PERFORMANCE INDICATORS

- Identify that healthy behaviors impact personal health.
- Demonstrate healthy practices and behaviors to maintain or improve personal health.

HEALTH GOALS

- I will learn symptoms and treatment of disease.
- I will choose habits that prevent cancer.

MATERIALS

The poem "Friend or Foe?"; sunglasses; hat; two umbrellas; long-sleeved shirt that buttons up the front; sunscreen with an SPF rating; a sheet of yellow construction paper that has been cut into the shape of the sun; a white sheet of paper cut into the shape of the moon; a gray sheet of paper cut into the shape of a large raindrop; TM-1, "Learn Health Facts," Appendix A

MOTIVATION

1 Begin the lesson by taping the paper sun, moon, and large raindrop on the chalkboard. Explain to students that these are three of their friends. Ask them why each is a friend. Why is the sun a friend? (The sun can keep you warm. You can play outside when it is sunny. You might go swimming when it is sunny.) Why is the moon a friend? (When the moon shines, you can see the sky. It is beautiful. The moon means it is bedtime and you can get some sleep.) Why is rain your friend? (The rain gives flowers and grass a drink of water. The rain fills up lakes and rivers with water. Some people like to swim in the lake. Some people take boats on the lake.)

2 Explain to students that you are going to read them a poem about one of these three friends. The poem is called "Friend or Foe?" A foe is someone who might harm you. Ask them to listen carefully to guess which of these friends might also harm them. After you have read the poem, ask the students if the foe was the sun, the moon, or the raindrop. (The sun can be both a friend and a foe.) What might harm them? (The sun's rays might harm them.) The sun's rays can harm the skin. The skin covers the body and is made of cells. A cell is the smallest part of a person's body. The sun can change the cells in harmful ways. Then a person gets skin cancer. Skin cancer is harmful changes in the skin.

3 Explain that there are ways to keep the skin safe from too much sun. Show students the following: hat, umbrella, long-sleeved shirt, and sunscreen with an SPF rating. Explain how each of these keeps the sun from the skin. Although there is hair on the head, the sun's rays can still reach the skin. The hat covers the head and keeps the skin on the head from getting too much sun. The hat also keeps sun off the face. (Put the hat on.) Say, "The umbrella can also keep the sun away from the skin. Look at how much of my skin is covered by the umbrella. If I put on this long-sleeved shirt, I also keep the sun from my skin. The long-sleeved shirt keeps my arms, shoulders, and back from getting too much sun." (Put on the long-sleeved shirt.)

4 Now show students the sunscreen. Show them the letters SPF. Explain that *SPF* means "sun protection factor." SPF is something in sunscreen that keeps the sun from harming the skin. An SPF rating is a num-

Communicable and Chronic Diseases

ber. It might be an 8, a 15, a 25, or a 30. The higher the number, the more it keeps the sun from harming the skin. (A product with an SPF rating of 30 keeps more sun from the skin than does a product with a rating of 8.) Take a drop of sunscreen and rub it on your arm. Tell the students that using sunscreen when you are going to be outside on sunny days keeps the sun from harming your skin.

5 Finally, explain that they will want to protect their eyes from the sun too. Too much sun can harm the eyes. You can put on the sunglasses.

EVALUATION

Divide the students into five groups. Give each group one of your props: hat, long-sleeved shirt, sunglasses, umbrella, and sunscreen. Begin with group 1 and say, "I am going to be in the sun, so I will wear . . ." They are to answer, "My hat." Then begin again, "I am going to be in the sun, so I will wear . . ." Groups 1 and 2 say, "My hat." And Group 2 is to add, "and long-sleeved shirt." Begin again, "I am going to be in the sun, so I will wear . . ." Groups 1, 2, and 3 say, "My hat and my long-sleeved shirt." And Group 3 adds, "and my sunglasses." Repeat. Groups 1, 2, 3, and 4 will say, "My hat, my long-sleeved shirt, and my sunglasses." Group 4 will add, "my umbrella." Repeat, and Groups 1, 2, 3, 4, and 5 will say, "My hat, my long-sleeved shirt, my sunglasses, and my umbrella." Group 5 will add, "and my sunscreen." Repeat again, "I am going to be in the sun, so I will use . . ." All five groups will respond, "My hat, my long-sleeved shirt, my sunglasses, my umbrella, and my sunscreen." Show TM-1, "Learn Health Facts," and ask students to describe how they used health facts in giving their answers.

Friend or Foe?

❖❖❖❖❖❖❖

I greet you in the morning
and watch you through the day.
When you look and see me,
you want to come and play.

I give you warmth and light
and help you tell the time.
I like to see you run and jump
and be a friend of mine.

But if you stay and play
and spend some time with me,
you must take special care
or you'll be unhappy.

Because while I mark the time
and keep you nice and warm,
you cannot keep safe from me
or the rays I send that harm.

❖❖❖❖❖❖❖

Don't Forget to Floss

HEALTH EDUCATION STANDARDS

- Students will comprehend concepts related to health promotion and disease prevention to enhance health.

PERFORMANCE INDICATORS

- Identify that healthy behaviors impact personal health.

HEALTH GOALS

- I will check out ways to learn facts.
- I will be neat and clean. (Personal Health and Physical Activity)
- I will take care of my teeth. (Personal Health and Physical Activity)

MATERIALS

Student master "A Flossing I Will Go"; a shoe box; thick colorful strip of yarn that is about eighteen inches in length; scissors; a gumdrop; TM-7, "Find Health Facts and Get Help," Appendix A

MOTIVATION

1 To prepare for this strategy, make a model set of teeth from a shoe box. Take the bottom of a shoe box and turn it on its side. On the actual bottom side of the shoe box, trace teeth from one end to the other. Then cut slits between the teeth so that the bottom of the shoe box becomes a set of teeth. Bring the shoe box to class.

2 Discuss the importance of brushing teeth. It is also important to discuss the fact that when people eat food, they get food caught between their teeth. Sometimes brushing with a toothbrush cannot remove food that is lodged between the teeth. Explain that one way to remove food that is stuck between teeth is to use dental floss. *Floss*

is a thin, stringlike substance that is slid between teeth. Using floss helps loosen and remove food trapped between teeth.

3 Tell students that you are going to demonstrate how to use floss by using yarn and the shoe box that you made into a set of teeth. Show students a strip of yarn that is approximately eighteen inches in length. Explain that they can use floss in strips of about the same length as the yarn. Wrap the floss several times around each index

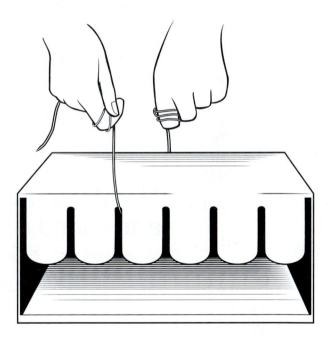

finger and slide it between two teeth. First, slide the floss up and down the side of one tooth pulling the floss slightly in the direction of that tooth. Then slide the floss along the side of the other tooth pulling it slightly to the side of that tooth. To make your demonstration easier, you can ask a student to help you by holding the shoe box as you demonstrate the flossing technique.

4 Explain that there are different kinds of floss. Some people have very tight teeth so that they may need a kind of floss that is waxed. Other people may want a kind of floss that does not have wax and can be used when teeth are not as close to one another.

Consumer and Community Health

5 Select student volunteers to come up to the front of the room and demonstrate the proper flossing technique that you demonstrated. Be sure they slide the floss up and down the side of the teeth.

EVALUATION

Distribute the student master "A Flossing I Will Go." Have students complete a smiling face on each tooth in the master for each day they floss. They are to draw a smile if they flossed or a frown if they did not floss. One tooth is drawn for each day of the week. Ask students to describe the proper way to floss teeth. Then ask them why flossing is important. (Their teeth will be clean, and students will be practicing good dental health.) Show TM-7, "Find Health Facts and Get Help," to identify dental health helpers in the community.

Student Master

A Flossing I Will Go

Name _____

Draw a smile (⌣) on the tooth if you flossed that day.
Draw a frown (⌢) on the tooth if you did not floss that day.

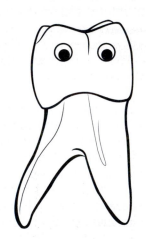  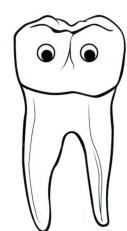 

Monday   Tuesday   Wednesday Thursday

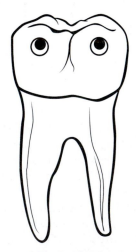  

Friday   Saturday   Sunday

Environmental Health

Messy Things

SCIENCE STUDIES · RESPONSIBLE CITIZEN

HEALTH EDUCATION STANDARD

- Students will demonstrate the ability to practice health-enhancing behaviors and avoid or reduce health risks.

PERFORMANCE INDICATOR

- Demonstrate healthy practices and behaviors to maintain or improve personal health.

HEALTH GOAL

- I will help protect my environment.

MATERIALS

Teaching master "Messy Things"; globe; three-by-five-inch index cards; crayons or markers; butcher paper; TM-1, "Learn Health Facts," Appendix A

MOTIVATION

1 Show students a globe and tell them it is a model of Earth. Let students examine the globe as you point out the areas that show water and the areas that show land. Explain that we often refer to the world as our home. Ask students what they think that means. (We live on Earth. All people share a home.) Ask students what they might do to take care of their home and keep it clean. (They might clean up after themselves; they might not litter.) Point out that it is easier to get sick or have accidents in a messy home.

2 Read the poem aloud. Ask students to name messy things they have seen around the school (papers on the streets, bottles and cans left on the ground). Ask students what might happen if no one cared about keeping Earth clean. (It might get messier and messier.) Explain that people use trash cans to help keep Earth clean. Tell students that putting trash where it belongs helps keep the world clean.

3 Take students on a short nature walk around the school neighborhood. Have them pay attention as they breathe in the fresh air. Explain that people, plants, and animals need fresh air and clean water to grow. Then send students on a litter patrol around the school. Tell students to observe what kinds of trash they see around the school grounds. Tell students not to touch the trash. (It is important that students do not touch any items they see on the ground because the items may be harmful.) When you return to the classroom, make a class list of the kinds of trash they saw.

4 Write the word *pollution* on the board. Read it aloud and then invite the class to read it along with you. Explain that pollution is dirt and gases that make Earth's water and air unsafe. Allow students who know examples of pollution to share what they know. Ask students what might happen if the air and water are dirty. (People might get sick. Plants and flowers might die.)

EVALUATION

Show TM-1, "Learn Health Facts," and have students brainstorm facts to help keep the environment clean. Review the list of kinds of litter students saw. Have students draw a picture using color markers or crayons of one of the pieces of litter that is on the list, or of another piece of litter that might be found on the ground. While students are drawing, tape a large piece of butcher paper on the wall. On the butcher paper draw a picture of a large trash can. Over the trash can write "Our class knows where litter belongs!" or "Our class helps keep Earth clean!" Have the students tape their pictures of litter inside the trash can to show that they know the proper way to dispose of solid waste. Also have students discuss which types of trash are suitable for recycling.

Messy Things

Messy things do bother me—
A can along the street,
a wrapper on the ground.
It's sad to think the earth
  should see
Such messy things around.

My friends and I can keep
  things clean—
the bottles with the glass,
the litter where it goes.
We want the world all blue and
  green
So that its beauty shows.

GRADE 1

Staying Below the Smoke Line

HEALTH EDUCATION STANDARD

- Students will demonstrate the ability to practice health-enhancing behaviors and avoid or reduce health risks.

PERFORMANCE INDICATORS

- Demonstrate healthy practices and behaviors to maintain or improve personal health.
- Demonstrate behaviors to avoid or reduce health risks.

HEALTH GOALS

- I will follow safety rules for home and school.
- I will get help in an emergency.

MATERIALS

Student master "Five Fire Facts"; several mats from the gymnasium (or you may take your class to the gymnasium); TM-24, "Practice Healthful Habits," Appendix A

MOTIVATION

1 Ask students if they have ever seen smoke from a fire or smokestack. Ask students what they noticed about the smoke. Students should say smoke usually rises. Explain that warm air rises. Smoke is in the air. Smoke rises with the air. Explain that this lesson is about being safe when in a fire. Many deaths due to home fires result not from burns, but from smoke the residents inhale. Therefore, it is important to know what to do in case students may need to escape from a fire and its smoke.

2 Have students imagine they are surrounded by smoke. Ask them what they should do. Students would need to keep low to the ground so that they are below the line of smoke. Bring mats to class (or take your students to the gymnasium). Lay several mats on the floor. Explain to students that they are to get down on their hands and knees (demonstrate this) and crawl. Have students pretend that they are escaping from a fire and there is smoke above. Tell students to crawl on their hands and knees from one end of the mats to the other.

3 There are many other safety rules students should know if they are trying to escape from a fire. If they are trying to get out of a room but must open a door to do so, explain that they need to feel the door before they open it. If the door feels hot, they are not to open it. Fire could burst into where they are if they open the door. If they can, they should get to a window. They can scream, "Fire!" Each student's family should also have fire escape plans for their homes and practice family fire drills at least twice each year. People need to practice escape routes and plan a place to meet outside the home. If people meet at the assigned place, everyone will know that all people have escaped safely. If someone is not at the meeting place, firefighters can be told that someone may yet be inside the home.

4 Review the following poem with students and have them say it with you. The title of the poem is "Five Fire Facts."

Five fire facts can help you be
Fabulous, safe, and healthy.

First, you need to understand,
In smoke you crawl and do not stand.

Second, you don't open a door
   that's hot,
For escape from fire, you will not.

Third, you need to have a plan,
So you can escape as quickly as
   you can.

Fourth, you'll need to pick a spot,
Outside the house, where it's not
   fiery hot.

Fifth, and finally, have fire drills,
So you can practice your fire
   escape skills.

5 This poem is on the student master "Five Fire Facts." Have students take the master home and share with their parents and other significant adults what they have learned in school. Students can encourage their parents to practice fire safety in the home.

the safety tips. Ask students what conditions might cause fires in the home (unsafe wiring, heaters, open flames, natural disasters such as earthquakes that cause gas leaks, etc.). Also ask them to identify sources of smoke in their community and to make suggestions for reducing the amount of smoke. Show TM-24, "Practice Healthful Habits," and ask students to act out how they would stay below the smoke line to escape from a fire.

EVALUATION

Read the first line of each part of the poem to students. Then have students say the second line. As they say this, they will be reinforcing

Student Master

Five Fire Facts

Dear Parent,

Your child has been learning about fire safety. The poem that follows focuses on escaping from a fire. Read this poem aloud with your child and review the five facts in this poem with him/her. It is important that you and your family have a fire escape plan for your home. Firefighters recommend that families practice fire drills in the home. Take this opportunity to work with your child to make a fire escape plan for your home.

Five Fire Facts

Five fire facts can help you be
Fabulous, safe, and healthy.

First, you need to understand,
In smoke you crawl and do not stand.

Second, you don't open a door that's hot,
For escape from fire, you will not.

Third, you need to have a plan,
So you can escape as quickly as you can.

Fourth, you'll need to pick a spot,
Outside the house, where it's not fiery hot.

Fifth, and finally, have fire drills,
So you can practice your fire escape skills.

Physical Stress

HEALTH EDUCATION STANDARDS

- Students will comprehend concepts related to health promotion and disease prevention to enhance health.
- Students will demonstrate the ability to practice health-enhancing behaviors and avoid or reduce health risks.

PERFORMANCE INDICATORS

- Recognize that there are multiple dimensions of health.
- Demonstrate behaviors to avoid or reduce health risks.

HEALTH GOAL

- I will practice life skills.

MATERIALS

Teaching master "The Effects of Stress on the Body"; transparency projector; inflated balloon; a pin; TM-27, "Manage Stress," Appendix A

MOTIVATION

1 Before the class enters, blow up a balloon and keep it under your desk out of sight of your students. After the students are sitting at their desks and are quiet, reach under your desk. Using a pin, burst the balloon. Obviously, there will be a loud noise, and the students will be startled momentarily.

2 Explain to students that when the balloon burst, certain things happened inside their bodies. Ask students to share what happened. For example, students may say that their heart raced. They may also indicate that they became frightened, and perhaps their muscles became tight because they jumped when the balloon burst.

3 Explain that when the balloon burst, they were temporarily stunned and reactions occurred inside their bodies. They were feeling the effects of stress. Explain that certain physical changes such as increased heart rate occur with stress. Explain that everyone experiences stress and that the body changes when stress occurs. Other physical signs that indicate a person is feeling stress may be sweating, having a dry mouth, feeling tired, and not being able to go to sleep.

4 Explain that there are many different causes of stress. Have students share ways stress may be caused in their lives. For example, they may have an argument with a friend; they may argue with a family member; their parents may have an argument; they may be moving to another neighborhood; they may be called a name by a friend. These are some reasons that a person may feel stress.

5 Explain that there are ways to deal with stress. How a person handles stress may depend on the cause of the stress. For example, if a student has an argument with a friend, he can speak to the friend to settle their differences. A counselor at school may help a student who is feeling the effects of stress. Ask students what they would do if friends called them names. Some answers may center around telling a friend that you feel hurt when you are called a name and asking the friend to stop. You may choose to discuss other reasons why a person might feel stress and how stress can be handled healthfully.

6 Show the teaching master "The Effects of Stress on the Body." Review the physical effects of stress on the body, shown on the teaching master. The pupils of the eyes widen. The *pupil* is the dark circle in the eye that opens and closes to control the amount of light entering the eye. The heartbeat rate speeds up. The stomach may feel as if it is tied up in knots. The muscles in the body

Mental and Emotional Health

may tighten. The mouth becomes dry. Explain that these all are signs of stress.

EVALUATION

Review information about stress by showing TM-27, "Manage Stress," and give examples of each of the four steps. Identify different situations that might cause stress for the students. Some examples may be forgetting to do homework, not having enough money to buy something that the student needs, having feelings hurt by a friend, worrying about a family member who is ill, or having a new baby in the family. Have students share ways to deal with each of these stressors. Remind students that dealing effectively with stress helps them maintain good health.

INCLUSION

Students with special needs can identify stressors they experience and share healthful ways to manage these stressors. For example, a student with a hearing impairment might feel stress when students place their hands in front of their mouths and talk. It is difficult to read lips. The student might ask other students to speak clearly, look directly at her, and not hold things in front of their mouths.

Teaching Master

The Effects of Stress on the Body

The pupils of the eyes widen.
The mouth becomes dry.

The muscles tighten.

The heartbeat rate increases.

The stomach feels as if it is tied up in knots.

Peaceful Flakes

HEALTH EDUCATION STANDARDS

- Students will demonstrate the ability to use interpersonal communication skills to enhance health and avoid or reduce health risks.
- Students will demonstrate the ability to practice health-enhancing behaviors and avoid or reduce health risks.

PERFORMANCE INDICATORS

- Demonstrate ways to respond when in an unwanted, threatening, or dangerous situation.
- Demonstrate behaviors to avoid or reduce health risks.

HEALTH GOAL

- I will work out conflict.

MATERIALS

Teaching master "Handling Disagreements"; transparency projector; empty cereal box (or shoe box) for each student; crayons; construction paper; TM-15, "Resolve Conflicts," Appendix A

MOTIVATION

1 To prepare for this strategy, have each student bring an empty cereal box from home. (An empty shoe box also could be used.)

2 Introduce the term *conflict*. A **conflict** is a disagreement between two or more people or between two or more choices. Explain that it is common for people to have occasional disagreements. The important thing is to learn how to respond to disagreements in healthful and responsible ways. A person can learn skills to resolve disagreements without getting angry and getting into a fight.

3 Explain that you are going to suggest some skills for handling disagreements without getting into a fight. Use the teaching master "Handling Disagreements" to discuss these skills with students:

- *Stay calm.* Speak softly. Do not get excited.
- *Be polite.* Show others that you want to treat them respectfully.
- *Take time to cool down.* If you are feeling angry, take time to get over the anger before you do anything.
- *Share your feelings.* Tell the other person why you feel the way you do about the disagreement.
- *Do not use put-downs.* A put-down is a remark about another person that is not nice.
- *Listen to the other person.* Listen and try to understand why the other person disagrees with you.
- *Pretend you are the other person.* Imagine that you are the other person. This often helps us to understand the other person's feelings.
- *Ask an adult for help.* Adults, such as a parent or a teacher, are available to help settle a disagreement.
- *Let others know when you are wrong.* If you take time to stay calm or to cool down, you may realize that you have made a mistake. When you admit that you are wrong, the disagreement will end.
- *Run away if someone threatens you or insists on fighting.* Realize that you might be harmed if you continue the disagreement.

4 Explain to students that they are going to design a box for a new kind of cereal. The name of the cereal is Peaceful Flakes. Explain that the Peaceful Flakes are going to represent ways of handling disagreements without fighting. Give a sheet of construction paper to each student. Students are to design the words and pictures that will appear on the box for the new cereal,

including the name and the kinds of "flakes," which are skills to handle disagreements without fighting. After they have finished their designs, they will paste the new design on one side of their empty cereal boxes. Students may add additional "flakes." Ask for volunteers to share their new cereal boxes with the class.

EVALUATION

Show TM-15, "Resolve Conflicts," and review the four steps in this master. Share examples of disagreements, such as two students who want the same book from the school library. As you state each example, call on students to choose a "flake" that would be a way to handle the disagreement without fighting. Students should demonstrate that they recognize harmful relationships and that they seek to resolve conflicts.

Teaching Master

Handling Disagreements

1. Stay calm.

2. Be polite.

3. Take time to cool down.

4. Share your feelings.

5. Do not use put-downs.

6. Listen to the other person.

7. Pretend you are the other person.

8. Ask an adult for help.

9. Let others know when you are wrong.

10. Run away if someone threatens you or insists on fighting.

GRADE 2

My Puppy

HEALTH EDUCATION STANDARD

- Students will demonstrate the ability to use interpersonal communication skills to enhance health and avoid or reduce health risks.

PERFORMANCE INDICATORS

- Demonstrate healthy ways to express needs, wants, and feelings.

HEALTH GOAL

- I will learn ways people age.

MATERIALS

Teaching master "My Puppy"; construction paper; paper; crayons or markers; stapler; TM-29, "Help Others to Be Healthy," Appendix A

MOTIVATION

1 Ask students what happens when something dies. (Students might say it stops breathing, it stops growing, it is not alive anymore.) Explain to students that dying is a natural part of life. Point out that the cycle of life is that living things are born (or sprout), grow, and die.

2 Read the poem aloud and ask students how they would feel if their puppy died.

(Students might say sad, lonely.) Ask students what the child in the poem did in order to feel better. (Students will say the child talked to a friend and told her how he misses the dog.) Explain that often when we feel sad, talking or crying helps us to feel better. Point out that when something very sad happens, such as when a pet dies, it is healthy to cry.

3 Tell students that when a person has sad feelings, sharing those feelings is the best way to start to feel better. Ask students why they think this might be true. (Students might say that other people have had sad feelings too and they might help, or that sometimes just talking about what happened can help us understand it better.)

EVALUATION

Write the poem on the board. Provide several sheets of paper for students, and have them draw a picture to illustrate the poem. Help students copy the appropriate lines of the poem under their pictures. Have students use another sheet of paper to draw a picture of a person whom they can talk to about their questions about death. Staple the sheets of paper inside a construction paper cover, and have students design a cover for their book. Allow time for students to share their books and their ideas with a friend. Show TM-29, "Help Others to Be Healthy," and use each of the four steps to describe how to help others.

Teaching Master

My Puppy

I loved my puppy,

a sunny, yellow, friendly dog.

And then, one day, he died.

I didn't know.

I didn't know.

My yellow dog would die and go.

And when I knew,

I cried.

I found a friend,

a gentle, caring kind of friend.

She listened and I let her.

I talked to her.

I talked to her.

I said I missed my puppy's fur.

And when she knew,

I felt better.

Pyramid Relay

HEALTH EDUCATION STANDARDS

- Students will demonstrate the ability to access valid information and products and services to enhance health.
- Students will demonstrate the ability to practice health-enhancing behaviors and avoid or reduce health risks.

PERFORMANCE INDICATORS

- Identify ways to locate school and community health helpers.
- Demonstrate healthy practices and behaviors to maintain or improve personal health.

HEALTH GOALS

- I will eat the recommended daily amounts of food from MyPyramid.
- I will follow the Dietary Guidelines.

MATERIALS

Student master "MyPyramid"; tape; legal-size envelopes; two paper bags; index cards (two sets, each set a different color); markers; chalk; TM-1, "Learn Health Facts," Appendix A

MOTIVATION

1 Use the student master "MyPyramid" as a guide for this teaching strategy. Review the information about how different foods are grouped. Then follow the outline of MyPyramid by drawing the outline of the food triangle on the chalkboard. Label the names of the food groups on the outside of the pyramid as shown on the master. Inside the pyramid that is drawn on the chalkboard, write the amount of food needed each day. Tape a legal-size envelope next to each of the five areas on the pyramid.

The amounts for your students are as follows:

Grains: 4 to 5 ounces
Vegetables: 1½ cups
Fruits: 1½ cups
Dairy (milk): 2 cups
Meat and beans: 3 to 4 ounces

2 Write the names of the following foods on index cards, using one card per food. Write the name of each food twice—once on one color index card, and once on the other color card. The cards will correlate to the correct amount of food in each of the areas on the pyramid. You will have eleven index cards for the Grain Group. The eleven food items for this group would include brown rice, whole-wheat bread, corn flakes, oatmeal, spaghetti, pita bread, lo mein noodles, barley, cracked wheat, bagel, and tortilla. The amount of food in the Vegetable Group would include carrots, potatoes, broccoli, green beans, and peas. The amount from the Fruit Group would include grapes, apples, kiwi fruit, and banana. The amount from the Milk Group would include skim milk, yogurt, and cheddar cheese. The amount from the Meat and Bean Group would include beef, turkey, and cashew nuts.

3 Place each set of index cards into a grocery bag. The two grocery bags will be in the front of the room. Divide the class into two teams. Team 1 and Team 2 will line up in single file. When you say "go," the race will begin. The first student in each team will run to the bag in front of his or her line. The student will pull a card from the bag, read it, and place it in the correct envelope. (If a student cannot read a word, you may help that student.) Thus, a student who pulls *banana* will place this card in the envelope that is attached to the Fruit Group. When the student completes this task, she or he will run back to the line and tag the next student in line. This continues until one team finishes.

4 The envelopes are now checked to be sure the foods were placed in the correct food groups. The team that finished first will get 15 points and the team that finished second will get 10 points. In addition, each food placed in the correct envelope will earn 2 points for that team. (You can determine the team who earns or loses points by checking the color of the index card.) For each card placed incorrectly in the envelope, you will subtract 2 points from the team's total points. As you check each envelope, review the foods and the correct food groups. Some foods identified are less common than other foods. Allow students to ask questions about the different kinds of foods with which they may not be as familiar.

EVALUATION

Use TM-1, "Learn Health Facts," to find information about healthful foods. Distribute a copy of the student master "MyPyramid" to each student. Tell the students to draw pictures of different foods their family eats so that the food falls inside the correct group on the master. Have students share their pictures. This is a good time to discuss the amount of food to eat and how to maintain desirable weight. It is also a good time to identify foods that may be specific to different cultures. You may follow up by having a "healthful snack day" and have students bring foods to class that are healthful. You also may follow up by having a "foods from different cultures day" and have students bring foods related to various cultures.

INCLUSION

If you have a student in your class who is in a wheelchair, ask another student to serve as a runner. The student in the wheelchair will stay near the bag and will tell the runner where to place the card.

Anatomy of MyPyramid

One size doesn't fit all

USDA's MyPyramid symbolizes a personalized approach to healthy eating and physical activity. The symbol has been designed to be simple. It has been developed to remind consumers to make healthy food choices and to be active every day. The different parts of the symbol are described below.

Proportionality

Proportionality is shown by the different widths of the food group bands. The widths suggest how much food a person should choose from each group. The widths are just a general guide, not exact proportions. Check the Web site for how much is right for you.

Variety

Variety is symbolized by the 6 color bands representing the 5 food groups of the Pyramid and oils. This illustrates that foods from all groups are needed each day for good health.

Gradual Improvement

Gradual improvement is encouraged by the slogan. It suggests that individuals can benefit from taking small steps to improve their diet and lifestyle each day.

Activity

Activity is represented by the steps and the person climbing them, as a reminder of the importance of daily physical activity.

Moderation

Moderation is represented by the narrowing of each food group from bottom to top. The wider base stands for foods with little or no solid fats or added sugars. These should be selected more often. The narrower top area stands for foods containing more added sugars and solid fats. The more active you are, the more of these foods can fit into your diet.

Personalization

Personalization is shown by the person on the steps, the slogan, and the URL. Find the kinds and amounts of food to eat each day at MyPyramid.gov.

MyPyramid.gov
STEPS TO A HEALTHIER YOU

GRAINS | VEGETABLES | FRUITS | OILS | MILK | MEAT & BEANS

USDA U.S. Department of Agriculture
Center for Nutrition Policy
and Promotion
April 2005 CNPP-16

USDA is an equal opportunity provider and employer.

GRADE 2

Check Me Out

HEALTH EDUCATION STANDARDS

- Students will comprehend concepts related to health promotion and disease prevention to enhance health.
- Students will demonstrate the ability to advocate for personal, family, and community health.

PERFORMANCE INDICATORS

- Identify that healthy behaviors impact personal health.
- Make requests to promote personal health.

HEALTH GOALS

- I will have checkups.
- I will keep a health record.
- I will cooperate with health helpers. (Consumer and Community Health)

MATERIALS

Teaching master "Check Me Out"; student master "The Checkup"; pencils or crayons; TM-7, "Find Health Facts and Get Help," Appendix A

MOTIVATION

1 Tell students you are going to read them a poem titled "Check Me Out." This poem is about having a checkup. A *checkup* helps a doctor learn about the health of your body. Read the poem out loud. Ask students if they have had a checkup.

2 Give students a copy of the student master "The Checkup." Read the poem again. After you read each of the following lines, stop and have students find the correct picture on "The Checkup" and circle it:

- Waiting while I get weighed (circle the scale)

- Sitting for my blood pressure (circle the blood pressure cuff)
- I'm still with the thermometer (circle the thermometer)
- Looks at my throat (circle the tongue depressor)
- She listens to me breathe (circle the stethoscope)
- She looks in my ears (circle the otoscope)

3 Review the following information about checkups with students. When you go to the doctor, the doctor may measure you. *Height* is a measure of how tall you are. The doctor wants to know how fast you are growing.

Weight is a measure of how heavy you are. The doctor wants to know if you are at a healthful weight. The doctor shines a light into your eyes to check them. The doctor may ask you to read letters on a chart to learn how well you see. The doctor shines a light into your ears to check them. The doctor will look to see if there is too much wax in your ears. This can keep you from hearing. The doctor may ask you to listen for sounds and raise your hand when you hear them. The doctor wants to know if you can hear well. The doctor will listen to your lungs. You will be asked to take a deep breath and blow out. The doctor also listens to your heart to see if your heart is healthy.

EVALUATION

Tell students that they will want to have regular medical checkups. Have students use the student master "The Checkup." Ask them to tell what a doctor does during the checkup. They are to take turns pointing to one of the pictures on the student master and saying one of the following: *checks to see how much I weigh, listens to my blood pressure, takes my temperature, looks in my throat, listens to my lungs, checks my ears.* Then show TM-7, "Find Health Facts and Get Help," to determine how to find medical help in the community.

Teaching Master

Check Me Out

by Patricia M. Dashiell

Sitting and waiting,
that's what I do.
Sitting and waiting,
outside on the chairs,
inside on the table.

It's boring on the chairs.
It's cold on the table.
I sit, and I wait.

Sitting and waiting,
that's what I do,
sitting and waiting.
Then, she walks in,
No more waiting!

Sitting and waiting,
that's what I do,
sitting and waiting,
waiting while I
get weighed,
sitting for my blood pressure
 (and my temperature).

I don't move on the scale.
I'm still with the
thermometer.
I sit, and I wait.

I say, "Ahhhhh."
She looks at my throat.
I cough.
She listens to me breathe.
I look right.
I look left.
She shines a light at me.
She looks in my ears.
She thumps my back.
She taps my knees.

Sitting and waiting,
that's mostly
what I do
whenever I come here.
I sit, and I wait,
wait for the doctor
to check me out!

Student Master

The Checkup

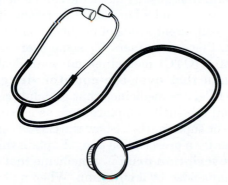

**Stethoscope
(Heart)**

**Tongue Depressor
(Tongue)**

**Scale
(Body Weight)**

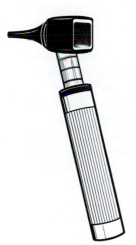

**Otoscope
(Ear)**

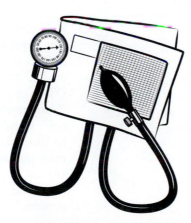

**Blood Pressure
Cuff (Arm)**

Thermometer

GRADE 2

Medicine Safety

HEALTH EDUCATION STANDARDS

- Students will demonstrate the ability to access valid information and products and services to enhance health.
- Students will demonstrate the ability to practice health-enhancing behaviors and avoid or reduce health risks.

PERFORMANCE INDICATORS

- Identify ways to locate school and community health helpers.
- Demonstrate healthy practices and behaviors to maintain or improve personal health.

HEALTH GOALS

- I will use medicine in safe ways.
- I will choose safe and healthful products. (Consumer and Community Health)

MATERIALS

Teaching master "A Prescription Drug Label"; student master "Medicine Safety Rules"; transparency projector; examples of containers for over-the-counter and prescription drugs; TM-1, "Learn Health Facts," Appendix A

MOTIVATION

1 Introduce the word *drug*. A **drug** is something that will change the way a person's body works. Explain that some kinds of drugs, such as medicine, can be helpful. A **medicine** is a drug that is given to help a person feel better if she or he is ill. There are many different kinds of medicines. Some medicines are pills. Some are given in shots, or injections. Some medicines can be breathed in, or inhaled, such as medicine sprays. Other medicines can be placed on the skin in the form of a patch. The patch has medicine that is absorbed,

or goes through the skin. From the skin, the medicine goes into the blood, where it is carried throughout the body.

2 Explain that, just as medicine can be helpful, it can also be harmful. Place containers for different kinds of medicine on your desk. Place containers for some over-the-counter (OTC) medicines on your desk. Explain that **over-the-counter drugs,** or **OTCs,** are medicines that an adult can buy off the shelf in a place such as a drugstore or supermarket. Show the class a container for a prescription drug. Explain that a **prescription drug** is a medicine that is recommended by a physician. When a physician thinks that a certain type of drug will help a person, the physician writes a special note called a prescription. The prescription is taken to a special worker called a pharmacist. A **pharmacist** is a person who fills the prescription. Explain that prescription drugs are more powerful than OTC drugs.

3 Explain to students that regardless of the type of medicine, a medicine should be given to students only by a responsible adult. Students should not take either OTCs or prescription drugs by themselves. Emphasize that medicines can be dangerous. Read the warnings on these labels to the class. For example, some warnings may indicate that the medicine can cause rashes. Other medicine can cause drowsiness and sleep. Some medicines can cause serious harm.

4 Have students differentiate between OTC labels and prescription labels. Pick up containers for different medicines and have students tell you if it is an OTC or prescription drug. Then distribute the student master "Medicine Safety Rules." You can review the information on this master before distributing it. In addition, review safety tips for taking medicine: (1) Take medicine only from a responsible adult. (2) Ask an adult to help you read the label so that the medicine is taken according to

directions. (3) Tell a responsible adult if the medicine produces a harmful effect such as a rash. Stop taking the medicine and have the responsible adult contact a physician to find out what to do. (4) Never take another person's medicine because, while it can help the other person, it can harm you. (5) Medicine should be placed away from the reach of small children so that they do not take it by mistake.

5 Show the teaching master "A Prescription Drug Label," and have students observe certain parts of the label. For example, point out that the name of the person for whom the medicine is prescribed is on the label. The physician's name is on the label. There is a place that shows a warning. Show students the directions one must follow in using the medicine. Emphasize that only the person for whom the medicine is intended should be taking the medicine.

EVALUATION

Have students take home the student master "Medicine Safety Rules" to share with a parent. Students are then to share ways they practice medicine safety in their homes. Students can also share tips with others to protect them from being harmed by medicine. Use TM-1, "Learn Health Facts," to brainstorm facts to know about medicine safety.

Student Master

Medicine Safety Rules

Dear Parent,

Your child has learned about medicines. Your child has learned the difference between an over-the-counter (OTC) medicine and a prescription drug. A copy of each label is shown below. Show your child OTC medicines and drugs that are in your home. Tell your child not to take any medicine unless you give it to him or her. Go over the medicine safety rules with your child.

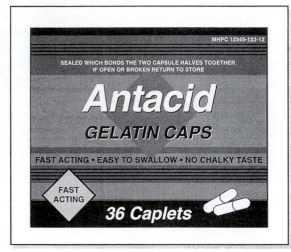

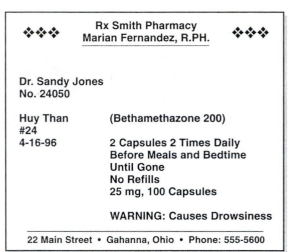

Medicine Safety Rules

1. Take medicine only from a parent or another responsible adult.

2. Read the label with an adult, and follow the directions.

3. Tell an adult if a medicine produces a harmful effect such as a rash. Stop taking the medicine, and have the responsible adult contact a physician to find out what to do.

4. Never take another person's medicine. It can help the other person, but it may harm you.

5. Keep medicine away from small children so they do not take it by mistake.

Teaching Master

A Prescription Drug Label

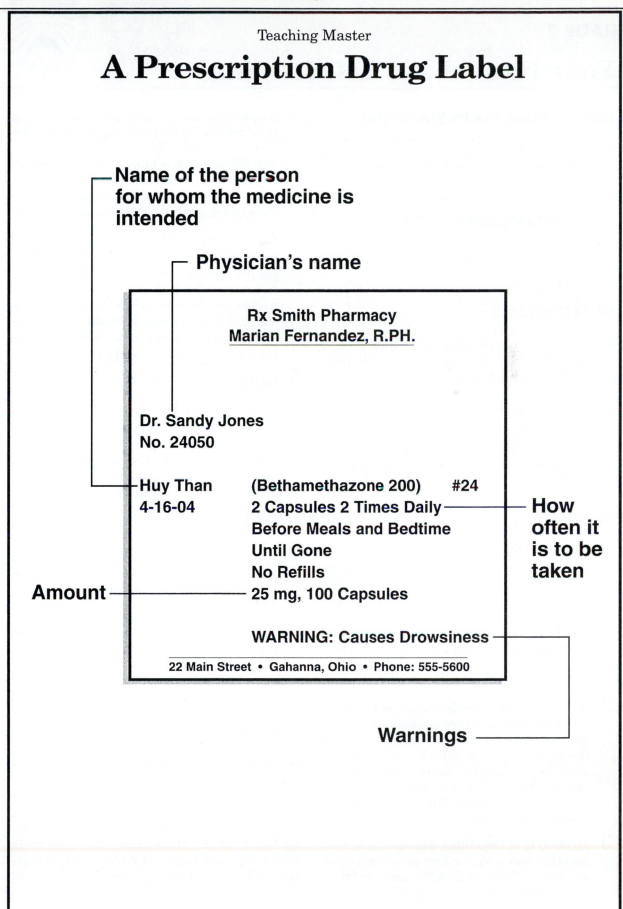

Name of the person for whom the medicine is intended

Physician's name

Rx Smith Pharmacy
Marian Fernandez, R.PH.

Dr. Sandy Jones
No. 24050

Huy Than   (Bethamethazone 200)   #24
4-16-04   2 Capsules 2 Times Daily
               Before Meals and Bedtime
               Until Gone
               No Refills
Amount   25 mg, 100 Capsules

               WARNING: Causes Drowsiness

22 Main Street • Gahanna, Ohio • Phone: 555-5600

How often it is to be taken

Warnings

GRADE 2

Your Handshake Is Glittering

HEALTH EDUCATION STANDARD

- Students will comprehend concepts related to health promotion and disease prevention to enhance health.

PERFORMANCE INDICATORS

- Describe ways to prevent communicable diseases.

HEALTH GOALS

- I will protect myself and others from germs.
- I will be neat and clean. (Personal Health and Physical Activity)

MATERIALS

Student master "Avoiding Other People's Germs"; glitter; TM-1, "Learn Health Facts," Appendix A

MOTIVATION

1 Begin this strategy by showing the class you have glitter. Empty a small amount of glitter on your right hand. Spread it all over your hand and ask for a volunteer who would like to shake your hand. Shake hands with this person and make sure the handshake is tight and held for a few seconds so the glitter is transferred to the student's hand.

2 Ask this student to do the same with another student, who then shakes hands with another student, and so forth. Stop when five students in the class have had an opportunity to shake hands. Then ask the last student to shake hands to show the class his or her hand. The class will notice glitter on the hand.

3 Explain that the glitter represented germs and that you were the first person who had the germs. Explain that five persons later, your germs showed up. Emphasize that

people who are ill have germs in and on their bodies. Through touch, the germs are spread to others. Suppose the people who had glitter on their hands (all five) touched their mouths with the hand with germs on it. The germs would have gotten inside their bodies and caused them to become ill.

4 Explain that one person can infect others without even touching them. For example, the fifth person who got the teacher's germs never even touched the teacher. Yet that person got the teacher's germs. This is one reason why people who have some illnesses, like the common cold, can infect many others without directly touching them.

5 Explain that the most common way germs are spread is through touch. The germs from one person's hands can be spread to another person when they touch or when they share an object. You can use another demonstration with the class to show how germs are spread. Ask to use another person's pencil. Take the pencil. Pretend to sneeze and cover your nose with the hand holding the pencil. The pencil now has the germs. Now hand the pencil back to the student. Suppose that student were to place her hand in her mouth. That student might become infected with your germs. That student might become ill.

6 Explain to students that if they are not feeling well, it may be important for them to stay home. If they have a cold and come to school, they can spread their cold germs to others.

EVALUATION

Distribute the student master "Avoiding Other People's Germs." Have students share this student master with a parent. It contains tips for avoiding the germs of others. Students can work with a parent to add ways to avoid the germs of others. Have students share their health tips with the class. Show TM-1, "Learn Health Facts," and review tips about ways to avoid germs at home.

Avoiding Other People's Germs

Dear Parent,

Your child has been learning about ways germs are spread. This master contains a list of ways your child can avoid the germs of others and keep from spreading germs.
Help your child add to the list.

1. I will not go near other people who are ill.
2. I will wash my hands after I use the restroom.
3. I will wash my hands with soap and water after I sneeze or cough.
4. I will not drink from the same cup as someone else.
5. I will cover my mouth when I cough.
6. I will cover my mouth when I sneeze.
7. I will stay home from school when I have a cold.
8. I will wash my hands before handling food.
9. I will not handle objects that a person who has a cold has touched.
10. I will not touch a used tissue.

11. _____

12. _____

13. _____

14. _____

15. _____

Don't Fall for It

HEALTH EDUCATION STANDARDS

- Students will demonstrate the ability to access valid information and products and services to enhance health.
- Students will analyze the influence of family, peers, culture, media, technology, and other factors on health behaviors.

PERFORMANCE INDICATORS

- Identify trusted adults and professionals who can help promote health.
- Describe how the media can influence health behaviors.

HEALTH GOALS

- I will check out ads.
- I will choose safe and healthful products.

MATERIALS

Student master "Make the Better Deal"; two paper cups; any two health-related products that can be purchased from a supermarket, such as aspirin, but one a name brand and the other a generic brand, each with exactly the same ingredients and weight but with different prices; TM-4, "Think about Your Health Choices," Appendix A

MOTIVATION

1 Begin this strategy by telling the class that you just discovered the most exciting product in the world. This product is called Incredible Ears. Bring two cups to class. However, tell students that although these two objects may look like cups, they are not. Explain that you just got these cups from a friend of yours who saw them advertised on television. Tell students that they will have the opportunity to buy a set of Incredible Ears too, but first you want to provide them with information so they know what they will be purchasing.

2 Begin by telling students that the Incredible Ears help people learn better because they help the brain understand any information very easily. Tell the class that other students who use Incredible Ears get A's in school. Incredible Ears have the ability to make any schoolwork easy to understand. And Incredible Ears work easily. Show students how they work by placing a cup over each ear and holding them in place with your hands. Tell students that if they want a pair, they will need to bring twenty-five cents from home tomorrow. If they do not, they will not be able to get a pair, because Incredible Ears will no longer be sold. Tell students that if they buy Incredible Ears, they will probably get all A's every year in school.

3 Ask students, by a show of hands, who plans to bring in twenty-five cents to school the next day. Many students will probably raise their hands.

4 Process the information you have just told to the class. Ask students why they would want to buy Incredible Ears. Students may indicate that they believe what you have said. They particularly believe you because you are the teacher. Explain that every day, many famous people such as movie stars and athletes appear on television to try to sell products. This is called an endorsement. However, an endorsement does not mean that the product being sold is something that the buyer may really need.

5 Explain to students that you made many false claims, and say that there is no product that is capable of making students understand everything and thus making it easy to get A's. The only way to get A's is to do all schoolwork and study hard. Even this will not guarantee that people will get A's. No product they can buy will help them to automatically get A's. Explain that you

made a false claim. A *false claim* is a lie that a company might tell so that people will buy its product.

6 Tell the class that you also mentioned that you needed the money by tomorrow because after that time Incredible Ears will no longer be available. Explain that when some people try to sell products, they say things like "the products will be available for only a short period of time." This pressures people into making choices without having the time to think about whether or not these products really work.

7 Explain to students that they have just seen how companies try to get people to buy their products. Most companies do not lie or pressure people to buy their products. However, some do. Also, people do not know if the products work. As a result, many people spend money on products they do not need or do not work. Explain to students that as they grow older, they will make decisions about products. They will need to analyze the information they receive about the product and determine if they need the product or if there is another product that may be a better purchase. Show the students the two products you purchased at the supermarket. Explain that the products are exactly the same, but one is the popular, or name brand, product and the other is the generic, or store brand, product. Read the labels to students. Read the claims made on the products. Tell the students how many items of each of the products are in the package. Then tell them the price. Have students tell you which product they should buy and why. Review why buying one product is a wiser choice than buying the other product.

EVALUATION

Distribute the student master "Make the Better Deal." Have students complete the master. Explain that many choices about health often are influenced by family beliefs and cultural aspects. Review TM-4, "Think about Your Health Choices," and discuss how culture influences health decisions. For example, people may eat different foods during holidays. Have students give examples.

Make the Better Deal

Name _____

Look at the two products. Answer the questions about the products. Decide which product is a better deal.

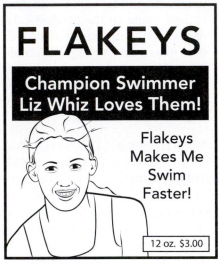

1. Which product contains an endorsement?

_____

_____

2. Which product has a false claim?

_____

_____

3. Which product has healthful ingredients?

_____

_____

4. Which product is a better deal? Why?

_____

_____

Environmental Health

GRADE 2

That's a Litter Bit Better

HEALTH EDUCATION STANDARD

- Students will comprehend concepts related to health promotion and disease prevention to enhance health.

PERFORMANCE INDICATOR

- Identify that healthy behaviors impact personal health.

HEALTH GOAL

- I will help keep my environment friendly.

MATERIALS

A large trash bag containing enough of the following items so that each student can have at least one item: crumpled papers, tissues, soda cans, candy wrappers, empty cereal boxes; TM-1, "Learn Health Facts," Appendix A

MOTIVATION

1 Before coming to class, take a trash bag and place different disposable items in it. The items should be clean and may include clean tissues, newspaper pages, sheets of paper, candy wrappers, and empty cereal boxes. Be sure to have at least one item for each student in the class.

2 Bring the filled trash bag to class. Before you begin this strategy, be sure the classroom is clean. Have students look around the room and notice how clean it looks. Emphasize that the room is clean. Tell students that you are going to have a grab bag. Explain that students will have the opportunity to select something from the bag you brought to school. Go around the room and have each student select an item and place that item on his or her desk. Students will

probably wonder why they are picking the items you have brought to class. Explain to students that they do not need to keep their items on their desks. Tell students that they should place their items on the floor. They do not need to place these items in the trash basket in the room.

3 Once students have placed their items on the floor, have them observe how the room now looks. Students will share that the room looks dirty. Ask them if they would mind if the room stayed like it is. Students may say that they do not wish to be in a room with trash all over. Explain to students that what they just did was litter. To *litter* means to throw trash in places that are not made to hold garbage. Explain that it is against the law to litter. Products such as crumpled papers and cereal boxes need to be disposed of, or thrown away, properly.

4 Have students pick up their litter and then place it in your trash bag. Tell students you will dispose of the litter. Explain to students that when they are in their community, they have a responsibility to dispose of trash in a responsible manner. This means throwing trash in litter baskets or garbage cans. It also means recycling. To recycle is to use something again.

5 Explain that litter can be harmful to health. For example, food that is thrown on the ground attracts insects and rodents such as flies and rats. Flies and rats carry germs that can cause people to become ill. For example, a fly is an insect. A fly can land on food or on other products that may contain germs. The fly then lands on a piece of food you will eat. The germs from the fly can enter your body when you eat that food and you can become ill. Tell students that litter can cause harm. Suppose the soda can has soda inside and it spilled on the floor in the classroom. A person walking by might fall because the floor would be slippery.

Environmental Health

EVALUATION

Review the information in TM-1, "Learn Health Facts," and apply this information to the task that follows. Have students take a small strip of paper and write the name of an item of waste that they may have seen on the street in their community. They are then to come to the front of the room and throw their crumpled paper in the trash. But they must first say the name of the item; for example, "This is an orange peel and it belongs in the trash." After each student has a turn, name the most common forms of litter and discuss what people can do to dispose of each of these properly. Ask students to name items that can be recycled.

Who's Calling?

HEALTH EDUCATION STANDARD

- Students will demonstrate the ability to practice health-enhancing behaviors and avoid or reduce health risks.

PERFORMANCE INDICATOR

- Demonstrate behaviors to avoid or reduce health risks.

HEALTH GOALS

- I will follow safety rules for home and school.
- I will protect myself from people who might harm me.

MATERIALS

Telephone (not hooked up); TM-1, "Learn Health Facts," Appendix A

MOTIVATION

1 Explain to students that it is not possible to tell, from looking at or listening to a person, if that person might try to harm them. Explain that one way to protect themselves is to be especially careful around strangers. A *stranger* is a person they do not know. Students need to know that most strangers will not harm children. However, some strangers may try to harm children. These strangers may not look different from other people and they may seem to be very friendly. Explain that it is important for students to learn to protect themselves.

2 Explain that you are going to illustrate one particular way that a person might try to harm a child. Ask for a volunteer to help you with a demonstration. Pretend you are a stranger who is calling the student. Share the following script with the volunteer so that she or he will answer your

questions in the way that a typical student might answer the telephone. Pretend to have the telephone ring and then proceed with the following conversation:

Student: Hello.
Stranger: Hi! Who is this?
Student: This is Fran.
Stranger: Hi, Fran. This is Mr. Smith. Is your mother at home?
Student: No.
Stranger: Do you know when she will be home?
Student: No.
Stranger: Is anyone else at home?
Student: No.
Stranger: Fran, I have a package your mom wanted me to deliver to your house and I lost your address. Would you give me your address, and I'll stop by in a little while to deliver her package?
Student: Sure. I live at 1234 Fifth Street.
Stranger: Thanks. When I come over, just open the door and I'll give you the package.

3 Ask students to identify the different items of information that were given to you, the stranger. They should list the child's name, the fact that the mother was not home, that the child did not know when she would be home, that no one else was at home, and the address. Explain that if the stranger wanted to harm a child, the student would be in possible danger.

4 With a volunteer, demonstrate another telephone conversation with the student giving the following different answers:

Student: Hello.
Stranger: Hello. Who is this?
Student: With whom do you wish to speak?
Stranger: Is your mother at home?
Student: She's busy right now and can't come to the phone. Can I take a message?
Stranger: I need to deliver a package for her, and I lost your address. Will you please give me your address so that I can deliver the package for her?

Student: If you leave me your name and phone number, my mother will call you back shortly.

Stranger: Never mind. Good-bye.

5 Discuss with students the reason that the second conversation protects the safety of the student. At the end of the conversation, the stranger had no information about the student. If the stranger was a person who wanted to harm a child, this student would be safe.

EVALUATION

Review TM-1, "Learn Health Facts," and apply the information on this master to answering the telephone when at home. Ask students to identify the information that was not given to the stranger in this conversation. They should say the child's name, that the mother was not home, and the address. Repeat this activity with different students and evaluate their responses. Review telephone safety rules.

Mental and Emotional Health

GRADE 3

Putting Your Best Foot Forward

HEALTH EDUCATION STANDARDS

- Students will demonstrate the ability to practice health-enhancing behaviors and avoid or reduce health risks.
- Students will demonstrate the ability to use goal-setting skills to enhance health.

PERFORMANCE INDICATORS

- Identify responsible personal health behaviors.
- Set a personal health goal and track progress toward its achievement.

HEALTH GOALS

- I will take responsibility for my health.
- I will practice life skills.

MATERIALS

One pair of shoes for each student; TM-25, "Practice Healthful Behaviors," Appendix A

MOTIVATION

1 On the day before you teach this strategy, ask students either to bring an extra pair of shoes from home or to wear a pair of shoes that they wore to a meaningful event and when they performed a healthful action. For example, a student may have worn a pair of shoes at a birthday party at which family members who had not visited for a long time gathered together and shared wonderful memories. The shoes can be any type, such as athletic shoes, dress shoes, or tap dance shoes.

2 Explain to students that it is important to be at their best to maintain and improve health status. Introduce the phrase *putting your best foot forward*. Have students share what they think this phrase means. Explain that "putting your best foot forward" means to do the very best you can at all times. This means doing your best when you perform tasks, interact with others, and make decisions.

3 Tell the class that student volunteers are going to participate in an activity called Putting Your Best Foot Forward. Ask for each student volunteer, in turn, to wear his or her chosen pair of shoes and come to the front of the room. Each student volunteer is to show her or his pair of shoes to the class and describe a situation in which the shoes were worn.

4 Discuss the situations in which the shoes were worn. Why was it important for the students to "put their best foot forward" in each of these situations?

EVALUATION

Ask students to name three life skills they will practice. Have them tell how each life skill shows a way to "put their best foot forward."

Show TM-25, "Practice Healthful Behaviors," and have students identify a healthful behavior. Then have them apply each step in the master.

MULTICULTURAL INFUSION

Have students wear or bring a pair of shoes that has a cultural significance. Perhaps the shoes were purchased in another country or were worn by people of another culture during a celebration or on a particular holiday. Have students share a life skill practiced by people of a specific culture.

Family and Social Health

GRADE 3

Want Ad: A Friend

HEALTH EDUCATION STANDARDS

- Students will demonstrate the ability to use interpersonal communication skills to enhance health and avoid or reduce health risks.
- Students will demonstrate the ability to advocate for personal, family, and community health.

PERFORMANCE INDICATORS

- Demonstrate effective verbal and nonverbal communication skills to enhance health.
- Encourage others to make positive health choices.

HEALTH GOALS

- I will work to have healthful friendships.
- I will encourage others to take responsibility for their health.

MATERIALS

Student master "Want Ad: A Friend"; teaching master "Making Responsible Decisions with Friends"; transparency projector; paper and pencil; newspaper; chalkboard; chalk; TM-30, "Be a Health Advocate," Appendix A

MOTIVATION

1 Discuss friendship. A **friend** is a person whom one knows and likes. Ask students to share qualities they feel are important in a friend. Student responses may include characteristics and behaviors such as these: tells the truth, does things with me, shares feelings with me, does not say unkind things about me, helps me, and is kind.

2 Introduce the idea of a want ad. Explain that a want ad is a printed notice that a person may write in order to find someone or sell something. You might explain that if a school is looking for a teacher, the principal may place a want ad in a newspaper. The want ad will tell people who read that newspaper that this particular school needs a teacher. The word *ad* is short for *advertisement*.

3 Explain to the students that they are going to write their own want ads. Distribute the student master "Want Ad: A Friend." Open a newspaper to the Help Wanted section. Read several Help Wanted advertisements. Explain to students that the ads in this section are notices for people who are needed for jobs. Read some of the copy in the ads. Have students notice the kinds of qualities for which companies are looking. Explain that the companies note the specific qualities that they need.

4 Tell students they also are going to have the opportunity to write want ads. But they are going to write want ads for a friend. Tell students that they are to think about the characteristics they would want in a good friend. A *characteristic* is a special quality or feature a person has. A characteristic might be that a person is funny or friendly. Other characteristics a friend may have might be caring about others or always sharing with others. Tell students to write five characteristics they think a good friend should have. They are to write these characteristics in the lines provided.

5 Have students share what they have written. Write the students' responses on the chalkboard. Do not list responses already mentioned. Afterward, have students read silently what you have written on the chalkboard. Then have the students discuss what they think might be the most important characteristics a friend should have. Eliminate the characteristics that do not appear to be among the most important.

EVALUATION

Show TM-30, "Be a Health Advocate," to demonstrate how each of the four steps can be related

558 © Copyright by The McGraw-Hill Companies, Inc.

to choosing a friend. Have students identify the five most important characteristics a friend should have. Then they are to tell ways to tell if a friend has these characteristics. Have students discuss how a good friend would treat them. Tell students that it is also important for them to choose friends who make responsible decisions. Explain that a **decision** is a choice. A responsible decision is a decision that protects health, safety, and laws; shows respect for oneself and others; follows guidelines set by responsible adults such as parents and guardians; and demonstrates good character and moral values. You can review responsible decision making by showing the teaching master "Making Responsible Decisions with Friends." Have students relate the importance of being a good friend and making responsible decisions.

INCLUSION

Emphasize that being a good friend is not related to how a person looks or what physical qualities a person has. Explain that being a good friend is related to how people treat each other. Explain that people who make fun of others or treat them unfairly because of how they look are not the kind of people who would make good friends. Good friends show respect for others. To show respect means to treat someone as if that person is important. Tell students that every student in the class is important. All people have characteristics that make them special.

Want Ad: A Friend

Write five characteristics you would want a good friend to have.

1. _____

_____

2. _____

_____

3. _____

_____

4. _____

_____

5. _____

_____

Teaching Master

Making Responsible Decisions with Friends

My actions should

• be safe

• be healthful

• follow my family's guidelines

• show good character

• follow rules and laws

• show respect for myself and others

Growth and Development

All of Me

SOCIAL STUDIES · EFFECTIVE COMMUNICATOR

HEALTH EDUCATION STANDARD

- Students will demonstrate the ability to practice health-enhancing behaviors and avoid or reduce health risks.

PERFORMANCE INDICATOR

- Demonstrate a variety of healthy practices and behaviors to maintain or improve personal health.

HEALTH GOAL

- I will be glad that I am unique.

MATERIALS

Teaching master "All of Me"; butcher paper (a five-foot length for each student and a longer sheet for any guest speakers); scissors; crayons or markers; blindfolds for half the students; TM-25, "Practice Healthful Behaviors," Appendix A

MOTIVATION

1 Read the poem "All of Me" to students. Assign students to pairs. Have one student in each pair wear a blindfold for fifteen minutes. Have students do an activity in pairs, such as work on a math problem or write a story. The student who is not blindfolded should provide help and guidance as the student who is blindfolded works. Then have partners change roles. Ask students the following question: What do you think would be different if you could not see?

2 Tell students that a physical challenge changes the body, not the person. Reread the poem with the class, and ask students to explain why the speaker is sad. Dim the lights and ask children to close their eyes as you read the poem aloud. Invite students to explain what the poem is saying. Ask students how the boy without sight learns. Have students describe how the two children are alike and how they are different.

3 Tell students that everyone has feelings, thoughts, and challenges. Define the word *challenges*. Challenges are tasks that are stimulating or difficult. Ask the class to name challenges the two children in the poem are facing. Explain that a physical challenge can be very noticeable (such as needing a wheelchair) or almost invisible (such as a learning disability). Help students brainstorm the kinds of physical challenges a person might face. Point out that people can react to a challenge differently. Have a student read the poem aloud and ask the class how each child reacted to his personal challenge. Allow students time to speculate as to why the two young people feel so differently about their challenges.

4 Give a five-foot length of butcher paper to each student. Have students work in pairs to trace their bodies to make life-size cutouts. Have students draw their faces and draw a T-shirt on their cutouts. Discuss the variety of characteristics people have. (Students might say physical characteristics such as their face or body or personality characteristics such as being friendly or funny.) Then ask students to write some of the traits, skills, and talents they have on the T-shirt of their cutouts. Once students begin writing, add traits and skills to each student's list. Encourage students to add traits and skills to other students' lists. Display the cutouts on walls throughout the classroom. Encourage students to add to their lists as they think of other traits and skills they have. Guide students to recognize that they are more than what they can do.

5 Tell students people with physical challenges are just that—people. Have a Challenge Day for the class. Invite people with disabilities to visit the class to talk about their lives, their friends, and what they want to tell people about their disabilities. Before guests arrive, have the class prepare a list of questions to share with the visitors. Guide students to include questions about guests' thoughts and feelings. Then have groups of students help guests make their own life-size butcher-paper figures and lists for the classroom wall.

EVALUATION

Have small groups work together to make up a play about a child with a physical challenge. Ask students to use their plays to show how all people have feelings, thoughts, and challenges. Show TM-25, "Practice Healthful Behaviors," and apply each of the four steps to helping another person who has a physical challenge.

Teaching Master

All of Me

I have a friend, whose eyes are dark—
who sees all of me.
His heart and mind see even more
than two bright eyes might see.

When he takes my hand to walk,
He says, "Your sadness shows."
And when I ask, "How could you tell?"
He says, "Oh, I just know."

And if we're at a baseball game,
He sees just how I feel.
And when I hate my wheelchair,
He says, "Some feet are wheels."

I have a friend whose eyes are dark—
who sees all I can be.
And when I ask, "How do *you* see?"
He says, "With all of me."

GRADE 3

Balloon-Toss Veggies

HEALTH EDUCATION STANDARDS

- Students will comprehend concepts related to health promotion and disease prevention to enhance health.
- Students will demonstrate the ability to practice health-enhancing behaviors and avoid or reduce health risks.

PERFORMANCE INDICATORS

- Identify responsible personal health behaviors.
- Describe the relationship between healthy behaviors and personal health.

HEALTH GOALS

- I will eat healthful meals and snacks.
- I will choose habits that prevent heart disease. (Communicable and Chronic Diseases)
- I will choose habits that prevent cancer. (Communicable and Chronic Diseases)

MATERIALS

Balloon; TM-2, "Understand Health Facts," Appendix A

MOTIVATION

1 Explain to students that their health habits today will influence how healthy they will be as adults. This means that it is important to eat correctly now and continue to eat correctly throughout life. Introduce the word *habit*. Explain that a habit is an action that is repeated so that it becomes automatic. Students may have picked up harmful habits in the past. For example, students who play sports may have developed habits that continue. When a habit continues, it can be hard to break. Perhaps a student may not dribble a ball correctly.

The longer a person dribbles incorrectly, the more difficult it becomes to dribble correctly. It can take a lot of time and practice to change an old habit.

2 Explain that eating healthfully can become a habit. If this habit is started early in life, it is easy to continue. But if a student has harmful eating habits now, these eating habits may continue throughout adulthood. The harmful eating habits may be difficult to break in adulthood. Emphasize that it is important to follow healthful eating habits now. One way to start is to eat healthful foods. One group of healthful foods is the vegetable group.

3 Explain that this strategy will help students name the many different kinds of vegetables they can eat.

4 Divide the class in half, and have the students form two equal lines. They are to face each other and line up in single file. Explain to students that they are going to play a game called Balloon-Toss Veggies. The game goes as follows: You will begin by standing in front of one line. Tap the balloon high in the air to the first student in the line. The student to whom the balloon is tapped must name a vegetable and tap the balloon to the first student in the other line. This student must then name another vegetable and tap it back. After students tap the balloon and name a vegetable, they go to the back of their team's line. The balloon gets tapped back and forth from student to student and must remain in the air. Students cannot repeat the name of a vegetable that has already been named. If a student incorrectly names or repeats the name of a vegetable, that student is out of the game and must leave the line and sit down. A team wins when it has the last student remaining.

5 Any number of vegetables can be named, including artichokes, asparagus, green beans, lima beans, navy beans, waxed

beans, beets, broccoli, brussels sprouts, cabbage, carrots, cauliflower, celery, chard, corn, cucumber, dandelion greens, eggplant, kale, kohlrabi, leeks, lettuce, mushrooms, okra, onion, parsnips, peas, peppers, potatoes, radishes, rutabagas, sauerkraut, spinach, squash, sweet potatoes, tomatoes, turnips, yams, and zucchini.

6 You can adapt this strategy to any of the different groups from MyPyramid. For example, you can ask students to name different fruits or meats.

EVALUATION

Keep count of the number of different vegetables students name. Then name the vegetables on the list in step 5 that have not been given. You can have students repeat this activity and compare the number of vegetables named the first time the game was played with the number of vegetables named the second time. Show TM-2, "Understand Health Facts," and apply the information in this master to learning about different kinds of vegetables.

Personal Health and Physical Activity

GRADE 3

O Two My CO$_2$

HEALTH EDUCATION STANDARDS

- Students will demonstrate the ability to practice health-enhancing behaviors and avoid or reduce health risks.
- Students will demonstrate the ability to use goal-setting skills to enhance health.

PERFORMANCE INDICATORS

- Demonstrate a variety of behaviors to avoid or reduce health risks.
- Set a personal health goal and track progress toward its achievement.

HEALTH GOAL

- I will get plenty of physical activity.

MATERIALS

Five index cards on which "O$_2$" is written; five index cards on which "CO$_2$" is written; five index cards on which "CO" is written; fifteen-foot strip of yarn; TM-25, "Practice Healthful Behaviors," Appendix A

MOTIVATION

1 Tell students they are going to play a game called the Exchange Game. The game will be played as follows: Take a fifteen-foot strip of yarn and place it on the floor to form an outline of a lung. Select five students to line up single file around the inside of the lung. Hand each student standing inside the lung an index card that says "CO$_2$." Have five more students line up in single file around the lung. These students are to hold cards that say "O$_2$."

2 Students often have difficulty understanding the exchange of gases inside the lungs. Explain to students that they are holding cards that represent gases in the air. These gases are used in the body. The cards that have "O$_2$" written on them represent oxygen. *Oxygen* is a gas in the air that is inhaled into the lungs and is carried by the blood to the cells. "CO$_2$" represents carbon dioxide. *Carbon dioxide* is a gas that is released as a waste product after oxygen is used by the cells. Carbon dioxide is carried away from the cells to the lungs by the blood and released from the body when a person exhales.

3 Explain to students that the following game will demonstrate how the exchange of gases in the lungs occurs. Have each student outside the lung holding an O$_2$ card enter the lung and line up opposite a student lining the inside of the lung. The students should be facing each other. Have them exchange cards with their partners. Now have the students who walked from the outside of the lung to the inside step outside the lung again. The O$_2$ cards will remain with the students who are inside the lung. The CO$_2$ cards are now with the students who are outside the lung.

4 Tell students that when a person inhales, oxygen is absorbed into the lining of the lungs. The oxygen is stored in the air sacs, or *alveoli,* of the lungs. The blood then picks up the oxygen and carries it to the cells. At the same time, blood brings CO$_2$ to the lungs to be exhaled. This exchange of gases was demonstrated by the students who walked into the lung holding O$_2$ cards and left holding CO$_2$ cards.

5 Explain that physical exercise can keep the heart and lungs healthy. A healthful exercise for the heart is called aerobic exercise. **Aerobic exercise** is exercise in which large amounts of oxygen are required continually for an extended period of time. For example, running for twenty minutes without becoming out of breath is an aerobic exercise. People who participate in aerobic exercise should do so without becoming out of breath.

6 Repeat the Exchange Game, but this time make the exchange of cards faster. You begin this activity by leading the class in clapping hands at the rate of about seventy beats per minute. As the class claps to your lead, students will step in and out of the lung and exchange their cards. Then introduce an aerobic exercise such as running, walking, or bicycle riding. Explain that when people exercise, the heartbeat rate increases. More blood is pumped by the heart; more oxygen is needed and must be sent to the cells inside the body. Clap your hands to approximately one hundred beats per minute so that students now must move much faster to exchange their cards. Explain that the heart muscle is working harder. It gets stronger with exercise.

7 Now demonstrate what happens when a person smokes. Use another five students. Three of these students will be given CO cards and two will be given O_2 cards. CO is **carbon monoxide,** which is a poisonous gas in cigarette smoke. CO takes the place of oxygen in the blood. Because the body cells cannot get the same amount of oxygen when CO enters the body, the heart must beat faster than normal to get the same amount of oxygen in the blood. Repeat the activity, but this time students will exchange their cards at a fast pace. Clap at a pace of about eighty-five beats per minute. Students will notice that the heart beats faster when a person smokes. The heart beats about fifteen more times each minute. Emphasize the importance of not smoking and of engaging in aerobic exercises.

EVALUATION

Have students identify different kinds of exercises in which they participate that strengthen the heart muscle. Have students share examples of exercises in which they participate. You can use this opportunity to have students develop a log to record how often they exercise. They can identify the exercises they do, the amount of time spent exercising, and how often they exercise. Have students share their logs with the class. Show TM-25, "Practice Healthful Behaviors." Have the class choose one exercise, then apply each of the four steps to that behavior.

Cigarette Tips

HEALTH EDUCATION STANDARDS

- Students will demonstrate the ability to use decision-making skills to enhance health.
- Students will comprehend concepts related to health promotion and disease prevention to enhance health.

PERFORMANCE INDICATORS

- List healthy options to health-related issues or problems.
- Describe ways to prevent common childhood injuries and health problems.

HEALTH GOALS

- I will not use tobacco.
- I will choose habits that prevent heart disease. (Communicable and Chronic Diseases)
- I will choose habits that prevent cancer. (Communicable and Chronic Diseases)

MATERIALS

Teaching master "How Smoking Affects Health"; transparency projector; old shoe box; sheets of paper; cellophane tape; pencil or pen; magazines; scissors; TM-25, "Practice Healthful Behaviors," Appendix A

MOTIVATION

1 Explain to students that tobacco use is a major health concern. **Tobacco** is a plant that contains a product called nicotine. **Nicotine** is a drug in tobacco that causes the parts inside the body to work harder than they normally should. Drugs that increase the speed at which the body parts work are called **stimulants.**

2 Review the harmful effects of cigarette smoke on the body. Explain that cigarette smoke contains nicotine, and that when a person smokes, nicotine enters the lungs. The smoke from the cigarette replaces the oxygen in the lungs. There is less oxygen in the lungs for the blood to carry to the body parts. Yet the body parts need oxygen. The nicotine also enters the blood. These actions cause the heart to work harder. The heart beats more often. This places stress on the heart.

3 Explain that tobacco also contains tar. **Tar** is a dark, sticky substance in tobacco that is very harmful. Tar can stick to the lining of the lung. The surface of the lungs has tiny air sacs that supply blood with oxygen. Tar can destroy these air sacs. Tar also can cause diseases of the lungs as a person grows older.

4 Explain that the smoke from a smoker's cigarette also is harmful. Tell students that if they are inside a room with people who are smoking, they will inhale the smoke. Explain that people who breathe smoke become ill more often than people who do not breathe smoke.

5 Present the following strategy to the class. Have students decorate a shoe box as if it were a large cigarette pack. The box should have a warning statement that says cigarettes are harmful. Students can cut pictures from magazines and combine these pictures to create sayings or pictures that show that smoking is harmful.

6 Give students a sheet of paper. Tell them to write a statement that indicates why smoking is harmful. They can also be given the option of writing a jingle about the dangers of cigarette smoking or why a person should never smoke.

7 After students write their statements, tell them to roll their sheets of paper into what appears to be a long cigarette. Use tape to attach the paper at the edge so that it remains closed. The paper will now look like a cigarette. Have students place their

"cigarettes" into the shoe box (cigarette box). Explain that the shoe box now contains cigarette tips. Have each student select a "cigarette tip" from the box and read it to the class. Write the different kinds of facts students identified on the chalkboard. Do not repeat similar tips.

EVALUATION

Review the information in TM-25, "Practice Healthful Behaviors," and relate it to smoking. Have students identify the harmful effects of cigarette smoking on the body. You can then show the teaching master "How Smoking Affects Health" and compare student responses to the responses on the teaching master. Have students add additional items they would place on this list.

Teaching Master

How Smoking Affects Health

People who smoke

- have yellow teeth.

- get tired easily.

- have increased heartbeat rate.

- are more likely to have diseases of the heart and blood vessels.

- increase their chances of getting diseases of the lungs.

- have clothes and breath that smell of stale smoke.

- cause nonsmokers to inhale the smoke from their cigarettes.

- can cause fires with their cigarettes.

- spend their money on cigarettes when they can spend it on more useful products.

- have more colds and respiratory diseases than people who do not smoke.

GRADE 3

Steady Flow

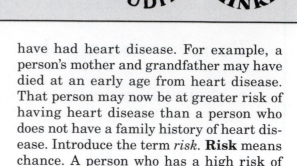

HEALTH EDUCATION STANDARDS

- Students will demonstrate the ability to practice health-enhancing behaviors and avoid or reduce health risks.
- Students will comprehend concepts related to health promotion and disease prevention to enhance health.

PERFORMANCE INDICATORS

- Demonstrate a variety of behaviors to avoid or reduce health risks.
- Describe ways to prevent common childhood injuries and health problems.

HEALTH GOAL

- I will choose habits that prevent the spread of germs.

MATERIALS

Teaching master "Health Habits for My Heart"; transparency projector; straw; hollow coffee stirrer; TM-8, "Access Health Facts, Products, and Services," Appendix A

MOTIVATION

1 Explain to students that heart disease is the leading cause of death. Often, heart disease is due to the health habits a person follows throughout life. Show students the teaching master "Health Habits for My Heart." Review the health habits a person can follow to reduce the risk of heart disease.

2 Explain that sometimes a person cannot completely control the risk of heart disease. For example, a person who belongs to a family that has a history of heart disease has a greater chance of getting heart disease. Explain that a "history of heart disease" means that one or more family members

have had heart disease. For example, a person's mother and grandfather may have died at an early age from heart disease. That person may now be at greater risk of having heart disease than a person who does not have a family history of heart disease. Introduce the term *risk*. **Risk** means chance. A person who has a high risk of having heart disease has a greater chance of having heart disease.

3 Explain that there are different causes of heart disease. The most common cause is when the artery gets narrow. An **artery** is a blood vessel that carries blood away from the heart. The narrower an artery is, the less blood can pass through it. To show what is meant by "narrow," hold your thumb and forefinger (pointer finger) so that they form a circle. (This is the same shape as when someone gives an okay sign using the thumb and forefinger.) Now, close up the circle by sliding your forefinger lower down your thumb. Show students that the opening is narrower. Explain that if they were looking inside an artery, they would notice that the opening can change sizes.

4 To demonstrate the difference between the flow of blood through a narrow and a healthy artery, ask two students to participate. Fill two identical beverage glasses to the halfway point with water. Give each student a beverage glass. Give one student a straw and the other student a hollow coffee stirrer. At your signal, have both students begin together to drink the water. They are to race to determine who can finish first. Stop the activity as soon as one person has emptied his or her glass. Now show the class what happened. (The student who used the straw finished drinking the water much sooner than the student who sipped the water through the stirrer.)

EVALUATION

Have the class discuss why the student using the straw finished sooner than the student using the stirrer. (The opening of the straw is wider than the opening of the coffee stirrer. More water was able to pass through it.) Now have students make an analogy to the functioning of the heart. (Narrowed arteries cannot allow as much blood to pass through them as arteries that are open.) Review the teaching master "Health Habits for My Heart," and have students give examples of each of the ways to keep their heart and arteries healthy. For example, for "exercise each day" students might say "ride a bicycle" or "run." Review TM-8, "Access Health Facts, Products, and Services," and identify organizations within the community that offer information about heart health. One example is the American Heart Association.

Teaching Master
Health Habits for My Heart

I will

- exercise each day.

- eat a healthful diet.

- have a medical checkup each year.

- eat few fatty foods.

- cope with stress.

- know my family history of heart disease.

- never smoke cigarettes.

- stay away from places where people are smoking.

- never use illegal drugs.

GRADE 3

A Hardening Experience

HEALTH EDUCATION STANDARD

- Students will comprehend concepts related to health promotion and disease prevention to enhance health.

PERFORMANCE INDICATORS

- Describe the relationship between healthy behaviors and personal health.

HEALTH GOALS

- I will check out sources of health information.
- I will follow a dental health plan. (Personal Health and Physical Activity)

MATERIALS

Teaching master "The Structure of a Tooth"; transparency projector; two eggs; white vinegar; two beverage glasses; water with fluoride; TM-8, "Access Health Facts, Products, and Services," Appendix A

MOTIVATION

1 Prepare one day before you teach this strategy in class. Place a whole egg in a glass that contains vinegar; place another egg in a glass that contains fluoridated water.

2 Tell students that it is important for them to follow dental health practices. Explain that there are many ways to care for teeth. They have learned about brushing and flossing. But it is also important to choose dental health products that promote healthy teeth.

3 Review the anatomy of a tooth. Show the teaching master "The Structure of a Tooth." Explain that you will review the different parts of a tooth and what the different parts of a tooth do. As you describe what each part does, have students write the information you present. You can also write the information on your overlay. The following is the information you will need to share with students:

- *Crown*—The crown is the surface of the tooth that is at the top.
- *Root*—The root is the part of the tooth that holds the tooth to the jawbone.
- *Enamel*—The enamel is the hard tissue that covers the tooth and protects it.
- *Dentin*—The dentin is the hard tissue that forms the body of the tooth.
- *Pulp*—The pulp is the soft tissue that contains the nerves and blood vessels.
- *Cementum*—The cementum is the hard tissue that covers the root portion of the tooth.

4 Review the importance of the enamel in protecting the tooth and preventing *decay,* or holes in the teeth. Explain to students that they need to use toothpaste that contains fluoride. **Fluoride** is a mineral that is added to water and helps protect teeth from decay. Show students the two eggs in the glasses. Explain that the shell of the egg is somewhat like the enamel on the teeth. The shell protects the egg just like the enamel protects the inside of the tooth. Tell students that one egg is in fluoride and the other is not. Remove the eggs, wipe them dry, and then have students feel them. Students will notice that one egg (the one in the vinegar that was not given fluoride) has a shell that is soft, if not dissolved. Explain that if this was a tooth, it would not be protected from decay.

5 Show the egg that was inside the fluoride. Explain that this egg has a hard shell. It is protected from decay. Emphasize that fluoride protects teeth from decay. Students should read the printing on tubes of toothpastes to see that the toothpaste contains fluoride. If you wish, you can bring a tube of toothpaste to class and show students where fluoride is printed on the label.

Consumer and Community Health

EVALUATION

Point to the different parts of the tooth on the teaching master "The Structure of a Tooth." Have students name each part and identify what each part does. They can also check their toothpaste at home to make sure it contains fluoride. Students can come to class and tell the brand they use and whether it contains fluoride. Show TM-8, "Access Health Facts, Products, and Services," and have students identify different community services that promote dental health.

Teaching Master

The Structure of a Tooth

Enamel

Dentin

Crown

Pulp

Root

Cementum

Environmental Health

GRADE 3

Go Fish

HEALTH EDUCATION STANDARDS

- Students will comprehend concepts related to health promotion and disease prevention to enhance health.

PERFORMANCE INDICATORS

- Describe how a safe and healthy school and community environment can promote personal health.

HEALTH GOALS

- I will help protect my environment.
- I will not waste energy and resources.

MATERIALS

Family master "Ways to Save the Planet"; student master "The Fish Pattern"; a paper clip; a stick at least three feet long; a three-foot string; a magnet; a large paper bag; TM-30, "Be a Health Advocate," Appendix A

MOTIVATION

1 Introduce the word *environment*. Explain that the **environment** is everything that is around us. This means the products we use, the cars we ride in, and the televisions we view. Tell students this activity is about the environment and the many ways we can keep it a healthful and safe place to live.

2 Share with students ways to keep the environment clean. Explain that you are going to give them ten tips for keeping the environment clean. Distribute the family master "Ways to Save the Planet." Define *planet* as the Earth on which people live. Review the ten tips with students, as well as the information highlighted about each tip. The tips are as follows:

1. Recycle products. To *recycle* means to reuse. Jars can be used to store objects instead of being thrown away. Newspapers can be saved and taken to *recycling centers*. The newspapers are collected and the paper is reused.
2. Ride a bike instead of riding in a car. A bike does not use gasoline. Cars burn gasoline. Chemicals created by burning gasoline can make the air dirty. This does not happen with a bike.
3. Do not litter. *Litter* is garbage and trash that is thrown on the ground. Litter attracts insects. Insects can spread disease.
4. Use paper rather than plastic bags. Plastic cannot be recycled. Paper can be recycled. Using plastic helps cause trash to accumulate faster than it would otherwise. This takes up space.
5. Encourage your parent(s) to fix leaks in faucets. Dripping water is wasted water.
6. Use sponges rather than paper towels to clean. Sponges are reused but paper towels are thrown away.
7. Use a cloth bag when shopping. Cloth bags can be reused.
8. Shut off the faucet when brushing teeth. This way, water is not used needlessly.
9. Use products that do not have aerosol sprays. Use pump sprays instead of aerosol sprays. Aerosol sprays such as those used in air fresheners have harmful products that pollute the air.
10. Use both sides of scrap paper. You can save paper this way.

3 Give each student two copies of the student master "The Fish Pattern." On one copy, have each student write a tip on the fish to help save the environment. On the other copy, have students decorate the fish. Give each student a paper clip. Have students cut out and glue each fish with a tip written on it to a decorated fish from the other sheet. As they do this, have them place the paper clip between the two parts of each fish to make a mouth for the fish.

4 Divide the class into two teams. Each team will select one person to be the person fishing. A stick will serve as a pole and a string as the line of the fishing pole. At the end of the string is a magnet. The person will "fish" for a tip on how to save the planet. When a student gets a fish attached to the line by the magnet, another person on the team who is assigned to be the helper will remove the fish from the line. As the fish is removed, the helper reads the tip to the student fishing. The student who is fishing must identify a way to follow that tip. These tips are from the family master "Ways to Save the Planet." A team gets one point for a correct tip. If a student selects a decorated fish and answers the question correctly, that team gets three points. An incorrect answer will earn no points. If someone misses an answer, the next person in line on the other team gets a chance to answer.

EVALUATION

The number of correct answers will serve as a way to assess what students know. After students have taken the family master home and shared it with a parent, ask them ways their families can help care for the environment. Begin this evaluation by referring to TM-30, "Be a Health Advocate," to share with students how they can perform each of the four steps listed.

Ways to Save the Planet

Dear Parent,

Your child is learning ways to care for the environment. Review these tips together.

1. Recycle products. *To recycle* means to reuse. Jars can be used to store objects instead of being thrown away. Newspapers can be taken to recycling centers where the newspapers are collected and reused.

2. Ride a bike instead of riding in a car. A bike does not use gas. Cars burn gas, and the air can become dirty. This does not happen with a bike.

3. Do not litter. Litter is garbage and trash that is thrown on the ground. Litter attracts insects. Insects can spread disease.

4. Use paper bags rather than plastic bags. Plastic cannot be recycled. Paper can be recycled. Using plastic helps cause garbage to pile up faster than need be. This takes up space.

5. Fix leaks in faucets. Dripping water is wasted water.

6. Use sponges rather than paper towels to clean. Sponges are reused, but paper towels are thrown away.

7. Use a cloth bag when shopping. Cloth bags can be reused.

8. Turn off the faucet when brushing teeth. This way, water is not used needlessly.

9. Use pump sprays instead of aerosol sprays. Aerosol sprays such as those used in air fresheners have harmful products that pollute the air.

10. Use both sides of scrap paper. You can save paper this way.

Student Master

The Fish Pattern

GRADE 3

Biking Safely

HEALTH EDUCATION STANDARDS

- Students will comprehend concepts related to health promotion and disease prevention to enhance health.
- Students will demonstrate the ability to practice health-enhancing behaviors and avoid or reduce health risks.

PERFORMANCE INDICATORS

- Describe ways to prevent common childhood injuries and health problems.
- Demonstrate a variety of behaviors to avoid or reduce health risks.

HEALTH GOALS

- I will follow safety rules for biking, walking, skating, and swimming.
- I will follow safety rules for sports and games. (Personal Health and Physical Activity)

MATERIALS

Student master "A Safe Biking I Will Go"; student master "Bicycle Safety"; a bicycle with the parts labeled correctly; TM-25, "Practice Healthful Behaviors," Appendix A

MOTIVATION

1 Begin this strategy by asking students how many of them ride bicycles. Most students will probably raise their hands. Explain that there are important rules to follow when a person rides a bicycle.

2 Give each student a copy of the poem "A Safe Biking I Will Go," and read the poem aloud.

3 Each section of the poem has information about bicycle safety. As you read each part of the poem, use the bicycle to point out many important safety facts. The first fact relates to the need to have a reflector

on the bike. Explain that a *reflector* allows lights from a car to bounce off it, creating light that a driver can see. The light from the car's headlights lights up the reflector. Most reflectors are red. The next important fact relates to brakes. Explain that, before riding, students should make sure the brakes on their bikes are in good working order. They should try to use brakes before they ride too fast or far.

4 The next safety fact concerns seats. It is important for the seat to be just the right height. Explain that, the balls of a person's toes should be resting on the ground when seated on the bike with both feet fully stretched to the ground. The distance to the handlebars should feel comfortable. The handlebars should be set straight ahead and kept tight.

5 Explain that the tires should have enough air inside them because, unlike a car, one does not carry a spare tire on a bike. If the tires feel soft when squeezed, they may need air. Tell students to ask an adult to help put air in a tire and to avoid using an air pump at a gas station. The air pumps at gas stations pump with a great deal of force. Gas station air pumps can cause a tire to burst.

6 Explain that their bikes should have a chain guard to prevent clothing from getting caught in the chain, thus causing them to fall. For students whose bikes do not have a chain guard, discourage them from wearing clothing that could become caught inside the chain. This means not wearing pants with loose cuffs.

EVALUATION

Distribute the student master "Bicycle Safety." Have students look at the picture of the bicycle and write a safety tip for each part. Collect student masters and review their answers. Have them take the master home to their parents. Show TM-25, "Practice Healthful Behaviors," and have them apply each of the four steps to bicycle safety.

Student Master

A Safe Biking I Will Go

❖❖❖❖❖❖❖❖❖

A safe biking I will go,
as my reflectors will glow.

My brakes will stop me in time.
In fact, they'll stop on a dime.

My seat will be set just right.
And my handlebars will be straight and tight.

The tires will have air,
for I do not carry a spare.

The chain guard will help stop
my chances of taking a flop.

It's to everyone's liking,
when safely I go biking.

Bicycle Safety

Look at the parts of the bicycle. Write a safety tip for each part.

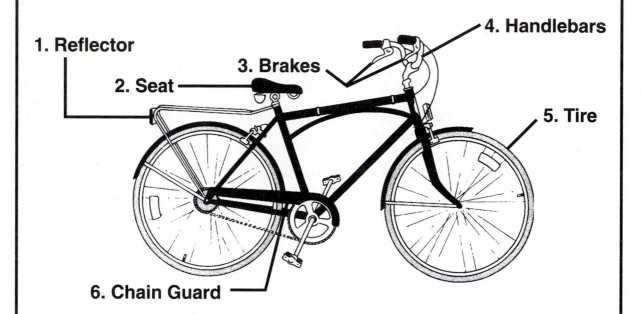

1. Reflector

3. Brakes

2. Seat

4. Handlebars

5. Tire

6. Chain Guard

1. _____

2. _____

3. _____

4. _____

5. _____

6. _____

GRADE 4

Hiding Hurt Feelings

HEALTH EDUCATION STANDARDS

- Students will analyze the influence of family, peers, culture, media, technology, and other factors on health behaviors.
- Students will demonstrate the ability to use interpersonal communication skills to enhance health and avoid or reduce health risks.

PERFORMANCE INDICATORS

- Describe how family influences personal health practices and behaviors.
- Demonstrate effective verbal and non-verbal communication skills to enhance health.

HEALTH GOALS

- I will choose behaviors to have a healthy mind.
- I will work to have healthful family relationships. (Family and Social Health)

MATERIALS

Apple; knife; paper; pencil; TM-25, "Practice Healthful Behaviors," Appendix A

MOTIVATION

1 Introduce the term *self-esteem*. Explain that **self-esteem** is the feeling a person has about himself or herself. **Positive self-esteem** is liking oneself and believing that one is worthwhile. **Negative self-esteem** is not liking oneself or believing one is worthwhile.

2 The day before this lesson, take a bright red apple and hit it once on a hard surface so it becomes bruised on the inside. About one hour before class, slice a fairly large wedge-shaped piece out of the apple from top to bottom. Make sure the slice is through the bruised part of the apple. Keep

the sliced wedge from the apple separate from the rest of the apple. Before students come to class, place both parts of the apple together.

3 Begin this lesson by showing the apple to students. Ask them to describe it to you. Students will make statements such as "It looks bright red" or "I'd like to eat it." After a number of students have had the opportunity to describe the apple, ask who would like to take a bite. Many students may volunteer, but choose only one. As you walk up to the student, separate the two pieces from the apple. The class will not have known that you sliced the apple. Show students the inside of the apple. The inside of the apple will look bruised. It will also have turned brown, and students will say that they would not want to take a bite of the apple.

4 Explain that this apple was bruised inside, and therefore what they saw on the outside was not representative of what the inside was like. Now make the analogy that people may appear to be feeling one way on the outside, but on the inside they may feel differently. This is a good opportunity to emphasize to students that sometimes people want others to think they feel great, so they act cheerful and pretend that nothing is wrong. Yet they may be angry, sad, depressed, or disappointed.

5 This also is a good opportunity to discuss the importance of sharing feelings with a trusted adult. Explain that a *trusted adult* is a person such as a parent whom the student knows will offer help. Explain that not feeling well or not sharing certain feelings can harm a person's health. A person may feel more stress. A person may feel nervous or not be able to concentrate. A person may feel angry or may start fights easily. This can also cause people not to feel good about themselves and have low self-esteem. There are many different people in school or in the community who can be of help. For example, in school, the teacher or the

Mental and Emotional Health

school nurse is available to help with different concerns. You can also identify other people in the school such as counselors who can be of help. Help students identify people in the community who can help such as workers in community health agencies or clergy.

6 Emphasize to students that help is available to them if they ever need it. Have students work in small groups. Each group is to identify sources of anger, sadness, depression, and disappointment in people their age. Then they are to discuss healthful ways to share these feelings.

EVALUATION

Have students fold a sheet of paper in half to create two columns. In the first column, they are to list "Five Ways Young People Get Bruised Inside." In the second column, they are to list "Five Ways to Deal with Bruised Feelings." Show TM-25, "Practice Healthful Behaviors," and have students tell what they can do to practice healthful behaviors.

Family and Social Health

GRADE 4

Older and Wiser

HEALTH EDUCATION STANDARD

- Students will demonstrate the ability to practice health-enhancing behaviors and avoid or reduce health risks.

PERFORMANCE INDICATOR

- Identify responsible personal health behaviors.

HEALTH GOALS

- I will work to have healthful family relationships.
- I will choose habits for healthful growth and aging. (Growth and Development)

MATERIALS

Petroleum jelly; pair of old glasses; wooden tongue depressors; strip of cellophane tape about five inches long; tape recording of muffled sounds; tape recorder; TM-11, "Use Communication Skills," Appendix A

MOTIVATION

1 Introduce the word *aging*. Explain that aging means getting older. Make an analogy between aging and older, beautiful trees in the community. Explain that as trees get older, they have more branches and their trunks become larger. This is an indication that a tree is aging. Explain that people age also. As people get older, their bodies grow bigger, but then they stop growing. For males, this may occur at about age twenty, but for females it may occur at age eighteen or nineteen. This varies with different people. Explain that people age in other ways. They age mentally. That is, they learn more and have had many different experiences throughout life that make them more aware of their surroundings.

2 Explain that as people grow older they have many different physical changes. For example, a tree that is older may have branches that may break easily. As a person ages, that person's body may have changes such as bones breaking more easily.

3 One part of the body that may be affected by aging is vision. Explain that vision is the ability to see. The following activity can help students become more aware of what it might feel like to begin to lose vision. Take the old pair of glasses and smear petroleum jelly on the outside of the lenses. Then ask a student volunteer to wear the glasses and try to read a book or look at an object at a distance. Have that student share what that experience may feel like. The student will probably indicate that his or her vision is not clear. The student probably cannot read the book. You can explain that many older people get blurred vision as they grow older. This happens because the muscles around the eye do not work as well as they once did and objects are not focused. This causes a person to wear glasses to correct the vision problems.

4 Have students cover their ears with their hands. Then play the tape recording of muffled sounds. After students listen to the muffled tape, ask them to share how they felt trying to understand the sound. Students will feel frustrated. You can make an analogy that people who are older may experience a hearing loss.

5 Take the tongue depressor and the piece of cellophane tape. Ask for a student volunteer. Put the tongue depressor behind one finger, and then tape two fingers together. Ask the student to try to do simple things like tying shoes or eating with a fork using the taped hand. Introduce the word arthritis. Explain that **arthritis** is a condition in which the joints are difficult to move. Arthritis is more common in older people than in younger people.

Family and Social Health

6 Explain to students that they have just experienced three different scenarios that a person who is aging may experience. Emphasize that the majority of people who are older than sixty-five do not have many of these conditions and that, in fact, these people are healthy. But it is important to be sensitive to the needs of older adults, especially family members who may have some of these conditions. Explain that there are many ways to be sensitive to older adults. Suppose a person cannot see clearly. Ask students what they might do to help this person. Answers may include the following: "Help to make sure enough light is present when that person is reading," "Help by reading to someone," and "Answer any questions this person may have." Suppose a person has difficulty hearing. One may speak more slowly, loudly, and clearly. A person who has arthritis may have difficulty moving. One can help this person to perform certain tasks or to move around.

7 Ask students if they have known someone who has died. Explain that it is normal to feel a deep sense of loss and sadness when someone they care about dies. Tell students that it is helpful to talk to other people about their loss.

EVALUATION

This is a good opportunity to have students identify physical or mental health concerns an older adult, perhaps someone in their family, may experience. Some of these conditions are mentioned in the strategy. Others may be conditions such as feeling tired often, not speaking clearly, dropping objects easily, or falling easily. Have students identify actions they can take when they are around an older person who has health problems. Emphasize to students that when they are helpful to others, they are also helpful to themselves. They have good feelings when they are helpful to other people. Have them tell you what they would say to a friend or adult if someone they care about dies. Have students write papers on "The Special Gifts and Special Needs of Older People." Use TM-11, "Use Communication Skills," to have students describe what they can do to better communicate with others.

Growth and Development

GRADE 4

Disjointed Movements

HEALTH EDUCATION STANDARDS

- Students will comprehend concepts related to health promotion and disease prevention to enhance health.
- Students will demonstrate the ability to practice health-enhancing behaviors and avoid or reduce health risks.

PERFORMANCE INDICATORS

- Describe the relationship between healthy behaviors and personal health.
- Identify responsible personal health behaviors.

HEALTH GOAL

- I will accept the way my body changes as I grow.

MATERIALS

Teaching master "The Skeletal System"; transparency projector; a coin such as a dime; TM-2, "Understand Health Facts," Appendix A

MOTIVATION

1 Explain to students that one major system of the body about which they will learn is the skeletal system. The **skeletal system** is the body system that is made up of all of the bones. The collection of bones inside the body helps give the body support. Explain that the bones serve as a frame. You can make an analogy of a building being constructed. Explain to students that usually a frame is built. The frame helps to support everything. The frame supports the roof. The frame also helps support the walls. The bones inside the body serve as a frame. *Skeleton* is another name for the bony frame of the body. The skeleton helps a person stand straight. It also helps a person move.

2 Explain that people can move because their bones have joints. A **joint** is a part of the body where two bones meet. Show students examples of different kinds of joints. Bend your knee. Bend your elbow. Explain that these joints can bend back and forth. Hold your arms straight out to the side. Now rotate your arms. Explain to students that you can do this because the joints in the shoulders enable you to move in many different directions such as in a circular fashion. Emphasize that different kinds of joints can help the bones move in different directions.

3 Have students pretend what their bodies would be like if they did not have any joints. Have students seated at their desks. Then ask them to stand while trying not to bend their knees. Students will observe that a simple task like standing is difficult. Have students try to pick up a coin from the floor while keeping the joints in their fingers locked. Students will not be able to do this and will develop an appreciation for how the joints help them move.

4 Explain that bones have functions in addition to supporting the body. Bones also contain a center part called marrow. **Bone marrow** is a part inside the bones that helps produce red blood cells. **Red blood cells** are cells that carry oxygen to the different parts throughout the body.

5 The following activity will enable students to identify the major bones inside the body. Use a transparency of the teaching master "The Skeletal System" to review the location of different bones inside the body, pointing to the corresponding areas on your body as you point to the bones.

6 After reviewing the bones on the master, tell the class you are going to play Simon Says. You can review the rules if students do not know how this game is played. The rules of this version will be similar. While keeping the transparency projected, you

589

will point to areas of the body that contain different kinds of bones. When you point to the area on the master, you will name the corresponding bone. For example, you may say, "Simon Says touch your patella," and students will point to their knee area. Following the rules of Simon Says, students will be eliminated if they do not point to the area you name or if they point to that area when you do not preface your statement with the words "Simon Says."

EVALUATION

Use TM-2, "Understand Health Facts," to have students identify five reasons why knowing about the bones in the body is important for achieving good health. By playing Simon Says, you will be able to determine how well students understand the names of the different bones in the body and where they are located. You can also use the same transparency, but cover the names. Identify certain bones inside the body and ask students to identify the location of the particular bones on the projected image. You can also assign a number to each bone while covering up the name. You may choose ten bones students will need to identify. Students can number down the side of a paper from one through ten. They must write the correct name of the bone that corresponds to the number on the transparency. This can be used as a test. Have students point to bones on their bodies that are most often injured in accidents, and ask them what they can do to prevent injury to these bones. In a discussion of taking care of their bones, students should indicate that proper nutrition is essential to bone growth and to healing should one of their bones become broken.

Teaching Master

The Skeletal System

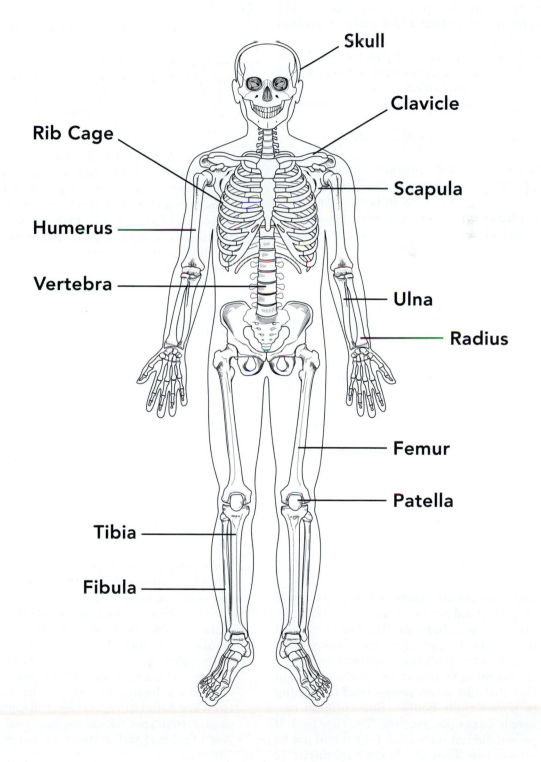

Skull

Clavicle

Rib Cage

Scapula

Humerus

Vertebra

Ulna

Radius

Femur

Patella

Tibia

Fibula

GRADE 4

Mineral Match

HEALTH EDUCATION STANDARDS

- Students will comprehend concepts related to health promotion and disease prevention to enhance health.
- Students will demonstrate the ability to practice health-enhancing behaviors and avoid or reduce health risks.

PERFORMANCE INDICATORS

- Describe ways to prevent common childhood injuries and health problems.
- Demonstrate a variety of healthy practices and behaviors to maintain or improve personal health.

HEALTH GOALS

- I will follow the Dietary Guidelines.
- I will eat the recommended dietary amounts of food from MyPyramid.
- I will read food labels.
- I will choose habits that reduce the risk of disease. (Communicable and Chronic Diseases)

MATERIALS

Teaching master "Important Minerals"; transparency projector; TM-25, "Practice Healthful Behaviors," Appendix A

MOTIVATION

1 Begin by asking students how a car would travel if it did not have gasoline in its tank. Students will indicate that the car would not be able to get anywhere if there were no gas in the tank because there would not be anything to power the engine. Explain that just like a car, people need something to power their bodies. But unlike a car, people do not use gasoline. They use food. If people did not have food, they would not be able to live. They would not have anything

to provide them with a source of energy. Their bodies would not be able to perform.

2 Explain that just having food is not enough. People need to have foods that contain nutrients. A **nutrient** is a substance in food that the body uses as a source of energy. Explain to students that there are six kinds of nutrients. These six nutrients are proteins, carbohydrates, fats, minerals, vitamins, and water.

3 Review the major points about each kind of nutrient. Begin with proteins. Explain that **proteins** are nutrients that help build and repair cells in the body. Proteins are also a source of energy. The kinds of foods that contain proteins include dairy products such as milk and meat such as beef, poultry, and fish.

4 Introduce the word **carbohydrate.** Carbohydrates are nutrients that serve as a main source of energy for the body. The two kinds of carbohydrates are starches and sugars. **Starches** are foods such as bread, rice, and potatoes that provide energy over a long period of time. **Sugars** are carbohydrates that provide very quick energy for the body. Some sugars are natural in that they are contained in healthful foods such as oranges, kiwi, and apples. Other foods contain sugar that is added. Sugars that are added to foods are called **processed sugars.** Cake and candy contain processed sugars. It is best to limit the intake of processed sugars.

5 Introduce the word *fats*. **Fats** are nutrients that help provide energy to the body as well as help the body to store vitamins. There are two kinds of fats. **Saturated fats** are fats in foods that come mostly from animals. Some examples of foods that contain saturated fats include pork, steak, eggs, whole milk, and butter. **Unsaturated fats** are more healthful than saturated fats and are found in vegetables, nuts, and fish. Emphasize that eating too much saturated fat is related to the development of heart disease.

6 Explain that **minerals** are nutrients that regulate many of the chemical reactions in the body. Minerals help the body grow and develop. Green leafy vegetables and meat contain different kinds of minerals. Distribute the teaching master "Important Minerals." Make a transparency of this chart and review content with students. Explain that you are going to play a game called Mineral Match with the class. After reviewing the material in the chart, have students put their charts away. Cover the last two columns on the chart. Only the names of the minerals and the headings in the other two columns should be showing. Identify content in one of the columns. For example, you may say, "This mineral helps a person grow and stay alert." The students will have to answer, "Zinc." You may say, "Bananas and green leafy vegetables are examples of this nutrient." Students will respond, "Potassium." Do this activity so that all of the information in the chart is covered.

7 Explain that **vitamins** are nutrients that help other chemical reactions in the body take place. Some people think they have to take vitamin pills to get all the vitamins they need. But most people following a healthful diet should not need to take vitamins in the form of pills.

8 Introduce the final nutrient, water. **Water** is a nutrient that is needed for all body pro-

cesses. An important function of water is controlling the temperature of the body. Emphasize to students that they should have the equivalent of between six to eight glasses of water each day. Many foods such as fruits and vegetables are made up of large amounts of water.

9 Explain that food should be prepared in ways that help keep the nutrients in them. Share some hints about ways to keep nutrients in foods, such as these: Keep foods cold, cook vegetables for a short period of time to avoid nutrient loss, do not soak vegetables before cooking, and eat foods fresh rather than keeping them around for long periods of time.

EVALUATION

Review the facts about minerals by giving students a blank chart similar to the one used in the strategy. Then have students fill in the blank areas inside the chart. Have students develop a daily menu for a week that includes breakfast, lunch, dinner, and snacks. Be sure they include food and beverage selections that indicate they are aware of diseases that can be caused by nutrient excesses and deficiencies. Use TM-25, "Practice Healthful Behaviors" to have students select a behavior to include nutritious foods in their diets.

Important Minerals

Name of Mineral	Purpose of Mineral	Examples of Foods
Iron	Helps produce red blood cells	Dried beans, peas, liver
Sodium	Helps muscles relax and contract	Salt, beets
Calcium	Helps build strong bones and teeth, helps blood clot	Milk, yogurt, green vegetables
Potassium	Helps cells maintain a balance of water	Bananas, green leafy vegetables
Zinc	Promotes growth and alertness	Wheat bran, eggs, oatmeal
Iodine	Helps make thyroid hormones and provides energy	Iodized salt, seafood

Personal Health and Physical Activity

GRADE 4

The Benefits of Fitness

HEALTH EDUCATION STANDARDS

- Students will demonstrate the ability to use goal-setting skills to enhance health.
- Students will demonstrate the ability to practice health-enhancing behaviors and avoid or reduce health risks.

PERFORMANCE INDICATORS

- Set a personal health goal and track progress toward its achievement.
- Demonstrate a variety of healthy practices and behaviors to maintain or improve personal health.

HEALTH GOALS

- I will get plenty of physical activity.
- I will follow safety rules for sports and games.

MATERIALS

Teaching master "Bee Wise and Exercise"; transparency projector; straw; small glass of water; TM-2, "Understand Health Facts," Appendix A

MOTIVATION

1 Start with a glass of water and a straw. Ask a student to drink a small amount of water through the straw. The student will notice that the water moved smoothly through the straw. You can make an analogy that the straw is like a healthy blood vessel in that this blood vessel was not clogged, and water (analogous to the blood) flowed easily.

2 Then pinch the straw and twist it around. Now ask the same student to drink the water through the straw. The student will notice that the water does not flow easily through the straw. Explain that this straw (blood vessel) is not healthy. The water (blood) could not flow through it easily.

3 Tell students that people who do not exercise and who participate in unhealthful behaviors can have problems with their circulation. Their blood vessels may be clogged and not allow blood to flow easily. Explain that being physically fit helps the blood vessels as well as the heart to stay healthy. Define **physical fitness** as the condition of the body as a result of participating in exercises that promote muscular strength, muscular endurance, flexibility, cardiovascular endurance, and a healthful percentage of body fat.

4 Explain that there are many benefits of physical fitness. Discuss these benefits by showing the teaching master "Bee Wise and Exercise." Provide students with the opportunity to add benefits to this list.

5 Explain that to get one's body into top condition it is important to develop the components of physical fitness. They are muscular endurance, muscular strength, cardiovascular endurance, flexibility, and a healthful percentage of body fat.

6 Introduce the term *muscular endurance*. **Muscular endurance** is the ability to use muscles for an extended period of time. A person who swims for a mile or who runs two miles demonstrates muscular endurance. Muscular endurance can be developed by participating in activities that require long periods of work. For example, a marathon runner will need to run many miles almost every day to develop the endurance needed to run a marathon.

7 Introduce the term *muscular strength*. **Muscular strength** is the ability of muscles to perform tasks with power such as pulling and pushing. For example, a person may be able to lift heavy weights, thereby showing that his or her muscles are strong.

8 **Cardiovascular endurance** is the ability to do exercises that require increased oxygen intake for an extended period of time. Aerobic exercises such as riding a bicycle over a long distance without getting tired indicates that a person has heart fitness.

9 **Flexibility** is the ability to bend easily at the joints and stretch muscles without too much effort. Touching your toes with your fingertips while your knees are locked straight shows you have flexibility. Being flexible helps keep the muscles in the body free from injury.

10 The reduction of body fat is important in becoming physically fit. Everyone has fat tissue, but some people have more fat tissue than others. **Lean tissue** is body tissue that has little or no fat. Becoming physically fit reduces the amount of fat tissue and increases the amount of lean tissue in the body. Aerobic exercises such as speed walking and long-distance running reduce the amount of fat tissue.

EVALUATION

After reviewing the five components of physical fitness, have students identify activities they can do to develop each one. For example, they may do toe touches each day to improve their flexibility. Provide students with the following health fact: "Walking helps you become physically fit." Then show TM-2, "Understand Health Facts," and have students apply this health fact to the four items in the master.

Teaching Master

Bee Wise and Exercise

Bee Wise says that exercise will

help you cope with stress,

help improve your self-concept,

help you feel rested and sleep well,

help your muscles become strong,

help you get along well with others,

help you concentrate in school more easily,

help reduce the chances of developing heart disease,

help the lungs work more easily,

help you have a healthful appearance,

help you perform better in many kinds of sports.

GRADE 4

It's a Difficult Task

HEALTH EDUCATION STANDARDS

- Students will comprehend concepts related to health promotion and disease prevention to enhance health.
- Students will demonstrate the ability to practice health-enhancing behaviors and avoid or reduce health risks.

PERFORMANCE INDICATORS

- Describe the relationship between healthy behaviors and personal health.
- Demonstrate a variety of behaviors to avoid or reduce health risks.

HEALTH GOALS

- I will not be involved in illegal drug use.
- I will say "no" if someone offers me a harmful drug.

MATERIALS

One pair of old eyeglasses; petroleum jelly; needle with tape covering the point; thread; TM-25, "Practice Healthful Behaviors," Appendix A

MOTIVATION

1 Explain that the use of illegal drugs can be harmful to many parts of the body. Opiates such as heroin and morphine are types of illegal drugs that can be abused. These drugs slow the actions of the central nervous system. Drugs that slow body actions are called depressants. Other drugs called stimulants speed up the actions of the body. Cocaine, amphetamines, and crack are stimulants. Stimulants can speed up actions of the body so much that a person can experience heart failure. Marijuana is a drug that is prepared from crushed leaves of the cannabis plant. People who smoke marijuana may experience amotivational syndrome. People

with **amotivational syndrome** lack the desire to perform common everyday tasks such as doing homework.

2 Explain that many body parts are affected when a person uses illegal drugs. The following activity will demonstrate how drugs affect muscle coordination and the ability of the brain to control muscle activity.

3 Place a light coating of petroleum jelly on the lenses of an old pair of eyeglasses. Select a volunteer to come to the front of the class. Give the volunteer a needle and a piece of thread. Tape should cover the point of the needle. Ask the volunteer to try to thread the needle while she or he is wearing the eyeglasses. The volunteer will have difficulty performing the task.

EVALUATION

Have the students in the class explain how using drugs might be compared to wearing eyeglasses that are coated with petroleum jelly. Explain that the blurred vision caused by the petroleum jelly prevented the student from threading the needle. (Using illegal drugs can interfere with vision, which makes the completion of simple tasks difficult.) Responses should indicate that students understand the many effects that different types of drugs can have on the body and that they will avoid the use of illegal drugs in any form. Have students identify a healthful behavior and explain how this behavior is important for good health. Use TM-25, "Practice Healthful Behaviors," as a guide.

Communicable and Chronic Diseases

GRADE 4

Wheel of Misfortune

LANGUAGE ARTS

CRITICAL THINKER

HEALTH EDUCATION STANDARDS

- Students will comprehend concepts related to health promotion and disease prevention to enhance health.
- Students will demonstrate the ability to use decision-making skills to enhance health.

PERFORMANCE INDICATORS

- Describe ways to prevent common childhood injuries and health problems.
- List healthy options to health-related issues or problems.

HEALTH GOALS

- I will recognize symptoms and get treatment for communicable diseases.
- I will choose habits that prevent the spread of germs.

MATERIALS

Student master "Terms Related to Communicable and Chronic Diseases"; paper; writing marker; TM-2, "Understand Health Facts," Appendix A

MOTIVATION

1 Explain to students that they will play a game called Wheel of Misfortune. Explain that the game will focus on diseases that, unfortunately, many people have. Terms related to diseases will also be given.

2 Explain that this game is played like the television show *Wheel of Fortune*. The class can be divided into teams. Each member of the team will have only one turn to select a letter and guess the disease or related term. Explain that the diseases will be either communicable or noncommunicable. You will need enough sheets of paper to hold the individual letters that will spell the words or terms that you use. The words or terms may be diseases that have been covered in previous lessons, or they may be related terms, diseases, or disorders that are listed on the Teaching Master "Terms Related to Communicable and Chronic Diseases." You can choose to distribute copies of this master to students and have them review the information on it. But students should not use this master to find answers to the words or terms. You can choose to assign certain categories for the diseases such as "A Communicable Disease" or "A Disease That Affects Children."

3 You can play several rounds of this game and declare the team that guesses the most words as the winner.

EVALUATION

You can use the information from the teaching master to design a quiz on the different kinds of diseases and terms related to these diseases and their definitions and characteristics. Use TM-2, "Understand Health Facts," to have students identify a health fact and apply the steps in this master.

Terms Related to Communicable and Chronic Diseases

Allergy—a hypersensitive reaction by the immune system to a foreign antigen (protein)

Alzheimer's Disease—a degenerative disease of the brain characterized by premature senility

Antibiotic—a medicine used to treat certain diseases

Antibody—protein produced by B cells that helps destroy pathogens inside the body

Arthritis—a general term that includes more than a hundred diseases, all of which involve inflammation

Athlete's Foot—a fungal infection that grows between the toes when feet are not kept dry

Bacteria—single-celled microorganisms that can produce illness

Cancer—a group of diseases in which there is uncontrolled multiplication of abnormal cells in the body

Chronic Disease—a disease that lasts a long time or recurs frequently

Common Cold—a viral infection of the upper respiratory tract

Communicable Disease—illness caused by pathogens that enter the body through direct or indirect contact

Cystic Fibrosis—a genetic disease that affects the mucous and sweat glands

Diabetes—a disease in which the body is unable to process the sugar in foods in normal ways

Disability—a physical or mental impairment

Epilepsy—a condition in which there is a disturbance of impulses in the brain leading to seizures

Fungi—single-celled or multicellular plant-like organisms, such as yeasts and molds, that are capable of causing disease to the skin, mucous membranes, and lungs

Hives—small, itchy bumps on the skin

Hypertension—high blood pressure

Immunity—the body's protection from disease

Influenza—a viral disease that affects the respiratory system

Leukemia—cancer of the blood

Mononucleosis—a viral infection that occurs most frequently to those in the fifteen-to-nineteen-year-old age group; also known as "mono"

Pathogen—disease-causing organism

Pneumonia—an inflammation of the lungs accompanied by fever, shortness of breath, headache, chest pain, and coughing

Protozoa—tiny, single-celled organisms that produce toxins that are capable of causing disease

Reye's Syndrome—a serious condition, which may follow influenza and chickenpox in children and adolescents, that is characterized by swelling of the brain and destruction of liver tissue

Rheumatic Fever—disease in which there is an acute fever, the joints swell, and the body temperature rises

Sickle-Cell Disease—a blood disease that gets its name from the shape of the abnormal red blood cell

Symptom—a change in a body function from a normal pattern

Tay-Sachs Disease—a genetic disease caused by the absence of a key enzyme needed to break down fats in the body

Consumer and Community Health

GRADE 4

Quack, Quack, Quack

HEALTH EDUCATION STANDARDS

- Students will demonstrate the ability to access valid information and products and services to enhance health.
- Students will demonstrate the ability to use decision-making skills to enhance health.

PERFORMANCE INDICATORS

- Identify characteristics of valid health information, products, and services.
- Choose a healthy option when making a decision.

HEALTH GOALS

- I will check out sources of health information.
- I will choose safe and healthful products.

MATERIALS

Construction paper; writing markers; scissors; variety of empty cans and bottles; children's clothes; TM-8, "Access Health Facts, Products, and Services," Appendix A

MOTIVATION

1 Distribute construction paper, scissors, and writing markers to students. Have students draw two ducks on the construction paper and cut them out.

2 Explain to students that they are going to learn about quackery. Explain that **quackery** is the selling of products or services using false information. Explain that **products** are materials that people may buy, such as cans of food or medicines. **Services** are ways that people are helped. For example, visiting a physician for a checkup is a service for which a person will pay.

3 Present the following tips that students should know to help identify quackery:

- Someone tells you that a product is a miracle cure for something.
- Someone tells you that there is a secret ingredient in a food or product.
- Someone comes to your door to sell you a product that should be sold in a supermarket or drugstore.
- Someone tells you that a product will cure many different illnesses.
- Someone tells you that you can be just like someone else if you buy the product.

4 Explain to students that you are going to sell them products. If they think you are using methods that a quack would use to sell products, they are to hold up their ducks and say, "quack, quack, quack."

5 The following are examples of products and ways to sell them:

- Hold up an empty bottle. "This miracle drug will make you grow up to be very tall." (quack, quack, quack)
- "This cereal has no sugar." Show a cereal high in sugar. (quack, quack, quack)
- "I am coming to your door because this food is so new that no one yet has the secret recipe to make it. You can be the first to try it." (quack, quack, quack)
- "If you wear this clothing, you will be just like . . ." Name a famous person students will admire. (quack, quack, quack)
- "If you wear these sneakers you will play basketball like an all-star." (quack, quack, quack)

6 Have students discuss the criteria they used in determining whether something was quackery or legitimate. Students can also share examples of quackery they have observed and tell why they considered something or someone as being associated with quackery.

EVALUATION

Use TM-8, "Access Health Facts, Products, and Services," to discuss general rules about being a responsible consumer. Divide the class into small but equal groups and have each group select a product from a magazine or make up its own product. Have half of the groups develop "quack" commercials that they will present to the rest of the class. Have the other half of the groups present an actual advertisement from the magazine. Have students determine which are the quack presentations and which are valid advertisements. Students are to discuss their reasons for their choices.

GRADE 4

Environmental Smash CD

HEALTH EDUCATION STANDARDS

- Students will comprehend concepts related to health promotion and disease prevention to enhance health.
- Students will demonstrate the ability to advocate for personal, family, and community health.

PERFORMANCE INDICATORS

- Describe how a safe and healthy school and community environment can promote personal health.
- Encourage others to make positive health choices.

HEALTH GOALS

- I will help protect my environment.
- I will help keep my environment friendly.

MATERIALS

Poster paper; color markers; glue; TM-30, "Be a Health Advocate," Appendix A

MOTIVATION

1 Explain to students that they are going to have the opportunity to use their creative talents to identify ways they can make the environment a more healthful place to live. Give students enough poster paper so they can glue two pieces together. They should form a thick poster that is to resemble a CD, but it will be much bigger so they can have room to write. Explain to students that they are to pretend that they are music producers who have the opportunity to produce a hit CD. However, the CDs they produce will be related to making the environment a more healthful place to live.

2 Tell students to think up a title for their CD and to use their markers to write the title on their CD poster. They should create a title that will focus on making the environment a healthful one for them. For example, they may create a title such as "Sweet Surroundings" or "Clean and Green." They are to create a name of a group that has recorded the songs. One example of a fictitious group might be Ozzie and the Ozones. Another example of a group might be Robby Reuse and the Recyclers. Students are then to design a cover for their album, focusing on a picture of the environment.

3 Tell students they are to take a sheet of paper and use it as sheet music. They are to write a ten-line song that identifies five facts that show the environment is important. Students should give their songs a title. If students wish, they can cut their paper in the form of a CD and write their song on it.

4 An alternative way to do this exercise is to have the students work in teams. Within teams, they can sing a song, thereby presenting different facts to the class. The students in the class must focus on what is being said so they can identify important information about the environment.

EVALUATION

Use TM-30, "Be a Health Advocate," to present this evaluation. Take notes about the different facts presented by the different groups. Use your notes to quiz students about the facts related to the environment. Ask students to identify environmental problems and issues in their community. Have them suggest the names of agencies they might contact to learn more about these problems and issues and to learn if and how students can be of help in addressing some of these environmental concerns.

GRADE 4

I Guard My Eyes

HEALTH EDUCATION STANDARD

- Students will demonstrate the ability to practice health-enhancing behaviors and avoid or reduce health risks.

PERFORMANCE INDICATORS

- Demonstrate a variety of healthy practices and behaviors to maintain or improve personal health.

HEALTH GOALS

- I will follow safety rules for my home and school.
- I will choose safe and healthful products. (Consumer and Community Health)
- I will prevent injuries during physical activity. (Personal Health and Physical Activity)

MATERIALS

Two unpeeled hard-boiled eggs; crayons; marble; glass of water; plastic wrap; magazines; posterboard; glue; paints; TM-25, "Practice Healthful Behaviors," Appendix A

MOTIVATION

1 Show the unpeeled eggs to students. Explain that each of the eggs represents an eye. Use a crayon or marker to draw the parts of the eye on each of the hard-boiled eggs. Place one of the hard-boiled eggs in a clear glass. Pour water over the egg so that water is barely covering it. Explain that a real eyeball is in a protected area. This protected area is the eye socket. Explain that an eyeball is protected by fluids also.

2 Take a marble and drop it on the egg that is in the glass of water. Students will notice that the shell on the egg cracks. Explain that this egg, or eyeball, was not protected. If this were a real eyeball and the marble hit it, the eyeball could have been injured. Vision could have been harmed or even lost.

3 Remove the cracked hard-boiled egg from the glass of water. Replace this egg with the other hard-boiled egg. Cover the top of the glass with clear plastic wrap. Again, drop the marble above the glass. This time, students will notice that the marble hit the plastic wrap and bounced off. The marble did not penetrate the plastic wrap and get to the egg or eyeball. Explain that the eyeball was protected because, in some respects, the cellophane wrap acted like an eyeguard. Eyeguards protect eyes just as the plastic wrap protected the egg. Eyeguards prevent objects from entering the eyes.

4 Explain to students that they are consumers. A **consumer** is a person who buys and uses products and services and who makes choices about how to spend time. Consumers need to make wise choices about products that help protect the health of individuals. For example, your students may participate in many different kinds of sports. They need to keep themselves protected from injury when they play these sports. To do this, they may need to buy special products. One part of the body that needs protection is the eyes. Not only do the eyes need protection during sports, but they also need protection when one is participating in other activities.

5 Explain to students that thousands of people each year lose some vision or are blinded because they injured their eyes doing certain activities. In most of these cases, loss of vision could have been avoided had the person been wearing eyeguards for protection.

6 Identify certain situations in which eyeguards would be recommended. For example, in certain sports such as racquet sports, eyeguards can offer protection from a ball that can hit the eyeball. Suppose a

person has already suffered an eye injury; that person would need to protect his or her eye from further harm. Ask students if they watch basketball on television. They may wonder why some basketball players wear eyeguards. Explain that some of these players may already have suffered an eye injury. They do not want another person's fingers or the ball coming in contact with their eyes. They wear the eyeguards for protection.

7 Tell students that they need to wear eyeguards at certain times. Some situations that call for the use of eyeguards are using sharp tools, being around areas where there may be flying substances such as wood chips flying when a power saw is being used, playing a sport such as racquetball, or using power lawn equipment.

EVALUATION

Introduce this evaluation by using TM-25, "Practice Healthful Behaviors." Have students brainstorm different activities they do or are around that may necessitate the use of eyeguards. Students can also share where they can purchase eyeguards. For example, sporting goods stores or hardware stores sell eye-

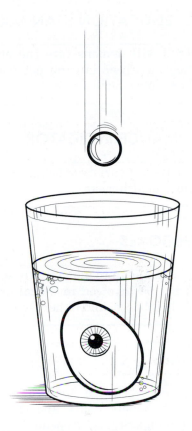

guards. Have students make a commitment to use eyeguards when necessary to protect their vision. You can evaluate students by giving them one point for each activity they identify that requires the use of eyeguards.

GRADE 5

Stress Test

HEALTH EDUCATION STANDARD

- Students will demonstrate the ability to practice health-enhancing behaviors and avoid or reduce health risks.

PERFORMANCE INDICATOR

- Demonstrate a variety of behaviors to avoid or reduce health risks.

HEALTH GOALS

- I will have a plan to manage stress.
- I will not be involved in illegal drug use. (Alcohol, Tobacco, and Other Drugs)

MATERIALS

Student master "Health Behavior Contract"; ruled paper; pencil; chalk and chalkboard; TM-28, "Manage Stress," Appendix A

MOTIVATION

1 Prior to beginning this strategy, students should not know what topic you plan to cover because the element of surprise is important. As soon as your class begins, place students in the following stressful situation. Tell students, "Take out a sheet of paper and number down the left-hand side from one to twenty. I told you that you were responsible for reading (whatever you are working on currently). I am going to see if you completed this assignment. And by the way, this test is going to be worth 50 percent of your grade for the course." Proceed to give students questions that will be almost impossible for them to answer. For example, you can say, "The first question has three parts. Name three effects of stress on the cerebral cortex." Choose three more difficult questions before stopping.

2 Tell students, "This is not a real test. However, when I told you that I was giving you a test, certain reactions occurred inside your body. What are some reactions that occurred?" Students will most likely mention increased heart rate, sweating, and dry mouth, for example.

3 Define the words *stress* and *stressor*. **Stress** is the response of a person's mind or body to stressors. A **stressor** is a physical, mental, emotional, social, or environmental demand. In the illustration, an example of stress was the increase in heart rate. This was one of the body's responses to the stressor. The stressor was the unannounced and difficult test. The test was a mental-emotional demand.

4 Review information regarding general adaptation syndrome. **General adaptation syndrome, or GAS,** is the body's response to a stressor. During the **alarm stage of GAS,** the body prepares for quick action as adrenaline is released into the bloodstream, heart rate and blood pressure increase, digestion slows, blood flows to muscles, respiration increases, pupils dilate, and hearing sharpens. The body is prepared to meet the demands of the stressor. As the demands are met, the resistance stage of GAS begins. During the **resistance stage of GAS,** pulse, breathing rate, and blood pressure return to normal. The pupils contract and muscles relax. If the demands of the stressor are met unsuccessfully, the GAS continues, and the exhaustion stage of GAS begins. During the **exhaustion stage of GAS,** the body becomes fatigued from overwork and a person becomes vulnerable to diseases.

5 Explain that people respond to stressors in different ways. **Eustress** is successful coping or a healthful response to a stressor. When a person experiences eustress, the resistance stage is effective in establishing homeostasis in the body because the demands of the stressor are met. **Distress** is

unsuccessful coping or a harmful response to a stressor. The exhaustion stage often accompanies distress.

6 Emphasize the importance of using stress-management skills. **Stress-management skills** are techniques that can be used to cope with stressors and to lessen the harmful effects of distress. Stress-management skills used to cope with stressors include talking with responsible adults about difficult life events and daily hassles, using the *Responsible Decision-Making Model* and resistance skills, and writing in a journal. Exercising, eating a healthful diet, and spending time with caring people also help with stress.

7 Outline reasons why using harmful drugs increases stress rather than relieves stress. Harmful drugs such as stimulants increase the body's response to stress. The heart beats faster, respiration increases, digestion slows, and the pupils dilate. Harmful depressant drugs such as barbiturates and alcohol depress the reason and judgment centers of the brain. It becomes more difficult to make choices about what to do about the stressors.

EVALUATION

Have students complete the student master "Health Behavior Contract" on the topic of stress management. Have them discuss the ef-fects of drug misuse and abuse on the ability of people under stress to cope with stressors. Show TM-28, "Manage Stress." Have students identify one stressor in their lives and then complete each step in the master.

MULTICULTURAL INFUSION

Ask students to describe stressors that they experience and that they believe are specific to their culture. Have the class brainstorm stress-management skills that might be used to ease the stress that may be caused by these stressors. Write students' ideas on the chalkboard. How might classmates help students with cultural stressors relieve stress?

INCLUSION

Ask students with special needs to describe stressors that they experience as a result of their specific disabilities. Have the class brainstorm stress-management skills that might be used to lessen the stress that may be caused by these stressors. Write students' ideas on the chalkboard. How might classmates help students with special needs relieve stress?

Student Master

Health Behavior Contract

Name _____

Life Skill: I will practice stress-management skills.

Effect on My Health:

_____

_____

_____

_____

My Plan to Manage Stress:

_____

_____

_____

_____

How My Plan Worked:

_____

_____

_____

_____

_____

My Relationships, My Future

HEALTH EDUCATION STANDARD

- Students will analyze the influence of family, peers, culture, media, technology, and other factors on health behaviors.

PERFORMANCE INDICATORS

- Identify how peers can influence healthy and unhealthy behaviors.

HEALTH GOALS

- I will show respect for all people.
- I will work to have healthful family relationships.
- I will work to have healthful friendships.

MATERIALS

A yardstick or a broomstick about three feet in length; cellophane tape; pen; two small pieces of paper about one-inch square; TM-11, "Use Communication Skills," Appendix A

MOTIVATION

1 Begin this strategy by introducing the term *relationship skills*. Define relationship skills as the ability people have to communicate and get along well with others. People who have good relationship skills promote the health of others. They help others make responsible decisions.

2 Take the yardstick or broomstick and two small pieces of paper that are about one-inch square. On one piece of paper, write "Your present," and tape that paper to the bottom of the broomstick (or yardstick). On the other sheet of paper, write "Your future." Tape this piece to the top of the broomstick. Then ask for a volunteer to come up to the front of the room. Explain that you want this person to balance the

broomstick on one finger. However, you are going to place certain restrictions on this task. The person must hold out a hand at about waist height and balance the stick on the finger only looking at where the broom meets the finger. Emphasize that the eyes must be focused on where the broomstick meets the finger. Tell the class that this yardstick represents a person and that this person must have a balanced life. The balanced life is indicated by how long this "life" can be balanced on the finger. Now ask the volunteer to begin to balance this "life" on a finger, looking only where the finger and broomstick meet. Count the number of seconds the person keeps the broomstick balanced. The class will observe that the broomstick, or "life," falls rather quickly.

3 Now have the volunteer repeat the task, but this time the volunteer can look anywhere.

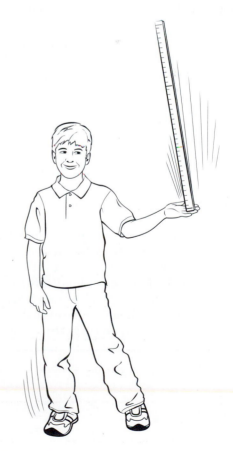

Tell the class they are to observe this person the second time and see what happens. The class will notice that the volunteer raised his or her eyes toward the top of the broomstick and that the "life" was balanced for a much longer period of time.

4 Explain what took place by asking students what they observed. Students will indicate that when the volunteer looked up, the "life" became balanced for a much longer period of time. Explain that when the volunteer looked up or ahead, she or he was looking at "your future." When looking only where the broomstick met the finger, the volunteer was looking at "your present." The yardstick or life became unbalanced very quickly when the volunteer looked only at "your present."

5 Introduce this concept to indicate that people who make decisions based only on what might feel good right now are not looking at the implications of their behavior for the future. But when people make decisions looking at the implications for the future, they are more balanced. They have looked at "your future."

6 Have students describe how they make decisions with friends and family members. For example, if a student agrees to the pressures from friends to smoke a cigarette, this student may think that it is all right for now to try to smoke. But choosing to smoke now may be a stepping stone for beginning to smoke as a regular habit. This student can look at the implications of smoking now by being aware that smoking can upset the balance of health because it is easy to become dependent on cigarettes. To be *dependent* means to need to do something. Thus, by thinking that smoking

might seem harmless now, the risk remains that smoking will become a regular habit. This regular habit can cause many health problems. Emphasize to students that they must look at the future results of their present actions.

7 Explain that people who have good relationship skills with others will be able to communicate in healthful ways. They will also support healthful actions for their friends and family members. This presents a good opportunity to have students discuss how they can deal with people who encourage them to engage in harmful behaviors. Have students share specific ways to handle some of the different pressures they may face. For example, ask students what they would do if they had a friend who wanted them to try to smoke. Discuss using resistance skills to avoid harmful behaviors. Discuss walking away from the situation and telling a family member or trusted adult who would be in a good position to provide guidance.

EVALUATION

Use TM-11, "Use Communication Skills," to have students proceed with the evaluation activity. Divide the class into two equal groups. Have one group identify a situation that people their age might face. The situation should involve family or friends. They are to present that situation to the other group. That group must identify healthful ways to handle that situation. Then have the groups reverse roles so that the first group responds to a situation and the second group presents a different situation for consideration. Assess the responses to indicate the use of responsible decision making.

GRADE 5

The Body Systems Game

HEALTH EDUCATION STANDARD

- Students will comprehend concepts related to health promotion and disease prevention to enhance health.

PERFORMANCE INDICATOR

- Describe the relationship between healthy behaviors and personal health.

HEALTH GOAL

- I will accept the ways my body changes as it grows.

MATERIALS

Twenty-five three-by-five-inch index cards; tape; one red marker; one green marker; pencil or pen; TM-2, "Understand Health Facts," Appendix A

MOTIVATION

1 To prepare for this activity, you will need twenty-five three-by-five-inch index cards. On each of these cards, print the following body systems and the parts associated with each of these systems. Print the names of the body systems in red. The parts that belong under these body systems can be printed in green.

- *Circulatory system*—heart, arteries, veins, blood
- *Digestive system*—liver, small intestine, stomach, large intestine
- *Respiratory system*—lungs, bronchial tubes, alveoli, bronchi
- *Nervous system*—axon, dendrite, neuron, brain
- *Skeletal system*—bones, kneecap, ribs, skull

2 Define the term *body systems*. A **body system** is a group of body organs that work together to perform certain functions. The **circulatory system** is the body system that provides all body tissues with a regular supply of oxygen and nutrients and carries away carbon dioxide and waste products. The **digestive system** is the body system that breaks food down into chemicals that the body can use for energy and to maintain cells and tissues. Included in this system are the stomach, liver, small intestine, and large intestine. The **respiratory system** is the body system responsible for carrying oxygen from the air to the bloodstream and for expelling the waste product carbon dioxide. Included in this system are the lungs, bronchial tubes, alveoli, and bronchi. The **nervous system** is the body system that gathers information from the external environment, stores and processes it, and initiates appropriate responses. Included in this system are the brain, axons, dendrites, and neurons. The **skeletal system** is the body system that forms a framework to support the body and to help protect internal soft tissues of the body. Included in this body system are the bones, kneecaps, ribs, and skull. You may want to review these five body systems with students before playing the Body Systems Game.

3 Tell students that they are going to play a game called the Body Systems Game. Explain to students that they will form a single line on one side of you. When they come up to you, they are to turn their backs so that you can tape a card with a name of a body system or the name of a part of that body system on their backs. Explain that they will not know what part of the body system is taped on their backs. One objective of this activity is for students to guess what is printed on the card on their backs. They are to do this by approaching other students. When they approach other students, they are to turn their backs so the person can read the card. Then the person will turn and ask a question. However,

students may only ask a question that will receive a yes or no response. For example, a student cannot approach another student and ask, "Am I above or below the waist?" Rather, the student is to ask, "Am I above the waist?" After receiving an answer, the student must then approach another person. Explain that each person may ask only one question. Explain that when someone correctly identifies the word on his or her back, that student is to tape the card in the front of his or her body. This will indicate to others that the student guessed what was printed on the card. However, this student must still be available to help others who have not guessed what is on their backs.

4 When most of the students have guessed what is on the card on their backs, stop the activity. Ask students who have not guessed what is on their backs to now take their cards and tape them to their fronts. Next, explain that they are to remain completely nonverbal. Explain to students that they each belong to one of five groups. Without allowing them to talk, have students sort themselves into the groups to which they belong. Have groups assemble across the room so that the groups are distinct.

5 After students assemble into groups, explain that you helped them assemble themselves into body systems by printing the names of the body systems in red and the names of the parts of each body system in green.

6 Now that students are in groups, explain that their group is going to have a task to perform. Tell students that they are going to look at ways to care for the body system their group represents. They can introduce any health facts they desire, but these facts must be presented as lyrics to a song. For example, students may sing about a body system using the lyrics they have written and singing to the tune of a popular song or nursery rhyme. Give students about fifteen minutes to prepare for this assignment. Explain that they are to think of a

name for their group and a title for their song. Then, they will come to the front of the room and sing the words to their song. Their song is to be from eight to ten lines in length. You can give students an example of how this would work by saying, "The name of our group is Denny and the Dendrites, and we are here today to sing the newest single from our CD titled 'I'm Nervous about That Impulse.'" The lyrics to the song may go as follows:

The nervous system has a brain.
If I touch something sharp, I'll feel the
  pain.
Hot and cold, soft and rough.
When my nervous system is healthy, I
sure am tough.

7 Have each group present its song. The class is to remember as many facts as possible. You can then use the information to review facts with the class about the care of the different body systems.

EVALUATION

Collect the index cards from students that were used to play the game the first time. Play the game again, but this time make sure students have different cards. Compare the length of time it took for students to guess what was on their backs and get into groups the second time you did this activity with the first time. Assess how accurate the students were in separating into groups. This will give you the opportunity to determine how familiar students are with the different body parts and the body systems to which they belong. In addition, you can assign students another body system. Have them write at least five facts about that body system and include at least one way to care for that system.

Use TM-2, "Understand Health Facts," and have students identify a health fact related to a disease that affects a body system. Then respond to each of the four items on the master.

GRADE 5

Read That Label

HEALTH EDUCATION STANDARDS

- Students will demonstrate the ability to access valid information and products and services to enhance health.
- Students will demonstrate the ability to practice health-enhancing behaviors and avoid or reduce health risks.
- Students will demonstrate the ability to advocate for personal, family, and community health.

PERFORMANCE INDICATORS

- Identify characteristics of valid health information, products, and services.
- Demonstrate a variety of healthy practices and behaviors to maintain or improve personal health.
- Encourage others to make positive health choices.

HEALTH GOALS

- I will follow the Dietary Guidelines.
- I will read food labels.
- I will choose habits that reduce the risk of cancer. (Communicable and Chronic Diseases)

MATERIALS

Teaching master "Nutrition Facts Label"; transparency projector; five different boxes of cereal; napkins; scissors; TM-30, "Be a Health Advocate," Appendix A

MOTIVATION

1 Obtain five different boxes of cereal. If you ask the manager of a large supermarket for damaged boxes of products such as cereals, you might get them for free. (You might also save and ask friends to save cereal boxes with one serving of cereal left in each one.) For this strategy, you will need the cereal from five different cereal boxes placed on five separate napkins on your desk. Do not let students know which cereal came from which box. Ask students if they can identify the most healthful cereal, the second most healthful cereal, and so on. Students will not be able to do this task. Ask them why they cannot do it. Students will probably respond that they have no information about the cereal because they do not have the cereal boxes.

2 Explain that information about different products can be obtained from the labels on their containers. If students had seen the labels, they would be able to answer the question regarding the most nutritious cereals. Explain to students you are going to review information about the food labels that are included on all packages. Show the teaching master "Nutrition Facts Label" to the class. Explain that this label is required on food products and contains important information about the foods inside a package.

3 Use the teaching master "Nutrition Facts Label" to review information about the product. Begin with the top line that says "serving size." The **serving size** is the amount of food that most people would eat, or a portion. Explain that the serving size comes in two measurements. On this label, serving size is written in cups (1 cup). But serving size can be written in grams (228 g). Using grams is a more precise way to measure the amount. Indicate that the number of servings in the package (2) is identified.

4 Point out that nutrients are listed next to the calories. A **calorie** is a unit of energy. The label tells the number of calories in a serving. The label also tells the number of calories that come from fat. Explain that 30 percent or less of a person's calories should come from fat each day. For example, a person who eats one hundred calories should have no more than thirty calories come from fat.

5 Explain that after the calories, nutrients are listed. Fats, cholesterol, and sodium are on the label because they are to be eaten in moderation. Eating a diet high in fats, cholesterol, and sodium is related to the development of heart disease. Explain that the percentages given at the ends of the lines for each nutrient make it easy to tell if a serving is high or low in nutrients. Usually, 5 percent or less is considered low.

6 After cutting the Nutrition Facts labels from the five cereals, divide the class into five equal groups. Each group will get one label. Cut an additional area from each cereal box around the space where the label was cut out so that students cannot match the labels with the boxes on the basis of the cutout label shape. Also, pass the cereal boxes to each group and have the groups read them. Then you can have the class pass the boxes from one group to another group after reviewing the information on the boxes for three minutes. Students are to match the labels to the correct cereal boxes by analyzing the nutrients listed on the label and the information on the cereal box. Have students share how they came to conclusions about matching the labels to the correct cereal boxes.

EVALUATION

Follow this activity by saving five labels and food packages. Hand out the labels to different students, and ask them to match the labels to the correct food packages. Evaluate students' knowledge by how accurately they match the labels to the food packages. Ask students to name diseases they might develop if they fail to make wise dietary choices. Show TM-30, "Be a Health Advocate," and use the items to outline how students can make responsible dietary choices with family members.

Nutrition Facts Label

Nutrition Facts

Serving Size 1 cup (265g)
Servings per Container 2

Amount per Serving

Calories 235   Calories from Fat 30

	% Daily Value*
Total Fat 3g	**5%**
Saturated Fat 1g	**5%**
Trans Fat 0.5g	
Cholesterol 30mg	**10%**
Sodium 775mg	**32%**
Total Carbohydrate 34g	**11%**
Dietary Fiber 9g	**36%**
Sugars 5g	
Protein 18g	

Vitamin A 25%	•	Vitamin C 0%	
Calcium 12%	•	Iron 20%	

*Percent Daily Values are based on a 2,000 calorie diet. Your daily values may be higher or lower depending on your calorie needs:

	Calories	2,000	2,500
Total Fat	Less than	65g	80
Sat Fat	Less than	20g	25g
Cholesterol	Less than	300mg	300mg
Sodium	Less than	2,400mg	2,400mg
Total Carbohydrate		300g	375g
Dietary Fiber		25g	30g

Calories per gram:
Fat 9 • Carbohydrate 4 • Protein 4

GRADE 5

Medical and Dental Checkups

HEALTH EDUCATION STANDARDS

- Students will comprehend concepts related to health promotion and disease prevention to enhance health.
- Students will demonstrate the ability to access valid information and products and services to enhance health.

PERFORMANCE INDICATORS

- Describe ways to prevent common childhood injuries and health problems.
- Locate resources from home, school, and community that provide valid health information.

HEALTH GOALS

- I will be well groomed.
- I will have regular checkups.
- I will check out sources of health information. (Consumer and Community Health)

MATERIALS

Teaching master "How to Floss"; teaching master "A Healthy Body"; transparency projector; classified telephone directory; paper; pencils; TM-2, "Understand Health Facts," Appendix A

MOTIVATION

1 Begin this strategy by asking students to open up a book and begin to read. As they are reading, turn the lights off in the room and close the shades on the windows. Students will say that they cannot read. Explain to students that their sight is very important and they need to take steps to protect their vision.

2 Tell students that they need to protect their eyes, and that one way to do this is to have vision screening. *Vision screening*

is having an eye exam to help detect any eye disorders. Emphasize to students that even if they think their eyes are healthy, they need eye checkups each year so that if any problems are present, they can be corrected. The sooner a health problem is detected, the more effectively it can be treated. Explain that there are many health helpers in the community who can help protect people's eyes. An **ophthalmologist** is a physician who can examine eyes and prescribe glasses and contacts as well as do surgery. An **optometrist** is a health care professional trained and licensed as a doctor of optometry who examines the eyes and detects vision and eye problems. An **optician** is the person who fills prescriptions for glasses and contact lenses.

3 Explain to students what happens during an eye examination. A medical professional can ask a person to read a special chart to see if the person can see objects clearly. The inside of the eyeballs may also be examined. By looking at the blood vessels and other areas in the eyeball, the health professional can determine the health of the eyes. Explain that eyes may be checked for nearsightedness and farsightedness. A person who is *nearsighted* can see objects up close clearly but distant objects are fuzzy. A person who is *farsighted* sees objects that are far away clearly but objects that are close are blurred. Distribute the teaching master "A Healthy Body," and review the tips for keeping the eyes healthy.

4 Begin to read and then lower your voice. Continue to lower your voice until it is no longer audible. Eventually you will be moving your lips and not saying anything. Explain to students that if they suffered hearing loss, they would not be able to hear sounds. Many young people suffer hearing loss but are not aware of it. Explain that hearing screening is important to help keep the ears healthy.

5 Introduce the word *audiologist*. An **audiologist** is a person who tests hearing. An

audiometer is a machine that assesses the range of sounds that a person can hear at various frequencies and intensities. The audiometer works by sending sounds through headphones that the person wears. At first the sounds are loud. Then they are made softer. The point at which no sound can be heard indicates to the audiologist how well a person can hear. Explain that there are many reasons for hearing loss. Among these might be damage to the eardrum from listening to constant, loud sounds or from infection. Pathogens also can enter the ears from the throat.

6 Explain that dental screening is important in helping to protect the teeth. Have students open a book and ask them to read aloud. Then have them stop and pretend they have no teeth. They can simulate this by puckering their mouths so that their lips are folded over their teeth. Now, ask them to read again. Students will notice that they cannot speak clearly. Explain that if they did not have teeth, they would not be able to speak clearly or to chew food. Explain that there are many people in the community who help protect teeth. A **dentist** is a person who is trained to provide care for the teeth, ranging from giving medical examinations to repairing teeth that are decayed. A **dental hygienist** is a person who cleans teeth, takes X-rays, and provides information about ways to care for the teeth.

7 Explain what happens during a dental exam. X-rays are often taken of the teeth. This helps determine how healthy teeth are on the inside. The teeth are inspected with certain instruments, as are the gums. A person's teeth should be cleaned twice a year. This helps remove calculus. **Calculus** is hardened plaque. **Plaque** is the sticky substance on the teeth that consists of saliva, bacteria, and food debris. Explain that not caring for teeth can result in dental disease. **Gingivitis** is a condition in which the gums bleed easily. Gingivitis can be caused by improper brushing and not flossing. Show the teaching master "How to Floss,"

and review the steps in flossing. Explain that another problem related to poor dental health is periodontal disease. **Periodontal disease** is a disease of the gums and other tissues that support the teeth. If the teeth lose their supporting tissue and underlying bone, they can fall out.

8 Introduce the word *braces*. **Braces** are devices that are placed on the teeth to straighten them. Sometimes teeth are crowded and teeth must be pulled to reduce overcrowding in the mouth. Usually braces are put on by an orthodontist. An **orthodontist** is a person who specializes in repositioning the teeth with braces.

9 Discuss grooming. **Grooming** is taking care of the body by following practices that help people look, smell, and feel their best. Explain to students that they should bathe regularly and keep themselves clean in order to reduce the risk of infection and disease.

EVALUATION

Introduce TM-2, "Understand Health Facts," to have students obtain health facts in their community. Students need to be aware of resources in the community that they can use to obtain medical care. Using the classified pages of the telephone directory, have students work in groups to make a list of health professionals in their community. It is also important to share with students the health services that may be available at their school. Have students make a health directory.

Teaching Master
A Healthy Body

Tips for Keeping Eyes Healthy
- Have regular eye checkups.
- Avoid rubbing the eyes.
- Do not use another person's washcloth.
- Avoid using sharp objects near the eyes.
- Give your eyes a rest when they feel tired.
- Wear sunglasses when in bright sunlight or when playing sports in which you look into the sun at times.
- Keep some lights on in a room when you watch television.

Tips for Keeping Ears Healthy
- Have regular hearing checkups.
- Do not place objects in the ears.
- Do not use headphones when listening to loud music.
- Keep the outer ear clean by using a washcloth.
- Allow a health professional to remove wax from the ears.
- Protect the eardrum by wearing a safety helmet when involved in contact activities.
- Seek medical help if sounds become more difficult to hear.

Tips for Dental Health
- Have a dental exam every six months.
- Contact a dentist if teeth are sensitive to hot or cold.
- Always brush after meals with a toothpaste that contains fluoride.
- Floss regularly.
- Eat foods such as cheese that contain calcium to harden teeth.
- Avoid foods that contain sugar and stick to teeth, such as marshmallows.

Teaching Master

How to Floss

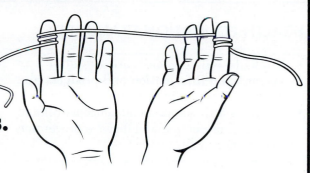

1. **Wrap dental floss around two fingers.**

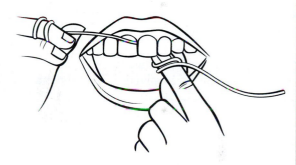

2. **Gently move floss between teeth to gum line.**

3. **Wrap floss around tooth and slide up and down.**

Alcohol, Tobacco, and Other Drugs

GRADE 5

Trying to Think Straight

SOCIAL STUDIES

SELF-DIRECTED LEARNER

HEALTH EDUCATION STANDARDS

- Students will demonstrate the ability to access valid information and products and services to enhance health.
- Students will comprehend concepts related to health promotion and disease prevention to enhance health.

PERFORMANCE INDICATORS

- Locate resources from home, school, and community that provide valid health information.
- Describe ways to prevent common childhood injuries and health problems.

HEALTH GOALS

- I will not drink alcohol.
- I will be not be involved in illegal drug use.

MATERIALS

Teaching master "How Alcohol Affects Well-Being"; transparency projector; sheet of paper; pencil; TM-25, "Practice Healthful Behaviors," Appendix A

MOTIVATION

1 Begin this strategy by asking students to write their names on a sheet of paper clearly in cursive. After they have written their names, ask them to move their chairs so that they can extend one foot in front of them. Their foot should be extended so that the knee is locked. They can use either the right or left foot to do this activity. Tell students that, while their foot is extended, they are to turn it in a wide circle continuously until you tell them to stop.

2 While students are turning their feet in a continuous circle, ask them to write their names in cursive again underneath the

name they wrote earlier. As students are doing this, observe their foot. You will notice that they are no longer turning their foot in a circle. Rather, they are moving their foot up and down and side to side. Say, "I see that you are having trouble keeping your foot going in a circle. Please move it in a circle while you are writing your name."

3 Students will be confused and probably laugh at the difficulty they are having. After students have completed this task, discuss what happened. Ask the following questions: "Was it easier to write your name the first time or the second time?" (the first time) "Did writing your name the first time take more or less time?" (less) "Did your name appear neater or sloppier the first time?" (neater) "What happened when you tried to keep your foot going in a circle while writing your name?" (the foot went side to side or up and down)

4 Explain to students that the task of writing a name became very difficult when they were asked to do a second task at the same time, such as moving the foot in a circle. The foot could not move in a circle and

Alcohol, Tobacco, and Other Drugs

the ability to perform an easy task such as writing a name became a problem. Explain to students that they just experienced what it might be like to function if they had alcohol in their body. Define alcohol. **Alcohol** is a harmful drug such as beer or wine that slows down how the body functions. Alcohol is classified as a depressant. A **depressant** is a drug that slows down the actions of the body. Explain to students that had they tried to perform tasks under the influence of alcohol, they would have had great difficulty. This is one reason why people who drink have many accidents and often become injured.

5 Show the teaching master "How Alcohol Affects Well-Being," and review the many ways alcohol harms health. All ten areas of health are affected by the use of alcohol.

6 Introduce the word *alcoholism*. **Alcoholism** is a disease that causes a person to be physically and mentally dependent on alcohol. In the case of alcohol and other drugs, to be dependent means to have a need for a drug. Alcohol causes two kinds of dependence. Physical dependence is a bodily need for a drug. Psychological dependence is a mental need for a drug. Explain that in many families, alcoholism is a problem. About 15 million families in the United States have a member who suffers from alcoholism; this results in many problems for the family. People who have alcoholism often become violent. They cause stress to family members. Children may be afraid to bring friends home because they feel embarrassed. Children may also feel guilty because they do not have the skills to know how to cope or stop the person from drinking. Schoolwork may suffer.

7 Explain to students that help is available for people who have alcoholism and for families who suffer the effects of a member who has alcoholism. Explain that **Alcoholics Anonymous (AA)** is a support group that helps people who have drinking problems. **Al-Anon** is a support group for family members or friends of someone with alcoholism. **Al-Ateen** is a support group for teens who are affected by a friend or family member's drinking. To familiarize students with resources in the community, show them a telephone directory that lists community agencies that offer help. Tell students that they can also see a counselor at school if they have concerns about alcohol and a family member.

EVALUATION

Identify an area of health that appears on the teaching master "How Alcohol Affects Well-Being," and have students identify how using alcohol can have an effect on this area. It is also important for students to understand the importance of being alcohol-free. Divide the class into groups of about five, and have each group write five tips to help people avoid the use of alcohol. For example, if they are at a party, they can leave if they notice someone drinking. Each group in the class is to present five tips to remain alcohol-free. These tips might include suggestions for school and community resources that could be used should there be a need for intervention and treatment. Make a list of these tips and write them in order from the tips most often given down to the one tip least often given. Make a note of how many times each tip was given. Explain to students that there are many alternatives to alcohol use. Show TM-25, "Practice Healthful Behaviors," and have students identify a healthful behavior and apply each of the four steps in the master.

Teaching Master

How Alcohol Affects Well-Being

Mental and Emotional Health
- Decreases learning and performance in school
- Intensifies moods and feelings
- Interferes with responsible decision making
- Causes various brain disorders including organic mental disorder
- Intensifies stress

Family and Social Health
- Interferes with effective communication
- Intensifies arguments
- Increases the likelihood of violence
- Causes fetal alcohol syndrome (FAS)
- Creates codependence and enmeshment

Growth and Development
- Destroys brain cells
- Decreases performance of motor skills
- Lowers body temperature
- Dulls the body senses
- Increases heartbeat rate and resting blood pressure

Nutrition
- Interferes with healthful appetite
- Interferes with vitamin absorption
- Causes niacin deficiency
- Causes thiamine deficiency

Personal Health and Physical Activity
- Decreases athletic performance
- Interferes with coordination
- Increases likelihood of sports injuries

Alcohol, Tobacco, and Other Drugs
- Depresses the brain and respiratory center
- Causes physical and psychological dependency
- Causes dizziness when combined with tranquilizers
- Can cause coma or death when combined with narcotics

Communicable and Chronic Diseases
- Causes cirrhosis of the liver
- Causes heart disease
- Increases the risk of cancers of the mouth, esophagus, larynx, and pharynx when combined with cigarette smoking
- Increases the risk of kidney failure

Consumer and Community Health
- Is an expensive habit to maintain
- Is taxed heavily in most states

Environmental Health
- Is costly due to an increased need for treatment centers and law enforcement
- Is linked to many missed days of work
- Contributes to environmental pollution

Injury Prevention and Safety
- Is linked to most violent crimes
- Is linked to many suicides and suicide attempts
- Increases the risk of being injured, drowning, or falling
- Is linked to many fires

Communicable and Chronic Diseases

Stuck for Life

HEALTH EDUCATION STANDARDS

- Students will comprehend concepts related to health promotion and disease prevention to enhance health.
- Students will demonstrate the ability to practice health-enhancing behaviors and avoid or reduce health risks.

PERFORMANCE INDICATORS

- Describe when it is important to seek health care.
- Identify responsible personal health behaviors.

HEALTH GOAL

- I will learn facts about HIV and AIDS.

MATERIALS

Teaching master "How HIV Attacks the Immune System"; transparency projector; two apples (one shiny and one bruised); a needle; red food coloring; TM-2, "Understand Health Facts," Appendix A

MOTIVATION

1 Make the following preparation for the lesson without students seeing what you are doing. Place the needle into the container of red food coloring. After removing the needle from the container, some of the red food coloring should remain on it. Then stick the needle into the shiny apple. Be certain that some of the red food coloring gets inside the apple.

2 Define HIV, AIDS, and intravenous drug use. **HIV,** or **human immunodeficiency virus,** is a pathogen that causes AIDS. **AIDS,** or **acquired immunodeficiency syndrome,** is the final stage of HIV infection during which there is a significant de-

crease in the disease-fighting cells inside the body. *Intravenous drug use* refers to the injection of a drug into a vein. Explain that people sharing needles for intravenous drug use are engaging in a risk behavior for becoming infected with HIV. Review how HIV affects the immune system by reviewing the teaching master "How HIV Attacks the Immune System."

3 Show students the two apples—one shiny and one bruised. Explain that each of the apples represents a person. Ask the class which one they believe is infected with HIV. In many cases, most students in the class will say that they believe the bruised apple is the one infected with HIV. Explain that appearance alone will not indicate whether or not a person is infected with HIV. It is not a person's appearance, gender, sexual orientation, or race that puts a person at risk. Rather, it is a person's behavior.

4 Cut a piece from the shiny apple near the spot where you inserted the needle with the red food coloring on it. Explain what you did earlier—that you stuck the apple with the needle that had previously been in the container of red food coloring. Further explain that you did this to demonstrate what happens when people share needles for intravenous drug use.

5 Explain that the transmission of HIV through intravenous drug use occurs when people who use drugs share needles. Sharing needles, whether used for anabolic steroids or narcotics, increases the risk of HIV infection. The process in which the needle is used—whether it be skin popping or subcutaneous, intramuscular (such as injecting steroids), or mainlining (directly into a vein)—makes no difference in a person's chances of becoming infected with HIV. HIV can enter the syringe when the drug user draws back on the plunger to see if the needle is inside the vein. A vein is tapped when blood is easily drawn into the syringe. Even if only a small amount of blood is trapped inside the syringe, this

blood can contain a large amount of HIV when drawn from an infected person. Even if this blood is "shot up," traces of HIV will remain. If another person uses the same syringe, there is a high probability that HIV will be transmitted and cause infection. One of the reasons for the high probability of infection is the fact that HIV is pumped directly into the bloodstream rather than through the skin.

6 Explain that, in the case of the apple that was stuck with red food coloring, enough of the apple might be cut off to get rid of the food coloring. But this is not true of people who are stuck with an HIV-infected needle. Once a person is infected with HIV, he or she is infected for life. Students should also explain that a person's appearance, race, religion, and sexual orientation are not risk factors; rather it is a person's behavior choices. They also should explain the importance of HIV testing for people who have engaged in risk behavior.

7 Cut off pieces from the bruised apple in several places. Explain to students that even though the bruised apple did not look as healthful or appealing as the shiny apple, it is not infected with HIV.

8 Discuss the importance of testing people who have shared needles or other injection equipment for intravenous drug use for HIV infection. The test most commonly used to detect HIV infection is called ELISA. **ELISA** is a test that detects antibodies developed by the human immune system in response to the presence of HIV. The **Western blot** is a blood test that is used to confirm the results of a positive ELISA.

EVALUATION

Have students write a paper with the theme "Stuck for Life." Students should include a discussion of how HIV transmission occurs when needles or other injection equipment are shared. They should explain that once a person is infected with HIV, he or she will always be infected. Students should also explain why appearance, race, and sexual orientation are not risk factors, but the risk factor is a person's behavior choices. They also should explain the importance of HIV testing for people who have engaged in risk behavior.

Show TM-25, "Practice Healthful Behaviors," and use it as a guide to have students determine how HIV can be prevented.

INCLUSION

Have students write a paper including at least ten sentences with the theme "Stuck for Life." Provide them with the following list of facts to include in their papers:

1. Intravenous drug use is a risk behavior for HIV infection.
2. A needle that is shared may have droplets of HIV-infected blood on it.
3. You cannot tell by appearance if a person is infected with HIV.
4. A person is not HIV positive because of his or her race, appearance, or sexual orientation.
5. A person who has engaged in risk behavior should be tested for HIV.
6. There are two tests for HIV: ELISA and Western blot.
7. A person who is infected with HIV will always be infected.

Communicable and Chronic Diseases

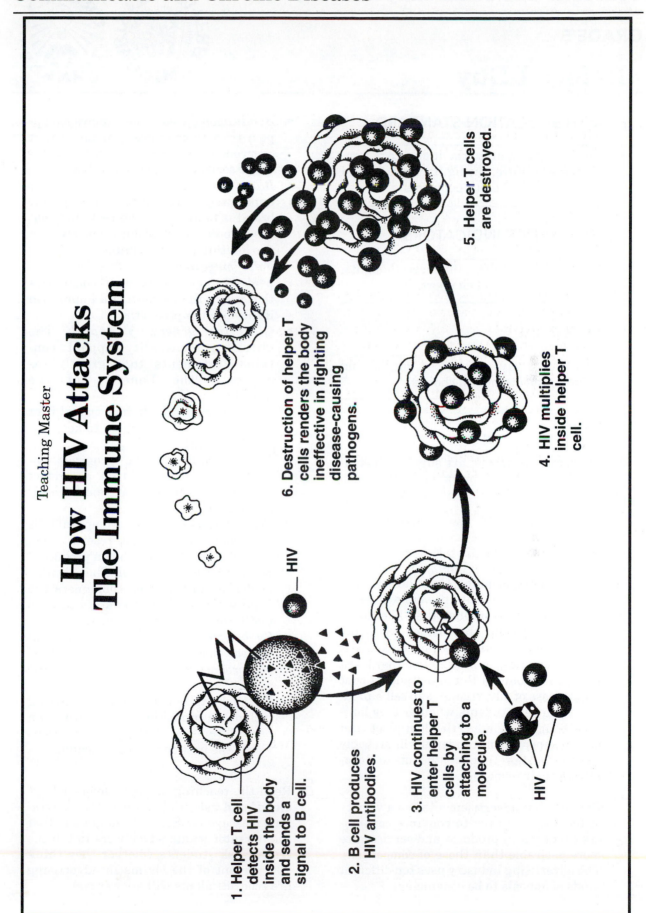

Teaching Master

How HIV Attacks The Immune System

— HIV

1. Helper T cell detects HIV inside the body and sends a signal to B cell.

2. B cell produces HIV antibodies.

3. HIV continues to enter helper T cells by attaching to a molecule.

HIV

4. HIV multiplies inside helper T cell.

5. Helper T cells are destroyed.

6. Destruction of helper T cells renders the body ineffective in fighting disease-causing pathogens.

Consumer and Community Health

GRADE 5

Before I Buy

HEALTH EDUCATION STANDARD

- Students will analyze the influence of family, peers, culture, media, technology, and other factors on health behaviors.

PERFORMANCE INDICATORS

- Explain how media influences thoughts, feelings, and health behaviors.

HEALTH GOAL

- I will check ways technology, media, and culture influence health choices.

MATERIALS

Newspapers; magazines; art supplies, including poster board and black markers; video camera (optional); TM-5, "Analyze What Influences Your Health," Appendix A

MOTIVATION

1 Ask students to name their favorite advertisements. (Student answers will vary.) Discuss with them what they like about the advertisements they named. (Students might mention humor, which makes ads more interesting, or information they learn about the product.) Remind students that the purpose of advertising is to sell a product. Then ask students whether they have ever bought an advertised product and been disappointed. (Students will probably say "yes.") Allow time for students to elaborate on their responses.

2 Explain that advertisements use a variety of techniques to try to convince consumers that certain products and services are more desirable than those of competitors. The advertising industry uses ten different kinds of appeals to be convincing.

- *Bandwagon appeal.* The bandwagon appeal tries to convince consumers that everyone else wants a particular product or service and they should too.
- *Brand loyalty appeal.* The brand loyalty appeal tells consumers that a specific brand is better than the rest, and that they would be cheating themselves to use anything but this brand.
- *False image appeal.* The false image appeal attempts to convince consumers that they will give a certain impression if they use the product.
- *Glittering generality appeal.* The glittering generality appeal contains statements that greatly exaggerate the benefits of the product.
- *Humor appeal.* The humor appeal uses a slogan, jingle, or cartoon to keep the consumer's attention.
- *Progress appeal.* The progress appeal tells consumers that a product is newer and better than one formerly advertised.
- *Reward appeal.* The reward appeal tells consumers that they will receive a special prize or gift if they buy a product.
- *Scientific evidence appeal.* The scientific evidence appeal gives consumers the results of survey or laboratory tests to instill confidence in a product.
- *Snob appeal.* The snob appeal convinces consumers that they are worthy of a product or service because it is the best.
- *Testimony appeal.* The testimony appeal includes a promotion by a well-known person who says that a product or service is the best one for the consumer.

3 Read the teaching master "Before I Buy" aloud, and ask students what the narrator's message is. (Students might say that the narrator wants advertisers to tell the truth.) Ask students whether they think 100 percent of the claims in advertising are true. (Students will answer no.)

4 Give small groups of students old magazines, newspaper, and art supplies. Have them cut out ads and write down television and radio jingles for health products, such as cold remedies or diet products. Have them glue the ads to the posterboard and decorate their work to make a collage.

5 When groups are finished, have them present their collages to the class. Work with the class to find claims in the ads that are exaggerated or untrue. Allow group members to use a black marker to write "NOT!" on any ad that has such claims. Ask students how such ads might be dangerous to a person's health. (Students may say that people might substitute going to a doctor with using a product.)

6 Point out that commercials and ads usually have an underlying message that implies that the product has many benefits. Ask students to give examples of how ads do this. (For example, students might mention a potato chip commercial that shows young people playing at the beach and say that it implies that if they eat these potato chips they will be popular.) For homework, ask students to write down three more examples of underlying messages in advertising. (Student answers will vary but should show they understand the hidden message an ad is sending, such as a commercial for perfume that implies that a person wearing it will be irresistible.)

EVALUATION

Have students work in pairs to present or videotape a hard-sell commercial for a common school item, such as a pencil. They are to include at least two of the appeals discussed in class. When students share their commercials with the class, have the class point out which statements were factual and which were misleading or false appeals. Have the class then compare the points the students made with the four items on TM-5, "Analyze What Influences Your Health."

Teaching Master

Before I Buy

❖❖❖❖❖❖❖❖

Ads in my magazines!
Commercials on TV!
Ads in the newspapers!
Bombarding me!

This will make you perfect!
This will make you thin!
This will make you stronger!
Send your money in!
Here's a cure for sickness!
Won't you even try it?
Melt that fatty fat away!
Buy our ice cream diet!
I won't be a target
for every ad I see.
Before I buy your product,
prove it works for me.

❖❖❖❖❖❖❖❖

Environmental Health

GRADE 5

Environmental Draw-and-Guess

HEALTH EDUCATION STANDARDS

- Students will comprehend concepts related to health promotion and disease prevention to enhance health.
- Students will demonstrate the ability to advocate for personal, family, and community health.

PERFORMANCE INDICATORS

- Describe how a safe and healthy school and community environment can promote personal health.
- Encourage others to make positive health choices.

HEALTH GOAL

- I will help keep the air, land, and water clean and safe.

MATERIALS

Student master "Glossary of Environmental Terms"; chalkboard; chalk; TM-2, "Understand Health Facts," Appendix A

MOTIVATION

1 Before beginning this strategy, distribute the student master "Glossary of Environmental Terms." This master contains many terms that will be used in this strategy. Have students silently read the vocabulary words and terms.

2 Explain to students that they are going to play a version of a well-known game. This game will be called Environmental Draw-and-Guess. Explain to students that they will need to identify a term based on another person's drawing that relates to that term.

3 Divide the class into two equal groups. Begin by asking one member from each team to come to the front of the room. Use a coin toss to indicate which person goes first. Show that person a term that is related to the environment. You can use any of the terms on the student master, or you may add terms. Tell students if you have added terms they can use.

4 After seeing the term, the student is to draw a picture that will help her or his teammates identify the term. The student's team will have one minute to identify the term. If it is not identified in the time allotted, the other team will have the opportunity to guess the term. The team that correctly guesses the term will receive one point. The teams will take turns drawing pictures. Each person on a team will have one turn to draw a picture.

5 You can adapt this game by playing a special round of Environmental Draw-and-Guess. In this round, one team decides on the term that the other team must guess. Give each team one point for identifying the term correctly. If a team does not guess correctly, the team providing the term will receive the point.

EVALUATION

You can assess this activity by evaluating the students' ability to identify the terms during the game. You can also use the student master to develop a vocabulary test by selecting terms and having students spell and define them. Also, you can ask students to tell ways they can protect the environment, using the terms in the glossary. Use TM-2, "Understand Health Facts" to have students discuss how understanding facts about the environment promotes health.

Glossary of Environmental Terms

acid rain: precipitation (rain, snow, sleet, hail) that contains high levels of acids formed from sulfur oxides, nitrogen oxides, and moisture in the air

air pollution: dirty air

asbestos: a fire-resistant mineral that is found in building materials

biodegradable: able to be decomposed through natural or biological processes into harmless materials

decibel (dB): a unit used to measure sound intensity

Environmental Protection Agency (EPA): a federal agency that is responsible for alleviating and controlling environmental pollution

fluorocarbons: chemicals used as propellants in aerosol-spray cans

hazardous waste: harmful substances that are difficult to discard safely

lead: an element that is found in many products used inside and outside the home

noise pollution: loud noises in the environment

ozone: a chemical variant of oxygen that is classified as a photochemical because it is created in the presence of hydrocarbons, nitrous oxides, and sunlight

particulate: particle in the air

pesticide: any substance that is used to kill or control the growth of unwanted organisms

radiation: term applied to the transmission of energy through space or through a medium

recycling: the process of reforming or breaking down waste products to their basic components so that they can be used again

solid waste: substances such as trash, unwanted objects, and litter that threaten the environment

thermal inversion: a condition that occurs when a layer of warm air forms above a cooler layer

thermal pollution: pollution of water with heat resulting in a decrease in the water's oxygen-carrying capacity

water pollution: dirty water

GRADE 5

Get That Breathing Started

HEALTH EDUCATION STANDARD

- Students will demonstrate the ability to advocate for personal, family, and community health.

PERFORMANCE INDICATOR

- Encourage others to make positive health choices.

HEALTH GOAL

- I will follow safety rules for my home and school.

MATERIALS

Teaching master "The Heimlich Maneuver"; transparency projector; a one-gallon plastic milk container; cork; a mannequin designed for practice rescue breathing; two mouth protectors; TM-25, "Practice Healthful Behaviors," Appendix A

MOTIVATION

1 Before beginning this strategy, prepare the following: Draw a pair of lungs on the surface of a one-gallon plastic milk container. Bring a cork that is big enough to fill the opening on the top of the milk container.

2 Begin this strategy by asking, "Have you ever been chewing some food and it lodged in your throat?" Many students will answer yes. Explain that almost everyone experiences having food stuck in the throat at some time. In almost all cases, the food will dislodge by itself and the air passage will open.

3 Explain that sometimes people are not so fortunate. On occasion, a piece of food that is stuck inside the throat may not become dislodged by itself. In this case, a person needs help to breathe. One method used to help a person breathe is the use of the Heimlich maneuver. The **Heimlich maneuver** is a technique in which external pressure is placed in the abdominal area to remove a blockage in the air passage.

4 Provide students with the following scenario. They are at a restaurant eating with a friend. The friend suddenly appears to be choking. Usually, people who are choking will place a hand on their throat. Their lips may be turning blue. If this person cannot cough, speak, or breathe, the Heimlich maneuver should be administered quickly. Show the teaching master "The Heimlich Maneuver." Use a student to demonstrate the position of the hands for the Heimlich maneuver. However, do not perform the thrust on the student, and do not let the students in the class perform it on each other. Demonstrate, but do not actually perform, the motions involved in the Heimlich maneuver: The person performing the maneuver is to move behind the standing or seated person and wrap his or her hands around the victim's waist. Place the thumb side of the fist against the victim's abdomen just below the tip of the breastbone and slightly above the navel. Grasp the fist with the other hand and press into the victim's abdomen with four quick upward thrusts. Each sharp thrust forces air out of the lungs; the air will push the object out. You can repeat giving thrusts if the initial attempts do not dislodge the object.

5 Show students the milk container with the cork that represents the food lodged inside the throat to demonstrate the result of the Heimlich maneuver. Squeeze the milk container until the cork flies out. This mimics what would happen if food were actually stuck in the air passage.

6 Explain that sometimes a person stops breathing because of illness or injury. In this case, rescue breathing is needed. **Rescue breathing** is a first-aid procedure in which a person who has stopped breathing

is given assistance to restore breathing. Rescue breathing is also known as artificial respiration or mouth-to-mouth resuscitation. Use the mannequin to simulate a victim to demonstrate rescue breathing. Describe and demonstrate on the mannequin the following steps:

Step 1—Check the victim's chest to see if it is moving up and down. Place your ear next to the victim's nose and mouth to feel for air being exhaled. If the victim's chest is not moving and there is no air coming from the nose and mouth, the person is not breathing and needs rescue breathing.

Step 2—Place the victim on his or her back and turn the head to the side. Remove anything that is inside the person's mouth.

Step 3—Place your hand underneath the victim's neck and rest your other hand against the forehead. Pull the neck up slightly and press the forehead down. This allows the passage into the lungs to be opened.

Step 4—Pinch the victim's nostrils closed. This will stop the air you will breathe into the victim from escaping through the nose. Take a deep breath and seal your mouth using the mouth protector over the victim's mouth and blow air into it. You will notice that the victim's chest rises.

Step 5—Place your ear by the victim's mouth so that you can listen for the exhaled air. If breathing resumes, do not blow any more air into the victim's mouth. If breathing did not continue, resume blowing air into the victim's mouth every four seconds until the person breathes on his or her own or until emergency help has arrived. If emergency help is needed, ask someone else to call the emergency service while you continue to monitor the person's condition.

EVALUATION

Introduce TM-25, "Practice Healthful Behaviors." Have students practice the steps of rescue breathing: Have one student practice the steps on the mannequin. Have the other students identify the steps while the student demonstrates. It is important that the student volunteer uses a clean mouth protector while demonstrating rescue breathing. Ask students how they will get emergency help if it is needed. Assess the order of the steps and the accuracy of the information given by the students.

Teaching Master

The Heimlich Maneuver

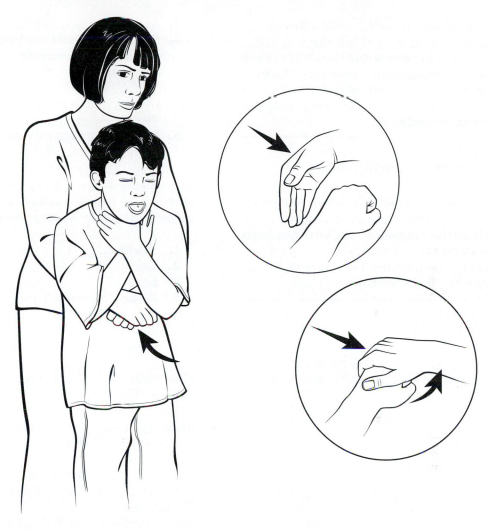

- **Wrap your arms around the person's waist.**
- **Make a fist.**
- **Place the thumb side of the fist on the middle of the person's abdomen just above the navel and well below the lower tip of the breastbone.**
- **Grasp the fist with your other hand.**
- **Press the fist into the person's abdomen with a quick upward thrust.**

GRADE 6

Stormy Weather

HEALTH EDUCATION STANDARDS

- Students will demonstrate the ability to use decision-making skills to enhance health.
- Students will comprehend concepts related to health promotion and disease prevention to enhance health.

PERFORMANCE INDICATORS

- Choose healthy alternatives over unhealthy alternatives when making a decision.
- Analyze the outcomes of a health-related decision.
- Examine the likelihood of injury or illness if engaging in unhealthy behaviors.

HEALTH GOALS

- I will make responsible decisions.
- I will use resistance skills when appropriate.

MATERIALS

Student master "The Responsible Decision-Making Model"; student master "Use Resistance Skills"; umbrella; construction paper; scissors; markers; tape; two chairs; index cards; TM-19, "Make Responsible Decisions," Appendix A

MOTIVATION

1 To prepare for this strategy, cut six large raindrops from the construction paper. Label each of the six large raindrops with one of the categories of risk behaviors identified by the Centers for Disease Control and Prevention (label with the underlined words only):

1. Behaviors that contribute to unintentional and intentional injuries—<u>injuries</u>
2. Tobacco use—<u>tobacco</u>

3. Alcohol and other drug use—<u>drugs</u>
4. Sexual behaviors that contribute to unintended pregnancy, HIV infection, and other STDs—<u>pregnancy, HIV, STDs</u>
5. Dietary patterns that contribute to disease—<u>diet</u>
6. Insufficient physical activity—<u>lack of exercise</u>

Cut six long strips of paper and label each with one of the six criteria from the *Responsible Decision-Making Model:*

1. Healthful
2. Safe
3. Legal
4. Respect for oneself and others
5. Follows guidelines of responsible adults
6. Demonstrates character

2 Give each student a copy of the student master "The Responsible Decision-Making Model." The **Responsible Decision-Making Model** is a series of steps to follow to ensure that the decisions a person makes lead to actions that promote health, promote safety, protect laws, show respect for oneself and others, follow guidelines set by responsible adults such as parents and guardians, and demonstrate good character. Explain that many benefits result from using the *Responsible Decision-Making Model.* Because the model contains guidelines for what is responsible behavior, students will always know how to evaluate behavior. Ask students to memorize the six questions asked to evaluate behavior.

3 Ask for two student volunteers. Have them sit next to one another in two chairs in front of the class. Give one of the students the umbrella. Explain that the two students are preparing for life. They learned that life skills are actions that promote health literacy, maintain and improve health, prevent disease, and reduce health-related risk behaviors. An important life skill is "I will make responsible decisions."

4 Explain that the student with the umbrella is prepared for the storms of life. This student makes responsible decisions and uses the six questions to evaluate her or his behavior. Review these six questions as you tape them to the top of the umbrella. Explain that the other student does not practice responsible decision making. This student does not ask these six questions to evaluate behavior before making decisions. The six questions are: Is it healthful? Is it safe? Is it legal? Does it show respect for oneself and others? Does it follow family guidelines? and Does it show good character?

5 Further explain that they are at an age when they will have many decisions to make. These decisions will involve whether or not to participate in risk behaviors. **Risk behaviors** are voluntary actions that threaten self-esteem, harm health, and increase the likelihood of illness, injury, and premature death. Discuss the six categories of risk behaviors identified by the Centers for Disease Control and Prevention. (These are identified in step 1 of this motivation.) Show students each of the six large raindrops that represent the six categories of risk behaviors.

6 Ask what will happen when each of the students encounters the storms of adolescence and must make responsible decisions. Demonstrate the following. Drop the raindrops on the student without the umbrella. Explain that this student might be affected by these risk behaviors because he or she doesn't have the umbrella (symbolizes a person who does not practice the life skill "I will make responsible decisions"). Collect the raindrops and allow them to drop over the student protected by the umbrella. This student with the umbrella symbolizes a person who is protected because she or he practices the life skill "I will make responsible decisions."

7 Give each student a copy of the student master "Use Resistance Skills." Explain that, in addition to practicing responsible decision making, students will need to practice the life skill "I will use resistance skills when appropriate." **Resistance skills** are skills that are used when a person wants to say "no" to an action or leave a situation. "Use Resistance Skills" is a list of suggested ways for effectively resisting pressure to engage in actions that threaten health, threaten safety, break laws, result in lack of respect for oneself and others, disobey guidelines set by responsible adults, and detract from character. Review and demonstrate the use of resistance skills.

EVALUATION

Use TM-19, "Make Responsible Decisions," and review the steps in the decision-making process. Give each student an index card. Ask students to write a situation on the index card that necessitates a decision. For example, a student might write, "A friend asks me to a party where there will be beer." Collect the index cards. Read them and discard inappropriate situations. Place the rest of the index cards in a pile. Have students take turns coming in front of the class and selecting an index card from the pile. Students are to evaluate the decision to be made using the six questions from the *Responsible Decision-Making Model*. Then they are to role-play with you how they would resist pressure to participate in the risk behavior.

Student Master

The Responsible Decision-Making Model

1. Describe the situation that requires a decision.

2. List possible decisions you might make.

3. Share the list of possible decisions with a responsible adult.

4. Evaluate the consequences of each decision. Ask yourself the following questions:
   Will this decision result in actions that
   - are healthful?
   - are safe?
   - are legal?
   - show respect for myself and others?
   - follow the guidelines of responsible adults, such as my parent or guardian?
   - demonstrate good character?

5. Decide which decision is responsible and most appropriate.

6. Act on your decision, and evaluate the results.

Use Resistance Skills

1. Say no in a firm voice.

2. Give reasons for saying no.

3. Be certain of your behavior.

4. Avoid situations in which there will be pressure to make wrong decisions.

5. Avoid being with people who make wrong decisions.

6. Resist pressure to do something illegal.

7. Influence others to make responsible decisions rather than wrong decisions.

GRADE 6

Gift of Friendship

HEALTH EDUCATION STANDARDS

- Students will analyze the influence of family, peers, culture, media, technology, and other factors on health behaviors.
- Students will demonstrate the ability to advocate for personal, family, and community health.

PERFORMANCE INDICATORS

- Examine how the family influences the health of adolescents.
- Demonstrate how to influence and support others to make positive health choices.

HEALTH GOALS

- I will develop healthful family relationships.
- I will practice abstinence.

MATERIALS

A shoe box for each student; wrapping paper; tape; ribbon; index cards; pens; TM-30, "Be a Health Advocate," Appendix A

MOTIVATION

1 Initiate a discussion about relationships and friendship. A **relationship** is the connection a person has with another person. Friendship is a special relationship. A friend is a person who one knows well and likes. Friends provide supportive relationships in which we can learn about ourselves and try new ways of interacting in order to grow personally. There are two important ingredients in friendship: affection and respect. Affection is a fond or tender feeling that a person has toward another person. It is experienced as emotional warmth or closeness. Respect is having esteem for someone's admirable characteristics and responsible and caring actions. In a health-

ful friendship, there is both affection and respect.

2 Identify some of the admirable characteristics and responsible and caring actions that make a young person of this age worthy of respect:

- Demonstrates self-loving behavior
- Is trustworthy and honest
- Expresses feelings in healthful ways
- Adheres to family guidelines
- Sets goals and makes plans to reach them
- Demonstrates interdependence
- Demonstrates balance when managing time for family, school, hobbies, and friends
- Avoids abusive behavior
- Is committed to a drug-free lifestyle
- Practices abstinence

3 Brainstorm other characteristics and responsible and caring actions that are important in friendship. Students may mention behaviors such as "keeps thoughts I share in confidence" and "encourages me to do well in school." Students may also mention qualities that they enjoy in others such as "has a sense of humor" and "has good listening skills." Sharing interests can bring people closer together. Explain that varied interests are a bonus to friendship.

4 Give each student a shoe box, wrapping paper, and tape (or have each student bring these items from home). Have students wrap their boxes. They should wrap the top and the bottom of the box separately so they can put something in the box later.

5 Give each student five index cards. Ask students to reflect for a moment on the characteristics and interests that they have that are valuable to a friendship. For example, a student might be a loyal person. Another student might be a cheerful person. Another student might have clear values and behave responsibly. Another student might be athletic and enjoy playing sports with

others. Another student might enjoy sharing his or her love of music. Ask students to make a list of the characteristics and interests that they have that are valuable to a friendship. From this list, they are to select five items and print each of the five items selected on a separate index card.

6 Have the students place the index cards in their wrapped boxes. Now have students tie a colorful ribbon around their boxes. Collect the boxes and place them in the center of the room.

7 Have each student take a box other than the one that belonged to him or her. Explain that each student has just received a gift. Ask students to describe what is meant by "gift." A *gift* is something special that is given to another person. It involves the act of giving or putting forth effort. A gift is only of value to a person if it is received. So a gift also involves the act of receiving.

8 Have students open the friendship boxes and read the index cards to learn about the gifts each has received. Then ask students to select one of the five gifts in their boxes. They are to tell the class which gift they selected as most valuable to them and why

they would like to receive this gift from a friend.

EVALUATION

Have students identify five gifts of friendship that they have to give and five gifts of friendship that they would like to receive. You might also explain that a gift of friendship includes not pressuring another person to do something that is a risk or harmful to physical, mental, or emotional health. You may have students discuss abstinence as a gift of friendship. Explain that being a health advocate is taking healthful action to communicate. Introduce TM-30, "Be a Health Advocate," and apply it to friendship.

MULTICULTURAL INFUSION

Initiate a discussion on the importance of having friends from different cultures. Have students share with classmates special gifts they possess because of their cultural heritage. Prior to sharing, you may want to have students discuss the positive aspects of their cultural heritage with their parents.

Growth and Development

Happy Birth-Day

HEALTH EDUCATION STANDARDS

- Students will comprehend concepts related to health promotion and disease prevention to enhance health.
- Students will demonstrate the ability to access valid information and products and services to enhance health.

PERFORMANCE INDICATORS

- Analyze the relationship between healthy behaviors and personal health.
- Describe situations that may require professional health services.

HEALTH GOAL

- I will learn about pregnancy and childbirth.

MATERIALS

Sock; small baby doll that can fit through the opening of the sock; scissors; TM-25, "Practice Healthful Behaviors," Appendix A

MOTIVATION

1 Explain to the class that you will describe how childbirth occurs. You can review the role of the uterus in the development of a baby. Explain that the uterus is the organ that each month during a female's reproductive years prepares to receive a fertilized ovum, supports the fertilized ovum during pregnancy, and contracts during childbirth to force delivery of the baby. Point to the approximate position of the uterus. Hold up a sock containing a small baby doll. Explain that the sock represents a uterus. Explain that the baby inside the uterus is ready to come out from the woman's body after growing and developing for about nine months.

2 Tell the class that muscles in the uterus are going to become tight. The body does this automatically when the baby is to be born. This tightening of the muscles of the uterus is called a contraction. When a baby is ready to be born, there are many contractions, one after another. Explain that the contractions push the baby down through the opening of the uterus. Push the baby slightly through the uterus, or sock. Explain that the opening of the sock represents the opening of the uterus, or cervix. As the baby's head pushes through the uterus, the opening of the uterus becomes fully widened, or dilated. The baby then moves completely through the uterus and into the birth canal, or vagina.

3 You can modify this strategy to use the neck of the sock as the vaginal canal. Explain that just as the neck of the sock stretches to allow the baby to pass through, so do the walls in the vagina stretch to allow a baby to pass through. Explain that, on occasion, the vaginal opening may not be able to stretch enough to allow the baby's head to pass through. You can use the sock to demonstrate an episiotomy. Cut a slit in the neck of the sock. Explain that this cut, or incision, widens the opening of the vagina so that the vagina will not overstretch. Then the neck of the sock, or vaginal opening, can be stitched. It is important to emphasize that the use of an episiotomy is not nearly as common today as it was years ago. Explain that episiotomies were performed unnecessarily in the past. In most cases, episiotomies are not needed.

4 You might also use this activity to explain a Cesarean section. In this surgical procedure, an opening is made through the abdomen into the uterus. The baby is removed through this opening. A Cesarean section is performed when vaginal delivery might be difficult for the baby, such as if the baby is not in a position to pass through the vagina easily.

Growth and Development

EVALUATION

Select a student to come to the front of the class. Ask this student to imagine that she or he is a physician who delivers babies. Tell the class that this kind of physician is called an obstetrician. Give the student the sock with the baby doll inside. Have the student use this visual aid to explain the process of childbirth, naming as many facts as possible. After completing this task, the class is to identify additional facts that this student may not have mentioned. You may want to include a discussion of conception at this time. Show TM-25, "Practice Healthful Behaviors." Select a healthful behavior and have students relate it to the information on this master. Have students explain why healthful behaviors now have important implications for adulthood.

GRADE 6

The ABC's of the New Dietary Guidelines for Americans

HEALTH EDUCATION STANDARDS

- Students will demonstrate the ability to use goal-setting skills to enhance health.
- Students will demonstrate the ability to practice health-enhancing behaviors and avoid or reduce health risks.

PERFORMANCE INDICATORS

- Assess personal health practices.
- Demonstrate healthy practices and behaviors that will maintain or improve the health of self and others.

HEALTH GOAL

- I will follow the Dietary Guidelines.

MATERIALS

Teaching master "The Dietary Guidelines for Americans—2005"; teaching master, "MyPyramid"; transparency projector; old magazines that contain pictures of food; scissors; masking tape; TM-19, "Make Responsible Decisions," Appendix A

MOTIVATION

1 Explain to students that the Dietary Guidelines for Americans were released in 2005. These guidelines differ from the previous guidelines, as evident by the teaching master, "The Dietary Guidelines for Americans—2005." Explain that the new guidelines are structured in an ABC for-mat, where A = Aim for Fitness, B = Build a Healthy Base, and C = Choose Sensibly.

2 Divide the class into three working groups. Each group is assigned a letter: A, B, or C. Each group is to have the following task. Group members are to develop lists of ten ways each of their categories can be met. For example, "Build a Healthy Base" can be accomplished by choosing to have a half cup of oatmeal each day.

3 Each group will then present its findings to the class. After each group has presented its findings, other class members can then add to that list. To help students get further information, refer them to the USDA Web site that contains the new dietary guidelines, www.health.gov/dietaryguidelines, where they can find detailed information.

4 Show students the teaching master, "My-Pyramid." Explain to students that they are to choose foods from each of the categories. Staying in their original groups, have students plan a menu for a seven-day week. Emphasize to students that they are to examine foods of different cultures and include them in their plans. Then have students share their choices with the rest of the class.

EVALUATION

Provide students with a choice they would need to make about food selection. Then show TM-19, "Make Responsible Decisions," and have them process the decision-making model steps in making a healthful decision.

Teaching Master

The Dietary Guidelines for Americans — 2005

Aim for Fitness
- Aim for a healthy weight.
- Be physically active each day for at least thirty minutes.

Build a Healthy Base
- Let MyPyramid guide your food choices.
- Choose a variety of grains daily, especially whole grains.
- Choose a variety of fruits and vegetables daily.
- Keep food safe to eat.

Choose Sensibly
- Choose a diet that is low in saturated fat and cholesterol and moderate in total fat.
- Choose beverages and foods to moderate your intake of sugars.
- Choose and prepare foods with less salt.
- If adults drink alcoholic beverages, they should do so in moderation. People your age should not drink alcohol.

Nutrition

Anatomy of MyPyramid

One size doesn't fit all

USDA's MyPyramid symbolizes a personalized approach to healthy eating and physical activity. The symbol has been designed to be simple. It has been developed to remind consumers to make healthy food choices and to be active every day. The different parts of the symbol are described below.

Activity

Activity is represented by the steps and the person climbing them, as a reminder of the importance of daily physical activity.

Moderation

Moderation is represented by the narrowing of each food group from bottom to top. The wider base stands for foods with little or no solid fats or added sugars. These should be selected more often. The narrower top area stands for foods containing more added sugars and solid fats. The more active you are, the more of these foods can fit into your diet.

Personalization

Personalization is shown by the person on the steps, the slogan, and the URL. Find the kinds and amounts of food to eat each day at MyPyramid.gov.

Proportionality

Proportionality is shown by the different widths of the food group bands. The widths suggest how much food a person should choose from each group. The widths are just a general guide, not exact proportions. Check the Web site for how much is right for you.

Variety

Variety is symbolized by the 6 color bands representing the 5 food groups of the Pyramid and oils. This illustrates that foods from all groups are needed each day for good health.

Gradual Improvement

Gradual improvement is encouraged by the slogan. It suggests that individuals can benefit from taking small steps to improve their diet and lifestyle each day.

MyPyramid.gov
STEPS TO A HEALTHIER YOU

GRAINS VEGETABLES FRUITS OILS MILK MEAT & BEANS

USDA U.S. Department of Agriculture
Center for Nutrition Policy
and Promotion
April 2005 CNPP-16

USDA is an equal opportunity provider and employer.

When I Grow Up

HEALTH EDUCATION STANDARDS

- Students will comprehend concepts related to health promotion and disease prevention to enhance health.
- Students will demonstrate the ability to access valid information and products and services to enhance health.

PERFORMANCE INDICATORS

- Analyze the relationship between healthy behaviors and personal health.
- Access valid health information from home, school, and community.

HEALTH GOAL

- I will have regular examinations.

MATERIALS

Teaching master "When I Grow Up"; copies of a blank team roster form; TM-30, "Be a Health Advocate," Appendix A

MOTIVATION

1 Ask students to define *teamwork*. (Students might say that teamwork is a group of people all working toward the same goal.) Have students give examples of teamwork they have experienced. (Student answers might include sports teams, band, dance groups, or speech teams.) Ask students if all members of a team have the same job. (Students will say "no.")

2 Have students explain why team members often have different jobs. (Students might say that each team member may be good at different things; by specializing, a team can have members who are good at working toward all facets of the team's goal.) Point out that teammates rely on each other to work toward the same good goal.

3 Distribute copies of a blank team roster to students. Explain that their task is to develop a "Health Team." Ask students what the goal might be for their personal health team. (Students might say to work together to keep them healthy.) Ask volunteers to give examples of people who might be part of their health team. (Students might answer their doctor, their parents, the school dietician.) Then ask students what a doctor's role is on the team. (Students might say to check on how they are growing; to find early symptoms of disease; to treat injuries and illnesses.) Have them think of all the health professionals who can contribute to the health team. (Student answers will vary but might include doctor, dentist, dental hygienist, school nurse, school psychologist, etc.)

4 Read the poem "When I Grow Up" aloud, and ask students why they should consider their doctor to be their friend. (Students may say because the doctor takes care of their health and is on their team.) Reread the poem and have students name examples from the poem that show the doctor's role. (Students will mention that the doctor helps people live healthful lives, keeps

people safe, and is available in an emergency.) Ask students to name their role as a member of the health team. (Students will say they must eat right, get enough sleep, get regular checkups, and have a checkup when they are sick.)

EVALUATION

Have groups of four or five students make up a cheer for their personal health team. In their cheers, they are to mention why they will have regular checkups. They are to name members of their health care team. Allow time for groups to perform their cheers for the class. Show TM-30, "Be a Health Advocate," and have students explain how they can be an advocate for their own health care.

Teaching Master

When I Grow Up

❖❖❖❖❖❖

I want a job
where I can
help folks
live their lives;
where I can
keep them
safe and healthy;
where I can
save them
from disease.
When I grow up,
I will be a doctor.
And you can call me
anytime,
day or night.
I will be there.
You can call me
to fix
what you've broken.
You can call me
to fix
what hurts.
You will call me
doctor,
but I hope
you will call me friend.

❖❖❖❖❖❖

Alcohol, Tobacco, and Other Drugs

GRADE 6

I Can't Understand You

HEALTH EDUCATION STANDARD

- Students will comprehend concepts related to health promotion and disease prevention to enhance health.

PERFORMANCE INDICATOR

- Analyze the relationship between healthy behaviors and personal health.

HEALTH GOAL

- I will not drink alcohol.

MATERIALS

A bag of marshmallows; TM-25, "Practice Healthful Behaviors," Appendix A

MOTIVATION

1 Review some of the possible physical effects that result when a person drinks alcohol. Examples are slurred speech, poor coordination of body muscles, liver damage, inability to think clearly, drowsiness, dizziness, and injury due to increased risk of accidents.

2 The following activity will demonstrate how alcohol affects coordination of body muscles. Select a volunteer to come to the front of the class and read a paragraph aloud from a book that is written at an appropriate reading level. Ask the class how clear the reading was. Most students should be able to follow what was read.

3 The volunteer will read the paragraph aloud again, but this time with a marshmallow in his or her mouth. This student cannot chew or eat the marshmallow; the marshmallow is to remain in the person's mouth. Again, ask the students how clear the reading was. Were they able to understand what the volunteer was reading? Students will indicate that the student was difficult to understand. The words were slurred.

4 Explain that the tongue is a muscle and that many muscles help the mouth move to form words. When a person drinks too much alcohol, muscles cannot work in a coordinated manner. Trying to read with a marshmallow in the mouth simulated how a person who drinks too much alcohol might sound.

5 You can have the class try another experiment. Have the students pair off. First, one partner will try reading to the other partner with a marshmallow in her or his mouth. Then the other partner will take a turn. Students might also remark that they felt frustrated as they tried to read with a marshmallow in their mouths. Explain that drinking alcohol also can cause a person to become frustrated.

EVALUATION

Have students name other activities requiring the use of coordinated muscles. Then have students share how drinking alcohol will interfere with the coordination needed for these activities. Show TM-25, "Practice Healthful Behaviors," and ask students to identify what can result if they do not practice healthful behaviors. For example, if they implement a behavior such as smoking, how might that affect them in the future?

Communicable and Chronic Diseases

GRADE 6

Defend That Line

HEALTH EDUCATION STANDARDS

- Students will comprehend concepts related to health promotion and disease prevention to enhance health.
- Students will demonstrate the ability to practice health-enhancing behaviors and avoid or reduce health risks.

PERFORMANCE INDICATORS

- Examine the likelihood of injury or illness if engaging in unhealthy behaviors.
- Explain the importance of assuming responsibility for personal health behaviors.

HEALTH GOALS

- I will choose behaviors to prevent the spread of pathogens.
- I will choose behavior to reduce my risk of HIV infection.

MATERIALS

Posterboard cut out in the shape of T-shirts; marker; string; strips of posterboard with the names of opportunistic infections written on them; TM-25, "Practice Healthful Behaviors," Appendix A

MOTIVATION

1 On each of five sheets of posterboard, draw an outline of a T-shirt with a marker. Punch two holes in the T-shirt on each side of the neck and insert string through each hole so that you can wear the T-shirt like a billboard. On the front of each of the T-shirts in large letters should be written one of five terms. The five terms are *skin, helper T cell, B cell, antibody,* and *macrophage.* Written on the back of each poster should be information about each term. For skin, you might write, "I'm the first line of defense." Helper T cell will state, "I send a signal to B cells to tell them to make antibodies." B cell will state, "I produce antibodies." Antibody will state, "I destroy pathogens so that macrophages can digest them." And macrophage will state, "I will surround pathogens and digest them." Be sure to number each T-shirt so it looks authentic. You can number the following: skin #40, helper T cell #58, B cell #60, antibody #65, and macrophage #72.

2 Select five students to come to the front of the room. Each is to wear a T-shirt. The teacher will introduce the T-shirt team and, as each member is introduced, state the function of each. Students may refer to the information on the back of the posters.

3 Ask for a volunteer and designate this volunteer as a non-HIV pathogen. First, line up the team in single file in the following order: skin, helper T cell, B cell, antibody, and macrophage. Have this volunteer gently try to "get into the body" by breaking through the skin. The skin is to prevent the person from getting through. Tell the class that the skin is the first line of defense in protecting us from pathogens. Then have the volunteer pretend to get through the skin, and have the helper T cell hug the pathogen to simulate that this type of cell will multiply and prevent harm by this pathogen. Have B cells arrive and produce antibodies, and the macrophage then digests the pathogen.

4 Now have another volunteer try to enter the body. Designate this volunteer as HIV. HIV breaks through the skin and attacks the helper T cell. Antibodies to HIV are produced, but the helper T cells are destroyed by HIV. Have three other students in the class pretend to be HIV that has multiplied in the body. Now that HIV has multiplied, they begin to call in their friends. To represent the friends of HIV, make opportunistic infection signs. Among the signs you can make up on strips of paper are *pneumocystis carinii pneumonia* (a type of pneumonia), *Kaposi's sarcoma* (a type of cancer), and

AIDS dementia complex (a mental disorder caused by the destruction of brain cells). Explain to the class that HIV destroys the helper T cells. The reduction in the number of helper T cells causes the immune system to become susceptible to the development of opportunistic infections and leads to the development of AIDS. Eventually, the opportunistic infections cause death.

5 You can modify this activity to introduce the roles played by B cells. Explain to the class that when a pathogen enters the body, helper T cells signal B cells to stimulate the production of antibodies. Suppose you were talking about the chickenpox virus. The antibodies to this virus would remain inside the body to prevent chickenpox from occurring again if that virus were to enter. But when HIV enters, helper T cells are destroyed, thereby interfering with the functioning of B cells. HIV multiplies and destroys the immune system. Even though HIV antibodies are present, they cannot protect the body from the increased multiplication of HIV that, in turn, destroys the immune system.

EVALUATION

Have the class divide into small groups of about five. Each group is to develop a skit that demonstrates how the immune system functions to protect the body and what happens to the immune system once it becomes infected with HIV. Have students identify the important facts they have included in their skits. Next, show TM-25, "Practice Healthful Behaviors," and have students do another skit that will address the points in the teaching master.

GRADE 6

The One

HEALTH EDUCATION STANDARD

- Students will demonstrate the ability to access valid information and products and services to enhance health.

PERFORMANCE INDICATOR

- Locate valid and reliable health products and services.

HEALTH GOAL

- I will develop media literacy.

MATERIALS

Teaching master "The One"; transparency projector; teaching master "Advertising Appeals"; advertisements cut from newspapers and magazines; TM-5, "Analyze What Influences Your Health," Appendix A

MOTIVATION

1 Ask students to bring in copies of advertisements for their favorite products. Then share the teaching master "Advertising Appeals" with the class. Have students determine which appeals each advertisement uses to convince consumers to buy the product.

2 Read the poem "The One" aloud. Have students use the chart of advertising appeals to determine how the poet is making each

purchase mentioned in the poem. (Students might say that the shampoo advertisement uses false image appeal; the jeans advertisement uses the brand loyalty appeal; the soft drink advertisement uses the glittering generality appeal.)

3 Point out to students that the underlying purpose of any advertisement is not to inform but to get consumers to buy. Ask students why advertisers use such a variety of ways to promote their products. (Students might say that different appeals will attract different consumers, that they want to try many ways to get consumers to buy.)

4 Explain that wise consumers analyze advertising to ensure that their purchases are a responsible use of money and that they will benefit them and meet their needs. Ask students to name examples of ways they can be responsible consumers of advertisements. (Students might mention that they can read ads and product labels before buying products; they can be aware of appeals to which they are vulnerable.)

EVALUATION

Have students find ads for three similar products and compare the ads for their type of appeal and for the information they give. Then have them explain which of the three products they would buy and on what basis they made that selection. Use TM-5 "Analyze What Influences Your Health," and describe how each of the four items on this master apply to the ads the students found.

Teaching Master

The One

❖❖❖❖❖❖❖

How do I choose
which shampoo I use?
Is it the ads on TV?

How do I know
it will make my hair glow?
How is it working on me?

How do I decide
which jeans I will try?
Do I decide by the fit?

If I saw the same tag
on any old rag,
would I make a point to buy it?

Why do I think
my favorite soft drink
tastes better than all the rest?

So many to try.
So why do I just buy
the one whose commercials are best?

❖❖❖❖❖❖❖

Teaching Master
Advertising Appeals

Bandwagon Appeal
Tries to convince consumers that everyone else wants a product and they should too.

Brand Loyalty Appeal
Tells consumers that a brand is better than the rest.

False Image Appeal
Convinces consumers that people who use the product give off a certain image.

Glittering Generality Appeal
Greatly exaggerates the benefits of the product.

Humor Appeal
Uses a slogan, jingle, or cartoon to keep consumers' attention.

Progress Appeal
Tells consumers that a product is new and improved compared to other versions.

Reward Appeal
Tells consumers that they will get a prize or gift if they buy the product.

Scientific Evidence Appeal
Gives consumers evidence of a survey or test that seems to prove the product is effective or reliable.

Snob Appeal
Tells consumers that they are worthy of the best products or services.

Testimony Appeal
Uses a well-known personality to say that a product or service is the best.

Environmental Health

GRADE 6

Environmental Mural

HEALTH EDUCATION STANDARDS

- Students will comprehend concepts related to health promotion and disease prevention to enhance health.
- Students will demonstrate the ability to advocate for personal, family, and community health.

PERFORMANCE INDICATORS

- Analyze how the environment impacts personal health.
- Work cooperatively to advocate for healthy individuals, families, and schools.

HEALTH GOALS

- I will stay informed about environmental issues.
- I will be a health advocate for the environment.

MATERIALS

Five-foot sheet of butcher paper; cellophane tape; colored markers; plastic trash bag with examples of trash that is clean and safe to handle and commonly found on streets, such as candy wrappers, soda cans, and crumpled tissues; TM-30, "Be a Health Advocate," Appendix A

MOTIVATION

1 Begin this strategy by laying a five-foot strip of butcher paper on the floor. Tell students that they are going to make a mural of the environment. Explain that this mural should consist of scenery that shows the environment at its best—that is, it should be free from any pollutants. Define **pollutants** as anything that makes the environment dirty, such as smoke or trash. Students can draw pictures of mountains, lakes, streams, people swimming, trees,

and any other scene that is pleasing to the eye. Have students use the colored markers to draw the mural.

2 Pick up the completed mural from the floor and tape it to the chalkboard or other long area at the front of the room. Have students observe the mural of the clean environment and provide you with feedback about how nice this environment looks.

3 Show students the bag of trash you have. Tell students that they are going to have the opportunity to select items from the trash bag. Explain that the trash inside your bag consists of items that are clean and safe to handle. Have each student select an item. The students will select items such as crumpled tissue papers, candy wrappers, aluminum soda cans, and other examples of discarded items. Explain that these items represent litter. *Litter* is trash that is thrown on the street, ground, or other places in the environment. Have each student take a piece of cellophane tape and attach his or her piece of trash to the mural. Have students describe how their mural of the environment looks now. Students will indicate that the environment looks dirty. Explain that the litter made the environment appear dirty. Explain that litter also attracts rodents and insects, which can carry disease. Encourage students to dispose of litter in litter cans or in other appropriate areas.

4 Explain that there are other sources of pollution in the environment. **Air pollution** is dirty air that is caused by automobile exhaust or other matter burned in the environment. Explain that the **Environmental Protection Agency (EPA)** is a federal agency that is responsible for alleviating and controlling environmental pollution. By following rules such as disposing of trash properly, students can help keep the environment clean. Explain that **water pollution,** which is dirt or waste in water, can be caused by the dumping of waste in rivers, lakes, and streams. Sometimes the water is

so dirty that swimming must be prohibited. Explain that it is important to avoid going into polluted water because pathogens from the water can enter the body. **Solid waste pollution** is the throwing away of substances such as trash, litter, and unwanted objects, some of which may be very large, in the environment. Many communities have solid waste buried in sanitary landfills. A **sanitary landfill** is an area where layers of solid waste are dumped and covered by layers of dirt. Introduce the word *pesticide*. A **pesticide** is any substance used to kill or control the growth of unwanted organisms. For example, a spray can of pesticide may be used to kill insects on a house plant. Explain that the pesticide can be harmful if inhaled or swallowed. Although pesticides can be helpful in controlling insects that harm the environment, they can also harm the environment by seeping into lakes and streams when it rains. This can kill fish and aquatic plants.

EVALUATION

Have students look through newspapers and magazines for one week and keep a log of different environmental issues that are described in news articles and editorials. In their logs, have students identify the type of pollution identified, the issue or issues involving this type of pollution, and what is being done to solve the issues. You can grade students' papers by referring to the number of articles they found and their summaries about the issues and solutions. Then use TM-30, "Be a Health Advocate," and have students identify an action they can take to help improve the environment.

GRADE 6

Introducing Maxine and the Matches

HEALTH EDUCATION STANDARD

- Students will demonstrate the ability to practice health-enhancing behaviors and avoid or reduce health risks.

PERFORMANCE INDICATOR

- Demonstrate healthy practices and behaviors that will maintain or improve the health of self and others.

HEALTH GOAL

- I will be skilled in first-aid procedures.

MATERIALS

Teaching master "First Aid: What You Should Know"; transparency projector; paper; pencil; TM-25, "Practice Healthful Behaviors," Appendix A

MOTIVATION

1 Begin this strategy by asking students if they have ever suddenly become ill or injured. Have students share what happened and how people responded to their situation. After students have shared their situations, explain that they probably received first aid. **First aid** is the immediate care given to an injured or ill person.

2 Explain that there are many different situations in which first aid may be given. To help present the information, show the teaching master "First Aid: What You Should Know." This master presents information about common emergencies; their causes, descriptions, signs and symptoms; and first-aid procedures to follow.

3 After reviewing the information on this master, divide the class into groups of about five. You can assign a different first-aid situation to each group. In turn, each group is to work together to develop a song that uses information from the master. The song is to be accompanied by a title and the name of the group who sang it. The group name is to relate to first aid or an injury associated with first aid. After students develop the lyrics to their songs, they are to sing their songs to the tune of a popular song. Or students can choose to create poetry and have a poetry reading. If they do choose to have a poetry reading, they also should give the poet a name. All of the students can sing or read the poetry together or different students can read different parts. Students should have between twenty to thirty minutes to prepare.

4 Tell students you want them to have ten lines to their poems or songs. Within the ten lines, they are to have at least five facts. You can give students the following as an example of a poem:

BURNED TO A DEGREE

by Maxine and the Matches

We're here today to tell you a way
That burns can make for an awful day.
We thought we would cook, that's certainly
    no sin,
Until that pot of boiling water poured onto
    our skin.
Those second-degree burns made our skin
    so red,
The pain was so severe we thought we were
    dead.
Those blisters and swelling were certainly
    bold,
But we relieved the pain by applying some-
    thing cold.
So a word of advice we want to say,
Be careful around heat and you'll have a
    great day!

5 After giving students the example of the poem, you can ask related questions, such as "What are the signs and symptoms of second-degree burns?" or "What can cause a second-degree burn?" For extra credit, you can have each group identify five questions the group can ask students about its poem or song.

EVALUATION

Have students present their songs or poems to the class. You can assess students' knowledge about the different first-aid situations by listening for the five facts in their songs or poems. You can develop questions based on the group presentations. You can also have students apply the information in this lesson by having them respond to each of the four steps in TM-25, "Practice Healthful Behaviors."

Teaching Master

First Aid: What You Should Know

SHOCK

Definition: A condition in which the rates of functions of the important organs in the body slow down.

Causes: Any injury or illness can cause shock. These include blood loss, a fracture, or sudden illness.

Signs and Symptoms: The early stages of shock will be evident by reduced blood flow to the skin that results in lowered body temperature. The skin may appear cold and clammy. The pulse may feel weak, and the breathing rate may increase. A person may feel nauseous. In the later stages of shock, a person may appear unresponsive. The eyes may appear sunken and the pupils of the eyes may be dilated.

First Aid: It is important to maintain body temperature. Keep the person lying down. Keep the head level with the body and raise the lower extremities about eight to twelve inches above the level of the heart. Do not raise the victim's feet if there is a head injury or a fracture in the leg. Keep the victim warm by covering him or her with a blanket. Do not give the victim anything to eat or drink and allow a medical professional to further treat the victim.

FRACTURE

Definition: A break or a crack in a bone.

Causes: A blow to a bone or a movement in an awkward position.

Signs and Symptoms: There may be pain, swelling, and loss of movement in the affected area. The injured area may be deformed. If the fracture is serious, the bone may protrude through the skin.

First Aid: Treat for bleeding and shock if necessary. Prevent the injured part from moving. For head injuries, keep the person still. Apply ice to prevent swelling, and get medical help immediately.

BLEEDING

Definition: A condition in which blood escaped from the vessels that naturally contain it.

Causes: Any accident in which the skin is opened.

Signs and Symptoms: A loss of blood from the injured area.

First Aid: Because blood carries oxygen and nutrients, a person needs to have the blood loss stopped as soon as possible. The most common way to stop bleeding is the application of direct pressure. Direct pressure is the force placed directly over the wound. This is done by placing a clean cloth over the cut and pressing down. If the cut is on a finger or arm, raise the body part above the level of the heart and apply direct pressure. If bleeding does not stop, place pressure on a supplying artery. A supplying artery is a major blood vessel that supplies blood to the affected part. The two supplying arteries recommended by the Red Cross are under the arm and inside the groin area.

HEAT CRAMPS

Definition: Muscle spasms that occur most often in the legs and arms due to excessive fluid loss through sweating.

Causes: Extended activity during warm weather.

Signs and Symptoms: A sharp pain will be felt around the muscle and it may be observed contracting. The muscle may also feel very hard.

First Aid: Heat cramps are easily treated with rest. Light massage to the affected area also is helpful. It is important to drink plenty of fluids during strenuous physical activity.

HEAT EXHAUSTION

Definition: Extreme tiredness due to the inability of the body temperature to be regulated.

Causes: Excessive physical activity at high temperatures.

Signs and Symptoms: A person will feel dizzy and have pale, cool, dry skin. Body temperature will be normal or above normal.

First Aid: Move the person to a cool, dry place, and lay him and her down. Give the person cool liquids and cool the body by applying cool water with a sponge.

HEAT STROKE

Definition: A sudden illness brought on by exposure to high temperatures.

Causes: The inability of the body to sweat causes it to have an elevated temperature.

Signs and Symptoms: The skin may be hot, red, and dry. The person may feel weak and have a headache.

First Aid: Move the person into the shade and sponge the skin with cool water. Take the person to the hospital immediately.

Teaching Master (continued)

FROSTBITE

Definition: The freezing of parts of the body. The parts of the body most often affected are the extremities such as the toes, fingers, and ears.

Causes: Overexposure to very cold temperatures.

Signs and Symptoms: At first, there is a tingling sensation in the affected body part. Pain may also be present. The body part may be numb and look waxy. A white, cold spot may appear.

First Aid: Place the affected body part in warm water for twenty minutes. Afterward it should be kept dry. Seek medical attention.

HYPOTHERMIA

Definition: A low body temperature.

Causes: Excessive exposure to cold, moisture, and wind for an extended period of time. The temperature can be as warm as fifty degrees Fahrenheit yet still cause a person to suffer from hypothermia.

Signs and Symptoms: A person may begin to feel chilled and eventually may become disoriented and weak.

First Aid: Bring the victim indoors and replace the clothing with clean, warm, and dry clothing. Give the victim warm fluids to drink.

Wiping Stress Away

HEALTH EDUCATION STANDARDS

- Students will comprehend concepts related to health promotion and disease prevention to enhance health.
- Students will demonstrate the ability to use interpersonal communication skills to enhance health and avoid or reduce health risks.

PERFORMANCE INDICATORS

- Describe the interrelationship of emotional, intellectual, physical, and social health in adolescence.
- Apply effective verbal and nonverbal communication skills to enhance health.

HEALTH GOALS

- I will follow a plan to manage stress.
- I will communicate with others in healthful ways.
- I will choose behaviors to reduce my risk of cardiovascular disease. (Communicable and Chronic Diseases)

MATERIALS

Teaching master "General Adaptation Syndrome"; tissue; two blank transparency overlays; transparency projector; one blue oil-based writing marker; one red water-based marker; a balloon; TM-11, "Use Communication Skills," Appendix A

MOTIVATION

1 Begin this strategy by asking students to define stress. After several students have given their definitions, review the correct definition. **Stress** is the response of the body to the demands of daily living. Explain that stressors are the sources or causes of stress. A **stressor** is a demand that causes changes in the body. Stressors

cause the body to respond. A stressor can be physical, mental, or social. Give examples of stressors, such as having an argument with a friend, being chased by a dog, and worrying about a test. Ask students to give other examples.

2 Explain to students that they do not always have the same response to stressors. Sometimes their responses are positive, while at other times they are not. **Eustress** is a healthful response to a stressor that produces positive results. For example, a student might experience stress before being in the school play. The student experiences excitement and performs very well. Ask students to share examples of eustress they have experienced. Then explain distress. **Distress** is a harmful response to a stressor that produces negative results. For example, some students might experience stress before a test and during the test be so anxious that they perform poorly. Ask students to share examples of distress they have experienced.

3 Explain that everyone experiences stressors. It is impossible to avoid stressors. Therefore, it is important to know how to manage stress. Make a transparency of the teaching master "General Adaptation Syndrome." Review the general adaptation syndrome. The **general adaptation syndrome (GAS)** is a series of changes that occur in the body when stress occurs. Refer to the written words on the left side of the figure. Explain that these are the responses of the body during the alarm stage of the GAS. The **alarm stage of GAS** is the first stage in which the body gets ready for action. During this stage, adrenaline is released into the bloodstream. Adrenaline is a hormone that helps the body get ready for an emergency.

4 Refer to the written words on the right side of the figure. Explain that these are the responses of the body during the resistance stage of the GAS. The **resistance stage of GAS** is the second stage in which the body attempts to regain balance and return to normal.

Mental and Emotional Health

5 Explain that there is a third stage of the GAS. The **exhaustion stage of GAS** is the third stage in which there is wear and tear on the body, lowered resistance to disease, and an increased likelihood of disease and death. People who experience the exhaustion stage frequently have a higher incidence of cardiovascular diseases and certain kinds of cancer.

6 Explain the importance of managing stress. **Stress-management skills** are techniques that can be used to cope with the harmful effects produced by stress. Do the following activity. Select one student who does not practice stress-management skills. Name this student "I. M. Stressed." Select another student who practices stress-management skills, and name this student "Stress Manager." Take two blank transparency overlays and place them on your desk. Give I. M. Stressed a blue, oil-based writing marker, and give Stress Manager a red, water-based writing marker. Ask the other students to identify at least eight stressors. As each stressor is identified, I. M. Stressed and Stress Manager are to list ways the body responds during the alarm stage of the GAS on the transparency.

7 Now explain that I. M. Stressed is going to show the class the importance of practicing stress-management skills. Give I. M. Stressed a tissue. Ask I. M. Stressed to "wipe away" the effects of the alarm stage of the GAS with the tissue. The effects cannot be wiped away. I. M. Stressed's body does not experience the resistance stage of the GAS, but instead the exhaustion stage of the GAS begins. Now give Stress Manager a tissue. Tell the class that you are going to identify stress-management skills that Stress Manager practices. Stress Manager is to wipe away one of the body's responses to the alarm stage of the GAS each time you mention a stress-management skill. The following are stress-management skills you might say: (1) using responsible decision-making skills, (2) getting enough rest and sleep, (3) participating in physical activities, (4) using a time-management plan, (5) writing in a journal, (6) having close friends, (7) talking with parents and other trusted adults, (8) helping others, (9) expressing affection in appropriate ways, (10) caring for pets, (11) changing outlook, and (12) keeping a sense of humor. Stress Manager wipes away the alarm stage of the GAS. Her or his body enters the resistance stage of the GAS and returns to normal. Review the importance to good health.

EVALUATION

Divide the class into groups of three students. For this cooperative learning experience, you may want to put students with strong language arts skills with those who need more help. Explain that each group is going to develop a ten-line poem that provides at least five stress-management skills. Give the groups an appropriate amount of time to write

their poems. Have a poetry reading in which each group reads its poem. Have the class review the stress-management skills included in each poem. Explain that situations that result in certain feelings, such as anger, disappointment, and worry, are stressors because they elicit the GAS. Have students list five stress-management skills they might practice when they experience these feelings. Explain that they will need to work through these feelings as well as practice stress-management skills. Refer to TM-11, "Use Communication Skills." Have students think of a time they have been angry. Then have them discuss each of the four steps in the master to show how they handled their anger.

Teaching Master

General Adaptation Syndrome

During the ALARM STAGE, the SYMPATHETIC NERVOUS SYSTEM prepares to meet the demand of the stressor.

During the RESISTANCE STAGE, the PARASYMPATHETIC NERVOUS SYSTEM attempts to return the body to a state of homeostasis.

ALARM STAGE

Pupils dilate

Hearing sharpens

Saliva decreases

Heart rate increases

Blood pressure increases

Bronchioles dilate

Digestion slows

Blood flow to muscles increases

Muscles tighten

RESISTANCE STAGE

Pupils constrict

Hearing is normal

Saliva increases

Heart rate decreases

Blood pressure decreases

Bronchioles constrict

Intestinal secretions increase to normal

Blood flow to muscles decreases

Muscles relax

Family and Social Health

Positive Parenting

HEALTH EDUCATION STANDARDS

- Students will analyze the influence of family, peers, culture, media, technology, and other factors on health behaviors.
- Students will comprehend concepts related to health promotion and disease prevention to enhance health.

PERFORMANCE INDICATORS

- Examine how the family influences the health of adolescents.
- Analyze the relationship between healthy behaviors and personal health.

HEALTH GOALS

- I will develop skills to prepare for marriage.
- I will make healthful adjustments to family changes.
- I will practice self-protection strategies. (Injury Prevention and Safety)

MATERIALS

Student master "Children Learn What They Live"; TM-11, "Use Communication Skills," Appendix A

MOTIVATION

1. Begin this strategy by introducing the saying "Do as I say, not as I do." Have students describe the meaning of this saying and give examples. You can clarify this saying by explaining that people may engage in risk behavior and at the same time express that risk behavior is inappropriate. For example, a person might admonish another person for starting a fight. Yet when this same person becomes angry, he or she might settle a disagreement by fighting. What the person says and what the person does are not the same. The person is inconsistent. Another example might be illustrative. Explain that a person who claims to be on a weight-loss diet might order a hamburger, french fries, and a milkshake for lunch. What the person says ("I am on a weight-loss diet") and what the person does (orders a high-calorie lunch) are not the same.

2. Ask students why it is important to practice the saying "Do as I do." Explain that this saying implies that people need to be consistent in what they say and do. This is because what a person does sends a strong message. Most of us have more meaningful learning experiences when we observe what someone does than when we listen to what someone says. Introduce the term *role model*. A role model is a person who teaches others by demonstrating specific behaviors. There are two types of role models. A positive role model demonstrates healthful and responsible behavior. A negative role model demonstrates harmful and irresponsible behavior. A negative role model may also demonstrate risk behavior.

3. Explain that the most significant role models in children's lives are their parents, guardians, or other people who raise them. Young children learn by observing their behavior. Ask students to imitate you, and then do the following: clap your hands, wave bye-bye, stomp your feet. Ask students if they have ever seen a baby do what they have just done. Now ask students if they have ever seen a small child scold a doll or treat another small child in the same way that an adult has treated him or her.

4. Give each student a copy of the student master "Children Learn What They Live." Divide the class into twelve groups. (There may be only two students in each group.) Assign each group one of the lines from the poem. Make these assignments randomly, and do not let the entire class know which group has which line. The students in each group are to develop a nonverbal skit to

demonstrate the line it was assigned. After an appropriate amount of preparation time, each group is to nonverbally act out its line for the other students in the class. The other students are to guess which line is being acted out. Be certain not to have the students act out the lines in the same order as the lines in the poem. After all groups have presented, discuss each line.

5 Explain that as they are developing and maturing, the students are learning from the significant role models in their lives. Discuss the kinds of relationships they are observing: male-female relationships, marriage relationships, parent-child relationships (significant adult/child). It is important for them to analyze the messages that they are learning. For example, they are learning ways that significant adults respond to family changes, such as having a new family member or having an ill family member. They are learning ways that significant adults rear children.

6 Explain that some significant adults may not be skilled in relationships. Refer to the student master. Significant adults who are not skilled in relationships might be critical and hostile. They might shame or ridicule others. They might be abusive. **Child abuse** is the harmful treatment of a person under the age of eighteen and includes physical abuse, emotional abuse, sexual abuse, and neglect. Further explain that young people who are treated in these ways and don't get help in understanding how they were treated might repeat these behaviors if they choose to be parents. This is why it is important to understand the effects of the behaviors of significant role models.

7 Identify other behaviors that might be modeled by significant adults. For exam-

ples, some adults might be drug-free while others might misuse or abuse drugs. Some adults might exercise regularly and practice stress-management skills, while others might be couch potatoes and be stressed.

EVALUATION

Have students write a "Positive Parenting Pledge" in which they identify at least ten behaviors for which they believe a parent should be a role model. Select students to read their pledges to the class. Have students share their pledges and their copies of "Children Learn What They Live" with the significant adults in their families. Then discuss how parents can be better communicators by referring to the information in TM-11, "Use Communication Skills."

MULTICULTURAL INFUSION

Use a globe or world map. Have several students point to different countries. After you have named different countries, introduce the concept that families around the world have much in common. The significant adults in all families are important role models. Have students identify five behaviors for which they believe significant adults in families from all cultures might be role models for their children.

INCLUSION

Explain how the behaviors and attitudes of significant adults affect young people with disabilities. When significant adults are patient and accepting, young people with disabilities develop positive self-esteem and are accepting of themselves.

Student Master

Children Learn What They Live

by Dorothy Law Nolte

If a child lives with criticism, (s)he learns to condemn.

If a child lives with hostility, (s)he learns to fight.

If a child lives with ridicule, (s)he learns to be shy.

If a child lives with shame, (s)he learns to feel guilty.

If a child lives with tolerance, (s)he learns to be patient.

If a child lives with encouragement, (s)he learns confidence.

If a child lives with praise, (s)he learns to appreciate.

If a child lives with fairness, (s)he learns justice.

If a child lives with security, (s)he learns to have faith.

If a child lives with approval, (s)he learns to like herself/himself.

If a child lives with acceptance and friendship, (s)he learns to find love in the world.

Growth and Development

GRADE 7

Steps toward Maturity

HEALTH EDUCATION STANDARDS

- Students will comprehend concepts related to health promotion and disease prevention to enhance health.
- Students will demonstrate the ability to use goal-setting skills to enhance health.

PERFORMANCE INDICATORS

- Analyze the relationship between healthy behaviors and personal health.
- Develop a goal to adopt, maintain, or improve a personal health practice.

HEALTH GOALS

- I will achieve the developmental tasks of adolescence.
- I will develop my learning style.

MATERIALS

Teaching master "Developmental Tasks of Adolescence"; transparency projector; four wastebaskets; eight sheets of paper plus one sheet of paper for each student; pencils; chalk, TM-22, "Set Health Goals," Appendix A

MOTIVATION

1 Make a transparency of the teaching master "Developmental Tasks of Adolescence." Review the information on the master with the students. Explain that a **developmental task** is an achievement that must be made during a particular period of growth in order for a person to continue growing toward maturity. The eight tasks identified on the transparency are the tasks that they are now attempting to master.

2 Divide the class into eight groups of students, one for each of the developmental tasks. Each group is to select one student to be its leader. The leader is to write the

assigned developmental task on a sheet of paper and crumple it into a ball. For example, the leader in group one would write "Achieving a new and more mature relationship with age mates of both sexes" on a sheet of paper and then crumple this sheet of paper into a ball.

3 Use chalk to make a starting point on the floor. In a direct line, place the first wastebasket three feet from the starting point. Place the second wastebasket six feet from the starting point. Place the third wastebasket nine feet from the starting point and the fourth wastebasket twelve feet from the starting point.

4 Ask the eight group leaders to line up in order of the developmental tasks (task 1, task 2, etc.) at the starting point. Explain that the wastebasket that is farthest from the starting point represents mastery of each of the developmental tasks written on the crumpled sheets of paper. The wastebaskets in between are "steps toward maturity" because they lead to mastery of the developmental tasks. Begin with the group leader who has task 1 written on the crumpled sheet of paper. Ask this student to toss the crumpled sheet of paper into the wastebasket that is twelve feet from the starting point. If the student misses, have the student pick up the crumpled paper. Repeat, asking the second student to follow the same directions. Repeat, having the remaining students representing their groups as leaders toss their crumpled sheets of paper into the farthest wastebasket. In many cases, none of the students will successfully toss their crumpled sheets of paper into the wastebasket.

5 Now begin again with different directions. The student who is the leader for task 1 is to toss the crumpled paper into the wastebasket that is three feet from the starting point. If the paper goes into the wastebasket, then the student is to remove it. Standing at the first wastebasket, the student is to toss it into the second wastebasket. If

Growth and Development

the paper goes into the second wastebasket, the student is to retrieve the paper, stand at the second wastebasket, and toss the paper into the third wastebasket. Finally, if successful at that, the student is to toss the crumpled paper into the fourth wastebasket. If the student misses at one of the wastebaskets, she or he remains at that wastebasket. Repeat, having the other students who are leaders for different tasks follow the same directions.

6 Finally, allow students who missed to make additional attempts so that they can move from one wastebasket to the next to get to the final wastebasket.

7 Explain that you have just demonstrated how to master the developmental tasks for their age group. Few, if any, students were able to toss their crumpled sheets of paper into the farthest wastebasket on the first try. Yet many students were successful when they followed the second set of directions and were allowed to progress from one wastebasket to the next. Explain that this is how developmental tasks are mastered—by taking one step at a time. For example, task 6 involves preparing for an economic career. This is not done quickly. It requires several steps, such as doing homework, attending school regularly, child-sitting or lawn mowing to earn money, and so on. Further explain that sometimes it is difficult to master a task and practice helps. Some students missed

the wastebaskets in between. You gave them additional tries. This is because trying is very important. For example, they may try to do math homework and some of their answers may be incorrect. They will want to do these math problems again.

EVALUATION

Show TM-22, "Set Health Goals," and review each of the four steps so students can complete the information that follows. Have students work in their assigned groups. Explain that a **goal** is something toward which a person works. The long-term goal of each group is to master the developmental task it was assigned. To reach this long-term goal, the group is to identify three short-term goals. (Long-term goal for task 6: preparing for an economic career; short-term goals: completing homework assignments, getting good grades, graduating from high school.) Have each group leader present the short-term goals by repeating the previous activity using the wastebaskets. Then have students use paper and pencils for the following evaluation. Have them list the eight developmental tasks and next to each identify an action they can take to move toward mastery.

INCLUSION

Have students with different learning styles, such as students with attention deficit hyperactivity disorder or dyslexia, work on an independent project with their parents. They are to set a long-term goal for their education and identify at least three short-term goals that will help them master their long-term educational goal.

Teaching Master
Developmental Tasks of Adolescence

Developmental tasks are achievements that need to be made during a particular period of growth in order for a person to continue growing toward maturity. For adolescents, the following developmental tasks have been identified:

Task 1: Achieving a new and more mature relationship with age mates of both sexes.

Task 2: Achieving a masculine or feminine social role.

Task 3: Accepting one's physique.

Task 4: Achieving emotional independence from parents and other adults.

Task 5: Preparing for marriage and family life.

Task 6: Preparing for an economic career.

Task 7: Acquiring a set of values and an ethical system as a guide to behavior—developing an ideology.

Task 8: Developing a social conscience.

Nutrition

GRADE 7

Nutrient Matchup

HEALTH EDUCATION STANDARDS

- Students will comprehend concepts related to health promotion and disease prevention to enhance health.
- Students will demonstrate the ability to practice health-enhancing behaviors and avoid or reduce health risks.

PERFORMANCE INDICATORS

- Analyze the relationship between healthy behaviors and personal health.
- Demonstrate healthy practices and behaviors that will maintain or improve the health of self and others.

HEALTH GOALS

- I will select foods that contain nutrients.
- I will eat the recommended dietary amounts of food from MyPyramid.

MATERIALS

Teaching master "The Six Basic Classes of Nutrients"; teaching master "MyPyramid Food Categories"; transparency projector; slips of paper; tape; red pen; blue pen; TM-25, "Practice Healthful Behaviors," Appendix A

MOTIVATION

1 Before beginning this strategy, you will need to prepare slips of paper with nutrients written on them. You will prepare six slips of paper by using a red pen to write one of the six basic classes of nutrients on each: proteins, carbohydrates, fats, vitamins, minerals, and water. Then you will use a blue pen to prepare the other slips of paper. Write examples of each of the six basic classes of nutrients on each slip of paper. The six basic classes of nutrients are listed here with the examples that you can use for the other slips of paper.

Proteins	Carbohydrates	Fats
meat	wheat bread	ice cream
chicken	rice	whole milk
tuna	pasta	french fries
dried	macaroni	butter
beans	noodles	corn oil
steak	cereal	
eggs	oatmeal	
nuts		

Vitamins	Minerals	Water
vitamin A	calcium	drinking
thiamine	chlorine	water
riboflavin	iodine	bottled
niacin	iron	water
folic acid	magnesium	fruit juice
ascorbic	phosphorous	soups
acid		fruits
		celery

2 Explain to students that they are going to be reviewing the nutrients and the importance of obtaining the nutrients they need for optimal health. Define nutrients. A **nutrient** is a chemical substance in food that furnishes fuel for energy, provides materials needed for building and maintaining body tissues, or supplies substances that function in the regulation of body processes. Explain that no one food contains all nutrients in the amounts needed for health. Identify the six basic classes of nutrients: proteins, carbohydrates, fats, vitamins, minerals, and water.

3 Use the teaching master "The Six Basic Classes of Nutrients" to review important information about each of the nutrients.

4 Tell students that they are going to play Nutrient Matchup. The directions for this activity are as follows. Students will form a line in front of you. They will turn so their backs are facing you. Tape a slip of paper on each of their backs. The slip of paper will have a word or words written on it. The word or words will either be the name of one of the six basic classes of nutrients or an example of one of the nutrients. Explain to students that they are not to look

at the slip of paper taped to their backs. Instead, they are to guess what is written on the slip of paper by asking their classmates questions. They can ask their classmates only questions that can be answered with yes or no. For example, a student can ask, "Am I a carbohydrate?" The student could not ask, "What kind of nutrient am I?" In addition, they can ask each student only one question. If they guess what is written on the slip of paper on their back, they are to take it off their back and tape it on their front. Allow students five to ten minutes for this part of the activity.

5 After enough time has passed, have students who have not guessed what was written on the slip of paper on their back take it from their back, read it, and tape it on their front. Explain that they are now ready for the second part of this activity. Further explain that each student belongs in a group. Have the six students who have the six basic classes of nutrients written in red ink on the slips of paper taped to them stand in front of the class. Without talking, the remaining students are to join one of these six students and form a group.

6 Some students may have more difficulty finding their correct groups. Explain that some words belong to more than one group. For example, steak contains fat, but it is also a source of protein. Check to see that students are in the groups identified in step 1 of this strategy.

EVALUATION

Ask students to write a song for their evaluation. Each student is to contribute at least one line to the group's song. The line should contain a fact pertaining to the word written on the slip of paper taped to the student. After an appropriate amount of time, have students sing their songs for the class. Use the teaching master "MyPyramid Food Categories." **MyPyramid** is a food-group guide to ensure a balanced diet. Explain that MyPyramid provides information about what foods Americans eat and how to make the best food choices. MyPyramid also stresses the amount of food that is recommended to be daily. Each food group provides some of the nutrients a person needs each day. Have students name foods they enjoy eating that belong to each of the food groups illustrated. Then have students identify one nutrition behavior they want to implement. Use TM-25, "Practice Healthful Behaviors," to implement their behavior.

MULTICULTURAL INFUSION

Place students in groups. Each group is to appoint a recorder. The recorder should fold a sheet of paper lengthwise to make two columns. The first column should be labeled "Foods" and the second column should be labeled "Food Groups." Each group is to brainstorm a list of foods from different cultures. The recorder will list these in the first column. Then each group is to identify the food group to which each food belongs. The food group should be written on the same line as the food but in the second column.

INCLUSION

Students who are gifted might be placed into a group for a cooperative learning experience. They are to use a foreign language dictionary, such as one written in Spanish, and create the slips of paper for each of the six basic classes of nutrients.

Teaching Master

The Six Basic Classes of Nutrients

NUTRIENT	FACTS	SOURCES
Proteins	• Essential for the growth, development, and repair of all body tissues • Form parts of muscle, bone, blood, cell membranes • Form hormones and enzymes • Made of amino acids	• Meat, chicken, tuna, dried beans, eggs, nuts
Carbohydrates	• Provide energy • Simple carbohydrates, such as fruit, enter the bloodstream rapidly for quick energy • Complex carbohydrates, such as rice, provide long-lasting energy	• Bread, wheat, rice, pasta, macaroni noodles, cereal, oatmeal
Fats	• A source of energy • Essential for making certain vitamins available • Stored as fat tissue, which surrounds and protects organs • Saturated fats, such as those in meat or dairy products, raise cholesterol levels • Unsaturated fats are found in plant products	• Ice cream, milk, cheese, butter, margarine, yogurt, meat, egg yolks, corn oil
Vitamins	• Facilitate chemical reactions	
	Vitamin A—night vision, bone formation	Carrots, sweet potatoes
	Thiamine—appetite	Nuts, cereals, peas, beans
	Riboflavin—metabolism, energy production, eyes and skin	Whole milk, cottage cheese, eggs
	Niacin—normal digestion, appetite, nervous system	Cereals, fish, peanuts
	Folic acid—blood formation, enzyme function	Whole-grain bread, broccoli
	Ascorbic acid—helps body resist infection, strengthens blood vessels	Oranges, limes, tomatoes

	Teaching Master (continued)	
NUTRIENT	**FACTS**	**SOURCES**
Minerals	• Assist in the regulation of chemical reactions	
	Calcium—strong bones and teeth, heartbeat	Milk, cheese, cottage cheese
	Chlorine—aids in digestion, keeps body limber	Table salt
	Iodine—energy, mental alertness, growth, manufacture thyroid	Table salt, seafood
	Iron—forms red blood cells, growth, prevents fatigue	Oatmeal, red meat, liver
	Magnesium—fights depression, insomnia, nervousness	Dark green vegetables, apples
	Phosphorus—healthy gums and teeth, growth and repair of cells	Whole grains, fish, poultry
Water	• Makes up blood • Helps digestion • Helps remove body wastes • Helps regulate body temperature	• Drinking water, bottled water, juices, soups, vegetables such as celery

Teaching Master

MyPyramid Food Categories

GRAINS	VEGETABLES	FRUITS	MILK	MEAT & BEANS
Make half your grains whole	Vary your veggies	Focus on fruits	Get your calcium-rich foods	Go lean with protein
Eat at least 3 oz. of whole-grain cereals, breads, crackers, rice, or pasta every day	Eat more dark-green veggies like broccoli, spinach, and other dark leafy greens	Eat a variety of fruit	Go low-fat or fat-free when you choose milk, yogurt, and other milk products	Choose low-fat or lean meats and poultry
1 oz. is about 1 slice of bread, about 1 cup of breakfast cereal, or 1/2 cup of cooked rice, cereal, or pasta	Eat more orange vegetables like carrots and sweet potatoes	Choose fresh, frozen, canned, or dried fruit	If you don't or can't consume milk, choose lactose-free products or other calcium sources such as fortified foods and beverages	Bake it, broil it, or grill it
	Eat more dry beans and peas like pinto beans, kidney beans, and lentils	Go easy on fruit juices		Vary your protein routine—choose more fish, beans, peas, nuts, and seeds

For a 2,000-calorie diet, you need the amounts below from each food group. To find the amounts that are right for you, go to MyPyramid.gov.

GRAINS	VEGETABLES	FRUITS	MILK	MEAT & BEANS
Eat 6 oz. every day	Eat 2 1/2 cups every day	Eat 2 cups every day	Get 3 cups every day; for kids aged 2 to 8, it's 2	Eat 5 1/2 oz. every day

Find your balance between food and physical activity

- Be sure to stay within your daily calorie needs.
- Be physically active for at least 30 minutes most days of the week.
- About 60 minutes a day of physical activity may be needed to prevent weight gain.
- For sustaining weight loss, at least 60 to 90 minutes a day of physical activity may be required.
- Children and teenagers should be physically active for 60 minutes every day, or most days.

Know the limits on fats, sugars, and salt (sodium)

- Make most of your fat sources from fish, nuts, and vegetable oils.
- Limit solid fats like butter, margarine, shortening, and lard, as well as foods that contain these.
- Check the Nutrition Facts label to keep saturated fats, *trans* fats, and sodium low.
- Choose food and beverages low in added sugars. Added sugars contribute calories with few, if any, nutrients.

MyPyramid.gov
STEPS TO A HEALTHIER YOU

U.S. Department of Agriculture
Center for Nutrition Policy and Promotion
April 2005
CNPP-15

Personal Health and Physical Activity

GRADE 7

Grooming Products Auction

HEALTH EDUCATION STANDARD

- Students will analyze the influence of family, peers, culture, media, technology, and other factors on health behaviors.
- Students will demonstrate the ability to access valid information and products and services to enhance health.

PERFORMANCE INDICATORS

- Analyze how messages from media influence health behaviors.
- Determine the accessibility of products that enhance health.

HEALTH GOALS

- I will be well groomed.
- I will evaluate sources of health information wisely. (Consumer and Community Health)

MATERIALS

Teaching master "Persuasion"; transparency projector; play money; grooming products or pictures of items such as cotton swabs, tissues, dental floss, toothbrush, powder, toothpaste, mouthwash, antiperspirant, lipstick, cotton balls, razor, soap, shampoo, nail file, nail polish, comb, brush, deodorant, perfume, after shave, conditioner, nail polish remover, nail polish, eyeliner, skin makeup, tweezers, toe clippers, cuticle scissors; magazines; calculators (optional); TM-6, "Analyze What Influences Your Health," Appendix A

MOTIVATION

1 Introduce the topic of grooming. **Grooming** is the practice of caring for the body in order to look, smell, and feel one's best. Good grooming practices require the regular cleansing of the body, including the care of the skin, hair, nails, and feet, as well as wearing clean clothes. Good groom-

ing practices help keep the physical body healthy by reducing the spread of germs from one part of the body to another and from one person to another.

2 Explain to students that there are many products for grooming. They are consumers when they make decisions about purchasing these products. A **consumer** is a person who chooses sources of health-related information and buys or uses health products and services. Explain that more than fifty cents of every dollar is spent on health products and services. It is important for them to learn to spend their money wisely. Companies that produce grooming products often advertise. **Advertising** is a form of selling in which individuals are informed of products and services. A **commercial** is an advertisement on television or radio.

3 Explain to students that sellers use a variety of techniques in their advertisements to try to convince consumers that their products and services are more desirable than those of their competitors. Use the teaching master "Persuasion" to review different advertising appeals.

4 Place the grooming products on a desk or table. Have students select one for the Grooming Products Auction. They will be asked to auction off this product when the auction begins. Give students time to prepare for the auction. Remind them that they can use one or more of the appeals from the teaching master "Persuasion." They may also tell the class facts about their products. For example, a student might auction off the tissues and suggest that the tissues are a good buy because they can be used when a person sneezes to prevent the spread of germs.

5 Give each student play money. Explain that they are to make the best buys possible. They need to decide which health products for grooming are most needed and to bid for these health products.

6 Select a student to begin the Grooming Products Auction. This student is to auction off his or her grooming product to the highest bidder. The student should try to get the highest price possible by convincing the bidders that the product is necessary and appealing.

7 After the auction, have students discuss the grooming products they bid on. Which products demanded the highest price? Why? Which products were not in demand? Why? What were some of the ways the auctioneers tried to persuade the bidders to raise their bids? Which appeals were most convincing?

EVALUATION

In this lesson, students learned about different ways advertisements can influence health. Review TM-6, "Analyze What Influences Your Health," by asking students to apply each of the four items. Have students bring a magazine advertisement for a grooming product from their homes. If students do not have magazines in their homes, you might ask those who do to share with those who do not. Students are to staple their advertisements to a sheet of notebook paper. They are to write two paragraphs on the notebook paper. The first paragraph is to discuss how this product is used for grooming. The second paragraph is to analyze the information and appeals used in the advertisement.

MULTICULTURAL INFUSION

If possible, obtain a foreign magazine that has an advertisement for a grooming product. The advertisement should be written in a language other than English. Ask students who are proficient in the other language not to tell the students what the ad says. Have students describe the appeal in the advertisement from its visual effect only. After they have had the opportunity to give answers, tell them the written words or have students who are proficient in the language read the words to them. Ask students if the same advertising appeals are used in magazines of different languages.

INCLUSION

Give students the opportunity to practice using calculators. As students bid on products, have them record the lowest bids and the highest bids. Then have them use the calculators to determine the difference.

Persuasion

Bandwagon Appeal. The bandwagon appeal tries to convince consumers that everyone else wants a particular product or service, and they should too.

Brand Loyalty Appeal. The brand loyalty appeal tells consumers that a specific brand is better than the rest and that they would be cheating themselves to use anything but this brand.

False Image Appeal. The false image appeal attempts to convince consumers that they will give a certain impression if they use the product.

Glittering Generality Appeal. The glittering generality appeal contains statements that greatly exaggerate the benefits of the product.

Humor Appeal. The humor appeal uses a slogan, jingle, or cartoon to keep the consumer's attention.

Progress Appeal. The progress appeal tells consumers that a product is a new and better product than one formerly advertised.

Reward Appeal. The reward appeal tells consumers that they will receive a special prize or gift if they buy a product.

Scientific Evidence Appeal. The scientific evidence appeal gives consumers the results of a survey or laboratory tests to provide confidence in a product.

Snob Appeal. The snob appeal convinces consumers that they are worthy of a product or service because it is the best.

Testimony Appeal. The testimony appeal includes a promotion by a well-known person who says that a product or service is the best one for the consumer.

GRADE 7

Stuck in the Middle

HEALTH EDUCATION STANDARDS

- Students will comprehend concepts related to health promotion and disease prevention to enhance health.
- Students will demonstrate the ability to use interpersonal communication skills to enhance health and avoid or reduce health risks.
- Students will demonstrate the ability to use decision-making skills to enhance health.

PERFORMANCE INDICATORS

- Analyze the relationship between healthy behaviors and personal health.
- Demonstrate refusal and negotiation skills to avoid or reduce health risks.
- Choose healthy alternatives over unhealthy alternatives when making a decision.

HEALTH GOALS

- I will not drink alcohol.
- I will avoid tobacco use and secondhand smoke.
- I will practice protection factors that help me stay away from drugs.
- I will use resistance skills if I am pressured to misuse or abuse drugs.
- I will make responsible decisions. (Mental and Emotional Health)

MATERIALS

Student master "The Consequences of Harmful Drug Use"; transparency of the teaching master "Resisting Harmful Drug Use"; transparency projector; twelve marshmallows; TM-13, "Use Resistance Skills," Appendix A

MOTIVATION

1 Make copies of the student master "The Consequences of Harmful Drug Use" for each student. Have students review the in-formation on the student master. Emphasize the consequences of harmful drug use. For example, violence may occur from the use of PCP.

2 Use a transparency made from the teaching master "Resisting Harmful Drug Use." Emphasize the importance of using resistance skills when pressured to use drugs. **Resistance skills** are skills that are used when a person wants to say "no" to an action or leave a situation that threatens health, threatens safety, breaks laws, results in lack of respect for oneself and others, disobeys guidelines set by responsible adults, or detracts from character.

3 Ask for two student volunteers. Have each of these students extend one arm and place the palm of the hand up. Place six marshmallows in the palm of each student's hand. The marshmallows represent peers. Explain that one student will use resistance skills when pressured by peers to use drugs. The other student will not. Ask the class to begin to pressure both students to use drugs. The one student will use resistance skills when pressured. The other will close the palm of her or his hand and squeeze tighter and tighter each time she or he is pressured. Have the class continue the pressure for several minutes.

4 Explain that the one student was able to withstand the pressure of peers by using resistance skills. This student has the six marshmallows in her hand. Although she is around peers, she made responsible decisions about drug use. Now have the student who made a tight fist open the fist. The marshmallows will be stuck together. Explain that this student did not use resistance skills. Now he is "stuck with the consequences" of what peers wanted him or her to do. Have students name some of the consequences. They can refer to the student master "The Consequences of Harmful Drug Use."

679

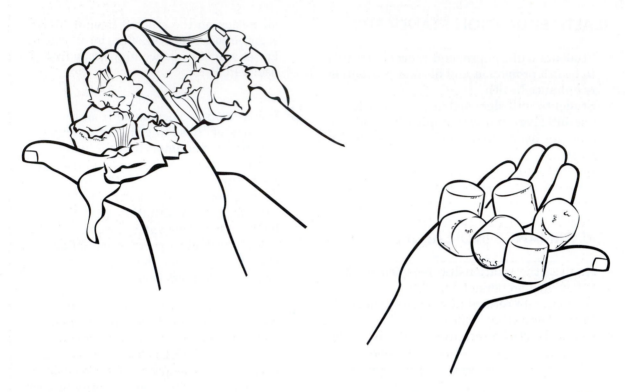

EVALUATION

Have students make their own Top Ten Reasons for Not Misusing or Abusing Drugs list. Explain that they are to recall at least ten facts from the student master "The Consequences of Harmful Drug Use." Then have two students role-play one pressuring the other to drink alcohol. Compare the resistance skills that were used by referring to the information on TM-13, "Use Resistance Skills."

INCLUSION

Students who have difficulty learning may use the student master when they make their Top Ten list.

The Consequences of Harmful Drug Use

Life Skill: I will not use alcohol.

Alcohol is a psychoactive drug that depresses the central nervous system. It slows reaction time and increases the likelihood of accidents. It intensifies feelings, increasing the risk of violence. **Cirrhosis** is a disease in which alcohol destroys liver cells and plugs the liver with fibrous scar tissue. It can lead to liver failure and death. **Alcohol dementia** is a brain impairment that causes intellectual decline. **Alcoholism** is a complex disease that is characterized by a preoccupation with drinking alcohol that has progressed to serious physical, social, occupational, and family consequences for the individual.

Life Skill: I will not use tobacco products.

Tobacco products include cigarettes and smokeless tobacco that contain many harmful ingredients. The estimated number of chemical compounds in tobacco smoke exceeds 4,000. **Tar** is a sticky, dark mixture in tobacco smoke that produces chronic irritation of the respiratory system and causes lung cancer. **Nicotine** is the psychoactive agent in tobacco. It increases heart rate and blood pressure and is addicting. Cigarette smoking causes lung cancer, emphysema, chronic bronchitis, and cardiovascular diseases. Use of smokeless tobacco causes oral cancer.

Life Skill: I will not misuse or abuse controlled substances.

A **controlled substance** is a drug that is illegal without a prescription. Many controlled substances are psychoactive drugs. A **psychoactive drug** is a substance that acts on the central nervous system and alters a user's moods, perceptions, feelings, personality, and behavior.

Cocaine is a drug that stimulates the central nervous system and causes dependence. People using this drug get a quick high but then slide into physiological depression. They may lose interest in work and other responsibilities, have delusions and hallucinations, and experience anxiety and panic. **Crack** is a form of cocaine that produces a rapid and intense reaction. The effects are believed to be ten times greater than cocaine.

Amphetamines are stimulants that speed up the central nervous system. They may produce euphoria, increased alertness, impaired judgment, and impulsiveness. They increase heart beat rate and blood pressure.
A **methamphetamine** is a stimulant drug that falls within the amphetamine family and produces behavioral and psychological effects similar to cocaine and other stimulants. **Crank** is an amphetamine-like stimulant with effects that last longer than crack or cocaine. **Ice** is an amphetamine-like drug that is smoked. Prolonged use of this drug results in serious lung and kidney damage.

Alcohol, Tobacco, and Other Drugs

A **hallucinogenic drug** is a substance that has the major effect of producing marked distortions in perception. Hallucinogens can cause euphoria, impair short-term memory, increase pulse rate, seem to make time pass very slowly, produce significant disturbances in judgment, and cause flashbacks. A **flashback** is the recurrence of the effects of a drug after it was taken. **LSD** is a synthetic drug that produces hallucinations. It is extremely potent and may produce "bad trips", in which a person experiences panic, fear, and physical symptoms. Flashbacks have been reported to reappear years after the drug was taken. **PCP** is a hallucinogen that is manufactured as a tablet or capsule, but it also can be smoked, swallowed, or sniffed. Small doses produce a feeling of intoxication, with staggering gait, slurred speech, numbness of extremities, and lowered sensitivity to pain. Increased doses may cause convulsions, coma, heart failure, lung failure, and stroke. People who use PCP often become violent. **Mescaline** is a hallucinogenic drug that comes from the Mexican peyote cactus. Its effects are similar to LSD. **Psilocybin** is a hallucinogenic drug derived from a specific type of mushroom that alters mood and perception. Its effects are similar to LSD.

Inhalants are chemicals that produce vapors, which cause psychoactive effects. The substances most likely to be abused include household chemicals such as aerosols, airplane glue, cleaning fluids, paint thinners, spray-can propellants, and gasoline. Inhalants are very dangerous. They travel quickly to the brain and cause disorientation, unconsciousness, sedation, and hallucinations. They may also harm the respiratory system, damage the kidneys and liver, produce seizures, and cause an irregular heartbeat. **Nitrous oxide** is a colorless gas that is abused as an inhalant.

Marijuana is a drug containing THC that impairs short-term memory and changes mood. This drug affects the nervous system by impairing coordination. It raises blood pressure and impairs the immune system. Use of marijuana may result in amotivational syndrome. **Amotivational syndrome** is a lack of desire by people to become motivated to perform daily responsibilities. **Hashish** is a drug that consists of the drug-rich resinous secretions of the cannabis plant. It is more potent than marijuana.

Narcotics are drugs that depress the central nervous system and block the feeling of pain. They are highly addictive. **Morphine** is a drug that is used to control pain. It is sometimes prescribed for the relief of pain. **Codeine** is a narcotic painkiller produced from morphine. **Heroin** is a narcotic drug derived from morphine that has no approved medical use. Heroin is injected into the vein. Sharing needles to inject heroin is a way that HIV is spread.

Sedative-hypnotic drugs are central nervous system depressants. **Sedatives** are drugs that have a calming effect on behavior. **Hypnotic** drugs are drugs that cause drowsiness and sleep. Use of these drugs can cause dependence. **Barbiturates** are depressant drugs used to induce sleep and relieve tension. They are extremely dangerous when taken with alcohol. People who become dependent on these drugs need medical supervision to stop taking them.

Teaching Master

Resisting Harmful Drug Use

1. **Say no in a firm voice.**

   Look directly at the person.
   Say no clearly and firmly.

2. **Give reasons for saying no.**

   Keep your reasons simple and clear.
   Repeat your reasons if necessary.

3. **Be certain your behavior matches your words.**

   Do not pretend to take a sip of alcohol or a puff from a cigarette to satisfy your friend.
   Look directly at the person, and look serious.

4. **Avoid situations in which there will be pressure to make wrong decisions.**

   Always think ahead, and if you suspect that drugs will be used, don't attend.

5. **Avoid being with people who make wrong decisions.**

   Peers who make wrong decisions often influence others to make the same wrong decisions.
   Others may think you use drugs if you are with friends who use drugs.

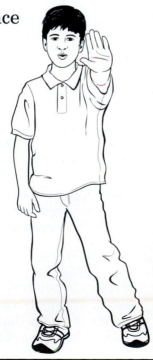

6. **Resist pressure to do something illegal.**

   You have a responsibility to follow laws and to be a responsible citizen.

7. **Influence others to make responsible decisions rather than wrong decisions.**

   Be a positive role model.

Communicable and Chronic Diseases

STD Scrabble

SOCIAL STUDIES

RESPONSIBLE CITIZEN

HEALTH EDUCATION STANDARDS

- Students will comprehend concepts related to health promotion and disease prevention to enhance health.
- Students will demonstrate the ability to practice health-enhancing behaviors and avoid or reduce health risks.

PERFORMANCE INDICATORS

- Describe the benefits of and barriers to practicing healthy behaviors.
- Explain the importance of assuming responsibility for personal health behaviors.

HEALTH GOALS

- I will choose behaviors to reduce my risk of infection with communicable diseases.
- I will practice abstinence. (Family and Social Health)

MATERIALS

Student master "STDs"; chalk; chalkboard; TM-25, "Practice Health Behaviors," Appendix A

MOTIVATION

1 Make a copy of the student master "STDs" for each student. Review the facts about each of the following STDs: chlamydial infections, gonorrhea, syphilis, genital herpes, genital warts, bacterial vaginosis, candidiasis, trichomoniasis, pediculosis pubis, and hepatitis B.

2 Review the facts by playing STD Scrabble. Using the chalk, print *SEXUALLY TRANSMITTED DISEASES* on the chalkboard. Then divide the class into two teams. Explain that the teams will take turns adding on letters to make words. The words must all be related to STDs. For ex-

ample, letters may be added vertically below the *S* to make syphilis. Then *ice* can be added to the *l* in syphilis to form the word *lice* (see the illustration). Each time letters are added to form a word, the student must use the word in a sentence. For example, suppose a student added the letters to form the word *syphilis*. Then this student might say, "Syphilis is an STD caused by a bacterium that penetrates the mucous membranes." Teams receive one point for a correct word and one point for a correct statement. They alternate turns.

```
SEXUALLY    TRANSMITTED    DISEASES
Y
P
H
I
LICE
I
S
```

3 Explain to students that they have just reviewed the facts regarding STDs. But there is another fact that they should know. The best way for them to avoid becoming infected with an STD is to practice abstinence. **Abstinence** is choosing not to engage in sexual intercourse. Encourage students to choose the following behaviors that support abstinence:

1. Be involved in activities that promote self-worth.
2. Establish goals.
3. Develop loving family relationships.
4. Be assertive and use decision-making skills.
5. Establish relationships with trusted adults.
6. Select friends who choose abstinence.
7. Date people who have chosen abstinence.
8. Avoid situations that are tempting.
9. Abstain from the use of alcohol and other drugs.
10. Select entertainment that promotes sex within a monogamous marriage.

Communicable and Chronic Diseases

EVALUATION

Explain to students that they have a pen pal who is their age. This pen pal lives in another area of the country. Many young people in this area are infected with STDs. Their pen pal writes them and expresses concern about STDs. They are to write back to the pen pal and explain why abstinence is a responsible choice and describe behaviors that support abstinence. In their letters, have students cover each of the four points listed in TM-25, "Practice Healthful Behaviors."

INCLUSION

You might modify STD Scrabble by giving some students a list of words that they might use. For example, the list might include *trichomoniasis, chancre, inflammation, urethra, culture, penicillin,* and so on. Students with special needs might use this list to locate words that will attach to a letter.

Student Master

STDs

CHLAMYDIAL INFECTIONS

Cause: the bacterium *Chlamydia trachomatis*
Transmission: sexual intercourse; from an infected mother to her baby during vaginal delivery
Symptoms in females: usually none; if symptoms occur, irritation and itching in the genital area, burning during urination, and a vaginal discharge
Symptoms in males: usually none; if symptoms occur, discharge and burning during urination; after many years, sterility
Diagnosis: microscopic examination of vaginal and urethral discharges
Treatment: antibiotics

GONORRHEA

Cause: the bacterium *Neisseria gonorrhoeae*
Transmission: sexual intercourse; from an infected mother to her baby during vaginal delivery
Symptoms in females: none; increased vaginal discharge, genital irritation, pain during urination
Symptoms in males: a discharge from the urethra, pain, increased urination
Diagnosis: culture test of mucous membranes in infected areas
Treatment: penicillin (there are some resistant strains)

SYPHILIS

Cause: the bacterium *Treponema pallidum*
Transmission: sexual intercourse; from a pregnant female to her fetus through the placenta
Symptoms in females and males: a chancre appears in the first stage and then goes away; a rash appears in the second stage and then goes away; in the late stage, organs such as the liver, heart, and brain are damaged
Diagnosis: culture of chancre in first stage; blood test
Treatment: penicillin G and doxycycline

GENITAL HERPES

Cause: herpes simplex virus
Transmission: sexual intercourse; contact with blisters
Symptoms in females and males: blisters in the genital area, fever, headaches, tiredness, swollen lymph nodes
Diagnosis: inspection and culture of fluid from the blisters
Treatment: no known treatment; genital herpes recurs; acyclovir relieves the symptoms

Communicable and Chronic Diseases

GENITAL WARTS

Cause: the human papillomavirus (HPV)
Transmission: sexual intercourse; direct contact with infected bed linen, towels, and clothing
Symptoms in females and males: painless warts that have a cauliflower shape appear on the genitals
Diagnosis: clinical inspection
Treatment: no treatment eradicates them completely; topical medications can be applied by a physician

BACTERIAL VAGINOSIS

Cause: the bacterium *Gardnerella vaginalis*
Transmission: sexual intercourse
Symptoms in females: a foul-smelling discharge, possible irritation of vaginal tissue, and burning during urination
Symptoms in males: inflammation of the foreskin, urethra, and bladder
Diagnosis: microscopic examination of discharge
Treatment: the antibiotic metronidazole

CANDIDIASIS

Cause: the fungus *Candida albicans*
Transmission: sexual intercourse
Symptoms in females: white, foul-smelling discharge and itching
Symptoms in males: itching and burning during urination
Diagnosis: examination by physician
Treatment: a cream, tablet, or vaginal suppository

TRICHOMONIASIS

Cause: a parasitic protozoan, *Trichomonas vaginalis*
Transmission: sexual intercourse; increased growth in vagina; sharing infected towels
Symptoms in females: half have none; frothy greenish yellow discharge that has an odor, itching, and burning
Symptoms in males: usually none
Diagnosis: microscopic examination of discharges
Treatment: metronidazole, a prescription drug

Communicable and Chronic Diseases

PEDICULOSIS PUBIS

Cause: the crab louse, *Phthirus pubis*
Transmission: close sexual contact; wearing infected clothing;
  sleeping in infected sheets; sharing infected towels
Symptoms in females and males: little black spots
Diagnosis: clinical inspection by physician
Treatment: lindane, a prescription drug

HEPATITIS B

Cause: hepatitis B virus
Transmission: sexual intercourse; sharing needles for IV drugs
Symptoms in females and males: profound fatigue, jaundice, nausea,
  abdominal pain; fatal in about 4 percent of cases; 5 to 10 percent
  become chronic carriers
Diagnosis: blood tests for hepatitis antibodies
Treatment: no effective treatment; bed rest and fluid intake;
  antibiotics treat secondary infections

Consumer and Community Health

You Can Count on Me

SOCIAL STUDIES

RESPONSIBLE CITIZEN

HEALTH EDUCATION STANDARD

- Students will demonstrate the ability to use goal-setting skills to enhance health.
- Students will demonstrate the ability to practice health-enhancing behaviors and avoid or reduce health risks.

PERFORMANCE INDICATORS

- Apply strategies and skills needed to attain a personal health goal.
- Demonstrate healthy practices and behaviors that will maintain or improve the health of self and others.

HEALTH GOALS

- I will develop media literacy.
- I will make a plan to manage time and money.

MATERIALS

Family master "Being a Volunteer"; student master "Health Behavior Contract"; computer with online service (optional); recording of "Count on Me," an oldie by the Jefferson Starship (optional); CD or cassette player; chalk and chalkboard; TM-22, "Set Health Goals," Appendix A

MOTIVATION

1 Before teaching this strategy, refer to your school district's policy on outside assignments such as volunteering. You may need to obtain school board clearance to use the Health Behavior Contract.

2 On the chalkboard, write the following column headings: *physical health, mental-emotional health, family-social health, no benefit.* Be certain to write these high enough on the chalkboard so that you will be able to make a list under each. Intro-

duce the topic of time management. Ask students to brainstorm ways that they spend their time. As students identify ways they spend time, ask them if there is a benefit to physical health, mental-emotional health, family-social health, or no benefit to health. Write the activities under the appropriate headings on the chalkboard.

3 Have students analyze the activities that are listed on the chalkboard. Students may learn that they have a balance of activities that promote health. They may learn that they neglect an area of their health. Introduce the idea that they are consumers when they make decisions about how to spend time. This is an important responsibility in the area of consumer health. To be a responsible consumer, they may want to have a time management plan. A time management plan is a plan that indicates how time will be spent on daily activities and leisure. An effective time management plan includes blocks of time set aside to promote physical, mental-emotional, and family-social health. To make a time management plan, a person identifies all daily activities on a calendar showing the hours of the day. Then a person might examine the activities and assess whether or not attention has been given to all areas of well-being.

4 Have the students review the lists on the chalkboard again. Explain that much of the emphasis in health education today is placed on personal responsibility for health. However, many health problems can be solved only by individuals working together and serving the needs of others. A volunteer is a person who undertakes or expresses a willingness to provide a service.

5 Divide the class into equal groups of students. Have each group brainstorm a list of ways that young people might volunteer to serve the health needs of others or the community. Give examples such as volunteering in school clubs, community organizations, and health agencies. Have students list ways they might volunteer

to help individuals such as a person who is shut in or disabled. If your school has computers with online service available, have students locate volunteer opportunities. For example, many services provide a special area for young people that contains online information they might use to locate volunteer opportunities. After an appropriate amount of time, have each group share its list with the class.

6 Give each student a copy of the student master "Health Behavior Contract" and the family master "Being a Volunteer." Explain to students that they are going to make a health behavior contract to volunteer in a school club, community organization, or agency to promote health or to help a specific individual or family. They are to give their parent or guardian the family master "Being a Volunteer" and obtain permission to perform the volunteer service identified in the Health Behavior Contract. Set a date for students to complete the Health Behavior Contract.

7 (Optional) If you are able to obtain the recording "Count on Me," by the Jefferson Starship, play it for the class. Discuss the words *You can count on me, count on my love.* Emphasize that we show love for others by providing those in need with service. Extending our love to others in this way helps us to feel more loving. It promotes self-esteem. It also helps others to feel more loved.

EVALUATION

For the evaluation, students will submit the two-page summary reports described on the "Health Behavior Contract." Check to see that students identified specific tasks they performed while volunteering. Check to see that students have identified ways that volunteering benefits them and why volunteering is a wise use of a consumer's time. Writing and fulfilling a health contract is a goal. Use TM-22, "Set Health Goals," to discuss how the "Health Behavior Contract" can be fulfilled.

MULTICULTURAL INFUSION

An appropriate volunteer activity might be for a student to help a younger child who is not proficient in English with homework and with reading. This volunteer activity promotes mental and emotional health. It promotes positive self-esteem. It also benefits the child by helping the child with mental alertness. The student can be a positive role model. In addition, the activity helps students to be more aware of the challenges faced by people who are not proficient in English.

INCLUSION

Students with special needs, such as those who have a physical disability or a learning disability, might volunteer to work with younger children who also have special needs. They can be role models of ways to promote physical, mental-emotional, and family-social health. For example, a student who uses a wheelchair might exercise with a child who uses a wheelchair. Explain that this relationship can be special for both the student and the child.

Family Master

Being a Volunteer

Dear Parent/Guardian:

In our health class, I have emphasized the importance of taking personal responsibility for health. However, many health problems can be solved only by individuals working together and serving the needs of others. We have been focusing on the importance of having volunteers in the community. I have explained to your child that a volunteer is a person who undertakes or expresses a willingness to provide a service. A young person might volunteer to visit elderly residents in a nursing home, read to someone who is visually impaired, or carry groceries for someone with a disability. A young person might also volunteer in a school club, community organization, or agency. Our class discussed a number of ways that young people might volunteer. Ask your child to share some of these ways with you.

As a follow-up to our lesson, I have asked your child to commit himself/herself to several hours of volunteer service. Your child is designing a Health Behavior Contract. I have asked your child to go over the Health Behavior Contract with you and to get your permission to perform a volunteer service.

Please return this letter to me so that I know that you are aware of the volunteer service and approve. If you have any questions or suggestions, please write them on the back of this letter and I will contact you.

I hope today finds you and your family in good health.

Sincerely,

My child has selected the following volunteer service:

_____

My signature indicates that I approve:

_____

Health Behavior Contract

Name_____

Life Skill: I will volunteer my services to a school club, community organization or agency, or to an individual or family to help promote health.

Effect on My Well-Being: Many volunteer services promote the health of individuals, families, and communities. When I participate in volunteer services, I promote the level of health for myself and others. I am a responsible, productive citizen. I feel good about myself. I help someone else by showing my care and concern. I learn about others.

My Plan: I will make a list of volunteer activities, such as visiting elderly residents of a nursing home, starting a recycling program, or teaching younger students about the dangers of drug use. I will speak with people in the community, such as those at organizations and agencies, to learn about volunteer possibilities. I will examine possible ways that I might help my neighbors. Then I will decide upon a service I want to perform, discuss it with my parent/guardian, and obtain approval. I will write the volunteer service I have selected in the space below.

_____

Results: I will keep a diary to record what I did and any insights that I had. I will write a two-page summary report identifying the tasks that I performed and how I felt performing them. I will describe how volunteering benefited my health and ways it promoted the health of another person(s) or my community.

Environmental Health

GRADE 7

Environment Calendar

HEALTH EDUCATION STANDARDS

- Students will comprehend concepts related to health promotion and disease prevention to enhance health.
- Students will demonstrate the ability to advocate for personal, family, and community health.

PERFORMANCE INDICATORS

- Analyze how the environment impacts personal health.
- Work cooperatively to advocate for healthy individuals, families, and schools.

HEALTH GOALS

- I will stay informed about environmental issues.
- I will help keep the air clean.
- I will help keep the water safe.

MATERIALS

Construction paper; markers; paint; stapler; magazines that contain pictures of healthful environments; photos students have taken (optional); transparency of the teaching master "Sources of Air Pollution"; transparency of the teaching master "Sources of Water Pollution"; transparency projector; computer with online service (optional); literature from environmental groups (optional); calendar with photo of landscape or ocean; TM-3, "Comprehend Health Concepts," Appendix A

MOTIVATION

1 Introduce the strategy by showing students the photo in the calendar. Ask students to imagine that they are in the surroundings depicted in the photo. Have them describe their feelings. Ask students how these surroundings might affect their health. De-

fine environment. The **environment** is the multitude of dynamic conditions that are external to a person. A healthful environment enhances the quality of life and allows people to achieve the highest levels of physical, mental-emotional, and family-social health.

2 Explain that concerned citizens have formed organizations to increase public awareness of environmental issues. These citizens want to guarantee that the environment is as depicted in the photo in the calendar that you showed them. Identify some of the issues about which these citizens are concerned: ozone layer deterioration, global warming, hazardous waste, oil spills, air pollution, acid rain, solid waste disposal, nuclear waste, contaminated water, forest destruction, endangered species and threats to wildlife, pesticide use, world population, radon gas, natural disasters, indoor air pollution. If your school has computers with online services, mention that people interested in environmental issues have information networks. Have students link to these information networks.

3 Use the transparency of the teaching master "Sources of Air Pollution" to discuss the life skill "I will keep the air clean."

4 Use the transparency of the teaching master "Sources of Water Pollution" to discuss the life skill "I will keep the water clean."

5 Divide the class into groups. Give each group construction paper, magazines, and markers. Explain that each group is going to make an Environmental Calendar. The calendar is to have twelve drawings, photos from magazines, or photos students have taken that depict a healthful environment. At least one of the photos or drawings should depict clean air while at least one other must depict clean water. Explain to students that a photo or drawing does not have to show a landscape, mountain, or ocean. A healthful environment might be depicted by a photo of a plastic bag in

which garbage has been collected. It might depict a clean bedroom or a clean school playground. Ask students to use their imaginations. Also, direct students to have a caption for each of the twelve pages of the calendar. The caption should be a creative statement about health, such as "I get high on clean air." Use TM-3, "Comprehend Health Concepts," to identify students' knowledge of environmental issues.

EVALUATION

Explain that each group is going to give its calendar as a gift to a person or organization in the community. Each student in the group is to write a letter to accompany the calendar. In the letter, students are to explain their concern for environmental issues. They are to express ways to keep the air and water clean.

Sources of Air Pollution

Life Skill: I will keep the air clean.

Air is needed to sustain life. Air pollution is one of the greatest environmental risks to human health. It may cause chronic bronchitis, pulmonary emphysema, lung cancer, bronchial asthma, and eye irritation. The major air pollutants are as follows:

Carbon monoxide is an odorless, tasteless, colorless, poisonous gas. Automobile exhaust is the main source. Carbon monoxide attaches to red blood cells in the body. Then the red blood cells carry less oxygen to the body's cells.

Sulfur oxides are pollutants that result from oxygen combining with by-products from the combustion of fuels containing sulfur. This gas may cause lung diseases.

Nitrogen oxides are gases produced by the high-temperature combustion of energy sources such as coal and oil. Automobile exhaust and cigarette smoke are sources. This gas irritates the eyes and the respiratory tract and causes lung diseases.

Hydrocarbons are chemical compounds that contain only carbon and hydrogen. Motor vehicles account for most pollutants produced from hydrocarbons. Hydrocarbons are a major contributor to smog.

Ozone is a chemical variant of oxygen and is the most widespread air pollutant. Fossil fuels that are burned and evaporated to form ozone. It causes irritation of the eyes, lungs, and throat. It produces headaches, coughing, and shortness of breath. In healthy, nonsmoking adults, two hours of exposure to ozone causes inflammation of the lungs and bronchial tubes.

Particulates are particles in the air, such as soot, ashes, dirt, dust, asbestos, and pollen. They can harm the surfaces of the respiratory system and increase the likelihood of persistent coughs, respiratory illness, and asthma attacks.

Acid rain is precipitation (rain, snow, sleet, hail) that contains high levels of acids formed from sulfur oxides, nitrogen oxides, and the moisture in the air. The burning of coal is the major contributor to acid rain. Acid rain can kill aquatic vegetation and animal life, creates toxic effects for soils and plant life, and corrodes statues and building materials.

Teaching Master

Sources of Water Pollution

Life Skill: I will keep the water clean.

After air, water is the most essential requirement of the human body. Humans can live without water for only a few days. Water pollution is a health hazard. In many parts of the world, dysentery is a major problem. Dysentery is a severe infection of the intestines, causing diarrhea and abdominal pain. Polluted water is often high in sodium. Drinking polluted water poses a health risk for people with high blood pressure. Polluted water contains mercury, which is toxic to humans and kills fish and shellfish. The major sources of water pollution are as follows:

Water runoff from farms, landfills, urban areas, mines, forestry activities, and construction areas contaminates water supplies, rivers, and lakes. It may contain oil, gasoline, pesticides, herbicides, fungicides, metals, bacteria, and viruses.

Sewage and animal waste increase the amount of nitrates in groundwater. Infants who drink water contaminated with nitrates can suffer from blood diseases.

PCBs are a class of organic compounds that contain chlorine. PCBs have been used in insulating materials in high-voltage electrical transformers. Discarded electrical equipment at dump sites have broken open and released PCBs into surrounding groundwater and drinking water supplies. PCBs accumulate in the fatty tissues and liver. They cause birth defects, reproductive disorders, liver and kidney damage, and cancerous tumors.

Thermal pollution is pollution of water with heat resulting in a decrease in the oxygen in the water. It is caused by dumping heater water from power plants into the environment. Fish and aquatic plants die.

Trihalomethanes are chemical by-products formed when chlorine attacks biological contaminants in the water. Any drinking water supply that has chlorine added contains these chemical by-products. These by-products slightly increase the risk of bladder and rectal cancer, birth defects, and central nervous system disorders.

Mercury is an element found in industrial waste. When people consume too much mercury through the food chain, they may suffer from mental retardation, numbness of body parts, loss of vision and hearing, and emotional disturbances.

Pesticides are substances used to kill or control the growth of unwanted organisms. **DDT** is a pesticide that was banned because it was found in food products after harvest. DDT accumulates in fat tissues and increases cancer risk.

Dioxins are a group of chemicals that were once used as insecticides. They are no longer produced for commercial use. However, they still occur because of incineration. **Agent Orange** is a substance containing dioxin that was sprayed on vegetation to kill it. It is believed to cause cancer, depression, liver damage, and miscarriages.

Lead is an element that may get into the water supply from lead pipes and water lines. Lead is also believed to cause mental retardation.

GRADE 7

The Weather Channel

HEALTH EDUCATION STANDARDS

- Students will comprehend concepts related to health promotion and disease prevention to enhance health.
- Students will demonstrate the ability to practice health-enhancing behaviors and avoid or reduce health risks.

PERFORMANCE INDICATORS

- Analyze how the environment impacts personal health.
- Demonstrate behaviors to avoid or reduce health risks to self and others.

HEALTH GOAL

- I will follow safety guidelines for severe weather and natural disasters.

MATERIALS

Student master "Weather Watch"; one copy for each student; computer with online service (optional); cable television (optional); weather forecast in the newspaper; map of the United States; index cards; TM-25, "Practice Healthful Behaviors," Appendix A

MOTIVATION

1 Explain to students the importance of practicing the life skill "I will follow safety guidelines for different weather conditions and natural disasters." Give each student a copy of the student master "Weather Watch." Review the information on the master. Explain that the guidelines on this master will help them to practice the life skill.

2 Explain that there are people with whom they can cooperate who protect their safety. If you have a computer with online service available, have students locate the weather service to learn weather conditions in different locations. Specifically, you may want them to find the weather forecast for your area for the next several days. If you have cable television in your school, have students locate the weather channel and listen to the forecast. Emphasize that these are services provided by people who help them protect their health and safety. If you do not have these options available, you may want to discuss them. Perhaps students can use the computer online service at home. They may have cable television at home. Show students the weather forecast in the newspaper.

3 Divide the class into seven groups. Assign each group one of the following: hot weather, cold weather, lightning, tornados, earthquakes, hurricanes, and floods. Explain that each group is going to prepare a report for its own weather channel. Each group is to select one person to be the meteorologist who will give the report. The group is to select an area in the country. When it presents its report, the group can use your map to show the location. The meteorologist is to give the weather report and then explain the safety guidelines to follow. Allow an appropriate amount of time for group work.

4 Have students present their reports. Discuss the different weather conditions and the recommended safety guidelines. Ask students to name the people in your community who are responsible for the weather report.

EVALUATION

Write each of the following on an index card: hot weather, cold weather, lightning, tornados, earthquakes, hurricanes, and floods. Place the index cards face down on your desk. Have students take turns selecting an index card and reviewing the safety guidelines aloud for the class. Have students identify a healthful behavior they learned and relate this to the information in TM-25, "Practice Healthful Behaviors."

conditions and natural disasters. Students also will feel good about helping you.

INCLUSION

Ask students who have difficulty learning to write the index cards for you. This allows them a further opportunity to review these weather

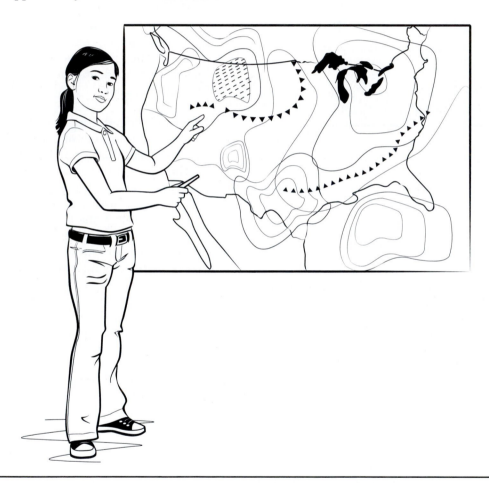

Weather Watch

HOT WEATHER SAFETY

Heat exhaustion is a condition in which the body loses large amounts of salt and water through sweating. **Heat stroke** is a condition that occurs when the body becomes so overheated that it no longer can sweat to cool off. To prevent these conditions, one should do the following:

1. Drink plenty of fluids.
2. Avoid overexertion.
3. Wear lightweight, loose-fitting clothing.
4. Stay in the shade or in the coolest area of an apartment, house, or building.

COLD WEATHER SAFETY

Hypothermia is low body temperature. **Frostbite** is a freezing of parts of the body. To prevent these conditions, one should do the following:

1. Wear layers of clothing.
2. Keep clothing as dry as possible.
3. Wear boots and gloves that are loose enough to allow the blood to circulate.
4. Stay inside when the windchill factor is very low. The windchill factor is a measure of the air temperature that takes into account the chilling effect of the wind.

LIGHTNING SAFETY

Lightning is the flashing of light caused by a discharge of electricity in the atmosphere. To stay safe during lightning, one should do the following:

1. Do not stand under a tree or out in the open during an electrical storm. If caught out in the open, try to find a ravine or low spot for shelter.
2. If swimming, immediately get out of and away from the water.
3. Stay away from metal objects, and avoid using the telephone.
4. Unplug electrical appliances during a severe thunderstorm, and stay away from the fireplace.

HURRICANE SAFETY

Hurricanes are tropical storms with heavy rains and winds in excess of seventy-four miles per hour. The southern Atlantic states are at risk for hurricanes. Most hurricanes occur during August, September, and October. Some hurricane safety precautions are the following:

1. Follow and heed the warnings issued by the National Hurricane Service, which are issued over television and radio stations.
2. In the event of a serious hurricane, evacuate the area if possible.

TORNADO SAFETY

Tornados are violent, rapidly spinning windstorms that have funnel-shaped clouds. Tornados are more common in Midwestern and Southern states, and most occur in the spring and early summer months. A **tornado watch** is a caution issued by the National Weather Service that the weather conditions are such that a tornado is possible. People in the area should be alert and prepared for possible danger. A **tornado warning** is a caution that a tornado has been sighted. It will be announced and broadcast over radio and television stations. Some tornado safety precautions are the following:

1. Seek shelter in a basement or underground cellar whenever possible. If no basement is available, move to the center of the ground floor, into a room with no windows such as a closet.
2. If possible, crawl under something solid such as a heavy piece of furniture.
3. If outside, seek shelter in a depression such as a ravine, gully, or ditch.

EARTHQUAKES

Earthquakes are violent shakings of the Earth's surface caused by the shifting of the plates that make up the Earth's crust. The greatest number of injuries occur from falling debris. Most areas of the United States are at risk for earthquakes. Some earthquake safety precautions are the following:

1. Stay calm.
2. Stay clear of any objects that can fall.
3. Stay away from broken power lines.
4. If inside a building, get under a table or desk.
5. Stay away from windows, which may shatter.
6. If riding in a car, stop and get out as soon as possible.
7. If riding or walking on a bridge, get off as soon as possible.

FLOODS

A **flood** is a rising and overflowing of a body of water onto normally dry land. Areas that receive heavy rainfall and are near a body of water are at risk for flooding. Some flood safety precautions are the following:

1. Leave your home and community if warned to do so by officials.
2. Keep a supply of batteries, flashlights, and a radio nearby.
3. Learn the safest and quickest route to take from your home to shelter.
4. Keep supplies of freshwater and food that does not need refrigeration or heat.
5. Turn off all electrical circuits in the home if a flood occurs.
6. Close all gas lines that lead into the home.
7. Move all valuables to the top floors in a home to help prevent them from being destroyed.
8. Maintain the family car in good working order and keep the gas tank filled so that you can leave the area quickly.
9. Have a first-aid kit available.
10. Do not drive where water is over the road.

Mental and Emotional Health

GRADE 8

Bean Self-Disciplined

HEALTH EDUCATION STANDARDS

- Students will comprehend concepts related to health promotion and disease prevention to enhance health.

PERFORMANCE INDICATORS

- Analyze the relationship between healthy behaviors and personal health.
- Describe the interrelationship of emotional, intellectual, physical, and social health in adolescence.

HEALTH GOALS

- I will take responsibility for my health.
- I will gain health knowledge.
- I will practice life skills for health.

MATERIALS

Teaching master "The Wellness Scale" (transparency); student master "Health Behavior Contract"; three beanbags; chalk; transparency projector; TM-22, "Set Health Goals," Appendix A

MOTIVATION

1 Define health. **Health** is the quality of life that includes physical, mental-emotional, and family-social health. Another term that describes health is *wellness. Physical health* is the condition of a person's body. *Mental-emotional health* is the condition of a person's mind and the ways that a person expresses feelings. *Family-social health* is the condition of a person's relationships with others. Ask students to give examples of physical, mental-emotional, and family-social health.

2 Make a transparency of the teaching master "The Wellness Scale." Review the information on this master. The **Wellness**

Scale depicts the ranges in the quality of life, from optimal well-being to high-level wellness, average wellness, minor illness or injury, major illness or injury, and premature death. Explain that there are at least nine factors that influence health and wellness over which a person has some degree of control. These factors are listed on the Wellness Scale. **Health status** is the sum total of the positive and negative influences of (1) the level of health knowledge a person has, (2) the behaviors a person chooses, (3) the situations in which a person participates, (4) the relationships in which a person engages, (5) the decisions a person makes, (6) the resistance skills a person has, (7) the protective factors a person possesses, (8) the degree to which a person is resilient, and (9) the degree of health literacy a person has achieved.

3 Review the following definitions. **Health knowledge** consists of information that one needs to become health literate, maintain and improve health, prevent disease, and reduce health-related risk behaviors. **Health-ful behaviors** are actions that promote health; prevent illness, injury, and premature death; and improve the quality of life. **Risk behaviors** are voluntary actions that threaten health, increase the likelihood of illness and premature death, and destroy the quality of the environment. **Healthful situations** are circumstances that promote health; prevent illness, injury, and premature death; and improve the quality of the environment. **Risk situations** are involuntary circumstances that threaten health; increase the likelihood of illness, injury, and premature death; and destroy the quality of the environment. **Healthful relationships** are relationships that promote self-esteem and productivity, encourage health-enhancing behavior, and are free of violence and drug misuse and abuse. **Destructive relationships** are relationships that destroy self-esteem, interfere with productivity and health, and may include violence and drug misuse and abuse. A **responsible**

decision is a decision that is healthful, safe, legal, respectful of oneself and others; follows guidelines of responsible adults; and demonstrates character. **Resistance skills** are skills that are used when a person wants to say "no" to an action or leave a situation. **Protective factors** are ways that a person might behave and characteristics of the environment in which a person lives that promote health, safety, or well-being. **Risk factors** are ways that a person might behave and characteristics of the environment in which a person lives that threaten health, safety, or well-being. **Resiliency** is the ability to prevent or to recover, bounce back, and learn from misfortune, change, or pressure. **Health literacy** is competence in critical thinking and problem solving, responsible and productive citizenship, self-directed learning, and effective communication.

4 Explain that people achieve a higher level of wellness on the Wellness Scale when they practice life skills for health. **Life skills** are actions that promote health literacy, maintain and improve health, prevent disease, and reduce health-related risk behaviors. Give examples of life skills such as wearing a safety belt, maintaining desirable weight, being drug-free, using conflict resolution skills, and having an escape plan for fire. Ask students to give examples of life skills they practice or want to practice.

5 Discuss the importance of being self-disciplined. **Self-discipline** is the effort or energy with which a person follows through on intentions or promises. It takes self-discipline to maintain desirable weight, wear a safety belt, maintain physical fitness, and so forth. A self-disciplined person recognizes that goals are achieved with effort. A **goal** is something desirable toward which a person works.

6 Play the game Bean Self-Disciplined. Have students identify a goal or life skill they want to achieve or practice. Now use chalk

to draw the following on the floor of your classroom. Draw a starting line. Two feet from the starting line, draw a circle with a circumference of two feet. Then draw another circle four feet from the starting line, another six feet from the starting line, and finally one that is eight feet from the starting line. Ask for three student volunteers. Give each a beanbag. Have each student take a turn. Each student is to stand at the starting line and throw the beanbag into the farthest circle (the one eight feet from the starting line). Most likely, one or more of the three students will miss.

7 Repeat, but this time give different directions. Each student is to throw the beanbag into the first circle (two feet from the starting line). Then the student proceeds to the first circle, stands there, and throws the beanbag into the next circle, which is two feet away. The student continues until she or he successfully throws the beanbag into the farthest circle.

8 Explain that being self-disciplined often requires taking small steps like these toward a goal. For example, a person cannot lose ten pounds or become physically fit overnight. A person must identify a life skill (set a goal) and then make a plan that involves setting small steps toward the mastery of the life skill. Then use TM-22, "Set Health Goals," to ascertain how that goal will be met.

EVALUATION

Give each student a copy of the student master "Health Behavior Contract." Students are to identify a life skill they want to master. They are to make a plan that involves setting small steps toward the mastery of the life skill. They are to write a two-page summary following the directions on the "Health Behavior Contract."

Mental and Emotional Health

Teaching Master

The Wellness Scale

Factors That Influence Health and Well-Being

Lack of health knowledge	Possession of health knowledge
Risk behaviors	Wellness behaviors
Risk situations	Healthful situations
Destructive relationships	Healthful relationships
Irresponsible decision making	Responsible decision making
Lack of resistance skills	Use of resistance skills
Lack of protective factors	Possession of protective factors
Lack of resiliency	Having resiliency
Lack of health literacy	Having health literacy

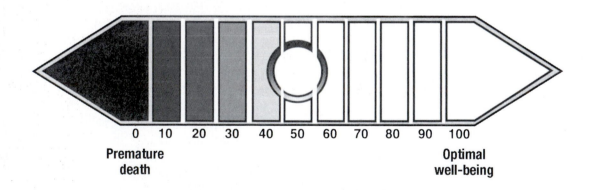

0   10   20   30   40   50   60   70   80   90   100

Premature death   Optimal well-being

Health status is the sum total of the positive and negative influence of these factors.

Student Master

Health Behavior Contract

Life Skill:

I will practice life skills for health.

Effect on My Well-Bcing:

Life skills are actions that promote health literacy, maintain and improve health, prevent disease, and reduce health-related risk behaviors. Practicing life skills shows that I have assumed responsibility for my health. I use self-discipline and attain a higher level of well-being on the Wellness Scale. I function better and enjoy life more fully.

My Plan:

I will identify a life skill for health that I want to practice regularly. I will write this life skill in the space below.

_____

Evaluating My Progress:

I recognize that mastery of this life skill requires self-discipline. I will set smaller goals and design a chart to record my progress. *(You may use the other side of this contract.)*

Results:

I will write a two-page summary and attach it to my completed plan. I will describe the health benefits of practicing the life skill. I will describe any difficulties I had following my plan. I will describe my plan for continuing to follow my life skill.

My Signature:

_____

Rainbow of Diversity

HEALTH EDUCATION STANDARDS

- Students will demonstrate the ability to use interpersonal communication skills to enhance health and avoid or reduce health risks.
- Students will comprehend concepts related to health promotion and disease prevention to enhance health.

PERFORMANCE INDICATORS

- Demonstrate effective conflict management or resolution strategies.
- Describe the interrelationship of emotional, intellectual, physical, and social health in adolescence.
- Describe the benefits of and barriers to practicing healthy behaviors.

HEALTH GOALS

- I will develop healthful family relationships.
- I will recognize harmful relationships.

MATERIALS

Ten-foot roll of white paper; tape; red marker; green marker; blue marker; purple marker; yellow marker; orange marker; black marker; TM-16, "Resolve Conflicts," Appendix A

MOTIVATION

1 Tape a five-foot roll of white paper across the chalkboard in the front of your classroom. Tape another five-foot roll of white paper across the chalkboard directly beneath the first. Explain to students that they are going to create a rainbow with six hues. They will use a marker to create a rainbow on the top roll of white paper that is taped to the chalkboard. Give the red marker to a student. Ask this student to draw one of the lines for the rainbow. Then give the red marker to another student and ask this student to draw another line for the rainbow. Repeat the previous directions asking four more students to draw lines for the rainbow. When the rainbow is completed, there will be five red lines to show the hues of the rainbow.

2 Now explain to students that they are going to create another rainbow. They will create this rainbow on the roll of paper that is directly beneath the first rainbow they created. Give the six markers (red, green, blue, purple, yellow, and orange) to six different students. Each is to take a turn drawing one of the lines on the rainbow. When the rainbow is completed, there will be six lines of color (red, green, blue, purple, yellow, and orange) to show the hues of the rainbow.

3 Ask students which rainbow they prefer and which one is most realistic. Although answers may vary, students will recognize that the rainbow with the six colors is more radiant and pleasing than the rainbow that is all red. In addition, they should recognize that the second rainbow is more realistic. Rainbows are multicolored, not just one color.

4 Explain that you have named the two rainbows. The first is called the "Rainbow of Duplication"; the second is called "The Rainbow of Diversity." Further explain that you created these rainbows to begin a discussion about the people with whom they interact. To duplicate means to copy. When students created the first rainbow, they duplicated the lines using the same color. The lines turned out exactly alike. To be diverse means to be different. When students created the second rainbow, they used different colors to create the lines.

5 Explain that society is like the second rainbow—it is created with diverse or different people. People not only differ in color, they differ in age, gender, and racial and ethnic heritage. (Depending on school district

guidelines, you may want to mention that people differ in sexual orientation.) However, all people are alike in that they want the respect of others. Everyone wants to be treated fairly. When people enjoy, appreciate, and respect everyone else in their environment, the result is synergy. **Synergy** is a positive outcome that occurs when different people cooperate and respect one another, and as a result, more energy is created for all. When there is synergy, people with different backgrounds, talents, and skills work together to produce better solutions than would be possible if everyone were exactly alike.

6 Explain that some people practice discriminatory behavior. They see themselves as belonging to the first rainbow. They accept others who belong to the first rainbow and who are just like them. When there are differences, they practice discriminatory behavior. **Discriminatory behavior** is behavior that makes a distinction in treatment or shows favor or prejudice against an individual or group of people. **Prejudice** is suspicion, intolerance, or irrational dislike directed at an individual or group of people. Both discriminatory behavior and prejudice divide people. These kinds of behavior are learned. Training in how to treat and respect people begins early in life.

7 Write "isms" on the red rainbow using the black marker. Explain that isms are beliefs, attitudes, assumptions, and actions that subject individuals or people in a particular group to discriminatory behavior. Common isms include ageism, sexism, and racism. As you define each of the following, use the black marker to write the term on the red rainbow. **Ageism** is behavior that discriminates against people in a specific age group. **Sexism** is behavior that discriminates against people because of their sex. **Racism** is behavior that discriminates against people of another race or color of skin.

8 Explain that discriminatory behavior and prejudice often result in violence. People who practice such behavior might become perpetrators or victims. A **perpetrator of violence** is a person who commits a violent act. A **victim of violence** is a person who is harmed by violence. A **hate crime** is a crime motivated by age, racial, ethnic, sexual orientation, or other biases. Hate crimes are sometimes called bias crimes and include violent attacks, and intimidation, and arson and other kinds of property damage. People who experience discrimination and prejudice may become angry. They may confront or fight back. This can result in serious injury.

9 Ask students to brainstorm ways to show respect for people who are different. Ask them how they might practice the life skill "I will avoid discrimination." Suggest the following: (1) Challenge stereotypes. A **stereotype** is a prejudiced attitude that assigns a specific quality or characteristic to all people who belong to a particular group. (2) Create synergy through diversity. Having friends who are different can enrich one's life. (3) Show empathy for all people. **Empathy** is the ability to share in another's emotions or feelings. (4) Avoid discriminatory comments. Words often cause emotional wounds that are more difficult to heal than physical wounds. (5) Ask others to stop discriminatory behavior. When people allow others to behave in a discriminatory way, they have their passive approval. (6) Learn about people who are different. As people learn about others, they gain appreciation.

EVALUATION

Ask students to write a Personal Pledge to Avoid Prejudice. The students' pledges should contain types of prejudice (isms) they will avoid and at least five actions they can take. Encourage students to be creative in their writing style. Their pledges might be written as poems. They might be designed as a cheer or a rap. Have selected students present their Personal Pledges to their classmates. Select some students to present their Personal Pledges to other classes or to community groups. Use TM-16, "Resolve Conflicts," to discuss what to do when a conflict arises.

MULTICULTURAL INFUSION

As an additional learning experience, have students discuss the diverse backgrounds of people in your community. Ask students if they have met someone who belongs to each culture, race, or age group mentioned. If not, ask students how they might have contact with people of diverse backgrounds in order to know and appreciate them.

INCLUSION

Discuss discriminatory behavior and prejudice that is directed at people who have special needs, such as people who are physically or mentally disabled. Have students include this type of prejudice on the first rainbow.

Family and Social Health

GRADE 8

Critical Thinker

OPTIONAL TEACHING STRATEGY: BIRTH CONTROL FACT-O

Examining facts about birth control methods helps teens prepare for adulthood when they might choose to marry and plan a family. Abstinence is the expected standard for teens. Abstinence reduces the risk of infection with HIV and other STDs and prevents pregnancy.

HEALTH EDUCATION STANDARD

- Students will comprehend concepts related to health promotion and disease prevention to enhance health.

PERFORMANCE INDICATOR

- Analyze the relationship between healthy behaviors and personal health.

HEALTH GOAL

- I will learn methods about birth control methods.

MATERIALS

- TM-3, "Comprehend Health Concepts," Appendix A; blindfold; student master "Birth Control FACT-O"

MOTIVATION

1 Ask for a student volunteer. Blindfold him or her. Explain to the student volunteer and to the class that you are going to put up a poster some place in the classroom. Then spin the student volunteer who is blindfolded and ask him or her to walk toward the poster. The student volunteer will not have enough information to walk toward the poster. Repeat the activity, but this time give the student volunteer some information concerning the location

of the poster (turn to the right, go to the left, etc.). Ask the class to explain why the student volunteer had a greater chance of walking toward the poster the second time. Students will say that the student volunteer had the information he or she needed. Facts helped the student volunteer move toward the goal—the poster.

2 Explain to students that this lesson will provide them with facts about birth control by playing a game called Birth Control FACT-O. Provide students with the following information on sixteen methods of birth control along with their definitions.

- *Combination pill.* A pill that combines estrogen and progesterone to change the natural menstrual cycle and to prevent ovulation. The combination pill differs from the progestin-only pill, or mini-pill, in that it contains estrogen. A female will resume her natural menstrual cycle if she stops taking the combination pill.
- *Progestin-only pill.* A pill that contains progesterone, which changes the natural menstrual cycle and prevents ovulation. The progestin-only pill differs from the combination pill in that it contains only a small dose of progestin and no estrogen. A female will resume her natural menstrual cycle if she stops taking the progestin-only pill.
- *Injectable progestin.* A shot of synthetic progesterone that is given every three months to change the natural menstrual cycle and to prevent ovulation.
- *Subdermal implants.* Flexible plastic tubes that are inserted under the skin in the upper arm and that release progestin.
- *Spermicides.* A foam, cream, jelly, film, or suppository that forms a barrier and contains a chemical that might kill some sperm.
- *Diaphragm.* A dome-shaped cup that fits over the cervix to provide a barrier to help prevent sperm from entering the uterus.

- *Cervical cap.* A rubber or plastic dome that fits snugly over the cervix to provide a barrier to help prevent sperm from entering the uterus.
- *Male condom.* A thin sheath of latex, natural skin, or polyurethane that is placed over the erect penis to collect semen during ejaculation.
- *Female condom.* A soft polyurethane pouch that is inserted deep into the vagina to collect semen during ejaculation.
- *Intrauterine device.* A small device that fits inside the uterus and helps prevent pregnancy.
- *Basal body temperature.* A birth control method in which a female uses her basal body temperature to predict ovulation.
- *Calendar method.* A birth control method in which a female records the length of her menstrual cycle on a calendar to predict her fertile period.
- *Mucous method.* The female records the changes in the mucous discharge from her vagina to predict her fertile period.
- *Tubal ligation.* A surgical procedure in which the fallopian tubes are closed off, cauterized, or cut.
- *Vasectomy.* A surgical procedure in which the vas deferens is cut, tied, or cauterized.
- *Douche.* The use of a solution to rinse out the vagina.

3 Distribute the Birth Control FACT-O sheet at the end of this lesson. This sheet has sixteen blank boxes. Write each of the sixteen methods of birth control on the chalkboard. Ask students to randomly fill in each box with a birth control method. They can place the methods in any order on their sheets. Explain that you will provide a definition of a birth control method and students are to place a check in the box that correctly corresponds to the birth control method. Just as in Bingo, the student who gets four across, down, or diagonally wins.

EVALUATION

Explain to students that they need to understand health facts. Review TM-3, "Comprehend Health Concept." Give eight students the definition of a birth control method written on a sheet of paper, and have students hold the definitions in front of them. Have eight other students each hold a birth control method. Without talking, each student has to match up with another student so that the correct definitions will match the appropriate birth control method. Those students who do not have sheets in front of them will act as observers and help move students to the correct positions.

Birth Control FACT-O

Knowing facts about birth control methods helps teens prepare for adulthood when they might choose to marry and have a family. Abstinence is the expected standard for teens. Abstinence reduces the risk of infection with HIV and STDs and prevents pregnancy.

Growth and Development

GRADE 8

My Hero

HEALTH EDUCATION STANDARDS

- Students will demonstrate the ability to advocate for personal, family, and community health.
- Students will demonstrate the ability to use interpersonal communication skills to enhance health and avoid or reduce health risks.

PERFORMANCE INDICATORS

- Identify ways that health messages and communication techniques can be altered for different audiences.
- Apply effective verbal and nonverbal communication skills to enhance health.

HEALTH GOAL

- I will develop habits that promote healthful aging.

MATERIALS

Student master "My Hero"; transparency projector; five flashcards with one of the following words written on each: *denial, anger, bargaining, depression,* and *acceptance;* CD or cassette of the sound recording "The Wind beneath My Wings" by Bette Midler (optional); CD or cassette player; paper; markers; TM-3, "Comprehend Health Concepts," Appendix A

MOTIVATION

1 Before beginning this strategy, prepare five large flashcards. On one side of each of the flashcards, print one of the following stages that appears in italics. On the other side, print the corresponding description for each stage.

Stage 1: *Denial*—People do not want to accept what is happening.

Stage 2: *Anger*—People are angry about what is happening.

Stage 3: *Bargaining*—People try to make deals thinking this will change the outcome.

Stage 4: *Depression*—People recognize that bargaining has not worked and begin to feel the loss and grieve.

Stage 5: *Acceptance*—People acknowledge the situation, talk about it, and feel a sense of peace.

2 Ask for a student volunteer. Explain that the class should pretend that this student is moving and will no longer attend the same school—in fact, the student is moving such a distance that classmates will most likely never see him or her again.

3 Divide the class into pairs or triads of students. Each pair or triad is to brainstorm ways to say goodbye to the student volunteer. Each is to select one of the students in the pair or triad who will come in front of the class and speak directly to the student volunteer expressing feelings and saying goodbye. After an appropriate amount of time, have the sharing session. Follow up by asking the students who played the role of saying goodbye to share how they felt. Then ask students if they have ever had this experience. How did they feel when they said good-bye to someone close?

4 Show students the transparency "My Hero." Ask students to explain the meaning of the poem. The poem is about a person who knows that "my hero" is dying. Explain that when a person is dying, those around him or her begin to say good-bye. Saying good-bye and being "with you in your fight" involve sharing different feelings.

5 Explain that people who are dying and those who love them often experience psychological stages that describe emotional feelings. Elisabeth Kübler-Ross identified these five stages as denial, anger, bargaining, depression, and acceptance. Use the flashcards to review these five stages. Show the students the side of each flashcard that identifies the stage and the emotional feelings most people experience. Then refer to what is written on the back of each flashcard as you describe each stage. You may want students to take notes on the five stages.

6 Discuss the importance of saying good-bye to someone who is dying. Explain that in some cases a person cannot say good-bye directly to the person who is dying. The person may be in a coma or may have died unexpectedly. It is still important to say good-bye. A funeral or memorial service is often performed so that people can gather together to say good-bye and to share feelings with others who were close to the person who has died.

7 Explain that after a death people may experience grief. **Grief** is the distress caused by the death of another person. Grief is a normal reaction to a death. People grieve in different ways. They may experience shock, numbness, disbelief, depression, or loneliness. These feelings are part of the recovery process. Ask students how they might show support for someone who is grieving. Give the following suggestions:

- Do something thoughtful for the person. Make a phone call, send a card, attend the funeral or memorial service, run errands, help with chores, offer meals.
- Be a good listener. Make yourself available to talk. Simply being a good friend is important.
- Allow the person the opportunity to grieve and express emotions.

- Accept your own limitations. Many situations can be difficult to handle. Seek advice from professionals or support groups if necessary.

8 Discuss the importance of memories. Explain that although people die, memories of them continue. After a period of grieving, these memories become the focus. If you have a CD or cassette of "The Wind beneath My Wings" by Bette Midler, play it for the class. Ask students why the person about whom Bette Midler sang was a hero. Ask students to describe the positive memories someone might have of such a hero.

9 Begin a discussion of people who are elderly. Explain the importance of sharing feelings with people of all ages, but especially of those who are elderly. It is important to share the positive memories experienced with these people.

EVALUATION

Show TM-3, "Comprehend Health Concepts" and have students identify the facts in this lesson that they can use to better understand how to communicate with different people. Have students design greeting cards to express their feelings to an elderly person about whom they care. Their message can be "I am glad you are here to share life's precious moments with me." They can write similar messages and then write personal notes. Show students the flashcards of the psychological stages that describe emotional feelings people experience when they or someone close to them are dying. On a sheet of paper, have students explain each of the five stages.

Student Master

My Hero

I've watched you all my life,
coming here and going there,
being everything to everyone,
a life the world could share.

I've seen you in my heart,
where you've found a place to live,
taking time to be my hero,
and there's nothing I can give.

Now I see you fading softly,
as you wander into the night.
It's my turn to be your hero—
I'll be with you in your fight.

GRADE 8

Shake the Salt Habit

HEALTH EDUCATION STANDARDS

- Students will comprehend concepts related to health promotion and disease prevention to enhance health.
- Students will demonstrate the ability to advocate for personal, family, and community health.

PERFORMANCE INDICATORS

- Describe ways to reduce or prevent injuries and other adolescent health problems.
- Identify ways that health messages and communication techniques can be altered for different audiences.

HEALTH GOALS

- I will follow Dietary Guidelines.
- I will evaluate food labels and food ads.

MATERIALS

Teaching master "The Dietary Guidelines for Americans—2005" (transparency); teaching master "The Food Label" (transparency); transparency projector; one empty salt shaker (unbreakable is preferable); coin; paper; pens and markers; computers and computer paper (optional); TM-3, "Comprehend Health Concepts," Appendix A

MOTIVATION

1 Review the dietary guidelines using a transparency of the teaching master "The Dietary Guidelines for Americans—2005." The **Dietary Guidelines for Americans—2005** are recommendations for diet choices for healthy Americans two years of age or older. The guidelines are a result of the research by the U.S. Department of Agriculture and the Department of Health and Human Services. Following the Dietary Guidelines, a person can improve the

chance of having better health and reduce the chance of getting certain diseases.

2 Use the transparency of the teaching master "The Food Label" to explain ways that information on food labels can help people follow the dietary guidelines. Explain to students that the information on the food label for sodium tells how much salt is in the food. This food label is for a food that contains 20 percent of the percent daily value for sodium in one serving size. The **percent daily value** tells how much of a day's worth of the nutrient is provided in the food product for a 2,000-calorie diet.

3 Remind students that it is important to use salt and sodium only in moderation. This helps reduce the risk of high blood pressure. High blood pressure is a chronic disease for many people. Have students brainstorm ways that they might reduce the amount of salt and sodium in their diets. Here are some suggested ways:

- Do not eat foods on which you can see the salt (pretzels).
- Do not place a salt shaker on the table.
- Use spices such as garlic, herbs, lemon juice, and flavored vinegars rather than salt to flavor food.
- Eat fresh foods rather than canned foods.
- If you eat canned foods, drain them, then rinse them for at least a minute. This removes almost 50 percent of the salt.
- Avoid eating cured, smoked, or highly processed foods.
- When dining in restaurants, ask that your food be prepared without salt.
- Taste your food before adding salt.
- Read food labels to determine the amount of sodium before purchasing foods.
- Purchase foods that are labeled "low sodium," "very low sodium," and "sodium free."
- Be aware that foods that are labeled "lite" or "reduced sodium" may still

contain too much sodium; read the label for the actual percent daily value.

• Identify foods that you eat that contain sodium and eat these foods less often.

4 Divide the class into two teams. Ask the students on each team to select a team captain and to stand in line behind this captain. Toss a coin to see which team goes first. Give the team captain the salt shaker. Explain that the team will have a two-minute time limit (you can vary this time limit depending on the number of students that are in your class). The team captain is to tell one way he or she might "shake the salt habit" (I will not salt my popcorn), shake the empty salt shaker, and then hand the salt shaker to the next student in line on the team. The second student on the team is to name another way to "shake the salt habit" (I will choose foods labeled "low sodium"), shake the empty salt shaker, and pass the salt shaker to the third student on the team, and so on. As the salt shaker is passed from student to student in the team line, each is to name a way to "shake the salt habit." However, no student can repeat what another team member has said. At the end of the two-minute time limit, count the number of students who have responded. This is team 1's score. Now students on the other team have a turn. They follow the same directions. They can repeat some of the ways to "shake the salt

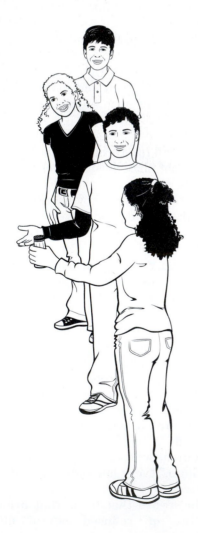

habit" that team 1 named; however, they cannot repeat what one of their team members has said. At the end of the two-minute time limit, count the number of students who have responded. This is team 2's score. Then have a second round. In the second round, team 2 goes first and then team 1. After the second round, compare the two teams' scores.

EVALUATION

Have students create their own Family Health Newsletters to take home to share with their families. They can use paper, pens, and markers. If your school has computers and computer paper available, this is an option. Their individual Family Health Newsletters should include a list and discussion of each of the Dietary Guidelines for Americans. They should include a personal plan for limiting the amount of sodium consumed by their family. Assess the individual Family Health Newsletters and allow students to make changes prior to taking them home to share with their families. By using TM-3, "Comprehend Health Concepts," have students show how their newsletters meet the guidelines in this master.

MULTICULTURAL INFUSION

Have students identify ethnic foods they enjoy. Refer to the dietary guidelines for Americans. Are these foods healthful? Which of these foods should be consumed in moderation? When students are writing their individual Family Health Newsletters, they can include a discussion of the ethnic foods their family enjoys. They can suggest limiting those that should be consumed in moderation.

INCLUSION

Mention that some students have difficulty with certain foods. For example, students with asthma may need to avoid specific foods that may increase respiratory problems. Students with geographic tongue (irregular patches on the surface of the tongue) may need to avoid very spicy foods to prevent the tongue from swelling. Students may volunteer to share foods they must eat in moderation to maintain optimal health. Although these dietary suggestions are not part of the Dietary Guidelines for Americans, they are important for the individual.

Teaching Master

The Dietary Guidelines
for Americans — 2005

Aim for Fitness
- Aim for a healthy weight.
- Be physically active each day for at least thirty minutes.

Build a Healthy Base
- Let MyPyramid guide your food choices.
- Choose a variety of grains daily, especially whole grains.
- Choose a variety of fruits and vegetables daily.
- Keep food safe to eat.

Choose Sensibly
- Choose a diet that is low in saturated fat and cholesterol and moderate in total fat.
- Choose beverages and foods to moderate your intake of sugars.
- Choose and prepare foods with less salt.
- If adults drink alcoholic beverages, they should do so in moderation. People your age should not drink alcohol.

Teaching Master

The Food Label

Nutrition Facts

Serving Size 1 cup (265g)
Servings per Container 2

Amount per Serving

Calories 235   Calories from Fat 30

	% Daily Value*
Total Fat 3g	**5%**
Saturated Fat 1g	**5%**
Trans Fat 0.5g	
Cholesterol 30mg	**10%**
Sodium 775mg	**32%**
Total Carbohydrate 34g	**11%**
Dietary Fiber 9g	**36%**
Sugars 5g	
Protein 18g	

Vitamin A 25%	•	Vitamin C 0%	
Calcium 12%	•	Iron 20%	

*Percent Daily Values are based on a 2,000 calorie diet. Your daily values may be higher or lower depending on your calorie needs:

	Calories	2,000	2,500
Total Fat	Less than	65g	80
Sat Fat	Less than	20g	25g
Cholesterol	Less than	300mg	300mg
Sodium	Less than	2,400mg	2,400mg
Total Carbohydrate		300g	375g
Dietary Fiber		25g	30g

Calories per gram:
Fat 9 • Carbohydrate 4 • Protein 4

GRADE 8

I Can't See What You Say

HEALTH EDUCATION STANDARDS

- Students will comprehend concepts related to health promotion and disease prevention to enhance health.
- Students will demonstrate the ability to practice health-enhancing behaviors and avoid or reduce health risks.

PERFORMANCE INDICATORS

- Analyze the relationship between healthy behaviors and personal health.
- Demonstrate healthy practices and behaviors that will maintain or improve the health of self and others.

HEALTH GOALS

- I will have regular examinations.
- I will prevent physical activity–related injuries and illnesses.

MATERIALS

Transparency of teaching master "Knowing about Your Vision"; transparency projector; paper; pencils; chalk; chalkboard; TM-3, "Comprehend Health Concepts," Appendix A

MOTIVATION

1 To prepare for this strategy, draw a design on a sheet of paper. The design should consist of line drawings of several different geometric shapes placed randomly on the sheet of paper.

2 To begin the strategy, ask students to have a sheet of paper and a pencil to participate in the following task. Then ask for a student volunteer. Show the student volunteer the design you have drawn. Do not show the other students the design. Explain that the student volunteer will describe the design. As the volunteer describes the design, the

students are to draw on their sheets of paper what the volunteer describes. They are to keep their eyes on their own papers and not ask fellow classmates for any help.

3 After this task is completed, share your design with the students. Then have students share the designs they have drawn. Are the designs exact duplications of your design? Whose design was most similar to yours? Why was it unlikely that one of the students would be able to duplicate your design with precision?

4 Explain that the students received information via the sense of hearing. The sense of hearing provided them with some information. Now have the students use the unused side of their sheets of paper. They can look at the design you have drawn as they draw the design again. Are their designs more similar to yours? Explain that the students received additional information via the sense of vision. Further explain the importance of caring for vision by protecting the eyes and having regular eye examinations. Define visual impairment. To have a *visual impairment* is to have difficulty seeing or to be blind.

5 Use a transparency of the teaching master "Knowing about Your Vision" to review information about kinds of eye doctors, kinds of visual problems, kinds of eye conditions, and ways to care for the eyes.

EVALUATION

The following quiz can be used to assess student knowledge needed to perform the life skills. Answers are provided on the teaching master "Knowing about Your Vision."

1. Name two kinds of eye doctors and tell what they do.
2. What condition exists when a person cannot tell the difference between red and green?

3. What condition exists when a person cannot see clearly at night?
4. What visual problem does a person have who can see distant objects clearly, but objects close by are fuzzy?
5. What visual problem does a person have who can see close objects clearly, but distant objects are fuzzy?
6. What is astigmatism?
7. What would you do if you had a sty?
8. How might conjunctivitis, or pinkeye, be spread to others?
9. What would you do if you were hit in the eye with a baseball?
10. What would you do if you got a small piece of dirt in your eye?

Have students write a paragraph on ways to care for the eyes. Use TM-3, "Comprehend Health Concepts," to guide students in answering each of the questions.

INCLUSION

Invite someone from a community agency to your class to discuss volunteer opportunities to help people who have visual impairment. You also may want to invite a person with visual impairment to class to describe ways that young people might assist people who have visual impairment. For example, students might read to people who have visual impairment.

Teaching Master

Knowing about Your Vision

Kinds of Eye Doctors

- An **ophthalmologist** is a medical doctor who specializes in the medical and surgical care and treatment of the eye. This doctor can diagnose and treat all types of eye disorders, test vision, and prescribe corrective lenses.

- An **optometrist** is a doctor who can test vision and prescribe corrective lenses.

Kinds of Visual Problems

- **Nearsightedness** is a defect in the shape of the eye that causes distant objects to be fuzzy.

- **Farsightedness** is a defect in the shape of the eye that causes objects that are close to be fuzzy.

- **Astigmatism** is the irregular curvature of the cornea that causes blurred vision.

- **Night blindness** is a condition in which a person cannot see clearly at night.

- **Color blindness** is a condition in which a person cannot tell the difference between red and green.

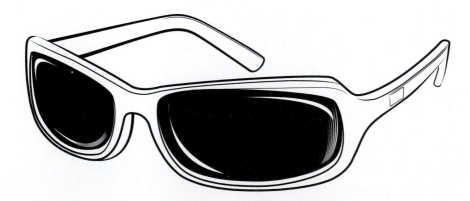

Teaching Master (continued)

Kinds of Eye Conditions

- A **sty** is an infection around the eyelash marked by swelling and pain; stys are treated by applying warm compresses to the eye. They usually heal in a week.

- **Conjunctivitis**, or pinkeye, is an inflammation of the membrane lining the eyelids and covering the eyeball. Pinkeye can be spread to others by sharing towels or washcloths. It is treated with medicines from a medical doctor.

- A **blow to the eye** should be treated immediately by applying an ice cold compress. An ophthalmologist should be seen.

- When **dirt or a small object** is in the eye, the eye should not be rubbed as this may damage the eye. By lifting the upper lid over the lower lid, the lashes can brush the object off the inside of the upper eyelid. Blinking can also be helpful in removing small particles from the eye. If this does not work, the eye should be kept closed until medical help is received.

Ways to Care for the Eyes

- Have regular eye checkups every eighteen months to two years. Wear corrective lenses (eyeglasses or contact lenses) if they have been prescribed for you. Follow guidelines for caring for eyeglasses or contact lenses. Contact lens wearers who notice any unusual redness, blurring or sudden change in vision, or persistent pain in or around the eye should remove the lenses and consult with their eye doctor.

- Wear safety glasses when using tools, when using chemicals, or when near flying debris.

- Wear safety glasses when playing sports such as racquetball or lacrosse.

- Wear sunglasses to protect the eyes from the sun's rays. Never look directly into the sun.

GRADE 8

Garbled

HEALTH EDUCATION STANDARDS

- Students will comprehend concepts related to health promotion and disease prevention to enhance health.
- Students will demonstrate the ability to access valid information and products and services to enhance health.

PERFORMANCE INDICATORS

- Describe ways to reduce or prevent injuries and other adolescent health problems.
- Access valid health information from home, school, and community.

HEALTH GOALS

- I will not drink alcohol.
- I practice protective factors that help me stay away from drugs.

MATERIALS

Transparency of the teaching master "Codependency and the Family"; transparency projector; marshmallow; interesting book; pamphlets describing community resources for intervention and treatment of drug dependency; yellow pages of a telephone directory; paper and pens; computers and computer paper (optional); TM-3, "Comprehend Health Concepts," Appendix A

MOTIVATION

1 Ask for a student volunteer to come forward and read from the interesting book you have brought to class. Allow the student to read several paragraphs. Then ask the student volunteer to place the marshmallow in his or her mouth. Tell the student volunteer not to bite down on the marshmallow. Explain to the class that the student volunteer now represents someone who has been drinking alcohol. Now ask the student volunteer to continue reading. Allow

the student to read several paragraphs. Most likely, the other students will begin to laugh as the words will be garbled. Explain to students that this teaching strategy is called "garbled." To *garble* is to alter or distort, to change the meaning of something, or to transmit in an inaccurate way. Further explain that the student volunteer began to garble as she or he read the second time. Drinking alcohol has this effect.

Dra wowon to-ed da ro-rice offi-huh...

2 Explain that the garbling effect increases as blood alcohol concentration (BAC) increases. **Blood alcohol concentration (BAC)** is the ratio of alcohol in a person's blood to the person's total amount of blood and is expressed as a percentage. As BAC increases, a person becomes increasingly affected. A person who is drinking is more likely to have accidents and more likely to be involved in violence (homicide, suicide, abuse, fighting). A person is more likely to make irresponsible decisions about his or her sexual behavior.

Alcohol, Tobacco, and Other Drugs

3 Show students the transparency of the teaching master "Codependency and the Family." Explain that at least one person in this family has alcoholism. **Alcoholism** is a complex disease that is characterized by preoccupation with drinking alcohol that has progressed to serious physical, social, occupational, or family consequences for an individual. Alcoholism has consequences not only on the dependent person directly involved but also on the children of parents who are dependent on alcohol.

4 Explain that alcoholism also has a garbling effect on the family. It distorts and changes family relationships. Family members may have codependence. **Codependence** is a mental disorder in which a person loses personal identity, has frozen feelings, and copes ineffectively. People who have codependence are called **codependent.** Have students discuss signs of codependence in these family members.

5 Refer to the young family member who abuses alcohol. Explain that children reared in families in which adults are chemically dependent may copy this behavior. They may abuse alcohol or other drugs. Research also indicates that the tendency for chemical dependency and alcoholism may be inherited. This means that a child who has a parent with alcoholism is at increased risk for this disease. The only way they can be certain not to have alcoholism is to never drink.

6 Introduce the topic of treatment. Explain that there are many school and community resources for intervention and treatment. If you have them available, share pamphlets describing community resources. Show students how to locate resources in the yellow pages of a telephone directory. Discuss support groups that are available to help families. **Alcoholics Anonymous,** or **AA,** is a support group in which people with alcoholism meet regularly to support one another to abstain from drinking alcohol. **Al-Anon** is a support group in which people who are

friends and family members with a person with alcoholism meet regularly to support one another and to change behaviors that are codependent. **Al-Ateen** is a support group for teenagers who are friends and family members of a person with alcoholism. Members of Al-Ateen meet regularly to support one another, to change codependent behavior, and to be drug-free.

EVALUATION

Have students develop pamphlets on alcoholism. They can use the library to gain information in addition to what was covered in class. If available, they can use computers to design their pamphlets and to assess information about alcoholism. Their individual pamphlets should include the following:

- A definition of the disease
- A list of signs of the disease
- An explanation of codependence, including a list of codependent behaviors
- A short description of treatment facilities in your community
- A description of Alcoholics Anonymous, Al-Anon, and Al-Ateen

Review TM-3, "Comprehend Health Concepts," to review how each of the five evaluation items are addressed.

INCLUSION

Explain that automobile accidents involving a person who has been drinking alcohol are a leading cause of injuries that result in disabilities. In addition, many falls that result in disabilities occur after a person had been drinking. Finally, violence that occurs due to drinking may result in people being disabled. Gunshot wounds have become a leading cause of disability. People who have been disabled in these ways have many lifestyle adjustments to make. Discuss ways to be supportive of people who are disabled after accidents caused by someone who had been drinking.

Teaching Master

Codependency and the Family

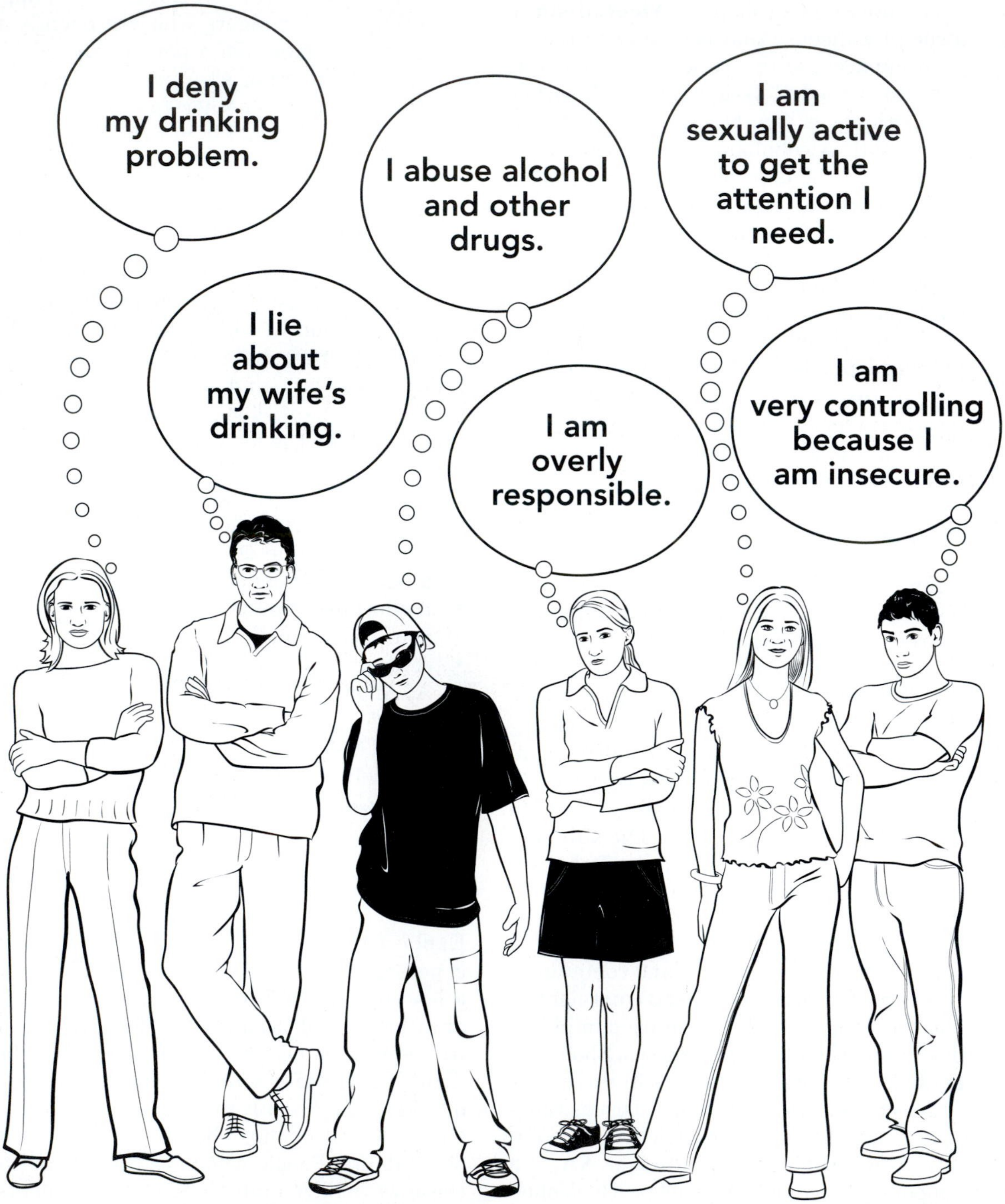

Communicable and Chronic Diseases

Sweet Success

HEALTH EDUCATION STANDARD

- Students will analyze the influence of family, peers, culture, media, technology, and other factors on health behaviors.
- Students will comprehend concepts related to health promotion and disease prevention to enhance health.

PERFORMANCE INDICATORS

- Examine how the family influences the health of adolescents.
- Describe how family history can impact personal health.

HEALTH GOALS

- I will choose behaviors to prevent the spread of pathogens.
- I will choose behaviors to reduce my risk of cardiovascular diseases.

MATERIALS

Transparency of the teaching master "Chronic Diseases"; transparency projector; test tube; sugar cubes or packets of sugar; water; small piece of felt; scissors; TM-3, "Comprehend Health Concepts," Appendix A

MOTIVATION

1 Before beginning this strategy, cut the piece of felt into a small circle. You may want to use the rim of an eight-ounce glass for the pattern. The piece of felt will be used to represent a body cell.

2 Begin the strategy by showing the students the sugar cube. Ask students to name foods they eat that contain sugar. They may mention cakes, pies, and candy. They may mention other foods such as oranges, apples, and ice cream. Explain that something must happen to foods in order for the sugar in them to be used by the body's cells. Empty a packet of sugar into the test tube. Explain that the **pancreas** is a gland in the digestive system that secretes insulin. **Insulin** is a hormone that promotes the absorption of blood sugar (glucose) into the muscle cells where it is used for energy. Thus, the pancreas must produce insulin for blood sugar to be absorbed by the body's cells. Pour some water from the measuring cup into the test tube. Mix the water and sugar by placing your finger over the opening of the test tube and shaking it. Then pour the water-sugar mixture on one of the felt pieces that represents a muscle cell. The water-sugar mixture will absorb into the felt. Then squeeze the felt. The water will drip off. Explain that the muscle cell has absorbed (soaked up) the blood sugar (glucose) and produced energy.

3 Repeat the demonstration in a different way. Empty a packet of sugar into the test tube. Do not add the water. Then pour the sugar onto the other piece (dry) of felt that represents a muscle cell. Students will notice that without the water (insulin), the sugar cannot be absorbed by the cell. Squeeze the felt. Students will notice that the sugar cannot be used to produce energy. The sugar remains unchanged and falls off the piece of felt. No energy can be squeezed from the felt muscle cell. Use this demonstration to discuss diabetes. In the first demonstration, the pancreas produced insulin. The insulin helped the muscle cell absorb the glucose or blood sugar. Then the muscle cell could produce energy. In the second demonstration, the pancreas produced little or no insulin. The sugar in the bloodstream remained unchanged and could not be absorbed by the muscle cell. **Diabetes** is a disease in which the body is unable to process the sugar in foods in normal ways. It occurs when the pancreas does not produce enough insulin to help the cells break down and use the sugar.

4 Use the transparency of the teaching master "Chronic Diseases" to review other facts

about diabetes. Explain that diabetes is a chronic disease. A **chronic disease** is a recurring or persistent disease. A **chronic health condition** is a recurring or persistent health condition. Review information about ulcerative colitis, diverticulosis, arthritis, systemic lupus, and chronic fatigue syndrome. Explain that people who have these chronic diseases and health conditions must learn to manage them. For example, a person who has insulin-dependent diabetes will take daily injections of insulin. This person may have a specific diet and exercise program. Managing his or her condition means being certain to get the injections and balance exercise and diet.

5 Explain to students that some chronic conditions and diseases are inherited. For example, diabetes can be inherited. Knowing one's family history of disease is important. It helps a person know his or her risk factors for developing specific diseases and conditions. For example, people who are at risk for developing diabetes need to practice certain health habits. They need regular physical examinations and blood tests. They need to eat a diet low in sugar. They need to have a regular exercise program. Having diabetes is a risk factor for cardiovascular diseases. By following these health habits, someone with a family history of diabetes reduces the risk of diabetes and cardiovascular diseases.

EVALUATION

Have students develop individual crossword puzzles using the terms on the teaching master "Chronic Diseases" and facts about them as clues. For example, the clue for osteoarthritis might be "may be caused by sports injuries or wear and tear on joints." Students must use ten of the eleven boldfaced words from the teaching master. Ask students how people with diabetes, irritable bowel syndrome, and chronic fatigue syndrome manage these chronic diseases. Have students select a chronic disease. Show TM-3, "Comprehend Health Concepts." Show how the information in this master can be used to address this disease.

INCLUSION

The evaluation might be completed as a cooperative learning activity. Pair students who might have difficulty designing an individual crossword puzzle with students who would not find this task to be demanding. Have them discuss a strategy for completing the evaluation as a team. What might each contribute to the task?

Teaching Master

Chronic Diseases

Diabetes

- **Diabetes** is a disease in which the body is unable to process the sugar in foods in normal ways. There are two types of diabetes.
- **Insulin-dependent diabetes** is diabetes in which the pancreas produces little or no insulin. People with this type of diabetes must have daily injections of insulin.
- **Noninsulin-dependent diabetes** is diabetes in which the pancreas produces some insulin, but the body cells are not able to properly use it. People control this type of diabetes with diet and exercise. Some people take oral medication.
- Symptoms of diabetes include frequent urination, abnormal thirst, weakness, fatigue, drowsiness, blurred vision, tingling, and numbness in the hands and feet, and slow healing of cuts.
- Complications include blindness and poor circulation, which can lead to gangrene.

Ulcerative Colitis

- **Ulcerative colitis** is an inflammatory disease of the walls of the large intestine.
- Symptoms include daily episodes of bloody diarrhea, stomach cramping, nausea, sweating, fever, and weight loss.
- People with this condition have an increased risk of colorectal cancer and often develop irritable bowel syndrome.
- **Irritable bowel syndrome** is a condition in which a person experiences nausea, gas, pain, attacks of diarrhea, and cramps after eating certain foods.
- Ulcerative colitis and irritable bowel syndrome are treated with a diet high in fiber and with certain medications.

Diverticulosis

- **Diverticulosis** is a disease in which the intestinal walls develop outpouchings called diverticula. It most often occurs in the small intestine.
- Symptoms include fecal material filling into the diverticula causing pain, discomfort, and infection. It can be life-threatening if bleeding and blockage occur.
- Diverticulosis is treated with surgery.

Communicable and Chronic Diseases

Arthritis

- **Arthritis** is a general term that includes more than one hundred diseases, all of which involve inflammation. There are two kinds of arthritis.
- **Osteoarthritis** is a wearing down of the moving parts of a joint. It occurs because of wear and tear, overweight, sports injuries, and heredity. It is treated with aspirin and pain relievers as well as exercise. Sometimes new joints are implanted in the body.
- **Rheumatoid arthritis** is a serious disease in which joint deformity and loss of joint function occur. It affects people between ages twenty and fifty-five. A careful exercise plan must be followed to avoid loss of joint function. Aspirin is used for pain. Cortisone may be used for inflammation. Surgery may be required.

Systemic Lupus

- **Systemic lupus erythematosus (SLE)** is a chronic disease of unknown cause that affects most of the systems in the body. The skin, kidneys, joints, muscles, and central nervous system may be affected. The onset occurs late in adolescence. The disease may progress to bleeding in the central nervous system. There may be heart and kidney failure. Treatment for SLE depends on the organs involved. Medications including steroids are used. Unfortunately, long-term use of steroids may cause bone disease, muscle wasting, and short stature.

Chronic Fatigue Syndrome

- **Chronic fatigue syndrome (CFS)** is a condition in which fatigue comes on suddenly and is relentless or relapsing, causing tiredness in someone for no apparent reason. The symptoms include headache, sore throat, low-grade fever, fatigue, weakness, tender lymph glands, muscle and joint aches, and inability to concentrate. CFS symptoms recur frequently and may persist for years. Currently, there is no effective treatment. People with CFS must maintain a healthful diet, get adequate rest and sleep, manage stress, and exercise at a comfortable pace.

GRADE 8

Chewing the Fat

HEALTH EDUCATION STANDARDS

- Students will comprehend concepts related to health promotion and disease prevention to enhance health.
- Students will demonstrate the ability to access valid information and products and services to enhance health.

PERFORMANCE INDICATORS

- Analyze the relationship between healthy behaviors and personal health.
- Analyze the validity of health information, products, and services.

HEALTH GOALS

- I will evaluate sources of health information wisely.
- I will make a plan to manage time and money.
- I will follow the Dietary Guidelines. (Nutrition)
- I will plan a healthful diet that reduces my risk of disease. (Nutrition)

MATERIALS

Teaching master "Saturated Sandwiches"; transparency projector; teaspoon; shortening; small clear plastic cup with lid; red food coloring; water; TM-9, "Access Valid Health Information and Products and Services," Appendix A

MOTIVATION

1 Write the following terms on the chalkboard: *egg salad, turkey with mustard, grilled cheese, Reuben, corned beef with mustard, vegetarian, ham with mustard, roast beef with mustard, BLT, turkey club, tuna salad,* and *chicken salad.* Take the shortening, teaspoon, and small clear plas-

tic cup with the lid. Explain that each of these sandwiches contains fat and saturated fat. Fat is an essential nutrient. The body needs fat to transport fat-soluble vitamins, to make hormones, and to regulate other body functions. However, too much fat, especially saturated fat, increases the risk of heart disease and cancer. A **saturated fat** is a fat from animal origin such as beef or dairy products. Ask students to rank the sandwiches written on the chalkboard beginning with the one that contains the least amount of saturated fat. Write the ranking given next to each sandwich.

2 Use the teaspoon, shortening, and clear plastic cup with a lid. Explain to students that one teaspoon of the shortening represents four grams of saturated fat. Place one-half teaspoon of shortening into the clear plastic cup. Tell students that the sandwich with the least amount of saturated fat in it contained two grams of fat. Look to see which one they ranked as having the least amount of saturated fat. Tell them that the sandwich made with turkey and mustard had the least amount of saturated fat. Now add another one-half teaspoon of shortening. Explain that there are now four grams of fat in the plastic cup. Then add four more teaspoons of shortening to the plastic cup. There will be a total of five teaspoons of shortening in the plastic cup, or (5 × 4) twenty grams of fat. The sandwich with the greatest amount of saturated fat in it contained twenty grams of saturated fat. Which sandwich did the students rank as having the greatest amount of saturated fat? Tell them that the Reuben had twenty grams of saturated fat.

3 Use the transparency of the teaching master "Saturated Sandwiches" to review the amount of fat and saturated fat in the sandwiches listed on the chalkboard. Ask students if they were surprised at how the sandwiches ranked. Most people are surprised to learn the amount of fat and saturated fat in a tuna sandwich. Often, people rank it as one of the sandwiches with the least amount of fat and saturated fat. Tuna is healthful and low in fat and saturated fat. However, one tablespoon of mayonnaise is loaded with eleven grams of fat and one hundred calories. A person could eat eighty potato chips to have the equivalent of the tuna sandwich. One way to cut the amount of fat and saturated fat when eating a sandwich is to use mustard rather than mayonnaise.

4 Add water and red food coloring to the clear plastic cup. Explain that the plastic cup is an artery. The red colored water is the blood and the shortening is the saturated fat from the Reuben. Explain to students that eating a diet high in saturated fat increases the risk of heart disease and cancer. Further explain that there are three ways to reduce the amount of fat in the blood. The first way is to reduce the intake of saturated fat. The teaching master "Saturated Sandwiches" offered information as to the amount of saturated fat that should be eaten. The other way is to engage in regular aerobic exercise. Cover the clear plastic cup with the lid and shake it vigorously. Note that some of the shortening dissolves. Explain that regular vigorous aerobic exercise clears some saturated fat from the bloodstream. A third way to lower the amount of fat in the bloodstream is to eat foods that are high in fiber. Whole-grain breads contain fiber. It is healthful to eat sandwiches made with whole grain, low-fat breads. Have students review an ad about food. Then have them use TM-9, "Access Valid Health Information and Prod-

ucts and Services." They are to use each of the steps to validate the ad.

EVALUATION

Have students write television commercials warning consumers to reduce the number of "saturated sandwiches" they eat. Their commercials should encourage consumers to make healthful choices when ordering sandwiches at fast-food restaurants. They should tell the number of grams of fat and saturated fat that adolescent females and males should eat to have a heart-healthy diet.

Teaching Master

Saturated Sandwiches

The Center for Science in the Public Interest examined the fat content of twelve common sandwiches. The Food and Drug Administration recommends daily limits of sixty-five grams of total fat and twenty grams of saturated fat for adults eating 2, 000 calories a day. Adolescent females consume approximately 2,200 calories per day. Their total fat should be less than seventy-three grams and their saturated fat should be twenty to twenty-four grams. Adolescent males consume approximately 2,800 calories per day. Their total fat should be less than ninty-three grams per day and their saturated fat should be twenty-five to thirty-one grams.

Fat Content of Common Sandwiches

GRAMS	FAT GRAMS	SATURATED FAT
Turkey with mustard	6	2
Roast beef with mustard	12	4
Chicken salad	32	6
Corned beef with mustard	20	8
Tuna salad	43	8
Ham with mustard	27	10
Egg salad	31	10
Turkey club	34	10
BLT	37	12
Vegetarian	40	14
Grilled cheese	33	17
Reuben	50	20

My Fair Share

HEALTH EDUCATION STANDARDS

- Students will comprehend concepts related to health promotion and disease prevention to enhance health.
- Students will demonstrate the ability to practice health-enhancing behaviors and avoid or reduce health risks.

PERFORMANCE INDICATORS

- Analyze how the environment impacts personal health.
- Demonstrate healthy practices and behaviors that will maintain or improve the health of self and others.

HEALTH GOALS

- I will protect the natural environment.
- I will practice life skills for health. (Mental and Emotional Health)
- I will not carry a weapon. (Injury Prevention and Safety)

MATERIALS

Construction paper; marker; chalk; scissors; pencils or pens; TM-25, "Practice Healthful Behaviors," Appendix A

MOTIVATION

1 Prepare for the strategy in the following ways. On a sheet of construction paper, use the marker to print the following words: *water, food, shelter, sewage facilities, medical care.* Using chalk, draw a large circle with a five-foot diameter on the floor.

2 Ask for five student volunteers. Have the five student volunteers stand inside the circle. Give one of the student volunteers the sheet of construction paper. Ask this student to read the words printed on the paper.

Explain that these are resources available in the environment in which these five student volunteers live. The student who has the paper is to share these resources with the other four students in the circle. The student can share the resources by tearing the sheet into five pieces, keeping one of the pieces.

3 Now explain that the population is growing. There are going to be more people living in the environment and sharing the resources. Ask two more students to join the circle. Of course, they must have a share of the resources, so two of the students who are already in the circle must tear off part of their torn sheets of paper and give them to the two new students. Allow two of the original five students to volunteer to share their resources.

4 Repeat step 3. Have two more students join the circle. Of course, two of the students in the circle must tear off part of their torn sheets of paper and give them to the two new students. The students in the circle will have to decide among themselves who shares resources and tears off a piece of their torn paper. Repeat step 3 again. Continue until no space is left in the circle.

5 Process what happened as the group became larger and more crowded. Obviously, decisions had to be made about who must give up resources (tear off their torn sheet of paper). And of course, there was the issue of how much paper to tear off or give away. Did everyone in the group agree as to how the resources were shared? Does anyone in the group feel cheated? Was anyone denied resources?

6 Explain that human health is greatly affected by population growth. More than 5 billion people inhabit the world, and the current rate of growth exceeds a net population gain of more than 90 million people per year. By the year 2029, the world's population will double unless something happens to slow population growth.

Environmental Health

7 Ask students to brainstorm ways that overcrowding and poverty will affect the environment. Explain that poverty, overcrowding, and poor housing are linked to poor health conditions. Poverty is related to an increased occurrence of depression, hostility, psychological stress, inadequate medical care, poor nutrition, infant mortality, child abuse, and crowded and unsanitary living conditions. In poor environments, more people smoke cigarettes, have harmful diets, are physically inactive, and abuse alcohol and other drugs. Young people their age who are reared in overcrowded and poor environments show a higher risk of doing poorly in school, dropping out of school, becoming adolescent parents, becoming delinquent, and using alcohol and other drugs. Four million youths in the United States live in poor, overcrowded neighborhoods.

8 Explain that there is another serious health consequence that occurs frequently in poor and overcrowded environments—violence. Because there is a lack of resources and an increase in substance abuse and stress, there is more conflict and crime. Young people living in poor and overcrowded environments need to practice behaviors to reduce the risk of being violent or being harmed by violence. Having an adult role model who can manage stress and who is nonviolent is essential. Learning to manage stress and communicate without fighting are important life skills. Participating in regular physical exercise, avoiding alcohol and other drugs, and keeping a sense of humor are helpful.

EVALUATION

Cut sheets of construction paper into four equal pieces. Give each student one of the pieces. On their sheets of paper, have students write as many words and terms as possible to describe what it would be like to live in a poor and overcrowded environment. They are to crowd the words and terms on the paper. Examples of words might be *stressful, dangerous, substance abuse, smoking cigarettes, drop out of school, adolescent parenthood, lack of medical care, lack of shelter, not enough food, inadequate sewage facilities, lack of water, depression, hostility, child abuse, infant mortality.* After an appropriate amount of time, ask students to turn their sheets of paper to the unused side. Have them list at least three life skills, that might be practiced by young people living in poor and overcrowded environments. Their answers might include having a role model who can manage stress, practicing stress-management skills, expressing feelings without fighting, participating in physical exercise, avoiding alcohol and other drugs, and keeping a sense of humor. They can use the information in TM-25, "Practice Healthful Behaviors," to help them identify ways to address these life skills.

GRADE 8

Sealed with Strength

HEALTH EDUCATION STANDARDS

- Students will comprehend concepts related to health promotion and disease prevention to enhance health.
- Students will demonstrate the ability to use interpersonal communication skills to enhance health and avoid or reduce health risks.

PERFORMANCE INDICATORS

- Describe ways to reduce or prevent injuries and other adolescent health problems.
- Demonstrate how to ask for assistance to enhance the health of self and others.

HEALTH GOALS

- I will practice protective factors to reduce the risk of violence.
- I will develop healthful family relationships. (Family and Social Health)

MATERIALS

Transparency of teaching master "Protective Factors That Prevent Violence"; transparency projector; two rubber balls; sealant or patch; small air pump; TM-25, "Practice Healthful Behaviors," Appendix A

MOTIVATION

1 Prepare for this strategy in the following way. Obtain two rubber balls similar to the ones that are used to play dodge ball. Put a small hole in one of the rubber balls. The other rubber ball should have air in it.

2 Show the two rubber balls to the class. Explain that each rubber ball is a young person. Allow the balls to drop to the floor. The ball with the small hole in it will not bounce back as high as the one without the hole. Explain that there is a difference be-

tween these two young people. The young person represented by the ball with the puncture or hole in it has been a survivor of violence. This young person has had the "wind knocked out of him or her."

3 Explain that a survivor of violence must participate in recovery in order to be "sealed with strength." Explain that a person who has experienced violence might

- be highly emotional
- feel depressed
- cry often
- not want to talk with others about what happened
- neglect everyday tasks
- have difficulty paying attention
- feel afraid
- sleep often or have difficulty sleeping
- have nightmares
- have flashbacks about what happened
- use alcohol and other drugs
- choose to stay away from others
- feel ashamed
- behave in violent ways

4 Further explain that although some survivors recover from physical injuries and emotional hurt without help, most do not. Often many experience difficulty for many years. **Post-traumatic stress disorder (PTSD)** is a condition in which a person relives a stressful experience again and again. Emphasize that people who are survivors of violence are at risk for behaving in violent ways. For example, grown-ups who abuse children often were abused when they were children. Many young people who commit crimes and join gangs have lived in homes where there has been domestic violence.

5 Further emphasize the importance of participating in survivor recovery if one has experienced violence. Define survivor recovery. *Survivor recovery* is a person's return to physical and emotional health after being harmed by violence. Place a seal over the puncture or hole in the rubber ball. As you mention each of the following suggestions for survivor recovery, pump a small amount of air into the ball:

- Talk about what happened.
- Get a complete medical examination.
- Seek counseling.
- Join a support group.
- Learn and practice self-protection strategies.

6 Bounce the rubber ball again. Explain that the rubber ball has been "sealed with strength" because this survivor of violence has participated in survivor recovery. Ask students to tell you what the strongest part of the ball is. They should recognize that the strongest part of the ball is the place where it has been sealed. Use this illustration to initiate a discussion about the importance of asking for and getting help. Emphasize that this is a sign of strength.

7 Explain that you have covered just one protective factor for violence. This protective factor is "I will participate in recovery if I am harmed by violence." Define protective factors. **Protective factors** are ways that you might behave and characteristics of the environment in which you live that promote your health, safety, or well-being. Use the transparency of the teaching master "Protective Factors That Prevent Violence" to review other protective factors.

EVALUATION

Divide the class into two teams. Have each team form a line. Give one of the rubber balls to a student at the beginning of one of the two team lines. This student is to name a way for a survivor of violence to become "sealed with strength," then bounce the ball to the first person in line for the second team, and then go to the end of the line. The first person in line for the second team is to repeat what the first student did. She or he is to name a way for a survivor of violence to become "sealed with strength," then bounce the ball back to the next person in line for the other team. Repeat. As you complete this evaluation activity, encourage students to be specific. For example, one survival skill is to "join a support group." A student might say, "join a support group at St. Stephens community center." You want students to identify specific people and places in your community. Each survival skill is a healthful behavior that can be practiced. Use TM-25, "Practice Healthful Behaviors," to serve as a guide to practice survival skills.

INCLUSION

If possible, invite a person from your community who has been disabled as a result of violence to speak with your class. Violence is a leading cause of disability. Ask the person to speak about survivor recovery. What were his or her feelings following the incident? In what survivor recovery efforts did she or he participate? You may also want to invite a person who has lost a family member or friend to violence. Explain that this person is also a survivor of violence and has survived the death of a loved one. What were his or her feelings following the incident? In what survivor recovery efforts did this person participate?

Teaching Master

Protective Factors That Prevent Violence

Protective factors are ways that you might behave and characteristics of the environment in which you live that promote your health, safety, or well-being. Practicing the following life skills will help protect you.

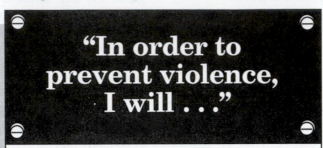

"In order to prevent violence, I will . . ."

- Recognize violent behavior.
- Develop positive self-esteem.
- Develop healthful family relationships.
- Overcome an adverse environment.
- Use social skills.
- Practice anger management skills.
- Practice stress-management skills.
- Participate in physical and recreational activities.
- Practice suicide prevention strategies.
- Practice conflict resolution and peer mediation skills.
- Avoid discriminatory behavior.
- Make responsible decisions.
- Practice resistance skills.
- Avoid alcohol and other drugs.
- Practice responsible behavior around weapons.
- Resist gang membership.
- Respect authority and abide by laws.
- Practice self-protection strategies.
- Participate in recovery if I have been a survivor of violence.
- Change my behavior if I have been a juvenile offender.

Mental and Emotional Health

GRADES 9–12

Internal Messages

HEALTH EDUCATION STANDARD

- Students will demonstrate the ability to practice health-enhancing behaviors and avoid or reduce risks.

PERFORMANCE INDICATORS

- Analyze the role of individual responsibility for enhancing health.
- Demonstrate a variety of healthy practices and behaviors that will maintain or improve the health of self and others.

HEALTH GOALS

- I will be resilient during difficult times.
- I will interact in ways that help create a positive social-emotional environment.

MATERIALS

Transparency of the teaching master "Internal Messages Heard by People Who Are Codependent"; transparency projector; blank cassette tapes; cassette player; spotlight (a flashlight might be used); TM-26, "Practice Healthful Behaviors: A Health Behavior Contract," Appendix A

MOTIVATION

1 Explain to students that they are going to be in the spotlight. Give them the following directions. One at a time, students are to come forward, step in the spotlight, and make a statement about something memorable they hope to do in the future. (A flashlight might be used if a spotlight is unavailable.) For example, a student might come forward, step in the spotlight, and say, "I am graduating from high school." A student might come forward, step in the spotlight and say, "I am shooting the winning basket in a basketball game." During their moment in the spotlight, they are to share something special that they picture themselves doing.

2 Explain to students that they have just shared a positive vision of themselves. Further explain that having a positive vision of oneself is essential to mental and emotional health. Self-esteem is what people think or believe about themselves. Explain that there are ways to develop positive self-esteem:

- Set goals and make plans to reach them.
- Develop a skill or talent.
- Make a list of things you do well.
- Work to do your best in school.
- Be involved in school clubs and community activities.
- Develop a trusting relationship with at least one adult.
- Choose friends who encourage others to do their best.
- Spend time with friends and adults who provide support.
- Volunteer to help another person.
- Keep a neat appearance.

3 Explain that mentally healthy people are people who feel good about themselves, have satisfying relationships, set realistic goals for themselves, and behave in healthful ways. Some people struggle with their mental health. They may have addictive behavior. Addictive behavior is behavior associated with repeated and continual connection with an activity or object that results in unhealthful effects on the person. These activities or objects may seem to have beneficial short-term effects but in the long run, they are harmful. Addictive behavior is compulsive; a person does not have control over it. In fact, a person who is addicted usually denies that the behavior is out of control. Kinds of addictions include codependence; money, clothes, shopping, and gambling addictions; workaholism;

are playing messages that interfere with positive self-esteem and with mental health.

EVALUATION

Have students make their own individual cassette tapes of positive internal messages that would contribute to their having positive self-esteem and mental health. These messages might be ones they hear or ones they would like to hear. The messages should include at least three of the ways to develop positive self-esteem that were stated in step 2. For example, a student might make a tape recording that says, "I have a good sense of humor. I am capable of doing well on tests. I keep a neat appearance. I am a member of the baseball team. I try my best." As students plan to make their cassette tapes of "Internal Messages," they may want to identify messages they want to reprogram. For example, a student who hears the internal message "I am safer if I keep my feelings to myself" will want to place a different message on the tape, such as, "It is safe to share my feelings with others." Ask students to listen to their tapes frequently. Remind them that it is important for some people to reprogram their internal messages to delete negative messages and learn new positive messages. Students can use the information in TM-26, "Practice Healthful Behaviors: A Health Behavior Contract," to complete this evaluation. The contract can serve as a guide in this task.

exercise addiction; relationship addiction; and eating disorders.

4 Further explain codependence. Codependence is a mental disorder in which a person loses personal identity, has frozen feelings, and copes ineffectively. The behavior of codependents is addictive. They usually learn and believe certain messages from their families. Review the transparency of the teaching master "Internal Messages Heard by People Who Are Codependent." Discuss why these messages interfere with self-esteem.

5 Explain that young people with positive self-esteem and who are mentally healthy have positive internal messages. It is as if a tape recording is playing inside their minds saying, "You are lovable. You are capable. You are trustworthy. It is safe to share your feelings. You can trust others." These messages are quite different than the messages that young people who are codependent hear. Their internal tapes

Teaching Master

Internal Messages Heard by People Who Are Codependent

"I would be better off continuing to behave the way that I am than attempting to deal with the dysfunction in my family."

"I am better off being dishonest because if I told others the truth, they might not like me."

"I am safer if I keep my feelings to myself."

"I am more comfortable being serious than playful and having fun."

"I cannot trust others."

"I should not talk to others about family problems."

"I do not deserve to be treated with respect."

"I should get others to believe that everything in my life is fine."

Family and Social Health

Mentor Match

HEALTH EDUCATION STANDARDS

- Students will analyze the influence of family, peers, culture, media, technology, and other factors on health behaviors.
- Students will demonstrate the ability to use interpersonal communication skills to enhance health and avoid or reduce health risks.

PERFORMANCE INDICATORS

- Analyze how family influences the health of individuals.
- Analyze the influence of personal values and beliefs on individual health practices and behaviors.
- Demonstrate how to ask for and offer assistance to enhance the health of self and others.

HEALTH GOALS

- I will develop healthful family relationships.
- I will work to improve difficult family relationships.

MATERIALS

Transparency of the teaching master "The Family Continuum"; transparency projector; puzzles made from the teaching master "Mentor Match"; cardboard paper; scissors; marker; paper; pencils; TM-11, "Use Communication Skills," Appendix A

MOTIVATION

1 Prepare for this strategy in the following ways. Divide the number of students in your class by six to determine the number of puzzles you will need to make. You will need to make six different sets of puzzles using the cardboard and scissors. Use a marker to outline the six pieces of each puzzle and to write the words on each of the six pieces. Make the first set of puzzles by cutting out the piece on the pattern labeled "A." Therefore, you will have a puzzle with one missing piece (refer to the illustration). Make the second set of puzzles by cutting out the piece on the pattern labeled "B," and continue until you have made the sixth set of puzzles by cutting out the piece on the pattern labeled "F."

2 Use the transparency of the teaching master "The Family Continuum" to review family relationships. Explain that family relationships are the connections one has with family members, including extended family members. Extended family members are family members in addition to parents, brothers, and sisters. The Family Continuum is a scale marked in units ranging from zero to one hundred that shows the quality of relationships within a family. A dysfunctional family is toward the zero end of the Family Continuum. A dysfunctional family is a family in which feelings are not expressed openly and honestly, coping skills are lacking, and family members do not trust each other. The quality of the relationships within a dysfunctional family is low. A healthful family is toward the one hundred end of the Family Continuum. A healthful family is a family in which feelings are expressed openly and honestly, coping skills are adequate, and family members trust each other. A family does not have to be at one end or the other of the continuum but could be somewhere in between. For example, a family might demonstrate some of the items listed under the dysfunctional family and at the same time demonstrate items listed under the healthful family.

3 Now divide the class into two groups. One group of students will consist of five-sixths of the class. Explain that they each will get a puzzle with a piece missing. Hand the puzzle to them with the blank side up. They will not see the outline of the pieces on the back. They will not read what the puzzles they are holding say. This group of students is to stand in one area of the classroom. The other one-sixth of the students are to be given one of the small puzzle pieces. Again, hand the pieces to the students with the blank side up. They are not to read the words on the other side. Explain to the students who are holding a puzzle with a missing piece that when you tell them to do so they are to find a student who has a small puzzle piece that will make their puzzle complete. They are to stand next to the person who has this piece. Allow an appropriate amount of time for students to find the matching pieces to their puzzles.

4 After students have found their matches, have them turn their puzzles over and read them. Explain the following. Each student who originally held the puzzle with a missing piece was holding a puzzle with five of the following six characteristics written on it: respect, trust, responsible behavior, no substance abuse, no violence, healthful communication. These students represented young people reared in families with many positive characteristics. Still, one of the characteristics of relationships in a healthful family was missing. Explain that you asked them to find another student who was holding the piece their puzzle was lacking in order to be whole. What you had asked them to do was to locate a person outside the family who might serve as a mentor. A mentor is a person who guides and helps a younger person. The mentor, or missing piece, they found to make their puzzle whole is a person who helps them learn the characteristic written on the piece. This characteristic makes them better equipped to have healthful relationships with others. Emphasize the importance mentors can play in teaching them how to have healthful relationships.

5 Have students return to their desks. Explain that the strategy they have done focused primarily on families that had healthful relationships. After all, these families demonstrated five of the six positive characteristics. Healthful relationships are relationships that enhance self-esteem, foster respect, develop character, and promote health-enhancing behavior and responsible decision making. Further explain that some young people are reared in dysfunctional families. They may have harmful relationships. Harmful relationships are relationships that threaten self-esteem, are disrespectful, indicate a lack of character, threaten health, and foster irresponsible decision making. Ask students what might have appeared on the six puzzle pieces for a dysfunctional family. They might answer lack of respect, distrust, irresponsible behavior, chemical dependency, violence, or harmful communication. Emphasize the importance of mentoring for young people reared in families with these characteristics.

6 Identify resources to improve relationships and family communication. Twelve-step programs focus on twelve steps that members take to recover from the past and gain wholeness. These programs change behavior by focusing on strengthening relationships—relationships with oneself, others, and one's personal beliefs. Getting professional help can also be an important step to recovery from harmful relationships. There are many different areas of mental health for which professional counseling programs are available.

EVALUATION

Have students develop individual Family Relationship Checklists. Their checklists should include ten characteristics of healthful families. Encourage students to include at least five characteristics from the Family Continuum. However, they might also include other characteristics they deem to be important. For example, a student might say, "Keeps a sense of humor." Explain that it is important that

Family and Social Health

students develop good communication skills. Use TM-11, "Use Communication Skills," to review steps to take to communicate effectively.

INCLUSION

Have students add characteristics to their Family Relationship Checklists that are especially important when family members have disabilities. For example, a student might say, "compassion" or "patience."

MULTICULTURAL INFUSION

Ask students to assess the Family Relationship Checklists they have developed and comment as to whether families with members of various cultures would select the same characteristics. Explain that families may differ in some ways; however, characteristics of healthful families seem to transcend the issue of culture.

Teaching Master
The Family Continuum

The Family Continuum depicts the degree to which a family promotes skills needed for loving and responsible relationships.

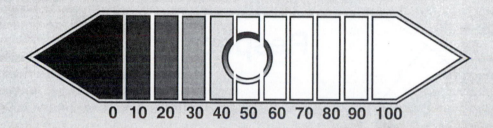

0 10 20 30 40 50 60 70 80 90 100

Dysfunctional Families   **Healthful Families**

Dysfunctional Families

1. Do not show respect for each other
2. Do not trust each other
3. Are confused about guidelines for responsible behavior
4. Are not punished or are punished severely for wrong behavior
5. Do not spend time with each other
6. Do not share feelings or do not share feelings in healthful ways
7. Do not have effective coping skills
8. Resolve conflicts with violence
9. Abuse alcohol and other substances
10. Abuse each other with words and actions

Healthful Families

1. Show respect for each other
2. Trust each other
3. Follow guidelines for responsible behavior
4. Experience consequences when they do not follow guidelines
5. Spend time with each other
6. Share feelings in healthful ways
7. Practice effective coping skills
8. Resolve conflict in nonviolent ways
9. Avoid alcohol and other substances
10. Use kind words and actions

Mentor Match

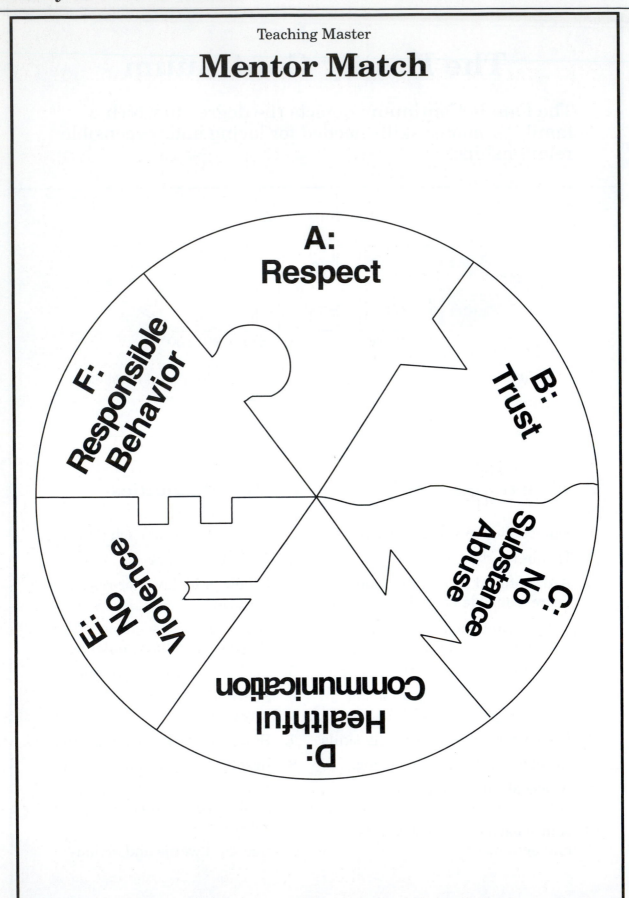

Critical Thinker

OPTIONAL TEACHING STRATEGY:
NAME THE BIRTH CONTROL METHOD

Examining facts about birth control methods helps teens prepare for adulthood when they might choose to marry and plan a family. Abstinence is the expected standard for teens. Abstinence reduces the risk of infection with HIV and other STDs and prevents pregnancy.

HEALTH EDUCATION STANDARD

- Students will demonstrate the ability to practice health-enhancing behaviors and avoid or reduce health risks.

PERFORMANCE INDICATOR

- Analyze the role of individual responsibility for enhancing health.

HEALTH GOAL

- I will learn about birth control methods.

MATERIALS

- Thirty-two index cards; TM-3, "Comprehend Health Concepts," Appendix A

MOTIVATION

1 Find a sentence in any textbook you may have on your desk. Open to any page and write one sentence from this book on the chalkboard. Then close the book and ask for a volunteer. Have this student come to the front of the room and tell him or her to open up the book and find this sentence. Obviously this student will not be capable of finding it. Then open up the book to the page in which this sentence appears and then ask the student to find the sentence by pointing to the paragraph in which this sentence appears. The student will then find the sentence.

2 Explain to the class that when information is not present, it is difficult to complete a successful action. Emphasize that having information about a task is important because this information serves as a guide. Tell students that they will learn about birth control. The information they will learn about birth control will help guide students to decisions they will make when they are responsible adults.

3 Take sixteen index cards and write the name of one birth-control method on each card. On another set of sixteen cards, write a fact about each. You will need a total of thirty-two cards. These methods and facts are as follows:

- *Combination pill.* A pill that combines estrogen and progesterone to change the natural menstrual cycle and to prevent ovulation. The combination pill differs from the progestin-only pill, or mini-pill, in that it contains estrogen. A female will resume her natural menstrual cycle if she stops taking the combination pill.
- *Progestin-only pill.* A pill that contains progesterone, which changes the natural menstrual cycle and prevents ovulation. The progestin-only pill differs from the combination pill in that it contains only a small dose of progestin and no estrogen. A female will resume her natural menstrual cycle if she stops taking the progestin-only pill.
- *Injectable progestin.* A shot of synthetic progesterone that is given every three months to change the natural menstrual cycle and to prevent ovulation.
- *Subdermal implants.* Flexible plastic tubes that are inserted under the skin in the upper arm and that release progestin.
- *Spermicides.* A foam, cream, jelly, film, or suppository that forms a barrier and contains a chemical that might kill some sperm.

- *Diaphragm.* A dome-shaped cup that fits over the cervix to provide a barrier to help prevent sperm from entering the uterus.
- *Cervical cap.* A rubber or plastic dome that fits snugly over the cervix to provide a barrier to help prevent sperm from entering the uterus.
- *Male condom.* A thin sheath of latex, natural skin, or polyurethane that is placed over the erect penis to collect semen during ejaculation.
- *Female condom.* A soft polyurethane pouch that is inserted deep into the vagina to collect semen during ejaculation.
- *Intrauterine device.* A small device that fits inside the uterus and helps prevent pregnancy.
- *Basal body temperature.* A birth control method in which a female uses her basal body temperature to predict ovulation.
- *Calendar method.* A birth control method in which a female records the length of her menstrual cycle on a calendar to predict her fertile period.
- *Mucous method.* The female records the changes in the mucous discharge from her vagina to predict her fertile period.
- *Tubal ligation.* A surgical procedure in which the fallopian tubes are closed off, cauterized, or cut.
- *Vasectomy.* A surgical procedure in which the vas deferens is cut, tied, or cauterized.

- *Douche.* The use of a solution to rinse out the vagina.

4 Select thirty-two students for this task. If you have fewer than thirty-two students, use fewer cards. Tell students they are not to talk at all. Tell students that they are to match with a partner by pairing the birth control method to the birth control fact. After they complete this task, have them introduce each other by asking them to name their birth control method, and then the partner will state the fact on his or her card.

EVALUATION

Review TM-3, "Comprehend Health Concepts," and do the following. Collect the thirty-two index cards and mix them up. Lay them on the floor, and have each student select a card. Have students take turns reading their cards. For example, one student will say the name of a birth control method. The student who has the appropriate match is to stand and then read his or her card, and the class is to determine if there is a correct match. You can also ask that with each initial card read, two students are to stand but only one would be the correct match. The class has to identify the correct match.

Growth and Development

GRADES 9–12

Snapping Back

HEALTH EDUCATION STANDARD

- Students will demonstrate the ability to advocate for personal, family, and community health.

PERFORMANCE INDICATORS

- Demonstrate how to influence and support others to make positive health choices.
- Work cooperatively as an advocate for improving personal, family, and community health.

HEALTH GOALS

- I will achieve developmental tasks of adolescence.
- I will develop healthful friendships. (Family and Social Health)
- I will recognize harmful relationships.

MATERIALS

Two rubber bands (short in length); two pencils; chalk; chalkboard; TM-3, "Comprehend Health Concepts," Appendix A

MOTIVATION

1 Explain to students that they are in a growth spurt. During this growth spurt, they are changing in many ways. There are mental-emotional, physical, and family-social changes. Define developmental tasks. Developmental tasks are achievements that must be made during a particular period of growth so that a person can continue growing toward maturity.

2 Identify one of the important developmental tasks of adolescence: task 4, achieving emotional independence from parents and other adults. Use the following illustration to clarify the meaning of this task. Take one of the pencils. Place the rubber band so that one end is touching a side of the pencil while the other end is not (see illustration). Explain that during adolescence, young people want to pull away from their parents. Begin to pull one end of the rubber band away from the pencil. Explain that this "pulling away" is natural and healthful. For adolescents to achieve emotional independence from parents and other adults, they must pull away.

3 Pull one end of the rubber band a little bit more. Then let it go so that it snaps back and hits the pencil. Explain that after a period of pulling away, adolescents often feel the need to "snap back." They will want to be very close to their parents. They will want their advice, help, and support. This is what adult intimacy is about—being independent and having feelings of closeness. Adolescents develop the ability to behave in this way over time. This is why "achieving emotional independence from one's parents" is considered a developmental task of adolescence.

4 Repeat the demonstration three times. As you repeat the demonstration, explain interdependence. Interdependence is a condition in which two people depend on each other yet have separate identities. During adolescence, they are learning to depend more on themselves, yet they still depend on their parents and other adults. Further explain that this can be confusing and trying at times. During this period, they may struggle with parents or other adults rearing them. At times, they will exert too much independence, and the adults will pull them back. At other times, they will want to depend heavily on parents. This is a part of growing to emotional maturity.

5 Further explain that this is also a growing period for their parents. Their parents are adjusting to them pulling away and snapping back. At times, their parents will want the closeness when they do not. At other times, their parents may expect

them to make adultlike decisions, and they may or may not count on parents to make the decisions. These adjustments in the parent-child relationship are necessary for adolescents to develop emotional maturity.

6 Now take the other pencil and wrap a rubber band very tightly around it (see illustration). Explain that this is another kind of parent-child relationship. Notice that the rubber band is wrapped so tightly around the pencil that it cannot pull away. Explain that this is not a healthful parent-child relationship. This is enmeshment. Enmeshment is a condition in which the identities of two people in a relationship have blended into one whereby at least one of the people cannot see himself or herself as having a separate identity. In the case of a parent-child relationship, either the parent or the child cannot see himself or herself as having a separate identity.

7 Ask one of the students to try to pull away the rubber band from the pencil. It will not be easy to do so. Explain that one or both people feel "strangled" when there is no opportunity to pull away and snap back. It is difficult for adolescents in this kind of parent-child relationship to have a sense of their own feelings. They become too

wrapped up in what the parents think and feel. Use the following example:

> A father was frustrated that he was not a good athlete. When his son was an adolescent, he began to pressure his son to excel in athletics. He wanted to live his dreams through his son's accomplishments. After a while, the son had difficulty knowing whether he really enjoyed playing football. He could not pull away and see whether he was playing football for his own enjoyment. He was so enmeshed with his father that his inner self was giving him the messages that his father was giving him: "To be worthwhile, you must be a good athlete."

It is impossible to be enmeshed and to master task 4, achieving emotional independence from parents and other adults. During adolescence, young people separate their thoughts and feelings from those of their parents. This does not mean that they will not have similar beliefs and attitudes to parents. It means that adolescents learn to own their own beliefs and attitudes.

8 Explain that the kind of parent-child relationship that was just illustrated was codependent. A person is codependent when she or he has no sense of personal identity. There are many resources to improve relationships and family communication, such as twelve-step programs and individual counseling.

9 Using chalk, list all eight developmental tasks on the chalkboard and discuss each task.

Task 1: Achieving a new and more mature relationship with age mates of both sexes.

Task 2: Achieving a masculine or feminine social role.

Task 3: Accepting one's physique.

Task 4: Achieving emotional independence from parents and other adults.

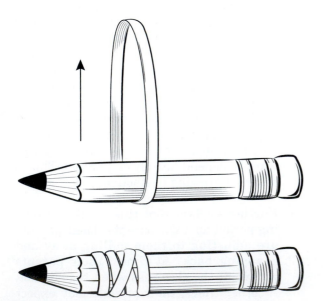

Task 5: Preparing for marriage and family life.

Task 6: Preparing for an economic career.

Task 7: Acquiring a set of values and an ethical system as a guide to behavior—developing an ideology.

Task 8: Developing a social consequence.

EVALUATION

Use TM-3, "Comprehend Health Concepts," to show students the importance of using health knowledge. Have students keep individual relationship journals for a week. Each day, have them write in their journals. They should describe times when they needed to pull away from parents or other significant adults responsible for rearing them. They should write the feelings they experienced during these times. They also should describe times when they wanted a special closeness with parents or other significant adults responsible for rearing them. They should write about the feelings they experienced during these times. Allow students to maintain privacy and confidentiality. Do not collect their journals. However, at the end of the week ask them to write a one- to two-page paper describing the importance and difficulty of mastering the developmental task of "Achieving emotional independence from one's parents." They are to include a discussion of how mastering this task will help them to prepare for future relationship choices. They also are to discuss ways that too much dependence or too little intimacy interferes with relationships. They might identify one place in the community that provides resources to improve family relationships. In addition, ask them to discuss one of the other developmental tasks covered in class.

GRADES 9–12

Name That Food

HEALTH EDUCATION STANDARDS

- Students will demonstrate the ability to advocate for personal, family, and community health.
- Students will demonstrate the ability to practice health-enhancing behaviors and avoid or reduce health risks.
- Students will demonstrate the ability to access valid information and products and services to enhance health.

PERFORMANCE INDICATORS

- Work cooperatively as an advocate for improving personal, family, and community health.
- Demonstrate a variety of behaviors to avoid or reduce health risks to self and others.
- Access valid and reliable health products and services.

HEALTH GOALS

- I will evaluate food labels.
- I will follow a healthful diet that reduces my risk of disease.
- I will make a plan to manage my time and money. (Consumer and Community Health)

MATERIALS

Transparency of teaching master "Name That Food"; transparency projector; chalk; chalkboard; marker; three grocery bags; purple and white licorice candy; artificial coffee sweetener; canned cat food; several food labels; paper; pencils; TM-9, "Access Valid Health Information, Products, and Services," Appendix A

MOTIVATION

1 To prepare for this strategy, use the marker to label the grocery bags. Label the first bag "1," the second "2," and the third "3." Place the purple and white licorice candy in the first grocery bag. Place the artificial coffee sweetener in the second grocery bag. Place the can of cat food in the third grocery bag. You may want to ask students to collect food labels from empty cans or cartons and bring them to class.

2 Use the transparency of the teaching master "Name That Food." Explain to students that they are going to play Name That Food. Tell the students that they are on a deserted island and they have three choices of foods to eat: food number 1, food number 2, and food number 3. You are going to give them a few minutes to choose one of these foods by examining the list of ingredients for each. You also want them to name the food after examining the ingredients.

3 After students have had time to examine the teaching master, write the following on the chalkboard: 1, 2, and 3. Then ask for a show of hands. Ask students how many of them would choose food number 1. Record the number next to the 1. Ask how many students would choose food number 2. Record the number next to the 2. Ask how many students would choose food number 3. Record the number next to the number 3.

4 Place the three grocery bags in view of the students. Begin with bag number 1. Ask students to name the food in this grocery bag. Have a student take the food out of the bag and show it to the class (purple and white licorice candy). Ask students to name the food in grocery bag number 2. Have a student take the food out of the bag and show it to the class (artificial coffee sweetener). Ask students to name the food in grocery bag number 3. Have a student take the food out of the bag and show it to the class (canned cat food). Many students will be surprised at the selections.

5 Ask students the basis for their food selections. They will respond that they made their selections based on the ingredients in the foods. Emphasize the importance of food labels. Food labels are designed to assist consumers with making healthful food choices. Food manufacturers must provide nutritional information that will be accurate, complete, and useful to consumers.

6 Give students copies of food labels. Have them look at the food labels as you explain the following. The title of the label is *Nutrition Facts*. The required information includes the following, always in this order:

- Total calories
- Calories from fat
- Total fat
- Saturated fat
- Cholesterol
- Sodium
- Total carbohydrates
- Dietary fiber
- Sugars
- Protein
- Vitamin A
- Vitamin C
- Calcium
- Iron

7 Explain that food manufacturers must list all the ingredients by weight in their products, beginning with the one that is present in the greatest amount. People should read the ingredients list carefully to determine the true amount of an ingredient. Further explain that by reading the food label and the list of ingredients, people can make food selections that reduce the risk of disease. For example, diet plays a major factor in the risk of heart disease. Diets high in fat and saturated fat increase the risk of heart disease. Vitamins C, E, and A may lower the risk of heart disease. Diets high in fat content also increase the risk of certain types of cancer. Diets that contain fiber and vitamins A and C tend to lower the risk of cancer.

8 Write the following words on the chalkboard: low fat, low calorie, lean, reduced, good source, and low sodium. Have students write the following definitions for each.

- *Low fat*—Three grams or less per serving
- *Low calorie*—Forty calories or less per serving
- *Lean*—Less than 10 grams of fat
- *Reduced*—25 percent less of a nutrient or of calories than the regular product
- *Good source*—One serving contains 10 to 19 percent of the daily value for a particular nutrient
- *Low sodium*—140 milligrams or less per serving

EVALUATION

Have each student write a Top Ten List of Reasons to read food labels. Their lists should include information as to what they will learn from reading food labels, such as "to learn the number of calories from fat." Their lists might also include benefits from reading food labels, such as "to spend money wisely" and "to reduce my risk of cancer." Check their lists for accuracy. Have students share their lists with the class. Then have students select a label from the back of a cereal box. They are to use TM-9, "Access Valid Health Information and Products and Services," to determine the validity of the cereal as it relates to promoting health.

Teaching Master

Name That Food

1 sugar, corn syrup, wheat flour, molasses, caramel color, licorice extract, corn starch, salt, artificial colors (including yellow #6), resinous glaze, anise oil, canuba wax, artificial flavors

2 corn syrup solids, partially hydrogenated vegetable oil, (may contain one or more of the following oils: coconut, cottonseed, palm, palm kernel, safflower, or soybean), sodium caseinate, mono- and di-glycerides (prevent oil separation), dipotassium phosphate, artificial flavor, and annato color

3 tuna, water sufficent for processing, vegetable oil, dicalcium phosphate, sodium tripolyphosphate, tricalcium phosphate, sodium chloride, vitamins A, B_1, B_6, E, and D_3 supplements, zinc sulfate, menadione soduim bisulfide, manganous sulfate, sodium nitrite, folic acid

Personal Health and Physical Activity

GRADES 9–12

Turn Off the Tube and MOVE!

HEALTH EDUCATION STANDARDS

- Students will demonstrate the ability to use goal-setting skills to enhance health.
- Students will demonstrate the ability to practice health-enhancing behaviors and avoid or reduce health risks.

PERFORMANCE INDICATORS

- Assess personal health practices and overall health status.
- Develop a plan to attain a personal health goal that addresses strengths, needs, and risks.
- Implement strategies and monitor progress in achieving a personal health goal.
- Analyze the role of individual responsibility for enhancing health.

HEALTH GOALS

- I will participate in regular physical-activity.
- I will develop and maintain health- and skill-related fitness.
- I will choose behaviors to reduce my risk of cardiovascular diseases. (Communicable and Chronic Diseases)
- I will choose behaviors to reduce my risk of cancer. (Communicable and Chronic Diseases)
- I will practice protective factors to reduce the risk of violence. (Injury Prevention and Safety)
- I will maintain a desirable weight and body composition. (Nutrition)

MATERIALS

Transparency of student master "Facts about Exercise" (optional); student master "Commitment to Exercise: Health Behavior Contract"; transparency projector (optional); five large index cards; notebook paper; pencils or pens; tape; TM-23, "Set Health Goals," Appendix A

MOTIVATION

1 To prepare for this strategy, reproduce the student master "Facts about Exercise." Cut the paper into five pieces so that each of the five facts about exercises are separate. Tape each to an index card.

2 Divide the class into five groups. Give each group an index card. Explain that each group is to identify three television programs that adolescents watch. The three programs are to be entertaining, not educational. After the groups identify the three programs, they are to create a news story that will be used to interrupt one of the programs. The news story will focus on the latest facts about exercise. Each group has an index card that contains facts that it can use to create an informative and creative news story. The entire group can be part of the news story or the group can design the news story and one or more group members can present it. Allow an appropriate amount of time for the groups to develop their news stories.

3 Have each group present its news story in the following manner. One group member is to tell the class the name of a popular television show. Students in the class are to pretend they are viewing this show. Then the same member or another member of the group is to say, "We interrupt . . . (name of show) . . . to bring you the latest reasons why you should "Turn off the tube and MOVE!" Then the group is to present its creative and informative news story. Have each group present its news story in this way.

4 After each group has presented its news story, review the facts about exercise that were presented. Ask students to take notes using notebook paper. You may choose to make a transparency of the student master "Facts about Exercise," although you can conduct a review without doing so.

5 Make a copy of the student master "Commitment to Exercise: Health Behavior

NEWS FLASH!

five components of physical fitness. Collect their journals to assess the benefits of exercise that they have identified. Students can also use TM-23, "Set Health Goals," in planning an exercise program.

INCLUSION

Have students with physical disabilities identify exercises they can do for each of the five components of physical fitness. If possible, invite a professional specializing in adaptive physical education to work with them on their physical fitness plans. Be certain that these plans have the support of parents, guardians, and other health professionals.

MULTICULTURAL INFUSION

Divide students into groups. Allow each group to select a foreign country. The groups should research information about the exercise habits of people living in the country selected. What factors influence the exercise choices? For example, people from Switzerland may choose snow skiing as a form of exercise because of the proximity of the Alps.

Contract" for each student or use a transparency of this student master and have students copy it. Review the five components of physical fitness that are defined in the "Effect on My Well-Being" paragraph. Have the class brainstorm examples of exercises that improve each of the five components of physical fitness. Set a date for students to complete this Health Behavior Contract.

EVALUATION

Collect the Health Behavior Contracts. Review them to evaluate whether or not students have identified exercises that develop each of the

Facts about Exercise

EXERCISE. . .

Strengthens the heart muscle.
Regular exercise strengthens the heart muscle and increases cardiac output. Cardiac output is the amount of blood pumped by the heart to the body each minute. Another way to say this is cardiac output is equal to the heart rate multiplied by the stroke volume. Heart rate is the number of times that the heart beats each minute forcing blood into the arteries. Stroke volume is the amount of blood the heart pumps with each beat. When the heart muscle is strong, the heart pumps more blood with each beat. This lowers resting heart rate and allows the heart to rest between beats. This is accompanied by lower resting blood pressure. There is less wear and tear on the arteries.

Increases the ratio of HDLs to LDLs.
Exercises that strengthen the heart muscle increase the ratio of HDLs to LDLs in the bloodstream. Lipoproteins are fats in the bloodstream. High-density lipoproteins or HDLs are fats that transport excess cholesterol to the liver for removal from the body. Low-density lipoproteins are fats that form deposits on the artery walls and contribute to the development of atherosclerosis.

Reduces the risk of chronic diseases.
Regular vigorous exercise reduces the risk of breast cancer, especially when a regular exercise routine is begun before adulthood. Regular physical activity also appears to reduce the risk of heart disease, diabetes, and osteoporosis

Helps control the effects of stress.
Regular exercise helps reduce stress by generating overall feelings of well-being. It uses the adrenaline that is secreted during the stress response and that causes an increase in heart rate and blood pressure. When a person continues a vigorous exercise program for at least three times per week for seven to ten weeks, his or her body secretes beta-endorphins. Beta-endorphins are substances produced in the brain that help reduce pain and create a feeling of well-being. Regular exercise also reduces feelings of anger and thereby lessens the likelihood that someone will act out and be violent when feeling stressed.

Promotes weight management.
The energy equation states that caloric intake needs to equal caloric expenditure for weight maintenance. A regular program of exercise changes the energy equation. During exercise, more calories are expended. People who exercise tend to burn more calories and eat less. Their bodies are leaner.

Improves female reproductive health.
Females who exercise regularly have milder menstrual cramps and shorter menstrual periods. They are less likely to feel sad or depressed during their periods.

Commitment to Exercise: Health Behavior Contract

Life Skill: I will achieve a desirable level of physical fitness.

Effect on My Well-Being: Physical fitness is the condition of the body as a result of participating in exercises that develop muscular strength, muscular endurance, flexibility, cardiovascular endurance, and a healthful percentage of body fat. Muscular strength is the amount of force the muscles can exert against resistance. Muscular endurance is the ability to use muscles for an extended period of time. Flexibility is the ability to bend and move the joints through a full range of motion. Cardiovascular endurance is the ability to do activities that require increased oxygen intake for extended periods of time. Healthful body composition is a high ratio of lean tissue to fat tissue. Physical activity and fitness strengthens the heart muscle, increases the ratio of HDLs to LDLs, reduces the risk of chronic disease, helps control the effects of stress, provides a physical outlet for angry feelings reducing the risk of violent behavior, promotes weight management, and improves female reproductive health.

My Plan: I will identify exercises I can do each day for one week for the different components of fitness.

Muscular strength:_____

Muscular endurance:_____

Flexibility: _____

Cardiovascular endurance:_____

Lean and trim body:_____

Evaluating Progress: I will develop a progress chart showing the exercises I will do each day during the week and recording whether or not I did them.

Results: I will keep a journal in which I write about my efforts to follow my plan. I will identify obstacles to doing my exercises as well as benefits. I will describe any modifications I need to make to my plan.

My Signature:

_____

GRADES 9–12

Sloppy Joe

HEALTH EDUCATION STANDARDS

- Students will demonstrate the ability to use goal-setting skills to enhance health.
- Students will demonstrate the ability to practice health-enhancing behaviors and avoid or reduce health risks.

PERFORMANCE INDICATORS

- Assess personal health practices and overall health status.
- Analyze the role of individual responsibility for enhancing health.

HEALTH GOALS

- I will not drink alcohol.
- I will choose a drug-free lifestyle to reduce the risk of HIV infection and unplanned pregnancy.
- I will make responsible decisions. (Mental and Emotional Health)
- I will choose to practice abstinence. (Family and Social Health)
- I will practice protective factors to reduce the risk of violence. (Injury Prevention and Safety)

MATERIALS

Transparency of the teaching master "Drugs and Sexuality"; transparency projector; watch with a second hand; paper; pencils; computers and computer paper (optional); TM-20, "Use the Responsible Decision-Making Model," Appendix A

MOTIVATION

1 Use the following activity to demonstrate to students how alcohol affects reaction time. First, have students use their dominant hand and write, "I will not drink alcohol" in script on a sheet of paper while you time their efforts. It will take them approximately ten to twelve seconds.

2 Now tell them to imagine that they did not follow this life skill. They drank alcohol at a party with peers. Then, have students use their other hand to write, "I will not drink alcohol," in script on the same sheet of paper while you time their efforts. It will take them approximately thirty to thirty-six seconds, or three times as long.

3 Discuss the results. Students should mention that after drinking alcohol they were not able to write as quickly or as neatly. In fact, each one became a "Sloppy Joe" or "Sloppy Josephine" when it came to writing ability. Explain that drinking alcohol results in a slower reaction time. Reaction time is the amount of time it takes to respond to a stimulus. Ask them to identify problems that may occur because of slowed reaction time. They might mention automobile accidents, injuries when playing sports, pedestrian accidents, and falls.

4 Then ask students to identify other ways that drinking alcohol affects the body. Mention the following:

- *Causes liver damage.* Cirrhosis is a disease in which alcohol destroys liver cells and plugs the liver with fibrous scar

759

tissue and can lead to liver failure and death.

- *Leads to abnormal heart functioning.* Cardiomyopathy is a degeneration of the heart muscle that is characterized by severe enlargement of the heart and inability of the damaged heart to pump blood effectively. Cardiac arrhythmia is an irregular heartbeat. Chronic alcohol consumption is also associated with a significant increase in high blood pressure and stroke.

- *Harms the stomach, mouth, and esophagus.* Alcohol injures the inner lining of the stomach, especially when combined with aspirin. It may cause inflammation of the esophagus and make existing peptic ulcers worse.

- *Causes pancreatitis.* Pancreatitis is inflammation of the pancreas that increases the risk of diabetes.

- *Causes neurological changes.* Heavy alcohol consumption may cause dementia, blackouts, seizures, hallucinations, and nerve destruction throughout the body. Alcohol dementia is brain impairment that is characterized by overall intellectual decline due to the direct toxic effects of alcohol.

- *May result in alcoholism.* Alcoholism is a complex disease that is characterized by a preoccupation with drinking alcohol that has progressed to serious physical, social, occupational, or family consequences for an individual.

- *During pregnancy, may cause fetal alcohol syndrome.* Fetal alcohol syndrome (FAS) is a characteristic pattern of severe birth defects present in babies born to mothers who drink alcohol during their pregnancy. Among the abnormalities are small eye slits, small head circumference, facial abnormalities, growth retardation, and mental retardation.

5 Use the following activity to demonstrate to students how alcohol affects decision making. Have students use their dominant hand and write, "I will not be sexually ac-

tive," in script on a sheet of paper while you time their efforts. It will take them approximately fifteen seconds.

6 Now have them imagine that they decided to drink alcohol. Then they were in a situation in which they were encouraged to be sexually active. Have students use their other hand to write, "I will not be sexually active," in script on the same sheet of paper while you time their efforts. It will take them approximately three times as long and their writing will be sloppy.

7 Process what happened. Explain that after drinking alcohol, it is difficult to respond quickly with the life skill. After drinking alcohol, their decision making is sloppy. It was not as clear that they were not going to be sexually active. Further explain that alcohol impairs the ability to think clearly and reduces inhibitions and defenses. People under the influence of alcohol have more difficulty sticking to the choices they have made for themselves and for their bodies. Alcohol use increases the risk of choosing behaviors that result in HIV infections, other STDs, and pregnancy because of impaired judgment. Alcohol use increases the risk of violence including sexual assault, suicide, and homicide because of impaired judgment. An alcohol-free mind is a protective factor against making unwise choices.

8 Use a transparency of the teaching master "Drugs and Sexuality" to review the importance of being alcohol-free and drug-free. If you do not want to make a transparency, you can discuss the information on this teaching master with students while they take notes.

EVALUATION

Have students design a one-page graphic that is an adaptation of the Wellness Scale showing a range of health from zero to one hundred. They are to provide their own clever title, such as "The Alcohol and Other Drug Scale." At the

Alcohol, Tobacco, and Other Drugs

zero end of the scale, they might use descriptors such as *liver damage, pancreatitis, sexual assault,* or *HIV infection*. At the one-hundred end of the scale, they might use descriptors such as *reduces risk of HIV infection, responsible decisions,* or *mental alertness*. Explain to students that after completing this task they will be asked to share their scales with the class. As they explain their scales, they must show information covering the following five life skills:

- I will not drink alcohol.
- I will choose a drug-free lifestyle to reduce the risk of HIV infection and unplanned pregnancy.
- I will make responsible decisions.
- I will practice abstinence.
- I will choose behaviors to reduce my risk of violence.

If computers are available at your school or students have them in their homes, you may want to have them design their scales using computer graphics. Ask students to imagine they are in a situation in which they are being pressured to drink alcohol. Show TM-20, "Use the Responsible Decision-Making Model," to determine how to resist the pressure to drink.

Teaching Master

Drugs and Sexuality

You can choose behaviors to reduce the likelihood that you will become infected with HIV and other STDs. You can choose behaviors to avoid becoming a teenage parent. You can choose behaviors to reduce the likelihood that you will be sexually assaulted or sexually assault another. Responsible behaviors include the following:

1. Be involved in activities that promote self-worth.

2. Establish goals.

3. Develop loving family relationships.

4. When family relationships are not strong, select a mentor who is alcohol-free and drug-free and who has clear values.

5. Select friends who are alcohol-free, drug-free, and choose to wait to have sex.

6. Select people to date who are alcohol-free, drug-free, and choose to wait to have sex.

7. Avoid being in situations and going to parties where there will be alcohol and other drugs.

8. Avoid being in situations where sexual feelings will be intense and you will be tempted to be sexually active.

9. Discuss pressure-packed situations, and get advice from trusted adults.

10. Choose entertainment carefully, and avoid movies, soap operas, music, and magazines that glamorize sex and drugs.

Communicable and Chronic Diseases

GRADES 9–12

Just One Look

SCIENCE STUDIES

SELF-DIRECTED LEARNER

HEALTH EDUCATION STANDARDS

- Students will comprehend concepts related to health promotion and disease prevention to enhance health.
- Students will demonstrate the ability to practice health-enhancing behaviors and avoid or reduce health risks.

PERFORMANCE INDICATORS

- Propose ways to reduce or prevent injuries and health problems.
- Compare and contrast the benefits of and barriers to practicing a variety of healthy behaviors.
- Demonstrate a variety of behaviors to avoid or reduce health risks to self and others.

HEALTH GOALS

- I will choose behaviors to reduce my risk of cancer.
- I will have regular examinations. (Personal Health and Physical Activity)

MATERIALS

Transparency of the teaching master "Cancer Clues"; transparency projector; several pairs of sunglasses; material to clean germs from sunglasses; several large mirrors; paper; markers; TM-3, "Comprehend Health Concepts," Appendix A

MOTIVATION

1 To prepare for this strategy, collect several pairs of sunglasses and mirrors, or ask students to bring sunglasses and mirrors to class. Be certain that when the sunglasses are worn, at least one pair is dark enough so that it is difficult to see the eyes through the lenses. Do not tell students that there is a difference in the darkness of the sunglasses or they may have a clue as to the purpose of this strategy.

2 Explain to students that you are going to have a sunglasses fashion show. Students can wear the sunglasses they have brought to class. If a student wears a pair of sunglasses you or another student has brought, be certain to clean the glasses before they are worn. The sunglasses fashion show will proceed as follows. Each student wearing sunglasses will parade in front of the class modeling the sunglasses for a few moments. The class will get "just one look" to determine how stylish the sunglasses are.

3 After each student wearing sunglasses has had a chance to parade in front of the class, have the class vote to determine which sunglasses they liked the best. Ask students to share the criteria they used for making their decisions. For example, they might say, "I liked metal frames," or "I liked the shape of the sunglasses," or "The sunglasses are the latest fashion."

4 Explain that there is an important factor to consider when choosing sunglasses. The sunglasses should block out ultraviolet radiation. Have students use the mirrors. Then ask them to look into the mirrors. Sunglasses should be dark enough to prevent the eyes from easily being seen. If not, they allow too much ultraviolet radiation through and the eyes may be damaged. Have each student who modeled the sunglasses stand and share with the class whether or not the sunglasses they mod-

eled blocked ultraviolet radiation. Emphasize the importance of wearing sunglasses that are dark enough to protect against ultraviolet radiation. Sunglasses should absorb at least 95 percent of UV-B rays and at least 65 percent of UV-A rays. Encourage students to purchase sunglasses that are rated by the American National Standards Institute (ANSI). ANSI ratings are determined by the amount of damaging UV rays that can penetrate the lens. Sunglasses rated "general purpose" are safe for most people, while "special purpose" should be worn by those participating in sports for long periods of time. Discuss wearing sunglasses when exercising outdoors.

5 Explain that ultraviolet radiation is also a cause of skin cancer. There is a definite link between exposure to ultraviolet radiation, whether from the sun's rays or tanning beds, and the development of skin cancer. Despite warnings, an estimated 1 million Americans are diagnosed with skin cancer each year (American Cancer Society 2007, National Cancer Institute, 2007). Side effects reported include burns, itching, dry skin, and nausea. Some young people go to tanning salons before taking a trip to a sunny area to get a base tan to protect their skin. However, the level of sun protection a salon "base tan" provides is the equivalent of wearing a sunscreen with a protective factor of 4, which is not enough protection from ultraviolet radiation. Recent studies suggest a higher likelihood of skin cancer for those who tan in the sun and with sunlamps than for those who are exposed to the sun only (American Cancer Society, 2007). There is now evidence that exposure to ultraviolet radiation is responsible for **malignant melanoma,** the most invasive of skin cancers.

6 Use the transparency of the teaching master "Cancer Clues" to review causes of cancer, the warning signs, and the kinds of treatment.

EVALUATION

Divide students into groups to design magazine advertisements for sunglasses. They are to design fashionable sunglasses. Their advertisements must creatively inform consumers that sunglasses must be worn to block ultraviolet radiation. They must encourage consumers to wear sunglasses when exercising outdoors. In a clever way, they can offer a free sunscreen containing an SPF of at least 15 with the purchase of a pair of sunglasses. Have students design individual crossword puzzles titled "Cancer Clues" using the information they recall from the teaching master with the same name. For example, a word in the crossword puzzle might be "bleeding" and the clue might be "a warning sign." Their individual crossword puzzles should contain at least ten facts from the teaching master. Have students identify a health fact. Then have them form a concept from this fact. Use TM-3, "Comprehend Health Concepts," to complete this task.

INCLUSION

Discuss the relationship between the development of cataracts and overexposure to ultraviolet radiation. A cataract is a clouding of the lens of the eye that obstructs vision and can lead to blindness. It is now believed that people who have not protected their eyes from ultraviolet radiation over the years are at increased risk of becoming visually impaired because of cataracts.

INCLUSION

You might also choose to have students paired for cooperative learning when developing the crossword puzzles to evaluate their recall of the "Cancer Clues" on the teaching master. Or you may choose to copy the teaching master for specific students and allow them to use it as they design their crossword puzzles.

Teaching Master

Cancer Clues

Causes of Cancer

Heredity
- Cancers of the breast, ovary, pancreas, and colon appear to run in families.

Viruses
- There is some link between viruses and the development of certain kinds of cancers such as leukemia.

Tobacco
- People who smoke cigarettes and use smokeless tobacco have an increased risk of developing cancer.
- According to one study, males who begin smoking during adolescence are twice as likely to develop lung cancer; females who begin at age twenty-five or younger are three times as likely.

Ultraviolet Radiation
- There is a definite link between exposure to ultraviolet radiation, whether from the sun's rays or tanning beds, and the development of cancer, especially skin cancer.

The Warning Signs

C hange in bowel or bladder habits

A sore that does not heal

U nusual bleeding or discharge

T hickening or lump in a breast or elsewhere

I ndigestion or difficulty swallowing

O bvious change in a wart or mole

N agging cough or hoarseness

Kinds of Treatment

Surgery
- The most common treatment method.
- Used to confine cancer to a particular site.

Radiotherapy
- X-rays are used kill cancer cells.

Chemotherapy
- The use of drugs to kill cancer cells inside the body.

Combination
- Any combination of surgery, radiotherapy, and chemotherapy.

Consumer and Community Health

GRADES 9–12

Health Fair

HEALTH EDUCATION STANDARDS

- Students will demonstrate the ability to access valid information and products and services to enhance health.
- Students will demonstrate the ability to advocate for personal, family, and community health.

PERFORMANCE INDICATORS

- Evaluate the validity of health information, products, and services.
- Utilize resources from home, school, and community that provide valid health information.
- Demonstrate how to influence and support others to make positive health choices.

HEALTH GOALS

- I will investigate public and international health needs.
- I will make responsible choices about health care providers and facilities.

MATERIALS

School board approval for having a health fair; parental permission for student participation in a health fair; a list of local agencies that are willing to participate; paper; pencils; chalk; TM-31, "Be a Health Advocate," Appendix A

MOTIVATION

1 Allow two months to plan and prepare for this strategy. Careful planning will include the following:

- Obtaining school board approval for having a health fair involving students and voluntary and public health agencies.
- Obtaining parental permission for student participation in the health fair.

- Securing a place and date for the health fair such as the school cafeteria, gymnasium, or a place in the community such as a shopping center or supermarket.
- Identifying voluntary health agencies that are willing to participate and work with students to deliver the health fair. (Refer to the Health Resource Guide for ideas.)
- Making and reproducing a copy of a list of the health agencies that are willing to participate, contact person, address, and telephone number. (Have this list approved by the appropriate people in your school district such as your school board to eliminate any conflicts of interest or controversy.)
- Arranging for a contact person from each of the health agencies on the approved list to participate in a scheduled class period to work with students.
- Identifying parents or guardians to help with supervision.
- Attending to all tasks associated with the health fair, such as transportation and liability.

2 Explain the following to students. Much of the emphasis in health education is on personal responsibility for health. However, many health problems can be solved or helped when individuals work together to serve the needs of others. A volunteer is a person who expresses a willingness to provide a service. Most voluntary health organizations need the services of volunteers. A voluntary health organization is an agency supported by funding other than taxes that usually focuses on a specific disease, health problem, or body organ. These agencies seek to educate the public and health care professionals about particular health conditions. They also raise funds for research and community health programs. Examples of voluntary health agencies are the following:

- American Cancer Society
- American Heart Association
- American Diabetes Association

Consumer and Community Health

- American Lung Association
- National Society for Prevention of Blindness
- March of Dimes
- American Red Cross
- National Safety Council
- Arthritis Foundation
- National Kidney Foundation

3 Explain that voluntary health agencies need the services of volunteers, particularly in the area of educating the public about particular health conditions and services provided. Further explain that voluntary health agencies often participate in health fairs. A health fair is a gathering designed to acquaint the public with health information and health services. Sometimes health screening is provided at a health fair. Health screening is an appraisal of a person's health status. For example, the American Heart Association or one of its state or local chapters may provide blood pressure screening at a health fair. Perhaps the health fair is being held at a shopping center. People coming to the shopping center to shop may stop at a table or booth and have a health screening to learn if their blood pressure is normal. If it is not, they are advised to see a physician. Further explain that information in the form of pamphlets and brochures is often given to people at a health fair.

4 Give students a copy of the list of voluntary health agencies that have agreed to participate in the health fair. Have them form groups based on their interests in doing volunteer work for a specific voluntary health agency. Explain that during the next class period, a contact person from the voluntary health agency will be available to work with the group on plans for the health fair.

5 Have the groups meet with the contact person from the voluntary health agency. They are to collaboratively make decisions on the goals of the health fair and the target population. They need to decide on the information that will be disseminated to the public. The students may decide to design pamphlets themselves. They may make posters, conduct interviews, and assist people from the voluntary health agency who are providing health screening. The contact person must approve all decisions. Review each group's final plans.

6 Have a discussion involving all of the contact people representing the voluntary health agencies and all of the students in the different groups. You might discuss ways to advertise the health fair, as well as ways to evaluate the health fair.

7 Conduct the health fair at the scheduled time. Be certain that you have parents or guardians present to help with supervision and unexpected situations. Provide time for students to visit the tables and booths of voluntary health agencies other than the one they chose for their group project.

8 Have a follow-up class meeting in which group members meet with the contact person from the voluntary health agency with whom they worked. During this follow-up meeting, ask each group to share experiences from the health fair and to evaluate its success in accomplishing its goals.

EVALUATION

Use chalk to draw a large circle on the floor. The circle should be large enough so that all students might step inside it. (You may want to do this outside or in the gymnasium of your school.) Have students stand around the outside of the circle. Explain that the inside of the circle represents their community. As a volunteer, they can step forward and get involved by expressing a willingness to provide a volunteer service. Taking turns, have each student identify a service that can be performed at one of the voluntary health agencies and step inside the circle. Ask students to avoid repeating what others have said. Explain that they can be specific, such as "I could hand out a pamphlet on juvenile diabetes" or "I could collect money for the heart association." Pause after several students have joined the circle to remark that as more volunteered, the community gained more benefits. When the circle is full, explain that every member of a community has some-

thing to offer. Explain that as they volunteered they became closer to others in the community. They gained a sense of community. Introduce the concept of being a health advocate. Show how the information in TM-31, "Be a Health Advocate," is used to address the aforementioned task in this evaluation.

Environmental Health

Environmental Link

HEALTH EDUCATION STANDARDS

- Students will comprehend concepts related to health promotion and disease prevention to enhance health.
- Students will demonstrate the ability to advocate for personal, family, and community health.

PERFORMANCE INDICATORS

- Analyze how environment and personal health are interrelated.
- Work cooperatively as an advocate for improving personal, family, and community health.

HEALTH GOALS

- I will stay informed about environmental issues.
- I will help keep the air clean.
- I will help keep the water safe.
- I will help keep noise at a safe level.
- I will help reduce and dispose of waste.
- I will protect the natural environment.

MATERIALS

Several sheets of colored construction paper (8½″ by 11″); stapler; scissors; blank white sheets of paper; pens or pencils; chalk; TM-3, "Comprehend Health Concepts," Appendix A

MOTIVATION

1 Prepare for this strategy in the following way. Cut each sheet of construction paper into four strips that are eleven inches long and two inches wide. You will need to have one strip of paper for each student.

2 Use this strategy to summarize what students have learned during other strategies focusing on environmental health. List the ten life skills for environmental health on the chalkboard:

1. I will stay informed about environmental issues.
2. I will help keep the air clean.
3. I will help keep the water clean.
4. I will help keep noise at a safe level.
5. I will precycle, recycle, and dispose of waste properly.
6. I will help conserve energy and natural resources.
7. I will protect the natural environment.
8. I will help improve my visual environment.
9. I will take actions to improve my social-emotional environment.
10. I will be a health advocate for the environment.

3 Divide the class into ten groups. Assign each group one of the ten life skills. The group members are to brainstorm actions they can practice to support the life skill that was assigned. For example, a group might be assigned "I will help keep the air clean." The group will brainstorm ways to keep the air clean such as "car pooling whenever possible" and "using roll-on deodorant rather than an aerosol." Allow the groups an appropriate amount of time to list as many actions as possible to promote the assigned life skills.

4 Give each student a strip of paper. Each student is to select an action that promotes the life skill his or her group was assigned and write it on the strip of paper. However, no two students in the same group can write the same action. For example, students in the group assigned the life skill "I will keep the air clean" must each write a different action on the strip of paper they were given.

5 Form the "Environmental Link" as follows. Have the students stand and move about the room so that they are not standing with members of their assigned groups. Then begin with one student. This student is to identify the action written on his or her strip of paper and the life skill it will promote. Staple the strip of paper in a circle, or link, as the student holds it. Now have a second student identify the action written on her or his strip of paper and the life skill it will promote. Have the student place the strip of paper through the chain link of the first student and staple it together to make another link. Repeat with the rest of the students (see the illustration). When the last student identifies the action written on her strip of paper and the life skill it will promote, she will need to slip her strip of paper through the previous student's chain link as well as the very first student's chain link. This will link all students together.

6 Ask students to discuss the "Environmental Link" that has been created. Why are the ten life skills linked so closely? What would happen if one of the links or life skills was removed? Why is it important to influence the decisions that others make about behaviors influencing the environment? How might they encourage others to practice these life skills?

EVALUATION

Erase the chalkboard so that students are not able to see the ten life skills. Give each student a blank sheet of paper. In the center of the paper, they are to draw or diagram aspects of their environment that they enjoy. In a creative way, they are to add the ten life skills to their drawings or diagrams illustrating their protective nature. For example, some students might draw their homes. The ten life skills might be written on a picket fence that surrounds and protects the home. Explain to students that they are using health knowledge to identify life skills. Use TM-3, "Comprehend Health Concepts," to show how having health knowledge promotes health.

Injury Prevention and Safety

GRADES 9–12

Buckle Up

HEALTH EDUCATION STANDARD

- Students will comprehend concepts related to health promotion and disease prevention to enhance health.

PERFORMANCE INDICATORS

- Predict how healthy behaviors can impact health status.
- Propose ways to reduce or prevent injuries and health problems.

HEALTH GOALS

- I will follow guidelines for motor vehicle safety.
- I will not drink alcohol. (Alcohol, Tobacco, and Other Drugs)

MATERIALS

Student master "Self-Protection while Driving and Riding in Cars"; enough clay to mold two balls the size of a softball; pencil or small stick; chalkboard; poster paper; markers; TM-26, "Practice Healthful Behaviors: A Health Behavior Contract," Appendix A

MOTIVATION

1 Ask for two student volunteers. Give each student a glob of clay to mold into a ball. Then give each student a pencil or small stick to use to carve a face into the ball. They can make the eyebrows, eyes, and a smiley face with teeth. You may choose to give each student extra clay to make a nose to mold into the face.

2 Have each student stand ten feet from the chalkboard. Explain to the class that they are about to witness two motor vehicle accidents. The two students are each holding a passenger in one of the motor vehicles that is involved in the accident. Neither is wearing a safety belt. Explain that a safety belt is a seat belt with a shoulder strap. Neither is riding in a motor vehicle that has an air bag. Explain that the first passenger is riding in a motor vehicle that is traveling fifty-five miles per hour. Have one student throw the clay ball as hard as she or he can at the chalkboard. Retrieve the clay ball from the chalkboard and show it to the students. The students will notice the damage. The passenger has sustained many injuries. Most likely the face that was inscribed into the clay has been damaged.

3 Now ask students what will happen to a passenger who is in an accident in a motor vehicle that is traveling only twenty-five miles per hour. Explain that many people do not wear safety belts when they are traveling at lower speeds such as while driving or riding in their neighborhoods. Have the second student gently toss his or her clay ball at the chalkboard. Retrieve the clay ball from the chalkboard and show it to the students. The students will notice the damage. Again, the passenger has sustained many injuries. Check the face that was inscribed into the clay. Most likely there are changes to the face.

4 Explain that more people die of motor vehicle injuries than any other cause of injury. Accidents in motor vehicles account for about half of all fatal accidents and about 20 percent of all injuries leading to disability. On the chalkboard, list the main factors that lead to motor vehicle injuries and deaths:

- Alcohol consumption
- Failure to use safety belts and seat belts (explain that newer cars have safety belts with seat belts and shoulder straps; older cars may have seat belts only)
- Speeding and reckless driving
- Poor driving conditions (heavy rainstorms, icy roads, reduced visibility)
- Disregarding traffic rules (failure to yield right of way)

- Poorly maintained motor vehicle (defective brakes, etc.)

5 Brainstorm a list of guidelines to reduce the risk of motor vehicle injuries and deaths:

- Avoid drinking and driving.
- Avoid riding in a car with someone who has been drinking.
- Avoid excessive speed.
- Heed warning signs.
- Anticipate what other drivers will do.
- Always use available safety devices such as safety belts or seat belts, and use safety restraints for small children.

6 Emphasize wearing a safety belt or seat belt, whichever is in the motor vehicle. Wearing a seat belt reduces the chance of being killed by 60 to 70 percent and the chance of being seriously injured by 50 percent. Seat belts are effective because they prevent or reduce the human collision. The human collision is a forceful collision experienced when an unbelted occupant is thrown against the motor vehicle's interior components, such as the dashboard, windshield, or steering wheel. Seat belts also prevent occupants from being ejected from the motor vehicle. Safety belts (seat belts with a shoulder strap) are much more effective in saving lives and preventing injuries than seat belts alone. Air bags are also effective motor vehicle safety devices. Air bags are cushions that inflate when activated by sensors in the dashboard and front bumpers within a fraction of a second between the first collision and the "human collision." They cushion the occupants in the front seat and prevent dangerous collisions with the car's interior components.

7 Emphasize the importance of not drinking alcohol and driving, as well as not riding in a motor vehicle with someone who has been drinking. Explain that the risk of a fatal crash, per mile driven, may be at least eight times higher for an intoxicated driver than for a sober one. Drinking alcohol and driving affects a person's ability to drive by impairing vision, perception, judgment, reaction time, and the ability to brake and control speed. The leading cause of death in adolescents and young adults is alcohol-related highway accidents.

8 Give students a copy of the student master "Self-Protection while Driving and Riding in Cars," and review other ways to stay safe.

EVALUATION

Organize a motor vehicle safety campaign for the school and community. Explain to students that as their evaluation, they will contribute to the campaign in two ways. Their first contribution will be done individually. They are to design a safety poster that focuses on one of the six guidelines for reducing the risk of motor vehicle injuries and deaths. Their second contribution to the school and community campaign will be a cooperative learning experience in which there is group participation. Divide the class into groups. Each group is to prepare a short skit, presentation, or message to be presented to (1) another class of students in the high school, (2) a group of students at a younger grade level, or (3) a community group such as a garden club or charity organization. They should present in a clever and creative way at least three methods for staying safe while driving or riding in a car. They can use the guidelines in TM-26, "Practice Healthful Behaviors: A Health Behavior Contract," to practice staying safe.

Student Master

Self-Protection while Driving and Riding in Cars

1. Always park in a safe and well-lit area where there are other people and other cars.
2. Take special note of exactly where you are parked in a large parking lot.
3. Lock your car at all times and keep your keys with you.
4. Have someone walk with you to your car whenever possible.
5. Check the front and back seats to make sure that no one is hiding inside before getting in your car.
6. Never leave infants or small children in an unattended car even if you are leaving for only a brief time.
7. Never leave the keys in the ignition or the engine running.
8. Always take your keys with you when leaving your car.
9. Keep wallets, purses, unattached stereos, and other valuables out of sight.
10. Do not allow yourself to run out of gas.
11. Plan ahead and fuel your car only during daylight hours.
12. Keep your car in good condition to prevent breakdowns.
13. Try to drive in safe, well-lit areas, especially at night.
14. Carry a cell phone to use in case of emergency.
15. Keep a sign in your car that says "Send Help" to display if your car breaks down.
16. Keep a flashlight and road flares in your trunk.
17. Stay in your car, keep your doors locked and windows rolled up, keep a lookout for passing police cars, and honk your horn if you see a police car when your car breaks down.
18. Do not get out of the car if someone other than a police officer stops and offers help. Roll the window down only a crack and ask the person to call the police.
19. Drive to a nearby phone and call 911 if you see someone in need of help.
20. Never pick up a hitchhiker.

21. Do not drive home if you think you are being followed. Go to a store, police station, or well-lit area where there are other people. Call the police and report that you were being followed.
22. Be cautious of anyone approaching your car when it is stopped.
23. Keep your car doors locked and windows rolled up at all times to prevent carjacking. If you need ventilation, roll the windows down only a crack. Keep your sunroof closed. Avoid driving in a convertible with the top down.
24. Keep your car in gear when at a stoplight or stop sign. Allow enough distance between your car and the car ahead to drive away.
25. If a person armed with a weapon demands your car or your keys, do not resist.
26. Do not give out your keys to other people.
27. Consider getting an inside latch for your trunk. If you are ever forced into the trunk, you could escape.
28. Do not rent cars that are marked as rental cars.
29. Be a courteous driver on the street. If another driver makes you angry, ignore this person. Never begin a fight.

SECTION FOUR 4

The Meeks Heit
K–12 Health Education
Curriculum Guide:

A Model for Implementing the National Health Education Standards

Using the Meeks Heit K–12 Health Education Curriculum Guide

The **comprehensive school health education curriculum** is an organized, sequential K–12 plan for teaching students the information and skills they need to become health literate, maintain and improve their health, prevent diseases, and reduce their health-related risk behaviors. This chapter identifies the components needed for a successful curriculum and includes a sample of a model curriculum, the *Meeks Heit K–12 Health Education Curriculum Guide.*

The Components in a Health Education K–12 Curriculum Guide Used to Implement the National Health Education Standards

The authors of this teacher resource book have worked closely with thousands of school districts throughout the United States, as well as in other countries, to produce curricula that emphasize individual responsibility for health. The authors have identified the essential components to be included in a health education curriculum guide

whose purpose is to teach students the information and skills they need to become health literate, maintain and improve their health, prevent diseases, and reduce their health-related risk behaviors. The following curriculum guide, the *Meeks Heit K–12 Health Education Curriculum Guide,* includes these sections:

- Goals and Philosophy
- NHES 1: Comprehend Health Concepts
- NHES 2: Analyze Influences on Health
- NHES 3: Access Valid Health Information and Products and Services
- NHES 4A: Use Communication Skills
- NHES 4B: Use Resistance Skills
- NHES 4C: Use Conflict Resolution Skills
- NHES 5: Make Responsible Decisions
- NHES 6: Set Health Goals
- NHES 7A: Practice Healthful Behaviors
- NHES 7B: Manage Stress
- NHES 8: Be a Health Advocate
- NHES 1-8: Demonstrate Good Character
- Abstinence Education
- *Totally Awesome Teaching Strategies*™
- Children's Literature
- Curriculum Infusion
- Health Literacy
- Inclusion of Students with Special Needs
- Service Learning
- Multicultural Infusion
- Family Involvement
- Evaluation
- The Meeks Heit K–12 Scope and Sequence Chart

The Meeks Heit
K–12 Health Education
Curriculum Guide

Goals and Philosophy

The *Meeks Heit K–12 Health Education Curriculum Guide* is an organized, sequential K–12 plan for teaching students the information and skills they need to become health literate, maintain and improve their health, prevent diseases, and reduce their health-related risk behaviors. The Meeks Heit Umbrella of Comprehensive School Health Education (Figure 16-1) illustrates concepts that describe the purpose of the curriculum. The Meeks Heit Umbrella of Comprehensive School Health Education protects students from the six categories of risk behaviors identified by the Centers for Disease Control and Prevention:

1. Behaviors that contribute to unintentional and intentional injuries
2. Tobacco use
3. Alcohol and other drug use
4. Sexual behaviors that contribute to unintended pregnancy, HIV infection, and other sexually transmitted diseases (STDs)
5. Dietary patterns that contribute to disease
6. Insufficient physical activity

At the top of the umbrella are three stripes, each of which illustrates an important component from which the comprehensive school health education curriculum is derived: Health Literacy, the National Health Education Standards, and the Performance Indicators (American Cancer Society, 2007).

- **Health literacy** is competence in critical thinking and problem solving, responsible and productive citizenship, self-directed learning, and effective communication. Health-literate students possess skills that protect them from the six categories of risk behaviors.
- The **National Health Education Standards** are eight standards that specify what students should know and be able to do. Students are protected from the six categories of risk behavior when they do the following:

1. Comprehend concepts related to health promotion and disease prevention to enhance health.
2. Analyze the influence of family, peers, culture, media, technology, and other factors on health behaviors.
3. Demonstrate the ability to access valid information and products and services to enhance health.
4. Demonstrate the ability to use interpersonal communication skills to enhance health and avoid or reduce health risks.
5. Demonstrate the ability to use decision-making skills to enhance health.
6. Demonstrate the ability to use goal-setting skills to enhance health.
7. Demonstrate the ability to practice health-enhancing behaviors and avoid or reduce health risks.
8. Demonstrate the ability to advocate for personal, family, and community health.

- The **performance indicators** are a series of specific concepts and skills students should know and be able to do in order to achieve each of the broader National Health Education Standards. Each health education standard has several performance indicators. The performance indicators designate what students should know and be able to do by grades 4, 8, and 11. Students need to be exposed to a curriculum that helps them master these performance indicators at these grade levels.

The Umbrella of Comprehensive School Health Education is divided into ten sections. These ten sections represent content areas for which young people need to gain health knowledge, learn and use life skills, work to achieve and maintain health goals, and master objectives. **Health knowledge** consists of information that a person needs to become health literate, maintain and improve health, prevent disease, and reduce health-related risk behaviors. **Life skills** are abilities that maintain and improve a person's health and promote the health of others. A **health goal** is a healthful behavior a person works to achieve and maintain.

FIGURE 16-1

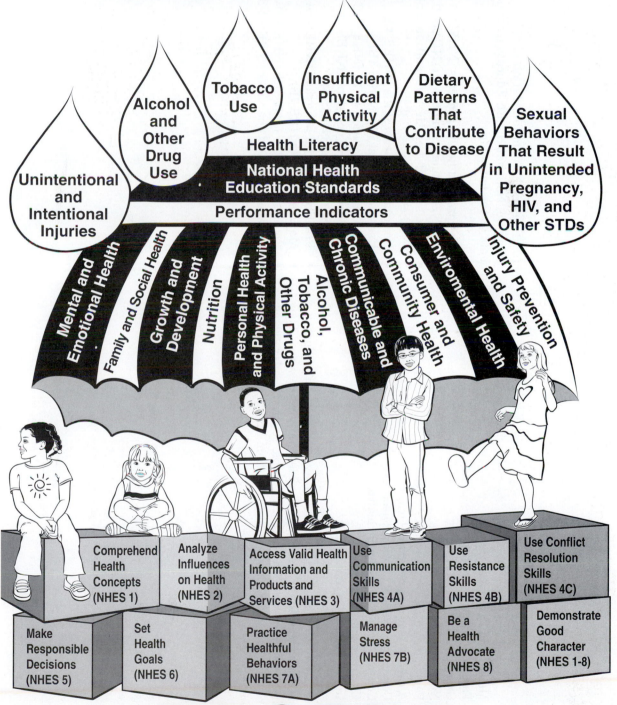

The Meeks Heit Umbrella of Comprehensive School Health Education

Health & Wellness

These are the ten content areas:

1. Mental and Emotional Health
2. Family and Social Health
3. Growth and Development
4. Nutrition
5. Personal Health and Physical Activity
6. Alcohol, Tobacco, and Other Drugs
7. Communicable and Chronic Diseases
8. Consumer and Community Health
9. Environmental Health
10. Injury Prevention and Safety

Students who participate in comprehensive school health education are enthusiastic, radiant, energetic, confident, and empowered. They are protected from risk behaviors (raindrops, severe thunderstorms, lightning) because the umbrella protects them and because they are

standing on the firm foundation of the skills they obtained by mastering the National Health Education Standards (NHESs). These students do the following:

- Comprehend health concepts (NHES 1)
- Analyze influences on health (NHES 2)
- Access valid health information and products and services (NHES 3)
- Use communication skills (NHES 4A)
- Use resistance skills (NHES 4B)
- Use conflict resolution skills (NHES 4C)
- Make responsible decisions (NHES 5)
- Set health goals (NHES 6)
- Practice healthful behaviors (NHES 7A)
- Manage stress (NHES 7B)
- Become advocates for health (NHES 8)
- Demonstrate good character (NHES 1-8)

Teaching Health Education Standard 1

Students will comprehend concepts related to health promotion and disease prevention to enhance health.

COMPREHEND HEALTH CONCEPTS

The *Meeks Heit K–12 Health Education Curriculum Guide* helps students learn how to comprehend health facts. Students can follow these steps to comprehend health facts and master National Health Education Standard 1 at different grade levels.

LEARN HEALTH FACTS (GRADES K–2)

1. Study and learn health facts.
2. Ask questions about health facts.
3. Answer questions about health facts.
4. Use health facts to achieve health goals.

Source: L. Meeks & P. Heit, *Health & Wellness K–8* (New York: Macmillan McGraw-Hill, 2008).

UNDERSTAND HEALTH FACTS (GRADES 3–5)

1. Study and learn health facts.
2. Ask questions if you do not understand health facts.
3. Answer questions to show you understand health facts.
4. Use health facts to promote health and prevent disease.

Source: L. Meeks & P. Heit, *Health & Wellness K–8* (New York: Macmillan McGraw-Hill, 2008).

COMPREHEND HEALTH CONCEPTS (GRADES 6–8) (GRADES 9–12)

1. Study health knowledge.
2. Ask questions about health knowledge that you don't understand. Make certain you get an answer you can understand.
3. Use health knowledge to form health concepts.
4. Use health concepts to promote health and prevent disease.

Sources: L. Meeks & P. Heit, *Health & Wellness K–8* (New York: Macmillan McGraw-Hill, 2008); L. Meeks, P. Heit, & R. Page, *Health & Wellness 9–12* (Columbus, OH: Glencoe/McGraw-Hill, 2008).

Teaching Health Education Standard 2

Students will analyze the influence of family, peers, culture, media, technology, and other factors on health behaviors.

ANALYZE INFLUENCES ON HEALTH

The *Meeks Heit K–12 Health Education Curriculum Guide* helps students learn how to analyze the influence of family, peers, culture, media, technology, and other factors on health. Students can follow these steps to analyze influences on health and master NHES 2 at different grade levels.

THINK ABOUT YOUR HEALTH CHOICES (GRADES K–2)

1. Name people and things that help you make choices about your health.

2. Tell which ones help make healthful choices. Tell which ones do not.

3. Choose ones that help you make healthful choices.

4. Stay away from ones that do not help you make healthful choices.

Source: L. Meeks & P. Heit, *Health & Wellness K–8* (New York: Macmillan McGraw-Hill, 2008).

ANALYZE WHAT INFLUENCES YOUR HEALTH (GRADES 3–5)

1. Identify people and things that might influence you.

2. Identify how these people and things might influence your choices.

3. Choose healthful influences.

4. Protect yourself from harmful influences.

Source: L. Meeks & P. Heit, *Health & Wellness K–8* (New York: Macmillan McGraw-Hill, 2008).

ANALYZE WHAT INFLUENCES YOUR HEALTH (GRADES 6–8) (GRADES 9–12)

1. Identify people and things that might influence you.

2. Evaluate how their influence might affect your health behavior and decisions.

3. Choose positive influences on health.

4. Protect yourself from negative influences on health.

Sources: L. Meeks & P. Heit, *Health & Wellness K–8* (New York: Macmillan McGraw-Hill, 2008); L. Meeks, P. Heit, & R. Page, *Health & Wellness 9–12* (Columbus, OH: Glencoe/McGraw-Hill, 2008).

Teaching Health Education Standard 3

Students will demonstrate the ability to access valid health information and products and services to enhance health.

ACCESS VALID HEALTH INFORMATION, PRODUCTS, AND SERVICES

The *Meeks Heit K–12 Health Education Curriculum Guide* helps students learn how to access health information, products, and services to enhance health. Students can follow these steps to access valid health information, products, and services and master NHES 3 at different grade levels.

FIND HEALTH FACTS AND GET HELP (GRADES K–2)

1. Tell when you need facts or help.
2. Tell where you can find health facts or help.
3. Find health facts or help.
4. Talk about what you found.

Source: L. Meeks & P. Heit, *Health & Wellness K–8* (New York: Macmillan McGraw-Hill, 2008).

ACCESS HEALTH FACTS, PRODUCTS, AND SERVICES (GRADES 3–5)

1. Identify the health facts, products, and services you need.
2. Find the health facts, products, and services you need.
3. Check out health facts, products, and services.
4. Take action when health facts, products, or services are not right.

Source: L. Meeks & P. Heit, *Health & Wellness K–8* (New York: Macmillan McGraw-Hill, 2008).

ACCESS VALID HEALTH INFORMATION AND PRODUCTS AND SERVICES (GRADES 6–8) (GRADES 9–12)

1. Identify the health facts and products and services you need.
2. Find health facts and products and services.
3. Evaluate health information and products and services.
4. Take action when health information is misleading or health products and services are unsatisfactory.

Source: L. Meeks & P. Heit, *Health & Wellness K–8* (New York: Macmillan McGraw-Hill, 2008).

Teaching Health Education Standard 4A

Students will demonstrate the ability to use interpersonal communication skills to enhance health and avoid or reduce health risks.

USE COMMUNICATION SKILLS

The *Meeks Heit K–12 Health Education Curriculum Guide* helps students learn how to use communication skills. Students can follow these steps to use communication skills and master NHES 4A at different grade levels.

COMMUNICATE (GRADES K–2)

1. Think about what you want to say.
2. Look at the person. Speak clearly.
3. Listen to the other person.
4. Make sure you understand each other.

Source: L. Meeks & P. Heit, *Health & Wellness K–8* (New York: Macmillan McGraw-Hill, 2008).

USE COMMUNICATION SKILLS (GRADES 3–5) (GRADES 6–8)

1. Choose the best way to communicate.
2. Express your thoughts and feelings clearly.
3. Listen to the other person.
4. Make sure you understand each other.

Source: L. Meeks & P. Heit, *Health & Wellness K–8* (New York: Macmillan McGraw-Hill, 2008).

USE INTERPERSONAL COMMUNICATION SKILLS (GRADES 9–12)

1. Choose the best way to communicate.
2. Express your thoughts and feelings clearly.
3. Listen to the other person.
4. Make sure you understand each other.

Source: L. Meeks, P. Heit, & R. Page, *Health & Wellness 9–12* (Columbus, OH: Glencoe/McGraw-Hill, 2008).

Teaching Health Education Standard 4B

Students will demonstrate the ability to use interpersonal communication skills to enhance health and avoid or reduce health risks.

USE RESISTANCE SKILLS

The Meeks Heit K–12 Health Education Curriculum Guide helps students learn how to use resistance skills. Resistance skills, or refusal skills, are skills used to say no to an action or to leave a situation. Students can follow these steps to use resistance skills and master NHES 4B at different grade levels.

SAY "NO"
(GRADES K–2)

1. Look at the person. Say, "No."
2. Tell why you are saying "no."
3. Do not change your mind.
4. Ask for help from an adult if you need it.

Source: L. Meeks & P. Heit, *Health & Wellness K–8* (New York: Macmillan McGraw-Hill, 2008).

USE RESISTANCE SKILLS
(GRADES 3–5)

1. Look at the person. Say, "No," in a firm voice.
2. Give reasons for saying "no."
3. Match your behavior to your words.
4. Ask an adult for help if you need it.

Source: L. Meeks & P. Heit, *Health & Wellness K–8* (New York: Macmillan McGraw-Hill, 2008).

USE RESISTANCE SKILLS
(GRADES 6–8)

1. Say, "No," in a firm voice.
2. Give reasons for saying "no."
3. Match your behavior to your words.
4. Ask an adult for help if you need it.

Source: L. Meeks & P. Heit, *Health & Wellness K–8* (New York: Macmillan McGraw-Hill, 2008).

LEARN HOW TO USE RESISTANCE SKILLS (GRADES 9–12)

1. Say, "No," with self-confidence.
2. Give reasons for saying "no."
3. Repeat your "no" response several times.
4. Use nonverbal behavior to match verbal behavior.
5. Avoid situations in which there will be pressure to make wrong decisions.
6. Avoid people who make wrong decisions.
7. Resist pressure to engage in illegal behavior.
8. Influence others to make responsible decisions.

Source: L. Meeks, P. Heit, & R. Page, *Health & Wellness 9–12* (Columbus, OH: Glencoe/McGraw-Hill, 2008).

Teaching Health Education Standard 4C

Students will demonstrate the ability to use interpersonal communication skills to enhance health and avoid or reduce health risks.

USE CONFLICT RESOLUTION SKILLS

The *Meeks Heit Health Education Curriculum Guide K–12* helps students learn how to resolve conflict. **Conflict resolution skills** are steps that can be taken to settle a disagreement in a responsible way. Students can follow these steps to resolve conflict and master NHES 4C at different grade levels.

RESOLVE CONFLICTS (GRADES K–2)

1. Stay calm.
2. Listen to the other person's side. Tell your side.
3. Talk about ways to work things out.
4. Agree on a way to work things out. Ask an adult for help if you need it.

Source: L. Meeks & P. Heit, *Health & Wellness K–8* (New York: Macmillan McGraw-Hill, 2008).

RESOLVE CONFLICTS (GRADES 3–5) (GRADES 6–8)

1. Stay calm.
2. Talk about the conflict.
3. Discuss possible ways to settle the conflict. Check out each way to settle the conflict. Use the Guidelines for Making Responsible Decisions.
4. Agree on a way to settle the conflict. You may need to ask a responsible adult for help.

Source: L. Meeks & P. Heit, *Health & Wellness K–8* (New York: Macmillan McGraw-Hill, 2008).

USE CONFLICT RESOLUTION SKILLS (GRADES 9–12)

1. Remain calm.
2. Set a positive tone.
3. Define the conflict.
4. Take responsibility for personal actions.
5. Listen to the needs and feelings of others.
6. List and evaluate possible solutions. Use the six questions from the Responsible Decision-Making Model.
7. Agree on a responsible solution.

Source: L. Meeks, P. Heit, & R. Page, *Health & Wellness 9–12* (Columbus, OH: Glencoe/McGraw-Hill, 2008).

Teaching Health Education Standard 5

Students will demonstrate the ability to use decision-making skills to enhance health.

MAKE RESPONSIBLE DECISIONS

The *Meeks Heit K–12 Health Education Curriculum Guide* helps students learn how to make responsible decisions. A **responsible decision** is a decision that leads to actions that promote health, protect safety, follow laws, show respect for oneself and others, follow guidelines set by responsible adults such as a person's parents or guardians, and demonstrate good character. Students can follow these steps to make responsible decisions and master NHES 5 at different grade levels.

MAKE WISE DECISIONS (GRADES K–2)

1. Tell what the choices are.
2. Ask questions before you choose:
   - Is it healthful?
   - Is it safe?
   - Do I follow laws?
   - Do I show respect for myself and others?
   - Do I follow family rules?
   - Do I show good character?
3. Tell what the wise decision is. Check this out with a parent or trusted adult.
4. Tell what happens if you make this decision.

Source: L. Meeks & P. Heit, *Health & Wellness K–8* (New York: Macmillan McGraw-Hill, 2008).

MAKE RESPONSIBLE DECISIONS (GRADES 3–5) (GRADES 6–8)

1. Identify choices.
2. Evaluate each choice. Use the Guidelines for Making Responsible Decisions.
   - Is it healthful?
   - Is it safe?
   - Do I follow rules and laws?
   - Do I show respect for myself and others?
   - Do I follow my family guidelines?
   - Do I show good character?
3. Identify the responsible decision. Check this out with your parent or trusted adult.
4. Evaluate your decision.

Source: L. Meeks & P. Heit, *Health & Wellness K–8* (New York: Macmillan McGraw-Hill, 2008).

USE THE RESPONSIBLE DECISION-MAKING MODEL (GRADES 9–12)

1. Describe the situation that requires a decision.
2. List possible decisions you might make.
3. Share the list of possible decisions with a parent, guardian, or other responsible adult.
4. Use six questions to evaluate the possible consequences of each decision:
   - Will this decision result in actions that promote health?
   - Will this decision result in actions that protect safety?
   - Will this decision result in actions that follow laws?
   - Will this decision result in actions that show respect for others and myself?
   - Will this decision result in actions that follow the guidelines of my parents and other responsible adults?
   - Will this decis on result in actions that demonstrate good character?
5. Decide which decision is most responsible and appropriate.
6. Act on your decision, and evaluate the results.

Source: L. Meeks, P. Heit, & R. Page, *Health & Wellness 9–12* (Columbus, OH: Glencoe/McGraw-Hill, 2008).

Teaching Health Education Standard 6

Students will demonstrate the ability to use goal-setting skills to enhance health.

SET HEALTH GOALS

The *Meeks Heit K–12 Health Education Curriculum Guide* helps students learn how to set health goals. A **health goal** is a healthful behavior a person works to achieve and maintain. Students can follow these steps to set health goals and master NHES 6 at different grade levels.

SET HEALTH GOALS (GRADES K–2)

1. Name one thing you want to do to stay healthy.
2. Make a plan for what you will do.
3. Keep track of what you do.
4. Tell how your plan worked.

Source: L. Meeks & P. Heit, *Health & Wellness K–8* (New York: Macmillan McGraw-Hill, 2008).

SET HEALTH GOALS (GRADES 3–5) (GRADES 6–8)

1. Write the health goal you want to set.
2. Explain how the goal will affect your health.
3. Describe a plan you will follow. Keep track of your progress.
4. Evaluate how your plan worked.

Source: L. Meeks & P. Heit, *Health & Wellness K–8* (New York: Macmillan McGraw-Hill, 2008).

SET HEALTH GOALS (GRADES 9–12)

1. Write your health goal.
2. Make an action plan to meet your health goal.
3. Identify obstacles to your plan.
4. Set up a time line to accomplish your health goal.
5. Keep a chart or diary in which you record your progress toward your health goal.
6. Build a support system.
7. Revise your action plan or time line, if necessary.
8. Reward yourself when you reach your health goal.

Source: L. Meeks, P. Heit, & R. Page, *Health & Wellness 9–12* (Columbus, OH: Glencoe/McGraw-Hill, 2008).

Teaching Health Education Standard 7A

Students will demonstrate the ability to practice health-enhancing behaviors and avoid or reduce health risks.

PRACTICE HEALTHFUL BEHAVIORS

The *Meeks Heit K–12 Health Education Curriculum Guide* helps students learn how to practice health-enhancing behaviors and avoid or reduce health risks. Students can follow these steps to practice healthful behaviors and master NHES 7A at different grade levels.

PRACTICE HEALTHFUL HABITS
(GRADES K–2)

1. Learn about a healthful thing to do.
2. Practice it.
3. Ask for help if you need it.
4. Make it a healthful habit.

Source: L. Meeks & P. Heit, *Health & Wellness K–8* (New York: Macmillan McGraw-Hill, 2008).

PRACTICE HEALTHFUL BEHAVIORS
(GRADES 3–5)
(GRADES 6–8)

1. Learn about a healthful behavior.
2. Practice the healthful behavior.
3. Ask for help if you need it.
4. Make the healthful behavior a habit.

Source: L. Meeks & P. Heit, *Health & Wellness K–8* (New York: Macmillan McGraw-Hill, 2008).

PRACTICE HEALTHFUL BEHAVIORS:
MAKE A HEALTH BEHAVIOR CONTRACT
(GRADES 9–12)

1. Write your name and the date.
2. Write the healthful behavior you want to practice as a health goal.
3. Write the specific statements that describe how this healthful behavior reduces health risks.
4. Make a specific plan for recording your progress.
5. Complete an evaluation of how the plan helped you achieve the health goal.

Source: L. Meeks, P. Heit, & R. Page, *Health & Wellness 9–12* (Columbus, OH: Glencoe/McGraw-Hill, 2008).

There are five parts to a health behavior contract.

Health Behavior Contract

Name: _____ Date: _____

1. Write your name and the date

Health Goal: I will eat healthful meals and snacks.

2. State the health goal you want to achieve

Effect on My Health: Eating healthful snacks will help me weigh what I should. I will be less likely to get cavities. I will get vitamins and minerals for growth.

3. Explain how it will reduce health risks

My Plan: I will choose foods from the list below. I will use a calendar. I will write the snacks I chose every day on my calendar.

4. Describe a plan you will follow and how you will keep track of your progress

				Snacks I Chose to Eat
milk	banana		Day	
low-fat cheese	apple	carrot sticks	Monday	_____
low-fat frozen yogurt	celery	plain popcorn	Tuesday	_____
low-fat granola bar	low-fat peanut butter		Wednesday	_____
cottage cheese			Thursday	_____
			Friday	_____
			Saturday	_____
			Sunday	_____

Evaluation: Did I choose healthful snacks every day? How can I make my plan work better?

5. Tell how your plan worked

Teaching Health Education Standard 7B

Students will demonstrate the ability to practice health-enhancing behaviors and avoid or reduce health risks.

MANAGE STRESS

The *Meeks Heit Health Education Curriculum Guide* helps students learn how to practice health-enhancing behaviors to avoid or reduce health risks. One way to avoid or reduce health risks is to practice health-enhancing behaviors that reduce the harmful effects of stress. Students can follow these steps to manage stress, reduce health risks, and master NHES 7B at different grade levels.

MANAGE STRESS (GRADES K–2)

1. Tell how stress feels.
2. Name things that cause stress.
3. Do something about things that cause stress.
4. Do something to keep healthy.

Source: L. Meeks & P. Heit, *Health & Wellness K–8* (New York: Macmillan McGraw-Hill, 2008).

MANAGE STRESS (GRADES 3–5) (GRADES 6–8)

1. Identify the signs of stress.
2. Identify the cause of stress.
3. Do something about the cause of stress.
4. Take action to reduce the harmful effects of stress.

Source: L. Meeks & P. Heit, *Health & Wellness K–8* (New York: Macmillan McGraw-Hill, 2008).

MANAGE STRESS (GRADES 9–12)

1. Identify the signs of stress.
2. Identify the cause of stress.
3. Do something about the cause of stress.
4. Take action to reduce the harmful effects of stress.

Source: L. Meeks, P. Heit, & R. Page, *Health & Wellness 9–12* (Columbus, OH: Glencoe/McGraw-Hill, 2008).

Teaching Health Education Standard 8

Students will demonstrate the ability to advocate for personal, family, and community health.

BE A HEALTH ADVOCATE

The *Meeks Heit K–12 Health Education Curriculum Guide* helps students learn how to use health-advocacy skills. **Health-advocacy skills are skills used to influence others' health decisions and behaviors and to emphasize health-related concerns and beliefs.** Students can follow these steps to become health advocates and master NHES 8 at different grade levels.

HELP OTHERS TO BE HEALTHY (GRADES K–2)

1. Choose a healthful action.
2. Find out more about it.
3. Find a way to tell others about it.
4. Tell others about it.

Source: L. Meeks & P. Heit, *Health & Wellness K–8* (New York: Macmillan McGraw-Hill, 2008).

BE A HEALTH ADVOCATE (GRADES 3–5)

1. Choose a healthful action to communicate.
2. Collect information about the action.
3. Decide how to communicate the information.
4. Communicate your message to others.

Source: L. Meeks & P. Heit, *Health & Wellness K–8* (New York: Macmillan McGraw-Hill, 2008).

BE A HEALTH ADVOCATE (GRADES 6–8) (GRADES 9–12)

1. Select a health-related concern.
2. Gather reliable information.
3. Identify your purpose and target audience.
4. Develop a convincing and appropriate message.

Sources: L. Meeks & P. Heit, *Health & Wellness K–8* (New York: Macmillan McGraw-Hill, 2005); L. Meeks, P. Heit, & R. Page, *Health & Wellness 9–12* (Columbus, OH: Glencoe/McGraw-Hill, 2008).

Character Education (NHES 1–8)

Refer to National Health Education Standards 1–8

DEMONSTRATE GOOD CHARACTER

The *Meeks Heit K–12 Health Education Curriculum Guide* contains an emphasis on good character and meets federal guidelines for purchasing materials to teach good character when using federal monies. **Good character** is the use of self-control to act on responsible values. Students can follow these steps to develop good character at different grade levels.

HEALTH EDUCATION STANDARDS 1–8 SHOW GOOD CHARACTER (GRADES K–2)

1. Do the right thing:
   - Be trustworthy.
   - Show respect.
   - Be responsible.
   - Be fair.
   - Show you care.
   - Be a good citizen.
2. Make wise choices.
3. Choose heroes who do the right thing.
4. Change wrong actions.

Source: L. Meeks & P. Heit, *Health & Wellness K–8* (New York: Macmillan McGraw-Hill, 2008).

HEALTH EDUCATION STANDARDS 1–8 SHOW GOOD CHARACTER (GRADES 3–5)

1. Act in responsible ways:
   - Be trustworthy.
   - Show respect.
   - Be responsible.
   - Be fair.
   - Show you care.
   - Be a good citizen.
2. Make responsible decisions.
3. Choose heroes who act in responsible ways.
4. Change wrong actions.

Source: L. Meeks & P. Heit, *Health & Wellness K–8* (New York: Macmillan McGraw-Hill, 2008).

HEALTH EDUCATION STANDARDS 1–8 DEMONSTRATE GOOD CHARACTER (GRADES 6–8)

1. Act on responsible values:
   - Be trustworthy.
   - Show respect.
   - Be responsible.
   - Be fair.
   - Show compassion.
   - Be a good citizen.
2. Make responsible decisions.
3. Choose role models who act on responsible values.
4. Correct wrong actions.

Sources: L. Meeks & P. Heit, *Health & Wellness K–8* (New York: Macmillan McGraw-Hill, 2005); L. Meeks, P. Heit, & R. Page, *Health & Wellness 9–12* (Columbus, OH: Glencoe/McGraw-Hill, 2008).

Abstinence Education

The *Meeks Heit K–12 Health Education Curriculum Guide* emphasizes abstinence from sex as the expected standard for teens. **Abstinence from sex** is choosing not to be sexually active. The content meets the criteria required by federal law for the funding of astinence education programs.

TEN REASONS TO CHOOSE ABSTINENCE

1. I want to follow family guidelines.
2. I want to respect myself.
3. I want to respect others.
4. I want to have a good reputation.
5. I do not want to feel guilty.
6. I am not ready for marriage.
7. I do not want to risk pregnancy.
8. I am not ready to be a parent right now.
9. I do not want to be infected with an STD.
10. I do not want to be infected with HIV.

Source: L. Meeks & P. Heit, *Health & Wellness K–8* (New York: Macmillan McGraw-Hill, 2008).

PRACTICE ABSTINENCE FROM SEX (GRADES 6–8) (GRADES 9–12)

1. Set limits for expressing physical affection.
2. Use resistance skills if you are pressured to be sexually active.
3. Avoid situations in which there might be pressure to be sexually active.
4. Stay away from peers who do not respect your limits.
5. Influence peers to choose abstinence.
6. Change your behavior if you have been sexually active.

Sources: L. Meeks & P. Heit, *Health & Wellness K–8* (New York: Macmillan McGraw-Hill, 2008); L. Meeks, P. Heit, & R. Page, *Health & Wellness 9–12* (Columbus, OH: Glencoe/McGraw-Hill, 2008).

Totally Awesome Teaching Strategies™ Contain

- **Clever title.** A clever title is set in boldfaced type on the left side of the page.

- **Designated content area.** In the upper left-hand corner appears the content area for which the teaching strategy is designed: Mental and Emotional Health; Family and Social Health; Growth and Development; Nutrition; Personal Health and Physical Activity; Alcohol, Tobacco, and Other Drugs; Communicable and Chronic Diseases; Consumer and Community Health; Environmental Health; Injury Prevention and Safety. A teaching strategy may include content from more than one content area. The additional content areas for which the teaching strategy is appropriate are identified in parentheses next to the health goals. One or more of the content areas include the six categories of risk behaviors identified by the Centers for Disease Control and Prevention: behaviors that contribute to unintentional and intentional injuries; tobacco use; alcohol and other drug use; sexual behaviors that contribute to unintended pregnancy, HIV infection, and other STDs; dietary patterns that contribute to disease; insufficient physical activity.

- **Designated grade level.** The grade level for which the teaching strategy is appropriate appears directly beneath the designated content area in the upper left-hand corner.

- **Infusion into curriculum areas other than health.** Infusion is the integration of a subject area into another area or areas of the curriculum. Teaching strategies are designed to be infused into several curriculum areas other than health education: art studies, foreign language, home economics, language arts, physical education, math studies, music studies, science studies, social studies, and visual and performing arts. The curriculum area into which the teaching strategy is designed to be infused is designated by a symbol that appears to the right of the boldfaced clever title.

- **Health literacy.** Health literacy is competence in critical thinking and problem solving, responsible and productive citizenship, self-directed learning, and effective communication (The Joint Committee on Health Education Standards, 1995). The teaching strategies are designed to promote competency in health literacy. Four symbols are used to describe the health literate individual: critical thinker, responsible citizen, self-directed learner, and effective communicator. The symbol designating one of the four components of health literacy appears to the right of the symbol designating curriculum infusion.

- **Health education standards.** Health education standards are standards that specify what students should know and be able to do. They involve the knowledge and skills essential to the development of health literacy (American Cancer Society, 2007). The health education standard(s) are listed under this boldfaced subheading.

- **Performance indicators.** Performance indicators are the specific concepts and skills students should know and be able to do in order to achieve each of the broader health education standards (The Joint Committee on Health Education Standards, 1995). The performance indicator(s) for the teaching strategy are listed under this boldfaced subheading.

- **Health goals.** A **health goal** is a healthful behavior a person works to achieve and maintain. The health goals for the content area are listed first under this boldfaced subheading. Health goals for other content areas covered in the teaching strategy appear in italics and are identified in parentheses.

- **Materials.** The materials are items that are needed to do the teaching strategy. The materials used in the teaching strategies are readily available and inexpensive. They are listed under this boldfaced subheading. Teaching masters that identify steps to follow to master the National Health Education Standards used in the evaluation also are listed under this boldfaced subheading.

- **Motivation.** The motivation is the step-by-step directions to follow when doing the teaching strategy. The motivation includes a creative way to teach the health knowledge and skills students need to master the health education standards, performance indicators, life skills, and health goals. The motivation is listed under this boldfaced subheading.

- **Evaluation.** The evaluation is the means of measuring the students' mastery of the health education standards, the performance indicators, the life skills, and the health goals. A suggested way to

Totally Awesome Teaching Strategies™ . . .

Totally Awesome Teaching Strategies™ are creative teaching strategies designed to help students become health literate and master the performance indicators established for each of the National Health Education Standards.

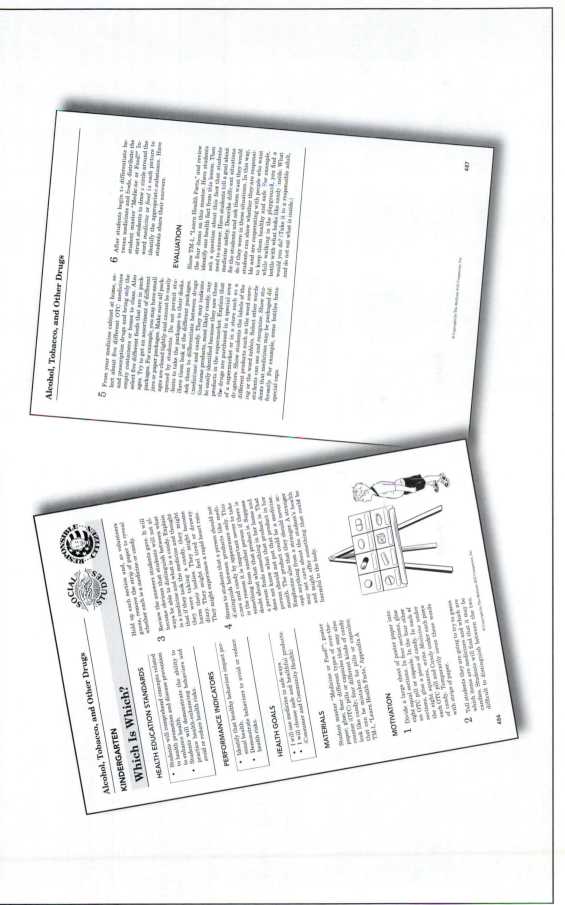

Alcohol, Tobacco, and Other Drugs

KINDERGARTEN

Which Is Which?

HEALTH EDUCATION STANDARDS

- Students will comprehend concepts related to health promotion and disease prevention to enhance health.
- Students will demonstrate the ability to practice health-enhancing behaviors and avoid or reduce health risks.

PERFORMANCE INDICATORS

- Identify that healthy behaviors impact personal health.
- Demonstrate behaviors to avoid or reduce health risks.

HEALTH GOALS

- I will use medicine in safe ways.
- I will choose safe and healthful products. (Consumer and Community Health)

MATERIALS

Student master "Medicine or Food?"; poster paper; glue; four different types of candy; four OTC pills or capsules that may also look like candy; fondant for pills or capsules; look-alike candy; fondant for pills or capsules that can be mistaken for pills or capsules; TM-1, "Learn Health Facts," Appendix A

MOTIVATION

1. Divide a large sheet of poster paper into eight equal sections. In the four other sections, glue an OTC pill or capsule. In each of the eight squares, write *Medicine* under each piece the eight OTC pill and *Candy* cover these words each OTC pill and *Candy*. Temporarily cover these words of candy. Temporarily cover these words with strips of paper.

2. Tell students they are going to try to guess which items are medicines and which may be candies. Students will find that it may be difficult to distinguish between the two.

Alcohol, Tobacco, and Other Drugs

486

physical education, math studies, music studies, science studies, social studies, and visual and performing arts.

- **Multicultural infusion.** Multicultural infusion is the adaptation of the teaching strategy to include ideas that promote an awareness and appreciation of the culture and background of different people. Suggestions for adapting the teaching strategy to incorporate learning about people of varied cultures and backgrounds are included under this boldfaced subheading.

- **Inclusion.** Inclusion is the adaptation of the teaching strategy to assist and include students with special learning challenges and may include enrichment suggestions for the gifted and reteaching ideas for students who are learning disabled. Suggestions for adapting the teaching strategy to assist students with special learning challenges are included under this boldfaced subheading.

Children's Literature

Several of the *Totally Awesome Teaching Strategies*™ contain children's literature. Students learn health knowledge and life skills as they examine short stories and poems. Children's literature is another medium through which students develop health literacy.

Curriculum Infusion

Skills needed to develop health literacy and to master the performance indicators for the National Health Education Standards are appropriately taught within the health education curriculum. However, today the trend in education is to infuse learning into many curriculum areas. Thus, the *Totally Awesome Teaching Strategies*™ are designed for infusion into the following curriculum areas other than health education: art studies, foreign language, home economics, language arts,

evaluate students' mastery of at least one of the National Health Education Standards is described under this boldfaced subheading.

Health Literacy

A focus for educational reform has been the need for health literacy. A **health-literate individual** is a critical thinker and problem solver, a responsible and productive citizen, a self-directed learner, and an effective communicator (Joint Committee on Health Education, 1995). The **Totally Awesome Teaching Strategies**™ are designed to promote health literacy.

A **critical thinker** is an individual who is able to examine personal, national, and international health problems and formulate ways to solve problems. This individual gathers current, credible, and applicable information from a variety of sources and assesses this information before making health-related decisions.

Service Learning

The *Meeks Heit K-12 Health Education Curriculum Guide* contains a focus on service learning. **Service learning** is an educational experience that combines learning with community service without pay.

Multicultural Infusion

A current trend in education is to include opportunities for students to gain awareness and appreciation of the culture and background of different people. Multicultural infusion promotes health literacy by helping students recognize how the strengths of people who are different can be blended to create synergy.

A **responsible citizen** is an individual who feels obligated to keep his or her community healthful, safe, and secure. This individual avoids behaviors that threaten the personal health, safety, and security of self and others.

The **self-directed learner** is an individual who gathers and uses health information throughout life as the disease prevention knowledge base changes. This individual embraces learning from others and continues to do so.

The **effective communicator** is an individual who is able to express and convey her or his knowledge, beliefs, and ideas through oral, written, artistic, graphic, and technological media. This individual is able to demonstrate empathy and respect for others.

Inclusion of Students with Special Needs

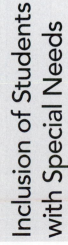

A current trend in education is to include students with special learning challenges as well as students who are gifted in the regular classroom. Inclusion is believed to promote health literacy as it gives students an opportunity to work together, socialize, and communicate. For inclusion to be effective, teachers may need to make adaptations to teaching strategies. These adaptations facilitate learning and bolster self-esteem in all students. Suggestions for inclusion accompany many teaching strategies.

tion Standards. Families might provide feedback as to attitudes and behaviors that are practiced and observed at home.

Family Involvement

The family can be involved in the *Meeks Heit K–12 Health Education Curriculum*. A Family Letter can be sent home to familiarize the family with the life skills and health goals that will be covered. *The Totally Awesome Teaching Strategies*™ contain suggestions for family involvement. Family members can participate in health behavior contracts and read and study health knowledge together. The family plays a significant role in the degree of health literacy achieved.

Evaluation

The *Meeks Heit K–12 Health Education Curriculum Guide* can be evaluated in several ways. *The Totally Awesome Teaching Strategies*™ contain suggestions for measuring students' mastery of the National Health Education Standards, the performance indicators, the life skills, and the health goals. Surveys might be developed and approved by the school board to gather information about students' behaviors. Portfolios might be used. Teachers might observe their students to determine attitudes and behaviors. Teachers might test students to see if they have mastered the steps for each of the National Health Educa-

The Meeks Heit K–12 Scope and Sequence Chart

The **Scope and Sequence Chart** serves as a blueprint for the *Meeks Heit K–12 Health Education Curriculum Guide.* The Scope and Sequence Chart is divided into separate charts for grades K–2, grades 3–5, grades 6–8, and grades 9–12. The **content areas** appear as headings within each of the separate charts. The ten content areas are Mental and Emotional Health; Family and Social Health; Growth and Development; Nutrition; Personal Health and Physical Activity; Alcohol, Tobacco, and Other Drugs; Communicable and Chronic Diseases; Consumer and Community Health; Environmental Health; and Injury Prevention and Safety. The chart for grades 9–12 has one additional content area, Life Skills. The Scope and Sequence Chart has the following columns:

Health Goals

The first column designates age-appropriate **health goals** for each of the ten content areas in each of the grade level spans: grades K–2, grades 3–5, grades 6–8, and grades 9–12. The chart for grades 9–12 begins with an additional content area that is titled **Life Skills.**

The National Health Education Standards

The second column identifies the **National Health Education Standards** that are associated with the health goals/life skills identified in the first column. The abbreviation *NHES* and a number is used.

- NHES 1: Students will comprehend concepts related to health promotion and disease prevention to enhance health behaviors.
- NHES 2: Students will analyze the influence of family, peers, culture, media, technology, and other factors on health behaviors.
- NHES 3: Students will demonstrate the ability to access valid information and products and services to enhance health.
- NHES 4: Students will demonstrate the ability to use interpersonal communication skills to enhance health and avoid or reduce health risks.
- NHES 5: Students will demonstrate the ability to use decision-making skills to enhance health.
- NHES 6: Students will demonstrate the ability to use goal-setting skills to enhance health.
- NHES 7: Students will demonstrate the ability to practice health-enhancing behaviors to avoid or reduce health risks.
- NHES 8: Students will demonstrate the ability to advocate for personal, family, and community health.

Objectives for Specific Grade Levels

The remaining columns identify **objectives** for specific grade levels. The objectives state what students should know and be able to do to achieve the designated health goals and to master the National Health Education Standards.

Grades K–2 Scope and Sequence Chart

Mental and Emotional Health

Health Goals	The National Health Education Standards	Grade K Objectives	Grade 1 Objectives	Grade 2 Objectives
I will take care of my health.	NHES 7	• Name the three parts of health.	• Name ways to stay in good health.	• Name ways to stay healthy.
I will show good character.	NHES 7	• Name six ways to show good character. • Show a way to be fair.	• Name six ways to show good character. • Show a way to be fair and a way to be caring.	• Give examples of the six actions that show good character. • Role-play what to do if you make a mistake.
I will make wise decisions.	NHES 5	• Tell what a wise decision is. • Show how to use the steps to Make Wise Decisions.	• Show how to use the steps to Make Wise Decisions.	• Demonstrate the steps to Make Wise Decisions.
I will say "no" to wrong decisions.	NHES 4	• Show how to say "no" to a wrong decision. • Name adults who can help you say "no."	• Show how to use the steps to say "no" to a wrong decision.	• Demonstrate how to say "no" to a wrong decision.
I will share feelings.	NHES 4	• Name feelings. • Show how to share feelings.	• Show how to share feelings. • Explain what to do when you feel angry.	• Demonstrate the steps to follow to Communicate. • Identify healthful ways to share feelings.
I will choose actions for a healthy mind.	NHES 1	• Discuss ways to cope with feelings.	• Name three things to do when you make a mistake.	• Discuss ways to have a good self-concept.
I will act in ways that show I am special.	NHES 1	• Name ways people are different and alike.	• Identify ways that you and others are special.	• Discuss ways to have a good self-concept.
I will manage stress.	NHES 7	• Tell what stress is. • Show how to use the steps to Manage Stress.	• Identify signs of stress. • Show how to use the steps to Manage Stress.	• Tell what stress can do to your body. • Make a health plan to Manage Stress.

GRADES K–2 SCOPE AND SEQUENCE CHART

HEALTH GOALS	THE NATIONAL HEALTH EDUCATION STANDARDS	GRADE K OBJECTIVES	GRADE 1 OBJECTIVES	GRADE 2 OBJECTIVES
I will bounce back from hard times.	NHES 1 NHES 7	• Name adults who can help you with hard times.	• Explain what to do if you make a mistake.	• Discuss what to do if you make a mistake.
Family and Social Health				
I will get along with my family.	NHES 4 NHES 7	• Explain how to be a responsible family member. • Make a health plan to show a family member you care.	• Discuss how families are alike and different. • Name things that can be learned in a family. • Make a health plan to help family members.	• Identify ways families are alike and different. • Make a health plan to spend time with family members and share work.
I will share feelings about family changes.	NHES 4	• Name different kinds of families. • Name family changes and feelings family members might have.	• Identify feelings related to changes in the family. • Identify trusted adults that children can talk to about family changes.	• Identify various ways a family can change. • Discuss feelings family members might have.
I will show respect for others.	NHES 4	• Explain how to be a responsible family member. • Name ways in which family members care. • Discuss ways to show respect for friends.	• Discuss ways to show respect for others. • Name ways to be a good friend.	• List the steps used to communicate. • Discuss various ways to show respect.
I will help others take care of their health.	NHES 8	• Show how to use the steps to Help Others to Be Healthy.	• Show how to use the steps to Help Others to Be Healthy	• Demonstrate steps to Help Others (a friend) to Be Healthy.

Grades K–2 Scope and Sequence Chart

Health Goals	The National Health Education Standards	Grade K Objectives	Grade 1 Objectives	Grade 2 Objectives
I will make wise decisions with friends.	NHES 6	• Show how to use the steps to Make Wise Decisions with friends.	• Show how to use the steps to Make Wise Decisions with friends.	• Discuss ways to be a good friend. • Identify six questions to ask and answer to Make Wise Decisions with friends. • Demonstrate how to "Say No" to wrong decisions with friends.
I will resolve conflict.	NHES 4	• Define *conflict*. • Show how to use the steps to Resolve Conflict.	• Give examples of conflict. • Show how to use the steps to Resolve Conflict.	• Identify ways to keep from fighting. • Demonstrate the steps to use to Resolve Conflict.
		Growth and Development		
I will learn ways my body changes.	NHES 1	• Name ways you grow and change.	• Describe ways people are unique in how they grow and learn.	• Identify stages of growth and development in childhood.
I will try different ways of learning.	NHES 6	• Name different ways to learn. • Set a Health Goal to try a new way to learn.	• Explain that some people need extra help to learn. • Set a Health Goal to try different ways of learning.	• Explain ways people can get help learning. • Set a Health Goal to try different ways of learning.
I will learn ways people age.	NHES 1	• Name ways people age.	• Explain ways people age.	• Identify stages of growth and development.
I will choose habits to grow up healthy.	NHES 6	• Show how to use the steps to Practice Healthful Habits.	• Show how to use the steps to Practice Healthful Habits.	• Identify healthful habits. • Demonstrate the steps to Practice Healthful Habits.

GRADES K–2 SCOPE AND SEQUENCE CHART

HEALTH GOALS	THE NATIONAL HEALTH EDUCATION STANDARDS	GRADE K OBJECTIVES	GRADE 1 OBJECTIVES	GRADE 2 OBJECTIVES
I will take care of my body.	NHES 1 NHES 6	• Name body parts and their functions. • Name ways to keep body parts healthy. • Name and describe the five senses.	• Explain ways senses are used. • Make a health plan to protect one of the senses. • Explain ways to care for bones and muscles, heart and lungs, stomach, and brain.	• Identify the name and function for each body system. • Make a health plan to strengthen bones and muscles. • Identify ways to care for the heart and lungs, stomach, and brain.

Nutrition

HEALTH GOALS	THE NATIONAL HEALTH EDUCATION STANDARDS	GRADE K OBJECTIVES	GRADE 1 OBJECTIVES	GRADE 2 OBJECTIVES
I will use MyPyramid.	NHES 1	• Name the healthful food groups. • Tell daily amounts of foods for MyPyramid.	• Name foods that belong to each of the healthful food groups. • Identify the correct food group for a list of snacks.	• Classify foods using MyPyramid. • Identify the correct food group for a list of foods.
I will follow the Dietary Guidelines.	NHES 1 NHES 6	• Tell what the Dietary Guidelines are. • Set a Health Goal to eat fewer fatty foods.	• Name each of the Dietary Guidelines. • Set a Health Goal to follow a Dietary Guideline.	• Identify the ways each Dietary Guideline helps health. • Plan a meal that follows each of the Dietary Guidelines.
I will find food labels.	NHES 3	• Point to the food label on different foods.	• Name the facts found on food labels.	• Explain how facts on food labels can be used.
I will eat healthful meals and snacks.	NHES 7	• Name foods for healthful meals and snacks.	• Plan a healthful meal. • Plan healthful snacks for one day.	• Make a grocery list of healthful snacks. • Write a menu for a healthful lunch and dinner.
I will check out food ads.	NHES 2	• Name food ads that influence food choices.	• Discuss ways ads can influence food choices.	• Use the steps to Think about Health Choices to check out food ads.

GRADES K–2 SCOPE AND SEQUENCE CHART

HEALTH GOALS	THE NATIONAL HEALTH EDUCATION STANDARDS	GRADE K OBJECTIVES	GRADE 1 OBJECTIVES	GRADE 2 OBJECTIVES
I will protect myself from germs in food.	NHES 7	• Explain how germs get into food. • Show how to wash hands.	• Name ways to keep germs out of food. • Show the correct way to wash hands.	• Identify ways to avoid food-borne illness. • Make a plan to prepare foods in safe ways.
I will use good table manners.	NHES 7	• Name good table manners.	• Show how to use good table manners.	• Discuss ways using table manners shows respect for others and keeps germs out of food.
I will stay at a healthful weight.	NHES 7	• Tell what eating foods with lots of fats and sugar might do to healthful weight.	• Explain how eating the correct servings sizes can help you have a healthful weight.	• Discuss ways to stay at a healthful weight.

Personal Health and Physical Activity

HEALTH GOALS	THE NATIONAL HEALTH EDUCATION STANDARDS	GRADE K OBJECTIVES	GRADE 1 OBJECTIVES	GRADE 2 OBJECTIVES
I will have checkups.	NHES 3	• Explain why you need checkups.	• Tell what happens in a medical checkup. • Tell what happens in a dental checkup. • Tell what tools a doctor or dentist uses.	• Tell what to expect at a medical and dental exam. • Tell what happens during an eye exam. • Name ways to protect your vision. • Tell what happens during an ear exam. • Name ways to protect your hearing.
I will learn about a health record.	NHES 8	• Tell what a health record is.	• Explain why your parents or guardian might keep a health record for you.	• Tell what is in a health record and why the doctor goes over it with your parent or guardian.

Grades K–2 Scope and Sequence Chart

Health Goals	The National Health Education Standards	Grade K Objectives	Grade 1 Objectives	Grade 2 Objectives
I will take care of my teeth.	NHES 7	• Show how to brush and floss teeth. • Name ways to care for teeth.	• Show the correct way to brush and floss teeth. • Name ways to protect the teeth from injury.	• Demonstrate the correct way to brush and floss teeth. • Name what to include in a dental health plan.
I will be neat and clean.	NHES 7	• Name ways to be neat and clean. • Show how to sit and stand tall.	• Name ways to be well groomed. • Tell why you need good posture.	• Name ways you can look sharp. • Show exercises to do for good posture.
I will get plenty of sleep and rest.	NHES 6 NHES 7	• Explain the difference between sleep and rest. • Set a Health Goal to get plenty of sleep.	• Name ways sleep and rest help the mind and body. • Set a Health Goal to get the amount of sleep you need.	• Name ways to help you sleep. • Name ways you can rest. • Set a Health Goal to get plenty of rest.
I will get plenty of exercise.	NHES 6 NHES 7	• Name ways exercise helps health. • Name kinds of exercises. • Make a health plan to get plenty of exercise.	• Name ways fitness helps the mind and body. • Name exercises that are a part of a fitness test. • Make a health plan for fitness.	• Discuss ways fitness helps the mind and body. • Explain how to build heart fitness. • Describe exercises to make muscles strong. • Make a health plan for heart fitness.
I will exercise in safe ways.	NHES 7	• Show exercises to warm up and cool down. • Explain how to stay safe during exercise. • Name sports equipment that will keep you safe.	• Show exercises to warm up and cool down. • Identify ways to stay safe during exercise.	• Explain how a warmup and cooldown prevent injury. • Identify safety equipment that is worn for sports and exercise.

GRADES K–2 SCOPE AND SEQUENCE CHART

HEALTH GOALS	THE NATIONAL HEALTH EDUCATION STANDARDS	GRADE K OBJECTIVES	GRADE 1 OBJECTIVES	GRADE 2 OBJECTIVES
I will follow safety rules for sports and games.	NHES 1	• Name rules for the games you play. • Tell what a good sport is.	• Name the safety rules for sports and games. • Role-play how to be a good sport and play fair.	• Identify safety rules for sports and games. • Explain why you need to be a good sport to have good character.

Alcohol, Tobacco, and Other Drugs

I will use medicines in safe ways.	NHES 3	• Explain the ways medicine can help people. • Name the safety rules for using medicine. • Name adults who can give you medicine.	• Identify ways medicine is used. • Identify safety rules for using medicine.	• Identify safety rules for using medicine. • Discuss warning labels. • Discuss side effects. • Identify safe ways to store medicine.
I will not drink alcohol.	NHES 4 NHES 7	• Tell what alcohol does to the mind and body. • Show how to "Say No" to drinking.	• Identify the harmful effects of alcohol on the mind and body. • Show how to "Say No" to drinking.	• Identify the harmful effects of alcohol on the mind, body, and relationships. • Demonstrate how to "Say No" to drinking.
I will tell ways people who use harmful drugs can get help.	NHES 3	• Name adults who can help someone who uses drugs in unsafe ways.	• Identify people and places that provide help for people who use harmful drugs.	• Discuss the four steps to follow to Get Help for people who use harmful drugs.
I will not use tobacco.	NHES 4 NHES 7	• Discuss ways tobacco use harms health. • Show how to "Say No" to tobacco use.	• Explain the harmful effects of tobacco use. • Show how to "Say No" to tobacco use.	• Identify the effects of tobacco use on the mind, body, and relationships.
I will stay away from secondhand smoke.	NHES 6 NHES 7	• Tell what secondhand smoke is. • Set a Health Goal to stay away from secondhand smoke.	• Explain why secondhand smoke is harmful. • Set a Health Goal to stay away from secondhand smoke.	• Identify diseases linked to secondhand smoke. • Set a Health Goal to stay away from secondhand smoke.

GRADES K-2 SCOPE AND SEQUENCE CHART

HEALTH GOALS	THE NATIONAL HEALTH EDUCATION STANDARDS	GRADE K OBJECTIVES	GRADE 1 OBJECTIVES	GRADE 2 OBJECTIVES
I will stay away from drugs that are against the law.	NHES 7	• Name drugs that are against the law. • Name adults to tell if someone uses drugs against the law.	• Discuss laws about the use of alcohol, tobacco, and other drugs. • Make a health plan to stay drug-free.	• Discuss laws about the use of alcohol, tobacco, and other drugs. • Make a health plan to stay drug-free.
		Communicable and Chronic Diseases		
I will learn symptoms and treatment for diseases.	NHES 1	• Tell what symptoms, treatment, and disease-are.	• Describe the symptoms and treatment for common childhood diseases.	• Discuss symptoms and treatment for infectious diseases.
I will protect others and myself from germs.	NHES 1 NHES 6 NHES 7	• Name ways germs are spread. • Make a health plan to not spread germs.	• Name types of germs and tell how they spread. • Make a health plan to prevent the spread of germs in your family.	• Identify the different kinds of germs. • Identify ways germs spread. • Make a health plan to protect yourself from the spread of germs.
I will choose habits that prevent heart disease.	NHES 6 NHES 7	• Name ways to prevent heart disease. • Set a Health Goal to choose habits that prevent heart disease.	• Identify foods and exercises that reduce the risk of heart disease. • Set a Health Goal to choose habits that prevent heart disease.	• Describe habits that prevent heart disease. • Set a Health Goal to choose habits that prevent heart disease.
I will choose habits that prevent cancer.	NHES 6 NHES 7	• Name ways to protect the skin from the sun. • Make a health plan to choose habits that prevent cancer.	• Name healthful habits that help prevent cancer. • Make a health plan to choose habits to prevent cancer.	• Discuss healthful habits that reduce the risk of certain cancers. • Make a health plan to choose habits that prevent cancer.

GRADES K–2 SCOPE AND SEQUENCE CHART

HEALTH GOALS	THE NATIONAL HEALTH EDUCATION STANDARDS	GRADE K OBJECTIVES	GRADE 1 OBJECTIVES	GRADE 2 OBJECTIVES
I will tell ways to care for asthma and allergies.	NHES 1	• Name things that make it hard for some people to breathe.	• Identify common causes of asthma and allergies. • Name ways to help control asthma and allergy symptoms.	• Identify some causes of allergies. • Identify ways to manage allergies. • Identify some asthma triggers. • Identify ways to treat asthma.
I will tell ways to prevent diabetes.	NHES 1	• Tell what diabetes is. • Name foods that are low in sugar.	• Explain how healthful diet and exercise help prevent diabetes.	• Discuss ways to prevent and treat diabetes.

Consumer and Community Health

HEALTH GOALS	THE NATIONAL HEALTH EDUCATION STANDARDS	GRADE K OBJECTIVES	GRADE 1 OBJECTIVES	GRADE 2 OBJECTIVES
I will check out ways to learn health facts.	NHES 3	• Show how to use the steps to Find Health Facts. Get Help.	• Show how to use the steps to Find Health Facts. Get Help.	• Demonstrate how to use the steps to Find Health Facts for health products.
I will check out ads.	NHES 2	• Tell what an ad is. • Show how to use the steps to Think about Your Health Choices when you check out an-ad.	• Show how to use the steps to Think about Your Health Choices when you check out an-ad. • Tell why you need to check out ads.	• Demonstrate how to use the steps to Think about Your Health Choices when you check out an ad. • Identify questions to help you check out an ad.
I will choose safe and healthful products.	NHES 3	• Name safe and healthful products.	• Make a list of safe and healthful products your family uses.	• Tell where to find safe and healthful products.
I will choose healthful entertainment.	NHES 2	• Tell what healthful entertainment is.	• Show how to use the steps to Think about Your Health Choices to choose healthful entertainment.	• Demonstrate how to use the steps to Think about Your Health Choices to choose a computer game.

Grades K–2 Scope and Sequence Chart

Health Goals	The National Health Education Standards	Grade K Objectives	Grade 1 Objectives	Grade 2 Objectives
I will make wise choices about time and money.	NHES 6	• Name ways to spend time and money on health.	• Name six questions to ask when you are choosing how to spend time and money.	• Set a Health Goal and make a plan to make wise choices about time.
I will cooperate with health helpers.	NHES 8	• Name health helpers in your school and community.	• Name ways health helpers in your school and community help-you.	• Name ways to cooperate with health helpers in your community.
I will check out jobs in health.	NHES 8	• Name jobs where people Help Others to Be Healthy.	• Describe the jobs of people who Help Others to Be Healthy.	• Name ways to help people with jobs that Help Others to Be Healthy.
		Environmental Health		
I will help protect my environment.	NHES 8	• Names ways to protect the environment.	• Make a poster that shows how to protect the environment.	• Design a pamphlet to show how to protect the environment.
I will help keep my environment friendly.	NHES 8	• Name ways to keep your neighborhood friendly.	• Name ways you can be friendly. • Name ways to be a good neighbor.	• Explain how to keep your environment friendly.
I will help stop pollution.	NHES 7 NHES 8	• Tell what litter is. • Tell what red tide is. • Name ways to stop pollution.	• Explain ways pollution harms the environment. • Tell ways red tide affects health. • Identify ways to keep Earth clean.	• Name ways to prevent land pollution. • Name ways to prevent water pollution. • Name ways to prevent air pollution. • Explain what to do when there is red tide. • Name ways to reduce noise pollution.

GRADES K–2 SCOPE AND SEQUENCE CHART

HEALTH GOALS	THE NATIONAL HEALTH EDUCATION STANDARDS	GRADE K OBJECTIVES	GRADE 1 OBJECTIVES	GRADE 2 OBJECTIVES
I will keep noise down.	NHES 6 NHES 7 NHES 8	• Tell what noise pollution is. • Make a health plan to protect your ears from noise.	• Discuss kinds of noise pollution. • Discuss the harmful effects of noise pollution. • Make a health plan to keep noise down.	• Discuss reasons to keep noise at a safe level. • Make a health plan to protect your ears from noise.
I will save energy and resources.	NHES 6 NHES 7	• Name ways to save energy and water.	• Discuss reason to save energy and water. • Make a health plan to save energy and water.	• Discuss ways to save energy, water, and other resources. • Make a health plan to reuse items to save resources.
I will follow safety rules for home and school.	NHES 1 NHES 7	**Injury Prevention and Safety** • Name the safety rules for home and school. • Explain the meaning of safety signs and symbols. • Name fire safety rules. • Show how to Stop, Drop, and Roll. • Show how to answer the phone in a safe way.	• Identify safety rules for school, home, and Internet use. • Discuss ways to store and use household products in safe ways. • Identify fire hazards and ways to prevent fires. • Show how to Stop, Drop, and Roll.	• Identify safety rules for school, home, and Internet use. • Discuss ways to store and use household products in safe ways. • Identify safety rules for guns. • Name the safety rules for fires, earthquakes, storms, tornadoes, and mudslides. • Demonstrate Stop, Drop, and Roll.

Grades K–2 Scope and Sequence Chart

Health Goals	The National Health Education Standards	Grade K Objectives	Grade 1 Objectives	Grade 2 Objectives
I will follow safety rules when I play.	NHES 7	• Name ways to keep from being injured when you play. • Explain how to stay safe when you play in or by the water. • Explain how to stay safe around animals. • Show how to cross the street in a safe way.	• Identify safety rules to stay safe during play. • Identify unsafe situations outdoors and how to stay safe. • Identify bicycle safety rules. • Show how to cross the street in a safe way.	• Identify safe places to play. • Identify safety rules and safety equipment to prevent injury. • Identify safety rules for the playground. • Demonstrate how to cross the street in a safe way. • Demonstrate bicycle safety rules and hand signals.
I will follow safety rules when I ride in a car or bus.	NHES 7	• Name the safety rules for riding in a car or bus. • Set a Health Goal to wear a safety belt.	• Identify safety rules for riding in a car or bus. • Set a Health Goal to wear a safety belt.	• Identify safety rules for riding in a car or bus. • Set a Health Goal to wear a safety belt.
I will follow safety rules for bad weather.	NHES 7	• Name the safety rules for bad weather.	• Identify ways bad weather can harm health. • Identify ways to stay safe in bad weather.	• Identify ways to stay safe in earthquakes, storms, tornadoes, and mudslides.
I will protect myself from people who might harm me.	NHES 7	• Name ways to stay safe around strangers. • Role-play what to do if a stranger in a car approaches you.	• Identify safety rules for being around strangers, using the Internet, and opening mail. • Discuss ways to keep from getting lost. • Make a plan for what to do if you get lost. • Discuss the difference between a safe and an unsafe touch.	• Identify safety rules for being around strangers and using the Internet. • Role-play what to do if mail is suspicious. • Discuss the difference between safe and unsafe touch. • Name adults to tell if you get an unsafe touch.

Grades K–2 Scope and Sequence Chart

Health Goals	The National Health Education Standards	Grade K Objectives	Grade 1 Objectives	Grade 2 Objectives
I will stay safe from gangs.	NHES 6	• Name ways to stay safe from gangs.	• Discuss reasons to stay away from gangs. • Tell ways to stay safe from gangs.	• Explain why it is a wise decision to stay away from gangs. • Identify ways to stay safe from gangs.
I will stay safe from gun injuries.	NHES 7	• List steps to use if you find a gun.	• Identify safety rules that help to prevent injury from guns.	• Identify safety rules that help to prevent injuries from guns.
I will learn first aid.	NHES 8	• Tell what first aid is. • Explain how to stop a nosebleed. • Explain what to do if you get a cut or scrape.	• Discuss first aid for cuts, nosebleeds, bee stings, and sunburn.	• Discuss first aid for nosebleeds, scrapes, cuts, punctures, poisoning, choking, fractures, bee stings, bruises, burns, blisters, objects in the eye, skin rashes from plants, and sunburn.
I will get help in an emergency.	NHES 3	• Show how to make an emergency phone call.	• Show how to make an emergency phone call.	• Demonstrate how to make an emergency phone call.

GRADES 3–5 SCOPE AND SEQUENCE CHART

HEALTH GOALS	THE NATIONAL HEALTH EDUCATION STANDARDS	GRADE 3 OBJECTIVES	GRADE 4 OBJECTIVES	GRADE 5 OBJECTIVES
		Mental and Emotional Health		
I will take responsibility for my health.	NHES 1 NHES 7	• Describe the three parts of health. • Define life skills. • Explain ways that practicing healthful behaviors protects health. • Demonstrate the steps used to Practice Healthful Behaviors. • Explain how practicing life skills can help you take responsibility for your health. • Identify ways risk behaviors harm health.	• Explain how total health reduces health risks. • Identify life skills to improve health and wellness. • Demonstrate the steps to use to Practice Healthful Behaviors.	• Discuss life skills to practice to take responsibility for health and wellness. • Explain how a healthful behavior and a risk behavior differ. • Demonstrate the steps to use to Practice Healthful Behaviors.
I will make responsible decisions.	NHES 5	• List questions to ask to Make Responsible Decisions. • Discuss ways to communicate with responsible adults about health decisions.	• Describe the difference between a responsible decision and a wrong decision. • Identify factors that influence your choices. • Demonstrate steps to use to Make Responsible Decisions.	• Demonstrate steps to use to Make Responsible Decisions. • Describe things that might influence your choices, including peer pressure.
I will use resistance skills when necessary.	NHES 4	• Describe when to use resistance skills. • Demonstrate how to Use Resistance Skills.	• Explain when to use resistance skills. • Demonstrate how to Use Resistance Skills.	• Demonstrate how to Use Resistance Skills if you are pressured to make wrong decisions.

GRADES 3–5 SCOPE AND SEQUENCE CHART

HEALTH GOALS	THE NATIONAL HEALTH EDUCATION STANDARDS	GRADE 3 OBJECTIVES	GRADE 4 OBJECTIVES	GRADE 5 OBJECTIVES
I will show good character.	NHES 6 NHES 7	• Set a Health Goal to show the six parts of good character. • Explain why your friends and heroes should have good character.	• Set a Health Goal to show the six parts of good character. • Role-play situations that show good character.	• Set a Health Goal to show the six traits of good character. • Identify role models who have good character.
I will choose actions for a healthful self-concept.	NHES 7	• Describe actions that help you have a healthful self-concept. • Describe how to show respect, including what to do if you do something wrong.	• Describe a healthful personality. • Explain how to use self-statements to remind yourself to act in responsible ways. • Describe ways to have a healthful self-concept.	• Explain the parts of a healthful personality. • Name actions that show you have a healthful self-concept.
I will communicate in healthful ways.	NHES 4	• Describe how to share emotions in healthful ways. • Explain how to use I-messages. • Demonstrate how to Use Communication Skills.	• Identify different kinds of emotions. • Describe healthful ways to express emotions. • Demonstrate how to Use Communication Skills.	• Describe strategies for coping with strong emotions. • Demonstrate how to Use Communication Skills.
I will choose behaviors for a healthy mind.	NHES 1 NHES 7	• Set a Health Goal and make a plan to choose behaviors for a healthy mind.	• Set a Health Goal and make a plan to prevent boredom.	• Set a Health Goal and make a plan to develop several coping strategies.

GRADES 3–5 SCOPE AND SEQUENCE CHART

HEALTH GOALS	THE NATIONAL HEALTH EDUCATION STANDARDS	GRADE 3 OBJECTIVES	GRADE 4 OBJECTIVES	GRADE 5 OBJECTIVES
I will have a plan to manage stress.	NHES 7	• Explain what a stressor is and identify the body changes caused by stress. • Discuss the difference between healthful and harmful stress. • Make a health behavior contract to Manage Stress.	• Describe how the body responds to stress. • Identify steps to use to Manage Stress. • Make a health behavior contract to Manage Stress.	• Describe ways stress affects the mind, body, and relationships. • Identify steps to use to Manage Stress. • Make a health behavior contract to Manage Stress.
I will bounce back from hard times.	NHES 7	• List ways to stay in a healthful mood. • Explain ways mood affects health.	• Explain the health benefits of a positive attitude.	• Describe ways to bounce back from hard times.
I will show respect for all people.	NHES 4	**Family and Social Health** • List ways to show respect for other people. • List ways to tell if others show respect for you. • Discuss what to do if someone does not show respect for you.	• Describe how to show respect in relationships. • Describe ways to develop self-respect.	• Identify kinds of relationships. • Describe how to show respect and earn the respect of others.
I will communicate in healthful ways.	NHES 4	• List healthful ways to communicate. • Role-play the steps to Use Communication Skills.	• Identify healthful ways to communicate. • Role-play the steps to Use Communication Skills.	• Identify the steps to follow when you Use Communication Skills. • Role-play ways to use non-verbal communication and active listening. • Describe ways to communicate emotions.

GRADES 3–5 SCOPE AND SEQUENCE CHART

HEALTH GOALS	THE NATIONAL HEALTH EDUCATION STANDARDS	GRADE 3 OBJECTIVES	GRADE 4 OBJECTIVES	GRADE 5 OBJECTIVES
I will work to have healthful friendships.	NHES 4 NHES 6	• Describe ways to build a healthful relationship. • Describe kinds of peer pressure and their effects. • Explain why you need friends. • List ways to make new friends. • Explain how friends can help each other make responsible decisions.	• List the actions of true friends. • Identify the influence peers can have on character. • Describe healthful ways to make friends. • List actions to take when you feel left out. • Describe what to do when others try to harm you.	• Describe the importance of friends in your neighborhood, school, and community. • Identify how to have strong friendships. • Explain how to avoid cliques. • Explain ways peers might pressure you. • Demonstrate how to Use Resistance Skills when pressured by peers.
I will work to have healthful family relationships.	NHES 2 NHES 4	• Explain what it means to be a family. • List ways to be a responsible family member. • Tell ways family members influence your health choices.	• Explain reasons for being close to family members. • Describe ways a family influences health. • Describe ways that family members help one another.	• Identify actions that help make family relationships strong. • Describe ways a family might influence the health of its members. • Describe activities in which families cooperate.
I will adjust to family changes in healthful ways.	NHES 7	• List changes that might occur in a family. • Describe how to adjust to family changes in healthful ways.	• Explain how family members can adjust to changes. • Describe ways to adjust if parents separate or divorce. • Describe changes that occur as a family grows.	• Explain how families can adjust to changes and challenges. • Discuss ways family members can Use Communication Skills as they discuss family changes.

Grades 3–5 Scope and Sequence Chart

Health Goals	The National Health Education Standards	Grade 3 Objectives	Grade 4 Objectives	Grade 5 Objectives
I will resolve conflicts in healthful ways.	NHES 4	• List the four steps to Resolve Conflict. • Role-play the four steps to use to Resolve Conflicts. • List ways to get along better with others.	• Define self-control. • List strategies to help you control angry feelings. • Describe ways to stay away from fights. • Role-play the four steps to use to Resolve Conflicts.	• Explain why and how conflicts develop. • Role-play the four steps to use to Resolve Conflicts. • Explain how a responsible adult can help with mediation of a conflict.
I will encourage others to take responsibility for their health.	NHES 8	• List four steps to use to Be a Health Advocate. • Discuss ways to help friends to be healthy.	• List four steps to use to Be a Health Advocate. • Discuss ways to help family members to be healthy.	• List four steps to use to Be a Health Advocate. • Discuss ways to help peers to be healthy.
		Growth and Development		
I will care for my body systems.	NHES 1 NHES 7	• Describe what parts of the —muscular system do. —skeletal system do. —respiratory system do. —circulatory system do. —digestive system do. —nervous system do. • Tell ways to care for your —muscles and bones. —heart and lungs. —digestive system. —nervous system. • List the five senses and ways to protect each of them.	• Explain how body systems work together. • Discuss the structure and function of the —skeletal system. —muscular system. —digestive system. —circulatory system. —respiratory system. —nervous system. —skin. • Discuss habits that —keep bones strong. —keep muscles strong and flexible. —improve digestion and circulation. —make it easy to breathe. —protect the brain and spinal cord. —protect the skin.	• Explain ways body systems work together. • Discuss the structure and function of the —skeletal system. —muscular system. —circulatory system. —respiratory system. —digestive system. —nervous system. —endocrine system. —urinary system. • Identify healthful habits to practice to protect each of the body systems.

GRADES 3–5 SCOPE AND SEQUENCE CHART

HEALTH GOALS	THE NATIONAL HEALTH EDUCATION STANDARDS	GRADE 3 OBJECTIVES	GRADE 4 OBJECTIVES	GRADE 5 OBJECTIVES
I will accept the ways my body changes as I grow.	NHES 1	• List signs that show that you are growing. • Explain how your body grows.	• List the factors that affect growth. • Explain ways you change in infancy, childhood, adolescence, and adulthood.	• Discuss ways you can expect to change in adolescence and adulthood.
I will choose habits for healthful growth and aging.	NHES 7	• List habits for healthful growth in childhood. • Use the steps to Practice Healthful Habits to work on a habit for healthful growth.	• List habits to practice for healthful growth and aging.	• Explain why you should practice healthful habits now to age in a healthful way.
I will learn the stages of the life cycle.	NHES 1	• List the stages of the life cycle.	• Describe changes that occur in each stage of the life cycle.	• Discuss the health needs of family members for each stage of the life cycle.
I will be glad that I'm unique.	NHES 1	• Explain what makes you special.	• Explain what makes you unique.	• Explain ways heredity makes you unique. • Discuss skills and talents that make you unique.
I will discover my learning style.	NHES 6	• Identify different ways in which people learn. • Set a Health Goal to read about health each day this week.	• Describe ways you learn best. • Set a Health Goal to help a friend who has difficulty learning.	• Identify different ways in which people learn. • Set a Health Goal to learn sign language.
Nutrition				
I will eat the recommended daily amounts of food from MyPyramid.	NHES 7	• Identify the nutrients your body needs. • Identify what foods are in food groups. • Explain how to use MyPyramid to make healthful food choices.	• Discuss what nutrients are found in foods in MyPyramid. • List the recommended daily amounts of food from MyPyramid.	• List nutrients, their functions, and foods that provide them. • Use MyPyramid to plan a healthful meal with at least one serving from each food group.

GRADES 3–5 SCOPE AND SEQUENCE CHART

HEALTH GOALS	THE NATIONAL HEALTH EDUCATION STANDARDS	GRADE 3 OBJECTIVES	GRADE 4 OBJECTIVES	GRADE 5 OBJECTIVES
I will follow the Dietary Guidelines.	NHES 7	• List the Dietary Guidelines. • Explain how to follow the Dietary Guidelines.	• List ways to follow the Dietary Guidelines. • Set a Health Goal to follow one Dietary Guideline.	• Explain ways that following the Dietary Guidelines promotes health and prevents disease.
I will read food labels.	NHES 3	• Describe what facts are found on food labels. • Use the steps to Access Health Information to find sugar on a food label.	• Explain reasons to read food labels. • Use the steps to Access Health Information to find salt on a food label.	• Describe what information is contained on a food label. • Use the steps to Access Health Information to find nutrients on a food label.
I will check out food ads.	NHES 2	• Identify influences on your food choices. • Use the steps to Analyze What Influences Your Health to check out a fast-food ad.	• Identify appeals found in food ads. • Use the steps to Analyze What Influences Your Health to check out a pizza ad.	• Identify and evaluate influences on food choices. • Use the steps to Analyze What Influences Your Health to check out food ads in magazines.
I will eat healthful meals and snacks.	NHES 6 NHES 7	• Explain how to use the Dietary Guidelines to choose healthful snacks. • Explain how to plan a menu for a healthful meal.	• Explain how to use the Dietary Guidelines to plan healthful meals. • Set a Health Goal to eat a healthful breakfast.	• Prepare a menu of meals and snacks for a day using the Dietary Guidelines. • Set a Health Goal to eat healthful snacks.
I will choose healthful foods when eating at fast-food restaurants.	NHES 7	• Identify Dietary Guidelines to follow when you choose foods at fast-food restaurants.	• Discuss ways to compare meals at fast-food restaurants.	• Explain how to use the Dietary Guidelines when you choose foods at fast-food restaurants.

Grades 3–5 Scope and Sequence Chart

Health Goals	The National Health Education Standards	Grade 3 Objectives	Grade 4 Objectives	Grade 5 Objectives
I will protect others and myself against germs in foods and beverages.	NHES 1 NHES 7	• Explain ways to keep germs out of foods and beverages. • List safety rules for preparing foods.	• Identify ways people may adversely react to foods. • Explain ways to prevent foodborne illness.	• Explain how pathogens can get into food. • Discuss ways to keep from spreading germs when you handle or prepare foods.
I will use table manners.	NHES 4 NHES 7	• Discuss table manners that protect health and help you get along with others.	• List table manners and reasons to practice each.	• Discuss ways that using table manners promotes physical and social health.
I will stay at a healthful weight.	NHES 7	• Discuss reasons to stay at a healthful weight.	• Explain how to balance food intake with physical activity. • Identify ways to maintain a healthful weight.	• Explain the parts of weight management. • Explain how to gain weight and how to lose weight.
I will work on skills to prevent eating disorders.	NHES 2	(Refer to: I will accept the ways my body changes as I grow.)	• Tell ways to have a positive body image. • Tell how TV might influence how you want to look.	• Identify people and things that influence your body image. • Describe the causes, signs, and treatment of eating disorders.

Personal Health and Physical Activity

Health Goals	The National Health Education Standards	Grade 3 Objectives	Grade 4 Objectives	Grade 5 Objectives
I will have regular checkups.	NHES 3	• Explain why you need checkups.	• List the role of each member of your health care team.	• List kinds of checkups, who does each, and what each includes.

GRADES 3–5 SCOPE AND SEQUENCE CHART

HEALTH GOALS	THE NATIONAL HEALTH EDUCATION STANDARDS	GRADE 3 OBJECTIVES	GRADE 4 OBJECTIVES	GRADE 5 OBJECTIVES
I will keep my eyes and ears healthy.	NHES 7	• Describe how to keep your eyes healthy. • Describe how to keep your ears healthy. • Explain how to protect your hearing.	• Describe ways to take care of your eyes. • Describe ways to take care of your ears.	• Describe the structure and function of the eye. • List some common vision problems and ways they can be corrected. • Describe the structure and function of the ear. • List some common hearing problems and ways they are corrected.
I will help my parents or guardian keep my personal health record.	NHES 8	• Explain what a personal health record is.	• Work with a parent or guardian to compile a personal health record.	• Work with a parent or guardian to compile a personal health record.
I will follow a dental health plan.	NHES 3 NHES 7	• Explain why you need to keep your teeth healthy. • Demonstrate how to floss and brush your teeth. • Make a dental health plan.	• Describe the structure and function of teeth. • List ways to care for teeth and gums. • Describe ways to protect teeth against injury.	• Describe the structure and function of teeth. • Describe conditions that can harm teeth. • Make a dental health plan.
I will be well groomed.	NHES 3 NHES 7	• Discuss rules for the safe use of grooming products. • Discuss ways to groom your skin, hair, and nails. • List the steps to use to Access Health Products for grooming.	• Explain how to choose grooming products. • Explain ways to care for your skin, hair, and nails. • Identify the steps to use to Access Health Products for grooming.	• Identify the steps to use to Access Health Products for grooming. • Discuss ways to use grooming products for skin, hair, and nails.

GRADES 3–5 SCOPE AND SEQUENCE CHART

HEALTH GOALS	THE NATIONAL HEALTH EDUCATION STANDARDS	GRADE 3 OBJECTIVES	GRADE 4 OBJECTIVES	GRADE 5 OBJECTIVES
I will get plenty of physical activity.	NHES 7	• Explain why you need to be physically active. • Describe how you can work on the five kinds of fitness. • Discuss fitness skills you use for sports and games. • Make a physical fitness plan.	• Describe the physical, mental, and social benefits of physical activity. • Explain why you need each of the five kinds of physical fitness. • Identify fitness skills you can use when playing sports and games. • List tests that measure fitness. • Identify seven exercises involved in a fitness test. • Describe the difference between aerobic and anaerobic exercise. • Identify lifetime sports you can enjoy now. • Make a physical fitness plan.	• Describe the social, emotional, and physical benefits of physical activity. • List the five kinds of health fitness. • Describe the kinds of fitness skills. • Explain how age, gender, heredity, and health behaviors affect fitness. • Explain how aerobic exercise benefits the heart and lungs. • Explain the FITT formula for fitness. • Discuss the need for frequent workouts. • Make a physical fitness plan.
I will follow safety rules for sports and games.	NHES 8	• Identify safety rules for sports and games. • Identify ways to be a good sport.	• Identify safety rules for sports and games. • Explain how you can be a good sport and a good teammate.	• Identify safety rules for sports and games. • Be a role model of a good sport for a younger child.
I will prevent injuries during physical activities.	NHES 1 NHES 3	• Discuss ways to prevent injuries during physical activity. • List safety equipment for physical activities.	• Discuss ways to prevent injuries during physical activities. • Describe ways to determine the safety equipment you need for physical activity.	• Describe safety precautions to take before, during, and after a workout. • Explain how to prevent and treat muscle strain and sprains. • List factors to consider when you choose safety equipment.

GRADES 3–5 SCOPE AND SEQUENCE CHART

HEALTH GOALS	THE NATIONAL HEALTH EDUCATION STANDARDS	GRADE 3 OBJECTIVES	GRADE 4 OBJECTIVES	GRADE 5 OBJECTIVES
I will get enough rest and sleep.	NHES 6 NHES 7	• Discuss ways to get enough rest and sleep. • Make a health behavior contract to get enough rest and sleep.	• Describe ways sleep affects performance. • Make a health behavior contract to rest when tired.	• Describe the health benefits of getting enough sleep. • Set a Health Goal to get enough sleep.

Alcohol, Tobacco, and Other Drugs

HEALTH GOALS	THE NATIONAL HEALTH EDUCATION STANDARDS	GRADE 3 OBJECTIVES	GRADE 4 OBJECTIVES	GRADE 5 OBJECTIVES
I will use over-the-counter (OTC) and prescription drugs in safe ways.	NHES 3	• List ways medicines can help health. • Explain how prescription and OTC drugs differ. • List safety rules to follow when using medicines.	• List safety rules for taking prescription drugs. • Name safety rules for taking over-the-counter drugs.	• Describe the differences among drugs, medicine, prescription medicine, over-the-counter (OTC) medicine, and illegal drugs. • List important safety precautions involved with taking medicines.
I will tell how someone who uses drugs in harmful ways can get help.	NHES 3	• Explain how someone who uses drugs in harmful ways can be helped.	• Describe types of help available for someone who has a drinking problem. • Describe how to quit tobacco use. • Describe ways to get help for someone who abuses drugs.	• List the kinds of help available for people who abuse drugs. • Identify places that offer smoking cessation programs. • Discuss recovery programs.

GRADES 3–5 SCOPE AND SEQUENCE CHART

HEALTH GOALS	THE NATIONAL HEALTH EDUCATION STANDARDS	GRADE 3 OBJECTIVES	GRADE 4 OBJECTIVES	GRADE 5 OBJECTIVES
I will say "no" if someone offers me a harmful drug.	NHES 4 NHES 8	• List ways to say "no" to drinking alcohol. • List ways to say "no" to tobacco use. • Tell how to say "no" to illegal drugs. • Use the steps to Be a Health Advocate to share with friends the benefits of a drug-free lifestyle.	• List ten reasons to say "no" to drinking alcohol. • List ten reasons to say "no" to tobacco use. • List ten reasons to say "no" to drug abuse. • Name protective factors that help you say "no" to abusing drugs.	• Describe ways to resist pressure to use drugs. • List some important Food and Drug Administration (FDA) regulations on tobacco, alcohol, and drugs. • Explain how to Use Resistance Skills to avoid drug abuse.
I will not drink alcohol.	NHES 4 NHES 7	• List ways that alcohol affects physical health. • Describe how alcohol affects the way a person thinks, feels, and acts. • Demonstrate how to Use Resistance Skills and say "no" to drinking.	• Describe ways that alcohol harms physical health, mental and emotional health, and family and social health. • Demonstrate how to Use Resistance Skills and say "no" to drinking.	• List the short- and long-term effects of alcohol use. • Explain why laws prohibit children from drinking alcohol. • Describe the link between drinking alcohol and injury and disease. • Demonstrate how to Use Resistance Skills and say "no" to drinking.
I will not use tobacco.	NHES 2 NHES 4 NHES 7	• Describe how smoking and smokeless tobacco harm health. • Explain ways ads try to-get people to use tobacco. • Demonstrate how to Use Resistance Skills and say "no" to tobacco use.	• Discuss ways tobacco use harms health. • Discuss the appeals found in ads for cigarettes. • Demonstrate how to Use Resistance Skills and say "no" to tobacco use.	• List several toxins found in tobacco smoke. • Describe the short- and long-term effects of tobacco use on the body. • Describe the laws governing tobacco use by a minor. • Explain the link between tobacco use and disease. • Demonstrate how to Use Resistance Skills and say "no" to tobacco use.

GRADES 3–5 SCOPE AND SEQUENCE CHART

HEALTH GOALS	THE NATIONAL HEALTH EDUCATION STANDARDS	GRADE 3 OBJECTIVES	GRADE 4 OBJECTIVES	GRADE 5 OBJECTIVES
I will protect myself from secondhand smoke.	NHES 7	• List ways secondhand tobacco smoke harms health.	• Explain ways secondhand smoke harms health.	• Explain how secondhand smoke can be harmful to health.
I will not be involved in illegal drug use.	NHES 7	• Explain ways caffeine can harm health. • List the harmful effects of illegal drugs: marijuana, cocaine, crack, and Ecstasy. • List the dangers of chemical inhalants.	• Describe ways marijuana harms health. • Identify ways that the misuse or abuse of stimulants and depressants harms health. • Explain why it is harmful to abuse inhalants and steroids.	• Discuss the effects of illegal drugs: stimulants, depressants, narcotics, inhalants, marijuana, steroids, and hallucinogens. • List prescription and over-the-counter drugs that should be taken with caution. • Describe reasons why people abuse drugs. • List sources of pressure to abuse drugs. • Explain ways drug abuse can affect someone's family and friends. • Explains ways family members, peers, and the school can help someone resist drugs.

GRADES 3–5 SCOPE AND SEQUENCE CHART

Communicable and Chronic Diseases

HEALTH GOALS	THE NATIONAL HEALTH EDUCATION STANDARDS	GRADE 3 OBJECTIVES	GRADE 4 OBJECTIVES	GRADE 5 OBJECTIVES
I will choose habits that prevent the spread of germs.	NHES 7	• Tell what causes disease. • Describe ways to prevent the spread of disease. • Identify ways the body keeps germs out. • Explain how the immune system fights disease. • Use the steps to Practice Healthful Habits to make washing hands a habit.	• List kinds of pathogens that cause disease. • Name ways that pathogens enter the body. • Describe habits that keep germs from spreading. • Explain how the body's defenses work. • Make a plan to Practice Healthful Habits that protect you from diseases spread by pathogens.	• Describe how pathogens spread and cause disease. • Explain how pathogens get into the body. • List the stages of disease. • Describe how the body fights pathogens. • Make a plan to Practice Healthful Habits that strengthen your immune system.
I will recognize symptoms and get treatment for communicable diseases.	NHES 1	• Explain how to treat flu, colds, and strep throat. • Discuss how head lice and scabies are spread and treated.	• List symptoms of communicable diseases. • List treatments for communicable diseases. • List the cause, symptoms, and treatment for some common childhood illnesses.	• Distinguish between communicable and noncommunicable diseases. • Describe typical symptoms of communicable diseases. • Identify some common communicable diseases and their treatments.
I will choose habits that reduce the risk of heart disease.	NHES 6 NHES 7	• Discuss ways to reduce the risk of heart disease. • Set a Health Goal and make a plan to eat foods that are low in fat.	• Define heart disease. • Explain what causes a heart attack. • List ways to reduce the risk of heart disease and premature heart attack. • Set a Health Goal and make a plan to get plenty of exercise.	• List symptoms of heart disease and heart attacks. • Explain how to reduce the risk of heart disease. • Set a Health Goal and make a plan to avoid secondhand smoke.

GRADES 3–5 SCOPE AND SEQUENCE CHART

HEALTH GOALS	THE NATIONAL HEALTH EDUCATION STANDARDS	GRADE 3 OBJECTIVES	GRADE 4 OBJECTIVES	GRADE 5 OBJECTIVES
I will choose habits that reduce the risk of cancer.	NHES 6 NHES 7	• Discuss ways to reduce the risk of cancer. • Set a Health Goal and make a plan to wear sunscreen.	• List ways to reduce the risk of skin cancer. • List ways to reduce the risk of lung cancer. • List ways to reduce the risk of colon cancer. • Set a Health Goal and make a plan to eat foods with fiber.	• Describe the effects of cancer on the body. • Explain ways to reduce the risk of and to treat cancer. • Set a Health Goal and make a plan to reduce the risk of cancer.
I will choose habits that reduce the risk of diabetes.	NHES 6 NHES 7	• Discuss ways to reduce the risk of diabetes.	• Describe ways to reduce the risk of Type 2 diabetes. • Describe ways to control diabetes.	• Explain what diabetes is, its causes, and how to manage it.
I will tell ways to manage chronic (lasting) health conditions.	NHES 1 NHES 8	• Define noncommunicable diseases. • Describe ways to prevent noncommunicable diseases. • Demonstrate ways to show care, concern, and respect for people with special needs.	• List and discuss common chronic diseases. • Discuss ways to show support for people who have a chronic disease.	• Define chronic disease. • Discuss the signs of diabetes, arthritis, and epilepsy, and explain ways these chronic health conditions are managed.
I will tell ways to manage asthma and allergies.	NHES 1	• Explain what causes an asthma attack. • List things you can be allergic to. • Discuss ways to lessen allergens.	• Describe causes of allergies and ways to reduce the risk of allergy attacks. • Describe ways to reduce triggers for asthma.	• Explain what asthma and allergies are and how to manage them.

GRADES 3–5 SCOPE AND SEQUENCE CHART

HEALTH GOALS	THE NATIONAL HEALTH EDUCATION STANDARDS	GRADE 3 OBJECTIVES	GRADE 4 OBJECTIVES	GRADE 5 OBJECTIVES
I will learn facts about HIV and AIDS.	NHES 1	*Optional* • Explain what HIV does to helper T cells. • Name ways HIV is spread. • Name ways HIV is not spread. • Discuss universal precautions.	*Optional* • Explain what HIV does to body defenses. • Discuss symptoms that appear in people who have HIV. • Explain how HIV leads to AIDS. • List ways HIV enters a person's body. • List ways to keep from getting HIV.	*Optional* • Discuss how HIV infection leads to AIDS. • Identify ways HIV is spread. • Identify ways HIV is not spread. • Identify ways to prevent HIV infection.

Consumer and Community Health

HEALTH GOALS	THE NATIONAL HEALTH EDUCATION STANDARDS	GRADE 3 OBJECTIVES	GRADE 4 OBJECTIVES	GRADE 5 OBJECTIVES
I will check out sources of health information.	NHES 3	• Identify ways to get health information. • Demonstrate the steps to use to Access Health Information when given a health topic.	• List sources of health information. • Demonstrate the steps to use to Access Health Information when given a health topic.	• Identify ways to get health information. • Demonstrate the steps to use to Access Health Information when given a health topic.
I will check out ways technology, media, and culture influence health choices.	NHES 2	• Explain ways to analyze the influence of commercials for health products.	• Discuss ways to analyze the influence of advertisements and commercials. • Explain the purpose of advertisements and commercials.	• Analyze the influence of technology on health and health care.

Grades 3–5 Scope and Sequence Chart

Health Goals	The National Health Education Standards	Grade 3 Objectives	Grade 4 Objectives	Grade 5 Objectives
I will choose safe and healthful products.	NHES 3	• Describe ways to be a responsible consumer. • Name safe and healthful products consumers buy. • List steps to follow to Access Health Products.	• List health products. • Describe how to make responsible choices about health care products and services.	• Identify and discuss health care products and services. • Describe how to make responsible choices about health care products and services. • Explain how government and private groups help protect consumers.
I will spend time and money wisely.	NHES 6	• Describe ways to organize your time and spend money wisely. • Set a Health Goal to spend time with your family.	• Describe responsible ways to spend money on health. • Describe responsible ways to spend time on health.	• List strategies to manage time and money. • Set a Health Goal to get plenty of exercise.
I will choose healthful entertainment.	NHES 2	• Describe different kinds of healthful community activities. • Use the steps to Analyze Influences on Health to decide if a TV show is a healthful influence.	• Explain how to choose healthful entertainment. • Use the steps to Analyze Influences on Health to decide if a computer game is a healthful influence.	• Describe how to make responsible entertainment choices. • Use the steps to Analyze Influences on Health to decide if a magazine is a healthful influence.
I will cooperate with community and school health helpers.	NHES 8	• Name where health helpers work. • List ways you can help others to be healthy.	• List places where health helpers work in the community. • List ways people volunteer.	• List some health needs of people who live in your community. • Describe ways health helpers assist people in your community in meeting their health needs. • Explain ways that volunteers can contribute to the health of the community.

GRADES 3–5 SCOPE AND SEQUENCE CHART

HEALTH GOALS	THE NATIONAL HEALTH EDUCATION STANDARDS	GRADE 3 OBJECTIVES	GRADE 4 OBJECTIVES	GRADE 5 OBJECTIVES
I will learn about health careers.	NHES 8	• Explain what health helpers do.	• List health careers that benefit the community.	• Explain where information about health careers is available. • List some jobs done by health workers. • Describe how to prepare for a health career.

Environmental Health

HEALTH GOALS	THE NATIONAL HEALTH EDUCATION STANDARDS	GRADE 3 OBJECTIVES	GRADE 4 OBJECTIVES	GRADE 5 OBJECTIVES
I will help protect my environment.	NHES 8	• Discuss what makes up the environment. • Use the steps to Be a Health Advocate to encourage family members to do something to protect the home environment.	• Describe a healthful environment. • Use the steps to Be a Health Advocate and encourage friends to do something to protect the school environment.	• Describe what makes a healthful environment. • Use the steps to Be a Health Advocate and encourage citizens to do something to protect the community.
I will help keep the air, land, and water clean and safe.	NHES 8	• Discuss ways your community is kept clean. • Discuss kinds of pollution. • Discuss red tide and its effect on health. • List ways to keep your community clean.	• Identify kinds of land, air, and water pollution. • Explain what to do when red tide occurs. • Explain how to keep land clean and safe. • Identify ways to keep the air clean and safe. • Describe ways to keep water clean and safe.	• Explain how air pollution affects the health of the environment. • Explain ways red tide affects the environment. • List sources of water and land pollution. • Describe ways to reduce water and land pollution.

GRADES 3–5 SCOPE AND SEQUENCE CHART

HEALTH GOALS	THE NATIONAL HEALTH EDUCATION STANDARDS	GRADE 3 OBJECTIVES	GRADE 4 OBJECTIVES	GRADE 5 OBJECTIVES
I will help keep noise at a safe level.	NHES 8	• Explain ways noise harms health. • Explain why noise increases the risk of accidents. • Name ways to encourage others to keep noise at a safe level.	• Explain how noise pollution can affect your health. • List ways to keep noise at a safe level to help others.	• Explain how noise pollution affects the health of the environment. • List ways to reduce noise in your community.
I will not waste energy and resources.	NHES 8	• Name ways to save resources, such as gas, electricity, and paper.	• Describe ways to save water. • List ways to reduce, recycle, and reuse. • Describe ways to save energy.	• List ways to conserve water. • List ways to conserve energy. • Explain what it means to precycle, reuse, and recycle.
I will help keep my environment friendly.	NHES 8	• Explain how you can keep your neighborhood looking nice. • Discuss ways you can enjoy the environment with others.	• Identify ways to keep your school and community environment friendly.	• Name characteristics of a positive environment. • List ways to keep your environment positive.
I will follow safety rules for my home and school.	NHES 7	**Injury Prevention and Safety** • List safety rules to follow to prevent falls. • List safety rules to follow in case of fire. • List ways to prevent poisoning. • Explain what computer safety means. • Discuss how to stay safe outdoors.	• List safety rules to follow to prevent falls. • List safety rules to follow in case of fire. • Describe the elements of a family fire escape plan. • List ways to prevent poisoning.	• List ways to eliminate common safety hazards at home. • List ways to eliminate common safety hazards at school. • Describe some common fire hazards and some rules for fire safety.

GRADES 3–5 SCOPE AND SEQUENCE CHART

HEALTH GOALS	THE NATIONAL HEALTH EDUCATION STANDARDS	GRADE 3 OBJECTIVES	GRADE 4 OBJECTIVES	GRADE 5 OBJECTIVES
I will follow safety rules for biking, walking, skating, and swimming.	NHES 7	• List safety rules to follow for walking, biking, riding a scooter, and swimming. • Describe how to keep safe around water.	• List safety rules to follow for walking, biking, riding a scooter, and swimming. • Explain how personal flotation devices and HELP and huddle methods prevent drowning. • Identify the meaning of different safety signs.	• Describe safety precautions pedestrians should follow. • Describe safety rules to follow when you ride bicycles, scooters, or skateboards. • List safety rules to follow in the water.
I will follow safety rules for riding in a car or bus.	NHES 6 NHES 7	• List ways to keep safe around cars and buses. • Set a Health Goal to wear a safety belt.	• List safety rules for riding in a car and a bus. • Set a Health Goal to wear a safety belt.	• Describe safety rules to follow when you ride in a car. • Set a Health Goal to wear a safety belt.
I will follow safety rules for hazardous weather conditions.	NHES 7	• Explain how to stay safe in bad weather.	• List ways to stay safe in cold and hot weather, earthquakes, thunderstorms, tornadoes, and floods.	• List safety rules to follow during different weather conditions.
I will follow safety rules to protect myself from people who might harm me.	NHES 7	• List safety rules for times when you are home with someone besides your parents or guardian. • List ways to stay safe from strangers. • Explain what to do if you get an unsafe touch.	• List ways to stay safe from strangers when home alone. • List ways to stay safe at school, in the community, and on the Internet. • Describe what to do if you get an unsafe touch.	• Identify ways to protect yourself from people who might harm you. • Explain what to do if someone is suspicious. • Differentiate between a safe and an unsafe touch.

GRADES 3–5 SCOPE AND SEQUENCE CHART

HEALTH GOALS	THE NATIONAL HEALTH EDUCATION STANDARDS	GRADE 3 OBJECTIVES	GRADE 4 OBJECTIVES	GRADE 5 OBJECTIVES
I will follow safety rules to protect myself against violence.	NHES 7	• List safety rules for times when you are home with someone besides your parents or guardian. • Explain what to do if you get an unsafe touch.	• List safety rules to protect yourself from violence. • List ways to recover if you are a victim of violence.	• List examples of violence. • Describe ways to express anger and resolve conflict without violence. • Explain where victims of violence and abuse can get help.
I will stay away from gangs.	NHES 6	• List ways to stay safe from a gang.	• List reasons to stay away from gangs. • Name ways to avoid gangs.	• Discuss ways to recognize gang members. • Explain why it is risky to belong to a gang.
I will follow safety rules to reduce my risk of injuries from guns.	NHES 7	• Explain why you should not pretend to have a gun. • List steps to take if you find a gun.	• List safety rules your school might have about guns. • Name safety rules to follow if you find a gun or someone around you has a gun.	• Explain safety rules to reduce the risk of injuries from guns and knives.
I will be ready for an emergency.	NHES 3 NHES 8	• Discuss steps to follow to help an injured person. • Demonstrate how to make an emergency telephone call.	• Explain steps to follow for an emergency or emergency alert. • Demonstrate how to make an emergency telephone call.	• Discuss ways to be prepared for an emergency. • Explain ways to assess an emergency situation. • Describe what safety measures to take in case of a natural disaster. • Demonstrate how to make an emergency telephone call.

GRADES 3–5 SCOPE AND SEQUENCE CHART

HEALTH GOALS	THE NATIONAL HEALTH EDUCATION STANDARDS	GRADE 3 OBJECTIVES	GRADE 4 OBJECTIVES	GRADE 5 OBJECTIVES
I will be skilled in first aid.	NHES 3 NHES 8	• List items that belong in a first aid kit. • Describe precautions to take when giving first aid. • Describe first aid for cuts, scrapes, nosebleed, bruises, burns, insect stings, animal bites, reactions to poisonous plants, and choking.	• Describe how to put together a first aid kit with a parent or guardian. • Describe how to administer first aid for small cuts, deep cuts, scrapes, and nosebleeds. • Explain how to follow universal precautions. • Describe first aid for sprains, burns, and choking. • Describe first aid for rashes from plants and insects.	• Explain where you should keep a first aid kit. • Explain how to use universal precautions when giving first aid. • List the steps to give first aid for nosebleeds, scrapes, cuts, punctures, poisoning, choking, fractures, bee stings, bruises, burns and blisters, objects in the eye, skin rashes from plants, and sunburn. • Discuss what is meant by CPR and rescue breathing.

GRADES 6–8 SCOPE AND SEQUENCE CHART

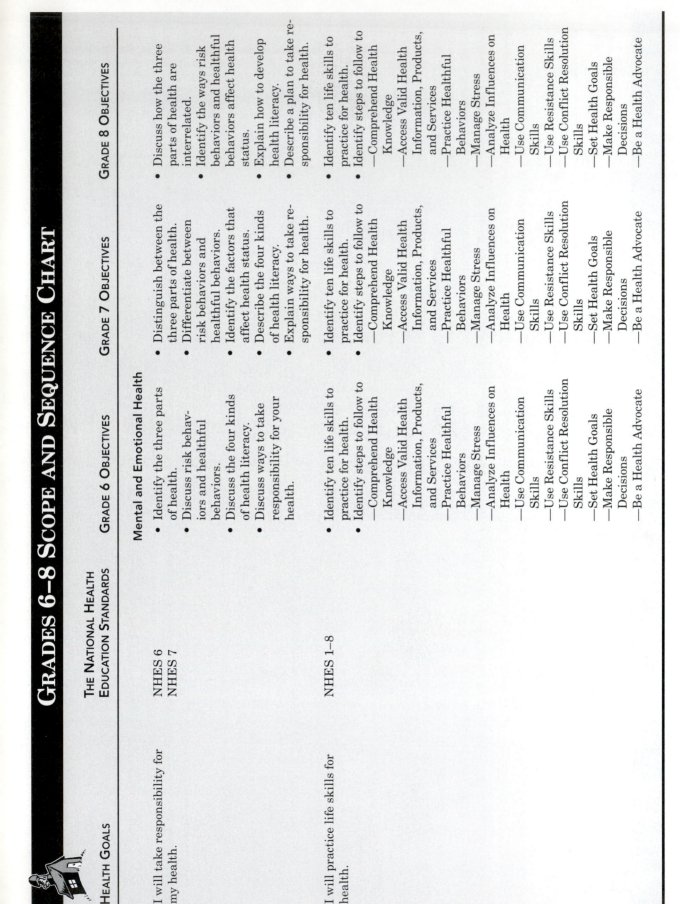

Mental and Emotional Health

HEALTH GOALS	THE NATIONAL HEALTH EDUCATION STANDARDS	GRADE 6 OBJECTIVES	GRADE 7 OBJECTIVES	GRADE 8 OBJECTIVES
I will take responsibility for my health.	NHES 6 NHES 7	• Identify the three parts of health. • Discuss risk behaviors and healthful behaviors. • Discuss the four kinds of health literacy. • Discuss ways to take responsibility for your health.	• Distinguish between the three parts of health. • Differentiate between risk behaviors and healthful behaviors. • Identify the factors that affect health status. • Describe the four kinds of health literacy. • Explain ways to take responsibility for health.	• Discuss how the three parts of health are interrelated. • Identify the ways risk behaviors and healthful behaviors affect health status. • Explain how to develop health literacy. • Describe a plan to take responsibility for health.
I will practice life skills for health.	NHES 1–8	• Identify ten life skills to practice for health. • Identify steps to follow to —Comprehend Health Knowledge —Access Valid Health Information, Products, and Services —Practice Healthful Behaviors —Manage Stress —Analyze Influences on Health —Use Communication Skills —Use Resistance Skills —Use Conflict Resolution Skills —Set Health Goals —Make Responsible Decisions —Be a Health Advocate	• Identify ten life skills to practice for health. • Identify steps to follow to —Comprehend Health Knowledge —Access Valid Health Information, Products, and Services —Practice Healthful Behaviors —Manage Stress —Analyze Influences on Health —Use Communication Skills —Use Resistance Skills —Use Conflict Resolution Skills —Set Health Goals —Make Responsible Decisions —Be a Health Advocate	• Identify ten life skills to practice for health. • Identify steps to follow to —Comprehend Health Knowledge —Access Valid Health Information, Products, and Services —Practice Healthful Behaviors —Manage Stress —Analyze Influences on Health —Use Communication Skills —Use Resistance Skills —Use Conflict Resolution Skills —Set Health Goals —Make Responsible Decisions —Be a Health Advocate

GRADES 6–8 SCOPE AND SEQUENCE CHART

HEALTH GOALS	THE NATIONAL HEALTH EDUCATION STANDARDS	GRADE 6 OBJECTIVES	GRADE 7 OBJECTIVES	GRADE 8 OBJECTIVES
I will gain health knowledge.	NHES 1 NHES 3	• Discuss what it means to be a self-directed learner. • Identify steps to follow to Comprehend Health Knowledge. • Use steps to Access Health Information to write a report on an assigned health topic.	• Explain ways to be a self-directed learner. • Identify steps to follow to Comprehend Health Knowledge. • Use steps to Access Health Information to investigate three journals on a health topic for a speech.	• Discuss reasons to be a self-directed learner throughout life. • Identify steps to follow to Comprehend Health Knowledge. • Use steps to Access Health Information to review three sources on the Internet for an assigned health topic.
I will make responsible decisions.	NHES 6	• Define a responsible decision. • Demonstrate the steps to use to Make Responsible Decisions.	• Differentiate between a responsible decision and a wrong decision. • Demonstrate the steps to use to Make Responsible Decisions. • Describe the benefits of making responsible decisions. • Explain how to take responsibility for wrong decisions.	• Describe three decision-making styles. • Describe internal and external influences that might affect decisions. • Demonstrate the steps to use to Make Responsible Decisions.
I will develop good character.	NHES 4 NHES 7	• Describe factors that influence personality. • Describe ways to demonstrate the six traits of good character.	• Describe personality traits that promote health. • Describe six traits that build character and promote health. • Identify influences on character and actions. • Discuss how to use resistance skills to maintain good character.	• Discuss the factors that influence personality. • Explain how to demonstrate traits of good character. • Explain how to advocate for good character.

GRADES 6–8 SCOPE AND SEQUENCE CHART

HEALTH GOALS	THE NATIONAL HEALTH EDUCATION STANDARDS	GRADE 6 OBJECTIVES	GRADE 7 OBJECTIVES	GRADE 8 OBJECTIVES
I will use resistance skills when appropriate.	NHES 7	• Explain how to resist negative peer pressure. • Demonstrate how to Use Resistance Skills.	• Demonstrate how to Use Resistance Skills. • Discuss how to Use Resistance Skills to maintain good character.	• List reasons to "Say No" to negative peer pressure. • Demonstrate how to Use Resistance Skills.
I will communicate with others-in healthful ways.	NHES 4	• Describe healthful ways to express emotions. • Describe the four levels-of verbal communication. • Describe how to use nonverbal communication. • Explain how to be an effective listener. • Demonstrate how to use I-messages to express feelings.	• Discuss the importance of using I-messages. • List strategies for effective communication. • Explain ways to communicate nonverbally. • Role-play how to Use Communication Skills to communicate nonverbally.	• Discuss interpersonal communication using I-messages. • Compare verbal and nonverbal communication. • Identify effective communication skills. • List guidelines for telephone, Internet, and written communication. • Explain effective communication for different audiences. • Role-play how to Use Communication Skills to express happiness, sadness, anger, and fear. • Explain how to manage anger and deal with fear.

GRADES 6–8 SCOPE AND SEQUENCE CHART

HEALTH GOALS	THE NATIONAL HEALTH EDUCATION STANDARDS	GRADE 6 OBJECTIVES	GRADE 7 OBJECTIVES	GRADE 8 OBJECTIVES
I will choose behaviors that promote a healthy mind.	NHES 6 NHES 7	• Describe factors that influence personality. • List ways to maintain positive self-esteem. • Set a Health Goal to choose behaviors that promote a healthy mind, such as reading each day.	• Describe personality traits that promote health. • Identify ways to improve self-esteem. • Explain how to deal with anxiety, insecurity, and depression. • Identify behaviors that indicate a person might be considering a suicide attempt and actions to take to get help. • Set a Health Goal to choose behaviors that promote a healthy mind, such as solving puzzles and playing concentration games.	• Discuss the factors that influence personality. • Define and give examples of addictive behaviors to avoid. • Set a Health Goal to choose behaviors that promote a healthy mind, such as learning something new each day.
I will follow a plan to manage stress.	NHES 6 NHES 7	• List the causes and signs of stress. • Identify the four steps to follow to Manage Stress. • Design a health behavior contract to Manage Stress.	• Describe the body's response to stress. • Examine the effects of prolonged stress on the body, mind, and relationships. • Describe different kinds of anxiety disorders. • Identify and change behaviors that are sources of stress. • Identify the four steps to follow to Manage Stress. • Design a health behavior contract to Manage Stress.	• Discuss how the body reacts to stressors. • Identify stress-management skills. • Identify the four steps to follow to Manage Stress. • Design a health behavior contract to Manage Stress.

GRADES 6–8 SCOPE AND SEQUENCE CHART

HEALTH GOALS	THE NATIONAL HEALTH EDUCATION STANDARDS	GRADE 6 OBJECTIVES	GRADE 7 OBJECTIVES	GRADE 8 OBJECTIVES
I will be resilient during difficult times.	NHES 6 NHES 7	• Describe healthful ways of dealing with depression and grief. • Identify suicide prevention strategies. • Set a Health Goal to develop a support system of adults and friends.	• Explain how to cope with stress and be resilient. • Discuss ways to deal with grief and depression. • Discuss suicide prevention strategies. • Set a Health Goal to develop a support system of adults and friends.	• Describe the five stages of grief and death and dying. • Discuss how to comfort a grieving person. • Discuss steps to help teens who are depressed. • List steps for suicide prevention. • Set a Health Goal to develop a support system of adults, friends, and mentors.
Family and Social Health				
I will develop healthful family relationships.	NHES 4 NHES 6	• Tell how family members communicate in healthful ways. • Set a Health Goal and make a plan to help a family member.	• List guidelines to follow to maintain healthful family relationships. • Set a Health Goal and make a plan to spend time with family members.	• Describe healthful family relationships. • Set a Health Goal and make a plan to listen more carefully to family members.
I will work to improve difficult family relationships.	NHES 3 NHES 4	• Discuss ways to cope with difficult family relationships, including abuse and violence. • Identify people and places that can help with family relationships.	• Identify kinds of problems families might have and how to get help for them.	• Discuss kinds of harmful family relationships. • Explain why teens who live in dysfunctional families might have difficulty in other relationships. • Summarize ways dysfunctional families can get help.

GRADES 6–8 SCOPE AND SEQUENCE CHART

HEALTH GOALS	THE NATIONAL HEALTH EDUCATION STANDARDS	GRADE 6 OBJECTIVES	GRADE 7 OBJECTIVES	GRADE 8 OBJECTIVES
I will make healthful adjustments to family changes.	NHES 7	• Discuss ways families might change. • Identify ways to adjust to family changes.	• Describe how you can adjust to changes within your family. • Discuss ways parents' divorce might affect school performance and relationships. • Summarize the special needs related to caring for older family members.	• Discuss healthful adjustments teens might make when there are family changes. • Discuss ways family changes might affect a teen's lifestyle.
I will use conflict resolution skills.	NHES 4	• Demonstrate how to Use Conflict Resolution Skills. • Explain what happens when you ask a trusted adult to help with mediation.	• Identify some causes of conflict. • Describe ways to resolve conflict using different conflict response styles. • Demonstrate how to Use Conflict Resolution Skills. • List steps that are used to resolve conflict by mediation.	• Describe common causes of conflict among teens. • Demonstrate how to use Conflict Resolution Skills. • Discuss steps to follow when using mediation.

GRADES 6–8 SCOPE AND SEQUENCE CHART

HEALTH GOALS	THE NATIONAL HEALTH EDUCATION STANDARDS	GRADE 6 OBJECTIVES	GRADE 7 OBJECTIVES	GRADE 8 OBJECTIVES
I will develop healthful relationships.	NHES 4	• Tell how you can make a new friend. • Describe how to maintain friendships. • Discuss why you should choose friends who make responsible decisions. • Discuss when and how to end a friendship. • Discuss how to resist negative peer pressure.	• Describe different types of relationships. • Discuss healthful ways to make new friends. • Explain how peer pressure influences decisions. • Discuss ways to practice abstinence from risk behaviors. • Discuss ways to Use Resistance Skills to reinforce healthful decisions within relationships.	• Identify social skills that promote healthful relationships. • Describe five qualities shared in healthful relationships.
I will develop skills to prepare for dating.	NHES 4	• List characteristics of a person with whom your parents would agree you could spend time. • Explain why abstinence from risk behaviors will be expected of you. • Demonstrate how to Use Resistance Skills if you are pressured to choose risk behaviors.	• List guidelines to help you prepare for group dating. • Identify the factors that contribute to a healthful dating relationship. • Demonstrate how to Use Resistance Skills if you are pressured to choose risk behaviors.	• Discuss activities for group dating. • List dating guidelines. • Explain reasons for setting limits for showing affection. • Demonstrate how to Use Resistance Skills if you are pressured to choose risk behaviors.
I will recognize harmful relationships.	NHES 4	• Contrast the effects of healthful and harmful relationships on you. • Discuss steps to take to improve or end a harmful relationship.	• Give examples of harmful relationships. • Explain what to do about harmful relationships.	• Explain when and how to end a relationship.

GRADES 6–8 SCOPE AND SEQUENCE CHART

HEALTH GOALS	THE NATIONAL HEALTH EDUCATION STANDARDS	GRADE 6 OBJECTIVES	GRADE 7 OBJECTIVES	GRADE 8 OBJECTIVES
I will practice abstinence.	NHES 4 NHES 6 NHES 7	• Explain why abstinence is expected of you. • List ten reasons to practice abstinence. • Explain the importance of setting limits and sticking to them. • Demonstrate how to Use Resistance Skills to say "no" to sex.	• Explain why abstinence from sex is a responsible decision. • Demonstrate how to Use Resistance Skills if pressured to be sexually active. • Identify choices that support the decision to practice abstinence.	• Outline reasons why practicing abstinence is a responsible decision. • Demonstrate how to Use Resistance Skills if you are pressured to be sexually active. • Identify and make a plan to practice behaviors that support the decision to practice abstinence. • List steps teens who have been sexually active can take to change their behavior.
I will develop skills to prepare for marriage.	NHES 6	• Explain how you handle commitments in relationships. • Identify reasons why teen marriage and parenthood is risky.	• Discuss skills needed for healthful marriage and parenthood. • Explain why teens who feel unloved are more at risk for teen marriage and parenthood.	• Explain the importance of honoring commitments in marriage and other relationships. • Outline responsibilities of adulthood for which married teens are not prepared.
I will develop skills to prepare for parenthood.	NHES 6	• Discuss the growth and development of infants, toddlers, and children in middle childhood. • Use steps to Access Health Information to learn five facts about the care of children. • Identify reasons why teen marriage and parenthood are risky.	• Discuss the responsibilities and skills needed for parenthood. • Explain why teens who feel unloved are more at risk for teen marriage and parenthood. • Use steps to Access Health Information to find facts for an oral report on the care of children.	• Identify the problems and risks of teen parenthood. • Use steps to Access Health Information to write a report about the care of children.

GRADES 6–8 SCOPE AND SEQUENCE CHART

HEALTH GOALS	THE NATIONAL HEALTH EDUCATION STANDARDS	GRADE 6 OBJECTIVES	GRADE 7 OBJECTIVES	GRADE 8 OBJECTIVES
		Growth and Development		
I will keep my body systems healthy.	NHES 7	• Explain how your body systems work together. • Discuss the functions of the body systems. • Discuss ways to care for the body systems.	• Detail the structure and function of the body systems. • Discuss ways to protect and promote the health of the body systems.	• Describe the structure and function of each body system. • Identify the physical changes that occur during puberty. • Explain ways to care for body systems.
I will achieve the developmental tasks of adolescence.	NHES 6	• Summarize the changes that occur throughout each stage in the life cycle. • Describe ways to care for the body during puberty. • Discuss the emotional, intellectual, and social changes that occur during adolescence.	• Identify ways in which individuals differ in growth and development. • Identify eight developmental tasks to work on right now. • Describe ways to become a responsible adult.	• Discuss the emotional and social changes that occur in adolescence. • Identify the eight developmental tasks of adolescence.
I will recognize habits that protect female reproductive health.	NHES 1 NHES 7	• Describe how the female body changes during adolescence. • Describe changes in feelings during adolescence.	• Identify the female secondary sex characteristics. • List and give the definition for each of the female reproductive organs. • Explain what occurs during the menstrual cycle. • Discuss habits a female can practice to protect reproductive health.	• Describe the functions of the endocrine and reproductive systems. • Identify physical changes that occur during puberty. • Trace the path of an unfertilized egg through the reproductive organs. • Describe the menstrual cycle. • Discuss habits a female can practice to protect reproductive health.

GRADES 6–8 SCOPE AND SEQUENCE CHART

HEALTH GOALS	THE NATIONAL HEALTH EDUCATION STANDARDS	GRADE 6 OBJECTIVES	GRADE 7 OBJECTIVES	GRADE 8 OBJECTIVES
I will recognize habits that protect male reproductive health.	NHES 1 NHES 7	• Describe how the male body changes during adolescence. • Describe changes in feelings during adolescence.	• Identify the male secondary sex characteristics. • List and give the definition for each of the male reproductive organs. • Discuss habits a male can practice to protect reproductive health.	• Describe the functions of the endocrine and reproductive systems. • Identify physical changes that occur during puberty. • Trace the path of a sperm cell through the male reproductive organs. • Discuss habits a male can practice to protect reproductive health.
I will learn about pregnancy and childbirth.	NHES 1	• Explain how a fertilized egg is formed and nourished. • Discuss why health care is important during pregnancy. • Explain why teen pregnancy and parenthood is risky.	• Explain what happens during pregnancy, labor, and childbirth. • Explain ways a mother-to-be's behaviors can affect the health of her baby. • Explain ways a male's behavior can affect the health of his baby. • Explain the risks of teen pregnancy and parenthood.	• Discuss conception and the stages of pregnancy. • Describe the development of a baby from conception through birth. • Discuss the importance of prenatal care. • Identify problems that can occur during pregnancy. • Discuss the processes of labor and delivery. • Explain the risks of teen pregnancy and parenthood.
I will provide responsible care for infants and children.	NHES 8	• Describe ways parents bond with their newborn baby. • List ways you can help provide responsible care for infants and children.	• Explain how parents can bond with their newborn baby. • Identify skills you need to be a child-sitter.	• Identify the skills a person needs to provide responsible care for infants and children.

GRADES 6–8 SCOPE AND SEQUENCE CHART

HEALTH GOALS	THE NATIONAL HEALTH EDUCATION STANDARDS	GRADE 6 OBJECTIVES	GRADE 7 OBJECTIVES	GRADE 8 OBJECTIVES
I will practice abstinence to avoid teen pregnancy and parenthood.	NHES 7	• Explain why teen pregnancy and parenthood is risky.	• Discuss reasons to practice abstinence and avoid teen pregnancy and parenthood.	• Discuss reasons why practicing abstinence is the best choice for teens.
I will develop habits that promote healthful aging.	NHES 7	• Explain how people age. • Use the steps to Practice Healthful Behavior to make a healthful habit for aging a habit.	• Identify habits that help a person maintain physical and mental health into late adulthood. • Use the steps to Practice Healthful Behavior to make a healthful behavior for aging a habit.	• Describe the four stages of adulthood. • Discuss differences in how people age. • Explain how practicing healthful habits now will help you age in a healthful way. • Use the steps to Practice Healthful Behavior to make a healthful behavior for aging a habit.
I will develop my learning style.	NHES 6	• Describe ways young people learn. • Set a Health Goal to improve your memory.	• Discuss habits that help you learn and stay mentally alert. • Set a Health Goal to improve your concentration.	• List suggestions to improve the way you learn. • Discuss the difficulties teens who have learning disabilities might have. • Set a Health Goal to study with a friend and to ask each other questions and share answers.

GRADES 6–8 SCOPE AND SEQUENCE CHART

HEALTH GOALS	THE NATIONAL HEALTH EDUCATION STANDARDS	GRADE 6 OBJECTIVES	GRADE 7 OBJECTIVES	GRADE 8 OBJECTIVES
I will share with my family my feelings about dying and death.	NHES 4 NHES 8	• List signs that a person might be grieving. • Discuss ways you can comfort someone who is grieving.	• Discuss healthful and harmful ways of grieving when someone close to you dies. • Explain why death of a young person is especially difficult for others. • Explain why you might grieve when a well-known person dies. • Give examples of how to comfort someone who is grieving.	• Describe the five stages of dying. • Identify people who are part of your support network. • Describe ways to comfort someone who is grieving.
Nutrition				
I will follow the Dietary Guidelines.	NHES 7	• Discuss why you need the six nutrients. • Explain how to follow the Dietary Guidelines.	• Identify types and sources of nutrients. • Discuss how to distinguish between foods that are healthful and those that do not contain many nutrients. • Describe how to use the Dietary Guidelines.	• List the Dietary Guidelines, and explain why each should be followed.
I will eat the recommended daily amounts of food from MyPyramid.	NHES 7	• List the five foods groups. • Tell what nutrients are found in foods. • Discuss how to use MyPyramid.	• Identify the recommended daily amounts of different foods from MyPyramid.	• Discuss nutrients that are in foods that belong to each of the five food groups. • List the recommended daily amounts of foods from MyPyramid.

GRADES 6–8 SCOPE AND SEQUENCE CHART

HEALTH GOALS	THE NATIONAL HEALTH EDUCATION STANDARDS	GRADE 6 OBJECTIVES	GRADE 7 OBJECTIVES	GRADE 8 OBJECTIVES
I will plan a healthful diet that reduces the risk of disease.	NHES 6	• Describe ways healthful eating habits reduce the risk of disease. • Set a Health Goal and make a plan to eat fewer fatty foods.	• Discuss diet choices that reduce the risk of developing premature heart disease. • Discuss diet choices that reduce the risk of developing cancer. • Set a Health Goal and make a plan to eat foods rich in fiber.	• Discuss how to choose foods that help reduce the risk of heart disease and cancer. • Identify healthful dietary choices for people who have diabetes and hypoglycemia. • Set a Health Goal and make a plan to reduce the amount of sugar in your diet.
I will evaluate food labels and food ads.	NHES 2 NHES 3	• Explain how to read a food label. • Explain how to compare nutritional value and the unit price of foods. • Discuss the purposes of food ads. • Use the steps to Analyze Influences on Health to determine the influence of advertising copy on a cereal box.	• List the information you can learn from reading a food label. • Compare food labels for two similar foods. • Discuss appeals found in food ads. • Use the steps to Analyze Influences on Health to determine the influence of a commercial for a fast-food meal.	• Interpret and evaluate the nutrition information found on food labels. • Analyze food ads for their mention of the Dietary Guidelines. • Use the steps to Analyze Influences on Health to determine the influence of a sports hero who recommends a specific beverage.
I will select foods that contain nutrients.	NHES 7	• Discuss why you need the six nutrients.	• Identify types and sources of nutrients. • Identify nutrients that are evaluated on a food label.	• Identify the functions of each of the six nutrients. • Give examples of foods that contain each of the six nutrients.

GRADES 6–8 SCOPE AND SEQUENCE CHART

HEALTH GOALS	THE NATIONAL HEALTH EDUCATION STANDARDS	GRADE 6 OBJECTIVES	GRADE 7 OBJECTIVES	GRADE 8 OBJECTIVES
I will develop healthful eating habits.	NHES 6	• Contrast healthful and harmful eating habits. • Set a Health Goal and make a plan to choose healthful snacks.	• Describe different eating styles. • Set a Health Goal and make a plan to eat a healthful breakfast. • Explain how to plan, shop for, and prepare healthful meals and snacks. • Describe how to plan healthful meals in a variety of settings.	• Discuss how to recognize healthful versus harmful eating habits. • List stressful situations for which teens might substitute harmful eating patterns for healthful ways of coping. • Set a Health Goal, and make a plan to eat healthful foods for lunch.
I will follow the Dietary Guidelines when I go out to eat.	NHES 6 NHES 7	• Discuss ways to follow the Dietary Guidelines when eating out. • Use the steps to Practice Healthful Behaviors to make eating less salty foods at fast-food restaurants a habit.	• Describe how to plan healthful meals in a variety of settings. • Use the steps to Practice Healthful Behaviors to make eating fewer fatty foods at restaurants a habit.	• Identify healthful food choices at fast-food restaurants. • Identify healthful food choices at ethnic restaurants. • Use the steps to Practice Healthful Behaviors to make ordering fewer high-sugar foods a habit.
I will protect myself from foodborne illnesses.	NHES 1 NHES 7	• Discuss ways to prevent foodborne illnesses. • Discuss ways to share food without spreading germs. • Discuss causes of food-allergies and intolerances.	• Identify different kinds of foodborne illnesses and their causes, symptoms, and treatments. • Discuss ways to reduce the risk of foodborne illnesses.	• Identify ways to reduce the risk of foodborne illnesses.

GRADES 6–8 SCOPE AND SEQUENCE CHART

HEALTH GOALS	THE NATIONAL HEALTH EDUCATION STANDARDS	GRADE 6 OBJECTIVES	GRADE 7 OBJECTIVES	GRADE 8 OBJECTIVES
I will maintain a healthful weight and body composition.	NHES 6	• List reasons to maintain a healthful weight. • Explain how to determine what a healthful weight is. • Summarize ways to maintain a healthful weight. • Explain how to maintain a healthful body composition.	• Determine healthful weight and body composition. • Assess the health risks associated with being overweight and underweight. • Identify strategies for healthful weight management. • Set a Health Goal to achieve a healthful percentage of body fat.	• Explain how to determine a healthful weight and body composition. • Describe strategies to achieve and maintain a healthful weight. • Discuss ways to achieve a healthful percentage of body fat.
I will develop skills to prevent eating disorders.	NHES 2	• Discuss ways you can recognize eating disorders. • Discuss treatments for eating disorders. • Analyze the influence of peer pressure and TV on body image.	• Identify signs and symptoms of eating disorders. • Describe the prevention and treatment of eating disorders. • Analyze the influence of ads for jeans and other clothing items on a teen's body image.	• Describe the causes, symptoms, related health problems, and treatment of eating disorders. • Identify factors that contribute to obesity and health problems caused by obesity. • Analyze the influence of stress on eating habits such as starvation and binging.

GRADES 6–8 SCOPE AND SEQUENCE CHART

HEALTH GOALS	THE NATIONAL HEALTH EDUCATION STANDARDS	GRADE 6 OBJECTIVES	GRADE 7 OBJECTIVES	GRADE 8 OBJECTIVES
Personal Health and Physical Activity				
I will have regular examinations.	NHES 3	• Explain what happens during a regular physical examination. • Explain causes and treatment for hearing loss. • Discuss vision problems and their correction.	• Explain the reasons to have a physical examination. • Identify vaccines and tell why and when they are recommended. • Explain how hearing loss is corrected. • Explain ways visual acuity is corrected.	• Discuss how a physician helps you to stay healthy. • List symptoms for which prompt medical treatment is needed.
I will follow a dental health plan.	NHES 3 NHES 7	• Explain how cavities and periodontal disease develop. • Demonstrate toothbrushing and flossing. • List diet guidelines to follow to keep teeth and gums healthy. • Explain why braces, rubber bands, and a retainer might be worn. • List actions to include in a dental health plan.	• Describe three ways crooked teeth can be straightened. • Make a health behavior contract for dental health.	• Describe ways a dentist helps you keep your teeth and gums healthy. • Explain the purpose of wearing braces. • Discuss proper brushing and flossing techniques.

Grades 6–8 Scope and Sequence Chart

Health Goals	The National Health Education Standards	Grade 6 Objectives	Grade 7 Objectives	Grade 8 Objectives
I will be well groomed and have correct posture.	NHES 2 NHES 3 NHES 7	• Identify health products for grooming. • Use the steps to Analyze Influences on Health to check out an ad for shampoo. • List the benefits of being well groomed. • Describe ways to care for your skin. • Describe ways to care for your hair and nails.	• List grooming habits for the care of the skin, hair, and nails. • Make a list of health products for grooming that you use. • Use the steps to Analyze Influences on Health to check out the claims made for a toothpaste.	• Summarize ways to care for the skin, nails, and feet. • Explain ways to care for your hair. • Make a health behavior contract to be well groomed. • Use the steps to Analyze Influences on Health to check out an ad for an acne product.
I will get adequate sleep and rest.	NHES 7	• Describe the benefits of rest and sleep.	• Discuss ways to get a good night's sleep. • Discuss ways to rest during the day.	• Explain how adequate rest and sleep promote health.
I will participate in regular physical activity.	NHES 6 NHES 7	• Discuss ways regular physical activity benefits the three areas of health. • Make a health behavior contract to participate in regular physical activity.	• Discuss the ways physical activity improves health. • Discuss ways that technology and other resources influence your physical activity choices.	• List the top ten reasons for being physically active. • Explain ways physical activity promotes well-being. • Explain ways physical activity can be used for stress management. • Explain ways physical activity promotes the development of social skills. • Describe ways physical activity teaches you about competition.

GRADES 6–8 SCOPE AND SEQUENCE CHART

HEALTH GOALS	THE NATIONAL HEALTH EDUCATION STANDARDS	GRADE 6 OBJECTIVES	GRADE 7 OBJECTIVES	GRADE 8 OBJECTIVES
I will develop and maintain health-related fitness.	NHES 6	• Explain how you can achieve the five kinds of health-related fitness. • Identify tests to measure health-related fitness. • Set a Health Goal and make a plan to improve muscular strength.	• Identify five kinds of health-related fitness. • Identify physical activities that help you achieve and maintain health-related fitness. • Describe exercises that are used in tests to measure health-related fitness. • Set a Health Goal and make a plan to improve flexibility.	• Describe how physical activity affects your heart, lungs, and blood vessels. • Explain how physical activity affects your bones, joints, muscles, weight, and body composition. • Discuss each of the five kinds of health-related fitness. • Practice for each of the health-related fitness tests. • Set a Health Goal and make a plan to improve cardiorespiratory endurance.
I will develop and maintain skill-related fitness.	NHES 6	• Discuss six fitness skills. • Set a Health Goal and make a plan to improve balance.	• Identify six fitness skills you can use in sports and games. • Set a Health Goal and make a plan to improve your speed running or skating.	• List the skills you need for skill-related fitness. • Set a Health Goal and make a plan to improve your agility.
I will follow a physical fitness plan.	NHES 6	• Describe resources to consider when making a physical fitness plan. • Identify tests to measure your level of physical fitness. • Discuss how to develop a physical fitness plan. • Make a physical fitness plan using a health behavior contract.	• Identify short-term and long-term goals to include in a physical fitness plan. • Identify tests to measure your level of physical fitness. • Make a physical fitness plan using a health behavior contract.	• Explain the meaning and purpose of training principles. • Describe factors to consider when making a physical fitness plan. • Identify tests to measure your level of physical fitness. • Make a physical fitness plan using a health behavior contract.

Grades 6–8 Scope and Sequence Chart

Health Goals	The National Health Education Standards	Grade 6 Objectives	Grade 7 Objectives	Grade 8 Objectives
I will prevent physical activity-related injuries and illnesses.	NHES 7	• Explain how to prevent and treat common injuries that occur during physical activities.	• Explain what is included in a sports physical. • Describe common physical activity–related injuries and illnesses. • Discuss ways to reduce the risk of physical activity–related injuries and illnesses.	• Explain the meaning and purpose of training principles. • Discuss ways to prevent injuries and illnesses when participating in physical activities.
I will be a responsible spectator and participant in sports.	NHES 8	• Explain how you can be safe when you watch or play sports. • Use the steps to Be a Health Advocate to advocate for sportsmanship.	• Discuss the health risks associated with anabolic steroid use in sports. • Discuss the role of coaches, sports officials, and spectators in maintaining a safe environment. • Use the steps to Be a Health Advocate to advocate for a spectator code of conduct for students at your school.	• Discuss rules for safe and responsible competition. • Use the steps to Be a Health Advocate to advocate for showing respect for sports officials at sporting events.

Grades 6–8 Scope and Sequence Chart

Health Goals	The National Health Education Standards	Grade 6 Objectives	Grade 7 Objectives	Grade 8 Objectives
		Alcohol, Tobacco, and Other Drugs		
I will follow guidelines for the safe use of prescription and over-the-counter (OTC) drugs.	NHES 3 NHES 7	• List ways medicines promote health. • Explain how drugs enter and affect the body. • Locate warnings on a label for an OTC drug. • Describe guidelines for using prescription and OTC drugs. • List way medicines promote health. • Explain how drugs enter and affect the body. • Locate warnings on a label for an OTC drug. • Describe guidelines for using prescription and OTC drugs.	• Classify drugs as prescription or OTC drugs. • Describe various prescription and OTC drugs. • Identify information found on a label for a prescription drug. • Identify guidelines for the responsible use of prescription drugs. • Identify guidelines for the responsible use of OTC drugs.	• Explain ways drugs enter the body. • Explain how drugs change the way the mind and body works. • Compare information on labels for prescription and OTC drugs. • Discuss guidelines for using prescription drugs. • Discuss guidelines for using OTC drugs.
I will not misuse or abuse drugs.	NHES 7	• Explain why drug misuse and abuse are dangerous. • Explain why some teens misuse or abuse drugs.	• Distinguish between drug misuse and abuse. • Discuss signs that a teen misuses or abuses drugs.	• Explain how drugs enter the body. • Identify factors that determine the effects of drugs on the body. • Discuss drug misuse, drug abuse, and drug dependence.

Grades 6–8 Scope and Sequence Chart

Health Goals	The National Health Education Standards	Grade 6 Objectives	Grade 7 Objectives	Grade 8 Objectives
I will be aware of resources for the treatment of drug misuse and abuse.	NHES 3	• Discuss how to recognize and get help for someone who abuses alcohol or other drugs.	• Discuss treatment and recovery for people who abuse drugs and the families of those who abuse drugs.	• Describe how drug misuse and abuse progress to drug dependence. • Describe the behaviors of denial and honest talk. • Discuss formal intervention and the resources available for the treatment of drug dependency.
I will choose a drug-free lifestyle to reduce my risk of violence and accidents.	NHES 4 NHES 6	• Discuss how alcohol and other drug abuse affects the individual, families, and society. • Set a Health Goal to choose a drug-free lifestyle. • Demonstrate how to Use Resistance Skills to maintain a drug-free lifestyle.	• Explain how drug misuse and abuse affects the three parts of health. • Explain how drug misuse and abuse affects society. • Explain why harmful drug use increases the risk of accidents and violence. • Identify ways to prevent drug slipping. • Set a Health Goal to choose a drug-free lifestyle. • Demonstrate how to Use Resistance Skills to maintain a drug-free lifestyle.	• Describe the risk factors and protective factors for drug misuse and abuse. • Explain how staying drug-free helps protect against violence, unintentional injuries, infection with HIV, and unintended pregnancy. • Set a Health Goal to choose a drug-free lifestyle. • Demonstrate how to Use Resistance Skills to maintain a drug-free lifestyle.

GRADES 6–8 SCOPE AND SEQUENCE CHART

HEALTH GOALS	THE NATIONAL HEALTH EDUCATION STANDARDS	GRADE 6 OBJECTIVES	GRADE 7 OBJECTIVES	GRADE 8 OBJECTIVES
I will choose a drug-free lifestyle to reduce my risk of HIV, STDs, and unintended pregnancy.	NHES 6	• Discuss how alcohol and other drug abuse affects the individual, families, and society. • Explain how a drug-free lifestyle reduces the risk of HIV, STDs, and unintended pregnancy. • Demonstrate how to Make Responsible Decisions if pressured to use drugs.	• Explain why harmful drug use increases the risk of HIV/STDs and unintended pregnancy. • Demonstrate how to Make Responsible Decisions if pressured to use drugs.	• Describe the risk factors and protective factors for drug misuse and abuse. • Explain how staying drug-free helps protect against violence, unintentional injuries, infection with HIV, and unintended pregnancy. • Demonstrate how to Make Responsible Decisions if pressured to use drugs.
I will practice protective factors that help me stay away from drugs.	NHES 7	• Name protective factors and risk factors for drug use.	• Describe protective factors and risk factors for drug use. • Discuss ways you can keep from being an enabler.	• Differentiate between risk factors and protective factors for drug misuse and abuse.
I will use resistance skills if I am pressured to misuse or abuse drugs.	NHES 4	• Demonstrate how to Use Resistance Skills if you are pressured to misuse or abuse drugs.	• Demonstrate how to Use Resistance Skills if you are pressured to misuse or abuse drugs.	• Summarize reasons for saying "no" to alcohol, tobacco, and other drug use. • Demonstrate how to Use Resistance Skills if you are pressured to misuse or abuse drugs.

GRADES 6–8 SCOPE AND SEQUENCE CHART

HEALTH GOALS	THE NATIONAL HEALTH EDUCATION STANDARDS	GRADE 6 OBJECTIVES	GRADE 7 OBJECTIVES	GRADE 8 OBJECTIVES
I will avoid tobacco use and secondhand smoke.	NHES 2 NHES 3 NHES 4 NHES 7	• Describe the effects of tobacco use on the body and mind. • Discuss the stages of nicotine addiction. • Explain why smoking, smokeless tobacco, and secondhand smoke are harmful to health. • Analyze the influence of tobacco ads. • Demonstrate how to Use Resistance Skills to say "no" to tobacco use.	• Identify types of tobacco products and their harmful ingredients. • Identify the harmful effects of using tobacco products. • Identify the harmful effects of secondhand smoke. • Analyze the influences on tobacco use. • Demonstrate how to Use Resistance Skills to say "no" to tobacco use. • Discuss how to Access Health Services to quit smoking.	• Discuss the harmful effects of the addictive drug nicotine. • Describe the short-term and long-term effects of tobacco use. • Summarize the effects of tobacco use on long-term goals and the health of your future family. • Summarize the risks of secondhand smoke. • List ways to reduce exposure to secondhand smoke. • Analyze the influence of advertisements and media to identify faulty thinking about tobacco use. • Demonstrate how to Use Resistance Skills to say "no" to tobacco use. • Discuss how to Access Health Services that provide tobacco cessation programs.

GRADES 6–8 SCOPE AND SEQUENCE CHART

HEALTH GOALS	THE NATIONAL HEALTH EDUCATION STANDARDS	GRADE 6 OBJECTIVES	GRADE 7 OBJECTIVES	GRADE 8 OBJECTIVES
I will not drink alcohol.	NHES 2 NHES 4 NHES 7	• Describe factors that affect blood alcohol concentration (BAC). • Discuss ways alcohol harms the body, the mind, and relationships. • Analyze beer ads for messages that include faulty thinking. • Discuss laws relating to alcohol. • Explain ways family members might respond to a family member who has alcoholism. • Demonstrate how to Use Resistance Skills to say "no" to drinking.	• Describe factors that affect blood alcohol concentration (BAC). • Describe the effects of varying levels of BAC. • Discuss the short-term and long-term effects of drinking on the mind and body. • Discuss the cause and effects of fetal alcohol syndrome (FAS). • Analyze ways commercials try to make drinking appealing. • Discuss alcoholism and its effects on families. • Demonstrate how to Use Resistance Skills to say "no" to drinking.	• Discuss factors that affect blood alcohol concentration (BAC). • Describe the effects of alcohol on the mind, the body, relationships, and pregnancy. • Analyze magazine ads for liquor to find appeals used in them. • Describe characteristics of problem drinking and alcoholism. • Discuss alcoholism: progression of the disease, effects on family members, treatment, and recovery programs. • Demonstrate how to Use Resistance Skills to say "no" to drinking.

GRADES 6–8 SCOPE AND SEQUENCE CHART

HEALTH GOALS	THE NATIONAL HEALTH EDUCATION STANDARDS	GRADE 6 OBJECTIVES	GRADE 7 OBJECTIVES	GRADE 8 OBJECTIVES
I will not be involved in illegal drug use.	NHES 4 NHES 6 NHES 7	• Identify reasons some teens abuse drugs. • Describe the short-term and long-term effects of using stimulants, depressants, narcotics, hallucinogens, marijuana, anabolic steroids, and inhalants. • Demonstrate how to Use Resistance Skills to say "no" to illegal drug use. • Set a Health Goal and make a plan to maintain a drug-free lifestyle.	• Discuss reasons why illegal use of the following drugs is harmful: marijuana, cocaine and crack, methamphetamine, LSD, MDMA, roofies, heroin, PCP, inhalants, and anabolic steroids. • Explain why drug mixing can cause injury, illness, and death. • Demonstrate how to Use Resistance Skills to say "no" to illegal drug use. • Set a Health Goal and make a plan to maintain a drug-free lifestyle.	• Differentiate between controlled drugs and illegal drugs. • Discuss the effects of commonly used controlled drugs. • Discuss the effects of stimulants, depressants, sedatives, hypnotics, narcotics, and hallucinogens. • Describe the source, composition, and effects of marijuana. • Explain why it is dangerous to use anabolic steroids without a prescription and to abuse inhalants. • Set a Health Goal and make a plan to maintain a drug-free lifestyle.
I will choose behaviors to prevent the spread of pathogens.	NHES 7	**Communicable and Chronic Diseases** • Discuss types of pathogens and ways they enter the body. • Explain how body defenses protect against pathogens.	• Discuss ways pathogens can be spread. • Describe how the immune system responds to pathogens. • List ways to keep the immune system healthy, including getting adequate rest.	• List different kinds of pathogens, and explain how they are spread. • Discuss ways to prevent the spread of pathogens. • Discuss ways that the body defends itself against disease. • Describe behaviors that keep the immune system healthy.

Grades 6–8 Scope and Sequence Chart

Health Goals	The National Health Education Standards	Grade 6 Objectives	Grade 7 Objectives	Grade 8 Objectives
I will choose behaviors to reduce my risk of infection with communicable diseases.	NHES 1 NHES 7	• Discuss the cause, symptoms, prevention, and treatment for the common cold, influenza, mononucleosis, hepatitis, strep throat, Lyme disease, anthrax, and West Nile virus. • Identify ways to reduce the risk of communicable diseases.	• Identify the causes, symptoms, diagnosis, and treatment for common communicable diseases. • Identify ways to reduce the risk of infection with communicable diseases.	• Describe the causes, symptoms, diagnosis, and treatment of common communicable diseases. • Summarize ways to reduce the risk of infection with communicable diseases.
I will keep a personal health record.	NHES 3	• Explain why you should keep a personal health record.	• Explain why you should keep a personal health record. • List the information you should keep in a personal health record.	• Explain why you should keep a personal health record. • List the information you should keep in a personal health record.
I will choose behaviors to reduce my risk of infection with sexually transmitted diseases.	NHES 6 NHES 7	• Identify the cause, signs, symptoms, diagnosis, treatment, and complications for STDs. • Discuss ways to reduce the risk of infection with STDs. • Demonstrate how to Make Responsible Decisions if pressured to be sexually active.	• Discuss the cause, signs, symptoms, diagnosis, treatment, and complications for STDs. • Discuss ways to reduce the risk of infection with STDs. • Demonstrate how to Make Responsible Decisions if pressured to be sexually active.	• Describe the facts and fallacies about how STDs are transmitted. • Outline the cause, signs, symptoms, diagnosis, treatment, and complications for STDs. • Discuss ways to reduce the risk of infection with STDs. • Demonstrate how to Make Responsible Decisions if pressured to be sexually active.

GRADES 6–8 SCOPE AND SEQUENCE CHART

HEALTH GOALS	THE NATIONAL HEALTH EDUCATION STANDARDS	GRADE 6 OBJECTIVES	GRADE 7 OBJECTIVES	GRADE 8 OBJECTIVES
I will choose behaviors to reduce my risk of HIV infection.	NHES 4 NHES 7	• Describe how HIV destroys the immune system. • Discuss risk behaviors and risk situations for HIV infection. • Explain why a person can infect others with HIV before testing positive. • Discuss treatment for HIV infection and AIDS. • Discuss ways to reduce the risk of infection with HIV. • Demonstrate how to Use Resistance Skills to say "no" to risk behaviors for HIV infection.	• List risk factors for HIV-infection. • Explain how HIV infection progresses to AIDS. • Discuss tests to determine HIV status. • Discuss ways to reduce the risk of HIV infection. • Identify ways HIV and AIDS threaten society and world health. • Demonstrate how to Use Resistance Skills to say "no" to risk behaviors for HIV infection.	• Explain how HIV destroys the immune system. • Describe signs of HIV infection. • Describe ways HIV is and is not spread. • Discuss tests for, treatment for, and prevention of HIV infection. • Discuss universal precautions that can be used to protect health care workers and others from HIV infection. • Demonstrate how to Use Resistance Skills to say "no" to risk behaviors for HIV infection.
I will choose behaviors to reduce my risk of cardiovascular diseases.	NHES 6 NHES 7	• List the causes, symptoms, treatment, and ways to prevent for cardiovascular diseases. • Set a Health Goal and make a plan to choose behaviors that reduce the risk of cardiovascular diseases.	• Identify risk factors for cardiovascular disease. • Discuss ways to reduce the risk of high blood pressure, stroke, and atherosclerosis. • Set a Health Goal and make a plan to choose behaviors that reduce the risk of cardiovascular diseases.	• Identify types of cardiovascular diseases. • Discuss treatment for cardiovascular diseases. • Discuss ways to reduce the risk of cardiovascular diseases. • Set a Health Goal and make a plan to choose behaviors that reduce the risk of cardiovascular diseases.

GRADES 6–8 SCOPE AND SEQUENCE CHART

HEALTH GOALS	THE NATIONAL HEALTH EDUCATION STANDARDS	GRADE 6 OBJECTIVES	GRADE 7 OBJECTIVES	GRADE 8 OBJECTIVES
I will choose behaviors to reduce my risk of cancer.	NHES 6 NHES 7 NHES 8	• List the warning signs of cancer. • Discuss ways to reduce the risk of cancer. • Use the steps to Be a Health Advocate to advocate behavior that reduces the risk of skin cancer.	• Identify common carcinogens. • Discuss ways to reduce the risk of cancer. • Use the steps to Be a Health Advocate to advocate for a diet that reduces the risk of cancer.	• Explain how cancers are classified. • List the early warning signs of cancer. • Discuss screening tests and treatment for cancer. • Discuss ways to reduce the risk of cancer. • Discuss coping strategies to use if a family member or friend has cancer. • Use the steps to Be a Health Advocate to advocate for a smoke-free environment.
I will recognize ways to manage chronic health conditions.	NHES 1	• Discuss chronic health conditions and ways to manage them.	• Differentiate between a chronic health condition and an acute health condition. • Discuss chronic health conditions and ways to manage them.	• Discuss possible causes of chronic health conditions. • Discuss the cause, symptoms, and treatment for allergies, arthritis, asthma, cerebral palsy, chronic fatigue syndrome, diabetes, epilepsy, headaches, muscular dystrophy, epilepsy, and multiple sclerosis.
I will recognize ways to manage asthma and allergies.	NHES 1	• Discuss what happens when a person has an allergic reaction. • Discuss ways a person can manage asthma and reduce the risk of an asthma attack.	• Discuss ways to manage and treat allergies. • Discuss asthma, including signs of an asthma attack, asthma triggers, and ways to avoid asthma triggers.	• Discuss the causes, symptoms, and treatment for allergies and asthma. • Discuss ways to prevent allergic reactions and asthma attacks.

GRADES 6–8 SCOPE AND SEQUENCE CHART

HEALTH GOALS	THE NATIONAL HEALTH EDUCATION STANDARDS	GRADE 6 OBJECTIVES	GRADE 7 OBJECTIVES	GRADE 8 OBJECTIVES
I will choose behaviors to reduce my risk of diabetes.	NHES 6 NHES 7	• Discuss the symptoms, treatment, and prevention of diabetes. • Set a Health Goal and make a plan to reduce sugar consumption.	• Discuss the symptoms, treatment, and risk factors for diabetes. • Set a Health Goal and make a plan to reduce sugar consumption.	• Discuss the symptoms, treatment, and risk factors for diabetes. • Set a Health Goal and make a plan to maintain a healthful weight.

Consumer and Community Health

HEALTH GOALS	THE NATIONAL HEALTH EDUCATION STANDARDS	GRADE 6 OBJECTIVES	GRADE 7 OBJECTIVES	GRADE 8 OBJECTIVES
I will evaluate sources of health information.	NHES 3	• List sources of valid health information. • Describe ways to stay safe when you access health information online.	• Identify types of valid health information. • Identify reliable sources of valid health information. • Explain ways to use technology to access valid health information.	• Explain how to evaluate sources of health-related information. • List professional and government groups that provide health-related information. • Describe ways you can use the computer, CD-ROMs, and Web sites to find health-related information. • State safety tips to use when you are online.
I will develop media literacy.	NHES 2	• Discuss what it means to be media literate. • Discuss messages in advertising that are intended to influence you. • Use the steps to Analyze Influences on Health to check out a commercial for a food.	• Discuss ways to evaluate the messages in media. • Use the steps to Analyze Influences on Health to check out an ad for a health product.	• Discuss the reasons to be media literate. • Describe appeals used in ads and commercials. • Use the steps to Analyze Influences on Health to check out an ad for a health service.

GRADES 6–8 SCOPE AND SEQUENCE CHART

HEALTH GOALS	THE NATIONAL HEALTH EDUCATION STANDARDS	GRADE 6 OBJECTIVES	GRADE 7 OBJECTIVES	GRADE 8 OBJECTIVES
I will make a plan to manage time and money.	NHES 6	• Discuss how to manage time. • Discuss how to manage money. • Set a Health Goal to make a time management plan.	• Explain why you need to have a time management plan. • Discuss ways money management can affect the quality of life. • Set a Health Goal to save money.	• Explain how to make a time management plan. • Describe how to make a budget. • Set a Health Goal to make a budget.
I will choose healthful entertainment.	NHES 2 NHES 6	• Explain ways to recognize shopping and entertainment addiction. • Discuss guidelines for choosing healthful entertainment. • Use the steps to Analyze Influences on Health to check the influence of a TV program.	• Discuss reasons to choose healthful entertainment. • Discuss guidelines for choosing healthful entertainment. • Use the steps to Analyze Influences on Health to check the influence of a computer game.	• Summarize guidelines for choosing healthful entertainment. • Identify signs of shopping and entertainment addiction. • Use the steps to Analyze Influences on Health to check the influence of a DVD.
I will recognize my rights as a consumer.	NHES 8	• Discuss quackery. • Explain your rights as a consumer.	• Identify the rights you can expect as a consumer. • List questions to ask before you buy something. • Discuss actions you can take if you are not satisfied with something you bought.	• Discuss what influences your purchases. • Discuss criteria to use when you comparison shop.

GRADES 6–8 SCOPE AND SEQUENCE CHART

HEALTH GOALS	THE NATIONAL HEALTH EDUCATION STANDARDS	GRADE 6 OBJECTIVES	GRADE 7 OBJECTIVES	GRADE 8 OBJECTIVES
I will take actions if my consumer rights are violated.	NHES 8	• Explain ways government agencies protect consumers. • Use the steps to Be a Health Advocate to teach others about government agencies who protect consumers.	• Identify and discuss agencies that protect your consumer rights. • Use the steps to Be a Health Advocate to teach others about consumer rights.	• Discuss how to recognize quackery. • Explain how to make a consumer complaint. • Use the steps to Be a Health Advocate to teach others how to make a consumer complaint.
I will make responsible choices about health care providers and facilities.	NHES 3	• Discuss how you can access health care and how the costs for health services are paid. • Explain health services in the community for people who have special needs.	• Identify types of health care facilities. • Explain how to select health care providers and insurance. • Discuss issues that might affect future health care and costs.	• Discuss preventive health care. • Explain how to choose health care providers. • Identify kinds of medical specialists. • Describe types of health care facilities. • Explain ways to pay for health care.
I will evaluate ways to pay for health care.	NHES 3	• Discuss how you can access health care and how the costs of health care are paid. • Discuss the role government plays in providing and paying for health care.	• Explain how to select health care providers and insurance. • Discuss issues that might affect future health care and costs.	• Explain how to choose health care providers. • Explain ways to pay for health care.
I will be a health advocate by being a volunteer.	NHES 8	• Describe ways you can volunteer.	• Identify ways you can be a volunteer in your community.	• Explain steps to get you started as a volunteer. • Identify ways you can be a volunteer in your community.

GRADES 6–8 SCOPE AND SEQUENCE CHART

HEALTH GOALS	THE NATIONAL HEALTH EDUCATION STANDARDS	GRADE 6 OBJECTIVES	GRADE 7 OBJECTIVES	GRADE 8 OBJECTIVES
I will investigate health careers.	NHES 3 NHES 8	• Describe reasons to choose a health career. • Describe ways to access information about health careers.	• Discuss influences that affect your choice of a career. • Describe work and training requirements for different health careers. • Identify ways to learn more about a health career that interests you.	• Discuss health careers. • Discuss ways to learn about health careers by having a mentor or shadowing.
		Environmental Health		
I will help keep the air clean.	NHES 8	• Explain why clean air is important. • Describe how air pollution changes air quality. • Describe how red tide affects air quality. • List ways to keep the air clean.	• Discuss ways air pollution affects the environment. • Explain what causes air pollution. • Explain ways red tide might harm health. • Explain ways indoor air pollution can harm health. • Discuss ways you can help keep the air clean.	• Name health conditions caused by airborne pollutants. • Discuss ways air becomes polluted. • Describe ways red tide affects the environment and health. • Discuss causes of indoor air pollution. • Discuss ways to keep the outside and inside air clean.
I will help keep the water safe.	NHES 8	• Discuss ways water pollution might harm health. • Discuss the relationship between water quality and water pollution. • List ways to keep water clean and safe.	• Discuss the health benefits of maintaining water quality. • Discuss ways the water becomes polluted. • Discuss guidelines for disposing of hazardous wastes. • Describe ways to keep water clean and safe.	• Discuss the relationship between the water cycle and water pollution. • Describe chemical and thermal pollution of water. • Outline ways to keep water clean and safe.

GRADES 6–8 SCOPE AND SEQUENCE CHART

HEALTH GOALS	THE NATIONAL HEALTH EDUCATION STANDARDS	GRADE 6 OBJECTIVES	GRADE 7 OBJECTIVES	GRADE 8 OBJECTIVES
I will help keep noise at a safe level.	NHES 8	• Describe ways noise pollution can affect health. • List ways to keep noise at a safe level.	• Discuss sources of noise pollution and its harmful effects. • Explain ways to keep noise at a safe level in your community.	• Identify the benefits of pleasant sounds. • Describe how to reduce noise pollution.
I will help reduce and dispose of waste properly.	NHES 8	• Explain how to reduce and dispose of waste properly.	• Discuss ways to precycle, reuse, recycle, and dispose of waste. • Discuss the causes and risks of land pollution. • Describe ways to protect land and dispose of hazardous waste.	• Explain ways to conserve land and rain forests. • Describe ways to dispose of waste.
I will help conserve energy and natural resources.	NHES 8	• List places in your community and nation where people enjoy the outdoors. • List activities that people enjoy outdoors. • Explain ways to conserve energy, land, and other resources.	• Discuss ways to protect the natural environment. • Discuss ways to conserve land and natural resources.	• Outline ways to conserve energy and natural resources.
I will be a health advocate for the environment.	NHES 8	• List agencies that help protect the environment. • Explain how the visual environment might affect health. • Use the steps to Be a Health Advocate to advocate for a pleasant visual environment.	• Discuss the role of environmental agencies. • Use the steps to Be a Health Advocate to advocate for conserving natural resources.	• Discuss federal, state, and local agencies that protect the environment. • Use the steps to Be a Health Advocate to advocate for the natural environment.

GRADES 6–8 SCOPE AND SEQUENCE CHART

HEALTH GOALS	THE NATIONAL HEALTH EDUCATION STANDARDS	GRADE 6 OBJECTIVES	GRADE 7 OBJECTIVES	GRADE 8 OBJECTIVES
I will stay informed on environmental issues.	NHES 3	• Use the steps to Access Health Information to identify environmental issues.	• Use the steps to Access Health Information to gather facts on environmental issues.	• Use the steps to Access Health Information to write a report on environmental issues.
I will take action to improve my visual environment.	NHES 8	• Explain ways that a pleasant visual environment promotes health.	• Describe how the visual and social-emotional environment affects health. • Identify ways to improve the visual environment.	• Identify benefits of a pleasant visual environment.
I will take actions to improve my social-emotional environment.	NHES 8	• Assess ways that the social-emotional environment affects health. • List coping strategies for dealing with a negative social-emotional environment. • Explain ways to improve the social-emotional environment.	• Describe ways the visual and social-emotional environments affect health. • List ways to promote a positive social-emotional environment.	• Discuss the benefits of a positive social-emotional environment. • Explain how having a support network can promote your health.

Injury Prevention and Safety

HEALTH GOALS	THE NATIONAL HEALTH EDUCATION STANDARDS	GRADE 6 OBJECTIVES	GRADE 7 OBJECTIVES	GRADE 8 OBJECTIVES
I will practice protective factors to reduce the risk of violence.	NHES 7	• List forms of violence. • Discuss responsible ways to manage anger. • Discuss protective factors to reduce the risk of violence in the school and community.	• Describe ways violence affects teens. • Discuss protective factors that reduce the risk of violence. • Describe ways to keep from being a victim of violence.	• Describe forms of violence. • Outline protective factors to reduce the risk of violence. • Describe ways to manage anger and stress.

GRADES 6–8 SCOPE AND SEQUENCE CHART

HEALTH GOALS	THE NATIONAL HEALTH EDUCATION STANDARDS	GRADE 6 OBJECTIVES	GRADE 7 OBJECTIVES	GRADE 8 OBJECTIVES
I will practice self-protection strategies.	NHES 7	• Discuss why people might harm themselves and others. • List warning signs that a person might be considering a suicide attempt. • Explain how to recognize abusive relationships.	• Identify self-protection strategies you can practice. • Discuss guidelines to follow to reduce the risk of rape.	• Describe self-protection strategies that help keep you safe.
I will respect authority and obey laws.	NHES 4	• Discuss reasons why you should respect authority and obey laws.	• Describe the behavior of a law-abiding citizen.	• Discuss ways to show respect for authority. • Identify laws that protect you and others from violence.
I will participate in victim recovery if I am harmed by violence.	NHES 3 NHES 7	• List people and places that can help someone who has been harmed by violence.	• Discuss the resources available for people who have been victims of violence.	• Explain the steps for victim recovery. • Discuss where to access health services for victim recovery.
I will stay away from gangs.	NHES 6	• Discuss ways you can stay away from gangs. • Demonstrate how to Make Responsible Decisions if asked to belong to a gang.	• Discuss reasons why you will stay away from gangs. • Explain how to protect yourself from gangs and bullies. • Demonstrate how to Make Responsible Decisions if approached by a gang member.	• Describe how you can protect yourself by avoiding gangs and respecting authority. • Demonstrate how to Make Responsible Decisions if asked to show disrespect for authority.

GRADES 6–8 SCOPE AND SEQUENCE CHART

HEALTH GOALS	THE NATIONAL HEALTH EDUCATION STANDARDS	GRADE 6 OBJECTIVES	GRADE 7 OBJECTIVES	GRADE 8 OBJECTIVES
I will not carry a weapon.	NHES 6	• Discuss reasons why not carrying a weapon helps keep you safe. • Set a Health Goal to tell a responsible adult if someone at school has a weapon.	• Summarize reasons for not carrying a weapon. • Set a Health Goal to tell a responsible adult if someone you know talks about using a weapon.	• Explain why carrying a weapon is a risk factor for violence. • Set a Health Goal to tell a responsible adult if someone mentions using a weapon to harm others.
I will follow safety guidelines to reduce the risk of unintentional injuries.	NHES 7	• Explain the difference between a risk that is worth taking and one that is not. • Describe ways to prevent falls, fires, electric shock, poisoning, and suffocation. • Discuss safety guidelines for riding in motor vehicles, walking, biking, skating, hiking, and swimming.	• Explain ways to reduce the risk of unintentional injuries from falls, using a microwave oven, poisoning, and using electrical appliances. • Explain ways to reduce the risk of unintentional injuries when you are at an amusement park and when you are engaging in celebrations. • Discuss ways to prevent near-drowning and drowning. • Make a fire escape plan for your house.	• Describe safety guidelines to help prevent injuries from falls, suffocation, fire, electric shock, and poisoning. • Design a family fire escape plan. • Describe safety guidelines for pedestrians, motor vehicle passengers, and people using bicycles, ATVs, scooters, skateboards, and inline skates. • Describe ways to prevent injuries on the farm and from animal bites. • Discuss rules for being safe when near water and camping.
I will follow guidelines for motor vehicle safety.	NHES 7	• Discuss safety guidelines for riding in a motor vehicle, walking, biking, skating, and hiking. • Set a Health Goal to wear a safety belt.	• Identify guidelines for motor vehicle safety. • Set a Health Goal to wear a safety belt.	• Describe safety guidelines for pedestrians, motor vehicle passengers, and people using bicycles, ATVs, scooters, skateboards, and inline skates. • Set a Health Goal to wear a safety belt.

GRADES 6–8 SCOPE AND SEQUENCE CHART

HEALTH GOALS	THE NATIONAL HEALTH EDUCATION STANDARDS	GRADE 6 OBJECTIVES	GRADE 7 OBJECTIVES	GRADE 8 OBJECTIVES
I will follow safety guidelines for severe weather conditions and natural disasters.	NHES 7	• List ways to stay safe during storms. • Identify ways to stay safe in hot and cold weather. • List ways to stay safe during natural disasters.	• Discuss ways to stay safe in a storm, tornado, hurricane, flood or flash flood, landslide, fires, earthquake, mudslide, severe temperature, and other natural disasters.	• Identify health conditions that might occur during hot and cold weather. • State ways to stay safe in hot and cold weather. • Explain safety guidelines to follow during a storm, hurricane, tornado watch or warning, earthquake, flood, fire, and mudslide.
I will be skilled in first aid procedures.	NHES 3 NHES 8	• Discuss the contents of a first aid kit. • Demonstrate how to make an emergency telephone call. • Discuss how to follow universal precautions. • Discuss how to check a victim. • Discuss how and when to perform abdominal thrusts. • Explain how to give rescue breathing and CPR. • Describe how to control bleeding and shock. • Describe how to give first aid for broken bones and sprains. • Explain how to recognize and treat first-, second-, and third-degree burns.	• Discuss the contents of a first aid kit. • Demonstrate how to make an emergency telephone call. • Explain how to follow universal precautions. • Explain how to check a victim and get consent to give first aid. • Explain first aid procedures for choking, rescue breathing and CPR, heart attack, stroke, bleeding, shock, poisoning, burns, fractures and dislocations, sprains and strains, vomiting, fainting, heat-related illnesses, frostbite, and hypothermia.	• Assemble contents for a first aid kit. • Demonstrate how to make an emergency telephone call. • Explain how to follow universal precautions. • Explain how to check a victim and get consent to give first aid. • Demonstrate the universal distress signal. • Explain first aid procedures for choking, rescue breathing and CPR, heart attack, stroke, bleeding, shock, poisoning, marine animal stings, tick bites, burns, injuries (to muscles bones, and joints), sudden illness, heat-related illnesses, and cold temperature–related illnesses.

GRADES 9–12 SCOPE AND SEQUENCE CHART

Unit 1 Life Skills

LIFE SKILLS	THE NATIONAL HEALTH EDUCATION STANDARDS	GRADE 9–12 OBJECTIVES AND LIFE SKILL ACTIVITIES
I will comprehend health concepts related to health promotion and disease prevention to enhance health.	NHES 1	**Lesson 1 Taking Responsibility for Health** • Draw and label the health triangle. • Discuss ten factors that affect health status. • Identify life skills to practice. • Discuss the steps to follow to comprehend health concepts related to health promotion and disease prevention. • Discuss four kinds of skills needed to be a health-literate person. **Activity: Using Life Skills** Comprehending Health Concepts: Skin Cancer Facts
I will access valid information and products and services to enhance health.	NHES 3	**Lesson 2 Accessing Valid Health Information, Products, and Services** • Discuss the steps to follow to access valid information, products, and services to enhance health. • Describe what should be included in a family health history. • Explain how to keep a personal health record. **Activity: Using Life Skills** Accessing Health Services: Making an Emergency Telephone Call
I will practice health-enhancing behavior and avoid or reduce health risks.	NHES 7	**Lesson 3 Practicing Healthful Behaviors** • Discuss the purpose of a health behavior inventory. • List the five parts of a health behavior contract. • Discuss healthful behaviors. • Discuss risk behaviors. • List the six risk behaviors categories for teens. • Discuss the steps to follow to practice health-enhancing behaviors and reduce or avoid health risks.
I will analyze the influence of family, peers, culture, media, technology, and other factors on health behavior.	NHES 2	**Lesson 4 Analyzing Influences on Health** • Discuss the steps to follow to analyze the influence of family, peers, culture, media, technology, and other factors on health behaviors. • Identify questions to ask when evaluating ads. • Explain why it is important to be media literate. • Identify ten appeals used in advertisements. **Activity: Using Life Skills** Analyzing Influences: Evaluating Ads

GRADES 9–12 SCOPE AND SEQUENCE CHART

Unit 1 Life Skills

LIFE SKILLS	THE NATIONAL HEALTH EDUCATION STANDARDS	GRADE 9–12 OBJECTIVES AND LIFE SKILL ACTIVITIES
I will use interpersonal communication skills to enhance health and avoid or reduce health risks.	NHES 4	**Lesson 5 Using Communication Skills** • Identify statements used to bring about responsible decisions. • Explain how to resist negative peer pressure. • Demonstrate how to use resistance skills. • Explain three steps you can take to be assertive and self-confident. • Describe types of conflict, conflict response styles, conflict resolution skills, and mediation.
I will use resistance skills when appropriate.	NHES 4	
I will use conflict resolution skills to settle disagreements.	NHES 4	• Demonstrate how to use conflict resolution skills. • Discuss ways to avoid discriminatory behavior. **Activity: Using Life Skills** Using Communication Skills: Sharpen Your Listening Skills
I will use goal-setting skills to enhance health. I will use decision-making skills to enhance health.	NHES 5, 6	**Lesson 6 Setting Health Goals and Making Responsible Decisions** • Discuss steps you can use to set and reach a health goal. • Discuss the two main goals of Healthy People 2010. • List the ten leading health indicators that will be used to measure the health of the nation over the next ten years. • Describe three decision-making styles. • Outline the six steps in the Responsible Decision-Making Model™. • Demonstrate how to use the Responsible Decision-Making Model™. • Explain four steps to take if you make a wrong decision. **Activity: Using Life Skills** Using Goal-Setting and Decision-Making Skills: Setting a Health Goal
I will advocate for personal, family, and community health.	NHES 8	**Lesson 7 Being a Health Advocate** • Identify four steps to follow to be a health advocate. • Discuss the benefits of being a volunteer. • Explain the healthy-helper syndrome. • List at least ten volunteer opportunities for teens. • Explain eight steps that can be taken to get involved as a volunteer. **Activity: Using Life Skills** Advocating for Health: Be a Volunteer

GRADES 9–12 SCOPE AND SEQUENCE CHART

Unit 2 Mental and Emotional Health

LIFE SKILLS	THE NATIONAL HEALTH EDUCATION STANDARDS	GRADE 9–12 OBJECTIVES AND LIFE SKILL ACTIVITIES
I will develop good character.	NHES 1–8	**Lesson 8 Developing Good Character** • Discuss two ways parents and guardians teach family values.
I will interact in ways that help create a positive social-emotional environment.	NHES 4, 7	• Identify traits and behaviors associated with having good character. • Describe responsible actions that promote positive self-esteem. • List and discuss ways to develop, maintain, or improve self-respect. • List ten ways a positive social-emotional environment improves health status. • List and discuss seven strategies to improve the social-emotional environment.
I will develop healthful personality characteristics.	NHES 7	**Lesson 9 Developing a Healthy Mind** • Identify personality characteristics that promote health. • Discuss ways addictions can affect health status.
I will choose behaviors to promote a healthy mind.	NHES 7	• Identify types and signs of addictions and ways to avoid addictions. • Discuss codependence. • Outline categories of mental disorders, giving examples of each. • Discuss mental-health services and treatment. • Identify strategies for coping with anxiety.
I will express emotions in healthful ways.	NHES 4	**Lesson 10 Expressing Emotions and Managing Stress** • Explain the mind-body connection. • Outline guidelines for expressing emotions in healthful ways.
I will use stress-management skills.	NHES 7	• Discuss hidden anger, anger cues, and anger-management skills. • Explain the bodily changes caused by stress during each of the three stages of the general adaptation syndrome. • Explain ways that prolonged stress can affect health. • Identify life changes that are most stressful for teens. • List and discuss stress-management skills. • Make a health behavior contract. **Activity: Using Life Skills** Using Goal-Setting and Decision-Making Skills: Managing Stress

GRADES 9–12 SCOPE AND SEQUENCE CHART

Unit 2 Mental and Emotional Health

HEALTH GOALS	THE NATIONAL HEALTH EDUCATION STANDARDS	GRADE 9–12 OBJECTIVES AND LIFE SKILL ACTIVITIES
I will be resilient during difficult times.	NHES 7	**Lesson 11 Dealing with Depression** • Discuss emotional responses used to cope with life crises.
I will seek help if I feel depressed.	NHES 3, 7	• Differentiate between kinds of depression, possible causes, symptoms, and treatments for depression. • Explain why being depressed puts teens at risk. • Identify strategies for coping with depression.
I will use suicide prevention strategies when appropriate.	NHES 3, 4, 7	• Identify warning signs for suicide and discuss suicide prevention strategies. • Discuss eight steps teens might take to be resilient. **Activity: Using Life Skills** Accessing Valid Health Information, Products, and Services Hotlines for Help
I will cope with loss and grief in healthful ways.	NHES 4	**Lesson 12 Dealing with Loss and Grief** • Identify causes of loss and grief. • Identify symptoms of loss and grief. • Identify the five stages of loss and grief. • Discuss healthful ways to respond when someone close to you is dying. • Discuss healthful ways to respond when someone you know is grieving a loss. • Discuss healthful ways to respond when you are grieving a loss.

GRADES 9–12 SCOPE AND SEQUENCE CHART

Unit 3 Family and Social Health

HEALTH GOALS	THE NATIONAL HEALTH EDUCATION STANDARDS	GRADE 9–12 OBJECTIVES AND LIFE SKILL ACTIVITIES
I will develop healthful family relationships.	NHES 4, 7	**Lesson 13 Developing Healthful Family Relationships** • Describe the roles of parents and guardians in promoting a healthful family.
I will work to improve difficult family relationships.	NHES 3, 4	• Discuss the roles of extended family members in promoting a healthful family. • Explain twelve behaviors and skills children learn in healthful families. • Discuss ten causes of dysfunctional family relationships, and identify steps to improve these relationships. • Discuss ten behaviors of codependent people. • Discuss the purposes of recovery programs. **Activity: Using Life Skills** Using Communication Skills: Conflict Resolution
I will make healthful adjustments to family changes.	NHES 4, 7	**Lesson 14 Adjusting to Family Changes** • Evaluate the effects divorce might have on teens and ways teens might adjust. • Discuss the effects of a single-custody family and ways teens might adjust. • Discuss effects of living in a stepfamily and ways teens can adjust. • Evaluate how a parent losing a job might affect teens, and discuss ways to adjust. • Discuss having a family member in the military and ways teens can adjust. • Evaluate the effects on teens if a parent is in jail, and discuss ways teens can adjust. **Activity: Using Life Skills** Using Communication Skills: Let's Talk
I will develop healthful friendships.	NHES 4, 7	**Lesson 15 Examining Dating and Friendships** • List four questions to ask before beginning a friendship.
I will develop dating skills.	NHES 4, 7	• Discuss ways to initiate a friendship and healthful ways to respond to rejection. • Learn communication skills that encourage conversation. • Analyze how the age at which a teen begins to date might affect his or her physical and emotional health. • Establish dating guidelines with parents. • Evaluate your dating skills using the Dating Skills Checklist. • Discuss ways that balanced and one-sided friendships affect health status.

GRADES 9–12 SCOPE AND SEQUENCE CHART

Unit 3 Family and Social Health

HEALTH GOALS	THE NATIONAL HEALTH EDUCATION STANDARDS	GRADE 9–12 OBJECTIVES AND LIFE SKILL ACTIVITIES
I will choose to practice abstinence from sex.	NHES 4, 6, 7	**Lesson 16 Practicing Abstinence from Sex** • Discuss how to set limits for expressing physical affection. • List resistance skills to use if you are pressured to be sexually active. • Analyze reasons why practicing abstinence is a responsible choice for teens. • Analyze the benefits of practicing abstinence to protect emotional health and to follow your family's guidelines. • Analyze the benefits of abstinence to prevent unintended pregnancy and infection with sexually transmitted diseases, including HIV. • Analyze the benefits of practicing abstinence when dating in order to promote responsibility within marriage. **Activity: Using Life Skills** Using Resistance Skills: How to Resist Pressure to Have Sex
I will recognize harmful relationships.	NHES 2, 4, 7	**Lesson 17 Recognizing Harmful Relationships** • Describe behaviors typical of people who relate in harmful ways, including the people pleaser, the enabler, the clinger, the fixer, the distancer, the controller, the center, the abuser, the liar, and the promise breaker. • Explain why some people get involved in harmful relationships. • Evaluate the negative effects harmful relationships might have on health status. • Outline steps to take to end or change harmful relationships.
I will develop skills to prepare for marriage.	NHES 4	**Lesson 18 Preparing for Marriage and Parenthood** • Explain the four kinds of intimacy in marriage. • Identify ten factors used to predict success in marriage.
I will develop skills to prepare for parenthood.	NHES 4	• Explain two ways to ensure that marriage will last. • Identify skills needed for responsible parenthood. • List and discuss six examples of faulty thinking that can result in teen pregnancy.
I will choose to practice abstinence from sex to avoid the risks of teen marriage and parenthood.	NHES 4, 6, 7	• List and discuss the risks associated with being a teen parent. • Discuss the risk associated with being a teen father. **Activity: Using Life Skills** Egg Baby Exercise

GRADES 9–12 SCOPE AND SEQUENCE CHART

Unit 4 Growth and Development

HEALTH GOALS	THE NATIONAL HEALTH EDUCATION STANDARDS	GRADE 9–12 OBJECTIVES AND LIFE SKILL ACTIVITIES
I will keep my body systems healthy.	NHES 7	**Lesson 19 Keeping Your Body Healthy** • Identify behaviors to keep your cardiovascular, nervous, and immune systems healthy. • List behaviors important to the health of your respiratory, skeletal, and muscular systems. • Identify behaviors important to the health of your endocrine and digestive systems. • List behaviors important to the health of your integumentary and urinary systems.
I will recognize habits that protect female reproductive health.	NHES 7	**Lesson 20 Learning about the Reproductive Systems** • Discuss physical and emotional changes during puberty. • Describe the functions of the female and male reproductive organs. • Identify concerns of reproductive health.
I will recognize habits that protect male reproductive health.	NHES 7	• Identify ways to protect reproductive health **Activity: Using Life Skills** Practice Healthful Behaviors: Breast Self-Exams **Activity: Using Life Skills** Practice Healthful Behaviors: Testicular Self-Exams
I will learn about pregnancy and childbirth.	NHES 1	**Lesson 21 Learning about Pregnancy and Childbirth** • Explain how a baby is conceived and how the baby's sex and inherited traits are determined. • Explain how pregnancy is determined. • Explain why prenatal care is important. • Describe the three stages of labor. **Activity: Using Life Skills** Accessing Valid Health Information: Research a Pregnancy Topic
I will learn about the growth and development of infants and children.	NHES 1	**Lesson 22 Caring for Infants and Children** • Describe what someone needs to know to be a good child-sitter. • Describe ways to care for infants and toddlers.
I will provide responsible care for infants and children.	NHES 1, 7	• Describe ways to care for young children.

GRADES 9–12 SCOPE AND SEQUENCE CHART

Unit 4 Growth and Development

HEALTH GOALS	THE NATIONAL HEALTH EDUCATION STANDARDS	GRADE 9–12 OBJECTIVES AND LIFE SKILL ACTIVITIES
I will develop my learning style.	NHES 6	**Lesson 23 Developing Learning and Planning Styles** • Discuss the four learning styles and tips for each. • List ways to achieve the eight developmental tasks of adolescence.
I will achieve the developmental tasks of adolescence.	NHES 6	• Discuss five keys to unlock the door to a successful future. • Explain how to set goals and make plans to achieve them. • Discuss four common learning disabilities and the learning support available for people who have learning disabilities.
I will develop habits that promote healthful aging.	NHES 7	**Lesson 24 Aging Healthfully** • Describe the physical, mental, and social changes that occur in middle and late adulthood.
I will share with my family my feelings about death and dying.	NHES 4	• Identify ten habits that promote healthful aging. • Discuss factors and resources to consider if you are a caregiver. • Discuss death and issues surrounding death, such as life support systems, living wills, and hospice care. **Activity: Using Life Skills** Advocating for Health: Volunteering to Help Older Adults

GRADES 9–12 SCOPE AND SEQUENCE CHART

Unit 5 Nutrition

HEALTH GOALS	THE NATIONAL HEALTH EDUCATION STANDARDS	GRADE 9–12 OBJECTIVES AND LIFE SKILL ACTIVITIES
I will select foods that contain nutrients.	NHES 7	**Lesson 25 Choosing Healthful Foods** • Identify the functions and sources of proteins, carbohydrates, and fats.
I will evaluate food labels.	NHES 3	• Identify the functions and sources of vitamins, minerals, water, and herbal supplements. • List and describe the five elements required on all food labels. • Discuss other information found on food labels. **Activity: Using Life Skills** Analyzing Influences on Health: Comparing Food Labels
I will eat the recommended daily amount of food from MyPyramid.	NHES 6, 7	**Lesson 26 Following Dietary Guidelines** • Discuss the recommended daily amounts of food in MyPyramid. • List examples of recommended daily amounts of food in MyPyramid.
I will follow the Dietary Guidelines.	NHES 6, 7	• Explain how to follow a vegetarian diet. • List and describe the ten Dietary Guidelines. • Explain how to use the Dietary Guidelines.
I will follow a healthful diet that reduces the risk of disease.	NHES 6, 7	**Lesson 27 Using Diet to Guard Against Disease** • Discuss dietary guidelines to reduce the risk of developing cancer. • Discuss dietary guidelines to reduce the risk of developing cardiovascular disease. • Discuss dietary guidelines to reduce the risk of developing osteoporosis. • Discuss diet recommendations for people with diabetes or hypoglycemia. • Discuss ways to avoid reactions to food allergies and intolerances, including lactose intolerance and celiac sprue, and reactions to MSG and yellow dye.
I will develop healthful eating habits.	NHES 7	**Lesson 28 Developing Healthful Eating Habits** • Explain the difference between hunger and appetite. • List guidelines to follow when planning healthful meals.
I will protect myself from food-borne illnesses.	NHES 7	• Discuss how some supplements and dietary behaviors affect performance in sports. • Discuss guidelines to follow when eating out. • List three examples of healthful foods that can be ordered at various ethnic restaurants.
I will follow Dietary Guidelines.	NHES 6, 7	• Outline ways to protect yourself from foodborne illnesses. • Explain five ways germs can be spread when people share food. **Activity: Using Life Skills** Practicing Healthful Behaviors: Planning a Day's Menu

GRADES 9–12 SCOPE AND SEQUENCE CHART

Unit 5 Nutrition

HEALTH GOALS	THE NATIONAL HEALTH EDUCATION STANDARDS	GRADE 9–12 OBJECTIVES AND LIFE SKILL ACTIVITIES
I will maintain a desirable weight and body composition.	NHES 6, 7	**Lesson 29 Maintaining a Healthful Weight** • Discuss ways to determine desirable weight and body composition. • Outline steps to follow for healthful weight gain and weight loss. • Evaluate common weight-loss strategies.
I will develop skills to prevent eating disorders.	NHES 7	• Discuss risks for developing eating disorders. • Discuss facts About anorexia nervosa and bulimia. • Discuss binge eating disorder and obesity: the causes, symptoms, associated health problems, and treatment. **Activity: Using Life Skills** Using Goal-Setting and Decision-Making Skills: Calculating Caloric Needs

GRADES 9–12 SCOPE AND SEQUENCE CHART

Unit 6 Personal Health and Physical Activity

HEALTH GOALS	THE NATIONAL HEALTH EDUCATION STANDARDS	GRADE 9–12 OBJECTIVES AND LIFE SKILL ACTIVITIES
I will have regular examinations.	NHES 3	**Lesson 30 Having Regular Physical Exams** • Identify what takes place during typical physical, eye, hearing, and dental examinations.
I will follow a dental health plan.	NHES 3, 7	• Identify symptoms that should prompt individuals to seek health care. • Identify ways to protect your eyes and conditions and diseases that can affect the eye. • Identify symptoms that indicate a need for an ear exam, factors that can lead to hearing loss, and ways to protect against hearing loss. • Identify how to keep teeth and gums healthy. **Activity: Using Life Skills** Accessing Valid Health Information, Products, and Services: Scheduling a Medical or Dental Exam
I will be well groomed.	NHES 3, 7	**Lesson 31 Being Well Groomed** • Discuss how to keep hair clean, what to do about dandruff, products for hair care, and hair removal. • Explain how you can prevent body odor, protect your skin, and care for your fingernails and artificial nails. • Discuss common foot problems, including athlete's foot, ingrown toenails, blisters, calluses, corns, bunions, and foot odor. • Discuss the causes and treatments of acne, warts, moles, and psoriasis. • Discuss the possible risks of tattoos, body piercings, and tanning beds.
I will get adequate rest and sleep.	NHES 6, 7	**Lesson 32 Getting Adequate Rest and Sleep** • Discuss the body changes that occur during the sleep cycle. • Explain why you need adequate rest and sleep to protect your health status. • Evaluate whether you are getting adequate sleep and rest. • List seven tips for getting a good night's sleep. **Activity: Using Life Skills** Using Goal-Setting and Decision-Making Skills: Keeping a Sleep Journal

GRADES 9–12 SCOPE AND SEQUENCE CHART

Unit 6 Personal Health and Physical Activity

HEALTH GOALS	THE NATIONAL HEALTH EDUCATION STANDARDS	GRADE 9–12 OBJECTIVES AND LIFE SKILL ACTIVITIES
I will participate in regular physical activity.	NHES 7	**Lesson 33 Participating in Physical Activity** • List eleven benefits of regular physical activity. • Identify at least ten ways to obtain a moderate amount of physical activity.
I will follow a physical fitness plan.	NHES 6, 7	• Outline six steps to design an individualized plan for health-related fitness. • List the four parts of the FITT formula. • Design a health behavior contract to develop health-related fitness. **Activity: Using Life Skills** Setting Health Goals: Creating a FITT-ness Plan
I will develop and maintain health- and skill-related fitness.	NHES 6, 7	**Lesson 34 Practicing Fitness** • Examine five kinds of exercise. • Using the FITT formula, examine how to develop cardiorespiratory endurance, muscular strength and endurance, and flexibility. • Examine six fitness skills.
I will be a responsible specta-tor and participant in sports.	NHES 4, 7, 8	• Examine the benefits of various lifetime sports and physical activities. • Examine the behaviors and characteristics of responsible sports spectators and participants. **Activity: Using Life Skills** Practicing Healthful Behaviors: Health-Related Fitness Assessment
I will try to prevent physical activity-related injuries and illnesses.	NHES 7	**Lesson 35 Exercising Safely** • List six training principles for physical activities. • Identify ten guidelines to follow to prevent physical activity-related injuries. • Explain the Fitness Training Zone. • Discuss how to prevent, recognize, and treat physical activity–related injuries. • Discuss precautions to take in physical activity during extreme weather conditions, at high altitudes, or in polluted air.

GRADES 9–12 SCOPE AND SEQUENCE CHART

Unit 7 Alcohol, Tobacco, and Other Drugs

HEALTH GOALS	THE NATIONAL HEALTH EDUCATION STANDARDS	GRADE 9–12 OBJECTIVES AND LIFE SKILL ACTIVITIES
I will follow guidelines for the safe use of prescription and over-the-counter drugs.	NHES 4, 7	**Lesson 36 Using Prescription and OTC Drugs Safely** • List and explain factors that influence the effects a drug will have on a person. • Discuss the ways that drugs are administered to the body. • Identify the difference between drug misuse and drug abuse. • Identify information that appears on prescription and OTC drug labels. • List ten guidelines for the safe use of prescription and OTC drugs. • Discuss the role of the Food and Drug Administration (FDA) in regulating OTC drugs, prescription drugs, and herbal supplements.
I will not drink alcohol.	NHES 4, 6, 7	**Lesson 37 Choosing an Alcohol-Free Lifestyle** • Discuss blood alcohol concentration (BAC) and the effects of alcohol on the different body systems. • Explain ways alcohol affects thinking and decision making and increases the risk of violence and illegal behavior. • Discuss the effects of alcohol on a developing fetus. • Explain how and why the drinking age came about. • Discuss causes, health problems, and treatment of alcoholism. • Discuss how advertisements may encourage drinking. • Practice resistance skills to resist peer pressure to drink. **Activity: Using Life Skills** Analyzing Influences on Health: Don't Be Fooled by Alcohol Advertising
I will avoid tobacco use and secondhand smoke.	NHES 2, 4, 7, 8	**Lesson 38 Choosing a Tobacco-Free Lifestyle** • Discuss the harmful physical and mental effects of nicotine. • Discuss laws regarding the sale and use of tobacco. • Discuss how tobacco companies try to convince minors to use tobacco products. • Understand the negative effects smoking has on a fetus. • Explain the harmful effects of secondhand smoke. • Outline eight ways to resist pressure to use tobacco products. • Outline steps to stop using tobacco products. **Activity: Using Life Skills** Advocating for Health Life Skill: I Will Use Interpersonal Communication Skills to Enhance Health and Avoid or Reduce Health Risks

GRADES 9–12 SCOPE AND SEQUENCE CHART

Unit 7 Alcohol, Tobacco, and Other Drugs

HEALTH GOALS	THE NATIONAL HEALTH EDUCATION STANDARDS	GRADE 9–12 OBJECTIVES AND LIFE SKILL ACTIVITIES
I will not be involved in illegal drug use.	NHES 1, 4, 7	**Lesson 39 Avoiding Illegal Drug Use** • Explain how illegal use of stimulants, sedative-hypnotics, narcotics, and hallucinogens harm health. • Describe the physical and emotional effects of marijuana. • Determine how the illegal use of anabolic-androgenic steroids harms health. • Explain the harmful effects of inhalants. • Practice resistance skills that can be used to resist peer pressure to use illegal drugs.
I will avoid risk factors and practice protective factors for drug misuse and abuse.	NHES 7	**Lesson 40 Avoiding Drug Dependence** • List risk factors and protective factors for drug use. • Explain reasons why drug use is risky. • Discuss drug dependence, including physical and psychological dependence. • Outline the five stages of drug use that can progress to drug dependence. • Discuss roles played by family members who are codependent: chief enabler, family hero, scapegoat, mascot, and lost child.
I will not misuse or abuse drugs.	NHES 4, 6, 7, 8	**Lesson 41 Resisting Pressure to Abuse Drugs** • Explain why teens who use drugs pressure their peers to use drugs. • Give examples of direct and indirect pressure to use drugs.
I will use resistance skills if I am pressured to misuse or abuse drugs.	NHES 4, 6	• Outline resistance skills that can be used to resist pressure to use drugs. • List reasons to say "no" when pressured by peers to use drugs. • List ways to be a drug-free role model. **Activity: Using Life Skills** Resistance Skills: Ways to Say "No" When Pressured to Use Drugs

GRADES 9–12 SCOPE AND SEQUENCE CHART

Unit 7 Alcohol, Tobacco, and Other Drugs

HEALTH GOALS	THE NATIONAL HEALTH EDUCATION STANDARDS	GRADE 9–12 OBJECTIVES AND LIFE SKILL ACTIVITIES
I will choose a drug-free lifestyle to reduce the risk of violence and accidents.	NHES 6, 7	**Lesson 42 Reducing Risk by Being Drug-Free** • Discuss ways drugs alter mood and behavior and increase the risk of violent behavior. • List ways to protect yourself from violence associated with drug use. • Explain how a safe and drug-free school zone decreases the risk of drug trafficking.
I will choose a drug-free life-style to reduce the risk of HIV infection and unplanned preg-nancy.	NHES 6, 7	• Explain reasons why teens who use drugs increase their risk of HIV infection and unplanned pregnancy and accidents. **Activity: Using Life Skills** Using Goal-Setting and Decision-Making Skills: Making a Responsible Decision
I will be aware of resources for the treatment of drug misuse and abuse.	NHES 3	**Lesson 43 Assessing Treatment Options** • Discuss steps teens can take to get help for someone who misuses or abuses drugs. • Discuss what happens during formal intervention. • Explain what happens during detoxification. • List the kinds of treatment for people who are drug dependent. • Discuss why family members and friends of people who are drug dependent may need treatment.

GRADES 9–12 SCOPE AND SEQUENCE CHART

Unit 8 Communicable and Chronic Diseases

HEALTH GOALS	THE NATIONAL HEALTH EDUCATION STANDARDS	GRADE 9–12 OBJECTIVES AND LIFE SKILL ACTIVITIES
I will choose behaviors that reduce my risk of infection with communicable diseases.	NHES 6, 7	**Lesson 44 Avoiding Communicable Diseases** • Identify types of pathogens that cause disease, and give examples of the types of diseases caused by the types of pathogens. • Discuss ways pathogens are spread.
I will be aware of immunizations that protect health.	NHES 1, 3	• Develop and analyze strategies to prevent infection with communicable diseases. • Explain how the immune system responds when a pathogen enters the body. • Discuss ways to develop active and passive immunity. **Activity: Using Life Skills** Practicing Healthful Behaviors: Avoiding Spreading Pathogens
I will choose behaviors to reduce my risk of infection with respiratory diseases.	NHES 7	**Lesson 45 Dealing with Respiratory Diseases, Asthma, and Allergies** • Analyze the causes, symptoms, diagnoses, and treatments of communicable respiratory diseases. • Analyze ways to prevent infection with communicable respiratory diseases.
I will recognize ways to manage asthma and allergies.	NHES 7	• Discuss asthma and ways to prevent and manage asthma attacks. • Describe common causes of allergies. • Describe ways to prevent or treat allergies. **Activity: Using Life Skills** Accessing Health Information, Products, and Services: Managing Asthma
I will choose behaviors to reduce my risk of infection with sexually transmitted diseases (STDs).	NHES 4, 6, 7	**Lesson 46 Reducing the Risk of STDs and HIV** • Discuss the causes and methods of transmission of common STDs. • Discuss the symptoms, diagnoses, and treatments of common STDs. • Analyze the long-term effects of common STDs. • Analyze ways to prevent infection from STDs.
I will choose behaviors to reduce my risk of HIV infection.	NHES 4, 6, 7	• Discuss the progression of HIV infection to AIDS. • List tests used to determine the presence of HIV. • Identify treatment and prevention strategies for HIV and AIDS.

GRADES 9–12 SCOPE AND SEQUENCE CHART

Unit 8 Communicable and Chronic Diseases

HEALTH GOALS	THE NATIONAL HEALTH EDUCATION STANDARDS	GRADE 9–12 OBJECTIVES AND LIFE SKILL ACTIVITIES
I will choose behaviors to reduce my risk of cardiovascular diseases.	NHES 6, 7	**Lesson 47 Reducing the Risk of Cardiovascular Diseases** • Identify characteristics of different cardiovascular diseases. • Identify cardiovascular disease risk factors that cannot be controlled. • Identify cardiovascular risk factors that can be controlled. • Describe medical diagnoses and treatments for heart disease. **Activity: Using Life Skills** Using Goal-Setting and Decision-Making Skills: Being Heart Healthy
I will choose behaviors to reduce my risk of diabetes.	NHES 6, 7	**Lesson 48 Managing Chronic Health Conditions** • Distinguish between the different types of diabetes. • Identify the risk factors for diabetes, and discuss ways to manage diabetes.
I will recognize ways to manage chronic health conditions.	NHES 6, 7	• Discuss ways to reduce the risk of diabetes. • Identify the incidence of chronic health conditions in young people. • Identify adjustments to make for different chronic health conditions. **Activity: Using Life Skills** Being a Health Advocate: Reducing the Risk of Diabetes
I will choose behaviors to reduce my risk of cancer.	NHES 6, 7	**Lesson 49 Reducing the Risk of Cancer** • Describe how cancerous cells grow and spread. • Describe the basic facts about common types of cancers. • Practice ways to reduce the risk of cancer. • Discuss different treatment procedures for cancer.

GRADES 9–12 SCOPE AND SEQUENCE CHART

Unit 9 Consumer and Community Health

HEALTH GOALS	THE NATIONAL HEALTH EDUCATION STANDARDS	GRADE 9–12 OBJECTIVES AND LIFE SKILL ACTIVITIES
I will acquire knowledge of laws to protect health.	NHES 1, 3 NHES 3, 8 NHES 6, 8	**Lesson 50 Acquiring Knowledge of Health Laws** • Explain the hierarchy of federal, state, county, and city laws. • Discuss consumer rights. • List steps that can be taken to be a successful consumer. • List questions that can uncover health fraud. • List steps to take if health fraud is suspected.
I will recognize my rights as a consumer.		• Discuss agencies and organizations that play a role in consumer protection. • Outline actions that can be taken when consumer rights have been violated.
I will take action if my consumer rights are violated.		
I will make a plan to manage my time and money.	NHES 6, 7	**Lesson 51 Managing Time and Money** • Identify twelve priorities for which a person needs to make time. • Explain how to make a budget. • Discuss reasons why a person must be careful when using credit cards. • Identify five criteria to use for comparison shopping. **Activity: Using Life Skills** Using Goal-Setting and Decision-Making Skills: How to Create a Schedule **Activity: Using Life Skills** Using Goal-Setting and Decision-Making Skills: Managing Your Money
I will choose healthful entertainment.	HES 2, 6, 7	**Lesson 52 Analyzing Media Messages** • Explain why adults are concerned with the amount of time teens spend on entertainment. • List guidelines to follow when choosing entertainment. • List eleven questions for evaluating entertainment media. • Discuss how to use television ratings and V-chips.
I will analyze ways messages delivered through technology might affect my health status.	NHES 2, 7	• List eight ways health can be harmed by inappropriate entertainment choices. • Explain why entertainment addiction is risky. • Give evidence for the link between media violence and violent behavior.

GRADES 9–12 SCOPE AND SEQUENCE CHART

Unit 9 Consumer and Community Health

HEALTH GOALS	THE NATIONAL HEALTH EDUCATION STANDARDS	GRADE 9–12 OBJECTIVES AND LIFE SKILL ACTIVITIES
I will make responsible choices about health care providers and facilities.	NHES 3, 6	**Lesson 53 Accessing Reliable Health Care** • List questions that can be used to evaluate a health care provider. • Discuss the credentials of various health care providers. • List two types of managed care programs, and discuss Medicare and Medicaid.
I will evaluate ways to pay for health care.	NHES 3	• Explain five types of coverage in health insurance plans. • List ten questions that can be used to evaluate health insurance coverage. • Discuss various health care facilities.
I will investigate health careers.	NHES 3	**Lesson 54 Investigating Health Careers** • List and discuss seven ways to investigate health careers. • Explain what it means to be licensed and have certification for a health career.
I will investigate public and in-ternational health needs.	NHES 3, 8	**Lesson 55 Learning about Public Health** • Describe why public health is a wise investment. • List public health agencies. • Explain why public health in the United States has improved during the past century. • List five important threats to today's public health. • Explain bioterrorism. • Explain the health risks that developing nations face.

GRADES 9–12 SCOPE AND SEQUENCE CHART

Unit 10 Environmental Health

HEALTH GOALS	THE NATIONAL HEALTH EDUCATION STANDARDS	GRADE 9–12 OBJECTIVES AND LIFE SKILL ACTIVITIES
I will stay informed about environmental issues.	NHES 3, 8	**Lesson 56 Accessing Valid Information about Environmental Issues** • List global environmental issues.
I will be aware of organizations that protect the environment.	NHES 3, 8	• Identify the connection between the population and the environment. • Discuss facts related to families and children who are homeless. • Describe the greenhouse effect and global warming. • List ways the ozone layer is being depleted. • Identify ways to stay informed about environmental issues.
I will help keep the air clean.	NHES 7, 8	**Lesson 57 Preventing Air and Water Pollution** • Identify sources of air pollution.
I will help keep the water safe.	NHES 7, 8	• Discuss how air pollution affects health. • Discuss the effects of indoor air pollution on health. • Discuss the effects of red tide on health. • List ways to keep the air clean. • Identify sources of water pollution. • Discuss how water pollution affects health. • Identify ways the government works to keep water clean. • List ways to help keep water safe.
I will help keep noise at a safe level.	NHES 7, 8	**Lesson 58 Preventing Noise and Visual Pollution** • Explain how noise affects health status. • Discuss ways to keep noise at a safe level.
I will improve the visual environment.	NHES 7, 8	• Contrast positive and negative visual environments. • Describe ways a positive visual environment improves health status. • Identify ways to improve the visual environment. **Activity: Using Life Skills** Practicing Healthful Behaviors: Avoiding Noise Pollution

GRADES 9–12 SCOPE AND SEQUENCE CHART

Unit 10 Environmental Health

HEALTH GOALS	THE NATIONAL HEALTH EDUCATION STANDARDS	GRADE 9–12 OBJECTIVES AND LIFE SKILL ACTIVITIES
I will conserve energy and natural resources.	NHES 7, 8	**Lesson 59 Practicing Recycling and Conservation** • Identify ways to recycle. • Identify ways to dispose of waste. • Identify sources of energy. • Practice ways to conserve energy. • Practice ways to conserve water.
I will help reduce and dispose of waste.	NHES 7, 8	
I will protect the natural environment.	NHES 7, 8	**Lesson 60 Protecting the Environment** • Explain how the natural environment protects health status. • List ways to protect the natural environment. • Discuss actions health advocates can take to protect the environment. • Describe ways to be a health advocate for the environment. **Activity: Using Life Skills** Advocating for Health: Create a Plan
I will be a health advocate for the environment.	NHES 7, 8	

Grades 9–12 Scope and Sequence Chart

Unit 11 Injury Prevention and Personal Safety

Health Goals	The National Health Education Standards	Grade 9–12 Objectives and Life Skill Activities
I will follow safety guidelines to reduce the risk of unintentional injuries.	NHES 7	**Lesson 61 Reducing Unintentional Injuries** • Analyze ways to reduce the risk of unintentional injuries in the home. • Analyze ways to reduce the risk of unintentional injuries in the community. • Analyze ways to reduce the risk of unintentional injuries in the workplace. • Analyze ways to reduce the risk of unintentional injuries in motor vehicles. • Analyze ways a person can reduce the risk of injury from road rage. **Activity: Using Life Skills** Using Goal-Setting and Decision-Making Skills: Contract for Motor Vehicle Safety
I will follow guidelines for motor vehicle safety.	NHES 7	
I will follow safety guidelines for severe weather, natural disasters, and national alerts.	NHES 7	**Lesson 62 Staying Safe during Severe Weather and Natural Disasters** • List five ways to prepare for severe weather and natural disasters. • Discuss ways to stay safe during a landslide, flood, earthquake, tornado, hurricane, wildland fire, electrical storm, winter storm, and terrorist attack.
I will practice protective factors to reduce the risk of violence.	NHES 7	**Lesson 63 Reducing the Risk of Violence** • List and discuss nine types of violence. • Identify twenty risk factors that increase the likelihood that a person will become a perpetrator or a victim of violence. • Identify twenty protective factors that reduce the likelihood that a person will become a perpetrator or a victim of violence. • Explain how passive, aggressive, and assertive behavior influence the risk of being a perpetrator or a victim of violence. **Activity: Using Life Skills** Setting Health Goals and Using Decision-Making Skills: Patterns of Behavior Self-Test
I will respect authority and obey laws.	NHES 6, 7, 8	**Lesson 64 Respecting Authority and Obeying Laws** • Explain how a person develops a moral code. • Explain why some teens challenge authority and break laws. • Discuss the consequences juvenile offenders may experience. • Identify ways juvenile offenders can change their behavior to show respect for authority and obey laws.

GRADES 9–12 SCOPE AND SEQUENCE CHART

Unit 11 Injury Prevention and Personal Safety

HEALTH GOALS	THE NATIONAL HEALTH EDUCATION STANDARDS	GRADE 9–12 OBJECTIVES AND LIFE SKILL ACTIVITIES
I will practice strategies to help protect myself from physical violence and abuse.	NHES 4, 7	**Lesson 65 Protecting Yourself from Physical Violence and Abuse** • List and discuss principles and strategies of self-defense. • Explain hazing. • Discuss bullying. • Identify signs of child abuse, and describe laws about mandatory reporting. • Identify warning signs of dating violence, and discuss defensive measures. • List six categories of mental and emotional abuse. • List the phases of a violent relationship and things that victims need to know. • Identify how victims and perpetrators can facilitate recovery.
I will practice strategies to help protect myself from sexual violence and abuse.	NHES 4, 7	**Lesson 66 Protecting Yourself from Sexual Violence and Abuse** • Explain the relationship between alcohol and other drugs and date rape. • Identify guidelines to follow to reduce the risk of date rape. • Identify signs of sexual abuse. • List steps to take if you are sexually harassed or stalked • Discuss the legal and ethical consequences of sexual assault, harassment, abuse, and rape. • Identify steps victims can take to better recover from sexual violence or abuse. **Activity: Using Life Skills** Resistance Skills: How to Reduce Your Risk of Date Rape
I will stay away from gangs.	NHES 2, 6, 7	**Lesson 67 Staying Away from Gangs** • Discuss characteristics of gang members. • Identify different roles of gang members. • Discuss reasons why it is risky to belong to a gang. • Explain how a gang can cause conflict in schools, families, and communities. • Analyze why teens join gangs. • Analyze strategies to avoid gangs. • Explain how a teen who belongs to a gang can leave the gang. • Discuss reasons why some teens have become antigang gang members.

GRADES 9–12 SCOPE AND SEQUENCE CHART

Unit 11 Injury Prevention and Personal Safety

HEALTH GOALS	THE NATIONAL HEALTH EDUCATION STANDARDS	GRADE 9–12 OBJECTIVES AND LIFE SKILL ACTIVITIES
I will follow guidelines to help reduce the risk of weapon injuries.	NHES 7	**Lesson 68 Reducing the Risk of Weapon Injuries** • Discuss laws regarding the sale of handguns and rifles to teens. • Analyze strategies for avoiding injury from weapons. • Discuss laws regarding carrying a concealed weapon. • Analyze how not carrying a weapon can help prevent accidental and deliberate injuries. • Discuss how a gun should be safely stored in a home. • Discuss safety actions you should take if you see a gun that is not safely locked up.
I will be skilled in common first aid procedures.	NHES 3, 7, 8	**Lesson 69 Performing Common First Aid Procedures** • Describe the contents of first aid kits and where they should be kept. • Distinguish between actual and implied consent. • Explain how to follow universal precautions. • Explain first aid procedures for sudden illnesses and burns. • Explain first aid procedures for injuries to muscles, bones, and joints. • Describe first aid procedures for cold temperature–related and heat-related illnesses.
I will be skilled in emergency first aid procedures.	NHES 7, 8	**Lesson 70 Performing Emergency First Aid Procedures** • Discuss steps to take when checking a victim. • Explain first aid procedures for choking. • Explain first aid procedures for rescue breathing. • Explain first aid procedures for shock. • Explain first aid procedures for CPR. • Describe first aid procedures for heart attack. • Describe first aid procedures for wounds. • Explain first aid procedures for poisoning.

APPENDIX A

National Health Education Standards: Teaching Masters

Table of Contents

NATIONAL HEALTH EDUCATION STANDARD 4C
Use Conflict Resolution Skills

NATIONAL HEALTH EDUCATION STANDARD 5
Make Responsible Decisions

NATIONAL HEALTH EDUCATION STANDARD 6
Set Health Goals

NATIONAL HEALTH EDUCATION STANDARD 7A
Practice Healthful Behaviors

NATIONAL HEALTH EDUCATION STANDARD 7B
Manage Stress

NATIONAL HEALTH EDUCATION STANDARD 8
Be a Health Advocate

Grades K–2
National Health Education Standard 1

Students will comprehend concepts related to health promotion and disease prevention to enhance health.

TEACHING MASTER-1

Learn Health Facts

1. Study and learn health facts.

2. Ask questions about health facts.

3. Answer questions about health facts.

4. Use health facts to set health goals.

Grades 3–5
National Health Education Standard 1

Students will comprehend concepts related to health promotion and disease prevention to enhance health.

TEACHING MASTER-2

Understand Health Facts

1. Study and learn health facts.

2. Ask questions if you do not understand health facts.

3. Answer questions to show you understand health facts.

4. Use health facts to promote health and prevent disease.

Grades 6–8
Grades 9–12
National Health Education Standard 1

Students will comprehend concepts related to health promotion and disease prevention to enhance health.

TEACHING MASTER-3

Comprehend Health Concepts

1. Study health knowledge.

2. Ask questions about health knowledge that you don't understand. Make certain you get an answer you can understand.

3. Use health knowledge to form health concepts.

4. Use health concepts to promote health and prevent disease.

Grades K–2
National Health Education Standard 2

Students will analyze the influence of family, peers, culture, media, technology, and other factors on health behaviors.

TEACHING MASTER-4

Think about Your Health Choices

1. Name people and things that help you make choices about your health.

2. Tell which ones help you make healthful choices. Tell which ones do not.

3. Choose ones that help you make healthful choices.

4. Stay away from ones that do not help you make healthful choices.

Grades 3–5
National Health Education Standard 2

Students will analyze the influence of family, peers, culture, media, technology, and other factors on health behaviors.

TEACHING MASTER-5

Analyze What Influences Your Health

1. Identify people and things that might influence you.

2. Identify how these people and things might influence your choices.

3. Choose healthful influences.

4. Protect yourself from harmful influences.

Grades 6–8
Grades 9–12
National Health Education Standard 2

Students will analyze the influence of family, peers, culture, media, technology, and other factors on health behaviors.

TEACHING MASTER-6

Analyze What Influences Your Health

1. Identify people and things that might influence you.

2. Evaluate how their influence might affect your health behavior and decisions.

3. Choose positive influences on health.

4. Protect yourself from negative influences on health.

Grades K–2
National Health Education Standard 3

Students will demonstrate the ability to access valid information and products and services to enhance health.

TEACHING MASTER-7

Find Health Facts and Get Help

1.   Tell when you need health facts or help.

2.   Tell where you can find health facts or help.

3.   Find health facts or help.

4.   Talk about what you found.

Grades 3–5
National Health Education Standard 3

Students will demonstrate the ability to access valid information and products and services to enhance health.

TEACHING MASTER-8

Access Health Facts, Products, and Services

1. Identify health facts, products, and services you need.

2. Find the health facts, products, and services you need.

3. Check out health facts, products, and services.

4. Take actions when health facts, products, or services are not right.

Grades 6–8
Grades 9–12
National Health Education Standard 3

Students will demonstrate the ability to access valid information and products and services to enhance health.

TEACHING MASTER-9

Access Valid Information and Health Products and Services

1. Identify information and health products and services you need.

2. Find information and health products and services.

3. Evaluate information and health products and services.

4. Take action when information is misleading or health products and services are unsatisfactory.

Grades K–2
National Health Education Standard 4A

Students will demonstrate the ability to use interpersonal communication skills to enhance health and avoid or reduce health risks.

TEACHING MASTER-10

Communicate

1. Think about what you want to say.

2. Look at the person. Speak clearly.

3. Listen to the other person.

4. Make sure you understand each other.

Grades 3–5
Grades 6–8
Grades 9–12
National Health Education Standard 4A

Students will demonstrate the ability to use interpersonal communication skills to enhance health and avoid or reduce health risks.

TEACHING MASTER-11

Use Communication Skills

1. Choose the best way to communicate.

2. Express your thoughts and feelings clearly.

3. Listen to the other person.

4. Make sure you understand each other.

Grades K–2
National Health Education Standard 4B

Students will demonstrate the ability to use interpersonal communication skills to enhance health and avoid or reduce health risks.

TEACHING MASTER-12

Say "No"

1. Look at the person. Say "no."

2. Tell why you are saying "no."

3. Do not change your mind.

4. Ask for help from an adult if you need it.

Grades 3–5
Grades 6–8
National Health Education Standard 4B

Students will demonstrate the ability to use interpersonal communication skills to enhance health and avoid or reduce health risks.

TEACHING MASTER-13

Use Resistance Skills

1. Look at the person. Say "no" in a firm voice.

2. Give reasons for saying "no."

3. Match your behavior to your words.

4. Ask an adult for help if you need it.

Grades 9–12
National Health Education Standard 4B

Students will demonstrate the ability to use interpersonal communication skills to enhance health and avoid or reduce health risks.

TEACHING MASTER-14

Use Resistance Skills

1. Say "no" with self-confidence.

2. Give reasons for saying "no."

3. Repeat your "no" response several times.

4. Use nonverbal behavior to match verbal behavior.

5. Avoid situations in which there will be pressure to make wrong decisions.

6. Avoid people who make wrong decisions.

7. Resist pressure to engage in illegal behavior.

8. Influence others to make responsible decisions.

Grades K–2
National Health Education Standard 4C

Students will demonstrate the ability to use interpersonal communication skills to enhance health and avoid or reduce health risks.

TEACHING MASTER-15

Resolve Conflicts

1. Stay calm.

2. Listen to the other person's side. Tell your side.

3. Talk about ways to work things out.

4. Agree on a way to work things out. Ask an adult for help if you need it.

Grades 3–5
Grades 6–8
National Health Education Standard 4C

Students will demonstrate the ability to use interpersonal communication skills to enhance health and avoid or reduce health risks.

TEACHING MASTER-16

Resolve Conflicts

1. Stay calm.

2. Talk about the conflict.

3. Discuss possible ways to settle the conflict. Check out each way to settle the conflict. Use the Guidelines for Making Responsible Decisions™.

4. Agree on a way to settle the conflict. You may need to ask a responsible adult for help.

Grades 9–12
National Health Education Standard 4C

Students will demonstrate the ability to use interpersonal communication skills to enhance health and avoid or reduce health risks.

TEACHING MASTER-17

Use Conflict Resolution Skills

1. Remain calm.

2. Set a positive tone.

3. Define the conflict.

4. Take responsibility for personal actions.

5. Listen to the needs and feelings of others.

6. List and evaluate possible solutions. Use the six questions from the Responsible Decision-Making Model™.

7. Agree on a responsible solution.

Grades K–2
National Health Education Standard 5

Students will demonstrate the ability to use decision-making skills to enhance health.

TEACHING MASTER-18

Make Wise Decisions

1. Tell what the choices are.

2. Ask questions before you choose.

   - Is it healthful?

   - Is it safe?

   - Do I follow laws?

   - Do I show respect for myself and others?

   - Do I follow family rules?

   - Do I show good character?

3. Tell what the wise decision is. Check this out with a parent or trusted adult.

4. Tell what happens if you make this decision.

Grades 3–5
Grades 6–8
National Health Education Standard 5

Students will demonstrate the ability to use decision-making skills to enhance health.

TEACHING MASTER-19

Make Responsible Decisions

1. Identify choices.

2. Evaluate each choice. Use the Guidelines for Making Responsible Decisions™.

    • Is it healthful?

    • Is it safe?

    • Do I follow rules and laws?

    • Do I show respect for myself and others?

    • Do I follow my family's guidelines?

    • Do I show good character?

3. Identify the responsible decision. Check this out with your parent or trusted adult.

4. Evaluate your decision.

Grades 9–12
National Health Education Standard 5

Students will demonstrate the ability to use decision-making skills to enhance health.

TEACHING MASTER-20

Use the Responsible Decision-Making Model™

1. Describe the situation that requires a decision.

2. List possible decisions you might make.

3. Share the list of possible decisions with a parent, guardian, or other responsible adult.

4. Use six questions to evaluate the possible consequences of each decision.

   • Will this decision result in actions that promote health?

   • Will this decision result in actions that protect safety?

   • Will this decision result in actions that follow laws?

   • Will this decision result in actions that show respect for myself and others?

   • Will this decision result in actions that follow the guidelines of my parents and of other responsible adults?

   • Will this decision result in actions that demonstrate good character?

5. Decide which decision is most responsible and appropriate.

6. Act on your decision and evaluate the results.

Grades K–2
National Health Education Standard 6

Students will demonstrate the ability to use goal-setting skills to enhance health.

TEACHING MASTER-21

Set Health Goals

1. Name one thing you want to do to stay healthy.

2. Make a plan for what you will do.

3. Keep track of what you do.

4. Tell how your plan worked.

Grades 3–5
Grades 6–8
National Health Education Standard 6

Students will demonstrate the ability to use goal-setting skills to enhance health.

TEACHING MASTER-22

Set Health Goals

1. Write the health goal you want to set.

2. Explain how the goal might affect your health.

3. Describe a plan you will follow. Keep track of your progress.

4. Evaluate how your plan worked.

Grades 9–12
National Health Education Standard 6

Students will demonstrate the ability to use goal-setting skills to enhance health.

TEACHING MASTER-23

Set Health Goals

1. Write your health goal.

2. Make an action plan to meet your health goal.

3. Identify obstacles to your plan.

4. Set up a time line to achieve your health goal.

5. Keep a chart or diary in which you record your progress toward your health goal.

6. Build a support system.

7. Revise your action plan or time line if necessary.

8. Reward yourself when you reach your health goal.

Grades K–2
National Health Education Standard 7A

Students will demonstrate the ability to practice health-enhancing behaviors and avoid or reduce health risks.

TEACHING MASTER-24

Practice Healthful Habits

1. Learn about a healthful thing to do.

2. Practice it.

3. Ask for help if you need it.

4. Make it a healthful habit.

Grades 3–5
Grades 6–8
National Health Education Standard 7A

Students will demonstrate the ability to practice health-enhancing behaviors and avoid or reduce health risks.

TEACHING MASTER-25

Practice Healthful Behaviors

1. Learn about a healthful behavior.

2. Practice the healthful behavior.

3. Ask for help if you need it.

4. Make the healthful behavior a habit.

Grades 9–12
National Health Education Standard 7A

Students will demonstrate the ability to practice health-enhancing behaviors and avoid or reduce health risks.

TEACHING MASTER-26

Practice Healthful Behaviors: A Health Behavior Contract

1. Write your name and the date.

2. Write the healthful behavior you want to practice as a health goal.

3. Write the specific statements that describe how this healthful behavior reduces health risks.

4. Make a specific plan for recording your progress.

5. Complete an evaluation of how the plan helped you achieve the health goal.

Grades K–2
National Health Education Standard 7B

Students will demonstrate the ability to practice health-enhancing behaviors and avoid or reduce health risks.

TEACHING MASTER-27

Manage Stress

1. Tell how stress feels.

2. Name things that cause stress.

3. Do something about things that cause stress.

4. Do something to keep healthy.

Grades 3–5
Grades 6–8
Grades 9–12
National Health Education Standard 7B

Students will demonstrate the ability to practice health-enhancing behaviors and avoid or reduce health risks.

TEACHING MASTER-28

Manage Stress

1. Identify the signs of stress.

2. Identify the cause of stress.

3. Do something about the cause of stress.

4. Take action to reduce the harmful effects of stress.

Grades K–2
National Health Education Standard 8

Students will demonstrate the ability to advocate for personal, family, and community health.

TEACHING MASTER-29

Help Others to Be Healthy

1. Choose a healthful action.

2. Find out more about it.

3. Find a way to tell others about it.

4. Tell others about it.

Grades 3–5
National Health Education Standard 8

Students will demonstrate the ability to advocate for personal, family, and community health.

TEACHING MASTER-30

Be a Health Advocate

1. Choose a healthful action to communicate.

2. Collect information about the action.

3. Decide how to communicate information.

4. Communicate your message to others.

Grades 6–8
Grades 9–12
National Health Education Standard 8

Students will demonstrate the ability to advocate for personal, family, and community health.

TEACHING MASTER-31

Be a Health Advocate

1. Select a health-related concern.

2. Gather reliable information.

3. Identify your purpose and target audience.

4. Develop a convincing and appropriate message.

APPENDIX B

Selected Healthy People 2010 Objectives That Relate to Schools and School-Age Youth

OBJECTIVES		BASELINE	2010 TARGET
7-2	Increase the proportion of middle, junior high, and senior high schools that provide comprehensive school health education to prevent health problems in the following areas: unintentional injury; violence; suicide; tobacco use and addiction; alcohol or other drug use; unintended pregnancy, HIV/AIDS, and STD infection; unhealthy dietary patterns; inadequate physical activity; and environmental health.	28%	70%
7-4	Increase the proportion of the nation's elementary, middle, junior high, and senior high schools that have a nurse-to-student ratio of at least 1:750.	26%–32%	50%
8-11	Eliminate elevated blood lead levels in children.	4.4%	0%
9-7	Reduce pregnancies among adolescent females.	72 per 1,000	46 per 1,000
9-8	Increase the proportion of adolescents who have never engaged in sexual intercourse before age 15.		
	Females	81%	88%
	Males	79%	88%
9-9	Increase the proportion of adolescents who have never engaged in sexual intercourse.		
	Females	62%	75%
	Males	57%	75%
9-10	Increase the proportion of sexually active, unmarried adolescents ages 15 to 17 years who use contraception that both effectively prevents pregnancy and provides barrier protection against disease.		
	Females who use condom	68%	75%
	Males who use condom	72%	83%
	Females who use condom plus hormonal	6%	9%
	Males who use condom plus hormonal	8%	11%
13-1	Reduce AIDS among adolescents and adults.	19.5 cases per 100,000 persons aged 13 and older	1.0 new cases per 100,000 persons
14-24	Increase the proportion of young children who receive all vaccines that have been recommended for universal administration for at least 5 years	73%	80%
14-27	Increase routine vaccination coverage for adults	No data	No specific target
15-31	Increase the proportion of public and private schools that require use of appropriate head, face, eye, and mouth protection for students participating in school-sponsored physical activities.	No data	No specific target
15-33	Reduce maltreatment and maltreatment fatalities of children.	13.9 victims per 1,000 children under 18	11.1 victims per 1,000 children under 18

OBJECTIVES		BASELINE	2010 TARGET
15-38	Reduce physical fighting among adolescents	37%	33%
15-39	Reduce weapon carrying by adolescents on school property.	8.5%	6%
16-3	Reduce deaths of adolescents and young adults.		
	Adolescents ages 10 to 14	21.8 per 1,000	16.8 per 1,000
	Adolescents ages 15 to 19	69.7 per 1,000	43.2 per 1,000
18-2	Reduce the rate of suicide attempts by adolescents.	2.6% in past 12 months	1.0% in past 12 months
18-7	Increase the proportion of children with mental health problems who receive treatment.	No data	No specific target
19-3	Reduce the proportion of children and adolescents who are overweight or obese.		
	Ages 6 to 11 years	11	5
	Ages 12 to 19 years	10	5
19-5	Increase the proportion of persons age 2 years and older who consume at least two daily servings of fruit.	28%	75%
19-6	Increase the proportion of persons age 2 years and older who consume at least three daily servings of vegetables, with at least one-third being dark green or deep yellow vegetables	3%	50%
19-7	Increase the proportion of persons age 2 years and older who consume at least six daily servings of grain products, with at least three being whole grains.	7%	50%
19-8	Increase the proportion of persons age 2 years and older who consume less than 10 percent of calories from saturated fat.	36%	75%
19-9	Increase the proportion of persons age 2 years and older who consume no more than 30 percent of calories from fat.	33%	75%
19-10	Increase the proportion of persons age 2 years and older who consume 2,400 mg or less of sodium daily.	21%	65%
19-11	Increase the proportion of persons age 2 years and older who meet dietary recommendations for calcium.	46%	75%
19-12	Reduce iron-deficiency anemia among young children and females of child-bearing age.		
	Nonpregnant females ages 12 to 49 years	11%	7%
19-15	Increase the proportion of children and adolescents ages 6 to 19 years whose intake of meals and snacks at schools contributes proportionally to good overall dietary quality.	No data	No specific target
21-1	Reduce the proportion of children and adolescents with dental caries experience either in their primary or permanent teeth.		
	Children ages 6 to 8	52%	42%
	Adolescents	61%	51%
21-2	Reduce the proportion of children, adolescents, and adults with untreated dental decay.		
	Children ages 6 to 8	29%	20%
	Adolescents	21%	15%
21-8	Increase the proportion of children who have received dental sealants on their molar teeth.		
	Children aged 8 years	23%	50%
	Adolescents aged 14 years	15%	50%
21-10	Increase the proportion of children and adults who use the oral health care system each year.	65%	85%

OBJECTIVES	BASELINE	2010 TARGET
21-12 Increase the proportion of children and adolescents under age 19 years at or below 200 percent of the federal poverty level who received any preventive dental service during the past year.	20%	57%
21-13 Increase the proportion of school-based health centers with an oral health component.	No data	No specific target
22-6 Increase the proportion of adolescents who engage in moderate physical activity for at least 30 minutes on 5 or more of the previous 7 days.	20%	30%
22-7 Increase the proportion of adolescents who engage in vigorous physical activity that promotes cardiorespiratory fitness 3 or more days per week for 20 or more minutes per occasion.	64%	85%
22-8 Increase the proportion of the nation's public and private schools that require daily physical education for all students.		
Middle and junior high	17%	25%
Senior high	2%	5%
22-9 Increase the proportion of adolescents who participate in daily school physical education.	27%	50%
22-10 Increase the proportion of adolescents who spend at least 50 percent of school physical education class time being physically active.	32%	50%
22-11 Increase the proportion of children and adolescents who view television 2 or fewer hours per day.	60%	75%
22-12 Increase the proportion of the nation's public and private schools that provide access to their physical activity spaces and facilities for all persons outside of normal school hours (that is, before and after the school day, on weekends, and during summer and other vacations).	No data	No specific target
24-1 Reduce asthma deaths.		
Children ages 5 to 14	3.2 per million	1.0 per million
Adolescents and adults ages 15 to 34 years	5.9 per million	3.0 per million
24-2 Reduce hospitalizations for asthma. Children and adults ages 5 to 64 years	13.8 per 10,000	8.0 per 10,000
24-5 Reduce the number of school or work days missed by persons with asthma due to asthma.	No data	No specific target
25-11 Increase the proportion of adolescents who abstain from sexual intercourse or use condoms if currently sexually active.	85%	95%
26-6 Reduce the proportion of adolescents who report that they rode, during the previous 30 days, with a driver who had been drinking alcohol.	37%	30%
26-9 Increase the age and proportion of adolescents who remain alcohol and drug free.		
Average age of first use of alcohol	13.1	16.1
Average age of first use of marijuana	13.7	17.4
Percent never using alcoholic beverages	19%	29%
Percent never using illicit drugs	46%	56%
26-10 Reduce past-month use of illicit substances.		
Adolescents not using alcohol or any illicit substances in past 30 days	77%	89%
Adolescents reporting use of marijuana in past 30 days	9.4%	0.7%

OBJECTIVES	BASELINE	2010 TARGET
26-11 Reduce the proportion of persons engaging in binge drinking of alcoholic beverages.		
High school seniors engaging in binge drinking in past 2 weeks	32%	11%
Adolescents ages 12 to 17 engaging in binge drinking during the past month	8.3%	3.0%
26-14 Reduce steroid use among adolescents.		
Steroid use in past year among 8th graders	1.2%	0.4%
Steroid use in past year among 10th graders	1.2%	0.4%
Steroid use in past year among 12th graders	1.2%	0.4%
26-15 Reduce the proportion of adolescents who use inhalants (in the past year).	4.4%	0.7%
26-16 Increase the proportion of adolescents who disapprove of substance abuse.		
Who disapprove of having one or two alcoholic drinks nearly every day:		
8th graders	77%	83%
10th graders	75%	83%
12th graders	69%	83%
Who disapprove of trying marijuana or hashish once or twice		
8th graders	69%	72%
10th graders	56%	72%
12th graders	52%	72%
26-17 Increase the proportion of adolescents who perceive great risk associated with substance abuse.		
Consuming five or more alcoholic drinks at a single occasion once or twice a week	47%	80%
Smoking marijuana once per month	31%	80%
Using cocaine once per month	54%	80%
27-2 Reduce tobacco use by adolescents.		
Tobacco products (past month)	43%	21%
Cigarettes (past month)	36%	16%
Spit tobacco (past month)	9%	1%
Cigars (past month)	22%	8%
27-3 Reduce initiation of tobacco use among children and adolescents.	No data	No specific target
27-4 Increase the average age of first use of tobacco products by adolescents and young adults.		
Adolescents ages 12 to 17 (age at first use)	12	14
27-7 Increase tobacco use cessation attempts by adolescent smokers.	73%	84%
27-9 Reduce the proportion of children who are regularly exposed to tobacco smoke at home.	27%	10%
27-11 Increase smoke-free and tobacco-free environments in schools, including all school facilities, property, vehicles, and school events.	37%	100%
27-14 Reduce the illegal buy rate among minors through enforcement of laws prohibiting the sale of tobacco products to minors.		
Number of states (and District of Columbia) with a 5% or less illegal buy rate among minors	0	51
27-16 Eliminate tobacco advertising and promotions that influence adolescents and young adults.	No data	No specific target
27-17 Increase adolescents' disapproval of smoking.		
8th graders	80%	95%
10th graders	75%	95%
12th graders	69%	95%

OBJECTIVES	BASELINE	2010 TARGET
28-2 Increase the proportion of preschool children ages 5 years and under who receive vision screening.	No data	No specific target
28-4 Reduce blindness and visual impairment in children and adolescents ages 17 years and under.	25 per 1,000 children and adolescents	22 per 1,000 children and adolescents
28-12 Reduce otitis media in children and adolescents.	344.7 visits per 1,000 under age 18	294 visits per 1,000 under age 18
28-17 Reduce noise-induced hearing loss in children and adolescents under age 17 years.	No data	No specific target

APPENDIX C

The Teacher's Encyclopedic Guide for Health Concerns of School-Age Youths . . . from A to Z

As a teacher, you will be called on to handle an increasing number of health situations, some of which were nonexistent only a few years ago, and an increasing number of students are coming to school with health-related concerns. To respond effectively, a teacher needs to know the nature of these situations and concerns, his or her limitations, when it is appropriate to request medical assistance, and where and how to obtain it. *The Teacher's Encyclopedic Guide for Health Concerns of School-Age Youths . . . from A to Z* addresses the major student health issues and concerns you will need to be well-informed about. Chapter 14's *Guide to First Aid Procedures* will also help you prepare for emergencies.

ACNE

Acne is a skin disorder characterized by inflammation of skin glands and hair follicles and the eruption of pimples. Pimples and blackheads (comedones) most often occur on the face, but they can also develop on the neck, shoulders, upper arms, chest, and trunk. Increased hormone production, which is characteristic of adolescence, and the presence of bacteria on the skin play important roles in the development of acne.

Nearly everyone will develop some form of acne during their lifetime, and it is most prevalent during the teenage years. It usually starts between the ages of ten and thirteen and lasts for five to ten years. Acne affects males and females about equally, but males are more likely to experience severe, long-lasting cases. Females are more likely to have intermittent acne due to hormonal changes associated with their menstrual cycles.

There are persistent misconceptions about acne that students and adults believe. Acne is not caused by poor hygiene or by stress. Neither is it the result of eating foods such as chocolate, sweets, milk, and fatty foods. Factors beyond a person's control, such as puberty, heredity, and hormonal changes, are responsible for acne's development. Teachers should provide accurate information about the nature of acne and how to treat it. They should instruct students to avoid vigorously scrubbing areas affected by acne when washing, and they should stress to students that the primary cause of acne is the flow of the hormones associated with puberty. In addition, students should be advised not to squeeze or rub pimples, because this can lead to secondary infections or scarring. Teenagers should be helped to realize that acne is a normal part of growing up and that it won't last forever.

Acne is one of the easiest skin conditions for teachers and school nurses to detect. Many young people are able to manage their acne with over-the-counter (nonprescription) treatments, such as cleansers, benzoyl peroxide, and salicylic acid. Students with severe cases of acne should be advised to seek medical care from a dermatologist. Medications such as antibiotics, vitamin A derivatives known as retinoids, or other medications might be prescribed. A dermatologist might also use other treatments in addition to medications. Health care professionals must be sure to address adolescents' emotional concerns about acne in addition to their physical concerns.

Young people hate the way acne makes them look. They suffer from impaired self-concept and poor body image. Proper treatment often can reduce the severity of acne and help improve the student's self-concept and body image. Some students may need psychological counseling, particularly those who have severe cases of acne that result in permanent scarring.

ADOLESCENT PREGNANCY

Adolescent pregnancy is pregnancy in the years between puberty and the end of the teen years. Each year in the United States, about 1 million adolescent females become pregnant and about a half million teens deliver babies. The United States has one of the highest rates of adolescent pregnancy in the developed world. Many pregnant adolescents do not seek early prenatal care. As a result, they have more problem pregnancies than adult females who do seek prenatal care. Adolescents are at a much higher risk than adult females of suffering from serious medical complications of pregnancy, including anemia, pregnancy-induced hypertension, toxemia, cervical trauma, and premature delivery. They are also at increased risk of giving birth to premature and low-birthweight infants. Even normal-birthweight infants of adolescent mothers have a higher rate of rehospitalization than infants of adult mothers.

Pregnant females and their partners have unique needs. Pregnant females need to understand what is happening to their bodies and what to expect during their pregnancy. They also need support. Fathers need this information too, as well as support in their own way. Adolescent fathers and mothers need counseling to help them handle the baby's needs as well as to help them with their relationship. They also need information on planning for the future. For example, they need to make financial plans for supporting the baby. Most states now require the male to make child-support payments if he does not marry the mother.

Through education, schools can play a significant role in preventing adolescent pregnancy. What to teach is an issue that is determined by each school district. The U.S. government promotes the teaching of abstinence in schools. Students need to be taught how to use resistance skills to say no to being sexually active.

Young women who give birth before completing high school are particularly at risk for severe economic and educational disadvantages. Schools can offer programs that address the multiple challenges facing teens who are becoming parents by providing academic and parenting instruction within the framework of a coordinated school health program. Alternative school programs can also help meet some of these needs.

ALCOHOL-RELATED PROBLEMS

Alcohol-related problems include abuse of alcohol by the student as well as a student's exposure to alcohol problems through alcohol abuse by a family member. Alcohol is one of the most commonly abused drugs of school-age youth. Youth who abuse alcohol might exhibit one or more of the following signs and symptoms:

- Drinking secretively
- Lying about drinking
- Drinking during times of stress and worry
- Gulping drinks
- Trying to find parties where alcoholic beverages will be served
- Preoccupation with drinking
- Declining grades
- Decrease in muscular coordination
- Not following through on class projects
- Becoming irritable too easily

Many students are affected by the drinking behavior of family members. One of every four families is affected by a family member who drinks. These students often come to school tense and poorly fed. They might withdraw in order to avoid calling attention to drinking problems at home. They might not invite friends to their home for fear of being embarrassed by a parent who is drunk. These students often have low self-esteem and, because of behavior they observe at home, are more likely to begin drinking themselves.

Alcohol-related problems involving youth require immediate intervention. The first step in helping young people with alcohol-related problems is to identify the problem. Teachers who are aware of the signs and symptoms of alcohol-related problems are often able to identify alcohol-dependent or alcohol-abusing youths who are at risk due to alcohol problems in the home. Once they recognize these problems, school professionals should intervene by linking students to available treatment services. This requires a team approach with parents, administrators, counselors, school nurses, and community treatment providers working with students. Some schools are able to offer school-based treatment or counseling services to students suffering from alcohol and other forms of drug abuse, and to students who are exposed to alcohol-related problems in the home. Other schools rely on school-linked treatment options with community programs or must make referrals to community-based programs. Follow-up and tracking of students throughout treatment are fundamental aspects of a responsible and effective intervention policy.

One approach used by many schools for dealing with alcoholism and the problems of children who have parents with alcoholism is the student assistance program. A **student assistance program** is a school-based approach to the prevention and treatment of alcohol abuse. This type of program is modeled after employee assistance programs in business and industry. Teachers and school personnel are trained to recognize alcohol and other drug involvement or related problems that interfere with a student's ability to function at school and then to use a referral process for getting appropriate help for the student. Students can also refer themselves to program services. The goals of student assistance programs include the following:

- Identifying early alcohol and other drug involvement or other problems
- Referring students to designated "helpers" within the school
- Providing in-school support or counseling services and groups
- Referring students to outside mental health, drug-treatment, and family services organizations and professionals

The key component in a successful student assistance program is the endorsement, support, and involvement of school officials and administrators, community leaders and organizations, parents, and students.

ALLERGIES

An **allergy** is a hypersensitive reaction by the immune system to a foreign antigen (protein). An allergen is a substance that stimulates the production of antibodies and subsequently results in allergic reactions. Many young people experience food allergies. Common food allergens are milk, strawberries, wheat, eggs, corn, nuts, citrus fruits, and shellfish. Airborne allergens include pollen, dust, and molds. Medications such as antibiotics and aspirin also can be allergens for some people. Allergic reactions can develop at any stage in the life cycle.

Although most allergic reactions are mild and localized, some people can experience a severe anaphylactic reaction to an allergen. An **anaphylactic reaction** is a sudden systemic reaction that can be life-threatening. Symptoms include dizziness, nausea, itching, hives, sudden weakness, a drop in blood pressure, and constriction of bronchial tubes that makes breathing difficult. A severe anaphylactic reaction requires immediate medical emergency care. Children and adolescents prone to these reactions should have quick access to kits that contain oral antihistamines and epinephrine-filled syringes to counteract the anaphylactic reactions. School professionals should be trained and prepared to assist or administer these medications according to school policies for administering medications.

Allergies should be listed on each student's health record, and teachers should be aware of each student's allergies. Teachers should be trained to recognize signs and symptoms of anaphylactic reactions and should be skilled in proper procedures for activating proper emergency care. Outdoor field trips increase the likelihood of exposure to allergens (e.g., bee stings, food), so teachers should be prepared with an emergency plan in case any students experience severe allergic reactions. This might require the emergency administration of epinephrine and other emergency measures. Reducing children's exposure to allergens is a preferred mode of allergy control, and action should be taken to remove any identified allergens from the school environment whenever such action is feasible and practical.

ANTHRAX

Anthrax is an infectious disease caused by a spore-forming bacterium. It most commonly occurs in hoofed mammals but can infect humans in two ways. First, the bacteria can proliferate in the lungs, causing a potentially fatal condition called *inhalation anthrax*. This condition can be cured with oral antibiotics if diagnosed early. Second, the bacteria can colonize on the skin, forming a treatable lesion called *cutaneous anthrax*. Anthrax is a rare infectious disease that is extremely unlikely to be spread from one person to another. The biggest threat from anthrax is due to bioterrorism. The disease has been spread to people through packages in the mail. For this reason, schoolchildren and school personnel should not open or handle any packages or envelopes that appear suspicious. Anyone who handles questionable mail should not shake it or hold it near the face, and the person should immediately report the mail to a security officer, law-enforcement official, or school official. Infection can be prevented with antibiotic treatment in people known to have been exposed to anthrax. An anthrax vaccine can also prevent infection. However, vaccination against anthrax is not recommended and not yet available to the general public.

ASTHMA

Asthma is an allergic disease of the lungs manifested by constriction of the small air passages called bronchioles. It is characterized by coughing, chest tightness, shortness of breath, and wheezing. Asthma usually starts in childhood. About three-quarters of people with asthma develop symptoms before age six. Asthma is often triggered by exposure to allergens such as dust mites, cockroach droppings, animal dander (dead skin flakes), pollens, molds, and tobacco smoke. Cold air or exertion during exercise can also trigger an attack. A tendency to have asthma seems to be inherited.

Asthma is a serious disease. It is the most common serious chronic childhood disease, affecting nearly 5 million children in the United States. It is estimated that there are, on average, two children with asthma per classroom. Hundreds of thousands of children are hospitalized each year because of asthma. Millions of days of school absenteeism are the result of asthma. About one-quarter of all school absences are due to asthma. Asthma kills 5,000 children and adults each year.

A doctor can prescribe certain medications and devices to help children manage asthma. A peak flow meter measures the ease of breathing. Older children can use metered-dose inhalers and dry-powder inhalers to deliver different types of asthma medication. Nebulizers, which deliver medication in a mist, are helpful for young children. They are also useful for young people whose asthma is not well controlled with other medications. For severe asthma, oral medications might be necessary. In general, there are two types of asthma medications. One type is medication taken to prevent or reverse inflammation. In adults, these drugs are often corticosteroids. However, because corticosteroids might slightly slow growth, children are usually first given nonsteroidal inhalants. The second type is medication that is to be taken only if the airways start to tighten up despite the anti-inflammatory drugs, or bronchodilators. Asthma medications can produce side effects that impair a child's concentration and ability to learn in school. These include headache, hand tremors, stomachache, and tiredness. Oral medications are more likely than inhaled medications to result in side effects.

These are some of the ways teachers and other school personnel can help asthmatic children:

- Identify children with asthma and inform all relevant school personnel of the child's asthma.
- Determine the asthma medications the child must take and their possible side effects.
- Allow the child to take required medications on schedule.
- Allow school-age children with asthma to carry metered-dose inhalers with them at all times and use them as appropriate.
- Treat children with asthma like other children.
- Provide inservice training for teachers and school staff about asthma management principles.
- Seek input and maintain communication with parents of asthmatic children.
- Encourage children with asthma to fully participate in activities.
- Be prepared to recognize when emergency measures are needed and take them.

The following signs could indicate that a young person is experiencing an asthma attack and that emergency measures might need to be taken:

- A hunched-over posture
- Tight neck and shoulder muscles
- Chronic, persistent coughing
- A feeling of tightness in the chest

- Chest discomfort after exertion
- Excessive breathlessness
- A pale, sweaty, agitated appearance
- A frightened or anxious look
- Difficulty walking or talking

ATTENTION DEFICIT HYPERACTIVITY DISORDER

Attention deficit hyperactivity disorder (ADHD) is characterized by developmentally inappropriate levels of attention, concentration, activity, distractibility, and impulsivity. It is the most commonly diagnosed behavioral disorder of children. The prevalence of ADHD is hard to determine; studies involving strict diagnostic criteria by mental health professionals report that 3 to 5 percent of students in the school-age population have ADHD. Teachers report ADHD prevalence rates between 10 and 20 percent, and rates are often even higher when parents report the incidence. A major controversy is over the use of psychostimulant drugs, particularly methylphenidate (Ritalin), to treat ADHD. Some believe there has been overuse and abuse of psychostimulant drug treatment for ADHD. Psychostimulant drugs are more readily available and are being prescribed more frequently than in the past. In the 1990s, prescriptions for stimulant medication for children increased severalfold. On a typical school day, 3.3 percent of all students now receive medications for ADHD (McCarthy, Kelly, & Reed, 2000). There has even been a dramatic increase in the number of two- to four-year-old children who are prescribed methylphenidate (Zito et al., 2000). Further, the U.S. Drug Enforcement Administration reports that 90 percent of the world's methylphenidate is consumed in the United States. Regions of the country vary significantly in the amount of stimulants prescribed by doctors to treat ADHD.

Symptoms of ADHD are often apparent to teachers. Students with ADHD are likely to display the following behavioral symptoms: difficulty concentrating on schoolwork or other tasks requiring sustained attention, difficulty sticking to play activities, being distracted, often failing to finish things they start, acting before thinking, shifting from one activity to another, requiring a lot of supervision, frequently calling out in class, difficulty waiting their turn in games or group situations, difficulty sitting still or staying seated, fidgeting excessively, and frequently engaging in random or aimless activity. These symptoms could indicate ADHD, but they are not diagnostic without referral and evaluation from a physician. There is no single test to diagnose ADHD. Physicians must assess several factors in determining an ADHD diagnosis, including school performance and behavior, family functioning, and adaptation. A team approach that includes parents, teachers, school psychologists, and other mental health specialists, along with a physician, facilitates accurate assessment and diagnosis of ADHD. However, such a time-intensive approach is not always followed, and physicians often make diagnostic decisions during the course of one or two office visits. Quick diagnoses of ADHD, without full assessment, is also associated with a response to prescribe medication for treatment. Unfortunately, medication is the only treatment prescribed. This has led to public concern about the overdiagnosis of ADHD and reliance on a quick-fix solution to a complex health condition.

Children with ADHD have pronounced difficulties and impairments that can result in long-term adverse consequences. ADHD appears to be associated with temper tantrums, low frustration tolerance, low self-esteem, difficulties with friendships and other interpersonal relationships, and poor academic achievement. Young people with ADHD often are very immature and have difficulty with their peers. As a result of their immaturity, they often associate with people younger than they are. Because of their impulsiveness, young people with ADHD often have difficulty in school. As children with ADHD grow older, they are more likely to engage in drug abuse and antisocial behavior and to have higher injury rates. For many individuals, the impact of ADHD continues into adulthood. Families of children with ADHD experience increased levels of parental frustration, marital discord, and divorce. Schools, social service agencies, criminal justice systems, and health care systems spend billions of dollars annually to deal with children who have ADHD.

There are no strategies for the prevention of ADHD, and research studies have discovered little about the causes of ADHD. Studies show that psychostimulant drugs and psychosocial treatments alleviate symptoms of ADHD in the short term (approximately three months). Currently it is not known what treatment for ADHD is effective over the long term. Scientific studies are under way that might help answer this question. Studies are also needed to determine the safety of psychostimulant drugs. Educators should attempt to keep current on research findings about ADHD.

It appears that educators can assist children with ADHD by providing structure and routine in order to alleviate distraction. Allowing enough time for these young people to process information is important. Using positive rewards instead of punishments helps bolster their self-esteem. Providing opportunities for positive peer interaction both in and outside the classroom is especially important. Being certain to assign these young people tasks that are very specific is a necessity.

CHILD ABUSE

Child abuse is maltreatment of a person under the age of eighteen. It is any act that endangers or impairs a child's physical or emotional health and development. There are different types of abuse. Each type of child abuse—physical abuse, emotional abuse, neglect, and sexual abuse—is described and discussed in a separate section in this encyclopedia.

It is difficult to get an accurate account for how common child abuse is because it most often occurs behind closed doors and goes unreported. However, in 2001 child protective service agencies received about 2.6 million reports of possible maltreatment, and there were 903,000 substantiated cases of the maltreatment of children (U.S. Department of Health and Human Services, 2003). About 1,300 children died of abuse or neglect.

Teachers are in a position to recognize cases of child abuse. Teachers can recognize appearance, behavior, and academic difficulties that could indicate possible abuse. Other school personnel such as coaches, bus drivers, school nurses, and office staff might also recognize signs of abuse.

By law, any teacher or educator must report suspected cases of abuse. Most school districts have specific policies about the reporting of abuse. A teacher who reports a case of suspected abuse has immunity from civil and criminal liability. When an abuse case is filed, the identity of the person reporting the abuse remains confidential. Reports of child abuse are often made to child welfare agencies or the police. Most reported cases of child abuse are investigated rapidly. If an investigation indicates that a child is in danger, that child will likely be placed in protective custody or in a foster home.

Child abuse occurs in families of all socioeconomic levels. In 85 to 90 percent of cases, the person who is abusing a child is a family member.

How would a teacher know if a student is being or has been abused? The student might confide that she or he is being abused. If this happens, it is extremely important to report the abuse to the principal or follow procedures established in your school district. Even though the student might share this information with you in strictest confidence, you have an obligation to report it promptly in order to protect the student and to abide by the law. In most cases of abuse, the student who has been abused tells no one and receives help only when an adult recognizes the signs and symptoms and obtains help for the student. Teachers need to be aware of these signs and symptoms and of the other characteristics that will help them assist students who are abused. The following behaviors are signs and symptoms that a child could be a victim of child abuse:

- Coming to school with dirty clothing, body odor, or unkempt appearance
- Having unexplained injuries
- Acting shy, withdrawn, or too eager to cooperate
- Arriving at school early and leaving late
- Not wanting to go home
- Wearing long-sleeved clothing in warm weather
- Talking about beatings
- Acting nervous, too active, or destructive
- Acting fearful of being touched by an adult
- Being absent from school with poor or no excuse
- Showing little hope of being comforted when in trouble
- Always searching for favors, food, or services

- Having problems getting along with other children

Teachers and other school personnel must know and follow their school's policy for reporting cases of suspected abuse. Childhelp USA is a national child-abuse hotline that provides information about reporting child abuse. Call the toll-free number (1-800-4-A-CHILD) to learn the reporting agency for your geographic area and your situation. Other information about child abuse is available through this organization's website at www.childhelpusa.org.

Additional related information is included under *emotional abuse, neglect, physical abuse,* and *sexual abuse.*

CHRONIC HEALTH CONDITIONS

Chronic health conditions are health conditions that recur or persist. It is estimated that 10 to 15 percent of students have a chronic health condition (McCarthy, Kelly, & Reed, 2000). More than three-quarters of teachers report teaching students with chronic health conditions during their career. However, many teachers feel that their professional training did not prepare them to deal with chronic health conditions in the classroom. The chronic health conditions most commonly seen in students are asthma, diabetes, epilepsy, cerebral palsy, heart disease, cancer, and spina bifida. Another chronic health condition of concern in children is HIV/AIDS.

A child with a chronic health condition requires school programs that are carefully planned to fit the child's condition and needs. It is important for children with chronic health conditions to lead as normal a life as possible. It is critical to balance academic needs with health care needs. As much as possible, the child should be encouraged to participate in regular classroom and school activities. Exemptions from specific activities should be allowed only when these are in the child's best interest. Sometimes it is necessary to make provisions for students who require technology (e.g., specialized electrical outlets, private areas for catheterization) or trained personnel to provide daily or emergency care. Schedules can be adjusted to accommo-

date rest periods and to enable the child to take care of personal needs. School programs for children with chronic health conditions should also do the following:

- Arrange for students to make up schoolwork.
- Develop individual education plans (IEPs) or Section 504 plans with parents and involved school staff.
- Employ specialized learning techniques.
- Have procedures to control and prevent infectious disease.
- Have teachers or other school personnel make home or hospital visits.
- Plan for emergency care.
- Have procedures for administering needed medications during school hours.
- Provide needed training to school personnel and students.
- Keep interruptions for medical and personal care interventions nondisruptive to the classroom or learning atmosphere.
- Maximize opportunities for educational success and social interaction and avoid limiting or isolating children with chronic health conditions.

Additional related information is included under *asthma, diabetes mellitus, HIV/AIDS,* and *seizure disorders.* Also see these sections of Chapter 2: "Confidentiality of Student Health Information," "School-Based Health Centers," "Accommodations for Special School Health Services," and "Administration of Medications at School."

CONJUNCTIVITIS

Conjunctivitis is an inflammation of the membrane lining the eyelids and covering the eyeball (the conjunctiva). Commonly known as "pinkeye," conjunctivitis is a highly contagious condition most often caused by a bacterial or viral infection. However, it also can be caused by allergies, certain drugs, or irritation from foreign objects. Conjunctivitis is rarely serious unless infection progresses to the deeper tissues of the eye, which might harm vision. The most common signs of this condition are redness and swelling of the eyes and significant tearing. A discharge might also be present. Students with conjunctivitis might complain of a gritty feeling in the eyes and of their eyelids sticking together upon waking from sleep.

A student who has conjunctivitis should be isolated and should not attend school, and the parents should be advised to seek medical consultation for their child. Most cases of conjunctivitis are treated effectively with antibacterial eyedrops or ointments. Over-the-counter medications are not effective. It is imperative that family members understand that conjunctivitis can easily spread from person to person through sharing the same towels and bedding. Careful handwashing is also helpful in preventing spread of infection. Students who have received treatment can usually return to school within a few days without risk of spreading infection.

DEATH

In humans, **death** is the permanent cessation of brain, heart, and lung function. At some time, a teacher will be faced with a student in class who has experienced the death of a loved one. A student's grandparent or parent might have died, or a pet might have been hit by a car or died of old age. At times, students might even be faced with the death of another student.

A student who suffers such a loss will experience any number of reactions. The death of a parent is the most stressful life event for a school-age student. How a student reacts can depend on the situation. For example, when a family member had a prolonged illness prior to death, a student might have already begun the grieving process. The family influences how a student adjusts to the death. A student whose family discusses death in an open and honest manner will be able to grieve openly and share feelings more easily than a student whose family does not discuss the death openly and honestly. A student's age also affects how he or she reacts to death. Very young students believe that death is temporary and like being asleep. Between the ages of five and nine, students begin to understand the finality of death and that death can be caused by an environmental force (e.g., car crash, gun shot, physical blow to the head). Students age nine and older can understand that death is a part of the life cycle and can happen to anyone.

Elisabeth Kübler-Ross identified five stages in the grieving process that accompanies dying and death. These stages are denial, anger, bargaining, depression, and acceptance. At first, students experience denial. They do not believe that someone they know or have been close to has died. When they realize that the person will not return, they are angry. Then they bargain, believing that the person can come back. They focus on it not being fair to have this loss. This stage is followed by depression and sadness. Guilt might accompany depression. The student will need much support. Young people also can be vulnerable to thoughts of their own death. Finally, the student will reach acceptance. But it is important to remember that in young people the grieving process is not short. Also, these stages are not necessarily sequential or linear: Students might not all progress through the stages in the same order, some might skip a stage altogether in the process of achieving acceptance, and some might return to a previous stage.

Here are some ways a teacher can help students who have experienced the death of someone they were close to:

- Do not shield students from or mislead them about death. Students need to know that death is not temporary and that it is not like sleeping.
- When students ask questions, give simple, direct answers. For example, a student might ask, "Why did *my* grandma die?" An appropriate answer is "Grandma was very ill for a long time, and her heart finally stopped beating." A student who is given a complex and long reply might become confused.
- Answer questions as they arise. If you do not have an answer to a question, say so. But you can tell the student that you will try to find an answer.
- Recognize that students need to grieve. Remember the five stages. Help students understand the grieving process. For example, if a student acts out in angry ways, you might say, "You are very angry that your father died. I can understand you feel it is unfair." This helps the student understand his or her feelings.
- Watch for signs of severe depression. Remember that students are especially vulnerable to depression if a parent or other loved one dies, and they need extra support and understanding.

DENTAL PROBLEMS

Dental problems are nontraumatic tooth-related conditions that exist as a result of structural problems, infection, or diet. Common dental problems in school-age students are cavities, tooth abscesses, need for extraction, gingivitis, and malocclusion. Dental caries, or cavities, are the most common health disorder in children and adolescents. A **cavity** is an area of decay in a tooth. Cavities that are detected and treated by a dentist usually do not represent a significant threat to health. However, not attending to a cavity might lead to an abscess and destruction of the tooth, requiring the need for tooth extraction by a dentist. An **abscess** is localized collection of pus. **Extraction** is surgical removal of a tooth. Tooth abscesses and extraction might be painful. When more than one tooth is involved, a student's nutritional status might be compromised because eating might be difficult. Poor dental hygiene also can lead to gingivitis. **Gingivitis** is inflammation of the gums. Severe gingivitis often results in ulceration and bleeding of the gums. Another dental problem frequently found in students is **malocclusion,** the improper alignment of teeth. This condition can destroy oral tissue if not corrected.

Some schools provide dental inspections upon school entry and at certain grade levels. Other schools do not, taking the view that this is the responsibility of students' families. Whether or not a school district offers inspections, teachers and other professionals are often in a position to observe signs and symptoms of dental problems, such as crooked teeth, bleeding gums, offensive breath, reports of toothache or other oral pain, poor hygiene, soreness or pain in the mouth upon eating, and visible caries on teeth. Students with signs or symptoms of dental problems should be referred to the school nurse, and their parents should be notified.

DIABETES MELLITUS

Diabetes mellitus is a chronic disease characterized by an excess of glucose (sugar) in the blood, resulting when the pancreas produces too little or no insulin. Insulin is a hormone produced in the pancreas that regulates the sugar in the blood. Glucose is the body's main source of energy, and insulin functions some-thing like a key that opens a door into the cells so the glucose can become fuel. Without insulin, glucose builds up in the blood, sometimes to dangerous levels. Diabetes cannot be cured, but it can be managed with proper diet, exercise, blood sugar monitoring, oral medication, and insulin injections.

There are two main types of diabetes. Type 1 diabetes, which used to be called juvenile diabetes, involves the destruction of the beta cells in the pancreas that produce insulin. As a result the pancreas produces too little or no insulin, and the Type 1 diabetic must take insulin. Type 1 diabetes is also called insulin-dependent diabetes because of the need for daily insulin injections. Most people with Type 1 diabetes are diagnosed between the ages of ten and twenty. In Type 2 diabetes, insulin is produced in insufficient quantity and the body doesn't use the insulin efficiently to move glucose into cells where it can be used as fuel. The symptoms of Type 2 diabetes build up slowly. Type 2 diabetes can be quietly damaging kidneys, eyes, and nerve endings before it is discovered. Diet, exercise, weight loss, and often, oral medication are used to control the disease. Some oral medications help the body use insulin; others increase insulin production. Some people with Type 2 diabetes need to take insulin. Rates of Type 2 diabetes are higher in American Indians, Hispanics, and African Americans than in Caucasians. Type 2 diabetes used to be called adult-onset diabetes, but it has increased sharply among children and adolescents. Therefore, the term *adult-onset diabetes* is no longer appropriate.

The symptoms of Type 1 diabetes include frequent urination, thirst, and loss of weight and appetite. There might also be blurred vision, itching, and infections of the skin. These symptoms can progress rapidly. If diabetes is suspected, a school nurse might be able to have a student take a urine test. School nurses have urine test paper strips that can be used to detect diabetes. Students who have Type 1 diabetes regularly need to take insulin—usually at home, in the morning before school and in the early evening after coming home from school. It is important that a student who has Type 1 diabetes follow a strict diet and take meals at specific times during the day.

It is important for teachers to understand that a student with diabetes can suffer from fluctuations in blood sugar levels. Any unusual behavior in a student with diabetes can be indicative of a blood sugar imbalance. Teachers need to be aware of complications that might occur. The most common complication is hypoglycemia, the most common problem in children with diabetes. **Hypoglycemia** is a condition in which the blood sugar is low as a result of excess insulin in the body. The signs and symptoms of hypoglycemia include pale skin, blurred vision, shakiness, dizziness, sweating, and rapid pulse. Behavioral signs associated with hypoglycemia can easily be mistaken for misbehavior. Behavior changes might include poor concentration, becoming withdrawn, confusion, restlessness, tantrums of sudden rage, crying, or even laughter.

Usually hypoglycemia is mild and can be easily treated. If symptoms occur and a student's blood sugar is not known, the student should immediately be given something sweet to eat (e.g., Life Savers, glucose tablets) or drink (e.g., juice, regular soda pop, milk). This will cause the sugar in the blood to rise. Do not send a child suspected of having low blood sugar to the nurse's office alone or unattended. Rather, send another student to get help. The blood sugar level needs to be checked after giving sweets. If the student still has symptoms of hypoglycemia, or the blood sugar level is below eighty after twenty to thirty minutes, additional sugar should be given. If a hypoglycemic student has difficulty swallowing or drinking, a glucose gel or cake icing (gel type) can be given. Rubbing the cheeks will help the sugar be absorbed. Signs of severe hypoglycemia are unconsciousness, unresponsiveness, convulsions, and failure to respond to glucose gel or cake icing (gel type). Severe hypoglycemia is a medical emergency and requires immediate emergency medical assistance.

Another complication of diabetes is hyperglycemia. **Hyperglycemia** is high blood sugar due to either too little insulin or too much food. Students with high blood sugar are often thirsty and have the need to urinate frequently. They sometimes appear sleepy or lethargic. When hyperglycemia is prolonged because of insufficient insulin, diabetic ketoacidosis might develop. **Diabetic ketoacidosis** is a serious condition in which there is a production of two abnormal acids or a lowering of the alkali in the blood as a result of faulty metabolism.

Diabetic ketoacidosis is treated with insulin and sugar-free fluids, such as water or diet soda. Students with diabetes should be given access to water and be free to use the bathroom as often as they need to.

Children with diabetes are entitled to full access to public schools and programs. This is often accomplished through the preparation of a plan that specifies how health care needs will be met in the school setting. The parents and school staff should work together to develop this plan.

Additional related information is included under *chronic health conditions*.

DRUG ABUSE

Drug abuse is drug use that impairs the user's ability to function normally or that harms the user or others. It is one of the most pressing health problems among school-age youth. You will learn more about drugs that young people abuse in Chapter 10. Drug use and abuse is a three-pronged problem affecting students from preschool through high school. Students may experience problems related to abusing substances by abusing them themselves, living in a drug- or alcohol-affected home, or being harmed as a result of the use of drugs by peers or others. Family problems can include child abuse, fetal alcohol syndrome, a change in the family dynamic that co-opts children in keeping the family secret, depression, feelings of guilt, and learning and academic problems, as well as genetic and environmental factors that increase the probability of substance abuse. Problems related to personal drug use can include legal difficulties, academic difficulties, truancy, dropping out of school, family difficulties, addiction, health problems, and morbidity and mortality related to accidental injury, homicide, and suicide. Drug use also poses the risk of being harmed and negatively impacted by the results of drug use such as being hit by a drunken or drug-impaired driver or getting into a fight as a result of someone else's drug use.

Problems associated with drug use often come to the attention of teachers and other school personnel. In the classroom, teachers are in a unique position to identify students who have problems that could signal drug use. Teachers and other school professionals should receive thorough inservice training in how to intervene when they suspect that a student is using drugs. Proper action on the part of teachers or others who suspect drug use is reinforced if a school has enacted clear policies regarding the use and possession of drugs. School staff members should be adequately trained in how to recognize drug use. The following are signs and symptoms that a student might be abusing drugs:

- Neglect of personal hygiene and appearance
- Depression, irritability, and mood swings
- Decline in academic performance
- Changes in friendships
- Inability to remain alert
- Fascination with drug-related music and drawings
- Stealing
- Possessing drug paraphernalia

For additional information on drug abuse, see *alcohol-related problems*.

EATING DISORDERS

Eating disorders are dysfunctional eating habits that harm the mind and body. Students typically develop eating disorders as a way of dealing with the conflicts, pressures, and stresses of their lives. Their eating disorders may be used as a way to express control when the rest of life seems out of control. Two types of eating disorders are anorexia nervosa and bulimia. **Anorexia nervosa** is an eating disorder characterized by an extreme reluctance to eat and a preoccupation with being excessively thin. **Bulimia** is an eating disorder in which a person has uncontrollable urges to eat excessively and then engages in self-induced vomiting or the excessive use of laxatives. These disorders are described more fully in Chapter 8.

Teachers and other school personnel need to know that eating disorders are serious conditions that can have long-lasting consequences. As a result, these conditions should never be taken lightly. Anorexia nervosa can result in cessation of menstruation, heart rhythm disturbances, osteoporosis, kidney failure, and

other serious and potentially fatal disorders. Bulimia can result in serious health hazards such as dehydration, electrolyte damage, bowel or esophagus damage, and even irregular heartbeat and cardiac arrest. The psychological problems associated with these disorders are so serious that they can result in feelings of profound depression, hopelessness, and contemplation or completion of suicide. Therefore, it is imperative that young people with eating disorders receive professional psychological and medical treatment. If untreated, the disorder will become part of a destructive cycle that can continue for years and may eventually lead to death. Teachers must identify people on the school staff, in the school district, or in the community to whom they can turn for advice concerning students suspected of having an eating disorder. Often, school counselors are helpful resources.

Educators should be aware that the following signs and symptoms could indicate an eating disorder in a young person (Renfrew Center, 2003):

- Obsessively concerned about weight
- Thin and keeps getting thinner, losing 15 percent or more of ideal body weight
- Continues to diet or restrict foods even though not overweight
- Has a distorted body image—feels fat even when thin or of normal weight
- Engages in binge eating and cannot voluntarily stop
- Preoccupation with food, calories, nutrition, or cooking
- Denies being hungry
- Exercises obsessively
- Weighs frequently
- Complains about feeling bloated or nauseated when eating normal—or less than normal—amounts of food
- Loses hair or begins to experience thinning hair
- Feels cold even though the temperature is normal or only slightly cool
- Stops menstruating
- Uses the bathroom frequently after meals
- Reacts to emotional stress by overeating
- Has swollen glands
- Has menstrual irregularities
- Experiences frequent fluctuations in weight

- Cannot voluntarily stop eating
- Attempts to adhere to diets, but generally fails
- Feels guilty or ashamed about eating
- Feels out of control
- Has depressive moods

EMOTIONAL ABUSE

Emotional abuse is maltreatment that involves nonphysical assault. For example, verbal assaults might take the form of threatening, yelling, belittling, and blaming. Ignoring a child and not communicating with the child in any way is also a form of emotional abuse. Emotional abuse might also involve bizarre or cruel forms of punishment such as severe isolation or locking a child in a dark closet. This type of abuse is the most difficult form of child maltreatment to identify because the signs are rarely physical. The effects of emotional injury are not as obvious as the bruises and lacerations of physical abuse. Signs that might indicate that a student is being emotionally abused include these:

- The student is depressed or apathetic.
- The student exhibits behavioral difficulties.
- The student withdraws from peers.
- The student reacts fearfully to persons in authority.
- The student exhibits behaviors such as facial tics or rocking motions.
- The student lags in development compared to same-age peers.
- The student verbally reports that she or he is being emotionally abused.

Just like physical abuse, emotional abuse is dangerous to the victim. The student might have low self-esteem and believe that she or he cannot succeed at anything. Students who are emotionally abused are more likely to attempt suicide. Unfortunately, determining emotional abuse can be difficult. Unlike other kinds of abuse, determining emotional abuse is more subjective. If a teacher suspects emotional abuse, the school psychologist or another responsible individual in the school should be notified. A teacher should be aware of the school's standard policy for reporting cases of suspected emotional abuse. Counseling might be recommended to assist the family in handling this situation.

EYE INJURIES

Eye injuries are irritations to the eye or damage to the eyeball. Sometimes foreign bodies such as dirt and sand get on the eyeball. If this happens, have the student blink several times. If the foreign body is still there, have the student flush the eye with water. Never rub the eye. If the object remains, the student needs prompt medical attention.

FAINTING

Fainting is partial or complete loss of consciousness due to reduced blood flow to the brain. Fainting is one of the most common sudden emergencies in the classroom. First aid for a student who has fainted begins with laying the student on the ground. Elevate the legs eight to twelve inches. Loosen any restrictive clothing, such as a collar or a belt. Do not give the student anything to eat or drink and do not splash water on the student's face.

HANTAVIRUS

Hantavirus is a virus that is found in the urine, saliva, or droppings of infected deer mice and some other wild rodents that can cause a rare but serious lung disease called Hantavirus Pulmonary Syndrome (HPS). The risk of hantavirus transmission in school is very low. An infected rodent can transmit the virus by biting, but this is extremely rare. The more common route of infection in humans is to touch something that has been contaminated with rodent urine, droppings, or saliva and then touch their nose or mouth, or to inhale dust from rodent droppings. Health experts also suspect people can contract the virus by eating food that is contaminated with virus-infected rodent urine, droppings, or saliva. For these reasons, it is important to disinfect rodent-infested areas. Hantavirus cannot be transmitted by an infected person to other people.

HEARING LOSS

Hearing loss is a reduction in the ability to detect sound. Hearing loss ranges from mild to profound deafness. There are many causes of hearing loss, including prenatal exposure to drugs or infection, premature birth, respiratory distress upon birth, birth defects, certain viral diseases early in life, middle ear infection, high fevers, and accidents. Recurring exposure to loud music, particularly through headphones and loud sound systems in vehicles, also can lead to hearing loss. Mild or moderate hearing impairment might be detected in the school setting by observation as well as through hearing tests. School professionals should be aware that the following might indicate hearing impairment in children: inattentiveness, turning the head to hear, talking loudly or in monotone, failure to respond to questions, and reports of dizziness, ringing in the ears, or earache.

Audiometry is the hearing test most frequently used in schools. An audiometer assesses the range of sounds that a student can hear at various frequencies and intensities. Hearing loss can be classified as either conductive or sensorineural. **Conductive hearing loss** occurs when sound waves are prevented from reaching the inner ear. Causes can be excessive earwax buildup, damage or malformation of ear structures, or middle ear infection. Hearing aids are most often used to remedy conductive hearing loss, and surgery is often necessary when damaged or malformed ear structures result in conductive hearing loss. **Sensorineural hearing loss** results when sound waves are effectively carried to the inner ear but are not conveyed to the brain. In some cases, sound impulses are carried to the brain but the brain fails to interpret the sound impulses. This type of hearing loss is also known as perception deafness. Frequently, little can be done to correct this type of hearing loss. However, recent advances in electrical implants, such as cochlear implants, allow some people to hear certain sounds.

HEMOPHILIA

Hemophilia is a hereditary disorder characterized by the impaired ability of the blood to clot. People with hemophilia have an increased tendency to bleed following external or internal injury. Hemophilia is much more likely to occur in males than females. School health services for people with hemophilia include injury prevention and early identification of and care for episodes of bleeding. External bleeding is easy to recognize, but internal bleeding is more difficult. Pain in a joint, restricted movement of an extremity, or a limp could indicate internal bleeding.

School professionals should encourage people with hemophilia to realize that they can pursue special interests, participate in a variety of interesting activities, and have fulfilling lives while still observing their special needs. Classroom teachers, physical education teachers, school nurses, guidance counselors, and other school personnel should be notified of people who have hemophilia. Encouragement and emotional support is often necessary for people with hemophilia and their families. During the 1980s, some people with hemophilia became infected with HIV, the virus that causes AIDS, from transfusions of HIV-contaminated blood or clotting factor. Today, however, because of blood-screening procedures implemented in 1985, the risk of HIV infection in the United States through blood transfusions is extremely low.

Additional related information is included under *HIV/AIDS*.

HIV/AIDS

Human immunodeficiency virus (HIV) is a pathogen that destroys the body's immune system, allowing the development of AIDS. **Acquired immunodeficiency syndrome (AIDS)** is the final stage of HIV infection during which there is a significant decrease in the disease-fighting cells inside the body. During this stage the immune system cannot defend the body, leaving the body vulnerable to opportunistic infections. AIDS is one of the most compelling health issues in recent times. Many people use the term *AIDS* when they mean infected with HIV. When HIV enters the body, a person is said to be infected with HIV. Being infected with HIV does not mean having AIDS. A person has AIDS when the immune system fails and opportunistic infections are present. The following are signs and symptoms that indicate possible HIV infection:

- Rapid weight loss for no apparent reason
- Recurring fever or night sweats
- Swollen lymph glands
- Diarrhea that lasts for more than one week

- White spots or unusual blemishes on the tongue, in the mouth, or in the throat
- Memory loss, depression, and other neurological disorders
- Persistent dry cough or shortness of breath
- Recent appearance of pink or purple blotches under the skin or inside the mouth, nose, or eyelids
- Recurring infections

HIV is transmitted in various ways. The major modes of transmission in adults include sexual contact with an infected partner and sharing an infected needle to inject intravenous drugs. Globally, heterosexual sexual contact is the most predominant cause of HIV transmission. In the United States, HIV is most commonly transmitted by male-to-male sexual contact, but the rate of heterosexual transmission is rapidly increasing. Intravenous drug use is the second most common method of transmission. The third most common is transmission by an infected pregnant woman to her baby, either through the placenta to the developing fetus (perinatal), during delivery, or through breast-feeding. The fourth most common mode of transmission is through transfusion of HIV-infected blood. Blood transfusion is no longer a common method of transmission in the United States and other industrialized countries, where all blood is screened before it is used in a transfusion. However, infected blood is a major source of HIV transmission in many parts of the world. Students who have recently immigrated to the United States from these parts of the world have a high risk of HIV infection, particularly if they received blood transfusions in their former countries.

School personnel must be educated about HIV disease (Committee on Pediatric AIDS, 2000). Teachers often have questions pertaining to HIV/AIDS: Should teachers teach about HIV/AIDS in school? Should students who have HIV or AIDS be permitted to attend school? Can other students in school become infected from the student who has tested positive for HIV or has AIDS? To best understand AIDS-related issues, the teacher needs basic information about this condition.

The federal government and most states have guidelines for school districts to follow regarding HIV/AIDS: Students who are infected with HIV should be allowed to attend school.

Students who are infected with HIV and who bite other children, vomit, or cannot control their bowel or bladder should not attend school. School personnel should follow guidelines to protect against infection. Surfaces where bodily fluids are spilled should be wiped immediately with a solution of one part bleach to one part water. If there is an outbreak of communicable diseases such as flu, students with HIV should not attend school because they have a weakened immune system. Becoming infected with a communicable disease can be serious for a person infected with HIV. Any student who must be excluded from school should receive an alternative education.

Because disclosure of a student's HIV infection can stigmatize the student and the family, confidentiality is a priority. The disclosure of a student's HIV status requires parental consent, and school staff members do not have a right to know a student's HIV status. Students with HIV infection may need medications administered during the school day. It is optimal for the school staff member who administers medication to an HIV-infected student to be informed of the HIV infection and familiar with the possible side effects of the medications being administered. This ensures that special requirements for taking certain medications are followed (e.g., drinking plenty of water, taking the medication after a meal) and that side effects are noticed. Having a responsible school staff member aware of the HIV infection can provide for better management of the health condition in the school setting (Committee on Pediatric AIDS, 2000).

To date, education is considered the best way to prevent HIV infection because no effective vaccine is currently available.

A good resource for schools on policies related to HIV is *Someone at School Has AIDS: A Complete Guide to Educational Policies Concerning HIV Infection*. This guide offers all the information and recommendations schools need for educational, health, sports, and confidentiality policies related to HIV. The publication contains sample policies that educators might find helpful in developing policies in their school systems. It is available through the National Association of State Boards of Education (see www.nasbe.org).

IMPETIGO

Impetigo is a highly contagious bacterial infection of the skin. Impetigo lesions are sores containing clear or yellow-colored fluid that eventually rupture and form a crust. Infection can spread through person-to-person contact as well as contact with contaminated clothing or bedding. With prompt medical treatment, which usually consists of antibiotic therapy, infected persons rarely suffer serious complications. Because of the highly contagious nature of impetigo, infected students should not attend school until they have taken antibiotics for at least twenty-four hours. School nurses should instruct family members of infected students in ways to reduce transmission of infection and ways to care for impetigo lesions.

INFECTIOUS DISEASES

An **infectious disease** is a disease caused by microorganisms. Several infectious diseases are communicable diseases that are readily and easily passed from one person to another. Children and adolescents are susceptible to a variety of infectious diseases. Children have a greater susceptibility than adults to many infectious illnesses. A child's immune system lacks the degree of immunity that adults have because it has not built up immunities through previous exposure to pathogens. Lack of exposure means that fewer antibodies are available to the immune system to fight the many viruses and bacteria children are exposed to. Susceptibility to communicable diseases also is heightened when children attend school because they are exposed to many germs there. Infectious diseases are discussed in greater depth in Chapter 11.

In addition to promoting immunizations, schools can help control infectious diseases by identifying infectious illness in students, enforcing policies for excluding students capable of infecting other children from school and determining when readmission is safe, and educating parents, staff, and students about procedures to reduce or prevent the spread of infectious disease. The threat of infectious diseases spreading in schools has caused school professionals to make infection-control procedures and policies in schools a priority. Most schools have well-defined policies and procedures for dealing with infectious diseases.

LEARNING DISABILITIES

A **learning disability** is a physical or psychological disorder that interferes with learning. Young people who have learning disabilities have special learning needs. Many schools offer individual education plans (IEPs) to meet the special needs of these students. Teachers and counselors work closely with the students' parents, stepparents, or guardians. These young people also need to learn coping strategies, because their frustration level is frequently high.

Students with learning disabilities often compare themselves unfavorably to peers who do not experience difficulty learning. They might also experience added pressures because they become overly concerned with their futures. It is important for educators to understand the needs of young people with learning disabilities and to give them the support and encouragement necessary to enhance their self-image. This can be accomplished by integrating them into school activities and helping them learn to interact with their peers in positive ways.

LICE

Lice are tiny insects that need human blood to survive. There are three types of human lice. The most common is the head louse *(Pediculus humanus capitis),* the second most common is the crab louse *(Phthirus pubis),* and the least common is the body louse *(Pediculus humanus corporis).* Head lice are about the size of a sesame seed. They cannot fly and do not have wings. Neither can they jump or hop to get around. They move around by crawling and grasping on human hair with their six legs. Each of these legs has a claw on the end for grasping the hair. The head louse is found only on humans. Head louse infestation cannot be contracted from dogs, cats, or other animals.

The head louse, which is common in lice outbreaks among students, attaches itself to the hair of the head, the hairy parts of the body, or clothing. The main method of transmission is by direct contact with a louse-infected person. Transmission can also occur by indirect contact with an infected person's belongings, such as hats, helmets, scarves, clothing, headphones, and perhaps combs or hairbrushes. Children ages six to eleven are the most likely to become infected with head lice. During these years, children are likely to engage in activities that result in prolonged head-to-head contact, such as taking nap breaks at school, wrestling with each other, and sharing personal items such as combs and hats.

Scratching is a possible sign of lice infestation. When lice feed, they pierce the skin and secrete a noxious salivary substance that results in itching and swelling. The scratching can be intense, resulting in open sores on the head where fingernails have penetrated the skin from scratching.

Many schools routinely conduct head inspection screenings for lice. Lice infestation can be detected by close and thorough inspection by school nurses and teachers. A thorough examination includes observing for lice eggs (nits) that attach themselves to hair shafts. Because lice depend on frequent blood meals for survival, lice are often found close to the scalp. When screening for lice, school nurses and teachers should use gloves, a strong light, and perhaps a magnifying glass.

Insecticidal products are available for head lice treatment. Several can now be purchased without a prescription. However, parents should be advised to consult a physician about treating lice and the choice of which products to use. These products are allergens to some children, and they might only reduce the number of live lice and not kill lice eggs (nits), which will prolong the infestation. Another drawback of these products is that lice are becoming increasingly resistant to these products. For these reasons, many physicians recommend thorough combing to remove lice and nits. The metal combs that are needed for effective removal can be purchased at most pharmacies. These special combs have long, tapered, stainless steel teeth set close enough together to remove both lice and nits. A plastic comb should not be used for lice removal. Thorough laundering of clothing, soaking of combs and brushes in hot water (130 degrees or higher) for at least ten minutes, and vacuuming of pillows, mattresses, furniture, and carpeting will help to control lice in an infected student's household.

School personnel should be prepared to dissuade parents from using ineffective home remedies for treating lice. Hair removal is not necessary and could make the child a focus of teasing by classmates. Vinegar, cooking oil, and mayonnaise are ineffective remedies, as is ordinary shampoo. Regrettably, some parents have applied dangerous chemicals, such as toxic pesticides or gasoline, to children's heads to kill lice. Toxic reactions and tragic accidents have resulted from these practices.

It is critical that students and families who experience lice infestation understand that lice can affect students of all socioeconomic levels and that lice infestation is not necessarily a matter of hygiene. Rather, lice infestation is a consequence of being exposed through direct or indirect contact.

NEGLECT

Neglect is maltreatment that involves lack of proper care and guidance. A parent, stepparent, or guardian might not follow practices that protect a child from injury. Those who are responsible for caring for children might not provide adequate food, shelter, clothing, or medical care. Neglect might involve not arranging for adequate supervision when adults are away from home. Adults who do not arrange for adequate supervision in their absence leave their children vulnerable to injury and violence. A student who is neglected might

- be hungry and appear sleepy,
- wear dirty, smelly, or tattered clothing, and
- need medical attention.

Neglectful families often appear to have many problems that they are not able to handle. Conditions in the neglected student's home might be unsatisfactory: food might be lacking or not nutritious, there might not be water or electricity, living areas might be untidy. Some of these conditions exist in many homes, but extreme cases indicate neglect. For the most part, school districts have specific policies about reporting neglect. Most reported cases of neglect are investigated rapidly. If an investigation indicates that a student is in danger, that student will likely be placed in protective custody or in a foster home.

Additional related information is included under *child abuse*.

PERFORMANCE-ENHANCING SUBSTANCES

Performance-enhancing substances are substances that increase the performance capacity of the human body beyond the level of one's natural abilities (Center on Addiction and Substance Abuse [CASA], 2000). School-age youth might be tempted to take performance-enhancing substances, including anabolic steroids and human growth hormones.

Anabolic steroids are powerful derivatives from the male hormones that produce muscle growth and can change health and behavior. Both male and female athletes have used steroids to build muscles and improve performance. However, steroids are now illegal and have been banned from use in sporting events. These drugs include the male hormone testosterone and its artificial derivatives. Anabolic steroids are taken orally or injected into muscles. Both males and females use anabolic steroids. The primary reason girls use anabolic steroids is to lose fat and gain lean muscle.

The continued use of anabolic steroids poses serious health consequences for both males and females. Males might experience testicular shrinkage and reduced sperm production. Females might experience breast reduction and sterility. Both females and males might experience liver tumors, kidney damage, and heart disease. Behavioral changes include aggression and violence. Even when steroid use is discontinued, the effects of steroids often cannot be reversed. Anabolic steroids can also stunt the growth of adolescents who use them.

Human growth hormone (hGH) is a growth hormone that is secreted by the pituitary gland. It appeals to athletes who are trying to increase muscular size and to train at a harder pace. Some adolescents believe that they can increase their height by taking hGH, but there is no scientific evidence to verify this belief (CASA, 2000). Young females are attracted to hGH because it does not produce the same masculine effects that anabolic steroids produce. Many side effects are associated with using

hGH as a performance-enhancing drug. One of these effects is the enlargement of the jaw and facial bones. The hands and the feet might become abnormally large. Enlargement of the internal organs (heart, liver, spleen, and kidneys) might occur. Currently, there is no reliable test to detect hGH abuse.

It is essential that schools include education about steroids and other performance-enhancing substances in the drug education curriculum. Students and educators alike need to recognize that the hazards and risks associated with use of performance-enhancing substances are serious and real. Drug education efforts should help students learn to evaluate the motivations to use steroids in light of the serious long-term consequences. Education should not be limited to students only; coaches, athletic trainers, nurses, administrators, parents, and others should be familiar with the hazards that steroids pose, the reasons young people use steroids, and how to recognize steroid abuse. Drug education programs face the challenge of countering the widespread use of anabolic steroids by high-profile athletes. Many of these athletes are role models for young aspiring athletes. Young people might believe that if it works for successful athletes, it will work for them. They might be willing to ignore the health risks of using performance-enhancing drugs.

PHYSICAL ABUSE

Physical abuse is maltreatment that harms the body. A student who is unusually bruised might be suffering from physical abuse. Bruises might appear on the back, genitals, face, eyes, or buttocks. Sometimes the outline of a hand or implement used to cause the bruise is evident. For example, a student might have an imprint of a stick or electrical cord where the contact was made. The bruises might be red or reddish blue in color. The bruises might be yellow or pale green, indicating that the healing process has begun. Sometimes heavy implements are used to inflict pain. A student might have been hit with a baseball bat or a heavy rubber tube. In these cases, bruises might not be evident, yet internal injury to the muscles and internal organs might be evident on an X-ray.

Burn marks are another indication of physical abuse. Burns might result from being forcibly held in hot water. Burns around the buttocks and genitals could be evidence that the student has been held in a jackknife position in hot water in a bathtub. Another common indicator of physical abuse is cigarette burns, which are often found on the palms of the hand, soles of the feet, and the back.

Biting is another way of inflicting physical abuse. Any part of the body can be bitten. Most bite marks are evident. Tooth impressions are often used as evidence in abuse cases. Other signs that a student has been physically abused include internal injuries, fractures (especially of the long bones), and abrasions on different body parts. By law, any teacher or health professional must report suspected cases of abuse. For the most part, school districts have specific policies about the reporting of abuse. A teacher who reports a case of suspected abuse has immunity from civil and criminal liability. When an abuse case is filed, the identity of the person doing the reporting remains confidential. Reports of child abuse are often made to child welfare agencies or the police. Most reported cases of child abuse are investigated rapidly. If an investigation indicates that a student is in danger, that student will likely be placed in protective custody or in a foster home.

Additional related information is included under *child abuse*.

REYE'S SYNDROME

Reye's syndrome, a serious condition that might follow influenza and chicken pox in children and adolescents, is characterized by swelling of the brain and damage to liver tissue. Reye's syndrome can lead to permanent brain damage and death. Children and adolescents who are given aspirin to treat their influenza or chicken pox are at increased risk for developing Reye's syndrome. School professionals should counsel parents about Reye's syndrome and the increased risk posed by administering aspirin to a child. Reye's syndrome generally occurs during recovery from an acute viral illness. Symptoms include severe vomiting, lethargy, and coma. A student who exhibits these symptoms needs prompt medical attention.

SCABIES

Scabies is an infectious skin disease caused by small parasitic mites that burrow under the skin. Scabies infection is found most often in children. Itching is the most common symptom. Frequent locations for scabies infestation are the waist, armpit, pubic area, face, scalp, arms, and between the fingers. Scabies is transmitted through skin-to-skin contact and through contact with contaminated clothing and other personal articles. Students infected with scabies should not attend school until successfully treated.

SCOLIOSIS

Scoliosis is a deformity of the spine in which the spine shows either a lateral or an S-shaped curvature. Scoliosis is found in approximately one in every fifty people. Scoliosis is more common in females than males and becomes most apparent in young people ages ten to sixteen. Untreated scoliosis can lead to permanent disfigurement. Detection of scoliosis in preadolescence and appropriate referral and treatment often prevent the need for surgery. The most accurate method of determining the presence and severity of scoliosis is an X-ray examination. However, because few children and adolescents visit physicians on a regular basis for physical examinations, and few have X-ray examinations when they visit physicians, many schools screen students for scoliosis. The most common screening technique is the bending test, and the screening is usually done in physical education classes. This simple test requires an examiner to observe the bare backs of students as they stand erect with feet together and arms hanging naturally to the side (females might wear brassieres). The observer checks to see if the left and right shoulders and shoulder blades are at an even height and to what degree the spine appears to be aligned. Next, the student is instructed to bend forward with the head and arms hanging in a relaxed position. This allows the observer to check for back symmetry and for unevenness on the surface of the back. Students with irregularities should be referred to a physician.

The value of school screening for scoliosis is controversial. Supporters of scoliosis screening argue that screening identifies scoliosis early enough to enable effective nonsurgical treatment. Opponents contend that screening results in too many children being referred to a physician for further evaluation and that few of those referred need treatment. A study in 1999 showed that out of 2,242 children screened for scoliosis, 92 were referred for medical evaluation and only 9 needed treatment (Yawn et al., 1999). The American Academy of Orthopaedic Surgeons and the American Association of Orthopaedic Surgeons continue to endorse school screening for scoliosis.

SEIZURE DISORDERS

A **seizure** is a change in sensation, awareness, or behavior brought about by a brief electrical disturbance in the brain. There are different kinds of seizures. A **generalized tonic clonic seizure** is a major convulsive seizure during which a person falls unconscious, exhibits jerking motions or body stiffening, and stops breathing temporarily or has shallow breathing. A child with this type of seizure might cry out and lose bladder and bowel control. These seizures, previously called grand mal, usually last one or two minutes. When consciousness returns, the child may be confused, fatigued, or even belligerent.

An **absence seizure** is a seizure in which a person experiences a momentary loss of awareness. A child experiencing an absence seizure, previously called petit mal, might drop whatever he is holding or, more often, exhibit a very small change such as staring into space, rolling his eyes, or losing his place in a sentence when reading. A teacher might view this lapse in a student as inattention or daydreaming rather than a seizure. Sometimes absence seizures are accompanied by blinking of the eyes, facial movements, or arm movements. Full awareness is usually achieved immediately after an absence seizure.

In complex partial seizures, a student might experience a jerking of the mouth or face. Consciousness is rarely lost, but the student may appear dazed, unresponsive, or drugged. Sometimes children experiencing complex partial seizures, previously called psychomotor seizures, get up from their desks and wander around in an aimless, undirected manner. They may

appear to be sleepwalking. Or they might feel terror and try to leave a classroom. Generally, this type of seizure lasts for one or two minutes. After the seizure, a child will feel confused and be unable to remember her actions during the seizure.

A single seizure can be caused by high fever, illness, lack of oxygen to the brain, lead poisoning, brain tumor, or severe head injury. When seizures continue to occur for unknown reasons or because of an underlying problem, the condition is known as epilepsy. **Epilepsy** is a permanent neurological condition in which, from time to time, there is a disturbance of impulses in the brain leading to seizures. In about seven out of ten people with epilepsy, the cause is unknown.

Witnessing a seizure can be frightening for a person who does not know what to do. When a student in a classroom has a convulsive or generalized tonic clonic seizure, the whole class is affected. Children who have witnessed the seizure are likely to become upset. They might fear for the welfare of the student having the seizure. The student having the seizure might be embarrassed. There is the potential that a child who has seizures will be shunned or teased by peers. For all these reasons, children need factual information about seizures and epilepsy. They need to know that seizures do not pose a danger for the student experiencing the seizure or other children in a classroom. The teacher or school nurse needs to promptly answer questions about seizures. The child who has experienced a seizure in the school setting should have the option to be included in classroom discussions about seizure episodes. If the child chooses not to participate in these discussions, she should be told what was discussed. Students should be allowed to ask questions and express their feelings in discussions about seizures. It is important for students to understand that epilepsy is not a disease and that it cannot be transmitted to other children. Also, children should understand that even though a person experiencing a convulsive seizure looks to be in serious danger, they are not. Even though a seizure may produce unusual behavior, it does not mean that a child experiencing a seizure is mentally ill. When bowel or bladder control is lost, children need to understand that the person having the seizure had no control.

It is important for teachers and students to understand that most seizures stop by themselves. Most generalized tonic clonic (convulsive) seizures in students with known epilepsy are not medical emergencies. However, it is important to keep a child safe during a seizure. Everyone needs to keep calm. If the seizure occurs in a classroom, teachers will need to reassure other students that everything will be okay. A student with a seizure should be protected from injury. The student should be assisted to lie on the floor, and objects that could cause injury (such as desks and tables) should be moved away. Something soft, such as a blanket, pillow, or coat, should be placed under the head to prevent banging against the floor during jerky movements. No attempts should be made to restrain the movements of the child having the seizure. The student should be gently turned onto his side to allow drainage of fluids from the mouth. The mouth should not be forced open, and nothing should be placed in the mouth between the teeth. Do not attempt to hold the victim's tongue. A person having a seizure rarely bites his tongue, and a victim cannot swallow his tongue during a seizure. When convulsions subside, allow the student to rest. Sometimes a child will be able to continue school participation shortly after a seizure. This should be encouraged whenever possible, because it is less difficult for the child psychologically. If bowel or bladder control has been lost during a seizure, the child should be allowed to go to the restroom. It is helpful for the child with epilepsy to keep a change of clothing in the health room or another location. When a child in a classroom has frequent seizures, the seizures should be treated as routine. Children in the classroom can rotate responsibilities for helping to deal with the seizure while other class members go about their schoolwork.

Additional related information is included under *chronic health conditions*.

SEXUAL ABUSE

Sexual abuse is maltreatment that involves inappropriate sexual behavior between an adult and a child. Sexual abuse can take many forms. It can consist of a single incident of sexual contact or prolonged sexual contact between an adult and a child. Kinds of sexual abuse include rape, incest, lewd acts upon a child, oral or genital intercourse, penetration of any object into the genitalia or anus, or any form of sexual molestation. Exploitation can consist of promoting minors to engage in sex acts, using minors to produce pornography, or encouraging and promoting prostitution.

Teachers should be aware of behaviors that indicate a student might have been sexually abused. Even if a student has only one of the behaviors or signs, sexual abuse might have occurred. If a student has more than one behavior or sign, the likelihood of sexual abuse increases. The behaviors and signs include the following:

- The presence of a sexually transmitted disease
- Pregnancy
- Itching or scratching in the genital or anal area
- A strong knowledge of sexual terms and behaviors
- Inappropriate sexual acting-out with friends and younger children
- A strong curiosity about sexual matters
- Indirect questions or statements about sexual abuse (for example, during a classroom discussion, a student says, "What could I do if I think a friend of mine is being abused sexually?" Often, students' third-person statements are reports of their own abuse).
- Problems with schoolwork
- Poor relationships with peers
- Crying and depression in school
- Attempted suicide
- Fear of using public showers or restrooms
- Difficulty walking or sitting due to pain in the genital area or anus
- Discharge or infection in the genital area

Incest is sexual abuse in which the abuser is a close relative of the child. Incest is the most common form of sexual abuse. Most often, heterosexual contact takes place between a father, stepfather, or mother's boyfriend and a young female. The second most common type of incest is homosexual contact involving male family members and a younger male. Incest involving a female adult and a child or adolescent is less common. Children often do not recognize incest as abuse; some might think it is an expression of favoritism.

A student who is sexually abused might have difficulty sharing information about this abuse. The student might fear that her or his parent will be penalized by law enforcement authorities. The student might worry that the family will break up. As a result, the student is reluctant to report the abuse. A student also might feel unjustly ashamed and guilty. However, television programs, articles in newspapers and magazines, and school-based educational programs on sexual assault prompt students to confide in someone if they have been sexually abused. A child might disclose sexual abuse immediately after an incident, or considerable time might pass before the abuse is disclosed or it is discovered by someone else. Several months or even years might pass before disclosure or discovery. Often children do not disclose sexual abuse out of fear that a perpetrator will harm them further. They are also likely to feel shame and embarrassment, which hinder disclosure.

By law, any teacher or health professional must report suspected cases of abuse. Most school districts have specific policies about reporting abuse. A teacher who reports a case of suspected abuse has immunity from civil and criminal liability. When an abuse case is filed, the identity of the person doing the reporting remains confidential. Reports of child abuse are often made to child welfare agencies or the police. Most reported cases of child abuse are investigated rapidly. If an investigation reveals that a student is in danger, that student will be placed in protective custody or in a foster home. Additional information is included under *child abuse.*

SEXUALLY TRANSMITTED DISEASES (STDs)

A **sexually transmitted disease (STD)** is a disease caused by pathogens that are transmitted from an infected person during intimate sexual contact. Many adolescents are engaging in behaviors that promote the spread of STDs. This has implications for teachers and health professionals.

A variety of STDs are prevalent in adolescents. The major types of STDs and their signs and symptoms, diagnosis, and treatment are reviewed in Chapter 11.

SMALLPOX

Smallpox is a highly contagious and sometimes fatal viral disease that produces high fever and distinctive pus-filled sores that crust over and fall off. In 1980, the disease was declared eradicated following worldwide vaccination programs. However, in the aftermath of the events of September and October 2001, the U.S. government is taking precautions to be ready to deal with a bioterrorist attack using smallpox as a weapon. A nationwide smallpox preparedness program has been established to protect Americans against smallpox as a biological weapon. This program includes the creation of preparedness teams that are ready to respond to a smallpox attack on the United States. Members of these teams—health care and public health workers—are being vaccinated so that they might safely protect others in the event of a smallpox outbreak. Government officials assure that there is enough smallpox vaccine to vaccinate everyone who would need it in the event of an emergency (Bioterrorism Preparedness and Response Planning, 2003). Additional related information is included under *anthrax, HIV/AIDS,* and *vaccine-preventable disease.*

SUICIDE

Suicide is the intentional taking of one's own life. It is a leading cause of death among children and adolescents. Suicide attempts have been reported in children as young as five years old. Suicide attempts among preteens are increasing. Children and adolescents attempt suicide for a number of reasons. They might be abused, have difficulty at school, lack love from their families, experience separation or divorce of parents, experience the death of a parent, or have poor peer relationships. Suicide can also result from untreated depression, health problems, a serious injury, or a buildup of events that are stressful or tragic.

Adolescents' reasons for attempting suicide commonly include these:

- Fights with parents
- High parental expectations

- Feelings of inferiority
- Difficulty making positive social adjustments
- Conflict with peers
- Difficulty at school
- Breakup of a romantic relationship
- Depression
- Academic failure
- Changes in the family
- Death of a parent or a family breakup

Children and adolescents who are thinking about attempting suicide will usually give indications. Some of these indications might be through conversations. They might mention they are thinking about attempting suicide. They might make statements such as "I sometimes wish I were dead" or "I'm not important to anyone, so why not take my life? No one will miss me." Certain behaviors can indicate that a student is considering a suicide attempt. A student who has made a previous attempt is at risk for making another attempt. Students who are contemplating a suicide attempt might plan for their death. They might do things such as give away their valuable possessions to peers or siblings. Other behavioral indicators include extreme changes in mood, feelings of guilt, truancy, involvement with drugs, reckless behavior, rapidly shifting moods, social isolation, promiscuity, quitting teams and after-school clubs and activities, and aggressive behavior.

A student might share with a teacher her intention to attempt suicide. If a student confides in you, you should follow the procedures outlined by your school. Usually this involves notifying the school counselor, who notifies the family. When a crisis is imminent, the student should not be left alone. Most of the time a student is seeking help, and telling a teacher is one way of asking for help. If a student indicates that he is thinking of suicide, do not panic. Tell the student you are really concerned about him and that you would like to offer your help. In addition to school personnel, many community health agencies, such as community mental health agencies, have trained personnel to help the student. The family, school personnel, and mental health professionals work together to support the student and teach the student additional coping strategies.

More information about suicide and suicide prevention is included in Chapter 5.

VACCINE-PREVENTABLE DISEASES

Vaccine-preventable diseases are infectious diseases for which effective vaccines or immunizations are available. School professionals should require that students have immunizations before entering school. In addition, school professionals should advocate that children younger than school age receive recommended immunizations as part of school readiness efforts. Immunizations are available for the following infectious diseases: diphtheria, pertussis (whooping cough), tetanus, measles, mumps, rubella (German measles), polio, hepatitis A, hepatitis B, *Haemophilus influenzae* Type b (Hib), varicella (chickenpox), influenza, and pneumococcal disease (Advisory Committee on Immunization Practices, 2003).

Additional related information is included under *infectious diseases.*

VISUAL DISORDERS

Visual disorders are conditions that adversely affect a person's sight. Several visual disorders affect school-age children and can affect school performance if not corrected. Through vision screenings, school professionals can detect the visual disorders that are discussed in this section. Teachers also are instrumental in detecting visual disorders from observing students who squint or frequently exhibit postural signs of not being able to see clearly. Poor academic progress, inattentiveness, headaches, reports of double vision, and itching and burning eyes also might be signs and symptoms of visual disorders.

Visual acuity is clearness of sight. A standard of visual acuity for distance that is frequently used is 20/20 vision. A student with 20/20 vision can read what the average student is able to read at twenty feet. Visual acuity for distance can be measured by standard vision charts, such as the Snellen chart. The **Snellen chart** is a chart used for testing visual acuity for distance. Letters, symbols, or numbers are organized in decreasing size from the top to the bottom of the chart. Vision charts are helpful in detecting myopia.

Myopia is a refractive error of the eye, usually due to elongation of the eyeball, that causes nearsightedness (e.g., a student cannot read numbers on a blackboard). Refractive errors are defects in the shape of eye structures that prevent images from being in focus on the retina. Myopia typically appears in students after age eight, and visual acuity can be achieved through the use of corrective lenses such as glasses or contact lenses. Two other refractive errors that reduce visual acuity for distance are astigmatism and hyperopia. **Astigmatism,** an irregular curvature of the cornea that results in blurred vision, is corrected with corrective lenses. **Hyperopia** is a refractive error that results in farsightedness (e.g., a student has difficulty reading a book). Corrective lenses also can be used for correcting the acuity of a hyperopic student. Visual acuity tests for distance do not effectively detect hyperopia.

Vision testing is recommended for preschoolers because undetected and untreated strabismus and amblyopia can lead to vision loss before age six. **Strabismus** is misalignment of the eyes and commonly referred to as "cross-eye." Misalignment is usually due to imbalanced muscles and leads to either a turning in or a turning out of an eye. When detected early in life, medical treatment (usually surgery) can correct imbalances in eye muscles. If left untreated, blindness in an eye can occur. Another important cause of blindness in students before age six is amblyopia. **Amblyopia** is a condition characterized by dimness of vision in one eye. These visual disturbances cause an amblyopic, or misaligned, eye to fail to develop and to stop functioning. The functioning eye might overcompensate, causing the student to become blind in one eye. Amblyopia is often treated by placing a patch over the functioning eye, which forces the nonfunctioning eye to develop. Corrective lenses and eye exercises are also treatments for amblyopia. The outlook for students who develop amblyopia and strabismus is positive if these conditions are detected early and treated promptly.

Bibliography

Advisory Committee on Immunization Practices. (2003). *Recommended childhood & adolescent immunization schedule.* Atlanta, GA: Centers for Disease Control and Prevention.

Bioterrorism Preparedness and Response Planning, Centers for Disease Control and Prevention. (2003). *Smallpox questions and answers: The disease and the vaccine.* Atlanta, GA: Centers for Disease Control and Prevention.

Center on Addiction and Substance Abuse. (2000, September). *Winning at any cost: A report by the CASA National Commission on Sports and Substance Abuse.* New York: Columbia University, National Center on Addiction and Substance Abuse.

Committee on Pediatric AIDS, American Academy of Pediatrics. (2000). Education of children with human immunodeficiency virus infection. *Pediatrics, 105,* 1358–1360.

McCarthy, A. M., Kelly, M. W., & Reed, D. (2000). Medication administration practices of school nurses. *Journal of School Health, 70,* 371–376.

Renfrew Center. (2003). Signs & Symptoms. Philadelphia, PA: Renfrew Center Foundation. Available at www. renfrewcenter.com/for-schools/signs-symptoms.asp.

U.S. Department of Health and Human Services, Administration on Children, Youth and Families. (2003). *Child maltreatment 2001.* Washington, DC: U.S. Government Printing Office.

Yawn, B. P., Hodge, D., Kurland, M., Shaughnessy, W. J., Ilstrup, D., & Jacobsen, S. J. (1999). A population-based study of school scoliosis screening. *Journal of the American Medical Association, 282,* 1427–1432.

Zito, J. M., Safer, D. J., dosReis, S., Gardner, J. F., Boles, M., & Lynch, F. (2000). Trends in the prescribing of psychotropic medications to preschoolers. *Journal of the American Medical Association, 283,* 1025–1030.

APPENDIX D

Health Resources

Many other resources can be used with this *Totally Awesome*™ teacher resource book on comprehensive school health education. The materials are designed so that other resources can easily be integrated with them. The following discussion focuses on ways to use this health resource guide.

Using Health Resources

This guide contains a listing of the names, telephone numbers, addresses, and websites of organizations and agencies that provide resources for coordinated school health education. This listing is divided into the following sections:

- Mental and Emotional Health
- Family and Social Health
- Growth and Development
- Nutrition
- Personal Health and Physical Activity
- Alcohol, Tobacco, and Other Drugs
- Communicable and Chronic Diseases
- Consumer and Community Health
- Environmental Health
- Injury Prevention and Safety
- Professional Health Organizations and Related National Organizations

The last section lists names, addresses, telephone numbers, and websites of important professional health organizations and agencies. A number of the agencies and professional organizations listed in this guide provide free or inexpensive materials, such as pamphlets, curricula, kits, videos, and films. They also may provide services such as speakers bureaus, support groups, screening programs, and hotlines. Individuals can phone hotlines to obtain immediate assistance. Teachers may want to share these hotline numbers with their students. They may want to have students write to these agencies and organizations to obtain further information when they are

writing reports or preparing oral presentations. Teachers also may want to have students explore health careers available at these agencies and organizations.

Mental and Emotional Health

American Mental Health Counselors Association
 801 North Fairfax Street, Suite 304
 Alexandria, VA 22314
 800-326-2642 or 703-548-6002

 www.amhca.org

American Psychiatric Association
 1000 Wilson Boulevard, Suite 1825
 Arlington, VA 22209-3901
 703-907-7300

 www.psych.org

American Psychological Association
 750 First Street NE
 Washington, DC 20002-4242
 800-374-2721

 www.apa.org

Child Welfare Information Gateway
 1250 Maryland Avenue SW, 8th Floor
 Washington, DC 20024
 800-394-3366

Federation of Families for Children's Mental Health
 9605 Medical Center Drive, Suite 260
 Rockville, MD 20850
 240-403-1901

 www.ffcmh.org

National Alliance on Mental Illness
Colonial Place Three
2107 Wilson Boulevard, Suite 300
Arlington, VA 22201-3042
800-950-6264 (Member Services)
703-524-7600 (Main)

www.nami.org

National Institute of Mental Health,
Public Information and Communications Branch
6001 Executive Boulevard
Room 8184, MSC 9663
Bethesda, MD 20892-9663
1-866-615-6464

www.nimh.nih.gov

National Mental Health Association
2001 North Beauregard Street, 12th Floor
Alexandria, VA 22311
800-969-6642 (Mental Health Resource Center)
703-684-7722

www.nmha.org

Family and Social Health

Alliance for Children and Families
11700 West Lake Park Drive
Milwaukee, WI 53224-3099
414-359-1040

www.alliance1.org

Children's Defense Fund
25 East Street NW
Washington, DC 20001
202-628-8787

www.childrensdefense.org

Child Welfare League of America
440 First Street NW, 3rd Floor
Washington, DC 20001-2085
202-638-2952

www.cwla.org

Family Resource Center on Disabilities
20 East Jackson Boulevard, Room 300
Chicago, IL 60604
800-952-4199

www.frcd.org

Health Resources and Services
Administration
U.S. Department of Health and Human Services
Parklawn Building
5600 Fishers Lane
Rockville, MD 20857

www.hrsa.gov

National Adoption Center
1500 Walnut Street, Suite 701
Philadelphia, PA 19102
800-TO-ADOPT

www.adopt.org

National Council on Family Relations
3989 Central Avenue NE, Suite 550
Minneapolis, MN 55421
888-781-9331

www.ncfr.org

Growth and Development

American Academy of Pediatrics
141 Northwest Point Boulevard
Elk Grove Village, IL 60007-1098
847-434-4000

www.aap.org

Centers for Disease Control and Prevention
U.S. Department of Health and Human Services
1600 Clifton Road
Atlanta, GA 30333
800-311-3435

www.cdc.gov

Division of Birth Defects, Child Development,
and Disability and Health
National Center for Environmental Health
Centers for Disease Control
and Prevention
1600 Clifton Road
Atlanta, GA 30333
800-311-3435

www.cdc.gov/ncbddd

National Council on Aging
Headquarters
1901 L Street NW, 4th Floor
Washington, DC 20036
202-479-1200

www.ncoa.org

Nutrition

American College of Nutrition
300 South Duncan Avenue, Suite 225
Clearwater, FL 33755
727-446-6086

www.amcollnutr.org

American Dietetic Association
120 South Riverside Plaza, Suite 2000
Chicago, IL 60606-6995
800-877-1600

www.eatright.org/

Center for Science in the Public Interest
1875 Connecticut Avenue NW, Suite 300
Washington, DC 20009
202-332-9110

www.cspinet.org

Food and Drug Administration
5600 Fishers Lane
Rockville, MD 20857
1-888-INFO-FDA
1-888-463-6332

www.fda.gov

Food and Nutrition Information Center
Agricultural Research Center, USDA
National Agricultural Library, Room 105
10301 Baltimore Avenue
Beltsville, MD 20705-2351
301-504-5719

www.nal.usda.gov/fnic/

International Food Information Council
Foundation
1100 Connecticut Avenue NW, Suite 430
Washington, DC 20036
202-296-6540

www.ific.org

School Nutrition Association
700 South Washington Street, Suite 300
Alexandria, VA 22314
703-739-3900

www.schoolnutrition.org

Society for Nutrition Education
7150 Winton Drive, Suite 300
Indianapolis, IN 46268
800-235-6690

www.sne.org

USDA Forest Service
1400 Independence Avenue SW
Washington, DC 20250-0003
202-205-8333

www.fs.fed.us

Personal Health and Physical Activity

American Alliance for Health, Physical
Education, Recreation and Dance
1900 Association Drive
Reston, VA 20191-1598
800-213-7193

www.aahperd.org

American College of Sports Medicine
401 West Michigan Street
Indianapolis, IN 46202-3233
317-637-9200

www.acsm.org

American Dental Association
211 East Chicago Avenue
Chicago, IL 60611-2678
312-440-2500

www.ada.org

American Medical Association
515 North State Street
Chicago, IL 60610
800-621-8335

www.ama-assn.org

Health Resources and Services Administration
U.S. Department of Health and Human Services
   Parklawn Building
   5600 Fishers Lane
   Rockville, MD 20857
   1-888-ASK-HRSA

   www.hrsa.gov

National Association for Health and Fitness
   c/o Be Active New York State
   65 Niagara Square, Room 607
   Buffalo, NY 14202
   716-583-0521

   www.physicalfitness.org

National Health Council
   1730 M Street NW, Suite 500
   Washington, DC 20036
   202-785-3910

   www.nhcouncil.org

National Dissemination Center for Children with Disabilities
   P.O. Box 1492
   Washington, DC 20013
   800-695-0285

   www.nichcy.org

National Pediculosis Association, Inc.
   50 Kearney Road
   Needham, MA 02494
   781-449-NITS

   www.headlice.org

Alcohol, Tobacco, and Other Drugs

Al-Anon Family Groups, Inc.
   1600 Corporate Landing Parkway
   Virginia Beach, VA 23454-5617
   888-4AL-ANON

   www.al-anon.alateen.org

Alcoholics Anonymous
   475 Riverside Drive, 11th Floor
   New York, NY 10115

   www.alcoholics-anonymous.org

American Academy of Addiction Psychiatry
   345 Blackstore Boulevard, 2nd Floor-RCH
   Providence, RI 02906
   401-524-3076

   www.aaap.org

Center of Alcohol Studies
   Rutgers, the State University
   607 Allison Road
   Piscataway, NJ 08854-8001
   732-445-2190

   www.alcoholstudies.rutgers.edu

Community Anti-Drug Coalitions of America
   625 Slaters Lane, Suite 300
   Alexandria, VA 22314
   1-800-54-CADCA

   www.cadca.org

International Commission for the Prevention of Alcoholism and Drug Dependency
   12501 Old Columbia Pike
   Silver Springs, MD 20904
   301-680-6719

   www.health20-20.org/ICPA.htm

National Council on Alcoholism and Drug Dependence, Inc.
   244 East 58th Street, 4th Floor
   New York, NY 10022
   212-269-7797
   Hope line: 800-NCA-CALL

   www.ncadd.org

National Institute on Drug Abuse
   6001 Executive Boulevard, Room 5213
   Bethesda, MD 20892-9561
   301-443-1124

   www.nida.nih.gov

Partnership for a Drug-Free America
   405 Lexington Avenue, Suite 1601
   New York, NY 10174
   1-888-575-3115

   www.drugfree.org

PRIDE Youth Programs
   4 West Oak Street
   Freemont, MI 49412
   800-668-9277

   www.prideyouthprograms.org

U.S. Department of Health and Human Services
and SAMHSA's National Clearinghouse for
Alcohol and Drug Information
   800-729-6686

   ncadi.samhsa.gov

Communicable and Chronic Diseases

Alzheimer's Association
   225 North Michigan Avenue, Floor 17
   Chicago, IL 60601-7633
   800-272-3900

   www.alz.org

American Anorexia/Bulimia Association
   P.O. Box 1287
   Longhorne, PA 19047
   215-221-1864

   www.aabaphila.org

American Cancer Society
   800-ACS-2345

   www.cancer.org

American Diabetes Association
   ATTN: National Call Center
   1701 North Beauregard Street
   Alexandria, VA 22311
   800-DIABETES

   www.diabetes.org

American Heart Association
   National Center
   7272 Greenville Avenue
   Dallas, TX 75231
   800-242-8721

   www.americanheart.org

American Lung Association
   61 Broadway, 6th Floor
   New York, NY 10006
   800-LUNGUSA

   www.lungusa.org

American SIDS Institute
   501 Augusta Drive
   Marietta, GA 30067
   800-232-SIDS

   www.sids.org

American Social Health Association
   P.O. Box 13827
   Research Triangle Park, NC 27709
   919-361-8400

   www.ashastd.org

Arthritis Foundation
   P.O. Box 7669
   Atlanta, GA 30357-0669
   800-568-4045

   www.arthritis.org

CDC National Prevention Information Network (NPIN)
   P.O. Box 6003
   Rockville, MD 20849-6003
   1-800-458-5231

   www.cdcnpin.org

Federation of Families for Children's Mental Health
   9605 Medical Center Drive
   Rockville, MD 20850
   240-403-1901

   www.ffcmh.org

Glaucoma Foundation
   80 Maiden Lane, Suite 1206
   New York, NY 10038
   212-285-0080

   www.glaucoma-foundation.org

Multiple Sclerosis Association of America
   706 Haddonfield Road
   Cherry Hill, NJ 08002
   856-488-4500

   www.msaa.com

National Alliance for Hispanic Health
   1501 16th Street NW
   Washington, DC 20036
   202-387-5000

   www.hispanichealth.org

National Cancer Institute, National
Institutes of Health

   www.nci.nih.gov

National Comprehensive Cancer Network, Inc.
   500 Old York Road, Suite 250
   Jenkintown, PA 19046
   215-690-0300

   www.nccn.org

National Institute of Diabetes and Digestive and
Kidney Diseases
   Office of Communications and Public Liaison
   NDDK, NIH
   Building 31, Room 9A 04 Center Drive
   MSC 2560
   Bethesda, MD 20892-2560

   www.niddk.nih.gov

National Institute of Environmental Health
Sciences
   P.O. Box 12233
   Research Triangle Park, NC 27709
   919-541-3345

   www.niehs.nih.gov

Overeaters Anonymous, Inc.
   World Service Office
   P.O. Box 44020
   Rio Rancho, NM 87174-4020
   505-891-2664

   www.oa.org

Consumer and Community Health

Center for Food Safety and Applied Nutrition
Food and Drug Administration
   5600 Fishers Lane
   Rockville, MD 20857
   1-888-INFO-FDA
   1-888-463-6332

   www.cfsan.fda.gov

Council of Better Business Bureaus, Inc.
   4200 Wilson Boulevard, Suite 800
   Arlington, VA 22203-1838
   703-276-0100

   www.bbb.org

National Council Against Health Fraud
   119 Foster Street, Building R, 2nd Floor
   Peabody, MA 01960
   978-532-9383

   www.ncahf.org

Office of Consumer Affairs, U.S. Food and Drug
Administration
   5600 Fishers Lane
   Rockville, MD 20857
   1-888-INFO-FDA

   www.fda.gov

Underwriters Laboratories, Inc.
   333 Pfingsten Road
   Northbrook, IL 60062-2096
   1-847-272-8800

   www.ul.com

Environmental Health

Action on Smoking and Health
   Information
   2013 H Street NW
   Washington, DC 20006
   202-659-4310

   www.ash.org

Asbestos Information Association/
North America
   1745 Jefferson Davis Highway
   PMB 114
   Arlington, VA 22202
   703-412-1150

National Center for Environmental Health
Centers for Disease Control and Prevention

   www.cdc.gov/nceh

U.S. Environmental Protection Agency/Lead
Office of Pollution Prevention and Toxics
   1200 Pennsylvania Avenue NW
   Mail code 7404T
   Washington, DC 20460
   202-566-0500

   www.epa.gov/opptintr/lead/
   www.epa.gov

Injury Prevention and Safety

American Burn Association
  Central Office—Chicago
  625 North Michigan Avenue, Suite 2250
  Chicago, IL 60611
  312-642-9130

  www.ameriburn.org

American Red Cross National Headquarters
  2025 E Street NW
  Washington, DC 20006
  202-303-4498

  www.redcross.org

Bicycle Helmet Safety Institute
  4611 Seventh Street South
  Arlington, VA 22204-1419
  703-486-0100

  www.bhsi.org

Children's Safety Network National Injury and
Violence Prevention Resource Center
  Education Development Center, Inc.
  55 Chapel Street
  Newton, MA 02458-1060
  617-969-7100 x2722

  www.childrenssafetynetwork.org

National Crime Prevention Council
  1000 Connecticut Avenue NW, 13th Floor
  Washington, DC 20036
  202-466-6272

  www.ncpc.org

National Fire Protection Association
  1 Batterymarch Park
  Quincy, MA 02169-7471
  800-344-3555

  www.nfpa.org

National Highway Traffic Safety Administration
Headquarters
  400 Seventh Street SW
  Washington, DC 20590
  1-888-327-4236

  www.nhtsa.dot.gov

National Safe Boating Council
  P.O. Box 509
  Bristow, VA 20136
  703-361-4294

  www.safeboatingcouncil.org

National Safety Council
  1121 Spring Lake Drive
  Itasca, IL 60143-3201
  630-285-1121

  www.nsc.org

Safe Kids Worldwide
  1301 Pennsylvania Avenue NW, Suite 1000
  Washington, DC 20004-1707
  202-662-0600

  www.safekids.org

Safe Sitter
  8604 Allisonville Road, Suite 248
  Indianapolis, IN 46250-1547
  317-596-5001

  www.safesitter.org

Professional Health Organizations and Related National Organizations

Academy for Educational Development
  1825 Connecticut Avenue NW
  Washington, DC 20009-5721
  202-884-8000

  www.aed.org

American Association for Health, Physical
Education, Recreation and Dance
  1900 Association Drive
  Reston, VA 20191-1598
  703-476-3400

  www.aahperd.org

American School Health Association
   7263 State Route 43
   P.O. Box 708
   Kent, OH 44240
   330-678-1601

   www.ashaweb.org

Council of Chief State School Officers
   1 Massachusetts Avenue NW, Suite 700
   Washington, DC 20001-1431
   202-336-7000

   www.ccsso.org

Directors of Health Promotion and Education
   1101 15th Street NW, Suite 601
   Washington, DC 20005
   202-659-2230

   dhpe.org

National Alliance of State and Territorial AIDS Directors
   444 North Capitol Street NW, Suite 339
   Washington, DC 20001
   202-434-8090

   www.nastad.org

Society of State Directors of Health, Physical Education and Recreation
   1900 Association Drive, Suite 1000
   Reston, VA 20101-1599
   703-390-4599

   www.thesociety.org

GLOSSARY

A

abdominal thrusts   a series of thrusts to the abdomen that force air from the lungs to dislodge an object

abrasion   a wound caused by rubbing or scraping away the skin

abscess   a localized collection of puss

absence seizure   a seizure in which a person experiences a momentary loss of awareness

abstinence   voluntarily choosing not to do something

abstinence from sex   voluntarily choosing not to be sexually active

abuse   harmful treatment of another person

acid rain   rain or another form of precipitation that has a high acid content

acne   a skin disorder characterized by inflammation of skin glands and hair follicles and the eruption of pimples

acoustic trauma   an immediate and permanent loss of hearing caused by a short, intense sound

acquaintance rape   a rape in which the rapist is known to the person who has been raped

acquired immunodeficiency syndrome (AIDS)   a disorder of the human immune system in a person infected with HIV, characterized by a severe breakdown of the immune system that leaves the person very susceptible to opportunistic infections

action plan   a detailed description of the steps to be taken to reach a goal

active immunity   resistance to disease owing to the presence of antibodies

active listening   a way of responding that shows that the listener hears and understands

actual consent   oral or written permission from a mentally competent adult to give first aid

acyclovir   an antiviral drug approved for the treatment of herpes simplex infections; relieves symptoms and prevents some recurrences of genital herpes

addiction   a compulsion to repeatedly take a drug or engage in a specific behavior

adrenal glands   endocrine glands that secrete several hormones, including adrenaline

adrenaline   a hormone that prepares the body to react during times of stress or in an emergency

Adult Children of Alcoholics (ACOA)   a recovery program for adult children who have one or more parents, a guardian, or a caregiver with alcoholism

adverse environment   an environment that interferes with a person's growth, development, and success

advertising   a form of selling products and services

aerobic exercise   exercise in which large amounts of oxygen are required continually for an extended period of time

affective disorder   a disorder involving extreme moods

affective domain   a category of objectives dealing with feelings and attitudes

afterbirth   the placenta that is expelled after delivery

aftercare   support and supervised services that juvenile offenders receive when they are released to live in the community

ageism   behavior that discriminates against people in a specific age group

Agent Orange   a substance containing dioxin that was sprayed on vegetation to kill it

aggressive behavior   the use of words or actions that are disrespectful toward others

agility   the ability to rapidly change the position of the body

AIDS dementia complex   a loss of brain function caused by HIV infection

Al-Anon   a recovery program for people who have friends or family members with alcoholism

alarm stage of GAS   the first stage of the generalized adaption syndrome (GAS) in which the body gets ready for quick action

Al-Ateen a recovery program for teens who have a family member or friend with alcoholism

alcohol a psychoactive drug that depresses the central nervous system, dulls the mind, impairs thinking and judgment, lessens coordination, and interferes with the ability to respond quickly to dangerous situations

alcohol dementia brain impairment that is characterized by overall intellectual decline, due to the direct toxic effects of alcohol

alcohol, tobacco, and other drugs the area of health that focuses on following guidelines for the safe use of prescription and over-the-counter drugs, not misusing or abusing drugs, avoiding risk factors and practicing protective factors for drug misuse and abuse, using resistance skills if pressured to misuse or abuse drugs, not drinking alcohol, avoiding tobacco use and secondhand smoke, not being involved in illegal drug use, choosing a drug-free lifestyle to reduce the risk of HIV infection and unwanted pregnancy, choosing a drug-free lifestyle to reduce the risk of violence and accidents, and being aware of resources for the treatment of drug misuse and abuse

alcohol withdrawal syndrome the reaction of the body when a person who has alcoholism suddenly stops drinking alcohol

alcoholic hepatitis inflammation of the liver resulting from excessive alcohol consumption

Alcoholics Anonymous (AA) a recovery program for people who have alcoholism

alcoholism a disease in which there is physical and psychological dependence on alcohol

allergen a substance that produces an allergic response

allergy an overreaction of the body to a substance that, in most people, causes no response

allied health professional a trained health care provider who practices under the supervision of a physician or health care practitioner, such as a nurse, audiologist, dental hygienist, pharmacist, and physical therapist

alveoli microscopic air sacs in the lungs

Alzheimer's disease a progressive disease in which the nerve cells in the brain degenerate and the brain shrinks in size

amblyopia a condition characterized by dimness of vision in one eye

amenorrhea the absence of menstruation

amnesia the inability to recall past experiences

amniocentesis a diagnostic procedure in which a needle is inserted through the uterus to extract fluid from the amniotic sac

amniotic sac a pouch of fluid that surrounds a fetus

amotivational syndrome a lack of desire to perform daily responsibilities by people who have abused drugs

amphetamines chemically manufactured stimulants that are highly addictive

amplitude the loudness of a sound

anabolic-androgenic steroid a steroid that is related to male sex hormones

anabolic steroids powerful derivatives from the male hormones that produce muscle growth, change behavior, and can affect helath adversely.

anaerobic exercise exercise that demands more oxygen than the body has available during exertion

analgesic a drug that relieves pain

analysis objectives objectives that require students to break drown into its component elements something that they have not broken down previously

anaphylactic reaction a sudden systemic reaction in the body that can be life-threatening

anaphylaxis a severe reaction to an allergen that results in serious symptoms, such as itchy tongue or mouth, tightening of the throat, wheezing, shock, and/or cardiac arrest

anemia a condition in which there is a deficiency in the red blood cells or hemoglobin that transports oxygen in the blood

aneurysm a weakened area of a blood vessel

anger an emotion varying in intensity from mild irritation to intense rage that is often accompanied by physiological changes that prepare the body for fighting

anger cue a body change that occurs when a person is angry, resulting in the fight-or-flight response so that the body is prepared for an emergency

anger-management skills healthful ways to control and express anger

anger trigger a thought or event that causes a person to be angry

angina pectoris chest pain that results from narrowed coronary arteries

annulment a legal way to end a marriage in which it is decided that the marriage was not legally binding

anorectic drug   a drug that decreases appetite

anorexia nervosa   an eating disorder involving self-starvation and being 15 percent or more below desirable weight

anthrax   an infectious disease caused by a spore-forming bacterium that can infect humans as well as hoofed mammals

antibiotic   a drug used to treat bacterial infections

antibody   a special protein that helps fight infection

anticipatory grief   grief experienced prior to a loss

anticonvulsant   a drug that is taken to prevent or relieve epileptic seizures

antidepressant   a drug used to treat depressive disorders

antiepileptic   a drug used to prevent and control epileptic seizures

antigang gang   a group of teens who stay together to avoid pressure and protect themselves from gang members

antihypertensive drug   a drug used to lower elevated blood pressure

antihypertensives   drugs that lower hypertension, or high blood pressure

antioxidant   a substance that protects cells from being damaged by oxidation

antiperspirant   a product used to reduce the amount of perspiration

antiretroviral drugs   drugs used to slow virus replication

antisocial personality disorder   a personality disorder in which a person disregards and violates other people's rights and safety

antiulcer drug   a drug used to treat the discomfort of ulcers

antivenom   a medicine that reduces the effects of the poison

anus   the opening to the outside of the body at the end of the rectum

anxiety disorder   a disorder in which real or imagined fears prevent a person from enjoying life

aorta   the main artery in the body

aortic aneurysm   a bulging, weakened area in the aorta

Apgar score   a rating of physical characteristics of an infant one to five minutes after birth

application objectives   objectives that require students to use the previously experienced procedures or knowledge in new situations

arrhythmia   a heart condition in which the heart sometimes beats very slowly or very fast for no obvious reason

arteriosclerosis   a general term for several conditions that cause hardening and thickening of the arteries

artery   a blood vessel that carries blood away from the heart; arteries have thick muscular walls that move the blood between heartbeats

arthritis   a painful inflammation of the joints

artifact   an actual sample of student work

asbestos   a heat-resistant mineral found in many building materials

assault   a physical attack

assertive behavior   the honest expression of ideas, feelings, and decisions without worrying or feeling threatened

assessment   the procedure used to measure the results or efforts toward a desired goal

assistive hearing device   a device that helps a person with hearing loss communicate and hear

asthma   a condition in which the bronchial tubes become inflamed and constricted, making breathing difficult

asthma attack   an episode of coughing, wheezing, and shortness of breath experienced by a person who has asthma

asthma triggers   substances that cause the airways to tighten, swell, and fill with mucus

astigmatism   a refractive error in which irregular shape of the cornea causes blurred vision

atherosclerosis   a disease in which fat, or plaque, accumulates on artery walls, narrowing the arterial passageways and reducing blood flow

athlete's foot   a fungus that grows on feet

atrium   one of the upper two chambers of the heart

attention deficit disorder (ADD)   a learning disability in which a person is restless and easily distracted

attention deficit hyperactivity disorder (ADHD)   a learning disability in which a person is easily distracted and is hyperactive

attestation   a document written about the work of the student by someone other than the student

audiologist   a specialist who diagnoses and treats hearing and speech-related problems

audiometer   a machine that measures the range of sounds a person hears

auditory learner   a person who learns best by listening or by discussing a topic

authority   the power and right to apply laws and rules

autoclave   to sterilize with steam under pressure

autoimmune disease   a disease that results when the immune system produces antibodies that turn against the body's own cells

avoidant personality disorder   a personality disorder in which a person avoids all social contact

avulsion   a wound in which skin or other body tissue is separated or completely torn away

axon   an elongated fiber that carries impulses away from the cell body to the dendrites of another neuron

B

B cell   a white blood cell that produces antibodies

bacteria   single-celled microorganisms that cause disease by releasing toxins

bagasse   a fibrous waste produced during the processing of sugarcane

bagging   inhaling fumes from a bag to get high

balance   the ability to keep from falling when moving or in a still position

balanced budget   a plan in which a person's income is equal to or more than expenses

balanced friendship   a friendship in which two people give to and receive from each other acts of kindness

ballistic stretching   rapidly stretching the muscle with a bouncing movement

barbiturate   a type of sedative-hypnotic drug that used to be prescribed to help people sleep and to reduce tension

basal body temperature method   a birth control method in which a female uses her basal body temperature to predict ovulation

basal metabolic rate (BMR)   the number of calories the body uses at rest

battering   intentional, harmful touching of another person without the person's consent

beach   the shore of a body of water covered by sand, gravel, or rock

beer   an alcoholic beverage that is made by fermenting barley, corn, or rye

behavior modification   a disciplinary technique in which positive rewards are used to encourage desirable behavior and negative consequences are used to stop undesirable behavior

behavioral objective   a statement of what a student should be able to do after completing a learning experience

benign tumor   a tumor that is not cancerous and does not spread to other parts of the body

benzodiazepines   sedative-hypnotic drugs that often are prescribed by physicians to treat anxiety

beta-endorphins   substances produced in the brain that create a feeling of well-being

bicuspids   the eight teeth in back of the cuspids; they have one or two roots and two cusps that tear and crush food

bidi   a small, hand-rolled, filterless cigarette made in India that contains more tar and nicotine than regular cigarettes

bifocals   lenses that correct for both close and distant vision

binge drinking   the consumption of large amounts of alcohol in a short amount of time

binge-eating disorder   an eating disorder in which a person cannot control eating and eats excessive amounts

biodegradable product   a product that can be broken down by living organisms into harmless and usable materials

biodiversity   the variety of life forms on Earth

biohazardous waste, or medical waste   infectious waste from medical facilities

biological age   a measure of how well a person's body systems are functioning

biomass   organic plant matter produced by solar energy from the sun's rays

bioterrorism   the use or threatened use of bacteria, viruses, or toxins as weapons

bipolar disorder, or **manic-depressive disorder**   a disorder in which a person's moods vary from extreme happiness to depression

birth control methods   ways to alter the conditions necessary for conception or pregnancy to occur

blackout   a loss of memory for what happened during a period of time

black-tar heroin   heroin produced in Mexico that is dark in color and sticky in texture

blended family, or **stepfamily**   a family consisting of the marriage partners, children that one or both of them had previously, and the children that they have by their marriage to one another

blister   a raised area containing liquid that is caused by a burn or by an object rubbing against the skin

blood alcohol concentration (BAC)   the amount of alcohol in a person's blood; BAC is given as a percentage

blood pressure   the force of blood against the artery walls

blood test   an analysis of blood for blood components, chemicals, pathogens, and antibodies

blotter acid   a small paper square that contains LSD

body composition   the percentage of fat tissue and lean tissue in the body

body frame   the approximate weight and density of the bone structure

body image   a person's perception of her or his body's appearance

body image distortion   having an inaccurate visual perception of one's body

body system   a group of organs that work together to perform a main body function

bone   the structural material of the skeletal system

bone marrow   the soft tissue in the hollow center area of most bones where red blood cells are produced

boot camp   a camp that uses rigorous drills, hard physical training, and structure to teach discipline and obedience

braces   devices that are placed on the teeth and wired together to help straighten teeth

brain   a mass of nerve tissue that acts as the control center of the body

brain death   the irreversible cessation of all functions of the entire brain, including the brain stem

brainstorming   an instructional strategy in which a variety of responses to the same question, problem, or trigger statement are requested

brand-name drug   a drug with a registered name or trademark given by a pharmaceutical company

breast self-examination (BSE)   a screening procedure for breast cancer in which a female checks her breasts for lumps and other changes

bronchi   two tubes through which air moves to the lungs

bronchioles   small tubes divided into alveoli

bronchodilator   a drug that widens air passages to facilitate breathing in people who have asthma

bruise   a wound in which damage to soft tissues and blood vessels causes bleeding under the skin

buccal absorption   the absorption of a drug between the cheek and gum

bulimia   an eating disorder in which a person binges and purges

bulletin board   a service that allows users to post and obtain messages

bully   a person who hurts or frightens people who are perceived to be smaller or weaker

bullying   an attempt by a person to hurt or frighten people who are perceived to be smaller or weaker

bunion   a deformity in the joint of the big toe that causes swelling and pain

buproprion   a prescription antidepressant drug approved by the Food and Drug Administration as a smoking cessation aid that does not contain nicotine

buzz group   an instructional strategy in which students discuss a topic or issue in small groups

C

caffeine   a stimulant found in chocolate, coffee, tea, some soda pops, and some prescription and over-the-counter drugs

caffeinism   poisoning due to heavy caffeine intake

calcium   a mineral that is needed for building bones and teeth and for maintaining bone strength

calculus   hardened plaque

calendar method   a birth control method in which a female records the length of her menstrual cycle on a calendar to predict her fertile period

callus   a thickened layer of skin caused by excess rubbing

caloric intake   the number of calories a person takes in from foods and beverages

calorie   a unit of energy produced by food and used by the body

calories from fat   the listing on the nutrition label of the number of calories from fat in one serving of the food

calories listing   the listing on the nutrition label of the number of calories in one serving of the food

Campylobacter   a bacterial pathogen that causes fever, diarrhea, and abdominal cramps

cancer   a group of diseases in which cells divide in an uncontrolled manner; these cells can form a tumor

capillary   a tiny blood vessel that connects arteries and veins

carbohydrate   a nutrient that is the main source of energy for the body

carbohydrate loading   an eating strategy in which a few days of a very low carbohydrate intake are followed by a few days of a very high carbohydrate intake

carbon monoxide   an odorless, tasteless gas that interferes with the ability of blood to carry oxygen

carcinogen   a substance that causes cancer in humans

cardiac muscle   muscle tissue found only in the heart

cardiac output   the amount of blood pumped by the heart each minute

cardiomyopathy   a disease in which the heart muscles weaken and enlarge and cannot pump blood effectively

cardiopulmonary resuscitation (CPR)   a first aid technique that is used to restore heartbeat and breathing

cardiorespiratory endurance   the ability of the circulatory and respiratory systems to supply oxygen during sustained physical activity

cardiovascular disease   a disease of the heart and blood vessels

cardiovascular disease risk factors   characteristics of people and ways they might behave that increase the possibility of cardiovascular disease

cardiovascular endurance   the ability to do activities that require increased oxygen intake over extended periods of time

caregiver   a person who provides care for a person who needs assistance

carjacking   motor vehicle theft by force or threat of force while the driver or passengers are still in the motor vehicle

cartilage   a soft, connective tissue on the ends of some bones

cataract   a clouding of the lens of the eye that obstructs vision

cavity   an area of tooth decay

CD4+ T cell count   a test that determines the number of CD4+ T cells in a sample of blood and indicates how well a person's immune system is working; used as a basis to determine how well treatment for HIV is working

C-reactive protein (CRP)   a protein produced by the liver as part of the normal immune system response to injury or infection

celiac disease, or **celiac sprue**   intolerance to gluten due to an unknown genetic defect

cell   the smallest living part of the body

Center for Science in the Public Interest (CSPI)   a nonprofit organization that conducts activities to improve government and industry policies regarding food, nutrition, and other health concerns

Centers for Disease Control and Prevention (CDC)   the lead federal public health agency for protecting the health and safety of people in the United States

central nervous system   the part of the nervous system that consists of the brain and spinal cord

cerebellum   the part of the brain that controls and coordinates muscle activity

cerebral palsy   a disorder of the nervous system that interferes with muscle coordination

cerebrum   the largest part of the brain; it controls the ability to memorize, think, and learn

certified athletic trainer   a specialist who works with athletes to maintain fitness and prevent and treat injuries

cervical cap   a rubber or plastic dome that fits snugly over the cervix to provide a barrier to help prevent sperm from entering the uterus

cervix   the lowest part of the uterus and connects the uterus to the vagina

Cesarean section   a procedure in which a baby is removed surgically from the mother's uterus

chancre   a painless, open sore that appears at the site where the spirochetes entered the body

character   a person's use of self-control to act on responsible values

characterizing objectives objectives that require students to act consistently in accordance with the values they have internalized at this level

chat   a real-time text conversation between people "in" a special online area, called a "chat room"

chemical burn   a burn that occurs when chemicals in a laboratory or in products get on the skin or into the eyes or body

chemotherapy   treatment with anticancer drugs

chewing tobacco   a tobacco product made from chopped tobacco leaves that is placed between the gums and cheek

child abuse   harmful treatment of a minor

chlamydia   an STD that is caused by the bacterium *Chlamydia trachomatis,* which produces inflammation of the reproductive organs; the most common STD in the United States

chlorofluorocarbons (CFCs)   a group of gases that, because they are easy to compress and expand, are used as propellants in aerosol sprays and as coolants in air conditioners, insulation, and refrigerators

choking   an emergency in which the airway is blocked

cholesterol   a fatlike substance made by the body and found in certain foods

chromosome   a threadlike structure that carries genes

chronic bronchitis   a recurring inflammation of the bronchial tubes

chronic disease   a recurring or persistent disease

chronic fatigue syndrome (CFS)   a condition in which recurring tiredness makes it difficult for people to function in normal ways

chronic health conditions   health conditions that recur or persist

chronic obstructive pulmonary disease (COPD)   a disease that interferes with breathing

chronological age   the number of years a person has lived

cigarette   dried and shredded tobacco wrapped in paper

cilia   hairlike structures that remove dust and other particles from inhaled air and prevent harmful substances from reaching the lungs

circumcision   the surgical removal of the foreskin from the penis

cirrhosis   a disease of the liver caused by chronic damage to liver cells

Clean Air Act   a law that allows the EPA to set standards for major air pollutants

Clean Water Act   a law that sets regulations on wastes going into water and on the operation of waste treatment plants and makes it illegal to release pollutants into the water

clinger   a person who is needy and dependent

clinical depression   depression characterized by long-lasting feelings of hopelessness, sadness, or helplessness

clinical psychologist   a psychologist who helps people deal with mental disorders, stressors, and life crises; provides individual, group, and family psychotherapy; and plans behavioral modification programs

clitoris   a small, highly sensitive structure located above the opening of the urethra in a female

closed fracture   a fracture in which there is no break in the skin

closed wound   an injury to the soft tissues under the skin

clove cigarette   a cigarette that has a mixture of ground cloves and tobacco

coal   a black or brown solid that contains stored energy from decayed plant material

cocaine   a highly addictive stimulant that is obtained from the leaves of the coca bush

cochlear implant   an electronic device that is implanted in the ear to restore partial hearing to someone who is deaf

codeine   a painkiller produced from morphine

codependence   a problem in which people neglect themselves to care for, control, or try to "fix" someone else

codependent   a person who wants to rescue and control another person

cognitive behavior therapy   a form of psychotherapy that involves behavior therapy and cognitive therapy

cognitive development   development of skills such as reasoning, language acquisition, problem solving, and knowledge acquisition

cognitive domain   a category of objectives dealing with thinking behavior

cold-temperature-related illnesses   conditions that result from exposure to low temperatures

color blindness   a condition in which a person cannot tell the difference between red and green

combination pill   a pill that combines estrogen and progestin to change the natural menstrual cycle and to prevent ovulation

commercial   an advertisement on television or radio

common cold   a respiratory infection caused by more than 200 different viruses

communicable and chronic diseases   the area of health that focuses on choosing behaviors to reduce the risk of infection with communicable diseases, choosing behaviors to reduce risk of infection with respiratory diseases, choosing behaviors to reduce risk of infection with sexually transmitted diseases, choosing behaviors to reduce risk of HIV infection, choosing behaviors to reduce risk of cardiovascular diseases, choosing behaviors to reduce risk of diabetes, choosing behaviors to reduce risk of cancer, recognizing ways to manage asthma and allergies, recognizing ways to manage chronic health conditions, and keeping a personal health record

communicable disease, or infectious disease   an illness caused by pathogens that can be spread from one living thing to another

communication   the exchange of feelings, thoughts, or information with one or more persons

communication skills   skills that help a person share feelings, thoughts, and information with others

community health educator   a health educator who focuses on educating people in a specific community

community park   an area of land kept for natural scenery and recreation

community water fluoridation   the process of placing fluoride in community water supplies to a level that is optimal for dental health

complete protein   a protein that contains all of the essential amino acids

complex carbohydrates   nutrients that are starches and fiber

compost   a mixture of decayed organic material generally used to fertilize and condition the soil

composting   the use of naturally occurring soil bacteria to break down plant remains into humus

Comprehensive Environmental Response, Compensation, and Liability Act   law that provides federal funding to clean up uncontrolled or hazardous waste sites and oil and chemical spills

comprehensive objectives   objectives that require students to reproduce or recall something previously experienced in a new form

comprehensive school health education curriculum   an organized, sequential K–12 plan for teaching students information and helping them develop life skills that promote health literacy and maintain and improve health, prevent disease, and reduce health-related risk behaviors

comprehensive tobacco control program   a statewide program designed to reduce disease, disability, and death related to tobacco use by preventing the initiation of tobacco use among young people, promoting quitting among young people and adults, eliminating nonsmokers' exposure to environmental tobacco smoke (ETS), and identifying and eliminating the disparities related to tobacco use and its effects among different population groups

computer   a machine that accepts, processes, and outputs data

concealed weapon   a weapon that is partially or fully hidden from view

conceit   excessive appreciation of one's worth

conception or **fertilization**   the union of an ovum and a sperm

conductive hearing loss   hearing loss that occurs when sound is not transported efficiently from the outer to the inner ear

conflict   disagreement between two or more people or between two or more choices

conflict avoidance   a conflict response style in which a person avoids disagreements at all costs

conflict resolution skills   steps that can be taken to settle a disagreement in responsible ways

congestive heart failure   a condition that occurs when the heart's pumping ability is below normal capacity and fluid accumulates in the lungs and other areas of the body

conjunctivitis   an inflammation of the eye membranes that causes redness, discomfort, and discharge

conservation   the saving of resources

conservatory   a greenhouse in which plants are grown and displayed to the public

constructed-response tests   tests made up of items to which students respond by constructing a few words, one or two sentences, or one or two paragraphs

consumer   a person who chooses sources of health-related information and buys or uses health products or services

consumer and community health   the area of health that focuses on choosing sources of health information wisely, recognizing one's rights as a consumer, taking action if one's consumer rights are violated, evaluating advertisements, making a plan to manage time and money, choosing healthful entertainment, making responsible choices about health care providers and facilities, evaluating ways to pay for health care, being a health advocate by being a volunteer, and investigating health careers

Consumer Information Center   a center that provides free and low-cost publications on numerous consumer topics

Consumer Product Safety Commission (CPSC)   a commission that establishes and enforces product safety standards, receives consumer complaints about the safety of products, and distributes product safety information

consumer rights   the privileges that a consumer is guaranteed

consumerism   the practice of obtaining valid information and reliable and tested products and services

Consumer's Union (CU)   an organization that tests products and publishes a magazine, *Consumer Reports,* that provides comparison ratings for product performance and safety

contract for life   a written agreement in which a person who is suicidal promises not to hurt himself or herself for certain period of time or until after he or she has received professional help

contraindication for use   a symptom or condition for which the OTC drug should not be used

controlled drug   a drug whose possession, manufacture, distribution, and sale are controlled by law

controlled substance   a drug whose possession, manufacture, distribution, and sale are controlled by law

controller   a person who is possessive, jealous, and domineering

conversion disorder   a disorder in which a person experiences sudden health changes as a result of an emotional state

cooldown   a period of five to ten minutes of reduced physical activity to help the body return to a nonexercising state

cooperative learning   an instructional strategy in which students work together to understand a particular concept or to achieve a health goal

coordinated school health program   a systematic approach schools use to meet the needs of the whole child and maximize the positive effect on students, schools, and communities

coordination   the ability to use the senses together with body parts during movement

co-payment   the portion of the medical fee an individual must pay

corn   a growth that results from excess rubbing of a shoe against the foot or from toes being squeezed together

coronary artery   a blood vessel that carries blood to the heart muscles

coronary collateral circulation   the development of additional arteries that can deliver oxygenated blood to the heart muscle

coronary heart disease (CHD)   a disease in which the coronary arteries are narrowed or blocked

coronary thrombosis   the narrowing of one of the coronary arteries by a blood clot

corpus luteum   a temporary gland that secretes progesterone

corticosteroids   drugs that are similar to cortisol

cortisol   a hormone produced by the adrenal glands that is activated when the body is under stress and serves other important roles in regulating body functions

could-be   a child or teen who is interested in belonging to a gang, perhaps to emulate a family member or friend who is a member

Council of Better Business Bureaus   a nonprofit organization that monitors consumer complaints and advertising and selling practices

counseling, psychological, and social services   services that provide broad-based individual and group assessments, interventions, and referrals that attend to the mental, emotional, and social health of students

covered expense   a medical expense that is paid for under the terms of a health insurance plan

Cowper's glands   two small glands located beneath the prostate gland that secrete a clear, lubricating fluid into the urethra

crack   purified cocaine that is smoked to produce a rapid and intense reaction

crank   an amphetamine-like stimulant

creative intimacy   the sharing of efforts to accomplish tasks and projects

credit card   a card used for payment that the owner of the card agrees to make later

critical thinker   a person able to examine problems and solve these problems

crowning   the appearance of the baby's head during delivery

culture   the arts, beliefs, and customs that make up a way of life for a group of people at a certain time

curfew   a fixed time when a person is to be at home

cuspids   the four teeth in the corners of the mouth that have a long, heavy root and a pointed cusp that tears food

custodial parent   the parent with whom a child or children live and the parent who has the legal right to make decisions about the health and well-being of a child or children

custom-made mouthguard   a mouthguard made from a cast model of a person's teeth

cuticle   the nonliving skin that surrounds the nails

cycle of abuse   the repeating of abuse from one generation to the next

cystic fibrosis   a condition in which large amounts of abnormally thick mucus are produced, particularly in the lungs and pancreas

D

daily food intake patterns   recommendations on what and how much to eat for good health

daily hassles   the day-to-day stressors of normal living

dandruff   a condition in which dead skin sheds from the scalp, producing white flakes

database   a collection of related information organized for quick access to specific items of information

date rape   rape that occurs in a dating situation

dating violence   violence in which one person in a dating relationship uses physical, emotional, or sexual abuse to control the other person

DDT   a pesticide that was banned because it was found in food products after harvest

death   the permanent cessation of function of all vital organs

debate   an instructional strategy in which an issue is presented and students identify and defend an approach, solution, or choice

debt   the condition of owing

decibel (dB)   a unit used to measure the loudness of sounds

decision   a choice

decision making   an instructional strategy in which students are given a situation for which a choice must be made and asked to apply a series of steps to determine which choice leads to responsible actions

decongestant   a drug used to relieve a stuffed-up nose

deductible   an amount to be paid by the insurance policyholder before the health insurance company makes any payment

deep-injection well   a well that pumps waste into porous rock far below the level of groundwater

deforestation   the destruction of forests

dehydration   a condition in which the water content of the body has fallen to a harmful level

delayed gratification the voluntary postponement of an immediate reward in order to complete a task before enjoying a reward

delinquent behavior illegal actions committed by a juvenile

delirium tremens a severe form of alcohol withdrawal syndrome in which a person has hallucinations and muscle convulsions

dementia a general decline in all areas of mental functioning

demonstration an instructional strategy in which the teacher demonstrates a concept or life skill

denial refusing to admit a problem

dental floss a string-like material used for flossing

dental health plan a plan for taking care of the teeth and gums that includes frequent brushing and flossing, reduction of cavity-promoting foods, avoidance of tobacco, protecting the teeth from injury, regular dental examinations, and cleaning of the teeth by a dental hygienist

dental hygienist a trained dental health professional who works under the direction of a dentist to provide dental care

dental plaque an invisible, sticky film of bacteria on teeth, especially near the gum line

dental sealant a thin, plastic coating painted on the chewing surfaces of the back teeth to prevent tooth decay

dental veneer a thin shell of ceramic material used to cover teeth

dentin the hard tissue that forms the body of the tooth

dentist a doctor of dental surgery (DDS) or a doctor of medical dentistry (DMD) who specializes in dental care

deodorant a product that reduces the amount of body odor, may reduce the amount of perspiration, and contains fragrance to cover up odor

dependent personality disorder a personality disorder in which a person cannot function without the advice and help of others

depilatories chemicals that dissolve hair at the skin's surface

depressant a drug that slows down the actions of the body

dermatologist a physician who specializes in the care of the skin

dermis a thick layer of cells below the epidermis that contains sweat glands, hair follicles, sebaceous (oil) glands, blood vessels, and nerves

desensitization the effect of reacting less and less to exposure to something

designer label a logo or name for a specific brand of clothing

desirable weight the weight that is healthful for a person

desktop publishing using a computer to produce high-quality documents

destructive relationship a relationship that destroys self-esteem, interferes with productivity and health, and may include violence and drug misuse and abuse

detoxification the process in which an addictive substance is withdrawn from the body

developed country a country that has achieved an acceptable standard of health conditions for its people

developing country a country that is working to achieve an acceptable standard of health conditions for its people

developmental milestones the physical or behavioral signs of development and maturation in infants and children

developmental task achievement that is necessary to be made during a particular period of growth in order that a person can continue growing toward maturity

diabetes, or diabetes mellitus a disease in which the body produces little or no insulin

diabetic ketoacidosis a serious condition in which there is a production of two abnormal acids or a lowering of the alkali in the blood as a result of faulty metabolism

diagnosis the determination of a person's condition or health status after taking a health history, studying symptoms, or getting test results

diaphragm a dome-shaped cup that fits over the cervix to provide a barrier to help prevent sperm from entering the uterus

dietary fluoride supplement a supplement containing fluoride that is prescribed by a dentist or physician to help prevent tooth decay

Dietary Guidelines for Americans recommendations for diet choices for healthy Americans two years of age and older

dietitian, or nutritionist a specialist who counsels people about diet and nutrition

digestion the process by which food is changed so that it can be absorbed by the body's cells

digestive system the body system that breaks down food into nutrients that can be used by the body

digital camera a camera that stores pictures in digital form on a small disk

digital rectal examination an examination in which the physician inserts a finger into the rectum and examines the internal reproductive organs and the rectum for irregularities

digital video disk (DVD) a special type of CD that can hold extensive amounts of computer data, audio, and video

dioxins a group of chemicals used in insecticides

disability insurance insurance that replaces income lost owing to accidents or illnesses requiring a period of recovery

discipline training that develops self-discipline and self-control

discretionary calorie allowance the remaining amount of calories in a food intake pattern after accounting for the calories needed for all of the food groups

discriminate to treat some people or groups of people differently from others

discriminatory behavior behavior that makes distinctions in treatment or shows behavior in favor of or prejudiced against an individual or group of people

dislocation the movement of a bone away from its joint

displacement the releasing of anger on someone or something other than the cause of the anger

dissociative disorder a mental disorder in which a person has memory loss, confused identity, or more than one identity

dissociative identity disorder a rare mental disorder in which two or more personalities coexist within the same person

dissolution a legal way to end a marriage in which the marriage partners decide the terms with respect to property, custody and support of children, and spousal support

distillation a process that uses a fermented mixture to obtain a beverage with a high alcohol content

distress a harmful response to a stressor that produces negative results

diuretic a drug or substance that increases the amount of urine excreted from the boxy

diversion an approach to rehabilitation that involves sending juvenile offenders somewhere to learn how to obey laws

diversity the quality of being different or varied

divorce a legal way to end a marriage in which a judge or court decides the terms with respect to property, custody and support of children, and spousal support

domestic violence violence that occurs within a family

dopamine a chemical that triggers feelings of pleasure

dowager's hump a severely rounded back due to reduced bone mass in the spine

Down syndrome a genetic disorder in which a child is born with an extra chromosome in each cell

drug a chemical substance that affects the way the body or mind functions

drug abuse the intentional use of a drug without medical or health reasons

drug addiction the compelling need for a drug even though it harms the body, mind, or relationships

drug metabolites chemicals that, when present in urine, indicate that the person has used a banned substance

drug misuse the incorrect use of a prescription or over-the-counter drug

drug-free lifestyle a lifestyle in which a person does not misuse or abuse drugs

drug-free role model a person who chooses a drug-free lifestyle, knows and follows laws and policies regarding drugs, and educates others about the risks of using drugs

drug-free school zone a defined geographic area around a school designated drug-free for the purpose of sheltering youth from the sale and use of controlled substances

drug trafficking   the illegal production, distribution, transportation, selling, or purchasing of drugs

dynamic blood pressure   the measure of the changes in blood pressure during the day. Sudden changes in blood pressure can cause stroke

dysentery   a severe infection of the intestines, causing diarrhea and abdominal pain

dysfunctional family   a family that does not promote loving, responsible relationships

dyslexia   a learning disability in which a person has difficulty spelling, reading, and writing

E

E. coli 0157:H7   a bacterial pathogen that lives in cattle and other similar animals

earthquake   a violent shaking of Earth's surface caused by the shifting of plates that make up Earth's crust

eating disorder   a mental disorder in which a person has a compelling need to starve, to binge, or to binge and purge

ectopic pregnancy, or **tubal pregnancy**   a pregnancy that occurs outside the uterus

educational technologies   teaching methods that involve the use of high-tech equipment, including computers, CD-ROMs, and online communication

effective communicator   a person able to express and convey his or her knowledge, beliefs, and ideas

ejaculatory duct   a short, straight tube that passes into the prostate gland and opens into the urethra in a male

elder abuse   physical, emotional, or psychological harm done to an older adult

electrical burn   a burn that occurs when electricity travels through the body

electrical storm   a storm that has lightning and thunder

electrocardiogram (ECG)   a record of the electrical impulses of the heart that is used to diagnose disorders of the heart

electrolysis   hair removal method that uses a hair-thin metal probe that delivers electricity to cause damage to hair follicles

electrolyte   a nutrient that becomes electrically charged when in a solution such as a body fluid

ELISA   a blood test used to check for antibodies for HIV

e-mail   the system of instantaneously transmitted electronic messages

embryo   the name given to a developing baby through the second month of growth after conception

emergency   a serious situation that occurs without warning and calls for quick action

emergency contraception   a method of preventing pregnancy after a contraceptive fails or after unprotected sex

emergency dispatcher   a person who decides whom to contact when there is a call for help

emergency medical technician (EMT)   a health care professional who gives health care to people in emergency situations before they reach the hospital

emergency planning committee   a committee established for the purpose of developing and implementing school emergency plans

emergency room   a facility within a hospital where emergency services are provided without an appointment

emotional abuse   putting down another person and making the person feel worthless

emotional development   the expression of feelings about oneself, others, and things

emotional environment   the feelings and sensibilities expressed in the set of expectations, interpersonal relationships, and experiences that affect the student's development

emotional security   a feeling of freedom from anxiety in which individuals feel that they can present and express themselves without fear of ridicule, threat, or belittlement

empathy   the ability to share in another person's emotions or feelings

emphysema   a condition in which the alveoli in the lungs lose most of their ability to absorb oxygen from inhaled air and pass it into the bloodstream or remove carbon dioxide from the bloodstream

employee assistance program   a work-site-based program designed to help identify and facilitate the resolution of behavioral, health, and productivity problems that may adversely affect employees' well-being or job performance

enabler   a person who supports the harmful behavior of others

Endangered Species Act   a law that protects animal and plant species that are threatened with extinction

endocrine system   glands that control many of the body's activities by producing hormones

endometrial implants   growths outside the surface of the uterus

endometriosis   a condition that occurs when tissue similar to the endometrium is found outside its normal location

endometrium   the tissue that lines the uterus

energy   the ability to do work

enriched food   a food in which nutrients lost during processing are added back into the food

entertainment   something that is designed to hold the interests of people

entertainment addiction   the compelling need to watch television or other entertainment media

environment   everything around a person

environmental health   the area of health that focuses on staying informed about environmental issues; keeping the air clean; keeping the water clean; keeping noise at a safe level; precycling, recycling, and disposing of waste properly; helping conserve energy and natural resources; protecting the natural environment; helping improve the visual environment; taking actions to improve the social-emotional environment; and being an advocate for the environment

Environmental Protection Agency (EPA)   a federal regulatory agency responsible for reducing and controlling environmental pollution

environmental tobacco smoke   the combination of sidestream smoke and the mainstream smoke exhaled by a smoker

enzyme   a protein that regulates chemical reactions

ephedrine   a stimulant that is found naturally in the ephedra plant

epidermis   the outer layer of skin cells

epididymis   a comma-shaped structure along the upper rear surface of the testes where sperm mature

epiglottis   a flap that covers the entrance to the trachea when a person swallows foods or beverages

epilepsy   a disorder in which abnormal electrical activity in the brain causes a temporary loss of control of the mind and body

episodic heavy drinking   drinking is which a person has five or more drinks on a single occasion

erection   a process that occurs when the penis swells with blood and elongates

esophagus   a tube connecting the mouth to the stomach

essential amino acids   the nine amino acids the body cannot produce

essential body fat   the amount of body fat needed for optimal health

estrogen   a hormone produced by the ovaries that stimulates the development of female secondary sex characteristics and affects the menstrual cycle

ethnic restaurant   a restaurant that serves food that is customary for people of a specific culture

eugenol   a chemical that numbs the back of the throat and reduces the ability to cough

eustachian tube   the tube that connects the middle ear and the back of the nose

eustress   a healthful response to a stressor that produces positive results

eutrophication   the buildup of excess nutrients in water

evaluation   the means of measuring a student's mastery of the health education standards, the performance indicators, and the life skills; the procedure used to measure the results of efforts toward a desired goal

evaluation objectives   objectives that require students to render judgments regarding something for which they have not rendered judgment previously

exercise   planned, structured, and repetitive bodily movement done to improve or maintain one or more components of physical fitness

exercise addiction   the compelling need to exercise

exercise-induced asthma (EIA)   a condition in which a person has difficulty breathing during or shortly after strenuous physical activity

exhaustion stage of GAS   the third stage of the generalized adaption syndrome (GAS) in which wear and tear on the body increases the risk of injury, illness, and premature death

expense   an amount of money needed to purchase or do something

extended care facility   a facility that provides nursing, personal, and residential care

extended family   a family including stepparents, stepbrothers, stepsisters, grandparents, aunts, uncles, and foster brothers and sisters; other significant adults may also be included as extended family

extinction   the death of all members of a species of animal or plant

extraction   the surgical removal of a tooth

F

fad diet   a quick weight-loss strategy that is popular for a short time

fainting   partial or complete loss of consciousness due to reduced blood flow to the brain

fallopian tube   a tube four inches (ten centimeters) long that connects an ovary to the uterus

family   basic unit of society that can include people related by blood, marriage, or other legal procedures

family and social health   the area of health that focuses on developing healthful family relationships, recognizing ways to improve family relationships, using conflict resolution skills, developing healthful friendships, developing dating skills, practicing abstinence, recognizing harmful relationships, developing skills to prepare for marriage, developing skills to prepare for parenthood, and adjusting to family changes

family continuum   a scale to show the degree to which a family promotes skills needed for loving, responsible relationships

family hero   a family member who tries to do everything right

family relationships   the connections between family members, including members of the extended family

family value   a standard that is held and copied by members of a family

farsightedness   a defect in the shape of the eye that causes objects that are close to be fuzzy

fast food   food that can be served quickly and is prepared in walk-in or drive-through restaurants

fat   a nutrient that provides energy and helps the body store and use vitamins

fat-soluble vitamin   a vitamin that dissolves in fat and can be stored in the body

Federal Bureau of Investigation (FBI)   a governmental agency responsible for federal criminal offenses, including investigation of health fraud such as insurance scams

federal law   a law that is enacted by the United States Congress

Federal Trade Commission (FTC)   a govermental agency that enforces consumer protection laws and monitors trade practices and the advertising of foods, drugs, and cosmetics

female condom   a soft, polyurethane pouch that is inserted deep into the vagina to collect semen during ejaculation

female reproductive system   a body system that consists of organs in the female body that are involved in producing offspring

fermentation   a process in which yeast, sugar, and water are combined to produce alcohol and carbon dioxide

fertile period   the days in a female's menstrual cycle during which having sexual intercourse can result in conception

fetal alcohol syndrome (FAS) the presence of severe birth defects in babies born to mothers who drank alcohol during pregnancy

fetus   the name given to a developing baby from the ninth week until birth

fiber   the part of grains and plant foods that cannot be digested

fibroadenoma   a lump that is formed when fluid becomes trapped in a lymph duct

field trip   an instructional strategy in which students visit a site outside the school to gather information

fighting   taking part in a physical struggle

finely coordinated movement objectives   objectives that require students to coordinate movements of the extremities, usually with the eye and ear

first aid   the immediate and temporary care given to a person who has been injured or suddenly becomes ill

first-degree burn   a burn of the top layer of skin

FITT formula   a formula in which each letter represents a factor for determining how to obtain fitness benefits from physical activity: F = frequency, I = intensity, T = time, and T = type

five stages of grief   five psychological stages of grieving: denial, anger, bargaining, depression, and acceptance; they describe the common grieving process

flash flood   a flood that occurs suddenly

flashback   a sudden hallucination a person has long after having used a drug

flexibility   the ability to bend and move the joints through the full range of motion

flood   an overflowing of a body of water onto normally dry land

fluoride   a mineral that strengthens the enamel of teeth

folate   a B vitamin found in many vegetables, beans, fruits, whole grains, and fortified breakfast cereals; helps to reduce the risk of cancer

food additive   a substance intentionally added to food; food additives may add nutrients, flavor, color, or texture

food allergy   an abnormal response of the immune system to food

Food and Drug Administration (FDA)   a governmental agency that monitors the safety of cosmetics and food and the safety and effectiveness of new drugs, medical devices, and prescription and over-the-counter drugs

food intolerance   an abnormal response to food that is not caused by the immune system

foodborne illness   an illness caused by consuming foods or beverages that have been contaminated with pathogens

formal intervention   an action by people, such as family members, who want a person to get treatment

fortified food   a food in which nutrients not usually found in the food have been added

fossil fuel   a fuel that is formed from plant or animal remains as a result of pressure over many years

foster care   an arrangement in which an unrelated adult assumes temporary responsibility for a child

fracture   a break or a crack in a bone

free weight   a barbell or dumbbell

freestanding emergency center, or **urgent care center**   a facility that is not part of a hospital that provides emergency care

freshwater   water that is not contaminated or salty

frostbite   the freezing of body parts, often the tissues of the extremities

full-service schools   schools that attempt to link the delivery of a full scope of educational, social, and health services through cooperative partnerships between schools and community agencies

fungi   single- or multicelled parasitic organisms

G

gallbladder   an organ that stores bile. The liver produces bile, which is transported to the small intestine

gambling addiction   the compelling need to bet money or other valuables

Gardasil   a vaccine given to females between the ages of nine and twenty-six to help prevent infection with some strains of human papillomavirus (HPV); reduces the risk of developing cervical cancer

garden   an area where trees, flowers, and other plants are grown and landscaping is maintained

gasohol   a blend of grain alcohol and gasoline that is used as a fuel source

gastric bypass surgery   a surgical procedure that removes a large portion of the stomach, makes a small pouch in the stomach, and then attaches the pouch with the small intestine so that the lower part of the stomach is bypassed when food travels through the digestive system

gene   a unit of hereditary material

general adaptation syndrome (GAS)   a series of body changes that result from stress

general anxiety disorder   a recurring state of anxiety, fear, restlessness, and tenseness

generalized tonic clonic seizure   a major convulsive seizure during which a person falls unconscious, exhibits jerking motions or body stiffening, and stops breathing temporarily or has shallow breathing

generational cycle of teen pregnancy   a term used when a teen whose mother was a teen parent becomes pregnant

generic drug   a drug that contains the same active ingredients as a brand-name drug

genetic counseling   a process in which a trained professional interprets medical information concerning genetics to prospective parents

genetic predisposition   the inheritance of genes that increase the likelihood of developing a condition

genital herpes   an STD caused by the herpes simplex virus (HSV), which produces cold sores or fever blisters in the genital area and mouth

genital warts   an STD caused by certain types of the human papillomavirus (HPV) that produces wartlike growths on the genitals

geothermal energy   heat transferred from underground sources of steam or hot water

gerontologist   a person who specializes in the study of aging

gerontology   the study of aging

gestational diabetes   diabetes that occurs in females pregnancy

GHB (gamma hydroxybutyrate)   a central nervous system depressant that was banned by the Food and Drug Administration in 1990

Giardia lamblia   a parasite that lives in the intestines of humans and other mammals and causes giardiasis

giardiasis   a stomach and intestinal infection that causes abdominal cramps, nausea, gas, and diarrhea

gingivitis   a condition in which the gums are red, swollen, and tender and bleed easily

gland   a group of cells or an organ that secretes hormones

glaucoma   a condition in which the pressure of the fluid in the eye is high and may damage the optic nerve

global environmental issues   environmental concerns that can affect the quality of life of people everywhere

global learner   a person who learns best by combining visual, auditory, and kinesthetic ways of learning

global warming   an increase in Earth's temperature

glucose   a simple sugar that is the main source of energy for the body

goal   a desired achievement toward which a person works

gonorrhea   an STD caused by the gonococcus bacterium *Gonorrhoeae niesseria* that infects the linings of the genital and urinary tracts of males and females

good character   the use of self-control to act on responsible values

Good Samaritan laws   laws that protect people who give first aid in good faith and without gross negligence or misconduct

government hospital   a hospital that is run by the federal, state, or local government for the benefit of a specific population

graduated license   a conditional license given to new drivers

graffiti   writing or drawings on a public surface

grand mal   a major seizure in which a person may have convulsions

grandparents' rights   the visitation rights with grandchildren that courts have awarded to grandparents in situations such as parental divorce, parental death, and children being born out of wedlock

greenhouse effect   a process in which water vapor and gases in the atmosphere absorb and reflect infrared rays and warm Earth's surfaces

grief   intense emotional suffering caused by a loss, disaster, or misfortune

grooming   keeping the body clean and having a neat appearance

gross bodily movement objectives   objectives that require students to move entire limbs

Group A carcinogen   a substance that causes cancer in humans

growth and development   the area of health that focuses on keeping body systems healthy, recognizing habits that protect female reproductive health, recognizing habits that protect male reproductive health, learning about pregnancy and childbirth, practicing abstinence to avoid the risks of teenage pregnancy and parenthood, providing responsible care for infants and children, achieving developmental tasks of adolescence, developing learning styles, developing habits that promote healthful aging, and sharing with family feelings about dying and death

guest speaker   a person with particular expertise on a topic who will speak to a class

guidance counselor   a specialist who assists students with personal, family, education, and career decisions and concerns

H

habitat   a place where an animal or plant normally lives

hair   a threadlike structure consisting of dead cells filled with keratin

hair follicle a pit on the surface of the skin that contains nutrients a hair needs to grow

halfway house a live-in facility that helps a person who is drug-dependent gradually adjust to living independently in the community

hallucinogenic drug a substance that has the major effect of producing marked distortions in perception

hallucinogens a group of drugs that interfere with the senses and cause hallucinations

hand-eye coordination the use of the hands together with the eyes during movement

hangnail a strip of skin torn from the side or base of a fingernail

hangover an aftereffect of using alcohol and other drugs

hantavirus a virus that is found in the urine, saliva, or droppings of infected deer mice and some other wild rodents that can cause a rare but serious lung disease called Hantavirus Pulmonary Syndrome (HPS)

hard drive a device that reads and enters data onto a hard disk

hard-core gang member a senior gang member who has the most influence

hardware electronic components that form a computer

harmful relationship a relationship that harms self-respect, interferes with productivity and health, and includes violence and drug misuse and abuse

hashish a drug that is made from marijuana

hashish oil the liquid resin from the cannabis plant

hate crime a crime motivated by prejudice

hay fever a common term for seasonal respiratory allergies

hazardous waste any solid, liquid, or gas that is harmful to humans or animal or plant life

hazing the physical or emotional abuse a person endures while trying to become or stay part of a group, regardless of that person's willingness to participate

hazing activity dangerous or demeaning acts in which a person is forced to participate in order to become a member of a club or group

health the quality of life that includes physical, mental-emotional, and family-social health

health advocacy taking responsibility to improve the quality of life by spending time and efforts to help in one's community

health advocacy skills skills used to influence others' health decisions and behaviors and to emphasize health-related concerns and beliefs

health advocate a person who promotes health for self and others

health advocate for the environment a person who promotes a healthful environment

health behavior contract a written plan to develop the habit of practicing a health goal

health behavior inventory a personal assessment tool that contains a list of health goals to which a person responds positively (+), "I have achieved this health goal," or to which a person responds negatively (−), "I have not achieved this health goal."

health care facility a place that provides health care

health care practitioner an independent health care provider who is licensed to practice on a specific area of the body

health care provider a trained professional who provides people with health care

health career a profession or occupation in the health field for which one trains

health center a facility that provides routine health care to a special population

health department clinic a facility in most state and local health departments that keeps records and performs services

health education standards standards that specify what students should know and be able to do

health education teacher a teacher who specializes in health education

health fact a true statement about health

health fraud the advertising, promotion, and sale of products and services that have not been scientifically proven safe and effective

health goal a healthful behavior a person works to achieve and maintain

health history a record of a person's health habits, past health conditions and medical care, allergies and drug sensitivities, and health facts about family members

health insurance financial protection that provides benefits for sickness or injury

health knowledge   the information and understanding a person has about health

health literacy   competence in critical thinking and problem solving, responsible and productive citizenship, self-directed learning, and effective communication

health-literate individual   a person who is a critical thinker and problem solver, a responsible and productive citizen, a self-directed learner, and an effective communicator

health maintenance organization (HMO)   a business that organizes health care services for its members

health product   something that is produced and used for health

health promotion   the science and art of helping people move toward an optimal state of health

health record   a file that includes a health history and the results of the physical examination

health service   the help provided by a health care provider or facility

health services manager and administrator   a professional who manages a health services organization

health status   the condition of a person's body, mind, emotions, and relationships; health status influences quality of life

healthful and safe school environment   a school environment that attends to the physical and aesthetic surroundings and the psychosocial climate and culture that maximize the health and safety of students and staff

healthful behavior   an action a person chooses that promotes health; prevents injury, illness, and premature death; or improves the quality of life

healthful body composition   a high ratio of lean tissue to fat tissue in the body

healthful family   a family that practices skills that promote loving, responsible relationships

healthful friendship   a balanced relationship that promotes mutual respect and healthful behavior

healthful relationship   a relationship that promotes self-respect, encourages productivity and health, and is free of violence and drug misuse and abuse

healthful situation   a circumstance that promotes health; prevents injury, illness, and premature death; and improves the quality of the environment

health-related fitness   the ability of the heart, lungs, muscles, and joints to function at optimal capacity

heart   a four-chambered muscle that pumps blood throughout the body

heart attack   the death of cardiac muscle caused by a lack of blood flow to the heart

heart rate   the number of times the heart contracts each minute

heart-healthy diet   a low-fat diet rich in fruits, vegetables, whole grains, nonfat and low-fat milk products, lean meats, poultry, and fish

heat cramps   painful muscle spasms in the legs and arms due to excessive fluid loss through sweating

heat detector   a device that sounds an alarm when the room temperature rises above a certain level

heat exhaustion   extreme tiredness due to the body's inability to regulate its temperature

heat-related illnesses   conditions that result from exposure to temperatures higher than normal

heat stroke   a life-threatening overheating of the body

Heimlich maneuver   a technique that makes use of abdominal thrusts to dislodge an object in the air passage of a conscious person who is choking

helminth   a parasitic worm

helper T cell   a white blood cell that signals B cells to produce antibodies

hemoglobin   an iron-rich protein that helps transport oxygen and carbon dioxide in the blood

hemophilia   an inherited condition in which the blood does not clot normally

heredity   the passing of characteristics from biological parents to their children

heroin   an illegal narcotic derived from morphine

herpes simplex virus Type 1 (HSV-1)   a virus that causes cold sores or fever blisters in the mouth or on the lips

herpes simplex virus Type 2 (HSV-2)   a virus that causes genital sores but also may cause sores in the mouth; the virus remains in the body for life

hidden anger   anger that is not recognized or is expressed in an inappropriate way

high blood pressure   blood pressure of 140/90 mm Hg (millimeters of mercury) or greater for an extended time

high-density lipoproteins (HDLs)   substances in the blood that carry cholesterol to the liver for breakdown and excretion

highly active antiretroviral therapy, or HAART   a triple drug combination treatment for HIV infection

high-risk driving   dangerous driving that can result in accidents

histrionic personality disorder   a personality disorder in which a person has emotional outbursts and constantly draws attention to himself or herself

HIV negative   a person who does not have antibodies for HIV present in the blood

HIV positive   a person who has antibodies for HIV present in the blood

HIV wasting syndrome   a substantial loss in body weight that is accompanied by high fevers, sweating, and diarrhea due to infection with HIV

holistic effect   the effect of the twelve factors that influence well-being on the whole person

holistic health   the connectedness of the twelve factors that influence health status, the ten areas of health, and the three domains of health

home health care   care provided within a patient's home

Homeland Security Advisory System   a system of the U.S. federal government to inform federal, state, and local authorities and the American people of the risk of terrorist acts

homicide   the accidental or purposeful killing of another person

honest talk   the straightforward sharing of feelings

hormone   a chemical messenger that is released directly into the bloodstream

hormone replacement therapy (HRT)   a combination of estrogen and progesterone that is taken to reduce the symptoms of menopause and to help prevent osteoporosis

hospice   a facility or home services for people who are dying and their families

hospital   a health care facility where people can receive medical care, diagnosis, and treatment on an inpatient or outpatient basis

hospitalization insurance   insurance that pays the cost of a hospital stay

hostility syndrome   a physical state in which the body is in the fight-or-flight state at all times

huffing,   or sniffing inhaling fumes to get high

human growth hormone (hGH)   growth hormone that is secreted by the pituitary gland

human immunodeficiency virus (HIV)   a pathogen that destroys infection-fighting T cells in the body

humus   a soil conditioner

hunger   the physiological need for food

hurricane   a tropical storm with heavy rain and winds in excess of seventy-four miles (118.4 kilometers) per hour

hybrid car   a car that uses a mixture of technologies such as internal combustion engines, electric motors, batteries, hydrogen, and fuel cells to improve gasoline mileage performance

hydrocarbons   chemical compounds that contain only carbon and hydrogen

hydroelectric power   electricity generated from flowing or falling water

hydrogen power   energy produced by passing electrical current through water to burn the hydrogen

hymen   a thin membrane that stretches across the opening of the vagina

hyperactive   a condition in which a person is not able to sit still or stand still

hyperglycemia   condition in which the blood sugar is high as a result of insufficient insulin in the body

hyperopia, or farsightedness   a refractive error in which close objects appear blurred and distant objects are seen clearly

hypnotic   a drug that produces drowsiness and sleep

hypochondria   a disorder in which a person is constantly worried about illness

hypoglycemia   a condition in which the pancreas produces too much insulin, causing the blood sugar level to be low

hypothermia   a reduction in body temperature to lower than normal

I

ice   a smokable form of pure methamphetamine

illegal drug use   the use of a controlled drug without a prescription

I-message   a statement that focuses on a specific behavior or event, how that behavior or event affects the speaker, and the emotions that result

immune system   a system of the body that removes harmful organisms from the blood and combats pathogens

immunity   the body's resistance to disease-causing agents

immunization, or vaccine   a substance containing dead or weakened pathogens that is introduced into the body to increase immunity

immunotherapy   a process in which the immune system is stimulated to fight cancer cells

impetigo   a highly contagious bacterial infection of the skin

incest   sexual abuse in which the abuser is a close relative of the child

incinerator   a furnace in which solid waste is burned and energy is recovered in the process

incision   a cut caused by a sharp-edged object, such as a knife, razor, scissors, or broken glass

incisors   the eight teeth in the front and center of the mouth that have a flat, sharp edge that cuts up food

inclusion   the adaptation of the teaching strategy to assist and include students with special learning challenges and may include enrichment suggestions for the gifted and reteaching ideas for students who are learning disabled

income   money received

incomplete protein   a protein from plant sources that does not contain all of the essential amino acids

indication for use   a symptom or condition for which the over-the-counter drug should be used

indoor molds   molds that grow on indoor surfaces that are wet

infection   a condition in which pathogens enter the body and multiply

infectious disease   a disease caused by microorganisms

inflammation   the process by which the body responds to injury

influenza, or the flu   a highly contagious viral infection of the respiratory tract

infusion   the integration of a subject area into another area of the curriculum

ingredients listing   the list of ingredients in a food

ingrown toenail   a toenail that grows into the skin

inguinal hernia   a hernia in which some of the intestine pushes through the inguinal canal into the scrotum

inhalants   chemicals that affect mood and behavior when inhaled

injectable progestin   a shot of synthetic progesterone that is given every three months to change the natural menstrual cycle and to prevent ovulation

injecting drug user   a person who injects illegal drugs into the body with syringes, needles, and other injection equipment

injury prevention and safety   the area of health that focuses on following safety guidelines to reduce risk of unintentional injuries, following safety guidelines for severe weather conditions and natural disasters, following guidelines for motor vehicle safety, practicing protective factors to reduce risk of violence, respecting authority and obeying laws, practicing self-protection strategies, staying away from gangs, not carrying a weapon, participating in victim recovery if harmed by violence, and being skilled in first aid procedures

inpatient care   treatment that requires a person to stay overnight at a facility

insomnia   the prolonged inability to fall asleep, stay asleep, or get back to sleep once a person is awakened during the night

instructional strategies   teaching methods that help students understand particular concepts and practice life skills

insulin   a hormone that regulates the blood sugar level

insurance policy   the legal document issued to the policyholder that outlines the terms of the insurance

integumentary system   the body system that covers and protects the body and consists of skin, glands associated with the skin, hair, and nails

intentional injury   an injury resulting from interpersonal violence and self-directed violence

interest   additional money that is paid for the use of a larger sum of money

Internet   an online telecommunications system that links most online networks worldwide

intimacy   deep and meaningful sharing between two people

intrauterine device (IUD)   a small device that fits inside the uterus and helps prevent pregnancy

invisible fat   fat that cannot be seen when looking at food

involuntary muscle   a muscle that functions without the person's control

iron   a mineral that is an important component of hemoglobin

isms   beliefs, attitudes, assumptions, and actions that subject individuals or people in a particular group to discriminatory behavior

isokinetic exercise   an exercise using special machines that provide weight resistance through the full range of motion

isometric exercise   exercise that involves muscle tightening for about five to eight seconds with no body movement

Isoniazid   a drug that helps prevent tuberculosis in people in close contact with people who are infected with tuberculosis

isotonic exercise   exercise in which a muscle or muscles move a moderate amount of weight eight to fifteen times

J

jaundice   yellowing of the skin and whites of the eyes

Joint Committee on Health Education Standards   a committee whose purpose was to identify the National Health Education Standards that incorporate the knowledge and skills essential to the development of health literacy

joint   the point where two bones meet

joint custody   an arrangement in which both previously married partners share legal custody of a child or children

jumping-in   an initiation rite in which a potential gang member is beaten by other members of the gang

juvenile detention   the temporary physical restriction of juveniles in special facilities until the outcome of their legal case is decided

juvenile offender   a minor who commits a criminal act

K

Kaposi's sarcoma (KS)   a type of cancer that affects people who are infected with HIV

keratin   a tough protein that makes up nails and hair

ketamine   a legal drug used as a veterinary sedative or as an anesthetic on humans; also known as Special K, Super K, KO, and Ket Kat

kidney   an organ that filters the blood and excretes waste products and excess water in the form of urine

kinesthetic learner   a person who learns best by acting out something, touching an object, or repeating a motion

knocked-out tooth   a tooth that has been knocked out of its socket

knowledge objectives   objectives that require students to reproduce or recall something that they have experienced previously in the same or similar form

L

labia majora   the heavy folds of skin that surround the opening of the vagina

labia minora   the two smaller folds of skin located within the labia majora

labor   the process of childbirth

laceration   a cut that causes a jagged or irregular tearing of the skin

lactase deficiency   a lack of lactase, an enzyme that breaks down the milk sugar present in the cells of the small intestine

lactic acid   a substance produced by the muscles during vigorous exercise that contributes to muscle cramps

lacto-ovo-vegetarian diet   a diet that excludes fish, poultry, and red meat

lactose intolerance the inability to digest lactose, which is found in most dairy products

lacto-vegetarian diet a diet that excludes eggs, fish, poultry, and meat

landfill a place where waste is dumped in layers and buried

landslide a rapid downward movement of a mass of earth or rock

large intestine a tube extending from the small intestine in which undigested food is prepared for elimination from the body

laser hair removal use of a laser to cause damage to hair follicles while sparing damage to surrounding tissues

late syphilis, or tertiary syphilis the final stage of syphilis in which spirochetes damage body organs

latent syphilis a stage of syphilis in which there are no symptoms but the spirochetes are still present and may damage tissues and organs

law a rule of conduct or action that is recognized to be binding and is enforced by a controlling authority

law of conservation of energy a scientific principle that says that energy cannot be created or destroyed but can be changed in form

laxative a drug that helps a person have a bowel movement

LCD projector a device that shows the material on the computer monitor on a larger screen

learner's permit an authorization to drive when supervised by a licensed driver of a certain age

learning disability a disorder in which a person has difficulty acquiring and processing information

learning style the way a person gains and processes information

lecture an instructional strategy involving a verbal communication

lecture and discussion an instructional strategy that combines verbal presentations with student dialogue

legal age of consent the age when a person is legally able to give permission

legal death brain death or the irreversible cessation of circulatory and respiratory functions

leisure time time free from work or duties

leukoplakia abnormal cells in the mouth that appear as white patches of tissue

lice insects that pierce the skin and secrete a substance that causes itching and swelling

licensed practical nurse (LPN), or licensed vocational nurse (LVN) a nurse, who under the direction of registered nurses or physicians, provides nursing care for people who are sick or injured

life crisis an experience that causes a high level of stress

life expectancy the number of years a person can expect to live

life skill an ability that maintains and improves a person's health and promotes the health of others

life-support system a mechanical or other means to support life

lifetime sport or physical activity a sport or physical activity that can be engaged in throughout a person's life

ligament a tough fiber that connects bones

light beer a beer that has fewer calories than regular beer but about the same alcohol content

lightning the flashing of light caused by a discharge of electricity in the air

Likert scale a technique used to measure beliefs and attitudes in which students react to statements with responses of strongly agree, agree, neutral, disagree, or strongly disagree

lipid-lowering drug a drug that lowers blood cholesterol levels

lipoprotein analysis a measure of two main types of lipoproteins in the blood

liquid diet a diet in which beverages are substituted for some or all meals

liquor an alcoholic beverage that is made by distillation

liver a gland that releases bile to help break down fats, maintain blood sugar level, and filter poisonous wastes

living will a legal document that tells what treatment a person wants in the event that she or he no longer can make medical decisions

local public health department a local government agency that offers programs and services aimed at protecting and promoting the health of a specific community

logical consequences discipline a disciplinary technique in which the child is allowed the opportunity to experience the results of undesirable behavior so that he or she will want to change the undesirable behavior

loneliness a condition that is characterized by unpleasant, painful, or anxious feelings as a result of having fewer or less satisfying relationships than desired

long-term goal something a person plans to achieve after a period of time

look-alike drug a drug manufactured to resemble another drug and mimic its effects

loss a feeling that occurs when someone dies or a life situation changes or ends

lost child a child who helps the family maintain balance by not causing problems or getting in the way

low birthweight a weight at birth that is less than 5.5 pounds (2.5 kilograms)

low-density lipoproteins (LDLs) substances in the blood that carry cholesterol to body cells

low-level radioactive waste any radioactive byproduct typically resulting from such activities as nuclear research and the development of nuclear medicines

LSD an illegal hallucinogen sold in the form of powder, tablets, liquid, or capsules

lungs the main organs of the respiratory system

lycopene the red-orange carotene pigment found primarily in tomatoes and tomato-based foods; may be protective against cancer

Lyme disease a bacterial disease transmitted by the bite of tiny infected ticks on field mice and deer

lymph a clear liquid that surrounds body cells and circulates in lymph vessels

lymph node a structure that filters and destroys pathogens

lymphocyte white blood cell that helps the body fight pathogens

M

macrophage white blood cells that surround and destroy pathogens

mainstream smoke smoke that is inhaled into the mouth and lungs of a person who is smoking

major medical insurance insurance that pays for extra expenses not covered by other insurance policies

malaria a serious, life-threatening parasitic disease transmitted by the bite of the female *Anopheles* mosquito

male climacteric a decrease in testosterone in males accompanied by symptoms such as hot flashes, depression, insomnia, and fatigue

male condom a thin sheath of latex, natural skin, or polyurethane that is placed over the erect penis to collect semen during ejaculation

male reproductive system a body system that consists of organs in the male body that are involved in producing offspring

malignant melanoma the form of skin cancer that is often fatal

malignant tumor a tumor that is cancerous and may spread to other parts of the body

malnutrition a condition in which the body does not get the nutrients required for optimal health

malocclusion the abnormal fitting together of teeth when the jaws are closed

malpractice insurance insurance that health care providers and health care facilities purchase to provide coverage for malpractice lawsuits

malt liquor beer that has a higher alcohol content than regular beer

mammogram the image of the breast tissue created by mammography and read by a qualified physician

mammography a highly sensitive X-ray screening test used to detect breast lumps and a highly effective tool in the early detection of cancer

managed care an organized system of health care services designed to control health care costs

mandatory reporter a person who is required by law to report suspected child abuse

marijuana the dried leaves and tops of the cannabis plant, which contains THC

marital conflict resolution a process in which married partners identify their problems, agree on solutions, and reestablish intimacy

marital separation a cessation of cohabitation between a married couple by mutual agreement or judicial decree

mascot a family member who relieves tension by acting in a funny or entertaining way

materials items that are needed to do the teaching strategy

maximum heart rate 220 beats per minute minus a person's age

MDMA a stimulant that also has mild hallucinogenic properties

media the various forms of mass communication, such as television, radio, magazines, and newspapers

Medicaid a health insurance plan for people with low incomes that is managed and paid for by the government

medical doctor a physician who is trained in a medical school and has a doctor of medicine (MD) degree

medical insurance insurance that pays physician's fees, laboratory fees outside a hospital, and fees for prescription drugs

medical writer a writer who specializes in the areas of medicine and health

Medicare a government health insurance plan for people sixty-five years of age and older and for people who have received Social Security disability benefits for two years

medicine a drug that is used to treat, prevent, or diagnose illness

Meeks Heit Umbrella of Comprehensive School Health Education a labelled drawing used to illustrate concepts that describe the purpose of comprehensive school health education

megadosing a practice in which a person takes vitamins in excessive amounts

melanin a pigment that gives the skin its color and protects the body from the ultraviolet rays of the sun

menstrual cycle a monthly series of changes that involve ovulation, changes in the uterine lining, and menstruation

menstruation the period in the menstrual cycle in which the unfertilized egg and the lining of the uterus leave the body in a menstrual flow

mental and emotional health the area of health that focuses on taking responsibility for health, practicing life skills for health, gaining health knowledge, making responsible decisions, using resistance skills when appropriate, developing good character, choosing behaviors to promote a healthy mind, expressing emotions in healthful ways, following a plan to manage stress, and being resilient during difficult times

mental disorder an illness of the mind that can affect the thoughts, feelings, and behaviors of a person, preventing him or her from leading a happy, healthful, and productive life

mental health clinic a facility that provides services for people who have mental disorders

mentor a responsible person who guides another person

mescaline illegal hallucinogen made from the peyote cactus

metabolism the rate at which food is converted into energy in body cells

metastasis the spread of cancer from one area of the body to another

methamphetamine a specific type of stimulant drug in the amphetamine family

methcathinone a stimulant that has effects similar to those of methamphetamine

methylphenidate a stimulant that is used to treat attention deficit hyperactivity disorder

microtrauma an injury that is not recognized or becomes worse as a person continues to work out

migraine severe head pain that is caused by dilation of blood vessels in the brain

mind-body connection the close relationship between mental and physical responses

mineral a nutrient that regulates many chemical reactions in the body

miscarriage the natural ending of a pregnancy before a baby is developed enough to survive on its own

mites tiny, eight-legged animals that resemble spiders

mixed message a message in which behaviors (verbal and nonverbal) do not match in meaning

Model of Health and Well-Being a model that shows the relationship among the three domains of health, the health content areas, and the twelve factors that influence health status

moderation placing limits to avoid excess

molars the twelve teeth in the back of the mouth; they have two or three roots and several cusps that grind food

monogamous marriage a marriage in which partners have sex only with each other; provides security and helps protect partners from infection with STDs, including HIV

mons veneris   the fatty tissue that covers the front of the pubic bone and serves as a protective cushion for the internal reproductive organs

morphine   a narcotic found naturally in opium that is used to control pain

motivation   the step-by-step directions to follow when doing the teaching strategy

mucous membrane   a type of tissue that lines body cavities and secretes mucus

mucus   a thick secretion that moistens, lubricates, and protects mucous membranes

mulching lawn mower   a lawn mower that cuts grass clippings into small pieces that can be left on the lawn to decompose naturally, thereby reducing yard waste and creating a natural lawn fertilizer

multicultural infusion   the adaptation of the teaching strategy to include ideas that promote an awareness and appreciation of the culture and background of different people

multimedia   any form of video or audio used with technology

multiple sclerosis (MS)   a disease in which the protective covering of myelin on nerve fibers in the brain and spinal cord is destroyed

mumps   a viral infection that affects the salivary glands

muscle cramp   the sudden tightening of a muscle

muscle strain   the overstretching of a muscle that may result in tearing of a muscle or tendon

muscular dystrophy   a genetic disease in which the muscles progressively deteriorate

muscular endurance   the ability of the muscle to continue to perform without fatigue

muscular strength   the maximum amount of force a muscle can produce in a single effort

muscular system   the system of the body that consists of muscles that provide motion and maintain posture

myocardial infarction (MI)   the medical term for heart attack

myopia, or **nearsightedness**   a refractive error in which distant objects appear blurred and close objects are seen clearly

MyPyramid   an educational tool designed to help individuals make healthful food and physical activity choices based upon the *2005 Dietary Guidelines for Americans*

N

narcissistic personality disorder   a personality disorder in which a person is boastful, conceited, and inconsiderate of others

narcolepsy   a chronic sleep disorder in which people are excessively sleepy even after adequate nighttime sleep

narcotics   a group of drugs that slow down the central nervous system and relieve pain

National Council Against Health Fraud (NCAHF)   an organization that provides legal counsel and assistance to victims of health fraud

National Environmental Policy Act   a law that requires all government agencies to consider and assess the impact on the environment before taking any action that might affect the environment

National Health Education Standards   standards that specify what students should know and be able to do regarding health

National Health Information Center (NHIC)   an agency that refers consumers to organizations that can provide health-related information

National Institute for Occupational Safety and Health (NIOSH)   a federal regulatory agency that conducts research on health hazards in the workplace

National Longitudinal Study of Adolescent Health (Add Health)   a federally funded initiative to study adolescent health, risk behaviors, resilience, and protective factors

national parks and **state parks**   government-maintained areas of land open to the public

National School Lunch Program (NSLP)   a federally assisted program that provides nutritionally balanced, low-cost or free lunches to children each school day

natural gas   an energy source that is found underground, above deposits of oil

nature preserve   an area restricted for the protection of the natural environment

natural resource   anything obtained from the natural environment to meet people's needs

nature trail   a path through a natural environment

nearsightedness   a defect in the shape of the eye that causes distant objects to be fuzzy

negative peer pressure   influence from peers to behave in a way that is not responsible

negative self-esteem   a person's belief that he or she is not worthy and does not deserve respect

neglect   the failure to provide proper care and guidance

negligence   the failure to conduct oneself in conformity with standards established by law for the protection of others against unreasonable risk of injury

nervous system   the body system that carries messages to and from the brain and spinal cord and all other parts of the body

neuron   a nerve cell that is the structural and functional unit of the nervous system

nicotine   a stimulant drug found in tobacco products, including cigarettes and chewing tobacco

nicotine addiction, or **nicotine dependence**   the compelling need for nicotine

nicotine chewing gum   chewing gum that releases nicotine when chewed and then held between the teeth and cheek

nicotine inhaler   a device that provides nicotine vapor when air is inhaled through the device

nicotine nasal spray   a spray that administers nicotine to the mucous membranes in the nose

nicotine patch   a patch worn on the skin of the upper body or arms that releases nicotine into the bloodstream at a slow rate

nicotine withdrawal syndrome   changes that occur in a person's body when he or she first stops using tobacco products

night blindness   a condition in which a person cannot see clearly at night

nitrogen oxides   nitrogen-containing chemicals that irritate the respiratory system and appear as a yellow-brown haze in the atmosphere

nitroglycerin   a drug that widens the coronary arteries, allowing more oxygen to get to cardiac muscle

nitrous oxide   a colorless gas known for its powerful analgesic and weak anesthetic effect that is abused as an inhalant drug

nits   tiny white lice eggs that attach to body hair

noise   a sound that produces discomfort or annoyance

noise-induced hearing loss   the slow loss of hearing caused by too much noise

noise-induced permanent threshold shift   a permanent loss of the ability to hear certain frequencies and amplifications

nonrapid eye movement (NREM) sleep   the period of sleep in which the eyes are relaxed

nonverbal communication   the use of behavior rather than words to express feelings

nonverbal communication objectives   objectives that require students to convey a message to a receiver without the use of words

nonviolence   the avoidance of the threatened or actual use of physical force to injure, damage, or destroy oneself, others, or property

norepinephrine   a substance that helps transmit brain messages along certain nerves

noroviruses   a group of viruses that cause the "stomach flu" (gastroenteritis) in people

nosebleed   a loss of blood from the mucous membranes that line the nose

nuclear energy   energy produced by splitting atoms of uranium into smaller parts

nutrient   a substance in food that helps with body processes, helps with growth and repair of cells, and provides energy

nutrient density   the amount of nutrients in a food as compared to the calories

nutrition   the area of health that focuses on selecting foods that contain nutrients, eating the recommended number of servings from the MyPyramid, following the Dietary Guidelines, planning a healthful diet that reduces the risk of disease, evaluating food labels, developing healthful eating habits, following the Dietary Guidelines when going out to eat, protecting against food-borne illnesses, maintaining a desirable weight and body composition, and developing skills to prevent eating disorders

Nutrition Facts   the title of the information panel that is required on most foods

nutrition services   services that provide students with nutritionally balanced, appealing, and varied meals and snacks in settings that promote social interaction and relaxation

O

obesity a body weight that is 20 percent or more above desirable body weight

objectives statements that describe what students need to know and do in order to practice life skills and achieve health goals

obsessive-compulsive disorder (OCD) a disorder in which a person has an urgent need to repeat a thought or an action

Occupational Safety and Health Act a law that sets a series of minimum safety and health standards that all employers must meet

Occupational Safety and Health Administration (OSHA) a federal regulatory agency responsible for workplace environment

occupational therapist a health professional who helps people who have disabilities learn to make adjustments

off-label drug use the use of a drug that a physician has prescribed for treatments other than those specified on the label

oil refinery a processing plant that produces gasoline, heating oil, diesel oil, or asphalt from petroleum

one-sided friendship a friendship in which one person does most of the giving and the other person does most of the receiving

open fracture a fracture in which there is a break in the skin

open wound an injury in which the skin's surface is broken

ophthalmologist a physician who specializes in medical and surgical care and treatment of the eyes

opportunistic infection an infection that develops in a person with a weakened immune system

Opportunity-to-Learn Standards standards that specify directions for the policies, resources, and activities to be conducted in schools, communities, institutions of higher education, and state and national education agencies in order to implement the National Health Education Standards (The Joint Committee on Health Education Standards, 1994)

optician a person who fills prescriptions for glasses and contact lenses

optimal health balanced physical, emotional, social, spiritual, and intellectual well-being

optometrist an eye care professional who is specially trained in a school of optometry

oral hairy leukoplakia an infection with fuzzy white patches found on the tongue

ordinance a law enacted by county and municipal governments through the authority granted to them by the state

organ a body part consisting of several kinds of tissue that do a particular job

organizing objectives objectives that require students to organize values into a system, determine the interrelationships among them, and establish dominant and pervasive ones

orthodontist a dental health professional who specializes in correcting malocclusion

osteoarthritis the wearing down of the moving parts of joints

osteopath a physician who is trained in a school of osteopathy and has a doctor of osteopathy (DO) degree

osteopathy a therapy that uses manipulation to treat a wide range of health problems directly or indirectly relating to the musculoskeletal system of the body

osteoporosis a condition in which the bones become thin and brittle

otolaryngologist (ENT) a physician who diagnoses and treats disorders of the ears, nose, and throat

out-of-order death the death of a person that occurs at an unexpected time in his or her life cycle

outpatient care treatment that does not require a person to stay overnight at a facility

ova egg cells, or female reproductive cells

ovaries female reproductive glands that produce ova and estrogen

overfat having too high a percentage of body fat that is not within a healthful range

over-the-counter (OTC) drug a drug that can be purchased without a prescription

overuse injury an injury that occurs from repeated use or excessive overload

overweight a body weight that is 10 percent or more over desirable body weight

ovulation the release of a mature ovum from one of the two ovaries

Oxycontin a narcotic drug that is prescribed for chronic or long-lasting pain

ozone a form of oxygen

P

pacemaker a device that is implanted near the heart to stimulate normal heart contractions

pancreas a gland that produces digestive enzymes and insulin

pancreatitis inflammation of the pancreas

panel discussion an instructional strategy in which two or more students research and report on a topic or issue

Pap smear a screening test in which cells are scraped from the cervix and examined to detect cervical cancer

paranoid schizophrenia a type of schizophrenia in which a person has delusions of either persecution or grandeur

parathyroid glands endocrine glands that secrete hormones that control the amount of calcium and phosphorus in the body

parent abuse the abuse of parents by their children; a type of elder abuse

Parkinson's disease a brain disorder that causes muscle tremors, stiffness, and weakness

parole conditional release from a sentence in a correctional facility

particulates tiny particles in the air

passive behavior holding back ideas, feelings, and decisions

passive immunity immunity that results from introducing antibodies into a person's bloodstream; the antibodies may be from another person's blood

passive-aggressive personality disorder a personality disorder in which a person uses overly compliant behavior to mask anger or resentment

pathogen a germ that causes disease

PCBs chemicals that contain chlorine

PCP (angel dust) a hallucinogen that can act as a stimulant, sedative-hypnotic, or painkiller

peak flow meter a small device that measures how well a person is breathing

peer leader an older student who teaches younger students about drugs and how to resist pressure to use them

peer pressure influence that people of similar age or status place on others to behave in a certain way

pelvic examination an examination of the internal female reproductive organs

pelvic inflammatory disease (PID) a serious infection of the internal female reproductive organs

penis the male sex organ used for reproduction and urination

people pleaser a person who constantly seeks the approval of others

peptic ulcer an open sore on the lining of the esophagus, stomach, or first part of the small intestine

percent daily value the portion of the recommended daily amount of a nutrient provided by one serving of the food

perfectionism the compelling need to do everything perfectly

performance activities activities designed for a single class period in which students participate and make a verbal or written response to indicate health knowledge, attitudes, or skills gained

performance-enhancing substances substances that increase the performance capacity of the human body beyond the level of one's natural abilities

performance indicators a series of specific concepts and skills students should know and be able to do in order to achieve each of the broader National Health Education Standards

performance projects projects designed to be completed outside of class over an extended period of time and require students to complete a product that reveals what they can and will do

perinatal transmission the transfer of an infection to a baby during pregnancy, during delivery, or after birth through breast milk

periodontal disease a disease of the gums and other tissues supporting the teeth

periosteum a thin sheet of outer tissue that covers bone

peripheral nervous system consists of nerves that branch out from the central nervous system to the muscles, skin, internal organs, and glands

peristalsis a series of involuntary muscle contractions

perpetrator of violence   a person who commits a violent act

personal health and physical activity   the area of health that focuses on having regular physical examinations, following a dental health plan, being well groomed, getting adequate rest and sleep, participating in regular physical activity, developing and maintaining health-related fitness, developing and maintaining skill-related fitness, preventing physical activity-related injuries and illnesses, following a physical fitness plan, and being a responsible spectator and participant in sports

personality   an individual's unique pattern of characteristics

personality disorder   a disorder in which a person's patterns of thinking, feeling, and acting interfere with daily living

pesticide   any substance that is used to kill or control the growth of unwanted organisms

petit mal   a small seizure in which a person loses consciousness for a few seconds

petroleum, or **crude oil**   a black liquid energy source that is trapped in rock beneath Earth's surface

pharmacist   an allied health professional who dispenses medications that are prescribed by certain licensed health professionals

pharmacologist   a specialist in the composition of drugs and their effects

pharmacy   a place where prescription drugs are legally dispensed

pharynx   the throat

philosophical intimacy   sharing of beliefs and values

phobia   an excessive fear of certain objects, situations, or people

photorefractive keratectomy   laser surgery that reshapes the cornea to improve myopia

physical abuse   harmful treatment that injures the body of another person

physical activity   any bodily movement produced by skeletal muscles that results in energy expenditure

physical development   physical changes in the body that involve changes in weight, height, motor skills, vision, hearing, and development of the senses and perceptions

physical education   a planned, sequential K–12 curriculum that provides cognitive content and learning experiences in a variety of activity areas including basic movement skills; physical fitness; rhythms and dance; games; team, dual, and individual sports; tumbling and gymnastics; and aquatics

physical examination   a series of tests that measure health status

physical fitness   the ability to perform physical activity and to meet the demands of daily living while being energetic and alert

physical fitness plan   a written plan of physical activities to develop each of the components of fitness and a schedule for doing them

physical health   the condition of a person's body

physical intimacy   the sharing of physical affection; includes a wide range of behaviors that express warmth and closeness

physical punishment   a disciplinary technique in which an act is used to teach a child not to repeat undesirable behavior

physical therapist   an allied health professional who helps people rehabilitate physical disabilities and injuries

physician   an independent health care provider who is licensed to practice medicine

phytochemicals   a wide variety of compounds produced by plants that may play a role in reducing the risk of cancer in humans

pipe tobacco   shredded tobacco that is smoked in a pipe

pitch   how high or low a sound is

pituitary gland   an endocrine gland that produces hormones that control growth and other glands

placenta   an organ that anchors the embryo to the uterus

Plan B   an emergency contraceptive measure that can be taken up to three days (seventy-two hours) after unprotected sex

plaque   hardened deposits

plasma   the liquid component of blood that carries blood cells and dissolved materials

platelet   a particle that helps the blood clot; blood clots stop the bleeding when blood vessels are injured

Pneumocystis carinii **pneumonia (PCP)**   a form of pneumonia that may affect people infected with HIV

pneumonia   an infection in the lungs caused by bacteria, viruses, or other pathogens

podiatrist   a doctor of podiatric medicine (DPM) who specializes in problems of the feet

poison   a substance that causes injury, illness, or death if it enters the body

poisoning   a harmful chemical reaction from a substance that enters the body

pollen   a yellowish powder made by flowers and grass

pollutants   harmful substances in the environment

pollution standard index (PSI)   a measure of air quality based on the sum of the levels of five different pollutants

portfolio   a representative collection of a student's work used to assess the student's progress or achievement of health knowledge, attitudes, and skills over time or in progress

positive peer pressure   influence from peers to behave in a responsible way

positive self-esteem   a person's belief that she or he is worthy and deserves respect

postpartum period   the span of time that begins after the baby is born

post-traumatic stress disorder (PTSD)   a condition in which the aftereffects of a past event keep a person from living in a normal way

poverty   a condition of not having sufficient resources to eat and live healthfully

power   the ability to combine strength and speed

precycling   a process of reducing waste that includes purchasing products in packages or containers that have been or can be broken down and used again, purchasing products that have little packaging, and repairing existing products rather than throwing them out and buying new ones

preexisting condition   a health problem that a person had before being covered by the insurance

preferred provider   a health care provider who appears on a list that has been approved by the health insurance provider

preferred provider organization (PPO)   a health insurance plan that has a contract with a group of health care providers who agree to provide health care services at a reduced rate

prejudice   suspicion, intolerance, or irrational hatred directed at an individual or group of people

premature birth   the birth of a baby before it is fully developed, or less than thirty-eight weeks from time of conception

premature death   death before a person reaches her or his predicted life expectancy

premature heart attack   a heart attack that occurs before age fifty-five in males and age sixty-five in females

premenstrual syndrome (PMS)   a combination of physical and emotional symptoms that affect a female a week to ten days prior to menstruation

premium   a specific amount of money that will guarantee that an insurance company will pay for health services as specified in the insurance policy

prenatal care   care given to the mother-to-be and baby before birth

presbyopia   a refractive error caused by weakening of eye muscles and hardening of the cornea

prescription   a written order from a physician or other licensed health professional

prescription analgesic   a prescription drug that relieves pain

prescription drug   a medicine that can be obtained only with a written order from a licensed health professional

prestige crime   a crime committed to gain status among other gang members

preventive discipline   training in which a parent explains correct behavior and the consequences of wrong behavior

primary care   general health care

primary syphilis   the first stage of syphilis

principle of cooldown   the principle that a workout should end with five to ten minutes of reduced exercise to help the heart rate, breathing rate, body temperature, and circulation return to the nonexercising state

principle of fitness reversibility   the principle that fitness benefits are lost when training stops

principle of overload   the principle that a workout must include exercise beyond what a person usually does to gain additional fitness benefits

principle of progression   the principle that the amount and intensity of exercise during workouts must be increased gradually

principle of specificity   the principle that a workout should include a specific type of exercise to obtain the desired fitness benefits

principle of warmup   the principle that a workout should begin with three to five minutes of easy exercise to increase blood flow, raise the temperature in muscles, stretch muscles, and increase joint lubrication

private hospital   a hospital that is owned by private individuals and operates as a profit-making business

probation   a sentence in which an offender remains in the community under the supervision of a probation officer for a specific period of time

product recall   an order to take a product off the market because of safety concerns

productions   works prepared by the student to document knowledge and skills

products   material goods, such as food, medicine, and clothing, that are made for consumers to purchase

progesterone   a hormone that changes the lining of the uterus

progestin   the synthetic form of the hormone progesterone.

progestin-only pill, or **mini-pill**   a pill that contains progestin, which changes the natural menstrual cycle and prevents ovulation

promise breaker   a person who is not reliable

proof   a measure of the amount of alcohol in a beverage

prostate gland   a gland that produces a fluid that helps keep sperm alive

protective factor   something that increases the likelihood of a positive outcome

protective order   an order of the court issued by a judge to prohibit a domestic violence offender from committing further acts of violence, harassing or threatening the victim, and going near the victim's home or place of work

protective school   a school that has a physical and psychological atmosphere that promotes healthy youth development

protein   a nutrient needed for growth; for building, repairing, and maintaining body tissues; and for supplying energy

protein-energy malnutrition (PEM)   undernutrition that results from inadequate calorie intake

protozoa   tiny, single-celled organisms that produce toxins that cause disease

psilocybin and **psilocyn**   hallucinogenic substances contained in certain mushrooms

psychoactive drug   a substance that acts on the central nervous system and alters a user's moods, perceptions, feelings, personality, and behavior

psychological dependence   a strong desire to continue using a drug for emotional reasons

psychological intimacy   the sharing of needs, emotions, weaknesses, and strengths

psychomotor domain   the category of objectives dealing with action behavior

psychosomatic disease   a physical disorder caused or aggravated by emotional responses

puberty   the stage of growth and development when the body becomes capable of producing offspring

pubic lice   infestation of the pubic hair by pubic, or crab, lice that survive by feeding on human blood

public health   the use of organized community efforts to prevent disease and injury and promote health

public health programs   planned activities that are carried out to prevent disease and injury and promote health

pulmonary artery   a blood vessel that carries blood from the heart to the lungs to pick up oxygen and release carbon dioxide

pulp   the living tissue within a tooth; if the pulp becomes irreversibly damaged or dies, a root canal must be performed

pulse   the surge of blood that results from the contractions of the heart

puncture   a wound produced when a pointed instrument or projectile pierces the skin

Q

quack   a person or company who is involved in health fraud

quackery   a consumer fraud that involves the practice of promoting or selling useless products and services

quality of life   the degree to which a person lives life to the fullest capacity

R

racism   behavior that discriminates against members of certain racial or ethnic groups

radial keratotomy   a type of surgery that improves myopia by changing the curve of the cornea

radiation therapy   a cancer treatment that uses high-energy radiation to kill or damage cancer cells

radiologic technologist   an allied health professional who works under the direction of a radiologist

radon   an odorless, colorless radioactive gas that is released by rocks and soil

random violence   violence over which a person has no control

rape   the use of physical force (threatened or actual) to force sex on a person without the person's consent

rape survivor   a person who has been raped and often requires treatment for both physical injuries and emotional damage

rape trauma syndrome   a condition in which a rape survivor experiences emotional responses and physical symptoms over a period of time

rapid eye movement (REM) sleep   the period of sleep during which virtually all dreaming occurs and that is characterized by rapid eye movements behind closed eyelids

reaction time   the time it takes a person to move after hearing, seeing, feeling, or touching a stimulus

receiving objectives   objectives that require students to recognize and receive certain phenomena and stimuli

recreational therapist   a health care professional who plans and directs medically approved recreational activities

recreational trail   a path designed for recreational activities, such as walking, jogging, in-line skating, biking, and hiking

rectum   a short tube at the end of the large intestine that stores wastes temporarily

recycling   the process of re-forming or breaking down a waste product so that it can be used again

red blood cell   a blood cell that transports oxygen to body cells and removes carbon dioxide from body cells; red blood cells contain large quantities of hemoglobin

red tides   caused by the rapid growth or "blooms" of certain microscopic algae that usually results in a marked discoloration of the water and released toxins in the air

reflex action   an involuntary action in which a message is sent to the brain via the spinal cord, is interpreted, and is responded to immediately

refractive error   a variation in the shape of the eyeball that affects the way images are focused on the retina and blurs vision

reframing   changing your outlook in order to see a situation in a more positive way

registered nurse (RN)   a nurse who is certified for general practice or for one or more of several nursing specialties

regular gang member   a person who belongs to a gang and obeys the hard-core gang members

regular physical activity   physical activity that is performed on most days of the week

regulatory agency   an agency that enforces laws to protect the general public

rehabilitation of juvenile offenders   the process of helping juvenile offenders reject wrong behavior and adopt responsible behavior

relapse   a return to a previous behavior or condition

relationship   a connection a person has with another person

relationship addiction   the compelling need to be connected to another person

repetitions   the number of times an exercise is performed in one set

repetitions maximum   the maximum amount of resistance that can be moved a specified number of times

repetitive strain injury (RSI)   an injury from repeated physical movements

reproductions   tangible evidence of student participation

rescue breathing   a way of breathing air into an unconscious victim who is not breathing but has a pulse

resiliency   the ability to adjust, recover, bounce back, and learn from difficult times

resilient   the trait or quality of being able to adjust, recover, bounce back, and learn from difficult times

resistance exercise   an exercise in which a force acts against muscles

resistance skills, or **refusal skills**   skills that help a person to say "no" to an action or leave a situation that threatens health, threatens safety, breaks laws, results in lack of respect for oneself and others, disobeys guidelines set by responsible adults, or detracts from character and moral values

resistance stage of GAS   the second stage of the generalized adaption syndrome (GAS) in which the body attempts to regain internal balance

respiratory system   the system of the body that provides body cells with oxygen and removes carbon dioxide that cells produce as waste

respite care   care provided by someone who is temporarily relieving a family member of caregiving responsibilities

responding objectives   objectives that require students to demonstrate a variety of reactions to stimuli

responsible citizen   a person who is committed to the expectation that all citizens deserve a high quality of life and work with others to maintain the health for others

responsible decision   a choice that promotes health and safety, abides by the laws, shows respect for oneself and others, follows the guidelines set by parents and other responsible adults, and demonstrates good character

Responsible Decision-Making Model   a series of steps a person can follow to assure that his/her decisions lead to actions that promote health, protect safety, and follow laws

responsible drug use   the correct use of legal drugs to promote health and well-being

rest   a period of relaxation

restitution   the act of making up for what has been taken, damaged, hurt, or done

restraining order   an order by a court that forbids a person from coming within a certain distance of the victim

retainer   a device that is worn to keep the teeth from moving back to their original locations

reteaching   the teaching that occurs when a teacher uses an alternate strategy for instruction after students were not able to garner the concept or life skill from the first instructional strategy

Reye's syndrome   a disease that causes swelling of the brain and deterioration of liver function

Rh incompatibility   a mismatch between the blood of a pregnant female and the blood of the developing baby

rheumatic fever   an autoimmune action in the heart that can cause fever, weakness, and damage to the valves in the heart

rheumatic heart disease   permanent heart damage that results from rheumatic fever

rheumatoid arthritis   a condition in which joints become deformed and may lose function

rhinovirus   a virus that infects the nose

rickettsia   pathogens that grow inside living cells and resemble bacteria

ringworm   a skin condition that causes small, red, ring-shaped marks on the skin

risk   a chance that a person takes without knowing what the outcome will be

risk behavior   an action a person chooses that threatens health; increases the likelihood of injury, illness, or premature death; or harms the environment

risk factor   something that increases the likelihood of a negative outcome

risk situation   a circumstance that threatens health; can cause injury, illness, or premature death; or harms the environment

road rage   violent and aggressive actions of drivers and passengers in motor vehicles toward other drivers

Rocky Mountain spotted fever   a potentially life-threatening disease carried by a tick

roid rage   an outburst of anger and hostility caused by using steroids

role play   an instructional strategy in which students are assigned roles to show how they might act in specific situations

role reversal   a technique used during role play in which a role assigned to one student is switched with the role of another student

root canal   a dental procedure performed to save a tooth in which the pulp has died or is severely diseased

rubric   a written scoring system for student works that measures both health knowledge and health skills, using a point system

runoff   water that runs off the land into a body of water

S

safe and drug-free school zone   a defined area around a school for the purpose of sheltering young people from the sale of drugs and use of weapons

Safe and Drug-Free Schools and Communities Act (SDFSCA)   a federal initiative that supports programs or efforts to reduce drug, alcohol, tobacco use, and violence through education and prevention activities

Safe Drinking Water Act (SDWA)   law that protects the quality of drinking water

safety belt   a seat belt and shoulder strap

saliva   a fluid that helps soften food so that it can be swallowed more easily

salivary glands   glands in the mouth that release saliva, which contains a chemical to begin the digestion of carbohydrates

Salmonella   a bacterium that is widespread in the intestines of birds, reptiles, and mammals

sanitary landfill   a waste disposal land site where solid waste is spread in thin layers, compacted, and covered with a fresh layer of dirt daily

sanitation   the protection of health and prevention of disease by removing filth and infectious material from the environment

saturated fat   a type of fat from dairy products, solid vegetable fat, meat, and poultry

savings   money set aside for future use

scabies   an infectious skin disease caused by small parasitic mites that burrow under the skin

scanner   equipment used to copy material from a hard copy source to a computer

scapegoat   a child who is blamed as the cause of problems in the family

schizophrenia   a disorder in which there is a split or breakdown in logical thought processes

school-based health center   an easily accessible location on a school campus where students can go for comprehensive preventive and primary health care services

School Breakfast Program   a federal entitlement program that provides funds to states that provide breakfast programs in schools

school health coordinator   the individual responsible for program administration, implementation, and evaluation of the coordinated school health program

school health services   services designed to appraise, protect, and promote the health of students

school psychologist   a psychologist who works with students, parents, school personnel, and teachers to solve learning and behavioral problems

school-site health promotion for staff   health promotion programming such as health assessments, health education, and health-related physical fitness activities that protect and promote the health of those on the school staff

scoliosis   a deformity of the spine in which the spine shows either a lateral or an S-shaped curvature

Scope and Sequence Chart   a chart that serves as a blueprint for the curriculum; it includes the components of health literacy, the National Health Education Standards, the performance indicators, the content areas and health goals, and the health topics

scrotum   a sac-like pouch that holds the testes and helps regulate their temperature

search engine   a program that looks for Web sites that include key words and provides a list of relevant Web sites

seasonal affective disorder   a type of depression that is caused by insufficient exposure to sunlight

sebaceous gland   a small, oil-producing gland that helps protect the skin

sebum   the oil produced by sebaceous glands

secondary sex characteristics   physical and emotional changes that occur during puberty

secondary syphilis   the stage of syphilis characterized by a skin rash; begins anywhere from three to six weeks after a chancre appears

second-degree burn   a burn of the top layers of the skin

secondhand smoke, or environmental tobacco smoke   exhaled smoke and sidestream smoke

secure landfill   a landfill that has protective liners to reduce or prevent leachate from escaping through water runoff

sedative   a drug that has a calming effect on a person's behavior

sedative-hypnotics a group of drugs that depress the activities of the central nervous system

sediments suspended solids that settle to the bottom of bodies of water

seizure a period in which a person loses control over mind and body

selected response tests or multiple choice tests tests made up of items that have a direct question or an incomplete question stem followed by four or five answer options, from which students must select the correct answer

self-appraisal a personal assessment tool that contains a list of actions to which a student responds

self-control the degree to which a person regulates his/her own behavior

self-defense strategies that can protect people from violence

self-directed learner a person who embraces learning throughout life

self-discipline the effort or energy with which a person follows through on intentions or promises; necessary for a person to develop self-responsibility

self-disclosure the act of making one's thoughts and feelings known to another person

self-efficacy a person's belief in his/her capacity or ability to perform a behavior or skill in a desired way

self-esteem one's belief about one's own worth

self-respect a high regard for oneself because one behaves in responsible ways

self-respecting behavior treating oneself in healthful and responsible ways

self-responsibility for health the priority a person assigns to being health-literate, maintaining and improving health, preventing disease, and reducing health-related risk behaviors

self-statements words a person can say to himself/herself when he/she experiences anger triggers and cues

semantic differential a technique used to measure beliefs and attitudes in which students are asked to circle a letter (A-B-C-D-E) to indicate their preference on a continuum

seminal vesicles two small glands that secrete a fluid rich in sugar that nourishes sperm and helps them move

seminiferous tubules a network of coiled tubules in which sperm are produced

semi-vegetarian diet a diet that excludes red meat

sensorineural hearing loss hearing loss that occurs when there is damage to the inner ear or acoustic nerve

serotonin a chemical in the body that helps regulate primitive drives and emotions

service learning an educational method by which people learn and develop through active participation in service

services work that is provided

serving size the listing on the nutrition label of the amount of food that is considered a serving

servings per container the listing on the nutrition label of the number of servings in the container or package

set a group of repetitions of an exercise followed by a rest period

severe acute respiratory syndrome (SARS) a viral respiratory illness caused by a coronavirus, called SARS-associated coronavirus (SARS-CoV)

severe thunderstorm warning a warning that is issued when a severe thunderstorm has been sighted or indicated by radar

severe thunderstorm watch a warning that is issued when the weather conditions favor the development of a severe thunderstorm

sex role socially prescribed behavior for being male or female

sexism behavior that discriminates against people of the opposite sex

sex-linked characteristics hereditary characteristics transmitted on the sex chromosomes

sexual abuse sexual contact that is forced on a person

sexual addiction the compelling need for sexual activity

sexual assault any type of unwanted sexual contact

sexual harassment unwanted sexual behavior ranging from making sexual comments to forcing another person into unwanted sex acts to which that person does not consent

sexually transmitted disease (STD) a disease caused by pathogens that are transmitted from an infected person to an uninfected person during intimate sexual contact

shin splint an overuse injury that results in pain in the front and sides of the lower leg

shock a dangerous reduction in blood flow to the body tissues

shopping addiction the compelling need to purchase things

short-term goal something a person plans to achieve in the near future

shyness a condition characterized by discomfort, inhibition, and awkwardness in social situations

sick building syndrome (SBS) an illness that results from indoor air pollution; very risky for the elderly, infants, and people who have asthma

sickle-cell anemia a condition in which the red blood cells are sickle shaped and are fragile and easily destroyed

side effect an unwanted body change that is not related to the main purpose of a drug

side stitch a dull, sharp pain in the side of the lower abdomen

sidestream smoke smoke that enters the air from a burning cigarette, cigar, or pipe

simple carbohydrates sugars that enter the bloodstream rapidly and provide quick energy

single custody an arrangement in which one parent keeps legal custody of a child or children

single-custody family a family in which a child or children live with one parent who has custody

skeletal muscle muscle tissue that is attached to bone

skeletal system the body system that serves as a support framework, protects vital organs, works with muscles to produce movement, and produces blood cells

skill-related fitness the capacity to perform well in sports and physical activities

skin patch a patch worn on the body that contains a drug that is absorbed through the skin

skin patch test putting allergens on a patch, taping the patch to the skin, and observing the reaction

sleep a state of deep relaxation in which there is little movement or consciousness

small intestine a coiled tube in which the greatest amount of digestion and absorption takes place

smallpox a viral disease that produces high fever and distinctive pus-filled sores that crust over and fall off; highly contagious and sometimes fatal

smegma a substance that forms under the foreskin consisting of dead skin and other secretions

smog the haze that results when water vapor in the air combines in the presence of sunlight with motor vehicle emissions and the smoke and particles from factories

smoke detector an alarm that sounds when it detects smoke

smokeless tobacco tobacco that is chewed or snorted but not smoked

smooth muscle involuntary muscle tissue found in many internal organs

Snellen chart a chart used for testing visual acuity for distance

snorting sniffing drugs through the nose so that they can be absorbed through the mucous membranes of the nasal passages

snuff a tobacco product made from powdered tobacco leaves and stems that is snorted or placed between the gums and cheek

social age a measure of a person's involvement in leisure activities

social conscience a desire to contribute to society and to live a socially responsible life

social development relating to others

social-emotional booster an interpersonal contact that helps a person feel encouragement and support, choose responsible behavior, and recognize options

social-emotional environment the quality of the contacts a person has with the people with whom he or she interacts

social-emotional pollutant an interpersonal contact that closes options or may cause a person to feel discouraged and alone or to choose wrong behavior

social worker a person who helps people with a wide range of social problems

sodium a mineral that regulates and maintains the balance of fluids in the body

software a computer program

solar energy the energy of the sun

solid waste discarded solid materials, such as paper, metals, plastics, glass, leather, wood, rubber, textiles, food, and yard waste

solid waste pollution   the throwing away of substances such as trash, litter, and unwanted objects, some of which may be very large, in the environment

somatoform disorder   a disorder in which a person has symptoms of disease for which no physical cause can be found

sound frequency   the number of sound waves produced per minute

sound waves   vibrations, or movements, of air

Special Milk Program   a federal program that provides milk to children in schools and child care institutions that do not participate in other federal child nutrition meal service programs

specialist   a professional who has specialized training in a particular area

speech objectives   objectives that require students to communicate through speech, such as public speaking

speech pathologist   an allied health professional who helps people overcome speech disorders

speed   the ability to move quickly

sperm   male reproductive cells

spermatogenesis   the process by which sperm are produced

spermicide   a foam, cream, jelly, film, or suppository that forms a barrier and contains a chemical that might kill some sperm

spirochete   a spiral-shaped bacterium

spleen   an organ on the left side of the abdomen that filters foreign matter from the blood and lymph

splint   material or a device used to protect and immobilize a body part

sprain   an injury to the ligaments, tendons, and soft tissue around a joint caused by undue stretching

spreadsheet   a table of numerical data arranged in columns and rows

stalking   following or lying in wait for a person with the intent to threaten, harm, or control that person

starch   a food substance that is made and stored in most plants

state health department   an official agency that has responsibility for providing health services and programs for people living within a state

state laws   laws that are enacted by state legislatures

static stretching   stretching the muscle to a point where a pull is felt and holding the stretch for fifteen to thirty seconds

status offenses   behaviors for which an adult would not be arrested, such as truancy, alcohol use, running away, defying parents or guardians, and breaking curfew

stereotype   a prejudiced attitude that assigns a specific quality or characteristic to all people who belong to a particular group

sterilization   any procedure by which an individual is made permanently incapable of reproduction

steroids   a group of drugs that are made from hormones

stillbirth   a fully developed baby that is born dead

stimulants   a group of drugs that speed up the activities of the central nervous system

stomach   an organ that releases acids and juices that mix with food and produce a thick paste called chyme

strabismus   misalignment of the eyes and commonly referred to as "cross-eye"

strain   an overstretching of muscles or tendons

strangulation   choking to death due to pressure on the throat

strep throat   a bacterial infection of the throat

stress   the body's response to the demands of daily living

stress fracture   a hairline break that results from repetitive jarring of a bone

stress-management skills   techniques to prevent and deal with stressors and to protect one's health from the harmful effects produced by the stress response

stressor   a source or cause of stress

stroke   a condition caused by a blocked or broken blood vessel in the brain

stroke volume   the amount of blood the heart pumps with each beat

student assistance program   a school-based program to help prevent and treat alcoholism and other drug dependencies

student presentation   an instructional strategy in which a student makes an oral presentation or demonstration on a health topic that has been researched in depth

sty an infection around the eyelash marked by swelling and pain

sublingual absorption the absorption of a drug when it is placed under the tongue

sudden illness an illness that occurs without warning

suffocation a condition in which there is lack of oxygen due to an obstruction to passage of air into the lungs

suicide the intentional taking of one's own life

suicide-prevention strategies techniques that can be used to help prevent a person from thinking about, attempting, or completing suicide

sulfur oxides sulfur-containing chemicals that irritate the nose, throat, and eyes and smell like rotten eggs

support group a group of people who help one another deal with an addiction, a particular disease, or difficult situation

suppository a wax-coated form of a drug that is inserted into the anus or vagina

surgical insurance insurance that pays for fees related to surgery

sweat gland a gland that helps cool the body by releasing sweat through the pores to evaporate on the surface of the skin

symptom a change in a body function from the normal pattern; a diagnosis is made after reviewing symptoms

synergy a positive outcome that occurs when different people cooperate and respect one another and create more energy for all

synovial fluid fluid that lubricates and provides nutrition to the cells on the surface of joints

synthesis objectives objectives that require students to put something together that they have not put together previously

syphilis an STD caused by the spirochete bacterium *Treponema pallidum*

systemic fluoride fluoride that is meant to be ingested into the body

systemic lupus erythematosus (SLE) an autoimmune condition in which connective tissue becomes inflamed

T

T cell a white blood cell that destroys pathogens

tamper-resistant package a package that is sealed to assure the buyer that the package was not opened previously

tar a sticky, thick substance that is formed when tobacco is burned

target heart rate a heart rate of 75 percent of maximum heart rate

teaching hospital a hospital that is associated with a medical school or school of nursing

teaching strategy a technique used by a facilitator or teacher to help a student (1) understand a particular concept or (2) develop and practice a specific life skill

technology the use of high-tech equipment to communicate information

television addiction the compelling need to watch television

temporary threshold shift (TTS) the temporary loss of the ability to hear certain frequencies and amplifications

tendinitis inflammation of a tendon

tendon tough tissue fiber that attaches muscles to bones

terrarium a transparent container that holds plants or small animals

testes male reproductive glands that produce sperm cells and testosterone

testicular self-examination a screening procedure for testicular cancer in which a male checks his testes for lumps or tenderness

testosterone a hormone that produces male secondary sex characteristics

tetanus, or **lockjaw** a bacterial infection that produces a strong poison that damages the nervous system and muscles

THC a drug found in the cannabis plant that produces psychoactive effects

therapeutical equivalence when two drugs are chemically the same and produce the same medical effects

thermal inversion a condition that occurs when a layer of warm air forms above a layer of cool air

thermal pollution a harmful condition caused by the addition of heated water to a water supply

third-degree burn a burn of all layers of the skin and some underlying tissues

thrill-seeking addiction the compelling need to take unnecessary risks

thrush a fungal infection of the mucous membranes of the tongue and mouth

thymus gland a gland that causes white blood cells to become T cells

thyroid gland an endocrine gland that produces thyroxine

thyroxine a hormone that controls metabolism and calcium balance in the body

time management organizing time to accomplish priorities

tissue a group of similar cells that work together

tobacco cessation program a program to help a person stop smoking or using smokeless tobacco

tobacco use the use of cigarettes, pipes, cigars, or smokeless tobacco

tolerance a condition in which the body becomes accustomed to a substance

topical fluoride a fluoride product that is applied directly to the teeth

tornado a violent, rapidly spinning windstorm with a funnel-shaped cloud

tornado warning a warning issued when a tornado has been sighted or indicated by radar

tornado watch a warning issued when weather conditions favor the development of tornadoes

Totally Awesome™ Health the highest level of health that a person can achieve

Totally Awesome™ Teacher a teacher who is committed to improving health literacy, improving health, preventing disease, and reducing health-related risk behaviors in students, and to creating a dynamic and challenging classroom where students learn and practice life skills for health

Totally Awesome Teaching Strategy™ a technique that a facilitator or teacher uses to help students become health literate and master the performance indicators established for each of the National Health Education Standards

toxemia of pregnancy a condition in a pregnant female characterized by increased blood pressure, swelling, and leakage of protein into the urine

toxic shock syndrome (TSS) a severe illness resulting from infection with toxin-producing strains of staphylococcus

Toxic Substances Control Act a law that authorizes the EPA to set standards for the manufacturing, use, transportation, and disposal of toxic substances

toxin a substance that is poisonous

trachea a tube through which air moves to the lungs

tracking disorder a learning disability in which a person has difficulty following a series of words or images

traditional marriage an emotional, spiritual, and legal commitment a man and woman make to one another

traffic violation any violation of the current traffic code

training principles guidelines to follow to obtain maximum fitness benefits and reduce the risk of injuries and illnesses

transdermal contraceptive patch, or Ortho Evra a skin patch applied to the lower abdomen, buttocks, or upper body that slowly releases progestin and estrogen into the bloodstream to prevent pregnancy

***trans*-fatty acids** fatty acids found in prepared foods containing partially hydrogenated vegetable oils (e.g., cookies, crackers, some margarines, commercially prepared fried foods)

trichomoniasis an STD caused by the single-celled protozoan *Trichomonas vaginalis*

trihalomethanes harmful chemicals produced when chlorine attacks pollutants in water

tropical rain forest a hot, wet forested area that contains many species of trees, plants, and animals

tubal ligation a method of female surgical sterilization that includes the use of clips, rings, and cauterization to block the fallopian tubes.

tuberculin skin test the injection of a protein substance under the skin in the forearm

tuberculosis a bacterial infection of the lungs

tumor an abnormal growth of tissue

turbine an engine that rotates

Type 1 diabetes the body produces little or no insulin

Type 2 diabetes a type of diabetes in which the body produces insulin but it cannot be used by cells

U

ulcer an open sore on the skin or on a mucous membrane; it is usually inflamed and painful

ultraviolet (UV) radiation a type of radiation that comes from the sun and also is emitted by sunlamps and tanning booths

umbilical cord a ropelike structure that connects the embryo to the placenta

undernutrition a deficiency in calories, protein, vitamins, or minerals as a result of inadequate diet and frequent infection

underweight a body weight that is 10 percent or more below desirable body weight

unintentional injury an injury caused by an accident

U.S. Department of Agriculture (USDA) a federal agency that enforces standards to ensure the safe processing of food and oversees the distribution of food information to the public; also publishes consumer pamphlets on nutrition and food safety topics

U.S. Postal Service (USPS) a federal agency that offers postal services and works to protect the public from crimes and fraud involving mail

universal distress signal a warning signal given by a person to indicate difficulty breathing and is shown by clutching at the throat with one or both hands

universal precautions steps taken to prevent the spread of disease by treating all human blood and certain body fluids as if they contain HIV, HBV, and other pathogens

unsaturated fat fat obtained from plant products and fish and is usually liquid at room temperature

uranium a radioactive substance that is mined and used to power nuclear reactors, which split atoms to produce steam; the steam is used to generate electricity

ureter a narrow tube that connects the kidneys to the urinary bladder

urethra a narrow tube extending from the urinary bladder to the outside of the body through which urine passes out of the body

urinalysis a set of urine tests that check for normal kidney function and urinary tract infections

urinary bladder a muscular sac that stores urine; as the urinary bladder fills with urine, it expands

urinary system the body system that removes liquid wastes from the body and maintains the body's water balance

urine a pale yellow liquid composed of water, salts, and other waste products

V

vaccine-preventable diseases infectious diseases for which effective vaccines or immunizations are available

vagina a muscular tube that connects the uterus to the outside of the body; the female sex organ; serves as the birth canal

vaginal contraceptive ring, or NuvaRing a flexible ring about two inches in diameter that is inserted in the vagina where it remains for three weeks, releasing progestin and estrogen to prevent pregnancy

valuing objectives objectives that require students to display a behavior with sufficient consistency

vas deferens two long, thin tubes that act as a passageway for sperm and a place for sperm storage

vasectomy a method of male sterilization in which the vas deferens is resected (cut off) and tied

V-chip a small electronic device that allows television programs to be blocked

vegan diet a diet that excludes foods of animal origin

vegetarian diet a diet in which vegetables are the foundation and meat, fish, and poultry are limited or eliminated

vein a blood vessel that returns blood to the heart

vena cava one of two large veins that returns blood rich in carbon dioxide to the right atrium

ventricle one of the lower two chambers of the heart

victim assessment a check of a person who is ill or injured to determine if he/she has an open airway, is breathing and has blood that is circulating, is severely bleeding, or has other injuries

victim of violence　a person who has been harmed by violence

victim recovery　a person's return to physical and emotional health after being harmed by violence

videoconferencing　a conference between people in different locations who can hear and see each other using electronic communications

villi　small folds in the lining of the small intestine

violence　the use of physical force to injure, damage, or destroy oneself, others, or property

viral hepatitis　a viral infection of the liver

viral load test　a test that measures the amount of HIV in a person's blood

virus　the smallest known pathogen

virus replication　the virus copying itself or reproducing or multiplying

visible fat　fat that can be seen when looking at food

visitation rights　guidelines set for the visitation of children by the parent who does not have custody

visual acuity　sharpness of vision

visual environment　everything people see around them

visual learner　a person who learns best by seeing or creating images and pictures

visual pollution　sights that are unattractive such as litter, graffiti, and dilapidated buildings

vitamin　a nutrient that helps the body use carbohydrates, proteins, and fats

vitamin C　a water-soluble vitamin found in many vegetables and fruits, particularly oranges, grapefruit, and peppers

voluntary hospital　a hospital that is owned by a community or organization and does not operate for profit

voluntary muscle　a muscle a person can control

W

walk-in surgery center　a facility where surgery is performed on an outpatient basis

wanna-be　a child or teen who is not a gang member but might wear gang clothing and engage in violent or criminal behavior to prove worthy of being a gang member

warmup　a period of three to five minutes of easy physical activity to prepare the muscles to do more work

wart　a contagious growth that forms on the top layer of the skin

water　a nutrient that is involved with all body processes, makes up the basic part of the blood, helps with waste removal, regulates body temperature, and cushions the spinal cord and joints

water pollution　contamination of water that causes negative effects on life and health

water runoff　runoff from farms, landfills, urban areas, mines, forestry activities, and construction areas that contaminates water supplies, rivers, and lakes; may contain oil, gasoline, pesticides, herbicides, fungicides, metals, bacteria, and viruses

water-soluble vitamin　vitamin that dissolves in water and cannot be stored in the body

waxing　applying hot wax to the skin

weapon　a device used for fighting

Web site　a collection of documents listed under one uniform resource locator (URL)

weight machine　an apparatus that provides resistance to a muscle or group of muscles

weight management　a diet and exercise plan to maintain or attain a desirable weight and body composition

weight management plan　a specific plan to maintain or attain a desirable weight and body composition based on caloric intake and caloric expenditure

weight training　a conditioning program in which free weights or weight machines provide resistance for muscles

wellness　the quality of life that results from a person's health status

Wellness Scale　a scale that depicts the range of quality of life, from optimal well-being to high-level wellness, average wellness, minor illness or injury, major illness or injury, and premature death

Western blot　a blood test used to check for antibodies for HIV and to confirm an ELISA

wheal　a round skin lump that indicates sensitivity to a particular allergen

white blood cell　a blood cell that attacks, surrounds, and destroys pathogens that enter the body and helps prevents them from causing infection

wildland fire   a fire that occurs in the wilderness

wildlife sanctuary   a place reserved for the protection of plants and animals

wind energy   energy from the wind

wine   an alcoholic beverage made by fermenting grapes or other fruits

wine cooler   a carbonated, fruit-flavored alcoholic beverage that is 1.5 to 6 percent alcohol

winter storm   a storm in the form of freezing rain, sleet, ice, heavy snow, or blizzards

withdrawal symptoms   unpleasant reactions that occur when a person who is physically dependent on a drug discontinues its use

word processing   using a computer to produce documents

work ethic   an attitude of discipline, motivation, and commitment toward tasks

workaholism   the compelling need to work to fill an emptiness

World Wide Web   a vast collection of linked Internet documents that use hypertext

wound   an injury to the body's soft tissues

Y

you-message   a statement that blames or shames another person

INDEX

Note: Page numbers followed by *f* indicate figures; those followed by *t* indicate tables; and those followed by *b* indicate boxed material.

A

AA. *See* Alcoholics Anonymous (AA)
AAA (American Automobile Association) Foundation for Traffic Safety, 415
AAHE (Association for the Advancement of Health Education), 25, 61
Abandonment in family, 146
Abdominal thrusts, 440–441
Abrasions, 444
Abscess, A-47
Absence seizure, A-57
Abstinence from sex
  avoiding risks of teen marriage and parenthood, 170–172
  benefits, 157–158, 173
  changing sexual behavior for, 160, 793
  definition, 157, 793
  facts about, 174*t*
  reasons for choosing, 793
  reproductive health and, 196, 199
  resisting negative peer pressure to be sexually active, 159–160, 793
  risk reduction for STDs and HIV infection, 344, 349
  setting limits for expressing physical affection, 158–159, 793
  statistics, 158
Abuse
  child abuse, 7, 416, 423–424, A-44–A-45
  cycle of abuse, 170
  definition, 169
  domestic violence, 7, 145, 301, 416–417
  elderly abuse, 170
  in family, 145–146, 416
  mental and emotional abuse, 169, 170, 423, 424, A-50
  neglect, 169, 170, 423, A-54
  parent abuse, 417
  physical abuse, 169–170, 423, A-55–A-56
  reporting of child abuse, 423, A-44, A-59
  sexual abuse, 145, 169, 170, 423, 429–430, A-58–A-59
Abuser, 162
Academy for Educational Development, A-68
Acceptance
  in coping with life crisis, 140
  as stage of grief, 137, 215
Accessibility, 43
Accident reports, 46–47
Accidents
  drug abuse and, 311–317, 319, 327
  tobacco use and fires, 305, 407
  See also Injuries; Injury prevention and safety
Accutane, 134
Acid rain, 390
ACIP (Advisory Committee on Immunization Practices), 333, 341
Acne, 134, 266, A-39
ACOA (Adult Children of Alcoholics), 302
Acoustic trauma, 396
Acquaintance rape, 301, 427–429

Acquired immunodeficiency syndrome. *See* AIDS
Action on Smoking and Health, A-67
Active lifestyle, 226
Active listening, 75, 127
Actual versus implied consent, 438–439
Acyclovis, 340
ADA (American Dental Association), 110*b*, 373, A-64
ADD (attention deficit disorder), 206
Addictions
  codependence and, 124, 146, 147*f*, 322
  definition and description, 120–121, 248
  depression and, 133
  in family, 145, 322, A-40
  formal intervention for, 121, 328
  pregnancy and, 200
  relapse, 121, 124
  signs of, 121
  treatment, 121, 327–329
  types and characteristics, 122–123*t*
  See also Alcohol; Drug use/abuse; Tobacco use
ADHD (attention deficit hyperactivity disorder), 206, 310, A-43–A-44
Adolescents
  developmental tasks of, 165–167, 206–210
  immunizations for, 332–333
  sleep and, 269–271
  See also specific health content areas; specific grades
Adrenal glands, 189
Adrenaline, 79, 129, 189
Adult Children of Alcoholics (ACOA), 302
Adverse environment, 320*f*
Advertising
  ad clutter, 398
  alcohol advertising, 302–303
  tobacco advertising, 306–307
Advisory Committee on Immunization Practices (ACIP), 333, 341
AED (automated external defibrillator), 37, 37*f*
Aerobic exercise, 275, 276, 282
Affection
  learning to express, in families, 143–144
  setting limits for expressing physical affection, 158–160
  See also Intimacy; Sexuality
Affective disorders, 124
Affective domain, 68–69
African Americans
  hair care, 265
  homicide as cause of death of, 7
Afterbirth, 201
Aftercare, 420
Aggressive behavior, 300, 418
Agility, 282
Aging
  biological age, 210
  chronological age, 210
  elder abuse, 417
  falls in home, 407
  gerontology and, 210
  habits promoting healthful aging, 213
  mental changes, 212
  physical changes, 210–212
  regular physical activity and, 274
  social age, 210
  social changes, 212
  theories about causes of, 210
Agriculture Department, U.S.
  consumer protection, 365
  Dietary Guidelines for Americans, 227
  Food and Nutrition Information Center, A-64
  Food and Nutrition Program, 55
  Forest Service, A-64
  National School Lunch Program (NSLP), 53–54

School Breakfast Program, 54
Special Milk Program, 54–55
AIDS
  CDC guidelines for prevention, 14
  definition, 325, A-51
  development of, following HIV infection, 10, 345
  drug use and, 9
  prevention, 159, 173
  treatment, 348–349
  as worldwide epidemic, 383
  See also HIV infection
AIDS dementia complex, 345
Air bags, 414
Air pollution
  actions for keeping air clean, 391
  air quality, 388–389
  asbestos, 390
  cancer and, 360
  definition, 389
  effects on children, 389
  effects on health status, 389
  fossil fuels, 389–390
  indoor air pollution, 390
  indoor molds, 391
  law against, 362, 388
  motor vehicle emissions, 390
  particulates, 390
  pollution standard index (PSI), 289
  radon, 390–391
  sick building syndrome (SBS), 391
  smog, 390
  sources, 389–391
Air Quality Index (AQI), 389
Airway obstruction, 408
Al-Anon Family Groups, Inc., 148, 302, A-65
Alarm stage of GAS, 129, 130, 277
Al-Ateen, 148, 302
Alcohol
  advertising, 302–303
  alcoholism as addiction, 145, 302
  binge-drinking, 297
  blackout, 300
  blood alcohol concentration (BAC), 295–297
  cancer and, 360
  definition, 9, 295
  depression and, 133
  dietary guidelines, 229*f*
  driving and, 5, 301–302, 414
  effects of, on the body, 297–298
  entertainment media and, 371
  episodic heavy drinking, 9
  family members' use of, 145, 322, A-40
  fetal alcohol syndrome (FAS), 200, 299
  hangover, 300
  hazing activity and, 297
  health goals, 23, 291
  as illegal for teens, 301
  loss and grief causing use of, 137
  motor vehicle related injuries and, 5
  pregnancy and, 200, 299
  rape and, 301, 428
  resources on, A-65–A-66
  risks associated with, 9, 301–302, 326
  sexuality and, 172
  signs and symptoms, A-40
  statistics, 9
  stress and, 130
  student assistance program, A-41
  thinking and decision making following use of, 299–300
  as toxin, 296
  treatment for alcoholism, 148, 302, A-40–A-41
  violence and illegal behavior as risks of, 301–302, 326
  See also Addictions; specific grades

B

X

Y

Z